GOWER'S

PRINCIPLES OF

MODERN COMPANY LAW

D1439644

AUSTRALIA

LBC Information Services
Sydney

CANADA and USA

Carswell
Toronto

NEW ZEALAND

Brooker's
Auckland

SINGAPORE AND MALAYSIA

Thomson Information (S.E. Asia)
Singapore

 WITHDRAWN

GOWER'S

PRINCIPLES OF

MODERN COMPANY LAW

SIXTH EDITION

By

PAUL L. DAVIES, M.A., LL.M

Professor of the Law of the Enterprise
Fellow of Balliol College, Oxford

With a contribution from

D.D. PRENTICE, M.A., LL.B., J.D.

Barrister
Allen & Overy Professor of Corporate Law
Fellow of Pembroke College, Oxford

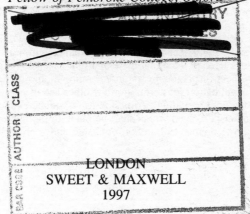

LONDON
SWEET & MAXWELL
1997

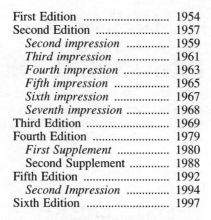

First Edition 1954
Second Edition 1957
   Second impression 1959
   Third impression 1961
   Fourth impression 1963
   Fifth impression 1965
   Sixth impression 1967
   Seventh impression 1968
Third Edition 1969
Fourth Edition 1979
   First Supplement 1980
   Second Supplement 1988
Fifth Edition 1992
   Second Impression 1994
Sixth Edition 1997

Published in 1997 by
Sweet & Maxwell Ltd, 100 Avenue Road,
Swiss Cottage, London NW3 3PF
Computerset by
Wyvern 21 Ltd, Bristol
Printed in Great Britain by
Clays Ltd, St Ives plc

No natural forests were destroyed to make this product:
only farmed timber was used and replanted

A CIP catalogue record for this book is available from the
British Library.

ISBN 0 421 52480 4 (P/b)
ISBN 0 421 52470 7 (H/b)

All rights reserved. U.K. statutory material in this
publication is acknowledged as Crown copyright.
No part of this publication may be reproduced or transmitted,
in any form or by any means, or stored in a retrieval system
of any nature, without prior written permission, except for
permitted fair dealing under the Copyright, Designs
and Patents Act 1988, or in accordance with the terms
of a licence issued by the Copyright Licensing Agency
in respect of photocopying and/or reprographic reproduction.
Application for permission for other use of copyright
material including permission to reproduce extracts in
other published works shall be made to the publishers.
Full acknowledgement of author, publisher and source must be given.

©
L. C. B. GOWER
1997

PREFACE

When Professor Gower asked me to produce a text of the sixth edition of his work on company law, it was in the expectation that he would be able to comment on what I produced and thus give me the benefit of his enormous experience and wisdom in the field of corporate law. Sadly, circumstances have permitted that plan to be followed only to a limited extent, and the sixth edition of *Gower's Principles of Modern Company Law* thus lacks a crucial input.

Nevertheless, I have attempted to remain faithful to the fundamental objectives of the book. In the preface to the first edition Professor Gower stressed the importance of expounding the principles of company law. Principles were contrasted with giving a full exposition of the detail of company law, on the one hand, and writing a mainly theoretical book, on the other. Some reviewers of the previous edition would have wished that the book had developed in a more theoretical direction, but, as Professor Brian Cheffins' recent book, *Company Law: Theory, Structure and Operation*, perhaps demonstrates, to do that successfully would have required the writing of a very different book. It seemed to me that the growing bulk of statutory company law and the arrival of comprehensive statutory regulation of the financial services area, both notable features of the subject since the first edition of this book was produced, have strengthened the case for an exposition of principles from a standpoint internal to the subject. It is that tradition which this edition attempts to carry forward.

Although the fifth edition of this work appeared as recently as 1992 and there has been no comprehensive legislative reform in the intervening period, the Government's addiction to "salami tactics" for reform of company law has produced a fairly long list of topics where changes have been made. Among the more notable are the introduction (at last) of a new regulatory regime for public offers of unlisted securities; the recasting of the insider trading provisions as part of the Criminal Justice Act 1993; the implementation, after one false start, of a system of electronic recording and transfer of title to securities; and the changes made in the areas of accounts and audits in favour of small companies (perhaps the most important of the reforms made by the Government in the name of "deregulation").

The Government's penchant for deregulation showed itself also in the very process of law reform. Thus, both the Cadbury and the Greenbury Committees were ostensibly private, but Government-supported, initiatives at the very heart of company law. Their output also, in so far as it was regulatory in content, was implemented largely in a non-statist fashion, that is, by additions to the Listing Rules of the Stock Exchange, which, consequently, have continued their move centre-stage as one of the leading sources of regulation of large companies.

Within the existing framework of the law, the efforts of the Insolvency Service, an Executive Agency of the Department of Trade and Industry, have continued to give the courts multiple opportunities, to develop a modern law of the duties of directors, especially in relation to creditors, at least for the period prior to insolvency; whilst private litigation under section 459 of the Companies Act has afforded a similar opportunity in relation to the restraints placed by the law upon the actions of the controllers of companies *vis-à-vis* minority shareholders. Both lines of case law suggest that it is no longer appropriate to see the judges as wedded to a wholly non-interventionist role as against corporate management. Equally, however, as the courts' continued adherence (to the despair of the Law Commission) to the rule in *Foss v. Harbottle* suggests, the old attitude has not been replaced by one in which the values underlying the policy of non-intervention have been thrown overboard. A more sophisticated analysis of judicial attitudes in the field of company law is called for.

This edition attempts to take account of these (and other) changes which have affected many of the Chapters of the previous edition. One structural change has also been made. Despite the arguments put forward to the contrary in the Preface to the first edition, and maintained ever since, this edition does depart from tradition to the extent of dealing with the formation of companies before the consequences of incorporation. The main advantage of this way of proceeding has been the possibility of thereby creating a separate Part Five devoted to companies and the securities markets, which reflects the growth of regulation specific to companies whose securities are traded on public markets. It might be thought that this process should have been carried further by the inclusion within this Part of the Chapter on takeovers. The problem of how best to present company law to first-time students is almost insoluble, and I should be grateful to receive readers' reactions to this particular attempt.

I am grateful to my colleague, Dan Prentice, for accepting Professor Gower's invitation to continue his involvement with the Chapter on company charges.

I have attempted to deal with the law as it stood at the end of 1996, although limited references to some later developments have proved possible.

Paul Davies
Oxford
SS Philip and James' Day, 1997

EXTRACT FROM PREFACE
TO FIRST EDITION

Company Law, to those who specialise in it, is among the most fascinating of legal subjects. But its fascination is not always readily apparent to general practitioners or to the students of law, economics and accounting who try to master its intricacies. Indeed, they often regard it as technical and dull. This, perhaps, is because they find difficulty in viewing it in its historical and economic context and in grasping its underlying principles. This book has been written in an attempt to meet their needs. Its aim is to supply essential background material, and to emphasise the principles of common law and equity on which this branch of the law is still based, rather than the statutory provisions which supplement and amend them in detail.

The book is not intended to be an exhaustive treatise on every branch of company law. In particular, no attempt is made to deal fully with the procedure on a winding up—a subject which requires a volume to itself or a large share of a volume on bankruptcy. It is concerned with the living law of living companies, in sickness and in health. But within these limits I think it is true to say that it discusses most of the important aspects of the subject. While it emphasises principles, it is not intended to be mainly theoretical; on the contrary an attempt has been made to concentrate on those principles which are still important in practice and to explain their purpose and how they operate. For this reason, and because of the discussion of certain problems which are ignored elsewhere, it is hoped that the book may be found useful by practitioners (lay and legal) as well as by students.

No attempt has been made to deal with systems of company law other than the English. On the other hand, attention is drawn to developments elsewhere (particularly in the USA) when these have seemed illuminating either by way of contrast or as pointers towards the possible solution of questions as yet unsolved in England. In general the footnotes have not been burdened with detailed references to American authorities as these can be readily found in any of the standard texts or casebooks.

CONTENTS

Part One

INTRODUCTORY

Part Two

FORMATION OF COMPANIES

Part Three

THE CONSEQUENCES OF INCORPORATION

Part Four

A COMPANY'S SECURITIES

Part Five

COMPANIES AND THE SECURITIES MARKET

Part Six

SHAREHOLDER AND CREDITOR PROTECTION

Part Seven

COMPANIES IN TRAUMA

Contents

TABLE OF CASES

TABLE OF STATUTES

TABLE OF STATUTORY INSTRUMENTS

TABLE OF EUROPEAN MATERIAL

TABLE OF RULES OF TAKEOVER CODE

Part One

INTRODUCTORY

CHAPTER 1

NATURE AND FUNCTIONS OF COMPANIES

SCOPE OF THE SUBJECT

ALTHOUGH company law is a well-recognised subject in the legal curriculum and the title of a voluminous literature, its exact scope is vague since "the word *company* has no strictly legal meaning".[1] It is clear, however, that in legal theory (though not, as we, shall see always in economic reality) the term implies an association[2] of a number[3] of people for some common object or objects. The purposes for which men and women may wish to associate are multifarious, ranging from those as basic as marriage and mutual protection against the elements to those as sophisticated as the objects of the Confederation of British Industry or a political party. But in common parlance the word "company" is normally reserved[4] for those associated for economic purposes, *i.e.* to carry on a business for gain.

English law provides two main types of organisation for such associations: partnerships and companies. Although the word "company" is colloquially applied to both,[5] the modern English lawyer regards companies and company law as distinct from partnerships and partnership law. Partnership law, which is now largely codified in the Partnership Act 1890, is based on the law of agency, each partner becoming an agent of the others,[6] and it therefore affords a suitable framework for an association of a small body of persons having trust and confidence in each other. A more complicated form of association, with a large and fluctuating membership, requires a more elaborate organisation which ideally should confer corporate personality on the association, that is, should recognise that it constitutes a distinct legal person,

---

[1] *Per* Buckley J. in *Re Stanley* [1906] 1 Ch. 131 at 134.

[2] *Pace* James L.J. in *Smith v. Anderson* (1880) 15 Ch.D. 247 at 273: "The word 'association,' in the sense in which it is now commonly used, is etymologically inaccurate, for 'association' does not properly describe the thing formed, but properly and etymologically describes the act of association together, from which act of associating there is formed a company or partnership."

[3] Since the implementation in the U.K. of Council Directive 89/667 on single-member private limited-liability companies a company need have only one member, and for many decades before that the interest in the company of only one of the members might have been more than nominal. Nor indeed does a public "company" automatically cease merely because, in the course of time, the number of members is reduced to one or none.

[4] But not universally; we still talk about an infantry company, a livery company and the "glorious company of the Apostles".

[5] So that it is common for partners to carry on business in the name of "—& Company".

[6] Partnership Act 1890, s. 5.

subject to legal duties and entitled to legal rights separate from those of its members.[7] This the modern company can obtain easily and cheaply by being formed under a succession of statutes culminating in the principal Companies Act of 1985 as amended in particular by that of 1989.

Briefly what occurs is that the promoters of a company prepare certain documents expressing their desire to be formed into a company with a specified name and objects and these documents are lodged with the Registrar of Companies. If the documents are in order, they are registered, the Registrar grants a certificate of incorporation, and the company is formed. The essential feature is public registration and this type of company is therefore described as a registered company.

Although today there is a clear-cut legal distinction between partnerships and incorporated companies and although the latter can now be formed almost as easily and cheaply as the former, this is a relatively modern development. Little more than a century-and-a-half ago corporate personality could be acquired only by the dilatory and expensive process of promoting a special Act of Parliament or acquiring a Royal Charter. Hence, the business world tried to adapt the partnership form to an organisation with a large and fluctuating membership and, as we shall see,[8] thanks to the equitable doctrine of the trust, their efforts met with considerable success. It was from these "deed of settlement" companies (rather than from chartered corporations) that the modern company was developed. Nearly all these unincorporated companies[9] have now either been wound up, registered under the Companies Acts, or become incorporated by statute or charter, but until recently several important insurance companies remained as examples of the once normal earlier form.[10]

Choice of partnership or company

The distinction between partnerships and companies is often merely one of machinery and not of function. If a small number of persons

---

[7] It is outside the scope of this book to discuss whether this recognition is of a pre-existing fact (as contended by the Realist school, associated with the name of Gierke) or of legal fiction. Legal personality, in the sense of the capacity to be the subject of legal rights and duties, is necessarily the creation of law whether conferred upon a single human being or a group and the Realist and other theories are of no direct concern to the lawyer (as opposed to the political scientist) except in so far as they have influenced the judges in the development of the law. See further H.L.A. Hart, (1954) 70 L.Q.R. 37 at pp. 49–60.

[8] Chaps. 2 and 3.

[9] An unincorporated company must not be confused with an unlimited incorporated company. The members may, if they wish, form an incorporated company but accept personal responsibility for its debts. In such a case they will reap all the other advantages of corporate personality which an unincorporated association necessarily lacks: see Chap. 5, below.

[10] The Sun Insurance Society and the General Life Assurance Company did not adopt the modern form until as late as 1926 and 1927 respectively. Insurance companies formed before 1844 or in 1855–1856 can lawfully remain organised in the old way, and it seems that a few mutual assurance societies still are.

wish to carry on business in common with a view to profit they may either form themselves into a partnership or a company. Normally the only restraint on their freedom of choice is that, if their numbers are too great for that mutual trust appropriate to a partnership, they must form a company. An arbitrary maximum of 20 is imposed by section 716(1) of the Companies Act 1985 (re-enacting similar provisions in the earlier Acts). However, this maximum does not apply to firms of solicitors, accountants qualified to audit company accounts or members of a recognised stock exchange[11]; and the Secretary of State may by regulations exempt other professions.[12] Several unincorporated firms of solicitors or accountants now have well over 100 partners.[13]

Types of company

Incorporation under the Companies Act is not the only way in which a company may be formed. Three types of company are recognised by section 716[14]:

(i) *Registered companies*
There is first the company formed under the Act in the manner briefly described above. This is the typical and infinitely the most important kind of company at the present day and that with which this book is primarily concerned.

(ii) *Statutory companies*
Bodies with special types of object which it has been thought desirable to encourage may be formed under general public Acts, such as the Friendly Societies, the Industrial and Provident Societies and the Building Societies Acts. Although some of these bodies, particularly building societies, or co-operative societies formed under the Industrial and Provident Societies Acts, closely resemble companies, they fall outside the scope of this book. A company properly so called may, however, be formed by a special Act. In the past, statutory incorporation by private Acts, of public utilities, such as railway, gas, water and

---

[11] s.716(2). There is a further exemption in subs.(5) of bodies approved for the purposes of the Marine and Aviation (War Risks) Act 1952 as re-insurers of war risks. In other cases Lloyd's underwriting syndicates are so organised as to avoid the implication that their members are "associated" in a business. Lloyd's itself is now a statutory corporation but does not itself undertake insurance business.

[12] By various Partnerships (Unrestricted Size) Regs. several types of partnership have been exempted. These include patent agents, surveyors, auctioneers, valuers, estate agents, actuaries, chartered engineers and architects. In practice, membership of, or recognition by, a professional association is a condition of exemption.

[13] Similar limits and exceptions apply to limited partnerships; see s.717.

[14] Earlier Acts referred also to a fourth type, "cost-book" companies engaged in working tin mines in the Cornish "Stanneries", but this reference was repealed by s.28 of the Companies Consolidation (Consequential Provisions) Act 1985, it having finally been concluded that no such companies now exists.

electricity undertakings, was comparatively common since the undertakings would require powers and monopolistic rights which needed a
special legislative grant. During the nineteenth century, therefore,
public general Acts[15] were passed providing for standard clauses
deemed to be incorporated into the private Acts, unless expressly
excluded. As a result of post-war nationalisation measures, most of
these statutory companies were taken over by public boards or corporations set up by public Acts (but many, if not most, of them have
now been "privatised" and become registered companies). These
boards and corporations also fall outside the scope of this book. But
some statutory companies remain and others may be formed. The statute under which they are formed need not incorporate them but today
this is invariably done.

(iii) *Chartered companies*

   Section 716 thirdly refers to companies formed in pursuance of
"letters patent".[16] This relates to companies granted a charter by the
Crown under the Royal Prerogative or special statutory powers.[17] Such
a charter normally confers corporate personality, but, as it was
regarded as dubious policy for the Crown to confer a full charter or
incorporation on an ordinary trading concern, it was empowered by
the Trading Companies Act 1834 and the Chartered Companies Act
1837 to confer by letters patent all or any of the privileges of incorporation without actually granting a charter.[18] Today an ordinary trading
concern would not contemplate trying to obtain a Royal Charter,[19] for
incorporation under the Companies Acts would be far quicker and
cheaper. In practice, therefore, this method of incorporation is used
only by organisations formed for charitable, or quasi-charitable,
objects, such as learned and artistic societies, schools and colleges,
which want the greater prestige that a charter is thought to confer.

---

[15] The Companies Clauses Acts 1845–1889. These Acts, containing the general corporate powers
and duties, were supplemented in the case of particular utilities by various other "Clauses
Acts", *e.g.* the Lands Clauses Consolidation and Railways Clauses Consolidation Acts 1845,
the Electric Lighting (Clauses) Act 1899, and numerous Waterworks Clauses Acts, and Gas-
works Clauses Acts.

[16] This is, of course, the same expression as is used in connection with inventions and historically
the two are closely connected. Just as the Crown might grant a monopoly of an invention by
grant under its letters patent, so might it grant a charter of incorporation and the charter might
confer a monopoly of trading in a particular territory.

[17] Under many ad hoc statutes the Crown has been granted power to grant charters in cases
falling outside its prerogative powers. Moreover, by the Chartered Companies Acts 1837 and
1884, the prerogative was extended by empowering the Crown to grant charters for a limited
period and to extend them. Thus the BBC charter was for 10 years and has been prolonged
from time to time.

[18] The Stock Exchange, when revising its "deed of settlement" constitution in the light of the
City of London's "Big Bang", at one time proposed to apply for privileges under the latter
Act, but instead registered under Part XXII, Chap. II of the Act.

[19] There are, however, still a few old-established trading companies incorporated by charter.

Many such organisations remain unincorporated for, as Maitland pointed out in his famous essay *Trust and Corporation*,[20] until recent years England, in contrast with the continental countries, made little use of corporations in connection with associations for purposes other than those of trade, preferring to rely on the English invention of the trust. By the trust, learned societies, clubs, and professional bodies could function satisfactorily without incorporation by vesting their property in a small body of trustees.[21] Many of the more important and wealthy, such as the leading public schools, colleges and universities, obtained Royal Charters, while others, as we have seen, became subject to special legislation. But many societies, clubs and professional bodies (including the Inns of Court) remain unincorporated to this day.

Although this book is primarily concerned with companies registered under the Companies Act 1985 (or one of the earlier Companies Acts and thus subject to the provisions of the 1985 Act[22]) it should be pointed out that certain provisions of that Act may apply to the other types of company previously mentioned and, indeed, to other bodies as well. Thus under section 718, certain "unregistered companies" are subject to the provisions specified in Schedule 22 if incorporated and having a principal place of business in Great Britain. Further, under Part XXIII a company incorporated outside Great Britain which establishes a branch or place of business here must comply with the obligations of that Part.[23]

The functions of company legislation

Company legislation has two main functions: (i) enabling and (ii) regulatory. The enabling function empowers people to do what they could not otherwise achieve—namely to create a body with a distinct corporate personality. The regulatory function prescribes the conditions which have to be complied with to obtain incorporation and the rules that thereafter have to be observed to protect members, creditors and the public against the dangers inherent in such a body.

In respect of neither function, and particularly the second, is the Companies Act 1985, despite its vast size,[24] a complete codification

---

[20] *Selected Essays* (ed. Hazeltine, Camb., 1936), p. 141.
[21] Until the legislation of the late 19th century, so did building societies, friendly societies, industrial and provident societies and trade unions. Even now some of these remain unincorporated and still rely primarily on the trust.
[22] See Part XXII of the Act.
[23] See Chap. 6 at pp. 127–130, below.
[24] It originally consisted of 747 sections and was supplemented by the Company Securities (Insider Dealing) Act (19 sections), Business Names Act (11 sections) and Companies Consolidation (Consequential Provisions) Act (35 sections and 2 Schedules) also enacted in 1985 as part of the consolidation exercise.

of English Company Law.[25] It is merely a consolidation of statutory provisions in the former principal Act of 1948, and in four subsequent major Companies Acts and other legislation. And, unhappily, it immediately ceased to be even a complete consolidation because subsequent Acts repealed and replaced many of its provisions and added many more. Behind it is a residual body of law and equity where some of the fundamental principles are still to be found.[26] However, there are now few of those general principles which are not affected in some way by the extremely detailed provisions of the Act whose bulk astonishes our partners in the European Community. Their legislation is expressed in relatively general terms which the courts are left to interpret purposefully; ours, even to a greater extent than in other common law countries, is expressed in meticulous detail attempting to cover every conceivable eventuality, and thus to become "judge-proof" when interpreted literally. Contrary to what an earlier generation was taught at Law School, in the Civil Law countries judges have greater freedom to make law (albeit on the basis of codified general principles) while in the United Kingdom it is increasingly made by statute and judges are inhibited from developing new principles by the extent and detail of the statutory intervention.

THE FUNCTIONS OF COMPANIES

Inadequacy of legal definitions

At the beginning of this Chapter it was said that "company" implied an association of a number of persons for a common object, that object normally being the economic gain of its members. But it is no longer practicable to restrict consideration to trading concerns. In the last 100 years incorporation has become so easy and so cheap that many non-profit-making bodies, which would hitherto have remained unincorporated, have become registered under the Companies Acts. Far from being designed to secure the economic profit of their members, these companies expressly prohibit it, and between them and normal trading companies there is nothing in common beyond the fact that they both adopt the same legal framework within which to function.[27]

Even as regards trading companies our description was legalistic

---

[25] For an attempt at a complete codification in a Commonwealth country with a company law based on the English model, see Ghana's Companies Code 1963 (Act 179). This was based on a report by Professor Gower: *Final Report of the Commission of Enquiry into the Working and Administration of the Company Law of Ghana* (Accra, 1961).

[26] In fact, since the Acts apply to Scotland as well as to England and Wales, the statutory rules are superimposed on two distinct common law systems. In some respects these differ widely. This book is primarily concerned with English (not Scottish) company law.

[27] As we shall see, the legal framework is modified slightly to meet their particular needs: below, p. 10.

rather than realistic. No doubt many of the smaller companies may properly be described as associations of a number of persons for the common object of mutual profit; if two partners convert their business into a limited company they may well continue to carry on business in common, just as they did before the incorporation. More questionable is the reality of this description when applied to large public companies. A holder of 100 shares in, say, Imperial Chemical Industries is a member of the company but it is fantasy to describe him as associating with the other members in running it. The running of the business is left to the directors, or probably to the managing directors, and the shareholder, although a member, is in economic reality but not in the eyes of the law, a mere lender of capital, on which he hopes for a return but without any effective control over the borrower.

The legal implications of this development were first explored in the United States by A.A. Berle and G.C. Means in their *The Modern Corporation and Private Property*,[28] which drew attention to the revolutionary change thus brought about in our traditional conceptions of the nature of property. Today the great bulk of industrial enterprise is in the hands not of individual entrepreneurs but of large public companies in which many individuals have property rights as shareholders and to the capital of which they have directly or indirectly contributed. Direct or indirect investment in companies probably constitutes the most important single item of property, but whether this property brings profit to its "owners" no longer depends on their energy and initiative but on that of the management from which they are divorced. The modern shareholder in a public company has ceased to be a quasi-partner and has become instead simply a supplier of capital. If he invests in the older forms of private property, such as a farm or his own shop, he becomes tied to that property.[29] The modern public company meets the need for a new type of property in which the relationship between the owner and the property plays little part, so that the owner can recover his wealth when he needs it without removing it from the enterprise which requires it indefinitely. "The separation of ownership from management and control in the corporate system has performed this essential step in securing liquidity."[30] Even when, as is increasingly the case, shareholding in large companies is concentrated in the hands of institutional shareholders, such as pension funds and insurance companies, which do have a more significant potential for intervention in management than individual shareholders, such participation is discontinuous and usually precipitated by some crisis in the company's affairs.[31]

---

[28] New York, 1933 (reprinted in 1968 with a new preface).
[29] Berle & Means, p. 284.
[30] *ibid.*, p. 285.
[31] See Davies, "Institutional Investors in the United Kingdom" in Prentice and Holland (eds.), *Contemporary Issues in Corporate Governance* (Oxford, 1993).

The modern public company is therefore one further piece of machinery (like the trust) whereby the property of individuals is managed by other individuals. In so far as there is any true association in the modern public company it is between management and workers rather than between the shareholders *inter se* or between them and the management. But the fact that the workers form an integral part of the company is largely ignored by the law.[32]

The three functions of the modern company

From a functional viewpoint there are today three distinct types of company:—

1. *Companies formed for purposes other than the profit of their members*, *i.e.* those formed for social, charitable or quasi-charitable purposes. In this case incorporation is merely a more modern and convenient substitute for the trust.

2. *Companies formed to enable a single trader or a small body of partners to carry on a business*. In these companies, incorporation is a device for personifying the business and, normally, divorcing its liability from that of its members despite the fact that the members retain control and share the profits.

3. *Companies formed in order to enable the investing public to share in the profits of an enterprise without taking any part in its management*. In this last type, which is economically (but not numerically) by far the most important, the company is again a device analogous to the trust, but this time it is designed to facilitate the raising and putting to use of capital by enabling a large number of owners to entrust it to a small number of expert managers.

For the first of these classes the Companies Act provides the company limited by guarantee. For the second and third it provides the company limited by shares. It also provides for the possibility of registering as an unlimited company (with or without a share capital) but as, in practice, great and perhaps exaggerated[33] importance is placed on the advantage of limitation of liability this is rarely resorted to except where the nature of the business is such that, though incorporation is permissible, limited liability is not.

Guarantee companies

The Companies Act does not permit a company to be created in which the members are free from any liability whatsoever, but, as an

---

[32] See, however, Companies Act 1985 ss.309 and 719, Insolvency Act 1986, s.187, and Chap. 4 at pp. 63–66, below.

[33] The members of a private company (or such of them as are directors) will find that they will be required to give personal guarantees to those who grant formal credit facilities to the company—thus rendering the limitation on liability illusory.

alternative to limiting their contribution to the amount payable on their shares, it enables them to agree that in the event of liquidation they will, if required, subscribe an agreed amount. The Act recognises two forms of company limited by guarantee, namely, the guarantee company without a share capital and the guarantee company with a share capital. The former is the guarantee company in its pure form, whereas the latter is something of a hybrid. Little use was made of the hybrid form, and the power to form such a company, or for a pure guarantee company to convert to one with a share capital, was abolished by the Companies Act 1980.[34] But the pure form was, and is, widely used by charitable and quasi-charitable organisations (such as schools, colleges and the ''Friends'' of museums and picture galleries) since incorporation with limited liability is often more convenient and less risky than a trust. A division of the undertaking into shares is inappropriate since no sharing of profits is contemplated and the incorporators may not wish initially to put any money into the concern, as they would have to if they subscribed for shares. The members are under no liability so long as the company remains a going concern; they are liable, to the extent of their guarantees,[35] only if the company is wound up and a contribution is needed to enable its debts to be paid.[36]

Companies limited by shares

A guarantee company is, however, unsuitable where the primary object is to carry on a business for profit and to divide that profit among the members. Just as a partnership agreement will need to prescribe the shares of the partners, so will a company's constitution need to define the shares of its members, and if these shares are to be transferable it will be convenient for them to be expressed in comparatively small denominations. Thus if the initial capital is to be £1,000 this will normally be divided into 1,000 shares of £1 each, even though there may initially be only two or three members. The members who subscribe for the shares will be under a duty to pay the company for them in money or money's worth, and the company is accordingly said to be ''limited by shares'', that is to say, the members' liability[37] to contribute towards the company's debts is limited to the nominal value of the shares for which they have subscribed, and once the shares have been ''paid up'' they are under no further liability. A funda-

---

[34] Now 1985 Act s.1(4). But a small number of such companies remain (for example theatre clubs and management companies for blocks of flats of which the tenants are members).

[35] Which, in practice, are minimal; usually only £1.

[36] In contrast, a member of one of the surviving guarantee companies with a share capital may be under a two-fold liability—as shareholder to pay up the price of his shares and, on winding up, as guarantor.

[37] In the case of private companies this liability may in practice be illusory as there is no minimum nominal value of shares or of total share capital. A company (estate agents) has been registered with a share capital of 1/2d. divided into two 1/4d.

mental distinction between this type of company and the pure guarantee company is that the law assumes that its working capital will be, to some extent at any rate, contributed by the members; their contributions float the company on its launching and are not a mere *tabula in naufragio* to which creditors may cling when the company sinks.

Public and private companies

The company limited by shares can be used whether the company is to be a small family concern or a large organisation to which the public is to be invited to contribute capital, but obviously some of the safeguards required in the latter case in the interests of the public investor, can be dispensed with in the former. In recognition of this the Companies (Consolidation) Act 1908 exempted from some of the normal requirements a "private company" which it defined as one which (a) limited the membership to 50, (b) restricted the right to transfer shares and (c) prohibited any invitation to the public of its shares. Companies not coming within this definition were normally described as "public companies".

This definition survived until the Companies Act 1980 although it had proved quite inadequate to distinguish small family concerns from other, so-called public, companies[38]; and although the two most prized advantages afforded private companies[39] had been removed by the Companies Act 1967.[40] However, the 1980 Act, implementing the E.C. Second Company Law Directive, adopted the more satisfactory approach of defining the public company as a company limited by shares (or by guarantee and having a share capital[41]) whose memorandum of association states that it is to be a public company and in relation to which the provisions of the Companies Act as to registration or re-registration are complied with.[42] These provisions prescribe that the suffix to its name must be "public limited company"[43] (or its abbreviation "plc"[44]) instead of "limited",[45] and that before it can do business it must have a prescribed minimum issued and paid up share capital.[46] All other companies are private companies. They are not subject to the minimum capital requirements but normally it is a criminal offence to issue an advertisement offering their shares or deben-

---

[38] A further attempt to achieve this aim was made by the Companies Act 1948, which subdivided private companies into "exempt" and "non-exempt", but this produced hideous complications and capricious results and, in accordance with the recommendations of the Jenkins Committee (Cmnd. 1749, paras. 55–68), was abandoned by the 1967 Act, s.2.

[39] Exemption from filing accounts and from the prohibition on loans to directors.

[40] 1967 Act s.2.

[41] New companies of this type cannot be formed: see above.

[42] See now 1985 Act s.1(3).

[43] s.25(1).

[44] s.27.

[45] Welsh equivalents can be adopted if its registered office is to be in Wales: ss.25(1) and 27.

[46] ss.117 and 118.

tures.[47] If limited companies, the traditional suffix "Limited" or "Ltd" normally remains mandatory.[48]

The result is that only some 12,000 companies are now registered as public ones while there are nearly 1 million private companies.[49] Some of the latter are large both in assets and in number of members (for the former limit of 50 on that number has now gone and the attempt to restrict private companies to small family concerns has been finally abandoned). On the other hand, the differences in the legal rules relating to public and private companies, which had by 1980 become minimal, have grown as a result of the Acts of 1980, 1981 and 1989 and seem likely to become greater in the future.[50] Moreover, the Act, in relation to financial disclosure, draws a three-fold distinction between large, medium and small companies.[51] In relation to the auditing of accounts, regulations have now added a fourth category of "micro" companies.[52] In essence, these categorisations involve drawing distinctions among private companies of varying sizes, so as to reduce the regulatory burden on the smallest. Unhappily, an attempt in 1981 to tackle the problem by providing a simpler form of incorporation for really small firms was abortive.[53]

THE COMPANY'S CONSTITUTION

Before proceeding further it may be useful to indicate in general terms the type of constitution adopted by companies to enable them to perform their economic or social functions as described above.

Today a company's original constitution is very much a matter for its promoters. This was not always so. When incorporation could be obtained only through a special statute or charter the promoters could petition for what they wanted but it rested with the legislature or the Crown to decide what they should actually have. In theory, this is still the case so far as statutory and chartered companies are concerned, but in practice the initiative has shifted to the promoters, who will draft and promote their private Bill or append a draft charter to their petition, and, although this may be rejected or amended, they will probably either fail completely or obtain very much what they themselves have put forward. And as regards a company registered under

[47] See p. 425, below.
[48] Once again with Welsh equivalents: 1985 ss.25(2) and 27.
[49] *Companies in 1995–96* (HMSO), Table A2. But there has been a steady rise in the proportion of public companies since 1984 from 0.4 per cent to 1.1 per cent: *ibid.*
[50] If only because some of the E.C. Company Law Directives which we shall have to implement need be applied only to public companies.
[51] See pp. 526–530, below.
[52] See below, pp. 530–532.
[53] See *A New Form of Incorporation for Small Firms* (1981 Cmnd. 8171). It received insufficient support to encourage the Government to proceed further. But legislation on somewhat similar lines has been enacted in South Africa.

the Companies Act—overwhelmingly the most common type—the
promoters have almost complete freedom, provided that the constitution is set out in the statutory form. This is because the modern company—as we shall see in the next two chapters—developed mainly
through the unincorporated partnership, the constitution of which
naturally depended on the agreement of the partners.

The modern registered company has, however, inherited one feature
from statutory and chartered corporations, namely that its constitution
has to be set out in two separate documents, its memorandum of association (corresponding to the statute or charter) and its articles of association (corresponding to the bye-laws which, in practice, the statute
or charter would empower the corporation to make to supplement its
provisions). This makes sense if it is desired to ensure that the basic
constitution of the body corporate shall be inflexible and not alterable
without the consent of Parliament or the Crown. In theory that inflexibility applies to registered companies. The memorandum of association, laying down the company's basic constitution, is alterable only
to the extent permitted by the Companies Act[54] and, under the early
Companies Acts, the company itself had virtually no power to effect
alterations. But today the constitution has become much more flexible
and in one way or another every provision of the memorandum (except
that fixing the country in which its registered office is to be situated)[55]
can be altered unless the memorandum expressly provides to the contrary. Moreover, the memorandum need only state the company's
name, objects, domicile, share capital (if any) and, if such be the case,
that the liability of the members is limited and that it is a public
company. Everything else is regarded as a matter of administration to
be dealt with in the second document, the articles of association. The
provisions of this, subject to some ill-defined restraints on abuse,[56] are
alterable by a special resolution of the company[57]; *i.e.* by a resolution
in general meeting passed by a three-fourths majority of members
voting after at least 21 days' notice has been given of the intention to
pass it as a special resolution.[58]

The company's organs

The form of articles of association has become largely standardised
under the influence of the model tables formerly appended to the Com-

---

[54] s.2(7).
[55] Even the country of registration may be changed from "England and Wales" to "Wales"
by special resolution: s.2(2).
[56] See Chap. 26. These restraints stop far short of any principle that "bye-laws must be reasonable".
[57] s.9.
[58] s.378(2).

panies Acts and now prescribed by regulations[59] and of specialist company lawyers and books of precedents. They may, and do, contain regulations on many matters—on the share capital, meetings, dividends, accounts and the like—but the most important are those relating to the company's organs.

A company has two primary organs: the members in general meeting and the board of directors. Here, again, an analogy may be found in constitutional law. In a parliamentary democracy such as ours, legislative sovereignty (subject to Community law) rests with Parliament, while administration is left to the executive Government, subject to a measure of control by Parliament through its power to force a change of Government. It is much the same with a company, except, of course, that a company is not sovereign but has a limited competence only. Within these limits, supreme rule-making authority (in theory) rests with a general meeting of the members. Generally a simple majority vote suffices, but in some cases a larger majority or other special formalities may be required. Thus the Companies Act provides that certain things can only be done by an extraordinary resolution, which requires a three-fourths majority, and others by a special resolution which requires longer than the normal notice, and, again, a three-fourths majority, and the constitution may entrench certain rights still further by embodying them in the memorandum and providing that they shall be unalterable.[60]

Although it would be constitutionally possible for the company in general meeting to exercise all the powers of the company, it clearly would not be practicable (except in the case of a small company which is in reality an incorporated partnership or sole trader) for day-to-day administration to be undertaken by such a cumbersome piece of machinery. Hence the articles will provide for a board of directors[61] and will say what powers are to be conferred on the board and how it is to be appointed and changed. Like the Government, the directors will be answerable to the "Parliament" constituted by the general meeting, but in practice (again like the Government) they will exercise as much control over it as it exercises over them. And the modern practice is to confer on the directors the right to exercise all the company's powers, except such as the Act, the memorandum and articles

---

[59] Companies (Tables A to F) Regulations 1985 (S.I. 1985 No. 805 as slightly amended by S.I. 1985 No. 1052). These include also model memoranda of association but unless and until the Act is amended to provide (as some Commonwealth Acts do) that a registered company has the capacity of a natural person, no memorandum will be found with an "objects clause" as short and sweet as those in these models. But see s.3A, inserted by the 1989 Act, which is intended to encourage such brevity.

[60] s.17(2).

[61] The name "directors" will not necessarily be used; in many guarantee companies the equivalent officers will be called "governors"; see the definition of "directors" in s.741(1).

or a special resolution expressly provide must be exercised in general meeting.[62]

Consequently, the directors of a modern company will undertake considerably more than detailed administration; it is certainly they who will make most policy decisions. Indeed, their position *vis-à-vis* the company is, in many ways, more powerful then that of the Government *vis-à-vis* the Parliament at Westminster. The theory of parliamentary sovereignty means that Parliament could (in theory) override anything done by the Government notwithstanding that this was clearly within its competence as a matter of pure administration. So originally could the members in general meeting; in fact the directors seem to have been treated as their agents. The modern theory, however, is somewhat different, for, provided that the act is within the powers delegated to the directors, the members in general meeting normally cannot interfere with it.[63] The most they can do is to dismiss the directorate and appoint others in their place, or alter the articles so as to restrict the powers of the directors for the future.

This wide delegation of the company's powers is, however, to the directors acting as a board, not to the individual directors. But, here again, it will obviously be impractical in the case of large companies for day-to-day management to take place at formal board meetings which will probably be held not more than once a month. In the meantime other officers of the company will have to ensure that the decisions of the board are implemented and its policy carried out; under the board and directly or indirectly responsible to and appointed by the board will be found the management and secretariate. In all probability some at least of the managers, and perhaps the secretary, will also be directors, for the normal practice today is to provide that directors may be appointed to other paid offices in the company.[64] And, in practice, these officers will do much more than merely carry out the decisions and policy of the board; they will themselves make policy decisions. In fact, many, and perhaps most, of the company's powers which have been primarily delegated to the board will be sub-delegated by them to the managing director or directors; a provision enabling this to be done has become common form in articles.[65]

It is in these managers that in reality we find the closest parallel to the executive government; this, indeed, is recognised by the common use of the expression "business executives" to describe, not directors as such, but the higher ranks of managers. The business of the directorate is coming more and more to be recognised as one of laying down policy in the most general terms and exercising an equally general

---

[62] Table A, art. 70.
[63] See further Chap. 9, pp. 183–187, below.
[64] Table A, art. 84.
[65] Table A, art. 72.

supervision over or monitoring of the way in which it is carried out; everything else is left to the managers assisted by the secretariate.

These distinctions between the functions of members in general meeting, boards of directors and management must not be exaggerated. They are of importance only in the case of the public company or the larger private company. In the one- or two-person private company the factual position will be the same as in a partnership, with the same few people exercising all these functions.[66] In practice they will probably not clearly distinguish between their actions in their various capacities and normally this will not matter much. In recent years company law has begun to recognise this reality about small companies.[67]

One of the main problems facing company law is to provide in relation to public companies an adequate system of checks and balances between the various organs—and here again there is an obvious analogy in the field of government. For the present, however, it is only necessary to point out that this division of functions between separate organs is one of the features which distinguishes a company from a partnership and which enables the public company to fulfil its economic role.

Interpretation of the constitution

The analogies which have been drawn with constitutional law must not be taken to imply that the courts, in interpreting the constitution of a company, adopt the same "large and liberal interpretation" that may be regarded as appropriate when construing the written constitution of a state.[68] Though they will strive to adopt a construction which gives "business efficacy"[69] to the company's regulations, they are bound by the strict letter of the words used and, if these words are unambiguous, an argument that they produce inconvenience,[70] or even absurdity, is unlikely to suceed.[71] The result is to produce even greater strictness than in normal cases of contract, for the written regulations cannot be rectified by the court even if they are not in accordance with the parties' intention.[72]

---

[66] Hence it was not until 1948 that a private company was required to have any directors. Only one is essential in their case—public companies must have at least two: 1985 Act, s.282— but a sole director may not also be the secretary: s.283(2) and (4).

[67] See pp. 91–96, below.

[68] *Edwards v. Att.-Gen. for Canada* [1930] A.C. 124, P.C., at 136–137.

[69] *Holmes v. Keyes* [1959] Ch. 199, C.A., *per* Jenkins L.J. at 215.

[70] *Worcester Corsetry Ltd v. Witting* [1936] Ch. 640, C.A., at 646.

[71] *Grundt v. Great Boulder Proprietary Mines Ltd.* [1948] Ch. 145, C.A. "'Absurdity' . . . like public policy, is a very unruly horse": Greene M.R. at 158. See also Vaisey J. in *Rayfield v. Hands* [1960] Ch. 1 at 4 and *cf. Bushell v. Faith* [1970] A.C. 1099, H.L.

[72] *Scott v. Frank Scott (London) Ltd* [1940] Ch. 794, C.A. Within limits they can, of course, be altered for the future if the necessary majority can be obtained for passing a special resolution.

CHAPTER 2

HISTORY OF COMPANY LAW TO 1825

THIS book is concerned with modern company law, but there are some branches of modern English law which cannot be properly understood without reference to their historical background, and company law is certainly one of them; indeed, of all branches of the law it is perhaps the one least readily understood except in relation to its historical development, a somewhat extended account of which is therefore essential.[1] Such an account falls conveniently into three periods: (1) until 1720 when the Bubble Act was passed; (2) from 1720 until the Bubble Act was repealed in 1825; and (3) from 1825 until the present day. The present Chapter deals with the first two of these periods.

Early forms of commercial association

Various forms of association were known to medieval law and as regards some of them the concept of incorporation was early recognised. At first, however, incorporation seems to have been used only in connection with ecclesiastical and public bodies, such as chapters, monasteries and boroughs, which had corporate personality conferred upon them by a charter from the Crown or were deemed by prescription to have received such a grant.[2]

---

[1] This account owes much to Formoy, *The Historical Foundations of Modern Company Law* (Lond., 1923); C.A. Cooke *Corporation, Trust and Company* (Manchester, 1950); Holdsworth, *History of English Law* Vol. 8, pp. 192–222; *Anglo-American Essays in Legal History*, Vol. 3, pp. 161–255 (Boston, Mass., 1909); W.R. Scott, *Joint Stock Companies to 1720* (Camb., 1909–1912)—especially Vol. 1; C.T. Carr, *Law of Corporations* (Camb., 1905) and *Select Charters of Trading Corporations* (Selden Society, 1913); C.M. Schmitthoff, *The Origin of the Joint Stock Company* (1939) 3 Toronto L.J. 74–96; A.B. DuBois, *The English Business Company after the Bubble Act, 1720–1800* (N.Y. 1938); H.A. Shannon, *The Coming of General Limited Liability*, and *The First 5,000 Limited Companies and their Duration* (1931–1932) Econ. Hist., Vol. 11, 267 and 396; B.C. Hunt, *The Development of the Business Corporation in England 1800–1867* (Harvard Economic Studies, 1936). The works of DuBois and Hunt are particularly fascinating accounts of the formative years which largely render obsolete earlier accounts of the periods to which they relate. Much old learning is to be found in J. Grant, *Law of Corporations* (Lond., 1850).

[2] While it is doubtful whether English law has ever unequivocally committed itself to the "fiction" theory of corporation, it seems to have fairly consistently adopted the "concession" theory—namely, that incorporation depends upon a State grant. But it has recognised the power of foreign States and it may be that until the Reformation a grant of incorporation could be conferred on an English religious body by the Pope. That incorporation might be granted by statute appears never to have been doubted (Holdsworth, H.E.L., Vol. 3, p. 476) but in fact it was not until the latter part of the 18th century that it became the practice for Acts of Parliament actually to effect the incorporation. Until then statutes were used only to amplify the royal prerogative by authorising the Crown to confer a charter of incorporation with privileges beyond those which the Crown alone could confer (this was done, for example,

In the commercial sphere the principal medieval associations were the guilds of merchants, organisations which had few resemblances to modern companies but corresponded roughly to our trade protection associations, with the ceremonial and mutual fellowship of which we can see relics in the modern Freemasons and Livery Companies. Many of these guilds in due course obtained charters from the Crown, mainly because this was the only effective method of obtaining for their members a monopoly of any particular commodity or branch of trade. Incorporation as a convenient method of distinguishing the rights and liabilities of the association from those of its members was hardly needed since each member traded on his own account subject only to obedience to the regulations of the guild.

Trading on joint account, as opposed to individual trading subject to the rules of the guild, was carried on through partnerships, of which two types were known to the medieval law merchant. The first of these, the *commenda*, was in fact a cross between a partnership and a loan whereby a financier advanced a sum of money to the active trader upon terms that he should share in the profits of the enterprise, his position being similar to that of a sleeping partner but with no liability beyond that of the capital originally advanced. In continental law the *commenda* developed into the *société en commandite*, a form of association which has played, and still plays, an important part in the commercial life of those countries which adopted it. But in England it never took root, possibly because we lagged behind the Continent in book-keeping technique.[3] Had it become an accepted institution of English law the history of our company law might well have been very different, but in fact it did not become legalised here until 1907[4] by which time complete limitation of liability could be obtained easily and cheaply by incorporation under the Companies Act.

The other type of partnership was the *societas*, a more permanent form of association which developed into the present-day partnership, each partner being an agent of the others and liable to the full extent of his private fortune for partnership debts. The full implications of the partnership relationship were not fully worked out by courts of equity until the eighteenth and nineteenth centuries but these two main elements of agency and unlimited liability were already appreciated during this period.

---

in the case of the Bank of English and the South Sea Co.). DuBois (*op. cit.*, pp. 87 and 88) quotes examples of incorporation granted by Scottish burghs during the 18th century when the question also arose of the extent to which the royal prerogative could be delegated to colonial governors. As Sir Cecil Carr pointed out long ago (*Law of Corporations*, pp. 173 *et seq.*) the concession theory has worn somewhat thin now that incorporation can be obtained by mere registration.

[3] See Cooke, *op. cit.*, p. 46.

[4] Limited Partnerships Act 1907. It was adopted in Ireland by statute in 1781 and it seemed for a time that it might take root in Scotland: DuBois, *op. cit.* pp. 224–225.

Merchant adventurers

The first type of English organisation to which the name "company" was generally applied was that adopted by merchant adventurers for trading overseas. Royal charters conferring privileges on such companies are found as early as the fourteenth century,[5] but it was not until the expansion of foreign trade and settlement in the sixteenth century that they become common. The earliest types were the so-called "regulated companies" which were virtually extensions of the guild principle into the foreign sphere and which retained much of the ceremonial and freemasonry of the domestic guilds. Each member traded with his own stock and on his own account, subject to obeying the rules of the company, and incorporation was not essential since the trading liability of each member would be entirely separate from that of the company and the other members. Charters were nevertheless obtained largely because of the need to acquire a monopoly of trade for members of the company and governmental power over the territory for the company itself.[6]

At a later stage, however, the partnership principle of trading on joint account was adopted by the regulated companies which became joint commercial enterprises instead of trade protection associations.[7] At first, in addition to the separate trading by each member with his own stock, and later instead of it, they started to operate on joint account and with a joint stock.

This process can be traced in the development of the famous East India Company,[8] which received its first charter in 1600, granting it a monopoly of trade with the Indies. Originally any member could carry on that trade privately, although there also existed a joint stock to which members could, if they wished, subscribe varying amounts. At first this joint stock and the profits made from it were redivided among the subscribers after each voyage. From 1614 onwards, however, the joint stock was subscribed for a period of years, and this practice subsisted until 1653 when a permanent joint stock was introduced. It was not until 1692 that private trading was finally forbidden to members. Until this date, therefore, the constitution of the East India Co. represents a compromise between a regulated company, formed primarily for the government of a particular trade, and the more modern type of company, designed to trade for the profits of its members. This new type was called a joint stock[9] company, a name which persists

---

[5] See C.T. Carr, *Select Charters of Trading Corporations* (Selden Society), pp. xi–xii.

[6] See the charter of the Levant Company (1600) in Hahlo, *A Casebook of Company Law* (2nd ed.), p. 8.

[7] For an account of this development and a comparison with similar developments on the Continent, see Schmitthoff (1939) 3 Toronto L.J., pp. 74 *et seq.*

[8] See Scott, *op. cit.* Vol. II, pp. 89–206.

[9] "Stock" is, of course, here used in the same sense as in "stock in trade" and not as in "stocks and shares".

until the present day, although few of those who use it realise that it was adopted to distinguish the companies to which it relates from a once normal, but now obsolete, form.

Companies and incorporation

It was not until the second half of the seventeenth century that the differentiation between the two types of company was firmly established. Nor was there, until very much later, any clear distinction between unincorporated partnerships and incorporated companies. Many joint stock companies were originally formed as partnerships by agreement under seal, providing for the division of the undertaking into shares which were transferable by the original partners with greater or less freedom according to the terms of the partnership agreement. At this time there was no limit to the number of partners, but in fact they were generally small in number and additional capital was raised by "leviations" or calls on the existing members rather than by invitations to the public.

On the other hand, incorporation had certain clear advantages. A corporation was capable of existing in perpetuity, it could sue outsiders and its own members, and possession of a common seal facilitated the distinction between the acts of the company and those of its members. Although the transferability of shares was in practice procurable under a skilfully drafted deed of co-partnership, its legality, except under a power expressly conferred in a charter, was not free from doubt, for choses-in-action were not assignable at common law. However, the fact that shares were essentially a form of chose-in-action was not clearly recognised until later. The shares of the New River Company[10] were, for example, held to be realty,[11] and so they remained until the twentieth century.

Rather surprisingly the most important advantage of all those conferred by incorporation—limited liability—seems only to have been realised as an afterthought. The fact that an individual member of a corporation was not liable for its debts had been accepted in the case

[10] Which originated in a statute of 1606 (3 Jac. 1, c. 18), was granted a charter in 1619, and became subject to no fewer than 13 later statutes culminating in the Metropolis Water Act 1902 which expressly preserved its shares as realty (s.9(1)) Board. In pursuance of a further statute the company registered under the Companies Acts in 1905 and later became an investment trust company. (The "new river" which it created still flows.) For a full history of the company, see Rudden, *The New River* (1985, Clarendon Press).

[11] *Townsend v. Ash* (1745) 3 Atk. 336. The theory seems to have been that a corporation held its assets on trust for its members; *cf. Child v. Hudson's Bay Co.* (1723) 2 P. Wms. 207. Later equity went a stage further by recognising, both in partnerships and companies, and implied trust for conversation under which the shares became personalty irrespective of the nature of the firm's assets. In many charters and statutes of incorporation this conversion was expressly provided for; see Companies Clauses Consolidation Act 1845, s.7, and Companies Act 1985, s.182(1).

of non-trading corporations as early as the fifteenth century,[12] and, not without some doubts, it was eventually recognised at the end of this period in the case of trading companies.[13] But, although it was recognised, it appears at first to have been valued mainly because it avoided the risk of the company's property being seized in payment of the members' separate debts,[14] rather than as a method of enabling the members to escape liability for the company's debts. This doubtless was because many charters expressly conferred a power on the company to make "leviations" (or calls) on the members and it was by no means clear that a company did not have this power even in the absence of an express provision.[15] This being so, limited liability was illusory; the company as a person was liable to pay its debts and in order to raise money to do so it would make calls on its members. Moreover, the creditors, by a process resembling subrogation, could proceed directly against the members if the company refrained from taking the necessary action.[16] But legal ingenuity was not long in appreciating the possibilities of expressly excluding or limiting the company's power to make levies by agreement to that effect between the company and its members. Such agreements seem to have been in use by both incorporated and unincorporated companies, and the fact that they were effective only in the case of the former was probably not clearly grasped by lawyers and certainly not by investors.

Growth of domestic companies

By the middle of the seventeenth century powerful monopolistic companies were already coming to be regarded as anachronisms; it was realised that their governmental powers were properly the functions of the State itself and that their monopolies were an undue restraint on freedom of trade. Most of them atrophied; but some survived for a time by converting, as did the Levant and Russia companies, from the joint stock to the regulated form (a strange reversal of the normal trend designed to allow greater freedom to their members) and others, like the Royal Africa Company, by completely relinquishing their monopolies.[17] After the Revolution of 1688[18] it seems

---

[12] Holdsworth, H.E.L., Vol. 3, 484.

[13] *Edmunds v. Brown & Tillard* (1668) 1 Lev. 237; *Salmon v. The Hamborough Co.* (1671) 1 Ch.Cas 204, H.L.

[14] See the common form provision in petitions for charters quoted by Carr, *Select Charters*, pp. xvii, xviii.

[15] See DuBois, *op. cit.*, pp. 98 *et seq.*

[16] *Salmon v. The Hamborough Co.*, above. But for a criticism of this interpretation of the decision, see Jenkins [1975] C.L.J. 308

[17] The Hudson's Bay Company did not do so until 1869 and still survives as a chartered company. The East India Co. also survived until the middle of the nineteenth century but as a State organ rather than as a trading concern.

[18] Previously it seems to have been assumed that the *Case of Monopolies* (1602) 11 Co.Rep. 84b, and the Statute of Monopolies 1623, had left unimpaired the Crown's power to grant a

to have been tacitly assumed that the Crown's prerogative was limited to the right to grant a charter of incorporation, and that any monopolistic or other special powers should be conferred by statute.[19]

The decline in the foreign-trading companies was, however, accompanied by an immense growth in those for domestic trade. Some of these were powerful corporations chartered under statutory powers (such as the Bank of England[20]) the objects of which resembled those of the public corporations of the present day, but most were public companies in the sense that they invited the participation of the investing public. As regards these, the close relation between incorporation and monopoly was still maintained, for most companies were incorporated in order to work a patent of monopoly granted to an inventor.[21]

By the end of the seventeenth century some idea had been gleaned of one of the primary functions of the company concept—the possibility of enabling the capitalist to combine with the entrepreneur. Share dealings were common and stock-broking was a recognised profession, the abuses of which the legislature sought to regulate as early as 1696.[22] But it would be entirely misleading to suggest that there was in any sense a company law; at the most there was an embryonic law of partnership which applied to those companies which had not become incorporated and, with modifications required by the terms of the charter and the nature of incorporation, to those which had. Both deeds of partnership (or "settlement", to use the later term) and charters owed much to the practices of the medieval guilds, particularly as regards the constitution of the governing body which generally consisted of a governor and assistant governors. From the end of the seventeenth century the term "directors" began to supersede "assistant governors". But the terminology varied and still varies.[23] It is interesting to note that although the invention of preference shares is generally attributed to the railway boom a century later, certain companies had already experimented with different classes of shares or of loan stock[24] (for the distinction between shares and debentures was not appreciated until much later).

---

monopoly for the regulation of foreign trade and this power had been upheld by the H.L. in 1684 in *East India Co. v. Sandys*, 10 St.Tr. 371. But *cf. Horne v. Ivy* (1668) 1 Ventr. 47, showing that the courts were already placing limitations on the extent of its exercise.

[19] Even earlier this had become the practice in the case of domestic companies requiring special powers; for example, the New River Co. (see n. 10, above).

[20] Incorporated, by charter preceded by statute, in 1694.

[21] See Cooke, *op. cit.*, Chap. 4.

[22] 8 & 9 Wm. 3, c. 32. It is interesting to note that this legislation followed a report of the Commissioners for Trade (the forerunners of the Board (later the Department) of Trade) which seems to be the first instance of this Department interesting itself in a branch of company law (see p. 34, below).

[23] Thus the Bank of England, the B.B.C. and most incorporated schools and colleges still employ the term "Governors" while some corporations use the expression "Managers".

[24] Scott, *op. cit.* Vol. I, pp. 364–365.

The South Sea Bubble

The first and second decades of the eighteenth century were marked by an almost frenetic boom in company flotations which led to the famous South Sea Bubble.[25] Most company promoters were not particularly fussy about whether they obtained charters (an expensive and dilatory process), and those who felt it desirable to give their projects this hallmark of respectability found it simpler and cheaper to acquire charters from moribund companies which were able to do a brisk trade therein.[26] An insurance company acquired the charters of the Mines Royal and the Mineral and Battery Works, and a company which proposed to lend money on land in Ireland and a banking partnership[27] in turn acquired the charter of the Sword Blade Company which had been formed to manufacture hollow sword blades.

Impetus was given to this boom by the grandiose scheme of the South Sea Company to acquire virtually the whole of the National Debt[28] (some £31 million) by buying out the holders or persuading them to exchange their holdings for the company's stock, the theory being that the possession of an interest-bearing loan owed by the State was a basis upon which the company might raise vast sums to extend its trade. This theory was not necessarily unsound—it was indeed a logical extension of the principle upon which the Bank of England, and the South Sea Company itself, had been originally formed—but unfortunately the company had precious little trade to expand. Moreover, it had to pay dearly for its privileges by outbidding and outbribing the Bank of England.[29]

When the flood of speculative enterprises was at its height, Parliament decided to intervene to check the gambling mania which the Government had itself encouraged by sanctioning the South Sea Company's scheme. Its attempt was, however, somewhat inept. A House

---

[25] The literature on the Bubble crisis is, of course, immense; the most scholarly treatment is still that of Scott, *op. cit.* Vol. I, Chaps. XXI and XXII. For popular accounts, see Carswell, *The South Sea Bubble* (Lond., 1960), and Cowell, *The Great Swindle* (Lond., 1960).

[26] We cannot afford to scoff at our predecessors, for a trade is still done in dormant companies. Two centuries hence, a generation which, for tax reasons, was prepared to pay more for those with accumulated losses will probably appear just as ridiculous.

[27] Which thereupon issued "sword blade" notes and bonds, and acted as bankers for the South Sea Company.

[28] The company was originally formed, by charter preceded by statute, in 1711, to incorporate the holders of the floating debt in exchange for a monopoly of trade with South America, a right which the power of Spain rendered something of a *damnosa hereditas*. The extended scheme seems to have been inspired by the financial experiments known as the Mississippi System introduced in France, with equally disastrous results, by John Law.

[29] It is interesting to speculate on what might have happened had the Bank of England outbid the company. Perhaps it would have been the former whose bubble reputation was so soon pricked, and the latter which acquired the mantle of respectability (with the final canon of nationalisation) in fact worn by "the old lady of Threadneedle Street".

of Commons Resolution[30] of April 27, 1720 ignored the causes and merely emphasised the effects of the rash speculation by drawing attention to the numerous undertakings which were purporting to act as corporate bodies without legal authority, practices which "manifestly tend to the prejudices of the public trade and commerce of the Kingdom". This was followed by the so-called Bubble Act[31] of the same year, which also made no attempt to put joint stock companies on a proper basis so as to further industry and trade and protect investors. Exactly what it did is, however, somewhat obscure.

The main section, 18, repeated the Resolution of the House of Commons and provided that all such undertakings as were therein described, "tending to the common Grievance, Prejudice and Inconvenience of His Majesty's subjects", should be illegal and void. The section then proceeded to give particular examples, namely the acting as a corporate body and the raising of transferable stock or the transfer of any shares therein without legal authority either by Act of Parliament or Crown charter, or acting or pretending to act under any obsolete charter. By section 21, brokers dealing in securities of illegal companies were to be liable to penalties. The remaining sections, however, exempted companies established before June 24, 1718 (which were therefore left to the common law, whatever that may have been), and also the East India and South Sea Companies and the two assurance companies authorised by the first part of the Act. Finally, in section 25, there was a vague proviso that nothing "shall extend . . . to prohibit or restrain the carrying on of any home or foreign trade in partnership in such manner as hath been hitherto usually and may be lawfully done according to the Laws of this Realm now in force".

This statute was our first attempt at a Companies Act[32] and it clearly reflected little credit on anyone concerned with it. As Holdsworth says,[33] "What was needed was an Act which made it easy for joint stock societies to adopt a corporate form and, at the same time, safeguarded both the shareholders in such societies and the public against frauds and negligence in their promotion and management. What was passed was an Act which deliberately made it difficult for joint stock societies to assume a corporate form and contained no rules at all for the conduct of such societies, if, and when, they assumed it." But in

---

[30] H.C. Jour. XIX, 351. This resolution was based upon the Report of a Committee appointed on 22 Feb. to inquire into certain of the projects: for its Report, see *ibid.*, pp. 341, *et seq.*

[31] 6 Geo. 1, c 18. This prolix and confusing statute, which, as Maitland said, "seems to scream at us from the Statute Book" (*Collected Papers*, Vol. 3, p. 390), is divided into two parts. The first (ss. 1–17) authorised the incorporation of the London and Royal Exchange Assurance Companies with a monopoly of the corporate insurance of marine risks. It is with the later sections only that we are at present concerned.

[32] Or, perhaps, more properly, a Prevention of Fraud (Investments) Act, such as that of 1939 or 1958.

[33] H.E.L., Vol. 8, pp. 219–220.

fact the authorities were faced with a new phenomenon and had no clear idea of the issues involved. Nor is it altogether fair to blame them; a further 120 years' experience was to be needed before anything on the right lines was enacted, and even today we find it necessary to amend our company law every few years. It was obviously too much to expect the Parliament of 1720 to rush through a Companies Act comparable to that of 1985 or even 1844. Where they seem most blameworthy is not for what they omitted to do, but for the vagueness of what they in fact did, and when the courts were called upon to interpret it they found it vague indeed. But this they were not called upon to do for many years.

The Bubble bursts

The passage of the Bubble Act, to which publicity was given by Royal Proclamation, and the events leading up to it must obviously have done much to sap public confidence. But what precipitated the disastrous collapse of 1720 was the institution of proceedings against some of the companies operating under obsolete charters with a view to these being forfeited.[34] This, as might perhaps have been foreseen,[35] led to a widespread panic from which the South Sea Company itself never fully recovered.[36] In June 1720 its stock had stood at over 1,000 per cent and immediately before the issue of the writs it was still at 850 per cent A month later it had fallen to 390 and by the end of the year it was quoted at 125. The Government was too much involved to allow the company to crash completely,[37] but the subsequent investigations disclosed fraud and corruption (in which members of the Government and the royal household were implicated) which ruined the company's reputation. With it fell many of its contemporaries, which, not being regularly chartered nor so fortunate as to have friends in high places, burst like the bubbles they were. But, although they disappeared, they were not forgotten, for public confidence in joint stock

---

[34] For an account of these proceedings and an attempted refutation of the generally accepted theory that they were instituted by the South Sea Company or its directors, see (1952) 68 L.Q.R. 214.

[35] Although the legitimacy of the birth of the South Sea Company was beyond reproach, it was employing as its bankers a company incorporated under the Sword Blade Charter. The failure of these bankers was one of the factors which frustrated the efforts to arrest the panic by an agreement between the South Sea Company and the Bank of England.

[36] The third volume of Scott, *op. cit.* contains a graph showing the fluctuations in the shares of the South Sea Company, the East India Company and the Bank of England between May and September 1720.

[37] In the words of Holdsworth (H.E.L., Vol. 2, p. 210) it "dragged out a struggling existence till 1807; and the faded splendours of its South Sea House survived long enough to secure immortality in the Essays of Elia". Later that House became for a time the home of the Baltic Exchange, and a building in the City of London bearing the name South Sea House survived the blitz of the Second World War more successfully than the company survived the financial "blitz" of an earlier century.

companies and their securities was destroyed so effectively that it was three-quarters of a century before there was a comparable boom. If the legislators had intended the Bubble Act to suppress companies they had succeeded beyond their reasonable expectations; if, as seems more probable, they had intended to protect investors from ruin and to safeguard the South Sea Company, they had failed miserably.

Prosecutions under the Act were few; only one[38] is reported until the beginning of the nineteenth century.[39] Nevertheless, it is clear that the Bubble Act was for long a sword of Damocles which exercised a restraining influence as potent as the memory of the great slump. DuBois's researches[40] have shown how existing companies and the promoters of new enterprises took counsel's opinion on the application to them of the Act, and it is to this Act that he attributes the first traces of the dominant part subsequently played by lawyers in the development of company law and practice.

Effect on incorporations

Joint stock companies did not disappear completely. On the contrary, many regularly chartered companies and a few unincorporated ones[41] had survived the panic and were living examples of the advantages of this type of organisation. Others, too, still succeeded in obtaining charters; but not many, for a lasting effect of the Bubble Act and the crisis of 1720 was to make the Law Officers of the Crown chary of advising the grant of charters,[42] and to insist on restrictive conditions in those that were granted.[43]

Nor at first was Parliament any more complaisant. It was not until towards the end of the century, with the growth of canal building, which necessarily involved an application to Parliament for special powers, that Parliament became less strict in its requirements and that

---

[38] *R. v. Cawood* (1724) 2 Ld.Raym. 1361. It decided nothing of importance on the interpretation of the Act.

[39] But contemporary news-sheets make it clear that others were instituted.

[40] *op. cit.*, pp. 3 *et seq.* He refers particularly to the influence of Sjt Pengelly who is known to have delivered opinions (which still survive) on no fewer than 27 companies and whose views foreshadow the judicial interpretation adopted in the succeeding century. Dubois's book, to which the author is greatly indebted, is not as well known as it deserves to be.

[41] Including the Sun Fire Office, established in 1709.

[42] For an account of the difficulties which company promoters had to surmount, see Dubois, *op. cit.*, pp. 12 *et seq.* "The law officers of the Crown, mindful of [the Act's] provisions, hesitated to approve of applications for charters which contemplated the creation of large stocks of transferable shares. Consequently, not only were the operations of unincorporated joint stock companies restricted by the Act, but the Act was used as an expression of policy to restrain the formation of business corporations": *ibid.*, p. 12.

[43] *ibid.* To this period can be traced conditions restricting the amount of capital which the company might raise. A further restraint on joint enterprise arose from the habit, introduced after 1720, of inserting in patents of invention prohibitions on assignment to more than five persons; *ibid.* pp. 21–24.

direct statutory incorporations became common.[44] It is to this statutory incorporation that we owe many of the features of modern companies: in particular the method of limiting liability of the members to the nominal value of their shares.

Hence throughout the century (and beyond) the shadow of 1720 retarded the development of incorporated companies. The official view is well represented by the oft-quoted words of Adam Smith,[45] writing as late as 1776, in which he stated that a joint stock company was an appropriate type of organisation only for those trades which could be reduced to a routine, namely, those of banking, fire and marine insurance, making and maintaining canals, and bringing water to cities; others, in his view, were bound to be inefficient as businesses as well as being contrary to the public interest. The great man thereby put the seal of his approval on the current legislative and administrative practice, for the authorities, in their wisdom, had incorporated precisely these four types and had (with rare exceptions) refused to incorporate others.

Resurgence of unincorporated companies

Had the authorities granted incorporation more readily, already in the eighteenth century incorporated companies might have become the dominant type of commercial enterprise. And had that policy been adopted, the Government, by its control over charters and statutes, could have shaped the development of company law 150 years earlier than it seriously attempted to do so. Instead, as we have seen, the authorities placed almost insuperable difficulties in the way of incorporation and left it to businessmen and their legal advisers to find an alternative device. This they found in the unincorporated association; paradoxically, the Bubble Act in the end caused a rebirth of the very type of association which it had sought to destroy. The history of the previous period had shown that it was perfectly feasible to trade with a joint stock without incorporation, and although the Bubble Act had struck at unincorporated companies it had expressly exempted partnerships carried on "in such manner as hath been hitherto usually and may be lawfully done".[46] This exemption clearly could not have covered every type of unincorporated company, for otherwise the Act became completely meaningless, but exactly how far partnerships could lawfully go was far from clear. The size of the membership could not be the decisive factor, for at this time there was not and never had been any upper limit on numbers.[47] Professional opinion at

---

[44] Over 100 statutory incorporations occurred during the last 40 years of the eighteenth century.

[45] *Wealth of Nations*, vol. V, Chap. 1, Pt. III, Art. 1.

[46] s.25.

[47] Except in the case of banking, as regards which the Bank of England's monopoly was protected by a prohibition, under a statute of 1708 (7 Anne, c. 30), of banking in England by

the time[48] took the view, in fact adopted by the courts in the nineteenth century, that the basic test of illegality was the existence of freely transferable shares and for a time such unincorporated associations as were formed (and the shock of the crash of 1720 caused there to be few for many years) were careful to place severe restrictions on transfers.[49] But from the middle of the century onwards it is clear that unincorporated joint stock companies, often with a large number of proprietors,[50] were operating to a gradually increasing extent and that (as the Bubble Act came to be regarded as a dead letter) complete freedom of transfer of shares was assumed to be permissible.

The deed of settlement company

Legal ingenuity enabled these unincorporated associations to operate with many of the advantages of incorporation by use of trusts.[51] The company would be formed under a "deed of settlement" (approximating to a cross between the modern articles of association and a trust deed for debentures or unit trusts) under which the subscribers would agree to be associated in an enterprise with a prescribed joint stock divided into a specified number of shares; the provisions of the deed would be variable with the consent of a specified majority of the proprietors; management would be delegated to a committee of directors; and the company's property would be vested in a separate body of trustees,[52] some of whom would often be directors also. Usually it would be provided that these trustees could sue or be sued on behalf of the company, and although the legal efficacy of such a provision was by no means clear, suit by the trustees in a court of equity seems to have been generally permitted.[53] As for liability to be sued, it will be appreciated that obscurity on this point was by no means an unmixed disadvantage from the point of view of the company.

Long before the end of the century certain types of commercial activity were dominated by companies organised on this basis, which, strangely enough, seems to have been encouraged rather than frowned

more than five persons in association. And under the first part of the Bubble Act itself the London and Royal Exchange Assurances had a monopoly of insuring marine risks by companies or societies.

[48] See DuBois, *op. cit*, pp. 3 *et seq.*

[49] In the light of this it is interesting to note that unincorporated companies were often described as "private" companies, in contradistinction to the incorporated "public" company; restriction on transfer was until 1980 an essential feature of the 20th-century private company. Use of the term "public company" to describe those formally incorporated is found in a statute of 1767 (7 Geo. 3, c. 48), which struck at the practice of splitting shareholdings to increase voting power, by disqualifying members from voting until they had held their shares for six months.

[50] The true extent of the numbers was sometimes disguised by the device of subpartnerships, *i.e.* the original few shares would be subsequently subdivided; see Dubois, *op. cit.*, pp. 78–79.

[51] For details, see *ibid.*, Chap. III.

[52] This was by no means unusual even in the case of incorporated companies: *ibid.*, pp. 115–116.

[53] In practice considerable use was made of arbitration: *ibid.*, p. 221.

upon by the Government, for frequent examples are found of refusal by the Law Officers to recommend charters of incorporation on the ground that "coparcenary" was a more appropriate form of organisation.[54] Unincorporated associations had a virtual monopoly of the growing activity of non-marine[55] insurance, both by companies trading for the profit of their members (where the old Sun had formed the model for the Phoenix, Norwich General, Norwich Union and a host of others) and by mutual and friendly societies.[56] They were also used extensively in the metal industries and the theatre, and were even used at times in canal building where statutory incorporation was more common. Indeed, the researches of DuBois into the eighteenth-century company records and counsel's opinions have made it clear that the use of joint stock companies was far more widespread than had hitherto been supposed on the basis of the paucity of incorporations and of reported cases on unincorporated companies.

On the other hand, we have to wait until the nineteenth century for any outbreak of speculation in shares comparable to that of 1720. Although the mechanism of the stock market was well understood and several rather half-hearted attempts were made by the legislature to check its abuses,[57] company shares do not seem to have been generally regarded as suitable investments or gambling counters[58] for the lay public, but rather as means of enabling members of the mercantile community to acquire a permanent stake in enterprises with which they were familiar. But the picture changed at the turn of the century, when first the exigencies of war and then the growth of the railways

[54] Thus on the Equitable Assurance petition in 1761 the Att.-Gen. (Yorke) said: "If the Petitioners are so sure of success there is an easy method of making the experiment by entering into a voluntary partnership of which there are several instances now subsisting in the business of insuring": quoted in DuBois, *op. cit.*, p. 30. Having regard to the size of these enterprises the Law Officers can hardly have been so naive as to suppose that the "partnership" would be other than on a joint stock basis. Indeed petitions were often made by existing unincorporated companies and it was unknown for such companies to take the opinion of the Law Officers on questions relating to their constitutions: *ibid.*, p. 313, n. 35 (Law Officers at that time were not forbidden to undertake private practice).

[55] The first part of the Bubble Act had given the London and Royal Exchange Assurance companies a monopoly of marine assurance by associations. During this period the value of this monopoly was diminished by individual insurances by underwriters who assembled at Lloyd's Coffee House and grew into the famous "Lloyd's of London" which was eventually incorporated, although policies continue to be underwritten not by the corporation but by individual underwriters.

[56] Friendly Societies became so common that they were authorised by statute in 1793 (33 Geo. 3, c. 54), the first general authorising Act from which sprang not only the modern Friendly Society but also Industrial and Provident Societies, and Building Societies. Under the Act the rules had to be approved by the local justices, who probably enjoyed ratifying the rule of the Beneficent Society of Tinwold (1793) that "None shall be admitted into this Society who are suspected of being friendly to the new fangled doctrines of LIBERTY AND EQUALITY AND THE RIGHTS OF MAN as set forth by Thomas Paine and his adherents."

[57] 7 Geo. 1, stat. 2, No. 8 (1721); 7 Geo. 2, c. 8 (1733); and 10 Geo. 2, c. 8 (1736).

[58] During the 18th century the lotteries met this need. Their abolition in 1826 under the Lotteries Act 1823 may well have encouraged share speculation. On these early lotteries, see J. Ashton, *A History of English Lotteries* (Lond., 1893), a most entertaining book.

led to an outbreak of company promotion and of general speculation comparable to that of the Bubble period. It was only then that the inherent disadvantages of the unincorporated type became fully apparent.

Disadvantages of unincorporation

As we have seen, one difficulty related to the power to sue or be sued. In law, these unincorporated companies were partnerships,[59] and this was before the time when legislation permitted suit in the firm's name. Actions at law[60] had to be brought by or against all the partners, and the difficulties[61] which this caused (particularly when there had been changes in the shareholdings) can be imagined. The only satis-factory, but expensive, solution was the promotion of a private Act of Parliament permitting the company to sue or be sued in the name of one or more of its officials. Such Acts became common towards the end of this period,[62] and the right was conferred on friendly societies by the (Public) Act of 1793. As will be appreciated, the members of the company would probably be concerned only with the possibility of suing and would be happy to find obstacles in the way of being sued, particularly as they would be personally liable without limita-tion.

This brings us to the second and most important disadvantage of the absence of incorporation—the members could not limit their personal liability. Until late in the century limited liability still seems to have been regarded as only a secondary consideration; DuBois[63] finds the earliest clear recognition of it as the motive for incorporation in the petition for incorporation by the Warmley Company in 1768. But increasingly from then on it became openly recognised as a factor of prime importance and one which incorporation alone could fully achieve. Unincorporated companies could strive to approximate to it by expressly contracting in every case that liability should be limited to the funds of the company—a solution only practicable where the contracts were of a formal type such as insurance,[64] for it was gener-

---

[59] But even the law could not shut its eyes to all the differences between a large company and a simple partnership. A shareholder in the former could obviously not bind the company, as a partner could the firm; anyone dealing with the company must be deemed to know that powers of management were restricted to the directors. Here we can detect the germ of the later rule in *Royal British Bank v. Turquand*; see Chap. 10, below.

[60] As we have seen, equity was somewhat more lenient and, even at common law if the contract was with the trustees, they could sue on it for the benefit of the company: *Metcalfe v. Brian* (1810) 12 East 400.

[61] They are well described in *George on Companies* (1825), pp. 19 *et seq.*, quoted by Formoy, *op. cit.*, pp. 33 *et seq.*

[62] DuBois, *op. cit.*, p. 142, quotes an example as early as 1730 but this was exceptional.

[63] *op. cit.*, p. 95.

[64] In the 19th century these stipulations became customary in the policies of unincorporated offices. Such an express contract was ultimately held to be effective: *Hallet v. Dowdall* (1852) 21 L.J.Q.B. 98.

ally believed that a statement to this effect in the deed of settlement
would be ineffective even if the creditor had notice of it.[65] Or, of
course, they could make a virtue of necessity, as did the Phoenix
Assurance which, when its rival, the incorporated Royal Exchange
Assurance, boasted of the advantages to policy-holders of a ready
remedy against the corporate stock, retorted by emphasising the
advantages to the public of the full responsibility of its members.[66]

In truth, however, unlimited liability, though a danger to the risk-
taker, was often a snare and a delusion rather than a protection to the
public and no handicap at all to the dishonest promoter. The difficulties of suing a fluctuating body and the even greater difficulties of
levying execution[67] made the personal liability of the members largely
illusory. Moreover, the investor was supposed to become a member
by signing the deed of settlement and until he did so his identity would
not be known by the creditors. But in fact "stags" would deal in
allotment letters or scrip certificates to bearer without signing the deed
and often before any formal deed was in existence, and dishonest
promoters, who alone might be under any legal liability, might disappear with the subscription moneys.[68] Many promotions were still-born
and others perished with the slumps[69] which followed each successive
boom. Some intervention by the State was inevitable but the question
was what form it should take.

State intervention

The first form was the characteristic English expedient of reviving
an old remedy—in this case prosecution under the almost forgotten
Bubble Act. In November 1807 the Attorney-General (at the instance
of a private relator) sought a criminal information against two recently
formed unincorporated companies,[70] both of which had freely transferable shares and advertised that the liability of the members would be
limited. Lord Ellenborough[71] dismissed the applications because of the
lapse of 87 years since the Act was previously invoked, but he issued
a stern warning that no one in the future could pretend that the statute
was obsolete and indicated that a "speculative project founded on

---

[65] But statements alleging limited liability were commonplace in both deeds of settlement and prospectuses: see Hunt, *op. cit.*, pp. 33–34, 72 and 99–101. They were eventually held to be ineffective in *Re Sea, Fire & Life Insurance Co.* (1854) 3 De G.M. & G. 459.

[66] DuBois, *op. cit.*, p. 96.

[67] These difficulties are well explained in Formoy, *op. cit.*, pp. 35 *et seq.* They did not disappear even it there was a private Act permitting the company to be sued in the name of its officers.

[68] The opportunities for fraud thus provided are immortalised by Charles Dickens's account of the "Anglo-Bengalee Disinterested Loan and Life Assurance Company" in the pages of *Martin Chuzzlewit*.

[69] These occurred particularly in 1808, 1825–1826, and 1844–1845: see Hunt, *op. cit.*, *passim*.

[70] The London Paper Manufacturing Co. and the London Distillery Co.

[71] *R. v. Dodd* (1808) 9 East 516.

joint stock or transferable shares" was prohibited.[72] Shortly afterwards two further associations were held illegal, apparently because their shares were transferable.[73]

These decisions caused alarm among investors and promoters and were probably contributory causes of the slump of 1808. However, despite further prosecutions, confidence was gradually restored and the years 1824–1825 witnessed a boom which was compared with that of 1719–1720 and which was followed by a similar slump. The various court cases[74] did little to clarify the law; the better view seemed to be that a company with freely transferable shares was illegal, but that one where the right to transfer was restricted was unlawful only if it had "a mischievous tendency". On the other hand, there were many who were opposed to the whole concept of joint stock enterprise, both incorporated and unincorporated, and until the middle of the nineteenth century bitter debates continued in which the virtues of healthy private enterprise were contrasted with the dead hand of monopolistic companies.[75] Lord Eldon, in particular, attacked the latter in both his legislative and judicial capacity. In the former he announced his intention of introducing further restrictive legislation but finally dropped this idea on the ground that the law as it stood was sufficiently strict.[76] Had his view of it prevailed, it certainly would have been strict, for he was apparently prepared to hold that assuming to act as a corporation[77] was an offence at common law as well as under the Act.[78]

Finally, the Government felt compelled to do something to bring the law more into accord with the facts; but just as their predecessors in 1720 could think of nothing more constructive than the Bubble Act, so now they could think of nothing better than its repeal. In 1825, its Indian summer was finally ended. The repealing statute[79] was spon-

---

[72] *ibid.*, at 526–528.

[73] *Buck v. Buck* (1808) 1 Camp. 547 and *R. v. Stratton* (1809) 1 Camp. 549n. As we have seen (above, p. 27, n. 40) this had been Sjt Pengelly's view.

[74] They were summarised by Hunt, *op. cit.*, Chaps. II and III, and in Cooke, *op. cit.*, Chaps. VII. The most instructive of those reported are: *R. v. Webb* (1811) 14 East 406; *Pratt v. Hutchinson* (1812) 15 East 511; *Josephs v. Pebrer* (1825) 3 B. & C. 639; and *Kinder v. Taylor* (1825) 3 L.J.Ch. 68. See further *Lindley on Companies* (6th ed., London, 1902), pp. 180–184.

[75] Accounts of these will be found in Hunt, *op. cit.*, passim. The arguments used by the supporters of "private" (as opposed to corporate) enterprise were astonishingly reminiscent of those later used by the opponents of nationalisation.

[76] Hunt, *op. cit.*, pp. 38 and 39.

[77] But Eldon himself was unable to give any clear account of what this meant. The Inns of Court come close to acting as corporations, even to the extent, or so it is generally said, of using common seals and this seems to have impressed Eldon and acted as a restraining influence: see *Lloyd v. Loaring* (1802) 6 Ves. 773 at 779. But query if the Inns do, in fact, use common seals: see Lloyd, *Law of Unincorporated Associations*, p. 51, n. (c).

[78] He did not get a very good press; the Morning Chronicle said it confirmed their view that his opinions "as a Politician were seldom worth much": March 30, 1825, quoted by Hunt, *op. cit.*, p. 39.

[79] 6 Geo. 4, c. 91. The marine insurance monopoly had been repealed a year earlier: 5 Geo. 4, c. 114.

sored by Huskisson, the President of the Board of Trade, and it is then that this Government Department first started to take an active part in the development of company law.

Influence of the Board of Trade

The Board[80] was the successor of the Commissioners for Trade and Plantations, the history of which, as an ad hoc or standing Committee of the Privy Council, can be traced back to the beginning of the seventeenth century and whose report on stock-jobbing in 1696 led to the first legislative attempt[81] to regulate brokers. Throughout the eighteenth century examples can be found of references to the Commissioners of petitions for charters of incorporation,[82] especially in cases where the object was colonial trade (for at this time the greater part of the Commissioners' work was concerned with the colonies rather than with domestic trade). But, in general, decisions were taken by the Law Officers[83] (which in practice must often have meant the Attorney-General's "devil"[84]) and it was not until the Board was re-created by Pitt in 1784 that the emphasis changed and that it gradually came to be recognised that the Board was the appropriate Government Department to advise on incorporations and to guide the development of company law. Since Huskisson repealed the Bubble Act a century-and-a-half ago, the Board, until it ceased to have an independent existence in 1970,[85] was responsible for all company legislation and was entrusted with gradually increasing supervisory powers over joint stock enterprises. It is appropriate that its first major intervention should have been an act of liberation rather than of control, for its policy throughout had been to allow the greatest possible freedom to

---

[80] The influence of the Board has been largely ignored by writers on the history of company law. For accounts of the Board's development, which, however, say little about its functions in connection with companies, see Llewellyn Smith, *The Board of Trade* (The Whitehall Series, 1928) and Prouty, *The Transformation of the Board of Trade 1830–1855* (Lond., 1957).

[81] 8 & 9 Wm. 3, c. 32.

[82] See DuBois, *op. cit.*, pp. 13, 57, 58, 60, 62, 66, 69, 70, 89 and 172. There are also occasional examples of applications to the Commissioners for investigation of the affairs of existing companies: *ibid.*, p. 126.

[83] DuBois, *op. cit.*, pp. 169–170, n. 135 says: "The usual procedure in the case of an application for incorporation was the presentation of a petition to the Privy Council. The Privy Council would refer the matter to a subcommittee, which, if it were favourably inclined to the plan after consideration, would submit the petition to the Attorney-General or Solicitor-General. On occasion the Commissioners of Trade and Planations would be consulted."

[84] Napier, *A Century of Law Reform* (Lond., 1901), p. 389.

[85] On the creation of the Department of Trade and Industry in 1970 it absorbed the Board but left it in existence, the Secretary of State for Trade and Industry retaining the additional title of President of the Board: S.I. 1970 No. 1537. In 1974 the Department split into separate Departments of Trade and of Industry which combined again in 1983. Today, some of its functions have been devolved to executive agencies, notably Companies House and the Insolvency Service.

private enterprise. As its official historian[86] rightly says: "Broadly speaking the part played by the Board of Trade in relation to the movement which has revolutionised the structure of industry has been that of a vigilant onlooker rather than of a continuous supervisor."

[86] Llewellyn Smith, *op. cit.*, p. 168.

CHAPTER 3

HISTORY OF COMPANY LAW SINCE 1825

Twenty years' vacillation

THE repeal, like the enactment, of the Bubble Act was followed by a disastrous slump further emphasising the need for some constructive measures of control. These, however, were still lacking; the only real advance made by the 1825 Act was a provision[1] enabling the Crown to declare the extent of the member's liability on the grant of charters, so that charters were no longer necessarily accompanied by a complete absence of liability on the part of the members for the company's debts. This provision might have been expected to encourage greater freedom in the grant of charters, but in fact the authorities remained as strict as ever. Applications for statutory incorporation, stimulated by the boom in railway promotion, fared better but their expense was prohibitive except in the case of the largest concerns.[2]

Hence, most promoters were thrown back on the unincorporated form, the legality of which was still in doubt, especially as Eldon had secured the inclusion in the repealing Act of an express recital that undertakings should be adjudged and dealt with according to common law. It was not until 1843 that it became reasonably clear what their position was at common law,[3] and even then little had been done to remove the disadvantages under which they laboured. But, despite these handicaps, joint stock banks,[4] insurance companies and a host

---

[1] s.2.
[2] Hunt, *The Development of the Business Corporation in England, 1800–1867* (Harvard Economic Studies, 1936) p. 82, quotes two railway incorporations which cost £72,868 and £40,588. Even the fees for a charter amounted to at least £402 which was a substantial sum in those days: *ibid.* The Report on Investments for the Savings of the Middle and Working Classes (1850 B.P.P., Vol. XIX, 169) quoted a chartered incorporation costing £1,134 which was alleged (surely mistakenly?) to be "greater even than that of obtaining an Act of Parliament".
[3] *Garrard v. Hardey* (1843) 5 M. & G. 471; *Harrison v. Heathorn* (1843) 6 M. & G. 81; not following *Duvergier v. Fellows* (1832) 5 Bing. 248 and *Blundell v. Winsor* (1835) 8 Sim. 601. Brougham L.C. on the Bench took a more liberal view than his predecessor (*Walburn v. Ingilby* (1832) 1 Myl. & K. 61) although in the House he was almost equally reactionary on this matter and received an equally unfavourable press. "The commercial part of the community have little reason to thank God, with Cobbett, that there is a House of Lord, and above all Brougham": *Morning Chronicle*, August 15, 1838 (cited in Hunt, *op. cit*, p. 84)— a reference to the prosecution of Cobbett in 1831 for criminal libel when he subpoenaed six members of the House of Lords and secured an acquittal largely because of the evidence of Brougham L.C.
[4] Guided by the experience of Scotland (where joint stock banks had flourished in contrast with the failures of the English private concerns) the monopoly of the Bank of England was whittled away by Acts of 1826 (7 Geo. 4, c. 46) and 1833 (3 & 4 Wm. 4, c. 98). These Acts

of other projects flourished as never before and joint stock companies came to play an important role in every part of the country's economy. Clearly some steps had to be taken to remove the legal confusion.

The first step was taken by the Trading Companies Act of 1834, which was intended to extend slightly the availability of corporate advantages. It empowered the Crown to confer by letters patent any of the privileges of incorporation without actually granting a charter, thus, in particular, obviating the need for special Acts enabling companies to sue and be sued in the names of their officers.[5] The major importance of this compromise was that it was the first general Act requiring public registration of members, but it contained no express provision that the letters patent might limit the members' liability and, indeed, expressly provided that judgments against the company should, with leave of the court, be enforceable against every member until three years after he had ceased to be a member. Moreover, its practical value was much diminished by the restrictive rules which the Board of Trade laid down for the granting of petitions under it.[6]

In 1837 the Board of Trade instructed a Chancery barrister, H. Bellenden Ker, to prepare a report on the law of partnership with particular reference to the expediency of introducing limited partnerships on the continental model.[7] His report[8] was pigeon-holed and the only result was the re-enactment of the 1834 Act in the Chartered Companies Act of 1837 but with the valuable clarification that personal liability of members might be limited by the letters patent to a specified amount per share. In the ensuing 17 years some 50 companies did in fact form under this Act, but most still preferred to rely on the *de facto* protection from personal liability conferred by the difficulties of suing and levying execution on the members of a fluctuating body. Many of these were from their inception fraudulent shams, particularly the bogus assurance companies such as those pilloried by Dickens in *Martin Chuzzlewit*,[9] and it was primarily the existence of these which led the Board of Trade to secure the appointment in 1841

---

provided that banking companies could sue or be sued in the names of their officers and, in anticipation of the Act of 1844, provided for registration of certain essential particulars.

[5] The difficulties with which a suitor might otherwise be faced have already been stressed; they are well exemplified in *Van Sandau v. Moore* (1825) 1 Russell 441, in which Lord Eldon, at 472, gave this as this principal justification for holding unincorporated companies to be illegal.

[6] They are quoted by Hunt, *op. cit.*, pp. 57–58. The progressive Huskisson had retired from the Board in 1827, and in 1830 had lost his life in an accident at the opening of the Liverpool and Manchester railway—a victim of the railway boom which he had himself done so much to promote. In the words of a contemporary poet:

"This fatal chance not only caused delay
But damped the joy that erst had crowned the day"!

T. Baker: *The Steam Engine*, canto X.

[7] John Austin was a staunch advocate of this proposal: see *1825 Parliamentary History and Review*, p. 711.

[8] 1837 B.P.P., Vol. XLIV, 399.

[9] First published in 1843.

of a Parliamentary Committee on Joint Stock Companies. In 1843
Gladstone, who had become President of the Board of Trade, assumed
the chairmanship of the Committee and widened the scope of its
inquiries. Its epoch-making report[10] and the Joint Stock Companies
Act 1844[11] which followed it were mainly due to his genius and
energy.

Gladstone's legislation of 1844 and 1845

The 1844 Act introduced three main principles which have constituted the basis of our company law from that time. In the first place
it drew a clear distinction between private partnerships and joint stock
companies by providing for the registration as companies of all new
associations with more than 25 members,[12] or with shares transferable
without the consent of all the members. Secondly, it provided for
incorporation by mere registration as opposed to a special Act or charter; but this it did by a system of provisional registration, which
authorised the company to function for certain strictly limited preliminary purposes, followed by complete registration on filing a deed of
settlement containing the prescribed particulars and other documents
when for the first time the company became incorporated.[13] Thirdly,
it provided for full publicity which ever since has been regarded as
the most potent safeguard against fraud. It is to this Act, too, that we
owe the Registrar of Companies[14] with whom particulars of companies' constitutions, and changes therein, and annual returns are filed.

Limited liability, however, was still excluded. Although the company became incorporated, the personal liability of the members was
preserved,[15] but their liability was to cease three years after they had
transferred their shares by registered transfer[16] and creditors had to
proceed first against the assets of the company.[17] Existing companies
were compelled to register certain particulars, but did not have the
privileges conferred by the Act unless they amended their deeds of

[10] 1844 B.P.P., Vol. VII.
[11] It contained 80 sections and nine Schedules and was by far the most elaborate piece of
company legislation attempted in England up to that time. It did not apply to Scotland which
was left to its common law (Scottish judges were distinctly more liberal than their English
colleagues) until the Act of 1856.
[12] Reduced to the present 20 by the Act of 1856. This provision was based on Ker's report of
1837 which suggested a maximum of 15. New assurance companies were also required to
register irrespective of the number of members or transterability of shares: s.2.
[13] We may detect resemblances to this "two-tier" arrangement in the present provisions for a
certificate of incorporation followed later, in the case of a public company, by a "trading
certificate" (Companies Act 1985, s. 117) but there is no historical connection between the
two sets of provisions.
[14] s.19
[15] s.25
[16] This provision was, of course, based on the Trading Companies Act 1834.
[17] s.66

settlement so as to comply with its provisions.[18] Winding up was dealt with by a separate Act[19] of the same date which made companies subject to the bankruptcy law. Banking companies were also dealt with by a separate Act,[20] the provisions of which were generally similar except that the maximum number of members of an unregistered partnership was six[21] (instead of 25) and that there were stringent requirements for a minimum nominal and paid-up capital. It is perhaps surprising that these latter conditions did not then become general requirements of English company law for they constitute an essential feature of continental practice and appear to be a fair price to pay for the boon of simple and cheap incorporation by registration.[22]

Finally, Gladstone prepared and introduced the Bill which was passed under his successor as the Companies Clauses Consolidation Act 1845.[23] This set out the standard provisions normally included in private statutes of incorporation. These provisions were thereafter to be incorporated by reference, thus materially shortening and cheapening the process of statutory incorporation—still necessary in the case of public utilities requiring powers of compulsory acquisition.

Gladstone, therefore, during his tenure of office as President of the Board of Trade, succeeded for the first time in placing joint stock companies on a sound legal footing; he may fairly be regarded as the father of modern company law. His legislation, however, only solved the legal and not the commercial problems. It gave a company the legal status of a corporation but denied its members the most sought-after advantage of it—freedom from personal liability. In the latter respect the only advance was the recognition that the company itself was primarily liable and that its bankruptcy did not necessarily involve bankruptcy of its members.

The winding-up Acts

The legislation of 1844 was passed at the height of the "railway mania" and led to promotions in other fields, thus bringing the man

---

[18] ss.58–59.

[19] 7 & 8 Vict. c. 111.

[20] 7 & 8 Vict. c. 113.

[21] Later it became 10.

[22] *cf.* O. Kahn-Freund "Some Reflections on Company Law Reform" (1945) 7 M.L.R. 54 at pp. 57–59. Such provisions were, in fact, included in the Limited Liability Bill of 1855, but were struck out in Committee. They were reintroduced by the H.L. in an emasculated form but deleted in the Act of 1856. However, there have been special capital requirements in relation to certain types of business (*e.g* banking and insurance) as there are now for all public companies.

[23] A separate Act of the same date dealt with Scottish statutory companies (8 & 9 Vict. c. 17). These Acts contained the general corporate powers and duties and Table A of later Acts owed much to them. They were supplemented in the cases of particular types of utility by other Acts of the same and later years. As Cooke points out (*Corporation, Trust and Company* (Manchester, 1950), p. 119), these were illustrations of a wider tendency to bring under

in the street into contact with companies as never before, and to an expansion of the stock markets both in London and the Provinces.[24] Inevitably, however, the boom was followed by a collapse a year later which changed the emphasis from promotions to liquidations. A winding-up Act applying to railway companies[25] was passed in 1846 and this was followed in 1848[26] and 1849[27] by Acts of general application conferring winding-up jurisdiction on the Court of Chancery. Unhappily the resulting conflicts of jurisdiction between the Courts of Bankruptcy and Chancery led to great confusion,[28] which, less unhappily, proved highly beneficial to the legal and the new-born accountancy professions.

At a later date the confusion was resolved by the total removal of incorporated companies from the bankruptcy jurisdiction[29] and by the discrete treatment of company insolvency in Companies Acts and of individuals in Bankruptcy Acts, a distinction which prevailed until they were reunited by the Insolvency Act 1986.

The struggle for limited liability

Several features of the Act of 1844 were open to criticism. In particular the cumbersome procedure of provisional and final registration[30] was attacked, but was left unaltered until 1856,[31] though frequently disregarded by unscrupulous promoters who dealt in scrip prior to complete registration.

But, of course, the main cause of complaint was the absence of limited liability, and the next 10 years saw the battle fairly joined on this issue. It is clear that public opinion began to harden in favour of the extension of limited liability, particularly when the slump of 1845–1848 drew poignant attention to the consequences of its absence. But

---

general legislation matters which had previously been left to private Bills; other examples will be found in the fields of divorce, naturalisation and municipal corporations.

[24] Hunt, *op. cit.*, pp 104 *et seq.*

[25] 9 & 10 Vict. c. 28.

[26] 11 & 12 Vict. c. 45.

[27] 12 & 13 Vict. c. 108.

[28] Accounts appear in Formoy, *The Historical Foundations of Modern Company Law* (Lond., 1923), pp. 93 *et seq.*, and Cooke, *op. cit.*, Chap. X. They illustrate their accounts principally by the Royal British Bank's liquidation (1856) 28 L.T. (O.S.) 224. It is, of course, to this company that we are indebted for the rule in *Royal British Bank v. Turquand* (below, Chap. 10).

[29] The Joint Stock Companies Act 1856 and the Companies Winding Up (Amendment) Act 1857.

[30] It is estimated that less than half the provisional registrations were ever followed by complete registration: Shannon (1931–1932) Econ. Hist., Vol. II, p. 397. See also *ibid.*, pp. 281–282. The defects were emphasised in the Report of the Select Committee on Assurance Associations, 1852–1853, B.P.P., Vol. XXI.

[31] A few amendments were made in 1847 (10 & 11 Vict. c. 78), notably the deletion of the need to file prospectuses, a retrograde step which was apparently taken without any reference to the Registrar: see his evidence before the Select Committee on Assurance Associations, above, at p. 13, Q. 160. It was not corrected until 1900.

it was less clear how and to what companies it should be extended. As a result of the 1844 Act there were three principal types[32] of commercial association:

1. Private partnerships of not more than 25 persons, and quasi-partnerships of unlimited size formed before 1844 which had not reformed under the Act of that year. These were unincorporated and the liability of the members was necessarily unlimited.

2. Chartered and statutory companies, which were incorporated and the members of which were normally free from liability or had their liability limited to a prescribed sum per share.

3. Companies formed or registered under the Act of 1844 which were incorporated but with unlimited liability.

The first question, therefore, was whether limited liability should be extended to private partnerships on the lines of the continental *sociétés en commandite*, to registered companies, or to both.

Bellenden Ker's report of 1837 had been directed primarily to private partnerships and the desirability of the *société en commandite*. The 1844 Report had given birth to the third type of association but had not extended limited liability to it; the object of the Commission was to control companies and discourage frauds, not to stimulate promotions. The *société en commandite* was outside the terms of reference of the 1844 Commission but was the main subject of consideration by the Select Committee of 1850 on Investments for the Savings of the Middle and Working Classes, which reported[33] that "the difficulties which affected the law of partnership operate with increasing severity in proportion to the smallness of the sums subscribed and the number of persons included in the association. . . . Any measures for the removal of these difficulties would be particularly acceptable to the Middle and Working Classes and would tend to satisfy them that they are not excluded from fair competition by laws throwing obstacles in the way of men with small capitals." The result, as Hunt[34] says, was that the argument for limited liability acquired a "tinge of social amelioration". One can detect more than a slight whiff of humbug when one reads the evidence of Chancery barristers accepting the invitation of M.P.s to persuade them that limited liability was desirable in the interests of the poor. In truth, as the evidence of working-class witnesses makes plain, what the working man required

---

[32] There were also companies granted letters patent under the Trading Companies Act 1834 and Chartered Companies Act 1837, which were unincorporated (unless they registered under the 1844 Act) but with most of the advantages of chartered incorporation except limited liability.

[33] 1850 B.P.P., Vol. XIX, 169.

[34] *op. cit.*, p. 120.

was an improvement in the law of friendly societies, particularly as regards housing trusts, co-operative societies and building societies—and this in fact soon came about.[35] John Stuart Mill, more realistically, pointed out[36] that "the great value of a limit of responsibility as it relates to the working classes would be not so much to facilitate the investment of their savings, not so much to enable the poor to lend to those who are rich, as to enable the rich to lend to those who are poor".

A year later a similarly constituted Select Committee considered the law of partnership. On the major issue of limited liability its report[37] was non-committal; it recommended that this vexed question should be referred to a Royal Commission "of adequate legal and commercial knowledge". It did, however, make one firm recommendation, namely, that it should be permissible to lend money at a rate of interest varying with the profits of a business without becoming a partner in the business. At this time it was still supposed that such a loan automatically made the lender a partner[38]; the Committee proposed that instead he should be a deferred creditor in the event of bankruptcy and thus placed in a position not dissimilar to that of a limited partner.

In accordance with the recommendations of the Committee the question was referred to a strong Royal Commission[39] containing representatives from England, Scotland and Ireland.[40] They were, however, quite unable to reach unanimity. They had, they said, "been much embarassed by the great contrariety of opinion. . . . Gentlemen of great experience and talent have arrived at conclusions diametrically opposite; and in supporting these conclusions have displayed reasoning power of the highest order. It is difficult to say on which side the weight of authority in this country predominates." In the result a bare majority of five[41] signed a Report, opposing the general extension of limited liability to joint stock companies or the introduction of the *société en commandite*, and stating that they were unable to agree on the 1851 Committee's proposal regarding loans. Bramwell and Hodgson (a merchant banker), on the other hand, were wholeheartedly in favour of all three proposals. They came out uncompromisingly in favour of laissez-faire. "If ever," said Bramwell,[42] "there was a rule established by reason, authority and experience, it is that the interest of a community is best consulted by leaving to its members, as

---

[35] Industrial and Provident Societies Acts 1852, 1854 and 1856; Building Societies Act 1874.
[36] In his evidence at p. 78.
[37] 1851 B.P.P., Vol. XVIII, 1.
[38] *Grace v. Smith* (1775) 2 Wm.Bl. 997.
[39] 1854 B.P.P., Vol. XXVII, 445. The same Commission was to consider the assimilation of the mercantile laws of the various parts of the U.K.
[40] The English legal representatives were G.W. Bramwell Q.C. (afterwards Baron Bramwell), Cresswell J. and J. Anderson Q.C. (afterwards an Official Referee).
[41] Including Cresswell J.
[42] 1854 B.P.P., Vol. XXVII, p. 23.

far as possible, the unrestricted and unfettered exercise of their own talents and industry.'' In his opinion the restraint on limited liability offended against this golden rule. He therefore recommended[43] that people should be allowed as of right to form partnerships limiting the liability of all or some by private agreement followed by registration; and that where the liability of all was to be limited the partnership should be incorporated and the word "Limited" added after the name. The remaining member, Anderson, was against the introduction of limited liability and *sociétés en commandite*, but in favour of the 1851 Committee's proposal regarding loans.

Although the majority against limited liability was six out of eight, the House of Commons immediately passed, without a division, a motion in favour of limited partnerships.[44] On this occasion the Government remained non-committal,[45] but in the following Session they introduced two Bills, the Partnership Amendment Bill allowing profit-sharing loans without partnership, and the Limited Liability Bill which provided for limited liability in the case of companies securing complete registration under the 1844 Act subject to certain safeguards. Their bold action in introducing the latter is the more surprising since almost all the prior discussion had related to limited partnerships and not to incorporated companies.

Both Bills secured a second reading in the Commons[46] without a Division, but thereafter the former fell a victim to time pressure and proceeded no further. Nevertheless, the Government determined to press on with the Limited Liability Bill, which was rushed through the Commons and given a third reading, again without a Division.[47] It was then sent to the Lords who were asked to pass it that same Session as a matter of urgency. Certain Lords protested vigorously,[48] and certainly it is difficult to see why the Government, which had sat on the fence for so long, should suddenly regard this as a matter of the utmost urgency at the most critical time of the Crimean War. Doubtless it was true that public opinion, at any rate as represented by the Press,[49]

[43] *ibid.*, p. 29.

[44] (1854) *Hansard*, 3rd Series, Vol. 134, at cols. 752 *et seq.*

[45] Commenting on the speech of Cardwell, the President of the Board of Trade, Cobden said (*ibid.*, col. 779) that ''all he could learn of the views of the right hon. gentleman was that he told them when he began that he would not offer an opinion, and he contrived very ingeniously to keep his word''.

[46] *Hansard*, 3rd Series, Vol. 139, cols. 310 *et seq.*

[47] Cols. 1709 *et seq.* (for Committee Stage, see *ibid.*, cols. 1348, 1378, 1445 and 1517).

[48] Fourteen voted against and nine of them minuted a formal protest (*ibid.*, col. 1918).

[49] By this time even *The Times*, formerly an uncompromising opponent, had come round. Lord Stanley of Alderley, in introducing the measure in the House of Lords, said that a hostile deputation had ''candidly admitted that, with the exception of the Leeds Mercury, there was no journal in the Kingdom which would admit an article against the principle of limited liability'' (*Hansard*, Vol. 139, col. 1896). This seems to be an exaggeration so far as the legal Press was concerned, for the *Law Times* was still most hostile—even to the extent of describing the Bill as the ''Rogues Charter''; see (1854) 24 L.T. 142; (1855) 25 L.T. 116 and 210; (1856) 26 L.T. 230; and (1858) 31 L.T. 14. Nor was it universally popular in business circles.

had at last come to favour the measure, but this hardly explains the almost indecent haste with which it was pushed through,[50] particularly as the official view still seemed to be that it was a question of abstract principle rather than of practical importance.[51] The Lords, having made various amendments, finally passed the Bill without a Division.[52] The Commons[53] reluctantly accepted the Lords' amendments and the Bill was given the Royal Assent in August 1855.

The attainment of limited liability

The Act[54] provided for the limited liability of the members of a company on complete registration if (a) the company had at least 25 members holding £10 shares paid up to the extent of 20 per cent, (b) not less than three-fourths of the nominal capital was subscribed, (c) "Limited" was added to the company's name, and (d) the Board of Trade approved the auditors. The directors were to be personally liable if they paid a dividend knowing the company to be insolvent or made loans to the members, and the company had to wind up if three-fourths of the capital was lost.[55] Banks and insurance companies were excluded. The method of limitation was that already used for chartered companies under the Act of 1837 and for statutory companies under the Companies Clauses Act of 1845, namely, the restriction of members' liability to the nominal (unpaid) value of their shares.

The Limited Liability Act only remained in force for a few months, as it was repealed and incorporated in the Joint Stock Companies Act 1856.[56] This Act, of 116 sections and a Schedule of Tables and forms, was the first of the modern Companies Acts. It did away with provi-

---

The Manchester Chamber of Commerce declared it "so subversive of that high moral responsibility which has hitherto distinguished our Partnership Laws as to call for their strongest disapproval": *Proceedings*, June 13 1855, cited by Redford, *Manchester Merchants and Foreign Trade* (Manchester, 1934), p. 215, and Cooke, *op. cit.*, p. 157.

[50] John Bright told the Manchester Chamber of Commerce in 1856 that the Bill was rushed through because the Palmerston administration wanted to be able to say that something had been done besides voting money for the War (Redford *op. cit.*, and Cooke, *op. cit.*) But Bright (an opponent of the War) was perhaps not an impartial witness.

[51] Both Pleydell-Bouverie (the Vice-President of the Board of Trade) in the Commons (col. 329), and Lord Stanley of Alderley (the President) in the Lords (col. 1919) said that they thought it would prove the wisdom of Adam Smith's view "that in ordinary trading undertakings Joint Stock Companies could not compete with private traders" but that there ought to be no legal impediments in the way of competition.

[52] Cols. 1895 *et seq.*, 2025 *et seq.* and 2123 *et seq.*

[53] Cols. 2127 *et seq.*

[54] 18 & 19 Vict. c. 133. It contained only 19 sections.

[55] An existing company could take advantage of the new Act on complete registration under the 1844 Act if it made the necessary alterations to its deed of settlement by a resolution passed by a three-fourths majority of shareholders voting at a special meeting, and obtained a certificate of solvency from the Board of Trade.

[56] The Government had reintroduced the Partnership Amendment Bill at the same time (*Hansard*, Vol. 140, cols. 110 *et seq.*) but this ill-fated measure was ultimately withdrawn (*ibid.*, col. 2201).

sional registration, superseded deeds of settlement by the modern memorandum and articles of association,[57] and incorporated provisions for winding up. Banks and insurance companies were still excluded but, unlike the earlier Acts, it applied to Scotland. Passed as it was in the heyday of laissez-faire, it allowed incorporation with limited liability to be obtained with a freedom amounting almost to licence; all that was necessary was for seven or more persons to sign and register a memorandum of association. Virtually all the safeguards prescribed by the 1855 Act were deleted; there was no minimum nominal or paid-up capital or share value; only the provision for winding up on the loss of three-fourths of the capital was retained; and this too disappeared in 1862. Board of Trade approval of auditors was not required and even their appointment was no longer compulsory.[58] Directors were still to be liable if they paid dividends knowing the company to be insolvent, but the only other requirements were the use of the word "limited" and provisions for registration and publicity.

In effect, the legislature had adopted Lord Bramwell's[59] recommendations and accepted his view that those who dealt with companies knowing them to be limited had only themselves to blame if they burnt their fingers. The mystic word "Limited" was intended to act as a red flag, warning the public of the perils which they faced if they had dealings with the dangerous new invention. It is because of the arbitrary coupling of personal liability and incorporation which had prevailed for 11 years that English companies still bear the label "Ltd"[60] instead of the more logical "Inc." of the United States.

The battle for incorporation with limited liability by simple registration was now won and the issue has never been seriously reopened, although the victory has at times been unpopular.[61] Its importance has sometimes been discounted. Certainly it is true that the various devices, already described, for acquiring *de facto* freedom from liability had become perfected, and this led *The Economist*[62] to regard the

---

[57] Model articles were appended in Table B which became the influential Table A of the 1862 and later Acts.

[58] Provisions regarding auditors were moved from the operative parts, where they had been in the Acts of 1844 and 1855, to the optional Table B. In fact these provisions continued to be adopted expressly or impliedly by most companies, so that the salutary practice of a professional audit remained customary although not again compulsory until 1900. It had been reintroduced as regards banks by the Companies Act 1879. For an account of the historical development of the accounting and auditing provisions of the Acts, see Littleton & Yamey (eds.) (London, 1956), *Studies in the History of Accounting*, pp. 356–379.

[59] He took great pride in having invented "Limited"; see his speech to the Institute of Bankers in 1888, *Journal of Inst.*, Vol. 9, pp. 373 *et seq.* and especially p. 397. Llewellyn Smith (*op. cit.*, p. 165) says that he even suggested playfully that the word should be inscribed on his tombstone.

[60] Or, now, "plc" in the case of public limited companies.

[61] The repeated bank failures during the second half of the 19th century caused renewed outbursts against limited liability; particularly on the failure of Overend Gurney Ltd. in 1866: see Hunt, *op. cit.*, pp. 153 *et seq.*

[62] (1854) Vol. XII, 698.

issue as of no great importance. Maitland[63] seems to have taken much the same view. "If", he said, "the State had not given way we should have had in England joint stock companies, unincorporated, but contracting with limited liability. We know nowadays that men are not deterred from making contracts by the word limited". We have no reason to suppose that they would have been deterred if that word were expanded into four or five lines printed at the head of the company's letter paper." Nevertheless it is clear that without the legislative intervention, limited liability could never have been attained in a satisfactory and clear-cut fashion, and that it was this intervention which finally established companies as the major instrument in economic development. Of this the immediate and startling increase in promotions is sufficient proof.[64]

Subsequent developments

The subsequent history of companies belongs to the modern law and can be sketched more briefly.[65] Its main feature has been a movement away from the complete freedom allowed by the 1856 Act and the imposition of greater controls and increased provisions for publicity—the basic policy of Gladstone's Act of 1844 which had suffered partial eclipse in later Acts.

In 1857 the Act of the previous year was slightly amended,[66] banks were brought within its scope by the Joint Stock Banking Companies Act 1857, but without limited liability which was not conceded until the following year,[67] and legislation was passed dealing with frauds by directors.[68] In 1862 the various enactments were consolidated and amended in an Act which is the first to bear the short title of "Companies Act",[69] and which, with numerous amendments,[70] remained the principal Act until 1908. It was considerably larger than the 1856 Act, consisting of no fewer than 212 sections and three Schedules. The additions were mainly amendments to the winding-up provisions and

---

[63] *Trust and Corporation*, Collected Papers, Vol. III, pp. 321, 392.

[64] Between 1844 and 1856, 956 companies were completely registered under the 1844 Act; in the six years following the 1856 Act no fewer than 2,479 were registered and their paid-up capital in 1864 was over £31 million; Shannon, *op. cit.*, p. 290. For further details, see the Table at *ibid.*, p. 421.

[65] Students of the history of this later period are referred to Dr J.B. Jeffreys' London Ph.D. Thesis: *Trends in Business Organisation in Great Britain Since 1856* which is unfortunately unpublished but is available in the London University Library. It contains an excellent account of the major trends and an invaluable bibliography.

[66] 20 & 21 Vict. c. 14.

[67] 21 & 22 Vict. c. 91.

[68] 20 & 21 Vict. c. 54. See also Larceny Act 1861, ss. 81–84.

[69] The poet W.H. Auden was somehow able to detect in this Act the symptoms of a modification of the pure liberal doctrine of laissez-faire: *Poets of tne English Language*. Vol. 5, p. xxiii.

[70] The most important were the Companies Acts of 1867, 1879 and 1880, the Companies Winding Up Act 1890, the Directors' Liability Act 1890, and the Companies Act 1900.

improved and more detailed drafting, but it included insurance companies[71] and also introduced the company limited by guarantee which, as already pointed out,[72] affords a convenient type of organisation for clubs and charitable or quasi-charitable associations.

Limited partnerships and private companies

Hence by 1862 two of the three functions[73] of the modern company had been catered for. Capitalists were encouraged to lend their money to industry without having themselves to operate the enterprise, and non-trading bodies formed for social or philanthropic purposes could conveniently adopt the company rather than the trust as their *modus operandi*. But, or so it was thought, the need for limited liability within the field of the ordinary partnership or one-man business had still not been met. By the Partnership Amendment Act 1865[74] (commonly known as Bovill's Act) it was ultimately provided that sharing of profits should not be conclusive evidence of partnership but that lenders, or sellers of goodwill, in consideration of a share of profits should be deferred creditors. At the time it was thought that this had effected a substantial advance by legalising something in the nature of limited partnerships. In fact, as the courts soon held,[75] it did no such thing; it protected the creditor only where he was not in truth associated in the running of the business, for, if he was, he became fully liable as a partner notwithstanding that he was described as a contributor "under Bovill's Act". It therefore made no advance on the decision of the House of Lords in *Cox v. Hickman*[76] which had already overruled the rule in *Grace v. Smith*.[77] Far from protecting such lenders, the Act merely worsened their position by making them deferred creditors on bankruptcy.

When this was realised there was a renewed outbreak of attempts to introduce full-fledged limited partnerships on the continental model, and it was from one such abortive attempt[78] that the Partnership Act 1890 resulted, although this in its final form merely codified the existing law. In fact, however, the Companies Acts enabled all the advantages of limited partnerships, and more besides, to be obtained; for the requirement of seven members did not mean that so many as seven had to be beneficially interested—some could be bare nominees for the others and all could thus acquire the benefits of limited

---

[71] Hitherto governed by the 1844 Act which had been revived for their benefit: 20 & 21 Vict. c. 1900.

[72] Above, Chap. 1, p. 10.

[73] Above, Chap. 1, p. 10.

[74] This was an amended version of the ill-fated Partnership Bill of 1855.

[75] *Syers v. Syers* (1876) 1 App.Cas 174, H.L.; *Pooley v. Driver* (1876) 5 Ch.D. 458.

[76] (1860) 8 H.L.C. 268.

[77] (1775) 2 Wm.Bl. 997, above.

[78] See the account by the original draftsman, Sir Frederick Pollock, in the preface to the 12th edition of his *Law of Partnership*.

liability.[79] When this was established, as a result of the House of Lords decision in the famous case of *Salomon* v. *Salomon*,[80] the need for limited partnerships had largely ceased, particularly as the legislature, far from discouraging "one-man" and other small "private companies", discriminated in their favour by the Companies Acts of 1900 and 1907 by exempting them from certain of the requirements of publicity.

Nevertheless, public opinion, in this instance lagging behind the law, caused limited partnerships to be legalised by the Limited Partnerships Act 1907. In practice this Act has not been much used because the private limited company involves little more trouble and expense to the members, and enables the liability of all of them to be limited, even if they take part in the management. However, the liability issue continues to be productive of controversy for those professions which continue to trade in the partnership form.[81]

Case law developments

As already pointed out, the Companies Acts are far from being a complete code and it would be misleading to give an impression that the major developments during the nineteenth century were entirely statutory. On the contrary, the courts, building on the foundations of agency, trust and partnership law, had for the first time evolved a coherent and comprehensive body of company law. Many of the most fundamental principles were worked out by the courts with little or no help from the statutes though some, but still not all, have since been codified, amended or eroded by later Companies Acts.

Twentieth-century reforms

By the end of the nineteenth century the Board of Trade had established the practice of appointing at intervals of about 20 years a Departmental Committee to review company law, implementing its recommendations by an amending Act with was then repealed and replaced by a consolidation of all company legislation in a Companies Act. This practice was followed during the first half of the twentieth century with

---

[79] The result, as has been well said (by O. Kahn-Freund in his notes to Renner, *The Institutions of Private Law* (London, 1948) at pp. 221 and 222) is that whereas in the 18th and early 19th centuries the law of partnership had been pressed into the service of joint stock enterprise, now the legal form of joint stock undertakings has come to annex the functions of the law of partnership. A similar reversal has taken place in the law of trusts into whose service the joint stock company is now pressed as a trust corporation: for a brief history of this development, see D.R. Marsh, "The Friendly Corporation" in (1951) IV Cambridge J. 451, and for a fuller account, the same author's *Corporate Trustees* (London, 1952).

[80] [1897] A.C. 22, H.L. Below, pp. 77–80.

[81] For a possible reform of this legislation to deal with the liability problems of accountants and other professional partnerships see pp. 560–561, below.

new consolidations in 1908,[82] 1929[83] and 1948.[84] Thereafter it ran into difficulties. The latest, and probably the last, Company Law Committee (the Jenkins Committee) was appointed in 1960 and reported in 1962.[85] While it was sitting, legislation was passed introducing into Scottish law the valuable English concept of the floating charge,[86] and shortly thereafter there were two further Acts. One attempted to curb the abuses flowing from a growing practice, by companies which were not recognised banks, of inviting the public to deposit money with them[87] and the other simplified somewhat the process of transferring stocks and shares.[88] But thereafter successive Governments proved dilatory in implementing the Jenkins Committee's recommendations.

A first step was taken in the Companies Act 1967 which, in addition to tightening the prudential regulation of insurance companies, abolished the 1948 Act's distinction between "exempt" and other (non-exempt) private companies[89] and made a few other amendments relating to companies generally. This was intended by the then Labour Government as a prelude to "wider reforms in the structure and philosophy of our company law" after a re-examination of "the whole theory and purpose of the limited joint stock company, the comparative rights and obligations of shareholders, directors, creditors, employees and the community as a whole".[90] Nothing as ambitious had been attempted by any Company Law Committee or Royal Commission; nor has it been attempted since. The succeeding Conservative Government introduced a Bill in 1973 which would have implemented most of the other recommendations of the Jenkins Committee and, had it been enacted and followed by a reconsolidation, our company law would have been more intelligible both to us and to our continental partners in the European Communities to which we had belatedly secured admission. Unfortunately the Bill lapsed with the defeat of the Conservative administration in the General Election of 1974 and

---

[82] Companies (Consolidation) Act 1908 (implementing the Report of the Loreburn Committee: 1906 Cmnd. 3052).

[83] Companies Act 1929 (implementing the Report of the Greene Committee: 1926 Cmd. 2657, and an earlier Report of the the Wrenbury Committee: 1918 Cd. 9138).

[84] Companies Act 1948 (implementing the Report of the Cohen Committee: 1945 Cmd. 6659).

[85] 1962 Cmnd. 1749.

[86] Companies (Floating Charges) (Scotland) Act 1961 (implementing a Report of the Scottish Law Reform Committee: (Cmnd. 1017). This, however, did not introduce receiverships which were also unknown to Scottish law. Following a Report of the Scottish Law Commission (1970 Cmnd. 4336) this omission was rectified by the Companies (Floating Charges and Receiverships) (Scotland) Act 1972.

[87] Protection of Depositors Act 1963 which was later superseded by the Banking Act 1979 and, now, 1987.

[88] Stock Transfer Act 1963. Further steps in this direction were later taken by the Stock Exchange (Completion of Bargains) Act 1976, by s.207 of the Companies Act 1989 and the Uncertificated Securities Regulations 1995 made under the 1989 Act and, in relation to the stocks of public authorities, by the Stock Transfer Act 1982.

[89] See Chap. 1 at p. 12, n. 39, above.

[90] H.C. Debs., Vol. 741, col. 359.

was never resuscitated. An Insolvency Act and a further Companies Act, dealing mainly with accounts and audit, were passed in 1976, but thereafter the legislative programme was dominated by the need to comply with our E.C. obligations.

The European Commission has an ambitious programme for harmonising the company laws of the Member States, and the United Kingdom is faced by the need to implement by legislation[91] a continuing flow of Directives, many of which are specifically designated as Company Law Directives or impinge closely on company law.[92] The European Communities Act 1972 attempted to comply with our immediate obligations in this respect and, in its section 9, to implement the First Company Law Directive relating to publicity, pre-incorporation contracts, the *ultra vires* doctrine and the authority of directors. In 1980 and 1981 two major Companies Acts were passed, primarily to implement respectively the Second Company Law Directive, relating to the formation of public companies and the maintenance of their capital, and the Fourth relating to accounts.

The fact that compliance with our international obligations made it necessary to find a niche for these implementing measures in the legislative programme provided an opportunity to include also provisions unrelated to the Directives but thought to be desirable (and overdue) domestic reforms. This opportunity was seized to a greater extent than the Government had initially envisaged, with the result that in each case the Act emerged some 50 per cent longer than the Bill as originally introduced. These Acts made very substantial changes relating, in particular, to duties of directors and conflicts of interest, insider dealing, remedies for members unfairly prejudiced, company names, acquisition by companies of their own shares,[93] providing financial assistance for the acquisition of their shares, and disclosure of interests in shares.[94]

The 1985 consolidation

This spate of legislation made the need for a new consolidation of the Companies Acts an urgent necessity—our company legislation was in a worse state than at any time this century.[95] In achieving this mam-

---

[91] The European Communities Act 1972 confers a limited power to use secondary legislation rather than an Act of Parliament but most Directives cannot be satisfactorily implemented except by the latter.

[92] See Chap. 4, below.

[93] On which a Consultative Document, *The Purchase by a Company of its Own Shares*, had been published as 1980 Cmnd. 7944.

[94] Both insider dealing and disclosure of interests in shares are matters now covered by community law, but domestic legislation on both of them preceded the Community initiatives by a considerable margin.

[95] By 1984 the Companies Acts 1948–1983 officially consisted of: the principal Act of 1948, Parts I and III of the Companies Act 1967, the Companies (Floating Charges and Receivers) (Scotland) Act 1972, s.9 of the European Communities Act 1972, ss.1 to 4 of the Stock Exchange (Completion of Bargains) Act 1976 (but not the Stock Transfer Acts 1963 and 1982), s.9 of the Insolvency Act 1976, the Companies Acts 1976, 1980 and 1981 and a short but highly technical Companies (Beneficial Interests) Act 1983.

moth task by 1985 the draftsman was assisted by prior use of the power, inserted in the Companies Act 1981,[96] for amendments, which the Law Commission and the Scottish Law Commission recommended as needed to produce a satisfactory consolidation, to be made by Orders in Council. He also had the courage not to follow slavishly the wording of the provisions to be consolidated and succeeded in improving both wording and arrangement. What emerged was a main Companies Act 1985, and three supplemental Acts of the same year, the Company Securities (Insider Dealing) Act, the Business Names Act and the Companies Consolidation (Consequential Provisions) Act.

Unfortunately the consolidation could not include important pieces of legislation then in preparation. These were, first, the Insolvency Acts 1985 and 1986. The 1985 Act, implementing the Report of the Cork Committee[97]—though not as comprehensively as the Committee had hoped—made major reforms both to the law of individual bankruptcy and to company winding-up. The second consolidated the new and the surviving earlier legislation on these subjects. The result was to remove from the Companies Act 1985 all the provisions relating to winding up and receiverships. This was followed by the Company Directors Disqualification Act 1986 which consolidated all the extant provisions empowering the courts to disqualify miscreants from acting as directors or being concerned in the management of companies—provisions which had previously been split between Insolvency Acts and Companies Acts. Secondly, there was the Financial Services Act 1986 which, in addition to repealing and replacing the Prevention of Fraud (Investments) Act 1958[98] by a detailed and sophisticated system of regulation of those professionally engaged in investment business, aimed to repeal and replace all the "prospectus provisions" of the Companies Act, amended a number of its other provisions, particularly in relation to takeovers, and replaced some sections of the Company Securities (Insider Dealing) Act. This left gaping holes in the Companies Act and unconsolidated insider dealing legislation.[99] It has, however, also led to a major, and desirable, reclassification of subject-matter, distinguishing company law from insolvency law and from securities regulation.

Reclassification of company law

Hitherto the winding up of companies had been seen as a branch of company law divorced from the bankruptcy law relating to individuals. Now both need to be regarded as branches of a single subject—

---

[96] s.116.

[97] (1982) Cmnd. 8558.

[98] For an analysis of the defects of the 1958 Act: see Gower, *Review of Investor Protection: A Discussion Document* (1982, HMSO).

[99] The domestic insider dealing legislation had to be later recast to take account of the Community Directive of 1989 on this topic and is now contained in Part V of the Criminal Justice Act 1993.

insolvency law. It is, perhaps, anomalous that members' voluntary winding up of solvent companies should be dealt with in the Insolvency Act; it might have been better if that had remained in the Companies Act (or, failing that, if the Insolvency Act had been entitled the Bankruptcy and Winding Up Act). But it is an advance to have recognised the essential unity of bankruptcy and insolvent liquidation and, accordingly, that company law should concentrate on the life, rather than the death and interment, of companies. That, of course, does not mean that companies (or books on company law) can wholly ignore what will happen if companies become insolvent.

Even more important are the implications of the Financial Services Act.[1] Many other common law countries have long recognised that what most of them call Securities Regulation is a distinct and important subject (and, incidentally, one in which it is lucrative to specialise). We, however, had treated it, in so far as we recognised it at all, as an unimportant adjunct to company law. That has changed now that the primitive Prevention of Fraud (Investments) Act 1958 (which was virtually identical with the pre-War Act of the same name) has been replaced by an up-to-date system modelled to a large extent on that of the United States. By whatever name it is called—Securities Regulation, Investment Regulation, Financial Services Regulation or whatever—and wherever one draws its precise boundaries, it has become an important subject in its own right and one on which books will need to be written and courses conducted at Law Schools.

This book does not attempt to deal with the new subject in so far as that is concerned with the regulation of those who carry on investment business—the financial services industry. But it has to deal with some of the matters covered by the Financial Services Act. Public issues, takeovers and insider dealing are rightly regarded as part of Securities Regulation since they relate to dealings with investments, whether or not these are the securities of companies. On the other hand, the most important types of investment in these respects are company securities. Hence such matters also have to be dealt with in books on Company Law and not left exclusively to those on Financial Services Regulation.

The Companies Act 1989

A further Companies Act[2] was passed in 1989. The primary purpose of this was to implement the Seventh E.C. Company Directive on

---

[1] The Act was largely based on the Gower Report, *Review of Investor Protection*, Part I (1984 Cmnd. 9125) and Part II (1985, HMSO) and on a White Paper, *Financial Services in the United Kingdom: A New Framework for Investor Protection*, 1985 Cmnd. 9432. For a brief (and "personal") account of the genesis of the Act and the main features of the regulatory system, see "*Big Bang and City Regulation*" (1988) 51 M.L.R. 1. Although in this area the influence of the E.C. had hitherto been less dominant, it had not been negligible (for example in relation to public issues). The E.C. has now embarked on a programme designed to lead to a unified European financial market. Happily the U.K. with a more advanced system than many of its partners has been able to influence these developments to a greater extent than it has with the Company Law Directives.

[2] Of 216 sections and 24 Schedules!

consolidated accounts and the Eighth on audits, but, once again, the opportunity was taken to include a number of domestic reforms (and to amend the Financial Services Act). The amendments to the Companies Act were substantial and, at the time of writing, there has not been an official reconsolidation.[3]

Unless that is undertaken promptly after each new Companies Act (for others will undoubtedly have to be enacted to implement further Company Law Directives) much of the good work which culminated in the 1985 consolidation will have been in vain.

Reorganisation at the DTI

The Department of Trade and Industry (the DTI) is now the Government Department responsible, among many other matters, for Company and Insolvency Law. Under the Secretary of State there is usually an Under-Secretary of State for Corporate Affairs. The Board of Trade has effectively ceased to exist as such—though its ghost haunts the Department's corridors and the Secretary of State sometimes wears his presidential hat on social occasions. For our purposes, the most relevant sections of the DTI are the Company Law and Investigations and Enforcement Directorates, and Companies House and the Insolvency Service. In 1988, the Companies Registration offices for England and Wales (located in Cardiff)[4] and for Scotland (located in Edinburgh) were converted into an Executive Agency[5] known as *Company House* with a view to affording them greater autonomy but without severing their relationship with the Department. In relation to financial services law, the Finance Regulation and Industry Directorate of the Treasury is the leading source of policy.

In 1978 the Department had re-established a standing Company Law Advisory Committee of outside experts but this was no more successful than earlier such efforts and it was disbanded in 1983.[6] The experiment of recruiting a part-time Adviser on Company Law, started in 1979, has now been replaced by the engagement of groups of consultants to review specific subjects.

---

[3] But unless officialdom is prepared to allow this to be done on consolidation retaining the existing numbering of the sections, the professions would probably prefer this to be left to the commercial publishers. Other countries do not boggle at sections numbered 35A, 35B (etc.) and there is no valid reason why we should.

[4] But with search facilities still available in London, a facility which it is intended to extend to other cities. A programme of computerisation of the Registries is in hand but, at present, is less advanced than in some other common law countries; in Singapore, for example, a lawyer or accountant can make searches and file all documents (including all those required on original registration) via his own office computers.

[5] As was the Insolvency Service in 1990.

[6] But see the Memorandum of the Law Society's Company Law Committee (approved by the Law Reform Committee of the General Council of the Bar): *The Reform of Company Law* (July 1991, No. 255). This, rightly, is highly critical of the present procedures for keeping Company Law up-to-date. It suggests the establishment of an independent Company Law Commission on the lines of those in some other Commonwealth countries (and which have produced consultative documents and reports the likes of which the DTI has been unable to match).

CHAPTER 4

CURRENT TRENDS AND FUTURE POSSIBILITIES

OVER the past 25 years the development of company law in the United Kingdom has been heavily influenced by European Community law. This will be mentioned when the relevant parts of our domestic law are analysed later in this book. Nevertheless, it seemed useful to bring together at this point some general remarks on this important source of company law. In addition, before plunging into the detail of British corporate law (and this is a subject where it is very easy to fail to see the wood for the trees) some comments will be made about a few of the fundamental problems facing company law, some of which the Member States have attempted to address at Community level and others they have not.

THE IMPACT OF COMMUNITY LAW[1]

The Community legislation which has had an impact upon domestic company law falls into two main categories. These are the specific Company Law Directives and the Capital Markets Directives, though there are some additional important measures which will be discussed below and which fall into neither category. The typical instrument of Community law in this field is thus the Directive, which is expected to be transposed into domestic law by an appropriate act of the domestic legislature. Nevertheless, the company lawyer cannot ignore the Community origins of those parts of the domestic law which give effect to the supranational law. National courts are under a *Community* law obligation to interpret national law so that it conforms, as far as possible, with the underlying Directive, as interpreted by the European Court of Justice, where relevant.[2] Further, if a Directive is transposed by the national legislator either not at all or imperfectly, it may be possible for a litigant in the national courts to sue upon the Directive against the person upon whom the Directive intended to lay the obligation in question, at least where the defendant is an emanation of the

---

[1] An excellent account of the state of play on Community Company law initiatives, which is constantly updated, is to be found in Part 16 of *Palmer's Company Law*.

[2] Case C–106/89, *Marleasing S.A. v. La Commercial Internacional de Alimentation S.A.* [1990] I E.C.R. 4135, a case arising out of the first Company Law Directive. See also Case C–234/94, *Tomberger v. Gebruder von der Wettern GmbH*, Opinion of A-G Tesauro, [1996] 2 BCLC 457.

state, and thus displace any domestic law to the contrary.[3] Alternatively, it may be possible to sue the national government in the national courts for the failure to transpose the Directive.[4]

The Company Law Directives

Article 54(3)(g) of the Treaty of Rome, as amended, permits the Council of Ministers by qualified majority vote, on a proposal from the European Commission and in co-operation with the European Parliament, to adopt Directives which aim to protect the interests of members "and others"[5] by "co-ordinating to the necessary extent the safeguards which ... are required by Member States of companies and firms ... with a view to making such safeguards equivalent throughout the Community". This power is probably best seen as a method of advancing freedom of establishment, one of the four fundamental commercial freedoms enshrined in the original Treaty of Rome.[6] Equivalence of company law in the Member States will facilitate the establishment by companies located in one Member State of subsidiaries in another.

In any event, armed with this power the Commission embarked upon an extensive programme of harmonisation. To date, the First,[7] Second,[8] Third,[9] Fourth,[10] Sixth,[11] Seventh,[12] Eighth,[13] Eleventh[14] and Twelfth[15] Directives have been adopted, though not necessarily in that order. In some cases the original Directives have been amended subsequently, the willingness of the Community legislator to re-visit Directives already adopted being an important development, for other-

---

[3] See the "*Karella*" cases: Joined Cases C–19 & C–20/90 [1991] I E.C.R. 2691, Case C–381/89 [1992] I E.C.R. 2111, and Cases C–134 and 135/91 [1992] I E.C.R. 5699; and Case C–441/93, *Panagis Pafitis v. Trapeza Kentrikis Ellados Est* [1996] 2 CMLR 551, all cases arising under the Second Company Law Directive.

[4] These three sentences summarise some very complicated Community law for the further elucidation of which the reader is referred to the standard works on Community law.

[5] Which has been taken to include at least creditors and employees.

[6] Wolff, "The Commission's Programme for Company Law Harmonisation" in Andenas and Kenyon-Slade (eds.), *EC Financial Market Regulation and Company Law* (London, 1993) at p. 22.

[7] Council Directive 68/151, [1968] O.J. 68. See below, p. 207.

[8] Council Directive 77/91, [1977] O.J. L26/1 (formation of public companies and the maintenance and alteration of capital). See below, Chaps. 11 and 12.

[9] Council Directive 78/855, [1978] O.J. L295/36 (mergers of public companies). See below, p. 762.

[10] Council Directive 78/660, [1978] O.J. L222/11 (accounts). See below, p. 512.

[11] Council Directive 82/891, [1982] O.J. L378/47 (division of public companies). See below, p. 762.

[12] Council Directive 83/349, [1983] O.J. L193/1 (group accounts). See below, p. 159.

[13] Council Directive 84/253, [1984] O.J. L126/20 (audits). See below, p. 538.

[14] Council Directive 89/666, [1989] O.J. L395/36 (branches established by oversea companies). See below, p. 128.

[15] Council Directive 89/667, [1989] O.J. L395/40 (single-member companies). See below, pp. 83, 150.

wise areas of national law which had fallen within the Community sphere might become ossified.

All these Directives have been at least partly implemented in the United Kingdom. They thus represent a substantial, if not comprehensive, body of company law reform. Obviously, the impact of the Directives in any Member State depends partly on the ambition of the Community legislator (the Twelfth Directive, for example, hardly seems of earth-shattering importance in any Member State), partly on how far that Member State's national law is reflected in the Community provisions and partly on how far the practices the Directive seeks to regulate are actually to be found in that Member State (the Third and Sixth Directives, for example, relate to forms of merger and de-merger rarely used in the United Kingdom). As far as the United Kingdom is concerned, the most significant on the list have probably been the Second Directive, which was much influenced by French and German law and which led to the reintroduction of some protections for creditors which the English law had abandoned in the nineteenth century,[16] and the Fourth Directive, which represents a somewhat uneasy combination of French, German and British approaches to the presentation of company accounts.

In recent years, however, the pace of Community company law harmonisation has slowed. Partly this is because some of the older proposals of the Commission have remained snared in the difficulties of resolving the fundamental problems facing company law. This is true of the Draft Fifth Directive on the structure of public companies and the Draft Tenth Directive on cross-border mergers of public companies (both caught up on the issue of worker representation)[17] and the Draft Ninth Directive on groups.[18] But it is also true that the Commission has added only one new proposal for company law harmonisation in the past decade and that is the controversial proposal, first made in 1989 and subsequently twice revised, for a Thirteenth Directive on takeover bids.[19] It may be that the new requirements of ''subsidiarity'' added by the Treaty on European Union in 1992, which requires the Commission to justify the need for Community action in any area, are having a chilling effect on the process or, more likely,

---

[16] See p. 45, above.

[17] See below, p. 63.

[18] See below, p. 69.

[19] Discussed in Chap. 29, below. However, the Commission is currently in preparatory work for a proposed directive concerning the transfer of the head office of a company from one Member State to another, a problem addressed as long ago as 1968 in the Convention on the Mutual Recognition of Companies and Firms, but not solved because the Convention was not ratified even by all the then Member States. Under the British Companies Act 1985 the statement in the memorandum as to the company's place of registration is the only condition contained in the memorandum which cannot in principle be altered. See p. 14, above. The work raises the tricky issue of the conflict between the place of incorporation rule and the headquarters rule (the *siège réel*) for determining the law applicable to a company.

that the Commission has turned its not unlimited resources to more pressing areas, such as capital markets law and the mutual recognition of Member States' banking, insurance and investment services regulation. However, it may be that the Community's new-found respect for the job-creation potential of small and medium-sized enterprises will give the company law harmonisation programme a new lease of life. Up until now it has been mainly, though not exclusively, concerned with public companies. The Twelfth Directive, unimportant though it is by itself, may be a harbinger of a more general concern on the part of the Community with private companies.

The Capital Markets Law Directives

Although often also based in part on Article 54(3)(g), these Directives are not included in the numbered company law series because they relate to all types of securities (including securities issued by governments or other public authorities) and not only to company securities. Nevertheless, company securities constitute the most important single type of instrument covered by the directives and so the company lawyer cannot ignore them. An important group of three Directives regulates the process of listing securities. They govern the admission of securities to listing on official stock exchanges,[20] the content, approval and distribution of listing particulars to be issued by companies when they are listed,[21] and the reporting requirements for companies once listed.[22] A further Directive covering prospectuses issued in connection with public offerings generally (whether by listed companies or not) came along later, in 1989,[23] even though logically it should have preceded the three listing Directives. In consequence, domestic law was in a state of uncertainty for a while, but it has now settled down.[24] At the end of the day, the four Directives can be seen to have had a considerable (and largely beneficial) impact upon the old prospectus provisions of the Companies Act 1985, on the legal status of the Stock Exchange and on the nature and contents of the Exchange's Listing Rules, through which a number of the provisions of the Directives are implemented.

The impetus in the late 1980s towards the completion of the internal market also saw the adoption of a Directive on insider dealing,[25] which, although it postdated the introduction of such legislation in the United Kingdom, did have the desirable consequence of precipitating

---

[20] Council Directive 79/279, [1979] O.J. L66/21.
[21] Council Directive 80/390, [1980] O.J. L100/1. It has been amended subsequently, mainly to deal with mutual recognition issues.
[22] Council Directive 82/121, [1982] O.J. L48/26.
[23] Council Directive 89/298, [1989] O.J. L124/8.
[24] The current law is discussed in Chap. 16, below.
[25] Council Directive 89/592, [1989] O.J. L334/30.

a re-casting of the domestic law as a piece of securities market regulation rather than of company law or even statutory fiduciary law, as it has previously been.[26] Also dating from this period is the Directive on the disclosure shareholdings in listed companies,[27] which, as we shall see, has had the effect of persuading the DTI, if not yet the legislature, that the existing domestic provisions should be refocused and simplified by concentrating on the objective of making transparent to the public share-dealing markets the location of voting rights in the companies there traded.[28]

Other measures

The two categories above do not contain all the examples of initiatives at Community level which are of relevance to domestic company lawyers. For example, the Member States of the Community have negotiated a convention on insolvency proceedings under Art. 220 of the Treaty, the convention dealing with the mutual recognition of companies and the enforcement of judgements on cross-border insolvency.[29] If ratified by all the Member States, it could have an important impact on companies' decisions on location, since national insolvency laws have not been harmonised.

Perhaps of more direct concern to company lawyers is the Regulation[30] adopted under Art. 235 of the Treaty, providing for the establishment of an entity to be recognised throughout the Community and known as a European Economic Interest Grouping (or EEIG). Based on the model of the French *Groupement d'Intérêt Economique*, the EEIG is designed to enable existing business undertakings in different member States to form an autonomous body to provide common services ancillary to the primary activities of its members. Any profits it makes belong to its members and they are jointly and severally responsible for its liabilities.

The basic requirements for the formation of an EEIG are simply the conclusion of a written contract between the members and registration at a registry in the Member State where it is to have its official address. The Regulation confers upon the EEIG full legal capacity, though whether it is afforded corporate personality is left to national law, which is also left with considerable scope to supplement the mandatory provisions of the Regulation. Hence, although the Regulation is

---

[26] For this argument in more detail see Davies (1991) 11 O.J.L.S. 92. The current law is discussed in Chap. 17.
[27] Council Directive 88/627, [1988] O.J. L348/62. This Directive is not contained in the numbered series and, though it is based only on Art. 54 and applies only to companies, does not refer specifically to Art. 54(3)(g).
[28] See pp. 485–486, below.
[29] Insolvency was excluded from the Brussels Convention on Jurisdiction and the Enforcement of Judgments in Civil and Commercial Matters 1968.
[30] Council Regulation 2137/85, [1985] O.J. L199/1.

directly applicable, it provided that EEIGs could not be set up before July 1, 1989 so as to allow Member States time to get their houses in order and their registration offices established. The United Kingdom has supplemented the E.C. Regulations by the European Economic Interest Grouping Regulations 1989[31] which nominate the Companies Registrar as the registering authority and the Secretary of State as the "competent authority". A number of the sections of the Companies Act[32] and the Insolvency Act[33] are applied to an EEIG as if it was a company registered under the Companies Act and it may be wound up as an unregistered company under Part V of the Insolvency Act.[34]

What use English companies will make of this, to us, novel type of body remains to be seen. They may find themselves required to use it if they wish to collaborate in joint operations with companies established in countries, especially France, where it is not so novel. Some English solicitors (partnerships not companies) have adopted it as a means of collaboration with lawyers elsewhere in the Community.[35]

The future

As we noted above, the programme of company law harmonisation, as such, seems to have lost a degree of momentum in recent years, but there is one initiative outside that programme which is of potential significance. This is the project for a European Company, an old proposal but one to which the completion of the internal market has given a renewed impetus. If the worker representation issues can be solved (see below), then the political support for a "European" form of incorporation, distinct from incorporation under the laws of any particular Member State, may bring the project to fruition. However, there is still debate about the utility of this new form of incorporation, especially as the successive drafts of the statute[36] for such companies have reduced the extent to which a comprehensive uniform corporate law is envisaged, as more and more matters have been delegated to the law of the Member State in which the company has its headquarters.

The proposal for a European Company is generally regarded as the brain-child of Professor Pieter Sanders of the University of Rotterdam[37] who aired the idea in a speech in 1959 and, in 1965, was invited by the Commission, on the initiative of the French Government, to lead a team which produced, with remarkable speed, a draft Statute

---

[31] S.I. 1989 No. 638.
[32] Reg. 18 and Sched. 4.
[33] Reg. 19 which applies to them Part III of the Insolvency Act relating to receiverships.
[34] In which event the Company Directors Disqualification Act applies to their managers: Reg. 20.
[35] On March 31, 1995 some 85 EEIGs were registered in Great Britain with their principal establishment in Britain: see *Companies in 1995–96* (DTI, 1996), Table E3.
[36] Currently envisaged as a Regulation to be adopted under Art. 100A of the Treaty and thus by qualified majority vote.
[37] Though the French claim co-paternity.

published in 1967. Subsequently, after further study, the Commission published a draft Regulation and a revised draft Statute. Thereafter the project was put on the back-burner where it remained until 1988, when the Commission, in a well-argued Memorandum, proposed its revival as a major contribution to the Single European Market, and to its economic and social programmes, and as a possible means of resolving the vexed worker-participation problem. Most Member States (but not the United Kingdom) favoured a resumption of work on the Statute and in August 1989 the Commission submitted formal Proposals[38] to the Council for a Regulation on a Statute for a European public limited company, to be known as a *Societas Europea* (SE), and a complementary Directive regarding the involvement of employees in SEs. In December 1989 the Departments of Trade and Industry and of Employment circulated a Consultative Document which included the texts of the Regulation and Directive[39] and the Commission's commentary thereon. In 1991[40] and 1992[41] further revisions of the proposal were produced.

As the Directive's provisions regarding worker-participation are in substance identical with those in the latest draft of the Fifth Company Law Directive and raise the same issues[42] no more need be said here than that the United Kingdom Government's opposition to them has been no less implacable[43] notwithstanding that they would relate to a Community body and not a British one. While the United Kingdom Government sees no need for the SE (but do not object in principle)[43a] the continental Member States (and the Commission) regard it as needed if the E.C. enterprises large enough to compete effectively with those of America and Japan are to emerge. The 1988 Draft permitted the use of an SE only in a restrictive range of circumstances when two or more companies in different Member States wished to merge[43b] or to form a joint subsidiary or holding company. But subsequent discussions have culminated in an amended Proposal[44] whereby two or more companies of different Member States may merge into an SE or a single company in one Member State may convert itself or form

---

[38] COM (89) 268 final [1989] O.J. C263.
[39] The Regulation and the Directive form a composite whole and must be applied together: Commission's Commentary (appended as Annex B to the Government's Consultative Document), p. 1.
[40] COM (91) 174 final [1991] O.J. C176/1, on which see DTI, *Revised Proposal for a European Company Statute*, January 1992.
[41] But not apparently officially published.
[42] On which, particularly in the present context, see Wedderburn, *The Social Charter, European Company and Employment Rights* (The Institute of Employment Rights, 1990).
[43] See para. 33 of its Consultative Document.
[43a] Consultative Document on the 1988 Draft, paras. 32 and 35.
[43b] Under the continental practice, mergers are effected by merging undertakings (takeovers of share capital are uncommon and hostile ones virtually impossible) but where the companies concerned are incorporated in different States this at present is impracticable.
[44] See n. 40, above.

an SE so long as it has a subsidiary or branch in another Member State.[45]

The draft Statute is, in effect, a skeletal Companies Act. It relies extensively on existing Community legislation (particularly the Company Law Directives which in some cases are incorporated by reference) and provides that matters not expressly mentioned shall be governed by the general principles on which the Regulation is based, and, if these do not provide a solution, by the law relating to public companies of the State in which the SE has its registered office. In the Government's Consultation Document on the 1988 Draft this reliance on national law was rightly identified as a serious flaw,[46] but the later amendments[47] increase the number of matters where that will be so. Nevertheless, it is a feature common to many E.C. Regulations and though a flaw it does not seem to be a fatal one. However, it is a feature of the proposal which will necessarily cause attention to focus on the provisions of the statute which govern the freedom of the SE to shift its legal base from one Member State to another.[48]

If the worker-participation issues connected with the European Company are solved, then it may be that the same technique could be applied to the Draft Fifth Directive on the structure of public companies and that that Directive could also make progress towards adoption. The Directive, even shorn of its worker-participation provisions, contains important initiatives for domestic company law. Although the latest version of the proposals[49] no longer make two-tier board structures compulsory,[50] nevertheless it contains provisions which could have significant effects upon the content of directors' duties and their enforcement and upon the freedom of companies to adopt whatever voting right structure they prefer.

FUNDAMENTAL PROBLEMS OF COMPANY LAW

To suggest that company law, despite the efforts of the domestic and Community legislators, faces fundamental problems which it has not resolved may seem churlish. Unquestionably the limited liability company has been a major instrument in making possible the industrial

---

[45] This comes close to the system in Canada where incorporators have the option of forming under the (federal) Canada Business Corporations Act or under the legislation of one of the Provinces. The ideal in a federation is federal pre-emption of company Law (as Australian is at last likely to achieve). But this is not yet practical politics in the quasi-federal E.C.

[46] para. 32.

[47] See n. 40, above.

[48] An issue which, see n. 19, above, has already proved difficult to resolve within the programme for the harmonisation of national company laws.

[49] See n. 65, below.

[50] Though it would appear that the combined effect of the Cadbury and Greenbury reports, with their emphasis on the distinct role of non-executive directors, has already been *de facto* to push domestic law away from a unitary board structure in its pure form. See p. 193, below.

and commercial developments which have occurred throughout the world. And our system of company law was, until recently, the model widely followed in the common law countries. That leading role has now been taken over by the United States[51] and we cannot hope to recover it. As a result of our membership of the European Community, our company law is increasingly diverging from that in the non-European, common law world and all we can do is to strive harder to influence the harmonisation programme of the European Community so as to ensure that the result preserves the best features of both the common law system and the civil law systems of our continental partners.[52]

Nor can it be said that our company legislation has not reacted to changing conditions; legislation which grew from 212 sections and three schedules in the Companies Act 1862 to 747 sections and 25 Schedules in the Companies Act 1985[53] cannot be accused of stagnation.[54] But if one looks at the major developments this century and at the problems that these have thrown up, it is difficult to avoid the conclusion that there has been a reluctance to recognise their implications for company law and that, when those implications have been recognised, the reaction has been to add to the existing framework without ever re-examining its foundations to ensure that they are still sufficiently sound to bear the weight of the expanding superstructure.

That sad conclusion can be illustrated by a brief look[55] at five of those developments and at how our company law has reacted, or failed to react, to them.

1. The growth of incorporated, and decline of unincorporated, businesses

When incorporation with limited liability was introduced in the nineteenth century it was envisaged that its use would be in relation to businesses for which entrepreneurs needed to raise capital for large-scale enterprises (*i.e.* in relation to what are now called public limited companies). By the end of that century it had been recognised that it could also be advantageously adopted by partnerships and sole traders. Today it is commonly used throughout industry and commerce, leaving the unincorporated form largely to the professions which, as pro-

---

[51] Whose business corporation laws influence Canada, Australia and New Zealand directly and the rest of the common law world mainly through the latter two.

[52] Perhaps other countries might then find it worthwhile to borrow from it.

[53] And this ignores the other three Acts forming part of the 1985 Consolidation and the many other enactments which compilations, such as Butterworth's *Company Law Handbook*, rightly include.

[54] A more legitimate criticism is that it has grown excessively; no other country's legislation goes into such detail.

[55] It must be brief, for the primary object of this book is to explain what the law is and not what ideally it ought to be.

fessional rules are relaxed to permit incorporation, are now also adopting the corporate form. The implications of this have not been wholly ignored by company law. On the contrary, ever since the distinction between public and private companies was introduced efforts have been made to adjust the companies' legislation to the needs of small businesses. But these efforts led only to vacillating concessions in favour of "private", "exempt private", "small" and "medium-sized" companies. A belated effort was made in 1981[56] to arouse interest in a separate form of incorporation which would recognise that a company in which there was no separation of ownership and control was, in principle and in its needs, a different animal from a public company. But the attempt failed, as did a later effort to raise the issue,[57] and placebos continue to be preferred to major surgery. The most promising of these[58] arose from an initiative by the Institute of Directors which resulted in the DTI in 1988 consulting on what came to be described as *The Elective Regime in Private Companies*. Under this, with the consent of the members, private companies would be enabled to contract out of the need to observe a number of provisions of the Companies Act, thus suspending their application to the company unless and until the members resolve to end that suspension. This proposal was adopted in the Companies Act 1989 under the rubric *De-regulation of Private Companies*[59] and is certainly a step in the right direction though it falls far short of giving such companies a simple Act of their own.

2. Employee participation

The notion that it is one of the roles of company law to deal with the place of the employees in the enterprise is one which is almost entirely foreign to British company law, though not to the company laws of a number of our European partners. As we have noted, the controversy whether this is an appropriate role for company law has led to a lack of agreement over the Draft Fifth Directive, the proposals for which originally envisage that all Member States would adopt a two-tier structure for the boards of public companies above a certain

---

[56] *A New Form of Incorporation for Small Firms: A Consultative Document* (1981 Cmnd. 8171).

[57] After examination the Law Commission concluded that a separate form of incorporation would not address the main problems facing small companies. See DTI, *Company Law Review: The Law Applicable to Private Companies*, November 1994, which contains the Law Commission's report, and Freedman (1994) 57 M.L.R. 555.

[58] And the least, that mooted in 1987 by the Inland Revenue and the DTI in a Consultative Document on *"Disincorporation"* suggesting that small incorporated businesses should be provided with facilities to convert to unincorporated form.

[59] Act, ss. 113–117 inserting new provisions in the 1985 Act. See below, p. 91. Special provisions for small companies have also been taken forward in the areas of financial reporting and auditing. See pp. 526–532, below.

size and that employees would be represented on the upper (or "supervisory") board.

These concepts originated in Germany. Since 1861, German public companies have had a two-tier board structure: a supervisory board to control the basic policy of the company and a management board to manage its operations. The supervisory board appoints the management board but otherwise the two are distinct and a member of one may not be a member of the other. After the 1939–1945 War, on the instigation of the occupation authorities in West Germany, representatives elected by the company's employees were, by law, given half the places on the supervisory boards of coal and steel companies and, in 1952, one third in the case of other large companies, a proportion increased for the largest companies to nearly one half in 1976. Representation at board level is underpinned by works councils providing for formal consultation and even co-decision with employees at lower levels. Less far-reaching approaches to this system of *Mitbestimmung* or "co-determination" have been adopted in some other European countries.[60]

The first Draft proposed comparable harmonised provisions throughout the Community in the case of the larger public companies.[61] To this, however, some Member States were strongly opposed. In the United Kingdom in the 1970s, under Labour Governments and when trade unions were more powerful, industrial democracy was the subject of heated debate and led to the appointment and report of the Bullock Committee[62] (which split three ways but with a majority favouring a unitary board and making detailed suggestions for worker representation) and to a Government White Paper proposing co-determination but under a two-tier board.[63] But the subsequent Conservative Government set its face firmly against worker participation other than on a voluntary basis, and in the light of the weakened position of the trade unions,[64] co-determination officially ceased to be regarded as a live issue.

However, later Drafts are no longer tied to the German concepts. Compulsory two-tier boards were abandoned in that published in 1983 and in the latest[65] all that is required is that a Member State must make provision for either one or both of a one-tier or a two-tier system and that if it makes provision for both it may permit each company to choose which to adopt. Moreover, worker-representation on the

---

[60] The Netherlands, Luxembourg, Sweden and Denmark, while France permits optional two-tier boards (which very few of its companies have adopted).

[61] In the latest Draft it would apply only to public companies with more than 1,000 employees.

[62] *Report of the Committee on Industrial Democracy*, (1977) Cmnd. 6076.

[63] *Industrial Democracy*, (1978) Cmnd. 7231.

[64] Whose attitude had always been somewhat ambivalent.

[65] 1988 Draft: appended to the DTI's Consultative Document, *Amended Proposal for a Fifth Directive on the Harmonisation of Company Law in the European Community*, Jan. 1990.

supervisory board, if there is one, or on the unitary board, if there is not, is not the only permitted method of providing worker-participation. There are three options: (i) board representation, (ii) a separate organ, representing employees only, with rights to be regularly given information and to be consulted, and (iii) a collective agreement concluded between the company (or an organisation representing the company) and an organisation representing the employees providing that the concluded agreement provides at least for (i) or (ii).[66] Since (ii) amounts to "consultation" rather than "co-determination", this is a far cry from the compulsory introduction of anything like the German system. It seems to be generally acceptable in most Member States, but the United Kingdom Government has remained implacably opposed, believing "that in the United Kingdom successful employee involvement depends on a spirit of cooperation rather than on formal machinery and that it is best introduced voluntarily".[67]

Similar difficulties have beset the discussions over the European Company statute, where, if anything, the conflict is more acute. If worker-participation is not part of the statute for SEs, there is a danger that Member States with domestic co-determination requirements will find that companies incorporated under domestic law re-incorporate as European Companies in order to escape those requirements. However, in a recent Communication the Commission has floated a proposal to break the log-jam.[68] The Commission's idea attempts to build on the success of the European Works Councils Directive,[69] adopted under the Social Agreement and thus not applicable in the United Kingdom. This Directive requires companies above a certain employee threshold and operating in more than one Member State (not taking the United Kingdom into account for these purposes) to establish a trans-national works council for the purpose of informing and consulting their employees over certain basic matters of corporate strategy. This Directive has undoubtedly been successful in encouraging the establishment of EWCs, which tend in fact to include representatives of the company's British employees (though the impact of EWCs in practice remains to be assessed).

The Commission now boldly proposes to drop the worker-participation provisions of the draft European Company statute on the grounds that such companies will be covered in any event by the

---

[66] The introduction of this third option caused the British trade unions to swing in favour of the proposal: *cf.* n. 64, above.

[67] See para. 4 of the DTI Consultative Document (n. 65, above). But does the British experience suggest that really meaningful employee involvement will be introduced on any scale without compulsion?

[68] *Communication from the Commission on Worker Information and Consultation*, November 1995, COM(95) 547 final.

[69] Council Directive 94/45, [1994] O.J. L254/64.

European Works Council Directive.[70] Similarly, the Commission envisages that the worker-participation provisions of the Draft Fifth Directive could be dropped if a separate directive were to be adopted requiring works councils with defined powers to be established at national level, so that purely domestic companies would be also be required to inform and consult representatives of their employees.[71] Whether these proposals will prove acceptable to the Member States, especially Germany, remains to be seen, but company lawyers should note that, if they are adopted, they would mark the end of the Community's efforts to provide for representatives of the employees' interest within the structure of company law and a decision to choose instead a representational mechanism existing outside the company and in the land of labour law.

3. Corporate governance

The issue of employee participation is part, though only a part, of the debate over ''corporate governance'', to use the modern term for an issue which is as old as the emergence of the large public company. The increasing economic power of public companies and the implications of the separation of ownership from control in such companies have thrown up a number of inter-related problems. Initially these were seen as restricted to finding means of ensuring that those who controlled and managed such companies did so for the benefit of the shareholders and were effectively accountable to them. This was generally described, particularly in the American literature, as the quest for ''stockholder democracy'', but that expression is now heard less often as it has come to be accepted that Athenian democracy is not the way to govern a large public company. Instead, this and a wider range of problems have come to be debated under the rubric *''Corporate Governance''*.[72] However, the quest for ''accountability'' to shareholders still continues and has always been recognised as a proper subject for company law. The traditional methods of seeking to secure it have mainly been by an increase both in the information which has to be disclosed to shareholders and in the matters that need to be ratified by them in general meeting. These methods can be effective only if the members (i) are sufficiently knowledgeable fully to understand the information, (ii) have large enough shareholdings to be able

---

[70] This of course is not true of the U.K., and the non-applicability of the EWC Directive in the U.K. thus casts some doubt over whether companies with their headquarters in the United Kingdom would be permitted to incorporate as European Companies.

[71] In fact, only the U.K. and Ireland seem not to have some system of this sort in place already.

[72] For recent contributions to an already huge literature, see Prentice and Holland (eds.), *Contemporary Issues in Corporate Governance* (Oxford, 1993) and Parkinson, *Corporate Power and Responsibility* (Oxford, 1993). For a comparative survey see Hopt & Teubner (eds.), *Corporate Governance and Directors' Liabilities* (de Gruyter, 1985).

to influence decisions, and (iii) are able and willing to resort to the courts if need be. In the United Kingdom the only shareholders likely to meet conditions (i) and (ii) are institutional investors—who today own some 80 per cent of listed shares (another major transformation this century). But they rarely meet condition (iii) because, though able, they are usually unwilling to litigate[73] and prefer either to support the managers or to sell their shares if they have lost confidence in them.

The basic problem here is that accountability cannot be secured by legal prescriptions unless these are enforced—in the last resort by the courts. In England,[74] the cost of litigation, even if successful, is such that shareholders are not able and willing to resort to the courts. The major contribution that English company law has made in this area is to recognise that what is needed is a watchdog empowered to take action on their behalf (by investigations, inspections and the institution of civil and criminal proceedings).[75] In the company law field that watchdog is the Department of Trade and Industry but in the related field of financial services the role is delegated to a self-standing body (the Securities and Investments Board). It is possible that one day its role may be extended to "corporate governance" also.

However, the Government has never been willing to shoulder the cost of making the DTI a day-to-day supervisor of company affairs, nor is the Department likely to be capable of doing that job. Perhaps for the above reasons the recent reports of the Cadbury[76] and Green-bury[77] Committees, whilst stressing the importance of greater reporting to shareholders, have placed their main emphasis on a larger role for non-executive members of the board in monitoring the performance of the company, including that of the executive directors. Whether the new approach will bring real changes, in the absence of a close link between the non-executive directors and the shareholders, which the two committees do not advocate, remains to be seen.

Until the 1930s, and despite the fact that it had become common-place for directors' reports to declare that they recognise that they owed duties not only to the shareholders but also the company's employees, customers and the community, it had not occurred to com-pany lawyers, at any rate in the common law world, that if there were any such duties they had anything to do with company law. Since

---

[73] And it must be said that on the rare occasions when they have litigated on behalf of the shareholders as a whole they have received precious little encouragement from the English courts: see, *e.g. Prudential Assurance v. Chatterley-Whitfield Collieries* [1949] A.C. 512, H.L., and *Prudential Assurance v. Newman Industries Ltd (No. 2)* [1982] Ch. 204, C.A.

[74] Contrast the USA, where different rules relating to liability for costs and lawyers' ability and willingness to take cases on a contingent fee, enable litigation to be undertaken with less risk of bankruptcy.

[75] See Chap. 25, below.

[76] *Report of the Committee on the Financial Aspects of Corporate Governance*, 1992.

[77] *Directors' Remuneration: Report of a Study Group chaired by Sir Richard Greenbury*, 1995.

then, however, stimulated by the writings of Berle and Means[78] and the debate between Berle and Dodds in the Harvard Law Review,[79] company lawyers have, often with misgivings, faced the possibility that these wider duties may be owed and that public companies may have developed social consciences.[80] This is coupled with a general recognition that public companies are not, in practice, carried on solely, or even mainly, with a view to the maximisation of profits for the benefit of shareholders but rather to increase the size and importance of the company and thereby the power and influence of its controllers and managers. And now these matters too are debated under the rubric "Corporate Governance".[81]

English company law, however, has proved resistant to the acceptance of such subversive notions. Although in the 1970s, as we saw above, we toyed with the idea of "co-determination" in the sense of worker-participation in corporate decision-making, this has ceased to be regarded as a live issue here, and is unlikely to become one until Community action succeeds in reviving it.[82] However, two small steps towards recognising that the employees are part of a company, and not just servants of it, were taken by the Companies Act 1980. This declared that "the matters to which directors . . . shall have regard . . . shall include the interests of the company's employees in general as well as the interests of its members",[83] though it carefully went on to ensure that employees, as such, had no power to enforce that duty.[84] And, perhaps more importantly, it declared that on the cessation or transfer of a company's business, the company might make provision for employees or former employees even though that might not be in the best interests of the company.[85] In general, however, the position of employees *vis-à-vis* the companies who employ them and on which their livelihood is likely to depend to a far greater extent than does that of the shareholders, is still not regarded as a matter for company law but for the law of master and servant, latterly given the less Victorian name of employment or labour law. Voluntary employee

---

[78] *The Modern Corporation and Private Property* (1932) and revised edition (1968): see Chap. 1, p. 9, above.

[79] (1932) 43 Harvard L.R. 1049; (1932) 45 Harvard L.R. 1145.

[80] See, *e.g.* Berle, *The 20th Century Capitalist Revolution* (London, 1955) and *Power without Property* (London, 1960).

[81] The subtitle of Hopt & Teubner: *loc. cit.* n. 72, above, is "Legal, Economic and Sociological Analyses on Corporate Social Responsibilities". There is an immense literature on all these topics. Those wishing to explore them further will find an exhaustive bibliography at the end of each contribution in that book: See also Herman, *Corporate Control, Corporate Power* (Camb., 1981) and Wedderburn, "The Social Responsibility of Companies" (1985) 15 *Melbourne University Law Review* 4 and "Trust, Corporation and the Worker" (1985) 23 Osgoode Hall L.J. 203.

[82] See pp. 63–66, above.

[83] s.46(1). Now Companies Act 1985, s.309(1).

[84] s.46(2). Now Companies Act 1985, s.309(2).

[85] s.74. Now Companies Act 1985 s.719 and Insolvency Act 1986, s.187. This reverses the effect of the decision in *Parke v. Daily News* [1962] Ch. 927. See p. 205, below.

share-ownership schemes have been encouraged by the Government by tax and other concessions. But these schemes stop far short of co-determination; if shareholders lack effective participation in decision-making, workers are not helped in that regard by becoming shareholders—though that may perhaps lead them to take a greater interest in enhancing the company's prosperity.

So far as concerns the wider social duties of public companies, English company law has made no movement at all. Whatever directors themselves may say, the law says that their duties are owed to the company which for this purpose and so long as the company is a going concern means the long-term interests of its members and, as a result of the recent grudging admissions, its employees. In the United Kingdom the possibility that this may be an anachronism is more widely debated by those who are not lawyers[86] than by those who are—and is less debated by anyone than it is in the United States.[87] And this despite the efforts of the Government to encourage wider business sponsorship of the arts and of other charitable activities.[88]

4. Mega-multinationals

The growing number, and power, of multinational groups, operating in many countries and, possibly, dwarfing all of them, is another phenomenon which has caused alarm and led some countries to take protective measures. Once again, such action as has been taken in the United Kingdom has not been through companies' legislation. Indeed, except in relation to tax avoidance, very little has been done. The fact that large areas of British commerce and industry (including the national press and financial services) are now dominated by multinationals, whose ultimate control is outside both the United Kingdom and the European Community, is treated with apparent equanimity, except in some cases in relation to the privatisation of nationalised industries—the final development to which reference needs to be made.

Indeed, British company law has failed, unlike German or U.S. law, effectively to come to grips with the problems posed even by purely domestic groups of companies. We still commence with the proposition that all the companies in a group are separate legal entities,[89] and only in the realms of tax law and financial reporting has any significant

---

[86] See, *e.g.* the one-man crusade of George Goyder in his *The Future of Private Enterprise* (1951), *The Responsible Company* (1961), *The Responsible Worker* (1975) and *The Just Enterprise* (1987).

[87] But the lawyers' contributions are growing: see n. 72, above.

[88] Fortunately, boards of directors do not seem to experience much difficulty in persuading themselves that generosity in this respect is for the good of the company. But the extent of the generosity is minimal in comparison with that in the USA.

[89] See pp. 166–173, below.

attempt been made to deal with the group as a whole. Nor, as we have seen, is this an area where the Community as a whole has had any greater success.[90]

5. Nationalisation and privatisation

In the United Kingdom the immediate post-War years were an era of nationalisation. Occasionally the Government achieved its aim by acquiring a controlling interest in the companies or groups whose business was being nationalised; more often a new type of corporate body, "the public corporation," was created by the nationalising statute and the undertakings and assets vested in that body. Either method produced material differences in "corporate governance"—particularly when the latter was adopted; any pretence that the directorate was answerable to the shareholders was abandoned since there were no shareholders. Instead the board became answerable to the appropriate Minister and he or she to Parliament. It was also hoped that nationalisation would lead to a more co-operative and less confrontational relationship between management and employees. In most cases the hoped-for advantages failed to materialise and we are now in an era of de-nationalisation or "privatisation".

When nationalisation had been achieved by acquisition by the Government of the share capital of the former companies, privatisation is a straightforward operation, not necessarily involving any legislative action; the Government merely has to dispose of the shares either by a public offering and listing on the Stock Exchange or by private deals. When the undertaking had been vested in a statutory public corporation the privatising *modus operandi* is somewhat more complicated; a new limited company has to be registered and the undertaking vested in it and, normally, a public offering made of its share capital. In either event, novel constitutional and legal questions are likely to arise.[91] This is principally because, although the Government may declare that it wishes to relinquish all political control, leaving the industry to the discipline of the market, this generally proves to be easier said than done, and because when, as in the case of public utilities, the company will have a monopoly, special arrangements need to be made to protect consumers.

Hence privatisation has led to interesting distortions of, and supplements to, company law. The distortions consist of special provisions in the company's articles of association (some of which would not be countenanced by the Stock Exchange in the case of normal listed companies) designed principally to enable the Government to prevent takeovers or other changes of control which it regards as undesirable.

---

[90] Above, p. 56.
[91] For a useful account, see Graham & Prosser, *Privatising Public Enterprises* (Oxford, 1991).

One such device[92] is the "golden share", retained by the Government, either for a limited period or indefinitely, and enabling it to outvote all others on certain types of resolution.[93] Another is a provision enabling the Government to nominate some of the directors. The supplements to company law, adopted to protect consumers in the cases where there is a monopoly, consist of consumer "watchdogs" independent of the company's management, the prototype being OFTEL which performs this role in relation to British Telecom.

Surprisingly, one constituency for which no special protective measures have been thought appropriate in the privatisation measures is that of the vastly increased body of individual, small, first-time investors whom the privatisation issues have been deliberately designed to attract—and with considerable success although most of them sell the shares once they have exhausted the special inducements offered them. Shareholders have no greater protection than they would in other public listed companies; in so far as there is control over the management it will be by the Government, or institutional investors if and when they choose to exercise it in their own interests.

CONCLUSION

It seems inevitable that developments in our company law over the next 25 years will follow much the same pattern as that of the past 25. Reforms will be piecemeal without any review of the basic structure and with a marked reluctance to tackle fundamental problems except to the extent forced upon us by the European Community. The latter's initiatives may result in major changes and if these are to be to our liking it behoves us to play a more constructive role in the preparatory stages of Community legislation than we generally have in the past. Domestically inspired changes to our companies' and related legislation are likely to be restricted mainly to technical matters, to the removal of flaws which have come to light in the legislation of 1985–1986, and to the closing of loop-holes revealed by scandals as yet unforeseen. Our company legislation will continue to increase in length and, since changes in our style of legislative drafting are most unlikely, will become still more complex and opaque. But cheer up: all this should provide grist to the mills of company lawyers.

---

[92] Others include provisions intended to ensure that no shareholder is beneficially entitled to an interest in more than a fixed proportion (say 15 per cent) of voting shares and disenfranchising his shares if he does have such an interest. So far none of these devices seems to have proved particularly effective.

[93] The legality of this device was upheld by the House of Lords in *Bushell v. Faith* [1970] A.C. 1099 which, ironically, the Government had proposed to overrule in its aborted Companies Bill 1973.

Part Two

FORMATION OF COMPANIES

INTRODUCTION

In Part One of this book we examined, in outline, the growth of British company law to its present state of sophistication and complexity. However, the fact remains that the use of the corporate form is not obligatory for those wishing to carry on business. It is a facility which the law makes available. There are alternative legal forms for the carrying on of a business and at least for small businesses the choice among them is not necessarily a foregone conclusion. A person may carry on a small business as an unincorporated small trader or in a partnership, the alternative when a small body of persons wishes to "carry on business in common with a view of profit".[1] Consequently, Chapter 5 discusses the practical advantages and disadvantages of carrying on business through an incorporated company as compared with the unincorporated forms. Chapter 6 then discusses the procedures for forming a company, on the assumption that a decision has been made that that is the most appropriate legal form for the activity in question; and Chapter 7 deals with the liabilities of those—the promoters—who help to create companies and who perhaps seek to sell to the company something which they own.

It must be stressed, however, that it does not follow that every unincorporated body lacks all the attributes which incorporation automatically provides. As we have seen,[2] statutes of the early nineteenth century enabled the Crown by letters patent to confer all or any of the advantages of incorporation without actually granting corporate personality, and similarly a statute may confer many of these privileges without actual incorporation. In fact, this has frequently been done, with the result that between the two extremes of an unincorporated club or society and a full-fledged corporation there are many hybrids, which, though formally unincorporated, possess a greater or lesser number of the attributes of a corporation. Among these hybrids, even partnerships ought perhaps to be included for the partners can now sue or be sued in the firm's name and, if insolvent, can be wound up in much the same way as an incorporated company.

Originally the main examples of hybrids were those that sprang from the nineteenth century's friendly societies, co-operative societies and trade unions. Most of these have now attained full corporate status (though still registered with the Registrar of Friendly Societies) and

---

[1] This is the definition of a partnership contained in s.1(1) of the Partnership Act 1890.
[2] Above, p. 37.

are subject to their own legislation and not regarded as "companies"—though in most cases they can be wound up as if they were. Thus, co-operative societies and housing associations, formed under the Industrial and Provident Societies Acts, and building societies, formed under the Building Societies Acts, have full corporate personality. Indeed the latter, as a result of the Building Societies Act 1986, may now extend their roles way beyond their traditional ones of providing savings facilities and loans for house purchase and they are subject to the general supervision of a new Building Societies Commission and to that of the Securities and Investments Board in relation to their "investment business" activities.[3] Only friendly societies and trade unions remain, somewhat anomalously, formally unincorporated though for most purposes they are treated as if they were distinct legal entities[4] but with their property vested in trustees. This reliance on the trust concept rather than on that of de jure incorporation, also played a part in the development of trustee savings banks until they were merged and converted into a "privatised" public company under the Trustee Savings Banks Act 1985.[5]

---

[3] Some have taken the next step and converted to being companies incorporated under the Act, sometimes as a prelude to their being taken over by another financial institution.

[4] An attempt was made by s.74 (1) of the Industrial Relations Act 1971 to require registered trade unions to become bodies corporate but this proved abortive as the unions refused to register under the Act. Accordingly the Trade Union and Labour Relations Act 1974 went to the opposite extreme by providing that "a trade union . . . shall not be, or be treated as if it were, a body corporate" although it went on to say that the union could sue or be sued in its own name and that any judgment should be enforceable against its property "to the like extent and in like manner as if the union were a body corporate" (now, Trade Union and Labour Relations Consolidation Act 1992, s.10). As a result it has been held that although a union may sue in tort it cannot sue for libel because it no longer has a "personality" to be defamed: *EETPU v. The Times* [1980] Q.B. 285.

[5] An operation which revealed, to most people's surprise, that, in contrast with other associations, the statutory Savings Banks had no members, that their depositors' rights were contractual and not as beneficiaries under a trust, and that the banks' assets belonged to the State: *Ross v. Lord Advocate and Others* [1986] 1 W.L.R. 1077 (H.L.Sc. & E.). But the trust concept played and, in the United Kingdom, continues to play a major role in relation to unit trusts.

CHAPTER 5

ADVANTAGES AND DISADVANTAGES OF INCORPORATION

Legal entity distinct from its members

As already emphasised, the fundamental attribute of corporate person-ality—from which indeed all the other consequences flow—is that the corporation is a legal entity distinct from its members. Hence it is capable of enjoying rights and of being subject to duties which are not the same as those enjoyed or borne by its members. In other words, it has "legal personality" and is often described as an *artificial person* in contrast with a human being, a *natural person*.[1]

As we have seen, corporate personality became an attribute of the normal joint stock company only at a comparatively late stage in its development, and it was not until *Salomon v. Salomon & Co.*[2] at the end of the nineteenth century that its implications were fully grasped even by the courts. The facts of this justly celebrated case were as follows:

Salomon had for many years carried on a prosperous business as a leather merchant. In 1892 he decided to convert it into a limited com-pany and for this purpose Salomon & Co. Ltd was formed with Salo-mon, his wife and five of his children as members and Salomon as managing director. The company purchased the business as a going concern for £39,000—"a sum which represented the sanguine expectations of a fond owner rather than anything that can be called a businesslike or reasonable estimate of value".[3] The price was satisfied by £10,000 in debentures, conferring a charge over all the company's assets, £20,000 in fully paid £1 shares and the balance in cash. The result was that Salomon held 20,001 of the 20,007 shares issued, and each of the remaining six shares was held by a member of his family, apparently as a nominee for him. The company almost immediately ran into difficulties and only a year later the then holder of the deben-tures appointed a receiver and the company went into liquidation. Its assets were sufficient to discharge the debentures but nothing was left for the unsecured creditors. In these circumstances Vaughan Williams J. and a strong Court of Appeal held that the whole transaction was

---

[1] A company, even if it has only one member, is a "corporation aggregate" as opposed to the somewhat anomalous "corporation sole" in which an office, *e.g.* that of a bishop, is personified.

[2] [1897] A.C. 22, H.L.

[3] *Per* Lord Macnaghten at 49.

contrary to the true intent of the Companies Act and that the company
was a mere sham, and an alias, agent, trustee or nominee for Salomon
who remained the real proprietor of the business. As such he was
liable to indemnify the company against its trading debts. But the
House of Lords unanimously reversed this decision. They held that
the company has been validly formed since the Act merely required
seven members holding at least one share each. It said nothing about
their being independent, or that they should take a substantial interest
in the undertaking, or that they should have a mind and will of their
own, or that there should be anything like a balance of power in the
constitution of the company. Hence the business belonged to the company and not to Salomon, and Salomon was *its* agent. In the blunt
words of Lord Halsbury L.C.[4]:

> "Either the limited company was a legal entity or it was not. If it
> was, the business belonged to it and not to Mr Salomon. If it was
> not, there was no person and no thing to be an agent at all; and it
> is impossible to say at the same time that there is a company and
> there is not."

Or, as Lord Macnaghten put it[5]:

> "The company is at law a different person altogether from the sub-
> scribers . . .; and, though it may be that after incorporation the busi-
> ness is precisely the same as it was before, and the same persons
> are managers, and the same hands receive the profits, the company
> is not in law the agent of the subscribers or trustee for them. Nor
> are the subscribers, as members, liable in any shape or form, except
> to the extent and in the manner provided by the Act."[6]

Of course this decision does not mean that a promoter can with
impunity defraud the company which he forms or swindle his existing
creditors. In the *Salomon* case it was argued that the company was
entitled to rescind in view of the wilful overvaluation of the business
sold to it. But the House held that in fact there was no fraud at all since
the shareholders were fully conversant with what was being done. Had
Salomon made a profit which he concealed from his fellow shareholders the position would have been different.[7] Nor was there any
fraud on Salomon's pre-incorporation creditors, all of whom were paid
off in full out of the purchase price. Otherwise they or Salomon's
trustee in bankruptcy might have been entitled to upset the sale.[8] And
today the charge securing the debenture might be invalidated if there

---

[4] At 31.
[5] At 51.
[6] For an early statutory recognition of the same principle, see 22 Geo. 3 c. 45, which disqualified
those holding Government contracts from election to Parliament but expressly provided (s.3)
that the prohibition did not extend to members of incorporated companies holding such contracts.
[7] See below, p. 133
[8] Under what are now ss.423 to 425 of the Insolvency Act 1986.

was a successful petition for a winding-up or an administration order within two years.[9] But, in this particular case, Salomon seems to have been one of the victims rather than the villain of the piece for he had mortgaged his debentures and used the money to try to support the tottering company. However, the result would have been the same if he had not, and even if he had been the only creditor to receive anything from the business which was "his" in fact though not in law.

This decision opened up new vistas to company lawyers and the world of commerce. Not only did it finally establish the legality of the "one-man" company and showed that incorporation was as readily available to the small private partnership and sole trader as to the large public company, but it also revealed that it was possible for a trader not merely to limit his liability to the money which he put into the enterprise but even to avoid any serious risk to the major part of that by subscribing for debentures rather than shares. This result seems shocking, and the decision has been much criticised.[10] The only justification for it is that the public deal with a limited company at their peril and know, or should know, what to expect. In particular a search of the company's file at Companies House should reveal its latest annual accounts and whether there are any charges on the company's assets.[11] But the accounts will probably be months out of date and, in the case of a small or medium sized company, may be expurgated editions of those circulated to the members.[12] Nor does everyone having dealings with a company have the time or knowledge needed to search the file. The experienced businessman with his trade protection associations can take care of himself, but the little man, whom the law should particularly protect, rarely has any idea of the risks he runs when he grants credit to a company with a high-sounding name,[13] impressive nominal capital (not paid up in cash), and with assets mortgaged up to the hilt.[14] Nor is it practical for the unemployed worker who is offered a job with a limited company, to decline it until he or she has first searched the company's file.[15]

Since the *Salomon* case, the complete separation of the company

---

[9] Insolvency Act 1986, s. 245.

[10] See, *e.g.* O. Kahn-Freund, "Some Reflections on Company Law Reform" (1944) 7 M.L.R. 54 (a thought-provoking article still well worth study) in which it is described as a "calamitous decision".

[11] But not necessarily the amount secured; most companies grant floating charges to their bankers to secure "all sums due or to become due" on their current overdrafts and the register of charges will not give any indication of the size of the overdraft at any particular time.

[12] Companies Act 1985, ss. 247–251: see below, Chap. 19.

[13] There are undoubtedly many who think that "Ltd" is an indication of size and stability (which "plc" may be but "Ltd" certainly is not) rather than a warning of irresponsibility.

[14] But no sympathy was wasted on him by the H.L. "A creditor who will not take the trouble to use the means which the statute provides for enabling him to protect himself must bear the consequences of his own negligence": *per* Lord Watson at 40.

[15] The likely result would be loss of social security benefits.

and its members has never been doubted. As we shall see later,[16] there are cases in which the legislature, and to a very small extent the courts, have allowed the veil of incorporation to be lifted, but in general it is opaque and impassable. The consequences, however, are not necessarily wholly beneficial to the members.[17] For example, if a trader incorporates his business he will cease to have an insurable interest in its assets even though he is the beneficial owner of all the shares. If therefore he forgets to assign the insurance policies, and to obtain any necessary consents of the insurers, nothing will be payable if the assets perish.[18] Similarly, a parent company will not have an insurable interest in the assets of its subsidiary companies even though wholly owned, for the rule that a company is distinct from its members applies equally to the separate companies of a group.[19] In Kahn-Freund's striking phrase,[20] "sometimes corporate entity works like a boomerang and hits the man who was trying to use it".

Limited liability

It follows from the fact that a corporation is a separate person that its members are not as such liable for its debts.[21] Hence in the absence of express provision to the contrary the members will be completely free from any personal liability. This is, in fact, the position as regards municipal and ecclesiastical corporations and the rapidly decreasing number of public corporations, and may be so as regards statutory and chartered companies, the members of which will be under personal liability only if, and to the extent that, the statute or charter so provides.

But as regards a company registered under the Companies Acts a complete absence of any liability is not permitted. Such a company can either be registered as unlimited, in which case the members are in effect guarantors of its obligations without any restriction on amount,[22] or it can be limited by shares or guarantee.[23] In the case of

---

[16] Below, Chap. 8.

[17] See especially Kiralfy, "Some Unforseen Consequences of Private Incorporation" (1949) 65 L.Q.R. 231, and Kahn-Freund, *loc. cit.* and below, Chap. 8.

[18] *Macaura v. Northern Assurance Co.* [1925] A.C. 619, H.L.; *Levinger v Licences, etc. Insurance Co.* (1936) 54 Lloyds L.R. 68.

[19] As will be pointed out later, inroads have been made into this principle, but it still remains the general rule though for tax purposes "group relief" had drawn its sting.

[20] *loc. cit.*, p. 56.

[21] This sentence was quoted and relied on by Kerr L.J. in *Rayner (Mincing Lane) Ltd. v. Dept of Trade* [1989] Ch. 72 at 176 as an accurate statement of English law although, as he pointed out, it is not accurate in relation to most Civil Law countries—including Scotland so far as partnerships are concerned—or to international law: at 176–183.

[22] "In effect" because, of course, the *modus operandi* is different; the creditor has no direct right against the member, as he would have against a surety on default by the principal debtor.

[23] The Companies Acts (now 1985 Act, ss. 306–307) have always provided that a limited company may have directors with unlimited liability. It is not surprising that these provisions have

a company limited by shares each member is liable to contribute when called upon to do so the full nominal value of the shares held by him in so far as this has not already been paid by him or any prior holder of those shares. In the case of a guarantee company each member is liable to contribute a specified amount to the assets of the company in the event of its being wound up while he is a member or within one year after he ceases to be a member. In effect the member, without being directly liable to the company's creditors, is in both cases a limited guarantor of the company.

When, therefore, obligations are incurred on behalf of a company, the company is liable and not the members, though the company may ultimately be able to recover a contribution from them to enable it to discharge its obligations. If the company is an unlimited one their liability to contribute will be unlimited; if it is limited by shares their liability will be limited to the unpaid nominal value of their shares and in practice their shares are today likely to be fully paid up so that they will be under no further liability. If the company is limited by guarantee they will be under no liability until it is wound up, and then, in practice, only for a derisory sum.[24] In contrast, an unincorporated association, not being a legal person, cannot be liable, and obligations entered into on its behalf can bind only the actual officials who purport to act on its behalf, or the individual members if the officials have actual or apparent authority to bind them. In either event the persons bound will be liable to the full extent of their property unless they expressly or impliedly restrict their responsibility to the extent of the funds of the association, as the officials may well do. Hence the extent to which the member will be liable depends on the terms of the contract of association. In the case of a club, and presumably the same applies to learned and scientific societies, there will generally be implied a term that the members are not personally liable for obligations incurred on behalf of the club. But very different is the position of members of a partnership, an association carrying on business for gain. Each partner is an agent of all the others and his acts done in "carrying on in the normal way business of the kind carried on by the firm" bind the partners.[25] Only if the creditor knows of the limitation placed on the partners' authority will the other members escape liability.[26] Moreover, an attempt to restrict the partners' liability to partnership funds by a provision to that effect in the partnership agreement will be ineffective even if known to the creditors[27]; they will only be

---

long been a dead letter except occasionally in relation to professions which permit their members to practise as incorporated companies but only if the directors accept personal liability.

[24] See Chap. 1, p. 11, n. 36, above.

[25] Partnership Act 1890, s.5. This applies equally to Scotland thus largely negativing the consequence of recognising the Scottish firm as a separate person.

[26] *ibid*, ss.5 and 8.

[27] *Re Sea, Fire and Life Insurance Co.* (1854) 3 De G.M. & G. 459.

able to restrict their financial liability, in respect of acts otherwise authorised, by an express agreement to that effect with the creditor concerned.[28]

There is, it is true, now a method whereby liability can be limited without forming an incorporated company; namely, by a limited partnership under the Limited Partnerships Act 1907. But this has many disadvantages in comparison with a company. In particular, it is not possible to limit the personal liability of all the partners but only some of them.[29] Moreover, even the limited partners lose their privilege of limited liability if they take any part in the management of the business.[30] This latter rule is especially inconvenient, for although a person who puts money into a business may be happy to leave the running of it to his colleagues while all goes well, he will probably want to be able to intervene if things go wrong. If a limited partner does so, his attempt to salvage the wreck may well result in the whole of his fortune sinking with it.

Hence a limited company is generally found preferable. It enables the liability of all the members to be limited without restriction on the part which they play in the management, and, although it involves somewhat greater formality, publicity and expense, these are not very onerous. In practice, therefore, limited partnerships are used only where for some reason an incorporated company is inappropriate (*e.g.* in the case of certain professions which companies are not allowed to practise) but one member of the firm is not prepared to accept full liability for its debts or the other partners do not want him to play any part in the management. This may occur on the retirement from active participation of a senior partner whom it is wished to retain as a consultant or for the prestige value of his name and reputation. Save in these rare cases where limited partnerships are appropriate, the only practical alternatives at present are either complete personal liability or limited liability through the medium of a company. The unattractiveness of both these options to the accountancy profession, in particular, has generated pressures for a review of the Limited Partnership Act, as we shall see below, which is being undertaken currently.[31]

The overall result of the broad recognition by the courts of the separate legal entity of the company and of the limited liability of its members and managers is to produce at first sight a legal regime which is very unfavourable to potential creditors of companies, a situation which they have naturally sought to readjust in their favour, so far as

---

[28] *Hallett v. Dowdall* (1852) 21 L.J.Q.B. 98. It is a criminal offence to carry on business under a name ending with "Limited" unless duly incorporated with limited liability: Companies Act 1985, s.34.

[29] Limited Partnership Act 1907, s.4(2).

[30] *ibid.*, s.6(1). They may only "advise with the partners".

[31] Chap. 20, pp. 560–561.

is in their power. For large lenders, especially banks, there are a number of possibilities, to be used separately or cumulatively. Apart from the obvious commercial response of charging higher interest rates on loans to bodies whose members have limited liability, such lenders may seek to leap over the barrier created by the law of limited liability by exacting as the price of the loan to the company personal guarantees of its repayment from the managers or shareholders of the company, guarantees which may be secured on the personal assets of the individuals concerned. Instead of or in addition to obtaining personal security by contracting around limited liability, large lenders may seek to improve the priority of their claims by taking real security against the *company's* assets. As we shall see later on in this Chapter, chancery practitioners in the nineteenth century were quick to respond to this need by creating the flexible and all-embracing instrument of the floating charge to supplement the traditional fixed charge mechanisms which were already available.

However, these self-help remedies may not be practicable for trade creditors or employees[32] and, even in the case of large lenders, there is a strong danger that, when things begin to go wrong, the controllers of the company will take risks with the company's capital which were not within the contemplation of the parties when the loan was arranged. For these reasons, although the legislature has not overturned *Salomon v. Salomon* and, indeed, under the influence of Community law, the one-person company is now expressly recognised by English law,[33] the Companies and Insolvency Acts are full of provisions whose purpose cannot be completely understood except against the background of limited liability. These range from the extensive publicity and disclosure obligations placed upon limited liability companies[34] to priorities for certain classes of unsecured creditors on the winding-up of a company, the which priorities override even floating (but not fixed) charges.[35] Recently added to these statutory weapons are the provisions relating to wrongful trading[36] and the expanded provisions on the disqualification of directors, especially on grounds of unfitness.[37]

---

[32] Unless and to the extent that they have a statutory preference, unsecured creditors are in the worst possible world. Limited liability normally stops them suing the shareholders or directors, whilst the fixed and floating charges of the big lenders often soak up all the available assets of the company.

[33] See Council Directive 89/667 on single-member private limited liability companies, [1989] O.J. L395, December 12, 1989, implemented in Britain by S.I. 1992 No. 1699, which introduced *inter alia* new s.1(3A) of the Act.

[34] See Chap. 19 below, but note s.254 whereby the directors of unlimited liability companies are not normally required to deliver accounts and reports to the registrar for general publication.

[35] See Insolvency Act 1986, ss.40, 175 and 386–387.

[36] See pp. 153–155, below.

[37] See Chap. 24, below.

Property

One obvious advantage of corporate personality is that it enables the property of the association to be more clearly distinguished from that of its members. In an unincorporated society, the property of the association is the joint property of the members. The rights of the members therein differ from their rights to their separate property since the joint property must be dealt with according to the rules of the society and no individual member can claim any particular asset. By virtue of the trust the obvious complications can be minimised but not completely eradicated. And the complications cause particular difficulty in the case of a trading partnership both as regards the true nature of the interests of the partners[38] and as regards claims of creditors.[39]

On incorporation, the corporate property belongs to the company and members have no direct proprietary rights to it but merely to their "shares" in the undertaking.[40] A change in the membership, which causes inevitable dislocation to a partnership firm, leaves the company unconcerned; the shares may be transferred but the company's property will be untouched and no realisation or splitting up of its property will be necessary, as it will on a change in the constitution of a partnership firm. Similarly, the claims of the company's creditors will merely be against the company's property and the difficulties which can arise on bankruptcy of partners will not occur.

Suing and being sued

Closely allied to questions of property are those relating to legal actions. The difficulties in the way of suing, or being sued by, an unincorporated association have been sufficiently stressed in the previous chapters, where it was pointed out that they were partially surmounted by the trust device and, more satisfactorily, by statutory intervention. The problem is obviously of the greatest practical importance in connection with trading bodies and in fact it has now been solved in the case of partnerships by allowing a partnership to sue or be sued in the firm's name.[41] Hence, there is now no difficulty so far as the pure mechanics of suit are concerned—although there may still be complications in enforcing the judgment.

In the case of other unincorporated bodies (such as clubs and

---

[38] See Partnership Act 1890, ss.20–22; *Re Fuller's Contract* [1933] Ch. 652.

[39] *ibid.*, s.23, and the Insolvent Partnerships Order 1986 (S.I. 1986 No. 2142).

[40] "Shareholders are not, in the eye of the law, part owners of the undertaking. The undertaking is something different from the totality of the shareholdings": *per* Evershed L.J. in *Short v. Treasury Commissioners* [1948] 1 K.B. 116, 122, C.A. (affd. [1948] A.C. 534 H.L.).

[41] R.S.C., Ord. 81. For the equivalent county court procedure, see C.C.R., Ord. 5 r.9 and the County Courts Act 1984 s.48.

learned societies) not subject to special statutory provisions, the problems of suit are still serious. Sometimes its committee or other agents may be personally liable or authorised to sue. Otherwise, the only course is a "representative action" whereby, under certain conditions, one or more persons may sue or be sued on behalf of all the interested parties. But resort to this procedure[42] is available only subject to compliance with a number of somewhat ill-defined conditions, and the law, which has been inadequately explored,[43] is obscure and difficult. The result is apt to be embarrassing to the society when it wishes to enforce its rights (or, more properly, those of its members) though it has compensating advantages when it wishes to evade its duties.[44] Needless to say, none of these difficulties arises when an incorporated company is suing or being sued; the company as a legal person can take action to enforce its legal rights and can be sued for breach of its legal duties. The only disadvantage is that if a limited company is the plaintiff it may be ordered to give security for costs.[45]

Perpetual succession

One of the obvious advantages of an artificial person is that it is not susceptible to "the thousand natural shocks that flesh is heir to". It cannot become incapacitated by illness, mental or physical, and it has not (or need not have) an allotted span of life.[46] This is not to say that the death or incapacity of its human members may not cause the company considerable embarrassment; obviously it will if all the directors die or are imprisoned or if there are too few surviving members to hold a valid meeting, or if the bulk of the members or directors become enemy aliens.[47] But the vicissitudes of the flesh have no direct effect on the disembodied company.[48] The death of a member leaves the

---

[42] Which is also of considerable importance in company law, *e.g.* where a member, on behalf of himself and the other members is suing the company to restrain an alleged "fraud on the minority" (see Chap. 23, below) or where a debenture-holder starts an action, on behalf of himself and the other debenture-holders, to enforce the security (see Chap. 15, below).

[43] But see *Prudential Assurance Co. Ltd v. Newman Industries Ltd* [1981] Ch. 257; *EMI. Records Ltd v. Riley* [1981] 1 W.L.R. 923; *Murray v. Hibernian Dance Club, The Times,* August 12, 1996.

[44] "An unincorporated association has certain advantages when litigation is desired against them": *per* Scrutton L.J. in *Bloom v. National Federation of Discharged Soldiers* (1918) 35 T.L.R. 50, 51, C.A.

[45] Companies Act 1985, s.726. The court has a discretion whether to order security and as to its amount: *Keary Development Ltd v. Tarmac Construction Ltd* [1995] 3 All E.R. 534, C.A.

[46] s.84(1)(a) of the Insolvency Act 1986, replacing s.572 of the Companies Act 1985 and a similar provision in earlier Companies Acts, envisages that the period of the company's duration may be fixed in the articles, but this is never done in practice and even if it were the company would not automatically expire on the expiration of the term; an ordinary resolution would be necessary. It is otherwise with chartered companies: see Chap. 1, above p. 6, n. 17.

[47] *cf. Daimler Co. v. Continental Tyre and Rubber Co.* [1916] 2 A.C. 307, H.L.

[48] As Greer L.J. said in *Stepney Corporation v. Osofsky* [1937] 3 All E.R. 289, 291, C.A.: a corporate body has "no soul to be saved or body to be kicked". This epigram is believed to be of considerable antiquity. Glanville Williams, *Criminal Law: The General Part* (2nd ed.),

company unmoved; members may come and go but the company can go on for ever.[49] The insanity of the managing director will not be calamitous to the company provided that he is removed promptly; he may be the company's brains but lobectomy is a simpler operation than on a natural person.

Once again, the disadvantages in the case of an unincorporated society can be minimised by the use of a trust. If the property of the association is vested in a small body of trustees, the death, disability or retirement of an individual member, other than one of the trustees, need not cause much trouble. But, of course, the trustees, if natural persons, will themselves need replacing at fairly frequent intervals and the need for constant appointment of new trustees is a nuisance if nothing worse. Indeed, it may be said that the trust never functioned at its simplest until it was able to enlist the aid of its own child, the incorporated company, to act as a trust corporation with perpetual succession.

Moreover, the trust obviates difficulties only when a member or his estate, has, under the constitution of the association, no right to be paid a share of the assets on death or retirement, which, of course, is the position with the normal club or learned society. But on the retirement or death of a partner, the partnership is automatically dissolved, so far at any rate as he is concerned,[50] and he or his estate will be entitled to be paid his share. The resulting dislocation of the firm's business can be reduced by special clauses in the articles of partnership, providing for an arbitrary basis of valuation of his share and for deferred payment, but cannot be eradicated altogether. With an incorporated company these problems do not arise. The member or his estate is not entitled to be paid out by the company. If he, or his personal representative, trustee in bankruptcy, or receiver, wishes to realise the value of his shares, these must be sold, whereupon the purchaser will, on entry in the share register, become a member in place of the former holder.[51]

p. 856, has traced it back to Lord Thurlow and an earlier variation to Coke. *cf.* the decree of Pope Innocent IV forbidding the excommunication of corporations because, having neither minds nor souls, they could not sin: see Carr, *Law of Corporation*, at p. 73. In *Rolloswin Investments Ltd v. Chromolit Portugal S.A.R.L.* [1970] 1 W.L.R. 912 it was held that since a company was incapable of public worship it was not a "person" within the meaning of the Sunday Observance Act 1677 so that a contract made by it on a Sunday was not void (the court was unaware that before the case was heard the Act had been repealed by the Statute Law (Repeals) Act 1969).

[49] During the 1939–1945 War all the members of one private company, while in general meeting, were killed by a bomb. But the company survived; not even a hydrogen bomb could have destroyed it. And see the Australian case of *Re Noel Tedman Holding Pty Ltd* (1967) Qd.R, 561, Qd.Sup.Ct. where the only two members were killed in a road accident.

[50] And, in the absence of contrary agreement, as regards all the partners: Partnership Act 1890, s.33.

[51] In practice, this may not be so easy as the company's articles may restrict transfer. For an unsuccessful attempt to use the unfair prejudice provisions to secure the return to the shareholder's estates of the capital represented by his shares see *Re A Company* [1983] Ch. 178

Until the Companies Act 1981 it was not permissible for the company itself to be the purchaser and this could be disadvantageous both to the would-be seller and to the company and the other members, especially in the case of private companies. The seller might not be able to find a purchaser and the other members might not have sufficient free capital to purchase the shares. Now, subject to stringent conditions, purchase by the company is allowed[52] as it has long been under the laws of many other countries.

The continuing existence of a company, irrespective of changes in its membership, is helpful in other directions also. When an individual sells his business to another, difficult questions may arise regarding the performance of existing contracts by the new proprietor,[53] the assignment of rights of a personal nature,[54] and the validity of agreements made with customers ignorant of the change of proprietorship.[55] Similar problems may arise on a change in the constitution of a partnership.[56] Where the business is incorporated and the sale is merely of the shares, none of these difficulties arises. The company remains the proprietor of the business, performs the existing contracts and retains the benefits of them, and enters into future agreements. The difficulties attending vicarious performance, assignments and mistaken identity do not arise.

Transferable shares

As was pointed out in Part I, incorporation, with the resulting separation of the business from its members, greatly facilitates the transfer of the members' interests. Even without formal incorporation much the same end was achieved through the device of the trust coupled with an agreement for transferability in the deed of settlement. But this end could only be approximately attained since the member, even after transfer, would remain liable for the firm's debts incurred during the time when he was a member. Moreover, in the absence of limited liability his opportunities to transfer would in practice be much restricted.

With an incorporated company freedom to transfer, both legally and

---

and see also the explanation of this case in *Re A Company* [1986] BCLC 382 and below, p. 746.

[52] Companies Act 1985, ss.162–181: see Chap. 11, below.

[53] *Robson v. Drummond* (1831) 2 B. & Ad. 303; *cf. British Waggon Co. v. Lea* (1880) 5 Q.B.D. 149.

[54] *Griffith v. Tower Publishing Co.* [1897] 1 Ch. 21 (publishing agreement held not assignable); *Kemp v. Baerselman* [1906] 2 K.B. 604, C.A. (agreement not assignable if question of one party's obligation depends on the other's "personal requirements"). *cf. Tolhurst v. Associated Portland Cement* [1902] 2 K.B. 660, C.A.

[55] *Boulton v. Jones* (1857) 2 H. & N. 564.

[56] See *Brace v. Calder* (1895) 2 Q.B. 253, C.A. where the retirement of two partners was held to operate as the wrongful dismissal of a manager. And see also Partnership Act 1890, s.18. In practice such difficulties are often avoided by an implied novation.

practically, can be readily attained. The company can be incorporated with its liability limited by shares, and these shares constitute items of property which are freely transferable in the absence of express provision to the contrary, and in such a way that the transferor drops out[57] and the transferee steps into his shoes. A partner has a proprietary interest which he can assign, but the assignment does not operate to divest him of his status or liability as a partner; it merely affords the assignee the right to receive whatever the firm distributes in respect of the assigning partner's share.[58] The assignee can be admitted into partnership in the place of the assignor only if the other partners agree[59] and the assignor will not be relieved of his existing liabilities as a partner unless the creditors agree, expressly or impliedly, to release him.[60]

Even in the case of an incorporated company the power to transfer may, of course, be subject to restrictions. In a private company some form of restriction was formerly essential in order to comply with its statutory definition[61] and it is still desirable if such a company is to retain its character of an incorporated private partnership. In practice these restrictions are usually so stringent as to make transferability largely illusory. Nor is there any legal objection to restrictions in the case of a public company, although such restrictions, except as regards partly paid shares, are unusual, and impracticable if the shares are to be marketed on the Stock Exchange.[62] But there is this fundamental difference: in a partnership, transferability depends on express agreement and is subject to legal and practical limitations, whereas in a company it exists to the fullest extent in the absence of express restriction. The partnership relationship is essentially personal; and in practice this is maintained in the case of the private company which in economic reality is often a partnership though in law an incorporated company.[63] On the other hand, the relationship between members of a public company is, as we have seen[64] essentially impersonal and

---

[57] Subject only to a possible liability under ss.74–76 of the Insolvency Act 1986 if liquidation follows within a year and the shares were not fully paid up.

[58] Partnership Act 1980, s.31.

[59] *ibid.*, s.24(7).

[60] *ibid.*, s.17(2) and (3).

[61] Companies Act 1948, s.28. Such restrictions are no longer obligatory under the new distinction between plcs and private companies resulting from the Companies Act 1980; see now Companies Act 1985, s.1(3).

[62] See the *Listing Rules*, para. 3.15. This requirement has not prevented the use of "golden shares" in privatisations, whose effect is to prevent takeovers of privatised companies without the government's consent, at least for a period after the privatisation. See the final sentence of para. 3.15.

[63] In recent years the courts have shown a welcome tendency to recognise the economic reality in applying the legal rules to such incorporated partnerships: see especially *Ebrahimi v. Westbourne Galleries Ltd* [1973] A.C. 360, H.L.: see Chap. 27, below.

[64] See Chap. 1, above.

financial and hence there is usually no reason to restrict changes in membership.

Borrowing

Hitherto we have considered only the advantages or disadvantages which flow inevitably, or at any rate naturally, from the fact of incorporation. There are, however, two further respects, borrowing and taxation, in which incorporation has important consequences.

At first sight one would suppose that a sole trader or partners, being personally liable, would find it easier than a company to raise money by borrowing. In practice, however, this is not so since a company is often able to grant a more effective charge to secure the indebtedness. The ingenuity of equity practitioners led to the evolution of an unusual but highly beneficial type of security known as the floating charge; *i.e.* a charge which floats like a cloud over the whole assets from time to time falling within a generic description, but without preventing the mortgagor from disposing of those assets in the usual course of business until something occurs to cause the charge to become crystallised or fixed. This type of charge is particularly suitable when a business has no fixed assets, such as land, which can be included in a normal mortgage, but carries a large and valuable stock-in-trade. Since this stock needs to be turned over in the course of business, a fixed charge is impracticable because the consent of the mortgagee would be needed every time anything was sold and a new charge would have to be entered into whenever anything was bought. A floating charge obviates these difficulties; it enables the stock to be turned over but attaches to whatever it is converted into and to whatever new stock is acquired.

In theory there is no reason why such charges should not be granted by sole traders and partnerships as well as by incorporated companies. But, until recently, there have been two pieces of legislation which have effectively precluded that. The first was the "reputed ownership" provision in the bankruptcy legislation relating to individuals.[65] This, however, under the reforms resulting from the report of the Cork Committee,[66] was repealed and not replaced in the Insolvency Act 1986. It never applied to the winding-up of companies. The second, which still remains, is that the charge, in so far as it related to chattels, would be a bill of sale within the meaning of the Bills of Sale Acts 1878 and 1882 which apply only to individuals and not to companies.[67] Hence

[65] Bankruptcy Act 1914, s.38(1)(c).
[66] (1982) Cmnd. 8558, Chap. 23. Its repeal had been recommended in the Report of the Blagden Committee 25 years earlier: (1957) Cmnd. 221.
[67] This was always accepted in relation to mortgages in the light of s.17 of the 1882 Act. It has now been held, after an exhaustive review of the conflicting authorities, that both Acts apply only to individuals: *Slavenburg's Bank v. International Natural Resources Ltd* [1980] 1 W.L.R. 1076.

it would need to be registered in the Bills of Sale Registry,[68] and, what is more important, as a mortgage bill it would need to be in the statutory form[69] which involves specifying the chattels in detail in a schedule. Compliance with the latter requirement is obviously impossible, since in a floating charge the chattels are, *ex hypothesi*, indeterminate and fluctuating.

When, belatedly, we get round to reforming, as many common law countries have done, our antiquated law relating to security interests in movables,[70] we shall be able to repeal the Bills of Sale Acts and thus make it practicable for unincorporated firms to borrow on the security of floating charges[71] or some comparable form of security on the lines of that provided by Article 9 of the American Uniform Commercial code.[72] In the meantime, use of this advantageous form of security is in practice restricted to bodies corporate. By virtue of it the lender can obtain an effective security on "all the undertaking and assets of the company both present and future" either alone or in conjunction with a fixed charge on its land.[73] If, in addition, the lender requires some personal security he can insist on the members, or some of them, (*e.g.* the directors) joining as guarantors. By so doing he can place himself in a far stronger position than if he merely had the personal security of the individual traders. It therefore happens not infrequently that a business is converted into a company solely in order to enable further capital to be raised by borrowing. And sometimes, as the *Salomon* case[74] shows, a trader by "selling" his business to a company which he has formed can give himself priority over his future creditors by taking a debenture, secured by a floating charge, for the purchase price.

Taxation

Once a company reaches a certain size the attraction of limited liability is likely to outweigh all other considerations when business people are considering in what form to carry on their activities.

---

[68] For some reason registration of a bill of sale against a tradesman destroys his credit, whereas registration of a debenture against a company does not. This can only be explained on the basis that the former is exceptional, whereas the latter is usual and familiarity has bred contempt.

[69] 1882 Act s.9. Nor could it cover future goods: see s.5. s.6(2) allows a limited power of replacement but not anything as fluid as a floating charge.

[70] As recommended in the Crowther Report on Consumer Credit (1971) Cmnd. 4596. Part V, and in the Review of Security Interests in Property which the DTI commissioned from Professor A.L. Diamond (HMSO, 1989).

[71] Farmers can already do so under the Agricultural Credits Act 1928 which permits individuals to grant to banks floating charges over farming stock and agricultural assets and excludes the application of the former reputed ownership provision and the Bills of Sale Acts: see ss.5 and 8(1), (2) and (4). Farming stock and agricultural assets are more readily distinguishable from a farmer's other assets (than, say, the stock of an antique dealer who lives over his shop) thus meeting the difficulty referred to above on p. 84.

[72] See the Reports referred to in n. 70, above.

[73] The implications of floating charges are discussed more fully in Chap. 15, below.

[74] [1897] A.C. 22, H.L. above, p. 77.

Investors are unlikely to be willing to put money into a company where their liability is not limited if they are to have no or little control over the running of the company.[75] However, with small businesses, where it is feasible to give all the investors a say in management, it is likely that tax considerations play a major part in determining whether the business shall be set up in corporate form or as a partnership, especially as in such cases, as we have seen, limited liability may not be available in practice *vis-à-vis* large lenders.[76] This is not the place to examine the tax considerations which may cut one way or another at different times on this issue. What we should note, however, is that in the case of small companies, the investors' return on their capital may take the form of the payment of directors' fees rather than dividends, so that participation in the management of the company may be the means for the investor both to safeguard the investment and to earn a return on it.[77]

Formalities, publicity and expense

Incorporation is necessarily attended with formalities, loss of privacy and expense greater than that which would normally apply to a sole trader or partnership. A sole trader is a person who already exists. A partnership cannot exist without some form of agreement, but this can be written on a half-sheet of notepaper or be an informal oral agreement. An unincorporated firm can conduct its affairs without any formality and publicity beyond that which may be prescribed by the regulations (if any) applying to the particular type of business. If the business is carried on under a name different from the true name of the sole trader or those of all the partners, it will have to comply with the provisions of the Business Names Act 1985 (as would a company trading under a pseudonym) but these are not onerous—registration in the former Business Names Register was abolished as a result of the Companies Act 1981. The business, unless it is insolvent, can eventually be wound up equally cheaply, privately and informally. An incorporated company, on the other hand, necessarily involves formalities, publicity and expenses at its birth, throughout its active life and on its final dissolution.

Private companies

On the original formation of a private company, the incorporators have only to complete and register a memorandum and articles of association and a few simple forms. These can be obtained at any law

---

[75] The recent history of Lloyds shows how unwise it is for investors to combine unlimited liability with very limited management control.

[76] As noted, in the case of professional businesses the rules of the governing professional body may require the partnership form, though in fact many professional bodies have become more flexible on this issue in recent years.

[77] See further Chap. 27, below.

stationers, and Table A can be adopted as its articles.[78] Alternatively, a ready-made company can be bought "off-the-shelf" from one of the agencies which make a business of forming companies and selling them to all-comers.[79] The heaviest expenses on incorporation are likely to be capital gains tax (if the rules for exemption are not strictly complied with) and professional fees—for it is rash to dispense with professional advice even if the intention is to buy a shelf company.

It is the formalities and costs of operating the company which, at present, are found excessively burdensome. Some of these so-called burdens are aimed at protecting those who deal with the limited liability company. These can and ought never to be entirely removed, for they are in part the proper price the incorporators pay for trading with limited liability. Nevertheless, there is scope for asking the question whether the requirements are not greater than is necessitated by the protective objectives underlying the legislation. In particular, is it the case that the Act, which begins from the position that the rules it contains ought to apply to all companies, great or small, lays upon small and medium-sized companies requirements which need to be applied in full only to public and perhaps even only to listed companies? Other provisions, whose scope is currently under question, relate to the internal affairs of the company and are often premised upon a separation between shareholders and managers, between "ownership" and "control". In companies where ownership and control are not separated, there may be considerable scope for disapplying these provisions, either in whole or in part.[80] In recent years, the legislature has become much more concerned with the need to tailor the companies legislation to the situation of small and medium-sized companies. The result so far has been a relaxation in three main areas of the administrative and accounting requirements applying to small companies, the first to be mentioned concerning rules aimed mainly at protecting third parties, and the second and third with the internal affairs of small companies.

First, as we shall see in Chapter 19, "small" and "medium-sized" companies, as defined, have been given certain exemptions from the full requirements of the Act in relation to the compilation and publication of annual accounts; and "micro" companies have been exempted

---

[78] Or Table C or E if limited by guarantee or unlimited. Table A, without substantial deletions and additions, is unlikely to be ideal for small private companies. The new s.8A (inserted by the 1989 Act) envisages a Table G for "partnership companies" but at the time of writing the needed Regulations have not been published. See however, DTI, *Model Articles for Partnership Companies (Table G): A Consultative Document*, March 1995.

[79] While they remain on the shelf they will be "dormant companies" able to take advantage of s.250, (as substituted by 1989 Act) regarding accounts and audit; and the assets transferred to them will be minimal and may need to be increased after the purchase.

[80] For a thought-provoking development of the distinction between these two types of legislation in the context of small companies, see Freedman, "Small Businesses and the Corporate Form: Burden or Privilege?" (1994) 57 M.L.R. 555.

from the requirement to have their accounts audited, either entirely or by way of substitution of an independent accountant's report for the audit.

Secondly, formal meetings had long tended to be fictional in the case of small companies, and in the Companies Act 1989 Parliament decided to bring the law into line with reality rather than to continue to insist upon small businesses complying with an unrealistic law. The 1989 Act inserted new sections and a new Schedule 15A into the principal Act enabling the to dispense in most cases with formal meetings and with the pretence that they had held them when frequently they had not. By the new section 381A(1) it is provided that anything which may be done by a private company by a resolution of the company in general meeting or by a resolution of a meeting of a class of members may instead be done, without a meeting and without any previous notice being acquired, by a resolution in writing signed by or on behalf of all members entitled to vote on that resolution.[81] This applies to all types of resolution—ordinary, extraordinary, special or "elective"[82] except for resolutions to remove a director[83] or an auditor[84] before the expiration of his period of office.[85]

However, section 381B provides that a copy of any proposed written resolution has to be sent to the company's auditors.[86] The provision previously in the legislation empowering the auditors to insist upon a meeting being held if the resolution concerned them as auditors has now been repealed.[87] Although this will undoubtedly facilitate the passing of written resolutions, especially as failure to send a copy of the proposed resolution to the auditors does not invalidate the resolution,[88] it may also weaken the position of auditors.[89] In any event, the statutory written resolution procedure seems to leave intact the common law rules which in most cases make the unanimous agreement of all the members entitled to vote the equivalent to a resolution in general meeting, whether the new statutory procedure is followed or not.[90] Further, it has now been made clear that, if the articles of a

---

[81] Signatures need not be on a single document provided that each is on a document which accurately sets out the proposed resolution: s.381A(2). It is deemed to be passed when the last member signs s.381A(5).

[82] s.381A(6). On "elective resolutions" see p. 94, below.

[83] Under s.303: see p. 189, below.

[84] Under s.391: see pp. 549–552, below.

[85] s.381A(7) and Sched. 15A Part I. Part II adapts certain sections of the Act which as drafted assume that a meeting will be held, so as to meet cases where a written resolution is used instead.

[86] s.381B(1), if the company has auditors (see above).

[87] The Deregulation (Resolutions of Private Companies) Order 1996 (S.I. 1996 No. 1471).

[88] s.381B(4). Criminal sanctions are provided: s.381B(2) and (3).

[89] See below, p. 547.

[90] s.381C(2); see Chap. 8, pp. 175–177, below. See also Higginson (1993) 109 L.Q.R. 18, raising a doubt about the scope of the common law rule in the light of the (pre-1986) statutory provisions.

particular company provide for an even less onerous method for adopting written resolutions, dispensing, say, with the requirement to give a copy of the proposed resolution to the auditors, the company may use that procedure rather than the statutory one.[91] Consequently, although dispensing with meetings may be regarded as a deregulatory achievement, the method chosen for reaching that result involves, ironically, rather complex regulation: the members of the company are presented with a choice of using the new statutory procedure, relying on the common law and devising their own mechanism.

Proceeding by way of a written resolution does not obviate the need to record the resolution in the company's minute book[92] or to send a copy to the Registrar within 15 days after it is passed.[93] But the omission to do either does not affect the validity of the resolution though it makes the company and its officers in default liable to penalties[94] and, in the former case, deprives them of the presumption that all the requirements of the Act have been complied with.[95]

Thirdly, the 1989 Act introduced an "elective regime" enabling private companies to dispense with or relax a number of the requirements of the principal Act. At present the requirements to which this applies[96] relate to the duration of the directors' authority to allot shares,[97] laying accounts and reports before a general meeting,[98] the need to hold annual general meetings,[99] the majority required to authorise short notice of a meeting,[1] and the need to appoint auditors each year.[2] In combination with section 381A, the effect is virtually to enable private companies to dispense completely with formal meetings if all the members want to. All that is needed is to pass an "elective resolution" in accordance with section 379A. On its face, this demands that the resolution shall be (a) passed at a general meeting of which at least 21 days' notice has been given stating that an elective resolution is to be proposed and setting out its terms and (b) agreed to at the meeting by all members entitled to attend and vote.[3] In fact,

---

[91] s.381C(1)

[92] s.382A(1).

[93] s.380.

[94] s.382(5) and s.382A(3).

[95] s.382A(2).

[96] See s.379A(1) lists the relevant sections. Somewhat mysteriously, s.379A(5) says that the provisions of the section (1) have effect notwithstanding any contrary provision in the company's articles but, in conspicuous contrast with s.381C(1), does not say "memorandum or articles". Is the intention that a company can contract out of the ability to pass elective resolutions by a provision in the memorandum? Or is it an oversight? Or a deliberate omission on the basis that it is unthinkable that any company would do so?

[97] 1985 Act, s.80A.

[98] *ibid.*, s.252.

[99] *ibid.*, s.366A.

[1] *ibid.*, ss.369(4) and 378(3).

[2] s.386.

[3] s.379A(1) and (2). Even the 21 days' notice may be waived by all the members. s.379A(2A).

however, as a result of section 381A[4] it can be passed by a written resolution under that section. The elective resolution can be rescinded by an ordinary resolution[5] and ceases to have effect if the company re-registers as a public company.[6] A copy of any elective resolution, or ordinary resolution revoking it, has to be sent to the Registrar.[7]

Furthermore, and, in the long term, perhaps most importantly, section 117 of the 1989 Act[8] empowers the Secretary of State to make provision by regulations[9] whereby additional requirements which appear to him "to relate primarily to the internal administration and procedure of companies" may be dispensed with or modified by elective resolutions[10] and to make consequential amendments to the principal Act.[11] If robust use is made of this power small companies may at long last be provided with a regime more suitable to their needs. One advantage of this way of proceeding is that it avoids many of the difficulties of defining what is meant by a small company. The elective regime applies to all private companies, which constitute some 98.9 per cent of the companies on the effective register,[12] and it is then a matter for unanimous decision by the members of the company whether the particular provisions of the Act are applied to their internal affairs or not. Provided there are appropriate safeguards,[13] the procedure constitutes a valuable addition to the freedom which the incorporators already have through the adoption of customised articles of association[14] or of shareholders' agreements outside the articles[15] to fashion the internal regulations of the company in the way which suits them best.

However, where the statutory provisions are aimed wholly or partly at the protection of third parties, it is obviously inappropriate to leave the decision on applicability totally in the hands of the members of the company.[16] It is noticeable that the choice of threshold for the

---

[4] See s.381A(6), above.
[5] s.379A(3). Which again can be a written resolution under s.381A.
[6] s.379(4).
[7] s.380 as amended.
[8] This provision is not inserted in the principal Act but presumably will be if and when there is another official consolidation.
[9] Subject to an affirmative resolution of both Houses: s.117(5).
[10] s.117(1).
[11] s.117(2) and (3).
[12] DTI, *Companies in 1995–96*, Table A2.
[13] In this respect it is somewhat disturbing to find that the Law Commission's Report (see n. 22 below at p. 23, n. 5) mentioned the unfair prejudice provisions as a potential candidate for the elective regime. It is submitted that it is precisely in relation to quasi-partnership companies that these provisions have had their greatest and most beneficial effect: see Chap. 27, below.
[14] See p. 107, below.
[15] See below, pp. 727–732.
[16] Indeed, the amendment of such provisions would appear not to fall within the scope of s.117 of the 1989 Act, but may be achievable by statutory instrument under s.1 of the Deregulation and Contracting Out Act 1994 or under the now numerous sections of the Companies Act

disapplication of the reporting and auditing requirements, mentioned above, has been set at a lower level than that of all private companies; in the case of the audit exemption at a significantly lower level.[17] Here, the difficult issue of defining "small" companies cannot be avoided, and it is a tricky one because the legislation covers, in fact, not two types of company, large and small, but a spectrum of different types and sizes of company, ranging "from the one person firm, through the husband and wife company, the family company, the private company which brings in outside finance, the unlisted public company and the quoted company to the multinational group".[18] The present approach of the legislature seems to be to pick different criteria for the application of different relaxations, according to the circumstances of the case. This has the merit of flexibility, though it does not conduce to simplicity of legislation.[19]

What is clear is that current trends are away from a separate form of incorporation for small firms. That was proposed in the early 1980s[20] but was not taken up with enthusiasm by the business and legal communities,[21] and the Law Commission has recently recommended against going down this path,[22] on the grounds mainly that the companies legislation did not constitute the major obstacle facing small firms and that it was not in the public interest to encourage access to limited liability on the part of under-capitalised businesses.

Public companies

It is unusual initially to incorporate a company as a public limited company. In the rare circumstances where this is done, the initial costs will be heavy since the new company must have a prescribed minimum share capital[23] and, before commencing business, must obtain a certificate from the Registrar that it has complied with the strict conditions regarding the allotment of its capital.[24] Normally, companies start as private ones and become public only when they wish their shares to be offered to the public. On conversion they have to comply with similarly strict provisions relating to capital.[25] In either event, the company on going public will, in addition, have to incur the heavy expense

---

which give the Secretary of State power to alter it by regulation. See, for example, s.257 in relation to the Act's accounting requirements.

[17] See below, p. 530.

[18] Freedman, *op. cit.*, n. 80, p. 559.

[19] In our current state of lack of precise knowledge about how many companies fulfil which criteria there is also an element of guesswork involved in the choice of exemption levels.

[20] Department of Trade, *A New Form of Incorporation for Small Firms*, Cmnd. 8171, 1981, putting forward for consultation a set of proposals by Professor Gower.

[21] Though Professor Gower's proposals did have a strong influence on the South African Close Corporations Act 1984.

[22] DTI, *Company Law Review: The Law Applicable to Private Companies*, November 1994.

[23] s.11.

[24] ss.117, 118.

[25] ss.43–48.

of complying with the statutory and Stock Exchange rules relating to public offerings.

As we have seen,[26] a public company is essentially one which is designed to enable entrepreneurs to raise capital from the public and one in which there is a separation of ownership and control. Hence, throughout its life it will be subject to a regime somewhat stricter than that applying to a private company. But this, in practice, is unlikely to be found unduly burdensome in the light of its greater resources.

CONCLUSION

The balance of advantage and disadvantage in relation to incorporation no doubt varies from one business context to another, at least as far as small firms are concerned; for large companies, the arguments in favour of incorporation are conclusive. It has been known for some time that in manufacturing and construction incorporation is the predominant method of doing business, whereas in service industries many small businesses happily continue as partnerships or sole traders.[27] This may reflect the firms' respective needs for capital to finance their operations. The main disadvantages of the corporate form are the statutory publicity requirements and a certain inflexibility of internal procedure, though, as we have seen, recent changes have done something to modify both these disadvantages. The main advantage is probably that of limited liability. Even if in practice major lenders of working capital to the company will negotiate their way around limited liability, that protection may still operate in relation to trade creditors and tort victims. There is, however, one group, namely the professions, for whom free choice of business form is not available, because professional rules or customs require the partnership form. Responding to the threat to such partnerships from large tort claims, the Government has proposed to make available to regulated professions a revised form of the limited liability partnership. Under this hybrid, all the partners would be free to be involved in the management of the firm, would benefit from limited liability and would retain complete freedom of internal organisation, but would have to accept some of the external protections which are applied to companies.[28]

---

[26] p. 9, above.

[27] Report of the Committee of Inquiry on Small Firms, Cmnd. 4811 (1971) (the Bolton Committee), para. 2.2.

[28] DTI, *Limited Liability Partnership: A New Form of Business Association for Professions*, Consultative Document, February 1997.

CHAPTER 6

FORMATION PROCEDURES

As we have seen,[1] today there are three basic types of incorporated company—statutory, chartered and registered, and the formalities attending formation vary fundamentally as between each type. Detailed consideration is necessary only in respect of the last, companies registered under the Companies Act, for these are overwhelmingly the most common and important.

STATUTORY COMPANIES

These are formed by the promotion of a Private Act of Parliament. Details of the procedure therefore appertain to the field of Private Bill legislation rather than to a manual of company law and the reader who is concerned in the formation of such a company should refer to the specialised works on the former topic. In practice the work is monopolised by a few firms of solicitors who specialise as parliamentary agents and by a handful of counsel at the parliamentary bar. The numbers of both promotions and specialist practitioners are dwindling, having regard to the curtailment of work resulting first from nationalisation and now from privatisation, both of which are achieved under Public Acts.

CHARTERED COMPANIES

It is unlikely that there will be any further creations of chartered trading companies but the grant of charters to charitable or public bodies is not uncommon. The procedure in such cases is for the promoters of the body to petition the Crown (through the office of the Lord President of the Council) praying for the grant of a charter, a draft of which is normally annexed to the petition. If the petition is granted the promoters and their successors then become "one body corporate and politic by the name of—and by that name shall and may sue or be sued plead and be impleaded in all courts whether of law or equity . . . and shall have perpetual succession and a common seal".

Sometimes a charter will be granted to the members of an existing guarantee company registered under the Companies Acts in which

---

[1] Above, p. 5.

98

event the assets of the company will be transferred[2] to the new chartered body, and the company wound up unless the Registrar can be persuaded to exercise his power to strike it off the register under section 652 of the Companies Act, thus avoiding the expense of a formal liquidation.[3]

REGISTERED COMPANIES

In the vast majority of cases the company, whatever its objects, will today be formed under the Companies Act, and it may be helpful to set out the practice in such cases in some detail. In what follows references will be made to the functions of the Registrar of Companies and of the Secretary of State in the formation of companies, but it should be noted that, in the modern fashion, power has been taken to delegate these functions to such persons as may be authorised by them.[4]

Choice of type

The promoters will first have to make up their minds which of the several types of registered company they wish to form, since this may make a difference to the number and types of documents required, and will certainly affect their contents.

First, they must choose between a limited and an unlimited company.[5] The disadvantage of the latter is that its members will ultimately be personally liable for its debts and for this reason they are likely to be wary of it if the company intends to trade. If, however, the company is merely to hold land or investments, the absence of limited liability may not matter and may confer certain advantages, for example, as regards returning capital to the members and escaping from having to give publicity to the company's financial position. The absence of limited liability may also render the company more acceptable in certain circles (for example, the turf).

If they decide upon a limited company they must then make up their minds whether it is to be limited by shares or by guarantee, and as already explained,[6] this is really a matter which will be decided for

---

[2] It is understood that it is not the practice of the Revenue to claim *ad valorem* stamp duty thereon.

[3] See Chap. 30 at pp. 846–848, below.

[4] Contracting Out (Functions in Relation to the Registration of Companies) Order 1995 (S.I. 1995 No. 1013) made under the Deregulation and Contracting Out Act 1994.

[5] An alternative, which in practice is very rarely adopted, is a limited company with unlimited liability on the part of the directors: s.306. A similar type of association is of considerable importance in some other legal systems, *e.g.* the German *Kommandit-Gesellschaft auf Aktien* and the French *société en commandite par actions*.

[6] See Chap. 1, above.

them by the purpose which the company is to perform. Only if it is to be a non-profit-making concern are they likely to form a guarantee company which is especially suited to a body of that type.

Overlapping these distinctions, but closely bound up with them, is the further point of whether or not the company should have a share capital. If, as is most probable, the company is to be limited by shares this question does not arise. Likewise if it is to be limited by guarantee.[7] But if the company is unlimited it may or may not have its capital divided into shares. Once more, the decision is dependent on the company's purpose; if the company is intended to make and distribute profits a share capital will be appropriate.

They will further have to make up their minds whether the company is to be a public or private one. As we have seen,[8] public and private companies essentially fulfil different economic purposes; the former to raise capital from the public to run the corporate enterprise, the latter to confer a separate legal personality on the business of a single trader or a partnership. Once again, therefore, the choice will in practice be clear-cut and normally it will be to form a private company. The incorporators may have the ultimate ambition of "going public" but, as we have seen,[9] rarely will they be in a position to do so immediately. If, however, they are, then the company will have to be a company limited by shares, the memorandum of association will have to state that it is to be a public company and special requirements as to its registration will have to be complied with.[10] Any other type of company will, perforce, be a private company. Theoretically therefore, the incorporators will have a choice of five types:

  (i) a public company limited by shares
 (ii) a private company limited by shares
(iii) a private company limited by guarantee and without a share capital
(iv) a private unlimited company having a share capital
 (v) a private unlimited company not having a share capital.

In practice, however, the choice is likely to be between (ii) and (iii) and will be determined for them according to whether they want the company to trade for the profit of the members or to perform some charitable or quasi-charitable purpose.

Name of company

The incorporators must next decide on a suitable name. This is of some importance in identifying an artificial person[11] and the Act pro-

---

[7] Since the coming into force of the Companies Act 1980 no further companies limited by guarantee and having a share capital can be formed: s.1(4).

[8] Chap. 1, above.

[9] See p. 96, above.

[10] s.1(3).

[11] Though less so now that the Registrar has to allot each company a registered number (s.705) which it has to state on its business letters and order forms: s.351(1)(a).

vides that it must be stated in the memorandum of association,[12] on the company's seal,[13] on business letters, negotiable instruments, and order forms[14] and must be affixed outside every office or place of business.[15] It is advisable, therefore, that it should be kept as short as possible. Nor, once the company has been registered, can it change its name as informally as can a natural person.

Major changes in the law relating to company names[16] were made by the Companies Act 1981 and the present position is now set out in Part 1 Chapter II of the Act[17] under which a name can no longer be refused registration merely because it is considered to be undesirable. There are, nevertheless, still restrictions on freedom of choice. The first of these is the obvious one, already referred to,[18] that if the company is a limited company its name must end with the prescribed warning suffix—"limited"—if it is a private company or "public limited company" if it is a public one.[19] These expressions may be abbreviated to "Ltd" or "plc"[20] and the company may subsequently use those abbreviations even if it has registered with the full suffix.[21]

To the requirement that a private limited company must have "limited" at the end of its name, section 30 provides an exemption in relation to a company limited by guarantee, the objects of which are to be "the promotion of commerce, art, science, education, charity or any profession"[22] and the memorandum of which forbids the distribution of profits or income and requires its assets on a winding up to be transferred to a body with like objects. Prior to the Act of 1981 a licence from the Department had to be obtained if this exemption was to be enjoyed.[23] This caused the Department a considerable amount of

---

[12] s.2.

[13] s.350 (if it decides to have one: see s.36A(3) inserted by the 1989 Act).

[14] s.349. See Chap. 8 at p. 157, below.

[15] s.348.

[16] And business names (the former register of busines names was abolished).

[17] *i.e.* ss.25–34.

[18] See pp. 12–13, above.

[19] s.25. If, however the company's memorandum states that its registered office is to be situated in Wales, the Welsh equivalents ("cyfyngedig" or "cwmni cyfyngedig cyhoeddus") may (not must) be used instead. It is an offence for any person to use any of the suffixes in carrying on business if the person is not a limited company or a public limited company: ss.33 and 34.

[20] s.27 (the Welsh equivalents are "cyf" or "c.c.c."). The abbreviations can be adopted whenever a company "by any provision of this Act is either required or entitled to include in its name" the prescribed suffix. But it will, of course, have to state in full in its memorandum that the liability of its members is limited and, if such be the case, that it is to be a public company.

[21] Or, presumably, vice versa though the section does not say so.

[22] Anomalously the objects have to be to "promote" rather than to "regulate" a profession. Hence to enable SIB to dispense with "limited", the Financial Services Act had specifically to extend ss.30 and 31 to "designated agencies" under that Act: FSA 1986 Sched. 9 para. 2.

[23] At that time licences could be granted to companies other than those limited by guarantee, though in practice it was only guarantee companies that applied for them. Any company limited by shares which may have obtained an exemption retains it under the new provisions: see s.30(2).

somewhat pointless labour.[24] The new system avoids much of that since the Registrar may accept a statutory declaration that the necessary conditions are fulfilled and may (and normally will) refuse to register without the suffix unless such a declaration is delivered to him.[25] From the company's point of view, exemption has the additional advantage that it also exempts from the requirements of the Act relating to the publication of its name[26] and the sending of lists of members to the Registrar with its annual return under section 364A (4).[27] It does not, however, exempt it from the requirement to state on business letters and order forms that it is a limited company.[28]

More important than what the name must contain is what it must not. Certain expressions are banned.[29] Thus the name must not include, except at the end, any use of "limited", "unlimited", "public limited company" or their abbreviations or Welsh equivalents.[30] And the name must not be the same as any name already on the Registrar's index of names.[31] This is likely to present the severest obstacle because there are about 1 million names on that index. Hence a Smith, Jones, Brown or Davies who has carried on an unincorporated business under his name may have difficulty in finding an available way of continuing to use that name on incorporating the business.[32]

Two further prohibitions differ somewhat from the foregoing since they depend upon the opinion of the Secretary of State (which means the Registrar in the first instance). If, in his opinion, the name is such that its use would constitute a criminal offence[33] or be "offensive",[34] it cannot be adopted.

Certain other names may be adopted only with the express approval

---

[24] When the Jenkins Committee asked the representatives of the Board of Trade why they wished to continue to perform this task their reply was "We have been doing it for a long time and have got rather to like it"!: Minutes of Evidence, 20th Day, Q6886.

[25] s.30(4) and (5). If it subsequently appears to the Secretary of State that the conditions for exemption are not being observed he may direct the company to change its name (by a resolution of the directors) so that it ends with "Limited": s.31(2).

[26] Under ss.348, 349.

[27] s.30(7).

[28] s.351(1)(d). This somewhat reduces the value of the cachet which the absence of "limited" is thought to confer but its effect is usually minimised by putting the statement inconspicuously at the bottom of the notepaper. For charitable companies stricter rules apply (see Charities Act 1993, ss.67 and 68) which are designed to ensure that the name and charitable status of the company are publicised in its correspondence, etc.

[29] s.26(1)(a), (b) and (c).

[30] This is primarily to prevent any blurring of the warnings implied by "Ltd" or "plc" but the inclusion of "unlimited" (for which, incidentally, there is no authorised abbreviation) would presumably prevent a moneylender from incorporating as "Unlimited Loans Ltd".

[31] In determining whether one name is the same as another, words such as "the", and "and Company" are to be ignored: s.26(3) and see s.28(2).

[32] Those with less common surnames can often surmount this difficulty by, for example, inserting an appropriate place-name: *e.g.* Gower (Hampstead) Ltd.

[33] s.26(1)(d). *e.g.* a name which holds out the company as carrying on a business which requires a licence or authorisation which the company does not have.

[34] s.26(1)(e).

of the Secretary of State. These are names which, in his opinion, would be likely to give the impression that the company is connected in any way with the Government or a local authority[35] or which include any word or expression for the time being specified in regulations made under section 29.[36] That section empowers the Secretary of State to specify the words or expressions for which his approval is required and, in relation to any of them, to state the Government Department or other body which has to be asked whether it objects and, if so, why. The relevant regulations[37] list some 90 words[38] and, in relation to about a third of them, specify a body which has to be invited to object.[39] The person making the statutory declaration of compliance[40] then has to send to the Registrar, when the incorporation documents are lodged, a statement that the body has been asked and a copy of any response.[41]

It will, therefore, be apparent that it may be difficult to find a name acceptable to both the incorporators and the Registrar or Secretary of State. But until it is achieved, it will be impossible to complete the documents required to obtain registration and unsafe to order the stationery which the company will need once it is registered. We have never introduced a system comparable to that in some other common law countries whereby a name can be reserved for a prescribed period. Prior to 1981, however, it was possible and usual to write to the Registrar submitting a name (or two or three alternative names) and asking if it was available. If the reply was affirmative it was usually safe to proceed so long as one did so promptly. Now, however, the incorporators or their professional advisers will have to search the index[42] and make up their own minds.

Even if they do secure registration under a particular name they cannot be certain that they will not be forced to change it. The main risk is that the Secretary of State, under section 28(2), will, within 12 months of the company's registration, direct it to change its name on the ground that it: "is the same as, or in the opinion of the Secretary

---

[35] s.26(2)(a).

[36] s.26(2)(b).

[37] The Company and Business Names Regs. 1981 (S.I. 1981 No. 1685) as subsequently amended. In addition, the Registrar has published *Notes of Guidance on Company and Business Names* and on *Sensitive Words and Expressions* (NG 8 and 9).

[38] Mainly those implying some official or representative status but ranging from "Abortion" to "Windsor" and including, for example "University", "Trade Union" and "Stock Exchange". A listed word should be avoided unless the incorporators are prepared to face delay and possible rejection.

[39] *e.g.* if the name includes "Charitable" or "Charity", the Charity Commission must be asked; if "Dental" or "Dentistry", the General Dental Council, and if "Windsor" (because of its royal associations) the Home Office or the Scottish Home and Health Dept.

[40] See below, p. 110.

[41] s.29(2) and (3).

[42] And, ideally, also the Register of Trade Marks to ensure that the name proposed is not someone's registered trademark.

of State, *too like*[43] a name appearing at the time of registration in the registrar's index of company names ... or which should have appeared in that index at the time''.

The object of section 28(2) is two-fold: (a) to enable a mistake to be rectified, when the name of an existing company has been registered either because the name had not then been entered on the index, or because the fact that it was the same as that of the new company had escaped detection, and (b) to extend, by the words italicised above, the ambit of ''the same as'' to ''too like'' that of another. If another company finds that the new company is trading with a name so similar to its own as to cause confusion and face it with unfair competition, that company can, as a cheaper alternative to a ''passing-off action'', complain to the Registrar asking that the Secretary of State should exercise his powers to direct the new one to change its name.[44] If the Secretary of State does so, the company will have to comply within such period as he may direct. But this course will be effective only if the complaint is in time for a direction to be made within 12 months of registration of the second company. Otherwise the only remedy available to the first company will be a passing off action[45] which will not be successful merely because the two names are identical or ''too like''. It will have to be established that both companies are carrying on the same of type of business and that the second is, in effect, cashing in on the reputation of the first and appropriating its goodwill and connection.[46] If that is established the new company will be enjoined from continuing to trade under that name and will either have to go out of business or change its name. Any company can now do the latter by passing a special resolution[47] but the new name will have to pass the same tests as those for a name selected on original registration.[48]

The Secretary of State may also direct the company to change its name if it appears to him that misleading information has been given in connection with the company's registration with a particular name or that undertakings or assurances have been given for that purpose which have not been fulfilled[49] and in this case the direction may be given within five years of registration.[50] And, finally, he may at any

---

[43] For a case where the names were not thought ''too like'' although they were sufficiently alike to have caused a petitioning creditor to obtain a winding up order against the wrong company with damaging consequences to it, see *Re Calmex Ltd* [1989] 1 All E.R. 485.

[44] 53 directions were made in 1995–1996. *Companies in 1995–96*, Table D4. But an interlocutory application in a passing off action may provide speedier relief: *Glaxo plc v. Glaxowellcome Ltd* [1996] F.S.R. 388.

[45] Unless the name conflicts with the older company's registered trademark, in which event it may also have a right of action in that respect.

[46] See. *e.g. Tussaud v. Tussaud* (1890) 44 Ch.D. 678: *Panhard et Levassor v. Panhard Levassor Motor Co.* [1901] 2 Ch. 513.

[47] s.28(1).

[48] *i.e.* ss.26 and 27 apply.

[49] This is likely to arise only when approval of the name has been obtained under ss.26(2) or 30.

[50] s.28(3)

time direct it to change its name if, in his opinion, it gives so misleading an indication of the nature of the company's activities as to
be likely to cause harm to the public.[51] Little use of this power has
been made; undoubtedly the names of many companies give totally
misleading indications of the nature of their activities but this, on its
own, has apparently not been thought "likely to cause harm to the
public".

On a change of name, whether voluntarily or because of a direction,
the Registrar enters the new name on the register in place of the old
and issues an amended certificate of incorporation.[52] The change is
effective from the date on which that certificate is issued.[53] But the
company remains the same corporate body and the change does not
affect any of its rights or obligations or render defective any legal
proceedings by or against it.[54]

The effect of the statutory provisions is to afford a registered company something approaching an exclusive right to corporate trading
under its registered name,[55] since another company should not be
registered with the same name and may be forced to change its name
if that is too like the name. That, however, does not protect it against
the use of the name by unincorporated businesses. These are free from
any statutory restraints so long as they use the true names of their
proprietors.[56] Alternatively, subject to observing the provisions of the
Business Names Act 1985 regarding disclosure of the identity of
the proprietors,[57] they can adopt any business name so long as it is
not one of those which are prohibited or require the approval of the
Secretary of State.[58]

There is nothing in the Business Names Act 1985 which empowers
the Secretary of State to direct the change of a business name because
it is the same as, or too like, the name of an existing business, corporate or incorporate. However, if a registered company carries on any
business under a name other than its own (for example because it has
acquired an existing business with a goodwill attached to its name) it
too will have to comply with the provisions of the Business Names

---

[51] s.32.
[52] See on this certificate, pp. 111–114, below.
[53] ss.28(6) and 32(5).
[54] ss.28(7) and 32(6). Hence contracts entered into prematurely under the new name will not be
pre-incorporation contracts on which, under s.36C, the individual who acted would be personally liable (see Chap. 7 at pp. 141–144). But if the new name was used prior to the date of
the issue of the certificate (or the old name used thereafter) there would be a risk of personal
liability under s.349 (4): see Chap. 8 at pp. 157–158, below.
[55] Hence companies have sometimes been registered in order to obtain an exclusive right to use
a name which the incorporators think they might wish to trade under at some future date.
And recently someone has apparently registered companies with the names of well-known
firms of solicitors which he then offers to sell to the firms!
[56] Business Names Act 1985, s.1.
[57] *ibid*, s.4.
[58] *ibid*., ss.2 and 3 (equivalent to ss.26(2) and 29 of the Companies Act).

Act, by disclosing on all business documents and at all its business premises its corporate name and an address in Great Britain at which documents can be served.[59] A breach of this obligation is not only an offence[60] but may prevent the company from suing on its contracts.[61]

Finally, in relation to company names, it should be mentioned that the controls exercisable under sections 26 and 27 of the Companies Act are extended by section 694 of that Act to the name under which overseas companies may trade from a place of business in Great Britain.[62] While the Secretary of State cannot compel a foreign company to change its corporate name, the section empowers him to prevent trading here under that name and to approve another which, for the purposes of our law, is treated as if it were the corporate name.

The memorandum and articles

The next step is to prepare the memorandum and articles. The Companies Act provides that, as regards each of the various types of company,[63] these documents shall be in the form specified by regulations[64] made by the Secretary of State "or as near to that form as circumstances admit".[65] This, however is treated with considerable latitude and so long as the documents submitted are in the same basic form as that specified and contain what the Act prescribes,[66] the widest variations of content are permitted.[67] Thus, as we shall see,[68] the practice has long been to produce memoranda much lengthier than the prescribed forms because of inflated objects clauses—a practice which conceivably may change as a result of the reforms of the *ultra vires* doctrine by the Act of 1989.

The present Regulations[69] contain five Tables of which Table A, prescribing model articles for a company (whether public or private) limited by shares, is the most important and differs in its effect from

---

[59] *ibid.*, s.4.

[60] *ibid.*, ss.4(6). (7) and 7.

[61] *ibid.*, s.5.

[62] This closes a loophole of which advantage was formerly taken; see, *e.g. Wallersteiner v. Moir* [1974] 1 W.L.R. 991, C.A., where the Liechtenstein registered "Rothschild Trust" had no connection with the well-known merchant banks.

[63] Except in relation to an unlimited company without a share capital when there are no prescribed forms.

[64] Under earlier Companies Acts the forms were Scheduled to the Act (but alterable by regulations) which made them more readily accessible (unless they were so altered).

[65] s.3 (as regards the memorandum) and s.8 (as regards articles).

[66] ss.2 and 7(2).

[67] *Gaiman v. National Association for Medical Health* [1971] Ch. 317.

[68] Below, pp. 203–204.

[69] The Companies (Tables A to F) Regs (S.I. 1985 No. 805 as amended by S.I. 1985 No. 1052). The new s.8A, inserted by the 1989 Act, envisages an additional Table G containing articles appropriate for "partnership companies". See DTI, *Model Articles of Association for Partnership Companies (Table G): Consultative Document*, 1995.

the others. Such a company does not have to register articles[70] (as opposed to the memorandum) and, if it does not, Table A (as in force at the date of the company's registration) becomes its articles.[71] Even if it does register articles, in so far as these do not exclude or modify Table A, its provisions will apply. Furthermore, it, and any other type of company (which will have to register articles) may, in them, adopt by reference any provisions of Table A.[72] In contrast, the model articles in Table C (relating to a company limited by guarantee without a share capital). Table D (relating to a company limited by guarantee and with a share capital[73]) and Table E (relating to an unlimited company having a share capital) are merely models which cannot he adopted by reference and will not apply to fill lacunae in the registered articles. Tables C and D also include model forms of memoranda for the types of company to which they relate as does Table B (for a private company limited by shares) and Table F (for a public limited company).

Before preparing the memorandum and articles, the draftsmen will need to obtain, from the promoters, information on matters such as the following:

1. *The nature of the business.*[74] This will be required in connection with the objects clauses of the memorandum unless the promoters are content to adopt the general purpose formula in section 3A.[75]

2. *The amount of nominal capital and the denomination of the shares into which it is to be divided* (assuming, of course, that it is to have a share capital). These will need to be stated in both the memorandum and articles. For the articles the draftsman will also require to know if the shares are to be all of one class and, if not, what special rights are to be attached to each class,[76] as these should be set out in the articles, but preferably not in the memorandum.[77] The capital of a public company will have to be not less than the authorised minimum.

3. *Any other special requirements which deviate from the normal as exemplified by the appropriate Table.* The most likely matters are quorums, and the minimum and maximum numbers of directors.

With the aid of this information the draftsman should have no

---

[70] s.7(1)

[71] s.8(2).

[72] s 8(1).

[73] Although these cannot now be formed it has been thought necessary to retain this Table to ensure that those registered prior to 1981 maintain the appropriate forms of memoranda and articles.

[74] Particular care will need to be taken if it is intended that the company shall obtain the advantage of charitable status. The courts will not look outside the memorandum to discover what the objects are, though it may look at surrounding circumstances to determine whether the stated objects are charitable: *Incorporated Council of Law Reporting v. Att. Gen.* [1972] Ch. 73, C.A.

[75] See Chap. 10, pp. 209–210, below.

[76] See further, Chap. 13, below.

[77] See Chap. 13, below.

difficulty in preparing drafts based on precedents from his own experience, reference books and the Tables. Moreover, most law stationers have their own standard forms set up in print, adaptation of which will reduce printing charges.

The main question for consideration is the extent to which Table A is to be adopted. The option of not registering any articles, which is permissible when the company is limited by shares, is rarely chosen because most such companies on initial registration will be private ones and the incorporators will wish to include the sort of restrictions on freedom to transfer shares which were a pre-condition for qualifying as a private company prior to the Companies Act 1980. The restrictions in Table A are limited to giving the directors a right to refuse to register a transfer when the shares are partly paid or the company has a lien upon them.[78] When the incorporation is a partnership or family business what will be wanted is an absolute discretion to reject transfers and, probably, provisions requiring the shares to be offered to the existing shareholders if a member wishes to sell. A common practice is to register articles which substitute alternative provisions for certain Table A provisions but adopt the rest. This reduces the length of the document and the printing costs.[79] But if this is done, care should be taken to specify exactly which provisions of Table A are excluded and not leave this to implication by some such formula as "Table A shall apply except in so far as it is varied by or inconsistent with the following provisions"—a formula which inevitably leads to trouble.

Unless economy is a serious consideration, however, it is far better to exclude Table A completely and to have self-contained articles, even if, as will almost certainly be the case, these in most respect merely duplicate the provisions of the Table. By so doing, the company's officer will not be faced with the task of extracting its regulations from two separate documents, one of which, Table A, may become progressively less accessible—for it will be appreciated that it is the Table extant at the time of incorporation which continues to govern.[80] Adoption of Table A is therefore often a false economy, particularly as the larger firms of company solicitors have their own standard forms which are kept in print by their stationers, thus minimising the costs to their clients.

In the case of a company whose memorandum states that its registered office is to be in Wales it is now permissible for the memor-

---

[78] Table A 1985, art. 24.

[79] Articles must be printed: s.7(2). The Act specifically requires memoranda to be printed only when they are subsequently altered (s.6(1)(a)) but, in practice, both documents are printed and bound up together. Section 706 provides for prescription of the form, size, durability, etc., of any documents delivered to the Registrar and s.707 facilitates the use of modern technology (on which see the DTI *Guidance Note on Company Information on Magnetic Tape*, N.G. 24).

[80] This is often overlooked when new articles are adopted; it is the original, not the current Table A which should be expressly excluded.

andum and articles (and other documents that have to be delivered for registration) to be in Welsh, but they have to be accompanied by certified English translations when delivered for registration or be translated into English by the Registrar.[81]

The distinction between the memorandum and the articles of association has already been dealt with.[82] The effect of the two documents as between the members and the company will be considered later.[83]

Lodgment of documents

The final step is to lodge certain documents at the Companies' Registry.[84] The first of these documents—the memorandum and articles—must each have been signed by at least two persons,[85] whose signatures must be attested by a witness.[86]

If the company has a share capital each subscriber to the memorandum must write opposite his name the number of shares he takes and must not take less than one.[87] In practice he will merely subscribe for one share in the first instance, irrespective of the number which eventually he intends to acquire, and more often than not clerks in the solicitors' office will sign as subscribers rather than the true promoters. On lodging the memorandum and articles they must be accompanied by two documents in the forms prescribed,[88] *i.e.* the *Statement of Particulars of the Directors and Secretary and Situation of Registered Office* and the *Declaration of Compliance*. The first of these[89] is required by section 10 of the Act. Under its subsection (2) the Statement must contain the names and "requisite particulars"[90] of the first directors and secretary of the company. An appointment made by the articles is void unless the appointee is named in the Statement.[91] The

---

[81] s.710B. The Companies (Welsh Language Forms and Documents) Regulations (S.I. 1994 No. 117, as amended by S.I. 1994 No. 727 and S.I. 1995 No. 734) determine whether the burden of translation falls on the company or the Registrar. The latter takes the burden in the case of the memo. and arts., unless the company is listed.

[82] Chap. 1, p. 14, above.

[83] pp. 115–122, below.

[84] Since 1976 this has been, for English and Welsh companies, at the Companies Registration Office, Maindy, Cardiff. Prior to that, the registry was at Companies House, City Road, London EC1, and search facilities have been retained there.

[85] Or one person in the case of a private company limited by shares or guarantee: s.1(34).

[86] ss.1(1), 2(6) and 7(3)(c). *Semble*, an infant can be a subscriber (*Re Laxon & Co. (No. 2)* [1892] 3 Ch. 555, C.A.) as can an alien resident abroad: *Reuss v. Bos* (1871) L.R. 5 H.L. 176. If more than the minimum number subscribe the memorandum they must also subscribe the articles.

[87] s.2(5).

[88] The various prescribed English language forms are in the Companies (Forms) Regs 1985 (S.I. 1985 No. 854 (as amended). This adopts, wherever possible, the helpful practice of numbering forms by the number of the relevant section of the Act. The forms are obtainable from any law stationer. Increasing, dual English and Welsh Language forms are being prescribed.

[89] Which combines in one form what were formerly two.

[90] See Sched. 1 to the Act (as amended by the 1989 Act).

[91] s.10(5). Table A 1985 makes no provision for the first appointments which, in effect, can be made only by naming the appointees in the Statement and obtaining their signed consents.

Statement may be signed either by or on behalf of the subscribers to the memorandum[92] but it must include a consent to act signed by each person named.[93] Finally, the Statement must also specify the intended situation of the company's registered office on incorporation. The memorandum will have stated whether this is to be in England and Wales, in Wales or in Scotland,[94] but it will not state its actual address, which can be moved within the relevant country as the company decides, so long as notice is given to the Registrar within 14 days.[95] But the company must, at all times, have a registered office to which all communications and notices may be addressed.[96]

The second of the two documents, the Declaration of Compliance, is required by section 12(3) and consists of a statutory declaration in the prescribed form, by either the solicitor or a director or secretary named in the Statement required under section 10, declaring that all the requirements of the Act in respect of registration and of matters precedent and incidental to it have been complied with.[97] Unless the Registrar is satisfied that the foregoing requirements have been complied with he is not entitled to register the company[98] but he may accept the declaration as sufficient evidence of compliance.[99]

Normally these will be the only documents required and all that will be needed in addition is payment of the registration fees.[1] However, as we have seen, a second declaration may be needed if the company is a guarantee company which wishes to dispense with "limited"[2]: and a further Statement will be required if the company's proposed name is one on which a Government Department of other body has to be consulted.[3]

Purchase of a shelf-company

If the incorporators have no immediate special requirements regarding the company's constitution or name, but want their business to be incorporated as rapidly as possible as a private company limited by shares, an alternative to registering a new company is to buy one off-the-shelf from one of the agencies which provide this service. This alternative is increasingly being adopted, somewhat to the horror of

---

[92] When the memorandum is lodged by their agent, (*e.g.* the solicitor or accountant) the Statement must give his name and address: s.10(4).

[93] s.10(3).

[94] s.2. This determines the company's domicil and cannot be altered except as provided in s.2(2) as regards Welsh companies.

[95] s.287.

[96] *ibid*. And the address must appear on its business letters and order forms: s.351(1)(*a*).

[97] s.12(3).

[98] s.12(1).

[99] s.12(3). And normally will unless a flaw is apparent from the documents lodged.

[1] See Companies (Fees) Regs. 1991 (S.I. 1991 No. 1206) as amended. The fee for initial registration is now only £20.

[2] pp. 101–102, above.

[3] p. 103, above.

traditional company lawyers. Its great advantage is speed because all the incorporators have to do is to pay the agency and to take transfers of the subscribers' shares and custody of the company's registers. They will, of course, then have to send to the Registrar notices of changes of the directors and secretary (with the required consents) and of the situation of the registered office. Any other changes (*e.g.* alterations of the articles or a change of name) can be effected at leisure. The main disadvantage is that until they make changes, the company's name is unlikely to bear any relationship to them or to the business being carried on. But with the recent virtual abolition of the *ultra vires* rule and the introduction of the all-purpose objects clause[4] there should be less risk that the objects clause of the memorandum of association will prove inappropriate.

Registration and certificate of incorporation

If the Registrar is satisfied that the requirements for registration are met and that the purpose for which the incorporators are associated is "lawful",[5] he issues a certificate of incorporation signed by him or authenticated under his official seal.[6] This states that the company is incorporated and, in the case of a limited company that it is limited[7]; it is, in effect, the company's certificate of birth as a body corporate on the date mentioned in the certificate.[8] Section 13(7) declares that the certificate is conclusive evidence:

"(a) that the requirements of this Act in respect of registration and matters precedent and incidental to it have been complied with and that the association is a company authorised to be registered and is duly registered under this Act,[9] and

(b) if the certificate contains a statement that the company is a public company, that the company is such a company."

The functions of the Registrar in deciding whether or not to register the company are administrative, rather than judicial, but a refusal to register can be challenged by judicial review, albeit with scant hope

---

[4] s.3A inserted by the 1989 Act.

[5] See s.1(1) which permits incorporation only by "any two or more persons associated for a lawful purpose". This is interpreted as banning both purposes which are criminal and those which are regarded as contrary to public policy: *R. v. Registrar of Joint Stock Companies* [1931] 2 K.B. 197, C.A.; *R. v. Registrar of Companies, ex p. H.M.'s Attorney-General*, below p. 112, n. 14. In the light of the decision in *Yuen Kun Yeu v. Att.-Gen. of Hong Kong* [1988] A.C. 175, P.C., it seems clear that a member of the public subsequently defrauded by the company could not successfully sue the Registrar on the ground that he was negligent in registering the company (or, in the case of a public company, issuing the trading certificate).

[6] s.13(1) and (2). He also causes notice of the issue to be published in the *Gazette* (s.711(1)(a)) allots the company a registered number (s.705), and enters its name on the index of company names (s.714).

[7] s.13(1).

[8] s.13(3).

[9] It has been held to be conclusive as regards the date of incorporation even when that was clearly wrong: *Jubilee Cotton Mills v. Lewis* [1924] A.C. 958, H.L.

of success.[10] However, normally, the registration of a company cannot be challenged because of the conclusive effect of the certificate. This, happily, has rendered English company law virtually immune from the problems arising from defectively incorporated companies which have plagued the United States and many continental countries.[11] But the decided cases on section 13(7) (or its predecessors under earlier Acts) and the recent review of them by the Court of Appeal in a case[12] concerning the, then, comparable provision relating to a certificate of registration of a charge on a company's property, show that this immunity is not complete. Since section 13 and its predecessors in earlier Companies Acts are not expressed to bind the Crown, the Attorney-General can apply to the court and may obtain certiorari to quash the registration.[13]

This was successfully done in *R. v. Registrar of Companies, ex p. H.M.'s Attorney-General*,[14] where a prostitute had succeeded in incorporating her business under the name of "Lindi St Claire (Personal Services) Ltd." (the Registrar having rejected her first preference of "Prostitutes Ltd" or "Hookers Ltd" and shown no enthusiasm for "Lindi St Claire (French Lessons) Ltd") and, with scrupulous frankness, she specified its primary object in the memorandum as "to carry on the business of prostitution".[15] The court, on judicial review at the instance of the Attorney-General, quashed the registration on the ground that the stated business was unlawful as contrary to public policy.[16] It is unlikely, however, that the Attorney-General (or any other Crown servant) will take action unless public policy is thought to be involved and will not do so if all that has occurred is a technical breach of the formalities of incorporation.

---

[10] *R. v. Registrar of Joint Stock Companies* [1931] 2 K.B. 197, C.A. where an application for mandamus to order the Registrar to register a company formed for the sale in England of tickets in the Irish Hospital Lottery was rejected on the ground that the Registrar had rightly concluded that such sales were illegal in England.

[11] See Drury, "Nullity of Companies in English Law" (1985) 48 M.L.R. 644. The First Company Law Directive contains three Articles dealing with Nullity.

[12] *R. v. Registrar of Companies, ex p. Central Bank of India* [1986] Q.B. 1114, C.A. Reversing the decision at first instance, the C.A. held that, even on judicial review, the effect of s.98(2) of the Companies Act 1948, under which the certificate of registration of a charge was "conclusive evidence that the requirements—as to registration have been satisfied", was to make evidence of non-compliance inadmissible, thus precluding the court from quashing the registration.

[13] *Bowman v. Secular Society* [1917] A.C. 406, H.L. where, however certiorari was denied as the Society's purposes were held not to be unlawful.

[14] [1991] BCLC 476.

[15] Had she been less frank, for example by stating the primary object as "to carry on the business of masseuses and to provide related services", she would probably have got away with it.

[16] Notwithstanding that, as she indignantly protested, she paid income tax on her earnings. Since prostitution can be carried on without necessarily committing any criminal offence and since she continued, without incorporation, to practise her profession (for which she has become a well-known spokeswoman), some may think that this was an example of the "unruly horse" of public policy unseating its judicial riders.

Nevertheless, there is one other situation in which the certificate does not seem to be conclusive of valid incorporation. This results from what is now section 10(3) of the Trade Union and Labour Relations (Consolidation) Act 1992 (repeating similar provisions in earlier Acts) which declares that the registration of a trade union under the Companies Acts, shall be void. In the past, parties other than the Crown have been held entitled to rely on this; for example as a defence to a claim by a registered company whose objects make it a trade union. The reported cases[17] related to versions of what is now section 13(7) which were less comprehensive and which were not thought to cover substantive matters but only ministerial acts leading to registration.[18] Hence, it seems doubtful if they would be followed today. However, the researches of Mr Drury[19] have unearthed a more recent example of a company's removal from the register because its objects made it a trade union. The company in question was one formed by junior hospital doctors to represent their interests. It was later realised that its objects made it a trade union within the statutory definition. The Department of Trade took the view that the labour law provision overrode what is now section 13(7) of the Companies Act and accordingly the Registrar removed the company from the register for "void registration".[20] This, apparently, was done without any court order[21] and without challenge by the doctors. Presumably this action by the Registrar could be regarded as having been taken on behalf of the Crown and as the correction of a mistake which he, or one of his predecessors, had made and therefore as rectifiable.[22]

Hence, it now seems probable, but not certain, that in no circumstances can anyone other than the Crown plead the nullity of a registered company unless and until it has been removed from the register as a result of action by or on behalf of the Crown. Removal as a result of that action is tantamount to a declaration that it never existed as a corporate body.[23] This is not likely to be a satisfactory

---

[17] *Edinburgh & District Water Manufacturers Assoc. v. Jenkinson* 1903 5 Sessions Cases 1159; *British Assoc. of Glass Bottle Manufacturers v. Nettlefold* [1911] 27 T.L.R. 527 (where, however, the company was held not to be a trade union).

[18] (1911) 27 T.L.R. at 528, 529.

[19] *loc. cit.*, n. 11, above, at pp. 649, 650.

[20] See *Companies in 1976*, Table 10.

[21] Notwithstanding that the First Company Law Directive provides by Art. 11.1(*a*) that "Nullity must be ordered by a decision of a court of law."

[22] But, presumably, unless the company agreed, he could not take this action unless the incorporation was void (as in the case of a trade union or where the purposes were unlawful), rather than voidable (which would seem to be the case where, for example, registration had been secured by fraudulent misrepresentations).

[23] Whether this retrospective effect could be avoided by the Att.-Gen. asking for relief in the nature of *scire facias* (instead of certiorari) is obscure. The writ itself seems to have been abolished by the Crown Proceedings Act 1947, s.13 and Sched. 1, and it was always doubtful whether it was available in relation to statutory incorporations.

outcome if it has in fact been carrying on business as what both its members and its creditors believed to be a registered company[24]; it should be wound up[25] rather than declared never to have existed.[26] All that can be said with some assurance is that Mr Drury[27] is right in concluding that, although cases of nullity of incorporation may be rare in England, they do happen and when they do the present law is unclear, unsatisfactory and not wholly consistent with our obligations under the First Company Law Directive which we purported to implement in 1972. Remedial legislative action is needed and it is a pity that the opportunity to provide it was not taken in the Companies Act 1989 which remedied defects in relation to the analogous problem of *ultra vires*.[28]

Commencement of business

From the date of registration mentioned in the certificate of incorporation, the company, if it is a private company, becomes "capable forthwith of exercising all the functions of an incorporated company". But when it is registered as a public company this is "subject . . . to section 117 (additional certificate as the amount of allotted share capital)".[29] In order to ensure that the company complies with the stringent requirements imposed on a public company regarding the allotment of the minimum share capital, as described in Chapter 11, it must not do business or exercise any borrowing powers until the Registrar has issued it with a certificate (commonly known as a "trading certificate") or it has re-registered as a private company.[30] Unless it does one or the other within a year from incorporation, it may be wound up by the Court and the Secretary of State may petition.[31]

In order to obtain the trading certificate the company must apply in the prescribed form supported by a statutory declaration in the prescribed form signed by a director or the secretary of the company.[32] This statutory declaration must state that the nominal amount of the allotted share capital is not less than the authorised minimum

---

[24] Their rights and obligations would be seriously affected (especially when the company was registered with limited liability) contrary to the First Company Law Directive, Art. 12.3.

[25] As the First Directive appears to envisage: see Art. 12.2.

[26] But as what? As a registered company, which it ostensibly is? Or as an unregistered compay under Part V of the Insolvency Act 1986?

[27] *loc. cit.*, p. 112, n. 11 above.

[28] See Chap. 10, below.

[29] s.13(4).

[30] s.117(1). In the more usual case where original registration was as a private company but it later converts to a public one, similar requirements will first have to be met (see ss. 43–48) but there is no suspension of business during the process of conversion: below, pp. 122–123.

[31] Insolvency Act 1986, ss.122(1)(b) and 124(4)(a).

[32] s.117(2).

and must specify the amount paid up, the preliminary expenses and to whom they were paid or payable, and any payment or benefit to a promoter and what it was for.[33] The Registrar may accept this statutory declaration as sufficient evidence of the matters stated in it.[34] He may, however, have rather more information to go on, since within one month of allotting the shares the company will have had to deliver another document, the Return of Allotments, required by section 88 and, as regards any shares issued for a non-cash consideration, a copy of the valuation report required by sections 103 and 108.[35] Hence, only if he issues the certificate before the latter documents are filed will he need to rely solely on the bald statement in the statutory declaration that the minimum capital has been duly allotted. If satisfied, he has to issue the certificate.[36]

The certificate is "conclusive evidence that the company is entitled to do business and exercise any borrowing powers".[37] However, by analogy with the decisions referred to above[38] in relation to the certificate of incorporation, it appears that, as this section is not expressed to bind the Crown, the Registrar's decision could be quashed on judicial review at the instance of the Attorney-General.[39] This, in contrast with quashing registration, would not have the undesirable effect of nullifying the incorporation. A more likely course, however, would be for the Secretary of State, if he had grounds for suspecting that the share capital had not been properly allotted, to institute an investigation under Part XIV of the Act[40] and, if his suspicions proved well founded, petition the court to wind up the company under section 124 or 124A of the Insolvency Act.

Contractual effect of the memorandum and articles

Section 14 of the Act provides that the memorandum and articles, "shall, when registered, bind the company and its members to the same extent as if they respectively had been signed and sealed by each member, and contained covenants on the part of each member to observe all" their provisions, and that money payable by a member to the company under the memorandum or articles shall be in the nature of a specialty debt.

The wording of this section can be traced back with variations to

[33] s.117(3).
[34] s.117(5).
[35] s.111. On ss.103 and 108, see Chap. 11 at pp. 239–241, below.
[36] s.117(2).
[37] s.117(6).
[38] See pp. 111–114, above.
[39] See p. 112, above.
[40] See Chap. 25, below.

the original Act of 1844 which adopted the existing method of forming an unincorporated joint stock company by deed of settlement (which did, of course, constitute a contract between the members who sealed it) and merely superimposed incorporation on registration. The 1856 Act substituted the memorandum and articles for the deed of settlement and introduced a provision on the lines of the present section. Unhappily, full account was not taken of the vital new factor (namely that the incorporated company was a separate legal entity) and the words "as if ... signed and sealed by each member" did not have added to them "and by the company". This oddity has survived into the modern Acts (with the result that debts due *from* the company to a member under the contract are not specialty debts).[41] Despite the odd wording, however, certain points are clearly established.

First, the memorandum and articles constitute a contract between the company and each member.[42] But it is a contract with various special characteristics. Section 14 expressly provides that it is "subject to the provisions of this Act".[43] Those provisions include sections which permit of alterations of the memorandum and articles of association by means of a special resolution. Thus, a member enters into a contract on terms which are alterable by the other party,[44] rather in the same way as a member of a club agrees to be bound by the club rules as validly altered from time to time, or a workman agrees to be employed on the terms of a collective agreement as occasionally varied by the employers and his trade union. That a majority of the members should normally be able to alter the articles and the memorandum by following a prescribed procedure and thus alter for the future the contractual rights and obligations of individual shareholders is hardly surprising. It reflects the fact that the company is an association and that some process of collective decision-making is needed, even in relation to its constitution, if it is to be able to adapt to changing circumstances in the business environment. The alternative would be constitutional change only with the consent of each individual shareholder, which would be very difficult to obtain in many cases and which would give unscrupulous individuals golden opportunities

---

[41] Hence sums due as repayment of share capital become statute-barred on the lapse of the shorter period applicable to simple contracts, in contrast with those due on express contracts under the company's seal, such as bonds or debentures: *Re Compania de Electricidad de Buenos Aires* [1980] Ch. 146 at 187.

[42] *Hickman v. Kent or Romney Marsh Sheepbreeders' Assoc.* [1915] 1 Ch. 881, where Astbury J. reviewed earlier cases in a judgment which has become the *locus classicus*. An article providing for a reference to arbitration of disputes between members and the company was held to be contractually binding.

[43] Articles cannot therefore contract out of the statutory requirement in s.183(1) (which expressly operates "notwithstanding anything in the company's articles") for a written instrument for the transfer of shares: *Re Greene* [1949] Ch. 333, C.A.

[44] *Shuttleworth v. Cox* [1927] 2 K.B. 9, C.A., *per* Atkin L.J. at 26; *Malleson v. National Insurance and Guarantee Corporation* [1894] 1 Ch. 200, *per* North J. at 205.

for disruptive behaviour. On the other hand, as we shall see in Chapter 26 below, where we examine the variation procedure in detail, there are corporate situations, notably joint ventures, where individual consent to constitutional change is an appropriate arrangement and is what the joint venturers need in order to give effect to their business plans. In other words, the law should provide for constitutional change by majority vote to be the "default setting", but also enable the incorporators to entrench individual rights to veto constitutional change, if they deliberately choose that option. As we shall see in Chapter 26, the question is whether company law meets this need in the way it should.

A further set of particularities relating to the section 14 contract stems from a different set of considerations: not the promotion of internal flexibility, as with the variation procedures, but the protection of new investors. They buy shares in the company or otherwise invest in it on the basis of the memorandum and articles of association which, as we have seen, are filed with the Registrar in order to be available for public inspection. The courts are thus reluctant to apply to the statutory contract those doctrines of contract law which might result in the memorandum and articles subsequently being held to have a content substantially different from that which someone reading the registered documents would have predicted. Thus, the Court of Appeal has held that articles cannot later be rectified to give effect to what the incorporators actually intended but failed to embody in the registered document, since the reader of the registered documents could have no way of guessing that any error had been made in transposing the incorporators' agreement into the document.[45] Equally, that Court has refused to imply terms into the statutory contract from extrinsic evidence of surrounding circumstances, since that evidence would probably not be known to potential investors who would thus have no basis for anticipating that any such implication was appropriate.[46] Further, in this case Steyn L.J. was of the view that for the same reasons the statutory contract "was not defeasible on the grounds of misrepresentation, common law mistake, mistake in equity, undue influence or duress".[47] These decisions by the courts on the meaning of the company's constitutional documents support the policy underlying the statutory provision on the conclusiveness of the certificate of incorporation.[48] Both

---

[45] *Scott v. Frank F. Scott (London) Ltd* [1940] Ch. 794, C.A.

[46] *Bratton Seymour Service Co. Ltd v. Oxborough* [1992] BCLC 693, C.A. In this case the majority were in effect seeking to avoid the prohibition on alterations to the constitution without individual shareholder consent which have the effect of increasing the shareholder's financial liability to the company. See s.16 and below, p. 709.

[47] *ibid.*, at 698. On the other hand, investor protection was not inconsistent with the implication of terms based on the construction of the language used in the memorandum and articles, for here the basis of the implication was available to those who read the company's constitution.

[48] Above, pp. 111–114. A further expression of this policy can be found in the reluctance of the courts to protect "legitimate expectations" under s.459 where these arise out of informal agreements outside the articles to which not all shareholders are party: *Re Blue Arrow plc* [1987] BCLC 585 (below, p. 744).

conduce to investor protection by enabling the investor to rely on what
he or she finds upon a search of the public registry.[49]

Secondly, the contract is enforceable among the members *inter se*.
The principal occasions on which this question is likely to be important arise when articles confer on members a right of pre-emption or
first refusal when another member wishes to sell his shares[50] or, more
rarely, impose a duty on the remaining members or the directors to
buy the shares of a retiring member.[51] A direct action between the
shareholders concerned is here possible; and for the law to insist on
action through the company would merely be to promote multiplicity
of actions and involve the company in unnecessary litigation.

Thirdly, the decisions have constantly affirmed that the section confers contractual effect on a provision in the memorandum and articles
only in so far as it affords rights or imposes obligations on a member
qua member.[52] As Astbury J. said in the *Hickman* case[53]:

> "An outsider to whom rights purport to be given by the articles in
> his capacity as such outsider, whether he is or subsequently
> becomes a member, cannot sue on those articles, treating them as
> contracts between himself and the company, to enforce those
> rights."

The same applies to the contract between the members *inter se*.[54] On
the wording of the section it would be difficult to interpret it as creating a contract with anyone other than the company and the members.
Furthermore, there is obvious sense in restricting the ambit of the
section to matters concerning the affairs of the company.[55] But there
is no obvious justification in the statutory wording for still further
restricting it to matters concerning a member in his capacity of
member.[56]) It may not matter much that the result is that a provision
that a promoter, who becomes a member, cannot enforce a provision
that the company shall reimburse the expenses he incurred[57] or that
solicitor, who becomes a member, cannot enforce a provision that he

[49] A further and important restriction on the *remedies* available in respect of breaches of the
corporate constitution, namely the supposed rule that damages were not available to a shareholder in an action against his company so long as he remained a member, seems to have
been removed by s.111A, inserted by the 1989 Act.

[50] *Borland's Trustee v. Steel* [1901] 1 Ch. 279 (member seeking declaration that rights of pre-
emption in articles were valid). *cf. Lyle & Scott v. Scott's Trustees* [1959] A.C. 763, H.L.

[51] *Rayfield v. Hands* [1960] Ch. 1, where Vaisey J. was prepared to make an order in effect for
specific performance.

[52] But not necessarily qua shareholder; in *Lion Mutual Marine Insurance v. Tucker* (1883) 12
Q.B.D. 176, C.A., the provision concerned the members' liabilities qua insurers.

[53] [1915] 1 Ch. 881 at 897.

[54] *London Sack & Bag Co. v. Dixon & Lugton* [1943] 2 All E.R. 763, C.A.

[55] If the solicitor had slipped into the articles, to which he and his wife were the subscribers, a
provision to the effect that he and his wife should no longer be bound to cohabit, it would be
absurd if this were treated as a deed of separation.

[56] The *Hickman* case may reflect the high regard in which the courts then held the doctrine of
privity of contract.

[57] *Re English & Colonial Produce Co.* [1906] 2 Ch. 435.

shall be the company's solicitor.[58] What does matter is that it apparently prevents a member who is also a director or other officer of the company from enforcing any rights purporting to be conferred by the articles on directors or of ficers. Only if he has a contract extraneous to the articles will he have contractual rights and obligations *vis-à-vis* the company or his fellow members. This, as we shall see in relation to directors' contracts of service,[59] does not mean that such an extraneous contract may not be interpreted in the light of the articles or adopt provisions in them but it presumably does mean (though there seems to be no reported decision to that effect) that a non-executive director without any express or implied contract with the company cannot sue to recover directors' fees.

It is highly anomalous to treat directors as "outsiders" since for most purposes the law treats them as the paradigm "insiders" (which members, as such, are not) and they will breach their fiduciary duties and duties of care if they do not act in accordance with the memorandum and articles. It also produces some strange results. *Hickman's* case[60] concerned a provision in the articles stating that any dispute between the company and a member should be referred to arbitration and this was enforced as a contract. But in the later case of *Beattie v. Beattie Ltd*[61] where there was a similar provision, the Court of Appeal, relying on the dictum in *Hickman*, held that a dispute between a company and a director (who was a member) was not subject to the provision because the dispute was admittedly in relation to the director qua director. In the still later case of *Rayfield v. Hands*,[62] the articles of a private company provided that a member intending to transfer his shares should give notice to the directors "who will take the said shares equally between them at a fair value". A member gave notice but the directors refused to buy. Vaisey J. felt able to hold that the provision was concerned with the relationship between the member and the directors as members and ordered them to buy.[63]

This difficult concept of "member in his capacity of member" has not been carried by the courts to what might be its logical conclusion, *i.e.* that, since a member need not be a shareholder[64] (or, more rarely, a shareholder a member[65]) the statutory contract does not embrace matters appertaining to him as a shareholder only. Rights conferred by the articles to attend general meetings, to speak thereat and to vote on a show of hands are clearly rights qua member.[66] Rights to vote on

[58] *Eley v. Positive Life Association* (1876) 1 Ex.D. 88, C.A.
[59] Chap. 9 at pp. 191–192, below.
[60] Above, n. 53.
[61] [1938] Ch. 708, C.A.
[62] [1960] Ch. 1.
[63] What he would have held if one of the directors had not been a member is unclear.
[64] He cannot be a shareholder if the company has no share capital.
[65] He need not be a member if he holds share warrants to bearer: see below, pp. 329–330.
[66] As in *Pender v. Lushington* [1877] Ch.D. 70.

a poll seem to be a mixture of both membership and shareholder rights since the number of votes exercisable will normally depend on the number of shares held as well as on membership. But rights to a return of capital,[67] to payment of a dividend duly declared and payable,[68] or to receive a share certificate[69] appear to affect a member solely as shareholder. Happily it has never been doubted that the statutory contract applies to all these cases.[70]

However, in addition to these relatively straightforward examples, section 14 is also important in relation to the rights of members to restrain corporate irregularities and to the so-called Rule in *Foss v. Harbottle*. This Rule is discussed in some detail in Chapter 23. Here it suffices to say that, subject to certain exceptions, if the irregularity complained of is a wrong done to the company, the company acting, normally, through its board of directors, is the only proper plaintiff in an action to prevent, or recover in respect of, the wrong, and that when, in exceptional circumstances, an individual member is allowed to sue he must do so in a "derivative action" suing on behalf of himself and the other members and joining the company as a defendant. None of this applies, however, if his personal rights have been infringed. In that event the only restriction is that he may not be allowed to sue if the irregularity complained of is one which could be put right by an ordinary resolution of the company.

In 1957, Lord Wedderburn, in his seminal article on *Foss v. Harbottle*,[71] pointed out that, in *Quinn & Axtens Ltd v. Salmon*,[72] the Court of Appeal and the House of Lords allowed a managing director, suing as a member, to obtain an injunction restraining the company from completing transactions entered into in breach of the company's articles which provided that the consent of the two managing directors was required in relation to such transactions. This, in effect, showed that a member had a personal right to require the company to act in accordance with its articles, which right could be enforced by the member even though the result was indirectly to protect a right which was afforded to him as director. If this is correct, the supposed principle, that there is a statutory contract between the company and its members only in respect of matters affecting members qua members,

---

[67] As in *Re Compania de Electricidad de Buenos Aires* [1980] Ch. 146, above p. 116, n. 41.
[68] As in *Wood v. Odessa Waterworks Co.* (1889) 42 Ch.D. 636.
[69] As in *Burdett v. Standard Exploration Co.* (1899) 16 T.L.R. 112.
[70] Nor was it argued in *Rayfield v. Hands* that the provision did not relate qua member to the member disposing of his shares. It also seems to be assumed that a provision in the articles entitling the holders of a class of shares to appoint a director is enforceable as a s.14 contract between the class members and the company. Where debenture-holders are given such a right it will normally be prescribed in the debentures and therefore enforceable as a contract extraneous to the memorandum and articles.
[71] "Shareholders' Rights and the Rule in Foss v. Harbottle" [1957] C.L.J. 193, especially at 210–215. See also Beck (1974) 22 Can.B.R. 157 at 190–193.
[72] [1909] 1 Ch. 311, C.A.; affd. [1909] A.C. 442, H.L.

is effectively outflanked—though presumably it still applies to the statutory contact between members *inter se*.

As we have seen, this has not caused the judges to cease to express the orthodox view[73] which, on the whole, continues to be espoused in the textbooks. It has, however, led to a fascinating and continuing debate in the law reviews,[74] in which the contributors, Goldberg, G.N. Prentice, Gregory and Drury, favour the Wedderburn view rather than the orthodox one but seek to refine it. Goldberg does this by narrowing Wedderburn's formulation so that it would provide that a member of a company has a contractual right under section 14 to have any affairs of the company conducted by the particular organ of the company specified in the Act or the company's memorandum or articles, even if its enforcement has the effect of, indirectly, enforcing outsider rights. That, he argues with force, would produce a conclusion desirable on policy grounds and would not conflict with decisions such as those in *Ely v. Positive Life Assurance* or *Beattie v. Beattie*, neither of which concerned what organ should conduct the company's affairs. Prentice takes a broadly similar view but expresses it somewhat differently. He argues that a member qua member can sue the company to compel it to observe those provisions which relate to the company's constitutional powers and their exercise, even if that indirectly enforces his rights as an outsider, and that the company can sue a member on any provision of the memorandum and articles relating to him qua member whether or not the provision relates to such constitutional matters. Gregory flatly denies that there is any extant rule that the statutory contract arises only when it affects members qua members and contends that the Court of Appeal decision in *Beattie v. Beattie* was plainly wrong in the light of the earlier House of Lord's decision in *Quinn & Axtens v. Salmon*,[75] Drury's conclusion is essentially similar to that of Wedderburn but with the gloss that an individual member should not be able to enforce rights relating to him as an outsider in disregard of the views and interests of other members, so that the matter should ultimately be decided, like other matters of internal management, by the members in general meeting.[76]

---

[73] But Wedderburn can point to later decisions which afford support for his interpretation of *Quinn & Axtens*: see, *e.g. Re Harmer Ltd* [1959] 1 W.L.R. 62 at 85 and 89, C.A., *Re Richmond Gate Property Co.* [1965] 1 W.L.R. 335, (see (1965) 28 M.L.R. 347 and (1966) 29 M.L.R. 608 at 612); *Hogg v. Cramphorn* [1967] Ch. 254; *Bamford v. Bamford* [1970] Ch. 212; *Re Sherbourn Park Residents Co. Ltd* (1986) 2 BCC 99.528; *Breckland Group Holdings v. London & Suffolk Properties* [1989] B.C.L.C. 100 (see (1989) 52 M.L.R. 401 at 407, 408); *Guinness plc v. Saunders* [1990] 2 A.C. 663, H.L.

[74] See, *pro tem.*, Goldberg, (1972) 33 M.L.R. 362; G.N. Prentice, (1980) 1 Co.Law 179; Gregory, (1981) 44 M.L.R. 526; Goldberg, (replying) (1985) 48 M.L.R. 121; and Drury, [1989] C.L.J. 219.

[75] In this he is not supported by Goldberg: see (1985) 48 M.L.R. 121.

[76] This gloss would seemingly come close to reducing the member's personal right to his position in a derivative action: *Smith v. Croft (No. 2)* [1988] Ch. 114, discussed in Chap. 23, pp. 673–675, below.

There, for the present, the matter rests and this book is not the appropriate place to carry the debate further. What clearly is needed is either a review of all the relevant authorities by the House of Lords or a revised version of section 14. And the latter would probably be desirable even if there were a definitive ruling by the Lords since, on the present wording of the section, it is difficult to see how any interpretation could cure all its imperfections. At the very least the section needs to be re-drafted so that it says that the memorandum and articles constitute a contract between the company, its members, directors and other officers, and also provides that whether that contract is sought to be enforced by or against the company, it should be treated similarly, either as a simple contract or as a contract under seal.

Re-registration of an Existing Company

A company may wish, at some stage, to convert itself into a company of a different type. This, in most cases, it may do without the expense of effecting a complete re-organisation of the types referred to in Chapter 28 below, and without having to form a brand new company. The circumstances and methods whereby conversions may be achieved are now collected together in Part 2 of the Act.

(i) Private company becoming public

Under sections 43 to 48 a private company limited by shares can become re-registered as a public company, by passing a special resolution that it should be so re-registered and applying to the Registrar in the prescribed form signed by a director or the secretary, accompanying the application by a number of documents designed to enable the Registrar to satisfy himself that the minimum capital requirements for a public company are complied with.[77] The special resolution must alter the memorandum of association to state that the company is to be a public company and must make such further alterations as are necessary to comply with the provisions of the Act in relation to public companies[78] (including the change of the suffix to its name from "Ltd" to "plc"[79]) and it must also make any needed alterations to its articles of association.[80]

The documents that must accompany the application are copies of:

(a) the altered memorandum and articles;
(b) a balance sheet dated not more than seven months before the

---

[77] s.43(1).
[78] s.43(2).
[79] Or the Welsh equivalents.
[80] s.43(2)(c).

application and the auditors' report thereon, which must be "unqualified"[81];

(c) a written statement by the auditors that that balance sheet showed that at its date the company's net assets were not less than the aggregate of its called up share capital and undistributable reserves;

(d) if, since the balance sheet date, shares have been allotted otherwise than for cash, the valuation report required under sections 103 and 108[82];

and these documents must be supported by

(e) a statutory declaration by a director or secretary of the company confirming that the special resolution has been passed, that the conditions of sections 44 and 45 have been complied with, and that no change has occurred since the balance sheet date resulting in the net assets becoming less than the called up capital and undistributable reserves.[83]

If the Registrar is satisfied that the company may be re-registered as a public company,[84] he issues a new certificate of incorporation,[85] the alterations in the memorandum and articles take effect, and the company becomes a public company.[86] In effect, the certificate is a combined certificate of incorporation and trading certificate which would have been needed had the company been initially registered as a public company.

If the private company, which wishes to convert to a public one, is an unlimited company it will, of course, have to become limited, that being one of the essential elements of the definition of a public company. This, by virtue of section 48, it is enabled to do in the conversion operation—and rather more simply than if it first re-registered as limited under (iv) below, and subsequently re-registered under section 43 as a public company. It merely has to add to the special resolution that the liability of the members is to be limited and what its share capital is to be and to make the appropriate alterations in the company's memorandum.[87]

---

[81] Defined in s.46, as amended by the 1989 Act.

[82] See pp. 240–241, below.

[83] s.43(3).

[84] He may accept the statutory declaration as sufficient evidence (s.47(2)) but must not issue the certificate if it appears that the court has made an order confirming a reduction of capital bringing the company's allotted share capital below the authorised minimum: s.47(3).

[85] Which is conclusive evidence that the requirements have been met: s.47(5). On "conclusiveness", see pp. 111–114 and 115, above.

[86] s.47(4).

[87] s.48(2).

(ii) Public company becoming private

To convert from public to private (an operation which must not be confused with "privatisation" in the sense of de-nationalisation) is comparatively simple unless there is disagreement among the members. Under section 53 it can convert to a private company limited by shares or by guarantee[88] by passing a special resolution making the necessary alterations to the memorandum and articles and applying, in the prescribed form, to the Registrar with a copy of the amended memorandum and articles. But special safeguards are prescribed since loss of public status may have adverse consequences to the members, especially as regards their ability to dispose of their shares. Hence, under section 54, members who have not consented to, or voted in favour of, the resolution can, within 28 days of the resolution, apply to the court for the cancellation of the resolution if they can muster the support of:

(a) holders of not less than 5 per cent in nominal value of the company's share capital or any class of it; or
(b) if the company is not limited by shares,[89] not less than 5 per cent of the members; or
(c) not less than 50 members.

The Registrar must not issue a new certificate of incorporation until the 28 days have expired without an application having been made or, if it has been made, until it has been withdrawn or dismissed and a copy of the court order delivered to the Registrar.[90] The court has powers similar to those on an application under sections 4 and 5 in relation to a resolution altering a company's objects.[91] Unless the court cancels the resolution, the Registrar issues a new certificate of incorporation with the usual conclusive consequences.[92]

A public company will have to re-register as a private company if, under section 137,[93] the court makes an order confirming the reduction of its capital which has the effect of reducing the nominal amount of its allotted share capital below "the authorised minimum". In such

---

[88] For obvious reasons it cannot, by this simple process, convert to an unlimited company: s.53(3). Nor can it become a company limited by guarantee but with a share capital: s.1(4).
[89] This is somewhat puzzling since, until the Registrar issues a new certificate, the company remains a public company (s.55(2)) which it could not be unless it had a share capital. Presumably (b) is to cater for an "old public company" which has still not re-registered under the transitional provisions, now in the Companies Consolidation (Consequential Provisions) Act 1985, ss.1–9. As there can now be few, if any, such companies that have not re-registered under the transitional provisions either as plcs or as private companies, this book ignores them.
[90] s.53.
[91] s.54(5), (6), (7) and (8).
[92] s.55.
[93] See Chap. 11 at pp. 247–251, below.

circumstances that order will not be registered and come into effect (unless the court otherwise directs) until the company is re-registered as a private company.[94] The court may (and, in practice will) authorise this to be done without the need to resort to section 53. Instead of the company having to pass a special resolution, the court will specify in the order the alterations to be made in the memorandum and articles[95] and, on application in the prescribed form signed by a director or the secretary, accompanied by a printed copy of the memorandum and articles as so altered,[96] the Registrar will issue the new certificate of incorporation.[97] In this case there can be no application to the court by dissenting members[98] since the company has no option but to become private.

(iii) Limited company becoming unlimited

The conversion which presents the greatest dangers to the members is, obviously, that from a limited company to an unlimited one. Nevertheless it is not completely banned since the members of a small private company may legitimately conclude that forfeiting the advantages of limited liability is worthwhile, as enabling them to operate with much the same flexibility (particularly as regards withdrawal of their capital) and privacy of their financial affairs as a partnership, while yet retaining all the advantages of corporate personality other than limited liability. Hence, under section 49 a private limited company[99] may re-register as an unlimited company if *all* the members agree.[1] As with other conversions, an application, in the prescribed form and signed by a director or the secretary, has to be lodged with the Registrar, together with supporting documents.[2] The application must set out the alterations to be made in the memorandum and articles,[3] and the supporting documents needed are[4]:

(a) the prescribed form of assent signed by or on behalf of all the members[5];
(b) a statutory declaration by the directors, confirming that assent and

---

[94] s.139(1) and (2).
[95] s.139(3).
[96] s.139(4).
[97] s.139(5).
[98] Under s.54, above.
[99] s.49(3).
[1] s.49(8)(a) and (b).
[2] s.49(4).
[3] s.49(5), (6) and (7).
[4] s.49(8).
[5] Including the personal representatives of any deceased member and the trustee in bankruptcy of any member: s.49(9). In the event of the company's subsequent liquidation, a past member is not liable to contribute to its assets to a greater extent (if any) than if the conversion had not occurred: Insolvency Act 1986, s.78.

stating that they have taken all reasonable steps to satisfy themselves that each person who signed on behalf of a member was empowered to do so;

(c) a printed copy of the altered memorandum; and

(d) if articles have been registered (as they normally will have been) a printed copy of them incorporating any alterations.

The Registrar then issues a new certificate of incorporation with the usual conclusive effect.[6]

(iv) Unlimited company becoming limited

In this, the converse of case (iii), it is not the members who need special safeguards but the creditors. Surprisingly, however, in section 51 of the Companies Act under which this conversion is effected (unless it is combined with a conversion from a private to a public company under section 43, *i.e.* under (i) above) the only protection afforded them is that the new suffix, "Ltd", to the company's name should alert them to the fact that it has become a limited company. Their real protection is afforded by what is now section 77 of the Insolvency Act 1986, which applies whether the conversion is achieved under section 43 or 51.[7] The effect of this is that those who were members of the company at the time of its re-registration remain potentially liable in respect of its debts and liabilities contracted prior thereto if winding up commences within three years of the re-registration.[8]

Section 51 permits re-registration as a company whether limited by shares or by guarantee. The first step is the passing of a special resolution stating which of these the company is to be and making the necessary alterations to its memorandum and articles.[9] A copy of this must (like all special resolutions) be forwarded to the Registrar within 15 days. With it, or subsequently, an application in the prescribed form, signed by a director or the secretary, and accompanied by printed copies of the altered memorandum and articles must be lodged with the Registrar[10] who then issues a new certificate of incorporation with the usual conclusive consequences.[11]

Ban on vacillation between limited and unlimited

What a company is not permitted to do is to chop and change more than once between limited and unlimited. Once a limited company has

---

[6] s.50.

[7] Insolvency Act s.77(1).

[8] *ibid.*, s.77(2)–(4) which, in a somewhat confusing manner, make the necessary adjustments to s.74 regarding the respective obligations of past and present members.

[9] s.51(1), (2), (3).

[10] s.51(4) and (5).

[11] s.52.

been re-registered as unlimited it cannot again re-register as a public company under section 43[12] or as a limited company under section 51[13] and once an unlimited company has been re-registered as a limited company under section 51, it cannot be re-registered as an unlimited company under section 49.[14] There is, however, no ban on switching back and forth between private limited company and public limited company.

TREATMENT OF UNREGISTERED COMPANIES

A matter which has caused the Department of Trade and Industry and Parliamentary Counsel agonies disproportionate to its practical importance is how to deal with "unregistered companies", *i.e.* bodies not formed under our past or present companies' legislation.[15] The solution has been to deal with them in four ways, only two of which, the third and fourth, require more than a mention here. The first has been to apply to all bodies incorporated and having a place of business in Great Britain[16] (other than (a) those formed under a public general Act, (b) those not formed for the purposes of gain, and (c) those exempted by a direction of the Secretary of State) an ever increasing number of the provisions of the Companies Act.[17] The second has been to subject to the winding-up jurisdiction of the courts[18] a still wider range of bodies, corporate or unincorporated.[19].

The third has been to include in the Companies Act special provisions whereby unregistered companies can re-register under the Act. The object of this is to enable (and, indeed, to encourage) the few remaining companies formed by deeds of settlement, Private Acts of Parliament or letters patent to register under the Companies Act without having to form a new company and wind up the old one. The *modus operandi* is dealt with in Chapter II[20] of Part XXII of the Act as supplemented by Schedule 21.[21] Subject to various qualifications and exceptions, any such company may register under the Act as an

---

[12] s.43(1).

[13] s.51(2).

[14] s.49(2) and (3).

[15] Companies formed under earlier companies' legislation are, if still surviving, subject to all the present provisions of the Act (see ss.675–677) except to the extent that these expressly provide (as occasionally they do) that they shall not apply to companies formed prior to a stated date.

[16] And to any surviving unincorporated bodies entitled by virtue of letters patent to any privilege conferred by the Chartered Companies Act 1837 (s.718(4)).

[17] s.718 and Sched. 22 (as amended by the 1989 Act) and the Companies (Unregistered Companies) Regs. 1985 (S.I. 1985 No. 680).

[18] Insolvency Act 1986, Part V.

[19] *i.e.* "any association and any company" except a railway company incorporated by Act of Parliament: *ibid.*, s.220.

[20] *i.e.* ss. 680–690. Only the salient features are dealt with here.

[21] As amended by the 1989 Act.

unlimited company, or as a company limited by shares or by guarantee.[22] A distinction is drawn between companies which were "joint
stock companies" (essentially those with a share capital)[23] and others.
Only the former may register as companies limited by shares[24] and
may do so either as private companies or, if they comply with the
normal conditions for registration as a public company and for
obtaining a trading certificate, as public companies.[25] On registration,
a deed of settlement company may substitute a memorandum and articles of association for the deed of settlement but need not do so.[26]
The procedural requirements for registration are a cross between those
required for initial registration and for re-registration as a different
type of company under the provisions dealt with above[27] and there are
similar controls over company names.[28] On registration the Registrar
issues a certificate which has the usual conclusive consequences.[29] The
details of the effect of registration, provisions for the automatic vesting
of property, savings for existing liabilities and rights and similar matters are dealt with in Schedule 21.[30]

The fourth solution is to develop special legal regimes for what
the Act calls "oversea companies", but regimes which follow those
applicable to companies incorporated in Great Britain and apply, *mutatis mutandis*, the same principles as apply to domestic companies. In
the area of formation of companies, this approach has been followed
especially in relation to the disclosure of information. The current
rules are to be found in Part 23 of the Act. For example, section
693 imposes on oversea companies' business communications similar
publicity requirements (with some additions) to those applicable to
domestic companies and, as we have seen, there is a similar control
over the name under which the oversea company carries on business
in Great Britain.[31]

However, the main topic dealt with in this Part is the delivery of
information to the Registrar by oversea companies. This area, always
somewhat obscure, has now become over-complicated as a result of
the way the United Kingdom has chosen to implement[32] the Eleventh

---

[22] s.680. If it has only one member it may re-register only as a private company limited by
shares or guarantee.
[23] s.683.
[24] ss.680(3), 684.
[25] s.685.
[26] s.690. The Stock Exchange when, as a result of the City's "Big Bang", it re-registered as a
limited company initially retained its deed of settlement.
[27] ss.681, 684, 685 and 686.
[28] ss.682, 687.
[29] s.688.
[30] s.689. See, in particular, Sched. 21 paras. 5 and 6 on how certain provisions in its constitution
(unless, in the case of a deed of settlement company, it substitutes a memorandum and articles)
have to be treated in future as if they were in a memorandum.
[31] Above, p. 106.
[32] In the Oversea Companies and Credit and Financial Institutions (Branch Disclosure) Regulations 1992 (S.I. 1992 No. 3179), which amended Part XXIII of the Act.

Company Law Directive[33] and the Directive on Bank Branches.[34] There are now *two*[35] somewhat different legal regimes which apply to such companies. The first are the "traditional" rules which apply to companies incorporated outside Great Britain and which have established a "place of business" in this country, a concept which requires something more than simply doing business in Great Britain. The second are the rules of Community origin which apply only where the company incorporated outside Great Britain has established a "branch" in this country. The implementing Regulations were drafted on the basis that the establishment of a branch is a more demanding threshold than the establishment of a place of business, so that a company might fall within the latter category but not in the former. On the other hand, the opposite was not true: a company with a branch in Great Britain would have established a place of business here. In this case the Community rules would apply, rather than the traditional ones, so that the dominant rules are now the ones derived from Community law.[36] The traditional rules will generally apply only in the narrow category of case where the oversea company has crossed from merely doing business in Great Britain to establishing a place of business here, but has not gone so far as to establish a branch of its business in Great Britain.

It is true that both the Community-derived and the traditional legal regimes are very similar. Both are based on the principle of disclosure, the former being somewhat more demanding overall than the latter. For present purposes, it will be sufficient to sketch out the rules derived from Community law for non-bank branches. A company establishing a branch in Great Britain must deliver certain information to the Registrar about both the company and the branch within one month of its opening, in particular a statement of the identity and authority of those who represent the branch in Great Britain and who can accept service on its behalf, translated copies of the company's constitution and its latest accounting documents.[37] That information must be kept up-to-date, which is crucial, of course, in relation to the accounts, and must be supplemented fairly substantially if the company which has established the branch becomes subject to winding-up proceedings.[38] The Registrar must keep a branch register, the information filed in which is naturally open to public inspection.

As stated, the traditional requirements are similar if less far-reaching

---

[33] Directive 89/666.

[34] Directive 89/117.

[35] Or even three, since the Community rules for bank etc. branches are rather more demanding than the Community rules for non-bank branches: compare Scheds. 21C and 21D to the Act.

[36] In particular, it should be noted that the Community-derived rules apply to all companies incorporated outside Great Britain and not just to those incorporated in other Community Member States: s.690A(1).

[37] Scheds. 21A and D.

[38] Chapter IV of Part 23.

in general. Nevertheless, the efficient conduct of business requires that it ought to be clear which regime applies.[39] Unfortunately, this is not the case. The criteria for the establishment of a business have always been somewhat uncertain, though some, if not complete, illumination has been shed on the matter by judicial decisions over the years.[40] Establishing a place of business, as opposed to merely doing business, in this country requires "a degree of permanence or recognisability as being a location of the company's business".[41] However, it is not fatal to the establishment of a place of business that the activities carried on there are only subsidiary to the company's main business, which is carried on outside Great Britain, or are not a substantial part of the company's overall business.[42]

If the tests for the establishment of a business are not absolutely clear, the situation is worse for the new concept of a "branch". That is defined in the Act as being a branch within the meaning of Directive 89/666,[43] but that Directive contains no definition of a branch! On the other hand, the Act, following Directive 89/117, does contain a definition of a bank branch, from which some guidance may be obtainable. That refers to a place of business which "conducts directly some or all of the operations inherent in the business".[44] So it may be that purely ancillary activities, such as warehousing or data processing, do not constitute the establishment of a branch though they could amount to a place of business.

The underlying principle behind these provisions of Part XXIII is relatively straightforward. An oversea company should not be able to avoid domestic requirements as to publicity by operating though an unincorporated branch rather than a subsidiary incorporated in Great Britain. More than that, there should be a "level playing field" in terms of the burden of disclosure as between these two methods of carrying on business. The present method of implementing that principle in this country is, however, far from straightforward, and the resulting complex regulation is likely to give company administrators headaches which they do not need or deserve.

---

[39] There are also criminal penalties for non-compliance (s.697) but some protection may be found for innocent mistakes in the fact that the breach must be committed "knowingly and wilfully".

[40] Many of the cases have involved interpretation of the phrase "has an established place of business" in the provisions relating to the registration of company charges, but the courts have accepted that the same criteria apply in this context.

[41] *Re Oriel Ltd* [1986] 1 W.L.R. 180, 184. See also *Cleveland Museum of Art v. Capricorn Art International* S.A. [1990] BCLC 546.

[42] *South India Shipping Corporation v. Export-Import Bank of Korea* [1985] 1 W.L.R. 585, C.A.; *Actiesselskabat Dampskib "Hercules" v. Grand Trunk Pacific Railway Co.* [1912] 1 K.B. 222, C.A.

[43] s.698(1)(b).

[44] s.699A(3).

CHAPTER 7

PROMOTERS

Meaning of "promoter"

IF, in a psychoanalyst's consulting room, we were asked to say what picture formed in our minds at the mention of the expression "company promoter", most of us would probably confess that we envisaged a character of dubious repute and antecedents who infests the commercial demi-monde[1] with a menagerie of bulls, bears, stags and sharks as his familiars, and who, after rising to affluence by preying on the susceptibilities of a gullible public, finally retires from the scene in the blaze of a sensational suicide or Old Bailey trial.[2] In other words, we should envisage someone whose profession it was to form bogus companies and foist them off on the public to the latter's detriment and his own profit. Such figures have existed and it is probably too much to hope that they will ever be entirely eradicated, but even in their Edwardian heyday they formed only the minutest fraction of those whom the law classifies as promoters. A much more typical, if less romantic, example, would be the village grocer who converts his business into a limited company. He, of course, is in no sense a professional company promoter, always and increasingly a rare bird,[3] but he would be the promoter of his little company, and a moment's thought will make it clear that the difference, however great, between him and a professional promoter is basically one of degree rather than of kind. Both create or help to create the company and seek to sell it something, whether it be their services or a business. Both are obviously so placed that they can easily take advantage of their position by obtaining a recompense grossly in excess of the true value of what they are selling.[4] The only difference is that the grocer is less likely than the professional to abuse his position since he will probably continue to be the majority shareholder in his company, whereas the promoter, if a

---

[1] Somehow associated in our minds with "the curb".

[2] It is perhaps a tribute to the law that we definitely picture him as coming to a sticky end; *cf.* Lord MacNaghten in *Gluckstein v. Barnes* [1900] A.C. 240, H.L. at 248.

[3] As pointed out in Chapter 16, the handling of public issues is now virtually monopolised by reputable merchant bankers. It is the close scrutiny by these and the Stock Exchange as much as the rigour of the law which has caused the virtual disappearance of the old-time promoter. Moreover, the nineteenth-century practice of seeking public subscription before the company is formed has been abandoned. A company seeking listing on the Stock Exchange, or even a quotation on A.I.M. must be able to show some track record. Consequently, the duties of the promoters are often swallowed up in such cases in those of the directors.

[4] A good (or rather, bad) example of the *modus operandi* is *Re Darby* [1911] 1 K.B. 95.

131

shareholder at all, will intend to off-load his holdings on to others as soon as possible.

It will have been apparent from the foregoing that the expression "promoter" covers a wide range of persons. Indeed it is still wider. Both the professional promoter and the village grocer are promoters to the fullest extent, in that each "undertakes to form a company with reference to a given project, and to set it going and . . . takes the necessary steps to accomplish that purpose".[5] But a person may be a promoter who has taken a much less active and dominating role; the expression may, for example, cover any individual or company that arranges for someone to become a director, places shares, or negotiates preliminary agreements.[6] Nor need he necessarily be associated with the initial formation of the company; one who subsequently helps to arrange the "floating off" of its capital (in the manner explained in Chapter 16) will equally be regarded as a promoter.[7] On the other hand, those who act in a purely ministerial capacity, such as solicitors and accountants, will not be classified as promoters merely because they undertake their normal professional duties[8]; although they may if, for example, they have agreed to become directors or to find others who will.[9]

Who constitutes a promoter in any particular case is therefore a question of fact.[10] The expression has never been clearly defined either judicially[11] or legislatively, despite the fact that it is frequently used both in decisions and statutes. So far as the promoter himself is concerned this imposes no particular hardship; as we shall see, his duty is merely to act with good faith towards the company and this he should do whether legally compelled or not. But from the point of view of the company the vagueness of the term is apt to be embarrassing when legislation requires promoters to be named or transactions with them to be disclosed.[12]

---

[5] *Per* Cockburn C.J. in *Twycross v. Grant* (1877) 2 C.P.D. 469 at 541, C.A.

[6] *cf. Bagnall v. Carlton* (1877) 6 Ch.D. 371, C.A.; *Emma Silver Mining Co. v. Grant* (1879) 11 Ch.D. 918, C.A.; *Whaley Bridge Printing Co. v. Green* (1880) 5 Q.B.D. 109; *Lydney & Wigpool Iron Ore Co. v. Bird* (1886) 33 Ch.D. 85, C.A.; *Mann v. Edinburgh Northern Tramways Co.* [1893] A.C. 69, H.L.; *Jubilee Cotton Mills v. Lewis* [1924] A.C. 958, H.L. and cases cited, below.

[7] *Lagunas Nitrate Co. v. Lagunas Syndicate* [1899] 2 Ch. 392 at 428, C.A.

[8] *Re Great Wheal Polgooth Co.* (1883) 53 L.J.Ch. 42.

[9] *Lydney & Wigpool Iron Ore Co. v. Bird* (1886) 33 Ch.D. 85, C.A.; *Bagnall v. Carlton* (1877) 6 Ch.D. 371, C.A.

[10] For an excellent discussion of this question, see J.H. Gross, (1970) 86 L.Q.R. 493, and his book *Company Promoters* (Tel-Aviv, 1972).

[11] For attempts, in addition to Cockburn C.J.'s description (above), see those of Lindley J. in *Emma Silver Mining Co. v. Lewis* (1879) 4 C.P.D. 396 at 407, and of Bowen J. in *Whaley Bridge Printing Co. v. Green* (1880) 5 Q.B.D. 109 at 111.

[12] *e.g.* under s.117(3)(d) (see p. 115, above) and the Stock Exchange *Listing Rules*, paras. 6.c. 21 and 18.10(j).

Duties of promoters

The early Companies Acts contained no provisions regarding the liabilities of promoters, and even today they are largely silent on the subject, merely imposing liability for untrue statements in listing particulars or prospectuses to which they were parties.[13] The courts, however, were conscious of the possibilities of abuse inherent in the promoter's position and in a series of cases in the last quarter of the nineteenth century they laid it down that anyone who can properly be regarded as a promoter stands in a fiduciary position towards the company with all the duties of disclosure and accounting which that implies; in particular he must not make any profit out of the promotion without disclosing it to the company. The difficulty, however, is to decide how he is to make this disclosure—the company being an artificial entity. The first leading case on the subject, *Erlanger v. New Sombrero Phosphate Co.*,[14] suggested that it was his duty to ensure that the company had an independent board of directors and to make full disclosure to it. In that case Lord Cairns said[15] that the promoters of a company:

"stand ... undoubtedly in a fiduciary position. They have in their hands the creation and moulding of the company; they have the power of defining how, and when, and in what shape, and under what supervision, it shall start into existence and begin to act as a trading corporation ... I do not say that the owner of property may not promote and form a joint stock company and then sell his property to it, but I do say that if he does he is bound to take care that he sells it to the company through the medium of a board of directors who can and do exercise an independent and intelligent judgment on the transaction. ..."

This rule, however, was obviously too strict; an entirely independent board would be impossible in the case of most private and many public companies, and since *Salomon v. Salomon*[16] it has never been doubted that a disclosure to the members would be equally effective. In that famous case it was held that the liquidator of the company could not complain of the sale to it at an obvious over-valuation of Mr Salomon's business, all the members having acquiesced therein. "After Salomon's case I think it impossible to hold that it is the duty of the promoters of a company to provide it with an independent board of

---

[13] FSA 1986, ss. 150–152 and the Public Offers of Securities Regulations 1995, regs. 13 to 16 (see below, pp. 426–433). But note s.150(6) which makes it clear that in respect of misstatements in listing particulars a promoter is in no worse position than any other person responsible for the listing particulars.

[14] (1878) 3 App.Cas. 1218, H.L.

[15] At 1236.

[16] [1897] A.C. 22, H.L.: see p. 77, above.

directors if the real truth is disclosed to those who are induced by the promoters to join the company.''[17] But the promoter cannot escape liability by disclosing to a few cronies, who constitute the initial members, when it is the intention to float off the company to the public or to induce some other dupes to purchase the shares. This was emphasised by the speeches of the House of Lords in the second great landmark in the development of this branch of the law—*Gluckstein v. Barnes.*[18] "It is too absurd", said Lord Halsbury with his usual bluntness, "to suggest that a disclosure to the parties to this transaction is a disclosure to the company. . . . They were there by the terms of the agreement to do the work of the syndicate, that is to say, to cheat the shareholders; and this, forsooth, is to be treated as a disclosure to the company, when they were really there to hoodwink the shareholders."

The position therefore seems to be that disclosure must be made to the company either by making it to an entirely independent board or to the existing and potential members as a whole. If the first method is employed the promoter will be under no further liability to the company, although the directors will be liable to the subscribers if the information has not been passed on in the invitation to subscribe; indeed, if the promoter is a party to this invitation,[19] he too will be liable to the subscribers.[20] If the second method is adopted disclosure must be made in the prospectus, or otherwise, so that those who are or become members, as a result of the transaction in which the promoter was acting as such, have full information regarding it. A partial or incomplete disclosure will not do; the disclosure must be explicit.[21]

It is sometimes stated that the duty of a promoter may be even heavier than that of making full disclosure of any profit made. The suggestion is that if he acquires any property after the commencement of the promotion he is presumed to do so as a trustee for the company so that he must hand it over to the company at the price he gave for it, unless he discloses not merely the profit which he proposes to make but also informs the company of its right to call for the property at its cost price. In theory this is undoubtedly sound. If the promoter broke his duty by attempting to acquire the property beneficially when he should have acquired it for the unborn company,[22] then his breach of

---

[17] *Per* Lindley M.R. in *Lagunas Nitrate Co. v. Lagunas Syndicate* [1899] 2 Ch. 392, C.A. at 426.

[18] [1900] A.C. 240, H.L. at 247.

[19] In which event he will find some difficulty in persuading the court that the directors were truly independent of him.

[20] See above n. 13 and Chap. 16, below.

[21] *Gluckstein v. Barnes*, above.

[22] There seems to be no objection in principle to the establishment of a trust in favour of an unformed company—for there can certainly be a trust in favour of an unborn child and this might have alleviated the problem of pre-incorporation contracts dealt with below at pp. 141–144, but the decisions display a reluctance to invoke this principle: *cf. Natal Land Co. v. Pauline Syndicate* [1904] A.C. 120, P.C.

duty was not merely failure to disclose his profit but was his attempted expropriation of the company's property. Indeed, if this is the situation, it appears that nothing short of unanimous consent of all the shareholders of the company, when formed, should entitle the promoter to retain his ill-gotten gains,[23] for not even a resolution of a general meeting can authorise an expropriation of the company's property.[24] But in fact the English decisions cited in support of this suggestion[25] do not go anything like so far (although certain dicta in them do[26]). There seems to be no case in which, *full disclosure of the profit having been made*, the promoter has been held liable to account. The judgments acknowledge the possibility that the promoter may have acquired the property as trustee, but they seem to require something more than the mere acquisition of property after the commencement of the promotion with the intention of re-selling it to the company.[27] In principle it should suffice if the company can show that the promoter acquired the property for himself when it was his duty to acquire it for the company.[28] But in practice all seems to turn on the intentions of the promoter at the time of purchase; on whether he intended to buy for himself for re-sale *to* the company or to buy initially *for* the company.[29] In the former case his only duty is to disclose; in the latter he cannot subsequently change his mind and seek to act as vendor rather than as trustee.

It seems clear that a promoter cannot effectively contract out of his duties by inserting a clause in the articles whereby the company and the subscribers agree to waive their rights.[30] Moreover, Article 11 of the Second Company Law Directive was intended to ensure that, when a public company acquired a substantial non-cash asset[31] from its promoters within two years of its entitlement to commence business, an independent valuation of that asset and approval by the company in general meeting should be required. But, as we shall see,[32] as implemented by the United Kingdom[33] this applies only to acquisitions from

---

[23] *cf. Cook v. Deeks* [1916] 1 A.C. 554, P.C.

[24] See Chap. 22, below.

[25] *Tyrrell v. Bank of London* (1862) 10 H.L.C. 26; *Re Ambrose Lake Tin Co.* (1880) 14 Ch.D. 390, C.A.; *Re Cape Breton Co.* (1885) 29 Ch.D. 795, C.A., affd. *sub nom. Cavendish Bentinck v. Fenn* (1887) 12 App.Cas. 652, H.L.; *Ladywell Mining Co. v. Brookes* (1887) 35 Ch.D. 400, C.A.

[26] See especially (1887) 35 Ch.D. at 413.

[27] See especially, *Omnium Electric Palaces v. Baines* [1914] 1 Ch. 332, C.A.

[28] *c.f. Cook v. Deeks*, n. 23, above.

[29] See especially, *per* Sargant J. in [1914] 1 Ch., 347.

[30] *Gluckstein v. Barnes*, above; *Omnium Electric Palaces v. Baines* [1914] 1 Ch., 247, *per* Sargant J. Such "waiver" clauses used to be common and, except as regards actual misrepresentations (on which see Misrepresentation Act 1967, s.3), there is still no statutory prohibition of them: s. 310 (invalidating exemption clauses) only covers offers and auditors.

[31] One for which the consideration paid by the company was equal to one-tenth or more of the company's issued share capital.

[32] Chap. 11 at pp. 241–242, below.

[33] Now s.104(1), (2) and (4)–(6).

the subscribers to the memorandum who need not be the true pro-moters and generally are not.[34] However, when a private company re-registers as a public one (a more common occurrence than initial formation as a public company) a similar requirement applies to such acquisitions from anyone who was a member on the date of re-registration[35] and that may well catch a promoter. This, therefore, affords an additional statutory protection[36] against the risk that pro-moters will seek to off-load their property to the company at an inflated price.

Remedies for breach of promoters' duties

Since the promoter owes a duty of disclosure to the *company*, the primary remedy against him in the event of breach is for the company to bring proceedings for rescission of any contract with him or for the recovery of any secret profits which he has made. So far as the right to rescind is concerned, this must be exercised on normal contractual principles, that is to say the company must have done nothing to show an intention to ratify the agreement after finding out about the non-disclosure or misrepresentation[37] and *restitutio in integrum* must still be possible.[38] In view of the wide powers now exercised by the court to order financial adjustments when directing rescission, it is doubtful whether the *restitutio in integrum* rule operates as any real restraint, at any rate where the promoter has been fraudulent or where he himself is responsible for the dealings alleged to have resulted in restitution being impossible.[39] The only circumstances where this requirement seems likely to impose a serious limitation is where innocent third parties have acquired rights to the property concerned, and even there a monetary adjustment will often enable the third parties' rights to be satisfied.[40] The mere fact that the contract had been performed never seems to have destroyed the right to rescind a contract of this type[41]

---

[34] See Chap. 6 at p. 109, above.

[35] s.104(3)–(6).

[36] But one which can be avoided by the promoters ceasing to be members prior to the re-registration.

[37] *Lagunas Nitrate Co. v. Lagunas Syndicate* [1899] 2 Ch. 392, C.A. Here again "the company" must mean the members or an independent board; clearly ratification by puppet directors cannot be effective.

[38] *Re Leeds & Hanley Theatre of Varieties* [1902] 2 Ch. 809, C.A.; *Steedman v. Frigidaire Corpn.* [1933] 1 D.L.R. 161, P.C.; *Dominion Royalty Corp. v. Goffatt* [1935] 1 D.L.R. 780 (Ont.C.A.), affd. [1935] 4 D.L.R. 736 (Can.S.C.).

[39] *Erlanger v. New Sombrero Phosphate Co.* (1878) 3 App.Cas. 1218, H.L., and *Spence v. Crawford* [1939] 3 All E.R. 271, H.L. These cases suggest that the courts have more restricted powers of financial adjustment when there is no fraud: *sed quaere, cf. Armstrong v. Jackson* [1917] 2 K.B. 822.

[40] As, perhaps, in *Re Leeds & Hanley Theatre of Varieties*, above, where the property had been mortgaged to a bank.

[41] As pointed out in the 10th Report of the Law Reform Committee (Cmnd. 1782), paras. 6–9, the extent, if any, of any such rule was doubtful except as regards contracts relating to land. The Misrepresentation Act 1967 is based on this Report.

and since the Misrepresentation Act 1967 any suggestion to that effect seems unarguable.[42]

If the contract is rescinded the promoter's secret profit will normally disappear as a result, but if he has made a profit on some ancillary transaction there is no doubt that this too may be recovered. Moreover, a secret profit may be recovered although the company elects not to rescind. The classic illustration of this is *Gluckstein v. Barnes*[43] itself. In that case a syndicate had been formed for the purpose of buying and reselling Olympia, then owned by a company in liquidation. The syndicate first bought up at low prices certain charges on the property and then bought the freehold itself for £140,000. They then promoted a company of which they were the directors, and to it they sold the freehold for £180,000 which was raised by a public issue of share and debentures. In the prospectus the profit of £40,000 was disclosed. But in the meantime the promoters had had the charges on the property repaid by the liquidator out of the £140,000 and thereby made a further profit of £20,000. This was not disclosed in the prospectus, though reference was there made to a contract, close scrutiny of which might have revealed that some profit had been made. Four years later the new company went into liquidation and it was held that the promoters must account to the company for this secret profit.

There is, however, authority for saying that if the property on which the profit was made was acquired before the promoter became a promoter, there can be no claim for the recovery of the profit as such.[44] According to this view it may be necessary for this purpose to make the, admittedly difficult, determination of the exact moment of time at which the promotion began.

Normally, however, this rule works fairly enough. If the company freely elects to affirm the purchase, there would be an element of injustice in making the promoter disgorge the whole of the difference between the price at which he bought—perhaps many years previously—and that at which he sold. No doubt the court could assess the market value at the date of the sale and on that basis force the promoter to account, but this, it has been argued,[45] would be to make a new contract for the parties. On the other hand, the rule could work grave

---

[42] s.1 of that Act expressly provides that a contract can be rescinded for misrepresentation notwithstanding that the misrepresentation has become a term of the contract or that the contract has been performed.

[43] [1900] A.C. 240, H.L. And see *Jubilee Cotton Mills v. Lewis* [1924] A.C. 958, H.L.

[44] *Re Ambrose Lake Tin Co.* (1880) 14 Ch.D. 390, C.A.; *Re Cape Breton Co.* (1885) 29 Ch.D. 795, C.A., affd, *sub nom. Cavendish Bentinck v. Fenn* (1887) 12 App.Cas. 652, H.L.; *Ladywell Mining Co. v. Brookes* (1887) 35 Ch.D. 400, C.A.; *Re Lady Forrest (Murchison) Gold Mine* [1901] 1 Ch. 582; *Burland v. Earle* [1902] A.C. 83, P.C.; *Jacobus Marler Estates v. Marler* (1913) 85 L.J.P.C. 167n.; *Cook v. Deeks* [1916] 1 A.C. 554 at 563, 564, P.C.; *Robinson v. Randfontein Estates* [1921] A.D. 168 (S.Afr.S.C.App.Div.); *P. & O. Steam Nav. Co. v. Johnson* (1938) 60 C.L.R. 189 (Austr.H.C.).

[45] *Re Cape Breton Co.* (1885) 29 Ch.D. 795, C.A.

injustice to the company on the rare occasions when *restitutio in integrum* had become impossible so that the company had lost the right to rescind through circumstances beyond its control. In practice the courts avoided this injustice either by finding that the promoter was fraudulent, and accordingly liable to an action for deceit, or that the promotion had commenced when he acquired the property; indeed, they have often found both.[46] They have even suggested that, in the absence of common law fraud, the promoter would be liable in damages for his failure to disclose,[47] or negligence in allowing the company to purchase at an excessive price,[48] the damages being the difference between the market value and the contract price. As a result of the Misrepresentation Act 1967 there is a clear legal basis for awarding damages in all cases where the promoter has made an actual misrepresentation and cannot prove that he had reasonable ground to believe, and did believe up to the time the contract was made, that the facts represented were true.[49] When there is any misrepresentation the Misrepresentation Act makes any exclusion clause ineffective to bar any remedy, "except in so far as it satisfies the requirement of reasonableness . . . ".[50]

In addition to the remedies of the company, the promoter may be liable to those who have acquired securities of the company in reliance on mis-statements in listing particulars or prospectuses to which the promoter was a party. The remedies available against him are the same as those against the officers of the company or others responsible for the listing particulars or prospectuses and are dealt with in Chapter 16 below.

Remuneration of promoters

A promoter is not entitled to recover any remuneration for his services from the company unless there is a valid contract to pay between him and the company. Indeed, without such a contract he is not even

---

[46] *Re Olympia, Ltd* [1898] 2 Ch. 153, affd. *sub nom., Gluckstein v. Barnes*, above; *Re Leeds and Hanley Theatre of Varieties*, above. But the mere non-disclosure of the amount of the profit is not misrepresentation: *Re Lady Forrest (Murchison) Gold Mine* [1901] 1 Ch. 582; *Jacobus Marler Estates Ltd* v. *Marler* (1913) 85 L.J.P.C. 167n.

[47] *Re Leeds & Hanley Theatre of Varieties*, above; see especially *per* Vaughan Williams L.J. [1902] 2 Ch. at 825.

[48] *Per* Lord Parker in *Jacobus Marler Estates v. Marler* (1913) 85 L.J.P.C. at 168.

[49] Misrepresentation Act 1967, s.2(1). Damages under s.2(1) are awarded on a tortious, rather than a contractual basis, but as if the tort committed were that of deceit: *Royscot Trust Ltd v. Rogerson* [1991] 2 Q.B. 297, C.A. Moreover, under s.2(2) damages may be awarded in lieu of rescission.

[50] *ibid.*, s.3, as substituted by s.8 of the Unfair Contract Terms Act 1977, s.11 of which defines the requirements of reasonableness for this purpose as "the terms shall have been a fair and reasonable one to be included having regard to the circumstances which were, or ought reasonably to have been, known to or in the contemplation of the parties when the contract was made". The onus is on those seeking to show that the requirement is satisfied: ss.8 and 11.

entitled to recover his preliminary expenses or the registration fees.[51] In this respect the promoter is at the mercy of the directors of the company. Until the company is formed it cannot enter into a valid contract[52] and the promoter therefore has to expend the money without any guarantee that he will be repaid. In practice, however, recovery of preliminary expenses and registration fees does not normally present any difficulty. Former Tables A contained an express provision authorising the directors to pay them[53] and, although this did not constitute a contract between the company and the promoter,[54] it empowered the directors to repay expenses properly incurred.[55] The corresponding article of Table A 1985[56] omits this express provision; presumably it was thought to be unnecessary. And this surely must be correct; the whole tenor of the Act assumes that preliminary expenses properly incurred will be borne by the company[57] and that the general delegation of the company's power to the board of directors suffices.

It may well be, however, that the promoter will not be content merely to recover his expenses; certainly if he is a professional promoter he will expect to be handsomely remunerated. Nor is this unreasonable. As Lord Hatherly said,[58] "The services of a promoter are very peculiar; great skill, energy and ingenuity may be employed in constructing a plan and in bringing it out to the best advantages." Hence it is perfectly proper for the promoter to be rewarded, provided, as we have seen, that he fully discloses to the company the rewards which he obtains. The reward may take many forms. The promoter may purchase an undertaking and promote a company to repurchase it from him at a profit, or the undertaking may be sold directly by the former owner to the new company, the promoter receiving a commission from the vendor. A once-popular device was for the company's capital structure to provide for a special class of deferred or founders' shares which would be issued credited as fully paid in consideration of the promoter's services.[59] Such shares would normally provide for

---

[51] *Re English and Colonial Produce Co.* [1906] 2 Ch. 435, C.A.; *Re National Motor Mail Coach Co.* [1908] 2 Ch. 515, C.A.

[52] *Kelner v. Baxter* (1866) L.R. 2 C.P. 174; *Natal Land Co. v. Pauline Syndicate* [1904] A.C. 120, P.C. Nor can it ratify a preliminary contract purporting to be made on its behalf: *ibid.* It must enter into a new contract and this ought to be by a deed since the consideration rendered by the promoter will be past.

[53] See, *e.g.* Table A 1948, art. 80.

[54] See Chap. 6 at p. 118, above.

[55] *Re Rotherham Alum Co.* (1883) 25 Ch.D. 103, C.A.; *Re Englefield Colliery Co.* (1877–1878) 8 Ch.D. 388, C.A.

[56] Art. 70.

[57] See *e.g.* s.117(3)(c) regarding the need to state the amount of the preliminary expenses in the statutory of declaration leading to the issue of the trading certificate: above, p. 115.

[58] In *Touche v. Metropolitan Ry Warehousing Co.* (1871) L.R. 6 Ch.App. 671 at 676.

[59] The promoter should obtain a contract with the company prior to rendering the services, for past services are not valuable consideration: *Re Eddystone Marine Insurance* [1893] 3 Ch. 9, C.A. Hence if the services are rendered before the company was formed the promoter will have to pay for the shares. Moreover, in the case of a public company an undertaking to

the lion's share of the profits available for dividend after the preference
and ordinary shares had been paid a dividend of a fixed amount. This
had the advantage that the promoter advertised his apparent confidence
in the business by retaining a stake in it; but all too often his stake
(which probably cost him nothing anyway) was merely window-
dressing. And if, in fact, the company proved an outstanding success
the promoter might do better than all the other shareholders put
together. Today, when the trend is towards simplicity of capital structures, founders' shares are out of favour and, in general, those old
companies which originally had them have got rid of them on a reconstruction.[60] A more likely alternative is for the promoter to be given
warrants or options entitling him to subscribe for shares at a particular
price, (*e.g.* that at which they were issued to the public) within a
specified time. If the shares have meanwhile gone to a premium this
will obviously be a valuable right.

Preliminary contracts by promoters

Until the company has been incorporated it cannot contract or enter
into any other act in the law. Nor, once incorporated, can it become
liable on or entitled under contracts purporting to be made on its behalf
prior to incorporation,[61] for ratification is not possible when the ostensible principal did not exist at the time when the contract was originally
entered into.[62] Hence, preliminary arrangements will either have to be
left to mere ''gentlemen's agreements'' or the promoters will have to
undertake personal liability. Which of these courses will be adopted
depends largely on the demands of the other party. If our village grocer
is converting his business into a private company of which he is to be
managing director and majority shareholder he will obviously not be
concerned to have a binding agreement with anyone. In such a case a
draft sale agreement will be drawn up and the main object in the
company's memorandum will be to acquire his business as a going
concern ''and for this purpose to enter into an agreement in the terms
of a draft already prepared and for the purpose of identification signed

---

perform work or supply services will no longer be valid payment: s.99(2), Chap. 11 at p. 239,
below. But provided the shares are given a very low nominal value this may not be a serious
snag.

[60] There have been many interesting battles between holders of founders' shares and the other
members. If the holdings of founders' shares are widely dispersed there is obviously a risk
of block being acquired on behalf of the other classes in the hope of outvoting the remaining
founders' shareholders at a class meeting to approve a reconstruction. To safeguard their
position, in a number of cases the founders' shareholders formed a special company and
vested all the founders' shares in it, thus ensuring that they were voted solidly at any meeting.

[61] *Kelner v. Baxter* (1866) L.R. 2 C.P. 174; *Natal Land Co. v. Pauline Syndicate* [1904] A.C.
120, P.C.

[62] Contrast the position when a public company enters into transactions after its registration but
before the issue of a trading certificate (s.117(8), above Chap. 6 at p. 114) or when a company
changes its name (above Chap. 6 at p. 105).

by . . .''. When the incorporation is complete the seller will ensure that the agreement is executed and completed.

If, however, promoters are arranging for the company to take over someone else's business, the seller will certainly, and the promoters will probably, wish to have a binding agreement immediately. In this event the sale agreement will be made between the vendor and the promoters and it will be provided that the personal liability of the promoters is to cease when the company in process of formation is incorporated and enters into an agreement in similar terms, which, once again, will be referred to in the memorandum.

Agreements of this nature will be a necessary feature of nearly every incorporation, and not only must the promoters make full disclosure to the company but, in addition, the company must give particulars of them in any listing particulars or prospectuses.[63] Generally speaking, all material contracts must be disclosed unless entered into more than two years previously and in particular all those relating to property acquired or to be acquired by the company.

Companies' pre-incorporation contracts

What, in practice, is a not infrequent source of trouble is that those engaged in the formation of a company cause transactions to be entered into ostensibly by the company but before it has in fact been formed. As we have seen, the company, when formed, cannot ratify or adopt the contract,[64] but prior to the European Communities Act 1972 the legal position of the promoter and the other party seemed to depend on the terminology employed. If the contract was entered into by the promoter and signed by him "for and on behalf of XY Co. Ltd" then, according to the early case of *Kelner v. Baxter*,[65] the promoter would be personally liable. But if, as is much more likely, the promoter signed the proposed name of the company, adding his own to authenticate it (*e.g.* XY Co. Ltd, AB Director) then, according to *Newborne v. Sensolid (Great Britain) Ltd*,[66] there was no contract at all.

However, on the entry of the United Kingdom to the European

---

[63] See Chap. 16, below.

[64] Unless it enters into a new contract. This, of course, does not mean that, in the absence of a new contract, the company or the other party can accept the delivery of the goods or payment without being under any obligation.

[65] See n. 61, above. If two (or more) promoters each enter into pre-incorporation contracts that will not in itself make them partners or liable as such on contract entered into by the other: *Keith Spicer Ltd v. Mansell* [1970] 1 W.L.R. 333, C.A.

[66] [1954] 1 Q.B. 45, C.A. In that case it was the promoter who attempted to enforce the agreement but it appears that the decision would have been the same if the other party had attempted to enforce it, as was so held in *Black v. Smallwood* [1966] A.L.R. 744 (Aust.H.C.): see also *Hawkes Bay Milk Corporation Ltd. v. Watson* [1974] 1 N.Z.L.R. 218, *cf. Marblestone Industries Ltd v. Fairchild* [1975] 1 N.Z.L.R. 529. But it is difficult to see why the promoter should not be liable for breach of implied warranty of authority.

Community we had to implement Article 7 of the First Company Law Directive. The relevant provision is now section 36c of the Act, which reads:

"(1) A contract which purports to be made by or on behalf of a company at a time when the company has not been formed, has effect, subject to any agreement to the contrary, as one made with the person purporting to act for the company or as agent for it, and he is personally liable on the contract accordingly."

The aim of this provision, in line with that of the first Company Law Directive, is to increase security of transactions for third parties by avoiding the consequences of the contract with the company being a nullity. This protection is provided by giving the third party an enforceable contractual obligation, not against the subsequently formed company, but against the promoter, unless the third party agrees to forego that protection. In its first decision on the new provision the Court of Appeal held that such consent could not be deduced simply from the fact that the promoter signed as the agent of the company; an express agreement, presumably either in the contract itself or subsequently, on the part of the third party that the promoter should not be personally liable was required.[67]

However, the presence of the statutory provision has also had an effect on the courts' perception of the common law in this area. In the same case, Oliver L.J. said that the "narrow distinction" drawn in *Kelner v. Baxter* and the *Newborne* case did not represent the true common law position, which was simply: "does the contract purport to be one which is directly between the supposed principal and the other party, or does it purport to be one between the agent himself— albeit acting for a supposed principal—and the other party?"[68] This question is to be answered by looking at the whole of the contract and not just at the formula used beneath the signature. If after such an examination the latter is found to be the case, the promoter would be personally liable at common law, no matter how he signed the document.

On this analysis the difference between section 36C and the common law is narrowed, but not eliminated. At common law, if the parties intend to contract with the non-existent company, the result will be a nullity and the third party protected only to the extent that the law of restitution provides protection. Under the statute, a contract which purports to be made with the company will trigger the liability of the promoter, unless the third party agrees to give up the protection. In other words, the common law approaches the question of the third party's contractual rights against the promoter as a matter of the par-

---

[67] *Phonogram Ltd v. Lane* [1982] 1 Q.B. 938, C.A.
[68] *ibid.*, at 945. This approach was applied by the Court of Appeal in *Cotronic (UK) Ltd v. Dezonie* [1991] BCLC 721 and in *Badgerhill Properties Ltd v. Cottrell* [1991] BCLC 805.

ties' intentions, with no presumption either way, whereas the statute creates a presumption in favour of the promoter being contractually liable. The common law is still important in those cases which fall outside the scope of the statute.[69]

Despite the improvements which section 36C has effected, there are still considerable problems with its operation. First, perhaps as a consequence of the legislature's concern with the promotion of third-party protection, the section does not make it clear whether the promoter acquires a right under the statute to enforce the contract, as well as contractual obligations. It is submitted that normal principles of contractual mutuality should lead to this latter result.[70]

Secondly, the section bites only when the contract "purports" to be made on behalf of a company which has not been formed. Both limbs of this proposition must be satisfied. Thus, where the parties thought the company existed, though it had in fact been struck off the register, the Court of Appeal held[71] that the contract did not purport to be made on behalf of the company of the same name which was hurriedly incorporated when the parties later discovered their mistake. Since all were in blissful ignorance when the contract was drawn up and signed, it could not be said that the contract purported to be on behalf of the company, the need for whose existence was not appreciated at the time. The contract in truth purported to be made on behalf of that company which had been struck off, but that was not a company of which it could be said it "has not been formed". Ensnared in this conundrum the plaintiff failed. Thus, the section has not been construed as protecting third parties in all situations where they in fact attempt to contract with non-existent companies, but only in those situations where the contract identifies a specific company as the purported contracting party and where that company is one which has not been formed.[72]

Thirdly, and undoubtedly the most serious,[73] the reforms have done nothing to make it simpler for companies to "assume" the obligations of a pre-incorporation transaction. While one can understand that the

---

[69] As was the situation in the two cases cited in the previous note.

[70] In *Cotronic* (above, n. 68) the "promoter" failed in his attempt to enforce the contract against the third party, but not because the court gave any indication that it thought the contract was in principle incapable of enforcement by such persons.

[71] In *Cotronic*, above, n. 68.

[72] See also *Badgerhill* (above, n. 68). On the other hand, it is submitted that the decision in *Oshkosh B'Gosh Inc. v. Dan Marbel Inc. Ltd* [1989] BCLC 507, C.A. that section 36C does not apply to a company which trades under its new name before completing the statutory formalities for change of name, is correct, since a change of name does not involve re-incorporation. See above, p. 105.

[73] Also serious from the point of view of the harmonising objectives of the First Directive is the decision of Harman J. in *Rover International Ltd v. Cannon Film Sales Ltd* [1987] BCLC 540 that s.36C does not apply to companies incorporated outside Great Britain, a view from which the Court of Appeal did not dissent ([1988] BCLC 710).

Directive preferred to leave that to each Member State, it is lamentable that we have not got round to doing anything about it.

Many common law countries have recognised, either by judge-made law or by statute that a company when formed can effectively elect to adopt pre-incorporation transactions purporting to be made on its behalf without the need for a formal novation and that the liability of the promoter ceases when the company adopts it. In 1962 the Jenkins Committee recommended[74] that we should do likewise (and clause 6 of the aborted Companies Bill 1973 would have implemented that recommendation) but we have still not done so. We have tried to make promoters personally liable on pre-incorporation transactions unless it is otherwise agreed or unless the company, after its incorporation, adopts the transaction. But at present the only way in which the company can adopt it is by entering into a post-incorporation agreement in the same terms. Even if the company does so, that will not relieve the promoters of personal liability (at any rate while the new agreement remains executory[75]) unless they are parties to the new agreement which expressly relieves them of liability under the pre-incorporation agreement. The need for all this is frequently overlooked. This may not matter much if all those concerned remain able and willing to perform their obligations under the pre-incorporation agreement. But it can be calamitous if one or more of them becomes insolvent or wants to withdraw because changes in market conditions have made the transactions disadvantageous to him or them.

As pre-incorporation transactions are inevitable features of every new incorporation we ought to make it as easy as possible to achieve what the parties intend (or would have intended if they had realised that the company was not yet incorporated and had understood the legal consequences). In this case, if not generally, the legal technicality that ratification dates back to the date of the transaction so that it is not effective unless, at that time, the ratifying person existed and had capacity to enter into the transaction, should not apply.

---

[74] Cmnd. 1749, para. 44.

[75] If the contract has been fully performed by the company, after incorporation, and by the other party, that clearly will end any liability under the contract.

Part Three

THE CONSEQUENCES OF INCORPORATION

INTRODUCTION

WE have seen that one of the main attractions of the corporate form to those wishing to run a business is the separate existence of the company from its members and the limited liability of the latter. Although some creditors, usually large ones, may seek to leap over the barrier of limited liability by seeking personal guarantees of those involved in the business, there is no doubt that this doctrine does restrict the extent of the recovery which many creditors can achieve upon the company's insolvency, at least if they have not been able to obtain a position of priority in relation to the company's assets by taking an appropriate security.[1] On the other hand, the doctrine of limited liability encourages public investment in companies by those who do not have the time continuously thereafter to monitor the activities of the company's management.

The argument in favour of limited liability was won decisively in the nineteenth century.[2] However, the law has been left with the question of whether limited liability, although the normal situation, should also be incapable of exception, say, in case of "abuse" or in relation to groups of companies, where the question is whether the single company or the group as a whole should be regarded as the legal entity.

With or without limited liability, the existence of the company as a separate legal entity within which a number, sometimes a large number, of people have come together to effectuate a common purpose, raises questions about how relations among this group are to be most effectively arranged and about how they are to organise the running of the business. In addition, how is the company, an artificial entity which can act only when the acts of human beings are attributed to it by the law, to represent and bind itself towards outsiders? These issues are discussed in the following two Chapters.

Finally, and returning to limited liability, the existence of this doctrine, by excluding creditor recourse to the assets of individual members or directors, forces the law to create special rules to protect the assets of the company for the benefit of the creditors. The last two Chapters of this part consider the application of this principle both at the point when the company raises capital and when, later, it is considering a distribution or return of capital to its members.

---

[1] See Chap. 15, below.
[2] See pp. 40–44, above.

CHAPTER 8

LIFTING THE VEIL

WHAT is generally described as "lifting the veil"[1] has until quite recently aroused little attention and even less theoretical discussion in this country.[2] Nevertheless, it has always been recognised that "the legislature can forge a sledgehammer capable of cracking open the corporate shell"[3] and even without the aid of a legislative sledgehammer the courts have sometimes been prepared to have a crack. To various illustrations we now turn. In the cases where the veil is lifted, the law either goes behind the corporate personality to the individual members or directors, or ignores the separate personality of each company in favour of the economic entity constituted by a group of associated companies. The latter situation is often merely an example of the former, the individual members being corporate, rather than human, beings but even when that is so the two situations are worth distinguishing since there seems to be a greater readiness to lift the veil in the latter.

Before dealing with exceptional situations in which the veil is lifted, it should be emphasised that the veil never means that the affairs of the company are completely concealed from view. On the contrary, the legislature has always made it an essential condition of the recognition of corporate personality with limited liability that it should be accompanied by wide publicity. Although third parties dealing with the company will normally have no right to resort against its members, they are nevertheless entitled to see who those members are, what shares they hold and, in the case of a listed company, the beneficial interests in those shares if substantial. They are also entitled to see who its officers are (so that they know with whom to deal), what its constitution is (so that they know what

---

[1] Etymologically "mask" might have been a better metaphor, since "persona" is derived from the name for a mask worn by a player in the Greek theatre.

[2] It is a favourite topic in the USA where the veil is lifted more readily (see Blumberg, *The Multinational Challenge to Corporation Law* (1993), especially Part II) and there is now a considerable body of comparative literature in English; see, *e.g.* Cohn & Simitis, "Lifting the Veil in the Company Laws of the European Continent" (1963) 12 I.C.L.Q. 189; Wooldridge, *Groups of Companies: Britain, France and Germany* (I.A.L.S. 1981); Hopt (ed.), *Groups of Companies in European Laws* (Berlin, 1982); Ottolenghi, "From Peeping behind the Corporate Veil to Ignoring it Completely" (1990) 53 M.L.R. 338, Schmitthoff & Wooldridge (eds.), *Groups of Companies* (London, 1991). Sugarman and Teubner (eds.), *Regulating Corporate Groups in Europe* (Baden-Baden, 1990); Wymeersch (ed.), *Groups of Companies in the EEC* (Berlin, 1993).

[3] *Per* Devlin J. in *Bank voor Handel en Scheepvaart N.V. v. Slatford* [1953] 1 Q.B. 248 at 278.

the company may do and how it may do it), and what its capital is and how it has been obtained (so that they know whether to trust it). And unless it is an unlimited company they are also entitled to see its accounts, or at least a modified version of them— again in order to know whether to trust it.

Normally, however, third parties are neither bound nor entitled to look behind such information as the law provides shall be made public; in addition to the veil of incorporation, there is something in the nature of a curtain formed by the company's public file, and what goes on behind it is concealed from the public gaze.[4] But sometimes this curtain also may be raised. For example, an inspector may be appointed to investigate the company's affairs,[5] in which case he will have the widest inquisitorial powers; indeed he may even be appointed for the purpose of going behind the company's registers to ascertain who are its true owners. It is not always easy to decide whether one is faced with a true example of lifting the veil or with a raising of the curtain and some of the examples[6] dealt with hereafter should perhaps be regarded as lifting the curtain (rather than the veil).

That, however, is not our primary concern, which is to examine the circumstances in which the fundamental principle of corporate personality itself is disregarded. Some of the major examples arising under the express words of a statute will be discussed first.

UNDER EXPRESS STATUTORY PROVISION

Reduction of number of members

Under what is now section 24 of the Companies Act, if a public[7] company carries on business for more than six months with fewer than two members any person who is a member after that six months may become liable, jointly and severally with the company, for the payment of its debts. This rule is the final and probably now insupportable remnant of a legislative policy which attached significance to the number of members of a company as a protection for those who deal with it. The Limited Liability Act 1855[8] applied only to companies with at least 25 members, and as late as 1980 public companies had to have at least seven members. But the requirement was effectively undermined by the decision in *Salomon*'s case,[9] and since Parliament

---

[4] *cf.* the rule in *Royal British Bank v. Turquand*, below, Chap. 10.
[5] See Chap. 25, below.
[6] *e.g.* the residence and ratification cases: see p. 175, below.
[7] More precisely, any company other than a private company limited by shares or guarantee.
[8] See above, p. 44.
[9] See above, p. 77.

chose not to reverse that decision, the requirement as to numbers has ever since been capable of being met through the use of bare nominees. The rule was all but abolished by the Twelfth Company Law Directive on single-member private limited liability companies which had the consequence that private companies limited by shares or by guarantee were excluded from section 24.[10]

This section does not operate to destroy the separate personality of the company; it still remains an existing entity even though there is one member only,[11] or, indeed, although there is none.[12] And the rights which the section confers on creditors are severely limited. It is only the member who remains after the six months that can be sued (not those whose withdrawal has led to the fall below the minimum[13]) and then only if he knows that it is carrying on business with only one member[14] and he is liable only in respect of debts contracted[15] after the six months and while he was a member. The crowning anomaly is that liability attaches only to a member and not to a director unless he is also a member.

Although the facts giving rise to a possible application of the section are of not infrequent occurrence[16] it seems rarely to be invoked, doubtless because of the limitations considered, and, with the exclusion of most private companies from the scope of the section in 1992, this situation is likely to continue. It constitutes an exception to the general rule of theoretical interest rather than practical importance.

---

[10] Council Directive 89/667, implemented in Britain by the Companies (Single Member Private Limited Companies) Regulations 1992 (S.I. 1992 No. 1699). Note the remark by Hoffmann L.J. in *Nisbet v. Shepherd* [1994] 1 BCLC 300, C.A. that s.24 "seems to serve no purpose in protecting the public or anyone else".

[11] *Jarvis Motors (Harrow) Ltd v. Carabott* [1964] 1 W.L.R. 1101. But the company can be wound up on this ground: Insolvency Act 1986, s.122(1)(e).

[12] Anomalously the section does not then bite, there being no member to make liable.

[13] Thus, if the members of a company are A and B and B dies and his executors fail to become registered as members, A will be liable for debts contracted six months after B's death (unless C is admitted to membership), and there can be no resort against B's estate. It seems that the deceased B cannot be counted as a member, although the shares are registered in his name: *Re Bowling & Welby's Contract* [1895] 1 Ch. 663, C.A.

[14] Which, if he was not an officer of the company, he might not know.

[15] This presumably means only contractual pecuniary obligations and not other liabilities; *cf.* "debts or other liabilities" in the sections referred to below under *Fraudulent or Wrongful Trading*.

[16] *e.g.* in the circumstances suggested in n. 13. There may be complications in regularising the position especially if there are no surviving directors. It may then be necessary to apply to the court under s.371 to order a meeting and to direct that one member shall suffice. If all the members have died the position is still more difficult. The Jenkins Committee recommended that for the purposes of that section the personal representatives of deceased members should be treated as members (Cmnd. 1749, para. 26) but this has not yet been implemented. *cf. Re Noel Tedman Holding Pty Ltd* (1967) Qd.R.561 (Qd.Sup.Ct), where a still wider provision in Table A of the Australian Act enabled the executors prior to obtaining probate (but not administrators prior to obtaining letters of administration) to act at a meeting ordered by the court.

Fraudulent or wrongful trading

An example of far greater practical importance has long been afforded by provisions which, until 1986, were in section 332[17] of the Companies Act 1948. This created a specific but widely defined criminal offence of carrying on the business of a company with intent to defraud. It further provided that, if the company was in the course of winding up, the court could declare that the culprits were to be personally responsible, without limitation of liability, for all or any of the debts or other liabilities of the company to the extent that the court might direct. In the legislative reforms of 1985–1986 the criminal offence became section 458[18] of the Companies Act but the civil sanction was moved to sections 213–215 of the Insolvency Act 1986 and, following the recommendations of the Cork Committee[19] extended to "wrongful trading" involving a lesser degree of moral culpability. It is with the latter sections that we are here concerned[20] and they constitute what is probably the most extreme departure from the rule in *Salomon's* case yet achieved in the United Kingdom.

These provisions recognise that the separate entity and limited liability doctrines are capable of being abused and that the benefit of them should be removed from the abusers. Abuse in the shape of hiding behind limited liability to effect fraud is easy to identify, as the long-standing provisions against fraudulent trading indicate. More significant are the recently added provisions on wrongful trading which, in effect, make access to limited liability dependent upon objective standards of competence on the part of controllers of companies, at least during the period when insolvency threatens and the controllers are under the greatest incentive to take advantage of the company's creditors. As we shall see below, this statutory innovation has had a significant impact upon the courts' development of the general common law duty of care to which directors are subject.[21]

Section 213, dealing with fraudulent trading, is generally the same as the relevant provisions of the former section 332 and decisions on the latter remain relevant. It provides that:

"(1) If in the course of the winding up of a company it appears that

---

[17] As amended by s.96 of the Companies Act 1981 which reversed the effect of the decision in *DPP v. Schildkamp* [1971] A.C. 1, H.L. holding that winding up of the company was an essential precondition to a criminal prosecution.

[18] Which, as did the amended s.332, applies whether or not the company is in liquidation.

[19] Cmnd. 8558 (1981), Chap. 44.

[20] But the criminal sanction is a useful deterrent and prosecutions will doubtless continue to be frequent since it has been regarded as less confusing to juries to face them with a single charge of fraudulent trading rather than with numerous charges of individual acts of fraud: see *R. v. Kemp* [1988] Q.B. 645, C.A. (pet. dis. [1988] 1 W.L.R. 846, H.L.). The section embraces fraud on future, as well as present, creditors: *R. v. Smith* [1996] 2 BCLC 109, C.A.

[21] See pp. 640–644, below.

any business of the company has been carried on[22] with intent to defraud creditors of the company[23] or creditors of any other person or for any fraudulent purpose . . .''
then;

''(2) The court on the application of the liquidator may declare that any persons who were knowingly parties to the carrying on the business in [that] manner are to be liable to make such contributions (if any) to the company's assets as the court thinks proper.''

Hence, unlike the criminal offence now in the Companies Act, it applies only if the company is in liquidation[24] and, in contrast with the former section 332,[25] applications for the declaration can be made only by the liquidator. But the class of persons against whom the declaration can be made is far wider than members or directors. Hence the Government[26] when less reluctant than it now is to rescue "lame ducks") and banks and parent companies have at times felt inhibited from providing finance to ailing companies, fearing that they may thereby fall foul of the provisions. Their fears, however, seem unfounded so long as they play no active role in running the company with fraudulent intent.[27]

To establish that intent, what has to be shown is "actual dishonesty involving, according to current notions of fair trading among commercial men, real moral blame".[28] That may be inferred if "a company continues to carry on business and to incur debts at a time when there is, to the knowledge of the directors, no reasonable prospect of the creditors ever receiving payment of those debts",[29] but cannot be

---

[22] It may be regarded as carrying on business notwithstanding that it has ceased active trading: *Re Sarflax Ltd* [1979] Ch. 592.

[23] It suffices if only one creditor in the course of one transaction is defrauded: *Re Cooper Chemicals Ltd* [1978] Ch. 262. Or if those defrauded are customers who are not actual, but only potential, creditors: *R. v. Kemp*, above. Or indeed if none is actually defrauded.

[24] But, in contrast with s.214 (below) not necessarily *insolvent* liquidation.

[25] Under which the application could also have been made by the official receiver, a creditor or a member.

[26] See Ganz, *Government and Industry* (Abingdon, 1977), pp. 97–100.

[27] In *Re Maidstone Building Provisions Ltd* [1971] 1 W.L.R. 1085 an attempt to obtain a declaration against the company's secretary, who was also a partner in its auditors' firm, failed because, although he had given financial advice and had not attempted to prevent the company from trading, he had not taken "positive steps in the carrying on of the company's business in a fraudulent manner". In *Re Augustus Barnett & Son Ltd* [1986] BCLC 170 an attempt against its parent company (Rumasa) failed on the same ground. But in *Re Cooper Chemicals Ltd*, above, it was held that a declaration could be made against a creditor who refrained from pressing for repayment knowing that the business was being carried on in fraud of creditors and who accepted part payment out of money which he knew had been obtained by that fraud.

[28] *Re Patrick Lyon Ltd* [1933] Ch. 786 at 790, 791.

[29] *Re William C. Leitch Ltd* [1932] 2 Ch. 71, *per* Maugham J. at 77. See also *R. v. Grantham* [1984] Q.B. 675, C.A., where the court upheld a direction to the jury that they might convict of fraudulent trading a person who had taken an active part in running the business if they were satisfied that he had helped to obtain credit knowing that there was no good reason for thinking that funds would become available to pay the debts when they became due or shortly thereafter.

inferred merely because they ought to have realised it. It is this need to prove subjective moral blame that had led the Jenkins Committee in 1962 vainly to recommend the introduction of a remedy for "reckless trading"[30] and the Cork Committee, 20 years later, successfully to promote it under the the name of "wrongful trading".

"Wrongful trading" is dealt with in section 214 of the Insolvency Act. It empowers the court to make a declaration similar to that under section 213[31] but only in one specific set of circumstances. It operates only when the company has gone into *insolvent* liquidation[32] and the declaration can be made only against a person who, at some time before the commencement of the winding up, was a director of the company and knew, or ought to have concluded, at that time, that there was no reasonable prospect that the company would avoid going into insolvent liquidation.[33] But the declaration is not to be made if the court is satisfied that the person concerned thereupon took every step with a view to minimising the potential loss to the company's creditors as, on the assumption that he knew there was no reasonable prospect of avoiding insolvent liquidation, he ought to have taken.[34] In judging what facts he ought to have known or ascertained, what conclusions he should have drawn and what steps he should have taken, he is to be assumed to be a reasonably diligent person having both the general knowledge, skill and experience to be expected of a person carrying out his functions in relation to the company[35] and the general knowledge, skill and experience that he in fact has.[36]

There are thus two questions which have to be answered, both on an objective basis. Should the director have realised there was no reasonable prospect of the company avoiding insolvent liquidation and, once that stage has been reached, did the director take all the steps he or she ought to have taken to minimise the loss to the company's creditors, especially, no doubt, by seeking to have the company cease trading? Both these judgments will depend heavily on the facts of particular cases: what sort of company was involved, what were the functions assigned to or discharged by the director in question, what outside advice was taken and what was its content?[37]

---

[30] Cmnd. 1749, para. 503(b).

[31] Insolvency Act 1986, s.214(1).

[32] *i.e.* when its assets are insufficient for the payment of its liabilities and the expenses of the winding up: *ibid.*, s.214(6).

[33] *ibid.*, s.214(2).

[34] *ibid.*, s.214(3).

[35] This includes functions entrusted to him even if he has not carried them out: *ibid.*, s.214(5). If he has failed the objective test he cannot be excused by the court, under Companies Act 1985 s.727, on the ground that he has acted honestly: *Re Produce Marketing Consortium Ltd* [1989] 1 W.L.R. 745.

[36] Insolvency Act 1986, s.214(4).

[37] The directors are likely to be treated with a particular lack of sympathy by the court if they have not abided by the statutory requirements for keeping themselves abreast of the company's financial position: *Re Produce Marketing Consortium Ltd (No. 2)* [1989] BCLC 520 at 550,

Moreover, and this is of considerable importance for a number of reasons, for the purpose of section 214 "director" includes "shadow director", *i.e.* a person, other than a professional adviser, in accordance with whose directions or instructions the directors of a company are accustomed to act. This considerably widens the class of persons against whom a declaration can be made. The two potential defendants of greatest interest are, once again, banks and parent companies. As far as the former are concerned, the courts have so far taken a cautious line, on the grounds that the definition of a shadow director requires that the board cede its management autonomy to the alleged shadow director and that the taking of steps by a bank to protect itself does not induce such a cession, if the company retains the power to decide whether to accept the restrictions put forward by the bank, even though the company may be thought to have no other practicable alternative.[38] In relation to parent companies, such a degree of cession of autonomy by the subsidiary may be more easily found, but much will still depend upon how exactly intra-group relationships are established. The degree of control exercised by parent companies may vary from detailed day-to-day control to virtual independence, with many variations in between. It would seem that the establishment of business guidelines within which the subsidiary has to operate would not make the parent inevitably a shadow director of the subsidiary.[39] Thus, whether the courts will take the opportunity afforded by the wrongful trading provisions to rationalise the legal position of groups of companies remains to be seen.

Section 214 is expressly stated to be "without prejudice" to section 213[40] and there may well be cases where the circumstances will justify an application by the liquidator under both. Indeed, section 215 contains certain procedural provisions common to both fraudulent and wrongful trading. Most of these repeat, in substance, provisions in the former section 332: for example, that on an application for a declaration the liquidator may give or call evidence[41] and that the court may add further directions for giving effect to any declaration it makes and, in particular, may direct that the liability of any person against whom the declaration is made shall be a charge on any debt due from the company to him or on any mortgage or charge in his favour on assets

---

which requirements Knox J. referred to as the "minimum standards". This case, the leading one to date, and the underlying statutory provisions are analysed by Oditah [1990] LMCLQ 205 and Prentice (1990) 10 O.J.L.S. 265.

[38] *Re Hydrodan (Corby) Ltd* [1994] 2 BCLC 180; *Re PFTZM Ltd* [1995] BCC 161; *cf. Re A Company, ex p. Copp* [1989] BCLC 13.

[39] In *Re Hydrodan (Corby) Ltd* [1994] 2 BCLC 180 the judge was prepared to treat the indirect parent as a shadow director, but that was because the directors of the company in question were both corporate bodies and so must have received their instructions from elsewhere. Even here, the directors of the indirect parent were held on the facts not to be shadow directors.

[40] Insolvency Act 1986, s.214(8).

[41] *ibid.*, s.215(1).

of the company.[42] And both sections 213 and 214 have effect notwithstanding that the person concerned may be criminally liable.[43] What is new and valuable is that section 215[44] also provides that the court may direct that the whole or any part of a debt, and interest thereon, owed by the company to a person against whom a declaration is made, shall be postponed to all other debts, and interest thereon, owed by the company.

It was accepted in *Re Produce Marketing*[45] that the jurisdiction under section 214 was primarily compensatory, in contrast to assessments under section 213 where a penal element may be appropriate.[46] The outer boundaries of the compensation are thus set by the amount by which the company's assets have been depleted by the director's conduct. Within that the court has a discretion to fix the amount to be paid as it thinks proper.[47] It seems that the contribution from the directors is to the assets of the company generally and not for the particular benefit of those who became creditors of the company during the period of wrongful trading. What is less clear is whether the contribution can be caught by a floating charge previously granted by the company. The better view is that it cannot[48]; certainly, the opposite view would defeat the policy espoused by the Cork Committee,[49] which was to improve the position of the unsecured creditor. On the other hand, the liquidator may be unwilling to sue except in the strongest cases,[50] and, if the contribution goes into the hands of the general creditors, the banks will have no incentive to fund it either.

Abuse of company names or employment of disqualified directors

The Insolvency Act 1986 added further examples of cases where the managers of a company may become liable for its debts and other liabilities. A common abuse had been for those responsible for the running of a company which had gone into insolvent liquidation to

---

[42] Including any assignees from that person: *ibid.*, s.215(2) and (3).

[43] *ibid.*, s.215(5).

[44] subs. (4).

[45] Above, n. 37.

[46] *Re A Company* [1991] BCLC 197.

[47] s.214(1).

[48] See Oditah, *op. cit.*, pp. 215–220. And see n. 50, below.

[49] See n. 19, above.

[50] The wrongful trading sections have certainly not generated a level of litigation equivalent to the disqualification provisions (see below, Chap. 24), where the public purse supports the applications. An assignment by the liquidator of the fruits of litigation under s.214 is champertous and is not saved from illegality by the liquidator's power under the Insolvency Act, Sched. 4, para. 6 to dispose of the company's property, because the right to sue under s.214, arising after the liquidation, is not part of the company's property: *Ward v. Aitken*, [1997] 1 All E.R. 1009, C.A. This decision deprives the liquidator of an obvious way of financing s.214 claims.

form another company, with an identical or very similar name,[51] which bought the undertaking and assets from the original company's liquid-ator[52] and through which they continued to trade. At best this was likely to mislead and confuse customers[53]; at worst it was a deliberate fraud. Section 216 of the Insolvency Act now makes it an offence for anyone who was a director or shadow director of the original company at any time during the 12 months preceding its going into insolvent liquidation to be in any way concerned (except with the leave of the court or in such circumstances as may be prescribed) during the next five years in the formation or management of a company, or business, with a name by which the original company was known or one so similar as to suggest an association with that company. The first, and most important, of the prescribed cases[54] is where the successor com-pany purchases the whole of the insolvent company's business from an insolvency practitioner acting for the company and gives notice of the name the successor company intends to use to all the creditors of the insolvent company. This suggests that the aim of the section is the protection of the creditors of the insolvent company rather than of the new company. The insertion of the insolvency practitioner is intended to ensure that the sale by the insolvent company is not at an undervalue and the notice to the creditors ensures that they are not misled into thinking that they may assert their claims against the new company.[55]

A person acting in breach of section 216 is, under section 217, personally liable, jointly and severally with that company and any other person so liable, for the debts and other liabilities of that com-pany incurred while he was concerned in its management in breach of section 216. So is anyone involved in its management who acts or is willing to act on the instructions given by a person whom he knows, at that time, to be in breach of section 216.[56]

Similar consequences apply to a person against whom a court order has been made under the Company Directors Disqualification Act

---

[51] The relaxation of the control over company names by the Companies Act 1981 (see p. 105, above) facilitated this.

[52] Or from a receiver and manager appointed by a debenture-holder. The sale was sometimes at a gross undervalue.

[53] Re-use of former names is not necessarily improper. So long as effective steps can be taken to avoid misleading future creditors of the second company, it may be justified if it enables such goodwill as the former company may have had to be preserved so that its undertaking can be sold at an enhanced price for the benefit of its creditors.

[54] These are set out in the Insolvency Rules (S.I. 1986 No. 1925), r. 4.228 to 4.230 and the Insolvency (Scotland) Rules (S.I. 1986 No. 1915), r. 4.78 to 4.82.

[55] See *Penrose v. Secretary of State for Trade and Industry* [1996] 1 W.L.R. 482, where the judge concluded that the protection of the creditors of the new company was to be ensured by applying the principles contained in the Directors' Disqualification legislation. See Chap. 24, below.

[56] For the purpose of both sections 216 and 217, "company" includes any company which may be wound up under Part V of the Insolvency Act, *i.e.* virtually any company or association: *ibid.*, s.220.

1986.[57] Section 15 of that Act provides that if such a person acts in the management of a company in contravention of the order, both he, and any other person concerned with the management of that company who is willing to act on his instructions despite knowing he is disqualified, are jointly and severally liable with the company for its debts contracted during that time.[58]

It will be observed that these sections, though similar in their consequences to sections 213–215 of the Insolvency Act, differ from them in that they apply without the need for an application to, and declaration by, the court—though the persons concerned may apply to the court to be granted leave. They differ also in that the sanctions apply to conduct, not in relation to the company that has gone into liquidation, but in relation to another company or business whether or not that goes into liquidation.

Misdescription of the company

On ordinary agency principles the officers of a company will, of course, make themselves personally liable, notwithstanding that they are acting for the company, if they choose to contract personally; for example by not disclosing that they are acting on behalf of the company. But the Companies Acts have gone further. What is now section 349(4) of the Companies Act 1985 provides that if any officer of the company or other person acting on its behalf:

"signs or authorises to be signed on behalf of the company any bill of exchange, promissory note, endorsement, cheque or order for money or goods[59] in which the company's name is not mentioned [in legible characters] . . . he is . . . liable to a fine; and he is further personally liable to the holder of the bill of exchange, promissory note, cheque or order for money or goods for the amount of it (unless it is duly paid by the company".

The result of this is that if the correct and full name of the company does not so appear, the signatory will be personally liable to pay if the company does not.[60] And it seems clear that it makes no difference

---

[57] See Chap. 24, below. A court may disqualify a person found liable under ss.213 or 214 (see p. 689, below) but it may also disqualify on grounds of unfitness a person who is in breach of ss.213 or 214 even though a liability order has not been made, provided unfitness is found. See p. 682, below and *Secretary of State v. Gash* [1997] 1 BCLC 341.

[58] And note s.14 as regards criminal sanctions.

[59] But not, it seems, an order for the supply of services even if they involve supplying goods!

[60] See *Atkins v. Wardle* (1889) 5 T.L.R. 734, C.A.; *Scottish & Newcastle Breweries Ltd v. Blair*, 1967 S.L.T. 72; *Civil Service Co-operative Society v. Chapman* [1914] 30 T.L.R. 679; *British Airways Board v. Parish* [1979] 2 Lloyd's Rep. 361. Contrast *Oshkosh B'Gosh Inc. v. Dan Marbel Inc. Ltd* [1989] BCLC 507, C.A. where a director, who had authorised the issue of an unsigned order for goods on which an incorrect name of the company was printed (the company was in process of changing its name to that printed but had not actually done so) was held not liable; he had not "signed or authorised" any signature.

that the third party concerned has not been misled by the description.[61] However, as a result of what is now section 27 of the Companies Act, the use of the authorised abbreviation "Ltd" or "plc" instead of the full prescribed suffix "limited" or "public limited company" (or the Welsh equivalent) is permissible. And the abbreviation of "Company" to "Co." has been held to be acceptable.[62] Furthermore the holder's conduct may estop him from enforcing the liability of the signatory; for example where he has written the document with the misdescription and submitted it for signature.[63] In any event the liability of the signatory is important only if the company is insolvent. If the signatory is authorised to act on its behalf, it will not escape liability, although misdescribed, so long as its identity can be established[64] and, if the signatory is successfully sued, he will be entitled to be indemnified by the company. On the company's insolvency, however, it affords the holder a remedy which may be wholly unmeritorious. It might be a useful reform to amend the subsection by affording the signatory a defence if he could establish that the holder had not been misled by the misdescription; the recent decisions display a marked disinclination to apply the provision when that is so.[65]

Premature trading

Another example of personal liability in the Companies Act is in section 117(8). Under the section, a public limited company, newly incorporated as such, must not "do business or exercise any borrowing powers" until it has obtained, from the Registrar of Companies, a certificate that it has complied with the provisions of the Act relating to the raising of the prescribed minimum share capital or until it has re-registered as a private company. If it enters into any transaction[66] in contravention of this provision, not only are the company, and its officers in default, liable to fines[67] but, if the company fails to comply with its obligations in that connection within 21 days of being called upon to do so,[68] the directors of the company are jointly and severally

---

[61] In the Scottish case of *Scottish & Newcastle Breweries Ltd v. Blair* (above) Lord Hunter (at 74) expressly approved this sentence.

[62] *Banque de l'Indochine v. Euroseas Group Finance Co. Ltd* [1981] 3 All E.R. 198.

[63] In *Durham Fancy Goods Ltd v. Michael Jackson (Fancy Goods) Ltd* [1968] 2 Q.B. 839 it was held that the abbreviation of the "Michael" to "M" breached the section but that the plaintiffs could not rely on it as they had submitted the document to the defendants with that abbreviation. But, in *Blum v. O.C.P. Repartition S.A.* [1988] BCLC 170 at 175a May L.J. reserved his position on the correctness of the decision.

[64] *Goldsmith (Sicklesmere) Ltd v. Baxter* [1970] Ch. 85.

[65] And when they feel compelled to do so, tend to blame Parliament: see *Lindholst v. Fowler* [1988] BCLC 166, C.A. and *Rafsanjan Pistachio Producers v. Reiss* [1990] BCLC 352.

[66] The validity of which is not affected: subs. (8).

[67] subs. (7).

[68] subs. (8), the wording of which does not make it crystal clear whether this means its obligations under the transaction or its obligations under the section to obtain the certificate or to convert to a private company. It presumably means the former, if only because it would be

liable to indemnify the other party in respect of any loss or damage suffered by reason of the company's failure to comply.

Whether this is a true example of lifting the veil is questionable; technically it does not make the directors liable for the company's debts but rather penalises the directors for any loss the third parties suffer as a result of the directors' default in complying with the section. But the effect is much the same. It is, however, unlikely to be invoked often since it is unusual for companies to be formed initially as public ones.

Company groups

Reference has already been made to the growth of groups of companies and to the failure of English company legislation to adapt adequately to this phenomenon.[69] Nevertheless, it has long been recognised that, in relation to financial disclosure, the phenomenon cannot be ignored if a "true and fair" view of the overall position of the group is to be presented and that accordingly when one company (the parent or holding company[70]) controls others (the subsidiary and sub-subsidiary companies) the parent company must present group financial statements as well as its own individual statements, thus avoiding the misleading impression which the latter alone might give.[71]

Having taken this step and prescribed criteria for determining when a parent–subsidiary relationship was established, use of the concept was extended to other areas. A further complication arose when it was thought desirable to provide for financial disclosure regarding some companies over which the degree of control was not such as to make them "subsidiaries" within the meaning of the statutory definition.[72] This is not the place to describe in detail the highly technical statutory

---

absurd that someone who has entered into the transaction in the belief that the company is a properly capitalised plc, entitled to do business as such, should forfeit any remedy against its directors if it succeeds in converting to a private company within the 21 days.

[69] See p. 69 but *cf.* p. 154, above.

[70] In practice the expressions "parent" and "holding" were used interchangeably. Until the Companies Act 1989, U.K. company legislation used the latter, but the E.C. Company Law Directives the former, which seems preferable since "holding" suggests that the sole function of the parent is to control the operations of subsidiaries whereas it too may well be undertaking one or more of the trading activities of the group. Now, in the Act, they have different meanings: see p. 162, below.

[71] To take a simplified example: if a parent company A has two wholly owned subsidiaries, B and C, and in a financial year B makes a loss of £100,000 while C makes a distributable profit of £10,000 all of which it pays to A by way of dividend, the individual accounts of A (assuming it has broken even) will show a profit of £10,000 whereas in fact the group has made a loss of £90,000.

[72] At this stage nomenclature went haywire. The Fourth and Seventh Directives describe the main class of such companies as "associated companies" and so do the accountancy bodies in *Statements of Standard Accounting Practice* (SSAPs). But Sched. 4 to the Companies Act called them "related companies" (an expression generally used to describe companies within the same group of parent and subsidiaries—and so used in the contemporaneous Companies Securities (Insider Dealing) Act—but which Sched. 4 described as "group companies").

provisions. It suffices to summarise, briefly and ignoring many refinements and qualifications, their general effect in the light of the changes resulting from the implementation of the Seventh Company Law Directive (83/349) by the Companies Act 1989,[73] which introduced a distinction between "parent and subsidiary undertakings" (relevant in relation to financial statements) and "holding company and subsidiaries" (relevant to other statutory provisions).

(i) *Financial statements*

Group accounts now have to be in the form of a consolidated balance sheet and a consolidated profit and loss account[74] for the parent and all its subsidiaries, so far as possible as if they were a single company and eliminating inter-group transactions.[75] Although this applies only if the parent is a company, a subsidiary may be any form of "undertaking," corporate or unincorporated (for example, a partnership).[76] Under section 258 and Schedule 10A (inserted by the Act of 1989) the parent–subsidiary relationship is established if any one (or more) of five criteria is met. Briefly summarised,[77] these criteria are that one undertaking (the parent):

(a) holds a majority of voting rights in another undertaking;
(b) is a member[78] of the other undertaking and has the right to appoint or remove a majority of its board of directors;
(c) by virtue of provisions in the constitution of the other undertaking or in a written "control contract", permitted by that constitution, has a right, recognised by the law under which that undertaking is established, to exercise a "dominant influence" over that undertaking (by giving directions to the directors of the undertaking on its operating and financial policies which those directors are obliged to comply with whether or not the directors are for the benefit of the undertaking)[79];
(d) is a member of another undertaking and alone controls, pursuant to an agreement with other members, a majority of the voting rights in that undertaking;

---

[73] Which made substantial amendments to the relevant provisions in Part VII of the Act and added a new Sched. 4A on consolidated accounts.

[74] Formerly they could be in another form if that was thought to be clearer but little use was made of this concession.

[75] Companies Act 1985, s.227 and Sched. 4A (as substituted by the 1989 Act). There are certain exceptions specified in ss.228 and 229.

[76] Formerly, subsidiaries had to be bodies corporate though not necessarily registered companies.

[77] This sumary, which ignores many of the detailed requirements, is of s.258 with such amplifications from ss.259, 260 and Sched. 10A as are needed to make it intelligible.

[78] For the extended meaning of "member", see s.258(3).

[79] s.258(2)(c) and Sched. 10A, paras. 4(1) and (2). It is difficult to see how a "control contract" could ever be regarded as "permitted by law" in relation to an English subsidiary; it would seem to be expressly forbidden by s.310: on which see Chap. 22 at pp. 623–625, below.

(e) has a "participating interest" in another undertaking (*i.e.* an interest in its shares which it holds for the purpose of securing a contribution to its (the parent's) own activities by the exercise of the control or influence arising from that interest)[80] and actually exercises a dominant influence over it[81] or there is unified management of both undertakings[82]

and sub-subsidiaries are to be treated as subsidiaries of the ultimate parent also.[83]

In addition to consolidating the figures so as to give, in the manner prescribed by Schedule 4A, a true and fair view of the parent and subsidiaries as a whole, details about the various undertakings have to be given in notes to the accounts.[84] In particular the parent company has to name all its subsidiaries, to state the countries where they are established and to specify the proportion of their shares or class of shares that it holds. And a subsidiary, in a note to its accounts, must name the body corporate[85] which its directors believe to be its ultimate parent and, if known to them, its country of incorporation.

However, as already mentioned, even though the parent–subsidiary relationship may not be established, some measure of financial disclosure, falling short of full consolidation, may be required. This is so in two sets of circumstances. The first is where the "quasi-parent" (to coin a name) has a "participating interest," as defined in section 260, in another undertaking.[86] That, under criterion (e) above, may cause that undertaking to become its subsidiary if it actually exercises its dominance. If it refrains from doing so, the undertaking will nevertheless be what the Act now calls "an associated undertaking"[87] and, in notes to the accounts, similar information to that required in the case of a subsidiary will have to be given. Moreover, separate figures relating to the quasi-parent's stake in it will have to be incorporated in its balance sheet and profit and loss account. The second circumstance is when the company owns 10 per cent or more of an undertaking. Information regarding the undertaking will then have to be given in notes to the accounts, the information varying according to whether more than 20 per cent is owned.

---

[80] This is presumed to be the purpose (unless the contrary is shown) if 20 per cent or more of the shares are held: s.260(2).
[81] Whether or not by the means specified in criterion (c): see Sched. 10A, para. 4(3).
[82] ss.258(4) and 260.
[83] ss.258(5).
[84] s.231 and Sched. 5, as substituted or amended by the Companies Act 1989. Part I of the Schedule specifies what has to be stated in the notes when the company is not required to prepare group accounts and Part II specifies what has to be stated when it is required to do so.
[85] Whether or not it is a "company" required to produce consolidated accounts.
[86] See above, n. 80.
[87] Thus coming into line with the Directives and SSAPs: see n. 72, above.

(ii) *Extension to other matters*

The Companies Acts have long used the concept of the parent–subsidiary relationship in areas other than that of financial disclosure. Clearly if one is to ban or control certain types of transaction between a company and its directors it is essential to ensure that this cannot be easily evaded by effecting the transactions with or through another company in the group. Hence many of the sections in Part X (Enforcement of Fair Dealing by Directors) so provide.[88] Similarly, the prohibition on financial assistance for the purchase of a company's own shares extends to financial assistance by any of its subsidiaries.[89]

Until the Companies Act 1989 a common definition of the parent–subsidiary relation applied to all references in the companies' legislation to holding or subsidiary companies. When, however, the Directives compelled us to change the definition for the purposes of accounts it was represented that to apply the whole of the extended definition to other cases would introduce an unreasonable degree of uncertainty.[90] Hence it was decided to omit two of the criteria in such cases and to use different terminology. As a result, in addition to the definition of parent and subsidiary undertakings for the purposes of consolidation[91] and related financial disclosure, we now have a simpler definition of holding and subsidiary companies which applies to other cases where we are not constrained by the Directives. While it is a pity that it was thought necessary to have different definitions for what are essentially the same concept, there is no doubt that both are considerable improvements on the previous definition[92] since they recognise that what counts is "control" and not majority shareholding which, because of non-voting shares or weighted voting, will not necessarily afford control.[93]

Under the substituted section 736(1) of the Companies Act 1985, the definition of "holding" and "subsidiary" company now is:

"A company is a 'subsidiary' of another company, its 'holding' company, if that other company

    (a) holds a majority of the voting rights in it, or

    (b) is a member of it and has the right to appoint or remove a majority of its board of directors, or

    (c) is a member of it and controls alone, pursuant to an

---

[88] See especially ss.319 (contracts of employment for more than five years), 320–332 (substantial property transactions), 323 (dealing in share options), 324–329 (disclosure of shareholdings) and 330–342 (loans and "quasi-loans").

[89] s.151.

[90] *e.g.* in relation to the prohibition on a subsidiary holding shares in its parent (s.23, as substituted by s.129 of the 1989 Act).

[91] For purposes of consolidation a measure of uncertainty is acceptable because, when in doubt, one can play safe and consolidate.

[92] 1948 Act, s.154.

[93] Under the former s.154(10)(a)(ii) holding more than half in nominal value of a company's equity share capital (voting or non-voting) made it a subsidiary.

> agreement with other shareholders or members, a majority of
> the voting rights in it,
> or if it is a subsidiary of a company which is itself a subsidiary of
> that other company."

The section goes on in subsection (2) to (7) to amplify and explain
this definition and a new section 736A empowers the Secretary of
State to amend the definition by regulations. The essential differences
from "parent" and "subsidiaries" under section 258 are that section
736 applies only when both the holding company and the subsidiaries
are "bodies corporate" and that, of the five criteria in section 258,[94]
only (a), (b) and (d)—and not (c) or (e)—are included in section 736.

(iii) *Overall result*

Although we now have some measure of recognition of the economic unity of a group, it does nothing to solve the major problems
referred to at page 69, above. The directors of each individual company in a group are still supposed to operate it in the best interests of
that company and not in the interests of the group. And the creditors
of each company can look only to that company for payment of its
debts and cannot rely on the parent bailing them out. As Templeman
L.J. (as he then was) said in 1979[95]:

> "English company law possesses some curious features, which may
> generate curious results. A parent company may spawn a number
> of subsidiary companies, all controlled directly or indirectly by the
> shareholders of the parent company. If one of the subsidiary com-
> panies ... turns out to be the runt of the litter and declines into
> insolvency to the dismay of its creditors, the parent company and
> other subsidiary companies may prosper to the joy of the share-
> holders without any liability for the debts of the insolvent subsidi-
> ary."

Since 1979 the position has improved somewhat as a result of the
Insolvency Act and, in particular, its provisions in relation to fraudulent or wrongful trading under which the parent may be liable as a
shadow director.[96] How far it has improved will depend on how ready
the courts will be to hold both (a) that the parent company was party
to the carrying on of the subsidiary's business with the required intent
and knowledge, and (b) that the directors of the subsidiary were accustomed to act in accordance with the parent's directions.

Apart from that, it can be argued that the extended provisions
regarding group disclosure have, in this respect, made matters worse
rather than better, for they are calculated to lead those who read group
annual reports to assume that there is group liability. Why, otherwise,

---

[94] pp. 160–161, above.
[95] *Re Southard & Co. Ltd* [1979] 1 W.L.R. 1198, C.A. at 1208.
[96] See above, p. 164.

should a subsidiary's reports be required to name its ultimate holding company?[97]

Miscellaneous statutory examples

In addition to the foregoing examples culled from the companies and related legislation, scattered throughout the statute-book are to be found many examples of modification of the corporate entity principle. This is particularly the case in relation to taxation; the Revenue, not surprisingly, has been astute to secure the passage of legislation "capable of cracking open the corporate shell"[98] when this is being used for purposes of tax avoidance and has occasionally done so to mitigate the burden of taxation if a strict application of the corporate entity principle would be unduly harsh or inhibiting.[99]

Mostly, statutory inroads have been in relation to groups (using the Companies Acts' definition of holding and subsidiary companies or some lesser degree of common control) or to situations arising on a change of control. Illustrations of both occur in the employment legislation relating to redundancy and unfair dismissal,[1] under which changes of employment within the group from one company to another or as a result of mergers are not treated as breaking the period of continuous employment. Another illustration occurs in relation to rights under business tenancies. Under the Landlord and Tenant Act 1954, as amended by the Law of Property Act 1969, when either the landlord or the tenant is a company its rights under the Act may enure for the benefit of other companies in the group[2] and, reversing a decision in which the court had refused to lift the veil,[3] an individual landlord may be able to recover possession if he requires it for the purpose of a business carried on, not by him, but by a company which he controls.[4]

Nevertheless, the courts have generally been reluctant to construe a statute as lifting the veil unless compelled to do so by the clearest words of the statute. The classic illustration is the refusal of the House of Lords in *Nokes v. Doncaster Amalgamated Collieries*[5] to construe what is now section 427 of the Companies Act 1985 as meaning that an order made thereunder transferring the property and liabilities of one company to another on a reconstruction could operate to transfer

---

[97] It is fanciful to suppose that this requirement has been retained to assist those who wish to avoid having investments in, or dealings with, a company in a group with interests in tobacco or armaments.

[98] See p. 148, above.

[99] *e.g.* in relation to "group relief".

[1] Presently in the Employment Rights Act 1996.

[2] Landlord & Tenant Act 1954, s.42.

[3] *Tunstall v. Steigmann* [1962] 2 Q.B. 593, C.A.

[4] Landlord & Tenant Act 1954, s.30(3).

[5] [1940] A.C. 1014, H.L. (reversing the unanimous decisions of the courts below).

a contract of personal service; and this notwithstanding that the section specifically provides that "property" includes property, rights and powers of every description. To Lord Atkin the contrary interpretation would have been "tainted with oppression and confiscation"[6] and would have subverted "the principle that a man is not to be compelled to serve a master against his will . . . [which] is deep-seated in the common law of this country".[7] Yet, had the whole share capital of the transferor company been transferred instead of the undertaking, the man would have been compelled to serve what, in reality, was a new master. The employee is better protected by recognising the continuation of the enterprise but providing him with rights to payments for redundancy or unfair dismissal if he is not kept on. And this is now recognised in respect of transfers of the undertaking (where the effect of the *Nokes* decision has been reversed[8]) under the influence of E.C. social law.[9]

UNDER CASE LAW

Efforts by the judges to lift the veil have, in general, been hamstrung by the *Salomon* case, which finally destroyed the possibility of regarding a "one-man company" as a mere alias of, or agent for, the principal shareholder. Perhaps the most extreme illustration of a refusal to lift the veil is afforded by *Lee v. Lee's Air Farming Ltd*.[10] There Lee, for the purpose of carrying on his business of aerial top-dressing, had formed a company of which he beneficially owned all the shares and was sole "governing director". He was also appointed chief pilot. Pursuant to the company's statutory obligations he caused the company to insure against liability to pay compensation under the Workmen's Compensation Act. He was killed in a flying accident. The Court of Appeal of New Zealand held that his widow was not entitled to compensation from the company (*i.e.* from their insurers) since Lee could not be regarded as a "worker" (*i.e.* servant) within the meaning of the Act. But the Privy Council reversed that decision, holding that Lee and his company were distinct legal entities which had entered into contractual relationships under which he became, qua chief pilot, a servant of the company. In his capacity of governing director he could, on behalf of the company, give himself orders in his other capacity of pilot, and hence the relationship between himself, as pilot, and the company was that of servant and master. In effect the magic

---

[6] *ibid.*, at 1030.
[7] *ibid.*, at 1033.
[8] See the Transfer of Undertakings (Protection of Employment) Regs. 1981 (S.I. 1981 No. 1794) implementing Directive 77/187 and construed by the House of Lords so as to give full effect to it: *Litster v. Forth Dry Dock* [1990] 1 A.C. 546, H.L. (Sc.).
[9] See n. 8, above.
[10] [1961] A.C. 12, P.C.

of corporate personality enabled him to be master and servant at the same time and to get all the advantages of both (and of limited liability).[11]

Nevertheless, there have been exceptional cases in which the courts have felt able to lift the veil and until recently there were perhaps signs of a greater willingness to do so. Indeed, as recently as 1985 a judgment of the Court of Appeal declared that:

"In our view the cases . . . show that the court will use its power to pierce the corporate veil if it is necessary to achieve justice irrespective of the legal efficacy of the corporate structure . . ."[12]

a view emphatically rejected by the Court of Appeal in the case of *Adams v. Cape Industries plc*[13] In that important case the Court in a mammoth judgment, involving a number of issues, subjected lifting the veil to the most exhaustive treatment that it has yet received in the English (or Scottish) courts.

The facts of the case were somewhat complicated but for present purposes it suffices to say that what the Court had ultimately to determine was whether judgments obtained in the United States against Cape, an English registered company whose business was mining asbestos in S. Africa and marketing it worldwide, would be recognised and enforced by the English courts. In the absence of submission to the foreign jurisdiction this depended on whether Cape could be said to have been "present" in the United States. On the facts, the answer to that question depended upon whether Cape could be said to be present in the United States through its wholly owned subsidiaries or through a company (C.P.C.) with which it had close business links.

In contending that Cape had been present in the United States the plantiffs raised three arguments.

The "single economic unit" argument

The first of these, described as the "single economic unit argument" proceeded as follows: Admittedly there is no general principle that all companies in a group of companies are to be regarded as one; on the contrary, the fundamental principle is unquestionably that "each company in a group of companies . . . is a separate legal entity possessed of separate rights and liabilities".[14] Nevertheless, it was

---

[11] However, in *Buchan v. Secretary of State for Employment* [1997] IRLR 80 the EAT refused to follow *Lee* on the grounds that such an approach would undermine the objectives of the legislation in question (*i.e.* legislation controlling dismissals, where the controlling shareholder would be able to determine whether the dismissal took place). Note also *Underwood v. Bank of Liverpool* [1924] 1 K.B. 775, C.A., which shows that third parties who are so ill-advised as to regard the members as the same as the company will not only fail to make the members liable to them, but may sometimes incur liability to the company.

[12] *Re A Company* (1985) 1 BCC 99.421, C.A.

[13] [1990] Ch. 433, Scott J. and C.A. (*pet. dis.* [1990] 2 W.L.R. 786, H.L.)

[14] At 532, quoting Roskill L.J. in *The Albazero* [1977] A.C. 744, C.A. and H.L., at 807.

argued, the court will, in appropriate circumstances, ignore the distinction between them, treating them as one. For this proposition a number of authorities were cited.

The first of these was *The Roberta*,[15] in which bills of lading had been signed on behalf of a subsidiary company but a concession was made at the trial that the parent company was responsible for the bills. The judge described the concession as properly made since the subsidiary was a separate entity from the parent (which owned all its shares and supplied two out of three directors) "in name only and probably for the purposes of taxation".[16] The second was *Holdsworth & Co. v. Caddies*[17] in which it had been argued that Caddies, who had been appointed managing director of Holdsworth, the parent company of the group, could not be ordered to devote his whole time solely to duties in relation to the affairs of the subsidiaries since these were separate legal entities under the control of their own boards of directors. This argument was rejected as too technical. Caddies' service agreement was "an agreement *in re mercatoria* and must be construed in light of the facts and realities of the situation".[18] The third authority was *Scottish Co-operative Wholesale Society Ltd v. Meyer*.[19] In that case it had been argued that the appellant could not be said to have conducted the affairs of the company in a manner oppressive to some part of the members within the meaning of section 210 of the Companies Act 1948[20] since it was not that company which had acted oppressively but a subsidiary which it had formed. The House of Lords had no hesitation in rejecting this argument since "every step taken by [the subsidiary] was determined by the policy of [the parent]"[21] and "the section warrants the courts in looking at the business realities of the situation and does not confine them to a narrow legalistic view".[22]

The above three authorities related exclusively to the interpretation of statutes or documents, an area in which further authority to the like effect can be found.[23] The fourth case relied on in support of the "single economic unit argument", *D.H.N. Food Distributors Ltd v.*

---

[15] (1937) 58 L.L.R.159.
[16] At 169.
[17] [1955] 1 W.L.R. 352, H.L.
[18] *Per* Lord Reid at 367.
[19] [1959] A.C. 324, H.L. (Sc.)
[20] Now replaced by ss.459–461 of the 1985 Act on which see Chap. 27, below.
[21] *Per* Lord Simonds at 342.
[22] These words were of Lord President Cooper on the first hearing of the case and quoted with approval by Lord Simonds at 343.
[23] See *e.g. Bird & Co. v. Thos. Cook & Son Ltd* [1937] 2 All E.R. 227, where the endorsement of a cheque in favour of Thos. Cook & Son Ltd was treated as an endorsement in favour of a group company, Thos. Cook & Son (Bankers) Ltd: and *Amalgamated Investment & Property Co. v. Texas Commercial Bank* [1982] Q.B. 84, C.A. (*pet. dis.* [1982] 1 W.L.R.I. H.L.) where a guarantee of repayment of loans made by a bank was construed as covering those made by a wholly owned subsidiary set up by the bank as its channel for making the loans.

Tower Hamlets L.B.C.[24] was rather different. D.H.N. had two wholly owned subsidiaries, in one of which the landed property of the group was vested, while D.H.N. carried on the business of the group, occupying the property as a licensee. According to the decision of the Lands Tribunal, on the compulsory purchase of the land, negligible compensation only was payable since D.H.N. had been deprived merely of a revocable license and the subsidiary had had no business to lose. The Court of Appeal reversed that decision on three grounds, the one relevant here[25] being expressed thus by Lord Denning M.R.[26]:

> "This group is virtually the same as a partnership in which all the three companies are partners. They should not be treated separately so as to be defeated on a technical point . . . They should not be deprived of the compensation which should justly be payable for disturbance. The three companies should, for present purposes, be treated as one and the parent company, D.H.N., should be treated as that one."

This, and the way in which it was put by Goff L.J.,[27] namely that "This is a case in which one is entitled to look at the realities of the situation and to pierce the corporate veil", show, surely, that the Court did not regard itself as construing a document or statute but was relying on what, in the judgment in *Cape*, is dealt with under its next head, "the corporate veil" point. And, surely, it was on that assumption that in the later case of *Woolfson v. Strathclyde Regional Council*,[28] Lord Keith of Kirkel said, in reference to the D.H.N. case,[29]

> "I have some doubts whether . . . the Court of Appeal properly applied the principle that is is appropriate to pierce the corporate veil only where special circumstances exist indicating that it is a mere façade concealing the true facts."

In none of the cases considered under the present heading[30] was the company concerned a "mere façade concealing the true facts". If it were only when that is so that the court, in construing a document or statute, could have regard to the economic realities there would be very few such cases.

It is therefore somewhat puzzling that the Court of Appeal in *Cape*, said[31]:

> "the relevant parts of the judgments in the D.H.N. case . . . must, we think, likewise be regarded as decisions on the relevant statutory

---

[24] [1976] 1 W.L.R. 852, C.A.

[25] The others being (i) that the subsidiary held the property on a resulting trust for D.H.N. which had supplied the money for its purchase and (ii) that D.H.N. had an irrevocable licence.

[26] At 860.

[27] At 861 D. See also Shaw L.J. at 867–868.

[28] 1978 S.L.T. 159, H.L.Sc.

[29] At 161 in a speech with which Lords Wilberforce, Frazer of Tullybelton and Russell of Killowen agreed.

[30] With the possible exception of *Scottish Co-operative v. Meyer*.

[31] At 536 E.

provisions for compensation even though these parts were somewhat broadly expressed and the correctness of the decision was
doubted by the House of Lords in *Woolfson* . . ."

The true position, it is submitted, is that a façade concealing the true
facts is *not* an essential element in interpretation cases; it is this which
distinguishes them from the "corporate veil" cases considered under
the next heading.

The fifth and sixth cases prayed in aid of the "single economic
unit" argument clearly were cases of interpretation. In the first, *Revlon
Inc. v. Cripp & Lee Ltd*,[32] the question arose as to whether goods were
"connected in the course of trade with the proprietor of the
trademark", within the meaning of section 4(3) of the Trade Marks
Act 1938. The proprietor of the trade mark was not Revlon Inc
(Revlon) but Revlon Suisse S.A. (Suisse). In holding that the goods
traded by Revlon were connected with Suisse, Buckley J., said[33]:

"Since . . . all the relevant companies are wholly owned subsidiaries
of Revlon, it is undoubted that the mark is, albeit remotely, an asset
of Revlon and its exploitation is for the ultimate benefit of no one
but Revlon . . . The mark is an asset of the Revlon group of companies regarded as a whole, which all belong to Revlon. This view does
not, in my opinion, constitute what is sometimes called piercing the
corporate veil; it recognises the legal and factual position resulting
from the mutual relationship of the various companies."

The sixth authority considered by the Court was the advice of Advocate General Warner in two related cases[34] before the European Court
of Justice (an illustration of the growing influence of E.C. law on
English law) on the question whether a parent company and its subsidiary were separate "undertakings" within the meaning of the competition Articles 85 and 86 of the Treaty. He pointed out[35] that neither
article referred to "persons" but to "undertakings, a much wider and
looser concept" and said that this is "what one would expect, because
it would be inappropriate to apply rigidly in the sphere of competition
law the doctrine referred to by English lawyers as that of *Salomon v.
Salomon & Co. Ltd*". In his view that doctrine existed basically in
order to preserve the principle of limited liability although it had been
applied, "with more or less happy results in other spheres". But "to
export it blindly into branches of the law where it had little relevance
could serve only to divorce law from reality". If a company, established outside the European Community, carried on business from a
branch office within the European Community it would be amenable
to the jurisdiction of the E.C. Commission and Court; it should make

---

[32] [1980] F.S.R. 85.
[33] At 105.
[34] *Instituto Chemioterapico SpA and Commercial Solvents Corp. v. The Commission* (Joined
Cases 6 & 7/73) [1974] E.C.R. 223.
[35] At 263–264. Cited in *Cape* at 535–536.

no difference if it did so through a subsidiary company whether wholly
owned or not. He therefore concluded that:
(i) "there is a presumption that a subsidiary will act in accordance
with the wishes of its parents because according to common experience they generally do so act; (ii) unless the presumption is rebutted,
it is proper for the parent and the subsidiary to be treated as a single
undertaking for the purposes of articles 85 and 86 . . . ."
After reviewing these authorities the Court in *Cape* expressed some
sympathy with the plaintiffs' submissions and agreed that:
"To the layman at least the distinction between the case where a
company trades itself in a foreign country and the case where it
trades in a foreign country through a subsidiary, whose activities it
has power to control, may seem a slender one."[36]
It also accepted that the wording of a particular statute or document
may justify the court in interpreting it so that a parent and subsidiary
are treated as one unit at any rate for some purposes.[37] It seems therefore that in aid of interpretation the court may have regard to the
economic realities in relation to the companies concerned. But that
now seems to be the extent to which the "single economic unit"
argument can succeed. The narrowness of this proposition needs to be
appreciated. It does not say that the court, when construing a statute
or document, must treat all the companies in a group as a single legal
entity. Whether the court does so will depend upon its conclusion as
to whether such a step is needed to effect the underlying purpose of
the statute or transaction.[38]

The "corporate veil" point

However, the Court accepted that:
"Quite apart from the cases where statute or contract permits a
broad interpretation to be given to references to members of a group
of companies there is one-well recognised exception to the rule
prohibiting the piercing of "the corporate veil".[39]
Since the House of Lords' decision in *Woolfson v. Strathclyde Regional
Council*[40] this exception has generally been expressed (and was in *Cape*)

---

[36] At 536B.
[37] At 536D.
[38] See *Re Polly Peck International plc (in administration)* [1996] 2 All E.R. 433 for a robust
rejection by the judge of the view that a subsidiary incorporated as a "single purpose finance
vehicle" in relation to the issue of bonds should be regarded as a single entity with its parent,
even though the creditors undoubtedly lent on the basis of the credit of the parent and even
though the effect of not applying the single entity doctrine was to give the bondholders two
bites at the cherry in the administration of the group, on the grounds that the court was
concerned with legal substance, not economic substance. See also *Acatos & Hutcheson plc v.
Watson* [1995] 1 BCLC 218, below, p. 249.
[39] At 539.
[40] Above, n. 8.

as permitting it when the corporate structure is a "mere façade concealing the true facts"—"façade"[41] having replaced an assortment of epithets[42] which judges have employed in earlier cases. The difficulty is to know what precisely may make a company a "mere façade".

Of the earlier cases, the one which the Court found the most helpful in this connection[43] was *Jones v. Lipman*.[44] In that case Lipman, having entered into a contract to sell land to Jones, attempted to defeat Jones' right to specific performance by forming a company and conveying the land to it. Russell J. made an order for specific performance against both Lipman and the company, holding that specific performance cannot be resisted by a vendor who has absolute ownership and control of the company in which the land is vested. This case showed, the Court held, that contrary to the views of Scott J. at first instance, where a façade is alleged the motives of the architects of the façade may be highly material.[45] It also shows that piercing the veil can be invoked against a controller of a company whether an individual or a company.[46]

Apart from *Jones v. Lipman* the Court felt that it was "left with rather sparse guidance as to the principles which should guide the court in determining whether or not the arrangements of a corporate group involve a façade . . ." but, unfortunately, it declined to "attempt a comprehensive definition of those principles".[47] It did, however, decide that one of Cape's wholly owned subsidiaries (AMC incorporated in Liechtenstein) was a façade in the relevant sense. Scott J. had found as a fact that arrangements made in 1979 regarding AMC and other companies concerned in the marketing of Cape's asbestos "were part of one composite arrangement designed to enable Cape asbestos to continue to be sold into the United States while reducing, if not eliminating, the appearance of any involvement therein of Cape or its subsidiaries".[48] Although he had thought that motive was irrelevant, the Court of Appeal, as we have seen, thought it might be highly relevant, though apparently this particular motive alone would not have sufficed to make AMC a mere façade.[49] What seems to have been regarded as decisive was the fact that AMC was not only a wholly owned subsidiary of Cape but also no more than a corporate

---

[41] Used, clearly in its secondary meaning (the primary one being "the face of a building"), *i.e.* "an outward appearance or front, especially a deceptive one."

[42] Such as "device", "sham", "creature", "stratagem", "mask", "puppet" and even (see *Re Bugle Press* [1961] Ch. 270, C.A., at 288) "a little hut".

[43] See at 542.

[44] [1962] 1 W.L.R. 832.

[45] At 540 C and 542 C. See also *Creasey v. Breachwood Motors Ltd* [1993] BCLC 480 where this principle was applied to the transfer of a business to an existing and established company in order to render the plaintiff's claim against the transferor company worthless.

[46] So could the "interpretation" exception (to which the "single economic unit" exception has been reduced) if that was a legitimate interpretation of the statute or document concerned.

[47] At 543D.

[48] At 478F, approved by the C.A. at 541G–H, 544A and B.

[49] See the discussion, which follows, regarding another related company, C.P.C.

name which Cape or its subsidiaries used on invoices.[50] However, the implications of that were not pursued because all the Court was concerned with was whether Cape could be regarded as present in the United States and ''on the judge's undisputed findings AMC was not in reality carrying on any business in the United States'',[51] and therefore could not cause Cape to be regarded as present there. Presumably, however, those who, as a result of the invoices, thought they were dealing with AMC would, if AMC failed to perform the contract, have been able to sue Cape.

What mattered in relation to establishing that Cape was present in the United States was whether another company, C.P.C., incorporated and carrying on business in the United States, was a façade. Despite the fact that C.P.C. was a party to the same arrangement as AMC and that it probably had been incorporated at Cape's expense, that did not in itself make it a mere façade. On the facts the Court was satisfied that it was an independent corporation, wholly owned by its chief executive and carrying on its own business in the States and not the business of Cape or its subsidiaries.

Moreover the Court declared[52] that it did not accept that:

''as a matter of law the court is entitled to lift the corporate veil as against a defendant company which is the member of a corporate group, merely because the corporate structure has been used so as to ensure that the legal liability (if any) in respect of particular future activities of the group (and correspondingly the risk of enforcement of that liability) will fall on another member of the group rather than the defendant company. Whether or not this is desirable, the right to use a corporate structure in this manner is inherent in our corporate law.''[53]

And the Court added[54]:

''[Counsel for the plaintiffs] urged on us that the purpose of the operation was in substance that Cape would have the practical benefit of the group's asbestos trade in the United States . . . without the risks of tortious liability. This may be so. However, in our judgment Cape was in law entitled to organise the group's affairs in that manner and (save in the case of AMC to which special considerations apply) to expect that the court would apply the principle of [the *Salomon* case].''

---

[50] At 479E and 543E.

[51] At 543G.

[52] At 544D, E.

[53] Hence Cape's *wholly owned* American subsidiary N.A.A.C. which, prior to the 1979 arrangements (when it was wound up) had performed a similar role to that undertaken thereafter by C.P.C. has equally to be regarded as a separate entity: see at 538.

[54] At 544E, F.

The agency argument

A company having power to act as an agent may do so as agent for its parent company or indeed for all or any of its individual members if it or they authorise it to do so. If so, the parent company or the members will be bound by the acts of its agent so long as those acts are within the actual or apparent scope of the authority.[55] But there is no presumption of any such agency relationship and in the absence of an express agreement between the parties[56] it will be very difficult to establish one. In *Cape* the attempt to do so failed.[57] While it was clear that C.P.C. rendered services to Cape and in some cases acted as its agent in relation to particular transactions, that did not suffice to satisfy the conditions which the Court had held to be necessary if Cape was to be regarded as "present" in the United States.[58] C.P.C. had carried on its own business from its own fixed place of business in the United States.[59]

The end result

Where then does this leave "lifting of the veil"? Well, considerably more attenuated than some of us would wish. There seem to be three circumstances only in which the courts can do so. These are:

(1) when the court is construing a statute, contract or other document;
(2) when the court is satisfied that a company is a "mere façade" concealing the true facts;
(3) when it can be established that the company is an authorised agent of its controllers or its members, corporate or human.

And (2) only is a true example of lifting the veil; in (1) and (3) the separate personality of the company is not denied but the practical effect on the parties' rights and liabilities is the same as if it had been. The court cannot lift the veil merely because it considers that justice

---

[55] See Chap. 10, below.
[56] As in *Southern v. Watson* [1940] 3 All E.R. 439, C.A., where, on the conversion of a business into a private company, the sale agreement provided that the company should fulfil existing contracts of the business as agents of the sellers, and in *Rainham Chemical Works v. Belvedere* [1921] 2 A.C. 465, H.L. where the agreement provided that the newly formed company should take possession of land as agent of its vendor promoters.
[57] Both in relation to C.P.C. (at 547–549) and to its predecessor, N.A.A.C., (n. 53, above) despite the fact that it had been Cape's wholly owned subsidiary (at 545–547).
[58] See above.
[59] Contrast *F.G. (Films) Ltd* [1953] 1 W.L.R. 483 and *Firestone Tyre and Rubber Co. Ltd v. Lewellin* [1957] 1 W.L.R. 464, H.L. which suggest that in tax cases there may be a greater readiness on the part of the English courts to hold that a foreign company is carrying on its business in the U.K. through its British subsidiary.

so requires.[60] Nor, unless the case falls within one or both of circumstances (1) and (2), can it have regard to the economic reality that most company groups are operated as if they were a single entity.

When the case falls within (1)—an "interpretation case"—the court may have regard to the economic reality and treat a group as if it were one entity if that is how the group operates. This gives scope for a measure of judicial activism by judges especially if they are prepared to adopt a purposive construction.[61] In doing so they will not be constrained by a need to find that the company is a mere façade as they will if they are to act under (2).

The difficulty about (2) is the lack of guidance on the principles for determining whether a company is a mere façade. The holding by the Court of Appeal in *Cape* that motive might be highly relevant is helpful. It also seems clear that a company can be a façade even though it was not originally incorporated with any deceptive intention; what counts is whether it is being used as a façade at the time of the relevant transactions.[62] But, apart from that, uncertainty and difficulties, remain.[63] If only for that reason, it is regrettable that the Court of Appeal and the House of Lords refused in *Cape* to give leave to appeal. It is to be hoped that the Lords will be afforded another opportunity of reviewing the law in this field. Having invented the "façade" test it behoves the Lords to tell us what it means. Perhaps one factor suggesting that a subsidiary is a mere façade for its parent is that the subidiary is obviously under-capitalised for the role that it is ostensibly performing as an independent entity. In the United States this is regarded as an important factor, as it was here in *Re F.G. Films Ltd.*[64]

Regarding circumstance (3), while it may be possible to establish that in particular transactions a subsidiary has acted as the authorised

---

[60] See *Cape* [1990] Ch. 433 at 537. English judges (apart from Lord Denning) have shown a marked reluctance to operate any such formula (for another example see Chap. 23, below, in relation to the rule in *Foss v. Harbottle*). Of course, the three categories identified in the text can overlap, as in *Re H* [1996] 2 All E.R. 391, C.A. where the court interpreted the legislation as overriding the use of the corporate form as a façade.

[61] *e.g.* to treat a new company as the same as its predecessor—as the C.A. did in *Willis v. Assoc. of Universities of the British Commonwealth* [1965] 1 Q.B. 140. But see *Re Polly Peck International plc*, above, n. 38.

[62] *cf. Creasey v Breachwood Motors Ltd* [1993] BCLC 480.

[63] *e.g.*: there are devices often employed by landlords to try to ensure that their tenants do not have the protection of statutory tenants under the Rent Acts. In *Antoniades v. Villiers* [1990] 1 A.C. 417, H.L. the landlord resorted to the device of incorporating in the lease a clause reserving to himself or his nominees a right to share occupation of a one-bedroom flat let to a young couple. This was held to be a mere sham and the landlord's efforts failed. In *Hilton v. Plustitle* [1989] 1 W.L.R. 149, C.A. *pet. dis.* at [1989] 1 W.L.R. 310, H.L. the device used was to interpose between the landlord and the real tenant a shelf company the sole purpose of which was to be the ostensible tenant. The company was held out not to be mere façade. Yet in both cases the motives were identical and the means seemingly equally deceptive.

[64] [1953] 1 W.L.R. 483. But *cf. Re Polly Peck International plc*, above n. 38, where a subsidiary with an issued capital of 25,000 Sfr. borrowed 700 million Sfr. for its parent, and was held not to be a façade.

agent of its parent (or vice versa) any prospect of establishing that it has general authority to carry on the latter's business is remote.

Hence while statutory inroads into the corporate entity principle continue to increase those by the judiciary have contracted.[65]

RATIFICATION OF DEFECTIVE CORPORATE ACTS

The matter to which we now turn relates not to lifting the veil but rather to the related question of raising the curtain over the internal operations of a company. As such, this seems to be an appropriate chapter in which to deal with what is a matter of considerable practical importance.

In a number of cases the question has arisen whether something less formal than a resolution duly passed at a properly convened meeting of the members can be regarded as equivalent to a resolution of the members in general meeting. In a comparatively early case[66] a strong Court of Appeal held in a judgment delivered by Lindley L.J. that:

"Individual assents given separately may preclude those who have given them from complaining of what they have sanctioned, but for the purpose of binding a company in its corporate capacity individual assents given separately are not equivalent to the assent of a meeting."[67]

In a series of later cases, however, the courts have come to recognise that "individual assents given separately" by all the members entitled to vote are "equivalent to the assent of a meeting" and that the assent may be no more than passive acquiescence in the result. This development started with a recognition that a resolution of a board meeting bound the company, notwithstanding that it was beyond the directors' powers, when the directors were the company's only members and all were present.[68] It was then extended to a recognition that the members might waive the normal period of notice for convening meetings[69]—a view adopted and extended by the companies legislation.[70] That also recognised that articles of association could effectively provide that a

---

[65] Note also the dictum of Browne-Wilkinson V.C. in *Tate Access Inc. v. Boswell* [1991] Ch. 512: "If people choose to conduct their affairs through the medium of corporations, they are taking advantage of the fact that in law those corporations are separate legal entities . . . In my judgment controlling shareholders cannot for all purposes beneficial to them insist on the separate identity of such corporations and then be heard to say the contrary" [when is it disadvantageous]; at 531H.

[66] *Re George Newman Ltd* [1895] 1 Ch. 674, C.A. The court also suggested that, in any case, the acts assented to were *ultra vires* and later cases have distinguished it on that ground.

[67] At 686.

[68] *Re Express Engineering Works Ltd* [1920] 1 Ch. 466, C.A.

[69] *Re Oxted Motor Co. Ltd* [1921] 3 K.B. 32.

[70] Companies Act 1985, s.369(3) and (4) repeating the 1948 Act, s.133(3). The consent of 95 per cent suffices (except for an AGM) and a private company may by an elective resolution reduce it to 90 per cent.

written resolution signed by all the members entitled to vote at general meetings was equivalent to one passed at a general meeting and, in the case of private companies, Table A Part II of the 1948 Act so provided and the latest Table A of 1985 so provides in the model articles for *all* companies limited by shares.[71] In relation to private companies, as a result of the Companies Act 1989 this now applies irrespective of any provision in the articles since, subject to a few qualifications, anything which could be done by a resolution in general meeting or a class meeting may be effectively done by written agreement of all members entitled to attend and vote and irrespective of the type of resolution.[72] And the courts have recognised that there need be no sort of "meeting" or "resolution", or, indeed, unanimous agreement of *all* members. It suffices if all the members entitled to vote on the matter concerned have informally ratified or acquiesced and this seems to be so irrespective of the nature of the resolution and the size of the majority that would have been needed had the formalities been observed.[73]

The only discordant note is that sounded by Nourse J. (as he then was) in *Re Barry Artist Ltd*.[74] This case concerned a resolution signed by all the members as a special resolution for the reduction of the company's capital. Though conceding that this was an effective resolution, the judge held that, on an application to confirm the reduction,[75] he was entitled to refuse confirmation unless and until the resolution was passed at a meeting. After an hour-and-a-half's argument he relented with great reluctance but warned that he "would not be prepared to do so in any similar case in the future". It is difficult to see why a unanimous written resolution should be regarded as any more objectionable in relation to capital reductions than in any other matter. In the light of the new section 381A(6) it clearly is permissible in relation to private companies and there is no apparent reason why it should be impermissible in relation to a public company with only a few members.[76]

---

[71] Table A 1985, art. 53. It is impracticable to use this procedure in the case of a widely held public company but not all plcs are widely held.

[72] See Chap. 5, pp. 93–94, above.

[73] *Parker & Cooper Ltd v. Reading* [1926] Ch. 975; *Re Pearce Duff & Co. Ltd* [1960] 1 W.L.R. 1014; *Re Duomatic Ltd* [1969] 2 Ch. 365; *Re Bailey Hay & Co. Ltd* [1971] 1 W.L.R. 1357; *Re Gee & Co (Woolwich) Ltd* [1975] Ch. 52; *Cane v. Jones* [1980] 1 W.L.R. 1451; *Re Moorgate Mercantile Holdings Ltd* [1980] 1 W.L.R. 227 at 242 G; *Multinational Gas Co. v. Multinational Gas Services* [1983] 1 Ch. 258, C.A. especially at 289.

[74] [1985] 1 W.L.R. 1305.

[75] Under what are now ss.136 and 137 of the Companies Act 1985.

[76] There may also be a singularly anomalous statutory exception: s.121 of the Act empowers a company to make certain innocuous alterations to its share capital (not involving a reduction of capital) by ordinary resolution and subs. (4) specifically provides that "the powers conferred by this section must be exercised by the company in general meeting". The wording of s.381A makes it clear that this does not prevent a private company from proceeding by a written resolution but it is arguable that a public one cannot, even though it has only a few members so that it would be practicable to do so.

What is not wholly clear is whether, in any circumstances, something less than agreement of all members entitled to vote can be treated as equivalent to a resolution passed at a general meeting. *Obiter dicta* in a decision of the Privy Council in 1937[77] suggest that it cannot. The decision which, at first sight, comes closest to holding that something less will suffice is *Re Bailey Hay & Co. Ltd.*[78] There a resolution was passed by two votes in favour and three abstaining at a meeting attended by all the members of the company but of which the requisite length of notice had not been given. One of the grounds for denying a challenge three years later to the validity of the resolution was delay (or "laches") in making the claim. The delay made it "practically unjust" now to upset the resolution (which had been for the appointment of a liquidator). This argument did not involve holding that the resolution was an act of the company, but simply that certain individuals, those who had delayed, could not bring proceedings to challenge the resolution. Happily, hints can be found that the courts might be prepared to hold that it could be "practically unjust" to allow anyone to complain of an irregularity if an unreasonable length of time had elapsed since the irregularity occurred.[79] If that is so, laches, unlike estoppel, would not merely ban proceedings by particular complainants but, like unanimous agreement of members, would, in effect, validate the transaction.

---

[77] *E.B.M. Co. Ltd v. Dominion Bank* [1937] 3 All E.R. 555 (cited with apparent approval by the H.L. in *Williams & Humbert v. W. & H. Trade Marks* [1986] A.C. 368 at 429).

[78] Above, n. 73.

[79] See *Phosphate of Lime Co. v. Green* [1871] L.R. 7 C.P. 43, where it was held that "acquiescence" by members of a company could be established without proving actual knowledge by each individual member so long as each could have found out if he had bothered to ask, and *Ho Tung v. Man On Insurance Co.* [1902] A.C. 232, P.C., where articles of association, which had never been adopted by a resolution but had been acted on for 19 years and amended from time to time, were held to have been accepted and adopted as valid and operative articles.

CHAPTER 9

THE COMPANY'S ORGANS AND OFFICERS

THE preceding Chapters attempted to show that a company is itself a legal person, with an existence independent of that of its members. Yet it remains an artificial person; its policy can be formulated and decided upon only by individual human beings, and can be put into effect and carried out only by human agencies.[1] So the question becomes: who is to be regarded as acting as or on behalf of the company and in which circumstances may they so act? Just as the legal position of unincorporated associations depends largely on the law of agency (especially is this so in connection with partnerships in which each partner automatically becomes the agent of the others and, as a necessary result, stands in a fiduciary position towards his co-partners) so also the law of agency is equally at the root of company law. But agency principles have undergone a number of modifications in their application to companies. The present chapter discusses the nature of these agencies and the relationship between them; the succeeding chapter will consider the extent to which a company may be held liable for their acts. Detailed consideration of the duties which they owe to the company and its members is left for later consideration.[2]

How a company's organs are appointed

The application of agency principles to companies meets an initial difficulty: since the company is an artificial person how is it to appoint its agents? This problem does not arise in connection with unincorporated societies for the question there is simply whether the members (natural persons) have appointed other persons as their agents. But, with a corporation, it is the incorporated company, not its members, which is the principal and somehow certain acts have to be regarded as those of the company itself if only in order to enable it to appoint agents. The early law of corporations seems to have tried to avoid this dilemma by a resort to formalism—the acts of the corporation were those which were authenticated by its common seal. This, however, merely begged the question without solving it, for someone had to affix the seal and if it was affixed without lawful authority the corporation would not be bound. Moreover, the insistence on the use of a seal which was appropriate only to contractual liability was, even there,

---

[1] "The company itself cannot act in its own person, for it has no person; it can only act through directors and the case is, as regards those directors, merely the ordinary case of principal and agent": *per* Cairns L.J. in *Ferguson v. Wilson* (1866) L.R. 2 Ch. 77 at 89.
[2] See Part Six, below.

totally unworkable under modern conditions[3] and has now been abrogated both as regards individuals[4] and companies.[5]

Hence a more satisfactory solution was found by regarding the decisions of the majority of the members of the company in general meetings[6] as the acts of the company itself.[7] But this rule too has had to be supplemented since it is normally impossible for all day-to-day decisions to be taken in general meeting. In practice the initial constitution of the company will provide for the appointment of a board of directors and expressly delegate all powers of management to it.[8] In such circumstances the theory seems to be that the company, as such, has, in its constitution, appointed its agents and clothed them with authority; the act which gives birth to the company operates as an appointment and delegation by the company.

It will be observed that authority to exercise the company's powers is delegated, not to individual directors, but only to the directors as a board; although it may be sub-delegated by the board to individual managing directors and to other officers.[9] Between the company and the board and the officers there is a relationship akin to agency, but there is none between the company and the members or between the members *inter se*. This is in marked contrast with the partnership in which each member becomes an agent of the others. The absence of any such relationship in the case of a company is one of its distinctive features and one which is essential if a public company is to perform its economic role.

The board of directors

All registered companies must now have directors and normally there must be at least two, though one suffices for a private company

---

[3] As recognised by the Corporate Bodies Contracts Act 1960.

[4] Law of Property (Miscellaneous Provisions) Act 1989.

[5] Companies Act 1985, ss.36, 36A and 36B (as substituted by the 1989 Act and later amended by the Requirements of Writing (Scotland) Act 1995). However, the new provisions seem not to be operating entirely smoothly. See Law Commission Consultation Paper No. 143, 1996.

[6] The functioning of general meetings is described in Chap. 21. Additionally, the unanimous decision of all the members entitled to vote, though not taken in general meeting, may be regarded as the act of the company: see above, at pp. 175–177.

[7] *Per* Hardwicke L.C. in *Att.-Gen. v. Davy* (1741) 2 Atk. 212: "It cannot be disputed that wherever a certain number are incorporated a major part of them may do any corporate act; so if all are summoned, and part appear, a major part of those that appear may do a corporate act . . . it is not necessary that every corporate act should be under the seal of the corporation . . ." This principle is at the root of the rule in *Foss v. Harbottle* (1843) 2 Hare 461 (see Chap. 23, below) in which Wigram V.-C. (at 493) referred to the members in general meetings as "the supreme governing body".

[8] Companies Clauses Consolidation Act 1845, s.90; Table A in the Companies (Tables A–F) Regs. 1985 (S.I. 1985 No. 805 as amended by S.I. 1985 No. 1052), art. 70. This Table A is hereinafter referred to as "Table A 1985". It must be borne in mind that it applies only to companies incorporated since the 1985 Act (without registering articles which exclude it) and to pre- or post-1985 companies which adopt it after 1985. Many, perhaps most, companies still have articles based on Table A of the 1948 Act or a still earlier Companies Act.

[9] Table A 1985, arts. 72 and 84.

or one registered before 1929.[10] On initial registration the company must send to the Registrar of Companies particulars of the first directors[11] with their signed written consents to act. Thereafter he must be sent particulars of any changes with signed consent to act by any new directors.[12] The Registrar must cause receipt of these notifications to be "officially notified" in the *Gazette*.[13] The company must also maintain a register giving particulars of its directors.[14] Hence the public can obtain information about who the directors are either from Companies House or from the company's registered office.

The Act itself says little more about the means of appointing the directors, leaving this to the articles of association. In particular, and contrary to popular belief, the Act requires neither that all directors be elected by the shareholders in general meeting nor that they submit themselves periodically to re-election by the shareholders. This may often be the case, though it is far from universal practice, but, if it is, it is a consequence of the provisions of the company's articles, not of the Acts requirements[15]. The articles normally provide for retirement by rotation of a certain proportion and for the filling of the vacancies at each annual general meeting.[16] The Act then provides that each appointment shall be voted on individually[17] except in the case of a private company or unless the meeting shall agree *nem. con.* that two or more shall be included in a single resolution. There is nothing in the Act to provide that an ordinary resolution suffices to elect a director, but this is the normal practice. However appointed, a director can be removed by ordinary resolution[18] in addition to any other means of removal that may be provided in the articles.[19] It is not uncommon in private companies for certain directors not to retire by rotation but

---

[10] s.282.

[11] s.10, and Sched. 1.

[12] s.288(2).

[13] s.711. This formality, somewhat pointless under English practice, is required to comply with the First Company Law Directive.

[14] ss.288, 289. It is no longer necessary to state the names of the directors on the company's letter-heading but if it states any it must state all: s.305.

[15] But there is nothing to prevent articles providing that directors can be appointed by a particular class of shareholders, by debenture holders or, indeed by third parties. Under the memo. and arts. of the Securities and Investments Board (a company limited by guarantee) all board members are appointed and dismissible by the Secretary of State and the Governor of the Bank of England (acting jointly) neither of whom is a member of the company.

[16] Table A 1985, art. 73. It is customary to empower the directors themselves to fill a casual vacancy and to appoint additional directors within the maximum prescribed by the articles (*ibid.*, art. 79). Normally directors appointed by the board come up for re-election at the next AGM (*ibid.*).

[17] s.272. This is designed to prevent the members being faced with the alternative of either accepting or rejecting the whole of a slate of nominees.

[18] s.303. See below, pp. 188 *et seq.* and on the functions of the general meeting see Chap. 21.

[19] These may, *e.g.* empower certain of the directors to remove others (see *Bersel Manufacturing Co. Ltd v. Berry* [1968] 2 All E.R. 552, H.L.) or provide for vacation of office on a request by his co-directors to resign: *Lee v. Chou Wen Hsien* [1984] 1 W.L.R. 1202, P.C.

to be appointed for life, or for as long as they hold some other office,[20] but these, too, can now be removed from their directorships by ordinary resolution.

It will, therefore, be appreciated that a member holding 51 per cent of the voting shares can be sure of electing the whole of the board or, at any rate, of having a veto over the constitution of the whole of the board. There is, in England, nothing comparable to the system of "cumulative voting" which is optional or compulsory in many states of the United States and which affords the shareholder the possibility of board representation proportional to his holding.[21] This system has now been extended, on an optional basis, to some other common law countries, but, though it has its advocates it seems unlikely to be introduced here.

Unless the articles so provide, directors need not be members of the company. At one time it was customary so to provide,[22] but now the possibility of a complete separation of "proprietors" and "managers" is recognised and Table A no longer provides for a share qualification. If, however, one is needed under the articles, the shares must be taken up within two months and his office will be vacated if they are not, or if they are later relinquished.[23]

Articles commonly provide for the vacation of office by directors in certain circumstances, including resignation, prolonged absence from board meetings or insanity.[24] The Cohen Committee also tried to ensure that directors should normally retire when they attained the age of 70,[25] but as finally enacted this provision is so riddled with exceptions that it has proved of little value.[26] Nor, it seems, is any minimum age required; presumably infant directors must be old enough to sign the required consent to act but that seems to be the only legal restraint.[27] Indeed, in contrast with the company secretary,[28] no

---

[20] *e.g.* that of managing director or other executive office: see Table A 1985, art. 84.

[21] Briefly, the number of votes which each shareholder has is multiplied by the number of directors to be elected and he can "cumulate" his votes on one or some nominees only instead of spreading them over the slate. This is of little benefit to a member with only a handful of votes but it does mean that one who holds one-third of the voting shares should secure one-third representation on the board and that one with 51 per cent should secure only one-half and not, as under our system, be able to elect the whole board.

[22] Companies Act 1929, Table A, art. 66.

[23] Companies Act 1985, s.291. The two month period runs from the declaration of the result of the vote electing the director: *Holmes v. Keyes* [1959] Ch. 199, C.A.

[24] Table A 1985, art. 81. But except as authorised by the articles the directors cannot exclude one of their number from the board and can be restrained by injunction from so doing (at any rate if the directorship carries fees): *Hayes v. Bristol Plant Hire Ltd* [1957] 1 W.L.R. 499.

[25] Cmd. 6659, para. 131.

[26] s.293. Note that the age limit does not apply to private companies unless subsidiaries of public ones (subs. (1)), that it can be excluded by the articles (subs. (7)), and that an over-age director can always be appointed if "special notice" (see below) is given (subs. (5)).

[27] A practical restraint is that if the infant was very young there would, presumably, be a "shadow director" behind him.

[28] See below, p. 197.

positive qualifications are required of directors—though, as we shall see, they may be disqualified on the ground of misconduct or unfitness. Nor need directors be natural persons; a body corporate can be appointed[29] and this has sometimes been done to enable a parent company to maintain complete control of a subsidiary by becoming its director.[30]

Sometimes the articles entitle a director to appoint an alternate director to act for him at any board meeting that he is unable to attend. The extent of the alternate's powers and the answer to such questions as whether he is entitled to remuneration from the company or from the director appointing him will then depend on the terms of the relevant article.[31] Some doubts have been expressed regarding the exact status of an alternate director and it was suggested to the Jenkins Committee that his position should be regulated in the Act. However, the Committee thought this unnecessary as they were satisfied that he was "in the eyes of the law in the same position as any other director".[32] The Committee also thought it unnecessary to do anything about the growing and potentially misleading practice of giving employees status without responsibility by appointing them "special" or "associate" directors.[33] The directors need not be so called; for the purposes of the Companies Act, "director" includes any person occupying the position of director, by whatever name called,[34] and directors of some guarantee companies are still called "governors" or the like.

De facto and shadow directors

While, *de jure*, people cannot be directors unless they have been properly appointed, they may, as we shall see later,[35] be able to bind the company although they have not. Moreover, they may be subject to liability as if they were directors because they have assumed that position,[36] or because an increasing number of legislative provisions expressly apply not only to directors, but also to "shadow directors", *i.e.* persons "in accordance with whose directions or instructions the directors of the company are accustomed to act" otherwise than only

---

[29] This is forbidden in some other countries and the Jenkins Committee recommended that it should be banned here: Cmnd. 1749, para. 84. It is somewhat surprising that this recommendation has not been implemented since liquidators, administrators and receivers must be natural persons.

[30] In the light of s.213 and s.214 of the Insolvency Act 1986 (see above pp. 151–155) it is less likely to be done now.

[31] See Table A 1985, arts. 65–69 which, if adopted, go far to clarify the alternate's position.

[32] Cmnd. 1749, para. 83.

[33] *ibid.*, para. 82. One difficulty is that it would be necessary to make exceptions for descriptions such as "director of research".

[34] s.741(1).

[35] Below Chap. 10 at pp. 224 *et seq.*

[36] *Re Lo-Line Electric Motors Ltd* [1988] Ch. 477.

because "the directors act on advice given ... in a professional capacity".[37] The difference between liability as a *de facto* director and as a shadow director is that the former has openly acted as if he had been validly appointed, whether or not there are other, properly appointed, directors, whereas the definition of shadow director "presupposes that there is a board of directors who act in accordance with instructions from someone else, the eminence grise or shadow director".[38] The last thing that the latter will want is to advertise the fact that he is exercising this improper influence and nor will the proper directors, who are breaching their duties by acting as his puppets.[39]

Division of powers between the general meeting and the board

Until the end of the nineteenth century it seems to have been generally assumed that the principle remained intact that the general meeting was the supreme organ of the company and that the board of directors was merely an agent of the company subject to the control of the company in general meeting. Thus, in *Isle of Wight Railway v. Tahourdin*,[40] the court refused the directors of a statutory company an injunction to restrain the holding of a general meeting, one purpose of which was to appoint a committee to reorganise the management of the company. Cotton L.J. said:

"It is a very strong thing indeed to prevent shareholders from holding a meeting of the company when such a meeting is the only way in which they can interfere if the majority of them think that the course taken by the directors, in a matter *intra vires* of the directors, is not for the benefit of the company."[41]

In 1906, however, the Court of Appeal in *Automatic Self-Cleansing Filter Syndicate Co. v. Cuninghame*,[42] made it clear that the division of powers between the board and the company in general meeting depended in the case of registered companies entirely on the construction of the articles of association and that, where powers had been vested in the board, the general meeting could not interfere with their exercise. The articles were held to constitute a contract by which the

---

[37] Companies Act 1985, s.741(2), Insolvency Act 1986, s.251, Company Directors Disqualification Act 1986, s.22(4) and (5); Financial Services Act 1986, s.207 (definition of "director").
[38] *Re Lo-Line Electric Motors Ltd* (above, n. 36 at 489). See also *Re Hydrodan (Corby) Ltd* [1994] 2 BCLC 180: "The terms do not overlap. They are alternatives, and in most and perhaps all cases are mutually exclusive" (*per* Millett J.).
[39] And, by failing to include him in the returns and register required by ss.288 and 289 (see above, p. 180) they will render the company and the officers liable to default fines (under s.288(4)) since, for the purposes of those sections, a shadow director is classed as a director of the company.
[40] (1883) 25 Ch.D. 320, C.A.
[41] At 329.
[42] [1906] 2 Ch. 34, C.A.

members had agreed that "the directors and the directors alone shall manage".[43] Hence the directors were entitled to refuse to carry out a sale agreement adopted by ordinary resolution in general meeting. *Tahourdin's* case was distinguished on the ground that the wording of section 90 of the Companies Clauses Act 1845 was different—though that section does not in fact seem to have been relied on in the earlier case.

The new approach, though cited with apparent approval by a differently constituted Court of Appeal in 1908,[44] did not secure immediate acceptance[45] but since *Quin & Axtens v. Salmon*[46] it appears to have been generally accepted that where the relevant articles are in the normal form exemplified by successive Tables A, the general meeting cannot interfere with a decision of the directors unless they are acting contrary to the provisions of the Act or the articles.[47]

In *Shaw & Sons (Salford) Ltd v. Shaw*,[48] in which a resolution of the general meeting disapproving the commencement of an action by the directors was held to be a nullity, the modern doctrine was expressed by Greer L.J. as follows[49]:

"A company is an entity distinct alike from its shareholders and its directors. Some of its powers may, according to its articles, be exercised by directors, certain other powers may be reserved for the shareholders in general meeting. If powers of management are vested in the directors, they and they alone can exercise these powers. The only way in which the general body of the shareholders can control the exercise of the powers vested by the articles in the directors is by altering their articles, or, if opportunity arises under the articles, by refusing to re-elect the directors of whose actions they disapprove.[50] They cannot themselves usurp the powers which by the articles are vested in the directors any more than the directors can usurp the powers vested by the articles in the general body of shareholders."

And, in *Scott v. Scott*[51] it was held, on the same grounds, that resolu-

---

[43] *Per* Cozens-Hardy L.J. at 44.

[44] *Gramophone & Typewriter Ltd v. Stanley* [1908] 2 K.B. 89, C.A.; see especially, *per* Fletcher Moulton L.J. at 98, and *per* Buckley L.J. at 105–106 (despite the fact that the then current edition of his book took the opposite view).

[45] *Marshall's Valve Gear Co. v. Manning Wardle & Co.* [1909] 1 Ch. 267.

[46] [1909] 1 Ch. 311, C.A.; [1909] A.C. 442, H.L.

[47] But for contrary views, see Goldberg (1970) 33 M.L.R. 177; Blackman (1975) 92 S.A.L.J. 286; and Sullivan (1977) 93 L.Q.R. 569. And see Chap. 6 at pp. 115–122, above, for the related dispute on the effect of what is now s.14 of the Act.

[48] [1935] 2 K.B. 113, C.A.

[49] At 134.

[50] They can now remove the directors by ordinary resolution: Companies Act 1985, s.303, below.

[51] [1943] 1 All E.R. 582. See also *Black White and Grey Cabs Ltd v. Fox* [1969] N.Z.L.R. 824, N.Z.C.A., where the cases were reviewed, as they were by Plowman J. at first instance in *Bamford v. Bamford* [1970] Ch. 212, C.A.

tions of a general meeting, which might be interpreted either as directions to pay an interim dividend or as instructions to make loans, were nullities. In either event the relevant powers had been delegated to the directors, and until those powers were taken away by an amendment of the articles the members in general meeting could not interfere with their exercise. As Lord Clauson[52] rightly said, "the professional view as to the control of the company in general meeting over the actions of directors has, over a period of years, undoubtedly varied".[53]

A remarkable feature of this development was that it came about in relation to companies in which the provisions of the relevant article were identical with, or based on, versions of Table A which, far from supporting the full extent of the case law, would seem to contradict it. Tables A of both the 1929 Act[54] and the 1948 Act,[55] having provided that, subject to the Act and the articles, the business of the company should be managed by the directors who might exercise all such powers as were not required to be exercised in general meeting, went on to qualify this by:

". . . *subject nevertheless to any regulation of these articles, to the provisions of the Act and to such regulations, being not inconsistent with the aforesaid regulations or provisions, as may be prescribed by the company in general meeting*[56]; but no regulation made by the company in general meeting shall invalidate any prior act of the directors which would have been valid if that regulation had not been made".

This, one would have thought, could only mean that the powers of the directors could be curtailed for the future by a resolution in general meeting[57]—though an act already undertaken by the directors could not be invalidated thereby. The decisions fail to give any satisfactory explanation for the words italicised,[58] which seem to have been deprived of any meaning.

However, in the present Table A[59] these words have been changed. The new version of the relevant article reads:

"Subject to the provisions of the Act, the memorandum and the articles *and to any directions given by special resolution*,[60] the business of the company shall be managed by the directors who may

---

[52] At 585D. Lord Clauson was sitting as a judge of the Ch.D.

[53] This is clearly seen if the judgments in the above cases are compared with that in *Foss v. Harbottle* (1843) 2 Hare 461; see especially at pp. 492–495. The modern view was reiterated at first instance in *Breckland Group Holdings Ltd v. London and Suffolk Properties Ltd* [1989] BCLC 100, noted by Wedderburn 52 M.L.R. 401 and Sealy [1989] C.L.J. 26.

[54] Table A 1985, art. 67.

[55] *ibid.*, art. 80.

[56] Italics supplied.

[57] As pointed out in the publications cited in n. 47, above.

[58] Though judges have tried: see Loreburn L.C. in [1909] A.C. at 444 and Lord Clauson in [1943] 1 All E.R. at 585A–D.

[59] *i.e.* Table A 1985, art. 70.

[60] Italics supplied.

exercise all the powers of the company. No alteration of the memorandum or articles and no such direction shall invalidate any prior
act of the directors which would have been valid if that alteration
had not been made or that direction had not been given . . .''[61]

This is an affirmation of the case law; but with a clarification or qualification in that it recognises that the general meeting may curtail the
future powers of the directors by a special resolution whether that
formally alters the memorandum or articles or merely gives "directions". Companies which incorporate under the 1985 Act and those
incorporated under earlier Acts which adopt new articles are likely to
follow the new formula.

It cannot be confidently predicted that the new formula will not raise
new questions. For example, can a "direction" by special resolution
effectively compel the directors to enter or not to enter into a transaction which is clearly part of the general management of the company's
business? Presumably it can, because the Act does not state that the
management *has* to be vested in the directors[62]; the articles could provide otherwise. But would the members then be "directors" within
the meaning of the Act which defines "director" as including "any
person occupying the position of director, by whatever name called"?
Not, presumably, unless all or a substantial part of "management"
was removed and vested in the members. Would it make any difference if the board had already resolved that the transaction should not,
or should, be entered into? Would that resolution be "a prior act" of
the directors which, under article 70, the special resolution cannot
invalidate? Probably it would. But the special resolution would not
"invalidate" it. The directors' resolution would remain valid as a resolution of the directors; what the special resolution would direct
(validly it seems) is that the directors should not act upon it. If, however, they had already acted upon it by entering into a binding contract
on behalf of the company, the special resolution could not invalidate
that. On the other hand, if the resolution had been that the transaction
should not be entered into, the special resolution could, it would seem,
force them to enter into it—assuming that that was still practicable.[63]

It is not clear whether the enhancement of the status of the board
of directors *vis-à-vis* the general meeting is wholly salutary. Where
the company is a public one it probably is, since management cannot
be undertaken by a vast body of small shareholders and will not be

---

[61] Art. 70 further states that "The powers given by this regulation shall not be limited by any
special power given to the directors by the articles" [thus excluding any risk of the application
of the *inclusio unius, exclusio alterius* rule] and that "a meeting of directors at which a
quorum is present may exercise all powers exercisable by the directors".

[62] As Corporation Laws of the USA do, and as it is arguable that we should have in order to
comply properly with E.C. Company Law Directives.

[63] Seemingly if, in *Shaw & Son (Salford) Ltd. v. Shaw* or *Scott v. Scott*, above, the relevant
article had been equivalent to art. 70 of the new Table A and the resolution had been a special
resolution, the decision in the former would have been the same but, in the latter, different.

undertaken by large institutional investors. Moreover, there is now an increasing number of situations in which the Act or the Stock Exchange requires major transactions to be ratified in general meetings.[64] Even so it seems strange that the members in general meeting can dismiss the board by an ordinary resolution[65] but cannot take a less extreme step except by a special resolution. And it is stranger still in the case of most small private companies which, as the courts have recognised,[66] are essentially incorporated partnerships. In them, one would have thought, the rule should be that unless otherwise agreed, "any differences arising as to ordinary matters connected with the partnership business may be decided by a majority of the partners, but no change may be made in the nature of the partnership business without the consent of all existing partners".[67] That is very different from article 70 of Table A; and, although the members may have legal remedies if their interests are being ignored by those quasi-partners who are the directors, it is clearly a handicap to them when they invoke those remedies.[68]

Default powers of the general meeting

Despite what has been said above, it seems that if for some reason the board cannot or will not exercise the powers vested in them, the general meeting may do so. On this ground, action by the general meeting has been held effective where there was a deadlock on the board[69]; where there were no directors[70]; where an effective quorum could not be obtained[71] or the directors were disqualified from voting.[72] Moreover, although the general meeting cannot normally abort legal proceedings commenced by the board in the name of the company,[73] it still seems to be the law that the general meeting can, in some circumstances, commence proceedings or ratify unauthorised proceedings already commenced by someone on behalf of the com-

---

[64] See Chap. 22 at pp. 626 *et seq.*, below.
[65] See below, p. 188 *et seq.*
[66] See Chap. 27, below.
[67] Partnership Act 1890, s.24(8).
[68] See Chap. 27, below.
[69] *Baron v. Potter* [1914] 1 Ch. 895. Contrast situations in which a board cannot do what the majority of the directors want because of the opposition of a minority acting within its powers under the articles: see, *e.g. Quin & Axtens v. Salmon* [1909] A.C. 442, H.L. and the decision of Harman J. in *Breckland Group Holdings v. London & Suffolk Properties* [1989] BCLC 100.
[70] *Alexander Ward & Co. v. Samyang Navigation Co.* [1975] 1 W.L.R. 673, H.L.Sc., *per* Lord Hailsham at 679 citing the corresponding passage from the 3rd edition of this book.
[71] *Foster v. Foster* [1916] 1 Ch. 532.
[72] *Irvine v. Union Bank of Australia* (1877) 2 App. Cas. 366 P.C.
[73] See *Breckland* case: n. 69, above. Even if the company had an article equivalent to Table A 1985, art. 70 (above) a "direction" by special resolution would seemingly be an ineffective attempt to "invalidate a prior act of the directors".

pany if the directors fail to pursue the claim.[74] These exceptions are convenient, but difficult to reconcile in principle with the strict theory of a division of powers. Their exact limits are not entirely clear.[75]

It is generally assumed that it is perfectly in order for the board of directors, if it so wishes, to refer any matter to the general meeting either to ratify what the board has done or to enable a general meeting to decide on action to be taken. It is quite clear, as was affirmed by the Court of Appeal in *Bamford v. Bamford*,[76] that an act of the directors which is voidable because, for example, it is in breach of their fiduciary duties, can be ratified by the company in general meeting if the act is within the powers of the company and the meeting acts with full knowledge and without oppression of the minority. It is, perhaps, less clear whether the board, without taking a decision on a matter within its powers, can initially refer it to the general meeting for a decision there. In an elaborate discussion at first instance in the *Bamford* case,[77] Plowman J. had held that the general meeting then had power to act under the residual powers, but he suggested that this might depend on the terms of the memorandum and articles of the company concerned. The Court of Appeal considered that this question was irrelevant to the issue before them and expressed no view on it. It seems absurd if the directors are forced to take a decision and then to ask the general meeting to whitewash them, but perhaps the safest course is for them to resolve on action "subject to ratification by the company in general meeting".

If the directors have purported to exercise powers reserved to the company in general meeting their action can be effectively ratified by the company in general meeting. And for the purpose of ratifying past actions of the board, as opposed to conferring powers on the board for the future, it is not necessary to pass a special resolution altering the article; normally an ordinary resolution will suffice.[78]

Removal of directors by the general meeting

One way in which the members can exercise ultimate control is by getting rid of the present directors and by appointing others more compliant. But until the 1948 Act this depended on the existence of powers to do so in the articles or on the members' ability to alter the articles.[79] In the absence of either, all they could do was to refrain

---

[74] See Chap. 23, below.
[75] In the words of Megarry J., "there are deep waters here"; *Re Argentum Reductions (U.K.) Ltd* [1975] 1 W.L.R. 186 at 189.
[76] [1970] Ch.D. 135, C.A.
[77] *ibid.*
[78] *Grant v. U.K. Switchback Rys* (1888) 40 Ch. D. 135, C.A.
[79] Which requires a three-quarters' majority of those voting. Under Table A of the 1929 Act a director could be removed by extraordinary resolution (a provision repeated in most articles at that time) but this too requires a three-quarters' majority.

from voting for the reappointment of directors if and when they came up for re-election. However, under section 303 of the Companies Act 1985, re-enacting section 184 of the 1948 Act, a director, subject to certain conditions, can be removed by ordinary resolution at any time. This expressly applies notwithstanding anything in the articles or in any agreement between the company and the director.[80] Notwithstanding this, it has been held by the House of Lords in *Bushell v. Faith*[81] that its object can be frustrated by a provision in the articles attaching increased votes to a director's shares on a resolution to remove him. This apparently indefensible decision can perhaps be justified on the ground that in a small private company[82] which is, in effect, an incorporated partnership, or in a joint-venture company it is not unreasonable that each "partner" should, as under partnership law, be entitled to participate in the management of the firm in the absence of his agreement to the contrary and to protect himself against removal by his fellow partners. Moreover, it has been recognised that the removal of a director in the case of such "quasi-partnerships" (as they have come to be called) may so strike at the essential underlying obligations of the members to each other as to justify the compulsory winding-up of the company on the ground that it is "just and equitable" to do so.[83] Nevertheless, the decision has been much criticised[84] and would have been reversed by the aborted Companies Bill 1973. At present, however, it remains the law and is probably likely to do so since, as we have seen,[85] the Government has used this device in relation to some of its privatisation measures.

Moreover, even where the articles contain no provisions as to weighted voting rights, the successful operation of the section requires some pretty stringent conditions to be met. Special notice has to be given of any resolution to remove a director[86] (that is to say the proposer must give 28 days' notice to the company of his intention to

---

[80] s.303(1).

[81] [1970] A.C. 1099, H.L. The shares in a private company were held equally by three directors and the articles provided that in the event of a resolution to remove any director the shares held by that director should carry three times their normal votes, thereby enabling him to outvote the other two. It was held that: "There is no fetter which compels the company to make voting rights or restrictions of general application and—such rights or restrictions can be attached to special circumstances and to particular types of resolution": *per* Lord Upjohn at 1109.

[82] A similar article would scarcely be practical in most other cases.

[83] See *Re Westbourne Galleries Ltd* [1973] A.C. 360, H.L., and Chap. 27, below. It also seems that the court could enjoin the breach of a binding agreement between members on how they should vote on any resolution to remove a director, thus, in effect, affording another method of circumventing s.303. On the endrenchment of shareholder rights in joint venture companies see Chap. 26, below, esp. pp. 727–732.

[84] See the forthright dissenting opinion of Lord Morris of Borth-y-Gest at 1106 and Prentice (1969) 32 M.L.R. 693 (a note on the C.A.'s judgments).

[85] At p. 70, above.

[86] s.303(2).

propose the resolution[87]) and the company must supply a copy to the director, who is entitled to be heard at the meeting.[88] Further, he may require the company to circulate any representations which he makes.[89] The object of these restrictions is to prevent a director from being deprived of an office of profit on a snap vote and without having had a full opportunity of stating his case.[90] This is fair enough. A more serious restraint on the members' powers of dismissal is the provision that the section shall not deprive a director of any claim for compensation or damages payable in respect of the termination.[91] If there is a contract of service between him and the company, as will be the case with managing and other executive directors, the probability is that the members will be able to sack him only at the risk of imposing on the company liability to pay damages or a sum fixed by the contract as compensation. This, it may be said, is also fair, because the company has freely bound itself by contract. But so far as the entry into service agreements is concerned it is normally the directors who will have the power to appoint and fix the terms of service of the executive directors.[92] The members may therefore find that the directors have entrenched themselves by contracts of service, as a result of which the company has to pay them substantial sums if it exercises its statutory power to dismiss them by ordinary resolution—or indeed dismisses them in any other way[93] other than for serious misconduct.

Formerly the members might know nothing about these contracts of service. In these respects their position has now improved; the contracts have to be available for their inspection[94] and, if the contract is for more than five years, during which it cannot be terminated by notice by the company, prior approval by a resolution of the general meeting is required.[95] As directors of public companies are unaccountably reluctant to have their service contracts submitted for approval by members of their companies, this has served to place some limit on the extent to which they entrench themselves. In the case of listed companies the *Listing Rules* extend the disclosure obligations in two

---

[87] s.379. The company must then give notice to the members in the notice convening the meeting or, if that is not practicable, by newspaper advertisement or other mode allowed by the articles, normally not less than 21 days before the meeting: *ibid.*

[88] s.304(1). In this case a private company cannot use a written resolution under s.381A; a meeting has to be held.

[89] s.304(2) and (3).

[90] But apparently he can be deprived of this protection if the articles contain an express power to remove a director by ordinary resolution and the company acts under that power; s.304(2) and (3) are expressly limited to removals "under this section".

[91] s.303(5).

[92] Table A 1985, art. 84.

[93] The board of directors can normally terminate a director's contract of service as an executive but, under Table A, so can the general meeting by removing him as a director: see *ibid.*

[94] s.318.

[95] s.319. It may also be necessary in some circumstances to obtain members' approval if compensation for loss of office is paid on termination resulting from a sale of the undertaking or a takeover: ss.312–316: see further Chap. 29 at pp. 812–815, below.

ways which will be of interest to shareholders contemplating the removal of directors. It requires the disclosure of "any other arrangements [*i.e.* not just the contract of service] which are necessary to enable investors to estimate the possible liability of the company upon early termination of the contract" and, following the Greenbury Committee's Report,[96] the Exchange now requires boards to report to the shareholders annually on the details of any director's service contract with a notice period of more than one year, "giving the reasons for such notice period".[97] However, despite recommendations now from both the Cadbury[98] and Greenbury[99] Committees, the length of the service contract for which shareholder approval is required has not been reduced below five years, either by the Exchange for listed companies or by statute for companies more generally.

It must be emphasised, however, that the dismissed director will have a legal claim for damages only if he has a binding contract entitling him either to hold his position for a fixed term or to be dismissed only after a prescribed or reasonable notice. As has been pointed out,[1] the articles alone do not constitute a contract between the company and a director. He will have to show that there is a separate contract of service or for services, whether formal or informal.[2] If there is such a contract, the company cannot evade its terms by altering the articles, unless, of course, the company has contracted on the basis that the terms of the contract will change automatically if the articles are altered.[3] If the alteration gives the company a power of dismissal contrary to the terms of an existing agreement, the exercise of this power will constitute a breach of contract.[4] This is so even though the articles at the time of his appointment provided that an "appointment shall be

---

[96] Directors' Remuneration: Report of a Study Group Chaired by Sir Richard Greenbury, 1995.

[97] Paras. 16.11(f) and 12.43(x)(vii). The latter applies also to "provisions for pre-determined compensation on termination which exceeds one year's salary and benefits in kind". The Act requires details to be given of amounts paid to directors as compensation for loss of office (see Sched.6, para. 8) but that occurs only after the removal from office has taken place.

[98] Report of the Committee on the Financial Aspects of Corporate Governance, 1992, which recommended in para. 4.41 that shareholders' approval be required in the case of contracts for three years or more.

[99] This Committee stated: "There is a strong case for setting notice or contract periods at, or reducing them to, one year or less." (Code of Best Practice, D2). However, initial research suggests that "only 15 per cent of companies have put all their executive directors on contracts running for one year or less" (*Financial Times*, May 7, 1996, reporting research by Arthur Andersen. See also *ibid.*, March 3, 1997, reporting research by Pirc.)

[1] Chap. 6 at pp. 115 *et seq.*

[2] For the complications which are liable to occur in the latter event, see *James v. Kent* [1951] 1 K.B. 551, C.A., and *Pocock v. A.D.A.C. Ltd* [1952] 1 All E.R. 294n.

[3] Even then, the alteration will normally operate only for the future: *Swabey v. Port Darwin Gold Mining Co.* (1889) 1 Meg. 385, C.A.; *Bailey v. Medical Defence Union* (1995) 18 ACSR 521 (H. Ct. Australia).

[4] *Southern Foundries v. Shirlaw* [1940] A.C. 701, H.L.; *Shindler v. Northern Raincoat Co. Ltd* [1960] 1 W.L.R. 1038 (Diplock J.). In the light of the observations in the earlier case it seems that the court will not grant an injunction to restrain the alteration of the articles. See further Chap. 26 at pp. 727–732, below.

automatically determined if he ceases from any cause to be a director'', since, on an appointment for a given period, there is an implied undertaking that the company will not during that period revoke his appointment as director. If, however, the director's contract does not contain any provisions about its duration and the articles of association at the time of his appointment provide that it shall cease automatically on his ceasing to be a director, it appears from the decision of the Court of Appeal in *Read v. Astoria Garage (Streatham) Ltd*,[5] that on his ceasing to be a director from any cause his contract will also be terminated without that being a breach of contract. Accordingly it would seem that the company in such circumstances can sack a managing director (without breaking the contract) by dismissing him as a director under section 303 (or under any other power in the articles) and that he can resign his directorship and then walk out without any period of notice—a surprising result. As stated, this difficulty can be dealt with by the director entering into a fixed-term service contract with the company, as is commonly done in large public companies. In any event, the current version of Table A (*Read* was decided under the 1929 version of Table A) attempts to remove the effect of that case. Although this provision is not free from difficulty,[6] it is submitted that its effect is that, although the appointment ceases if the director ceases to be a director, the contract with him is to be interpreted without any other reference to the article. Consequently, even if the contract is not one for a fixed term, it will nevertheless be lawfully terminable only on giving reasonable notice or the notice specified in the service agreement.

In fact, as the reports of the Cadbury and Greenbury Committees testify, at least in listed companies the current problem is perceived not to be that of the director who can be dismissed on a moment's notice without compensation, but rather that of the director with a long, perhaps also a rolling, fixed-term or with a contract of indefinite duration terminable only on very long notice,[7] whose dismissal will be very costly for the company even though his performance as director has been less than outstanding. It has yet to be seen whether the recommendations of these committees, both in relation to the termination of directors' service contracts and as to levels of directors' remuneration more generally, will be effective. In any event, it seems clear

---

[5] [1952] Ch. 637, C.A.
[6] These are discussed in the 5th edition of this book, at pp. 156–158, along with a comparison of the provisions of the versions of Table A from 1929, 1948 and 1985.
[7] In *Runciman v. Walter Runciman plc* [1992] BCLC 1084 the directors' service contracts required five years' notice for lawful termination, a provision which had been increased from three years in the face of the prospect of a takeover bid. On the potential conflicts of interest in the area of directors' remuneration see pp. 630–635, below.

that governmental plans in this area are at present confined to limited additional disclosure requirements for listed companies.[8]

Executive and non-executive directors

It will have been apparent from the foregoing that directors may be either non-executive or executive. The former are directors expected to do little or nothing other than to attend a reasonable number of board meetings and, perhaps, some of the committees that the board may establish.[9] As such they will be modestly rewarded by directors' fees resolved upon by the company in general meeting.[10] Executive directors are those who, in addition to their roles as directors, hold some executive or managerial position to which, as we have seen, they are appointed by the board, which will determine their emoluments and "perks".[11] Between them and the company there must therefore be some sort of contract although, even in the case of public companies, it may be no more formal than a board resolution communicated to the director or an exchange of letters. In the case of small private companies (quasi-partnerships) there may well be nothing in writing at all; the member directors will work out what each is to do and decide from time to time how much the company can afford to pay and how it should be divided between them.

The top executive directors are the managing director or directors. In the case of public companies, however, the growing practice is not to call all of them "managing directors" but to describe one as "Chief Executive",[12] a description frequently preceded by "Chairman and" (unless the board elects a non-executive director as its chairman). This is a development with which draftsmen of Table A have not caught up. And indeed it is rare to find any reference in articles to a "chief executive"; the assumption is that a power to appoint a managing director includes a power to call him or her a chief executive instead.

Public companies generally have both executive and non-executive directors and are encouraged to have a reasonable proportion of the latter. Indeed, one of the central aims of the Cadbury Committee[13] was to strengthen the influence of non-executive directors on the boards of

---

[8] DTI, *The Company Accounts (Disclosure of Directors' Emoluments) Regulations 1996: A Consultative Document*, January 1996. See further below, p. 632, n. 97.
[9] The articles invariably make provision for delegation to committees: see Table A 1985, art. 72.
[10] *ibid.*, art. 82.
[11] *ibid.*, art. 87. It was held in *Re Richmond Gate Property Co.* [1965] 1 W.L.R. 335 that in the absence of a determination there can be no claim on a *quantum meruit*. But see (1965) 28 M.L.R. 347 and (1966) 29 M.L.R. 608.
[12] The practice in the USA is to call him the "President" but in the U.K. this title does not imply any executive responsibilities but is sometimes conferred as an honorary title on a retiring chief executive.
[13] Above, n. 98.

listed companies. Although the Code of Best Practice, which accompanied its report, did not unequivocally recommend the division of the positions of chairman of the board and chief executive (with a non-executive director taking the former role) it did require "a clearly accepted division of responsibilities at the head of a company, which will ensure a balance of power and authority, such that no one individual has unfettered powers of decision" (paragraph 1.2). It also made recommendations to increase the number, quality and independence from executive management of non-executive directors generally ("The board should include non-executive directors of sufficient calibre and number for their views to carry significant weight in the board's decisions": paragraph 1.3). They should play an especially important part in the areas of executive director remuneration (there should be a remuneration committee made up "wholly or mainly" of non-executives: paragraph 3.3) and auditing (an audit committee should be established "of at least 3 non-executive directors": paragraph 4.3). Many companies have implemented these structural changes[14] but remains unclear what impact there has been on the quality of board decision-making. There seems to have been no downward pressure on executive remuneration, perhaps not surprisingly in view of the fact that many non-executive directors are executive directors of other companies and so could be expected to share a culture of high rewards for executives. More generally, their position can be somewhat individious since the executive directors will inevitably know so much more about the company's business. Hence effective non-executives are difficult to find[15] though some worthy souls collect an ever-increasing number of such directorships, often, apparently, without regard to the possibility that there must be some limit to the number in which any man or woman can be really effective.

A question which sometimes arises is whether it is permissible for the board to give contracts to non-executive directors providing emoluments additional to their fees. The answer seems to be that if the director is not intended to undertake any work for the company other than to perform the modest role for which the company has elected him, it cannot be justified as a bona fide exercise of the board's business judgment but will be an improper device to entrench the director[16] or to pay him more than the fees that the general meeting has resolved upon for that work. If, however, he is to "undertake any

---

[14] Listed companies incorporated in the U.K. are now required by the *Listing Rules*, para. 12.43(j), to report on the extent of their compliance with most aspects of the Cadbury Code, and to "give reasons for any non-compliance". Interestingly, companies are not required to report on their compliance with the recommendation that directors' service contracts should not exceed three years without shareholder approval. See above, p. 191.

[15] Inspired by the Bank of England, an organisation, PRONED (an acronym for "promotion of non-executive directorships") has been set up to help find them.

[16] See further, Chap. 22 at pp. 605–608, below.

services outside the scope of the ordinary duties of a director",[17] (for example, to be the board's chairman or deputy chairman or to act as a consultant in matters in which he has particular expertise albeit without becoming a full-time or part-time executive) that seems unobjectionable (as article 84 of Table A 1985 implies) unless the articles otherwise provide.

However, directors, like trustees, are not entitled to any remuneration unless the articles or a resolution of the company provides for it (as the articles always do except in the case of charitable companies) and the provisions of the articles must be strictly observed. Thus when a director with special expertise was appointed a member of a committee of the directors to act for the company in connection with a takeover and the committee agreed to his receiving additional remuneration on terms which enabled him to claim and be paid £5.2 million, it was held[18] that he had to return it to the company. Under the relevant articles, special remuneration could be granted only by the full board. Nor was he entitled to be paid anything on a *quantum meruit* or otherwise since that would conflict with the articles.[19]

Exercise of directors' powers

Where powers are conferred on the directors under articles such as those considered above in the Tables A, they are conferred upon the directors collectively as a board. Prima facie, therefore, they can be exercised only at a board meeting of which due notice has been given and at which a quorum is present. In contrast with general meetings, where the procedure is laid down in some detail,[20] directors are normally left very much to settle their own procedure.[21] But, unless the regulations provide to the contrary, due notice must be given to all of them and a quorum must be present at a meeting[22] which must be convened as such. Notice here merely means reasonable notice having regard to the practice of the company,[23] and if all in fact meet without notice they may waive this requirement if they wish, but are not bound to do so.[24] And although majority decision prevails, a meeting of the

---

[17] Table A 1985, art. 84 above.
[18] *Guinness plc v. Saunders* [1990] 2 A. C. 663, H. L.
[19] See further on this case, Chap. 22 at pp. 612–615, below.
[20] Chap. 21, below.
[21] See Table A 1985, arts. 88–98
[22] It seems clear that this does not necessarily involve meeting under one roof so long as they can discuss and vote: *Byng v. London Life Association Ltd* [1990] 1 Ch. 170, C.A. (see below Chap. 21, pp. 591–594) which related to a general meeting. With the aid of modern technology a meeting is possible despite the fact that physically the "meeters" are far apart. Nevertheless, articles commonly provide that notice of meetings need not be given to a director who is absent from the U.K.: Table A 1985, art. 88.
[23] *Browne v. La Trinidad* (1887) 37 Ch.D. 1, C.A. If the practice is for the directors to meet at fixed times, further notice may be unnecessary.
[24] *Barron v. Potter* [1914] 1 Ch. 895.

majority without notice to the minority is ineffective, for it could be
that the persuasive oratory of the minority would have induced the
majority to change their minds.[25] But if all are agreed, a meeting may
be a waste of time and hence it is usual to provide that a resolution in
writing signed by all the directors shall be as valid and effectual as if
it had been duly passed at a meeting.[26]

It follows that prima facie neither an individual director nor any
group of directors has any powers conferred on him or them. It seems
that in the absence of an express authorisation in the articles or other
appropriate constitutional document the board will not be entitled to
delegate such powers.[27] Nor will the individual director, even a managing director, have any powers unless and to the extent that the board
has exercised its authority to delegate.[28] The board will, of course, be
able to appoint executive agents or servants[29] of the company but must
not delegate the exercise of its discretion. Although it is very doubtful
whether the board of a registered company ought any longer to be
regarded as a delegate, nevertheless, the maxim *delegatus non potest
delegare* is regarded as applying.[30]

Today, in the case of public companies it is normally the executive
directors who manage the business of the company, with the board as
a whole exercising only a supervisory role. To some extent, therefore,
the practice of English public companies resembles that of continental
companies with two-tier boards—despite the hostility which the
English business world customarily displays towards the suggested
introduction of the two-tier system. This tendency has been intensified
by the Cadbury Committee's emphasis on the supervisory role of non-
executive directors. There are, however, major differences. Under the
continental system there is no overlapping membership of the supervisory board and the management board. In contrast, in England executives on the unitary board (even after Cadbury) normally outnumber
the non-executives and, even if they do not, tend to dominate it
because of their closer acquaintance with the company's affairs. Moreover, the division of powers between the various organs of the company is left to be determined not by the law but by provisions in the
articles of association and by the extent and terms of the delegation
to executives which the board has chosen to make. Hence there is
nothing in the law which ensures that the board holds the whiphand

---

[25] *Per* Jessel M.R. in *Barber's Case* (1877) 5 Ch. D. 963, C.A., at 968; and see *Re Portu-
guese Consolidated Copper Mines* (1889) 42 Ch. D. 160, C.A.

[26] Table A, 1985, art. 93.

[27] *Cartmell's Case* (1874) L. R. 9 Ch.App. 691.

[28] *Breckland Group Holdings Ltd v. London and Suffolk Properties Ltd* [1989] BCLC 100;
Mitchell & Hobbs (UK) Ltd v. Mill [1996] 2 BCLC 102.

[29] But it seems that in the absence of an express power (which the articles invariably confer)
one of the directors must not be appointed: *Kerr. v. Marine Products* (1928) 44 T.L.R. 292.

[30] By contrast, in the USA the board of directors is generally regarded as possessing original
and undelegated powers, which are capable of delegation.

over the executives. The Cadbury Committee recommended that there should be "a formal schedule of matters specifically reserved to it for decision to ensure that the direction and control of the company is firmly in its hands",[31] but that is not a requirement of the law. Admittedly, it is still customary for the terms of appointment, even of chief executives and managing directors, to provide that they shall perform such duties and exercise such powers as from time to time are assigned to them by the board. When that is so, the board can maintain a firm grip on them and curtail the range of their activities as it sees fit. But Table A articles[32] expressly permit delegation "either collaterally with or to the exclusion of their own powers." If the delegation was made to the exclusion of the board's own powers, until it was revoked[33] the effect quite clearly ought to be that both the board, in respect of its residual powers not delegated and the executive director should be treated as primary organs of the company. But, as we shall see from the next chapter, although the courts are prepared to recognise that executives may be organs rather than mere agents,[34] the legislature is not.[35]

The company secretary

A word must be said about another important officer of the company—the secretary.[36] Speaking generally the secretary's functions are purely ministerial and administrative and he is not, as secretary, charged with the exercise of any managerial powers. As was said in one case[37]:

"So far as the position of a secretary as such is concerned, it is established beyond all question that a secretary, while performing the duties appropriate to the office of secretary, is not concerned in the management of the company. Equally I think he is not concerned in carrying on the business of the company."

On the other hand it is he that will be charged with the primary responsibility of ensuring that the documentation of the company is in order, that the requisite returns are made to Companies' House, and

---

[31] Code of Best Practice, above p. 193, para. 1.4.

[32] Table A, 1948, art. 109; Table A 1985, art. 72.

[33] Table A expressly recognises that the delegation may be revoked by the board but, even if the relevant articles did not, it would be implicit in the general delegation of the company's powers to the board. The revocation might, however, be a breach of the executive's contract: see above. And query what the position would be if the powers exclusively sub-delegated included those to appoint and dismiss executives.

[34] pp. 230 *et seq.*, below.

[35] p. 232, below.

[36] The position of another important official—the auditor—is discussed in Chap. 20, below.

[37] *Per* Pennycuick V.C. in *Re Maidstone Buildings Provisions Ltd* [1971] 1 W.L.R. 1085 at 1092.

that the company's registers are properly maintained.[38] Moreover, it is he that will in practice be referred to in order to obtain authenticated copies of contracts and resolutions decided upon by the board, and the articles will generally provide that he is one of those in whose presence the company's seal (if it has one) is to be affixed to documents.[39]

The Act provides that every registered company must have a secretary who must not be the sole director.[40] It also provides that anything required to be done by a director and the secretary shall not be done by the same person acting as both.[41] But the secretary can be appointed with less formality than a director; the appointment will be made by the board—not by the general meeting—and any officer of the company may be authorised by the board to act in the absence of a formally appointed secretary.[42] Further it has been recognised that those dealing with the company will be concerned to know who the secretary is, and hence the register of directors has been expanded into a register of directors and secretaries. Copies of the particulars in this register must be filed at Companies' House and are available for inspection by the public both there and at the company's office.[43]

As a result of back-bench pressure, a new provision was inserted in the 1980 Act requiring qualifications for secretaries of public companies. This is now section 286 of the 1985 Act, which provides that it is the duty of directors to take all reasonable steps to secure that the secretary or each joint secretary of such a company "is a person who appears to them to have the requisite knowledge and experience to discharge the functions of secretary of the company" and who, in addition, fulfils requirements regarding previous experience or membership of specified professions or professional bodies.

Although all this amounts to little more than saying that the directors should not appoint someone unless they think he is capable of undertaking the task, it is interesting as a further recognition of the rising professional status of the secretary—and renders it still more anomalous that no qualifications are required of directors (an anomaly of which the Institute of Directors is very conscious). Despite this statutory recognition of the increasingly important status of the secretary the courts until recently continued to treat him as a subordinate servant, without ostensible authority to commit the company by his actions apart from such matters as the engagement of clerical staff. However, in *Panorama Developments (Guildford) Ltd v. Fidelis Furnishing Fabrics Ltd*,[44] the Court of Appeal held the defendant com-

---

[38] Sometimes a separate professional firm is appointed to act as registrar to maintain the registers of members and debenture-holders.

[39] Table A 1985, art. 101. Generally, too, he will be authorised to countersign cheques.

[40] s.283(1) and (2).

[41] s.284.

[42] s.283(3).

[43] ss.288 and 290.

[44] [1971] 2 Q.B. 711, C.A.

pany liable to a car hire company where the secretary had fraudulently ordered self-drive cars for his own use but ostensibly for the business purposes of his employers. In the words of Lord Denning M.R.[45]:

"But times have changed. A company secretary is a much more important person nowadays than he was in 1887.[46] He is an officer of the company with extensive duties and responsibilities. This appears not only in the modern Companies Acts, but also by the role which he plays in the day-to-day business of companies. He is no longer a mere clerk. He regularly makes representations on behalf of the company and enters into contracts on its behalf which come within the day-to-day running of the company's business. So much so that he may be regarded as held out as having authority to do such things on behalf of the company. He is certainly entitled to sign contracts connected with the administrative side of a company's affairs, such as employing staff, and ordering cars and so forth. All such matters now come within the ostensible authority of a company's secretary."

It is arguable, therefore, that the secretary has also graduated as an organ of the company; he is an officer of the company with substantial authority in the administrative sphere and with powers and duties derived directly from the articles and the Companies Act. And in the performance of his statutory duties he is clearly entitled to resist interference from the members, board of directors or managing director. Where he differs from them is that he has no responsibility for corporate policy, as opposed to playing an administrative role in ensuring that the policy decisions are implemented.

Organs of ailing companies

Since the aim of this book is to deal primarily with healthy, rather than sick, companies, this chapter has concentrated on the organs of a company while it remains a solvent going concern. When, however, it has become insolvent or needs for some other reason to cease business, the organs described above are likely to be largely superseded by another organ—an administrative receiver,[47] an administrator[48] or a liquidator.

A description of these "crisis organs" (to coin a collective description) is left to later chapters.[49] Here it suffices to say that, when any of them is appointed, the management of the company's business vests in him and is carried on for the following purposes: in the case

---

[45] At 716–717.

[46] The reference is to *Barnett, Hoares and Co. v. South London Tramways Co.* (1887) 18 Q.B.D. 815, in which Lord Esher M.R. said: "A secretary is a mere servant; his position is that he is to do what he is told, and no person can assume that he has any authority to represent anything at all . . ."

[47] The new description given to a "receiver and manager" by the Insolvency Act 1986, Part III.

[48] A new type of officer introduced by the Insolvency Act, Part II.

[49] In the case of administrative receivers, to Chap. 15 dealing with Company Charges and in the case of administrators and liquidators to Chap. 30.

of an administrative receiver, to realise the appointing creditor's charge over the company's undertaking and assets; in the case of an administrator, to restore, if possible, the company's fortunes and to avoid its liquidation; and, in the case of the liquidator, to achieve an orderly winding up. In each case the role of the board of directors (and of any executive directors if their services are retained) will cease to be dominant and will generally be vestigial. The role of the general meeting, too, will alter and, except in the case of a member's voluntary liquidation, will be greatly reduced.

The position of the crisis organs differs from that of the normal organs in another important respect. As we have seen, the method of appointment and the powers of the latter depend on the company's memorandum and articles and on resolutions of the general meeting and of the board of directors,[50] rather than on statutory provisions. In contrast, the position in these respects of the crisis organs depends on statutory provisions[51]; exclusively in relation to administrators and liquidators and largely in relation to administrative receivers.[52]

---

[50] The Second Company Law Directive (which we purported to implement in 1980) required in its Art. 2.d that the constitution of a public limited company with a share capital shall give information concerning the "allocation of powers" among the company's organs in so far as that is not "legally determined." It is difficult to see how perusal of U.K. memoranda and articles is likely to give that information.

[51] And, of course, on reported decisions interpreting those provisions.

[52] In relation to an administrative receiver it depends also on the terms of the instrument under which he is appointed.

CHAPTER 10

AGENCY AND ULTRA VIRES

As pointed out in the previous Chapter, one consequence of the artificial nature of a company as a legal person is that inevitably decisions for, and actions by, it have to be taken for it by natural persons. Decisions on its behalf may be taken either (a) by its primary organs (the board of directors or the members in general meeting) or (b) by officers, agents or servants of the company; acts done on its behalf will perforce be by (b). In either event a question may arise as to whether the decisions or acts have been taken or done in such a way that they can be attributed to the company. Similar problems of attribution arise where the question is simply whether the company "knew" about a certain fact or situation: whose knowledge in which circumstances should be attributed to the company?

As far as third parties are concerned, the answer to these questions depends upon the normal principles of vicarious liability and agency, which it is not the purpose of this book to expound in detail. The relevant principles can be summarised as follows:

(i) A principal is bound by the transactions on his behalf of his agents or servants if the latter acted within either
   (a) the actual scope of the authority conferred upon them by their principal prior to the transaction or by subsequent ratification[1]; or
   (b) the apparent (or ostensible) scope of their authority.[2]
(ii) A principal, *qua* employer, may also be vicariously liable in tort for acts of his employees which, though not authorised, are

---

[1] Actual authority may be conferred expressly or impliedly. Authority to perform acts which are reasonably incidental to the proper performance of an agents' duties will be implied unless expressly excluded and an agent who, on previous occasions, has been allowed to exceed the actual authority originally conferred upon him may thereby have acquired actual authority to continue so to act. Ratification of a contract entered into by an agent in excess of his authority enables the principal to sue the other party if the agent had disclosed that he was acting for an identifiable principal.

[2] This consists of (i) the authority which a person in his position and in the type of business concerned can reasonably be expected to have and (ii) the authority which the particular agent has been held out by the principal as having unless, in either case, the other party knows or ought to have known that the agent was not actually authorised. The liability of the principal in both cases rests on estoppel; but in case (ii) the principal cannot be estopped unless the other party knows that the agent is acting as agent whereas in case (i) the other party may believe the agent to be the proprietor of the business and the principal, having allowed him to appear as such, is estopped from denying his power so to act: see *Watteau v. Fenwick* [1893] 2 Q.B. 346.

nevertheless within the scope of their employment but, in general, is not criminally liable for their acts.[3]

Obviously, application of these principles is more complicated when the principal is a body corporate which cannot confer authority on agents or servants except through the action of natural persons who constitute its organs or agents. But to those inevitable complications English company law added others which were not inevitable. Happily, two of these additional complications have now been largely removed as a result of the Companies Act 1989. Unhappily, however, they cannot be wholly ignored mainly because the new statutory provisions cannot be properly understood without an appreciation of the earlier position with which those provisions had to deal. Nevertheless they can now be disposed of relatively briefly.

ULTRA VIRES

The first of the two former complications was the *ultra vires* doctrine in its relation to companies. *Ultra vires* is a Latin expression which lawyers and civil servants use to describe acts undertaken beyond (*ultra*) the legal powers (*vires*) of those who have purported to undertake them. In this sense its application extends over a far wider area than company law. For example, those advising a Minister on proposed subordinate legislation will have to ask themselves whether the enabling primary legislation confers *vires* to make the desired regulations.

In its application to bodies of persons, *ultra vires* is habitually used in three different senses which ought to be kept distinct. When used in the strict sense, essentially what is in question is whether the body as such has capacity to act. Unless the body is incorporated, and thus has a personality distinct from its members, this question will normally not arise; the body is simply an association of human beings all or most of whom will have full capacity. Hence *ultra vires* in this sense does not arise in relation to partnerships. And the early case of *Sutton's Hospital*[4] is generally taken to have established that it also has no application to chartered corporations despite the fact that they do have a legal personality distinct from that of their members.[5] In these cases

---

[3] Unless he has initiated, or participated in, the crime.

[4] (1612) 10 Co. Rep. 1a. 23a.

[5] See *British South Africa Co. v. De Beers* [1910] 1 Ch. 354, C.A.; *Bonanza Creek Gold Mining Co. v. R.* [1916] 1 A.C. 566, P.C.; *Jenkin v. Pharmaceutical Society* [1921] 1 Ch. 392; *Pharmaceutical Society v. Dickson* [1970] A.C. 403, H.L. The Att.-Gen. may take proceedings to restrain it from abusing its charter or for forfeiture of the charter if it exceeds the objects for which it was chartered; meanwhile its acts remain fully effective. But the strict *ultra vires* doctrine applies if the charter is granted under statutory powers which restrict the activities which the corporation may carry on: *Hazell v. Hammersmith & Fulham L.B.C.* [1990] 2 Q.B. 697, C.A.; [1991] 2 W.L.R. 372, H.L. and cases there cited. Anomalously the

the only question is whether those who have acted are deemed to be authorised to do so in accordance with the normal agency principles summarised above. Nevertheless, it is customary to say that when those so acting (for example, the governing body) have exceeded their authority they have acted *ultra vires*. Thirdly, the courts have an unfortunate habit of describing as *ultra vires* any activity which a company cannot lawfully undertake (for example one which infringes the capital maintenance provisions dealt with in Chapters 11 and 12.

It was not until the latter part of the nineteenth century that it was clearly established that the strict type of *ultra vires* applied to companies. Until 1844 the most common type of company—the deed of settlement company—had no corporate personality; that was enjoyed only by chartered companies (to which the strict doctrine did not apply) and by companies directly incorporated by statute (a rare breed until the railway boom). After the Joint Stock Companies Act 1856, deed of settlement companies became superseded by registered incorporated companies with limited liability and memoranda of association which had to specify their objects.[6] Only then were the courts forced to decide whether or not the *ultra vires* doctrine applied. And in the landmark decision in *Ashbury Carriage Company v. Riche*[7] the House of Lords finally decided that it did. If a company, incorporated by or under a statute, acted beyond the scope of the objects stated in the statute or in its memorandum of association, such acts were void as beyond the company's capacity even if ratified by all the members. The House, mindful no doubt of the abuses that had occurred at the time of the South Sea Bubble, thought that the decision would not only prevent trafficking in company registrations but would afford some protection to members and creditors who had to face the risk of loss if the company became insolvent in the course of its known and declared business but should not have to face the risk that it might embark on wholly different activities.

It was not, however, a decision that proved popular with the business world which, with the aid of its advisers, sought means of circumventing it. This was done by ensuring that the objects clauses of memoranda of association did not follow the succinct models in the Tables to successive Companies Acts but instead specified a profusion of all the objects and powers[8] that the ingenuity of their advisers could

---

doctrine applies to trade unions although they are not incorporated: see *Taylor v. N.U.M.* (1985) 14 I.R.L.R. 99: and Wedderburn (1985) 14 I.L.J. at 127–129.

[6] See Chap. 3, above.

[7] (1875) L.R. 7 H.L. 653. In relation to statutory companies it had become generally accepted that the *ultra vires* rule applied but that all the members could effectively ratify an *ultra vires* act. Shortly afterwards it was decided that they could not: *Att.-Gen. v. Great Eastern Railway* (1880) 5 App.Cas. 473, H.L.; *Baroness Wenlock v. River Dee Co.* (1885) 10 App.Cas. 354, H.L.

[8] The model memoranda in the Tables show that it had not been the intention that powers should be specified and the House of Lords in *Att.-Gen. v. Great Eastern Railway*, above, held that every ancillary power reasonably incidental to the specified objects was to be implied.

dream up. The courts sought to narrow the scope of the resulting *vires* by distinguishing between "objects" (in the sense of types of business) and "powers" and, applying the *ejusdem generis* rule of construction, ruling that the powers could be used only in relation to the objects. But that too was circumvented by the device of ending the "objects" clause by stating that each of the specified objects or powers should be treated as independent and in no way ancillary or subordinate one to another,[9] and, at a later date, by also inserting a power "to carry on any other trade or business whatsoever which can, in the opinion of the board of directors, be advantageously carried on by the company in connection with or as ancillary to any of the above businesses or the general business of the company . . ."[10]

The result of these devices was to destroy any value that the *ultra vires* doctrine might have had as a protection for members or creditors; it had become instead merely a nuisance to the company and a trap for unwary third parties. The nuisance to the company was reduced somewhat when the Companies Act 1948 made it possible for objects clauses to be altered without the need to obtain the court's consent.[11] But all too often companies launched into new lines of business without realising that changes in their objects clauses were needed and, as a result, wholly innocent people who had granted them credit might find themselves without a remedy.[12] So might the company on contracts which it had entered into, for, as a crowning absurdity, it seems that, such contracts being void, in contrast with the normal rules in cases of incapacity not only could the incapable company not be sued but it could not sue the other party.[13]

---

[9] The House of Lords in *Cotman v. Brougham* [1918] A.C. 514 felt reluctantly compelled to uphold the validity of such a provision, with the result that it was held to be *intra vires* for a rubber company to underwrite an issue of shares of an oil company by virtue of an "independent" general power to underwrite securities. But as recently as 1969 it was held by the C.A. that whatever the memorandum might say a power to borrow could not be treated as an independent object: *Introductions Ltd v. National Provincial Bank* [1970] Ch. 199, C.A. which concerned a company incorporated at the time of the Festival of Britain in 1951, with the object of providing foreign visitors with accomodation and entertainment but which later devoted itself solely to pig-breeding (an activity which those who drafted its memorandum had not foreseen) and granted its bank a debenture to secure the substantial overdraft which built up prior to its insolvent liquidation. It was held to have acted *ultra vires* so that the bank could not enforce the debenture or claim in liquidation.

[10] A provision upheld in *Bell Houses Ltd v. City Wall Properties Ltd* [1966] 2 Q.B. 656, C.A. See also *Newstead v. Frost* [1980] 1 W.L.R. 135, H.L., where the company had a general object "To carry on business as bankers, capitalists, financiers, concessionaires and transactions as an individual capitalist may lawfully undertake and carry out." It was held that this made it *intra vires* to enter into a partnership with Mr David Frost which minimised his U.K. tax on earnings in the USA.

[11] Prior to that Act the objects clause could be altered for one or more of seven specific reasons by a special resolution subject to its confirmation by the court. Thereafter confirmation by the court was not needed unless dissenting members petitioned within 21 days.

[12] See, *e.g. Introductions Ltd v. National Provincial Bank*, above, and *Re Jon Beauforte (London) Ltd* [1953] Ch. 131.

[13] See *Bell Houses Ltd v. City Wall Properties Ltd* at first instance [1966] 1 Q.B. 207 and the discussion by the C.A. at [1966] 2 Q.B. at 693, 694.

Moreover, the legal position became still more confused because courts failed to draw a clear distinction between strict *ultra vires* (in the sense of the company's lack of capacity) and illegality or lack of authority of the company's officers or agents. Moreover, they held that an activity not bona fide designed to enhance the financial prosperity of the company would necessarily be *ultra vires*: "charity", it was said, "cannot sit at the boardroom table" and "there are to be no cakes and ale except for the benefit of the company".[14] This did not necessarily ban charitable (or, indeed, political) donations or the grant of pensions to retired employees; while the company remained a going concern all that might well be good for business.[15] But in *Parke v. Daily News*,[16] it was held that to use the proceeds of sale of the defunct *News Chronicle* and *Star* newspapers to compensate employees who lost their jobs was *ultra vires* since the company's business had ended. This led to an outcry and belatedly to legislative action on this particular point.[17] But the general confusion continued, until later decisions[18] narrowed the formerly perceived scope of *ultra vires* and showed that many of the cases which had been decided on the assumption that they raised that issue should have been decided as involving only excess of the directors' authority or breach of their duty to act bona fide in the interests of the company.[19]

A further complication was that although *ultra vires* transactions were said to be void, the question whether a third party was affected by the voidness depended in some circumstances on the state of his knowledge. This, though perhaps difficult to justify in principle, was eminently reasonable. If, for example, a company had power to borrow or to buy office furniture (as almost every company has, expressly or by implication) a third party cannot be expected to check that the money or furniture is to be used by the company for an *intra vires*

---

[14] *Hutton v. W. Cork Ry* (1883) 23 Ch.D. 654, C.A., *per* Bowen L.J. at 673.
[15] *Evans v. Brunner Mond & Co.* [1921] 1 Ch. 359; *Re Lee Behrens & Co.* [1932] 2 Ch. 927.
[16] [1962] Ch. 927.
[17] Companies Act 1980, s.74. Now 1985 Act, s.719 and Insolvency Act 1986, s.187: see pp. 219–220, below.
[18] *Charterbridge Corporation Ltd v. Lloyds Bank* [1970] Ch. 62; *Re Halt Garage Ltd* [1982] 3 All E.R. 1016; *Re Horsley & Weight Ltd* [1982] Ch. 442, C.A.; *Rolled Steel Ltd v. British Steel Corp.* [1986] Ch. 246, C.A.; *Brady v. Brady* [1988] BCLC 20, C.A., revd. [1989] A.C. 755, H.L. They established, it is thought, that (i) *ultra vires* should be restricted to the question whether the company has acted within its capacity, (ii) this depended solely on the construction of its objects clause, (iii) if it had acted within those objects and the express and implied powers, the act was *intra vires*, whether or not it was done bona fide for the benefit of the company and for a proper purpose (that was relevant only in connection with the related question of whether the organ which acted for it had authority to do so) (iv) an exercise of an express power could never be *ultra vires* unless, perhaps, the power was not stated to be an independent object, and its exercise was undertaken in pursuance of activity beyond its objects.
[19] Yet, despite the exhortations of the C.A. in *Rolled Steel* (see *per* Browne-Wilkinson L.J. at [1986] Ch. at 302G–303A), the courts are still apt to describe unlawful reductions of capital as *ultra vires* the company: see, *e.g. Aveling Barford Ltd v. Perion Ltd* [1989] BCLC 626 at 631b.

object. But, unfortunately, the protection thus afforded was often illusory. This was because of the second of the, now discarded, complications which the courts introduced.

CONSTRUCTIVE NOTICE

This second rule, established even before the strict *ultra vires* doctrine was held to apply, was that anyone dealing with a registered company was deemed to have notice of the contents of its "public documents." Precisely what that included was never wholly clear[20] but it certainly included the memorandum and articles of association,[21] thus introducing a further distinction between partnerships and companies. It meant that anyone having dealings with a company was deemed to have knowledge of the contents of its objects clause. In *Re Jon Beauforte (London) Ltd*[22] (where the insolvent company's stated objects were to manufacture dresses but it had for some time instead been making veneered panels) a combination of actual knowledge of the business being carried on by the company and of constructive notice of its stated objects resulted in all but one of its creditors' claims being *ultra vires*. Even the claim of the supplier of heating fuel, who argued that this would have been needed whatever the company's business, was met by the answer that he had actual knowledge of the present nature of the business, since the fuel had been ordered on the company's notepaper which described it was "veneered panel manufacturers", and constructive knowledge that this was *ultra vires*! The result, therefore, of this constructive notice rule was that where the businesses being carried on by the company were known to the third party and, whether he actually knew it or not, were *ultra vires*, he would be unable to sue the company. And, as already pointed out, nor, it seems, would the company be able to sue him. The only remedy of either would be to recover money or property paid or transferred under the void transaction to the extent to which it was possible to trace it[23] or, in the case of a lender, to be subrogated to the claims of *intra vires* creditors to the extent that this money had been used to pay them.[24]

---

[20] Presumably one was not deemed to have knowledge of everything in the annual returns that companies have to file at Comapnies House.

[21] *Royal British Bank v. Turquand* (1856) 6 E. & B. 327, Exch.Ch.; *Ernest v. Nicholls* (1857) 6 H.L.C. 401, H.L.

[22] [1953] Ch. 131. Some of the creditors had in fact obtained judgments against the company in default of appearance or by consent but this did not avail them since the courts had not specifically adjudicated on the *ultra vires* issue and nor had there been any bona fide compromise on that issue.

[23] Either in law or in equity: see *Sinclair v. Brougham* [1914] A.C. 398, H.L.; *Re Diplock* [1948] Ch. 465, C.A. affd. *sub nom. Minister of Health v. Simpson* [1951] A.C. 251; and the helpful discussion in *Agip (Africa) Ltd v. Jackson* [1991] Ch. 547, C.A.

[24] *Sinclair v. Brougham*, above: *Re Airdale Co-op. Worsted Society* [1933] 1 Ch. 639. The difficulties that could be faced by a liquidator of a company, particularly if it had carried on both *intra* and *ultra vires* businesses, were horrendous.

In relation to *ultra vires*, improperly so called, where the directors or other organs or agents of the company acted beyond their authority, the effect of the constructive notice rule was mitigated by yet another refinement of normal agency principles. Under the so-called rule in *Royal British Bank v. Turquand* (on which see more below), although those dealing with a company were deemed to have notice of the contents of its memorandum and articles, they were not required to satisfy themselves that all the internal regulations set out therein had been complied with. This, however, was no help when the transaction was beyond the company's capacity.

The 1972 reforms

That the strict *ultra vires* doctrine in relation to companies should be abolished had long been recognised. But we made very heavy weather of doing so, partly because it took us long to recognise that it would do little good to abolish it unless we also abolished the constructive notice doctrine.[25] So long as that remained, the only consequence of abolishing *ultra vires* would be that, while transactions outside the company's stated objects and powers would not be void because of the company's incapacity, they would not bind the company, unless ratified by the company in general meeting, since they would be beyond the actual and apparent authority of the company's organ which acted on its behalf.

It was not until our entry into the European Community that we belatedly did anything effective and then only to the minimum extent thought necessary to comply with our obligations under the First Company Law Directive.

Section 9(1) of the European Communities Act 1972, later re-enacted as section 35 of the Companies Act 1985, attempted to dispose of all the problems posed in two short subsections, the first of which provided that, in favour of a person dealing with a company in good faith, any transaction decided on by the directors should be deemed to be within the capacity of the company and free from any limitations under the memorandum and articles on the directors' powers, and the second of which relieved the other party of any obligation to inquire about those matters.

Although this was a considerable step forward it was widely criticised as failing fully to implement the Directive and as leaving much to be desired on policy grounds. It covered only "transactions

---

[25] This was the excuse for not implementing, in 1948, the Cohen Committee's recommendation that, in favour of third parties, companies should have all the powers of a natural person; 1945 Cmd. 6659, para. 12. There was less excuse for not implementing those of the Jenkins Committee: 1962 Cmnd. 1749, paras. 35–42, which would have abolished constructive notice also.

decided on by the directors",[26] and protected only a third party
"dealing with the company in good faith".[27] And it did nothing to
protect the company against invocation of *ultra vires* by the other
party.[28] The few reported cases[29] on the section show that the courts
did their best to construe it sensibly and consonantly with the Directive, but it was recognised that more needed to be done. Hence, anticipating further company legislation in 1989, the Department of Trade
and Industry commissioned Professor Dan Prentice to undertake a
review of the position and to make recommendations. His report,
delivered in 1986, was circulated as a Consultative Document,[30] and
what the Department described as a "refined" (*i.e.* a more complicated but less far-reaching) version of his recommendations was
enacted in the Companies Act 1989.

The 1989 reforms
(a) *Objects clauses*

Professor Prentice had recommended that companies should be
afforded the capacity to do any act whatsoever and should have the
option of not stating their objects in their memoranda. Unfortunately
this straightforward solution was not adopted, notwithstanding the precedents for it in some other common law countries. Some of those
countries, however, were not subject to two complications which arose
here. First, our companies, as we have seen,[31] are not necessarily
"business corporations"; on the contrary most of those limited by
guarantee are formed to enable the advantages of corporate personality
and limited liability to be obtained by those undertaking activities
which are not the carrying on of business with a view of profit. Such
companies are entitled to dispense with "Ltd" as the suffix to their
names[32] and many of them are recognised, both by the Charity Com-

---

[26] Many, and in the case of public companies most, transactions will not in fact be decided on
by the board of directors. Art. 9.1 of the Directive (corresponding to s.35(1)) refers to "acts
done by the organs" and "organs" was certainly intended to cover more than the board of
directors. Moreover, Art. 9.2 further provides that: "The limits on the powers of the organs
of the company, arising under the statutes [*anglice* memorandum and articles] or from a
decision of the competent organs, may never be relied on as against third parties, even if they
have been disclosed."

[27] This expression had been deliberately omitted from the Directive because its meaning varied
between Member States.

[28] The Directive does not specifically deal with this point, presumably because prior to the entry
of the common law countries it did not occur to anyone concerned with the Directive that
any legal system could be so asinine as to allow a third party to invoke *ultra vires* against
the company.

[29] The main ones are: *International Sales & Agencies Ltd v. Marcus* [1982] 2 C.M.L.R. [1982]
3 All E.R. 551 (the former report is the better); *Barclay's Bank v. TOSG Trust Fund* [1984]
BCLC at 16–18 (the *ultra vires* point was not pursued on appeal: [1984] 2 W.L.R. 49, C.A.
and [1984] A.C. 626, H.L.); *T.C.B. Ltd v. Gray* [1986] Ch. 621 affd [1987] Ch. 458, C.A.

[30] *Reform of the Ultra Vires Rule: A Consultative Document*

[31] See Chap. 1, pp. 10–11, above.

[32] See Chap. 6, pp. 101–102, above.

mission and by the Inland Revenue, as charities. In all these cases the Department of Trade and Industry and, in the case of charities, the Charity Commission and the Inland Revenue, will need to be satisfied that they have stated objects and keep within them. But that need not have prevented the adoption of Professor Prentice's recommended solution which would have permitted companies to register objects if they wanted or needed to and which was expressly not intended to derogate in any way from the relevant authority's powers to intervene.[33]

The second complication (from which non-E.C. countries are free) was that the Second Company Law Directive requires that, in the case of public companies, the statutes or instruments of incorporation shall state the objects of the company.[34] But total abolition of limitations on capacity was in no way dependent on abolition of objects clauses and, if the Directive precluded the latter, it certainly did not preclude the former. In deciding not to go that far the Department may have been influenced by the argument that there are, obviously, certain acts, (*e.g.* marriage, the procreation of children and, according to a recent decision,[35] the driving of a lorry) which an artificial person is physically unable to do. But physical inability should not be confused with legal incapacity.

Whatever the reasons may have been, what the 1989 Act did[36] was rather different. First, without amending section 2 of the 1985 Act, which requires the objects of the company to be stated in its memorandum, it inserted a new section 3A providing (a) that a statement that the company's object is to carry on business as a "general commercial company" means that its object is to carry on any trade or business whatsoever, and (b) that then the company has "power to do all such things as are incidental or conducive to the carrying on of any trade or business by it". And secondly, it substituted a new section 4 providing simply that a company may, by special resolution, alter its memorandum with respect to the statement of the company's objects but that if an application is made under section 5 the alteration is not to have effect except in so far as it is confirmed by the court.

The object of section 3A is to encourage the use of simple general statements of objects. So far as objects in the sense of types of business are concerned, it may perhaps succeed in that aim in the case of some companies limited by shares[37] and it could be a boon to the marketers of shelf companies.[38] It is doubtful, however, whether it will lead to

---

[33] As the Charity Commission and the Inland Revenue manage to do when the charity is run by natural persons of full capacity under a trust instead of through a body corporate.

[34] Art. 2.1(*b*).

[35] *Richmond Borough Council v. Pinn & Wheeler Ltd* [1989] R.T.R. 354.

[36] By its s.110.

[37] It is wholly inappropriate for guarantee companies.

[38] On which see Chap. 6 at pp. 110–111, above.

the hoped-for disappearance of the present long list of what are really powers but which are stated to be independent objects. It seems more likely that, regrettably, the present practice will continue of naming certain businesses at the beginning of the objects clause, following that with a long list of specific "independent" powers,[39] and adding a general statement on the lines of section 3A(b)—perhaps expressing it subjectively (*i.e.* "all such powers as, *in the opinion of the directors*,[40] are incidental or conducive . . .") rather than objectively as the section does. If that fear proves well founded, objects clauses may become still longer.

The importance of the new section 4 is in what it omits, namely the former provision that alteration of the objects is to be for one or more of seven specified reasons only. That had long been a pretty ineffective restraint since it could be ignored unless there was a likelihood that there would be an application under section 5. That section remains unchanged[41] and entitles holders of 15 per cent of the company's issued share capital or any class of it or, if the company is not limited by shares, 15 per cent of the members[42] (provided in either case that they have not consented to, or voted for, the resolution[43]) to apply to the court within 21 days of the passing of the resolution which then does not take effect except to the extent that it is confirmed by the court.[44] Previously the court was constrained to refuse confirmation unless it was satisfied that the alteration could be justified under one of the seven reasons[45] and might refuse even if it was—though in that event it would be likely instead to exercise one of the wide powers given to it.[46] Now it has a discretion in all cases and, in the light of

---

[39] There is, however, a school of thought which argues that on the wording of s.3A a company cannot be a "general commercial company" unless that is stated as its sole object. If that is held to be correct, it is not likely to encourage the use of the section. Surely a company formed to acquire an existing business can state that as one of its objects as well as that of carrying on business as a general commercial company. And cannot it expressly exclude certain types of business?

[40] As in *Bell Houses Ltd* v. *City Wall Properties Ltd*, p. 204, n. 10, above.

[41] Notwithstanding that the anomalies in the section mentioned in nn. 42 and 43, below, were pointed out by the Jenkins Committee in 1962 with recommendations that they be removed: Cmnd. 1749, paras. 49(i) & (iii).

[42] Or a similar proportion of holders of debentures, secured by a floating charge first issued prior to December 1, 1947: s.5(2)(*b*) and (8). Notice of the proposed special resolution has to be given to such debenture holders: s.5(8); notice to the trustees for them will not do: *Re Hampstead Garden City Trust Ltd* [1962] Ch. 806. But anomalously, such notice does not have to be given to members without rights to attend and vote at the meeting so that they may not learn of the resolution until it is too late to exercise their right to apply to the court.

[43] This has the unfortunate effect that a nominee shareholder who has voted in favour on the instructions of some of his beneficiaries, but against on the instructions of others, cannot apply on behalf of the latter.

[44] s.4(2)

[45] *Re Hampstead Garden City Trust*, above.

[46] These include powers: to impose such terms and conditions as it sees fit and to adjourn in order that arrangements may be made to its satisfaction; to order the purchase of the interest of dissentients (s.5(4)); to provide for that purchase by the company, even if that involves a reduction of capital; to alter the memorandum and articles (s.5(5)); and to require the company

the statutory acceptance, by the new section 3A, of generalised objects clauses and the fact that the change will have been approved by the requisite three-fourths majority of those voting, the court is unlikely to refuse confirmation save in very exceptional circumstances. Under section 6 (also unchanged) the validity of the alteration cannot be challenged on any ground unless proceedings are taken, under the section or otherwise, within 21 days of the passing of the resolution.[47]

(b) *Virtual abolition of* ultra vires

Having thus attempted to simplify objects clauses (probably in vain) and (more successfully) to make it easier to alter them, the second step taken was to attempt to remove the consequences of exceeding any limitations on a company's capacity without actually admitting that it had full capacity. This the 1989 Act did[48] by substituting for the original section 35 of the 1985 Act new sections 35, 35A and 35B.

Subsection (1) of the new section 35 reads as follows:

"(1) The validity of an act done by a company shall not be called into question on the ground of lack of capacity by reason of anything in the company's memorandum."[49]

This is obviously an improvement on the former section 35(1). Unlike that, it deals discretely with the effects of lack of capacity instead of attempting, with confusing consequences, to deal in the same subsection also with acts in excess of directors' powers. It omits the former words "in favour of a person dealing with a company" and thereby does not merely remove the uncertainties flowing from "dealing with" but makes it clear that neither the company nor a third party can any longer invoke strict *ultra vires*. Had the section stopped there the only question that would have remained was whether the acts done failed to bind the company because those acting for it had acted outside their actual or apparent authority. Short of admitting that companies have full legal capacity we could hardly have done better.

In fact, however, the section went on to add qualifications. Subsection (2) provides:

"(2) A member of the company may bring proceedings to restrain the doing of an act which but for subsection (1) would be beyond

---

not to make further alterations to the memorandum and articles without the court's leave: s.5(6).

[47] s.6(4) and (5). s.6(1), (2) and (3) provide for notice to the Registrar whether no application is made (in which case a printed copy of the amended memorandum also has to be delivered to him) or if an application is made (in which case once an order is made an office copy of it and, if it alters the memorandum, a printed copy of the memorandum as altered, will also have to be delivered to him).

[48] By its s.108.

[49] Note that this is not restricted to the *objects clause* of the memorandum; it applies, for example, to a separate clause saying that the company shall *not* undertake certain types of business and to any provision in the memorandum imposing limitations on the company's powers and thereby on its "capacity".

the company's capacity; but no such proceedings shall lie in respect of an act done in fulfilment of a legal obligation arising from a previous act of the company.''

But for an idiosyncrasy of English company law this subsection would not have been necessary. If the proposed act breaches the provisions of the memorandum or articles it would necessarily be a breach of the company's constitution and in excess of the actual authority of those so acting. Hence a member ought to be able to bring proceedings to restrain that act from being undertaken. But, owing to the so-called rule in *Foss v. Harbottle*, he generally cannot. That notorious rule is dealt with more fully in a later Chapter.[50] Here it suffices to say that normally the only proper plaintiff to restrain corporate irregularities is the company itself, acting through its appropriate organ which, as we saw in the previous chapter, is likely to be the board of directors or, on their default, the general meeting. There are, however, exceptions to this rule, a well-established one being that a single member may sue to restrain an act that is *ultra vires*. Subsection (2) preserves that exception.

However, under the proviso to subsection (2) a member cannot bring proceedings to restrain an act of the company which, but for subsection (1), would be beyond its capacity, if that act is to be done in fulfilment of a legal obligation arising from a previous act of the company. Hence if, say, the company has entered into a contract which is beyond its powers, but which, as a result of subsection (1), cannot be questioned, the company cannot be restrained from performing its obligations to a bona fide third party under that contract. If, however, that contract was one under which, say, the company, bought an option to purchase, a member could take proceedings to restrain it from exercising the option since it would not be under a legal obligation to do so. Thus, overall, the policy of protecting third parties' legal rights is given priority to that of holding the company to its constitution.

The second qualification is made by subsection (3), which provides that:

"(3) It remains the duty of the directors to observe any limitation on their powers flowing from the company's memorandum and action by the directors which, but for subsection (1), would be beyond the company's capacity may only be ratified by the company by special resolution.

"A resolution ratifying such action shall not affect any liability incurred by the directors or any other person; relief from any such liability must be agreed to separately by special resolution.''

This subsection was included because of the Government's declared policy to abolish *ultra vires* in relation to external relations but, so far as possible, to maintain the status quo for internal relations between

---

[50] Chap. 23.

the company and its directors. Had that been carried to its logical conclusion it would have been provided that ratification by the company should not affect any liability which the directors had incurred to the company by causing it to enter into a transaction beyond its powers under its memorandum. Rightly recognising that this would go too far, it is instead provided that, in this case (in contrast with ratifying an act within the company's capacity but beyond the directors' actual or apparent authority—when an ordinary resolution suffices)[51] a special resolution is needed and, if this is to absolve "the directors or any other person" from liability which, but for subsection (1), they would have incurred, there must, it seems, be both a special resolution ratifying the transaction and a separate special resolution agreeing to absolve them.

There might have been some justification for this if the adverse consequences or moral blameworthiness were necessarily greater where the directors had caused the company to act in excess of its capacity than when they had exceeded their authority. But that is not the case. A better solution might have been to require a special resolution in both cases.

However, subsection (3) qualifies subsection (1) only in respect of the *liabilities* incurred by the directors and "other persons" (words presumably inserted to catch officers of the company who participated in the directors' act). It enables their action, which formerly could not be ratified even by the unanimous consent of the members, to escape liability only if their action is ratified by a special resolution in accordance with the subsection. It does not detract from the protection afforded to the other party to the transaction. Under subsection (1) the company's act cannot be called into question on the grounds of lack of capacity. So far as the other party is concerned, ratification by special resolution is of relevance only if it took place before any legal obligation to him was incurred (in which event it would preclude a member from bringing an action under subsection (2)) or when he is unprotected by section 35A because he has acted in bad faith (in which event the members would be unlikely to ratify).

(c) *Lack of authority and constructive notice*

These two matters are intertwined and were dealt with by inserting three further sections into the 1985 Act. These are sections 35A and 35B (inserted, like the substitute section 35, by section 108 of the 1989 Act) and section 711A (inserted by section 142, but not yet in force) in Part XXIV of the Act.

Subsection (1) of section 35A provides:

"(1) In favour of a person dealing with a company in good faith,

---

[51] *Grant v. U.K. Switchback Rys* (1880) 40 Ch.D. 135; s.35A (below) does not affect this when only absence of authority is involved.

the power of the board of directors[52] to bind the company, or authorise others to do so, shall be deemed to be free of any limitations under the company's constitution.''[53]

This, too, is an improvement on the wording of the former section 35 in that it omits the restriction to "transactions decided on by the directors''[54] and thus recognises that many transactions will be decided upon by executive officers appointed by the board of directors. But it is not free from difficulties. The first difficulty is that, as we saw in the previous chapter, our Companies Acts have never said what the powers of directors are; this is left to the constitution, *i.e.* normally the memorandum and articles of association.[55] To make sense of the subsection it seems that it has to be read as if it said:

"In favour of a person dealing with the company in good faith the board of directors shall be deemed to have authority to exercise all the powers of the company, except such as the Act requires to be exercised by some other organ, and to authorise others to do so, notwithstanding, in either event, any limitations in the company's constitution on the board's authority."

Only if the courts so construe it,[56] will it achieve its aim.

A more serious objection is that section 35A(1) fails to afford any protection when the third party has dealt with another organ of the company. There are companies which, under their constitutions, reserve certain powers to the general meeting and the general meeting is unquestionably an organ of the company within the meaning of the First Company Law Directive. It should also be noted that, whereas the section says that in favour of a person dealing with the company the board shall be deemed to have power to authorise other persons to bind the company, it does not say that the board shall be deemed to have exercised that power. To the consequences of that we shall revert later.[57]

---

[52] Under Prof. Prentice's proposals this would have read "the board of directors *or any individual director*" (see his Report, Chap. IV, para. 50 (iii)). This would have improved the position of a third party (see pp. 224 *et seq.*, below) and would, it is submitted, have given effect to the intention of the Directive.

[53] The substitution of "constitution" for the former "memorandum or articles" recognises that the sections apply to companies within the meaning of ss. 680 & 718 of the Act (see pp. 127 *et seq*, above) and that these will probably not have memoranda and articles.

[54] Lawson J. in *International Sales & Agencies Ltd v. Marcus*, n. 29, above, felt able to treat a single effective director as "the directors" within the meaning of the former version of the section. Under the new one, if the company has a board of directors, it will hardly be possible to construe "board of directors" as including a managing director or chief executive; he is one of the "others" whom the board has power to authorise to bind the company. Yet he would almost certainly be an "organ" of the company within the meaning of Art. 9.1. of the First Company Law Directive. If, as permitted in relation to private companies, there is only one director, he will, however, be "the board of directors".

[55] See Chap. 9, above.

[56] Which they should since they can refer to the Directive in aid of interpretation: *Litster v. Forth Dry Dock* [1990] 1 A.C. 456, H.L.

[57] See pp. 224–228, below.

Subsection (1) of section 35A retains the expressions ("dealing with the company" and "in good faith") which caused some difficulty in the earlier version of section 35. But happily subsection (2) gives help in their interpretation. It provides:

"(2) For this purpose—

(a) a person "deals with" a company if he is a party to any transaction or other act to which the company is a party;

(b) a person shall not be regarded as acting in bad faith by reason only of his knowing that an act is beyond the powers of the directors under the company's constitution; and

(c) a person shall be deemed to have acted in good faith unless the contrary is proved."

Subsection (2)(a) provides a straightforward test of whether a person is "dealing with a company". He will be, so long as he is a party to a transaction (*e.g.* a contract) or an act (*e.g.* a payment of money) to which the company is also a party. It no longer matters whether the person is an insider or an outsider, as it did under the *Turquand* rule.[58] A member or employee of the company is more likely than a complete outsider to know when an act is beyond the board's authority. But knowledge is not decisive of bad faith. That is expressly stated in subsection (2)(b). If he knew, the likelihood is that he acted in bad faith, and if he did not know the likelihood is that he acted in good faith. But that is all. As Nourse J. concluded on the wording of the former section, good faith is a subjective test: "A person acts in good faith if he acts genuinely and honestly in the circumstances of the case."[59] And, as in the former version of section 35, a person is presumed to have acted in good faith unless the contrary is proved.[60]

Section 35A(3) makes it clear that "any limitation under the company's constitution" includes not only a limitation in the memorandum and articles (or the equivalent) but also one deriving from an agreement or resolution of the members or a class of members even if it does not formally alter the memorandum or articles themselves. That such resolutions should be expressly covered is the more necessary because, as we have seen in the previous Chapter,[61] in companies with an article corresponding to Article 70 of Table A 1985, it is possible for the general meeting to curtail the directors' powers by "directions" given by special resolution.

---

[58] See p. 221, below. And as it still does if the other party is a director or connected with a director: see s. 322A, below, pp. 217–218.

[59] *Barclays Bank Ltd v. TOSG Trust Fund* [1984] BCLC at 18.

[60] But, on the authority of a case decided on the 1972 version of the provisions but seemingly unaffected by the latest version, the onus is on the third party to establish that he "dealt with" the company: *International Sales & Agencies Ltd v. Marcus* [1982] 2 C.M.L.R. 46; [1982] 3 All E.R. 551.

[61] At pp. 183–187, above.

Subsections (4), (5) and (6) are equivalent to subsections (2), (3) and (4) of the new section 35 except that subsections (4) and (5) omit any reference to ratification. Hence, an act in excess of the directors' powers or officers' authority can be ratified by ordinary resolution,[62] although if the act is beyond the *company's* powers, it will need under section 35(3) to be a special resolution if it is to relieve the directors from liability.

Turning now to constructive notice, the doctrine that those having dealings with a company are deemed to have notice of its public documents by reason of their registration, will be abolished by the new section 711A, subsection (1) of which provides that:

"(1) A person shall not be taken to have notice of any matter merely because of its being disclosed in any document kept by the registrar of companies (and thus available for inspection) or made available by the company for inspection."

The result of this is that those dealing with the company are no longer deemed to have notice of the contents of any document[63] merely because it is one of the company's documents available for inspection at Companies House or the company's registered office.[64] Of particular importance in the present context is the fact that thereby they are not saddled with notice of anything in the memorandum and articles, or of special resolutions or of anything on the register of directors and secretaries. Subsection (1) is, however, qualified by subsection (2) which reads:

"(2) This does not affect the question whether a person is affected by notice of any matter by reason of a failure to make such inquiries as ought reasonably to be made."

At first glance this might appear seriously to diminish the protection afforded by section 35A to a person dealing with the company in good faith. That, however, is not so, for two reasons. First, section 35B provides that a party to a transaction with the company is not bound to enquire whether it is permitted by the company's memorandum or as to any limitation on the powers of the board to bind the company or to authorise others to do so. Thus, the form of constructive notice arising from failure to enquire, which is in principle preserved by section 711A(2), is specifically excluded in the area covered by section 35B, which, it should be noted, applies to any person dealing with the company, whether via the directors or through an officer of the company. Secondly, in favour of a person dealing with the company in good faith via its directors or someone authorised by them, section 35A itself provides, as we have seen, that "the power of the board of

---

[62] See n. 5, above.
[63] Defined in subs. (3) as including "any material which contains information" (*e.g.* on a computer).
[64] On rights of public inspection see Chap. 19, below.

directors to bind the company or authorise others to do so" is deemed to be free of any limitation contained in the company's constitution and the third party is not regarded as acting in bad faith "by reason only of his knowing that an act is beyond the powers of the directors". In saying that, it is not suggested that a failure to make such inquiries as ought to be made may not be evidence of bad faith; if he has deliberately decided not to make inquiries, knowing that, if he does, it is likely to confirm his suspicions that the board is exceeding its powers, that may well be treated as equivalent to actual knowledge and, in consequence, as probable bad faith. But negligent failure to make inquiries cannot, in itself, constitute bad faith.

(d) *Transactions involving directors*

The new section 322A, which the 1989 Act[65] inserts in the 1985 Act Part X (enforcement of fair dealing by directors) constitutes an important qualification to sections 35 and especially 35A. It applies where the transaction exceeds a limitation on the powers of the board of directors under the company's constitution and the other parties include a director of the company or its holding company, or a person connected with[66] such a director, or a company with which such a director is associated.[67] In such circumstances the transaction is voidable at the instance of the company[68] and, whether or not it is avoided, such parties and any director who authorised the transaction, knowing that it exceeded the board's powers, are liable to account to the company for any gains they make and to indemnify the company against any loss it suffers.[69] The transaction ceases to be voidable in any of the four events[70] set out in subsection (5) but this, apparently, does not affect the company's right to be indemnified,[71] at any rate unless the transaction is ratified by the company in general meeting "by ordinary or special resolution or otherwise as the case may require".[72] Presumably this means that, if the transaction exceeds the company's capacity, ratification must be in accordance with section 35(3), *i.e.* by a special resolution, but that an ordinary resolution suffices if it is otherwise beyond the board's authority so that section 35A only is

---

[65] By its s.109.

[66] As defined in s.346(2) & (3).

[67] As defined in s.346(4).

[68] s.322A(1) and (2). s.322A(4) provides that nothing in the section shall exclude "the operation of any other enactment or rule of law by virtue of which the transaction may be called in question, or any liability to the company may arise."

[69] s.322A(3).

[70] (a) *restitutio in integrum* is no longer possible, (b) the company has been indemnified, (c) rights of a bona fide purchaser for value (other than a party to the transaction) would be affected or (d) the transaction is ratified by the company.

[71] This seems to follow from subss. (3) and (5).

[72] subs. (5)(d).

relevant.[73] The section does not affect the operation of section 35A in relation to any party to the transaction other than a director or a person with whom he is connected or associated but where that other party is protected by section 35A the court may make such order affirming, severing or setting aside the transaction on such terms as appear to be just.[74]

The effect of section 322A, therefore, is to preserve to some extent the distinction, drawn in relation to the rule in *Royal British Bank v. Turquand*,[75] between "insiders" who are not protected by that rule and "outsiders" who are. Directors and their associates, as insiders, should not be permitted to plead ignorance of the company's constitution and, indeed, should be under a duty to ensure that the company abides by the provisions of the memorandum and articles. But the meaning of "insider" is now clearly defined as it was not in relation to the *Turquand* rule.

(e) *Charitable companies*

The 1989 Act also made special provision regarding charitable companies. The broad effect of what is now section 64 of the Charities Act 1993 seems to be that where a charity is a company or other body corporate having power to alter its constitution, no exercise of that power which has the effect of the body ceasing to be a charity will affect the application of any of its existing property unless it bought it for full consideration in money or money's worth. In other words, although the company is not prevented from changing its objects (so long as it obtains the prior written consent of the Charity Commission[76]) in such a way that they cease to be exclusively for charity, its existing property obtained by donations continues to be held for charitable purposes only.[77] In effect, the company will be in an analogous position to an individual trustee of a charitable trust; part of its property will be held for charitable purposes only and part of it not. And, presumably, it will have to segregate the former.[78]

---

[73] But it could mean that liability to account for gains and to indemnify against losses remains despite ratification. There is a similar obscurity in ss.320–322 (major property transactions): see below, pp. 635–637.

[74] subs. (7).

[75] See below, p. 221. In a case on the *Turquand* rule (*Hely-Hutchinson v. Brayhead* [1968] 1 Q.B. 549) Roskill J., as he then was, held that a director was an "insider" only if the transaction with the company was so intimately connected with his position as a director as to make it impossible for him not to be treated as knowing of the limitations on the powers of the officers through whom he dealt. s.322A contains no such qualification.

[76] s.64(2)

[77] One cannot say "on charitable trusts" because it seems that a charitable corporation does not hold its property on a trust in the strict sense, see *Liverpool Hospital v. Att.-Gen.* [1981] Ch. 193 and cases there reviewed. These are waters too deep to be fathomed here.

[78] The result seems to be that if the Charity Commission consents to a change of objects which results in the company being empowered to undertake both charitable and non-charitable activities, any future donations which it receives will not be regarded as charitable donations *vis-à-vis* either the donors or the company unless the donors specifically direct that the gifts

Section 65 of the Charities Act 1993 provides that sections 35 and 35A of the Companies Act do not apply to acts of a company which is a charity except in favour of a person who either (i) gives full consideration in money or money's worth and does not know that the act is not permitted by the company's memorandum or is beyond the powers of the charity or (ii) does not know that the company is a charity. Under subsection (2), however, subsection (1) does not affect the title of any person who subsequently acquires an interest in property transferred by the company so long as he gave full consideration and did not have actual notice of the circumstances affecting the validity of the transfer. It is clear that "know", in subsection (1) connotes actual (not constructive) knowledge and subsection (3) provides that in any proceedings the burden of proving knowledge lies on the party alleging it. That burden, especially in relation to whether he knew that the company was a charity, should be lightened if the company complies with section 68.[79] This requires a company, which is a charity, but has a name which does not include the word "charity" or "charitable", to state on all business documents in English in legible characters that it is a charity. Proof that the party concerned has received such documents should go a good part of the way to discharging that burden.

Finally section 65(4) provides that, in the case of a company which is a charity, ratification of an act under the Companies Act, section 35(3) or to which section 322A applies shall be ineffective without the prior written consent of the Charity Commission.

The Charities Act does not extend to Scotland. Hence, section 112 of the 1989 Act makes comparable provisions applying to Scotland only.

(f) *Provision for employees*

Mention has already been made of the special provisions made by the Companies Act 1980 to reverse the effect of the decision in *Parke v. Daily News*.[80] Those provisions subsequently became section 719 of the Companies Act 1985 and section 187 of the Insolvency Act 1986. The 1989 Act did not alter these—though section 719 now sits rather uncomfortably with the new sections. It provides that the powers of a company include "if they would not otherwise do so apart from this section", power to make provision for employees or former employees of the company or any of its subsidiaries in connection with the cessation or transfer of the undertaking of the company or

---

are to be held by the company for its charitable objects. In practice, donations to it are likely to dry up since the *company* will not longer be recognised by either the Commission or the Revenue as a charity.

[79] If it fails to comply, it will commit an offence and it and its officers will be liable to fines in accordance with section 349(2)–(4) of the Companies Act: s.68(3)

[80] [1962] Ch. 927. See p. 205, above.

that subsidiary.[81] This power may be exercised notwithstanding that it is not in the best interests of the company.[82] Before the commencement of the winding up of the company,[83] provision may be made out of profits available for dividend.[84] But, if made "by virtue only of subsection (1)" it may be exercised only if sanctioned by an ordinary resolution of the company or, if the memorandum or articles so require, a resolution of some other description or compliance with other formalities in accordance with those requirements.[85]

Unless the memorandum or articles have made special provisions regarding this matter (and none of the 1985 Tables does), a board of directors is likely to find some difficulty in construing this section in the light of the new sections 3A, 35 and 35A. Presumably neither the new general purpose objects clause permitted by section 3A nor a similar clause at the end of the list of objects and powers[86] will suffice to authorise the board to exercise the power without the sanction of a resolution of the general meeting. But, under section 719(3), this resolution can, in the absence of contrary provision in the memorandum or articles, be an ordinary resolution, whereas under section 35 it would have to be a special resolution. Presumably section 719, dealing with a specific situation, prevails over section 35, with the apparent result that, if the memorandum includes a specific power to provide for employees and this is a power not excluded in the articles from those which can be exercised by the board, it will be able to exercise it without the sanction of the general meeting,[87] and that, if the memorandum does not include such a power, an ordinary resolution will suffice notwithstanding section 35(3).

In any event, the employees[88] once they have received their golden handshakes will be protected (unless they are directors[89]). The only risk they run is that a member will intervene,[90] or that the company will go into liquidation,[91] before any decision has been made.

---

[81] s.719(1).

[82] s.719(2).

[83] Then s.187 of the Insolvency Act confers similar powers on the liquidator.

[84] s.719(4).

[85] s.719(3).

[86] *Parke v. Daily News* had held that when the trade or business of the company is ending, gratuitous generosity cannot be "incidental or conducive to the carrying on of any trade or business by it".

[87] The transaction will be one within the powers of the company apart from s.719 and not one which it could exercise only by virtue of subs. (1); and, the directors will be authorised by the articles.

[88] They will be "dealing with" the company within the meaning of s.35A.

[89] When s.322A will apply.

[90] Under s.35(2) or s.35A(4).

[91] Under s.187 of the Insolvency Act the liquidator may implement and decision previously made by the company and if none has, may, after all the company's liabilities have been met, exercise a similar power to that which the company had by virtue only of s.719. But he must receive the sanction of members and, on a winding up by the court, any creditor or member may apply to the court.

THE RESULTING POSITION

The objective of the foregoing statutory changes was to draw the sting of the *ultra vires* and constructive notice doctrines, thus improving the position of those who dealt with the company externally, while making as few alterations as possible to the position as between the company and its members, directors and other agents. This limited objective appears to have been achieved reasonably satisfactorily. But it did not attempt to provide a complete code defining when a third party can safely assume that those dealing with him on behalf of a company have power to bind the company.

Normally, as a result of the new sections, if a transaction with a third party acting in good faith is effected on behalf of a company by the board of directors or by a person who, in fact, the board has authorised, the transaction will bind the company. But, except where the company is very small or the transaction is very large, the third party will probably not have had dealings through the board. His dealings will be in practice more often with someone who is an executive of the company or even a comparatively lowly employee of whom the members of the board of directors may never have heard. Nor will the third party be likely to know whether in fact that executive or employee has actually been authorised by the board. Is he then entitled to assume that the board has, in fact, authorised that person to bind the company? And that the board has imposed no limitations on the exercise of that person's authority? And what is his position if in fact there is no legally constituted board of directors? The new sections 35A and 35B give no answers. For them we have to turn to the basic common law principles of agency[92] as refined in relation to companies by the rule in *Royal British Bank v. Turquand*.[93]

The rule in Turquand's case

This rule was enunciated by the courts to mitigate the effects of the constructive notice doctrine. As that doctrine has now been abolished the rule is no longer often of direct relevance when the third party has dealt with the company through the board of directors.[94] Its importance now is in situations where, instead, the third party's dealings have been with some officer or agent other than the board. However, the

---

[92] Summarised with, it is hoped, sufficient accuracy for present purposes at p. 201, nn. 1 and 2, above.

[93] (1856) 6 E. & B. 327, Exch. Ch.

[94] As in the *Turquand* case itself. There, under the company's deed of settlement, the board could borrow on bonds such sums as from time to time should be authorised by a resolution of the company in general meeting. The court held that a third party "finding that the authority might be made complete by a resolution . . . would have a right to infer the fact of a resolution authorising that which on the face of the document appeared to be legitimately done": at 332. Today he would be protected by the new sections.

rule is relevant to those dealing with the board in one situation. This is best illustrated by the leading case of *Mahoney v. East Holyford Mining Co.*[95] The question to be decided was whether the liquidator of an insolvent company could recover from its bank money paid on cheques drawn on the company's account. The company's articles provided that cheques should be signed in such manner as the directors should determine. The bank had received a copy, signed by the "secretary", of an alleged board resolution that cheques should be signed by any two of three named "directors" and by the secretary. The cheques had been signed by those named. In fact, the directors had never been formally appointed and no formal directors' or members' meetings had ever been held. The Lords took the opinion of the judges and upheld their unanimous conclusion that the liquidator could not recover. As Lord Hatherly said[96]:

> "When there are persons conducting the affairs of the company in a manner which appears to be perfectly consonant with the articles of association, those so dealing with them externally are not to be affected by any irregularities which may take place in the internal management of the company."

Dealing with the board or those authorised by it

Lord Hatherly's dictum (substituting, now, "perfectly normal" for "perfectly consonant with the articles of association") remains, it is submitted, the guiding principle which the courts should bear in mind in interpreting the new statutory provisions. And it affords an answer to one of the questions that those provisions leave unanswered: "the board of directors" for the purpose of the new sections means "the persons occupying the position of the board of directors" whether or not they have been validly appointed.

For that proposition there is, indeed, additional statutory, support. The Companies Acts[97] have long provided that: "The acts of a director or manager[98] are valid notwithstanding any defect that may afterwards be discovered[99] in his appointment or qualification." To this the 1985

---

[95] (1875) L.R. 7 H.L. 869.

[96] At 894.

[97] Now s.285 which applies only to registered companies. It is normally supplemented by an article on the lines of Table A 1985, Art. 92 which, however, could not be invoked by a third party unless he actually knew of it and had relied upon it. Note also s.382(2) and (4) which could strengthen reliance on the *Turquand* rule when minutes of meetings have been kept.

[98] The "or manager" is probably only a relic of the days when "manager" was sometimes the name given to a director. Especially in the light of the recent addition to this section (s.292 relates only to the appointment of directors) it is unlikely that any court would construe it as including "sales manager" or the like.

[99] This apparently means "discovered by the other party": *Kansen v. Rialto (West End) Ltd* [1944] Ch. 346, C.A. But this point was left open by the H.L.: *sub nom. Morris v. Kanssen* [1946] A.C. 459.

Act added: "and this provision is not excluded by section 292(2) (void resolution to appoint)".[1]

This, however, seems to add little to the protection afforded by the common law rule[2] since the House of Lords had held in *Morris v. Kanssen*[3] that it applies only when there has been a valid appointment which has not been vacated and not where there has been "no appointment". This presumably still remains the law (subject to the new statutory exception) despite the difficulty, illustrated by the case itself,[4] of distinguishing between the two situations.

It can no longer be argued that a person having dealings with a company is deemed to have notice of who the true directors are (this being shown by its "public documents", *i.e.* by the register of directors required to be maintained by the company and the notices of changes therein which it is required to send to Companies House[5]). The new section 711A will dispose of that argument. It does not, however, dispose of a possible argument based on section of the Act.[6] That section provides that a company is not entitled to rely against other persons on the happening of certain events which have not been officially notified in the *Gazette*, unless these events are actually known by him at the material time. Among these events are changes among the directors. It could be argued that section 42 implies that if the events are notified in the *Gazette*, the company can rely on them. However it would be absurd if section 42 was held to have that effect and the Court of Appeal has held that it does not.[7]

Hence, a third party, who has dealt with the company through its board of directors (*de jure* or *de facto*) or with someone authorised by that board, will be protected so long as he has acted in good faith. The combined effect of the new sections and the *Turquand* rule produces that result.

---

[1] s.292 requires each director's appointment to be voted on individually (unless the meeting otherwise agrees *nem. con.*) and says that otherwise the resolution is void.

[2] Except that the section can be relied on by the director himself (*Channel Collieries Trust v. Dover Light Ry Co.* [1914] 2 Ch. 506, C.A.) whereas under the *Turquand* rule, as an insider, he normally could not.

[3] Above, n. 99. The approach of *Morris v. Kanssen* was followed by Oliver J. in *Re New Cedas Engineering Co. Ltd* [1994] 1 BCLC 797, a case decided in 1975.

[4] There an originally valid appointment had expired without being renewed and this was treated as "no appointment at all" when the director continued to act as such.

[5] ss.288 and 709. But if the directors with whom the third party dealt were those shown on the register at the material time, and that was known to and relied on by the third party, it might further enhance his protection as a holding out by the company that they were the directors (unless there had been a change within the previous 14 days: see s.288(2). A similar estoppel by holding out (see below, pp. 227–228) might occur if the company was one which still names its directors on its notepaper. This was formerly required by the Companies Act 1948, s.201, but is not under s.305 of the 1985 Act which replaced it.

[6] Originally s.9(4) of the European Communities Act, implementing Art. 3.5 of the First Directive.

[7] *Official Custodian v. Parway Estates* [1985] Ch. 151.

Dealing with officers not so authorised

What of the more common case where the third party has not dealt with the board or an agent authorised by the board? If the third party acted in good faith he or she is entitled to rely on the fact that the board had unlimited power to authorise another person to exercise the powers of the company. But the new sections do not say that he is entitled to assume that the board has done so or that, to the extent that it has done so, it has not imposed any limitations on that person. Yet in many, perhaps most, cases unless he is entitled to make some such assumptions the new statutory provisions will be precious little help to him. But if he is to be entitled to make any such assumptions it can only be by reliance on the general law of agency and the rule in *Turquand*'s case and not on section 35A of the Act. This needs emphasising because it seems often to be overlooked. Equally, however, it would be absurd if he could safely assume, say, that authorisation to sell the company's premises had been conferred on the office-boy, the lift attendant or someone who had no apparent connection with the company.[8] Despite the apparent width of the *Turquand* rule as expressed in the dicta in *Turquand* and *Mahony* quoted above[9] (and despite the fact that the rule will be freed from the limitations on it under the constructive notice doctrine), the later cases on the *Turquand* rule make it clear that these assumptions can be made only in one or both of two sets of circumstances on the basis of a holding out by the company, often taking the form of an appointment to a particular employment. A very similar result would be reached by applying normal principles of agency.

Where the person through whom the third party dealt occupies a position in the company[10] such that it would be usual for an occupant of that position to have authority to bind the company in relation to the transaction concerned, the company will be bound. The third party dealing with the company in good faith will be entitled to assume that that person has authority unless he knows the contrary or knows of facts which would have put a reasonable person on inquiry.[11] Thus if the person acting for the company is its chief executive or managing

---

[8] In these extreme cases the company would, no doubt, have little difficulty in persuading the court that the third party had not dealt in good faith.

[9] See p. 222, text and n. 94, above.

[10] Whether formally appointed to it or merely allowed by the company to assume it; that is a matter of "internal management".

[11] When dealing with someone other than the board or someone authorised by it, the third party is not necessarily protected merely because he acted in good faith. If there are suspicious circumstances, he should, as under s.711A, "make such inquiries as ought reasonably to be made" and he will be protected only if the suspicions of a reasonable person would be allayed by the answers to his inquiries: *Underwood Ltd v. Bank of Liverpool* [1924] 1 K.B. 715, C.A.; *Houghton & Co. v. Nothard, Lowe & Wills* [1927] 1 K.B. 48, C.A., affd, on other grounds, [1928] A.C. 1, H.L.

director, then, despite the fact that the Act refuses to treat him as an "organ" of the company equivalent to the board of directors, unless there are suspicious circumstances, or the transaction is of such magnitude as to imply the need for board approval, he may safely be assumed to be authorised. In practice, he will probably have actual authority[12] but, even if he has not, he will have ostensible authority and his acts will bind the company.[13]

Much the same applies to other executive directors except that, if the descriptions of their posts suggest particular areas of responsibility ("finance director", "sales director" or the like), they cannot be assumed to have authority outside those areas. Even though individual non-executive directors have no managerial responsibility unless the board delegates it to them,[14] they may be assumed to have some individual authority, beyond that of sharing in the exercise of the board's collective authority at meetings of the board or its committees. It is usual, for example, for them to be authorised signatories of the company's cheques[15] or attestors of the affixing of its seal.[16] And the new section 36A[17] (which removes the need for a company to have a common seal[18]) provides that in favour of a purchaser[19] a document shall be deemed to be duly executed by a company if it purports to be signed by a director and the secretary or by two directors and that, where it makes it clear on its face that it is intended to be a deed, to have been "delivered".[20]

Moreover, it is not uncommon for the board of directors to allow one of their number to assume the position of managing director even though he has never been formally appointed to that position and in these circumstances the courts have treated him as if he were the managing director.[21] Some decisions have even suggested that a non-executive chairman of the board has, as such, individual authority equating with that of a managing director.[22] But why the right to take

[12] *Hely-Hutchinson v. Brayhead Ltd* [1968] 1 Q.B. 549, C.A.
[13] *Freeman & Lockyer v. Buckhurst Park Properties Ltd* [1964] 2 Q.B. 480, C.A., especially the judgment of Diplock L.J. at 506.
[14] *Rama Corporation v. Proved Tin & General Investments Ltd* [1952] 2 Q.B. 147.
[15] See *Mahoney v. Holyford Mining Co.*: above.
[16] Articles normally provide that the seal shall be affixed only pursuant to a resolution of the board or a committee of the board and attested by a director and the secretary or a second director: Table A 1985, Art. 101. But this seems clearly to be a matter of the company's internal management despite suggestions to the contrary in *S. London Greyhound Racecourses Ltd v. Wake* [1931] 1 Ch. 496: see *County of Gloucester Bank v. Rudry Merthyr Colliery Co.* [1895] 1 Ch. 629, C.A.
[17] Inserted by the 1989 Act, s.130(2).
[18] s.36A(3).
[19] Defined as "a purchaser in good faith for valuable consideration [including] a lessee, mortgagee or other person who for valuable consideration acquires an interest in property".
[20] s.36A(6). This extends s.74 of the L.P.A. 1925.
[21] See, *e.g. Biggerstaff v. Rowatt's Wharf Ltd* [1896] 2 Ch. 93, C.A.; *Clay Hill Brick Co. v. Rawlings* [1938] 4 All E.R. 100; *Freeman & Lockyer v. Buckhurst Park Properties Ltd*, above.
[22] *B.T.H. v. Federated European Bank* [1932] 2 K.B. 176, C.A.; *Clay Hill Brick Co. v. Rawlings*, above. It is a popular misconception, shared by lawyers and laymen alike (and apparently by

the chair should imply a right to manage out of the chair is difficult to understand and the proposition has been doubted.[23]

When the third party deals with an officer or employee below the level of director the position is more problematical and, until recently, the courts have shown a marked reluctance to recognise any ostensible authority even of a manager.[24] But this is now changing and it may be taken that a manager, even if he does not have actual authority, will generally have ostensible authority to undertake everyday transactions relating to the branch of business which he is managing (though probably not if they are really major transactions[25]) and that the secretary will similarly have such authority in relation to administrative matters.[26] Indeed, almost every employee of a trading company must surely have apparent authority to bind the company in some transactions, though the extent of that may be very limited. For example, the men or women behind the counter in a departmental store clearly have apparent authority to sell the goods on display for cash and at the marked prices. Whether their apparent authority extends beyond that (for example, to accept a cheque not supported by a cheque-card or to take goods back if the customer returns them) we shall probably never know, for it is unlikely to be litigated—at any rate against the customer. But clearly the fact that, under section 35A, the board of directors might have authorised them to exercise all the company's powers (including that to sell the store itself) cannot estop the company from denying that it has done anything so crazy. Hence, when the employee or agent of the company does not occupy a position in the company in which it would be usual for him to have delegated authority to bind the company in relation to the transaction concerned, the company will not be bound, unless he has actual authority or has,

the legislature: see 1985 Act, Sched. 6, Pt 1, para. 3) that the chairman is some sort of overlord and remunerated as such; he often is but may be merely an ornamental figurehead.

[23] In *Hely-Hutchinson v. Brayhead* [1968] 1 Q.B. 549, C.A., *per* Roskill J. at first instance at 560D, and Lord Wilberforce at 586G.

[24] *Houghton & Co. v. Nothard, Lowe & Wills* [1927] 1 K.B. 246, C.A., affd. on other grounds [1928] A.C. 1, H.L.; *Kreditbank Cassel v. Schenkers* [1927] 1 K.B. 826, C.A.; *S. London Greyhound Racecourses v. Wake* [1931] 1 Ch. 496; see also the observations of Willmer L.J. in *Freeman & Lockyer v. Buckhurst Park Properties Ltd* [1964] 2 Q.B. at 494.

[25] See *Armagas Ltd v. Mundogas S.A.* [1986] A.C. 717, H.L. There an employee who bore the title of "Vice-president (Transportation) and Chartering Manager" was held not to have authority to bind his company to charter-back a vessel which it was selling. But there were complicating factors in that case for the employee was colluding with an agent of the other party in a dishonest arrangement and did not purport to have any general authority to bind the company but merely alleged that he had obtained actual authority for that particular transaction. Contrast *First Energy (UK) Ltd v. Hungarian International Bank Ltd* [1993] BCLC 1409, C.A., where a senior manager was held to have ostensible authority to communicate to a third party head office approval of a loan application, even though he did not have ostensible authority to contract on the bank's behalf.

[26] *Panorama Developments Ltd v. Fidelis Furnishing Fabrics Ltd* [1971] 2 Q.B. 711, C.A. (above, p. 198). How far, if at all, his apparent authority extends to the commercial side of the company's affairs is still unclear; see, *per* Salmon L.J. at 718.

in some other way, been held out as having authority to bind it in relation to that transaction.

The fact that, prior to the recent reforms, the third party was deemed to have notice of the contents of the memorandum and articles did not mean that he could rely on something in those documents to estop the company from denying the authority of an officer of the company who would not usually have had authority. Constructive notice was a negative doctrine curtailing what might otherwise be the apparent scope of the authority and not a positive doctrine increasing it.[27] The position may be different, however, if the third party had actual knowledge of the memorandum and articles and had relied on some provision in them. What, however, is clear is that mere knowledge that the board of directors might have delegated does not estop the company from denying that it has done so. It would be necessary for the other party also to establish that "the conduct of the board, in the light of that knowledge, would be understood by a reasonable man as a representation that the agent had authority to enter into the contract sought to be enforced".[28]

Obviously, it will be unlikely that the board will so conduct itself if it has neither conferred that authority nor decided to ratify what the agent has done. It is, no doubt, theoretically possible to conceive of a provision in the memorandum or articles which, if known to and relied on by the third party, might estop the company, but there seems to be no reported case in which that has occurred. If this sort of estoppel is to be relied on it will generally be because of conduct by the company's organs and not because of any provision in its memorandum or articles. An example is afforded by *Mercantile Bank of India v. Chartered Bank of India*[29] There the board of directors had caused the company to appoint agents under powers of attorney which authorised them to borrow on the security of charges on the company's property. The directors imposed limits on the extent to which those agents could borrow but these limitations did not appear in the powers of attorney.

---

[27] Any doubt on this point was finally dispelled by the C.A. in *Freeman & Lockyer v. Buckhurst Park Properties Ltd*, above; see especially Diplock L.J. at [1964] 2 K.B. at 504. It had formerly led to much judicial (and academic) disputation: see *Houghton v. Nothard Lowe & Wills* [1927] 1 K.B. 826, C.A.; *B.T.H. v. Federated European Bank* [1932] 2 K.B. 176; *Clay Hill Brick Co. v. Rawlings* [1934] 4 All E.R. 100; *Rama Corporation v. Proved Tin & General Investments* [1952] 2 Q.B. 147; and, finally, *Freeman & Lockyer v. Buckhurst Park Properties Ltd.*, above. For the academic discussion see (1934) 50 L.Q.R. 469; (1956) 11 Univ. of Toronto L.J. 248; (1966) 30 Conv. (N.S.) 128; (1969) 18 I.C.L.Q. 152.

[28] *Per* Diplock L.J. in *Freeman & Lockyer v. Buckhurst Park Properties*, above, at 508. See also Atkin L.J. in *Kreditbank Cassel v. Schenkers*, above, at 844.

[29] [1937] 1 All E.R. 231. The headnote is misleading in suggesting that it was the fact that the articles expressly empowered the board to delegate by powers of attorney (which today would be implied and, under s.35A, an exclusion in the articles would not affect a bona fide third party) that brought about the estoppel. It was the powers of attorney that did so. The only relevance of the articles (of which, at that time, third parties were deemed to have notice) was that they did not preclude the grant of such powers of attorney.

A charge to secure a borrowing in excess of the limitations was held to bind the company in favour of a lender who had relied on the powers of attorney. An officer or agent of the company cannot, however, confer ostensible authority on himself by representing that he has actual authority.[30] It can be conferred only by conduct of the company, acting through an organ or agent of the company, such as the board or the managing director, with actual or apparent authority to make representations as to the extent of the authority of the company's officers or agents. If the company has made such representations on which the third party has acted in good faith, the company may be estopped.[31]

It will therefore be seen that protection afforded to a third party who has dealt with an employee is considerably less than that afforded to one who has dealt with the board of directors, or with someone actually authorised by the board. The statutory reforms have improved his position by the modifications of *ultra vires* and constructive notice but section 35A helps him only to the extent that he may safely assume that the board had power to delegate to that employee. That will not protect him unless the board has actually done so or is estopped from denying that it has or has ratified what he did. If it has not, he will be unprotected unless the employee has acted within his apparent authority; and he will lose that protection not only if he has not acted in good faith but also if he negligently failed to make proper inquiries or if he actually knew or ought to have known that the officer had exceeded his authority.

There is one further respect in which the statutory reforms may lead to clarification of a grey area of the law. The cases establish that in some circumstances a third party becomes a constructive trustee of any property of the company which passes to him under a transaction which is in breach of the directors' fiduciary duties. But what has been unclear is precisely what those circumstances are.[32] The new emphasis in section 35A on lack of good faith should enable the courts to hold that the sole criterion is that the third party has acted in bad faith.[33]

---

[30] *Armagas Ltd v. Mundogas S.A.* [1986] A.C. 717, H.L.: see p. 226, n. 25, above.

[31] Contrary to what was thought at one time, this is so even if the officer or agent has forged what purported to be a document signed or sealed on behalf of the company: *Uxbridge Building Society v. Pickard* [1939] 2 K.B. 248, C.A., explaining dicta in *Ruben v. Great Fingall Consolidated* [1906] A.C. 439, H.L.; *Kreditbank Cassel v. Schenkers*, above; and *S. London Greyhound Racecourses v. Wake*, above.

[32] See, *e.g. Selangor United Rubber Estates Ltd v. Cradock (No. 3)* [1968] 1 W.L.R. 1555; *Karak Rubber Co. v. Burden (No. 2)* [1972] 1 W.L.R. 602; *Belmont Finance Corp. Ltd v. Williams Furniture Ltd* [1979] Ch. 250, C.A.; *International Sales & Agencies Ltd v. Marcus* [1982] 2 C.M.L.R. 46; *Rolled Steel Ltd v. British Steel Corp.* [1986] Ch. 246, C.A.; *Smith v. Croft (No. 2)* [1988] Ch. 114; *Agip (Africa) Ltd v. Jackson* [1990] Ch. 265.

[33] Which, in this context, should mean participating knowingly in an act of the directors which constitutes a breach of their fiduciary duties and not merely an act in excess of their authority. This, as revealed in the Debates under probing by Lord Wedderburn, was, it seems, the Government's intention: see O.R. (H.L.) Vol. 505, cols. 1234–1247 (April 6, 1989).

ATTRIBUTION IN OTHER CONTEXTS

So far, we have examined the rules which attribute to the company the acts and states of mind of individuals in a transactional context. Our main concern has been to answer the question of whether those rules give an appropriate degree of protection to third parties dealing with the company, normally by way of contracting with it. However, the attribution rules may need to be applied in a non-transactional context. In such a context questions of both criminal and civil liability may arise, but the question is particularly acute in the area of criminal law[34] because of the traditional reluctance of the courts to apply in the criminal sphere the notion of vicarious liability which, as we have seen, constitutes one of the fundamental bases of attribution in civil law.

Of course, Parliament may override the presumption against vicarious criminal liability and it is therefore a matter of construction of the statutory offence in question whether Parliament intended to do so. In the case of regulatory offences based on strict liability, it will be relatively easy to convince the court that this is indeed what Parliament intended. In an important recent decision the Court of Appeal was prepared to go further and find that vicarious liability was intended in the case of a hybrid offence, where the strict liability was qualified by a "reasonably practical" defence.[35] Where vicarious liability is imposed, then on usual principles the fact that the employees were acting contrary to their instructions does not necessarily provide the company with a defence.[36]

However, if the crime clearly does require *mens rea* on the part of the company, the courts will not attribute the necessary guilty state of mind to the company by using the doctrine of vicarious liability.[37] Similar issues may arise under statutes dealing with civil law matters, a fruitful source of litigation having been attempts to limit liability under the merchant shipping legislation where this was possible only

---

[34] The general principle of corporate criminal liability, which has troubled and still troubles some continental jurisdictions, had been relatively easily accepted in Britain, the difficulties, now no longer with us, being procedural rather than in principle. See Stessens (1994) 43 I.C.L.Q. 493.

[35] *R. v. British Steel plc* [1995] I.C.R. 586, C.A. This case only opens up the potential for imposing vicarious liability for hybrid offences. Whether a particular statute does so is again a matter of construction. See the Court of Appeal's distinguishing of the decision in *Tesco Supermarkets Ltd v. Nattrass* [1972] A.C. 153 as concerning a differently worded statute in a different area of regulation (consumer protection as against health and safety at work). See also *Seaboard Offshore Ltd v. Secretary of State for Transport* [1994] 1 W.L.R. 541, H.L. (not imposing liability) and *Tesco Stores Ltd v. Brent LBC* [1993] 2 All E.R. 718, C.A., imposing it.

[36] *Re Supply of Ready Mixed Concrete (No. 2)* [1995] 1 A.C. 456, H.L.

[37] Though this approach has been adopted in many United States jurisdictions, provided the crime in question is of a type for which companies may be held liable. See Law Commission, *Legislating the Criminal Code: Involuntary Manslaughter*, Law Com. No. 237, H.C. 171, 1996, para. 7.28.

if the damage was caused without "actual fault or privity"[38] on the part of the person seeking to limit liability. If vicarious liability is not to be used, what rules of attribution are available? It is always possible to look at what was known to the company's organs, especially its board of directors. Rules of attribution derived from the company's own constitution have been referred to, indeed, as the "primary" rules of attribution.[39] However, if the company's knowledge were to be confined to what its organs knew, then the operation of many rules of law, not least in the criminal sphere, would be unacceptably narrow in their relation to companies.

In consequence, from the beginning of the century onwards the courts began to develop rules of attribution which in appropriate cases "identify"[40] the acts and knowledge of those in control of the company as those of the company. Developed first in the area of civil law,[41] in the period immediately after the Second World War the same idea was applied in the criminal law.[42] The effect of this development was to create a set of rules of attribution which operated more broadly than the primary rules but more narrowly than rules based upon the general notions of agency and vicarious liability. The crucial question is, precisely where in the gap between the primary and the general rules are the rules of identification intended to operate or, in other words, what is the theory behind the idea of identification?

It is possible to find in the cases varying formulations of the underlying principle, and the most recent definitions suggest that the courts are prepared today to give the rule of attribution based on identification a somewhat broader scope. In the original formulation in the *Lennard's Carrying Company* case[43] Lord Haldane based identification on a person "who is really the directing mind and will of the corporation, the very ego and centre of the personality of the corporation".[44] Recently, however, such an approach has been castigated by the Privy Council through Lord Hoffmann in the *Meridian Global*

---

[38] These were the words used in the Merchant Shipping Act 1894. See *Lennard's Carrying Co. Ltd v. Asiatic Petroleum Co. Ltd* [1915] A.C. 705, H.L.; *The Truculent* [1952] P. 1; *The Lady Gwendolen* [1965] P. 294, C.A.

[39] *Meridian Global Funds Management Asia Ltd v. Securities Commission* [1995] 2 A.C. 500, 506, P.C.

[40] Law Commission, *op. cit.*, para. 6.2.

[41] See *Lennard's Carrying Co. Ltd v. Asiatic Petroleum Co. Ltd*, above, n. 38.

[42] *DPP v. Kent & Sussex Contractors Ltd* [1944] K.B.146; *R v. ICR Haulage Ltd* [1944] K.B. 551, C.C.A.; *Moore v. Bresler* [1944] 2 All E.R. 515. The application of the principle in the criminal law was approved by the House of Lords in *Tesco Supermarkets Ltd v. Nattrass*, above, n. 35.

[43] Above, n. 38.

[44] *Lennard's Carrying Co. Ltd v. Asiatic Petroleum Co. Ltd*, above, n. 38, at 713. See also *Bolton (Engineering) Co. Ltd v. Graham & Sons* [1957] 1 Q.B. 159, 172, C.A., *per* Lord Denning. Lord Haldane's dictum was probably influenced by the clear distinction drawn between agents and organs in German company law, Haldane having studied in his youth in Germany.

case[45] as a misleading "general metaphysic of companies". The true question in each case was who as a matter of construction of the statute in question, or presumably other rule of law,[46] is to be regarded as the controller of the company for the purpose of the identification rule. In appropriate cases, that might be a person who was less elevated in the corporate structure than those Lord Haldane had in mind. In *Meridian* itself, where the question was whether the company was in breach of the New Zealand laws requiring disclosure of substantial shareholdings knowingly held by an investor,[47] the controllers were held to be two senior investment managers who were not even members of the company's board. Given the purpose of the statute—speedy disclosure of shareholdings—it was appropriate to treat those in charge of dealing in the markets on behalf of the company as its "controllers" in this respect.

The result of this approach is a potentially powerful tool for holding companies liable. This is especially so when it is combined with the doctrine of "aggregation", whereby knowledge attributed to the company in one way is combined with an act attributed to it in another, so as to make the company liable in circumstances in which neither of the individuals is liable. Although aggregation has been rejected in the criminal law[48] and in civil cases based on fraud,[49] it is not otherwise ruled out in the civil law. As we shall see, it was fear of the operation of this doctrine that led the legislature to confine the newly created offence of insider dealing to individuals.[50]

Welcome and more straightforward though the new approach is, it inevitably leaves uncertainty as to who will be regarded as the relevant person within the corporate hierarchy for the purposes of the identification rule in any particular case. That it should not be any agent or employee of the company acting within the scope of his or her authority is clear, for, as we have seen, there is need to resort to the identification rule of attribution only where the general rules of attribution based on agency and vicarious liability are inappropriate in the particular context. Since, however, a precise answer to the question of whose acts and knowledge are to be attributed to the company depends *ex hypothesi* on an analysis of the context of the particular rule with which the court is dealing, it is doubtful whether more certainty can be provided at a general level.

---

[45] Above, n. 39, at 509. The case is noted by Sealy [1995] C.L.J. 507, Wells (1995) 14 I.B.F.L. 42 and Yeung [1977] CFILR 67.

[46] See *El Ajou v. Dollar Land Holdings plc* [1994] 2 All E.R. 685, C.A., where the Court of Appeal, including Hoffmann L.J., as he then was, applied a similar approach to the question of whether a company was in equity in knowing receipt of trust property.

[47] For the equivalent British rules see pp. 484–492, below.

[48] The need to overcome this point seems to have been the main reason leading the Law Commission to propose a new offence of "corporate killing": *op. cit.*, Part VIII.

[49] *Armstrong v. Strain* [1952] 1 K.B. 232, C.A.

[50] See below, p. 458.

The identification theory has been carried to the logical conclusion that a company and an individual, who is its directing will, cannot be successfully indicted for conspiracy since this requires the meeting of two or more minds.[51] But it has not been carried to absurd extremes. If those who constitute the controllers are engaged in defrauding the company they cannot successfully defend a civil action by the company[52] or a criminal prosecution[53] by saying "we were the controlling organs of the company and accordingly the company knew all about it and consented". Were such a defence to prevail, it would wholly negate the duties which the controllers owe to the company. So far as concerns the internal relationship between the company and its officers, dishonest acts directed against the company by its organs are not attributed to the company—though they may well be in favour of a third party dealing with the company in good faith.

CONCLUSION

A company's liability to third parties no longer depends solely on principles of agency or *respondeat superior*. Section 35A, though it does not use the word "organ", has, in effect, recognised that the board of directors is not a mere agent of the company but an organic part of it so that third parties can treat acts of the board as acts of the company itself. The section, however, has not, it seems, gone so far as to treat any other officers of the company as its organs. If third parties deal with the company through another officer they will not be entitled, under section 35A, to treat his acts as those of the company itself and the company will be bound only if that person is acting within his actual or apparent authority (or, where relevant, within the scope of his employment) or the company ratifies what he has done or the company is estopped. The courts, however, have gone further. They have recognised that where managerial powers have been delegated by the board to other officers, those officers also may be treated as organs, rather than agents or servants, of the company so that their acts can be regarded as those of the company itself and not merely as acts of the officers for which it is liable vicariously. As yet, however, they have adopted that theory only in relation to tortious and criminal liability of the company and in cases of contractual liability have generally been content to apply normal agency principles modified only by the *Turquand* rule and, now, by the statutory reforms.

On the face of it, it is anomalous that when an executive of the company signs a contract on behalf of the company its liability

[51] *R. v. McDonnell* [1966] 1 Q.B. 233.

[52] *Belmont Finance Corp. v. Williams Furniture Ltd* [1979] Ch. 250, C.A.

[53] *Att.-Gen.'s Reference (No. 2 of 1982)* [1984] Q.B. 624, C.A.; *R. v. Phillipou* (1989) 89 Cr.App.R. 290, C.A.; *R. v. Rozeik* [1996] BCC 271, C.A.

depends upon whether he has acted within the actual or apparent scope of his authority as an agent of the company, whereas if he negligently or fraudulently injures a third party, the company may be liable civilly or criminally on the basis that the company itself has acted. But this has come about because the courts have felt that, in the latter case, the company ought to be made liable even though on normal principles of vicarious liability it would not be. In contractual cases, however, normal principles of agency as elaborated by the Rule in *Turquand's* case work well enough.

Moreover, the new statutory rules and the courts' theory identification only apply externally and do not affect the liabilities of the organs in their internal relationships with the company; the members of the board are still regarded *vis-à-vis* the company as its fiduciary agents whose liability to the company the Act specifically preserves.[54]

The present position may be somewhat lacking in coherent logic and a few ghostly relics of *ultra vires* continue to haunt us, but at last we seem to have reached a pragmatic result which is generally defensible.

---

[54] See the rejection of an attempt to use the identification theory to deprive the company of the benefit of section 320 in *BRDC v. Hextall Erskine & Co. (a firm)* [1996] 3 All E.R. 667.

CHAPTER 11

THE RAISING AND MAINTENANCE OF CAPITAL

MEANING OF CAPITAL

THE concept of capital is of fundamental importance to a proper under-standing of company law in general, and in particular to an appreci-ation of the distinction between individual traders and partnerships on the one hand, and incorporated limited liability companies on the other. Unhappily "capital" is a word of many different meanings,[1] and even in the legal, economic[2] and accounting senses with which we are concerned, it is used loosely and to describe different concepts at different times, although its users do not always recognise the fact.

Expressed at its simplest, we may say that whenever anyone starts a business he will put certain property into it. This property may be tangible—money, land, furniture or stock-in-trade—or intangible—patents, copyrights, trade secrets or the goodwill and connection of a going concern. Whatever the form of this property it will probably be convenient to place a monetary value upon it, if for no other reason than because this will facilitate the preparation of accounts and enable the proprietor to see what return he is getting for the property sunk in the business. Especially is this so if two or more persons are trading in partnership; the monetary valuation of their respective contributions will then become desirable in order to quantify the shares in which they are respectively entitled. Hence the owners of the business start with a fund of capital and their aim is to use this fund so that it increases and provides profits. These profits may either be taken out by the proprietors, or left in the business which, in the latter case, will start the next trading period with a larger capital. Of course, the object of the proprietors may be defeated; the assets may not be increased by profits but diminished by losses. In this event the business will start the next year with a reduced capital unless the proprietors decide to bring in further assets.

So far as concerns the business of an individual trader or partnership this concept of capital is merely a matter of convenience and account-

---

[1] *cf.* capital punishment, capital letter, capital ship, capital city, capital of a pillar, capital and labour, capital and income, and "capital!".

[2] No attempt is here made to deal with the economist's analysis of capital; such an attempt would take us into the higher flights of economic theory for which the writers have no quali-fications.

ing practice. Except to the extent that the bankruptcy and tax laws and those regulating particular activities require accounts to be kept and profits or losses to be calculated, there is no legal requirement that the assets brought into the business should be given a money value and credited to the proprietors as their capital, and there is nothing to prevent capital being increased or withdrawn by the proprietors at any time. If they decide that the business is over-capitalised they are free to withdraw part of the assets and reduce the capital accordingly. Since the proprietors are fully liable without limitation of liability it makes little difference to creditors whether their personal wealth is treated as business capital or not; it remains liable for payment of debts in any event. The trust to be reposed in the proprietors has therefore little relation to the capital in the business as such. It does not even depend solely on the present wealth of the proprietors; third parties may be prepared to place trust in them because of their character and reputation irrespective of their existing fortunes, for, like Sir Walter Scott, they may be willing to slave for the rest of their lives to discharge the liabilities of the business.

With an incorporated company limited by shares all this is altered. But, unless trust is reposed in it, it will be unable to survive in competition with its rivals. It may need to raise by loans more money than that subscribed by its members, or to buy on credit; in any event it will be vital, if it is to dispose of its goods or services, that third parties shall be able to trust it properly to fulfil its contracts. The creditworthiness of the company depends on the adequacy of its capital,[3] and this being so it is essential that capital should be more clearly defined and inviolable than is the case with an individual or partnership.

Hence the law has worked out certain principles relating to the raising and maintaining of capital. In effect, capital has ceased to be a name given to the fluctuating net worth of the business and has become a yardstick fixing the minimum value of the assets which must be raised initially and then, so far as possible, retained in the business. These principles have no application to unlimited companies and have been worked out in relation only to companies limited by shares— though most of them apply to the few remaining companies limited by guarantee and having a share capital. They are primarily intended for the protection of creditors (and it is upon this aspect that the following discussion concentrates) but, as was the now defunct *ultra vires* rule, are also designed to protect shareholders, present and future, against action by the directors which might covertly diminish the value of their shares as long-term investments.

Until recently these principles were largely judge-made and were

---

[3] And the high rate of failure of small private companies is due to the fact that so many of them are under-capitalised.

lax in comparison with those of the civil law countries of the European Community. As a result of the need to implement[4] the Second Company Law Directive, they are now mainly statutory and far stricter. Although the Directive only compelled us to adopt these principles in respect of public companies, an option of which we took some advantage, the opportunity was seized to rationalise, in relation to both public and private companies, the former confusing mixture of judge-made law and statutory glosses and exceptions, so that something approaching a comprehensive code of the law relating to share capital can now be found in Parts IV and V of the Companies Act 1985.[5]

RAISING CAPITAL

Authorised share capital

In the case of a company with a share capital (unless it is an unlimited company) its memorandum must "state the amount of the share capital with which [it] proposes to be registered and the division of that share capital into shares of a fixed amount".[6] These amounts are normally expressed in United Kingdom currency. But, as was held in *Re Scandinavian Bank*,[7] except for the "authorised minimum"[8] required (now) in the case of a public company, they can be denominated in a foreign currency or in a number of different currencies.[9] Even if denominated in United Kingdom currency, the "fixed amount" of each share can be too small to be legal tender (for example a half-penny[10]). The amount of the authorised capital in itself is of no importance as an indication of creditworthiness.[11] All that the foregoing long-standing statutory provisions achieve is to prescribe the maximum number of shares which the company can issue without increasing its authorised capital and the nominal value which it has chosen to place upon the shares into which the share capital is

---

[4] Originally by the Companies Act 1980.
[5] However these Parts contain sections dealing with some matters (*e.g.* "pre-emptive rights", class rights, and debentures) which are dealt with in later Chapters of this book.
[6] s.2(5)(a).
[7] [1988] Ch. 87.
[8] See below, p. 243.
[9] As the Scandinavian Bank wished, and was permitted, to do. According to the evidence of the Registrar, at least 125 English registered companies already had foreign currency share capital and, probably, two had multi-currency share capital. What appears not to be permissible is to denominate a share as, for example, "£1 or 3DM"; it must be one or the other.
[10] And one public company listed on the Stock Exchange had its share capital divided into shares with a nominal value of 0.1p.
[11] Since the unsophisticated may not realise this and be misled by the (apparently) impressive amount of the authorised capital, if, on the company's stationery or order forms, there is any reference to the amount of its share capital it must be to paid-up capital: s.351(2).

divided.[12] It is not even true to say, as one tends to,[13] that the nominal value of the shares fixes the maximum liability of the shareholders; shares may be, and frequently are, issued at a premium which they will be contractually liable to pay.[14]

Issued share capital

All that is of any importance (and it may be very little in the case of a private limited company) is its issued capital. It was established by the courts in the nineteenth century[15] that shares must not be issued at a discount to their nominal par value. This is now stated in the Act,[16] which specifically provides that if the shares should be so issued the allottee is liable to pay to the company the amount of the discount with interest.[17] Payment by way of commissions, brokerage or the like to any person in consideration of his subscribing or agreeing to subscribe is prohibited, even if the shares are issued at a premium,[18] except to the limited extent permitted by section 97.[19] Hence those dealing with the company have some assurance that the company has received, or will be entitled to receive, from its members payment of the price at which the shares are issued and that this price is not less than the nominal value of the issued capital. Formerly it was common for shares to be issued on the basis that part of the price would be paid on allotment and the balance when called upon, thus introducing a distinction between paid-up capital and uncalled capital. Today the price is almost invariably payable on or shortly after allotment except that, to encourage small investors to respond to privatisation issues, payment in such cases may generally be made in two or three instalments, spread over about two years. Long-term uncalled capital

[12] And, if authorised by the articles, the authorised capital can be increased, and the nominal value of its shares can be increased or diminished by consolidation or sub-division. An ordinary resolution suffices: s.121.

[13] See pp. 11–12, above. It does, however, fix their minimum liability since shares cannot be issued at a discount.

[14] But, as we shall see (pp. 243–245, below) the premium is not technically *share* capital though it is now treated for most purposes as if it was.

[15] Finally by *Ooregum Gold Mining Co. v. Roper* [1892] A.C. 125, H.L. It was there held that discounts were forbidden even though the existing shares of the same class were quoted at a discount. This does not mean that a company whose existing shares stand at a discount cannot issue any more; it can by exercising the powers under s.121 (n. 12, above) to create shares of a different class which can be issued at or above this nominal value because of their preferential rights.

[16] s.100.

[17] A subsequent holder is also liable, jointly and severally, unless he is, or claims through, a purchaser for value without notice of the contravention (s.112(1) and (3)) but, unlike the original allottee, he may be granted relief under s.113, on which see pp. 242–243, below.

[18] s.98.

[19] This limits the permitted commission to 10 per cent of the share price or such lesser percentage fixed by the articles. But s.98 prohibits only the payment of commission out of capital. So would a higher commission payable out of distributable profits be lawful? Or would it be caught by s.151 (see below, pp. 263 *et seq.*)?

(though it could be a valuable indication of creditworthiness since, in effect, it affords a personal guarantee by the members[20]) is now virtually a thing of the past.[21] How far those dealing with a limited company can derive comfort from the assurance that its paid-up capital has been raised depends on that capital being more than negligible. As we shall see,[22] this is now necessarily the case in relation to public companies. But it is not so in relation to private ones which may carry on business with a paid-up capital of £2 or even less.[23]

Moreover, payment does not have to be in cash; it can instead be made in kind[24] and very frequently is.[25] But, except (now) in relation to public companies, it seems that the parties' valuation of the non-cash consideration will be accepted as conclusive[26] unless its inadequacy appears on the face of the transaction[27] or there is evidence of bad faith.[28] Hence on an issue for a non-cash consideration it is possible to "water" the shares by agreeing to accept payment in property which is worth less than the nominal value of the shares. The only protection against this in relation to private companies is that, under what is now section 88, companies have to send the Registrar a "Return of Allotments" which distinguishes between shares allotted for cash and those allotted for non-cash and that, in relation to the latter, this return has to be accompanied by the relevant contract, or particulars of it if it is oral. However, the wording of the section suggests that this is intended for the protection of the Revenue[29] rather than the public and, in any case, it is often avoidable by the device of two ostensibly distinct agreements between the proposed allottee and the company—one for him to supply the company with property or services for £X and the other for him to subscribe for shares at the price of £X.[30]

---

[20] The Act still provides (ss.120 and 124(b)) that a limited company may determine that any part of its uncalled capital shall not be called-up except in the event and for the purposes of its winding up and formerly banks, and the like, often took advantage of this.

[21] For obvious reasons long-term investors in public companies fight shy of partly paid shares. Not infrequently, however, members of private companies are lax in actually paying for their shares.

[22] See p. 243, below.

[23] See p. 11, n. 38, above.

[24] s. 99(1) restates the general rule that "shares allotted by a company may be paid-up in money or money's worth (including goodwill and know-how)" but this is followed by exceptions and qualifications relating to public companies only.

[25] For example, when the proprietor of a business incorporates it by transferring the undertaking and assets to a newly formed company in consideration of an allotment of its shares.

[26] *Re Wragg* [1897] 1 Ch. 796, C.A.; *Park Business Interiors Ltd v. Park* [1992] BCLC 1034.

[27] *Re White Star Line* [1938] Ch. 458.

[28] *Tintin Exploration Syndicate v. Sandys* (1947) 177 L.T. 412.

[29] By ensuring that any appropriate stamp duty is paid: see s.88(2)(b)(i), (3) and (4).

[30] The company and the other party then exchange cheques or rely on mutual set-off. Such an arrangement was held in *Spargo's Case* (1873) L.R. 8 Ch.App. 407 to be an issue for cash and s.738(2) appears to confirm that it is. But query whether the new statutory provisions on the valuation of non-cash consideration (see pp. 239–243, below) can be avoided by this device: *Re Bradford Investments plc (No. 2)* [1991] BCLC 688 at 695. Technically, a bonus

Until the Companies Act 1980, implementing the Second Company Law Directive, the foregoing rules were all that the law prescribed regarding raising share capital.[31] Then, however, in what probably amounts to the most fundamental adoption so far by English company law of civil law practices, there was a long overdue tightening-up *in relation to public companies.* The changes fall under two heads: (1) far stricter rules relating to issues for a non-cash consideration and (2) prescription of a minimum share capital.

Public companies: non-cash issues or transactions

Before turning to the regulation of non-cash issues, however, it is important to note the width of the definition of "cash" in section 738 (2), for the new regulations do not apply where the consideration falls within this section. It includes an undertaking to pay cash to the company in the future, thus putting the company at risk of the insolvency of the shareholder,[32] and also the release of a liability of the company for a liquidated sum. The latter is a useful provision in facilitating equity for debt swaps whereby the secured creditors of an insolvent company forego their claims as debtors against the company in exchange for the issue to them of equity shares. The company is thereby released from an often crippling burden of interest payments and the removal of the debt may even produce by itself a surplus of assets over liabilities. This will be to the immediate benefit of the shareholders and unsecured creditors, though if the company prospers in the future the original shareholders will naturally find that their equity interest has been extensively diluted. It seems that no infringement of the rule forbidding discounts occurs where the face value of the debt is taken for the purposes of paying up the new shares, even though the market value of the debt at the time of the swap was less than its face value because of the debtor's insolvency.[33]

A public company may not accept, in payment for its shares or any premium on them, an undertaking by any person that he or another will do work or perform services for the company or any other person.[34] If

---

issue (see below, p. 246) is a non-cash issue and, although for the purposes or many of the sections referred to in what follows it is expressly treated as if it was not, this is not so in relation to s.88. On a bonus issue it will not be practicable to adopt the avoiding device (hence Table A 1985, art. 110(d)).

[31] Apart from the rationalisation in the 1948 Act of the treatment of share premiums. see below, pp. 243–245.

[32] There is no apparent limit on the future date which may be fixed for the actual payment, for the five-year limit in s.102 (see below, p. 240) applies only to non-cash payments, but the undertaking must be one given to the company in consideration of the allotment of the shares: *System Controls plc v. Munro Corporation plc* [1990] BCC 386.

[33] *Re Mercantile Trading Co., Schroeder's Case* (1871) L.R. 11 Eq. 13; *Pro-Image Studios v. Commonwealth Bank of Australia* (1990–1991) 4 ACSR 586, though it should be noted that in this case both the debt and the consideration for the new shares were immediately payable.

[34] s.99(1) and (2). But neither these sections nor ss.102 and 103 (below) prevent the company from enforcing the undertaking: s.115. If a private company wishes to convert to a plc such undertakings must first be performed or discharged: s.45(3).

it should do so, the holder of the shares[35] is liable to pay the company an amount equal to the nominal value of the shares plus the premium or such part of that amount as has been treated as paid up by the undertaking.[36] Nor may it allot shares as fully or partly paid-up if the consideration is *any* sort of undertaking which need not be performed until after five years from the date of the allotment.[37] If the undertaking should have been performed within five years but is not, payment in cash then becomes due immediately.[38] And (though this is of minimal importance[39]) shares taken by a subscriber to the memorandum of association in pursuance of his undertaking in the memorandum must be paid for in cash.[40]

Finally, the possibility of "share-watering" by placing an inflated value on the non-cash consideration is tackled by requiring it to be independently valued. Under section 103 a public company may not allot shares as fully or partly paid-up (as to their nominal value or any premium) otherwise than in cash unless:—(i) the consideration has been valued in accordance with section 108, (ii) a report is made to the company in accordance with that section during the six months immediately preceding the allotment and (iii) a copy is sent to the proposed allottee.[41] To this there are exceptions in relation to bonus issues[42] and in relation to most types of takeovers and mergers[43] or schemes of arrangement with creditors.[44] But, in other cases, if the allottee has not received the copy of the valuation report or there is some other contravention of section 103 or 108, which he knew, or ought to have known, amounted to a contravention, once again he is liable to pay in cash with interest.[45]

Under section 108 the valuation has to be made by a person "qualified to be appointed, or continue to be, an auditor of the company".[46] He may, however, arrange for and accept a valuation from another person who appears to him to have the requisite experience and knowledge and who is not an employee or officer of any company in the

---

[35] Including not only the registered holder but also the beneficial owner: s.99(5).

[36] s.99(2) and (3). Bonus issues are excluded: s.99(4).

[37] s.102. If contravened the consequences are similar to those for contravention of s.99.

[38] s.102(5) and (6). And see s.45(4) regarding a private company converting to a plc.

[39] The English practice is for two persons to subscribe for only one share each and the subscribers are generally two clerks of the professional advisers (who will hold each share as a nominee for the promoters): see Chap. 6, p. 109, below. The promoters themselves may suffer more serious consequences under ss.104 and 105: below.

[40] s.106.

[41] s.103(1).

[42] s.103(2).

[43] s.103(3)–(5). The rules of the Takeover Panel or the Stock Exchange will normally ensure that there has been professional assessment of value in such cases.

[44] See s.103(7) as amended by the Insolvency Act 1986.

[45] s.103(6). As is a subsequent holder unless he is or claims through a purchaser for value without notice: s.112. See *Re Bradford Investments* [1991] BCLC 224.

[46] s.108(1). For these qualifications, see Chap. 20, pp. 539–544, below.

group.[47] In practice, therefore, the report will be by the company's auditor supported by another professional valuation of any real property or other consideration which the auditor does not feel competent to value on his own. The report has to go into considerable detail[48] and must support the conclusion that the aggregate of the cash and non-cash consideration is not less than the nominal value and the premium.[49]

A private company proposing to convert to a public one cannot evade these valuation requirements by allotting shares for a non-cash consideration shortly before it re-registers as a public one. In such a case, the Registrar cannot entertain the application to re-register unless the consideration has been valued and reported on in accordance with section 108.[50]

In addition, during an initial period of two years from the date when the company was entitled to carry on business as a public company, sections 104 and 105 apply similar valuation requirements to certain transactions with anyone who was a subscriber to the memorandum on the company's formation or a member of it on its conversion to a public company. The transactions in question are those under which such a person is to transfer to the company (or to anyone else) a non-cash asset[51] and the price to be paid (in cash or kind) by the company is equal in value at the time of the agreement to one tenth or more of the company's nominal issued capital at that time.[52] This is aimed at a mischief rather different from that tackled by section 103; not at an issue of shares by the company at a concealed discount but at a purchase by the company of property from the promoters at an excessive price.

Unless the transaction is in the ordinary course of the company's business or the agreement is entered into under the supervision of the court,[53] the following conditions will have to be complied with:

(i) the consideration to be received by the company and any consideration (other than cash[54]) to be given by the company must be independently valued under section 109, which adapts section 108 to meet this different situation[55];

---

[47] s.108(2) and (3).
[48] See s.108(4)–(7). Subs. (7) deals with the complication where the consideration payable to the company is partly for the shares and partly for some other consideration given by the company.
[49] s.108(6)(d).
[50] s.44.
[51] Defined in s.739.
[52] s.104(1), (2) and (3).
[53] s.104(6).
[54] If the consideration includes an issue of shares, s.103 will also have to be complied with: s.104(5)(b).
[55] The value of the consideration to be received by the company is the value of the non-cash asset, if that is to be transferred to another person: s.104(5)(a).

(ii) the valuer's report must have been made during the six months immediately preceding the agreement;

(iii) the terms of the agreement must have been approved by an ordinary resolution; and

(iv) not later than the giving of the notice of the meeting at which the resolution is to be proposed, copies of the agreement must have been circulated to members and to the other party to the agreement.[56]

If these conditions are not fulfilled, the agreement, so far as not carried out, is void.[57] Moreover, the company can normally recover the consideration given by it or its value.[58] If the agreement included provision for the allotment of the company's shares, that provision is not void but the consequences are similar to those on contravention of section 103.[59]

Whether the valuation is under section 103 or 104, the valuer is entitled to require from the officers of the company such information and explanation as he thinks necessary[60] and it is an offence if false or deceptive replies are made knowingly or recklessly.[61] However, when, under sections 99, 102, 103, 105 or 112 or by virtue of an undertaking given to the company, a person is liable to pay-up shares he may apply to the court to be relieved of that liability and the court may exempt him to the extent that it considers just and equitable.[62] But the court must have regard to two "overriding principles", namely:

(a) that a company which has allotted shares should receive money or money's worth at least equal in value to the aggregate of the nominal value of those shares and the value of the premium or, if the case so requires, so much of that aggregate as is treated as paid-up,[63] and

(b) that when the company would, if the court did not grant exemption, have more than one remedy against a particular person it should be for the company to decide which remedy it should remain entitled to pursue.[64]

---

[56] s.104(4).

[57] s.105(1)(a) and (2).

[58] But, if the other party has received the valuer's report, only if he knows or ought to have known of the contravention: s.105(1)(b) and (2).

[59] s.105(1)(b) and (2).

[60] s.110(1).

[61] s.110(2) and (3).

[62] s.113(1) and (2).

[63] *Re Bradford Investments plc (No. 2)* [1991] BCLC 688.

[64] s.113(5). For other matters which the court should take into account, see subss. (3) and (4). When proceedings are brought by one person (*e.g.* a holder of the shares) against another (*e.g.* the original allottee) for a contribution in respect of liability the court may adjust the extent (if any) of the contribution having regard to their respective culpability in relation to that liability: s.113(6) and (7). And see s.113(8) for exemption from liability under s.105(2).

Public companies: minimum capital

The "authorised minimum" share capital of a public company is £50,000 or such other sum as the Secretary of State may specify by statutory instrument.[65] In practice most public companies and all those whose shares are listed will have a considerably larger share capital than the minimum. A company formed as a public company cannot commence business until it has satisfied the Registrar that it has allotted and issued shares to the nominal value of not less than the authorised minimum,[66] of which at least one quarter[67] and the whole of any premium has been paid up either in cash or (to the extent permitted and subject to the independent valuation as described above) in kind.[68] He has similarly to be satisfied that these conditions are met when a private company re-registers as a public one.[69] The formalities that have to be complied with in order that he may be satisfied are described in Chapter 6, above. On any subsequent issue of shares the same requirements regarding payment-up have to be met, *i.e.* the shares must be paid-up at least to the extent of one quarter of their nominal value and the whole of any premium.[70]

Share premiums

Prior to 1948, when companies issued shares at a premium (*i.e.* at above their nominal value), the premiums were treated totally differently from share capital. Share capital was regarded as determined by the nominal par value of the shares; if they had been issued at a price above par the excess was not "capital" and, indeed, constituted part of the distributable surplus which the company, if it wished, could return to the shareholders by way of dividend.[71] This was ridiculous. If the price paid for the shares was £100,000, the true capital of the company was £100,000 and it should have made no difference to the company or to the shareholders whether the £100,000 was obtained by issuing 100,000 £1 shares at par or by issuing 10,000 £1 shares at £10. This absurdity, however, was mitigated by section 56 of the 1948

---

[65] s.118(1). Should an increase be specified, the S.I. may require any public company with capital less than that specified to conform or to convert to a private company: s.118(2).

[66] s.117(1) and (2).

[67] In view of the unpopularity of partly paid shares (see above, n. 21) the strong probability is that the full nominal value will be paid up.

[68] s.101. This does not apply (see s.101(2)) to shares allotted under an employees' share scheme (defined in s.743) but unless they are paid up to that extent they may not be taken into account in determining the nominal value of allotted share capital: s.117(4).

[69] ss. 43–45.

[70] s.101. If the company allots a share in contravention of s.101 it is treated as if this sum had been received (s.101(3)) and the allottee (and any subsequent holder, unless he is, or claims through, a purchaser for value without notice—see s.112) is liable to pay it with interest: s.101(4). Neither subs. (3) nor (4) applies to an issue of a bonus share unless the allottee knows or ought to have known of the contravention: s.101(5).

[71] *Drown v. Gaumont British Corp.* [1937] Ch. 402.

Act, now replaced by section 130 of the 1985 Act. This provides that a sum equal to the aggregate amount or value of the premiums shall be transferred to a "share premium account" which, in general, has to be treated as if it were part of the paid-up share capital.[72] But, anomalously, it is still necessary to refer expressly to both, and for the company, in its annual accounts and reports, to distinguish between them. What, if it were not for arbitrary par values, would be a single item—capital—has to be treated as two distinct items, albeit for most purposes treated identically.

Moreover, the two are not treated as wholly identical. Section 130 provides for two "exceptions"[73] and two "reliefs".[74] The first exception is that a company may apply the share premium account in paying up bonus shares. It would, of course, be impossible thus to apply issued capital but to apply share premium account is wholly unobjectionable since the only effect is to convert it, or a part of it, to share capital proper. The second exception is that it may be applied in writing off the company's preliminary expenses or the expenses of, or the commissions paid or discount allowed on, any issue of the company's shares, or in providing for the premium payable on redemption of debentures of the company. It is difficult to justify this second exception (and the reference to "discount allowed on any issue of shares" is puzzling since payment of such a discount is now proscribed in relation to both public and private companies[75]). The exceptions, however, are not of great importance. More important (and more interesting) are the "reliefs".

Section 130 (as did its predecessor, section 56) expressly applies to issues at a premium "whether for cash or otherwise". The result of this was held to be that if, say, on a merger one company (A) acquired the shares of another (B) in consideration of an issue of A's own shares and the true value of B's shares exceeded the nominal value of those issued by A, a share premium account had to be established in respect of the excess.[76] The result of this was that B's undistributed profits formerly available for distribution by way of dividend ceased to be distributable. This caused something of a furore in commercial circles which, in such circumstances, wanted to continue to avoid that consequence by employing so-called "merger", instead of "acquisition", accounting.[77] Although the decision was thought to be correct by the majority of the legal and accountancy professions there was at

---

[72] s.130(1) and (3).
[73] s.130(2).
[74] s.130(4).
[75] s.100: see p. 237, above. And commissions are permitted only to the limited extent provided in ss.97 and 98.
[76] *Head & Co. Ltd v. Ropner Holdings Ltd* [1952] Ch. 124.
[77] These alternative methods of accounting are explained in paras. 7–12 of the new Sched. 4A inserted by the 1989 Act.

least one well-known set of Chambers which disputed it. Hence, relying on Opinions obtained from that source,[78] merger accounting often continued to be employed, thus avoiding the creation of a share premium account. However, in 1980 the question was again litigated and the earlier decision fully upheld.[79] Faced with two decisions, the Chambers had to capitulate but joined the City in demanding that some relief should be afforded in the envisaged Companies Act 1981. This, to the extent thought to be reasonable and consonant with the Second Company Law Directive, was forthcoming. Hence, sections 131 and 132 now provide for "merger relief" (section 131) and "relief in respect of group reconstructions" (section 132).

The general effect of section 131 is that section 130 does not apply when, pursuant to a merger arrangement, one company has acquired at least 90 per cent of each class of equity shares of another in exchange for an allotment of its equity shares at a premium. The general effect of section 132 is to exclude the application of section 130 in the case of issues at a premium by a wholly owned subsidiary in consideration of a transfer to it of non-cash assets by another company in the group comprising the holding company and its wholly owned subsidiaries. If section 132 applies, section 131 does not.[80] The Secretary of State is empowered by section 134 to make regulations providing further relief from section 130 in relation to premiums other than cash premiums or for modifying any relief provided by sections 131–133.

Increase of capital

"Capital", in the sense of the net worth of a business, will fluctuate from time to time according to whether it makes profits and ploughs them back or suffers losses. But a company's capital, *i.e.* the issued share capital plus share premium account (if any) does not automatically fluctuate to reflect this. It remains unaltered until increased by a further issue of shares, which must be made in conformity with the rules dealt with above, or reduced in accordance with the rules dealt with below.[81] While a reduction is potentially dangerous, an increase of capital is to be encouraged and merely involves increasing the authorised share capital, if all that has been issued, and finding one or more persons willing to take up the new shares. If, however, the com-

---

[78] One of the few advantages of a divided profession is that, by shopping around, solicitors can generally obtain Counsel's Opinion supporting the course which their clients want to pursue.

[79] *Shearer v. Bercain Ltd* [1980] 3 All E.R. 295.

[80] Anyone wishing to take advantage of these reliefs will need to study carefully the sections themselves in the light of the supplementing provisions in s.133; they are more complicated than the above summary may imply. (Note that the erroneous cross-reference (to s.132(4) instead of s.132(8)) in s.131(1) was corrected by Sched. 19, para. 1 to the 1989 Act.)

[81] At pp. 247 *et seq.*

pany has made profits and not distributed them as dividends, a normal issue of further shares will not bring the "capital" of the company into balance with the net worth of the company. Although it will increase the share capital and the share premium account (if any), the price received will initially increase the net assets to a corresponding extent and it will still be necessary in the balance sheet to have a further (notional) liability in order to balance the "assets" and "liabilities". This is normally described as a "reserve", an expression which may confuse those unaccustomed to accounting practice since it may suggest (falsely) that the company has set aside an actual earmarked fund to meet some potential or actual liability.

The only way in which a profit-rich company can effectively bring its "capital" more into line with its increased capital, in the sense of its net worth, is by making a "bonus" or "capitalisation" issue[82] to its shareholders. The former expression is likely to be used by the company when communicating with its shareholders (in the hope that they will think that they are being treated generously by being given something for nothing) and the latter when communicating with the workforce (which might otherwise demand a bonus in the form of increased wages). In fact such an issue is merely a means of capitalising reserves by using them to pay-up shares newly issued to the shareholders. For example, suppose that before the issue the net worth (taking book values) of the company was £2 million and the issued capital one million shares of £1 each. The shares, on book values, will be worth £2 each.[83] The company then makes a one-for-one bonus issue paid up out of the share premium account or free reserves. The only effect on a shareholder is that for each of his former £1 shares worth £2 he will now have two £1 shares each worth £1.[84] And the only effect on the company is that, insofar as the bonus issue is paid up out of share premium account, that, as part of the "capital yardstick", is reduced or eliminated and replaced by issued share capital and, insofar as it is paid out of free reserves, these are reduced or eliminated and, again, replaced by issued share capital.

To a small extent the same effect can be achieved by the practice, increasingly common among listed companies, of allowing the shareholders to opt to take shares in lieu of dividends. This may appeal to shareholders whose concern is capital appreciation only. But it has disadvantages unless the dividends are very large; fractions of shares cannot be allotted, shareholders will end up with lots of share certific-

---

[82] The two expressions mean the same thing and, indeed, so does a third ("scrip" issue) which is sometimes used.

[83] This does not mean that listed shares will be quoted at that price; that will depend on many other factors, including in particular the expected future profits and dividends. And the book values, of fixed assets in particular, may not reflect their present values.

[84] The *quoted* price, is not likely to fall by a half because it is to be expected that the company will seek to maintain approximately the same rate of dividend per share as before the issue.

ates for small numbers of shares (unless they have opted for dematerialisation), and they will be liable to tax as if they had received the cash dividend. Nor is it likely to result in any simplification and rationalisation of the company's capital structure.

Maintenance of capital

Clearly all the foregoing provisions regarding raising of capital would be pointless if the company, having raised capital, had complete freedom to reduce it. But here we are faced with the ambiguity of the expression "capital". In saying that it should not be reduced, do we mean that the notional liability shown under that head in the company's balance sheet should not be reduced? If so, there is no difficulty about that; all that is needed is to say so or, indeed, merely to provide no means whereby that can be done. Or does it mean, instead or in addition, that the company must not allow the value of its net assets to fall below the figures representing "capital"? In fact, as finally enacted as a result of implementing the Second Company Law Directive,[85] it now means (at any rate in relation to public companies) something approaching both of these possibilities without, however, going quite so far as either.

Formal reductions of capital
Generally speaking, the capital yardstick represented by issued share capital plus share premium account (and, as we shall see shortly, any capital redemption reserve[86]) cannot be reduced except under an order of the court. By what is now section 135 of the 1985 Act, a company may, if so authorised by its articles,[87] reduce its share capital "in any way"[88] so long as confirmation by the court is obtained under sections 136–138 (dealt with in Chapter 28, below). Not only may the capital yardstick then be reduced[89] but that may be accompanied by a repayment of capital to the shareholders,[90] thus reducing both the capital yardstick (a notional liability) and the assets of the company to a corresponding extent.

If the result of the reduction thus made is that the nominal value of a public company's allotted share capital falls below the authorised minimum, the court's order is not registered by the Registrar, and so

---

[85] Initially by the Companies Act 1980.
[86] See below, pp. 252 *et seq.*
[87] If the articles do not so authorise, it can alter them by passing a special resolution.
[88] s.135(1).
[89] Thus, perhaps, enabling the company to resume the payment of dividends which might otherwise be prohibited by the dividend rules; see below, Chap. 12.
[90] See s.135(2)(c). It may also extinguish or reduce any uncalled capital (s.135(2)(a)) but in both such circumstances there are special protections (in s.136(3)–(6)) for creditors.

does not become effective,[91] until the company re-registers as a private company.[92]

Loss of capital

The mere fact that the company incurs losses so that the value of its net assets falls below the capital yardstick does not mean that it must cease trading. It would be going too far to demand that since it will still be fully solvent in every sense so long as its true assets exceed its true liabilities and it is able to pay its debts as they fall due. The only immediate effect of the loss of capital is that normally the company will not be able to pay dividends. However, in the case of a public company, section 142 requires that if the net assets[93] become half or less of its called-up share capital it must, within 28 days of that becoming known to a director, convene an extraordinary general meeting for not later than 56 days thereafter "for the purpose of considering whether any, and if so what, steps should be taken to deal with the situation".[94] Since the general meeting is not compelled to take any steps and is given no greater powers than it would otherwise have, the requirement seems somewhat fatuous[95] but a director who knowingly and wilfully authorises a failure to comply is liable to a fine.[96]

Acquisition of its own shares

It was held by the House of Lords in the nineteenth century that a company could not purchase its own shares, even though there was an express power to do so in its memorandum, since this would result in a reduction of capital.[97] Assuming that on purchase the shares were cancelled and nothing put in their place this would necessarily reduce the capital yardstick represented by issued share capital and could also be regarded as objectionable as a diversion of the company's assets to the shareholder whose shares were purchased. Nevertheless, the rule thus laid down was stricter than in some common law countries (for

---

[91] s.138(2).

[92] s.139.

[93] "Net assets" for the purposes of s.142 is not defined. Presumably it has the same meaning as elsewhere, *i.e.* "the aggregate of the company's assets less the aggregate of its liabilities (liabilities to include any provision for liabilities or charges within paragraph 89 of Schedule 4)": see ss.152(2) and 264(2). Or should the words in brackets be omitted?

[94] s.142(1) and (3).

[95] We were required to enact it, in respect of public companies, by the Second Company Law Directive but we did not extend it to private companies, most of which are mainly financed by bank overdrafts repayable on demand (and thus "liabilities") so that they might have had to convene such a meeting almost immediately after they were launched.

[96] s.142(2).

[97] *Trevor v. Whitworth* (1887) 12 App.Cas. 409, H.L. In addition, s.23 provides that, with very limited exceptions, a company cannot be a member of its holding company, either directly or through a nominee, and any allotment or transfer of shares in the holding company to the subsidiary or its nominee is void.

example the United States and Canada) and many civil law ones (and than was required by the Second Directive). Nor did either objection apply if, for example, the shares were given to the company and held by a nominee for it,[98] or if a company with uncalled capital forfeited shares for non-payment of calls—as has always been recognised as permissible. Moreover, increasingly over the years the legislation has empowered the courts to order a company to buy its shares in certain circumstances.

By the Companies Acts 1980 and 1981 the rule and an extended number of exceptions to it were codified and are now to be found in sections 143–181 of the 1985 Act. The following pages of this chapter attempt to explain their effect, not always adopting the order in which they appear in the Act. Before beginning, however, it is worth noting the recent judgment of Lightman J. in *Acatos & Hutcheson plc v. Watson*[99] in which he held that neither the common law nor section 143 prohibited the purchase by company A of the shares of company B, thereby acquiring control over the shares in company A held by company B, even where that shareholding represented both a substantial proportion of the issued share capital of company A and of the assets of company B. This is at first sight a surprising result, for a so-called "fundamental principle" of company law is side-stepped by a transaction which has the same economic effect on company A and its creditors as if it had bough the shares directly. However, to have held otherwise would have provided companies with a cast-iron anti-takeover defence, namely the purchase of shares in potential bidders,[1] unless the court was prepared to embark upon the tricky task of distinguishing between substantial and insubstantial shareholdings. Moreover, the "fundamental principle" was not left entirely without support: company A's directors would still need to act bona fide in the interests of their company, and if company B had been created simply to avoid the rule, the court would be able to ignore its separate legal personality as being a sham.[2]

Section 143(1)[3] lays down the general rule that a company "shall not acquire its own shares whether by purchase, subscription or otherwise." If it purports to do so, the company and every officer in default is liable to a fine and the purported acquisition is void.[4] This, however, is subject to the succeeding provisions of the Act. Section 143(3) mentions five exceptions some of which are elaborated or qualified in later sections. These five are:

---

[98] Held to be permissible in *Re Castiglione's Will Trust* [1958] Ch. 549.
[99] [1995] 1 BCLC 218.
[1] See below, Chap. 29, p. 783.
[2] See above, p. 174.
[3] Which applies to a company, public or private, whether limited by shares or by guarantee if it has a share capital.
[4] s.143(2).

(i) the acquisition of fully paid shares otherwise than for valuable consideration,[5]

(ii) the redemption or purchase of shares in accordance with sections 159 to 181,[6]

(iii) the acquisition of shares on a formal reduction of capital confirmed by the court,[7]

(iv) the purchase of shares in pursuance of an order of the court under section 5 (contested alteration of objects),[8] section 54 (litigated objection to conversion from public to private company),[9] sections 459–461 (relief to members unfairly prejudiced),[10] or

(v) forfeiture of shares (or acceptance of their surrender) for non-payment of calls.

Section 144 then contains further provisions relating to cases where (a) shares are issued to a nominee of the company or (b) are acquired by the nominee from a third party as partly paid. In either of such cases the shares are to be treated as held by the nominee for his own account and the company as having no beneficial interest in them; the nominee is liable to pay them up (as to their nominal value and any premium) when called upon to do so.[11] Section 145 provides certain exceptions principally designed to deal with problems faced by public companies in relation to shares acquired by the trustees of a company's employees' share scheme or pension scheme.[12]

Sections 146–149 deal with the treatment of the shares held by or for a public company when the acquisition of them is not void under section 143. In most cases, under section 146 the shares, or any interest of the company in them, must be disposed of or the shares cancelled before the end of "the relevant period"[13] which, according to the circumstances in which they were acquired, is either one year or three years.[14] If cancelled, the issued share capital must be reduced by the nominal value of such shares.[15] This, under section 147, can be done

---

[5] Thus adopting *Re Castiglione's Will Trust*, above, and apparently extending it by not compelling the vesting of the shares, if fully paid, in a nominee for the company.

[6] See pp. 251–263, below.

[7] See p. 247 above and Chap. 28 below.

[8] See Chap. 10 at p. 210, above.

[9] See Chap. 6 at p. 124, below.

[10] See Chap. 27 at pp. 747 *et seq.*, below.

[11] s.144(1). If he was a subscriber to the memorandum he and other subscribers become jointly and severally liable, as do the directors at the time of acquisition in other cases (s.144(2)) but the court may grant relief similar to that under s.113 (above, p. 242): s.144(3) and (4).

[12] These problems were originally tackled by the Companies (Beneficial Interests) Act 1983: see now the 1985 Act, ss.145, 146 and 148 and Schedule 2. The acquisition of such shares is likely to be financed by the company and the company may have a residuary beneficial interest in them which, under Schedule 2, may be disregarded.

[13] s.146(1) and (2).

[14] s.146(3).

[15] s.146(2).

by a resolution of the general meeting without the need for a formal reduction of capital. But if the effect is to reduce the allotted capital below the authorised minimum the company must apply for re-registration as a private company[16] in accordance with section 147(3) and (4).[17]

Furthermore, so long as the shares are held by or for the company no voting rights may be exercised and any purported exercise is void.[18] Were it not for this, the directors would be able to decide on how the shares should be voted, thus enhancing their own voting strength as shareholders. And if the value of the shares is shown in the company's balance sheet as an asset,[19] an amount equal to the value of the shares (or, where appropriate, the value to the company of its interest in them) must be transferred out of profits available for dividend to a reserve not available for distribution.

Section 148(1) and (2) applies provisions similar to those of sections 146, 147 and 149 to a private company which re-registers as a public one at a time when its shares were held by or for it, but with the modification that "the relevant period" for the purposes of section 146 runs from the date of re-registration.

Redeemable shares

Far more extreme examples of exceptions to the rule that a company limited by shares may not acquire its own shares, are afforded by what is now Part V, Chapter VII, of the Act[20] dealing both with redemption of shares issued as redeemable and with purchase of shares whether or not issued as redeemable. We deal first with redeemable shares, which have been permissible since the Companies Act 1929. This introduced a method whereby redemption could take place without a reduction of the capital yardstick—a method which was adopted when, many years later,[21] companies were empowered to purchase their own shares, whether or not they were issued as redeemable.

Prior to the 1981 Act only preference shares could be issued as redeemable. Now, however, section 159 of the 1985 Act provides that a company, if authorised by its articles, may issue shares of any class which are to be redeemed or are liable to be redeemed, whether at the option of the company or the shareholder.[22] They may not be issued

---

[16] If it fails to do so it is nevertheless treated as if it was a private company so far as offering of its shares are concerned and the company and its officers in default are liable to fines: s.149.

[17] s.146(2)(b).

[18] s.146(4).

[19] s.148(4). It is not normal practice to show them as assets.

[20] ss.159–181.

[21] By the Companies Act 1981.

[22] s.159(1).

unless the company also has issued shares which are not redeemable.[23] Nor may they be redeemed until they are fully paid.[24] In order to protect the shareholders whose shares are not to be redeemed, the terms and manner of the redemption must be set out in the company's articles.[25] At one time it was thought that this provision unduly restricted the directors' discretion in dealing with these matters and in the 1989 Act an amending section, which was intended to introduce a new section 159A into the 1985 Act, was hurriedly included. On close examination, however, the new section was found to be equally defect-ive and the original provision not so restrictive as originally thought; hence the amendment was never brought into force, and there seem to be no immediate plans for alternative reform.[26]

Subject to an exception relating to private companies,[27] they can be redeemed only out of distributable profits or out of the proceeds of a fresh issue of shares made for the purpose.[28] And any premium pay-able on redemption must be paid out of distributable profits.[29] On redemption the shares are cancelled and the issued share capital reduced by their nominal amount.[30] But the authorised capital is not reduced and can be utilised either for the new issue for the purpose of the redemption or for a future issue.[31] When redeemed out of the proceeds of a fresh issue the capital yardstick will be maintained as a result of the issue. This, however, is not so if shares are redeemed out of profits. The effect of that method is that not only are the company's assets reduced by the repayment to the shareholders but, without more, so would be the issued share capital.

The answer found to avoid that result is now stated in section 170. It provides that if shares are wholly redeemed out of profits the amount by which the issued share capital is diminished shall be transferred to a reserve called "the capital redemption reserve"[32] and that, if they

---

[23] s.159(2). This minimises the risk that redemption might result in the company having no members—though there are no very strong reasons why that should matter if s.24 of the Act and s.122(1)(e) of the Insolvency Act 1986 were repealed.

[24] s.159(3). Thus avoiding redemption wiping out the personal liability of the holders in respect of uncalled capital.

[25] s.160(3).

[26] DTI, *Terms and Manner of Redemption of Redeemable Shares*, 1993.

[27] s.171: see below, p. 258.

[28] s.160(1).

[29] s.160(1)(g). But where the shares were issued at a premium any premium payable on redemp-tion may be paid out of the proceeds of a fresh issue up to an amount equal to the aggregate of the issue premiums or the current amount of the share premium account, whichever is the less, the share premium account being appropriately reduced: s.160(2).

[30] s.160(4).

[31] s.160(5).

[32] s.170(1). Prior to the 1981 Act this was misleadingly called "the capital redemption reserve *fund*" which was apt to lead students into believing that companies could not redeem shares out of distributable profits unless these totalled at least twice the redemption price. This, of course, is not so. The capital redemption reserve is, and always was, merely a notional liability not an earmarked fund of assets.

are redeemed partly out of profits and partly out of the proceeds of a new issue and the aggregate amount of those proceeds is less than the nominal value of the shares redeemed, the amount of the difference shall be so transferred.[33] Like the share premium account this reserve is treated as if it was paid-up capital of the company but may be applied in paying up a bonus issues,[34] thus converting it to paid-up share capital. Unless and until this is done the "capital" will consist not just of issued share capital plus share premium account (if any) but of issued share capital plus share premium account (if any) plus capital redemption reserve. The result is that the company's former "capital" is not reduced (although, if the redemption is out of profits, the company will have a smaller amount (if any) of distributable profits out of which to pay dividends). There is no reduction of the capital yardstick; one type of "capital" is substituted for another.

As a result of the reforms introduced by the 1981 Act, there are circumstances in which the foregoing capital maintenance require-ments on redemption are relaxed in relation to private companies. But as the provisions in question apply both to redemption and to pur-chases other than redemptions, they are left for consideration in what follows.

Purchase of own shares

Until the 1981 Act, redemption of preference shares was the only type of purchase by a company of its own shares permitted by English Law without a court order. So far as capital maintenance is concerned there was no reason for so restricting it; the solution adopted in relation to redeemable shares could equally well be applied to other purchases. But undoubtedly the opportunities for other abuses are then greater; for example, the directors, by causing the company to repurchase shares of other members, could, without any personal expense, enhance the value of their own holdings and their control of the company. But these dangers too could be guarded against and it was widely felt that the former restrictions were anachronistic. Hence, in 1980 the Department of Trade pub-lished a Consultative Document (a Green Paper)[35] canvassing the possibility of widening a company's powers. This met with an enthusiastic reception and was implemented by the 1981 Act,[36] both in relation to private companies and, to the extent permitted by the Second Company Law Directive, to public companies. The power

---

[33] s.170(2) but with an exception in relation to private companies: ss.170(3) and 171, below.
[34] s.170(4).
[35] *The Purchase by a Company of its own Shares*: Cmnd. 7944.
[36] Now 1985 Act, Part V, Chap. VII which contains provisions relating to both redemption and purchase.

has been widely used by both and seems to have given rise to few problems.[37]

The essential difference between redemption and purchase is that, under the latter, agreement of the parties (the selling shareholder and the buying company) will be needed at the time of the purchase. Neither party can force the other to sell or buy if he or it does not want to and if he or it does want to, the terms and conditions will have to be agreed at the time of the purchase. In contrast, as we have seen, in the case of redeemable shares the terms and conditions of redemption will have been set out in advance in the company's articles at the time the shares were issued. Subject to that difference, the two transactions are, broadly speaking, treated alike.

Section 162 provides that: subject to the following provisions, a company, if authorised to do so by its articles, may purchase its own shares (including redeemable shares[38]); that sections 159 and 160 apply as they do to redemptions; but that a repurchase cannot be made if the result would be that there were no longer any members of the company holding non-redeemable shares.[39] Similarly, section 170, relating to the establishment of the capital redemption reserve, expressly applies to both redemptions and purchases; in other words, on a purchase "capital" has similarly to be maintained. And, in contrast with the practice in the United States, shares which are re-purchased have to be cancelled[40] and cannot be held as "treasury shares" which can be re-sold by the company. It was decided not to countenance the latter practice, which, in effect, would have enabled a company to trade as a market-maker in its own shares and which would have given rise to accounting and tax complexities.

However, in relation to matters other than capital maintenance, stricter provisions apply to purchases. These provisions vary according to whether the purchase is to be an "off-market" or a "market" purchase, as these terms are defined in section 163.[41] For practical purposes what this means is that if the Stock Exchange[42] has listed the relevant shares or afforded facilities for dealings in them to be undertaken on its Alternative Investment Market[43] and the purchase is so made it is a "market purchase"; otherwise it is not. Market purchases

---

[37] But an essential first step is to clear the transaction with the Inland Revenue to ensure that it will not be regarded as a "distribution". There is some evidence that re-purchases have been driven by their advantages for tax-exempt institutional shareholders.

[38] Thus enabling the company to "redeem" them prior to a date fixed in the terms and conditions if it can do so at a lower price.

[39] *cf.* s.159(2) and n. 23, above.

[40] s.162(2) applying s.160(4) and (5).

[41] As amended by the FSA 1986.

[42] The section refers to "any recognised investment exchange" other than "an overseas investment exchange".

[43] See below, Chap. 16.

create fewer risks of abuse since the rules of the Exchange will apply and purchases will be effected at an objectively determined market price. If there is no market, a shareholder who needs to sell is likely to find that the company (or its directors) is the only potential purchaser and the shareholder will have to accept the price that it is prepared to pay.

Off-market purchases

Under section 164 an off-market purchase can be made only in pursuance of a contract the terms of which have been authorised by a special resolution of the company before it is entered into.[44] The authorisation can subsequently be varied, revoked or renewed by a like resolution.[45] In the case of a public company the resolution must specify a date on which it is to expire and that date must not be later than 18 months after the passing of the resolution.[46]

Moreover, on any such resolution, whether of a public or private company, a member, any of whose shares are to be purchased, may not exercise the voting rights of those shares and if the resolution would not have been passed but for his votes the resolution is ineffective.[47] This is an interesting (and rare) example of the extension of the rule that directors must not vote at directors' meetings on matters in which they have a personal financial interest—a rule which normally does not apply to members voting as such. The resolution is also ineffective unless a copy of the contract or a memorandum of its terms is available for inspection by members at the meeting and for not less than 15 days before it is held.[48] The same requirements apply on a resolution to approve any variation of the contract.[49]

Section 165 provides that a company may purchase in pursuance of a "contingent purchase contract", *i.e.* one which does not amount to a binding contract to purchase shares but under which the company may become entitled or obliged to purchase them.[50] Similar requirements regarding prior approval of the contract by special resolution have to be observed.[51] Hence, although the Act does not expressly say

---

[44] s.164(1) and (2).
[45] s.164(3).
[46] s.164(4).
[47] s.164(5) which also provides (a) that it applies whether the vote is on a poll or by a show of hands, (b) that, notwithstanding any provision in the company's articles, any member may demand a poll and (c) that a vote and a demand for a poll by a member's proxy is treated as a vote and demand by the member. For the adaptations when a private company uses a written resolution under s.381A, see Sched. 15A, para. 5(2).
[48] s.164(6). The names of members holding shares to which the contract relates must be disclosed. For adaptations when a written resolution under s.381A is used, see Sched. 15A, para 5(3).
[49] s.164(7). For adaptations, see *ibid*.
[50] s.165(1)
[51] s.165(2) and s. 164(3)–(7) which it expressly applies.

so,[52] a purchase under a contingent purchase contract cannot be effected as a market purchase of traded options or futures since prior approval of the terms of individual market contracts is impracticable.[53] Where contingent purchase contracts may be particularly useful is to enable the company to bind or entitle itself to purchase the shares of a director or employee when his employment ends, or, as an alternative to the creation of a new class of redeemable shares, to meet the requirements of a potential investor in an unquoted company who wants assurance that he will be able to find a purchaser if he needs to realise his investment.

Market purchases

Under section 166 a company (which, in practice, will be a public one) cannot make a market purchase of its own shares unless the making of such purchases has first been authorised by the company in general meeting.[54] An ordinary resolution suffices[55] but, as in the case of a special resolution,[56] a copy of this and of any other resolution required by the section has to be sent to the Registrar within 15 days.[57] The authorisation may be general or limited to shares of any particular class or description and may be conditional or unconditional[58] but it must specify the maximum number of shares to be acquired, the maximum and minimum prices,[59] and a date on which it is to expire which must not be later than 18 months after the passing of the resolution.[60]

In the case of market purchases there is no requirement for the prior approval by members of the actual contracts of purchase.[61] What, in practice, will happen is that the company in general meeting will pass a resolution that x number of shares may be purchased at prices within a stated bracket, and the board of directors will instruct the company's stockbrokers to buy on the Stock Exchange when quoted prices make that possible. In order to provide some degree of equality of treatment

---

[52] And, indeed, the definition of "contingent purchase contract" seems wide enough to cover those types of traded options and futures relating to shares under which actual delivery may be required (though it rarely is) as opposed to contracts for differences which have to be settled in cash.

[53] See *Market purchases*, below.

[54] s.166(1). As in the case of off-market purchases, the authority may be varied, revoked or renewed by a like resolution: s. 166(4). As regards listed companies, see the *Listing Rules*, Chap. 15.

[55] Presumably to enable the company to act quickly (21 days' notice is needed for a special resolution but 14 days' suffices for an ordinary resolution).

[56] s.380.

[57] s.166(7).

[58] s.166(2).

[59] These may be determined either by specifying particular sums or by providing objective formulae for calculating the prices: s.166(6).

[60] s.166(3) and (4). But the purchase may be completed after the expiry date if the contract to buy was made before that date and the authorisation permitted the company to make a contract which would or might be executed after that date.

[61] But the members will, as a result of s.169 (below, p. 258) be able to find out precisely what was done.

of shareholders in relation to substantial market repurchases, which might affect the balance of power within the company, the *Listing Rules* require repurchases of more than 15 per cent of the company's equity shares to be either by way of a partial offer to all shareholders or by way of a tender (advertised in two national newspapers at least seven days in advance) at a fixed or maximum prices.[62]

Additional safeguards

Section 167(1) provides that the rights of a company under a contract to purchase its own shares are not capable of being assigned. This, once again, is designed to minimise the risk that the company will speculate in its own shares or attempt to rig the market. And, by section 167(2), an agreement by the company to release its rights under an off-market purchase is void unless approved in advance by a special resolution in relation to which the requirements of section 164(3) to (7) are observed.[63] The sort of abuse struck at here is when the company has agreed, contingently or otherwise, to purchase the shares of a director who, when the time to complete the purchase arises, finds that he has made a bad bargain and persuades his fellow directors to release him. A variation of the contract would require prior approval by special resolution; so should a release. There is no similar requirement in the case of market purchases; it is not needed since a bargain once struck on the Stock Exchange cannot be cancelled at the whim of the parties.[64]

As we have seen, the price for any of its shares purchased by the company must normally be paid out of distributable profits or the proceeds of a new issue of shares made for the purpose.[65] Section 168 applies a similar, but stricter, rule to any payment (other than the purchase price) made by the company in consideration of:

(a) acquiring any right (for example an option) to purchase under a contingent purchase contract,
(b) the variation of any off-market contract, or
(c) the release of any of the company's obligations under any off-market or market contract.

Although such payments are not strictly part of the purchase price,[66] none of them is normal expenditure in the course of the company's

---

[62] paras. 15.7 and 15.8.
[63] In the case of a private company which has proceeded by a written resolution, see me adaptations in Sched 15A.
[64] But if, in consideration of a payment made by the company, the contract is reversed, s.168 will apply.
[65] See above, p. 254.
[66] Though, in case (a), the division of the total price between that paid for the option and that paid on its exercise may be arbitrary.

business but rather a distribution to a member or members, and the payment would not have been made but for the fact that the company was minded to agree to purchase its shares. Such payments ought therefore to be treated, so far as practicable, in the same way as the purchase price. It is highly unlikely that a company would contemplate making a new issue of shares for the purpose of financing any such payment.[67] Hence the section provides that they must be paid for out of distributable profits only. If this is contravened, in cases (a) and (b) above, purchases are not lawful, and in case (c) the release is void.[68]

Finally, section 169 provides company law's traditional prophylactic—disclosure of precisely what has occurred. It requires both detailed returns to the Registrar within 28 days of the delivery to the company of shares purchased by it[69] and retention by the company of contracts, or memoranda of them, for 10 years at its registered office where they are to be open to inspection by any number and, if it is a public company, by any other person.[70]

Private companies: redemption or purchase out of capital

It was recognised that it would frequently be impossible for a private company to redeem or purchase its own shares unless it could do so out of capital[71] and without having to incur the expense of a formal reduction of capital with the court's consent. The whole concept of raising and maintaining capital is, in relation to such companies, of somewhat dubious value and will remain so unless and until a prescribed minimum share capital (realistic but, no doubt, less than that for public companies) is introduced in relation to them also. Hence it was decided that, subject to safeguards, they should be empowered to redeem or buy without maintaining the former capital yardstick. The relevant provisions are now contained in sections 171 to 177 of the 1985 Act.

Section 171 provides that, subject to what follows, a private company may, if so authorised by its articles, make a payment in respect of the redemption or purchase of its shares otherwise than out of its distributable profits or the proceeds of a fresh issue of shares.[72] The extent of any such payment (a "payment out of capital"[73]) must, however, be restricted to what the section describes as "the permissible

---

[67] Which, in case (a) and perhaps (b), would be made some time before any actual purchase and which in cases (a) and (c) might never be made at all.

[68] s.168(2) which qualifies "not lawful" by "under this Chapter" thus recognising that it may be "lawful" under provisions not included in Part V, Chapter VII of the Act; *e.g.* where a court so orders under s.461.

[69] s.169(1)–(3).

[70] s. 169(4)–(9) as amended by 1989 Act, s.143(2) in relation to subs. (5).

[71] This was particularly so prior to the relaxation of the tax provisions which discouraged "close companies" from retaining profits.

[72] s.171(1).

[73] s.171(2).

capital payment".[74] Subsections (3)–(6) define how one calculates what the permissible capital payment is and what adjustments to the company's issued capital and undistributable reserves have to be made when it is used. The permissible capital payment is the amount by which the price that the company has to pay (A) exceeds its "available profits"[75] and the proceeds of any fresh issue made for the purposes of the redemption or purchase (B). It is only if, and to the extent that, A exceeds B that a capital payment may be made.[76] If the permissible capital payment is less than the nominal value of the shares redeemed or purchased the amount of the difference must be transferred to the capital redemption reserve,[77] but if it should be more than that nominal value, the amount of the issued share capital and undistributable reserves[78] may be reduced by sums not exceeding in the aggregate the extent of the excess.[79]

Section 172 deals with the meaning of "available profits" for the purposes of section 171. Subsection (1) states that it means "the company's profits which are available for distribution (within the meaning of Part VIII[80])". However, it then goes on to say that for the purposes of section 171 "it shall be determined . . . in accordance with the following subsections instead of sections 270 to 275 in that Part". As in the case of the latter,[81] the profits must be calculated on the basis of specified items as shown in the "relevant accounts" of the company,[82] but in this case, these accounts must be specifically prepared for the purpose of determining the permissible capital payment and must give the position as at a date within a period of three months ending with the date of the statutory declaration which the directors are required to make under section 173.[83] The available profits so determined have then to be treated as reduced by any lawful distributions made by the company since the date of the accounts and before the date of the statutory declaration.[84]

Further safeguards

The effect of the foregoing concessions is that a private company may be able to make a return to one or more of its members which

[74] s.171(3).
[75] See s.172, below.
[76] s.171(3).
[77] s.171(4) and (6).
[78] *i.e.* paid up share capital, share premium account, and capital redemption reserve (and any "revaluation reserve" on which see Chap. 12, below).
[79] s.171(5) and (6). The overall effect of s.171 is to ensure that neither the permissible capital payment nor the reduction of the capital yardstick is greater than is necessary.
[80] *i.e.* the dividend rules, on which see Chap. 12, below.
[81] See pp. 286 *et seq.*, below.
[82] s.172(2).
[83] s.172(2), (3) and (6).
[84] s.172(4) and (5): "distributions" include payments made for the purchase of its share, or under s.168, above, and any lawful financial assistance under s.154 or s.155: below, pp. 263 *et seq.*

will exhaust its accumulated profits available for dividend and reduce both its assets and its capital yardstick. This presents potential dangers both to the members and to the creditors, present and future, of the company. Hence safeguards are needed, additional to those prescribed under the sections of the Act already dealt with, and these are provided by sections 173 to 177.

Section 173(1) states that, subject to any order of the court under section 177, payment by a private company for the redemption or purchase of its shares is not lawful unless the requirements of sections 173, 174 and 175 are satisfied. The first step required is that the directors must make a statutory declaration specifying the amount of the permissible capital payment and stating that, having made full inquiry into the affairs and prospects of the company, they have formed the opinion[85] that:

(a) immediately following the payment there will be no grounds on which the company could then be found unable to pay its debts, and
(b) for the year following, the company will be able to continue to carry on business as a going concern and to pay its debts as they fall due throughout that year.[86]

This declaration must be in the prescribed form[87] and contain such information with respect to the nature of the company's business as may be prescribed.[88] Annexed to it there must be a report by the company's auditors stating that they have enquired into the company's affairs, that the amount stated as the permissible capital payment is, in their view, properly determined in accordance with section 171 and 172 and that they are not aware of anything to indicate that the opinion expressed by the directors is unreasonable.[89]

Section 173(2) then requires the capital payment to be authorised by a special resolution of the company (or a written resolution under section 381A). Under section 174 this resolution must be passed on, or within a week immediately following, the making of the statutory declaration and the payment out of capital must be made no earlier than five nor more than seven weeks after the date of the resolution.[90] Once again,[91] the member of the company whose shares are to be redeemed or bought may not vote and if he does the resolution will

---

[85] A director who makes such a declaration without having reasonable grounds for the opinion commits an offence: s.173(6).
[86] s.173(3) and (4).
[87] Form No. 173.
[88] s.173(5).
[89] *ibid.*
[90] s.174(1).
[91] *cf.* s.164(5) above, p. 255.

be ineffective if it would not have been passed without his votes.[92] It will also be ineffective unless the statutory declaration and auditors' report were available for inspection by members attending the meeting.[93]

To protect creditors, section 175 requires that within a week following the passing of the resolution the company must cause to be published in the *Gazette* and, unless it notifies each of its creditors in writing, in an "appropriate national newspaper",[94] a notice giving details about the resolution and the intended purchase or redemption out of capital and stating that any creditor may within five weeks of the resolution apply to the court under section 176 for an order prohibiting the payment.[95] Not later than the date of the first publication of the notice the company must deliver to the Registrar a copy of the directors' statutory declaration and the auditors' report and the originals of these must be kept at the company's registered office for the next five weeks and be open to inspection by any member or creditor.[96]

Section 176 entitles any member of the company, who has not consented to or voted for the resolution, and any creditor of the company, within five weeks of the passing of the resolution to apply to the court for the cancellation of the resolution.[97] The company must then forthwith give notice to the Registrar and, within 15 days from the making of any order, deliver an office copy of it to the Registrar.[98] On the hearing of any such application the court is given the widest powers by section 177. For example, it can cancel the resolution, confirm it, or make such orders as it thinks expedient for the purchase of dissentient members' shares or for the protection of creditors, and may make alterations in the company's memorandum and for the reduction of its capital.[99]

Supplementary provisions

Finally, Chapter VII deals with certain questions which can arise in relation to redemption or purchase, whether by public or private companies and in the case of the latter, whether or not the redemption or purchase is out of capital. For example, section 179 empowers the Secretary of State to modify by regulations certain of the foregoing

---

[92] s.174(2) and see subss. (3) and (5).

[93] s.174(4). Here again Sched. 15A prescribes the adaptations when the company has used a written resolution: para. 6.

[94] *i.e.* an English or Scottish "national" according to whether the company is registered in England and Wales or in Scotland: s.175(3).

[95] s.175(1) and (2).

[96] s.175(4), (5) and (6). If inspection is refused, the company and its officers are liable to fines and the court may order an immediate inspection: s.175(7) and (8).

[97] s.176(1) and (2).

[98] s.176(3).

[99] *cf.* the powers of the court on an application under s.5 (alteration of objects) or ss.459–461 (unfair prejudice).

provisions[1] and section 180 contains a few transitional provisions relating, in particular, to the redemption of preference shares created prior to the 1981 Act. Only section 178 needs more than a mention in a book of this sort. That section deals with questions which could well have arisen prior to the 1981 Act in relation to redeemable preference shares, but upon which there was no clear authority, and which became of increasing importance on the introduction of new powers to purchase shares and to redeem equity shares.

The first such question is: What are the remedies of a shareholder if the company does not perform the contract to redeem or purchase his shares? This may occur because it decides to break the contract or because it cannot lawfully perform it since the new issue of shares has not raised the proceeds expected and the company has inadequate available profits.[2] Section 178[3] provides first that the company is not liable in damages in respect of any failure on its part to redeem or purchase.[4] It was thought that damages were not an appropriate remedy; that would result in the seller retaining his shares in, and membership of, the company and yet recovering damages (paid perhaps out of capital) from the company.[5] Instead the section provides[6] that the shareholder shall retain any other right to sue the company but that the court shall not grant an order for specific performance (perhaps a more appropriate discretionary remedy) "if the company shows that it is unable to meet the costs of redeeming or purchasing the shares in question out of distributable profits".[7] Apart from making it clear that the right to sue for specific performance is a right that the

---

[1] This power is becoming increasingly common in legislation especially when, as here, new practices are being introduced. For a still wider power, see s.117 of the 1989 Act: above, p. 95.

[2] The company could, presumably, protect itself from being in breach by expressly providing in the contract that the purchase is conditional upon its having the needed proceeds or sufficient profits. But then, perhaps, the contract would have had to be approved as a "contingent purchase contract"?

[3] Applying to purchases, or redeemable shares issued, after June 15, 1982.

[4] s.178(2).

[5] In any event, s.178 does not protect the company against paying damages in all cases as a result of its failure to redeem. See *British & Commonwealth Holdings plc v. Barclays Bank plc* [1996] 1 W.L.R. 1, C.A., where a consortium of banks had promised to take the shares from the shareholder if the company could not redeem them and the company had promised to indemnify the banks in respect of actions by it which made it impossible for it to redeem. It was held that the section did not prevent the banks suing the company on the covenants, even though the aim of the whole scheme was to ensure that the shareholder would be able to redeem even if the company had no distributable reserves. The case strongly suggests, but does not finally decide, that section 178 is concerned only with the range of remedies available to the shareholder rather than with ensuring that a company never in effect redeems shares out of capital. If so, this is somewhat odd in the light of the abolition by s.111A of the rule in *Houldsworth v. City of Glasgow Bank* (1880) 5 App. Cas. 317, H.L., which was understood to impose a general restriction upon the award of damages against a company and in favour of a shareholder.

[6] s.178(3).

[7] This ignores the possibility that it has adequate proceeds of a fresh issue but has nevertheless decided to break the contract. Surely the seller should then be entitled to specific performance?

shareholder retains, the section gives no indication of what "other rights" he might have. There is little doubt that these would include the right to sue for an injunction restraining the company from making a distribution of profits which would have the effect of making it unlawful for the company to perform its contract.

The second and related question which section 178 answers is: What is the position if the company goes into liquidation before the shares have been redeemed or purchased? Generally, the terms of redemption or purchase may then be enforced against the company and when the shares are accordingly redeemed or purchased, they are cancelled.[8] This, however, is not so if the terms of redemption or purchase provided for performance to take place at a date later than that of the commencement of the winding-up; nor, if during the period beginning with the date when redemption or purchase was to take place and ending with the commencement of the winding-up, the company did not have distributable profits equal in value to the redemption or purchase price.[9] Moreover, even if these exceptions do not apply, the shareholder will gain little or nothing by enforcing the contract if the winding up is an insolvent liquidation since any claim in respect of the purchase price is postponed to the claims of creditors—and, indeed, to those of other shareholders whose shares carry rights (whether as to capital or income) which are preferred to the rights as to capital of the shares to be redeemed or purchased.[10] Subject to that, however, his claim as a creditor ranks ahead of those of other members as such.[11]

Financial assistance by a company for the purchase of its shares

Superficially, for a company to provide finance to enable someone else to buy its shares may seem to resemble a purchase by the company itself and to be similarly objectionable as reducing the company's capital.[12] In fact it raises completely different issues and in no way affects "capital" in the sense of issued share capital, share premium

---

[8] s.178(4). Hence in respect of these shares the seller will cease to be a member or "contributory" and will become a creditor in respect of the price.

[9] s.178(5).

[10] s.178(6).

[11] *ibid.* The overall effect is that when he is entitled to enforce the contract (*i.e.* when subs. (4) applies and neither exception in subs. (5) does), his claim in the liquidation for the price is deferred to the claims of all other creditors but, if there is anything left after they have been paid in full, he is preferred to the claims of members unless they hold shares of a class which ranks ahead of his (in which event his claim is deferred to theirs).

[12] The Greene Committee (Cmd. 2657 (1926)), on whose recommendation the ban on the practice was imposed by the 1929 Act, thought that it offended against the spirit, if not the letter, of the rule in *Trevor v. Whitworth*, but the Jenkins Committee commented that had the ban "been designed merely to extend that rule we should have felt some doubt whether it was worth retaining": Cmnd. 1749 (1962), para. 173. Nevertheless, in the 1985 Act it still appears in Part V which is entitled "Share Capital, Its Increase, Maintenance and Reduction".

account or capital redemption reserve; nor does it necessarily result in a reduction of the value of the company's net assets.[13] Nevertheless, it is a practice which is open to the gravest abuses[14] abuses which have continued to this day despite prohibiting legislation (originally section 45 of the 1929 Act which was re-enacted with amendments as section 54 of the 1948 Act). That section, despite its relative brevity, became notorious as unintelligible and liable to penalise innocent transactions while failing to deter guilty ones. The Jenkins Committee[15] suggested an alternative approach very similar to that now adopted in relation to private companies, but at the time no action was taken on that suggestion and, when the Second Company Law Directive was adopted, it became impracticable in relation to public companies.[16]

However, in 1980 two reported cases[17] caused considerable alarm in commercial and legal circles, suggesting, as they did, that the scope of the section was even wider, and the risk of wholly unobjectionable transactions being shot down even greater, than had formerly been thought. Hence it was decided that something had to be done about it in the 1981 Act which was then in preparation. Probably more midnight oil was burnt on this subject than on all the rest of that Act and the resulting elaborate provisions are certainty some improvement on section 54. They are now to be found in Part V, Chapter VI (sections 151 to 158) of the 1985 Act.

The prohibition

Sections 151 and 152 apply to both public and private companies, but subject to a relaxation in relation to private companies if they comply with sections 153 to 158. The earlier legislation did not distinguish between assistance given prior to the acquisition and that given

---

[13] If the assistance is in the form of an adequately secured loan it merely substitutes one asset for another of equal or greater value.

[14] Particularly (but not exclusively) in relation to takeovers on which see Chap. 29, below. The classic abuse is financing the takeover by a bridging loan and immediately repaying it by raiding the cofferes of the cash-rich company which is taken over: on variations of this see *Selangor United Rubber Estates v. Cradock (No. 3)* [1968] 1 W.L.R. 1555; *Karak Rubber Co. v. Burden (No. 2)* [1972] 1 W.L.R. 602; and *Wallersteiner v. Moir* [1974] 1 W.L.R. 991, C.A. *(pet. dis.)* [1975] 1 W.L.R. 1093, H.L. A more sophisticated abuse is where the target company lends money to, or indemnifies against loss, known sympathisers who buy its shares; or where, on a share-for-share offer, either or both of the target and predator companies do so to maintain or enhance the quoted price of their own shares. Even if the predator does not provide financial assistance it runs the risk that its sympathisers may become its "associates" and fall foul of the Takeover Code; this cost *Guinness* an extra £95m on its takeover of *Distillers* (see p. 775, n. 24, below).

[15] Cmnd. 1749 (1962), paras. 170–186.

[16] See Art. 23 of Directive 77/91, [1977] O.J. L26/1.

[17] *Belmont Finance Corp. v. Williams Furniture Ltd (No. 2)* [1980] 1 All E.R. 393, C.A.; *Armour Hick Northern Ltd v. Whitehouse* [1980] 1 W.L.R. 1520.

afterwards. Section 151 does.[18] Its subsection (1) says that, subject to the exceptions in section 153:

"where a person is acquiring or is proposing to acquire[19] shares in a company, it is not lawful for the company or any of its subsidiaries[20] to give financial assistance directly or indirectly for the purpose of that acquisition before or at the same time as the acquisition takes place".

Subsection (2) provides that, subject to the same exceptions, when a person has acquired shares in a company and any liability has been incurred (by him or any other person[21]) for that purpose it is not lawful for the company or any of its subsidiaries to give financial assistance, directly or indirectly, for the purpose of reducing or discharging that liability.

Section 152 contains specific definitions of various expressions used in Chapter VI. Among those that are of relevance in understanding section 151, the first is the extremely wide meaning given to "financial assistance",[22] In addition to such obvious assistance as gifts, loans, guarantees, releases, waivers and indemnities,[23] it includes: any loan *or other* agreement under which the obligations of the company giving the assistance are to be fulfilled before the obligations of another party to the agreement,[24] and the novation of a loan or of such other agreement; or the assignment of rights under it.[25] If the assistance is of one or more of those types listed in section 152(1)(a)(i), (ii) or (iii) it is irrelevant whether or not the net assets of the company are reduced by reason of the assistance.[26] However, paragraph (a) concludes with "(iv) any other financial assistance given by a company, the net

---

[18] On the other hand, the drafters seem to have thought of financial assistance, whether given before or after the event, as a one-off-transaction. For the difficulties involved in calculating the impact of the assistance on the company's net assets where the assistance is continuing, see *Parlett v. Guppys (Bridport) Ltd* [1996] 2 BCLC 34, C.A.

[19] In contrast with the former s.54, which used the expression "purchase or subscription", the new section refers to "acquire" or "acquisition" thus extending the ambit of the section to non-cash subscriptions and exchanges.

[20] The sections do not apply to financial assistance by a holding company for the acquisition of shares in its subsidiary; in such a case there is less likelihood of prejudice to other shareholders or to creditors.

[21] Thus, if A lends B £1m to enable B to make a takeover of a company and C guarantees repayment, it will be unlawful for any financial assistance to be given by the company, when taken over, to A, B or C towards the repayment of the £1m.

[22] s.152(1)(a).

[23] Other than one in respect of liability resulting from the company's neglect or default, (*e.g.* the customary indemnity given to underwriters of a share issue): s.152(1)(a)(ii).

[24] *e.g.* where a company which is a diamond merchant sells a diamond to a dealer for £100,000, payment to be 12 months hence, the intention being that the dealer will sell the diamond at a profit or borrow on its security thus putting him in funds to acquire shares in the company.

[25] s.152(1)(a)(iii).

[26] In some cases (*e.g.* gifts) they will be; in others (*e.g.* loans or guarantees) they may or may not.

assets[27] of which are thereby reduced to a material extent, or which has no net assets".[28] The effect of this is that, even if the financial assistance does not fall within the specific types that the draftsman, and those instructing him, were able to foresee, it will nevertheless be unlawful if the company has no net assets or if the consequence of the assistance is to reduce its net assets "to a material extent".

Clearly "materiality" is to be determined to some extent by the relationship between the value of the assistance and the value of the net assets; assistance worth £50 would reduce the net assets materially if they were only £100 but immaterially if they were £1 million. But how far is that to be taken? A company with net assets of £billions might regard a reduction of £1 million as immaterial, but it seems unlikely that judges (most of whom are not accustomed to disposing of £millions) would so regard it.

Assistance, however, will not be unlawful unless it is "financial".[29] Merely giving information (even financial information) is not financial assistance.[30]

Moreover, even if financial, the assistance must fall within section 152(1) if it is to be unlawful. In other words, the definition of "financial assistance" seems intended to be exhaustive. Thus, timely repayment of a debt due, even if done in order to assist the creditor in the purchase of the debtor's shares, would not seem to be caught, but it might be if the debt were paid early because it could then be said to have an element of gift in it.[31] Finally, the impugned transaction must actually assist the acquirer to obtain the shares. This requirement may lead to the drawing of some fine lines, as in the *British & Commonwealth Holdings* case,[32] where promises, made by the company to banks which could be required to acquire the shares from the shareholder if the company did not redeem them, were regarded as an "inducement" to the shareholder to acquire the redeemable shares in the first place but not as financial assistance to it to do so.

The second definition in section 152 which is relevant to section 151(2) is to be found in section 152(3). It provides that a reference to a person incurring a liability includes

"his changing his financial position by making an agreement or arrangement (whether enforceable or unenforceable and whether

---

[27] Defined as "the aggregate of the company's assets, less the aggregate of its liabilities" and "liabilities" includes any provision for anticipated losses or charges: s.152(2).

[28] s.152(1)(a)(iv).

[29] The wording of s.152(1)(a) emphasises this.

[30] But reimbursement of the costs of digesting and assessing the information could be.

[31] See *Plaut v. Steiner* (1988) 5 BCC 352, but note also the insistence by the Court of Appeal in *British & Commonwealth Holdings plc v. Barclays Bank plc* [1996] 1 W.L.R. 1, C.A. that the terms used in the definition must be given their technical meaning (in this case in relation to the meaning of an "indemnity").

[32] Above, n. 5.

made on his own account or with any other person[33]) or by any other means";

and it adds that reference to a company giving financial assistance to reduce or discharge a liability incurred for the purposes of acquiring shares includes giving assistance for the purpose of wholly or partly restoring the financial position of the person concerned to what it was before the acquisition. This results in an enormous extension of the normal meaning of "liability" and seems to mean that before a company can give any financial assistance to *any* person (whether or not the acquirer) it must assess his overall financial position before and after the acquisition[34] and if, afterwards, it has deteriorated, must refrain from any form of financial assistance which is not covered by one of the exceptions—at any rate if there is a causal connection between the deterioration and the acquisition.

The exceptions

Section 153 provides a number of exceptions to the prohibitions. Those in subsections (3),[35] (4) and (5)[36] are more or less what one would have expected. They include allotment of bonus shares, transactions under other sections of the Act in accordance with a court order and redemptions or purchases of shares in accordance with Part V, Chapter VII of the Act.[37] Also excepted are lending money in the ordinary course of business when lending is part of the company's ordinary business, and contributions to employees' share schemes and the like[38]; but, in the case of a public company, only if it has net assets[39] which are not thereby reduced or, to the extent that they are thereby reduced, if the assistance is provided out of distributable profits.[40] It should be noted, however, that also excluded is "a distribution[41] of a company's assets by way of dividend lawfully made or a distribution made in the course of a company's winding-up".[42] Hence,

---

[33] The words "or with any other person" are somewhat puzzling; one would have expected "or that of any other person". Can there be an agreement or arrangement which is not made with some other person? And, if there can, would it not be covered by "or by any other means"?

[34] The difficulty of doing this after a takeover is mind-boggling.

[35] As amended by the Insolvency Act 1986.

[36] The FSA 1986 added a new subs. (4)(bb) and a new subs. (5) extending the ambit of the exception relating to employees' share schemes.

[37] s.153(3).

[38] s.153(4) and (5) (as amended by s.132 of the 1989 Act).

[39] For this purpose (*cf.* s.152(2)) "net assets" means the amount by which the aggregate of the company's assets exceeds its liabilities, taking those amounts to be as stated in the company's accounting records, and "liabilities" includes provisions for expected liabilities or losses: s.154(2).

[40] s.154(1). "Distributable profits" for the purposes of the Chapter is defined in s.152(1)(b) as "profits out of which the company could lawfully make a distribution equal in value to that assistance", including, if the assistance comprises a non-cash asset, any profit available for the purpose of a distribution in kind under s.276: see Chap. 12 at p. 286, below.

[41] As defined in s.263(2): s.152(1)(c). On s.263(2) see below, Chap. 12 at p. 282.

[42] s.153(3)(a).

if those taking over a company obtain control, they may be able lawfully to recoup the whole or part of the cost of doing so out of dividends paid by the company or by putting it into liquidation. But the dividends must be lawfully made in strict accordance with the rules in Part VIII of the Act and the provisions of the company's articles.[43]

The main change which section 153 makes to the former section 54 is to be found in section 153(1) and (2) intended to allay the fears aroused by the two decisions in 1980.[44] Subsection (1) says that section 151(1) does not prohibit a company from giving financial assistance if:

(a) the company's principal purpose in giving the assistance is not to give it for the purpose of acquisition of shares of the company or its holding company, or, if the giving of the assistance for that purpose is but an incidental part of some larger purpose of the company, and

(b) the assistance is given in good faith in the interests of the company.

Subsection (2) provides similarly that section 151(2) does not prohibit assistance given subsequently to the acquisition if:—(a) the principal purpose is not to reduce or discharge any liability incurred for the purpose of acquiring such shares, or the reduction or discharge of any such liability is but an incidental part of some larger purpose of the company, and (b) the assistance is given in good faith in the interests of the company.

On the meaning of these difficult subsections[45] we now have an authoritative ruling from the House of Lords in the case of *Brady v. Brady*,[46] a case remarkable both because of the extent of the judicial disagreement to which it gave rise and because it was ultimately decided on a ground not argued in the lower courts. It related to prosperous family businesses, principally concerned with haulage and soft drinks. The businesses were run and owned in equal shares by two brothers, Jack and Bob Brady, and their respective families, through

---

[43] See below, Chap. 12.

[44] *Belmont Finance Corp. v. Williams Furniture Ltd (No. 2)* and *Armour Hick Northern Ltd v. Whitehouse*: above, p. 264, n. 17.

[45] Which hardly seem to be compatible with Art. 23 of the Second Directive.

[46] [1989] A.C. 755, H.L. This case is an illustration (of which *Charterhouse Investment Trust v. Tempest Diesels Ltd* [1987] BCLC 1, is another) of how, all too often, parties agree in principle to a simple arrangement which on the face of it raises no question of unlawful financial assistance but then refer it to their respective advisers who, in their anxiety to obtain the maximum fiscal and other advantages for their respective clients, introduce complicated refinements which arguably cause it to fall foul of s.151. In the *Charterhouse* case, where the former s.54 applied, Hoffmann J., by exercising commonsense in interpreting the meaning of "financial assistance", was able to avoid striking down an obviously unobjectionable arrangement. But the elaborate definition of that expression in the present s.152 leaves less scope for commonsense.

a parent company, T. Brady & Co. Ltd (Brady's), and a number of subsidiary and associated companies. Unfortunately Jack and Bob fell out, resulting in a complete deadlock. It was clear that unless something could be agreed amicably, Brady's would have to be wound-up—which was the last thing that anyone wanted. It was therefore agreed that the group should be re-organised, sole control of the haulage business being taken by Jack and that of the drinks business by Bob. As the respective values of the two businesses were not precisely equal, this involved various intra-group transfers of assets and shareholdings which became increasingly complicated as the negotiations proceeded. It suffices to say that, in the end, one of the companies had acquired shares in Brady's and the liability to pay for them thus incurred was to be discharged by a transfer to it of assets of Brady's. Bob, however, contended that further valuation adjustments were needed and refused to proceed further unless they were made. Jack then started proceedings for specific performance which Bob defended on various grounds which were ultimately reduced to two: (i) that the transfer would be *ultra vires*[47] and (ii) that it would be unlawful financial assistance under section 151. Only the second concerns us here.

It was conceded that the transfer of assets would be unlawful financial assistance under section 151 (2) unless, in the circumstances, that was disapplied by section 153 (2). On the face of it one might have thought that the circumstances afforded a classic illustration of the sort of situation that section 153 (1) or (2) was intended to legitimate. And, at first instance, that view prevailed. In the Court of Appeal,[48] however, while all three judges thought that the conditions of paragraph (a), relating to "purpose", were satisfied, the majority thought that those of paragraph (b), relating to "good faith in the interests of the company", were not. In contrast, in the House of Lords[49] it was held unanimously that paragraph (b) was complied with but that (a) was not. Hence the contemplated transfer would be unlawful financial assistance if carried out in the way proposed.

Lord Oliver, in a speech concurred in by the other Law Lords, subjected the wording of paragraph (a) to detailed analysis.[50] He pointed out that "purpose" had to be distinguished from "reason" or "motive" (which would almost always be different and wider) and that paragraph (a) contemplated alternative situations. The first is where the company has a principal and a subsidiary purpose; the question then is whether the principal purpose is to assist or relieve the

---

[47] In relation to *ultra vires* the case has now been overtaken by the reforms in the Companies Act 1989. With one exception all the judges held the transaction not to be *ultra vires*.

[48] [1988] BCLC 20, C.A.

[49] [1989] A.C. 755, H.L.

[50] [1989] A.C. at 778, *et seq*. Agreeing with O'Connor L.J. in the C.A. ([1988] BCLC at 25) he described the paragraph, with commendable restraint, as "not altogether easy to construe".

acquirer or is for some other corporate purpose. The second situation is where the financial assistance is not for any purpose other than to help the acquirer but is merely incidental to some larger corporate purpose. As regards the first alternative, he accepted that an example might be where the principal purpose was to enable the company to obtain from the person assisted a supply of some product which the company needed for its business.[51] As regards the second, he offered no example, merely saying that he had "not found the concept of ılarger purpose' easy to grasp" but that:

"if the paragraph is to be given any meaning that does not provide a blank cheque for avoiding the effective application of section 151 in every case, the concept must be narrower than that for which the appellants contend".[52]

The trial judge, and O'Connor L.J. in the Court of Appeal,[53] had thought that the larger purpose was to resolve the deadlock and its inevitable consequences and Croom-Johnson L.J.[54] had found it in the need to reorganise the whole group. But if either could be so regarded, it would follow that, if the board of a company concluded in good faith that the only way that a company could survive was for it to be taken-over, it could lawfully provide financial assistance to the bidder—the very mischief that the legislation was designed to prevent.

The logic is, of course, impeccable and the House of Lords is infallible. But the result seems to reduce section 153 (1) and (2) to very narrow limits indeed and to make one wonder whether the midnight oil burnt on the drafting of the two subsections has achieved anything worthwhile.

Having reached the foregoing conclusion "with a measure of regret",[55] the House gave permission for Jack to raise further points of law not argued in either of the courts below.

The successful argument on these proceeded as follows: When an arrangement can be implemented in alternative ways, one lawful and one unlawful, it is to be presumed that the parties intend it to be carried out in the lawful manner unless it is clear that they have agreed on the other.[56] There was nothing in the terms of the arrangement which prevented its being implemented perfectly lawfully under the relaxation for private companies to which we turn next. Brady's (and each of the other companies involved) was a private company with

---

[51] A situation envisaged by Buckley L.J. in his judgment in the *Belmont Finance* case [1980] 1 All E.R. at 402, as giving rise to doubts under the former s. 54.

[52] At 779.

[53] [1988] BCLC at 26.

[54] *ibid.*, at 32.

[55] [1989] A.C. at 781.

[56] For another application of this principle to save an agreement from the operation of the financial assistance prohibition, see *Parlett v. Guppys (Bridport) Ltd* [1996] 2 BCLC 34, C.A.

ample distributable profits and thus able lawfully to effect the arrangement under the relaxed regime for private companies.[57] Hence, upon
obtaining an undertaking to comply strictly with the terms of sections
155 to 158, it was declared that the proposed transaction was not
unlawful.[58] Having regard to the wealth of legal and accountancy
talent available to the parties, it seems almost incredible that this
course had not occurred to anyone earlier.[59]

Moreover, the (eventually) successful outcome in the particular case
does not get rid of the awkward issues raised by it. The DTI[60] has
floated the ideas of substituting "predominant reason" for "principal
purpose" or relying solely on the test of good faith in the interests of
the company. Quite apart from the question whether the Second Directive gives us the freedom to apply such a broad exemption in the
case of public companies, these suggestions do nothing to address the
arguments put forward in the House of Lords in favour of giving
section 153(2) a strict interpretation, if section 151 is to remain a
meaningful restriction.

Relaxation for private companies

While the Second Company Law Directive curtailed our freedom
in relation to public companies, it did not in relation to private companies and, therefore, as in the case of purchase of shares, it was
possible for us to adopt a more relaxed regime for them based on that
suggested by the Jenkins Committee.[61] This was done by what are now
sections 155–158. While sections 152–153, dealt with above, apply to
private companies, the prohibitions in section 151 do not if a private
company is able to proceed instead under sections 155–158.

These sections maintain the basic principle that "financial assistance may only be given if the company has net assets, which are not
thereby reduced or, to the extent that they are reduced, if the assistance
is provided out of distributable profits".[62] There is also a restriction
on the use of the sections by subsidiary private companies in a group

---

[57] In a later case, *Plaut v. Steiner* [1989] BCC 352, the parties failed to establish the "wider
purpose" exception and were not able to take advantage of the private company relaxation.

[58] [1989] A.C. at 782, *et seq*.

[59] It seems to suggest that the professions were still not as familiar with the relevant provisions
introduced in 1981 as they ought to be and perhaps justifies what readers may regard as the
overlong treatment here. It was suggested by Lord Oliver that in fact the explanation was not
ignorance of the law but a misunderstanding of the facts, it having been thought that "the
transfers alleged to infringe the section had already taken place rather than being . . . still
uncompleted": *ibid.*, at 782. But why then did Jack sue for specific performance?

[60] *Company Law Reform: Proposals for Reform of Sections 151–158 of the Companies Act
1985*, 1993.

[61] See p. 264, n. 15, above.

[62] s.155(2). "Net assets" are as defined in s.154(2) and "distributable profits" as defined in
s.152(1)(b), above.

with public companies.[63] Subject to that, however, the conditions are not unduly onerous—though somewhat time-consuming.[64]

The first step is for the directors of the company and, where the assistance is for the acquisition of shares in its holding company, the directors of the holding company and any intermediate holding company, to make statutory declarations (similar to those required when private companies seek to redeem or purchase their shares out of capital[65]) complying with section 156.[66] Under the latter section these declarations must identify the person to whom the assistance is to be given[67] and must state that, in the directors' opinion, immediately following the assistance there will be no grounds on which the company could then be found unable to pay its debts; and either:

(a) if it is intended to commence the winding-up of the company within 12 months of the assistance, that it will be able to pay its debts in full within 12 months of the commencement, or
(b) in any other case, that the company will be able, during the year following the assistance, to pay its debts as they fall due.[68]

Each declaration must have annexed to it a report of the company's auditors stating that they have enquired into the state of affairs of the company and that they are not aware of anything to indicate that the directors' opinion is unreasonable in the circumstances.[69]

The second step is to secure the approval of the assistance by a special resolution (or written resolution under section 381A) of the company proposing to give it.[70] This can be dispensed with if the company is a wholly owned subsidiary[71] (when it could serve no purpose[72]) but, if the shares to be acquired are of its holding company, the latter and any intermediate holding company (other than a wholly owned subsidiary) must also approve by special (or written) resolution.[73] These special resolutions must be passed on, or within a week

---

[63] s.155(3). This is intended to prevent the relaxation being abused by indirectly enabling public companies to avail themselves of it.

[64] The courts have done their best to save schemes where the company concerned got some of the detail wrong: *Re S.H. & Co. (Realisations) 1990 Ltd* [1993] BCLC 1309; *Re N.L. Electrical Ltd* [1994] 1 BCLC 22.

[65] See pp. 260–261, above.

[66] s.155(6).

[67] s.156(1).

[68] s.156(2). They are required to take into account actual, contingent and prospective liabilities like a court determining whether a company should be wound up on the ground that it is unable to pay its debts: s.156(3) as amended by the Insolvency Act 1986.

[69] s.156(4). *British & Commonwealth Holdings v. Quadrex Holdings* [1989] Q.B. 942, C.A., illustrates how delays in obtaining the declaration and report may wreck a corporate reorganisation scheme.

[70] s.155(4).

[71] *ibid.*

[72] See the definition of "wholly owned subsidiary" in s.736(6), as substituted by the 1989 Act.

[73] s.155(5).

of, the day on which the directors made the statutory declarations,[74] and are not effective unless the declarations and auditors' reports are available for inspection by members at the meetings.[75]

The third step is to deliver to the Registrar a copy of each statutory declaration and annexed auditors' report. This has to be done within 15 days of the declaration and, if a special (or written) resolution of that company is required,[76] must be accompanied by a copy of the resolution which, like any other special (or section 381A) resolution, has to be delivered to the Registrar under section 380.[77]

Where any special (or section 381A) resolution was needed, the approved financial assistance must not be given before the expiration of four weeks beginning with the date on which the resolution was passed or, if more than one was passed, the date on which the last of them was passed, unless each member entitled to vote at general meetings voted in favour.[78] This is to provide time for members who did not consent or vote in favour to apply to the court to cancel the resolution under section 157.[79] If there is an application under that section the financial assistance must not be given before the final determination of that application unless the court otherwise directs.[80] Nor, unless there is such an application and the court otherwise directs, may it be given after the expiration of eight weeks from the time when the directors of the company proposing to give the assistance made their statutory declaration or, where declarations were made by the directors both of that company and of any of its holding companies, after the expiration of eight weeks from the date of the earliest declaration.[81] This is to prevent the assistance being given so long after the statutory declaration and auditors' report that they can no longer be relied on. If no resolution was needed, or if all members voted in favour, the assistance may be given immediately after the delivery to the Registrar of the statutory declaration and auditors' report but must not be given after the expiration of the eight week period, unless the court otherwise orders.[82]

Under section 157, which corresponds to sections 176 and 177 in relation to redemption or purchase by a private company out of capital

---

[74] s.157(1).

[75] s.157(4)(a). For adaptations when a written resolution is used under s.381A, see Sched. 15A, para. 4.

[76] A special (or written) resolution of at least one company will be required unless the financial assistance is to be given by a wholly owned subsidiary for the acquisition of its own shares (which the holding company will be able to stop if it wants to).

[77] s.155(6).

[78] s.158(2).

[79] See below.

[80] s.158(3).

[81] s.158(4).

[82] This is the effect of s.158(2) and (4).

(except that it protects only members and not creditors[83]) an application may be made to the court for the cancellation of the resolution:

(a) by the holders of not less in the aggregate than 10 per cent in nominal value of the company's issued share capital or any class of it, or

(b) if the company is not limited by shares,[84] by not less than 10 per cent of the company's members.

But it cannot be made by any member who has consented to, or voted in favour of, the resolution.[85] The court must either confirm or cancel the resolution, in either event being afforded the widest powers comparable to those under section 177.[86]

The DTI has recently put forward ideas for simplifying the more relaxed regime for private companies, ranging from making the time limits more flexible to reducing the obligations upon both directors and auditors in relation to the statutory declaration and abolishing the restriction that net assets may not be reduced (unless payments are made out of distributable profits).[87]

Civil remedies for breach of the prohibition

The only sanctions prescribed by the Act for breaches of section 151 are fining the company[88] and fining or imprisoning (or both) its officers in default.[89] But more important are the consequences in civil law resulting from the fact that the transaction is unlawful. Unfortunately, precisely what these consequences are has vexed the courts both of England and of other countries which have adopted comparable provisions[90] and it is a pity that the 1981 Act did not attempt to clarify the position as, to some extent, the 1989 Act did in relation to acts by the board of directors in excess of the company's objects or the board's powers.[91]

---

[83] Creditors are protected by ss.155(1) and 156, above.

[84] The company whose shares are to be acquired will be a company limited by shares but a subsidiary giving financial assistance for the purchase of shares of its holding company might be limited by guarantee.

[85] s.157(2).

[86] s.157(3) which, unlike s.177, does not set out these powers but incorporates them by applying s.54(3)–(10) relating to applications to cancel a resolution converting a public to a private company (on which see Chap. 6, p. 124, above).

[87] DTI, *op.cit.*, n. 60.

[88] Since s.151 is intended to protect the company and its members and creditors it is difficult to conceive of a more inappropriate sanction than to reduce the company's net assets (still further than the unlawful financial assistance may have done) by fining the company.

[89] s.151(3). See also s.156(7) making directors liable to fines for making statutory declarations without having reasonable ground for the opinions expressed.

[90] For a valuable account of the Australian and New Zealand decisions, see *Farrar's Company Law* (3rd ed., 1991, London) at pp. 198–200.

[91] See Chap. 10, above. Under s.277, a shareholder who has received a distribution paid in contravention of Part VIII of the Act (Chap. 12, below) is liable to repay it if he knew or had

What has caused the courts to make heavy weather of this is the somewhat curious wording of section 151 and its predecessors. Since the object of the section is to protect the company and its members and creditors, one would have expected it to say that it is not lawful for any person who is acquiring or proposing to acquire shares of a company to receive financial assistance from the company or any of its subsidiaries; that would have pointed the courts in the right direction to work out the consequences. But instead it declares that it is unlawful for the company to give the assistance, and follows that by imposing criminal sanctions on the company and (the one thing that makes good sense) on the officers of the company who are in default. This could be taken to imply (and was so taken by Roxburgh J. in *Victor Battery Co. Ltd v. Curry's Ltd*[92]) that the object was not to protect the company but to punish it and its officers by imposing fines (the maximum then being only £100!). This calamitous decision continued to be accepted in England, and was cited with apparent approval by Cross J. (subsequently a Law Lord) 20 years later,[93] though rejected by the Australian Courts whose decisions helped those in England eventually to see the light. The decision has now been disapproved or not followed in a series of cases[94] and is accepted to be heretical.

Freed from the fetters of that heresy the courts have since given the section real teeth and it is submitted that the following propositions can now be regarded as reasonably well established:

(a) *An agreement to provide unlawful financial assistance being unlawful is unenforceable by either party to it.* This proposition is undoubted and infallible authority for it is the decision of the House of Lords in *Brady v. Brady.*[95]

(b) *However, the illegality of the financial assistance given or provided by the company normally does not taint other connected transactions*, such as the agreement by the person assisted to acquire the shares; it would be absurd if, for example, a takeover bidder which had been given financial assistance by the company, or by a subsidiary

---

reasonable grounds for believing that it was paid in contravention of that Part but that section expressly does not apply to financial assistance in contravention of s.151 or in respect of redemption or purchase: see s.277(2).

[92] [1946] Ch. 242.

[93] *Curtis's Furnishing Stores Ltd v. Freedman* [1966] 1 W.L.R. 1219. But he ignored it in *S. Western Mineral Water Co. Ltd v. Ashmore* [1967] 1 W.L.R. 1110.

[94] *Selangor United Rubber Estate Ltd v. Cradock (No. 3)* [1968] 1 W.L.R. 1555; *Heald v. O'Connor* [1971] 1. W.L.R. 497; and Lord Denning M.R. in *Wallersteiner v. Moir* [1974] 1 W.L.R. at 1014H–1015A. The modern view helped Millett J. to conclude in *Arab Bank plc v. Mercantile Holdings Ltd* [1994] Ch. 330 that the legislation applies to assistance provided by a subsidiary of an English company only where the subsidiary is not a foreign company, on the grounds that the protection of the shareholders and creditors of a company is a matter for the law of the place of incorporation. By the same token, the giving of assistance by the English subsidiary of a foreign parent ought to be regulated by the Act, though it is by no means clear that it is.

[95] Above, p. 268.

of the company, could escape from the liability to perform purchase contracts which it has entered into with the shareholders. Clearly it cannot.

(c) *This, however, may be subject to a qualification if the obligation to acquire the shares and the obligation to provide financial assistance form part of a single composite transaction.* The obvious example of this would be an arrangement in which someone agreed to subscribe for shares in a company (or its holding company) in consideration of which the company agreed to give him some form of financial assistance. In such a case the position apparently depends on whether the terms relating to the acquisition of shares can be severed from those relating to the unlawful financial assistance. If they can, those relating to the acquisition can be enforced. If they cannot, the whole agreement is void.

The authorities supporting this proposition are the decisions of Cross J. in *South Western Mineral Water Co. Ltd v. Ashmore*[96] and of the Privy Council in *Carney v. Herbert.*[97] In essence the facts of both were that shares of a company were to be acquired and payment of the purchase price was to be secured by a charge on the assets of, in the former case, that company and, in the latter, its subsidiary. The agreed security was, of course, unlawful financial assistance. In the former case, the shares had not been transferred or the charge executed; in the latter, they had. In the former it was held that unless the sellers were prepared to dispense with the charge (which they were not) the whole agreement was void and that the parties must be restored to their positions prior to the agreement. In the latter it was held that the unlawful charge could be severed from the sale of the shares and that the sellers were entitled to sue the purchaser for the price. Despite the different results, the Privy Council judgment, delivered by Lord Brightman, cited with approval the decision of Cross J. in the earlier case. In both cases a fair result seems to have been arrived at and certainly one preferable to that for which the assisted share-purchaser contended in *Carney*, namely that he should be entitled to retain the shares without having to pay for them.[98] It is therefore to be hoped that even in a single composite transaction the courts will permit severance or order *restitutio in integrum* unless there are strong reasons of public policy[99] why the whole transaction should be treated as so unlawful as to preclude the court from offering any assistance to any party to it.

(d) *If the company has actually given the unlawful financial assistance, that transaction will be void.* The practical effect of that depends

---

[96] [1967] 1 W.L.R. 1110.
[97] [1985] A.C. 301, P.C., on appeal from the Sup. Ct. of N.S.W.
[98] Yet Lord Brightman seemed to think that this would be the consequence if severance was not possible: see [1985] A.C. at 309.
[99] In support of this caveat, see [1985] A.C. at 313 and 317.

on the nature of the financial assistance. If it is a mortgage, guarantee or indemnity of the like, the party to whom it was given cannot sue the company upon it.[1] It is he who suffers,[2] and the company, so long as it realises in time that the transaction is void, need do nothing but defend any hopeless action that may be brought against it. If, however, the unlawful assistance was a completed gift or loan, the company will need to take action if it is to recover what it has lost. And a long line of cases has established that, in most circumstances, this it will be able to do.[3]

Its claim may be based on misfeasance, when recovery is sought from the directors or other officers of the company, or on restitution, conspiracy, or constructive trust, when the claim is against them or those to whom the unlawful assistance has passed or who have otherwise actively participated in the unlawful transaction. The most popular basis seems to be constructive trust[4]; the argument being that the directors committed the equivalent of a breach of trust when they caused the company's assets to be used for the unlawful purpose and the recipients became constructive trustees thereof.

What is still not wholly clear is precisely what degree of fault has to be established if claims on any of the grounds are to succeed. The earlier decisions held that the company's officers would be liable on a misfeasance claim even though they had no idea that the transaction was unlawful,[5] and that other participants would be liable if they had knowledge, actual or constructive, which should have led them to realise that they were taking part in an unlawful or dishonest activity.[6] The more recent decisions suggest that (as seems to be the case with participants in acts of the directors in excess of the company's powers[7]) the essential condition for liability is bad faith. And, notwithstanding *Steen v. Law*, it may be that the same test should apply in an

---

[1] See the cases discussed under (c) and *Heald v. O'Connor* [1971] 1. W.L.R. 497, where the unlawful assistance was a mortgage on the property of the company whose shares were being acquired, the purchaser guaranteeing the payment of sums due under the mortgage. The mortgage was unlawful. Hence the purchaser escaped liability on the guarantee (though that was lawful) since no payments were lawfully due under the mortgage. It would have been different had the guarantee been an indemnity.

[2] Since the mortgage is illegal and void (not merely voidable) presumably a bona fide purchaser of it without notice could not enforce it either.

[3] *Steen v. Law* [1964] A.C. 287, P.C.; *Selangor United Rubber Estates v. Cradock (No. 3)* [1968] 1 W.L.R. 1555; *Karak Rubber Co. v. Burden (No. 2)* [1972] 1 W.L.R. 602; *Wallersteiner v. Moir* [1974] 1 W.L.R. 991, C.A.; *Belmont Finance Corp. v. Williams Furniture Ltd (No. 2)* [1980] 1 All E.R. 393, C.A.; *Smith v. Croft (No. 2)* [1988] Ch. 114; *Agip (Africa) Ltd v. Jackson* [1991] Ch. 547, C.A.

[4] See below, pp. 652 *et seq.*

[5] "[W]here directors have used their directorial powers to part with moneys of their company in a manner or for a purpose which the law forbids, it is not a defence . . . to plead merely that they acted in ignorance of the law": *Steen v. Law*, above, at 300.

[6] See the *Cradock* and *Burden* cases: n. 3, above.

[7] See Chap. 10, pp. 215–217, above. In principle it seems that the two situations should be treated alike; they are distinguishable only in that breach of s.151 is a criminal offence, while the other, without more, is not.

action against officers based on misfeasance. An officer commits an offence under section 151 only if he is "in default",[8] *i.e.* when he "knowingly and wilfully authorises . . . the contravention".[9] Even if that is established, the court may relieve him of civil liability if he has acted honestly and reasonably and ought fairly to be excused.[10] The probability is that an officer who has acted in good faith will not be "in default" (and, even if he is, he may be excused).

(e) *In the light of propositions* (a)–(d) *it would also seem to follow that if the unlawful assistance given by the company is a loan secured by a mortgage or charge on the borrower's property*[11] *then, so long as the company has rights of recovery from the borrower under proposition* (d), *it should be able to do so by realising its security.* This would certainly be so if the mortgage or charge could be severed from the unlawful loan—which, however, might be regarded as impossible since the consideration given for the mortgage or charge *was* the unlawful loan. But, since the effect of the recent case law is to recognise that the object of section 151, despite its wording, is to protect the company, the courts ought not to boggle at the conclusion that the security given to the company can be realised to recover what is due to it by the borrower.

It will therefore be seen that we have come a long way from the time when it was believed that the only likely sanctions were derisory fines on the company and its officers in default. These developments have caused the banking community some alarm, for there is no doubt that banks could find themselves caught out—as indeed they have been in the past.[12] The fact that money passing in the relevant transactions is likely to do so through banking channels inevitably exposes banks to risks.[13] But, if the above propositions are correct, these risks will generally be avoided so long as banks (or, in practice, their managers) act in good faith—or do not behave with such naivety and gullibility that a court cannot accept that they have so acted. Apart from that, perhaps the greatest risk they run is that they may innocently lend money on the security of a debenture with a charge on a company's property,

---

[8] s.151(3).

[9] s.730(5).

[10] s.727(1).

[11] Unless the company is a public company and the charge is on shares in it, for then the charge may be void under s.150: see below.

[12] See, for example, the *Cradock* and *Burden* cases, n. 3 above.

[13] But they are afforded special protection since section 151 does not invalidate a loan: "Where the lending of money is part of the ordinary business of the company" and the loan is "in the ordinary course of its business": s.153(4). This, as interpreted in *Steen v. Law* above, only avails banks and similar "moneylending" institutions (and then only if the transaction is in the ordinary course of that business). It does not avail a company which may incidentally lend money and may be expressly empowered to do so in its objects clause. But it recognises that it would be absurd if, a on a public issue of shares by one of the major High Street banks, its branches had to refuse to honour applicants' cheques if they were customes who had been granted overdrafts.

which, unbeknown to the bank, was issued by the company to enable the borrower to raise finance for the purpose of acquiring its shares or those of its holding company and which is therefore unlawful and void. But that is no more than the risk, which any lender faces, that there may be a defect in the borrower's title to the property offered as security.

Charges to a company on its shares

If, except as above, a company cannot purchase its own shares, one might have supposed that equally it cannot take a mortgage or charge on such shares. This, however, was not the view taken by the English courts and it was not uncommon for articles of association to provide that the company should have a lien on its shares, not only in respect of any money due in payment for the shares but for any sums due to the company from shareholders in any capacity.[14] However, the Second Company Law Directive took a different view which was implemented by the 1980 Act—though in relation to public companies only. The relevant section (now section 150 of the 1985 Act) provides that a lien or other charge on its own shares is void[15] unless:

(i) the shares are not fully paid and the charge is for any amount payable in respect of the shares,[16] or
(ii) the company's ordinary business includes the lending of money, providing credit or the bailment of goods under a hire-purchase agreement

and the charge arises in connection with a transaction entered into in the ordinary course of its business.[17]

The position of private companies remains unchanged.

CONCLUSION

This discussion of the raising and maintaining of capital is logically incomplete without a discussion of the extent to which a company can distribute its assets to its members by way of dividend; for much of what has gone before is an essential prelude to that. But this Chapter is already over-long and it seems better to postpone that to the next Chapter.[18] But one concluding observation:

It will have been apparent from the foregoing pages that what makes

---

[14] If, however, the shares were to be listed on the Stock Exchange the latter would not permit that.
[15] s.150(1).
[16] s.150(2).
[17] s.150(3). This protects hire purchase finance companies.
[18] The Act goes still further by postponing it from Part V to Part VIII.

the concept of share capital unnecessarily complicated and confusing is the insistence that shares shall be given a fixed nominal value and that the amount of the company's share capital shall be determined exclusively by that nominal value. The nominal value of a share need not bear any relationship to its true value even at the time of its issue and is most unlikely to do so after the company has been trading for some time. Nor does the nominal value of issued share capital provide the yardstick for determining whether the company can lawfully make a distribution to its members. When shares have been issued at a premium that will depend on the amount of the issued share capital plus its share premium account and, when shares have been redeemed or repurchased, on the aggregate amount of its issued share capital plus its share premium account plus its capital redemption reserve.

All this could be avoided if, like some countries (notably the United States and Canada) we permitted the issue of no-par-value shares. In 1954 the Gedge Committee recommended the legalisation of no-par equity shares[19] and in 1962 the Jenkins Committee[20] recommended it in respect of any class of shares. An attempt was made to introduce legislative provisions to that effect in what became the 1967 Act; but without success. And there is now little likelihood of their being introduced since nominal par values are required under the E.C. Directives. This is regrettable; particularly so in the light of the Government's efforts to increase individual share ownership, for no-par would render the true position more readily intelligible to unsophisticated investors and protect them from being misled.[21] There would, however, be little point in introducing them unless they were made compulsory.[22] If par and no-par existed side-by-side, confusion would be worse confounded and the unscrupulous would continue to adopt par shares when they wished to mislead.

---

[19] Cmd. 9112. The Committee had been appointed to consider this one topic.

[20] Cmnd. 1749, paras. 32–34.

[21] *e.g.* (as in an actual case) by describing shares as 9.5 per cent £1 Preference Shares and issuing them to the public at £1.25, (with the result that the true rate of dividend on the price paid was only 7.6 per cent and, on a winding-up or the return of capital, only £1 per share was repayable).

[22] As in the Ghana Companies Code 1963 (Act 179), s.40.

CHAPTER 12

CAPITAL AND DIVIDENDS

THE elaborate rules dealt with in the previous Chapter would achieve their primary purpose only if they controlled the extent to which any return of the company's assets could be made to its members. As that Chapter should have shown, this they do if the return is of capital not only when that is by a formal reduction of capital approved by the court but also when it is by a redemption or purchase by the company of its shares or by the company giving financial assistance for the subscription or purchase of its shares. But a far more common type of distribution to shareholders is in the form of periodical dividends. It defeats the purpose of the capital maintenance rules if dividends can be paid despite the fact that the value of the net assets of the company is, or would become as a result of the payment, less than the value of the capital yardstick of issued share capital plus share premium account (if any) plus capital redemption reserve (if any).

PRE-1981 POSITION

Nevertheless, under the largely judge-made law prevailing prior to the 1980 Act that was not prevented. True, the courts declared that dividends must not be paid out of capital. But that was meaningless; "capital" as an item in the company's accounts exists only as a notional liability and nothing can be paid out of a liability—actual or notional. More meaningfully, they declared that dividends could be paid only out of profits; but then discovered that "profits" was an elusive and baffling concept better left to accountants and businessmen.

Unfortunately, however, when litigation ensued it had to be decided by lawyers after listening to the expert evidence of accountants. The result was often one which baffled lawyers, accountants and businessmen alike.

What the courts seem to have decided can be briefly summarised as follows:

(a) So long as the properly presented accounts of the company showed a trading profit for the accounting period (normally a year) that could be distributed by way of dividend without regard to losses made in previous years; in other words "nimble dividends", as the Americans describe payments in such circumstances, were permissible.

(b) A realised profit made on the sale of a fixed asset[1] could also be so distributed and, according to the English courts[2] (but not the Scottish[3]) so could an unrealised profit on a revaluation of fixed assets.
(c) Accumulated profits of previous years could also be so distributed unless they had been capitalised by a bonus issue or transfer to the capital redemption reserve.

Had companies taken full advantage of these rules (which fortunately most public companies did not) it would have made nonsense of the whole capital concept. Happily, the Second Company Law Directive made it incumbent on us to tighten up our rules—at any rate in relation to public companies[4]—and this the 1980 Act did in relation to both public and private companies but to a greater extent as regards public ones. The resulting legislative provisions, as amended by the 1981 Act, are now to be found in Part VIII of the 1985 Act.[5]

PRESENT POSITION

Part VIII starts with section 263 which applies to companies whether public or private and to any distribution of its assets to its members, whether in cash or otherwise, except[6]

(a) an issue of shares as fully or partly paid bonus shares,
(b) redemption or purchase of a company's own shares in accordance with Chapter VII of Part V of the Act,[7]
(c) a formal reduction of capital, and
(d) a distribution of assets on a winding-up.

At common law the courts took a wide view of the meaning of a distribution, looking at the substance, not the form of the transaction, and this approach will presumably carry over into the interpretation of the statute. Thus, the sale by a company lacking profits of an asset at

---

[1] *i.e.* its lands, buildings, plant, office furniture, etc., as opposed to current assets turned over in the course of its trade.
[2] *Dimbula Valley (Ceylon) Tea Company v. Laurie* [1961] Ch. 353, not following the Scottish decision cited in n. 3.
[3] *Westburn Sugar Refineries v. I.R.C.* 1960 S.L.T. 297; [1960] T.R. 105. Both the English and the Scottish courts accepted that such profits could be used to pay-up a bonus issue. Buckley J. in *Dimbula* did not see how that could be possible unless the profits were distributable by way of dividend.
[4] It enunciated the basic principle that "No distribution to shareholders may be made when . . . the net assets are, or following such distribution would become, lower than the amount of the subscribed capital plus those reserves which may not be distributed under the law or the statutes" (art. 15.1 (a)) and prescribed detailed rules to give effect to that principle.
[5] *i.e.* ss.263–281 (as amended by the 1989 Act).
[6] s.263(2)(a), (b), (c) and (d).
[7] On which see Chap. 11, above.

an undervalue to another company controlled by its main shareholder has been held to be a distribution, although the transaction did not take the form of the declaration of a dividend.[8]

Any distribution, other than an excepted one, shall not be made otherwise than "out of profits available for the purpose".[9] It then defines "profits available for the purpose" as the company's "accumulated realised profits, so far as not previously utilised by distribution or capitalisation, less its accumulated, realised losses, so far as not previously written off in a reduction or reorganisation of capital duly made".[10] This results in two fundamental changes of the three rules summarised above.[11]

First, no longer may "nimble dividends" be paid out of profits for the year, ignoring losses for previous years; there must be a surplus of profits for the current and past years (so far as they are retained) over losses for those years (so far as they have not been lawfully written off). Secondly, the profits must be realised; although unrealised profits can be applied to pay up a bonus issue,[12] they can no longer be used to pay a dividend.[13]

It will be observed that, for the purpose of section 263, no distinction is drawn between revenue (trading) profits and capital profits. Such a distinction is relevant only in the case of "investment companies",[14] or when the company's articles restrict dividends to payments out of revenue profits only.[15] The sole test for the purposes of section 263, applicable to both public and private companies, is whether there are accumulated realised profits net of accumulated realised losses.

The main difficulty about this is precisely how one determines whether at a particular date there are realised profits or losses and in the Act's attempt to define those terms for the purposes of the account-

---

[8] *Aveling Barford Ltd v. Perion Ltd* [1989] BCLC 626, following *Ridge Securities Ltd v. I.R.C.* [1964] 1 W.L.R. 479 and *Re Halt Garage (1964) Ltd* [1982] 3 All E.R. 1016. The statute encourages such an approach since it defines a distribution as "every description of distribution of a company's assets to its members, whether in cash or otherwise" other than the excepted cases mentioned in the text: s.263(2).

[9] s.263(1).

[10] s.263(3). This is subject to the provision made by sections 265 and 266 for investment and other companies" on which see below, p. 286.

[11] At pp. 281–282.

[12] This being excepted by s.263(2)(a) above. But unrealised profits cannot be used to pay up amounts unpaid on issued shares for this would conflict with the policy of ss.98 and 99 (see Chap. 11, pp. 237–242, above) and is not a payment from "sums available for this purpose" within the meaning of s.99(4); nor can they be used to pay up debentures (s.263(4)) which, though it would not be a distribution to members as such, would be even more objectionable: s.263(4).

[13] *i.e. Westburn* is adopted rather than *Dimbula*: see nn. 2 and 3, above.

[14] See ss.265 and 266: below, p. 286.

[15] s.281 expressly recognises that the memo. and arts may restrict, though they cannot widen, the sums out of which, or the cases in which, a distribution may be made. See *Re Cleveland Trust plc* [1991] BCLC 424.

ing provisions in Part VII there is a note of frustrated desperation.[16] Nor have prolonged efforts successfully ensured that the profits or losses shown are adjusted to take account of inflation.[17]

As a result of section 263, the law, in relation to both public and private companies, now goes much of the way towards adopting the basic principle prescribed for public companies by the Second Directive. But it does not go all the way; it would still permit a public company to pay a dividend notwithstanding that its net assets are, or will be as a result of the payment, worth less than the amount of the issued share capital and undistributable reserves. Hence, in relation to public companies, we had to go further.

Public companies

The necessary extension is made by section 264. This provides that a public company may not make a distribution at any time unless, in addition to compliance with section 263, the amount of its net assets is not less than its called up share capital and undistributable reserves and would not become less as a result of the distribution.[18] For this purpose "net assets" means the aggregate of the company's assets,[19] less the aggregate of its liabilities and, although "liabilities" means real liabilities (and not notional ones like "free reserves") it includes "provisions" within the meaning of paragraph 89[20] of Schedule 4.[21] Moreover, "undistributable reserves" includes not only those which companies are prohibited by the Act from distributing, *i.e.* (a) share premium account and (b) capital redemption reserve (which, as we saw in the previous Chapter, are treated for most purposes as share capital) but also:

> "(c) the amount by which the company's accumulated unrealised profits, so far as not previously utilised by capitalisation,[22] . . . exceed its accumulated unrealised losses (so far as not previously .

---

[16] s.262(3) (as inserted by the 1989 Act) says: "References in this Part to 'realised profits' and 'realised losses', in relation to a company's accounts, are to such profits or losses of the company as fall to be treated as realised for the purpose of those accounts in accordance with principles generally accepted as the time when the accounts are prepared, with respect to the determination for accounting purposes of realised profits or losses"; *i.e.* the legislature, as the judges had done, tries to leave it to the accountants. But the subs. goes on to recognise that in some cases the Act makes specific provision, to which the foregoing is "without prejudice".

[17] The optional "alternative accounting rules" referred to in Chap. 19 at p. 516, do not go far in that direction.

[18] s.164(1). This, like s.263 (see n. 10, above) is subject to the modifications in ss.265 and 266 in relation to "investment companies."

[19] Not including uncalled share capital: s.264(4).

[20] *i.e.* "any amount retained as reasonably necessary for the purpose of providing for any liability or loss which is either likely to be incurred or certain to be incurred but uncertain as to amount or as to the date on which it will arise."

[21] s.264(2).

[22] Except by a post-1980 transfer to capital redemption reserve and thus falling under (b).

written off in a reduction or reorganisation of capital duly made) and

(d) any other reserve which the company is prohibited from distributing by any other enactment (other than one contained in this Part) or by its memorandum or articles.'[23]

Reserves of class (c) and (d) differ from (a) and (b) dealt with in the previous chapter (*i.e.* share premium account and capital redemption reserve), in that to them the rule does not necessarily apply that they cannot be reduced except by a formal reduction of capital or by their being converted into issued share capital by a bonus issue. Nevertheless, for the purpose of the capital yardstick measuring the extent to which the company can make distributions to members, they have, while they remain, to be treated as constituents of that yardstick.

Class (c) reserves would include the so-called "revaluation reserve" which companies, under the accounts rules in Schedule 4,[24] may have to set up when there is a revaluation of fixed assets.[25] An amount may be transferred from that reserve (i) to the profit and loss account, if previously charged to that account or it represents realised profits or (ii) on capitalisation by a bonus issue. The reserve is then reduced to the extent that the amounts transferred to it are no longer needed for the purposes of the valuation method used; but except to that extent it is an irreducible reserve.[26]

Class (d) reserves include those which banks and similar financial institutions, under legislation relating to them, may be required to maintain and those that a company may be required to establish by a provision in its memorandum or articles. The extent to which such reserves can be reduced will then depend on the provisions of the enactment or memorandum and articles, as the case may be.

Development costs

Normally, development costs are not shown as an asset in the company's accounts[27] and they can be only if the reasons for so doing are explained in a note to the accounts. Section 269 provides that the amount of the costs is then to be treated as a realised loss for the purposes of section 263 and as a realised revenue loss for the purposes of section 265.[28] This, however, does not apply to any part of that amount representing an unrealised profit made on a revaluation of those costs or if there are special circumstances justifying their not

---

[23] s.264(3).
[24] Sched. 4, para. 34, as amended by 1989 Act, Sched. 1, para. 6.
[25] On which see further s.275.
[26] Sched. 4, para. 34(3)(3A) and (3B).
[27] Normally research costs and development costs are not distinguished and it is not permissible to treat research costs as an asset.
[28] s.269(1).

being treated as a realised loss and, in the notes to the accounts, an explanation is given of the circumstances relied on to justify the directors' decision to that effect.[29]

Special cases

What has been described above are the general rules on distributions. The Act contains special rules for investment companies[30] and insurance companies carrying on business on what is called a "long-term" basis, *i.e.* life insurance and pensions business.[31] It is not proposed to analyse these provisions, although the investment company scheme is interesting because it draws a distinction between revenue profits and capital profits.[32]

RELEVANT ACCOUNTS

It will have been apparent from the foregoing that, in determining whether there are profits from which distributions can be made in accordance with the rules, what counts are the relevant figures in the company's accounts. Nevertheless, the provisions relating to accounts and audits in Part VII of the Act need to be supplemented by additional provisions in Part VIII, if only because companies may make distributions at a time when there are no, or no justifying, annual accounts prepared under Part VII. Accordingly sections 270 to 276 contain additional accounting provisions for determining whether a distribution may be made by a company "without contravening sections 263, 264 or 265".[33]

They start with a statement that the amount which may be distributed is to be determined by reference to the following items in the "relevant accounts":

(a) profits, losses, assets and liabilities,
(b) provisions of any of the kinds referred to in paragraphs 88 and 89[34] of Schedule 4, and
(c) share capital and reserves (including undistributable reserves).[35]

The relevant accounts for this purpose are normally the company's last annual accounts, prepared and presented to the members in

---

[29] s.269(2).
[30] ss.265–267.
[31] s.268.
[32] See the fifth edition of this book at pp. 247–250 for an analysis of the rules relating to investment companies.
[33] s.270(1).
[34] para. 88 refers to provisions for depreciation of assets. For para. 89 see n. 20, above.
[35] s.270(2).

accordance with Part VII of the Act.[36] When that is so, the distribution is lawful so long as it is justified by reference to those items[37] and the accounts have been properly prepared in accordance with the Act, or have been properly prepared subject only to matters not material for determining whether the distribution would be lawful.[38] These accounts must have been duly audited and, if the auditors' report is qualified, the auditors must also state in writing whether the respect in which the report was qualified is material in determining whether the distribution would be lawful. This statement must have been laid before the company in general meeting, or sent to the members when there is an election to dispense with a meeting.[39]

In two cases, however, special accounts will be needed. The first is where the distribution would contravene section 263, 264 or 265 if reference was made only to the last annual accounts. In that event the company will have to prepare additional "interim accounts". The second is where it is proposed to declare a dividend during the company's first accounting period or before any accounts have been presented in respect of that period. In that event it will have to prepare "initial accounts". The interim or initial accounts must be "those necessary to enable a reasonable judgment to be made as to the amounts of items mentioned" in section 270(2).[40] So far as *private* companies are concerned, that is the only requirement laid down in Part VIII regarding interim or initial accounts; presumably it was thought that it sufficed in relation to them and that it would be unreasonable to impose on them the specific obligations (which include auditing in relation to initial accounts) appropriate (and necessary to comply with the Directive) in relation to public ones.

Before turning to these latter obligations one point needs to be stressed. The use of the expression "interim accounts" might lead one

---

[36] s.270(3). Among the amendments to Part VII made by the 1989 Act are two new sections 252 and 253 which enable members of a private company, subject to stringent conditions, to elect to dispense with laying accounts and reports before a general meeting so long as they are sent to members and others in accordance with s.238(1) (though a member or the auditor may then require a meeting to be held). When such an election operates the wording of ss.270(3) and (4) and 271(4) is modified accordingly: see s.252(3).

[37] *i.e.* item (a) (b) and (c), above.

[38] s.271(1) and (2). Subs. (2) specifically refers to the need to ensure that the balance sheet and profit and loss account present "a true and fair view". If the directors knew or ought to have known of a serious defect in the company's accounts, they will not be "properly prepared" nor give a true and fair view, so that any distribution by the company will be unlawful: *Re Cleveland Trust plc* [1991] BCLC 424.

[39] s.271(3) and (4) (and see n. 36, above). This statement may be made whether or not a distribution is proposed at the time when the statement is made and may refer to all or any types of distribution; it will then suffice to validate any distributions of the types covered by the statement: s.271(5). The need for the auditors' statement is frequently overlooked and if the company has gone into liquidation before the omission is discovered it seems that nothing can be done to render the distribution lawful: *Precisions Dippings Ltd v. Precious Dippings Marketing Ltd* [1986] Ch. 447, C.A. Subss. 271(3) to (5) do not apply to companies exempted from the audit requirement (see pp. 530–532, below): s.249E(1)(c) and (2)(c).

[40] s.270(4).

to suppose that such accounts are needed whenever it is proposed to declare interim or special dividends in addition to the normal dividend for the year. That is not so. So long as the company has duly complied with its obligations under Part VII in respect of its annual accounts for the past year it can, in the current year, pay interim or other special dividends in addition to the final dividend for that year so long as these dividends, in total, do not exceed the amount (as determined from the relevant annual accounts) which it can distribute without contravening sections 263, 264 or 265.[41] It is only when the last annual accounts would not justify a proposed payment that it is necessary to prepare interim accounts. This might occur, for example, when a realised profit had been made on the sale of fixed assets after the date of the last annual accounts and the company wanted to distribute part or all of it to its shareholders without waiting until the next annual accounts are prepared. It could also occur if the net trading profits in the current year are seen to be running at a rate considerably higher than formerly and the directors wished to give the shareholders early concrete evidence of this by paying an immediate interim dividend.[42] In both these examples the last year's accounts might well not justify the payment and would have to be supplemented by interim accounts. Normally, however, it will not be necessary to prepare interim accounts merely because the company pays quarterly or half-yearly interim dividends in anticipation of the final dividend for the year to be declared by the company when the year's accounts are presented.[43]

As regards both interim and initial accounts, section 272 (interim accounts) and section 273 (initial accounts) specifically provide that in the case of a *public* company the accounts must have been properly prepared in accordance with Schedule 4, with such modifications as are necessary because the accounts are not prepared in respect of the company's accounting reference period, or have been so prepared subject only to such matters as are not material for determining whether the proposed distribution would contravene the relevant section.[44] In particular, the balance sheet and the profit and loss account must give a "true and fair" view.[45] And, like annual accounts, a copy of the accounts must be delivered to the Registrar[46] with an English translation if they are in a foreign language.[47] Initial accounts must be audited and, if the auditors' report is qualified, must, as in the case of annual accounts,[48] be accompanied by a written statement on whether the

---

[41] See s.274, below, p. 289.
[42] As articles normally authorise them to do: see Table A 1985, art. 103.
[43] See Table A 1985, art. 102, under which the dividend "shall not exceed the amount recommended by the directors".
[44] ss.272(2) and (3), 273(2) and (3).
[45] ss.272(3), 273(3).
[46] ss.272(4), 273(6).
[47] ss.272(5), 273(7).
[48] See ss.271(3)–(5), above, p. 287.

qualifications are material in relation to determining whether section 270 is complied with.[49] There are no such auditing requirements in relation to interim accounts.[50] Hence a public company with listed shares is unlikely to be put to much additional expense in preparing interim accounts when they are needed since it will have to prepare half-yearly financial statements in order to comply with the Stock Exchange's listing regulations.[51] Unless the requirements of sections 270 to 273 are duly complied with the distribution will be deemed to contravene sections 263 to 265 and the distribution will be unlawful.[52]

Section 274 deals, in respect of both public and private companies, with the method of applying section 270 in relation to successive distributions in reliance on the same relevant accounts, whether they be annual, interim or initial. As previously mentioned,[53] such reliance is permissible, but all previous such distributions have to be treated as added to that proposed for the purpose of determining whether the latter will be lawful. For this purpose, "distributions" include not only dividends but also payments, made since the date when the relevant accounts were prepared, in respect of financial assistance for the acquisition of the company's shares[54] or as the purchase price for the acquisition by the company of its own shares[55] (unless such payments were lawfully made otherwise than out of distributable profits[56]).[57]

Distributions in kind

Distributions within the meaning of Part VIII can be made in kind as well as in cash.[58] Section 276 then makes another (though minor) exception to the general rule that distributions can be made only out of realised profits. It provides that if a distribution is of, or includes, a "non-cash asset"[59] and any part of the stated value of that asset in

---

[49] s.273(4)(5) and (6).
[50] But, in contrast with initial accounts, there will be published audited annual accounts which the interim accounts supplement.
[51] *Listing Rules*, para. 12.46.
[52] s.270(5).
[53] See p. 288, above.
[54] On which see Chap. 11 at pp. 263 *et seq.*, above.
[55] On which see Chap. 11 at pp. 253 *et seq.*, above.
[56] Or, in the case of financial assistance, do not reduce its net assets or increase its net liabilities: s.274(2)(c).
[57] s.274(2) and (3). These subss. are deemed to be included in Chap. VII of Part V (redemption or purchase of shares) for the purpose of the Secretary of State's powers under s.179 to make regulations modifying that Chapter: s.274(4).
[58] s.263(2), above, p. 282. Whether this is so in respect of "distributions" excluded by s.263(2)(b) from those to which Part VIII applies is not wholly clear. If the terms of redemption of redeemable shares provided for their redemption otherwise than in cash there seems to be nothing in Part V, Chapter VII to prevent that (but if the consideration was another class of share, those redeemed would be "convertible" rather than "redeemable" shares). As regards purchase of shares, the wording of the relevant sections, which refer throughout to "purchase" and not "exchange", appears to require the company to pay cash.
[59] Defined in s.739 as "any property or interest in property other than cash; and for this purpose "cash includes foreign currency." When shares are denominated in foreign currency (see

the relevant accounts represents an unrealised profit, it will nevertheless be treated as if it were a realised profit for the purposes of determining whether the distribution is lawful and whether that profit can be included in, or transferred to, the profit and loss account, despite the fact that Schedule 4[60] provides that that can be done only with realised profits. The reason for this section was to facilitate de-mergers which had been rendered practicable without adverse tax consequences by the Finance Act 1981. Such operations will often involve distributions of the property or shares of the demerging company or of other companies in the same group. These distributions might be impossible to the extent needed unless some unrealised profits relating to the non-cash assets concerned could be treated as realised (and, in a sense, it can be said that the distribution by the de-merging company is equivalent to a realisation). However, the concession is not restricted to de-mergers and advantage of it could be taken whenever a non-cash distribution is made.

Effects of the "relevant accounts" rules

The fact that normally the legality of the distribution will have to be supported by accounts is certainly some protection against distributions to the members which place the creditors, present or future, at risk. Particularly is this so when the accounts concerned have to be audited, as is normally the case; they are then more likely to be accurate than if matters were left to the creative accountancy of the company's officers and scrutiny by the directors through rose-tinted spectacles. This is so despite the fact that accountancy is not an exact science and, as post-mortems after takeovers have frequently revealed, auditors of comparable expertise and reputation, faced with the same books of account, may arrive at widely different conclusions on what the "true and fair" results are.

A further consequence is that the answer to the question whether and what dividend can lawfully be paid depends primarily on the situation as at the date of accounts which, if the "relevant accounts" are the latest annual accounts, is likely to be at least seven months before the dividend is actually paid.[61] Hence the wording of sections 263, and, especially, 264 and 265, is somewhat misleading. It suggests that whether a distribution can lawfully be made depends upon the company having the requisite profits (and, in the case of public companies, net assets) available at the time of payment and not on the position some months before.

What then is the position if, before the date of actual payment, the

---

Chap. 11 at p. 236) dividends are likely to be paid in that currency—though they do not have to be unless the articles so provide.

[60] paras. 12(a) and 34(3)(a).

[61] See s.244 (as inserted by 1989 Act).

directors realise that the company is not going to meet those conditions at that time? The normal practice regarding dividend payments is that reflected in article 102 of Table A 1985, *i.e.* "Subject to the provisions of the Act, the company may by ordinary resolution declare dividends in accordance with the respective rights of the members but no dividend shall exceed the amount recommended by the directors."[62] The directors will make their recommendation in the notice of the meeting[63] at which dividends are to be declared. Whether they should, in the light of their then knowledge, not recommend a dividend will depend on the nature of that knowledge. If they have discovered that the relevant accounts were so seriously inaccurate that they did not in fact give a true and fair view of the state of the company's affairs and its profits or losses at the time the accounts were signed,[64] they clearly should not recommend a dividend, and, should withdraw any recommendation they have made; for the dividend, if paid, would be unlawful.[65] If, however, the relevant accounts truly reflected the position as at their date and the only reason why the requisite conditions are no longer met is some calamity occurring thereafter, payment of the dividend would not seemingly, be unlawful—unless the effect of paying it would be to reduce the company to insolvency.[66] That is not to say that the originally proposed dividend should necessarily be declared and paid; if the directors would not have recommended it had they foreseen what was to befall, it clearly would be wiser and safer if it were not declared.

CONSEQUENCES OF UNLAWFUL DISTRIBUTIONS

In contrast with unlawful financial assistance for the purchase by a company of its own shares[67] (where the Act provides only for criminal sanctions, leaving the courts to work out the civil law consequences), no criminal sanctions are provided in the case of unlawful distributions covered by Part VIII but something (though precious little) is said about the civil consequences. This is done by section 277 which

---

[62] Note also art. 103 as regards their own powers to pay interim dividends.

[63] Normally the AGM. If a private company has elected to dispense with meetings presumably the recommendation will be made when the accounts are sent to the members.

[64] *Re Cleveland Trust plc* [1991] BCLC 424.

[65] ss.270(3), 271(2) and (3), 272(2) and (3). And the accounts should be revised; there are now statutory provisions for this: see ss.245–245C.

[66] This, assuming that the payment was justified by the "relevant accounts", would not be one which the Act specifically makes unlawful but the pre-1980 case-law presumably survives: for an interesting illustration see *Peter Buchanan Ltd v. McVey* [1955] A.C. 516, H.L. (Ir.) at 521–522. It would certainly render the directors vulnerable to claims based on misfeasance (or on "wrongful trading" (see pp. 153–155, above) and clearly they should not exercise their own discretion to pay interim dividends: *Lagunas Nitrate Co. v. Schroeder & Co.* (1901) 85 L.T. 22.

[67] See Chap. 11, p. 274, above.

provides that, when a distribution[68] is made to a member which he then knows, or has reasonable cause to believe, is made in contravention (in whole or in part) of Part VIII, he is liable to repay it or, if the distribution was otherwise then in cash, its value.[69] In other words, the payment, though "unlawful", is neither void nor voidable but can nevertheless be recovered from any recipient of it who knew or ought to have known that it was unlawful.

Except in relation to small private companies (which rarely pay dividends) it is obviously unlikely that the prescribed actual or constructive knowledge could be established unless the member was an officer of the company.[70] Hence the occasions when the section will bite are likely to be few. It is true that the section further provides that it is "without prejudice to any obligations imposed apart from this section on a member of a company to repay a distribution unlawfully made to him"[71] but it is difficult to identify any such obligation on members, as such, in respect of dividends.[72]

A more powerful civil sanction is the possibility of recovering from the directors and other officers who were responsible for the making of the unlawful distribution. Clearly they may well have broken their duties of care and diligence and possibly those of good faith[73] and in that event the extent of their liability will not be limited to what they themselves have received by way of unlawful dividend but will extend to restoration of the loss which the company suffered as a result of the unlawful payments.[74] But in practice it is unlikely that action will be taken against them by the company unless there is a change in those controlling the company or unless it goes into liquidation,[75] administration or receivership. Until any of these events occur, nothing

---

[68] Other than financial assistance for the acquisition of the company's own shares given in contravention of s.151 or any payment made in respect of the redemption or purchase of shares in the company s.277(2).

[69] s.277(1).

[70] It seems fanciful to suppose that any court would hold that "Sid" and "Aunt Agatha" should study the relevant accounts and the documents accompanying them and read with understanding Part VIII of the Act to check that their dividends are lawfully payable.

[71] s.277(2).

[72] At common law, shareholders appear to be liable to repay only if they actually knew that the dividend was unlawful and it seems clear that, at best, the common law liability is no greater than that under s.277: see *Moxham v. Grant* [1900] 1 Q.B. 85, C.A. But in the *Precision Dippings* case (p. 287, n. 39, above) the C.A. avoided the need to construe what is now s.277(1) by holding that the unlawful payment was *ultra vires* (an example of the continuing loose use of that expression (see p. 202, above) and that the recipient of the dividend (the company's parent) was liable, as a constructive trustee, to restore it. See also *Aveling Barford Ltd v. Perion Ltd* [1989] BCLC 627, and *Re Cleveland Trust* [1991] BCLC 424 where the doctrine of common mistake was prayed in aid. In this case, however, which involved unlawful distributions by three companies in a group, the distribution by the sub-subsidiary was indeed *ultra vires*, by virtue of a provisions in its memo.

[73] On which see Chap. 22, below.

[74] *Dovey v. Cory* [1901] A.C. 477, H.L.

[75] When a misfeasance summons under what is now s.212 of the Insolvency Act 1986 might be successful: *Re Sharpe, Re Bennett* [1892] 1 Ch. 154, C.A.

is likely to happen, except perhaps an attempt to recover damages for alleged professional negligence against the firm of auditors that reported on the relevant accounts.[76]

CAPITALISATION AND THE DIVIDEND RULES

The final section of Part VIII to which reference needs to be made is section 278. But a short preamble is necessary. As we have seen, prior to 1981, according to the English courts, whether profits could be capitalised by making a bonus issue depended on there being profits out of which a dividend could be paid.[77] Now, however, a clear distinction is drawn between profits which can be distributed (generally only net realised profits) and profits which can be capitalised. Accordingly Part VIII of the Act excludes, from its definition of "distributions",[78] an "issue of shares as fully or partly paid bonus shares".[79] The only remaining connection between capitalisation and distributable profits is that once profits are capitalised, whether by a bonus issue or by a transfer to the capital redemption reserve, they cease to be profits and become, in the first case, share capital, and, in the second case, "undistributable reserves". This will affect the ability to pay dividends, both because the former profits are no longer "distributable profits"[80] and because, in relation to public companies, the capital yardstick will have been increased thereby.[81]

So far so good. But then comes section 278 which at first sight is curious and misleading. It provides that where, before December 1980, a company was authorised by its articles to apply its unrealised profits in paying up bonus shares "that provision continues (subject to any alteration of the articles) as authority for those profits to be so applied after that date". This seems to imply, in contradiction of what is said above, that only a company, with pre-1981 articles which expressly authorised it, can capitalise unrealised profits. In fact, however, the object of the section is not that at all.

Why it was thought (rightly) that some such provision was needed is because of the idiosyncrasies of English Companies Acts which, as we saw in Chapter 9, frequently empower companies to do various things but leave it to the companies' articles to say when, whether and

---

[76] Another possibility, of greater theoretical than practical importance, is that a member, if he acted in time, could obtain an injunction to restrain the company from paying an unlawful dividend. In such a case action by a member on behalf of the company would not seem to be precluded by the *Foss v. Harbottle* rule, on which see Chap. 23, below.

[77] See above, p. 282, n. 2.

[78] s.263(2). What makes a bonus issue a "distribution of a company's assets to its members" is not the issue of the shares (a company's shares are not its assets) but the fact that the company parts with its assets in paying them up.

[79] s.263(2)(a)

[80] For the purposes of s.263.

[81] Thus increasing the restrictive impact of s.264.

through which of their organs they shall do it. Part VIII affords an example of this. It prescribes when, so far as the Act is concerned, dividends may or may not be paid and makes it clear that companies may, and in some cases must,[82] capitalise profits. But it expressly recognises that its provisions are "without prejudice to . . . any provision of a company's memorandum or articles restricting the sums out of which or the cases in which a distribution may be made.[83] Nor does it say anything about which organs of a company are to exercise its powers to distribute profits or to capitalise them. Hence articles invariably contain provisions about these powers.[84] Since, prior to the 1980 Act, it was believed that profits, whether realised or unrealised, could be distributed, it was customary for the capitalisation article to refer to "profits available for dividend".[85] If nothing had been done, companies with such articles would have lost the right to capitalise unrealised profits when the 1980 Act (now section 263 of the 1985 Act) made them not "available for dividend". Hence the Act did two things. It first inserted[86] a new article 128A in Table A 1948 which enabled a company formed thereafter with Table A articles to capitalise any or all of its reserves. This, however, did not help those formed prior to the coming into force of that Act, most of which would probably not have realised that they had lost the ability to capitalise unrealised profits unless they altered their articles. Secondly, therefore, it contained a provision corresponding to the present section 278, the intention being to entitle such companies to continue to be authorised to capitalise unrealised profits without having to alter their articles. It is a pity that this intention could not have been more clearly expressed.[87]

However, as regards companies with an article equivalent to Table A 1985, article 110, there is no problem; it is carefully worded so as to enable the directors, with the authority of an ordinary resolution of the company, to capitalise profits "whether or not they are available for distribution."

CONCLUSION

While, perhaps, lawyers and businessmen, may fairly complain that not all the present capital maintenance and dividend rules, described in this and the previous Chapter, are expressed in a way which is

---

[82] *i.e.* where a company is required to transfer profits to capital redemption reserve or to the revaluation reserve.

[83] s.281.

[84] Table A 1948, arts. 114–122 (dividends) and 128, 129 (capitalisations); Table A 1985, arts. 102–108 (dividends) and 110 (capitalisations).

[85] As did art. 128 of Table A 1948.

[86] Companies Act 1980, Sched. 3.

[87] Particularly as the wording ignores the fact that unrealised capital profits of a Scottish registered company would not have been "profits available for dividend" unless and until the

readily intelligible to anyone other than a specialist corporate account-ant, at long last we have rules which on the whole are logical and sensible. For this we have to thank our membership of the European Community. It should again be emphasised, however, that while these rules afford protection against the risk that a public company's assets will not be milked by distributions to its members to the detriment of its creditors, they afford little protection in relation to private compan-ies—and will not do so unless they too are required to raise and main-tain a minimum capital and are made subject to section 264. Of that there is no immediate likelihood.

It must also be repeated that, in the case of most private companies, members who are also directors extract their rewards in the form of remuneration which will be paid whether or not there are profits or the members' capital is intact.[88] Moreover, in practice, companies (public or private) raise their working capital not only in the form of share capital but also from borrowings, secured or unsecured. When this loan capital is raised by an issue of secured debenture-stock or unsecured loan-stock, the subscribers will not think of themselves as wholly different animals from the members who have subscribed for shares.[89] But in law they will be wholly different—they will be cred-itors not members. And the rules relating to the raising and mainten-ance of capital or to distributions will have no application. Loan capital is a true liability, and, as such, it may reduce the company's net assets and payment of interest on it may reduce the distributable profits.[90] To that extent it affects the application of the rules relating to capital maintenance and to distributions to members—but not otherwise. And when the loan capital is secured on the undertaking and assets of the company, it may seriously reduce the protection which the capital concept is supposed to afford to trade creditors against the dangers of limited liability.

This is not to suggest that the capital concept is a chimaera; only that it still has its limitations.

Scottish courts overruled *Westburn Sugar Refineries v. I.R.C.* 1960 S.L.T. 297; [1960] T.R. 105: see p. 282, nn. 2 and 3, above. Section 278 achieves its object only if one assumes that *Westburn* was wrong on this point and *Dimbula Valley (Ceylon) Tea Company v. Laurie* [1961] Ch. 353, right (a view which few share).

[88] And members who are not directors will be lucky if they are paid anything.

[89] As the Act seems to recognise, since provisions relating to debentures are included in Part V notwithstanding that this is entitled "Share Capital, Its Increase, Maintenance and Reduc-tion".

[90] On the other hand, from the company's viewpoint operating on borrowings may prove a sound investment since (a) it will hope to earn more from employment of the money borrowed than the interest it has to pay, (b) the interest will be deductible in assessing its income for tax purposes, and (c) the money it will ultimately have to repay will, almost certainly, be worth less in real terms than the sum borrowed.

Part Four

A COMPANY'S SECURITIES

CHAPTER 13

THE NATURE AND CLASSIFICATION OF COMPANY SECURITIES

FREQUENT references have been made to the securities which a company can issue. It is now necessary to look a little more closely at the exact nature of these securities and to indicate the various forms they may take.

They fall into two primary classes which legal theory tries to keep rigidly separated but which in economic reality merge into each other. The first of these classes is described as shares; the second as debentures. The basic legal distinction between them is that a share constitutes the holder a member of the company,[1] whereas the debenture-holder is a creditor of the company but not a member of it.

LEGAL NATURE OF SHARES

What, then, is the exact juridical nature of a share? At the present day this is a question more easily asked than answered. In the old deed of settlement company, which was merely an enlarged partnership with the partnership property vested in trustees, it was clear that the members' "shares" entitled them to an equitable interest in the assets. It is true that the exact nature of this equitable interest was not crystal clear, for the members could not, while the firm was a going concern, lay claim to any particular asset or prevent the directors from disposing of it. Even with the modern partnership, no very satisfactory solution to this problem has been found, and the most one can say is that the partners have an equitable interest, often described as a lien, which floats over the partnership assets throughout the duration of the firm, although it crystallises only on dissolution. Still, there is admittedly some sort of proprietary nexus (however vague and ill-defined) between the partnership assets and the partners.

At one time it was thought that the same applied to an incorporated company, except that the company itself held its assets as trustee for its members.[2] But this idea has long since been rejected. Shareholders have ceased to be regarded as having equitable interests in the com-

---

[1] A person may, however, become a member without being a shareholder—the company may not have a share capital.

[2] *Child v. Hudson's Bay Co.* (1723) 2 P. Wms. 207. As in the case of partnerships it was clear long before the express statutory provisions to this effect (see now s.182(1)(a)) that shares were personalty and not realty even if the company owned freehold land.

pany's assets; "shareholders are not, in the eyes of the law, part owners of the undertaking".[3] As a result, the word "share" has become something of a misnomer, for shareholders no longer share any property in common; at the most they share certain rights in respect of dividends, return of capital on a winding up, voting, and the like.

Today it is generally stated that a share is a chose in action.[4] This, however, is not helpful, for "chose in action" is a notoriously vague term used to describe a mass of interests which have little or nothing in common except that they confer no right to possession of a physical thing, and which range from purely personal rights under a contract to patents, copyrights and trade marks.

It is tempting to equate shares with rights under a contract, for as we have seen[5] the memorandum and articles of association constitute a contract of some sort between the company and its members and it is these documents which directly or indirectly define the rights conferred by the shares. But a share is something far more than a mere contractual right *in personam*. This is sufficiently clear from the rules relating to infant shareholders, who are liable for calls on the shares unless they repudiate the allotment during infancy or on attaining majority,[6] and who cannot recover any money which they have paid unless the shares have been completely valueless.[7] As Parke B. said,[8]

> "They have been treated, therefore, as persons in a different situation from mere contractors for then they would have been exempt, but in truth they are purchasers who have acquired an interest not in a mere chattel, but in a subject of a permanent nature . . ."[9]

The definition of a share which is, perhaps, the most widely quoted is that of Farwell J. in *Borland's Trustee v. Steel*[10]:

> "A share is the interest of a shareholder in the company measured by a sum of money, for the purpose of liability in the first place, and of interest in the second, but also consisting of a series of mutual covenants entered into by all the shareholders inter se in

---

[3] *Per* Evershed L.J. in *Short v. Treasury Commissioners* [1948] 1 K.B. 122, C.A.

[4] See, *e.g. per* Greene M.R. in [1942] Ch. 241, and *Colonial Bank v. Whinney* (1886) 11 App.Cas. 426, H.L.

[5] Above, Chap. 6 at pp. 115 *et seq.*

[6] *Cork & Brandon Ry v. Cazenove* (1847) 10 Q.B. 935; *N.W. Ry v. M'Michael* (1851) 5 Exch. 114. If they repudiate during infancy it is not clear whether they can be made liable to pay calls due prior thereto: the majority in *Cazenove*'s case thought they could, but Parke B. in the later case (at 125) stated the contrary.

[7] *Steinberg v. Scala (Leeds) Ltd* [1923] 2 Ch. 452, C.A.

[8] (1851) 5 Exch. at 123.

[9] Later he suggested that the shareholder had "a vested interest of a permanent character in all the profits arising from the land and other effects of the company" (at 125). This can hardly be supported in view of later cases.

[10] [1901] 1 Ch. 279 at 288. Approved by C.A. in *Re Paulin* [1935] 1 K.B. 26, and by H.L. *ibid.*, *sub nom. I.R.C. v. Crossman* [1937] A.C. 26. See also the other definitions canvassed in that case.

accordance with [section 14]. The contract contained in the articles
of association is one of the original incidents of the share. A share
is not a sum of money . . . but is an interest measured by a sum of
money and made up of various rights contained in the contract,
including the right to a sum of money of a more or less amount.''
It will be observed that this definition, though it lays considerable
and perhaps disproportionate stress on the contractual nature of the
shareholder's rights, also emphasises the fact that he has an interest *in*
the company. The theory seems to be that the contract constituted by
the articles of association defines the nature of the rights, which, however, are not purely personal rights but instead confer some sort of
proprietary interest in the company though not in its property. The
company itself is treated not merely as a person, the subject of rights
and duties, but also as a *res*, the object of rights and duties.[11] It is the
fact that the shareholder has rights in the company as well as against
it, which, in legal theory, distinguishes the member from the debenture-holder whose rights are also defined by contract (this time the
debenture itself and not the articles) but are rights against the company
and, if the debenture is secured, in its property, but never in the company itself. Farwell J.'s definition mentions that the interest of a shareholder is measured by a sum of money. Reference has already been
made to this[12] and it has been emphasised that the requirement of a
nominal monetary value is an arbitrary and illogical one which has
been rejected in certain other common law jurisdictions. The nominal
value is meaningless and may be misleading, except in so far as it
determines the minimum liability. Even as a measure of liability, it is
of less importance now that shares are almost invariably issued on
terms that they are to be fully paid up on or shortly after allotment
and are frequently issued at a price exceeding their nominal value. But
reference to liability is valuable in that it emphasises that shareholders
qua members may be under obligations to the company as well as
having rights against it.

This analysis may seem academic and barren, and to some extent it
is, for a closer examination of the rights conferred by shares and
debentures will show the impossibility of preserving any hard and fast
distinction between them which bears any relation to practical reality.
Nevertheless, the matter is not entirely theoretical, for in a number of
cases the courts have been faced with the need to analyse the juridical
nature of a shareholder's interest in order to determine the principles
on which it should be valued. The most interesting of these cases is
Short v. Treasury Commissioners[13] where the whole of the shares of

---

[11] ''A whole system . . . has been built up on the unconscious assumption that organisations,
which from one point of view are considered individuals, from another are storehouses of
tangible property'': Arnold, *The Folklore of Capitalism* (New Haven, Conn., 1959) p. 353.
[12] Above, Chaps. 11 & 12.
[13] [1948] 1 K.B. 116, C.A., affd. [1948] A.C. 534, H.L.

Short Bros. were being acquired by the Treasury under a Defence Regulation which provided for payment of their value "as between a willing buyer and a willing seller".[14] They were valued on the basis of the quoted share price, but the shareholders argued that, since all the shares were being acquired, stock exchange prices were not a true criterion and that either the whole undertaking should be valued and the price thus determined apportioned among the shareholders, or the value should be the price which one buyer would give for the whole block, which price should then be similarly apportioned. The courts upheld the method adopted and rejected both the alternatives suggested, the first because the shareholders were not "part owners of the undertaking" and the second because the regulation implied that each holding was to be separately valued. It was conceded that had any individual shareholder held a sufficient block to give him "control" of the company then he might have been entitled to a higher price than the total market value of his shares,[15] since he would then have been selling an item of property—control—additional to his shares. But as no one shareholder had control to sell, the Government was able to acquire control of the company's assets for a fraction of their true value (and for a fraction of what it would have had to pay on a takeover bid[16]).

One thing at least is clear: shares are recognised in law, as well as in fact, as objects of property which are bought, sold, mortgaged and bequeathed. They are indeed the typical items of property of the modern commercial era and particularly suited to its demands because of their exceptional liquidity. To deny that they are "owned" would be as unreal as to deny, on the basis of feudal theory, that land is owned—far more unreal because the owner's freedom to do what he likes with his shares in public companies is likely to be considerably less fettered. Nor, today, is the bundle of rights making up the share regarded as equitable only. On the contrary, as the next chapter will show, legal ownership is recognised and distinguished from equitable ownership in much the same way as a legal estate in land is distinguished from equitable interests therein. Nor must this emphasis on the proprietary and financial aspects of a shareholder's rights obscure the important fact that his shareholding causes him to become a member of an association, normally with rights to take part in its deliberation by attending and voting at its general meetings.

---

[14] This popular formula is much criticised by economists who argue with some force that the willingness of the buyer and seller depends on the price and not vice versa.

[15] Hence in *Dean v. Prince* [1953] Ch. 590 (reversed on the facts [1954] Ch. 409, C.A.) Harman J. held that the "fair value" of a block of shares conferring control must include something above the "break-up" value of the assets, in respect of this control.

[16] On which, see Chap. 29, below.

THE PRESUMPTION OF EQUALITY BETWEEN SHAREHOLDERS

The typical company—one limited by shares—must issue some shares, and the initial presumption of the law is that all shares confer the same rights and impose the same liabilities. As in partnership[17] equality prevails in the absence of agreement to the contrary. Normally the shareholders' rights will fall under three heads: (i) dividends, (ii) return of capital on a winding up (or authorised reduction of capital) and (iii) attendance at meetings and voting, and unless there is some indication to the contrary all the shares will confer the like rights to all three. So far as voting is concerned this is a comparatively recent development, for, on the analogy of the partnership rule, it was long felt that members' voting rights should be divorced from their purely financial interests in respect of dividend and capital, so that the equality in voting should be between members rather than between shares. A stage intermediate between these two ideas was reflected in the Companies Clauses Act 1845[18] which provided that in the absence of contrary provision in the special statute every shareholder had one vote for every share up to ten, one for every additional five up to a hundred and one for every ten thereafter, thus weighting the voting in favour of the smaller holders. However, attempts to reduce the proportion of voting rights as the size of holdings increased were doomed to failure since the requirement could be easily evaded by splitting holdings and vesting them in nominees. It is now recognised that if voting rights are to vary, separate classes of shares should be created so that the different number of votes can be attached to the shares themselves and not to the holder. Even today, however, the older idea still prevails on a vote by a show of hands, when the common law rule is that each member has one vote irrespective of the number of shares held; a rule which, although it can be altered by the constitution, is normally maintained,[19] if only because the number of a human being's hands cannot be more than two.

For many years it was thought that in the absence of express provision in the original constitution the continued equality of all shares was a fundamental condition which could not be abrogated by an alteration of the articles so as to allow the issue of shares preferential to those already issued.[20] This idea was, however, finally destroyed in *Andrews v. Gas Meter Co.*[21] which established that in the absence of a prohibition in the memorandum, the articles could be altered so as to authorise such an issue.

---

[17] Partnership Act 1980, s.24(1).
[18] s.75.
[19] For the law and practice regarding voting at meetings, see Chap. 21, below.
[20] *Hutton v. Scarborough Cliff Hotel Co.* (1865) 2 Dr. & Sim. 521.
[21] [1897] 1 Ch. 361, C.A.

There is a similar presumption of equality in relation to shareholders' liabilities but it too can be altered by provisions in the memorandum and articles. In the case of a company limited by shares, normally the only liability imposed on a shareholder as such will be to pay up the nominal value of the shares and any premium in so far as payment has not already been made by a previous holder. This, however, does not mean that all the shares, even if of the same nominal value and of the same class, will necessarily be issued at the same price, or that, even if they are, all shareholders will necessarily be treated alike as regards calls for the unpaid part. Section 119 provides that a company if so authorised by its articles may: (a) make arrangements on an issue of shares for a difference between shareholders in the amounts or times of payments of calls; (b) accept from any member the whole or part of the amount remaining unpaid although it has not been called up; or (c) pay a dividend in proportion to the amount paid up on each share where a larger amount is paid up on some shares than on others.[22] Subject to that, however, calls must be made *pari passu*.[23]

Directors' authority to allot shares

The principle of equal treatment was carried a stage further when the Second Company Law Directive[24] was implemented by the Companies Act 1980. This introduced a system whereby existing shareholders had, in some circumstances, to be afforded pre-emptive rights on an issue of further shares. But as a preliminary to an explanation of the statutory pre-emption provisions it is necessary first to refer to a further reform introduced at the same time, *i.e.* to restrictions placed on the authority of directors to allot shares at their whim and pleasure. This was dealt with relatively simply in what is now section 80 of the 1985 Act to which the 1989 Act added section 80A. Section 80 provides that directors shall not exercise any power of the company to allot shares in the company or rights to subscribe for, or convert into, shares in the company unless they are authorised to do so by the company in general meeting[25] or by the company's articles.[26] This in

---

[22] Table A 1985 appears to authorise (a) only (see art. 17) probably rightly in view of the complications which (b) and (c) would cause a public company.

[23] *Galloway v. Halle Concerts Society* [1915] 2 Ch. 233.

[24] Council Directive 77/91 of December 13, 1976: [1977] O.J. L26/1. The principle itself was affirmed in Art. 42: "For the purposes of the implementation of this Directive the laws of the member States shall ensure equal treatment to all shareholders who are in the same position."

[25] *i.e.* by an ordinary resolution, which in the case of a private company can be a written resolution signed by all the members entitled to vote: s.381A. But a copy of it has to be sent to the Registrar under s.380: s.80(8).

[26] s.80(1). This does not apply to shares taken by subscribers to the memorandum or shares allotted in pursuance of an employees' share scheme (s.80(2)) but otherwise it applies to all classes of shares and all types of issues. The section describes those shares and rights to which it applies as "relevant securities" (not to be confused with "relevant shares" in ss.89–96 dealing with pre-emptive rights).

itself would have achieved little. What makes it more meaningful is that any such authority, whether given in the articles or by a resolution, must state the maximum number of securities which can be issued under it[27] and the date at which the authority will expire. That date must not be later than five years from the date of the relevant resolution or, if conferred in the original articles, from the date of incorporation,[28] though it may be renewed by the company in general meeting for successive periods not exceeding five years.[29] Moreover, it may at any time be varied or revoked by an ordinary resolution even if that involves an alteration of the articles.[30] Authority may be given for a particular exercise of the power or for its exercise generally (a distinction of some importance in relation to pre-emptive rights) and may be unconditional or subject to conditions.[31] Contravention of the section does not affect the validity of any allotment made[32] but any director, who "knowingly and wilfully" permits it, is liable to a fine.[33]

Section 80 is one of the provisions that a private company may relax by an elective resolution under section 379A.[34] If it does so the provisions of section 80A apply instead of those in subsections (4) and (5) of section 80 and the authority can be given for any fixed period or indefinitely though it can be revoked at any time.[35] Should the elective resolution cease to have effect, if the authority has lasted for five years or more before the election ceases to have effect, it expires forthwith: otherwise it has effect as if it had been given for a fixed period of five years.[36]

Pre-emptive rights

In contrast with the relative simplicity of sections 80 and 80A, the provisions relating to pre-emptive rights (now sections 89 to 96) are complicated and confusing—and also controversial. However, the basic principle which they enshrine is simple enough. It is that a shareholder should be able to protect his proportion of the total equity by

---

[27] In relation to allotments of rights to subscribe or to convert, what has to be stated is the maximum number of shares that can be allotted pursuant to the rights: s.80(6).

[28] s.80(4). But, if the authority so given permitted the directors to make an offer or agreement which would or might require an allotment to be made after the authority expired and the directors make such an offer or agreement before the authority expires, they may allot accordingly: s.80(7). But for this, directors who had lawfully allotted rights such as options, warrants or convertible bonds might find themselves precluded from allotting the shares when the rights were exercised.

[29] s.80(5).

[30] s.80(4).

[31] s.80(3).

[32] s.80(10).

[33] s.80(9).

[34] See Chap. 5, p. 94, above.

[35] s.80A(2) and (3).

[36] s.80A(7).

having the opportunity to subscribe for any new issue for cash of equity capital or securities having an equity element. In short, the Act requires companies, which wish to raise new capital, in certain circumstances to do so by means of a "rights" issue[37] to existing shareholders (or through an equivalent procedure in the case of a private company) rather than by a general offer of the shares.

There are two main reasons why a shareholder might be opposed to the dilution of his or her holding of equity shares. First, if new voting shares are issued and a shareholder does not acquire that amount of the new issue which is proportionate to his or her existing holding, his influence in the company may be reduced because he now has control over a smaller number of votes. In listed companies this is likely to be of concern only to large, often institutional, shareholders. Here, pre-emption rights operate as a potential limit on the freedom of the directors to effect a shift in the balance of control in the company by issuing new equity shares carrying voting rights.[38]

Secondly, large issues of new shares by a company are likely to be at a discount to the existing market price of the securities, in order to encourage their sale. Once the new shares are allocated, all the shares of the relevant class, new and old, will trade on the market at a price normally somewhere between the issue price and the previous market price, the new market price depending upon the size of the discount and the market's view of the company's plans for its new resources. If an existing shareholder does not acquire the relevant proportion of the new shares, the loss of market value of the existing holding, attributable to the discount, will not be compensated for by the increase in the value of the new shares above the offer price. The new shareholders, in effect, will have been let into the company too cheaply, and the existing shareholders will have paid the price for that decision. A rights issue will protect an existing shareholder against this financial dilution even if he cannot afford to take up the shares on offer. The shareholder may accept the right to acquire the new shares and then assign (or "renounce") the right for payment to someone who wishes to buy the new shares. In this way, an existing shareholder may compensate himself for the loss in value of his existing shareholding, even if he is not in a position to maintain its proportionate size.[39] Protection against both forms of dilution is what sections 89 to 96 seek to achieve.

---

[37] Rights issues are described in Chap. 16, pp. 399–400.

[38] See also Chap. 22, p. 605 on the collateral purposes doctrine which has a similar effect but operates only when the directors' predominant purpose is an improper one.

[39] The "discount" referred to in this paragraph is a discount to the prevailing market price of the shares, not to their par value, which is not permitted (see p. 237, above). If the shareholder's concern is with voting dilution, financial inability to acquire the new shares will be a problem for him. In the case of small companies, in such a situation the shareholder may be able to challenge the decision to issue new shares under s.459. See *Re A Company* [1986] BCLC 362 and *Re Sam Weller Ltd* [1990] Ch. 682 and below Chap. 27, p. 742.

In contrast with sections 80 and 80A, which apply to all issues, whether for cash or otherwise, and to rights to all classes of shares,[40] the ambit of the pre-emptive provisions extends only to issues for cash of "equity securities" as defined (by a somewhat tortuous process) in section 94. Subsection (2) of that section says that "equity security" means "a relevant share" in the company (other than one taken by a subscriber to the memorandum or a bonus share) or the right to subscribe for or convert into "relevant shares" in the company. Subsection (5) defines "relevant shares" as: "shares in the company other than—(a) shares which as respects dividends and capital carry a right to participate only up to a specified amount[41] in a distribution,[42] and (b) shares which are held by a person who acquired them in pursuance of an employees' share scheme or, in the case of shares which have not been allotted, are to be alloted in pursuance of such a scheme".

And subsection (4) defines "relevant employee shares" as "shares of the company which would be relevant in it but for the fact that they are held by a person who acquired them in pursuance of an employees' share scheme".

In the light of these definitions, section 89(1) becomes intelligible. What it provides is that a company proposing to allot equity securities shall not allot them to any person unless it has first offered, on the same or more favourable terms, to each person who holds relevant shares or relevant employee shares, a proportion of those equity securities which is as nearly as practicable equal to his existing proportion in nominal value of his aggregate holdings of relevant shares and relevant employee shares.[43] The effect of this is that equity shares, or rights to them, can be allotted as subscribers' shares, bonus shares or pursuant to an employees' share scheme[44] without first offering pre-emptive rights. But, if equity shares or rights to them are to be issued in other circumstances, they first have to be offered to all equity shareholders in proportion to their holdings whether or not these were acquired as subscribers' shares, bonus shares or pursuant to an employees' share scheme. This is clearly as it should be. Employees'

---

[40] Other than subscribers' shares and those subject to an employees' share scheme.

[41] There is no upper limit to this amount (and it would be impracticable to set one) with the result that it is possible to prescribe amounts so high that the holders would in fact be entitled to the whole or the lion's share of the equity (unless subsequent issues were made) without affording them pre-emptive rights.

[42] The test under (a) of whether or not shares are "relevant" (*i.e.* "equity capital" as defined in s.744) depends solely on their financial rights; voting rights are irrelevant. Pre-emptive rights are particularly important in relation to non-voting equity shares since sections 80 and 80A afford their holders no protection and they will have no say on whether the proposed issue should be made.

[43] On a date specified in the pre-emptive offer, which date must not be more than 28 days before that of the offer: s.94(7).

[44] Even if those scheme members may be entitled to renounce or assign their rights so that, if they do, the shares when allotted will not be "held in pursuance of the scheme."

share schemes, for example, would be unworkable if, every time a further allotment was to be made pursuant to them, all equity shareholders had to be offered pre-emptive rights. If, however, equity shares have been allotted under the scheme, the employee holders should have the same rights to protect their proportion of equity as any other shareholder.

Only one pre-emptive offering has to be made; if it is not accepted in full, shares not taken up may be allotted to anyone[45]; accepting existing shareholders do not have to be given further pre-emptive rights in respect of those unaccepted shares. The procedure whereby the pre-emptive offer is to be communicated to the shareholders is laid down in section 90. The offer must be in writing, must state a period of not less than 21 days within which it can be accepted and withdrawal of the offer before the end of the stated period is forbidden.[46]

All this is on the assumption that the proposed issue is exclusively for cash[47]; when it is proposed to allot shares as consideration payable to the vendor on the acquisition of a business or real property, it would be impossible to make an offer to the existing shareholders on the same terms. Nevertheless, the restriction of the statutory pre-emption provisions to cash issues, even if compelled by necessity, does make a severe hole in the principle of protecting shareholders against dilution, especially dilution of their voting position. In relation to financial dilution some alternative protection is provided by section 103, requiring an independent valuation report in the case of share issues by public companies for a non-cash consideration,[48] but, even so, that section does not confer individual rights upon shareholders in the way that section 89 does. In fact, the section does not even require the approval of shareholders as a whole to the proposed non-cash issue.

Moreover, the exclusion of issues which are wholly or partly other than for cash (section 89(4)) gives rise to possibilities of manipulation so as to avoid the pre-emption rules. For example, if any part of the consideration, even a minor part, is not cash, then it appears that the pre-emption rules are excluded. This may be of particular interest to private companies. In other cases it may well be possible to restructure the transaction so that the cash is provided otherwise than to the issuer

---

[45] s.89(1)(b). But in the case of listed companies see p. 311, below.

[46] This, being a statutory provision, overrides the common law rule that an offer may be withdrawn until it has been accepted.

[47] See s.89(4).

[48] See Chap. 11, p. 240. But section 103 does not apply to private companies or to share issues even by public companies in connection with takeover offers or mergers (s.103(3) and (5)), where there is in fact a considerable risk of financial dilution. Listed companies are somewhat more tightly regulated. Where a listed company proposes to enter into a transaction involving the issue of equity shares for a consideration (whether in cash or otherwise) equivalent to 25 per cent or more of the existing market value of its equity shares, that will be a "Super Class 1" transaction and the prior approval of the shareholders will be required: *Listing Rules*, paras. 10.4, 10.5 and 10.37.

in exchange for its shares. Thus, where company A wishes to acquire part of the business of company B, the latter wishing to receive cash, the obvious way to proceed would be for company A to issue new shares to raise the necessary money, if it does not have sufficient available cash, thus attracting the pre-emption provisions. Instead, however, company A may issue its shares to company B, in exchange for the latter's assets and thus without attracting the pre-emption provisions, company A having previously arranged for a merchant bank to offer to buy the shares from company B at a fixed price and to place them with interested investors. Such a "vendor placing" gives company B the cash it wanted, whilst relieving company A of the need to abide by the pre-emption rules.[49]

However, despite section 89, the statutory pre-emptive rights are far from being entrenched; in certain circumstances they can be modified or waived. Under section 91, the need to offer pre-emptive rights may be excluded by a provision in the memorandum or articles of a private company—either wholly or in relation to allotments of a particular description.[50] This seems unfortunate since pre-emptive rights are particularly needed in relation to those private companies which are essentially incorporated partnerships and it is difficult to see why, here, the Act could not have treated private companies in the same way as public ones.[51]

Section 95 deals with the position of public companies and with private companies to the extent that they have not excluded the statutory provisions in their memoranda or articles. The position differs according to the extent of the authority which has been conferred on the directors under section 80 to allot shares. If the directors are authorised generally, they may also be given power, by the articles or by the resolution, to allot equity securities as if section 89(1) did not apply or applied with such modifications as the directors determine.[52] When they are authorised, whether generally or in relation to a particular allotment, the company may resolve by special resolution that section 89(1) shall not apply to a specified allotment under that authority or shall apply with such modifications as are specified in the resolution.[53] In either event, the power to exclude or modify pre-emptive rights ceases with the expiration or revocation of the authority con-

---

[49] It is difficult to regard this scheme with great disapprobation, since, if company B had been prepared to take the shares of company A in exchange for its assets, no question of pre-emption would have arisen.

[50] s.91(1). A provision in the memorandum or articles which is inconsistent with s.89(1) or any subsection of s.90 has effect as an exclusion of that subsection: s.91(2).

[51] Happily, Table A 1985 does not disapply pre-emptive rights and appears to contain nothing that is inconsistent with them.

[52] s.95(1). Whereupon "sections 89 to 94 have effect accordingly", *i.e.* only to the extent that they are consistent with the disapplication in the articles or resolution.

[53] s.95(2). Again with like consequences to those in s.95(1).

ferred under section 80[54] (or 80A), though it can be renewed by special resolution when, and to the extent that, the authority is renewed.[55] However, a special resolution required under the section may not be proposed unless it has been recommended by the directors, and there is circulated to members entitled to notice of the meeting a written statement by the directors of their reasons for making the recommendation, the amount to be paid to the company in respect of the proposed issue, and the directors' justification of that amount.[56]

The result of sections 91 and 95 is that the statutory pre-emptive rights can be disapplied with relative ease and afford an individual equity shareholder precious little assurance that his existing pre-emptive rights will be preserved unless his shares carry sufficient votes to block the passing of a special resolution.

Finally, a civil (but not a criminal) sanction is provided by section 92. When there has been a contravention of subsection (1) of section 89 or of any of subsections (1) to (6) of section 90, the company and every officer of it who knowingly authorised or permitted the contravention are jointly and severally liable to compensate any person to whom an offer should have been made under the subsection or provision, for any loss, damage, costs or expenses.[57] Where under section 95, the statutory provisions are validly modified by a company resolution this will equally apply to a contravention of the modified provisions since "sections 89 to 94 have effect accordingly".[58] Section 92 does not invalidate an allotment of shares made in breach of the pre-emption provisions, no doubt in order to protect the legitimate interests of third parties. However, in *Re Thundercrest Ltd*[59] the judge was prepared to rectify the register under section 359[60] as against the directors of a small company, with only three shareholders, where the directors responsible for the breach of the pre-emption provisions had allotted the shares in dispute to themselves.

Where the company is listed on the Stock Exchange the protection

---

[54] s.95(3). But with a like power to that in s.80 (see n. 28, above) to permit allotments in pursuance of a contract entered into prior to the expiration of the authority: s.95(4).

[55] s.95(3).

[56] s.95(5). Any person who knowingly or recklessly permits the inclusion of a statement misleading in a material particular commits an offence: s.95(6). Where a private company uses a written resolution in accordance with ss.381A and 381B the directors' statement has to be supplied to each relevant member at or before the time when the resolution is supplied to him for signature: Sched.15B, para. 3.

[57] s.92(1). Proceedings must be commenced within two years of the filing of the relevant return of allotments under s.88 or, where rights to subscribe or convert are granted, within two years from the grant: s.92(2).

[58] See s.95(1) and (2), under which ss.89 to 94 "have effect accordingly". The issue of the relationship between the statutory provisions and pre-emption provisions in the company's memorandum or articles is dealt with in ss.89(2) and (3) and 90(7) and with pre-emption provisions contained elsewhere (possible only in relation to "pre-1982" arrangements) in s.96.

[59] [1995] 1 BCLC 117.

[60] See Chap. 14, p. 331.

afforded shareholders is greater than under the Act. In the first place, the Exchange's rules require that the authority to dispense with an offer of pre-emptive rights shall not last beyond the expiration of 15 months or until the next annual general meeting whichever occurs first.[61] Secondly, they require a listed company to obtain the consent of its shareholders if any of its major subsidiaries makes an issue for cash of securities having an equity element which would materially dilute the percentage equity interest of the company and its shareholders in that subsidiary.[62] Thirdly, while both the Act and the Stock Exchange rules allow fractional entitlements to be ignored,[63] they differ as regards the treatment of rights that are not taken up. The effect of section 89(1) is that the shares concerned may then be offered to anybody. Under the Stock Exchange rules regarding rights issues, the rights must normally be sold for the benefit of the non-accepting shareholders unless arrangements to the contrary have been specifically approved by the shareholders in general meeting and the Stock Exchange has been consulted.[64] However, where the amount to which the shareholders will be entitled is small, they may be sold for the benefit of the company or, if no premium exists, allotted to the underwriters.[65] A final difference between the Act and the Stock Exchange rules is that the latter specifically permit pre-emptive offers to exclude holders of shares when the directors "consider it necessary or expedient . . . on account of either legal problems under the laws of any territory or the requirements of any regulatory body".[66] The nearest approach to this in the Act is section 93 under which sections 89 to 92 are "without prejudice" to any enactment by virtue of which the company is prohibited (either generally or in specified circumstances) from offering or allotting equity securities to any person. This, however, is designed to make it clear that offer must not be made to those whose shares are subject to a restriction order under Part XV of the Act[67]; for the situation to which the Stock Exchange rule is directed,

---

[61] *Listing Rules*, para. 9.20. Under the Act the combined effect of ss.80 and 95 is that it may last for 5 years though it can be revoked by ordinary resolution at any time.

[62] *ibid.*, paras. 9.22 and 9.23.

[63] s.89(1) (which only requires the offer to be *"as nearly as practicable"* equal to his proportion) and the *Listing Rules*, para. 9.19(a). Hence, if there is a one-for-ten rights issue, a shareholder with, say, 475 shares will be offered only 47 new shares.

[64] *Listing Rules*, para. 4.19.

[65] *ibid.*

[66] *ibid.*, para. 9.19(b). This is primarily designed to deal with the situation where a company has shareholders resident in the USA. Under the Federal securities legislation it may have to register with the S.E.C. if it extends the offer to such shareholders. Hence the present practice is to exclude such shareholders and to preclude those to whom the offer is made from renouncing in favour of a U.S. resident. This practice was upheld in *Mutual Life Insurance of N.Y. v. Rank Organisation* [1985] BCLC 11, but a fairer arrangement would surely be for the rights of the American shareholders to be sold for their benefit?

[67] On which see Chap. 18 at pp. 495–497, below.

companies have to rely on the "as nearly as practicable" in section 89 (1), and *Mutual Life Insurance of N.Y. v. Rank Organisation.*[68]

The overall picture which emerges of the combined effect of the statutory and Stock Exchange rules is that the individual rights to participate in share issues, which the Act apparently creates, may be quite easily removed by collective decision of the shareholders, and this remains true of listed companies, even though the *Listing Rules* insist upon more frequent shareholder votes than the Act and are more alert to possible circumvention of the pre-emption requirement. So the matter becomes one of collective shareholder decision whether to displace the prima facie rule in favour of pre-emption which the Act creates. This is an area in which the growth of institutional shareholding[69] has made itself felt. Institutional shareholders are strongly opposed to dilution of their position, both in relation to voting and the value of the shares held, without their individual consent. In addition to influencing the Stock Exchange rules on this matter, they have agreed informal guidelines with the Stock Exchange which commit them to vote in favour of disapplication proposals only if the company in question limits the number of shares to be issued on a non pre-emptive basis to 5 per cent of the issued capital of the company in any one year and to 7.5 per cent in any rolling period of three years, and restricts the discount to 5 per cent of the market price.[70]

These restrictions have not proved popular with companies which think that rights issues increase the cost of raising capital, though it would seem that the real issue is more to do with the level of underwriting fees and whether the fees connected with capital issues should go predominantly to the institutions, in their capacity as underwriters of rights issues, or to merchant banks carrying out book-building exercises in connection with general issues, than with the inherent costs of rights issues as against general issues.[71] It seems sometimes to be forgotten in these discussions that, at least in relation to public companies, the Second Company Law Directive requires the pre-emption principle to be included in domestic law, though it also permits its displacement by decision of the shareholders as a whole.[72] So the matter is likely to continue to revolve around the institutions' ability

---

[68] See n. 66. Nor is it clear that the Directive permits this exception unless Art. 42 (above, n. 24) can be construed as qualifying the obligation laid down in Art. 29.

[69] See further below, Chap. 21, pp. 565–567.

[70] See "Pre-emption Rights" (1987) 27 *Bank of England Quarterly Bulletin* 545; Davies, "Institutional Investors in the United Kingdom" in Prentice and Holland (eds.), *Contemporary Issues in Corporate Governance* (Oxford, 1993), pp. 86–87; and Stapledon, *Institutional Shareholders and Corporate Governance* (Oxford, 1996) pp. 56–58. Interestingly, the institutional guidelines apply also to vendor placings which, as we have seen, fall outside the statutory provisions.

[71] See P. Marsh, *Underwriting of Rights Issues*, Research Paper 6, Office of Fair Trading, 1994 and *Underwriting of Equity Issues: A Second Report by the Director-General of Fair Trading*, 1996.

[72] Second Council Directive 77/91 of December 13, 1976, Art. 29.

to maintain a common front in relation to the types of non-rights issues which they are willing, or can be persuaded, to countenance.

CLASSES OF SHARES

As will have been apparent, the prima facie equality of shares can be modified by dividing the share capital into different classes with different rights as to dividends, capital or voting or with different nominal values. By permutations of these various incidents the number of possible classes is limited only by the total number of shares.

On the whole it is not the present fashion for public companies to complicate their capital structures by having a large number of share classes—though much ingenuity is displayed in devising the most attractive methods of marketing issues and in creating types of company securities other than shares, but with rights to convert into shares.[73] But, both in the case of public and private companies, there may well be two or three different classes and sometimes more. The division of shares into classes and the rights attached to each class will normally be set out in the company's memorandum or articles (generally the latter) but, in contrast with the Companies Acts of some other common law countries, that is not compulsory.[74] Instead, steps have been taken to ensure that the classes and their rights can be ascertained from the company's public documents. The effect of what is now sections 128 of the Act[75] is that if particulars of such rights are not set out either in the memorandum or articles, or in a resolution or agreement (a copy of which has to be sent to the Registrar under section 380) they must be given in a statement, in the prescribed form, sent to the Registrar within a month of allotment of the shares.[76] If a class is assigned a name or other designation, that too must be given in the statement.[77] The same applies if and when there is any variation of the class rights.[78]

---

[73] It is beyond the scope of this book to do more than draw attention to a further recent (and disturbing) development, namely the extent to which investors are being beguiled into including in their investment portfolios "futures", options, and contracts for differences whereby they speculate in, or bet on, fluctuations in the price of shares or indices of such prices.

[74] Except as regards rights of redemption: see s.159A (Chap. 11 at p. 252, above).

[75] Originally s.33 of the 1980 Act, section 129 contains similar provisions regarding companies without a share capital. In their case there will be no question of differences in respect of rights to dividends or return of capital but the members may nevertheless be of different classes in respect of voting rights.

[76] s.128(1). This statement is not required if shares are allotted which are uniform with shares previously allotted in all respects except in relation to dividends during the 12 months following the new allotment: s.128(2).

[77] s.128(4).

[78] s.128(3). The question of how class rights may be varied is left to Chap. 26 since it essentially concerns the extent to which class rights of members (whether or not shareholders) may be varied. Here it suffices to warn that the drafting of the Act (which assumes that, when a company has a share capital, any class rights will be attached to the shares rather than to the

Preference shares

Where the differences between the classes relates to financial entitlement, *i.e* to dividends and return of capital, the likelihood is that they will be given distinguishing names, though these may be no more informative than "preference" and "ordinary" (perhaps, in the case of the former, preceded by "first" or "second" where there are two classes of preference shares). If a potential investor should assume that "preference" means that he should prefer them to the ordinary shares he would be sorely in need of professional advice. The advice that he would receive would probably not be couched in terms of relative merits and de-merits of preference and ordinary shares but of security and levels of risk. And if the client's needs suggested the former, he would probably be advised to invest not in shares but in debentures. For preference shares may often be virtually indistinguishable from debentures except that they afford less assurance of getting one's money back or a return on it until one does. On the other hand, if in addition to being "preferential" they are also "participating" (*i.e.* have a right to share in the profits of the company after the ordinary shareholders have received a specified return), they may be a form of equity shares with preferential rights over the ordinary shares (and in consequence should be, and often are, designated "preferred ordinary"). Section 744 defines the company's equity share capital as all its issued share capital except that part which "neither as respects dividends nor as respects capital, carries any right to participate beyond a specified amount in a distribution".[79] Participating preference shares will thus normally fall within the definition of equity capital.

The truth of the matter is that an enormous variety of different rights, relating to dividends, return of capital, voting, conversion into ordinary shares,[80] redemption and other matters, may be attached to classes of shares, all of which are conventionally described as "preference" shares. What these rights are in any particular case and whether any particular issue of preference shares is located more at the debenture end or the ordinary share end of the spectrum will depend on the construction of the memorandum, articles or other instrument creating

---

holder of them) has faced the courts with problems: see *Cumbrian Newspapers Group Ltd v. Cumberland Newspaper Co. Ltd* [1987] Ch. 1.

[79] This definition seems to be of equivalent effect to the differently phrased definition of "relevant shares" for the purpose of the pre-emption rules (above, p. 307), which excludes "shares which as respects dividends and capital carry a right to participate only up to a specified amount in a distribution": s.94(5)(a).

[80] The apparently simple matter of converting preference shares into ordinary shares can become one of considerable complexity, at least where the nominal value and number of the ordinary shares into which the preference shares are to be converted differ from those of the preference shares to be converted, so that there is a danger that the transaction will involve an unauthorised return of capital, on the one hand, or the issue of shares at a discount, on the other. For a clear explanation of the ways of avoiding this result, see (1995) VI *Practical Law for Companies* (No. 10) at p. 43.

them. Unfortunately, in the past the drafting of the creating documents
has often been deplorably lax.[81] Hence the courts have had to evolve
various canons of construction which, even more unfortunately, have
fluctuated from time to time, thus overruling earlier decisions and
defeating the legitimate expectations of investors who purchased preference shares in reliance on the construction adopted earlier.[82] In
former editions of this book the story of these vacillations was traced,
in some detail,[83] starting with the virtually irreconcilable decisions
of the House of Lords[84] and the Court of Appeal[85] relating to the
winding-up of the *Bridgewater Navigation Company* in 1889–1891.
Since, at long last, a reasonably clear finale now appears to have
been reached, there is no longer a justification for that indulgence,
especially in view of the present unpopularity of preference shares.
It suffices to summarise what the present canons of construction
appear to be.

Canons of construction

1. Prima facie all shares rank equally. If, therefore, some are to have
priority over others there must be provisions to this effect in the terms
of issue.
2. If, however, the shares are expressly divided into separate classes
(thus necessarily contradicting the presumed equality) it is a question
of construction in each case what the rights of each class are.[86]
3. If nothing is expressly said about the rights of one class in respect
of either (a) dividends, (b) return of capital, or (c) attendance at meetings or voting, then, prima facie, that class has the same rights in that
respect as the residuary ordinary shares. Hence, a preference as to
dividend will not imply a preference as to capital (or vice versa).[87]
Nor will an exclusion of participation in dividends beyond a fixed
preferential rate necessarily imply an exclusion of participation in capital (or vice versa) although it will apparently be some indication of
it.[88]
4. Where shares are entitled to participate in surplus capital on a winding-up, prima facie they participate in all surplus assets and not merely

---

[81] Even to the extent of simply providing that the share capital is divided into so many X%
Preference Shares and so many Ordinary Shares and issuing them without further clarification.
[82] The classic illustration is the overruling, by the H.L. in *Scottish Insurance v. Wilsons & Clyde
Coal Co.* [1949] A.C. 462, of the C.A. decision in *Re William Metcalfe Ltd* [1933] Ch. 142.
[83] 4th ed. (1979), pp. 414–421.
[84] *Birch v. Cropper* (1889) 14 App.Cas. 525, H.L.
[85] *Re Bridgewater Navigation Co.* [1891] 2 Ch. 317, C.A.
[86] *Scottish Insurance v. Wilsons & Clyde Coal Co.* above, n. 81; *Re Isle of Thanet Electric Co.*
[1950] Ch. 161, C.A.
[87] *Re London India Rubber Co.* (1868) L.R. 5 Eq. 519; *Re Accrington Corp. Steam Tramways*
[1909] 2 Ch. 40.
[88] This is implied in the speeches in the *Scottish Insurance* case, above, and in *Dimbula Valley
(Ceylon) Tea Co. Ltd v. Laurie* [1961] Ch. 353.

in that part which does not represent undistributed profits that might have been distributed as dividend to another class.[89]

5. If, however, any rights in respect of any of these matters are expressly stated, that statement is presumed to be exhaustive so far as that matter is concerned. Hence if shares are given a preferential dividend they are presumed to be non-participating as regards further dividends,[90] and if they are given a preferential right to a return of capital they are presumed to be non-participating in surplus assets.[91] The same clearly applies to attendance and voting[92]; if they are given a vote in certain circumstances (*e.g.* if their dividends are in arrears), it is implied that they have no vote in other circumstances. It is in fact common to displace the preference shareholder's presumed equality in relation to voting by expressly restricting their voting rights to situations in which their dividends have not been paid for a period of time, on the basis that only in such cases will the preference shareholders need to assert their voice in the management of the company.[93]

6. The onus of rebutting the presumption in 5 is not lightly discharged and the fact that shares are expressly made participating as regards either dividends or capital is no indication that they are participating as regards the other—indeed it has been taken as evidence to the contrary.[94]

7. If a preferential dividend is provided for, it is presumed to be cumulative (in the sense that, if passed in one year, it must nevertheless be

---

[89] *Dimbula Valley (Ceylon) Tea Co. Ltd v. Laurie*, above: *Re Saltdean Estate Co. Ltd* [1968] 1 W.L.R. 1844. These cases "distinguished" *Re Bridgewater Navigation Co.*, above, (on the basis that the contrary decision of the C.A. depended on the peculiar wording of the company articles) but it is thought that *Bridgewater* can now be ignored; in *Wilsons & Clyde Coal Co.* Lord Simonds pointed out the absurdity of supposing that "parties intended a bargain which would involve an investigation of an artificial and elaborate character into the nature and origin of surplus assets": [1949] A.C. at 482.

[90] *Will v. United Lankat Plantations Co.* [1914] A.C. 11, H.L.

[91] *Scottish Insurance v. Wilsons & Clyde Coal Co.* above; *Re Isle of Thanet Electric Co.*, above.

[92] *Quaere* whether attendance at meetings and voting should not really be treated as two separate rights. It seems, however, that express exclusion of a right to vote will take away the right to be summoned to (or presumably to attend) meetings: *Re MacKenzie & Co. Ltd* [1916] 2 Ch. 450. If, under this canon they have votes but the articles do not say how many, the effect of s.370(6) appears to be that they have one vote per share or, if their shares have been converted to stock (on which see p. 321, below) per each £10 of stock and that if the company has no share capital each member has one vote.

[93] See, for example, *Re Bradford Investment Ltd* [1991] BCLC 224. The *Listing Rules* insist that, where preference shares are listed, their holders msut have voting rights if their dividends are more than six months in arrears and upon any resolution to wind up the company: para. 13 (App. 1). 4.

[94] *Re National Telephone Co.* [1914] 1 Ch. 755; *Re Isle of Thanet Electric Co.*, above and *Re Saltdean Estate Co. Ltd*, above. This produces strange results. If as the H.L. suggested in the *Scottish Insurance* case, the fact that shares are non-participating as regards dividends is some indication that they are intended to be non-participating as regards capital (on the ground that the surplus profits have been appropriated to the ordinary shareholders) where the surplus profits belong to both classes while the company is a going concern, both should participate in a winding-up in order to preserve the status quo.

paid in a later one before any subordinate class receives a dividend).[95]
This presumption can be rebutted by any words indicating that the
preferential dividend for a year is to be payable only out of the profits
of that year.[96]

8. It is presumed that even preferential dividends are payable only if
declared.[97] Hence arrears even of cumulative dividend are prima facie
not payable in a winding-up unless previously declared.[98] But this
presumption may be rebutted by the slightest indication to the contrary.[99] It may thus be advantageous to specify that the dividend is
automatically payable on certain dates (assuming profits are available)
rather than upon a resolution of the directors or shareholders. When
the arrears are payable, the presumption is that they are to be paid
provided there are surplus assets available, whether or not these represent accumulated profits which might have been distributed by way
of dividend,[1] but that they are payable only to the date of the commencement of the winding-up.[2]

The effect of applying these canons of construction has been, as
Evershed M.R. pointed out,[3] that over the past 100 years

"the view of the courts may have undergone some change in regard
to the relative rights of preference and ordinary shareholders . . .
and to the disadvantage of the preference shareholders whose position has . . . become somewhat more approximated to [that] of
debentureholders".

Unless preference shareholders are expressly granted participating
rights they are unlikely to be entitled to share in any way in the
"equity" or to have voting rights except in narrowly prescribed circumstances. Yet they enjoy none of the advantages of debenture-
holders; they receive a return on their money only if profits are earned[4]

---

[95] *Webb v. Earle* (1875) L.R. 20 Eq. 556.

[96] *Staples v. Eastman Photographic Materials Co.* [1896] 2 Ch. 303, C.A.

[97] *Burland v. Earle* [1902] A.C. 83, P.C.; *Re Buenos Ayres Gt Southern Ry* [1947] Ch. 384; *Godfrey Phillips Ltd v. Investment Trust Ltd* [1953] 1 W.L.R. 41. *Semble*, therefore, non-cumulative shares lose their preferential dividend for the year in which liquidation commences: *Re Foster & Son* [1942] 1 All E.R. 314; *Re Catalina's Warehouses* [1947] 1 All E.R. 51. But, if the terms clearly so provide, a prescribed preferential dividend may be payable so long as there are adequate distributable profits in accordance with Chap. 12, above: *Evling v. Israel & Oppenheimer* [1918] 1 Ch. 101.

[98] *Re Crichton's Oil Co.* [1902] 2 Ch. 86, C.A.; *Re Roberts & Cooper* [1929] 2 Ch. 383; *Re Wood, Skinner & Co. Ltd* [1944] Ch. 323.

[99] *Re Walter Symons Ltd* [1934] Ch. 308; *Re F. de Jong & Co. Ltd* [1946] Ch. 211, C.A.; *Re E.W. Savory Ltd* [1951] 2 All E.R. 1036; *Re Wharfedale Brewery Co.* [1952] Ch. 913.

[1] *Re New Chinese Antimony Co. Ltd* [1916] 2 Ch. 115; *Re Springbok Agricultural Estates Ltd* [1920] 1 Ch. 563; *Re Wharfedale Brewery Co.*, above, not following *Re W.J. Hall & Co. Ltd* [1909] 1 Ch. 521.

[2] *Re E.W. Savory Ltd*, above.

[3] *Re Isle of Thanet Electric Co.* [1950] Ch. at 175.

[4] This necessarily follows from the principle laid down in s. 263(1) that "a company shall not make a distribution except out of profit available for the purpose". See Chap. 12, p. 282.

(and not necessarily even then), they rank after creditors on a winding-up and they have less effective remedies against the company. Suspended midway between true creditors and true members they may get the worst of both worlds, unless the instrument creating the preference shares is carefully drafted.

Ordinary shares

Ordinary shares (as the name implies) constitute the residuary class in which is vested everything after the special rights of preference classes, if any, have been satisfied. They confer a right to the "equity" in the company and, in so far as members can be said to own the company, the ordinary shareholders are its proprietors. It is they who bear the lion's share of the risk and they who in good years take the lion's share of the profits (after the directors and managers have been remunerated). If, as is often the case, the company's shares are all of one class, then these are necessarily ordinary shares, and if a company has a share capital it must perforce have at least one ordinary share whether or not it also has preference shares. It is this class alone which is unmistakably distinguished from debentures both in law and fact.

But as we have seen, the ordinary shares may shade off imperceptibly into preference, for, when the latter confer a substantial right of participation in income or capital, or *a fortiori* both, it is largely a matter of taste whether they are designated "preference" or "preferred ordinary" shares. Moreover, distinctions may be drawn among ordinary shares, ranking equally as regards financial participation, by dividing them nevertheless into separate classes with different voting rights. In this event they will probably be distinguished as "A" "B" "C" (etc.) ordinary shares. Many public companies have issued non-voting A ordinary shares. By this device, control may be retained by a small proportion of the equity leading to a further rift between ownership and control. This disturbing development (a response to the threat of takeover bids[5]) gave rise to demands that the Stock Exchange should refuse to list such shares, or, failing that, that the legislature should intervene. The Jenkins Committee was divided on this issue. The majority took the view that the case for banning non-voting ordinary shares had not been made out but that such shares should be clearly

---

[5] See Chap. 29, below. After the initial battle in the 1950s for control of Savoy Hotel Ltd. the capital of the company was reorganised so that £21,198 B ordinary stock could outvote £847,912 A ordinary stock. There the A stock had voting rights but the votes were so weighted in favour of the B class that over 97 per cent of the equity could be outvoted by the remainder! Over 40 years later, despite changes in the share capital, the balance of power remained much the same and the continued efforts of the holders of a large majority of the equity to wrest control from the minority did not succeed. However, at the end of 1989 a truce was declared when the majority was allowed representation on the board.

labelled[6] and that their holders should be entitled to receive notices of all meetings so as to be kept informed.[7] A minority of three recommended that all equity shareholders should have a right to attend and speak at meetings and that there should be a prohibition on the listing of non-voting or restricted-voting equity shares.[8] No legislative action has been taken on either recommendation. However, opposition of institutional investors has caused issues of non-voting shares to be less frequent and many companies have enfranchised their non-voting shares.

Redeemable shares

As we have seen,[9] all classes of shares may now be issued as redeemable, at the option of the company or the shareholder, in accordance with Part V, Chapter VII of the Act. When that is done, those that are redeemable necessarily constitute a class separate from those not issued as redeemable, even though they may be identical in every other respect. In contrast with the power of a company to purchase its own shares in accordance with that Part,[10] the power to issue redeemable equity shares has been little used and when redeemable shares are to be found, they will normally be preference shares. The statutory scheme for redemptions is analysed in Chapter 11. All that needs to be added here is that if, in the case of redemptions at the option of the company, the terms of redemption merely provided for their redemption at par, their holders would be highly vulnerable; for if interest rates fell after the date of issue it would clearly pay the company to redeem them and to borrow money at a lower rate of interest than the fixed dividend. This, following the House of Lords decision in *Scottish Insurance v. Wilson & Clyde Coal Co*[11]. was, in effect, done by capital reductions even though the shares were irredeemable and quoted at above par, for the Lords decided in that case, and in *Prudential Assurance v. Chatterley-Whitfield Collieries*[12] in the same year, that the courts had to confirm the reductions since the preference shareholders were being treated in strict accordance with their class rights.[13] The obvious unfairness of this led to the practice of providing, on issues of non-participating preference shares by public

---

[6] The Stock Exchange requirements now provide that non-voting shares must be so designated and that the designation of equity shares with restricted votes must include the word "restricted voting" or "limited voting": *Listing Rules*, para. 13 (App. I). 2–3.

[7] Cmnd. 1749, paras. 123–140.

[8] *ibid.*, pp. 207–210.

[9] Chap. 11, p. 251, above.

[10] *ibid.*, pp. 253 *et seq.*, above.

[11] [1949] A.C. 462.

[12] [1949] A.C. 512.

[13] Though, in the first case, only as a result of its overruling of the decision of the C.A. in *Re William Metcalf Ltd* [1933] Ch. 142.

companies, that on redemption or any return of capital the amount repaid should be tied to the average quoted price in the months before. This, so-called "Spens formula",[14] affords reasonable protection in the case of listed companies but preference shareholders in unquoted companies still remain at risk.

Special classes

Although in most cases the shares of a company will fall into one or other of the primary classes of preference or ordinary, it is, of course, possible for the company to create shares for particular purposes and containing terms which cut across the normal classifications. An example of this is afforded by employees' shares. Frequent references have already been made to "employees share schemes". Under the present definition of such schemes,[15] the beneficiaries of them may include not only present employees of the company concerned, but also employees, or former employees, of it or any company in the same group, and the spouses, widows or widowers, children or step-children under the age of 18, of any such employees. When employees' share schemes first came to be introduced here, the normal practice was to create a special class of shares with restricted rights regarding, in particular, votes and transferability; only in relation to share option schemes, designed as incentives to top management, were ordinary voting equity shares on offer. Now, however, that is usual in all cases[16] in order that employees' share schemes may enjoy the special tax concessions conferred on "approved profit-sharing schemes" or "approved savings-related share option schemes". Hence today such schemes will rarely lead to the creation of a special class of share; it is only in relation to their allotment, financing, and provision for re-purchase by the company or the trustees of the scheme that there will be special arrangements which the Act facilitates by exclusions from the normal restrictions on purchase of own shares and on the provision of finance by a company for the acquisition of its shares.[17]

Unclassified shares

In recent years it has become common, when the whole of the stated authorised share capital is not intended to be issued initially, to designate the unissued shares as "unclassified shares". This practice, bor-

---

[14] Named after its inventor.

[15] s.743.

[16] But it would be rare indeed for this to have led to employees controlling a large public company—as has occurred in the USA.

[17] See Chap. 11 at pp. 256, 267. And note also the special treatment in relation to pre-emptive rights: above, p. 307.

rowed from the United States, recognises that until shares are issued they confer no rights at all, and that the rights ultimately attached to them depend on the company's decision at the time when they are issued.

Conversion of shares into stock

Once the shares or any class of them are fully paid, the company may convert them into stock[18]; in other words the company may merge the relevant share capital, say 10,000 shares of £1 each into £10,000 of stock. Formerly, when each share had, throughout its life, to bear a distinctive number, there were practical advantages in so doing. But the Companies Act 1948 (now the 1985 Act, section 182(2)) enables numbers to be dispensed with once shares are fully paid. Since, in relation to shares (as opposed to debentures[19]) there were no other practical advantages in conversion, this now rarely takes place, though many major public companies which date back to before the 1948 Act still have stock. For the purposes of the Act "shares" includes "stock"[20] and the distinction between them is merely a source of confusion.[21]

LEGAL NATURE OF DEBENTURES

The difficulty in the case of shares is to fit them into any normal legal category; but one is unlikely to be left in doubt whether something is or is not a share. The converse is the case in relation to debentures. The legal relationship between a company[22] and its debenture-holders is simply the contractual relationship of debtor and creditor, coupled, if the debt is secured on some or all of the company's assets, with that of mortgagor and mortgagee. In contrast with a shareholder, the debenture-holder is in law not a member of the company having rights in it, but a creditor having rights against it. In reality, however, the difference between him and a shareholder may not be anything like as clear-cut, for the debenture may give the holder a contractual rights akin to those of a shareholder, for example, to appoint a director; to a share of profits (whether or not available for dividend); to repayment

---

[18] s.121(2)(c). Stock can be re-converted into shares: *ibid*.

[19] See below, pp. 324–325.

[20] s.744.

[21] As the Jenkins Committee recognised: Cmnd. 1749, para. 473. The aborted Companies Bill 1973 would have banned future conversions.

[22] The word "debenture" is not restricted to securities of companies or bodies corporate. Clubs not infrequently issue debentures and the name may even be applied to bonds issued by an individual; *e.g.* to those issued by the Tichborne Claimant to finance his attempt to establish his right to the Tichborne inheritance. Lord Maugham (the Law Lord, not the novelist) was one of many who have written accounts of this fascinating chapter in legal and social history. See his *The Tichborne Case* (London, 1936).

at a premium; to attend and vote at general meetings[23] and even to convert his debentures into equity share.[24] Covenants in the loan instrument may also give the debenture-holders considerable influence over the way in which the company is managed. Moreover, where the debenture is secured by a floating charge on all the undertaking and assets of the company, the holder will have a legal or equitable interest in the company's business, albeit of a different kind from that of its shareholders.

Difficulty of defining

The difficulty, however, is to determine whether or not the transaction between the debtor company and the creditor is such as to make the latter a debenture-holder, for no one has yet succeeded in defining "debenture". As Chitty J. lamented over a century ago:

> "I cannot find any precise definition of the term, it is not either in law or commerce a strictly technical term, or what is called a term of art."[25]

It is, nevertheless, a term frequently used in statutes—including the Companies Act which contains, in Part V, Chapter VIII, eight sections[26] under the heading *Debentures* as well as frequent references throughout the Act to debentures and debenture-holders. One would therefore expect to find an attempt to define what debentures are. But all one gets is:

> "In this Act, unless the contrary intention appears . . . 'debenture' includes debenture stock, bonds and other securities of a company, whether constituting a charge on the assets of the company or not."[27]

This attempt to "define" by inclusions has been carried a stage further by the Financial Services Act which, for its purposes, employs both inclusions and exclusions.[28] While neither Act can be said to define

---

[23] But his vote should not be counted if the Act requires the resolution to be passed by "members"—as in the case of extraordinary or special resolutions: s.378(1) and (2).

[24] In which case he will be holding an "equity security" and when he exercises the right will become an equity shareholder. To issue at a discount debentures which can be immediately converted into shares of the full par value would be a colourable device to evade the prohibition on issuing shares at a discount (*Moseley v. Koffyfontein Mines* [1904] 2 Ch. 108, C.A.) but appears to be unobjectionable if covertible only when the debentures are due for repayment at par since the shares will then be paid up in cash "through the release of a liability of the company for a liquidated sum": s.738(2). See also p. 239 on debt/equity swaps.

[25] *Levy v. Abercorris Slate & Slab Co.* (1887) 37 Ch. 260 at 264. See also Lindley J. in *British India Steam Navigation Co. v. I.R.C.* (1881) 7 Q.B.D. at 172 and Warrington L.J. in *Lemon v. Austin Friars Trust* [1926] Ch. 1, C.A. at 17 and the H.L. in *Knightsbridge Estates Co. v. Byrne* [1940] A.C. 613.

[26] ss.190–197.

[27] s.744. A "definition" which has remained substantially unchanged since the 1929 Act.

[28] Sched 1, para. 2 of the FSA says that "debentures" means:—"Debentures, including debenture stock, loan stock, bonds, certificates of deposit and other instruments creating or acknowledging indebtedness . . .
Note This paragraph shall not be construed as applying—
(a) to any instrument acknowledging or creating indebtedness for, or for money borrowed to

what is the primary meaning of "debentures", both give some pointers to what, both in law and in commerce, would for most purposes be regarded as their essential feature; namely that debentures are a type of transferable security (in this respect resembling shares) whereby a company can raise finance in the form of loan capital instead of share capital.

In practice, the absence of a precise definition has given rise to surprisingly few problems and to even fewer reported cases. That may change; for, in recent years, developments in banking and commercial circles have led to the invention of a remarkable array of new and highly sophisticated types of "securitised" loan investments as a result of which finance, which would formerly have been raised by a straightforward bank loan (for most purposes not a debenture), may be obtained through the issue of instruments, some of which for most purposes unquestionably are debentures and others of which may or may not be.

However, if the courts display the commonsense approach that the House of Lords did in the one relevant reported case of any importance, the probability is that we shall get by without much trouble. That case, *Knightsbridge Estates Ltd v. Byrne*[29] concerned a mortgage on houses, shops and a block of flats by a company to secure a loan of £310,000. The loan was to be repayable by 80 half-yearly instalments spread over 40 years but became immediately repayable if the mortgagor should sell the equity of redemption. The company was forbidden from selling any of the properties free from the mortgage or from granting leases for more than three years without the consent of the mortgagee. Five years later the company wished to pay off the mortgage in full and argued that the term making the mortgage irredeemable for 40 years was void as a clog on the equity of redemption. Under what is now section 193 of the Act,

"a condition contained in debentures . . . is not invalid by reason only that the debentures are thereby made irredeemable or redeemable only on the happening of a contingency (however remote) or on the expiration of a period (however long) any rule of equity to the contrary notwithstanding".

The question therefore was whether this mortgage was a debenture. The speeches in the House of Lords pointed out that one would have expected to find this section in a Part of the Act dealing with company

---

defray, the consideration payable under a contract for the supply of goods or services;

(b) to a cheque or other bill of exchange, banker's draft or a letter of credit, or

(c) to a bank note, a statement showing a balance in a current, deposit or savins account or (by reason of any financial obligation contained in it) to a lease or other disposition of property, inheritable security or an insurance policy."

The inclusion of "certificates of deposit" is interesting since it was generally thought that they were not "debentures"; hence the need for the Protection of Depositors Act 1963 (now superseded by the Banking Act 1987).

[29] [1940] A.C. 613.

charges[30] rather than in that dealing with debentures,[31] and accepted that the mortgage would not be a "debenture", for the purposes of some of the other sections.[32] Nevertheless, it was held that the legislative intention must have been to exclude from the equitable rule any mortgage by a company. In the words of Lord Romer,[33]

"if it is thought desirable that debentures in their popular meaning may be made irredeemable, it would seem to be both absurd and inconsistent to forbid a company to make its ordinary mortgages of land also irredeemable".

Accordingly the mortgage was a "debenture" for the purposes of section 193.

The normal debenture, however, is very different from a single mortgage of land., It generally consists of one of a series of securities ranking *pari passu* with each other. The expression "debenture" is applied indiscriminately to the instrument creating or evidencing the indebtedness and to the debt itself and the bundle of rights vested in the holder to secure its payment. These rights, as we have seen, may include a charge on all or some of the company's assets. If there is no such charge it will normally be described as a "bond" or a "loan note" but, as the "definitions" in the Companies Act and the Financial Services Act at least make clear, it will in law be a "debenture". When there is a charge, it will probably be a floating charge, the peculiar features of which are left to Chapter 15 on Company Charges.

Debenture stock

Reference has already made to the, largely meaningless, distinction between "shares" and "stocks".[34] There is a similar distinction between "debentures" and "debenture stock" but here it is far from meaningless and debenture stock has considerable practical advantages. If a public company wishes to raise £1 million it could seek to do so by an issue of a series of, say £1, £10, £100, or £1,000 debentures, each representing a separate debt totalling in aggregate £1 million. This would result in an enormous bundle of paper for the company to process and subscribers to handle. And, if a subscriber for a single debenture wanted to sell half of it, he would not be able to make a legal transfer of that half. If, however, the company creates £1

---

[30] Where, indeed, it (and s.196) should be; the trouble is that there is no Part dealing with Company Charges—only one dealing with Registration of Charges.

[31] *Per* Lord Romer at 628.

[32] *Per* Viscount Maugham at 624. Clearly such a mortgage does not have to be registered in the company's register of debenture-holders under s.190 in addition to registration of the mortgage under Part XII.

[33] At 629. The other Law Lords concurred with the speeches of Lords Maugham and Romer.

[34] Above, p. 321.

million of debenture stock it can issue it[35] to subscribers in such amounts as each wants,[36] giving each a single certificate[37] and he can sell and transfer any fraction of it.[38] A further advantage is that, whereas with a series of debentures with a charge on the company's assets it will be necessary to say expressly in each debenture that it is one of a series each ranking *pari passu* in respect of the charge,[39] debenture stock achieves that result without express provision.

Trustees for debenture-holders

The deed required on the creation of debenture stock may be a deed poll executed by the company alone, but it is now invariable practice[40] for the deed to be made with trustees. This, too, is normally done when there is an issue of a series of debentures. In other words, trustees, normally a trust corporation,[41] are interposed between the company and the debenture-holders. Any charge can then be in favour of the trustees who hold it on trust for the debenture-holders. Such an arrangement has many advantages.

In the first place it will enable the security to be by way of specific legal mortgage or charge on the company's land as well as by way of equitable floating charge on the rest of the assets. Clearly the ideal security is one so constituted, but a legal interest cannot be vested in thousands of debenture-holders,[42] nor can the deeds be split up amongst them. If, however, there are trustees, the legal mortgage can be vested in them, on trust for the beneficiary debenture-holders, and the trustees retain custody of the title deeds. Again, if there is to be a specific charge on shares in subsidiary companies (which may be a necessary precaution) trustees are needed in order that someone independent of the holding company shall be able to exercise the voting rights attached to the shares.

Secondly, it will provide a single corporation or a small body of persons charged with the duty of watching the debenture-holders'

---

[35] Debenture stock can be created *de novo*; there is no need to create debentures and then to convert them to debenture stock as there is in relation to shares and stock.

[36] In practice there is likely to be a prescribed minimum amount which can be subscribed for or transferred.

[37] A simple document of one sheet, similar to a share certificate, in contrast with a debenture which will, unless there is a trust deed (see below) have to set out all the terms.

[38] But see n. 36, above.

[39] Without this their respective priorities might depend on the dates when each debenture was issued.

[40] Except with unsecured loan stock.

[41] Formerly it was common for banks to undertake this work but they have tended to fight shy of it since *Re Dorman Long & Co.* [1934] Ch. 635 drew attention to the conflict of interest and duty which might arise when the bank was both a creditor in its own right and a trustee. Today, therefore, the duties are generally undertaken by other trust corporations, such as insurance companies, though sometime by the separate trustee companies formed by certain banks. Very occasionally individual trustees are still employed.

[42] Since 1925 a legal estate in land cannot be vested in more than four persons.

interests and of intervening if they are in jeopardy. This is obviously far more satisfactory than leaving it to a widely dispersed class of persons each of whom may lack the skill, interest and financial resources required if he is to take action on his own.[43] It will also be possible, by the trust deed, to impose on the company or its directors additional obligations, regarding the submission of information and the like, which might not otherwise be practicable.[44] Similarly, the trustees can be empowered to convene meetings of the holders in order to acquaint them with the position and to obtain their instructions.

Complaints have been made in the past that the trustees are all too often content to act as passive recipients of their remuneration rather than as active watchdogs. The Cohen Committee admitted that these complaints were not altogether unfounded[45] but all that has resulted is section 192 of the Act which invalidates provisions in trust deeds (or elsewhere) which purport to exempt a trustee from, or to indemnify him against, "liability for breach of trust where he fails to show the degree of care and diligence required of him as a trustee having regard to the provisions of the trust deed conferring on him any powers, authorities or discretions".[46] There is here a conspicuous contrast with the stricter rules under Federal legislation in the United States and with the duties imposed on trustees of unit trusts under the Financial Services Act.

CONCLUSION

As will have become abundantly clear, it is extremely difficult to make significant statements about the *necessary* differences between ordinary and preference shares and debentures, although it is possible to identify *typical* patterns of entitlements which are attached to these securities in certain business situations. On the financial side, it is true that what shareholders receive, whether ordinary or preference, is dividends, for the payment of which profits must be available,[47] whereas a debenture-holder receives interest. So the latter is perhaps

---

[43] Although there are trustees, an individual stockholder can take steps to enforce the security but he is not regarded as a creditor with the latter's personal remedies against the company: *Re Dunderland Iron Ore Co.* [1909] 1 Ch. 446.

[44] See the facts which gave rise to the litigation in *New Zealand Guardian Trust Co. Ltd v. Brooks* [1995] 1 W.L.R. 96, P. C.

[45] Cmd. 6659, paras. 61–64.

[46] But note the exceptions and qualifications in subss.(2)–(4). In the case of listed debt securities, the Stock Exchange requires that, unless it otherwise agrees, there must be a trustee or trustees, at least one being a trust corporation with no interest in, or relation to, the company which might conflict with the position of trustee; and, unless the debenture-holders have a general power to remove and appoint trustees, any appointment must be approved by an extraordinary resolution of the holders. It also specifies provisions which trust deeds must contain: *Listing Rules*, para. 13.12 and 13 (App.2).

[47] s.263 and see Chap. 12, p. 282, above.

concerned only with the company's cash-flow, whereas a shareholder is interested too in the level of its profits. But this does not distinguish preference from ordinary shareholders. On the financial side, perhaps the most useful generalisation which can be offered relates not to the level of the entitlement attached to these securities but to their priority. These securities all represent claims on the company's cash-flow and assets but with differing degrees of seniority, the debenture having the most senior claim and the ordinary share the most junior. Even so, one must add the qualification that not every element of the entitlement must be ranked in this way. There is no legal requirement that preference shareholders must have a preference over the ordinary shareholders in relation to dividend or to return of capital, though it would be an odd preference share which did not have one or the other. Thus, to take an extreme example, in a split capital investment trust, the company may issue preference shares with a zero dividend entitlement, but with a substantial priority as to return of capital when the trust (which, despite its name, operates as a company) is wound up. In this case, the preference share is deliberately deprived of any priority as to dividend, which is paid out entirely on the ordinary shares.

As to control, again the apparently firm distinction between shareholders, who are members of the company, and debenture-holders, who merely have rights against it, begins to dissolve once one appreciates the range of covenants controlling the actions of the company which may be built into loan instruments and that preference (and even ordinary) shareholders may have votes only in restricted circumstances or not at all. The truth of the matter is that company law in this area is not in the business of prescribing a set of standard-form contracts which must be used as they stand. Rather, it provides a very flexible set of building blocks which can be used by those involved in particular transactions to create the scheme best suited to their financing needs. The limits on what can be done are probably established more by the intellectual ingenuity of practitioners in corporate finance (which is considerable) and by the needs of their clients than by the law.[48]

---

[48] The flexibility which emerges from this Chapter is only enhanced by the ability of the company's debenture-holders to create a hierarchy of claims amongst themselves through various forms of "subordinated debt": see Philip Wood, *The Law of Subordinated Debt* (London, 1990).

CHAPTER 14

ACQUISITION AND DISPOSAL OF COMPANY SECURITIES

BECAUSE of the peculiar nature of company securities, particularly shares,[1] their acquisition and disposal raise issues which need to be dealt with as a branch of company law. This Chapter discusses the most important of them.

BECOMING A SHAREHOLDER

The Act assumes that, in the case of a company with the share capital, becoming a shareholder is the same as becoming a member. That is not necessarily so in relation to the few surviving companies limited by guarantee and having a share capital.[2] And there is no inherent reason why it should be so with companies limited by shares; indeed a very sensible method of promoting voluntary "co-determination"[3] would be to provide means whereby employees could become members without also having to buy shares in the company, thus risking the loss of their savings as well as their jobs if their employer-company becomes insolvent. But while the Act does not specifically prohibit a constitution on those lines, it clearly does not contemplate it.

The basic principle which the Act lays down[4] is that to become a member, and thereby a shareholder, there must be agreement and entry on a register of members which every type of registered company is required to maintain and which, in relation to a company with shares is also a register of shareholdings.[5] Until entry on the register an acquirer is not, in law, yet a member or shareholder. To this, there are two exceptions. The first relates to subscribers' shares. Each subscriber to the memorandum of a limited company with a share capital is required to take at least one share and against the name of each must be shown the number of shares that he takes.[6] The subscribers are then "deemed to have agreed to become members of the company and on

---

[1] Which, as we saw from the last Chapter, are difficult to place in any traditional type of "property".

[2] Such companies can no longer be formed: see s.1(4).

[3] See Chap. 4, p. 63, above.

[4] s.22. On which, see *Re Nuneaton Football Club* [1989] BCLC 454, C.A., holding that "agreement" requires only assent to become a member.

[5] ss.352–362.

[6] s.2(5)(b) and (c).

its registration shall be entered in such in its register of members".[7]
The effect of this has been held to be that, even if the company omits
to put them on the register, they become members and holders of the
number of shares stated.[8] This is of little importance since in practice
only two shares will be subscribed for.

The second exception relates to share-warrants to bearer. Section
188[9] provides that a company, if so authorised by its articles, may
issue with respect to any fully paid shares a warrant stating that the
bearer of the warrant is entitled to the shares specified in it. If similarly
authorised, it may provide, by coupons attached to the warrant or
otherwise, for the payment of future dividends.[10] Title to the shares
specified then passes by manual delivery of the warrant,[11] which is a
negotiable instrument.[12] On their issue, the company removes from its
register of members the name of the former registered holder and
merely states the fact and date of the issue of the warrant and the
number of shares (or amount of stock) to which it relates.[13] The bearer
of the warrant from time to time is unquestionably a shareholder but
to what extent, if at all, he is a member of the company depends on
a provision to that effect[14] in the articles.[15] Hence shareholding and
membership are not necessarily co-terminous if share warrants are
issued. However, again subject to the articles, the bearer of the warrant
is entitled, on surrendering it for cancellation, to have his name and
shareholding re-entered on the register.[16] In practice this second exception is unimportant because bearer securities have never been popular
with a English investors or English companies and are rarely issued

---

[7] s.22(1). Since it is the invariable practice for the memorandum to conclude with "We, the
subscribers . . . agree to take the number of shares shown opposite our respective names" one
would have thought that they had expressly agreed and that no "deeming" came into it. But
perhaps it was thought necessary to preclude any argument that one cannot have a binding
agreement with a company which does not yet exist: see Chap. 7 at pp. 140–144. But see n.
4, above, where the member's "assent" was after the formation.

[8] *Evans' Case* (1867) L.R. 2 Ch.App. 247; *Baytrust Holdings Ltd v. I.R.C.* [1971] 1 W.L.R.
1333 at 1355–56. But if the company allots all the authorised share capital to others the courts
have had to accept the inevitable consequence that the subscribers did not become members
or shareholders: *Macley's Case* (1875) 1 Ch.D. 247; *Baytrust Holdings Ltd v. I.R.C.*, above,
where a statement to this effect in an earlier edition was cited with approval.

[9] As substituted by Sched. 17, para. 6 of the 1989 Act.

[10] s.188(3). Share-warrants to bearer must be distinguished from what is perhaps the more
common type of warrant, which gives the holder the right to buy shares in the company at a
specific price on a particular date or within a particular period. Such warrants are a form of
long-term call option over the company's shares. They may be traded, but their transfer simply
gives the transferee the option and does not make him or her a member until the option is
exercised.

[11] s.188(2).

[12] *Webb, Hale & Co. v. Alexandria Water Co.* (1905) 21 T.L.R. 572.

[13] s.355(1).

[14] Table A 1985 contains no provisions at all about share warrants.

[15] A "bearer of a share warrant may, if the articles so provide, be deemed a member of the
company within the meaning of this Act, either to the full extent or for any purposes defined
in the articles": s.355(5).

[16] s.355(2).

and hardly ever in respect of shares, as opposed to bearer bonds (*i.e.* debentures) which are sometimes issued to attract continental investors who have a traditional liking for securities in bearer form. It is fortunate that bearer shares are such a rarity for if they became common it would play havoc with many provisions of the Act.[17]

THE REGISTER

Since, in practice, shares in British companies are "registered" and not "bearer" and since the process of becoming (or ceasing to be) a member and shareholder is incomplete until entry on the register, the statutory provisions regarding its maintenance are of importance. In summary, they are as follows.

In addition to showing the name and address of every member and the date on which he was registered as a member or ceased to be a member,[18] in the case of a company with a share capital the register must also state the number and class[19] of shares (or amount of stock) held by him and the amount paid-up on each share.[20] In the case of a private company there must also be noted on the register the fact and the date of the company becoming, or ceasing to be, a single-member company.[21] If a company permits the holding of shares in uncertificated form (on which see below), the register must indicate how many shares each member holds in certificated and uncertificated form respectively.[22] The register may be kept at the company's registered office or at another office of the company or at the office of professional registrars to which the company has delegated this task,[23] but, if kept otherwise than at the company's registered office, notice must be given to the Registrar of the place where it is kept and of any change of that place.[24] If the company has more than 50 members

---

[17] *e.g.* those relating to purchase of own shares (see Chap. 11 at pp. 253–263, above, and especially, those relating to disclosure of share-ownership and dealings: see Chap. 18, below.

[18] s.352(1). The entry may be removed after 20 years of his ceasing to be a member: s.352(6).

[19] In the case of a company without a share capital but with different classes of membership the register now has to state the class to which each member belongs: s. 352(4). This fills the lacuna revealed in *Re Performing Right Society Ltd* [1978] 1 W.L.R. 1197.

[20] s.352(3).

[21] s.352A.

[22] Uncertificated Securities Regulations 1995 (S.I. 1995 No. 3272), reg. 19(1).

[23] s.353(1). Use of professional registrars (normally a subsidiary of a clearing bank) is now usual in the case of listed public companies. Where it is adopted, the professional registrar is liable to the same penalties for default in compliance with the statutory provisions as if it were an officer of the company: s.357. It is also common in such cases, as ss.722 and 723 permit, for the register to be held in electronic form.

[24] s.353(2) and (3). The place must be in England or Wales if the company is registered in England and Wales or in Scotland if it is registered in Scotland. But if the company carries on business in one of the countries specified in Sched. 14 to the Act it may cause to be kept an "overseas branch register" in that country: s.362. This, in effect, is a register of shareholders resident in that country, a duplicate of which will also be maintained with the principal register: see Sched. 14, Part I.

then, unless the register is kept in such form as to constitute an index of names of the members, such an index must also be kept in the same place as the register. The register and index have to be open for inspection during business hours by any member without charge and by any other person on payment of a small fee and a copy of it or any part of it has to be supplied to anyone on payment of a modest charge.[25] This is a legitimate help to any member who wishes to communicate with any of his fellow members and to a takeover bidder. But unfortunately it also enables traders who wish to attempt to sell their wares by "junk-mail", or telephone calls, to obtain, more cheaply than in any other way, a "sucker-list" of potential victims by buying a copy of the membership register of, say, British Telecom or British Gas.

A company may close the register for any time or times not exceeding in total 30 days in any year.[26] Advantage of this can be taken by widely held public companies to enable them temporarily to freeze the list of those who are entitled to receive an annual dividend or to vote at an annual general meeting. In the case of securities held in uncertificated form, the consent of the operator of the system is also required for the closure of the register.[27] However, companies participating in the electronic transfer system may adopt a simpler method than closure of the register to deal with attendance and voting at general meetings. Such companies are entitled to specify a time not more than 48 hours before the meeting by which a person must have been entered on the register in order to have the right to attend and vote at the meeting and may similarly choose a day not more than 21 days before notices of a meeting are sent out for the purposes of determining who is entitled to receive the notice.[28] This way of proceeding enables transfers to continue in the period before the meeting (thus reducing the risk to transferees) without landing the company in the position of having to deal with a constantly changing body of shareholders.

The register is "prima facie evidence of any matters which are by this Act directed or authorised to be inserted in it".[29] It is not, however, conclusive evidence for, as we have seen, membership is dependent both on agreement to become a member and entry in the register, and it may be that other requirements in the company's articles have to be met. If they are not, it seems that the registered person does not

---

[25] s.356.
[26] s.358. It must give notice of this in a newspaper "circulating in the district in which company's registered office is situated".
[27] Uncertificated Securities Regulations 1995, reg. 22.
[28] *ibid.*, reg. 34.
[29] s.361. This rule also applies in relation to registration of securities held in uncertificated form, provided the transfer occurs in accordance with the Regulations: Uncertificated Securities Regulations 1995, reg. 20(1).

become a member.[30] In any event, if the entry does not truly reflect the agreement or other requirements, the register ought to be rectified. Hence section 359 provides a summary remedy whereby:

> "(a) the name of any person is without sufficient cause entered in or omitted from a company's register of members, or
>
> (b) default is made or unnecessary delay takes place in entering on the register the fact of any person having ceased to be a member, the person aggrieved or any member of the company, or the company may apply to the court for rectification of the register."[31]

This wording is defective because it ignores the fact that the register is not just a register of members but also a register of shareholdings and that a likely error is in the amount of a member's shareholding. However, commonsense has prevailed and in *Re Transatlantic Life Assurance*[32] Slade J. felt able to hold that "the wording is wide enough in its terms to empower the court to order the deletion of some only of a registered shareholder's shares".[33] It must follow that it is similarly empowered to order an addition to the registered holding.[34]

On an application the court may decide any question relating to the title of any person who is a party to the application whether the question arises between members or alleged members,[35] or between members or alleged members on the one hand and the company on the other hand,[36] and may decide "any question necessary or expedient to be decided for rectification . . .".[37] Moreover, the court may order payment by the company of "damages sustained by any party aggrieved".[38]

There is some uncertainty as to the extent to which the company can rectify the register without an application to the court. But in practice here again common sense prevails. Sections 352, 354 and 355 clearly envisage, and indeed demand, alterations without which the register could not be kept up-to-date and fulfil its purpose, and

---

[30] *POW Services Ltd v. Clare* [1995] 2 BCLC 435. This issue of restrictions in the articles is not one which arises in relation to listed companies or companies whose share are held in uncertificated form, since the *Listing Rules* and the rules of CREST, see nn. 57 and 67, below, require such shares to be freely transferable.

[31] s. 359(1). This power operates equally in relation to shares held in uncertificated form: Uncertificated Securities Regulations 1995, reg. 21(1)(b).

[32] [1980] 1 W.L.R. 79. The case arose because the allotment of some shares was void because Exchange Control permission had not been obtained as at that time was necessary.

[33] At 84F–G.

[34] But the wording of s.359(1) ought to be amended to make it clear that the court can rectify "any matters which are by this Act directed or authorised to be inserted in" the register. A court following Slade J. would presumably so construe the subsection but its present wording would mislead anyone unfamiliar with his judgment.

[35] *e.g.* when A and B are disputing which of them should be the registered holder.

[36] *e.g.* when there is a dispute between the company and A or B on whether either should be.

[37] s.359(3).

[38] s.359(2). "Compensation" would clearly be a better word than "damages" and "party aggrieved" is an expression which courts have constantly criticised, but apparently without convincing Parliamentary Counsel responsible for drafting Government Bills.

although there is no express provision for alterations of members' addresses that takes place all the time. Indeed it would be quite absurd if companies cannot correct any mistake if all interested parties agree. The Uncertificated Securities Regulations 1995 also clearly contemplate that a company may rectify the register other than by order of a court, but, in order to preserve the integrity of the electronic transfer system, require the company in such a case to have the consent of the operator of the system and to notify it and the system-members concerned immediately the change is made.[39]

It must be emphasised, however, that although the register provides prima facie evidence of who its members are and what their shareholdings are, it provides no evidence at all, either to the company or anyone else, of who the beneficial owners of the shares are. The registered member may well be a trustee or nominee but of that the company neither knows nor is entitled to let anyone know; for "No notice of any trust, expressed, implied or constructive shall be entered on the register or be receivable by the Registrar" in the case of companies registered in England and Wales.[40] It has now been recognised that often the company, and indeed the regulatory authorities and the public, may need to be able to find out who the beneficial owners are and other sections, dealt with later,[41] seek to enable them to find out. But the register with which we are presently concerned is of little help; in the case of a listed company the majority of the shares will probably be registered in the names of nominees. As we shall see below, the introduction of uncertificated securities is likely to reinforce this tendency.

The register, like other records that a company is required to maintain, may be kept either in bound books or by recording the matter in any other way[42] and, in particular, may be on a computer or other electronic device so long as the material can be reproduced in legible form and is so reproduced for purposes of inspection or supply of a copy.[43] It is also subject to the powers of the Secretary of State to make provision by regulations as to obligations of a company under

---

[39] Reg. 21

[40] s.360. The omission from this section of Scotland is not because, as English laywers tend (mistakenly) to believe, Scots law (as a civil law system) does not recognise trusts. On the contrary it is because the traditional Scottish practice is for trustees to be registered as "trustee disponees". This, apparently, does not affect the relationship between the company and the registered trustees (the company is no more concerned with what the trusts are than it would be if this section did apply) but it affords the beneficiaries greater protection *vis-à-vis* the trustees since it identifies the holding as that of a trust. It would seem to have much to commend it. In the case of shares held in uncertificated form a similar rule in relation to the non-recognition of trusts is applied to the operator of an electronic transfer system: Uncertificated Securities Regulations 1995, reg. 33(3) and (4).

[41] See Chap. 18, below.

[42] s.722.

[43] s.723. See Companies (Registers and Other Records) Regs. (S.I. 1985 No. 724) made under its subs.(4)).

the Act to make documents available for inspection or to provide copies of them.[44] The wording of the section[45] suggests that this power could not be used to restrict the right to inspect or obtain copies, for example by requiring good cause to be shown thus preventing share registers being used as "sucker-lists",[46] but is intended to ensure that the matter is reproduced in a way which is as "user-friendly" as possible without imposing undue burdens on the company.[47]

ACQUISITIONS FROM THE COMPANY

Shares may be acquired either (a) from the company itself on an issue by it[48] or (b) by taking a transfer from an existing shareholder. Dealing first with (a), the normal *modus operandi* in the case of new issues by public companies is described in Chapter 16. A would-be shareholder will apply in response to the prospectus, listing particulars or circular; if the application is accepted, he will be sent an allotment letter[49]; and this completes the needful agreement to become a member and shareholder.[50] But he will not yet be either, since he will not at that stage have been "entered on the register" and it may be that he never will be. In practice, the letter of allotment will be renounceable; *i.e.* for a short period stated in it, his rights can be renounced in favour of someone else. Printed on the back of the letter there will be forms enabling the allottee to renounce, and the person to whom they are ultimately renounced to confirm that he accepts the renunciation and agrees to be entered on the register. Normally the original allottee will not insert the name of the person to whom they are to be renounced and the effect is then to produce something similar to a short-term share-warrant to bearer; it is not a negotiable instrument but once the renunciation is signed by the original allottee, the rights can be assigned by manual delivery of the allotment letter without a formal transfer. Before the stated period ends, however, it will be necessary for the name of the ultimate holder to be inserted, his signature

---

[44] s.723A, inserted by the 1989 Act. See the Companies (Inspection and Copying of Registers, Indices, and Documents) Regs. (S.I. 1991 No. 1998).

[45] See in particular subss.(1), (2), (3) and (6).

[46] See p. 33, above.

[47] Subs.(1) refers only to the obligation of the company and says that if it fails to comply with the regulations it shall be deemed to have refused inspection or failed to have supplied a copy. Nowhere in the section is there anything to suggest that regulations can impose conditions on the applicant.

[48] Or, of course, by subscribing the memorandum of association though that is an option available only to the promoters and the advisers.

[49] For the purposes of the Act "shares shall be taken ... to be allotted when a person acquires the unconditional right to be included in the company's register of members in respect of those shares": s.738(1). If that right is conditional, say, upon a further payment, the allotment letter will not be an "allotment" in that sense; it will be equivalent to a letter of rights on a rights issue: see Chap. 16 at pp. 399–400.

[50] See p. 328, above.

obtained, and the allotment letter lodged with the company or its registrars.

Only when the allottee,[51] or the ultimate person to whom his allotment has been renounced, has been entered on the register will anyone became a shareholder and member. "The Act of 1985 preserves the distinction in English law between an enforceable contract for the issue of shares (which contract is constituted by an allotment) and the issue of shares which is completed by registration. Allotment confers a right to be registered. Registration confers [legal] title."[52] Even when registered, the shareholder will find difficulty in selling the shares, if they are to be held in certificated form, until, later still, he or she receives a share certificate from the company. If the shares are to be held in uncertificated form,[53] then by definition no share certificate will be issued. Instead, the company, by computer instruction, will inform the operator of the electronic transfer system of the identity of those to whom the shares have been issued and of the number of shares issued to each person.[54] The lapse of time between registration in the company's share register and informing the operator of the electronic transfer system of what the company has done should be very much shorter than the gap between registration and the issue of share certificates, where the Act gives the company up to two months to complete the process.[55]

Becoming a member and shareholder on an issue by a private company (or a closely held public company whose shares are not listed or dealt in on the A.I.M.) is subject to the same legal requirements of agreement plus entry on the register but in practice both will be achieved with less formality and, in the case of private companies, without the issue of allotment letters. If someone wants to become a shareholder and the company wants him to, he will be entered on the register and issued with a share certificate without more ado.

ACQUISITIONS FROM A SHAREHOLDER

We now turn to the second method of becoming a member and shareholder, *i.e.* by taking a transfer of shares form an existing member and shareholder. Once again, the transaction will not be complete until the transferee is entered on the company's register as the holder of the

---

[51] If the original allottee does not wish to sell his rights he need do nothing apart from retaining the allotment letter in safe custody until he ultimately receives a share certificate.
[52] *Per* Lord Templeman in *National Westminster Bank plc v. I.R.C.* [1995] 1 A.C. 111 at 126, H.L. From this Lord Templeman reasoned that shares were not "issued" (the Companies Act does not define the term) for the purposes of a taxing statute until the applicants for the shares were registered as members of the company.
[53] See below, pp. 337 *et seq.*
[54] Uncertificated Securities Regulations 1995, reg. 28.
[55] s.185.

shares (and until then the transferor will not cease to be a member or the legal holder of the shares). Neither the agreement to transfer nor delivery of a signed transfer form will pass the legal title.[56] Registration can be confidently expected to occur in due course unless the company's articles impose restrictions on the transferability of its shares. This is most unlikely if the shares are listed[57] but very probable if the company is a private one. If there are any restrictions, a purchaser should not pay until he is satisfied that he will be registered, for there is no implied warranty to that effect by the seller.[58] In other circumstances all that needs to be done if the transaction is a domestic one, whereby, say, a shareholder transfers his holding as a gift to a member of his family or sells it to an acquaintance, is for the transferor to hand over to the transferee a signed share transfer[59] together with the share certificate which the transferee will lodge with the company and the register will then be amended by adding the transferee and noting that the transferor has ceased to be a member or shareholder in respect of the shares.[60]

Generally, however, anyone wishing to buy or sell listed shares will want to do so at the best price obtainable and for that purpose to use the facilities of the Stock Exchange instead of himself seeking out a willing counterparty. He will then enlist the services of a member firm of the Stock Exchange. The former mandatory distinction, between brokers, who acted only as agents for their clients, and jobbers who acted only as market-making principals, has disappeared; as a result of "Big Bang", firms may now act as either, so long as they disclose to the client whether they are acting as agents or principals. By pressing the appropriate buttons on their office computers linked to the Exchange's automated quotations system (SEAQ) they can execute their clients' instructions at the best available price quoted by market-makers in the shares concerned.

This, however, merely produces a contract to sell the shares. It is

---

[56] But the beneficial interest may pass to the transferee prior to registration. See pp. 347 *et seq.*, below.

[57] *Listing Rules*, paras 3.15 and B(App.1) 6–7.

[58] His only obligation is not to do anything to prevent the purchaser, or someone claiming through the purchaser, from being registered: *Hooper v. Herts* [1906] 1 Ch. 549, C.A.

[59] As a result of the Stock Transfer Act 1963 it is not necessary for the transferee to sign unless the shares are only partly paid.

[60] Alternatively the two documents may be lodged by the transferor (s.183(4)) and in the case of a gift this might well be done. On a sale, however, the purchaser will normally want to receive documents on payment. It is unlawful for the company to register a transfer of shares held in certificated form unless "a proper instrument of transfer has been delivered to it": s.183(1). This was primarily designed to ensure that payment of stamp duty on the transfer was not evaded by provisions in the company's articles dispensing with the need for a written document. However, the courts have regarded failures to complete the transfer form fully as mere irregularities, even when the failures included an omission to state the consideration: *Nisbet v. Shepherd* [1994] 1 BCLC 300, C.A.

still necessary for the buyer to transfer to the seller the purchase price
and for legal title to the shares to be transferred by the seller to the
buyer. This process is referred to as that of "settlement" of the transaction. Despite advances which have been made in recent years in
speeding up the process of settlement, and thus in reducing the risk of
either party becoming, or being revealed to be, unable to complete his
or her side of the bargain during the settlement period, share transfers
through the Stock Exchange are still not instantaneous transactions.
However, it may be that in future it will be possible to make payment
for and transfer of title to the shares events which occur simultan-
eously with the agreement to trade them.

A major obstacle to shortening the settlement period, let alone abolishing it, has been the need to transfer the share certificates from seller
to buyer. For this reason, an important recent development in facilitating quick settlement, as well as making the process of transfer more
efficient, has been the introduction of the possibility of "dematerialis-
ing" share certificates. This enables title to shares to be transferred by
means of instructions sent between computers rather than by the physical movement of transfer forms and certificates. However, in order
for this to happen, there must obviously be a system in place capable
of effecting the electronic transfer of title and the share certificate must
be replaced by an electronic record within that system (hence the share
certificates must be "dematerialised" and the securities must become
"uncertificated"). This is now achieved by the Uncertificated Securities Regulations 1995,[61] made under section 207 of the Companies Act
1989, which permits the relevant Treasury Minister to make regulations "for enabling title to securities to be evidenced and transferred
without a written instrument", and by the CREST computer system
which has been established under the Regulations.

Although Part II and Schedule I of the Regulations, which require
an Operator and its electronic transfer system to be approved by the
Treasury in relation to their financial resources, competence and capabilities, envisage the existence of a number of competing operators,
there is at present only one, namely CrestCo. Indeed, given the earlier
ignominious failure of the Stock Exchange to develop an effective
electronic transfer system (under the name of TAURUS), the immediate focus is on whether even one system can be made to work satisfactorily. CREST was developed under the guidance of the Bank of England, though it is owned by some 70 financial institutions, and so a
divorce has been created between the processes of trading listed securities, which still occurs predominantly through the facilities provided
by the Stock Exchange, and the settlement of trades, which will be
effected increasingly through CREST.

This is not the place to go into a full exposition of the new settle-

---

[61] S.I. 1995 No. 3272.

ment system, but a few of its implications for company law need to be highlighted. First, unlike TAURUS, CREST is not a compulsory system. In fact, the transfer of shares through CREST will require the prior approval of all three of CrestCo. (the company which operates the system), the issuer of the class of shares in question and the individual shareholder. Once the system is fully operational, CrestCo. will have an obvious financial incentive to admit to its system all classes of eligible shares. The Regulations allow for the electronic transfer of both shares and of interests in them (and indeed of other types of securities, such as rights under a depository receipt),[62] provided the securities are governed by the laws of England and Wales, Scotland or Northern Ireland.[63] The Regulations are thus not confined to listed securities, though it remains to be seen to what extent trades in unlisted securities (other than those of companies quoted on A.I.M.) will be settled through CREST.

Given the advantages of the new system for large shareholders (on which see below) and for companies themselves through the lower costs of maintaining share registers where transfers are effected electronically, issuers too will have an incentive to permit their shares to be traded through CREST. Moreover, the introduction of CREST is expected to lead to the demise of the Stock Exchange's existing TALISMAN system, so that trading in classes of shares which have not been accepted for the CREST system may be difficult for or unattractive to investors. Indeed, the Regulations are drafted so as to facilitate corporate decisions in favour of CREST. Classes of share are in principle admissible to CREST only where the holding of shares in uncertificated form and their transfer electronically is permitted by the company's articles of association,[64] which may well not be the case if the articles require the company to issue shareholders with a certificate of their holding.[65] Regulation 16 permits such provisions in the articles to be disapplied by resolution of the directors, rather than by the normal route for altering the articles by resolution of the shareholders,[66] provided the shareholders are given prior or subsequent notice of the directors' resolution. The Regulations then provide that the shareholders by ordinary resolution may vote to overturn the directors' resolution, but, unless they do so, the articles will be modified *pro tanto* without the shareholders' positive approval.

---

[62] See the definition of "securities" in reg. 3(1).

[63] This does not mean that shares governed by foreign law cannot in fact be handled by the CREST system, but rather, as far as issuers are concerned, that the conditions of access to the system will be determined by the foreign law. It seems that transactions in Irish securities will be capable of being settled through CREST: Companies Act 1990 (Uncertificated Securities) Regulations 1996 (S.I. 1996 No. 68 (Ireland)). Alternatively, a depository receipt arrangement, governed by U.K. law, could be established for the foreign securities.

[64] Reg. 15.

[65] See, for example, Table A 1985, art.6.

[66] See above, p. 116.

Once the resolution is in force, any provisions in the company's articles which are inconsistent with the provisions of the Regulations relating to the holding and transfer of uncertificated shares will cease to have effect. This would apply, for example, to restrictions relating to the nationality of shareholders or on the size of shareholdings by any one shareholder.[67] It seems that the effect of the directors' resolution is confined to the holding and transfer of securities in uncertificated form. In the case of convertible or redeemable shares changes in the articles may need to be made to enable these events to occur electronically and that such changes must occur through the normal procedures for amending the articles.

The third element of consent which is required is that of the individual shareholder. Even if the class of share which he or she holds has been admitted to CREST, the individual may choose to continue to hold the shares in certificated form.[68] Since, however, trading in certificated form will be more expensive than uncertificated trading, there will be pressure on all shareholders, except those who very rarely trade,[69] to move to uncertificated holding. This may have an unanticipated additional consequence. Although dematerialisation does not by itself break the direct relationship between shareholder and company, the pressures towards dematerialisation may tend in fact to break that link by encouraging those who opt for uncertificated holdings to do so through nominee accounts.

A small shareholder who wishes to hold shares in uncertificated form may do so either by becoming a sponsored member of CREST[70] or by transferring his or her shares into a nominee account run by a broker without becoming sponsored members of CREST. The latter may well turn out to be the less expensive course of action, but it would break the link between the company and the investor. The nom-

---

[67] The inconsistency with the Regulations arises because breach of the company's articles is not one of the situations in which a company is entitled to refuse to respond to an operator-instruction to transfer title to shares nor is the need to produce conformity with the articles one of the cases where a company may register a transfer of title without an operator-instruction (see pp. 340–341, below). This does not mean that companies may not include such provisions in their articles, to the extent that the Stock Exchange's *Listing Rules* permit it, or may not enforce them, for example by disenfranchising shares held in breach of the articles, but it does mean that they will not be able to enforce these restrictions by refusing to register transfers in breach of the provisions or by disposing of such shares without a court order.

[68] Nor, if the choice is made for uncertificated holding, is it irrevocable: see Sched. 1, para. 13 and regs. 26 and 27.

[69] For example, those who have picked up a few shares in privatisation issues and have put the certificates in a drawer and more-or-less forgotten about them, of whom there are many thousands. The reason why trading of certificated securities will be more expensive is that the shares must first be dematerialised to be processed by CREST and then rematerialised.

[70] That is, a member sponsored by a broker, the broker being a "sponsoring system participant" within reg. 3(1). With sponsored membership the beneficial owner of the shares will remain their registered holder. The third option of full membership is open to a shareholder, but would require him or her to have the computer equipment and software necessary to interface with the CREST system (see the definition of "system-participant") which is unlikely in the case of small shareholders—or even, for that matter, large ones.

inee will now appear on the company's share register and the broker will receive the communications from the company and be entitled to vote at its meetings. Although there are ways of re-constituting the link between beneficial owner and the company, they involve inserting an extra set of communications, *i.e.* between nominee and beneficial owner, and this is likely to be inefficient and thus to cut against recent proposals that companies should make greater use of the general meeting as a way of communicating with their shareholders.[71] In the case of institutional shareholders, their holdings are already often held in nominee accounts of their fund-managers. It seems likely that the advent of CREST will reinforce this tendency, so that the register of members of the company will become even less revealing about who is beneficially interested in its securities.[72] The statutory provisions requiring that beneficial holdings above a certain size be declared to the company and to the market[73] and enabling companies to require information to be given to them about the beneficial ownership of shares[74] will thus have their importance enhanced.

Where shares are held in uncertificated form, the process of transferring the shares ends with a computer instruction to the issuer requiring it to put the shares into the name of the new holder, an instruction to which the company, or its independent registrar, is itself likely to respond by making a change electronically in its share register. In order to preserve the integrity of the system the principle is that, within the system, only the operator of the system can give such an instruction to the issuer, so that system-participants may not directly instruct companies to alter their share registers. However, the Regulations recognise that in limited circumstances the company may have to respond to an instruction coming from outside the system, such as a court order (for example, to rectify the register) or an instruction made in or under legislation.[75] The regulations also permit the company to alter its register to take account of the transmission of shares by operation of law.[76] A transfer by the company outside these categories, other than in response to an operator-instruction, is of no effect[77] and the company is liable for breach of statutory duty at the suit of any person who suffers loss as a result of its breach of the regulations.[78]

Conversely, the company is under an obligation to register a transfer

---

[71] See below, Chap. 21, p. 564 and DTI, *Private Shareholders: Corporate Governance Rights*, Consultative Document, November 1996.

[72] See p. 333, above.

[73] See Chap. 18, pp. 483–492, below.

[74] See Chap. 18, pp. 492–500, below.

[75] Reg. 23(5), which also deals with compulsory acquisition under s.430 of the Act: see below, p. 806.

[76] Reg. 23(6). See below, p. 352.

[77] Reg. 23(7).

[78] Reg. 37(1), which liability is in addition to any the company may have outside the Regulations: reg. 37(2).

of title in response to an operator-instruction, except in very limited circumstances. These include where the transfer is prohibited by a court order in the United Kingdom[79] or by or under an enactment; or where the company has actual knowledge that the transfer is to a deceased person, to an entity which is not a legal or natural person or to a minor; or where the company has actual knowledge that the information contained in the operator-instruction is inaccurate, that the operator did not in fact send the instruction or that the operator did not have the authority of the person on whose behalf the instruction was sent to send it.[80] In addition the company must confirm to the operator whether the transfer has been registered in accordance with the operator-instruction.[81] Failure to give notice renders the company liable for breach of statutory duty.[82] As noted above, registration by the company where the company is not under an obligation to make the transfer as a result of the operator-instruction (assuming none of the other permitted bases for transfer is present) also renders the company liable for breach of statutory duty and the transfer itself ineffective.[83] However, mere failure to respond to an operator-instruction, provided that failure is notified, does not seem to attract liability for breach of statutory duty, though it would be no doubt a breach of the rules of CREST which the company accepted when joining the system.[84]

Obviously a major risk with an electronic system is that instructions to register transfers will be given which appear to come from the operator but which do not in fact do so.[85] The Regulations make it a condition of approval of the system that it should be designed so as to minimise the possibility of unauthorised instructions,[86] but the possibility cannot be eliminated entirely. Where the company knows the instruction is unauthorised, the situation is easy to deal with and, as we have seen, the Regulations do oblige the company not to make the transfer in this case. However, the company will often be unaware that the instruction is unauthorised. In this situation the Regulations provide for limited compensation to be paid, normally by the operator, to those who suffer loss.

Where an operator-instruction is induced either by a "forged dematerialisation instruction", which in this context means simply an

---

[79] See Chap. 18, p. 496, below.

[80] Reg. 23(1) to (3).

[81] Reg. 23(4).

[82] Reg. 37(1).

[83] Reg. 23(7).

[84] Sched. 1, para. 19(a). The Treasury, but not the person injured, may seek an injunction or restitution order against a person who acts in breach of the CREST rules on the same principles as those set out in s. 61 of the FSA: see reg. 9 and Chap. 17, p. 481, below.

[85] Or that some earlier step in the process of transfer will have been unauthorised. This account concentrates on operator instructions, but reg. 30 deals with all "forged" or unauthorised computer instructions generated within the system.

[86] Sched. 1, para. 5.

instruction not sent from a computer forming part of the overall system, or by a "causative act", which means an act other than a dematerialised instruction[87] which unlawfully causes the operator to send an operator-instruction,[88] the operator is prima facie liable in damages if an inaccurate entry is made on the share register or a change of entry is not made. The operator may shift the prima facie responsibility by identifying the person responsible for the forged dematerialised instruction or the causative act (even if the person who suffers loss cannot in fact recover compensation from the person so identified) or by showing that the company was in breach of duty by registering a transfer of title when it should not have done so. Otherwise, the court may order the operator to pay to each person who has suffered loss and in respect of each induced operator-instruction up to £50,000, the actual amount to be determined by the court's view of what is just and equitable having regard to the loss sustained by the applicant, subject to a duty on the part of the applicant to mitigate the loss and to a possibility of reduction of compensation on the grounds that the applicant caused or contributed to the loss to any extent.[89]

It will be apparent from the above account that Regulation 30 does not apply when the unauthorised act which induced the operator-instruction came from a computer which is part of the system. Thus, it does not apply, for example, in the case of the employee of a broker, a member of the system, who without authority issues a dematerialised instruction which results in an operator-instruction to the company to alter its share register. The operator would not be liable to pay compensation in this situation. This is a deliberate omission and reflects a general policy which underlies the Regulations, to the effect that all system participants should normally be able to rely without more ado on properly authenticated dematerialised instructions generated by the system.[90] The result, however, is to leave the client of the broker unprotected as far as these regulations are concerned. The issue is dealt with instead by making the sending of dematerialised instructions of behalf of another into investment business for the purposes of the FSA,[91] so that those employed by direct members to manage the

---

[87] Or other than an act which causes a dematerialised instruction to be sent from the computer of a system-participant.

[88] Reg. 30(1).

[89] Reg. 30(4) to (6). These provisions in fact echo those concerning compensation for unfair dismissal by an employer (Employment Rights Act 1996, s. 123) except that there the upper limit is the very much lower one of £11,300. The compensation scheme, contained in the Regulations, is without prejudice to any other remedy the applicant may have against any other person: reg. 30(8).

[90] See reg. 29 for the principle and its limited exceptions.

[91] The Financial Services Act 1986 (Uncertificated Securities) (Extension of Scope of Act) Order 1996 (S.I. 1996 No. 1322) makes the addition to para. 16 of Sched. 1 to the FSA and sets out some exceptions.

CREST computer facilities will have to be authorised under the FSA and the FSA protections will be available to the client.[92]

SHARE CERTIFICATES

Although the Regulations[93] expressly forbid a participating issuer to issue a share certificate in relation to uncertificated shares and provide that, if it does, section 186 (see immediately below) shall not apply to the document, share certificates will obviously not disappear entirely under the new system of transfer, even if they will become much less common. Some shareholders in companies which permit uncertificated holdings will prefer to hold on to their certificates, and in other cases whole classes of shares will not be allowed into the new transfer system because either the company or the operator decides not to permit it. So the law relating to share certificates will continue to be important, especially in relation companies whose securities are not not traded on public markets.

Where a company is not prohibited by the Regulations from issuing a share certificate, section 185(1) of the Act provides that, unless the terms of issue of the securities otherwise provide, a company shall, within two months of allotment or receipt of a transfer, complete and have ready for delivery certificates resulting therefrom. Section 186, as amended, provides:

"A certificate under the common seal of the company specifying any shares held by a member is—
    (a) in England and Wales, prima facie evidence, and
    (b) in Scotland, sufficient evidence unless the contrary is shown,
        of his title to the shares."

The wording of this is very curious, since it suggests that the section applies only if the certificate is under the common seal. This, however, cannot be correct since section 36A, inserted by the 1989 Act, provides that a company need not have a common seal[94] and that whether it has or not "a document signed by a director and the secretary of the company or by two directors and expressed (in whatever form of words) to be executed by the company has the same effect as if executed under the common seal of the company".[95] Moreover, section 40 (as amended by the 1989 Act) enables a company, which has a common seal, instead to use for sealing documents evidencing

---

[92] Reg. 29(9) expressly preserves whatever remedies the client may have which arise outside the Uncertificated Securities Regulations.

[93] See reg. 32(2) and (3). These provisions do not prevent, for example, a broker from issuing from time to time to its clients written statements of the dematerialised securities held on the clients' behalf, but they do deprive those written statements of any privileged legal status.

[94] s.36A(3). This was part of the general abolition of the need for deeds to be sealed: s.1 of the Law of Property (Miscellaneous Provisions) Act 1989.

[95] s.36A(4).

securities, an "official" seal which is the replica of its common seal with the addition of the word "Securities". Hence section 186 applies so long as the certificate is authenticated as executed by the company by the use of the common seal, the official seal or signatures of two directors or one director and the secretary.[96]

Since, like the membership register, a share certificate is prima facie evidence only, it is far from being a document of title in the sense that a share-warrant is. Where there is a conflict between the register and the certificate, the former is stronger prima facie evidence than the latter but neither is decisive; ownership of the shares depends on who is *entitled* to be registered. Suppose, say, that A, who is registered and is entitled to be registered, loses his certificate, obtains a duplicate from the company[97] and transfers to B who is registered by the company. Subsequently A finds the original certificate and, either because he has forgotten about the sale to B or because he is a rogue, then purports to sell the shares to C. The company will rightly refuse to register C whose only remedy will be against A (who may by this time be a man-of-straw) unless he can successfully invoke against the company the so-called doctrine of *estoppel by share certificate*.

A share certificate will contain two statements on which the company will know that reliance may be placed. The first is the extent to which the shares to which it relates are paid up. The second is that the person named in it was registered as the holder of the stated number of shares. The company may be estopped from denying either statement if someone in reliance upon it has changed his position to his detriment. This will rarely benefit an original recipient of the incorrect certificate because receipt of his certificate normally marks the conclusion of the transaction and is not something on which he relied in deciding to enter into it and because he should be aware of the true facts. But in exceptional circumstances it may do so.[98] More commonly, it may afford a transferee who, in reliance on the transferor's share certificate, has bought what he believed, wrongly, to be fully paid shares a defence if the company makes a call upon him.[99] The

---

[96] s.186(2) makes the position clear in relation to the Requirements of Writing (Scotland) Act 1995.

[97] Companies do this readily enough so long as the registered holder makes a statutory declaration regarding the loss and supplies the company with a bank indemnity against any liability it may incur. Since the risk is negligible (see below, n. 2) and what banks charge for this service is not, this must be a profitable activity for the banks.

[98] In *Balkis Consolidated Co. v. Tomkinson* [1893] A.C. 396, H.L., the facts were similar to the example in the text, except that the company (wrongly) issued a certificate to C but (rightly) did not put him on the register. When C tried to sell the shares to D the company (rightly) refused to register the transfer to D, and C, to complete his bargain had to buy other shares in the company. It was held that C could recover from the company the price he had paid.

[99] *Burkinshaw v. Nicholls* (1878) 3 App.Cas. 1004, H.L.; *Bloomenthal v. Ford* [1897] A.C. 156, H.L. If the reason why the shares were not fully paid up is because of a contravention of the provisions regarding payment in ss.97 *et seq.* of the Act (see Chap. 11 above at p. 237) a bona fide purchaser and those securing title from him will be exempted from liability to pay calls by virtue of s.112(3) and will not have to rely on estoppel.

company will also be estopped if the transferee has relied on a false statement in his transferor's certificate that the transferor was the registered holder of the shares on the date stated in the certificate.[1] But the certificate is not a statement that the named shareholder has continued to be a shareholder since that date.[2] Hence the company will not be estopped in the example given above; it has not made any false statement.

Already the estoppel doctrine has little or no relevance to transactions on the Stock Exchange under the old TALISMAN system; and when CREST is in full operation, it will cease to have any relevance to an even wider range of shares.

RESTRICTIONS ON TRANSFERABILITY

Of far greater practical importance are questions which may arise when the company's articles of association impose restrictions on the freedom of transferability of its shares. Except in relation to partly paid shares this is unlikely in the case of listed companies[3]; but is almost invariably done in relation to private companies. Generally, the directors will be empowered to refuse to register transfers and frequently this will be accompanied by provisions affording the other members or the company[4] rights of pre-emption, first refusal or even compulsory acquisition. Such provisions require the most careful drafting if they are to achieve their purpose; and have not always received it, thereby facing the courts with difficult questions of interpretation. However, the following propositions can, it is thought be extracted from the voluminous case law.

(a) The extent of the restriction is solely a matter of construction of the articles of association. But, since shareholders have a prima facie right to transfer to whomsoever they please, this right is not to be cut down by uncertain language or doubtful implications.[5] If, therefore, it is not clear whether a restriction applies to any transfer or only to a

---

[1] *Dixon v. Kennaway & Co.* [1900] 1 Ch. 833. This, in contrast with resisting a call, may seem to be committing the heresy of using estoppel as a sword rather than a shield. The justification is that a purchaser who has bought from the registered owner has a prima facie right to be registered in his place and that the company is estopped from denying that the transferor was the registered owner.

[2] *Rainford v. James Keith & Blackman Ltd.* [1905] 2 Ch. 147, C.A. "The only representation is that at the date of the certificate the person named therein was the owner of the shares": *per* Romer L.J. at 154. Hence companies which issue a duplicate certificate seem to run no risk thereby so long as it is a replica of the original accurate one.

[3] See n. 57, above. Similar requirements are to be found in the CREST rules.

[4] Acquisition by the company itself will, of course, be lawful only if it is able to comply with the conditions enabling a private company to buy its own shares: see above Chap. 11 at pp. 258–259. Less usually, the provision may impose an *obligation* on other members to buy.

[5] *Per* Greene M.R. in *Re Smith & Fawcett Ltd* [1942] Ch. 304, C.A., at 306. See also *Re New Cedos Engineering Co. Ltd* [1994] 1 BCLC 797 (a case decided in 1975); *Stothers v. William Steward (Holdings) Ltd* [1994] 2 BCLC 266.

transfer to, say, a non-member,[6] or to any type of disposition or only to a sale[7] the narrower construction will be adopted.

(b) On the other hand, the courts will not carry a literal construction of the articles so far as to defeat their obvious purpose. In one case[8] the articles conferred a right of pre-emption on the other shareholders when any shareholder was "desirous of transfering his ordinary shares". Certain shareholders sold their shares to a takeover bidder, received the purchase price and gave him irrevocable proxies to vote on their behalf, but, in the light of the articles, transfers were not to be lodged for registration. The House of Lords held that in the context "transferring" obviously meant assigning the beneficial interest and not the technical process of having a transfer registered.[9] The shareholders had clearly manifested an intention to sell their shares and could not continue with the sale without giving the other shareholders a right to exercise their option under the articles. But this decision was distinguished in a later case[10] where, in all relevant respects, the wording of the article was similar but the shares were held by the executors of a deceased shareholder. The administration of the estate was completed and the executors now held the shares as bare trustees for two beneficiaries. Neither had any wish that the shares should be transferred to him but it was argued that, on the basis of the House of Lords' decision, the passing of the beneficial interest to them was a "transfer" of which notice should have been given, thus entitling other members to acquire the shares at a fair price. Vinelott J. and the Court of Appeal refused to construe the provisions as extending to that situation.

(c) Where the regulations confer a discretion on directors with regard to the acceptance of transfers, this discretion, like all the directors' powers, is a fiduciary one[11] to be exercised bona fide in what they consider—not what the court considers—to be in the interest of the company, and not for any collateral purpose. But the court will presume that they have acted bona fide, and the onus of proof of the contrary is on those alleging it and is not easily discharged.[12]

(d) If, on the true construction of the articles, the directors are entitled to reject only on certain prescribed grounds and it is proved

---

[6] *Greenhalgh v. Mallard* [1943] 2 All E.R. 234, C.A.; *Roberts v. Letter "T" Estates Ltd* [1961] A.C. 795, P.C.

[7] *Moodie v. Shepherd (Bookbinders) Ltd* [1949] 2 All E.R. 1044, H.L.Sc.

[8] *Lyle & Scott Ltd v. Scott's Trustees* [1959] A.C. 763, H.L.Sc.

[9] This distinction is all too often overlooked in the drafting of the relevant article.

[10] *Safeguard Ltd v. NatWest Bank* [1981] 1 W.L.R. 286; [1982] 1 W.L.R. 589, C.A.

[11] For the application of the fiduciary principle to the transfer of shares in the context of takeover bids, see Chap. 29, pp. 785–788, below.

[12] In *Re Smith & Fawcett Ltd* above, the directors refused to register but agreed that they would register a transfer of part of the shareholding if the transferor agreed to sell the balance to one of the directors at a stated price. It was held that this was insufficient evidence of bad faith but it might today be "unfairly prejudicial" under s.459: see Chap. 27, below.

that they have rejected on others, the court will intervene.[13] And interrogatories may be administered to determine on which of certain prescribed grounds the directors have acted, but not as to their reasons for rejecting on these grounds,[14] and not if the articles provide, as they often do, that they shall not be bound to state their reasons.[15] If the directors do state their reasons the court will investigate them to the extent of seeing whether they have acted on the right principles and will overrule their decision if they have acted on considerations which should not have weighed with them, but not merely because the court would have come to a different conclusion.[16] If the regulations are so framed as to give the directors an unfettered discretion the court will interfere with it only on proof of bad faith[17] and since the directors will not be bound to disclose either their grounds or their reasons, the difficulty of discharging the onus of proof is especially great.

(e) If, as is normal, the regulations merely give the directors power to refuse to register, as opposed to making their passing of transfers a condition precedent to registration,[18] the transferee is entitled to be registered unless the directors resolve as a board to reject. Hence in *Moodie v. Shepherd (Bookbinders) Ltd*[19] where the two directors disagreed and neither had a casting vote, the House of Lords held that registration must proceed. The directors have a reasonable time in which to come to a decision,[20] but since section 183(5) of the Act imposes an obligation on them to give to the transferee notice of rejection within two months of the lodging of the transfer, the maximum reasonable period is two months.[21]

The positions of transferor and transferee prior to registration

In the case of an off-market transaction it may be of importance to determine the precise legal position of the transferor and transferee pending registration of the transfer which, if there are restrictions on

---

[13] *Re Bede Steam Shipping Co.* [1917] 1 Ch. 123, C.A.
[14] *Sutherland v. British Dominions Corp.* [1926] Ch. 746.
[15] *Berry & Stewart v. Tottenham Hotspur Football Co.* [1935] Ch. 718.
[16] *Re Bede Steam Shipping Co.*, above; *Re Smith & Fawcett Ltd*, above. Indeed, if there are rights of pre-emption at a fair price to be determined by the auditors the court can investigate the adequacy of this price only if the auditors give a "speaking valuation" stating their reasons: *Dean v. Prince* [1954] Ch. 409, C.A.; *Burgess v. Purchase & Sons Ltd* [1983] Ch. 216.
[17] *Re Smith & Fawcett Ltd*, above; *Charles Forte Investments Ltd v. Amanda* [1964] Ch. 240.
[18] It is common to state that transfers have to be passed by the directors but under normal articles that is not so (see, *e.g.* Table A arts. 24 and 25) and in the light of s.183(4) and (5) it is doubtful if the articles could make the directors' approval a condition precedent.
[19] [1949] 2 All E.R. 1044, H.L.Sc.
[20] *Shepherd's Case* (1866) L.R. 2 Ch.App. 16.
[21] *Re Swaledale Cleaners Ltd* [1968] 1 W.L.R. 1710, C.A. And normally it seems that they will not be treated as acting unreasonably if they take the full two months: *Re Zinotty Properties Ltd* [1984] 1 W.L.R. 1249 at 1260.

transferability, may never occur. As we have seen, only if and when the transfer is registered will the transferor cease to be a member and shareholder and the transferee will become a member and shareholder. However, notwithstanding that registration has not occurred, the beneficial interest in the shares may have passed from the transferor to the transferee. In the case of a sale the transaction will normally go through three stages:—(1) an agreement (which, particularly if a block of shares conferring *de facto* or *de jure* control is being sold, may be a complicated one) (2) delivery of the signed transfer and the certificate by the seller and payment of the price by the buyer and (3) lodgment of the transfer for registration by the company. Notwithstanding that the transfer is not lodged for registration or registration is refused, the beneficial interest in the shares will, it seems, pass from the seller to the buyer at the latest at stage (2) and, indeed will do so at stage (1) if the agreement is one which the courts would order to be specifically enforced.[22] The seller then becomes a trustee for the buyer and must account to him for any dividends he receives and vote in accordance with his instructions (or appoint him as his proxy).[23] This, however, begs several questions. The first arises because at stage (2) delivery of the documents may not necessarily be matched by payment of the full price; the agreement may have provided for payment by instalments[24] and the seller will then retain a lien on the shares as an unpaid seller. This will not prevent an equitable interest passing to the buyer but the court will not grant specific performance unless the seller's lien can be fully protected,[25] and until paid in full he is entitled to vote the shares as he thinks will best protect his interest.[26] Instead of being a bare trustee his position is analogous to that of a trustee of a settlement of which he is one of the beneficiaries.

The second begged question is whether the foregoing can apply when the articles provide for rights of pre-emption or first refusal when a shareholder wishes to dispose of his shares. In such a case the

---

[22] The fact that the agreement is subject to fulfilment of a condition beyond the control of the parties will not prevent it from being specifically enforceable, notwithstanding that the condition has not been fulfilled, if the party for whose benefit the condition was inserted is prepared to waive it. In *Wood Preservation Ltd v. Prior* [1969] 1 W.L.R. 1077, C.A., where the condition was for the benefit of the buyer, the court was prepared to hold that the seller ceased to be "the beneficial owner" on the date of the contract notwithstanding that the buyer did not become the beneficial owner until he later waived the condition. In the interim, beneficial ownership was, apparently, in limbo! In the case of CREST transfers, although the time between bargain and settlement will be very short (three days is the aim), an equitable interest is acquired by the transferee at the moment an operator-instruction is generated requiring the company to register the transfer of title: Uncertificated Securities Regulations 1995, reg. 25.

[23] *Hardoon v. Belilios* [1901] A.C. 118, P.C.

[24] The normal practice then is to provide that the transfer and share certificate shall be held by a stake-holder and not lodged for registration until released to the buyer on payment of the final instalment.

[25] *Langen & Wind Ltd v. Bell* [1972] Ch. 685.

[26] *Musselwhite v. Musselwhite & Son Ltd* [1962] Ch. 964; *JRRT (Investments) Ltd v. Haycraft* [1993] BCLC 401.

transferor (perhaps with the full knowledge of the transferee[27]) has breached the deemed contract under section 14 between him and the company and his fellow shareholders. There are observations of the House of Lords in *Hunter v. Hunter*[28] to the effect that accordingly the transfer is wholly void, even as between the transferor and transferee. However, in two later cases[29] courts have refused to follow this and, it must surely be right (at any rate if the price has been paid) that the buyer obtains such rights as the transferor had. This will not benefit the buyer if all the shares are taken up when the transferor is compelled to make a pre-emptive offer, but it does not follow that all of them will be taken up and, if not, the transferee has a better claim to those shares not taken up than has the transferor.

When the transaction is not a sale but a gift, there need be no agreement. Even if there is, it will not be legally enforceable under English law because there will be no valuable consideration and because, under the so-called rule in *Milroy v. Lord*,[30] "there is no equity to perfect an imperfect gift". One might have supposed, therefore, that if the donor has chosen to make the gift by handing to the donee a signed transfer and the share certificate, rather than by a formal declaration of trust in favour of the donee, the gift would not be effective unless and until the transfer was registered. In two modern cases,[31] however, it has been held that so long as the donor has done all he needs to do, the beneficial interest passes from him to the donee.[32]

Priorities between competing transferees

In the case of off-market transactions questions may also arise in determining the priority of purported transfers of the same shares to different people. In answering these questions the courts[33] have relied on two traditional principles of English property law: *i.e.* (1) that as between two competing holders of equitable interests, if their equities are equal the first in time prevails and (2) that a bona fide purchaser for value of a legal interest takes free of earlier equitable interests of which he as no notice at the time of purchase. In applying these prin-

---

[27] As in *Lyle & Scott Ltd v. Scott's Trustees* [1959] A.C. 763, H.L.Sc.

[28] [1936] A.C. 222 H.L.

[29] *Hawks v. McArthur* [1951] 1 All E.R. 22; *Tett v. Phoenix Property Co.* [1986] BCLC 149, where the C.A. was not required to rule on this point because the appellants did not argue that the decision on it at first instance was wrong.

[30] (1862) 4 De G., F. and J. 264.

[31] Both, purely coincidentally apparently, named *Re Rose*, respectively reported in [1949] Ch. 78 and [1952] Ch. 499, C.A.

[32] Thus, until the transfer is registered, placing the donee in the same position as if the donor had instead made a declaration of trust.

[33] The leading cases are *Shropshire Union Ry v. R.* (1875) L.R. 7 H.L. 496; *Société Generale v. Walker* (1885) 11 App.Cas. 20, H.L.; *Colonial Bank v. Cady* (1890) 15 App.Cas. 267, H.L. Among more recent decisions, see *Hawks v. McArthur*, above, n. 29, and *Champagne Perrier-Jouet v. Finch & Co.*, below, n. 44.

ciples to competing share transfers, a transferee prior to registration is treated as having an equitable interests only but registration converts his interest into a legal one.[34] Hence if a registered, shareholder, A, first executes a transfer to a purchaser, B, and later to another, C, while both remain unregistered B will have priority over C. If, however, C succeeds in obtaining registration before B, he will have priority over B so long as he had no notice, at the time of purchase, of the transfer to B. If C did have notice, although he has been registered, his prima facie title will not prevail over that of B, who will be entitled to have the register rectified (assuming that there are no grounds on which the company could refuse to register B) and in the meantime C's legal interest will be subject to the equitable interest of B.[35] If both transfers were gifts, the position would presumably be different; the gift to B[36] would leave A without any beneficial interest that he could give to C and, not being a "purchaser", C could not obtain priority by registration; his legal interest, on his becoming the registered holder, would be subject to the prior equity of B.

It should perhaps be pointed out once again that even registration affords only prima facie evidence of title. If the registered transferor, A, was not entitled to the shares, what will pass when he transfers to B or C is not, strictly speaking, either a legal or equitable interest but only his imperfect title to it, which will not prevail against the true owner. If, for example, the transfer to A was a forgery the true owner will be entitled to be restored to the register.[37] Hence a transferee can never be certain of obtaining an absolute title in the case of an off-market transaction. But his risk is slight so long as he promptly obtains registration of the transfer. And this he can do unless there are restrictions on the transferability of the shares or unless there are good reasons for failing to apply for registration.

The principal example for the latter occurs when the shareholder wants to borrow on the security of his shares. This can be done by a legal mortgage, under which the shareholder transfers the shares to the lender (who registers the transfer) subject to an agreement to retransfer them when the loan is repaid. Generally, however, this suits

---

[34] Notwithstanding a suggestion by Lord Selbourne (in *Société Generale v. Walker*, above, at 28) that "a present absolute right to have the transfer registered" might suffice, it seems that nothing less than actual registration will do. In *Ireland v. Hart* [1902] 1 Ch. 521 the transfer had been lodged for registration and the directors had no power to refuse but it was held that the legal interest had not passed.

[35] *France v. Clark* (1884) 26 Ch.D. 257, C.A.; *Earl of Sheffield v. London Joint Stock Bank* (1888) 13 App.Cas. 332, H.L.; *Rainford v. James Keith & Blackman* [1905] 2 Ch. 147, C.A.

[36] So long as it has been "perfected"—as interpreted in the two *Re Rose* cases: see above p. 349, n. 31.

[37] The transferee will have no remedy against the company based on estoppel by share certificate: it made no false statement: see p. 344, above. The Forged Transfers Acts 1891 and 1892 enabled companies to adopt fee-financed arrangements for compensating innocent victims of forged transfers but this is purely voluntary and seems to have been virtually a dead-letter since its inception.

neither party; the lender normally has no wish to become a member and shareholder of the company and the borrower does not want to cease to be one. Hence a more usual arrangement is one whereby the shareholder deposits with the lender his share certificate and, often, a signed blank transfer, this usually being accompanied by a written memorandum setting out the terms of the loan. The result is to confer an equitable charge which the lender can enforce by selling the shares if he needs to realise his security. Custody of the share certificate is regarded as the essential protection of the lender.[38] In the case of shares[39] dealt with through CREST, its rules provided for uncertificated shares to be held in "escrow" balances, which provision appears to give the bank an equivalent security.[40]

THE COMPANY'S LIEN

As we have seen,[41] a public company is no longer permitted to have a charge or lien on its shares except (a) when the shares are not fully paid and the charge or lien is for the amount payable on the shares, or (b) the ordinary business of the company includes the lending of money or consists of the provision of hire-purchase finance and the charge arises in the course of a transaction in the ordinary course of its business. Neither exception is of much importance in the present context. Hence it is only in respect of private companies that problems are still likely to arise when their articles provide, as they frequently do, that "the company shall have a first and paramount lien on shares, whether or not fully-paid, registered in the name of a person indebted or under any liability to the company". Since the decision of the House of Lords in *Bradford Banking Co. v. Briggs, Son and Co.*[42] it appears to be accepted that the effect of such a provision is that:

(a) Once a shareholder has incurred a debt or liability to the company, it has an equitable charge on the shares of that shareholder to secure payment which ranks in priority to later equitable interests and, it seems, to earlier ones of which the company had no notice when its lien became effective; and (b) in determining whether the company had notice,[43] section 360 has no application; if the company knows of

---

[38] Banks usually grant their clients overdrafts on the security of an equitable charge by a deposit of share certificates without requiring signed blank transfers.

[39] Shares not listed or dealt with on the A.I.M. are rarely accepted as security for loans because of their illiquidity and, usually, restrictions on their transferability. Banks will instead want a charge on the undertaking and assets of the company itself plus, probably, personal guarantees of the members or directors.

[40] See Evans (1996) 11 BJIBFL 259.

[41] Chap. 11 at p. 279, above.

[42] (1886) 12 App.Cas. 29, H.L.

[43] It is not altogether clear why notice should be relevant. Since the company's lien is merely an equitable interest, its priority *vis-à-vis* another equitable interest should depend on the respective dates of their creation. But the decisions seem to assume that the company's lien

the earlier equitable interest (because, for example, a transfer of the shares has been lodged for registration even if that is refused) it cannot improve its own position to the detriment of the holder of that known equitable interest.

An interesting modern illustration is afforded by *Champagne Perrier-Jouet v. Finch & Co.*[44] There the company's articles provided for a lien in the above terms. One of its shareholders[45] had been allowed to run up substantial debts to the company resulting from trading between him and the company and it had been agreed that he could repay by instalments. Another creditor of the shareholder subsequently obtained judgment against him and a charging order on the shares by way of equitable execution. It was held that the company's lien had become effective when the debts to it were incurred (even though they were not then due for repayment) and as this occurred before the company had notice of the charging order,[46] the company's lien had priority.[47]

As this case shows, an equitable charge on shares in a private company with articles conferring a lien on the company is likely to be an even more undesirable form of security than shares in private companies always are. It may, however, be the only security obtainable, for an attempt to obtain a legal charge will almost certainly be frustrated by the refusal of the directors to register the transfer. If, *faute de mieux*, it has to be accepted, notice should immediately be given to the company, making it clear that this is a notice which it cannot disregard in relation to any lien it may claim, and an attempt should be made to obtain information about the amount, if any, then owed to the company.

TRANSMISSION OF SHARES BY OPERATION OF LAW

The Act[48] recognises that shares may be transmitted by operation of law and that, when this occurs, the prohibition on registering unless a proper instrument of transfer has been delivered does not apply.[49] The

---

will have priority over an equitable interest if the company has not received notice of the latter.

[44] [1982] 1 W.L.R. 1359.

[45] He had also been a director and it was argued that the debt he incurred to the company was a loan unlawful under what is now s.330(1) so that the company could not have a valid lien. It was held that it was not a loan; it would, however, today be "a quasi-loan" as defined in s.331 and as such unlawful if the company was a "relevant company" (*e.g.* a subsidiary of a public company) as defined in s.331.

[46] It also ante-dated the charging order but the court seems to have regarded the date of notice as decisive: see at 1367B–E.

[47] It was also held that if the company enforced its lien by selling the shares it would have to comply with provisions in the articles conferring pre-emptive rights on the other members of the company.

[48] And see Table A 1985, arts. 29–31.

[49] s.183(2). In the case of shares held in uncertificated form, "operation of law" is one of the "extra-system" bases upon which a participating company may register a transfer of title,

principal examples of this are when a registered shareholder dies or becomes bankrupt. As regards the death of a shareholder, the Act further provides that a transfer by the deceased's personal representative, even if he is not a member of the company, is as valid as if he had been.[50] The company is bound to accept probate or letters of administration granted in any part of the United Kingdom as sufficient evidence of the personal representative's entitlement.[51] However, he does not become a member unless he elects to apply to be registered and is registered as a member. In the meantime, the effect is, as Table A, article 31 puts it, that he has:

"the rights to which he would be entitled if he were the holder of the share, except that he shall not, before being registered as the holder of the share, be entitled in respect of it to attend or vote at any general meeting of the company or at a separate meeting of the holders of any class of shares in the company".

If the shares are those of a listed company, this anomalous position can be ended rapidly because, unless the shares are not fully paid, there will not be any restrictions on transferability and the personal representative will either obtain registration of himself or execute a transfer to a purchaser or to the beneficiaries. In relation to a private company, however, it may continue indefinitely and prove detrimental to the personal representative, the deceased's estate and, sometimes, the company. The personal representative may suffer because it may not be possible for him fully to wind up the estate and to obtain a discharge from his fiduciary responsibilities. The estate may suffer because it may be impossible for the personal representative to sell the shares at their true value, especially if any attempt to dispose of them would trigger rights of pre-emption or first refusal.[52] The company may suffer because, as we have seen,[53] unless such rights have been most carefully drafted, they will not come into operation so long as no action regarding registration is taken by the personal representative. Clearly, in relation to private companies, reform of this branch of the law is urgently needed. At the least, this should include an obligation on directors who refuse to register personal representatives or

---

but the company is not obliged to register the transfer in such a case: Uncertificated Securities Regulations 1995, reg. 23(6) and see above, p. 340.

[50] s.183(3).

[51] s.187. If it does so without such production of the grant it may become liable for any tax payable as a result of the transmission (*NY Breweries Co. v. Att.-Gen.* [1899] A.C. 62, H.L.) but in the case of small estates, companies may be prepared to dispense with production of a grant if the Revenue confirms that nothing is payable. If the deceased was one of a number of jointly registered members, the company, on production of a death certificate, will have to recognise that he has ceased to be a member and shareholder and that the others remain such. But the whole beneficial interest in the shares will not pass to them unless they and the deceased were beneficial owners entitled jointly rather than in common.

[52] If there are any restrictions on transfers when Table A, art. 30 applies, all the articles relating to restriction on transfers apply both to a notice that the personal representative wishes to be registered and to a transfer from him.

[53] *Safeguard Ltd v. NatWest Bank*, above, p. 346, n. 10.

transferees from them to state their reasons.[54] All that statutory reforms have done as yet is to make piecemeal extensions of the remedies afforded to members so that they can be invoked by personal representatives of members.[55]

The position on bankruptcy of an individual shareholder[56] is broadly similar. His rights to the shares will automatically vest in the trustee in bankruptcy as part of his estate.[57] But, as in the case of a personal representative, until he elects to become registered and is so registered, he will not become a member of the company entitled to attend meetings and to vote. In contrast, however, with the position on the death of a member, the bankrupt will remain a member and be entitled to attend and vote—though he will have to do so in accordance with the directions of the trustee. As in the case of personal representatives, the company's articles will probably provide that any restrictions on transferability apply on any application to be registered and to any transfer by him[58] and these restrictions may handicap the trustee in obtaining the best price on a sale of the shares, particularly if the articles confer pre-emption rights.[59] If a personal representative or trustee in bankruptcy elects to be registered, and is, he becomes personally liable for any amounts unpaid on the shares and not merely representationally liable to the extent of the estate. Trustees in bankruptcy, but not personal representatives, may disclaim onerous property,[60] which the shares might be if they were partly paid or subject to an effective company lien.

APPLICABILITY TO DEBENTURES

The foregoing discussion in this Chapter has been primarily directed to the acquisition and disposal of shares. But much of it is equally applicable to debentures and many of the statutory provisions expressly apply equally to them, though it is clear that when they do

---

[54] As recommended by the Jenkins Committee Cmnd. 1749 (1962), para. 212(g).
[55] See, in particular, s.459(2) which makes it possible for personal representatives to invoke the "unfairly prejudicial" remedy which might well be effective if it could be shown that the directors were exercising their powers to refuse transfers in order to enable themselves or the company to acquire the shares of deceased members at an unfair price: see Chap. 27, below.
[56] On winding up of a corporate shareholder there is no transmission of the company's property; it remains vested in the company but most of the directors' powers to manage it pass to the liquidator.
[57] Insolvency Act 1986, ss.283(1) and 306. But not if the shareholder held his shares as a trustee for another person: *ibid.*, s.283(3)(a).
[58] See Table A 1985, art. 30. Both this article and art. 31 expressly apply to both personal representatives and trustees in bankruptcy.
[59] In *Borland's Trustee v. Steel Bros.* [1901] 1 Ch. 279, a provision in the articles that in the event of a shareholder's bankruptcy (or death) his shares should be offered to a named person at a particular price was held to be effective and not obnoxious to the bankruptcy laws.
[60] Insolvency Act 1986, s.315. Disclaimer puts an end to the interest of the bankrupt and his estate and discharges the trustee from any liability: *ibid.*, s.315(3).

so, "debentures" is usually used in its narrow sense of debenture stock or a series of identical debentures and not in its wider meaning of a single mortgage, charge or bond.[61] So far as the former are concerned, the Act (as does the Financial Services Act) assumes that public issues of debentures will be undertaken by the same methods as issues of shares and it provides that a contract to take up debentures, like one to take up shares, may be enforced by an order for specific performance.[62] It also assumes that debentures or debenture stock will be transferred in much the same way as shares. Hence, subsections (1), (2), (5) and (6)[63] of section 183 (relating to the need for written transfers, except when the transmission is by operation of law, and to the recognition of personal representatives) expressly apply. So do sections 184 (certification of transfers) and 185 (duty to issue certificates). And estoppel, similar to estoppel by share certificate, clearly could arise from statements in certificates of debenture stock or in debentures. Equally, the Uncertificated Securities Regulations, as the use of the word "securities" rather than the word "shares" suggests, permit the transfer of title to debentures held in uncertificated form.[64]

One could also be faced with problems, similar to those in relation to shares, regarding equitable and legal ownership of debentures and the priority of competing transferees. But the great difference here is the lesser role played by registration. Unlike with members, a company is not compelled to maintain a register of debenture-holders. At least this is the traditional rule. In relation, however, to debentures held in uncertificated form the company is now required to maintain in the United Kingdom a register of the names and addresses of those holding debentures in this way, together with a statement of the size of the individual holdings.[65] Even in relation to certificated debentures, the Act assumes that a company probably will maintain a register if it issues debenture stock or a series of debentures and the Act contains provisions, similar to, but not identical with, those relating to the membership register, concerning where the register shall be kept[66] and who shall be entitled to inspect and obtain copies of it.[67] But it says nothing about the register being evidence of ownership, and it is not clear what role, if any, it plays in converting an equitable interest to a legal one. On general principles relating to assignments of choses-in-action, a transfer of a debenture should be an equitable assignment only, until

---

[61] See Chap. 13 at pp. 321–325, above.
[62] s.195.
[63] But not subss.(3) and (4) which relate only to "members" which debenture-holders are not.
[64] Reg. 18 and the definition of "security" in reg. 3(1).
[65] Uncertificated Securities Regulations 1995, reg. 19(3). If the terms of issue of the debentures require the company to maintain a register of holders in the U.K., then the information is to be provided by addition to that register: reg. 19(2).
[66] s.190.
[67] s.191.

it becomes a legal assignment when the company receives notice of it. In principle, therefore, the legal interest should pass from transferor to transferee when the company is given notice of it, and that date, rather than the later date of actual registration, should be the relevant one in determining its priority over earlier unnotified transfers.

Other differences flow from the fact that, whereas the rights of shareholders depend mainly on the provision of the company's articles, which will have been drafted in the interests of the company, those of debenture-holders depend upon the terms of a contract between lender and borrower and its terms will have to be acceptable to the lender. Hence in practice there will be no problems arising from restrictions on transferability or from a company's lien; debentures will invariably provide that the money expressed to be secured will be paid, and that the debentures are transferable, free from any equities or claims between the company and the original or any intermediate holder.[68] It is possible that the terms of issue of the debentures will be inconsistent with their being held in uncertificated form, in which case they will need to be altered if the company wishes to make this form of holding debentures available.[69] The Regulations do not provide a simple shortcut to the necessary amendments, as they do in the case of shares, but they do something to encourage trustees to agree to such amendments without holding a meeting of the debenture-holders. A trustee for debenture-holders is not to be chargeable with breach of trust by reason only of his assenting to changes in the trust deed necessary to enable the debenture-holders to hold the debentures in uncertificated form or to transfer them or exercise any rights attached to them electronically.[70] Another contrast with shares is that if shares are redeemed or re-purchased by the company they have to be cancelled, whereas the Act provides that, unless it is otherwise agreed, redeemed debentures may be re-issued with their original priority.[71] The great contrast, however, is that debentures secured by charges on the company's property throw up problems regarding the priority between conflicting charges. These problems are dealt with in the next Chapter.

---

[68] Without this, debenture-holders and their transferees would be in grave danger, for a debenture, unless in bearer form and thus a negotiable instrument, would, as a chose-in-action, be transferable only subject to the state of the account between the company and the transferor. As stressed throughout this chapter, neither shares (unless in the form of share warrants to bearer) nor debentures (unless bearer bonds) are negotiable instruments like bills of exchange. Although the Admission to Listing Directive requires listed shares and debt securities to be "freely negotiable" (Scheds. A & B II 2) this is interpreted as "freely transferable" and not as prescribing that they must be "negotiable instruments" in full sense.

[69] See reg. 18 and above, p. 338.

[70] Reg. 33(2), provided notice is given to the holders at least 30 days before the changes become effective.

[71] s.194. Note subs.(3) which is designed to remove the technical difficulties revealed in *Re Russian Petroleum Co.* [1907] 2 Ch. 540, C.A. when a company secures its overdraft on current account by depositing with the bank a debenture for a fixed amount.

CHAPTER 15

COMPANY CHARGES

BORROWERS are often obliged to provide security for the repayment of their debts and in this respect a company is no different from any other borrower. Almost invariably, debentures issued by a company will be secured by a charge over the company's assets. However, there are sufficiently unique features associated with the granting of security by a company that justify it being treated as a separate topic. In particular, the floating charge is practicable only if created by a body corporate,[1] there is a separate system for the registration of company charges,[2] there are distinct statutory procedures for the enforcement of the floating charge,[3] certain provisions of the Insolvency Act 1986 affecting company charges are unique to corporate insolvency,[4] and the floating charge can be used tactically in order to veto the making of an administration order.[5] Coupled with these, the granting of security by a company is subject to the law relating to corporate capacity and director's duties.[6] As regards these latter matters, it will be assumed for the remainder of the Chapter, unless the contrary is stated, that a company has capacity to grant the security and that the directors were not acting in breach of their duty to the company or exceeding their authority. Some comment is also needed on nomenclature. "Charge", "security" or "security interest" will be used interchangeably in the sense of any form of security, fixed or floating, over a company's property present or future.[7]

The legal nature of security interests

It is necessary to deal briefly with what is a complex area of the law and that is the types of security interests recognised by English law.[8] Some knowledge of this topic is essential in order to understand the nature of the rights conferred on a secured charge holder, the priorities of charges, and the system for the registration of company

---

* As stated in the Preface, this Chapter has been contributed by Professor D.D. Prentice.
[1] See pp. 89–90.
[2] See pp. 376 et seq.
[3] See pp. 382 et seq.
[4] In certain situations there are analogues in the case of personal bankruptcy.
[5] See Insolvency Act 1986, s.9(3).
[6] See pp. 202 et seq. and Chap. 22.
[7] As will be seen later, "charge" can have a more restricted technical meaning in equity.
[8] There is a considerable volume of literature on this vast and vexed topic. See Oditah, *Legal Aspects of Receivables Financing* (London, 1991), Chap. 1 and Goode, *Commercial Law.* (2nd ed., London, 1996), Chap. 22, for helpful analyses.

charges. Although a number of security interests are clearly accepted as being recognised by English law, there is some doubt at the penumbra as to what constitutes a security interest and, in particular, as to whether there is a *numerus clausus* of such interests. Browne-Wilkinson V.-C., without claiming that it was comprehensive, accepted the following as a description of a security interest:

"Security is created where a person ('the creditor') to whom an obligation is owed by another ('the debtor') by statute or contract, in addition to the personal promise of the debtor to discharge the obligation, obtains rights exercisable against some property in which the debtor has an interest in order to enforce the discharge of the debtor's obligation to the creditor."[9]

This brings out what is perhaps the essential feature of a security interest, namely that ultimately it gives the holder of the security a proprietary claim over assets, normally the debtor's, to secure payment of the debt. The position of a secured creditor is to be contrasted with that of an unsecured creditor who merely has a personal claim to sue for the payment of his debt and to invoke the available legal processes for the enforcement of any judgment that he may obtain.[10]

Security interests can be divided broadly into consensual and non-consensual securities. As the name implies, consensual security interests arise by way of agreement of the parties. There is general acceptance that as regards consensual security English law recognises at least the following: the mortgage, the charge, the pledge and the lien.[11] In contrast to consensual security interests are those security interests that arise by operation of law. The classification of this category is not free from difficulty but it includes at least a common law lien and a lien arising by operation of law.[12]

It is not possible in a text of this nature to go into the details of security interests in any great depth but a number of questions arise with respect to the creation of such interests by a company.

---

[9] *Bristol Airport plc v. Powdrill* [1990] Ch. 744 at 760. The only significant refinement that one might want to add to this description is that the property of a third party can also be made available by way of security. See also *Re Curtain Dream plc* [1990] BCLC 925 at 935–937; *Welsh Development Agency v. Export Finance Co. Ltd* [1992] BCLC 148; Insolvency Act 1986, s.248. A charge can be created not only to secure the payment of a monetary obligation but also to secure other types of obligations: *Re Cosslett (Contractors) Ltd* [1996] 4 All E.R. 46 at 56.

[10] See Goode, *op. cit.*, at pp. 640–642. An unsecured creditor may be able to invoke certain types of court procedures which make a party's assets security for his claim: for the nature of these procedural securities see Goode, *op. cit.*, at pp. 671–673.

[11] See Bell, *Modern Law of Personal Property in England and Ireland* (London, 1989), Chap. 6; Oditah, *op. cit.*, at pp. 85–88; Goode, *Legal Problems of Credit and Security* (2nd ed., London, 1988), at pp. 10–15.

[12] Bell, *op. cit.*, at pp. 138–141. Section 246 of the Insolvency Act 1986 deprives certain types of merely possessory liens of effect against an administrator or liquidator; *Re Aveling Barford Ltd* [1989] 1 W.L.R. 360 at 364–365.

(i) First, is the charge fixed or floating? An example of the fixed charge is the mortgage and no more need be said about it here. The floating charge will be dealt with later.

(ii) Secondly, is the interest created by the charge equitable or legal? This has a bearing on the priorities of different chargees and of course the equitable charge holder can be defeated by the bona fide purchaser for value.

(iii) Thirdly, is the security interest possessory in the sense that possession, either actual or constructive, of the property subject to the security is necessary in order to confer a security interest on the security holder? Obviously, if all security interests had to be possessory it would make secured borrowing virtually impossible as a debtor would be deprived of the ability to use the assets subject to the security in the course of business (but English law has for long recognised non-possessory security interests). The classic example of a possessory security is the pledge which involves the pledgee (the security holder) taking possession of the goods of the debtor (the pledgor) until the debt is paid or the pledgee takes steps to enforce the pledge. The lien also in many situations is possessory although it is possible to have a non-possessory lien.

(iv) Fourthly, what type of "proprietary" interest is vested in the chargee by the charge? This has a direct bearing as to remedies. The remedies of the floating charge holder will be dealt with in greater detail later. But some brief comment is needed on the remedies available to the holders of other types of security interests. First is to be contrasted the mortgage and the charge and in this context charge is being used in its technical meaning and not in the broader sense set out at the beginning of this Chapter. Although the words "charge" and "mortgage" are often used interchangeably, there is technically an essential difference between them: "a mortgage involves a conveyance of property subject to a right of redemption, whereas a charge conveys nothing and merely gives the chargee certain rights over the property as security for the loan".[13] The essential difference between an equitable charge and a mortgage is as regards remedies; since a charge, unlike the mortgage, does not involve a conveyance of a proprietary interest, a chargee cannot foreclose or take possession. The remedy of a chargee is to apply to the court for an order for sale or for the appointment of a receiver.[14] The principal remedy of a pledgee is that of sale of the pledged goods and he

---

[13] See *Re Bond Worth Ltd* [1980] Ch. 228 at 250. Such a charge is, however, a present existing charge. For some of the difficulties in distinguishing an equitable charge from a mortgage in terms of the quality of the security granted, see Oditah, *op. cit.*, at pp. 94–96.

[14] See Megarry and Wade, *The Law of Real Property* (5th ed., London, 1984) at p. 953. The point is that a chargee does not have an estate.

can also sub-pledge the goods.[15] A lien holder merely has the right to detain the goods subject to the lien until the debt has been paid.[16]

(v) Fifthly, is the security interest one that is created by the act of the parties or is it one created by operation of law? This point has already been referred to above. It is of critical importance with respect to the registration of company charges since charges created by a company over its assets are treated differently from charges over a company's assets arising other than by the creation of the company. This point will be dealt with in greater detail later.

(vi) Lastly, is the charge registrable under the provisions for the registration of company charges? Again this will be dealt with in greater detail later.

The above is a very compressed survey of what constitutes a security interest. To complicate the picture even further, there are a number of other devices which, although not strictly security interests in the sense of vesting some type of proprietary interest in the creditor or which give him possessory control over assets of the debtor company, nevertheless act as security. These devices often put a creditor in a position superior to that of other unsecured creditors in the event of a company's insolvent liquidation. Two illustrative examples of such devices are (i) the negative pledge clause in unsecured lending, and (ii) retention of the title by a seller of goods. The first of these is an agreement by a debtor company and its unsecured creditor that the company will not create any securities which have priority to the claim of the creditor. Although this does not vest a security interest in the creditor, it has been claimed (rightly) that it "behaves"[17] like a security interest since it is an attempt to preclude the debtor from freely using its assets and thus, as with a security interest, it provides the creditor with a measure of protection. The retention of title is an arrangement whereby the seller of goods retains title to the goods until at least the buyer of the goods pays for them.[18] Some of the problems raised by this type of security will be dealt with later in the discussion on registration.[19]

---

[15] See Bell, *op. cit.*, at pp. 136–137.

[16] The lienee will normally have the right to sell by contract and where this is the case some argue that it is tantamount to a pledge. Other charge holders may of course take subject to the lien: *George Barker (Transport) Ltd v. Eynon* [1974] 1 W.L.R. 462.

[17] See Oditah, *op. cit.*, at p. 11. For a list of other types of quasi-security interests see Oditah, *ibid.*, at p. 11. See also Goode, *op. cit.*, Chap. 22.

[18] See generally, McCormack, *Reservation of Title* (2nd edn, London, 1995). This, rightly it is submitted, is seen as a matter of commercial substance as being a chattel mortgage securing a loan: Diamond, *A Review of Security Interests in Property* (DTI, 1989), at para. 3.6; *Welsh Development Agency v. Export Finance Co. Ltd* [1991] BCLC 936 at 950; [1992] BCLC 148.

[19] There are also self-help remedies such as set-off, abatement, rejection of goods and forfeiture of deposit, all of which firm up the position of a creditor: see Harris, *Remedies in Contract and Tort* (London, 1988), Chap. 2.

The purpose of taking security

There are a number of compelling reasons for a creditor to obtain a charge and not rely solely on his personal action against a debtor company. First, in the event of the insolvency of a company a secured creditor will at least have priority to unsecured creditors and will, according to the seniority of his claim, have priority over any less senior security holders. This is a direct consequence of the fact that a security interest confers some type of proprietary interest on its holder. Priority-gaining in the event of a company's liquidation is one of the principal reasons for taking security.[20] Secondly, the secured creditor may have the right of pursuit. This arises where a company in violation of the rights of a chargee disposes of the property subject to the charge and it entitles a chargee to pursue his claim into the proceeds of the disposition.[21] Thirdly, a security interest gives its holder the right of enforcement. What this entails is that once a charge becomes enforceable, the chargee may thereupon take whatever steps are available to enforce the charge since English law places no significant impediments in the way of the right of enforcement of a charge.[22] This right of enforcement is further enhanced by the fact that English insolvency law permits a chargee to remain outside the insolvency proceedings and to enforce his charge independently of such proceedings.[23] Lastly, a charge affords a chargee a measure of control over the business of the debtor company. The company may have to report regularly to the chargee and if the company gets into financial difficulties, the chargee may be made privy to management decisions.[24] In addition, the charge may be so all-embracing that it confers on the chargee as a matter of fact the exclusive right to supply the debtor company with credit.[25] A charge will obviously deter a second financier from providing the company with funds where its charge would rank after a charge that the company has already created over its assets. Also, unsecured creditors will often be deterred from seeking a winding-up since such creditors would readily appreciate the futility of such action where the company's assets were charged up to the hilt.[26]

---

[20] See Cork Report, Chap. 35.

[21] He may also be able to assert a claim against the property subject to the security unless it is acquired by a bona fide purchaser for value.

[22] The right has to some extent been circumscribed by statute: See Insolvency Act 1986, s.11(3) and s.43.

[23] *Sowman v. Samuel (David) Trust Ltd* [1978] 1 W.L.R. 22; *Re Potters Oils Ltd* [1986] 1 W.L.R. 201.

[24] Although the chargee has to be careful not to become a shadow director and thus, *e.g.*, potentially liable under the Insolvency Act 1986, s.214. The chances of this are, on the whole, minimal: see *Re Hydrodam (Corby) Ltd* [1994] 2 BCLC 180.

[25] For an unsuccessful attempt to challenge a charge precluding the creation of charges in favour of third parties as being in violation of Arts. 85 and 86 of the E.C. Treaty, see *Oakdale Richmond Ltd v. National Westminster Bank plc* (1996) BCC 919.

[26] See generally Wood, *Law and Practice of International Finance*, Chap. 6 which sets out the reasons for various types of bond covenants that can be taken by a creditor.

The floating charge

The general nature of a floating charge has already been explained[27]; it is an equitable charge on some or all of the company's present and future property which leaves the company free to deal with the property subject to the charge in the ordinary course of business. Such a charge is, therefore, a particularly valuable means whereby a business concern can raise money without removing any of its property from the business. Also, it facilitates the granting of security over assets which in the normal course of a company's business are circulating, for example, stock in trade. The charge remains floating and the company free to use the assets subject to the charge until the charge is converted into a fixed charge. This is referred to as the crystallisation of the charge. The normal crystallising event is the taking of steps to enforce the charge but there are others and these will be dealt with later.[28] No particular form of words is necessary to create a floating charge; it suffices if the intention is shown (a) to impose a charge on assets both present and future, (b) the assets are of such a nature that they would be changing in the ordinary course of the company's business, and (c) the company is free to continue to deal with the assets in the ordinary course of its business.[29] The phrase "ordinary course of business" is construed widely[30]: it may even cover the sale of the company's whole undertaking in exchange for securities in another company provided such sale is authorised by the objects clause in the company's memorandum.[31]

For a clear grasp of the nature of a floating charge, two important

---

[27] See pp. 89–90. For valuable analyses of the floating charge see Goode, *Commercial Law* (2nd edn), Chap. 25; Gough, *Company Charges*, (2nd ed., London, 1996), Chap. 5. Floating charges and receivers in Scotland are dealt with by Part XVIII of the 1985 Act and Part III, Chap. II of the 1986 Act.

[28] See pp. 367 *et seq.*

[29] *Re Yorkshire Woolcombers' Association Ltd* [1903] 2 Ch. 284 at 295; *Illingworth v. Houldsworth* [1904] A.C. 355, H.L. In practice it is usual to state specifically that the charge is "by way of floating charge" but it suffices if it is expressed to be on the "undertaking" or the like: *Re Panama Royal Mail Co.* (1870) L.R. 5 Ch.App. 318; *Re Florence Land and Public Works Co.* (1879) 10 Ch.D. 530, C.A.; *Re Colonial Trusts Corp.* (1880) 15 Ch.D. 465. The fact that a charge is called a "fixed" charge does not necessarily make it so; if the company is free to use the assets in the normal course of its business then it will be treated as a floating charge: *Re Armagh Shoes Ltd* [1984] BCLC 405, Ch.D. (N.I.).

[30] See *Hamilton v. Hunter* (1982–83) 7 A.C.L.R. 295; *Re Bartlett Estates Pty Ltd* (1988–1989) 14 A.C.L.R. 512 where the court found that the company had acted outside its normal course of business. To be affected by this, the person dealing with the company will probably have to be aware of this fact, and that it constitued a breach of the terms of the floating charge.

[31] *Re Borax Co.* [1901] 1 Ch. 326, C.A. It is important to note that the company in that case had not ceased to carry on business. It is not clear whether because of s.35 of the 1985 Act the disposition of a company's assets in a manner not authorised by its objects would result in the person who acquires an interest in the assets taking them subject to the floating charge. However, s.35 deals with the issue of validity of the transaction whereas the question under discussion is one of priority between the floating charge holder and the person who acquires the property outside the company's normal course of business. In this latter situation the question should be determined by the normal rules of priority.

factors must be kept in mind. First, probably the most significant feature for identifying the floating charge is that the company retains management autonomy with respect to the assets subject to the charge. Thus the essence of the charge is not determined by the nature of the property over which it is created but rather by the degree of freedom accorded to the company to deal with this property in the normal course of business. This is illustrated by *Siebe Gorman & Co. Ltd v. Barclays Bank Ltd*[32] in which the court held that the company had created a fixed charge over its book debts in favour of its bank. The charge provided that the company could not assign or charge the debts and the proceeds of the debts had to be paid into a designated bank account with the bank. It is submitted that the essence of the floating charge is the degree of management autonomy accorded to the company with respect to the charged assets.[33] If the company can use the charged assets in the normal course of its business then the charge is more likely than not a floating charge.[34] Also, of relevance in characterising a charge are the nature of assets subject to the charge,[35] and the extent to which the characterising of the charge as fixed would result in the company not having sufficient uncharged cash flow to enable it to carry on business.[36]

There have been a number of recent cases where the courts have held a charge to be fixed despite the fact that the company has been accorded considerable management autonomy with respect to the charged assets. It has been held that a charge over sub-rentals in favour of a bank whereby the company could use the rentals until the bank intervened was a fixed charge.[37] Obviously, the characterisation of a charge can give rise to reasonable dispute, but the ability of the company to use the proceeds of the charged assets until the chargee intervened, is very much the hallmark of a floating charge.

The second factor of importance with respect to the nature of a floating charge is that although a floating charge relates to future assets it is a present charge and not a future one. In *Re Margart Properties*

---

[32] [1979] 2 Lloyd's Rep. 142. In *Supercool Refrigeration and Air Conditioning v. Hoverd Industries Ltd* [1994] 3 N.Z.L.R. 300 at 321 the court, while accepting the principle of *Siebe Gorman* that it was possible to create a fixed charge over book debts, considered that the it had not successfully been done in the latter case since the company was free to operate its account.

[33] *Royal Trust Bank v. National Westminster Bank plc* [1996] BCC 613 at 619.

[34] *Re Cimex Tissues Ltd* [1995] 1 BCLC 409. This case shows that a limited power to deal with the assets in the normal course of business does not necessarily result in the charge being a floating charge. Likewise, some restrictions on the power of the company to deal with the assets, for example, a prohibition on factoring book debts subject to the charge, does not prevent it from being a floating charge: *Re Brightlife Ltd* [1987] Ch. 200.

[35] *e.g.* do they change from time to time?

[36] *e.g.* a fixed charge on all the company's sales proceeds would stultify its business.

[37] *Re Atlantic Computer Systems plc* [1992] Ch. 505. See also *Re Atlantic Medical Ltd* [1993] BCLC 386.

Ltd[38] a bank enforced its floating charge after the commencement of the company's winding up and the liquidator argued that the payment of the proceeds of the realisation was invalid because of what is the equivalent of section 127 of the Insolvency Act 1986 which invalidates any disposition of a company's property after the commencement of winding-up. The argument failed for the very good reason that the disposition of the company's property took place when the charge was created[39] and not when the charge was enforced; the floating charge is an existing charge and not one arising in the future when the charge is enforced or when it crystallises.

The third point about the floating charge is that the courts have emphasised its flexibility. Its terms are those that are agreed upon by the parties and there is little judicial intervention with this process. As Nourse L.J. stated in *Re New Bullas Trading Ltd*[40]: "An equitable assignment, whether it takes effect as an out and out assignment or . . . by way of charge, is a creature of exceptional versatility, malleable to the intention of its creditors, adaptable to the subject matter assigned." The result of that case was, however, somewhat odd. The company had created a fixed charge over its book debts and a floating charge over their proceeds. The issue before the court was whether it was possible to split the fruit (the proceeds) from the tree (the book debts) in this way.[41] The Court of Appeal held that it was, but in the course of doing so it did not explain how the proceeds, which were simply the mirror of the book debts, could be detached so as to constitute a distinct subject matter for the purpose of granting security. In a subsequent case, Millett L.J. stated that while it was possible to split a capital asset from its income, it simply was not possible "to separate a debt or other receivable from the proceeds of its realisation".[42]

Vulnerability of the floating charge

The holder of a floating charge is not solely concerned with the rights which it provides against the company but equally importantly he is concerned with the priority it provides against other charge holders. As regards the latter aspect, the floating charge provides less than perfect security. Because of the management autonomy accorded to

---

[38] [1985] BCLC 314 (this was a decision of the Supreme Court of New South Wales but it is submitted that it reflects English law): see also *Re French's (Wine Bar) Ltd* [1987] BCLC 499; *Evans v. Rival Granite Quarries Ltd* [1910] 2 K.B. 979 at 999 ("A floating security is not a future security; it is a present security . . .").

[39] This is of course only determines the relationship between the company and the floating charge holder and does not provide an answer to the issue of priority as between charges.

[40] [1994] 1 BCLC 485 at 491. See Berg (1995) J.B.L. 433; Goode (1994) 110 L.Q.R. 492.

[41] This device is of considerable importance for the providers of venture capital. Since venture capitalists do not operate a retail banking service they cannot tie up the proceeds as can the High Street clearers.

[42] *Royal Trust Bank v. National Westminster Bank plc* [1996] 2 BCLC 682 at 704. This was strictly obiter as the parties conducted the case on the assumption that the charge was fixed. Millett L.J. refused to accept this assumption.

the company with respect to the charged assets, the company can create security interests that have priority to the floating charge[43]: a floating charge will be deferred to any subsequent fixed legal or equitable charge created by the company over its assets.[44] Similarly, if debts due to the company are subject to a floating charge, the interest of the floating charge holder will be subject to any lien or set off that the company creates with respect to the charged assets prior to crystallisation,[45] for a floating charge is not regarded for this purpose as an immediate assignment of the chose in action,[46] it becomes such only on crystallisation.[47] If a creditor has levied and completed execution[48] the debenture-holders cannot compel him to restore the money, nor, until the charge has crystallised, can he be restrained from levying execution.[49] The floating charge holder will take the company's property subject to the rights of anyone claiming by title paramount. However, once the floating charge crystallises,[50] this effects an assignment of the assets subject to the charge with the result that the assets are no longer those of the company.[51]

To firm up their security against subsequent security interests created by the company and which would otherwise have priority, floating charges almost invariably contain a provision that restricts the right of the company to create charges that have priority to or rank equally with the floating charge (called a negative pledge clause). Such restrictions, which are quite common but strictly construed,[52] limit the company's actual authority to deal with its assets and accordingly remove the basis on which floating charges are postponed to later charges. Nevertheless, it has been held that a floating charge may still be postponed to later mortgages, notwithstanding the limitation of the

[43] The charge holder runs the risk that the company may dissipate the assets subject to the charge, arguably the most serious risk that the charge holder faces.

[44] *Wheatley v. Silkstone and Haigh Moor Coal Co.* (1885) 29 Ch.D. 715. See also *Robson v. Smith* [1895] 2 Ch. 118 at 124 (any dealing with the property subject to a floating charge "will be binding on the debentureholders, provided that the dealing be completed before the debentures cease to be merely a floating security").

[45] Even though, if *George Barker (Transport) Ltd v. Eynon* [1974] 1 W.L.R. 462, C.A. is rightly decided, the lien or set off has not actually accrued.

[46] *Biggerstaff v. Rowatt's Wharf* [1896] 2 Ch. 93, C.A.; *Rother Iron Works Ltd v. Canterbury Precision Engineers Ltd* [1974] Q.B. 1, C.A.; *George Barker (Transport) Ltd v. Eynon* [1974] 1 W.L.R. 462, C.A.

[47] See *Cretanor Maritime Co. Ltd v. Irish Marine Management Ltd* [1978] 1 W.L.R. 966, C.A. where the company's assets were subject to an injunction, against their removal from the jurisdiction, obtained by an unsecured creditor. On the application of the holder of the debenture whose charge had crystallised the court discharged the injunction. See also *Capital Cameras Ltd v. Harold Lines Ltd* [1991] 1 W.L.R. 54 (successful application of a receiver to dismiss a *Mareva* injunction).

[48] Seizure alone does not suffice: *Norton v. Yates* [1906] 1 K.B. 112, C.A.

[49] *Evans v. Rival Granite Quarries* [1910] 2 K.B. 979, C.A.

[50] On crystallisation, see pp. 367 *et seq.*

[51] *Re ELS Ltd* [1994] 1 BCLC 743.

[52] *Brunton v. Electrical Engineering Corp.* [1892] 1 Ch. 434; *Robson v. Smith* [1895] 2 Ch. 118.

company's actual authority. If the later mortgage is legal, the mortgagee will obtain priority by virtue of his legal interest unless he has notice not only of the floating charge but also of the restriction in it.[53] If it is equitable, the chargee may be preferred on the ground that the company has been allowed to represent that it is free to deal with the assets in the normal course of business as though they were unencumbered. For example, if the title deeds are left with the company, an equitable mortgagee by deposit will take priority.[54]

Mere knowledge of the existence of a floating charge,[55] or of its registration at the Companies' Registry, is not sufficient to give notice of any restriction on the creation of other charges,[56] but it is normal practice for the debenture-holders (or their trustees) to ensure that the registered particulars include a note of the restriction. The efficacy of this practice has been questioned[57] on the ground that constructive notice cannot extend to matters beyond those which are required to be inserted in the registered particulars. What is needed is actual knowledge of the restriction before the priority of a subsequent charge holder is affected.[58] It is, in any event a wise precaution to deprive the company of the title deeds of its properties—this is another advantage of having trustees who can take charge of the deeds.

Most of the problems in this area would be resolved by a requirement that undertakings by a company not to create subsequent charges having priority to an existing charge be registered in the company's register of charges and this will constitute notice to any person who is taking a charge which also has to be registered. A reform to enable this to be done was introduced by the Companies Act 1989.[59] However, this reform in all probability will not be implemented.[60]

Some limit was placed on the company's power to create charges having priority to the floating charge by the decision of Sargant J.[61] that a company could not create a floating charge on the same assets ranking in priority to or *pari passu* with the original floating charge. This decision was subsequently approved by the Court of Appeal,[62] but limited to cases where the assets comprised in both charges are

---

[53] *English & Scottish Mercantile Investment Co. Ltd v. Brunton* [1892] 2 Q.B. 700, C.A.

[54] *Re Castell & Brown Ltd* [1898] 1 Ch. 315; *Re Valletort Sanitary Steam Laundry* [1903] 2 Ch. 654.

[55] cf. *Ian Chisholm Textiles Ltd v. Griffiths* [1994] 2 BCLC 291 at 303–304.

[56] *Wilson v. Kelland* [1910] 2 Ch. 306. cf. *Re Mechanisations (Eaglescliffe) Ltd.* [1966] Ch. 20 and *Re Eric Holmes (Property) Ltd* [1965] Ch. 1052. L.C.A. 1925, s.10(5), and L.P.A. 1925, s.198, do not appear to affect this.

[57] See Gough, *op. cit.*, Chap. 10.

[58] It is submitted that the dictum of Morritt J. that such restrictions do not affect priorities as a matter of property law is wrong: see *Griffiths v. Yorkshire Bank plc* [1964] 1 W.L.R. 1427 at 1435. See also *Ian Chisholm Textiles Ltd v. Griffiths* [1994] 2 BCLC 291 at 303–304.

[59] Section 103 inserting s.415(2)(a) into the Companies Act 1985.

[60] See p. 376.

[61] *Re Benjamin Cope & Co.* [1914] 1 Ch. 800.

[62] *Re Automatic Bottle Makers Ltd* [1926] Ch. 412, C.A.

the same, and it appears that a general floating charge on the whole of the undertaking may be postponed to a subsequent floating charge on a particular class of assets where the first charge contemplates the creation of the later charge.[63] In Scotland, however, where the same property (or any part of the same property) is subject to two floating charges they rank according to the time of registration unless the instruments creating the charges otherwise provide.[64] Also, where the company subsequent to granting a floating charge containing a negative pledge provision purchases property leaving part of the purchase secured by a mortgage, the mortgagee will take priority, even if the mortgage has actual notice so long as what the company acquired was the equity of redemption subject to the mortgage.[65]

Given the vulnerability of the floating charge the question arises as to why a creditor should bother to obtain one. While obviously the fixed charge accords superior protection, there are sound reasons for taking a floating charge. First, where a subsequent holder of a registrable charge is deemed to have notice of a negative pledge clause then this accords priority to the floating charge holder. Secondly, the charge provides security against unsecured creditors. Thirdly, the floating charge holder will be able to take steps to enforce the charge and, as will be seen, this accords him considerable control over the company's affairs. Fourthly, the holder of a floating charge will have some measure of control over the company even without taking any steps to enforce it.[66] Lastly, the holder of a floating charge will be able to block the appointment of an administrator.[67]

Crystallisation

Crystallisation is the term used to describe the process by which a floating charge is converted into a normal fixed charge. A crystallised charge will bite on all the assets covered by the charge since normally a floating charge does not provide for crystallisation over part only of

---

[63] *Re Automatic Bottle Makers Ltd, ibid.*, implies that this depends on the wording of the charge and of the express provision, if any, relating to the creation of further charges.

[64] s.464(3) and (4) of the 1985 Act (as amended by s.140 of the 1989 Act). But when the first chargee receives written notice of the registration of the later charge his priority is restricted to present advances and future advances which he is legally required to make plus interest and expenses: s.464(5).

[65] *Re Connolly Bros. Ltd (No. 2)* [1912] 2 Ch. 25, C.A.; *Abbey National Building Society v. Cann* [1991] 1 A.C. 56, H.L. This directly addresses the issue of priority but does not, however, deal with the separate issue of registration and hence voidness. It is submitted that there is a sufficient degree of involvement by the company so as to make the charge one "created" by it and thus void for non-registration if not registered within 21 days of its creation: see *Tatun (UK) Ltd v. Gorlex Telesure Ltd* (1989) 5 BCC 325 at 327, *et seq.*; *Stroud Architectural Systems Ltd v. John Laing Constructions Ltd* [1994] 2 BCLC 276.

[66] See p. 361.

[67] See Goode, *Legal Problems of Credit and Security* (2nd ed.), at p. 50 where these points are developed.

the assets to which it relates.[68] The effect of crystallisation is to deprive the company of the autonomy to deal with the assets subject to the charge in the normal course of business. The events of crystallisation, on which there is general agreement, are[69] (i) the making of a winding-up order,[70] (ii) the appointment of an administrative receiver,[71] (iii) the company's ceasing to carry on business,[72] (iv) the taking of possession by the debenture-holder[73] and (v) the happening of an event expressly provided for in the debenture, often referred to as "automatic crystallisation". Automatic crystallisation is not a term of art but covers at least two situations which at first blush appear dissimilar; one is where the charge is made to crystallise on the happening of an event provided for in the charge without there being any need for a further act by the chargee,[74] and the other is where the charge is made to crystallise on the serving of a notice of crystallisation on the company. However, these events have one important common feature and that is they will normally not be known to a person dealing with the company and therefore it seems appropriate to treat them together. Although there was some doubt as the validity of automatic crystallisation provisions, the matter seems to be settled beyond dispute by the judgment of Hoffmann J. in *Re Brightlife Ltd*[75] upholding the validity of a provision enabling the floating charge holder to serve a notice of crystallisation on the company. He saw crystallisation as being a matter of agreement between the parties and on this reasoning there can be no objection to a charge being made to crystallise on the happening of a specified event. In so far as insolvency law is committed to the principle that property within the apparent ownership of the company should be treated as the company's in the event of its insolvent liquidation,[76] permitting party autonomy to effect automatic crys-

---

[68] There is no reason why partial crystallisation should not be provided for by agreement. It is submitted that *Robson v. Smith* [1895] 2 Ch. 118 is not authority against this since the floating charge in that case did not confer any such right.

[69] See Goode, *Legal Problems of Credit and Security* (2nd ed.) at pp. 59–77.

[70] *Wallace v. Universal Automatic Machines* [1894] 2 Ch. 547, C.A.; *Re Victoria Steamboats Ltd* [1897] 1 Ch. 158. Even if the winding-up is for purposes of reconstruction: *Re Crompton & Co.* [1914] 1 Ch. 954. It is the making of the order and not, for example, the presentation of the petition since there is always the chance that the court will decline to make the winding-up order. In Scotland the charge crystallises on the commencement of the winding-up of the company: section 463 (as amended) of the 1985 Act.

[71] *Evans v. Rival Granite Quarries Ltd* [1910] 2. K.B. 979. The same applies to the appointment of a receiver by the court.

[72] *Re Woodroffes (Musical Instruments) Ltd* [1986] Ch. 366 (it is the cessation of business and not ceasing to be a going concern assuming the latter is different). Express provisions for crystallisation will only exclude this implied provision for crystallisation if they expressly do so: *Re The Real Meat Co. Ltd* [1996] BCC 254.

[73] *Evans v. Rival Granite Quarries Ltd* [1910] K.B. 979 at 997.

[74] The crystallising event could, for example, be the failure by the debtor to pay any moneys due or to insure the charged property.

[75] [1987] Ch. 200.

[76] English insolvency law is not wholeheartedly committed to this policy but to some extent it achieves it by requiring registration of non-possessory securities. It does not, however, require registration of title retention clauses and assets in possession of the company which are subject to a trust do not form part of the company's assets in a winding-up.

tallisation undermines this policy. It has been claimed that automatic crystallisation is unfair in the sense that it could prejudice subsequent chargees who do not know, and indeed who may have no way of knowing, that the charge has crystallised.[77] Whether this is indeed the case is not clear cut. As Professor Goode has pointed out, the fact that the charge has crystallised will affect the relationship between the chargee and the company but it does not necessarily affect a third party since if the company is left free to deal with the assets in the normal course of its business then the chargee should be estopped from denying the company's authority to do so.[78] Even if this argument is unsuccessful, it should be kept in mind that it is not all security interests which will be prejudiced by automatic crystallisation but only those lacking priority to a crystallised floating charge.[79]

Provision was made in the Companies Act 1989 to empower the Secretary of State to pass regulations to require the giving of notice to the Registrar of events which would crystallise a floating charge and such events of crystallisation were to be ineffective until such notice had been given.[80] Since the 1989 Act provisions on charges are most unlikely to be brought into effect,[81] this beneficial reform will not be implemented.

It is unclear as to whether the making of an administration order crystallises a floating charge. Arguably the appointment of an administrator for the more advantageous realisation of the company's assets than a winding up has this effect since this constitutes a virtual cessation of business. Although there is no authority on this, it is submitted that this is not the case since the provisions on administration (particularly the right of the floating charge holder to block the appointment of an administrator[82]) obviously envisage that crystallisation must arise from the act of the floating charge holder or the terms of the charge.[83] Also, it would frustrate an administration where an

---

[77] It is common when taking a fixed charge or purchasing an asset of the company to serve on it inquiries as to whether any floating charge has crystallised. This provides limited protection since the company can lie or, more likely, it may not appreciate that the charge has crystallised.

[78] Goode, *op. cit.*, at pp. 70–71; a similar point is made by Gough, *op. cit.*, at pp. 255–256. For this approach to work, the company must be treated as free to deal even though the chargee is ignorant that the charge has crystallised.

[79] The primary charges in this category are the subsequent equitable chargee, charge over chattels and execution creditors: see Gough, "The Floating Charge: Traditional Themes and New Directions" in Finn (ed.), *Equity and Commercial Relationships* (Sydney, 1977), p. 239 at p. 262.

[80] Companies Act 1989, s.102.

[81] See p. 376.

[82] See p. 367. Floating charges normally contain a provision enabling the chargee to appoint an administrative receiver if a petition for the appointment of an administrator is presented. See Insolvency Act 1986, Sched. 11, para. 1 which inserted such a clause in floating charges created before the Act came into effect.

[83] Where a charge has crystallised it is unclear if it can be decrystallised by the charge holder renewing the company's licence to deal: see Lightman and Moss, *The Law of Receivers of Companies* (2nd ed., London, 1994) at paras. 3.42–3.45. It is difficult to see why de-crystallisation should not be treated as the creation of a new charge since it consitutes an

administrator is appointed for the purpose set out in section 8(3)(a) of the 1986 Act.

There are certain events that do not cause crystallisation. Default in the payment of interest or capital are not crystallising events[84] although, given the validity of an automatic crystallising clause, there is no objection in principle to a charge by its terms being made to crystallise on the happening of a stipulated event of default. However, even though default may not result in crystallisation, the company will be in breach of contract and the chargee will have appropriate contractual remedies. In many situations the chargee may have a contractual remedy even though the charge has not crystallised; for example, the holder of an uncrystallised charge can always "intervene and obtain an injunction to prevent the company from dealing with its assets otherwise than in the ordinary course of its business".[85] The crystallisation of an earlier floating charge does not crystallise a subsequent floating charge since the subsequent chargee may pay off the earlier charge or agree to indemnify the company which continues to carry on business despite the crystallisation of the earlier charge with respect to any liability incurred towards the earlier chargee.[86]

Statutory limitations on the floating charge

There are certain statutory provisions that further add to the vulnerability of the floating charge. These provisions relate to (i) preferential creditors—which affects the priority of the charge; (ii) defective floating charges—which affects the validity of the charge; (iii) the right of an administrator to override a floating charge—which affects the enforcement rights of the charge; (iv) costs of the liquidation—which diminishes the assets available for the floating charge holders. It is proposed to deal with these matters seriatim.

(i) **Preferential creditors.** As a matter of policy, insolvency law has to determine (a) what constitutes insolvency proceedings, and (b) whether any particular class of creditors should be given protection in the insolvency of a company[87] and accorded a statutory preference

---

alteration of the nature of the chargee's proprietary interest. What is clear is that the reverse would appear not to be possible, namely, the subsequent creation of a fixed charge as a floater as otherwise this would enable the rights of the preferential creditors to be overridden.

[84] *Government Stock and Other Securities Investment Co. Ltd v. Manila Ry Co. Ltd* [1897] A.C. 81.

[85] *Re Woodroffes (Musical Instruments) Ltd* [1986] Ch. 366 at 378.

[86] *ibid.* It would follow from this that the crystallisation of a later floating charge would not crystallise an earlier one. It is important to note that crystallisation does not affect priorities: see Picarda, *The Law Relating to Receivers, Managers and Administrators* (2nd ed., London 1990) at pp. 36–39.

[87] The same policy decisions have to be made with respect to bankruptcy: see, *e.g.* Insolvency Act 1986, s.336 dealing with the matrimonial home.

over some or all of the company's creditors.[88] The relevance of this policy to the rights of floating charge holders is that the procedure for enforcement of a floating charge is to some extent treated as an insolvency proceeding.[89] Also, as already pointed out, debenture-holders with a floating charge closely resemble shareholders and form a class of those interested in the company rather than of those who merely have claims against it. Consequently, it has been thought unjust that they should obtain priority over employees (one of the categories of preferential creditor) who have priority to the shareholders in the event of the company's liquidation.[90] Hence it is provided that on winding up, a voluntary arrangement, or appointment of an administrative receiver under a floating charge,[91] preferential debts, which include certain payments to employees, will have priority over the claims of ordinary creditors and shall similarly have priority over any floating charge. The preferential debts of the employees are set out in Schedule 6 to the Insolvency Act 1986 and include four months' wages and accrued holiday remuneration.[92] In the case of a floating charge, the relevant date for quantifying the preferential debts is the date of the appointment of the receiver by the debenture-holders.[93] Anyone who has advanced money for the payment of the employee debts which would have been preferential is subrogated to the rights of the employee.[94] It is important to note that the preferential creditors are given priority where a receiver is appointed with respect to a charge "which, as created, was a floating charge"[95]; thus the fact that the charge has crystallised at the time a receiver is appointed does not result in preferential debts being denied their statutory priority.[96] The

---

[88] This of course constitutes a departure from the normal principle of insolvency law that the pre-insolvency entitlements of creditors should be respected in liquidation.

[89] *e.g.* the enforcement of the floating charge is dealt with in Part III of the Insolvency Act 1986; administrative receivers have to be qualified insolvency practitioners (s.230(2)); and s.247(1) defines insolvency as including the appointment of an administrative receiver.

[90] Another argument made in favour of employees is that they have no way of obtaining security for the payment of their salary which is normally made after the provision of the services. This is not strictly correct since money to pay employees could be placed in a trust account to be paid on the appropriate date. But this would be cumbersome and as a matter of practice does not happen.

[91] ss.40, 175, 386 of and Sched. 6 to the Insolvency Act 1986 and s.196 of the 1985 Act are the most relevant for the subordination of the floating charge.

[92] See paras. 9 and 10 of Sched. 6.

[93] s.387(4)(a) of the 1986 Act. For the date of the appointment see s.33 of the 1986 Act.

[94] Sched. 6, para. 11 to the 1985 Act. This enables the company to be kept going where it is in financial difficulties but there is some chance that it can trade out of its difficulties. For case law on the previous statutory provisions see *Re Primrose (Builders) Ltd* [1950] Ch. 561; *Re Rutherford (James R.) & Sons Ltd* [1964] 1 W.L.R. 1211; *Re Rampgill Mill Ltd* [1967] Ch. 1138.

[95] s.40(1) of the 1986 Act.

[96] Under the old law the crystallisation of the charge prior to the appointment of a receiver resulted in the preferential creditors being denied their priority: see *Re Brightlife Ltd* [1987] Ch. 200. This alteration of the old law has made an automatic crystallising clause less attractive.

Secretary of State for Employment is required to pay employees unpaid remuneration and other entitlements and entitled to recover this in priority to the debenture-holder.[97]

More controversially, the Crown for certain unpaid taxes and other levies is also accorded the status of preferential creditor. It is argued that these are debts owed to the community and as such should be accorded a preference. This was roundly rejected by the Cork Committee who considered that the wrong done to individual creditors could well outweigh any prejudice to the community in depriving the Crown of its preference.[98] As regards withholding taxes (*e.g.* VAT and PAYE), where the company acts as a tax collector rather than a taxpayer, the Cork Committee considered that the Crown should be given a preference as other creditors had no legitimate expectation of payment from this source. The Insolvency Act 1986 embodies these reforms and the Crown's preferred position is confined to taxes or social security contributions collected by the company for transmission to the Government.[99]

The provisions relating to the payment of preferential creditors creates a statutory duty and if a debenture-holder or a receiver realises assets he will be personally liable to the extent of these assets if preferential creditors are not paid.[1] Where the company can exercise the right of set-off against a preferential creditor who is also owed a non-preferential debt by the company, the set-off must be exercised against the debts rateably in proportion to the amounts of the preferential and non-preferential claims of the creditor.[2]

(ii) **Defective floating charges.** It has also been thought unjust to allow

---

[97] Employment Rights Act 1996, Part XII. Such payments include wages (but for a limited period), holiday pay and any basic award for compensation for unfair dismissal: see Employment Rights Act 1996, ss.182–190. The Secretary of State is subrogated to the employee's rights as a preferential creditor: section 189. For a case involving the predecessor legislation to the 1996 Act, see *Re Urethane Engineering Products Ltd* [1991] BCLC 48, C.A. This type of wage-earner protection fund enables the employee to be promptly paid and accords the administrative receiver or liquidator a certain freedom to realise the assets of the company: see *The Law Reform Commission of Australia* (Discussion Paper No. 32), Chap. 14; see generally Davis, *Acquired Rights, Creditors' Rights, Freedom of Contract, and Industrial Democracy* (1990) 9 Y.B.E.L. 21.

[98] Cork Committee Report, Chap. 32.

[99] See the 1986 Act, Sched. 6, paras. 1–8. Levies under the ECSC Treaty are also given a preference: see para. 6. Where the holder of a fixed and floating charge exercises his rights under s.101 of the L.P.A. 1925 any surplus must be paid to the liquidator: *Re G.L. Saunders Ltd* [1986] 1 W.L.R. 215. Had there been another floating charge holder in that case the outcome would have been different. For an erudite discussion of this issue see Picarda, *The Law Relating to Receivers, Managers and Administrators* (2nd edn) at pp. 253–256.

[1] *I.R.C. v. Goldblatt* [1972] Ch. 498. The receivers' duty to pay preferential creditors does not disappear merely because the debenture-holder has been paid: *Re Pearl Maintenance Services Ltd* [1995] 1 BCLC 449.

[2] *Re Unit 2 Windows Ltd* [1985] 1 W.L.R. 1383. If the company's assets are insufficient to meet the claims of the preferential creditors, such creditors rank equally and their claims must abate in equal proportions: s.175(2) of the 1986 Act.

an unsecured creditor to obtain priority to other creditors by obtaining a floating charge when he realises that solvent liquidation is imminent. The temptation and the opportunities to attempt to salvage something out of the wreck are particularly great in the case of the directors themselves. So long as assets remain available they will have caused the company to borrow on mortgage, but when the company's credit is exhausted they may attempt to keep the company afloat by themselves making unsecured loans to it. Finding that their efforts are doomed to failure, what is more natural than that they should cause the company to execute a floating charge in their favour to secure the loans so that if anything is left, after the claims of the prior chargees are satisfied, they take it rather than the unsecured creditors?[3] To prevent this, section 245 of the Insolvency Act 1986[4] provides that a floating charge created in favour of an unconnected person within 12 months[5] of the commencement of the winding up or the making of an administration order[6] shall be invalid (except to a prescribed extent) unless it is proved that the company was solvent immediately after the creation of the charge.[7] If these conditions are not satisfied the charge is valid only to the extent of any new value in the form of cash, goods or services supplied to the company,[8] or the discharge of any liability of the company, where these take place "at the same time as, or after, the creation of the charge".[9] It has been held that the phrase in quotations requires the new value to be provided contemporaneously with the creation of the charge.[10] Any delay, no matter how short, in the execution of the debenture after the advance has been made, will result in the new value falling outside section 245.[11] Hence those who take a floating charge from a company which cannot be proved to be solvent,[12] and which does not survive for a further year, cannot thereby obtain protection in respect to their existing debts, but only to the

---

[3] In some cases the company has been deliberately floated with the intention of defrauding creditors by granting floating charges to the promoters and then winding up, the charge attaching to goods which the company has purchased on credit: see Cohen Report, Cmd. 6659, para. 148.

[4] This applies to Scotland: s.245(1).

[5] The period was three months in the 1908 Act and six months in the 1929 Act: each was found to be inadequate in view of the ingenuity displayed in staving off liquidation.

[6] s.245(3)(*b*) and (5).

[7] The test of solvency is that laid down in s.123 of the 1986 Act: s.245(4).

[8] The value of the goods or services is their market value: s.245(6).

[9] s.245(2)(a) and (b).

[10] *Power v. Sharpe Investments Ltd* [1994] 1 BCLC 111.

[11] *ibid.*, at 123a–b. If the delay is *de minimis*, for example, a coffee-break, it can be ignored: *ibid.* The inconvenience of this can be avoided by the parties creating a present equitable right to security rather than a promise to create security in the future: see *Re Jackson & Bassford* [1906] 2 Ch. 467.

[12] There is nothing in the section to displace the normal rule that he who asserts must prove and thus the burden of proof would be on the liquidator or administrator. This should cause no great hardship as they will normally have sufficient information to found their action.

extent that they provide the company with new value[13] and thus potentially increase the assets available for other creditors. The directors, in the example given previously, cannot retrospectively convert themselves into secured creditors in respect of moneys which they have previously advanced without demanding security. Nor will it avail them to advance further money on a floating charge on the understanding that this is to be used to repay existing loans; a creditor cannot by use of the floating charge transmute an unsecured into a secured debt by attempting to manipulate the saving provisions of section 245.[14] It is important to note that not all value is "new value" for the purpose of section 245 as the latter is confined to money, goods or services and excluded are, for example, intellectual property rights and rights under a contract.[15]

Where the floating charge is in favour of a "connected person" it is easier for an administrator or liquidator to challenge the charge. The period within which the charge is vulnerable is two years after its creation[16] and there is no need to show that at the time the charge was created the company was insolvent. The definition of connected person is somewhat complex but it includes a director, the director's relatives and companies within a group.[17]

The statutory limitations in (i) (preferential creditors) and (ii) (defective floating charges) only apply to floating charges and not to fixed charges. The policy justification for this has been questioned. The Cork Committee considered that section 245 should not be extended to fixed charges since such a charge would relate to the company's existing assets whereas the floating charge could cover future assets.[18] Why this should make a critical difference is far from clear since a company can create a fixed charge of accounts receivable or a mortgage of future property. The exclusion of fixed charges from section 245 arguably reflects the favouritism shown to secured cred-

---

[13] For interesting illustrations of the way in which the rule in *Clayton's Case* ((1816) 1 Mer. 572) may protect a bank when the charge secures a current account, see *Re Thomas Mortimer Ltd* (1925) now reported at [1965] Ch. 186n; *Re Yeovil Glove Co. Ltd* [1965] Ch. 148, C.A. The Cork Committee recommended that *Re Yeovil Glove Co. Ltd* be reversed by statute (paras. 1561–1562) but why this should be so is far from clear since the bank by permitting the company to continue to draw on its overdrawn account is providing it with new value: see Goode (1983) 4 Co.L. 81.

[14] *Re Destone Fabrics Ltd* [1941] Ch. 319 (this would now be a transaction with a connected person, on which see below); *Re G.T. Whyte & Co. Ltd* [1983] BCLC 311. It is submitted that the transactions in these cases would not fall within s.245(2)(*b*) as there would be no discharge as a matter of substance of the debts at the time of the creation of the charge. Contrast *Re Mathew Ellis Ltd* [1933] Ch. 458, C.A. The test seems to be whether the company receives what is genuinely new value.

[15] See Goode, *Principles of Corporate Insolvency Law* at p. 181.

[16] s.245(3)(a).

[17] See ss.249 and 435 of the 1986 Act and p. 637, above.

[18] Cmnd. 8558 at paras. 1494 and 1553. The other reason given was that the extension of s.245 to fixed charges would compel creditors to seek repayment if fixed security could not be granted. This argument could also be applied to the restriction in s.245 to obtaining a floating charge.

itors in English company law, although to make a secured charge subject to the claims of preferential creditors would obviously affect both the terms of credit and the amount of credit available, and this may justify the present position. A fixed charge may of course be attacked as a preference where it is given to secure past value[19] but not as a transaction at an undervalue since the assets of the company are not diminished by the creation of the charge.[20] Both these statutory limitations may affect companies other than those registered under the Act if, but only if, they are being wound up under it.[21]

(iii) Powers of administrator. The third statutory limitation on the right of a floating charge holder is section 15 of the Insolvency Act 1986 which empowers an administrator to sell property subject to a charge which as created was a floating charge without the need to obtain a court order.[22] As protection, the floating charge holder is given the same priority with respect to any property representing directly or indirectly the property disposed of as he would have had with respect to the property subject to the floating charge.[23] However, this quali-fication of the floating charge holder's rights does not constitute a serious erosion of the rights of the floating charge holder since he can block the making of an administration order by appointing an administrative receiver.[24]

(iv) Costs of liquidation. The last statutory limitation on the rights of the floating charge relates to costs of the liquidation. It is a principle of insolvency law that the expenses of a company's liquidation are payable out of the assets[25] of the company in priority to all other claims.[26] And since these costs can be substantial, it is important to determine what constitutes the company's assets out of which such

---

[19] For preferences, see p. 844. The principal difference between preferences and defective float-ing charges is that the time within which a preference in favour of an unconnected person can be challenged is six months. Also, a preference can involve a diminution of the company's assets whereas a floating charge constitutes a claim on them.

[20] *Re M.C. Bacon Ltd* [1990] BCLC 324.

[21] *i.e.* a floating chargee who appoints a receiver of a statutory or chartered company will not be subject to the claims of preferential creditors unless the company goes into compulsory liquidation under Part V of the 1986 Act.

[22] s.15(1) and (3).

[23] Where the charge has crystallised, the priority will be that of a fixed equitable charge.

[24] s.9(3) of the 1986 Act; *Re Croftbell Ltd* [1990] BCLC 844.

[25] The assets must, however, be the assets of the company and not, for example, assets held on trust. In certain limited circumstances the court can order liquidation expenses to be paid out of assets the beneficial interest in which is not vested in the company: *Re Berkeley Applegate (Investment Consultants) Ltd* [1989] BCLC 28.

[26] For voluntary winding up see section 115 of the 1986 Act; this section has been held to be a priority section and does not deal with the question of what constitute properly incurred expenses in a liquidation: see *Re M.C. Bacon Ltd* [1991] Ch. 127. The position as regards court-ordered winding up is not so explicit but a combination of section 156 and Insolvency Rules 1986, rr. 4.218 and 4.220 produces this effect.

costs can be paid. In *Re Portbase Clothing Ltd*[27] the court held that assets subject to a charge which as created was a floating charge constituted assets of the company for the purpose of paying the costs of the liquidation.[28] These costs, combined with the claims of the preferential creditors, entail a substantial erosion of the entitlement of the floating charge holder.[29]

Registration of charges

Introduction. Part XII of the Companies Act 1985 contains provisions requiring a company to register certain charges with the Registrar of Companies. This requirement has been a feature of the Companies Acts since 1990.[30] The Companies Act 1989 contains a new Part XII which was to replace the existing Part XII in the 1985 Act. This has not been brought into effect and probably will not be.[31] Accordingly, the references to the registration provisions are to those in the 1985 Act and not those in the reforms introduced by the 1989 Act.

Registration of charges fulfils a range of purposes. It provides a picture of the state of the incumbrances on a company's property, something which is obviously of interest to those contemplating entering into a secured lending transaction with the company. Registration is also of interest to credit analysts, liquidators, receivers, shareholders and prospective investors. In addition, registration operates to protect the security-holder by providing him with a certain degree of protection as to the validity and priority of his charge once it is registered; this in turn benefits the company by enabling it to give the chargee the guarantee of such protection.[32] Also, if registration creates, at the minimum, a presumption that the charge has been validly registered, this facilitates the chargee assigning the charge either outright or by way of security. It is to be doubted if unsecured trade creditors have much, if any, interest in the state of encumbrances on a company's property as they normally will only be interested in whether the company can pay its debts as they fall due. Also, the position of an unsecured creditor who extends credit can be weakened by the subsequent granting of security by the company.

---

[27] [1993] Ch. 388 at 407–409.

[28] This was because of the definition of floating charge in section 251 of the Insolvency Act 1986.

[29] Attempts to extend the *Portbase* principle decision have not been successful. In *Re M.C. Bacon Ltd* [1991] Ch. 127 the court held that the costs of the liquidator in bringing an action under s.214 of the 1986 Act and to challenge a transaction as a preference were not costs of realising the company's assets and thus did not enjoy the priority accorded to such expenses in a winding-up. See also, s.19(4) and (5) of The 1986 Act.

[30] First introduced by the Companies Act 1900, s.14.

[31] See *Company Law Review: Proposals for Reform of Part XII of the Companies Act 1985* (DTI, A Consultative Document, Nov. 1994).

[32] See Diamond, *A Review of Security Interests in Property* (DTI, 1989), Chap. 21.

The mechanics of registration. It is the duty of the company to submit particulars of a charge requiring registration to the Registrar[33] who, in turn, is under a statutory obligation to maintain a register setting out certain prescribed particulars.[34] The register of charges is open for public inspection and any person for a fee is entitled to a certified copy of it.[35]

What has to be registered. Section 396, which sets out the charges that have to be registered, enumerates a list of registrable charges and any charge not on the list does not have to be registered. It would equally be possible to require the registration of all charges (with perhaps some specified exceptions) but this approach, while guaranteeing comprehensiveness, is not free from difficulties. It is not possible to predict the types of security interests that will be created in the future, and requiring registration of some such unforeseen interests could be unnecessarily burdensome; even with respect to the known types of legal charge, particularly those conferring the right to possession, it would produce overkill. And lastly it is claimed that to require the registration of all charges could dry up certain types of secured borrowing.[36] Also, at the end of the day there may not be a great deal of difference between a system which requires all charges subject to exceptions to be registered as opposed to the present one which requires specified charges to be registered.

Part XII does not contain a generic definition of what constitutes a charge. Charge probably covers any type of security interest. As was pointed out earlier, there is some uncertainty as to what constitutes a security interest; it is submitted that the courts will adopt something along the lines of the definition of Sir Nicolas Browne-Wilkinson V.-C. set out at the commencement of this Chapter.[37] The uncertainties caused by what constitutes a security interest are greatly reduced by the fact, as pointed out above, that it is a *numerus clausus* of charges that has to be registered so if a charge is not within the list it is not registrable. Most of the major types of charge have to be registered and these on any definition are clearly security interests. Thus a charge

---

[33] s.399; the normal practice is for the chargee's solicitors to register the charge and s.399(1) provides that any person interested in the charge may register it. This, of course, must mean legal interest.

[34] s.401.

[35] s.401(3). See also s.709.

[36] See Jenkins Committee at para. 301; Diamond Report, *op. cit.*, at para. 21.3.6. This could happen if the security interest is transient and thus the need to register it could curtail its usefulness.

[37] See p. 358. *Quaere* would the court in this context find, as did the court of the purpose of s.11(3) (c) of the 1986 Act, that the right of re-entry for non-payment of rent constituted the enforcement of security: *Exchange Travel Agency Ltd v. Triton Property plc* [1991] BCLC 396. It is submitted that it probably will not, as security has to be given a purposive interpretation for the purpose of section 11(3)(c) and a right of re-entry does not as such vest any interest in the company's property in the lessor.

on land,[38] a charge which if created by a person would need registration as a bill of sale,[39] a floating charge on the company's undertaking or property[40] and a charge on goodwill or intellectual property,[41] all have to be registered. Registration is also required of any property acquired by a company which is subject to a charge of a class requiring registration.[42]

What need not be registered. There are a range of charges that do not need to be registered. Charges arising by operation of law (to be contrasted with those created by the company) fall into this category.[43] A deposit of a negotiable instrument by way of security to secure payment of a book debt does not have to be registered.[44] Also not included in the list of registrable charge are fixed charges on bank accounts[45] and, more importantly, fixed charges on shares held in a subsidiary. As to the latter, the Jenkins and Diamond Reports took diametrically opposed positions. Diamond came out against such registration on the grounds, *inter alia*, that it could mislead in circumstances where shares subject to a fixed charge are held in a company which becomes a subsidiary after the charge has been created.[46] This is an undoubted problem, but to use it to preclude registration of a charge of shares in a subsidiary is to make the best the enemy of the better. Lastly, it must always be kept in mind that there will be no need to register financing devices which the law of personal property does not treat as charges; for example, title retention clauses provided of course they are not, as a matter of legal form, charges.[47]

The question remains as to whether the register of charges maintained by the Registrar of Companies accurately reflects the extent of the incumbrances on a company's property. Although not exhaustively comprehensive, it does give a reasonably accurate picture and its most serious defects arise not from the register as such but because English law lacks a satisfactory system for classifying personal property security interests. Also, at the end of the day it is arguable that all the register needs to show are the principal charges over the company's property since anyone dealing with the company can seek to find out the full extent to which the company's property has been charged once

---

[38] s.396(1)(d) (excluded is a charge for rent or for the payment of some other periodical sum).
[39] s.396(1)(c).
[40] s.396(1)(f).
[41] s.396(1)(j).
[42] s.400.
[43] *London and Cheshire Ins. Co. Ltd v. Laplagrene Property Co. Ltd* [1971] Ch. 499.
[44] s.396(2). The reason for this is that it would destroy the negotiability of the instrument.
[45] A deposit at the bank is normally not be a book debt, although not necessarily in all situations: see *Re Permanent Houses (Holdings) Ltd* [1988] BCLC 583; *Northern Bank Ltd v. Ross* [1991] BCLC 401, C.A. (N.I.).
[46] Diamond report, *op. cit.*, at para. 23.8.
[47] See McCormack, *Reservation of Title* (2nd ed.), Chap. 6.

put on notice that *some* charges have been created. There is always the chance that the company will not give honest answers, but the extent to which debtor dishonesty is a danger should not be exaggerated.

Effect of (i) non-registration (ii) late registration and (iii) defective registration

(i) **Non-registration.** Failure to comply with the various registration requirements leads, as one would expect, to liability to fines.[48] But the most potent sanction is that non-registration in the register maintained by the Registrar of charges created by the company (as opposed to existing charges on property acquired by the company) destroys the validity of the charge.[49] Unless the prescribed particulars of the charge are delivered to the Registrar within 21 days of the creation of the charge, it will be void against the administrator, liquidator[50] or any creditor of the company.[51] The sufferer is, of course, the chargee, not the company; hence the provision previously mentioned allowing any person having an interest in the charge to register it. If, however, the company or the chargee fails to do so[52] the consequences are grave indeed for the chargee; in effect, he loses his security. To reduce this hardship, the Act provides that if the charge is void to any extent for non-registration the whole of the sum thereby secured becomes immediately repayable on demand.[53] This, of course, also provides the company with an incentive to register.

It is important to note that a void charge still remains valid against the company and there is no reason why the chargee should not take steps to enforce it.[54] An unsecured creditor has no standing to prevent the holder of a void charge from enforcing it[55] but, somewhat anomalously, such a creditor gets protection against an unregistered charge if the company goes into liquidation or administration. Since an administrator and liquidator (particularly the latter) are more or less statutory

---

[48] s.399(3).

[49] More accurately, it is the failure to deliver particulars of the charge to the Registrar that results in the charge being rendered void but this will be referred to as non-registration. Non-registration in the company's own register has no such sanction.

[50] s.395(1).

[51] For this purposes, creditor means secured creditor: *Re Teleomatic Ltd* [1994] 1 BCLC 90 at 95. Of course, if the company goes into liquidation or administration the charge is unenforceable and this *pro tanto* protects the interests of the unsecured creditors: see *R. v. Registrar of Companies, ex p. Central Bank of India* [1986] Q.B. 1114 at 1161–1162.

[52] This happens surprisingly often; *e.g.* because of failure to realise that the charge is of the registrable class, or because both the company and the lender assume that the other will register.

[53] s.395(2).

[54] If he does so then the charge is spent and there is no way in which a liquidator or administrator could retrospectively challenge the enforcement of the charge.

[55] *Re Ehrmann Bros. Ltd* [1906] 2 Ch. 697, C.A.

trustees for unsecured creditors, it could be argued that there is nothing anomalous about this. This, however, begs the question of what are the "trust" assets. The justification for this is probably that it provides the chargee with an additional incentive to ensure that his charge is registered.

(ii) Late registration. Section 404 enables the holder of a registrable charge which has not been registered within 21 days from its creation to apply to the court for an order extending the period for the registration of the charge. The jurisdiction of the court is very wide[56] but normally the court will not make an order under section 404 once a winding up has commenced.[57] The reason for this is that winding up is a procedure for the benefit of unsecured creditors and the registering of a charge after the commencement of winding-up would defeat their interests. The court may also refuse to exercise its descretion to order an extension of time where the company is insolvent.[58] Normally, the charge will be registered on terms that it is not to prejudice the rights of parties acquired between the date of the creation of the charge and its registration.[59]

(iii) Defective registration. It may be that the prescribed particulars as registered are defective. They may, for example, fail to state accurately the property subject to the charge or the amount secured by the charge.[60] Where a charge is registered, the Registrar has to issue a certificate of registration and this is made conclusive evidence that the requirements of the 1985 Act have been complied with.[61] Hence the charge is effective even though the registered particulars are inaccurate.[62] In English law,[63] there are no provisions for registering changes in the registered particulars except where the whole or part of the

---

[56] However, the chargee, once the failure to register is discovered, must act expeditiously and the court will not exercise its discretion favourably where the chargee hangs back to see which way the wind blows: *Re Teleomatic Ltd* [1994] 1 BCLC 30.

[57] *Re S. Abrahams and Sons* [1902] 1 Ch. 695. However, in exceptional circumstances the court may make an order even though winding-up has commenced: *Re R.M. Arnold & Co. Ltd* [1984] BCLC 535.

[58] See *Re Ashpurton Estates Ltd* [1983] Ch. 110.

[59] See *Gore-Browne on Companies* at para. 18–026.

[60] See generally, Prentice, *Defectively Registered Charges* (1970) 34 Conv. (N.S.) 410.

[61] s.404(3). In the case of English companies a copy of the certificate has to be endorsed on any debenture. The Jenkins Committee recommended that this burdensome requirement be abolished: Cmnd. 1749, para. 303.

[62] *National Provincial and Union Bank v. Charnley* [1924] 1 K.B. 431, C.A. (where property charged incorrectly stated); *Re Mechanisations (Eaglescliffe) Ltd* [1966] Ch. 20 (amount secured misstated); *Re Eric Holmes (Property) Ltd* [1965] Ch. 1052; *Re C.L. Nye Ltd* [1971] Ch. 442 (date of creation misstated).

[63] In Scotland, there needs to be registered an instrument of alteration which prohibits or restricts the creation of any fixed seciurty or other floating charge having priority over, or ranking *pari passu* with an existing floating charge, or varies or regulates the ranking of the charge in relation to other securities or charges: s.466(4) (For the proposed repeal, see 1989 Act, s.140.).

secured debt has been paid or part of the property released,[64] and even in that case there is no legal obligation to apply for registration. Accordingly, if the charge is capable of covering further advances it will validly cover such advances whether or not they are mentioned in the registered particulars,[65] and there is no means of registering particulars of those further advances when made.[66] At the best, a searcher will know only that further advances may have been made which will be covered by the security, and will not know even that if the registered particulars omitted to mention them. Similarly if there is a charge to a bank to secure "all sums due or to become due" the searcher will not be able to tell from the register how much is actually secured.

Also, a defect which is caused by the Registrar's officials (happily a rare event) will not affect the validity of a charge. This is because (as we have seen)[67] registered particulars means the particulars delivered for registration and where these are accurate the chargee will not be prejudiced by any defects arising from transcribing the submitted particulars on to the register.[68]

Effect of registration

Registration does not cure any flaw in the charge itself as between the parties so that the validity of the charge remains challengeable by the company. In addition, registration does not create a priority point in the sense that the chargee is guaranteed priority from the date of registration; this is because if A registers a charge on January 21 he has no guarantee that the company has not created a charge prior to this which may be registered within 21 days and thus have priority. Registration does, however, have considerable importance:

(i) first, while registration may not be a priority point, failure to register, as we have seen, renders the charge void and therefore registration is a necessary, although not sufficient, condition to obtain priority;

(ii) as we have already seen, the Registrar is obliged to issue a

---

[64] s.403.

[65] *Re Mechanisations (Eaglescliffe) Ltd* [1966] Ch. 20.

[66] *Archibald Campbell, Hope & King Ltd* 1967 S.C. 21; but for the position in Scotland, see s.414 of the 1985 Act. If, however, further property is charged, even if it is to secure the same debt, there will be a new charge which, if of a registrable class, can and must be registered: *Cornbrook v. Law Debenture Corp.* [1904] 1 Ch. 103, C.A. But *Cunard SS. Co. v. Hopwood* [1908] 2 Ch. 564 appears to establish that this does not apply if other property is substituted under provisions in a trust deed particulars of which have been registered under s.397 or s.466(4): *sed quaere.*

[67] See p. 379, n. 49.

[68] Whether the Registrar would be liable to anyone suffering damages must be open to doubt despite *Ministry of Housing and Local Government v. Sharp* [1970] 2 Q.B. 223: see *Davis v. Radcliffe* [1990] 1 W.L.R. 821, H.L. and the cases cited therein; *Banque Keyser Ullmann S.A. v. Skandia (U.K.) Insurance Co. Ltd* [1990] 1 Q.B. 665 at 796–798 (on appeal [1991] 2 A.C. 449).

certificate of registration which is conclusive that there has been compliance with the registration of charges provisions.[69] This provides assurance to transferees of the security that the validity of its registration cannot be challenged.

(iii) thirdly, and perhaps most importantly, any person taking a registrable charge over the company's property (and only such persons) will have notice of any matter requiring registration and disclosed.[70] To take an example, a person taking a charge on a bank account (assuming it is not a book debt) is not affected by the register since this is not a registrable charge but a person taking a floating charge would be.

Enforcement of debentures: receivers

The methods of enforcing a security interest depend upon the nature of the rights which it confers and are often in no way peculiar to company law. However, company law does provide a distinct procedure for the enforcement of a floating charge by the appointment of an administrative receiver. Almost invariably the first step in the enforcement of a charge is for the debenture-holders or their trustee to obtain the appointment of a receiver.[71] This appointment will normally be made by the debenture-holder under an express or implied[72] power in the debenture, or by the court. Where the appointment is pursuant to a provision in the debenture then it must be clear that the conditions justifying the appointment have arisen, otherwise the receiver will be a trespasser and also liable for conversion.[73] Once the conditions for the enforcement of a charge have arisen English law places few constraints on the right of the security holder to enforce his charge and in this respect it is pro-security holder. Thus if the chargee is entitled to payment on demand he is not required to give the company a reasonable time in which to raise the funds to make payment and is only required to give the company time in which to put into effect the mechanics of payment.[74] However, if the debtor company makes it

---

[69] See p. 380.

[70] s.401

[71] If the state of the company is so parlous that it is doubtful whether there will be enough to cover the receiver's remuneration it may be necessary for the trustees to take possession. If the "debenture" is just an ordinary mortgage of particular property the debenture-holder may, of course, exercise his power of sale without the preliminary step of appointing a receiver.

[72] *i.e.* under the L.P.A. 1925, s. 101 when applicable.

[73] Where the appointment is defective the court can order the person making the appointment to indemnify the receiver: s.34 of the 1986 Act. See also s.232 which deals with the validity of acts of a defectively appointed administrative receiver and s.234 dealing with the seizure or disposal of property by an administrative receiver which does not belong to the company and generally *Re London Iron and Steel Co. Ltd* [1990] BCLC 372; *Welsh Development Agency v. Export Finance Co. Ltd* [1992] BCLC 148.

[74] *Bank of Baroda v. Panessar* [1987] Ch. 335; this is normally a matter of hours during normal banking hours. In addition the company may be estopped by its conduct from challenging the validity of the appointment of a receiver, and the appointment of a receiver on invalid grounds may be subsequently cured if grounds justifying the appointment are subsequently discovered:

clear that the required funds to pay its debts are not available, this constitutes a sufficient act of default and there is no need to allow the debtor any time before treating it as being in default.[75] In addition, the chargee is not obliged to refrain from exercising his rights merely because by doing so he could avoid loss to the company,[76] nor does failure to exercise them when the security is declining in value constitute a breach of any duty that he may owe to the company.[77] If nothing has occurred to render the security enforceable but the debenture-holder's position is, nevertheless, in jeopardy, an application to the court may be necessary, for the court has a discretionary power to appoint a receiver in such circumstances.[78] The normal procedure is for one of the debenture-holders, on behalf of himself and all other holders to commence a debenture-holder's action, the first step of which will be the appointment of a receiver. "Jeopardy" will be established when, for example, execution is about to be levied against the company,[79] or when it proposes to distribute to its members its one remaining asset.[80] It would be tempting to say that, when there is a floating charge, "jeopardy" should be assumed whenever the circumstances make it unreasonable, in the interests of the debenture-holder, that the company should retain power to dispose of the property subject to the charge. This is in fact the statutory definition under Scottish law,[81] but the English decisions hardly go so far, for the fact that the assets on realisation would not repay the debentures in full has been held insufficient.[82]

In cases where appointment out of court is possible this is certainly preferable from the viewpoint of the debenture-holders as a body. The procedure in a debenture-holders' action is lamentably expensive and dilatory, since the receiver, as an officer of the court, will have to work under its closest supervision and constant applications will have

---

Bank of Baroda at 352–353 and *Byblos Bank SAL v. Al-Khudairy* [1987] BCLC 232 respectively. There is no need for the debenture-holder to specify the exact sum due in any demand: see *NRG Vision Ltd v. Churchfield Leasing Ltd* [1988] BCLC 624.

[75] *Sheppard & Cooper Ltd v. TSB Bank plc* [1996] 2 All E.R. 654.

[76] *Re Potters Oils Ltd* [1986] 1 W.L.R. 201; *Standard Chartered Bank Ltd v. Walker* [1982] 1 W.L.R. 1410.

[77] *China and South Sea Bank Ltd v. Tan* [1990] 1 A.C. 536, P.C.; of course it will always be in the commercial interests of the chargee to exercise his rights if the security is declining in value. On other aspects of the receiver's duties to the company and others, see p. 386.

[78] But the court will not normally have any power to appoint a receiver unless the debentures are secured by a charge: *Harris v. Beauchamp Bros.* [1894] 1 Q.B. 801, C.A.; *Re Swallow Footwear Ltd, The Times*, October 23, 1956. Also the court will not imply a term into a debenture empowering a chargee to appoint a receiver where his security is in jeopardy: see *Cryne v. Barclays Bank plc* [1987] BCLC 548, C.A.

[79] *McMahon v. North Kent Co.* [1891] 2 Ch. 148; *Edwards v. Standard Rolling Stock* [1893] 1 Ch. 574; and see *Re Victoria Steamboats Co.* [1897] 1 Ch. 158.

[80] *Re Tilt Cove Copper Co.* [1913] 2 Ch. 588.

[81] s.52(2) (for the purpose of appointing a receiver), s.122(2) (for the purpose of making a winding-up order) of the 1986 Act.

[82] *Re New York Taxicab Co.* [1913] 1 Ch. 1.

to be made in chambers throughout the duration of the receivership, which may last years if a complicated realisation is involved. Since the 1986 Act allows a receiver, even though appointed out of court, to obtain the court's directions,[83] it is difficult to envisage circumstances in which an application to the court can be justified if the cheaper alternative is available, and the professional adviser who recommended it would be laying himself open to grave risk of criticism. In the discussion which follows, it will be assumed that what is being referred to is a receiver appointed out of court. A receiver appointed out of court can be either a receiver or an administrative receiver, the difference between them being that the latter is a receiver appointed under a charge which as created was a floating charge.[84]

Function and status of receiver and administrative receiver

Part III of the 1986 Act regulates both types of receiverships, although the provisions applicable to them are not identical. As the administrative receiver is unique to company law (and is probably the most common type of receiver appointed with respect to companies) it is proposed to concentrate on this type of receiver. The 1986 Act views the appointment of an administrative receiver as being in some respects similar to insolvency proceedings and regulates it accordingly[85]. Thus administrative receivers must be qualified to act as insolvency practitioners[86] and can only be removed from office by the court.[87] Also, like the liquidator, the administrative receiver can compel those involved in the affairs of the company to provide him with information relating to the company's affairs[88] and is also obliged to report to the Secretary of State if he forms the opinion that the conduct of a director makes him unfit to act as a director of a company.[89] However, the appointment of a receiver must not be equated with that of a liquidator: (i) where a receiver is appointed the company need not go into liquidation[90] and if it does the same person who acted as receiver will normally not be appointed liquidator; (ii) liquidation is a class action designed to protect the interests of the unsecured

---

[83] s.35.

[84] s.29(2) and s.251 of the 1986 Act. The floating charge (along with any other securities) must be over the whole, or substantially the whole, of the company's assets. As to whether there can be more than one administrative receiver (other than joint appointments) see Oditah, "Lightweight Floating Charges" [1991] J.B.L. 49.

[85] See s.247(1) for the definition of "insolvency".

[86] s.388(1) of the 1986 Act. A body corporate, an undischarged bankrupt, or a person disqualified to act as a director may not act as an insolvency practitioner: see s.390(1) and (4). For other receivers see ss.30 and 31.

[87] s.45(1) of the 1986 Act; they can resign, *ibid.*

[88] ss.47 and 236; *Re Aveling Barford Ltd* [1989] 1 W.L.R. 360; *Cloverbay Ltd (Joint Administrators) v. BCCI S.A.* [1991] Ch. 90.

[89] Companies Directors Disqualification Act 1986, s.7(3)(d).

[90] See Insolvency Act 1986, s.247(2). Although generally a receiver should not be seen as a doctor but rather as an undertaker.

creditors whereas, as we shall see, receivership is designed to protect the interests of the security-holders who appointed the receiver and it is for this reason that a receiver can be appointed even where the company is in liquidation[91]; (iii) liquidation terminates the trading power of the company[92] whereas this is not the case with receivership; (iv) a liquidator has power to disclaim onerous property,[93] something not possible in the case of receivership; (v) a liquidator in a compulsory winding up is an officer of the court[94] whereas this is not the case with a receiver unless appointed by the court[95]; (vi) lastly, it is easier to obtain recognition of liquidation as opposed to receivership in proceedings in foreign courts.[96] These are the most important differences but there are others particularly with respect to liability on contracts.[97]

An administrative receiver might be considered to be the agent of those who appointed him but this is not the case; section 44 of the 1986 Act makes him the agent of the company.[98] The reason for this is to avoid those who appointed the administrative receiver being treated as mortgagees in possession[99] or being held liable for the receiver's acts which would be the case were the receiver to be treated as their agent.[1] As many have pointed out, the receiver's agency is a peculiar form of agency. This is because the primary responsibility of the receiver is to protect the interests of the security holders and to realise the charged assets for their benefit.[2]

The powers of the administrative receiver are extensive and he will have complete control over the assets subject to the change under which he was appointed.[3] In addition he can apply to the court for an

---

[91] *Re Potters Oils Ltd* [1986] 1 W.L.R. 201.

[92] Also without the leave of the court legal proceedings cannot be brought against the company: see s.130 of the 1986 Act.

[93] See s.178 of the 1986 Act.

[94] *Parsons v. Sovereign Bank of Canada* [1913] A.C. 160.

[95] It is contempt of court to interfere with the exercise of power by a court-appointed receiver without the leave of the court.

[96] s.72 of the 1986 Act permits an English or Scottish receiver to act throughout Great Britain provided local law permits this.

[97] See pp. 387 *et seq.*

[98] Also the debenture will invariably provide that irrespective of the type of receiver appointed by the charge holder he is to be the agent of the company. A receiver appointed by the court is not an agent of anyone but an officer of the court: see *Moss SS. Co. v. Whinney* [1912] A.C. 254, H.L.

[99] The duties of a mortgage in possession are onerous: see Megarry and Wade, *The Law of Real Property* (5th ed.) at pp. 942–943.

[1] If the chargee interferes with the receiver's discharge of his duties this could, provided the interference is sufficiently pervasive, result in the receiver being treated as the agent of the chargee: see *American Express International Banking Corp. v. Hurley* [1985] 3 All E.R. 564.

[2] The receiver would not, for example, be considered to be participating in the management of the company since he is not managing the company but the assets of the company: *Re B. Johnson & Co. (Builders) Ltd* [1955] Ch. 634; *Re North Development Pty Ltd* (1990) 8 ACLC 1004. *cf. Leyland DAF* case, p. 386, n. 12, below.

[3] s.42 of the 1986 Act confers on an administrative receiver the powers set out in Schedule 1 to the Act in so far as they are not inconsistent with the terms of the debenture. There are 23 powers enumerated and they are very wide; for example, number 14 confers on an

order empowering him to dispose of property subject to a prior charge.[4] In the exercise of his powers a receiver is under a duty to the debtor company to take reasonable care to obtain the best price reasonably possible at the time of sale[5]; this duty is also owed to a guarantor of the company's debts.[6] However, as the receiver in exercising his power of sale is in a position analogous to that of the mortgagee, he is not obliged to postpone sale in order to obtain a better price or to adopt a piecemeal method of sale.[7] The basis of the receiver's duty set out above was initially considered to involve the extension of the common law of negligence to supplement equity,[8] but the courts now treat it as something which flows from the nature in equity of the relationship between the mortgagee and mortgagor.[9] In *Downsview Nominees Ltd v. First City Corp.*[10] the Privy Council (dealing with a receiver) held that the law of negligence did not apply to the receiver. However, the extent to which this case goes in relieving any type of receiver from damage caused by his negligence is far from clear. It is difficult to imagine, for example, that a receiver who failed to give notice with respect to a rent review clause in a lease, the subject matter of the security, would not be liable in negligence.[11] It has been held that a receiver could be liable for fraudulent trading.[12] However, given that the receiver stands in the right of the security-holder, it is difficult to see how he would be liable for fraudulent trading when realising the assets subject to the charge. This he has both the right and the duty to do.

A person dealing with an administrative receiver in good faith is not bound to inquire if the receiver is acting within his powers.[13] Unlike a winding up,[14] the board of directors does not become *functus officio*

---

administrative receiver "Power to carry on the business of the company". An ordinary receiver does not have such powers but normally they will be conferred on him by appointing him as a manager.

[4] s.43 of the 1986 Act. The rights of the security holder are protected in the same way as they are under section 15: see p. 375.

[5] *Cuckmere Brick Co. Ltd v. Mutual Finance Ltd* [1971] Ch. 949; *Bishop v. Bonham* [1988] 1 W.L.R. 742.

[6] *Standard Chartered Bank Ltd v. Walker* [1982] 1 W.L.R. 1410; *American Express International Banking Corp. v. Hurley* [1985] 3 All E.R. 564.

[7] *Tse Kwong Lam v. Wong Chit Sen* [1983] 1 W.L.R. 1349.

[8] See Lightman and Moss, *op. cit.*, Chap. 7.

[9] *Parker-Tweedale v. Dunbar Bank plc* [1991] Ch. 12, C.A. (mortgagee owes no duty to beneficiary of mortgaged property); *Downsview Nominees Ltd v. First City Corp.* [1993] A.C. 295.

[10] [1993] A.C. 295; Lightman and Moss, *The Law of Receivers of Companies* (2nd ed.), at pp. 112–118.

[11] See, *e.g. Knight v. Lawrence* (1991) BCC 411 (decided before *Downsview*). See also *Bristol & West Building Society v. Mothew* [1996] 4 All E.R. 638 at 711.

[12] *Re Leyland DAF Ltd (No. 2)* [1994] 2 BCLC 760 at 771–772 (*i.e.* liability under section 213 of the 1986 Act).

[13] s.42(3). If an administrative receiver is seen as being an organ of the company, then this provision is arguably not in compliance with Article 9(2) of the First Directive.

[14] See pp. 840–842.

on the appointment of a receiver, but the directors' powers are substantially superseded since they cannot act so as to interfere with the discharge by the receiver of his responsibilities and accordingly their powers are suspended "so far as is requisite to enable a receiver to discharge his functions".[15] Given the extent of the powers of the administrative receiver, the directors will have a minuscule aperture within which they are free to exercise their powers. However, they do possess certain residual powers and, for example, it has been held that they can bring an action on behalf of the company against a debenture-holder for the improper exercise of his powers.[16] This authority has been doubted because of the conflict that would arise were the receiver and the directors to have different views on whether an action should be brought and also on the handling of any counterclaim.[17] Whatever the status of the *Newhart*[18] decision, it is clear that it will be confined to very narrow limits since to allow any such action would interfere with the primary duties of the receiver to protect the interests of the security-holder.[19]

Also, as the directors remain in office, the receiver would probably be under an obligation to provide the directors with the information that they need to know to enable them to comply with their reporting obligations under the Companies Act.[20] The receiver will be obliged at the end of his receivership to hand over to the company any documents belonging to the company but not those brought into existence for the discharge of his own professional duties or his duties to the chargee.[21]

---

[15] *Re Emmadart Ltd* [1979] Ch. 540 at 544; see also *Gomba Holdings UK Ltd v. Homan* [1986] 1 W.L.R. 1301.

[16] *Newhart Developments Ltd v. Co-operative Commercial Bank Ltd* [1978] Q.B. 814, C.A. (it is important to note that in that case the company was indemnified for any costs that it might incur and the receiver had decided not to bring any action against his appointor).

[17] *Tudor Grange Holdings Ltd v. Citibank N.A.* [1992] Ch. 53. As Browne-Wilkinson V.-C. pointed out in that case, it would be more appropriate for receivers or their appointor to use s.35 of the 1986 Act. *Tudor Grange* has itself come in for criticism: see *Re Geneva Finance Ltd* (1992) 7 ACSLR 415 at 426–432.

[18] It could be argued that the right to bring an action against the debenture-holder could not be an asset covered by the charge. This, however, proves too much since it would mean that the directors, would always be in a position to bring an action against the debenture-holder even when the special factors in *Newhart* were not present. And while this argument rightly emphasises the scope of the receiver's authority it fails to give effect to his functions. Also the agency of the receiver may have sufficient content to impose on him a duty to seek redress against a debenture-holder in appropriate cases.

[19] See also *Gomba Holdings U.K. Ltd v. Homan* [1986] 1 W.L.R. 1301; *Watts v. Midland Bank plc* [1986] BCLC 15 (a case which illustrates that since the power to use the corporate name in litigation is normally vested in the directors a shareholder will normally be precluded from bringing a derivative action against a receiver).

[20] *Gomba Holdings U.K. Ltd v. Homan*, n. 19, above; see also 1305–1306 where Hoffmann J. points out that equity may impose on a receiver a duty to account which is wider that his statutory obligations.

[21] *Gomba Holdings U.K. Ltd v. Minories Finance Ltd* [1988] 1 W.L.R. 1231, C.A. Once a receiver has sufficient funds to pay off the debt and his own expenses he should cease managing the company's assets: *Rottenberg v. Monjack* [1993] BCLC 374.

The receiver's liability with respect to contracts

This raises two separate issues. The first relates to contracts already in existence when the receiver is appointed. As the administrative receiver is the agent of the company, his appointment does not terminate the company's contracts. Thus, for example, contracts of employment are not terminated unless the receiver does something which is inconsistent with the continuation of the contract,[22] for example a sale of the company's business.[23] The receiver is not, however, obliged to fulfil existing contracts and because of this it is claimed that in this regard he is better placed than the company which, of course, must stand by its contracts.[24] The reason for this is one of priorities; if the receiver were obliged to fulfil existing contracts it would mean that the unsecured creditors would be in a position to require fulfilment of their contracts before the receiver could realise the security. Such an outcome would place priorities on their head and, accordingly, the receiver should be seen as acting in the right of the debenture-holder.[25] As a matter of policy, it would be desirable to impose a limited duty on the receiver to continue to trade where this would not jeopardise the chargee's interests and a failure to do so would impose gratuitous damage on the company.[26] Not to extend his duty in this way would stretch the pro-creditor bias of receivership to ridiculous lengths. However, it is now doubtful if such a duty is compatible with the reasoning in *Downsview*.[27]

Where the receiver enters into a new contract this will be binding on the company. More importantly, the receiver is liable on any contract that he enters into on behalf of the company unless the contract otherwise provides.[28] As regards contracts of employment, it is provided that he is to be liable on any contract of employment adopted by him but nothing he does or omits to do in the first 14 days of his appointment is to be taken as adoption of the contract.[29] What this

---

[22] *Griffiths v. Secretary of State for Social Services* [1974] Q.B. 468. The appointment of the receiver by the court does terminate contracts of service: *Reid v. Explosives Co. Ltd* (1887) 19 Q.B.D. 264; *cf. Sipad Holding v. Popovic* (1995) 19 ACSR 108.

[23] *Re Foster Clark's Ltd's Indenture Trusts* [1966] 1 W.L.R. 125.

[24] *Airlines Airspares Ltd v. Handley Page Ltd* [1970] Ch. 193. The receiver cannot interfere with existing equitable rights of a third party, for example under a contract which is specifically enforceable: see *Freevale v. Metrostore (Holdings) Ltd* [1984] Ch. 199 and *cf. Ash & Newman Ltd v. Creative Devices Research Ltd* [1991] BCLC 403.

[25] See *Edwin Hill v. First Federal Finance Corporation plc* [1989] 1 W.L.R. 225; as this makes clear the question is whether the chargee has a superior right to the person with a contractual claim and the answer to this will normally be in the affirmative.

[26] See Lightman and Moss, *op. cit.*, at pp. 112–118; *Knight v. Lawrence* [1991] BCC 411 at 418: "Though he may be appointed by one party his function is to look after the property of which he is a receiver for the benefit of all those interested in it."

[27] See nn. 9 and 10 and the text thereto.

[28] s.44(1)(b) of the 1986 Act as amended by the Insolvency Act 1994, s.2. He is entitled to indemnification out of the assets of the company (s.44(1)(c)), and can also contract for indemnification by those who appointed him (s.44(3)). See s.37 of the 1986 Act for other receivers.

[29] s.44(1)(b) and (2).

means is far from clear. Adoption is different from novation and also appears to be distinguishable from merely acting as though the contract were binding on the company. What it appears to import is some positive act which is short of entering into a new contract and as such it does not fit neatly into the conceptual apparatus of contract law.[30]

Publicity of appointment and reports

Where a receiver or manager is appointed then this must be stated in various business documents relating to the company.[31] Also, all receivers have to make prescribed returns to the Registrar[32] and the administrative receiver has to report to creditors including unsecured creditors.[33] A receiver who fails to comply with his reporting obligations can be ordered to do so[34] and, more importantly, he can be disqualified from acting as a receiver or manager.[35] There is no similar obligation to report where a debenture-holder enters into possession and it has been recommended that this omission be corrected.[36]

Other registers

There are a number of other registers that are relevant with respect to certain specialist charges; the most important of these registers are those maintained under the Land Registration Act 1925 and the Land Charges Act 1972. It is not intended to go into them in any detail here.[37] It is important to note that a company must itself maintain a register of charges which is more extensive than that maintained by the Registrar of Companies (since it covers all charges irrespective of type) but failure to register a charge in it does not invalidate the charge.[38]

---

[30] *Powdrill v. Watson* [1995] 1 BCLC 386 at 403–405. The meaning of adoption was not affected by the Insolvency Act 1994.

[31] s.39 of the 1986 Act.

[32] s.38 (receivers) and s.48 (administrative receivers) of the 1986 Act.

[33] s.48 of the 1986 Act.

[34] s.41 of the 1986 Act. Also of relevance are the Insolvency Rules 1986, Part 3.

[35] Company Directors Disqualification Act 1986, ss.1(1)(c), 3 and 22(7); see *Re Artic Engineering Ltd (No. 2)* [1986] 1 W.L.R. 686.

[36] Jenkins Committee, para. 306(k).

[37] See Diamond Report, Chap. 12. Registration in these registers does not eliminate the need to register in the companies register should it be a type of charge that needs to be so registered.

[38] s.407. This is open for inspection and copies can be obtained on payment of a fee: see s.408.

Part Five

COMPANIES AND THE SECURITIES MARKETS

INTRODUCTION

WE saw in an earlier part of this book that the strongest argument for the limited liability of companies is that it enables members of the public to invest in them without insisting upon being closely involved in the management of the enterprise. In this Part we look more closely at how companies raise capital by making offers of their securities to the public and at the regulation of this activity. However, public willingness to buy company securities will depend not only on their understanding of the quality of the securities which are being offered to them but also on the possibilities afforded to those who have bought corporate securities subsequently to dispose of them. Since, as we saw in Chapter 11, the law severely limits the freedom of companies to buy back securities they have previously issued (and the needs of corporate finance are normally an even bigger constraint), organised secondary markets on which security-holders can trade their securities with other investors are a crucial adjunct to the ability of companies to raise capital from the public. Although the regulation of the securities markets and of financial services more generally is becoming a separate branch of the law, a company lawyer must grapple with it to some degree. In particular, he or she should appreciate that the *Listing Rules* of the Stock Exchange constitute in many respects a specialist set of company laws for the largest of our companies, namely those listed on the London Stock Exchange.[1]

---

[1] Listing on the Exchange is not, of course, confined to companies incorporated in Great Britain, and a significant number of foreign companies have chosen to list in London as well as, or less often instead of, in the country of incorporation.

CHAPTER 16

PUBLIC OFFERS OF SECURITIES

INTRODUCTION

THIS Chapter is concerned with a subject which is now rightly regarded as a branch of Securities Regulation rather than company law. Nevertheless, it is not a subject which books on company law can ignore; students of that subject need to have some understanding of how public companies go about raising their share and loan capital from the investing public and of the legal regulations that have to be complied with when they do. An elaborate discussion of this specialised branch of legal practice is inappropriate in a book of this sort but an outline is essential.

Partly because of the interaction between domestic law and the law of the European Communities this is an area of regulation which has become complex in recent years. Nevertheless, the dominating principle of the law, both domestic and European, is easy enough to define. It is that members of the public who are offered company securities are entitled to full disclosure to them of the nature of what is on offer before they make a financial commitment, and to effective remedies to redress any loss incurred as a result of failure on the part of the company to make complete or accurate disclosure.

Before turning to an analysis of the various ways in which English law gives effect to this principle, it is necessary to give some factual information about the ways in which companies may seek to raise capital from the public and, in particular, about the role of the Stock Exchange[1] in this process. Although there is no legal obligation upon a company, as we shall see,[2] to ensure that a market is available to the investors in its securities, on which they may subsequently trade the securities which they have obtained from the company, nevertheless it is obvious that a company which is aiming to raise large amounts of money will be able to do so more easily and at a better price if, after the "primary issue" of the securities by the company, investors have a "secondary market" upon which they may liquidate their investment when they so choose. It is the main purpose of the Stock Exchange to provide such markets.

However, the Stock Exchange is more than just a provider of mar-

---

[1] Its full title is the International Stock Exchange of the United Kingdom and the Republic of Ireland Ltd but will be referred to in this Chapter as simply the Stock Exchange or the Exchange. Of its 300-odd members the most influential are the large investment banks.
[2] Below, p. 418.

kets in securities. As a result of the City of London's "Big Bang" and the Financial Services Act 1986 (FSA), the Exchange has completed its transformation from a club to a statutorily-recognised regulatory body, and, moreover, one with a special status. Whereas the self-regulating organisations (SROs) under the FSA are subject to the surveillance of the Securities and Investment Board (SIB) in relation to the authorisation and supervision of their members' investment business, the Exchange is the "competent authority" for the purposes of the E.C. Directives in this field and the FSA. In relation to the regulation of issues entered on the Exchange's "official list" it is not subject to the surveillance of the SIB.[3]

Although, institutionally, there is only one Stock Exchange, in fact it operates two markets in securities. In addition to the "Official List" of large and established companies, which is of considerable antiquity, the Exchange, alarmed by the growth of public issues of securities which were not "listed", decided in 1980 to institute a regulated lower-tier market. The current version of that market is the Alternative Investment Market (A.I.M.), which replaced the previous Unlisted Securities Market (U.S.M.) in 1995. The purpose of the lower-tier market is to provide a home for young companies which do not have the track record for admission to the Official List. However, the Stock Exchange does not have a monopoly of trading in securities. Section 37 and Schedule 4 to the FSA gives the Secretary of State a general power to recognise "investment exchanges" which meet the criteria of the Act and so permit them to operate in this country. The other recognised investment exchanges are more specialised or limited than that constituted by the Official List. In addition, the securities of large companies may be quoted on exchanges in other countries as well as in London, so that those other exchanges may provide competition for the Stock Exchange. Indeed, within the European Community it is sometimes feasible for a British company to list only on an exchange in another Community country.

Methods of public offering

A company may have a choice of various methods whereby its securities can be offered to the public. In practice, it will normally engage the services of an issuing house (a merchant bank) and a stockbroker as sponsors of the issue and the method chosen will depend on their advice. One of the changes resulting from "Big Bang" is that, whereas formerly there were a small number only of British merchant

---

[3] The status of "competent authority" is conferred upon the Exchange by s.142(6) of the FSA. However, in order to be authorised to carry to carry on investment business, the members of the Exchange have to be directly authorised by SIB to do so or, more likely, authorised through membership of the appropriate SRO, *i.e.* the Securities and Futures Authority (SFA).

banks specialising in this work as members of the Issuing Houses Association (and an even smaller number as members of the still more elite Accepting Houses Committee), there is now a far wider choice of British and multi-national concerns. While this has resulted in increased competition between them, so that they may have to expose themselves to a "beauty contest" to persuade the company to engage them rather than one of their rivals, it is less clear that it has led to reductions in the charges that they demand.[4]

Initial offers

On an initial public offering, a company's choice of method will be severely restricted. If the issue is of any size it will have to proceed by way of an offer for sale or subscription[5] coupled with an introduction to listing[6] (or admission to the A.I.M.). An offer to investors without an introduction of the securities to a public market will rarely be commercially practicable since the securities will then lack liquidity. And an introduction without an offer will not raise any new money for the company. Hence, unless the company's securities have somehow become sufficiently widely held (which is unlikely but conceivable[7]) to make it possible to raise the new money needed by a rights or open offer[8] to its existing shareholders, the only option will normally[9] be an offer for sale with an introduction to listing. That will prove to be an expensive and time-consuming operation. The company's finance director (and probably other executives) and representatives of the issuing house and of the company's and the sponsor's solicitors will for weeks or months devote most of their time to working as a planning team. At a later stage the services of the New Issues Department of one of the major banks will generally be needed to handle applications and the preparation and dispatch of allotment letters. The offer will have to be made by a lengthy prospectus which will have to be published. To ensure that the issue is fully subscribed, arrangements will have to be made for it to be underwritten. Today this is normally achieved by the sponsoring issuing house agreeing to subscribe for the whole issue and for it, rather than the company, to

---

[4] It has always been denied that there was ever any sort of price-fixing cartel but issuers, appalled by the proposed charges of their first choice, who shopped around to find another that would charge less, generally suffered disappointment—and probably still do.

[5] Generally this will be an offer for sale by the sponsoring issuing house which will have agreed with the company to subscribe. Hence, we hereafter describe it as an "offer for sale".

[6] The senior market operated by the Stock Exchange is called the "Official List" of the Exchange, and the process of "listing" involves gaining admission to that Official List. The Stock Exchange's rules governing admission to and maintenance of membership of the list are contained in its *Listing Rules* (sometimes referred to, by reason of the colour of the covers, as the "Yellow Book").

[7] Since the Companies Act 1980 there has been no upper limit on the number of members of a private company.

[8] On which see below, pp. 399–400.

[9] Unless a "placing" is permitted by the Stock Exchange: see below, pp. 398–399.

make the offer. In major offerings, such as the Government's privatis-ation issues,[10] a syndicate of issuing houses may be employed. The issuing house or houses will endeavour to persuade other financial institutions to sub-underwrite. Ultimately the cost of all this, including the commissions payable to underwriters and sub-underwriters,[10a] will have to be borne by the company.

The most ticklish decision that will have to be made is the price at which the securities should be issued and, for obvious reasons, this is normally left to the last possible moment. If it proves to have been set too low, so that the issue is heavily over-subscribed, the company will be unhappy, while, if it is set too high so that much of the issue is left with the underwriters, it is they who will be unhappy since their commission rates will have assumed that they will end up with a hand-some profit and not be left with securities that, initially, they cannot sell except at a loss. Nor, probably, will the company be best pleased since it is generally believed that an under-subscribed issue will reduce the company's prospects of raising further capital in the future.[11] The nightmare of all concerned is that there will be an unforeseen stock-market collapse between the date of publication of the prospectus and the opening of the subscription list.[12] The sweet dream is that the issue will be modestly over-subscribed and that trading will open at a small premium.

If the issue is over-subscribed it will obviously be impossible for all applications to be accepted[13] in full. Hence, the prospectus will need to say how that situation will be dealt with. Normally this will be by accepting in full offers for small numbers of shares and scaling down large applications, balloting sometimes being resorted to. The company will probably wish to achieve a balance between private and institutional investors. To succeed in that aim multiple applications by the same person will probably be expressly prohibited.[14] An abuse

---

[10] Most of the privatisation offers were not primary distributions (*i.e.* offers of securities by the company) but secondary distributions (*i.e.* offers by a large or sole shareholder of its shares to the public). This Chapter is concerned mainly with the raising of capital by a public offer by the company.

[10a] On which see p. 312, n. 71, above.

[11] The only obvious reason why they might be is that the sponsoring houses who have burnt their fingers might be reluctant to risk that again. But in view of what they charge they surely should take the rough with the smooth, especially as it is they who will have decided on what the issuing price should be.

[12] Which came true in the case of one of the privatisation issues on the "Crash of 1987". Yet thousands of small investors continued to put in applications notwithstanding that the media were warning them that trading would open at a massive discount.

[13] The so-called "offer" is normally not an offer (as understood in the law of contract) which on acceptance becomes binding on the offeror. It maybe in the case of a rights issue (see below) but on an offer for sale it is an invitation to make an offer which the issuer may or may not accept.

[14] Breaches are difficult to detect where applications are made in different names but that abuse will doubtless become less common now that culprits have been successfully prosecuted. The decision that they had committed a criminal offence and not merely a breach of contract was something of a surprise both to them and others.

which also needs to be guarded against is that "stags" will apply but seek to withdraw and stop their cheques if it seems likely that dealings will not open at a worthwhile premium to the offer price. However, offer documents will require applications to be accompanied by cheques for the full amount of the securities applied for, the cheques being cleared immediately on receipt and any refund sent later. This means that an applicant may not only fail to get all or any of the shares he hoped for but may, for a period, lose the interest that he was earning on his money.[15]

The offer price is normally stated as a fixed and pre-determined amount per share. It can however, be determined under a formula stated in the offer.[16] Or applicants can be invited to tender on the basis that the shares will be allocated to the highest bidders (this, however, is rarely used in relation to issues of company securities). Nevertheless, a variation of it became popular in the early 1980s. Under this, a minimum price will be stated and applicants invited to tender at or above that price, an issue price then being struck at the highest price which will enable the issue to be subscribed in full, all successful applicants paying the same price, and those applicants who tendered below the striking price being eliminated. This, however, did not prove to have the advantages expected of it and is now seldom used though it still has its advocates.[17]

Obviously, the expense of an offer for sale plus introduction to listing is prohibitive unless a very large sum of money is to be raised. The Stock Exchange was concerned about this and made changes to the listing rules, allowing greater use of an alternative method known as a "placing".

Under this method the sponsor obtains firm commitments, mainly from its institutional-investment clients (instead of advertising an offer to the general public) coupling this with an introduction to listing. The absence of the need for newspaper advertisements, "road-shows" and the like makes this a much less expensive procedure. On the other hand, it prevented the general public from acquiring shares at the issue price. Hence the Exchange had been reluctant to permit it except in the case of small issues and, when it did, normally insisted that 25 per cent was made available to the market when trading began.

However, that rule was relaxed and then in 1995 the Exchange moved to the general position that "essentially, the Listing Rules will allow a new applicant to bring securities to listing by whatever method

---

[15] This causes bona fide applicants who are unsuccessful understandable resentment.

[16] As is common in euro-security issues which are addressed to "professionals" rather than to the public: see below, pp. 401–403.

[17] See the Stock Exchange Report, *Initial Public Offers* (1990), pp. 17 and 18, where the pros and cons are summarised.

it and its advisers select, subject to certain disclosure requirements".[18] In consequence, the main substantive limitation on a placing now is where the placing involves equity securities of a class already listed. Here, unless the Exchange agrees, the pricing of the securities must not involve a discount of more than 10 per cent from the prevailing market price, a rule designed to prevent the dilution of the interests of those already holding listed shares of the class involved in the placing.[19]

Another way of proceeding is the "intermediaries offer", defined as "a marketing of securities . . . by means of an offer by, or on behalf of, the issuer to intermediaries for them to allocate to their own clients".[20] This way of proceeding should be only marginally more expensive than a straightforward placing, but has the advantage that it is more likely to result in a wide spread of shareholders and a more active and competitive subsequent market.

Subsequent offers

Once a company has made an initial public offering it will have additional methods whereby it can raise further capital and, even if it proceeds by an offer for sale, this will be less expensive if the securities issued are of the same class as those already admitted to listing or to the A.I.M. More often, however, it will make what is called a "rights issue" and, if it is an offering of equity shares[21] for cash, it will generally have to do this unless the company in general meeting otherwise agrees. This is because of the provisions of sections 89–96 of the Companies Act[22]. The object of those provisions is to protect the existing shareholders from having their aliquot share of the equity diluted without their consent. Hence the sections require that they be offered pre-emptive rights to subscribe in proportion to their existing holdings.

The practice is to make a rights issue at a price which represents a discount (often substantial) to the quoted price of the existing shares, thus increasing the likelihood that the rights will be taken up either by the existing shareholders or by those to whom they have renounced their rights.[23] Nevertheless, it is customary for the issue to be under-written, not only to guard against the risk of a market crash but also because there will always be some shareholders who, out of apathy or

---

[18] Stock Exchange, *Amendment 5 to the Listing Rules. Covering Letter*, August 1995.
[19] *Listing Rules*, para. 4.8. The rule is relaxed if the company is in severe financial difficulties or there are other exceptional circumstances. On dilution, see p. 306, above.
[20] *ibid.*, para. 4.10.
[21] Rights issues may be made of non-equity securities but in their case it is optional.
[22] Discussed at pp. 305–313, above.
[23] The shareholders will receive renounceable "letters of right" corresponding to renounceable allotment letters that successful applicants receive on an offer for sale.

because they have moved from their registered addresses or because the rights are being quoted at a minimal or no premium, have neither taken up nor renounced their rights.[24]

In one sense a rights issue is considerably less expensive than offer for sale; circulating the shareholders is cheap in comparison with publishing a lengthy prospectus in national newspapers and mounting a sales pitch to attract the public. But in another sense it may be dearer; if the issue price is deeply discounted the company will have to issue far more shares (on which it will be expected to pay dividends) in order to raise the same amount of money as on an Offer.

Analogous to, but distinguishable from, rights issues are Open Offers. Under these an offer is made to the company's existing security holders, not necessarily pro rata to their existing holdings and not affording them rights to renounce. Such offers are less common than rights issues[25] and, when they relate to cash offers for equity securities, will be practicable only if the offer is pro rata or pre-emptive rights have been waived in accordance with the statutory provisions referred to above. Other methods of issue, which can be used in appropriate circumstances, include exchanges or conversions of one class of securities into another, issues resulting from the exercise of options or warrants, and issues under employee share-ownership schemes—though these will not necessarily raise new money for the company. Nor, of course, will capitalisation issues, dealt with in Chapters 11 and 12, above.

Two other types of issue deserve mention. The first of these is a Vendor Consideration Issue, *i.e.* one made as consideration for, or in connection with, an acquisition of property.[26] If the vendor is willing to take by way of consideration an allotment of equity shares of the acquiring company, there will be no need to offer the existing equity shareholders pre-emptive rights; the issue to the vendor is not for cash.[27] But investors, and institutional ones in particular, became alarmed at the extent to which vendor consideration issues were being used even when the vendor wanted cash and the acquiring company raised it by a new issue of equity shares without offering its shareholders pre-emptive rights. The *modus operandi* was a tripartite arrangement whereby the vendor sold in consideration of an allotment of shares which a merchant bank then placed on behalf of the vendor who thereby received the desired cash. This had advantages for all the parties (the company because it made it easier for it to adopt merger

---

[24] In one rights issue in 1990 only 6 per cent of the rights were taken up and 94 per cent left with the underwriters.

[25] The *Listing Rules* regulate the timetable for such offers (which must be open for at least 15 business days), the information to accompany the offer and the price (to the extent of applying the "10% discount" rules here also), *Listing Rules*, para 4.22–4.26.

[26] Frequently on a takeover or merger but not necessarily so.

[27] And it world, of course, be impracticable to offer the shares to the existing shareholders ou like terms.

accounting[28]). And so long as the acquiring company did not have to increase its authorised capital and its directors had been given general authority to issue capital[29] all this could usually be done without any reference to its members in general meeting. However, in 1987 a committee consisting of representatives of listed companies, institutional investors and the Stock Exchange produced Guidelines which, if observed, will appease the Stock Exchange and the institutions but which, if not followed, will require the company to discuss with the investment committees of the National Association of Pension Funds and the Association of British Insurers and to obtain their prior approval if trouble is to be avoided.[30] Approval may involve what is known as a "claw-back", arrangement. Under this, instead of the merchant bank placing the shares with its associates, it will first make what is known as a "Vendor Rights Offer" enabling the acquiring company's shareholders to take up their pro rata entitlement at the issue price.

The second type is a Euro-Security Issue. Such an issue is sometimes used by a major company as a means of raising capital by an international offering of what are variously described as "euro-bonds", "euro-securities" or "euro-currency securities". "Euro" is a misnomer since the securities and the methods of issue have no particular connection with either Europe as a whole or with the European Community[31]—except that the largest concentration of the primary dealers is in London, that in so far as there is a regulatory or representative body it is the Association of International Bond Dealers (the AIBD) with headquarters in Switzerland, and that issues are generally listed on the Luxembourg Stock Exchange.[32] The only reason for listing is that under the laws of some countries certain institutions may not invest in unlisted securities. Transactions do not in fact take place on any stock exchange for the market is exclusively an international "over-the-counter" one, conducted by telephone or telex (and largely dominated by American and Japanese investment banks).

Originally the securities traded were pure debt securities—hence the original term "euro-bonds". But increasingly those of companies have come to contain an equity element—hence the growing use of "euro-equities" or "euro-securities".[33] No one as yet has succeeded in satis-

---

[28] See Chap. 11 at p. 244, above.

[29] See Chap. 13 at pp. 304–305, below.

[30] As we have seen (above, p. 312), companies regard rights issues as an expensive way of raising capital.

[31] It has been suggested that "euro" came to be adopted because that formed part of the name of the first body that made such an issue—but that seems to be apocryphal. The probable explanation is that it was adopted by American investment banks to distinguish such issues from U.S. domestic issues.

[32] Somewhat to the chagrin of the Stock Exchange; but Luxembourg is cheaper and is said to adopt a more "pragmatic" attitude to applications for listing.

[33] Terminology varies (the Stock Exchange favours "euro-currency" which, misleadingly, suggests that the securities are necessarily denominated in ECUs). This book uses "euro-securities".

factorily defining such securities; or is ever likely to, for the securities themselves do not have any unique features which distinguish them from other bonds or debentures, with or without conversion or similar rights to a share in the equity. Their distinguishing mark is the way in which they are marketed on issue and here the best attempt so far to distinguish them from other international issues is that in Article 3(f) of the Prospectus Directive,[34] which reads:

> "Euro-securities shall mean transferable securities which:—are to be underwritten and distributed by a syndicate, at least two of the members of which have their registered offices in different States,—are offered on a significant scale in one or more States other than that of the issuer's registered office, and—may be subscribed for or initially acquired only through a credit institution[35] or other financial institution."[36]

All one need add is that the value of the business conducted on the market is enormous (far greater than that on any stock exchange); that when trading starts[37] it will normally be in lots exceeding $(US) 25,000; and that there are efficiently organised clearing systems.

When we turn (as we are about to) to the legal regulation of public issues little will be said about euro-issues. This is because the attitude of the United Kingdom (and of other countries) has been studiously to exclude them from regulation;[38]—an attitude acquiesced in by the European Commission. The arguments of the AIBD and its members which have led to this "hands-off" treatment are (i) that the market is used by "professionals only" and (ii) that if attempts were made to regulate it more strictly the centre of its operations would move from London to somewhere else in the European time zone (say Zurich),[39] thus depriving the United Kingdom (and, perhaps, the Community)[40] of one of its more valuable financial assets. Neither argument is convincing. While it is true that the primary distributions will be to "professionals only", as a result of secondary dealings euro-securities can, and sometimes do, end up in the hands of private investors.[41] Nor is it really believable that the major dealers would

---

[34] Directive 89/298.

[35] E.C.-ese for "banks".

[36] This is an improvement on U.K. efforts such as FSA, s.152(6) but does not seem adequately to distinguish "euro" issues from other international offers such as those undertaken on some of the Government's privatisation issues.

[37] Which it frequently does before the listing particulars are even filed at the Luxembourg Exchange.

[38] Apart from the need for those dealers carrying on business in the U.K. to be authorised to carry on investment business.

[39] Since the euro-market is a global 24-hour market it is important that its centre should be in the time zone midway between that of Japan and the USA.

[40] Switzerland is not a member of the Community.

[41] While a minimum price of $25,000 would deter many private investors, on the secondary market odd-lots are obtainable for a little as $500. And "pools" or mutual funds afford another avenue.

uproot themselves from London and flee to Switzerland; only gross over-regulation would cause them to contemplate that. Nevertheless, until there is a major scandal in the market (so far there have only been relatively minor ones) the likelihood is that it will remain the most lightly regulated of the world's major capital markets.[42]

Regulation of public issues
Introduction

The legal regulation of offers by companies of securities to the public falls into two main divisions. Part IV of the FSA regulates public offerings of securities which are to be listed on the Official List of the Stock Exchange, and the Public Offers of Securities (POS) Regulations[43] control public offers of securities which are not to be listed. Thus, offers of securities which are to be traded on A.I.M., as well as offers in respect of which no trading arrangements are to be made by the company, fall within the POS Regulations. The reasoning behind this division of regulatory effort seems to be two-fold. First, in the case of companies whose securities are not admitted to the Official List it was thought that a lesser degree of disclosure was acceptable than in the case of securities so admitted. Secondly, in the case of listed securities it is possible, and indeed it was thought posit-ively desirable, to place part of the regulatory burden on the Stock Exchange, which was more than happy to accept it since regulation of the market in listed securities is a central part of its *raison d'être*. Consequently, the extent of the protection of the public in offerings of securities to be listed can be deduced only from reading the provi-sions of the FSA together with the appropriate parts of the Listing Rules of the Stock Exchange. In fact, in the case of listed securities, there are *three* levels of regulation, which, in descending order of legal status, are: Community law, which is implemented in the United Kingdom by Part IV of the FSA, which, however, establishes only a framework of regulation, because much of the detail of the task has been delegated to the "competent authority", *i.e.* the Exchange.

In the case of securities not to be admitted to the Official List, however, the relevant Community Directive[44] did not permit such a sharing of regulatory competence and, in any event, there could be no guarantee that such securities would be traded on any market. Thus, for these public offers the regulatory task falls almost entirely on the

---

[42] The Public Offers of Securities Regulations 1995 (see below, p. 418) contain a specific exemp-tion for euro-securities which are "not the subject of advertising likely to come to the attention of persons who are not professionally experienced in matters relating to investment" (reg. 7(2)(s) and the equivalent provision in FSA, Sched. 11A, para. 3(1)(r)). However, in practice some of the many other exemptions in the Regulations may be of more use to issuers of euro-securities, such as the "professionals", "50 offerees", "restricted circle", "minimum consideration" or "minimum denomination" exemptions.

[43] S.I. 1995 No. 1537.

[44] See n. 47, below.

POS Regulations.[45] So here there are only two levels of regulation: Community law and the implementing United Kingdom regulations, though the Exchange does play a limited role even in relation to offers of unlisted securities.[46]

However, it is important not to overestimate the differences in principle between the two sets of rules. Both reflect the need to implement in the United Kingdom the provisions of Council Directive 89/298[47] (the Prospectus Directive), which provides that Member States shall ensure that *any offer* of transferable securities to the public (whether the securities are to be admitted to the Official List or not) is subject to the publication of a prospectus by the person making the offer (Article 4). Although that Directive permits Member States to have somewhat different regulatory structures and requirements for securities to be admitted to the Official List and those which are not, the underlying principle in both cases is that a prospectus should be published which will enable investors "to make an informed assessment of the assets and liabilities, financial position, profits and losses, and prospects of the issuer and of the rights attaching to the transferable securities".[48]

Structure and scope

The structure of this part of the Chapter will follow that of the applicable legal rules. Thus, we shall examine first the European Community, FSA and Stock Exchange rules relating to public offers of securities to be listed, and then move on to analyse the POS Regulations governing offers of unlisted securities. It should be noted, however, that there are certain provisions of the FSA, not contained in Part IV of the Act, which are relevant to both types of offer. Examples are section 47 on misleading statements and practices[49] and section 56 which in principle prohibits "cold calling", *i.e.* making unsolicited calls for the purpose of selling securities.

In order to delimit the scope of this Chapter it is proposed to state at the outset what will and what will not be covered. First, the focus is naturally upon the issue of securities by companies rather than by issuers in general. Thus, it is not proposed to deal with debt securities issued by government, central or local, though debt securities issued by companies are covered within this Chapter. Secondly, it is proposed to concentrate upon securities issued by companies rather than upon securities offered by shareholders in companies. It may well happen

---

[45] See below, p. 424 for the limited role of the Exchange under the POS Regs.

[46] See p. 424, below.

[47] [1989] O.J. L124/8.

[48] Art. 11 (1) of the Prospectus Directive and the very similar provisions in Art. 4 (1) of Council Directive 80/390, the Listing Particulars Directive. The latter specifically refers to the information needs of investment advisers as well as of investors.

[49] See p. 433, below.

that a large shareholder decides to off-load some of its investment by offering the securities to the public. Many of the privatisations effected by Government in recent years have taken this form, the offeror being the Government rather than the company itself (and thus with the Government rather than the privatised company keeping the proceeds of the offer). Such "secondary" offerings raise many issues in common with "primary" issues by companies, but it is not proposed to explore the particular difficulties which they raise.[50]

Thirdly, and most important, in the case of listed securities it is proposed to assume that the application for listing is part of a single operation in which the securities are also offered to the public. This method of approach had two consequences. (a) We shall put on one side the situation where the company is not raising any new capital at all but is simply "introducing" to the Official List a class of securities which has been issued sometime previously. In this situation the company does not have to produce a prospectus in relation to the securities[51] but rather listing particulars.[52] (b) We shall be assuming that, even where the company is raising new capital, it is doing so by a method which amounts to "an offer to the public" within the meaning of Schedule 11A to the FSA. Again, if this is not the case, what the company has to produce is listing particulars rather than a prospectus.

This way of proceeding may seem cavalier, especially point (b) in the previous paragraph. Because of the many exceptions to the prima facie definition of a public offer contained in Schedule 11A to the FSA, it is quite feasible for, say, a company to structure a placing so that no offer to the public is made and so no prospectus need be produced. However, if the shares so placed are to be admitted to listing, listing particulars will have to be produced, and the differences between the requirements for prospectuses and for listing particulars are, from the perspective of this book, only minor. This situation arises because Article 7 of the Prospectus Directive states that when an offer to the public is coupled with an application for listing, it is the provisions of Council Directive 80/390[53] (the Listing Particulars Directive)

---

[50] Usually the offer by the Government was of securities to be listed, but sometimes the offer was of securities already listed. Thus, when in 1995 the Government sold off the holdings which it had retained upon the initial privatisation of National Power and PowerGen, the document offering the shares for sale was not a prospectus nor did it constitute listing particulars, since the securities were already listed. The applicable rules were in fact those relating to investment advertisements (see below, p. 420), though in practice the content of the offer document was not very different from what it would have been had Part IV of the FSA applied.

[51] s.144(2) requires a prospectus only where an application for listing is made in respect of securities "to be offered" to the public.

[52] See s.144(2A), requiring listing particulars in any situation of admission to the list not falling within s.144 (2).

[53] [1980] O.J. L100/1. The wording of Art. 7 is reflected in para. 5(1)(d) of the *Listing Rules* and s.154A of the FSA, which both apply the listing particulars requirements, *mutatis mutandis*, to prospectuses.

which are to govern the contents of the prospectus and the procedures for scrutinising and distributing it "subject to the adaptations appropriate to the circumstances of a public offer".

In other words, even where a prospectus is required, it is the rules relating to listing particulars which largely determine what the prospectus must contain and how it must be distributed. Thus, the regulatory rules governing prospectuses and listing particulars are similar, and *provided there is an application for listing*, it matters little from our perspective whether the listing particulars rules apply directly or via their incorporation into the requirements for prospectuses.[54] Where the definition of a "public offer" *is* crucial is in relation to offers of securities which are *not* to be listed. In that situation, if a prospectus is not required because there is no public offer, there is naturally no question of listing particulars being needed instead. In fact, the applicable regulatory regime in that situation is, as we shall see, that relating to "investment advertisements", which turns out to be not very demanding. However, for the reason given, we shall postpone our discussion of the definition of a public offer to that part of the Chapter where we deal with offers of unlisted securities.

Offers of securities to be listed
(i) *The form and content of prospectuses*

In the case of securities to be offered to the public before admission to the Official List, section 144(2) of the FSA states that it shall be a condition of admission first, that a prospectus be submitted to and be approved by the "competent authority" (*i.e.* the Exchange); secondly, that the prospectus be in the form and contain the information specified in the Listing Rules, and thirdly, that the prospectus be published. This immediately makes clear the central role of the Exchange in regulating the form and content of the prospectus in these cases and the need to examine the Stock Exchange's Listing Rules in order to find a full statement of the applicable regulations. However, the Exchange does not have by any means a completely free hand in setting the relevant rules. In devising the rules the Exchange is discharging the obligations accepted by the United Kingdom under Directive 80/390 (the Listing Particulars Directive), as applied by Article 7 of Directive 89/298 (the Prospectus Directive). The Schedules to the former Directive lay out in considerable detail mandatory requirements for the form and content of prospectuses.[55] That the Exchange may not fall below the standards required by the Directive is clear. Moreover, since the Directive is expressed to be a "co-ordinating" or "harmonising" Directive, rather than one laying down simply min-

---

[54] In particular situations, these differences could be important, especially in relation to exemptions, for they do not fall within Art. 7 of the Prospectus Directive.
[55] See especially Schedule A relating to the admission of shares to listing.

imum standards, it should also be the case that the Exchange is not wholly free to depart from the Directive's standards in an upwards direction, except where the Directive expressly permits such variations.[56]

In addition to compliance with the detailed provisions contained in the Listing Rules, section 146(1) of the FSA, implementing Article 4(1) of the Listing Particulars Directive, adds the very important "sweeping up" requirement that the prospectus submitted to the Exchange "shall contain all such information as investors and their professional advisers would reasonably require and reasonably expect to find" for the purpose of assessing the financial position of the issuer and the nature of the securities on offer.[57] This comes close to making contracts resulting from public offers into contracts of the utmost good faith demanding disclosure by the offerors of all material facts. In principle, this has much to commend it—and indeed seems to go no further than the view adopted by the English courts in the nineteenth century.[58]

However, section 146(2) excludes from the obligation of disclosure matters not within the knowledge of the persons responsible for the prospectus[59] or which it would not be reasonable for them to obtain by making inquires. This is probably a more restrictive exemption than the common law allowed (the dictum of Kindersley V.-C., quoted in note 58, refers to an obligation to disclose only facts known to those putting out the prospectus), but Article 4 of the Listing Particulars Directive in fact contains no exemption from the obligation to include all relevant information. Article 4(2) simply requires that "Member States shall ensure that the obligation referred to in paragraph 1 is incumbent upon the persons responsible for the [prospectus]".

In determining what information among that known to or knowable by those responsible for the prospectus should be included under this

---

[56] The Listing Rules now helpfully indicate in a marginal note beside each para. or subpara. of the Listing Rules which provision of which directive the para. is intended to implement. If the rule is not one which implements a Community obligation of the U.K., the Exchange may freely waive compliance with it. If the rule is an implementing rule the Exchange will not be able to so waive, unless the relevant Directive permits this.

[57] s.154A applies the provisions of ss.146 to 152 and 154 to prospectuses, although the provisions themselves refer only to listing particulars.

[58] "Those who issue a prospectus, holding out to the public the great advantages which will accrue to persons who will take shares . . . and inviting them to take shares on the faith of the representations therein contained, are bound to state everything with strict and scrupulous accuracy and not only to abstain from stating as fact that which is not so, but to omit no one fact within their knowledge, the existence of which might in any degree affect the nature, or extent, or quality of the privileges and advantages which the prospectus holds out as inducements to take shares" : *per* Kindersley V.-C. in *New Brunswick & Canada Ry Co. v. Muggeridge* (1860) 1 Dr & Sm. 363 at 381. This "golden legacy" (as the dictum was described by Page Wood V.-C. in *Henderson v. Lacon* (1867) L.R.5 Eq. 249 at 262) was adopted by Lord Chelmsford in *Central Ry of Venezuela v. Kisch* (1867) L.R. 2 H.L. 99 at 113.

[59] The definition of the persons "responsible" for the prospectus is discussed below at pp. 431–433.

general obligation, section 146(3) permits regard to be had not only to the nature of the issuer and of the securities but also to the nature of the persons likely to consider acquiring the securities, the knowledge which their professional advisers may be expected to have and to information already in the public domain by virtue of its publication under statutory requirements or the requirements of the Stock Exchange. The general disclosure obligation is not one upon which the Stock Exchange has chosen to elaborate. The Listing Rules simply state, rather unhelpfully: "Issuers should be aware of the provisions of section 146 of the FSA (general duty of disclosure)."[60]

Under section 147, if after the preparation of a prospectus but before dealing in the securities on the Exchange begins,[61] there is any change (including developments in areas not previously dealt with) significant for the purposes of making an informed assessment, the company must submit to the Exchange a supplementary prospectus for approval and, if it is approved, must publish it. The same applies if there is any subsequent change relevant to the supplementary prospectus. If the company is not aware of the change, it is not required to comply with this obligation, but any person responsible for the prospectus who does know of the change is under a duty to notify it to the company.[62]

As stated, the detailed rules governing the form and content of prospectuses are laid out in the Exchange's Listing Rules. It is not proposed to go into the information required at length. Suffice it to say that the main requirements are set out in Chapter 6 of the Listing Rules, which consists of some 30 pages of detailed rules, which in some cases are supplemented in other chapters of the Listing Rules, notably Chapter 12 relating to financial information.[63] Some idea of the scope of the Exchange's requirements can be gleaned by looking at the main sub-divisions of Chapter 6. Information is required concerning:

(a) the persons responsible for the listing particulars, the auditors and other advisers;
(b) the shares which are being offered to the public and for which admission to listing is being sought;
(c) the issuer and its capital;

---

[60] *Listing Rules*, Chapter 5, "Scope".
[61] Once dealings begin disclosure may still be required of the company, but now under the "continuing obligations" imposed by Chap. 9 of the *Listing Rules*. See p. 416, below.
[62] In some cases, of course, knowledge by the person responsible for the prospectus will be treated also as knowledge by the company. See above, pp. 229–232.
[63] Chapters 18 to 26 set out additional or alternative requirements for particular types of company, such as property companies, mineral companies and scientific research based companies.

(d) the group's activities[64];
(e) the issuer's assets and liabilities, financial position, and profits and losses;
(f) the management;
(g) the recent development and prospects of the group.

It should be noted that the effect of Chapters 6E and 12 is that a company offering to the public securities which are to be listed must produce audited accounts for at least the three previous years, so that very recently formed companies are excluded from the Official List, though they may be able to float on A.I.M. Consequently, it is not uncommon for new companies, whether entirely new or formed by management buy-outs from established companies, to fund themselves initially through funds supplied by venture capitalists, both the venture capitalists and the management concerned hoping to reap rich rewards when the company is later floated, after a demonstrable period of successful trading.

(ii) *The vetting of prospectuses*

As we shall see below,[65] the law provides *ex post* remedies for those who suffer loss as a result of omissions or inaccuracies in a prospectus or supplementary prospectus. However, it is obviously more desirable if the law or regulation can provide *ex ante* mechanisms designed to ensure that the information as provided is complete and accurate. A number of such mechanisms are to be found in the Listing Rules or the FSA. First, the directors of the issuer must declare collectively in the prospectus that they have taken all reasonable care to ensure that the information in the prospectus is indeed complete and accurate. Individually, they must provide letters to the Exchange stating that the prospectus contains all the information known to them or obtainable by them on inquiry which is relevant within the terms of section 146 of the FSA, discussed above.[66] Secondly, the annual accounts for the three previous years, which provide the basis for the financial information on the company which must be contained in the prospectus, must have been audited and the auditors are required to report on certain other financial information contained in the prospectus.

Thirdly, some types of statement in the prospectus are subject to multiple controls. For example, the requirement to state in the prospectus the "prospects" of the group aims to provide potential investors with information which directly addresses their concerns, *i.e.*

---

[64] Note this implicit acknowledgment that in the case of large companies it is rare that the issuer is a stand-alone company and entirely normal for it to be part (usually the parent) of a group of companies.

[65] See p. 428, below.

[66] *Listing Rules*, paras. 5.2 to 5.5 and 6.A.3.

how well is the company likely to do in the future? Historical information only partially addresses this question. On the other hand, a requirement to state the company's prospects gives the directors a golden opportunity to present the company in a rosy light for the future, without the check which historical data provides on their accounts of the past. Accordingly, the Exchange, like the City Panel in the takeover context,[67] is keen to expose to public light and professional scrutiny the assumptions upon which statements about the future are based. This is especially true of profit forecasts, which are likely to be especially influential with unsophisticated investors. These the Listing Rules subject to a three-fold control. The assumptions underlying profit forecasts contained in prospectuses must be stated and the assumptions are limited to matters outside the control of the directors. The company's auditors or reporting accountants must confirm that the forecast has been properly compiled on the basis stated in the forecast; and finally the sponsor[68] of the company applying for listing must confirm that it is satisfied that the forecast has been made only after due and careful inquiry by the issuer.[69]

Finally, the prospectus must be vetted by the Listing Department of the Stock Exchange. Following the requirements of the Listing Particulars Directive, the Listing Rules requires the submission of a draft prospectus, and indeed various other documents, to the Listing Department at least 14 days prior to the intended publication date. The Listing Rules then envisage a process of comment by the Exchange and amendment by the issuer before the prospectus is formally approved by the Exchange for publication.[70] The purpose of the vetting is to put the Exchange in a position to assure itself that the information is complete before it is published.[71] Inevitably, given the time and resources available, the Exchange cannot concern itself with the accuracy of the information put forward by the company, except perhaps for glaring inaccuracies appearing on the face of the document. Nor can the Exchange guarantee even completeness, except to the extent of seeing that something is said on all the matters upon which the Listing Rules require information and that, once again, the information is not obviously inadequate. Nevertheless, the obligation upon the issuer to obtain the prior approval of the Exchange is, no doubt, a valuable discipline upon the issuer and its professional advisers. It should also be noted that section 187(4) protects the Exchange and its officers from liability in damages for acts and omissions in the discharge of the functions conferred upon them by Part IV of the FSA, unless bad

---

[67] See p. 798, below.
[68] See above, p. 395.
[69] *Listing Rules*, paras. 6.G.2, 12.22, 12.23 and 2.15.
[70] paras. 5.9 to 5.12.
[71] para. 5.12.

faith is shown, so that it will be rare for the Exchange to be worth suing if the prospectus turns out to be incomplete or inaccurate.[72]

Under section 148 of the FSA, implementing Article 7 of the Listing Particulars Directive, the Exchange also has the power to grant limited exemptions from the full disclosure obligations which would otherwise apply. It may authorise the omission of information on grounds of the public interest, in relation to which it is entitled to rely without further inquiry on a Governmental certificate as to what the public interest requires, or on the grounds that the inclusion of the information would be "seriously detrimental" to the issuer. In the latter case, but not in the former, the omission of information may not be authorised if it would be misleading to potential investors in relation to information which it is essential for them to have to make a judgement on the offer. So the company's interests are not preferred to those of potential investors in relation to essential information, but the Act would seem to contemplate that it could be in the public interest for investors to be misled on such matters![73] Following Article 6 of the Public Offers Directive, the Exchange has also taken power to permit the publication of an abbreviated prospectus where the issuer has in the previous 12 months issued a full prospectus in relation to other of its securities (even if those other securities were not of the same class as those now on offer). The abbreviated prospectus need contain only the changes which have occurred since the full prospectus was published, but this dispensation is subject to the proper qualifications that the earlier full prospectus must be republished and that the "sweeping up" disclosure obligation of section 146 of the FSA still applies.[74]

(iii) *Publication of prospectuses and other material*

All the effort involved in drawing up a prospectus and having it approved by the Exchange is, of course, simply a prelude to its publication when the securities are offered to the public. This matter is regulated by Chapter 8 of the Listing Rules which stipulates that publication involves making the prospectus available "in printed form and free of charge to the public in sufficient numbers to satisfy public demand"[75] at the issuer's registered office in the United Kingdom, the

---

[72] Reg. 23(1) of the POS Regs. makes the same provision in relation to the (limited) functions of the Exchange under those provisions.

[73] There is also a special exemption in the section for, in effect, the euro-bond market and other specialised debt securities: s.148(1)(c) and see above, p. 401. These FSA powers are implemented by the Exchange in paras. 5.17 to 5.22 and 23.7 of the *Listing Rules*. Para. 5.18(a), following Art. 7 of the Listing Particulars Directive, also permits the omission of information of "minor importance" which is "not such as will influence assessment" of the offer, in which case it is not clear why there is any prima facie obligation to include the information in the first place.

[74] para. 5.23.

[75] para. 8.4.

Company Announcement's Office of the Stock Exchange and at the office of any paying agent of the issuer in the United Kingdom. They must be available for a period of at least 14 days commencing with the earliest date on which the company can be said to have made the offer public. The Exchange has not taken up the option contained in Article 20 of the Listing Particulars Directive to require publication of the prospectus in a national newspaper, though issuers often do this in their own interest of publicising the offer. However, the Exchange does require that some announcement appear in at least one national newspaper, even if it is only "formal notice" stating that a prospectus has been published and where it is available to the public.[76] In addition, section 149 of the FSA requires a copy of the prospectus to be delivered before publication to the Registrar of Companies, a requirement which no doubt helps the registrar to keep a complete file on companies incorporated in the United Kingdom or established or having a place of business in the United Kingdom, though the section is not well drafted.[77]

Despite the requirement in paragraph 5.7 of the Listing Rules, echoing Article 5 of the Listing Particulars Directive, that the information contained in the prospectus must be presented "in as easily analysable and comprehensible a form as possible", there is in fact a growing divergence between, on the one hand, the goal of providing comprehensive information and, on the other, that of providing comprehensible information and of advancing the understanding of potential investors of the risks which they face. The Directives and the Listing Rules, it may be said, have opted for the former, no doubt because it is an easier policy to embody in regulation. It is no doubt the case that for large, especially institutional, shareholders the two objectives largely coincide, since they have the resources to devote to an analysis of the extensive information now contained in prospectuses where the securities are to be listed.[78] No doubt, too, the comprehensive information contained in the prospectus is analysed by professional advisers and by financial journalists, from whom its distilled essence may flow, though this cannot be guaranteed, into the minds of smaller investors.

From the point of view of issuers, as well, the forbidding nature of the prospectus may be thought to hinder communication with small investors, and it is perhaps not surprising that, at least in large offerings, the prospectus has been supplemented by a number of sim-

---

[76] para. 8.10.

[77] On "oversea" companies see above pp. 127–130, and on the criticisms of s.149 see the fifth edition of this work at p. 326.

[78] On the other hand, it might also be said that such large investors do not need the protection of regulation since they are powerful enough to require issuers to provide whatever information they need. However, the standard form laid out in the *Listing Rules* could be defended on the grounds that it saves issuers from having to deal with each potential large investor individually and that it thus promotes efficiency in public offers.

pler documents. Indeed, it may be doubted whether in large issues the majority (by number) of investors make use of more than a small fraction of the information contained in the prospectus or even rely directly on it at all. Section 146(2) of the FSA (and the Community directives and the Listing Rules) require that prospectuses be published and be made available to the public, but they do not require them to be placed in the hands of the investor before he or she invests, nor that, even if this does happen, that the prospectus be read and understood before the investment decision is taken.

No doubt, the regulations could hardly demand these things with any degree of effectiveness, but the possibility (indeed certainty) arises of investors taking decisions wholly on the basis of documents other than the prospectus, and so the question arises as to how these other documents should be regulated. In this context, it is useful to distinguish between two types of non-prospectus material which an issuer may wish to put out. The first is advertisements and other "warm-up" material put out in advance of the public offer, in order to generate interest in what is to come, and the second is mini-prospectuses and other truncated versions of the prospectus which may be put out contemporaneously with the full prospectus.

As far as the former is concerned, there are two types of protection. First, section 156B makes it unlawful to offer securities to the public before the time of publication of the prospectus required by Part IV. So any "warm-up" material will have to stop short of actually offering the securities to the public, "offer" being defined for these purposes as including an invitation to treat.[79] This seems only right in principle; otherwise the whole point of having the prospectus produced could be subverted by securing acceptances of the offer before the prospectus was in circulation. Secondly, section 154 requires the approval of the Exchange for advertisements issued in connection with public issues of listed securities. "Advertisement" is widely defined in section 207(2) of the FSA and in any event section 154 also applies to "other information of a kind specified" by the Exchange. Section 154 requires the prior submission of the advertisement to the Exchange and gives the Exchange the power either to approve the contents of such documents or to authorise their issue without approval of the contents. In the case of documents issued in advance of the formal offer, the Exchange has chosen the latter, less demanding course, though the advertisement must state the extent of the approval the Exchange has given and provide a statement that a prospectus will be published and when and where it will be available.[80]

In the case of documents contemporaneous with the offer the terms

---

[79] FSA, s.142(7A).
[80] *Listing Rules*, paras. 8.24 and 8.25. Although it was previously unclear, it seems that "pathfinder" prospectuses are included within para. 8.24.

of section 156B are by definition satisfied, but section 154 still applies (*i.e.* this latter section is not confined to documents issued in advance of the prospectus). Here the Exchange has been rather more adventurous in the use of its powers, especially in relation to mini-prospectuses, the essential features of which are that they are abbreviated versions of the full prospectus and do contain an application form for the shares on offer.[81] Although they too are authorised for issuance by the Exchange without approval of their contents, the permissible contents of the mini-prospectus are in fact limited to information drawn from the prospectus and it must contain a statement by the directors that they are satisfied that the mini-prospectus contains a fair summary of the key information set out in the prospectus.[82] For many "retail" investors it is the advertisements issued in advance of the public offer, often in the form of a "pathfinder" prospectus, and the mini-prospectus issued at the time of the offer which provide the information for their decisions, together with some more or less well-informed newspaper comment. For them, the effective regulation of these documents is more important than increasingly complex full prospectuses.

(iv) *Admission to and maintenance of listing*

Although the public offer of securities and the admission of those securities to listing are in principle separate activities and although, since this is a book on company rather than securities market law, we are primarily concerned with the former, nevertheless the process of admission to and maintaining listing should be briefly dealt with, since the availability of a Stock Exchange quotation may be an important inducement for an investor to subscribe for shares of the company. Indeed, until the idea was lost in the recent reforms in this area, sections 86 and 87 of the Companies Act used to provide that, where the prospectus stated that an application was to be made for the securities to be listed on any stock exchange and admission to listing was not obtained within fairly narrow time-limits, then any allotment of the securities was void and the monies paid by the investors were to be repaid and in the meantime held by the company on a form of statutory trust for the investors. Those provisions no longer apply to securities covered by Part IV of the FSA, but it is to be hoped that they will be reintroduced in due course.[83]

Once again, there is a three-tiered set of regulations: Community law (this time in the shape of Council Directive 79/279—the Admission Directive), which is implemented in the United Kingdom by Part IV of the FSA and Chapters 1 to 3 of the Listing Rules. The overall purpose of

---

[81] para. 8.12.

[82] paras. 8.13 and 8.24. The mini-prospectus must also state that only the prospectus contains full details and say how it may be obtained.

[83] ss.86 and 87 have been repealed to the extent set out in S.I. 1986 No. 2246, paras. 5(a) and (b) and S.I. 1988 No. 740, para. 2 and Sched.

the regulation is to limit listing on the Official List to companies and securities of a certain quality. Not surprisingly, the task of implementing that policy in the United Kingdom is very largely once again in the hands of the Stock Exchange, with the FSA giving the Exchange a very broad mandate. In this case, Article 5 of the Admission Directive specifically grants Member States the power to impose more stringent conditions than are to be found in the Directive itself.

The relevant rules are set out largely in Chapter 3 of the Listing Rules. That is concerned to ensure the liquidity of the future market in the company's securities, and so requires the securities to be listed be freely transferable, the market value of the shares of any class which are to be listed to be at least £700,000 and, normally, at least 25 per cent of the class of shares to be listed to be distributed to the public.[84] The Chapter also seeks to ensure the quality of the company listed by requiring that it have an established trading record, under the same management, of at least three years' duration, that the directors have the appropriate expertise and experience for a business of the type in question,[85] and, if there is a shareholder who controls either the composition of the board or more than 30 per cent of the votes, that the board can act independently of that shareholder (and thus protect the interests of minority shareholders who buy the company's securities on the market).[86]

The role of the FSA in setting the conditions for admission is minimal. That Act[87] does insist upon the issuer's consent to an application for listing, so that a large shareholder cannot secure the listing of the company's securities without the company's consent. It also requires the Exchange to respond to applications for listing within six months. Nevertheless, the thrust of the Act is to grant the Exchange broad powers of regulation in this area. It may refuse listing if "it considers that by reason of any matter relating to the issuer the admission of the securities would be detrimental to the interests of investors".[88] The Exchange, in the interests of investor protection, may also subject particular applications for listing to special conditions.[89] Under section 145 the Exchange also has power subsequently to discontinue the company's listing if it thinks that there are "special circumstances which preclude normal regular dealings in the securities" and to suspend listing "in accordance with the listing rules".

Temporary suspension of a company's listing, often at the request

---

[84] See paras. 3.15 to 3.21.
[85] Contrast the lack of qualification requirements for directors at common law or under statute, where the only controls are *post hoc*, *i.e.* disqualification in the case directors proving themselves to be unfit. See below, Chap. 24.
[86] paras. 3.3, 3.7 to 3.9 and 3.12 to 3.13.
[87] s.143(2) and 144(4).
[88] s.144(3).
[89] See Art. 10 of the Admissions Directive, s.144(1)(b) of the FSA and para. 3.1 of the *Listing Rules*.

of its board, is a not uncommon event while matters central to the market in its shares are clarified. But a lengthy suspension against the board's wishes and, still more, the refusal of admission or the discontinuance of its listing are clearly matters of great moment to the company and, especially, its shareholders. Although it may be the misdeeds of the directors which cause the Exchange to take such action, it is the shareholders who will suffer through the loss of (or failure to obtain) a market on which to trade their shares. Given the enormous width of the Exchange's powers in relation to all three stages of admission, suspension and discontinuance, the question of legal remedies for companies and other interested parties aggrieved by the Exchange's decision is of paramount importance. Article 15 of the Admission Directive requires competent authority decisions as to listing and discontinuance (though not, surprisingly, suspension) to be "subject to the right to apply to the courts". However, the FSA makes no specific provision in this regard, so that Article 15 is implemented in the United Kingdom only by way of an application for judicial review, to which the decisions of the Exchange in this area are clearly subject.[90] Unfortunately, in its first decision on such matters the Court of Appeal held that the Admission Directive conferred upon shareholders (as opposed to the company itself) no right either to be consulted before a decision to discontinue was taken or to seek review of that decision in the courts.[91]

(v) *Continuing obligations*

In order to maintain their listing on the Exchange, listed companies are required not merely to continue to comply with the conditions necessary to secure admission to listing but to comply in addition with a wide range of further obligations relating to the way in which they conduct their business thereafter, especially in terms of the conduct of relations with their shareholders and the market more generally. The authority to impose such requirements is contained in section 153 of the FSA and it is expressed in wide terms. Once again, the Act is in part reflecting Community law, notably this time Council Directive 82/121 on information to be published on a regular basis by listed companies—the Continuing Obligations Directive.[92] However, the

---

[90] Chapter 1 of the *Listing Rules* provides an internal appeal procedure against decisions to suspend or discontinue (though not refusal decisions), distinguishing between such decisions taken as a sanction for breach of the Listing Rules and those taken purely to maintain a smooth market. The right of appeal is vested in the issuer and, it seems, in a disciplinary case any director of the issuer who is disciplined.

[91] *R. v. International Stock Exchange of the United Kingdom and the Republic of Ireland Ltd, ex p. Else (1982) Ltd* [1993] Q.B. 534. The Court was mainly concerned by the restriction on the Exchange's freedom to take speedy action which the shareholders' arguments were seen to entail. See for a similar policy towards the Takeover Panel, below, p. 775.

[92] Art. 13 of the Admission Directive also requires issuers to supply to the competent authorities and to publish all information "appropriate in order to protect investors or ensure the smooth operation of the market".

requirements imposed by Chapters 9 to 16 of the Listing Rules go far beyond what the Directives require. They relate to such matters as preemption rights, share repurchases and reductions of capital, notification of directors' interests and share dealings by directors, shareholder consent to large transactions, related-party transactions, as well as the more obvious matter of regular disclosure of financial information by listed companies.

A chapter on public offers of securities to be listed is not the appropriate place to investigate these matters in detail. All that needs to be noticed here is that the continuing obligations of listed companies constitute in effect an additional layer of regulation which applies to large public companies and which in many respects fills lacunae to be found in the statutory regulation of companies. Since these continuing obligations are enforceable ultimately by the powerful sanctions of suspension or discontinuance of listing (discussed above), there is no doubt that a complete picture of the regulatory universe in which listed companies operate must take into account the provisions of the Listing Rules.[93]

Accordingly, the substance of the continuing obligations will be dealt with in the appropriate parts of this work. All that needs to be noted here is that the tendency in recent years has been to put more and more weight on regulation via the Listing Rules. In part this reflects the increasing influence of institutional shareholders, who may find it easier to bring their influence to bear on the rule-making processes of the Stock Exchange than on those of Government.[94] However, Government, too, has shown an increasing penchant for this type of regulation. For example, the regulatory aspects of both the Cadbury Report on corporate governance and the Greenbury Report on directors' remuneration were implemented mainly by means of amendments to the Listing Rules.[95] Part of the motivation is that the choice of listed companies for regulation enables the regulator to isolate the largest companies and to impose upon them rules which might not be at all appropriate for smaller companies. In this respect, regulation confined to listed companies is part of the inevitable fragmentation of company law as it becomes ever more specialised. However, there is no reason why legislation should not choose to confine itself in appropriate cases to listed companies.[96] The additional decision to proceed by way of amendments to the Listing Rules rather than legislation applying only to listed companies no doubt reflects the preferences of the Exchange and its listed companies (for they may feel that such

---

[93] s.153(1) makes it clear that the Exchange may also adopt the less draconian sanction of publishing the fact that the issuer has not complied with a continuing obligation.
[94] See, for example, Davies, "Institutional Investors in the United Kingdom" in Prentice and Holland (eds.), *Contemporary Issues in Corporate Governance* (Oxford, 1993) at pp. 85–87.
[95] See pp. 191 and 194, above, and 632, below.
[96] See, for example, the disclosure requirements discussed below at p. 486.

regulation will be more flexible) and of Government, wishing to throw the costs of regulation upon others or to avoid the handling of a "hot potato", such as the appropriate levels of directors' remuneration.

Regulation of offers of unlisted securities

The legal regulation of unlisted issues by the Public Offers of Securities Regulations 1995 can be dealt with more briefly, for the disclosure they require follows the structure of the Listing Rules, whilst being less extensive than the latter. The structural similarity of the two sets of rules is no accident. The Prospectus Directive, which the 1995 Regulations implement, states in its preamble that in relation to all transferable securities "full, appropriate information" must be provided in the interests of investor protection, but nevertheless that in relation to securities which are not to be listed, "less detailed information can be required so as not to burden small and medium-sized issuers unduly". In short, the same types of information must be provided in the two cases but in less detail in relation to unlisted securities.

Yet, in some cases the offerees of unlisted securities need more, or at any rate different, information from that made available in the case of listed securities. For example, in the case of unlisted securities it will be vital to know what arrangements, if any, have been made to provide a trading market in the securities, so that the potential purchaser can form an opinion whether it is likely he or she will be able to sell the securities in the future at a fair price.[97] Again, whatever level of information it is decided to provide to potential purchasers of unlisted securities, it is crucial that the information actually provided in any particular case be complete and accurate. As we shall see below, in relation to both listed and unlisted issues the law provides *ex post* controls in the form of actions for compensation or criminal penalties, but the *ex ante* control of approval by the Exchange before issue is not available in respect of prospectuses relating to unlisted securities.[98] However, it must be recognised that the disclosure now required by the 1995 Regulations in relation to unlisted issues is more extensive than that demanded previously in this area under Part III of the Companies Act 1985, which the 1995 Regulations repealed.

(i) *The scope of the Regulations*

The 1995 Regulations apply to corporate securities which are not listed nor subject to an application for listing in accordance with Part

---

[97] para. 16 of Sched. 1 to the 1995 Regulations requires a statement to be made in the prospectus about whether the securities will be admitted to trading on a recognised investment exchange (*e.g.* A.I.M.) and, if not, a brief description of any other dealing arrangements which are to be made.

[98] With one exception dealt with in relation to the mutual recognition provisions, below at p. 425.

IV of the FSA, but which are being offered to the public for the first time in the United Kingdom.[99] The Regulations thus apply to securities which are to be dealt with on the Alternative Investment Market or which are not even to be traded on the lower-tier market, as well as to foreign listed securities which are being offered to the public in the United Kingdom without being listed on the London Stock Exchange.[1] They require the publication of a prospectus which must be made available to the public free of charge and a copy of which must be delivered to the Registrar of Companies.[2] They also require the publication of a supplementary prospectus in the same circumstances as those discussed above in relation to offers of listed securities (and with the same defence)[3] and also in the (additional) situation where "there is a significant inaccuracy in the prospectus".[4]

As with offers of listed securities, however, there is no obligation actually to ensure that a prospectus is placed in the hands of a person before he or she accepts the offer of the securities.[5] Moreover, the Regulations do not prohibit the use, in addition to the prospectus, of other advertisements or documents announcing a public offer of securities covered by the Regulations, provided such communications state that a prospectus has been or will be published and give an address from which it may be obtained.[6] Thus, the pathfinder and mini-prospectus may be used in relation to offers of unlisted securities, as they are in offers of listed securities, even though there is no requirement of prior authorisation of such documents in unlisted offers.[7] A pathfinder prospectus and other "warm-up" material will have to avoid making any offer of securities within the meaning of the Regulations,[8] but a mini-prospectus, issued contemporaneously with the prospectus and containing an application form for the securities, will be in the clear as far as the 1995 Regulations are concerned, provided only that the existence and availability of the full prospectus are indicated in the mini-prospectus. There is no equivalent in the Regulations to the restrictions on the contents of the mini-prospectus imposed by the Listing Rules[9] in the case of offers of securities to be listed.

In effect, the most significant regulation of advertisements, etc., in connection with offers of unlisted securities is not to be found in the

---

[99] An offer is made "in the United Kingdom" if it is made "to persons in the United Kingdom" (reg. 6), so that an offer made from outside the U.K. but to the public in the U.K. is covered by the Regulations, whereas the contrary situation is not.

[1] For the mutual recognition provisions see below, p. 425.

[2] Regs. 3(1) and 4.

[3] See above, p. 408.

[4] Reg. 10. Of course, the offeror must be or become aware of the inaccuracy for this obligation to bite: reg. 10(4). The supplementary prospectus must also be registered.

[5] Reg. 2 requires only that the prospectus be made "available to the public free of charge".

[6] Reg. 12.

[7] For listed offers see above, p. 413.

[8] Since otherwise the requirement in reg. 4 for a prospectus to accompany public offers will not have been complied with.

[9] para. 8.13, above, p. 414.

1995 Regulations, but in section 57 of the FSA (Part I). This prohibits the issuance of "investment advertisements"[10] unless they have been approved by a person authorised to carry on investment business, and lays down extensive civil and criminal sanctions in case of contravention. However, the impact of the requirement of authorised person approval will depend very heavily on the efficacity of the enforcement of the SIB and SRO rules to which authorised persons are subject.[11] In short, the effectiveness of the regulation of advertisements (other than the prospectus itself) in connection with offers of unlisted securities remains to be proved, and the rules may well allow the unscrupulous to obtain acceptances of offers from persons who have seen only very inadequate documentation.

The Regulations apply both to offers in the contractual sense (*i.e.* whose acceptance would give rise to contracts for the issue or sale of securities) and to invitations to treat. In either case, the "offeror" is defined as the person who makes the offer as principal (and "offer" is construed likewise),[12] so that where a merchant bank or broker solicits investors to subscribe for new shares to be issued by a company, it is the company which is the "offeror", but where a bank or broker offers to the public shares in a company it has acquired, say, as part of an underwriting commitment, it will be the latter which is the offeror.[13] Thus, the Regulations apply in principle to both primary and secondary offerings of securities, *i.e.* both to offers made by or on behalf of the issuer of the securities (the company) and one made by a security holder on its own behalf.[14] The correct identification of the offeror is necessary for a number of purposes under the Regulations; for example, the duties mentioned above to ensure that a prospectus is published, is made available to the public and is registered with the Registrar fall on the offeror.[15]

---

[10] "Any advertisement inviting persons to enter or offer to enter into an investment agreement ...": s.57(2). s.207(2) then gives a very broad interpretation to the word "advertisement". The prospectus itself is excluded from the operation of s.57 by art. 14(1) of the Financial Services Act (Investment Advertisments) (Exemptions) (No. 2) Order 1995 (S.I. 1995 No. 1536). s.58 of the FSA excludes prospectuses and advertisements issued in connection with offers of listed securities.

[11] Further, advertisement in connection with public offers of unlisted securities which confine themselves to limited factual information are excluded from the application of section 57 by the Financial Services Act 1986 (Investment Advertisements) (Exemptions) (No. 2) Order 1995 (S.I. 1995 No. 1536), art. 14.

[12] Reg. 5.

[13] However, if the shares were acquired in the underwriting of a public offer by the company, the underwriter would presumably be able to argue that it was not offering the shares to the public "for the first time" and so was not within the scope of the Regulations.

[14] Hence the reference in reg. 5 to an offer being one which "would give rise to a contract for *the issue or sale* of the securities".

[15] Where the offeror is not the issuer of the securities, the former may have difficulty in obtaining from the issuer all the information required to be included in the prospectus. Reg. 11(2) simply permits the offeror in these circumstances to omit the information (apparently no matter how important it is to potential investors), provided he has made reasonable efforts to obtain it from the issuer and provided the offeror is not acting in pursuance of an agreement

(ii) *What is the public?*

This is a crucial limiting concept in the Regulations. The Prospectus Directive applies only to offers of securities to the public and yet its preamble rather disarmingly states that "so far, it has proved impossible to furnish a common definition of the term 'public offer' and all its constituent parts". So the problem is passed on to the Member States. Since there is no guarantee that the unlisted securities on offer will be admitted to any investment exchange, there can equally be no guarantee that an exchange will regulate the offer if it falls outside the scope of a "public offer", as defined in the Regulations. In fact, as we shall see, if the Regulations do not apply, the protection available to investors from the law is in fact very limited.

The technique adopted in the Regulations to define a public offer consists in laying down an initial very broad definition and then qualifying it through an extraordinarily long list of "exemptions". The initial statement includes within the definition of a public offer an offer made to "any section of the public, whether selected as members or debenture holders of a body corporate, or as clients of the person making the offer, or in any other manner".[16] There then follow 21 exemptions,[17] of which only the more important will be mentioned here. Thus, exempted are offers to persons whose ordinary business activities involve "acquiring, holding, managing or disposing of investments (whether as principal or agent)".[18] This so-called "professionals" exemption will cover a wide range of fund-managers, insurance companies and broker-dealers and is presumably based on the premise that, as professionals, they do not need the aid of the law to assess the risks associated with particular types of security. However, it should be noted that there is another specific exemption for offers to "a restricted circle of persons whom the offeror reasonably believes to be sufficiently knowledgeable to understand the risks involved in accepting the offer".[19] This makes the point that a number of the exemptions overlap and that many of them constitute different ways of trying to identify those who can look after themselves and who thus do not need—or, rather, should not be entitled to—the protection of the Regulations. In the same vein are the exemptions for offerings "In connection with a

---

with the issuer (for otherwise this exception could be used by the issuer as a way to avoid the obligations imposed by the Regulations).

[16] Reg. 6. Section 59 of the Companies Act (now repealed) used similar wording.

[17] Listed in reg. 7(2)(a) to (u).

[18] Or who it is reasonable to expect will acquire etc. the securities for the purpose of their business or where the securities are "otherwise offered to persons in the context of their trades, professions or occupations" (reg. 7(2)(a))—the latter being a particularly obscure phrase.

[19] Reg. 7(2)(d), but information supplied by the offeror, except about the issuer, is to be disregarded in assessing knowledgeability: see reg. 7(7).

bona fide invitation to enter into an underwriting agreement''[20] and for euro-securities, discussed above.[21]

Other exemptions seem to tackle the same problem of defining those who can take care of themselves by reference to cruder indicators, but ones which are therefore easier to apply. Thus, where the minimum consideration "which may be paid for securities acquired pursuant to the offer" is at least the equivalent of 40,000 ECU,[22] there is an exemption, presumably on the grounds that only investors who can take care of themselves would make commitments of this size.[23] Again, there is an exemption[24] if the securities are denominated in amounts of at least the equivalent of 40,000 ECU—so-called "heavy-weight" securities—since that figure will then indicate the minimum amount the investor is committed to paying for each security purchased, though it seems unlikely that many issues of equities (by way of contrast with debt securities) will be issued in denominations of this size. Another crude indicator used is the number of people to whom the offer is made: if it is fewer than 50, there is an exemption.[25]

Other offers prima facie within the definition of a public offer are exempted presumably because they are not within the purposes of the regulation. Thus, bonus issues of shares are excluded,[26] as are, perhaps more questionably, offers confined to the employees of the company.[27] Further tranches of shares of the same issue, where a prospectus has been produced, will not need a separate prospectus.[28] Finally, it should be noted that the offers of shares in a takeover are prima facie within the scope of the Regulations, since "sale" includes "any disposal for valuable consideration",[29] but regulation 7(2)(k) then exempts them, thus reproducing the effect of the old law.[30] By contrast, if the offer

---

[20] Reg. 7(2)(e).

[21] p. 402.

[22] About £32,000 at the time of writing.

[23] Reg 7(2)(i). This implements in the U.K. Art. 2(1)(d) of the Prospectus Directive, which makes it clear that it refers to 40,000 ECU per investor. It is unclear whether the U.K. Regulations intend to apply the stronger rule of 40,000 ECU per security, which presumably they are entitled to do. This exemption should be sharply distinguished from the *de minimis* exemption in reg.7(2)(h), where the figure of 40,000 ECU again appears, but this time as indicating the total consideration payable for the all securities on offer.

[24] Reg. 7(2)(j).

[25] Reg. 7(2)(b).

[26] Reg. 7(2)(m), as being securities "offered free of charge to any or all the holders of shares in the issuer".

[27] Reg. 7(2)(o) and (12).

[28] Reg. 7(2)(t). This relates to offers of securities issued at the same time as the securities in respect of which a prospectus has been published. If the offer is of securities to be issued later, but is made within 12 months of an offer of securities of the same class in relation to which a prospectus has been issued, the original prospectus may be re-used together with a limited additional prospectus pointing out the differences which have subsequently arisen. This provision even extends to subsequent issues of different classes of security. See reg. 8(6).

[29] Reg. 2(1).

[30] *Government Stock and other Securities Investment Co v. Christopher* [1956] 1 W.L.R. 237. However, the exemption in reg. 7(2)(k) applies only to takeover offers falling within s.428

by the bidder is of securities to be listed, the bidder will have to comply with the Listing Rules' provisions[31] as well as the disclosure rules of the City Code on Takeovers and Mergers.[32]

Given the range of exemptions on offer, it would hardly be surprising if part of an offer fell within one exemption and another part or parts within others. In principle, the Regulations permit the cumulation of exemptions, so as to produce exemption for the whole of the offer. However, some of the exemptions may be used only in a free-standing way, that is, either they operate so as to exempt the whole of the issue or they cannot be used at all to secure exemption. In this category fall the minimum consideration, minimum denomination, the offer to employees and the euro-securities exemptions.[33] One can easily imagine the hours which will be spent in the major City law firms over devising methods of distributing securities which will make best use of the exemptions on offer. In general, however, it may be said that offers of unlisted securities by way of placings or intermediaries' offers should be capable of being brought within one or more of the exemptions, especially the "professionals", "no more than 50 investors" and the "restricted circle of knowledgeable investors" exemptions, all of which may be combined.

It follows from the above that a considerable number of what are prima facie public offers fall outside the scope of the Public Offer Regulations. The content of offer documents in such cases may not be entirely unsupervised. Like advertisements accompanying offers which do fall within the Regulations, non-public offers fall in principle within the investment advertisement regime of section 57 of the Act. In such cases the authorised person approving the advertisement will have to ensure that the offer document meets the standards for such documents laid down in the rules of the relevant SRO or by SIB. However, a large number of situations have been specified, paralleling those identified in the POS Regulations, in which offers of securities have been exempted from the investment advertisement regime as well, and in such cases only the general provisions of the Financial Services Act apply, such as section 47 relating to misleading statements.[34]

---

of the Companies Act 1985 (see below, p. 806), extended to included partial offers: reg. 7(10). The important point is that the 1985 Act requires all shareholders of the same class to be treated equally if the requirements of its definition are to be met.

[31] paras 5.1(b) and 8.15. The *Listing Rules* permits the circulation to shareholders of summary particulars in this case, but full listing particulars must still be produced: paras. 5.32 and 5.33.

[32] See below, p. 797. Although an offer of listed securities in connection with a takeover offer is not a public offer (see FSA, Sched. 11A. para. 3(1)(j)), nevertheless, if the securities are to be listed, listing particulars will have to be produced, subject only to the very limited exemption contained in para. 5.23A(a) of the *Listing Rules*, implementing Art. 6(1) of the Listing Particulars Directive.

[33] Reg. 7(3) and (4).

[34] See p. 433, below, on s.47 and above, p. 419 on the regulation of investment advertisements. The exemptions from the investment advertisement regime are to be found in the Financial

(iii) *The content of the prospectus*

The rules on the content of prospectuses in unlisted issues need not be reviewed in detail, since the headings under which information is required, as laid down in Schedule 1 to the Regulations, are similar to those governing prospectuses relating to offers of listed securities, though the requirements are overall less demanding. We have already noted that prior approval of the prospectus by the Stock Exchange is not a requirement in unlisted issues, and the requirement of registration of the prospectus with the Registrar of Companies is simply that: the Registrar carries out no review of either the accuracy or completeness of the prospectus. The absence of pre-vetting by an independent body is a most importance difference in the regulation of public offers of listed and unlisted securities.[35] The information is to be provided in "as easily analysable and comprehensible a form as possible"[36] and, as under the FSA, there is a general duty to disclose "all such information as investors would reasonably require and reasonably expect to find" for the purpose of making an informed assessment of the offer.[37]

(iv) *The role of the Stock Exchange.*

Issues of securities governed by the 1995 Regulations may or may not be intended to be admitted to trading on A.I.M. Where this is the case, the issuer must comply with the rules of A.I.M., which supplement the 1995 Regulations in various respects. In this case the Stock Exchange also has a role in the administration of the Regulations, although a much lesser one than in relation to listing particulars. The Exchange's role is to administer a small number of exemptions from the Regulations, for example, in relation to rights issues and issues of shares amounting to less than 10 per cent of a class of shares already traded on A.I.M.[38] Further, the Exchange also has one important role in relation to all prospectuses governed by the 1995 Regulations,

---

Services Act 1986 (Investment Advertisements) (Exemptions) Order 1996 (S.I. 1996 No. 1586).

[35] Since pre-vetting is an essential requirement for mutual recognition of prospectuses, an option to choose this had to be made available for those seeking to use a U.K. prospectus in another Member State, even where listing was not being sought here: see below, p. 425.

[36] Reg. 8(3).The policy underlying this provision seems to have persuaded the Government not to make general use of the derogation in Art. 13(3) of the Prospectus Directive that information may be omitted from a prospectus if it is available to investors from other documents. In such a case an investor might have to consult a number of documents in order to obtain an overall view of the company.

[37] Reg. 9. Perhaps reflecting the more informal nature of some unlisted distributions, however, the reference to what "professional advisers" would reasonably require, which appears in s.146 of the FSA, is omitted from reg. 9; and under reg. 9, in judging what is to be included, regard is to be had only to the nature of the securities and of the issuer and not to any knowledge which professional advisers might be expected to have (*cf.* s.146(3), above, p. 407).

[38] Regs. 8(4) and (5). In both cases it is a condition of exemption that up-to-date equivalent information be available as a result of the A.I.M. rules.

whether concerning securities to be traded on A.I.M. or not. As the competent authority under Part IV of the FSA, it is entrusted with the task of authorising omissions of information from the prospectus on the grounds that the inclusion of such information would be seriously detrimental to the issuer but that its omission would not be likely to mislead investors.[39]

Mutual recognition of prospectuses

It is a central plank of the policy of the European Community in the financial services field to promote mutual recognition of regulatory regimes. This means that a body or document authorised in one Member State (the "home" state) should be able to operate freely or be accepted (subject to translation) in another Member State without a fresh regulatory approval in the "host" state having to be obtained. The Listing Particulars Directive was amended by Directive 87/345 and the Prospectus Directive by Directive 90/211 in order to promote mutual recognition of prospectuses. As far as outgoing United Kingdom prospectuses are concerned, a significant point is that the Community rules require pre-vetting in the home state before the benefits of mutual recognition have to be accorded to them. As we have seen,[40] this is not part of the mandatory procedure for prospectuses issued in connection with unlisted securities. Consequently, section 156A and the Listing Rules[41] introduce an optional form of vetting for prospectuses intended to be used for an offer to the public in the United Kingdom, even though it is not intended to seek a listing for the securities on the London Stock Exchange. In such a case the more extensive form and content requirements of the Listing Rules will generally apply.[42] The rules for the recognition in the United Kingdom of prospectuses approved in another Member State are set out in paragraphs 17.68 to 17.78 of the Listing Rules and in Schedule 4 to the Public Offers Regulations.

Offers by private companies

It might be thought that it was inherent in the nature of private companies that they may not make public offers of their securities. This is almost what the current law says, but not quite. Section 143

---

[39] Reg. 11(3). This is the equivalent to the defence found in s.148 of the FSA, discussed above, p. 411. Reg. 11(1) contains a "public interest" exception, similar to the one to be found in the Act, but this time administered directly by the Treasury or Secretary of State.

[40] Above, p. 418.

[41] See the "Rules for approval of prospectuses where no application for listing is made", inserted at the end of the chapters and before the schedules contained in the Listing Rules.

[42] s.156A(2) of the FSA, and so the content provisions of the Regulations are disapplied in this case: reg. 4(3).

of the FSA prohibits applications for listing by private companies, so that no private company may make an effective offer of securities to be listed, whether to the public or otherwise. Section 81 of the Companies Act, which now applies only to offers of unlisted securities, makes it a criminal offence for a private company limited by shares to offer securities to the public, either directly or via an offer for sale, though the validity of any agreement to sell or allot securities or of any sale or allotment is not affected by breach of the section. However, the definition of what is a public offer for the purpose of section 81 is not identical to that used in the POS Regulations. For the purpose of section 81 the old definition of a public offer, to be found in sections 59 and 60 of the Companies Act, applies. In particular, that definition excludes from the scope of a public offer one which ''can properly be regarded, in all the circumstances, as not being calculated to result, directly or indirectly, in the shares or debentures becoming available for subscription or purchase by persons other than those receiving the offer or invitation . . .''. The exemption, which has no exact equivalent in the Regulations, appears to require no limit to be set on the number of people who receive the offer nor to impose any qualification as to their experience or qualifications. In other words, a private company might make what is a public offer for the purposes of the Regulations without contravening the criminal prohibition contained in section 81. In such a case, of course, it would have to comply with the requirements of the POS Regulations.[43]

Liabilities in relation to public issues

An important role for the law in relation to prospectuses, and indeed the area of greatest importance as far as litigation is concerned, has always been to provide *ex post* civil and criminal liabilities against those involved in the making of public issues, if they fail to comply with the statutory procedures contained in the FSA or the Regulations, or induce subscriptions by false or misleading representations, or engage in other improper practices. These potential liabilities are of particular importance in relation to issues which are not to be listed or dealt with on the lower-tier market since they then provide the only sanctions for breaches of the rules, the Exchange having no *locus standi* to impose sanctions. However, even where the securities are to be listed, the legal rules are of the utmost importance because they open up the possibility of those who have suffered loss being awarded compensation, something for which the Listing Rules do not provide. Accordingly, we shall examine together in this section the positions in relation to both listed and unlisted securities.

---

[43] Unless it can find an appropriate exemption in the Regulations, such as reg. 7(2)(f). On the operation of s.60, see *Government Stock v. Christopher*, above, n. 30.

We shall look first at the statutory provisions dealing specifically with prospectuses and the associated documents often produced in the course of a public offer; then examine the operation of section 47 of the FSA, which is a general provision but one with particular relevance to public offers; and finally and briefly consider the relevance of the general law about misrepresentation to public offers.

(i) *Failure to comply with the statutory procedures*

Non-compliance is dealt with comprehensively under the Regulations, but not in relation to the Act. This is because in relation to public offers of listed securities non-compliance can often be left to be dealt with by the Exchange.[44] However, where sanctions for non-compliance are provided, then under both the Act and the Regulations considerable use is made of the technique of invoking the sanctions provided by or under the FSA in respect of contraventions by persons authorised to carry on investment business.

(a) Listed securities. The Act provides a criminal sanction for failure to deliver a copy of the prospectus to the Registrar of Companies[45] (who is of course an official of the DTI and not of the Exchange). More interesting are the sanctions provided for breach of section 154 (requirement to submit advertisements, etc., issued in connection with prospectuses to the Exchange before publication),[46] where the culprit may not be a member firm of the Exchange. Hence, section 154(2) provides that, if the culprit is an authorised person, he shall be deemed to have breached the rules of conduct to which he is subject as an authorised person, thus exposing him to the risk of losing his authorisation and to possible civil liability under section 61 or 62 of the FSA. By contrast, the company itself will normally not be an authorised person but it, and others, may well be responsible for the contravention and, if so, under subsection (3) it and those others will be guilty of an offence.[47]

Similarly, the prohibition in section 156B on offering listed securities to the public before the publication of a prospectus may well be infringed by those not amenable to the discipline of the Exchange. Consequently, the section provides criminal sanctions against unauthorised persons, whilst treating those authorised to carry on investment business as having broken the conduct of business rules.

---

[44] The Exchange's powers are set out in particular in Chapter 1 ("Compliance with and Enforcement of the Listing Rules") and Chapter 2 ("Sponsors and Listing Agents") of the *Listing Rules*.

[45] s.149(3).

[46] See above, p. 413.

[47] There is a defence to the criminal liability for a person who, in the ordinary course of non-investment business, issues an advertisement to the order of another person if he believes on reasonable grounds that its issue had been authorised by the Exchange: s.154(4).

However, in this case it is specifically provided in addition that a person who contravenes the prohibition commits a breach of statutory duty which is actionable at the suit of any person who suffers loss as a result of the contravention.[48] Consequently, unauthorised as well as authorised persons are civilly liable in the case of breach of this section.

(b) Unlisted securities. As stated, the Public Offer Regulations, which cannot rely on the procedures of the Exchange, contain their own comprehensive provisions on the matter, but use the techniques described in the previous paragraph. Thus, regulation 16 provides that an authorised person who commits a breach of regulation 4(1)—containing the central obligation to publish and make available a prospectus—or regulation 4(2)—containing the requirement to deliver it to the Registrar—or of regulation 12—requiring advertisements etc. to contain a statement about the availability of the prospectus—will be regarded as in breach of the rules of conduct applicable to him or her as an authorised person, whilst an unauthorised person who breaks the same provisions will commit a criminal offence, punishable on indictment with up to two years' imprisonment. These sanctions are applied also to authorised and unauthorised persons who assist others to contravene these Regulations; for example, professional advisers or bankers involved in the flotation, who may indeed be more amenable to the sanctions than those immediately involved in the management of a company whose flotation has been irregular and which has collapsed in the process. As with section 156B of the Act, these sanctions are buttressed by a general civil liability on the part of the contraveners (but not, apparently, those who assist them) to "a person who suffers loss as a result of the contravention".[49]

Liability under both regulation 16 and section 156B is stated not to arise "by reason only" of the prospectus not having fully complied with the requirements of the Regulations or the Listing Rules "as to its form and content". In other words, these provisions are not intended to deal with liability for false or misleading prospectuses, but that is because the liability arising in this latter situation is dealt with elsewhere in the Regulations and the FSA. It is to those provisions which we now turn.

(ii) *Compensation for misleading prospectuses*

Fortunately for the student, the provisions on this matter in both the Act and the Regulations follow each other very closely and can be

---

[48] s.156B(5): "subject to the defences and other incidents applying to breaches of statutory duty". This general provision as to civil liability mirrors the provisions of reg. 16(4) of the 1995 Regulation with regard to offers of unlisted securities to the public. See below.

[49] Reg. 16(4), "subject to the defences and other incidents applying to actions for breach of statutory duty".

dealt with together. The relevant provisions are sections 150 to 152 of the Act and regulations 13 to 15 of the 1995 Regulations.[50] Both sets of rules follow and improve upon the format set by the Directors' Liability Act 1890, passed as a result of the decision in *Derry v. Peak*[51] which, by insisting upon at least recklessness, exposed the inadequacy of the common law tort of deceit as a remedy for investors who suffered loss as a result of misleading prospectuses.

(a) **Liability to compensate.** Subject to the exemptions in (b), below, those responsible for the prospectus (or supplementary prospectus) are liable to pay compensation to any person who has acquired any of the securities to which it relates and suffered loss as a result of any untrue or misleading statement in it or of the omission of any matter required to be included under the Act or the Regulations.[52] The same applies when a person has suffered loss as a result of a failure to publish a supplementary prospectus as required by the Act or the Regulations.[53]

This is a considerable improvement on the former provisions of the Companies Act 1985, which applied only to those who subscribed for shares and therefore excluded from protection those who bought on the market when dealings commenced.[54] Now anyone who has acquired[55] the securities whether for cash or otherwise and whether directly from the company or by purchase on the market and who can show that he or she suffered loss as a result of the misstatement or omission will have a prima facie case for compensation.[56] In addition, whereas the former version applied only to misleading "statements", the new provisions specifically include omissions. The provisions do not require the claimant to show that he or she relied on the misstatement in order to establish a cause of action, but obviously a causal connection between the misstatement or omission and the loss will

---

[50] The Regulations and the Act deal with the three issues in a different order, the Regulations discussing in turn the persons responsible for the prospectus, the circumstances in which compensation is prima facie payable and the defences. This is probably the better order, but the text will follow the established pattern of the Act, which puts the issue of the persons responsible last.

[51] (1889) 14 App. Cas. 337, H.L.

[52] s.150(1) and reg. 14(1). Where the rules require information regarding a particular matter or a statement that there is no such matter, an omission to do either is to be treated as a statement that there is no such matter: s.150(2) and reg. 14(2).

[53] s.150(3) and Reg. 14(3).

[54] It will also in principle cover those who exchange their sharers in a takeover, but see above, p. 422 for the different impact of the Act and the Regulations on takeovers.

[55] "Acquire" includes contracting to acquire the securities or an interest in them: s.150(5) and reg. 14(5).

[56] To be assessed presumably on the tort measure, *i.e.* to restore the claimant to his or her former position: *Clark v. Urquart* [1930] A.C. 28, H.L. It is unclear whether the plaintiff will always be limited to the difference between the price paid and the value of the securities at the date of acquisition: *cf. Smith New Court Securities Ltd v. Scrimgeour Vickers (Asset Management) Ltd* [1996] 4 All E.R. 769, H.L. (a case of fraud). See n. 96, below.

have to be proven. So, for example, market purchasers who buy after such a lapse of time that the prospectus or particulars would no longer have any influence on the price of the securities will not be able to satisfy this causal test.

On the other hand, as far as public offers are concerned, the statutory provisions under discussion apply only to misstatements in prospectuses. As we have seen, both the Act and the Regulations distinguish between prospectuses and advertisements, etc., issued in connection with the public offer, whether in advance of, or contemporaneously with, the prospectus.[57] In relation to advertisements, etc., it would seem that the statutory provisions as to civil liability do not apply. This would seem to be the case even in relation to the mini-prospectus.[58] However, since the mini-prospectus, at least in offers of listed securities, may include only information drawn from the full prospectus, an action for damages could probably be based on the equivalent statements in the full prospectus. It is also possible that other bases for civil liability, say at common law or under the Misrepresentation Act, might be available in the case of misstatements in documents which are not prospectuses,[59] but, as the origins of the current legislation suggest, investors in that situation will in all likelihood benefit from a lower level of protection than if they could invoke the civil liability provisions of the FSA or the Public Offers Regulations.[60]

(b) Defences. Section 151 and regulation 15 then provide persons responsible for the misstatement or omissions with what the headings to the sections describe as "exemptions", but which are really defences that may be available if a claim for compensation is made.

The overall effect[61] of these defences is that the defendant escapes liability under section 150 or regulation 14 if, but only if, he can satisfy the court (a) that he reasonably believed that there were no

---

[57] See s.154 and reg. 12 (above, pp. 413 and 419).

[58] Thus, s.154A of the FSA applies the civil liability provisions only to prospectuses "required by listing rules", and the publication of a mini-prospectus is not so required.

[59] Indeed, s.154(5) seems expressly to contemplate this by providing that, when the information in the advertisement has been approved by the Exchange, neither those persons issuing it nor those responsible for the listing particulars shall "incur any civil liability by reason of any statement in or omission from the information if that information and the listing particulars, taken together, would not be likely to mislead persons of the kind likely to consider the acquisition of the securities in question". The significant fact is that this protection is not confined to those responsible for the listing particulars but extends to those issuing the advertisement.

[60] Where the advertisement is issued in connection with an offer of securities which are not to be listed and so will normally need the approval of an authorised person under s.57 unless an exemption applies (see p. 420, above), then if the authorised person approves the advertisement in breach of the rules of conduct applying to him or her, that could give rise to an action for damages against the authorised person by a private investor under s.62 of the FSA, as modified by s.62A.

[61] This sentence merely summarises the very complex drafting of s.151 and reg. 15.

misstatements or omissions and that he had done all that could reasonably be expected to ensure that there were not any and that, if any came to his knowledge, they were corrected in time or (b) that the plaintiff acquired the securities with knowledge of the falsity of the statement or of the matter omitted. This not only reverses the onus of proof which, at common law, the plaintiff would have to discharge but considerably curtails the defences which, at common law, defendants would have under the increasingly narrow view taken by the courts of the extent of the duty of care owed to those who rely on a prospectus.[62]

(c) Persons responsible. The legislation then deals with the sensitive question of who are "persons responsible" and thus liable to pay the compensation. Section 152(1) and regulation 13 provide that they are:

(a) the issuer (*i.e.* normally the company)—a further improvement on earlier versions which did not afford a remedy against the company itself,
(b) the directors of the issuer,
(c) each person who has authorised himself to be named, and is named, as having agreed to become a director, whether immediately or at a future time,
(d) each person who accepts, and is stated as accepting, responsibility for, or for any part of, the prospectus,[63]
(e) each other person who has authorised the contents of the prospectus or any part of it, and
(f) the offeror of the securities where it is not the issuer.[64]

We have noted above[65] that the Exchange and its officials are given statutory protection against civil liability, except when bad faith is shown, but, apart from this, the above list would make almost everybody who had played any part in the preparation of the prospectus responsible for the whole of it. Accordingly, its scope is narrowed by the subsequent subsections. Section 152(2) and regulation 13(2) provide that a person is not responsible under (c) if the document was published without his knowledge and consent and, when he became aware of it, he forthwith gave reasonable public notice of that. Section 152(3) and regulation 13(3) restrict the responsibility of a person under (d) or (e) to that part of the document for which he has accepted responsibility or has authorised, and only if it is included substantially in the form and context to which he agreed. The somewhat opaque

[62] See below, p. 438.
[63] *i.e.* the reporting accountant and any other "experts".
[64] This takes account expressly of secondary offers: FSA, s.154(b), reg. 13(e) and (f), the latter dealing with the matter rather more clearly and explicitly including the directors of the offeror.
[65] p. 410.

section 152(4), which has no counterpart in the Regulations, is designed to avoid duplication of responsibility when, as described at page 400, above, "claw-back" arrangements within a vendor rights issue are made to preserve the pre-emptive rights of equity share-holders; the general effect is to enable each of the companies involved, and its directors, to be held responsible only for the parts which relate to that company.

Section 152(5), which also has no counterpart in the Regulations, enables the Exchange to exclude a director from responsibility under paragraph (b) or (c) by certifying that, by reason of his having an interest or of other circumstances, it was inappropriate for him to be responsible. It would clearly be unreasonable to face a director with the alternative of resigning or accepting responsibility for a document in the prepara-tion of which he was unable to play any part because of a conflict of interest or, for example, illness or absence abroad on the company's business. (yet this seems to be the position if the securities are not to be listed). Section 152(5) also excludes paragraphs (b) and (c) on a euro-security issue[66] which would be quite monstrous but for the fact that no one seems to rely on the prospectus in relation to such issues.

Sections 152(8) and regulation 13(4) provide that nothing in either section shall be construed as making a person responsible by reason only of his giving advice in a professional capacity. This is generally regarded as excluding the lawyers involved[67]—though confidence in this belief may be misplaced; the leading firms of solicitors admittedly carry on investment business, "arrange" as well as "advise" and are authorised persons under the Act. It clearly does not exclude the spon-sor required by the Listing Rules.[68] A crucial problem facing misled investors is to identify all the "persons responsible" so as to be in a position to decide whether any of them is worth powder-and-shot. The Public Offers Regulations now deal with that matter by simply requir-ing the prospectus to state the names and addresses and functions of all those responsible within the meaning of regulation 13, specifying the part of the prospectus for which they are responsible if it is only a part.[69] The Listing Rules achieve a similar result but by stipulating particular cases, and so may leave some gaps.[70]

Attention should also be drawn to sections 150(4) and (6). Section

---

[66] Described as an issue of "international securities" and defined (inadequately) in s.152(6). The absence of this provision in the Regulations is presumably because of the euro-securities exemption in the definition of a public offer (see above, p. 422).

[67] Though they seem to be less enthusiastic than formerly in being named prominently on the front of the listing particulars or prospectus.

[68] Above, p. 395.

[69] Sched. 1, para. 9.

[70] para. 6.A.1 requires a statement of the name, address and function of the directors and para. 6.A.8 the names and addresses of "the issuer's bankers, legal advisers and sponsor, legal advisers to the issue, reporting accountants and any other expert to whom a statement or report included in the listing particulars has been attributed".

150(4) says that the section "does not affect any liability which any person may incur apart from this section", but section 150(6) limits the effect of that by providing that no person, by reason of being a promoter or otherwise, shall incur any liability for failing to disclose in listing particulars information which he would not have had to disclose if he had been a person responsible for those particulars or, if he was a person responsible, which he would have been entitled to omit by virtue of section 148. Hence, it seems, section 150 pre-empts and overrules any duty, which a promoter or other fiduciary might be under, to disclose in the listing particulars of matters additional to those required under sections 146–148 and the Listing Rules.

There are no similar provisions in the Regulations.

(iii) *Section 47 of the Financial Services Act*

Some of the relevant provisions in other Parts of the FSA have already been mentioned but a further word needs to be said about section 47 and the exception to its subsection (2) placed, singularly infelicitously,[71] in section 48. Subsection (1) of section 47 is a revised version of section 13 of the repealed Prevention of Fraud (Investments) Act 1958. Under it, it is a criminal offence knowingly or recklessly to make a statement promise or forecast or to conceal material facts for the purpose of inducing, or reckless as to whether it may induce, any other person to enter into or refrain from entering into an investment agreement or to exercise or refrain from exercising any rights conferred by an investment. This is a useful weapon in the prosecutor's armoury since only recklessness (not fraud) needs to be established and promises and forecasts (not just statements or omissions of facts) are covered.

Subsection (2) is new.[72] It reads:

"A person who does any act or engages in any course of conduct which creates a false or misleading impression as to the market in, or the price or value of, any investments is guilty of an offence if he does so for the purpose of creating that impression and of thereby inducing another person to acquire, dispose of, subscribe for, or underwrite those investments or to refrain from doing so, or to exercise or refrain from exercising any rights conferred by those investments."

To this, subsection (3) provides a defence if he proves that he reasonably believed that his act or conduct would not create an impression

---

[71] s.47 applies to "any person" but s.48 only to conduct of business by authorised persons (see s.48(1)). Yet s.48(7) and (7A) purport to disapply s.47(2) by rules made under s.48 and to empower the S. of S. to amend subs. (7) by orders. The basic mistake was placing provisions relating to misconduct by *any person* in a Chapter of the Act dealing primarily with conduct of business by authorised persons.

[72] It was borrowed, though not verbatim, from the Federal securities legislation of the USA.

that was false or misleading.[73] The section says nothing about civil liability and it was a disputed question whether the former section, corresponding to subsection (1), gave rise to a civil action at the suit of the victim. Now the position seems to be that he cannot sue directly under section 47(1) or (2) for breach of statutory duty.[74] If, however, the offence is committed by an authorised person and involves a contravention of the rules of conduct to which that person is subject, there could be a damages remedy under section 62 of the Act.[75] This liability does depend upon a provision equivalent to section 47(1) or (2) having been included in the rule-book of the relevant Self-Regulating Organisation, since section 47 is not itself listed in section 62 as one of the sections breach of which can give rise to damages under the section.

More promising in relation to civil liability, at least at first sight, is section 61, which expressly mentions section 47 as one of the provisions which it is intended to support. Section 61, however, does not confer a private right of action upon investors; rather it is the Secretary of State or the SIB which are the potential plaintiffs on behalf of investors. The section thus has the advantage of being a form of class action, with the costs of the litigation falling on a public body, but the disadvantage is that the persons injured do not control the initiation or conduct of the litigation. Apart from an injunction to prevent future breaches, the SIB may seek an order against the person who has broken section 47 requiring that person "and any other person who appears to the court to have been knowingly concerned in the contravention[76] to take such steps as the court may direct to remedy it". However, in *SIB v. Pantell (No. 2)*[77] Scott L.J. doubted whether this provision empowered the court to order a contravener or a person concerned to make repayment to an investor of money paid by the latter pursuant to a transaction induced by a breach of section 47, for the transaction did not constitute the breach of the section but rather its result.

The judge may have been influenced to take this narrow view of the restitutionary remedy contained in section 61(1) because later subsections expressly provide for the disgorgement of profits made or the payment of compensation for losses suffered by investors as a result of breaches of, *inter alia*, section 47. Hence, SIB may apply to the court for an order for the recovery from the contravener (not here extended to any person "knowingly concerned") of such sum as seems to the court to be just having regard to the profits made by the

---

[73] Which suggests that all the prosecution has to establish is that the defendant acted with the intention to create *an* impression as to the market, price or value.

[74] In the context of an Act which specifically provides a civil remedy when that is intended, this seems to be the inevitable conclusion. On the other hand, the facts may give rise to civil liability at common law.

[75] See s.62(1) and (2).

[76] A very useful provision if the contravener is outside the jurisdiction but his advisors are not: see *SIB v. Pantell SA (No. 2)* [1993] Ch. 256, C.A.

[77] *ibid.*

culprit or the losses suffered by investors as a result of the contravention. The sums recovered are then to be divided among such persons as the court may direct "being persons appearing to the court to have entered into transactions with that person a result of which" the profit was made or the losses suffered.[78] In other words, the investors who may ultimately benefit from SIB's actions are only those in privity of contract with the contravener. This requirement may not prevent SIB from acting effectively, say, where the misleading statements in a public offer are contained in advertisements etc. put out by or on behalf of the issuer, but in the more general market rigging cases falling within section 47(2) the privity restriction may indeed prove a real handicap to effective investor protection.

Section 47(2) is aimed particulary at market manipulation. To what extent that is a common law offence is unclear but it appears to be if false rumours are passed or "false and fictitious acts" are undertaken with the object of causing a rise or fall of market prices.[79] It is clearly an offence under the new section.[80] However, two situations are excepted from the prohibition. The first concerns manipulation to stabilise the price of new issues during the offer period, which is not customary in United Kingdom domestic issues but is common in international public issues. This is permitted provided the stabilisation takes place in accordance with the rules adopted by SIB.[81] Secondly, anything done under the conduct of business rules relating to "Chinese walls"[82] is protected from both subsections of section 47.[83] Since the purpose of such rules is to prevent the free flow of information within financial conglomerates, it is not at all unlikely that they may result in persons in the firm making misleading statements or concealing material facts or creating a false or misleading impression.

(iv) *Liabilities under other legislation or at common law*

In addition to liabilities under the Financial Services Act, there is always the possibility that there will be contraventions of provisions in other Acts, such as the Companies Act[84] or the Theft Act 1968,[85]

---

[78] s.61(3) to (6).

[79] See *R. v. Beranger* (1814) 3 M. & S. 67 (where there had been a conspiracy to cause the price of gilts to rise by mounting an elaborate charade designed to spread false rumours that Napoleon had died) and *Scott v. Brown Doering & Co.* [1892] 2 Q.B. 724.

[80] For the application of a similar Australian section to an illicit share support scheme, see *North v. Marra Developments* (1981) 56 A.L.J.R. 106. The U.K. was in fact very slow to adopt a statutory prohibition on market manipulation, being perhaps the last common law jurisdiction with a developed securities market to do so.

[81] s.48(7) to (10). The securities must be listed or to be listed on a recognised investment exchange or "any other exchange of repute" and the cost of the investments on offer must be at least £15 million.

[82] See below, p. 458.

[83] s.48(6).

[84] *e.g.* of its s.151: see pp. 263 *et seq.*, above.

[85] See especially s.19 (false, misleading or deceptive statements made by an officer of a company with intent to deceive its members or creditors), on which see *R. v. Kyslant* [1932] 1 K.B. 442.

or at common law. This is particularly likely when there have been false or misleading statements in prospectuses and sections 150 and regulation 14 (above) expressly recognise this by saying in their respective subsections (4) that: ''This section does not affect any liability which any person may incur apart from this section.'' At common law[86] if there have been misrepresentations, there are likely to be remedies in tort or contract available to a misled investor entitling him to damages or rescission or both. Formerly, there was one peculiarity when the defendant was the company because the decision of the House of Lords in *Houldsworth v. City Glasgow Bank*[87] apparently established that a shareholder could not recover damages from the company unless he had first rescinded and thus ceased to be a member of the company. Happily, any such rule has now been abolished by section 131 of the Companies Act 1989 which inserts a new section 111A in the 1985 Act declaring that:

''A person is not debarred from obtaining damages or other compensation from a company by reason only of his holding or having held shares in the company or any right to apply or subscribe for shares or to be included in the company's register in respect of shares.''[88]

However, even after the abolition of the *Houldsworth* rule, a shareholder who subscribes for or is allotted shares and seeks damages for a misrepresentation which induced the application for the shares may face a difficulty if the company goes into liquidation. By virtue of the ''members last'' principle, now contained in section 74(2)(f) of the Insolvency Act 1986, a claim for damages in respect of such a misrepresentation may be regarded as not enforceable in competition with the other creditors of the company. It will be capable of enforcement only amongst the contributories *inter se* (*i.e.* only after all the creditors have been paid) and that in all probability will render the claim worthless.[89]

We shall now turn to a brief examination of the general law relating to misrepresentation, but is not intended to prolong this chapter by providing more than a sketch of the relevant principles as they apply to misstatements in prospectuses.

(a) **Damages.** The common law provides civil remedies for misrepres-

---

[86] Or as a result of the Misrepresentation Act 1967.

[87] (1880) 5 App. Cas. 317. See also *Re Addlestone Linoleum Co.* (1887) 37 Ch.D. 191, C.A.

[88] The wording of the section (and its insertion in a Chapter of the Act dealing with allotments) seems to assume that the rule applied only to ''shareholders'' and not to other members (*e.g.* of a guarantee company) who were not members.

[89] However, the earlier authorities to this effect (*Re Addlestone Linoleum Co.* (1887) 37 Ch.D. 191, Ch.D. and C.A. and *Webb Distributors (Aust.) Pty v. State of Victoria* (1993) 11 A.C.S.R. 731, Aust. H.C.) were doubted in *Soden v. British and Commonwealth Holdings plc* [1996] 3 All E.R. 951, C.A., where, however, the misrepresentee was a transferee of, not a subscriber for, the shares.

entations which have caused loss to those who have relied upon them. A misrepresentation is understood at common law as being a misstatement of fact rather than an expression of opinion or a promise or forecast. There must be a positive misstatement rather than an omission to state a material fact. However, this rule is heavily qualified by further rule that an omission which causes a document as a whole to give a misleading impression or falsifies a statement made in it is actionable.[90]

Historically, the common law has provided a damages remedy only for fraudulent misstatements, which require knowledge of the falsity of the statement or, at least, recklessness as to its truth. As we have seen, it was the decision of the House of Lords to this effect in *Derry v. Peek*[91] which led to the introduction of the predecessor of the statutory provisions relating to misstatements in prospectuses which we discussed above. Since then, however, there have been two significant developments. Section 2(1) of the Misrepresentation Act 1967 introduced a statutory remedy for negligent misstatement, which also reverses the burden of proof. The 1967 Act was in effect a generalisation of the principle contained in the statutory provisions relating to prospectus liability, and will therefore be of use where the misstatement was not contained in a prospectus but in some other document issued in connection with the offer. However, the generalisation in section 2(1) extends only to misstatements made by a party to the subsequent contract[92] and gives a cause of action only to the other party to it, so that it would seem impossible to use it to sue directors or other experts or advisers who are involved in public offers of shares by the company. The company itself may be sued, certainly in an offer for subscription or a rights issue or an open offer and perhaps even on an offer for sale, since a new contractual relation between a purchaser and the company comes into existence when the purchaser is registered as the holder of the securities. Where the subsection applies, it makes the misrepresenter liable as if he had been fraudulent. This had led the Court of Appeal to conclude that the measure of damages under section 2(1) is a tortious, rather than a contractual, one, but that the rules of remoteness are those applicable to actions in deceit, so that the person misled can recover for all losses flowing from the misstatement.[93]

---

[90] *R v. Kylsant* [1932] 1 K.B. 442, C.C.A.

[91] (1889) 14 App. Cas. 337.

[92] Or his agent, but even then not so as to make the agent liable but only the principal: *The Skopas* [1983] 1 W.L.R. 857.

[93] *Royscot Trust v. Rogerson* [1991] 2 Q.B. 297, C.A. However, in *Smith New Court Securities Ltd v. Scrimgeour Vickers (Asset Management) Ltd* [1996] 4 All E.R. 769 the House of Lords refused to commit themselves to acceptance of the proposition laid down in the *Royscot Trust* case. That decision of the House of Lords also held that it was no longer an inflexible rule that in deceit the shares acquired had to be valued on the basis of the market price at the time of the transaction. In that case the shares acquired as a result of the deceit of the defendants

Because of these limitations on the new statutory cause of action, it can be said that the more significant development in recent times has been the acceptance of liability for negligent misstatement at common law following the decision of the House of Lords in *Hedley Byrne & Co. Ltd v. Heller & Partners Ltd.*[94] This is a general principle of liability, not confined within the precise words of statutory formulation, and so capable of being used against directors and advisers as well as the company itself in the case of negligent misstatements in prospectuses and other documents associated with public offers. However, the common law liability does require a finding by the courts that the defendants owed a duty of care to those wishing to invoke the principle, and this is a matter towards which the courts have taken a restrictive attitude in recent years.

It was established in the nineteenth century that in an action for deceit the prima facie rule is that, where the false statement is contained in a prospectus, only those who rely upon it to subscribe for shares in the company have a cause of action, and subsequent purchasers in the market do not, even though they may have relied upon the prospectus.[95] The purpose for which the prospectus was issued was to induce subscriptions of shares and that purpose circumscribed the range of plaintiffs who could sue in respect of false statements contained in it. That this is only the prima facie position is demonstrated by the subsequent decision of the Court of Appeal in *Andrews v. Mockford*[96] where the jury were held to be entitled to conclude that the false prospectus was only one of a series of false statements made by the defendants, whose purpose was not simply to induce subscriptions but also to encourage purchases in the market when dealings began. There, the subsequent market purchasers could maintain their claims.

This emphasis upon the purpose of the statement and the nature of the transaction in issue has now entered the law of negligent misstatement following the decision of the House of Lords in *Caparo plc v. Dickman*[97] and is illustrated by the subsequent holding in *Al-Nakib Investments Ltd v. Longcroft*[98] that allegedly misleading statements in a prospectus issued in connection with a rights issue could form the basis of a claim by a shareholder who took up his rights in reliance upon the prospectus but not when the (same) shareholder purchased

---

were in fact worth much less than the market thought at the time of acquisition because of an independent and unconnected fraud which had been committed against the company, and misrepresentee was able to have damages assessed on the basis of the share price at the later time when the unconnected fraud became known to the market.

[94] [1964] A.C. 465.
[95] *Peek v. Gurney* (1873) L.R. 6 H.L. 377, H.L.
[96] [1892] 2 Q.B. 372.
[97] [1990] 2 A.C. 605. See below, p. 552.
[98] [1990] 1 W.L.R. 1390.

further shares on the market. Although this too is presumably a prima facie rule, it seems that the presumption will be hard to rebut if all that can be pointed to is the false statement in the prospectus. While *Caparo* is part of a more general move in the law of tort to restrict liability for negligent statements causing purely economic loss, it has to be said that the consequence in this area of drawing a distinction between subscribers and market purchasers in the immediate period after dealings commence is, in commercial terms, highly artificial. Companies have an interest not only in the issue being fully subscribed but also in a healthy after-market developing so that subscribers can easily dispose of their shares, if they so wish.[99] The statutory provisions on liability for misstatements recognise the force of this argument.[1] Perhaps the way forward in the common law would be for the courts to take a more inclusive view of the issuer's purposes.[2]

(b) Rescission. The common law has traditionally provided the remedy of a right to rescind contracts entered into as a result of a misrepresentation, whether that misrepresentation be fraudulent, negligent or wholly innocent. This right is a useful supplement to the right to claim damages, even when an extensive damages remedy is provided by the special provisions relating to prospectuses. In many cases, all the investor may wish or need to do is to return the securities and obtain back his or her money. The value of this right has been somewhat reduced by the provision of section 2(2) of the Misrepresentation Act 1967, giving the court a discretion in appropriate cases to substitute damages for the right to rescind, a provision included largely for the benefit of misrepresentors.[3] It might be invoked, for example, where the court thought that the rescission was motivated by subsequent adverse movements in the Stock Market as a whole rather than the impact of the misrepresentation as such. However, it is still an important weapon in the investor's armoury.

---

[99] "The issue of a prospectus establishes a basis for valuation of the securities and underpins the development of a market in them, irrespective of the precise circumstances of the initial offer": DTI, "Listing Particulars and Public Offer Prospectuses: Consultative Document", July 1990, para. 10.

[1] See above, p. 429.

[2] A recent indication of judicial willingness to take this view is the decision of Lightman J. in *Possfund Custodian Trustees Ltd v. Diamond* [1996] 2 BCLC 665 refusing to strike out a claim that an additional and intended purpose of a prospectus issued in connection with a placing of securities was to inform and encourage purchasers in the aftermarket, in this case the U.S.M. At the time the relevant provisions of the Companies Act 1985 conferred a statutory entitlement to compensation only upon subscribers.

[3] However, in *Thomas Witter Ltd v. TBP Industries Ltd* [1996] 2 All E.R. 573 there is a dictum of Jacob J. to the effect that the court's power to award damages under s.2(2) is not limited to situations where the misrepresentee still has the right to rescind, thus opening up the possibility of damages under the statute for non-negligent misstatements, a development which would benefit misrepresentees.

The right will be exercisable against the company,[4] if the contract for the securities is with the company, or against the transferor if the acquisition is from a previous holder. In the case of rescission against the company, it will be necessary to show, of course, that the misrepresentation was in fact made by the company, but in the case of statements included in the prospectus, even those made by experts, it seems that the company will be prima facie liable for them and that it carries a heavy burden to disassociate itself from them.[5]

The most important limitations on the right to rescind arise out of the various "bars" on its exercise. Although section 1(b) of the 1967 Act has removed the bar which was once thought to exist that an executed contract could not be rescinded, nevertheless the investor is still well advised to act quickly once the truth is discovered. If he or she accepts dividends, attends and votes at meetings or sells or attempts to sell the securities after the truth has been discovered, the contract will be taken to have been affirmed,[6] and even mere delay may defeat the right to rescind. The reason for this strictness is that the company may well have raised credit from third parties who have acted on the basis of the capital apparently raised by the company, which appearance the rescission of the shareholder's contract would undermine. A rescission claim is also defeated by the liquidation of the company (at which point the creditors' rights crystallise), or even perhaps by its becoming insolvent but before winding up commences,[7] so that the shareholder must have issued a writ or actually had his name removed from the register before that event occurs.[8] Finally, inability to make *restitutio in integrum* will bar rescission, though in the case of shares that principle would seem to be relevant mainly where the shareholder has disposed of the securities before discovering that a misrepresentation has been made.[9]

---

[4] Even if, as is today very unusual, the prospectus was issued by promoters prior to the formation of the company: *Karburg's Case, Re Metropolitan Coal Consumers' Association* [1892] 3 Ch. 1, C.A.

[5] *Mair v. Rio Grande Rubber Estates Ltd* [1913] A.C. 853, H.L.; *Re Pacaya Rubber Co.* [1914] 1 Ch. 542, C.A.

[6] *Sharpley v. Louth and East Coast Railway Company* (1876) 2 Ch.D. 663; *Scholey v. Central Ry of Venezuela* (1869) L.R. 9 Eq. 266n; *Crawley's Case* (1869) L.R. 4 Ch.App. 322.

[7] *Tennent v. The City of Glasgow Bank* (1879) 4 App.Cas. 615.

[8] *Oakes v. Turquand* (1867) L.R. 2 H.L. 325; *Re Scottish Petroleum Company* (1882) 23 Ch.D. 413. Whether this would apply in the case of rescission as against a transferor (rather than the company) is less clear, but the liquidator's consent would be needed for the re-transfer: Insolvency Act 1986, s.88.

[9] Even in this context one should note the dictum of Lord Browne-Wilkinson in *Smith New Court Securities Ltd v. Scrimgeour Vickers (Asset Management) Ltd* [1996] 4 All E.R. 769 at 774: "... if the current law in fact provides ... that there is no right to rescind the contract for the sale of quoted shares once the specific shares purchased have been sold, the law will need to be carefully looked at hereafter. Since in such a case other, identical shares can be purchased on the market, the defrauded purchaser can offer substantial *restitutio in integrum* which is normally sufficient." However, this comment was made in the context of a purchase from a shareholder, not a subscription of shares issued by the company.

(c) Breach of contract. Finally, in the general law of contract it not uncommonly occurs that the courts treat a misrepresentation as having been incorporated in the subsequent contract concluded between the parties. The advantage of establishing this would be that the misrepresentee would have a claim to damages to be assessed on the contractual basis, rather than on a tortious basis as is the position with claims based on the statutory prospectus provisions, the Misrepresentation Act[10] or, of course, the *Hedley Byrne* principle. In particular, the shareholder might be able to claim for the loss of the expected profit on the shares. However, a difficulty facing such claims against the company is that the processes of allotment of shares and entry in the register are to be regarded as a complete novation, *i.e.* the substitution of a new contract for the old contract based on the prospectus.[11] It has to be said, too, that prospectuses normally stop short of making explicit promises about future value or performance, so that the basis for finding a promise to be enforced may not be available.

CONCLUSION

There is little doubt that the new regime for the regulation of public issues is an improvement on the old, but defects remain, especially in relation to the public offering of unlisted securities. Here, pathfinder prospectuses are controlled only to the extent that they must stop short of making an offer of securities. However, this provision does not remove the risk of an outbreak of pathfinder prospectuses for unlisted securities, which extol the advantages of the proposed issue without adequate disclosure of the risks and which invite recipients to register for the receipt of a mini-prospectus when one is issued. When it is, it may come with an application form for shares but little more information than where to obtain full copies of the prospectus. The contents of the pathfinder and mini-prospectus will be controlled only to the extent that an authorised person must have approved their issue, and it remains to be seen how effective that control will be. By contrast, such documents in an offer of listed securities require the approval of the Exchange (though even then the Exchange does not approve their contents) and the Listing Rules impose some controls over the substantive content of mini-prospectuses. For unlisted securities, however, the principle that prevention is better than cure is being lost sight of, and a misled investor will often not have any "cure" unless the

---

[10] See above, p. 437.
[11] The possibilities and problems arising out of breach of contract claims against the company are illustrated by *Re Addlestone Linoleum Co.* (1887) 37 Ch.D. 191, C.A., which, however, must now be read in the light of the abolition of the rule that a shareholder cannot recover damages against the company unless the allotment of shares is also rescinded. See p. 436, above.

statutory liability provisions apply to the document which has misled the investor. Furthermore, with unlisted securities a wide range of regulatory bodies is involved in the policing of the system—the DTI, SIB, one or more SROs and the Stock Exchange. The potential for overlapping rules and roles of different authorities to lead to regulatory failure are great.

CHAPTER 17

INSIDER DEALING

THIS Chapter deals with the legal and regulatory controls that exist in relation to insider dealing, which we can define for working purposes as trading in securities whilst in possession of price-sensitive information which is not available to the person with whom one is contracting (in face-to-face transactions) or to other participants in the securities market (in the case of transactions on an exchange) at the relevant time. The information may be used by the person who has it to buy securities at their current price before the information in question becomes public and causes the price to rise, or to sell securities at their current price before their value falls upon the publication of the information. Why is this practice thought to be in need of control? Disparities of information among those who deal in securities are endemic. It is precisely because the acquisition of information about the performance of companies and economies makes it possible to come to better investment decisions that a breed of professional securities analysts and fund managers has arisen and has come to dominate decision-making in this area. But it is one thing to conclude that equality of information among investors is a chimaera and quite another to say that any informational advantage, however obtained, is unobjectionable. Despite the urging of Professor Manne,[1] it is difficult to see the public policy arguments in favour, say, of allowing a director, who because of his office knows that his company is about to publish disastrous financial results, to unburden him- or herself of shares in the company before this tale of woe becomes public knowledge.[2] In other words, the law may wish to distinguish between the legitimate and the illegitimate informational advantage, and to permit trading on the basis of the former and not on the latter.[3]

However, the argument in favour of the regulation of insider dealing is not simply the negative one that the undeserving should be deprived of gains made or losses avoided. There is a positive argument in favour of regulation, which is the promotion of public confidence in the securities markets.[4] Governments may have an interest in developing such

---

[1] H.G. Manne, *Insider Trading and the Stock Exchange* (New York, 1966).
[2] *ibid*. He thought the practice was an efficient way of rewarding risk-taking, but it might instead be a way of rewarding incompetence. In any event, it is wholly unclear whether opportunities for insider dealing correlate in any systematic way with enterpreneurship, as opposed to the simple holding of a position which gives one access to inside information.
[3] Which is not to say that the distinction between the two is always an easy one to draw.
[4] This is the argument stressed in the preamble to Council Directive 89/592 co-ordinating regulations on insider dealing, [1989] O.J. L334/30 (November 18, 1989), which is discussed more fully below.

confidence, perhaps in order to encourage their citizens to invest in the securities markets, either directly or via collective investment vehicles of one sort or another, or in order to encourage companies, including foreign companies, to list their shares on what can be presented as a well-regulated stock exchange. It will be noted that these arguments stress the advantages of regulating insider dealing on stock exchanges and other publicly available markets rather than controlling all contracting to buy or sell securities. Consistently with this, the most important measure in the United Kingdom aimed at controlling insider dealing, the Criminal Justice Act 1993, is in fact directed at trading on "regulated markets" or at least at trading through or by professional intermediaries.[5] Face-to-face transactions between private individuals are thus excluded. The decision to aim control of the practice at insider dealing on securities markets is significant, too, for the types of sanction likely to be employed in support of the regulation. With trading on public markets it is often difficult to identify any particular investor as having incurred a loss as a result of the insider's activities.[6] The Criminal Justice Act 1993 thus deploys purely criminal sanctions to back up its prohibitions, and we shall see that difficult issues arise in making the civil sanctions (especially damages), which are theoretically available under the Financial Services Act 1986 in some cases of insider trading, work satisfactorily in this context.

The first country to tackle insider trading effectively was the United States.[7] In the United Kingdom we agonised over it for several decades, but did not legislate against it until 1980. In 1989 the European Community adopted a directive in the área,[8] and the British legislation consequently had to be revised, a task achieved by the 1993 Act. Before turning to an analysis of the 1993 Act and of other provisions which directly address the regulation of insider dealing, we must briefly look at those legal rules which control the practice indirectly. By indirect regulation we mean either general principles of liability which, whilst not developed primarily with insider trading in mind, seem capable of being applied to at least some examples of the practice, or statutory provisions which, while not prohibiting insider dealing, aim to discourage the practice by exposing it to the public gaze.

INDIRECT RESTRAINTS

(i) General fiduciary principles

Those most likely to have confidential price-sensitive information affecting the securities of a company are its directors and officers.

---

[5] Below, p. 455.

[6] This point in developed more fully below at pp. 479–482.

[7] For the current situation, see Loss and Seligman, *Fundamentals of Securities Regulation* (3rd ed., Boston, Mass., 1995), pp. 759–875.

[8] See n. 4, above.

As pointed out in Chapter 22,[9] if they make use of it for their personal advantage they will breach their fiduciary duties to the company and be liable to account to it for any profits they have made. A great advantage of the civil suit brought by the company for breach of fiduciary duty is that it does not have to show that it has suffered loss as a result of the insider dealing, simply that the insider fiduciaries have made an undisclosed profit.[10] In practice, however, it is unlikely that the company will call them to account unless and until there is a change of control. If this occurs as a result of a takeover, those who will benefit from any recovery of the profits are the successful takeover bidders and not the members of the company at the time of the directors' breach—as *Regal (Hastings) Ltd v. Gulliver*[11] illustrates. If only one director has committed the breach, the others may cause the company to take action against him—as in *Industrial Development Consultants Ltd v. Cooley*[12]—but most public companies are likely to avoid damaging publicity by persuading the errant director to resign "for personal reasons" and to go quietly.

It is also possible that, for example, in relation to a takeover of a small company,[13] the directors may place themselves in the position of acting as agents negotiating on behalf of the individual shareholders and thereby, despite *Percival v. Wright*,[14] owe fiduciary duties to the shareholders. If so, they would breach those duties if they persuaded any shareholder to sell to them at a price which they knew (and the shareholders did not) was materially lower than that which the bidder was likely to offer. It is, however, highly unlikely that the directors of a listed company would create such a relationship. If they did[15] engage in insider dealing, it would be by dealing, through a nominee, on a stock exchange so that no seller would be able to link up his sale with a purchase by a director.[15]

Hence, the general equitable principle is, on its own, rarely an effective deterrent. Moreover, the law relating to directors' fiduciary duties is simply incapable of applying to the full range of insiders and, except in the rare case where the decision in *Percival v. Wright* can be overcome, it has the demerit of concentrating on the

---

[9] At pp. 615–623, below.

[10] The leading case is the decision of the New York Court of Appeals in *Diamond v. Oreamuno* 248 N.E. 2d 910 (1969), on which see Loss and Seligman, *op. cit.*, pp. 771–777. The precise situation has not yet arisen in an English court. The fiduciary principle is probably wide enough to catch senior employees who are not directors: *Brophy v. Cities Serv. Co.* 31 Del. Ch. 241 (1949).

[11] [1967] 2 A.C. 134n, H.L. See pp. 615–617, below.

[12] [1972] 1 W.L.R. 443: p. 617, below.

[13] For an early example of the directors constituting themselves agents in this way, see *Allen v. Hyatt* (1914) 30 T.L.R. 444, P.C.

[14] [1902] 2 Ch. 421: see p. 599, below.

[15] But it would be an offence under the insider dealing legislation and a breach of the Stock Exchange's *Model Code* and of the *Code on Takeovers and Mergers*: see below.

relationship between the director and the company rather than on the relationship between the director and other traders in the market.

Somewhat similar criticisms can be made of the second source of fiduciary obligation which is relevant here, namely that imposed by the receipt of information from another person where the recipient knows or ought to have known that the information was imparted in confidence. However, the range of persons potentially covered by this fiduciary obligation is much wider that those covered by the fiduciary duties applying to directors and officers of companies. It will extend to the professional advisers of companies who, say, are involved in preparing a takeover bid which the company is contemplating, and to the employees of such advisers, since no contractual link between the confider and the confidant is necessary to support this fiduciary obligation. Indeed, the obligation extends to anyone who receives information knowing that they are receiving it in breach of a duty of confidentiality imposed upon the person communicating the information.[16]

If the duty attaches, the holder of the information may not use it (for example, by trading in securities) or disclose it (for example, to another person so that that person may trade)[17] without the permission of the confider. Breach of the duty gives rise to a liability to account for the profits made, potentially the most useful civil sanction in the case of insider dealing on securities markets, and, though much less certainly in this situation, to an action for damages (because it is far from clear that the confider actually suffers any loss if the confidant uses the information for the purposes of insider dealing and does not, in so doing, communicate the information to other persons). However, the cause of action again lies in the hands of the person to whom the fiduciary obligation is owed (*i.e.* the confider) not in the hands of the person with whom the confidant has dealt in the securities transaction or other participants in the market at the time. This might not matter if in fact the duty of confidence was routinely used to deprive insiders of their profits,[18] but, although much inside information must also be received in confidence and although the law in this area has achieved much greater prominence in recent years than it had previously, there are no reported cases of its use against insider dealers. This may be because the difficulties of detection and proof, which abound in this area, operate so as to deprive confiders of the incentive to use their

---

[16] For both these propositions see *Schering Chemicals Ltd v. Falkman Ltd* [1982] Q.B. 1, C.A.

[17] And by virtue of the *Schering Chemicals* case (see previous note) the recipient of the information (the ''tippee'') would also be in breach of duty by using or disclosing the information if aware that it had been communicated in breach of the duty of confidence imposed on the tipper.

[18] That is, one might be more concerned with depriving the insiders of their profits than with working out who precisely are the best persons to receive them.

private law rights to secure the transfer of insider dealing profits from the insiders to themselves.

(ii) Misrepresentation

When in 1989 the Government was considering its response to the Community's Directive on insider dealing, it decided to continue its policy of not providing civil sanctions under the insider dealing legislation partly on the grounds that these worked satisfactorily only in face-to-face transactions and that the general law already provided remedies in that situation.[19] Apart from the insider's liability to the company, discussed above, the Government referred to liability for fraudulent misrepresentation. Misrepresentation-based liability, however, whether for fraudulent, negligent or innocent misrepresentation, faces a formidable obstacle in relation to insider trading. This is the need to demonstrate either that a false statement has been made or that there was a duty to disclose the inside information to the other party to the transaction. As to the former, the insider can avoid liability by not making any statements to the other party relating to the area of knowledge in which he holds the inside information, so that the liability of the insider comes to depend upon the other party having the good luck or the right instinct to extract a false statement from the insider by probing questions. Liability in such cases seems likely to be quite haphazard.

As to non-disclosure, the current legislation does not adopt the technique contained in some earlier proposals for insider dealing legislation: requiring insiders in face-to-face transactions to disclose the information before dealing.[20] Consequently, the potential plaintiff has to fall back on the common law, which imposes a duty of disclosure in only limited circumstances. The most relevant situation would be where the insider was in a fiduciary or other special relationship with the other party, but, as we have seen above, even as between directors and shareholders, the current law recognises such a relationship only exceptionally, whilst many insiders and their counterparties are simply not in the relationship of director and shareholder at all.[21] There is also little evidence at present of a willingness on the part of the courts to expand the categories of fiduciary or other special relationships in this area[22] or to bring securities contracts within the category of contracts *uberrimae fidei*.

---

[19] DTI, *The Law on Insider Dealing: A Consultative Document* (1989), paras. 2.11–2.12.
[20] Companies Bill, Session 1978/79, H.C. Bill 2, cl. 59.
[21] For example, where the director is selling shares in the company to a person who is not presently a shareholder or where the insider is not a corporate fiduciary at all.
[22] See *Chase Manhattan Equities v. Goodman* [1991] BCLC 897, discussed below, p. 453, where the judge passed up the opportunity to use the Stock Exchange's *Model Code for Securities Transactions by Directors of Listed Companies* as the basis of an extended duty of disclosure.

(iii) **Disclosure of dealings by directors and their families**

This type of disclosure is dealt with in Part X of the Companies Act. Its section 323 was, in effect, our first limited attack on insider dealing by prohibiting directors from buying put or call options in the listed securities of the company or another in the same group; a practice which could conceivably be undertaken without the director making use of his price-sensitive information but which is likely to involve just that.

Part X of the Act does not forbid directors from buying or selling, otherwise than by way of put or call options, the company's securities; on the contrary, it is generally regarded as desirable that they should show their confidence in the company by becoming shareholders of it and as unreasonable to prevent them from realising their investment if they need to. But it does require them to disclose their holdings and dealings. By section 324(1) a person who becomes a director, whether of a listed company or not, is obliged to notify the company in writing of both his interest in any shares or debentures of the company or of any other company in the same group and of the number or amount of each class in which he is interested. Thereafter, under section 324(2), he is under a like obligation to notify the company of: (a) any event occurring while he is a director as a result of which he becomes or ceases to be so interested; (b) his entering into any contract to sell any such shares or debentures; (c) any assignment by him of a right granted to him by his company to subscribe for any such shares or debentures and (d) the grant to him by another company in the group of a right to subscribe for its shares or debentures and the exercise or assignment of such rights.[23] The notification must state the number or amount and class of the securities involved.

A detailed Schedule 13 to the Act amplifies the two subsections. It is crucial to note that "interested in" is defined elaborately and widely. In general, it includes an interest "of any kind whatsoever"[24] and whether actual or contingent.[25] It extends to shares or debentures held not by the director but by any body corporate of which he is a shadow director or is entitled to exercise or control the exercise of one-third or more of the voting power at general meetings.[26] There are, however, certain exceptions,[27] of which, perhaps, those of most

---

[23] Rights to *subscribe* for shares or debentures are excluded from the prohibition on directors taking options over shares in their company (s.323(5)), the latter being exercisable against other traders in securities. Rights to subscribe for shares of one's company on favourable terms have nevertheless, become controversial in recent years. See below, p. 632. Such rights to subscribe are often referred to as directors' "share options".

[24] Sched. 13, Part I, para. 1.

[25] *ibid.*, paras. 1–8.

[26] *ibid.*, paras. 4.

[27] *ibid.*, paras. 9–13. Under s.324(3) other exceptions may be added by statutory instrument—and have been; see S.I. 1985 No. 802, below.

general importance relate to nominees and to trustees. When securities are held by nominees, the nominees are not deemed to be "interested"[28]; it is the person for whom the nominee holds as a bare trustee who is. Hence, while a director cannot escape notification by vesting his shares in nominees, he will not have to notify if he holds the shares as a nominee for another person (not being a member of his family[29]). If, however, he holds them as trustee of a family trust (of which all the beneficiaries are not absolutely entitled[30]), he will have to notify.[31] Whether or not he is a trustee, he will have to notify if he is one of the beneficiaries unless his interest is only in reversion to that of another person entitled to the income during his (or another person's) life.[32] There are also, under the Schedule or the Companies (Disclosure of Directors' Interests) (Exceptions) Regulations,[33] exceptions in relation to special types of trust where it would be unreasonable[34] or unnecessary[35] to require notification.

Part II of Schedule 13 prescribes the period within which notification has to be made. In relation to section 324(1) (*i.e.* on the director's initial appointment), the period allowed is normally five days beginning on the day after that on which he becomes a director.[36] Owing, however, to the width of the definition of "interest" it could be that the director will not know until later that he has a notifiable interest.[37] In that event the five days begin on the day after he finds out.[38] In relation to section 324(2) (*i.e.* as regards subsequent acquisitions or cessations of his interest), there are similar periods of five days beginning the day after the occurrence or, if he did not then know of the occurrence, beginning the day after he finds out.[39] It is perhaps surprising that the Act does not require disclosure of interests of which, in all the circumstances, the director ought to have been aware. In all cases Saturdays, Sundays and bank holidays in any part of Great Britain[40] are to be disregarded.

---

[28] They are "bare trustees" excluded by *ibid.*, para. 10.

[29] See s.328 below.

[30] So that the trustee is a "bare" trustee.

[31] But, if he wishes, he can indicate that his interest is merely as a trustee: see Sched. 13, para. 23, below.

[32] *ibid.*, paras. 9.

[33] S.I. 1985 No. 802.

[34] *e.g.* where the interest is in units of an authorised unit trust, the portfolio of which happens to include shares in the director's company: Sched. 13, para. 11(a).

[35] See Sched. 13, paras. 11(b), (c) and 12 and Regs. 2 and 3.

[36] Sched. 13, para. 14(1).

[37] This could easily happen as a result of the extension in s.327 to interests of his spouse and his infant children. If a husband and wife are living apart they may well not acquaint each other with their investment decisions or the directorships which they hold. Nor will a teenager necessarily tell his parents that he has subscribed for shares in a privatisation issue of shares in a company of which his father or mother is a director.

[38] Sched. 13, para. 14(2).

[39] Sched. 13, para. 15(2) and (2).

[40] Since Scottish bank holidays are not identical with those in England and Wales this may afford directors one or two (undeserved) extra days.

Part III of Schedule 13 is entitled "Circumstances in which obligation imposed by section 324 is not discharged". This is a euphemism. What it in fact does is to add the requirement which directors are likely to find the most distasteful; namely that the price or other consideration paid or received must be disclosed in the notification—a requirement which section 324 studiously avoids stating. It also requires certain other information in some circumstances[41] but disclosure of the price is the bitterest pill to swallow.

Returning to section 324 itself, subsection (5) says that the obligation to notify is not discharged unless the notification is expressed to be given pursuant to section 324. The object of this is to help the company's secretariat in maintaining the register required under section 325 (to which we are about to turn). Subsection (6) crams two unrelated matters into a single sentence: first the section applies to shadow directors as to directors; and secondly, the section does not require notification in relation to shares in a wholly owned subsidiary. Since all the wholly owned subsidiary's shares will necessarily be owned by the holding company or its other wholly owned subsidiaries or by bare nominees for it or them,[42] notification by it of transactions relating to its shares would serve no purpose.[43]

Finally, subsection (7) says that any person who fails to discharge within the proper period an obligation to notify or who, in purported compliance, makes a statement which he knows to be false or makes it recklessly is guilty of an offence.[44]

Under section 325 every company has to keep a register in which must be entered the information received from each director and the date of the entry.[45] The company is also obliged, when it grants to a director a right to subscribe for its shares or debentures, to enter on the register the date on which the right was granted, the period during, or the time at which, it is exercisable, the consideration (or, if none, that fact) and a description of the securities involved, their number or amount and the price or consideration to be paid when the rights are taken up.[46] When the rights are exercised by the director the company must enter against his name on the register the number or amount of shares or debentures, the names of the persons in whose names the securities are registered and the number or amount in the name of each.[47]

---

[41] Sched. 13, para. 17, 19.

[42] See s.736(2) as inserted by the 1989 Act.

[43] And would, in general, be excluded anyway under Sched. 13. All that is relevant are transactions in the holding company's shares, and in wholly owned subsidiaries' debentures.

[44] For which he can be prosecuted only with the consent of the Secretary of State or the DPP: ss.324(8) and 732.

[45] s.325(1) and (2).

[46] s.325(1) and (3). This would apply on a rights issue (if the director was already a shareholder) and to a grant of warrants or options.

[47] s.325(4).

Part IV of Schedule 13 prescribes how the register shall be kept and contains the customary provisions for its inspection by both members and any other interested person, and the obtaining of copies.[48] The company has to fulfil its obligations within three days beginning with the day after the obligation arises.[49] The nature and extent of the director's interest must, if he so requires, be recorded[50] but this does not put the company on notice as to the rights of any person.[51] Section 326 imposes liability to fines on the company, and any officer of it in default, in the event of failure by the company to comply with section 325 or Part IV of the Schedule.

In relation to the recently controversial matter of directors' options to subscribe for shares in their company, usually at a level well below the market price at the date the director chooses to exercise the options, the register maintained under the Act does enable shareholders and others to establish the extent of the options held by particular directors and, most important, the price at which the options are exercisable, for, as we have seen, this information is required to be delivered to the company under section 325 (4). However, the shareholder will obtain this information only if he or she inspects the register or learns of it from someone, such as a financial journalist, who has done so. Curiously, in the Directors' Report, which is circulated automatically to all shareholders each year,[52] less detailed information about options is required and, notably, the exercise price does not have to be stated.[53] However, as a result of the Greenbury Committee's report,[54] the Listing Rules of the Stock Exchange now require an annual report to the shareholders by the remuneration committee of the board which details *inter alia* the exercise price of all options and the market price of the company's shares at the date of exercise of any of the options.[55]

Section 327 extends the banning of dealings in options in the company's listed shares[56] to dealings by the spouse or infant children or step-children of the director and section 328 similarly extends the ambit of the disclosure obligation imposed by section 324. But whereas section 327 does so by making those members of the director's family personally liable on a contravention of the prohibition,[57]

---

[48] See Chap. 19 at pp. 509–510, below. It also has to be produced at the commencement of the company's AGM and to remain open and accessible to any person attending the meeting: Sched. 13, para. 29.

[49] With the exclusion of Saturdays, Sundays and bank holidays: Sched. 13, para. 22. Ten days are allowed for dispatch of copies.

[50] Sched. 13, para 23.

[51] *ibid.*, para. 24.

[52] See p. 517, below.

[53] Sched. 7, para. 2B.

[54] See p. 632, below.

[55] Stock Exchange, *Listing Rules*, para. 12.43(x)(iv), operating by reference to Abstract 10 of the Urgent Issues Task Force of the Accounting Standards Board.

[56] By s.323. mentioned at p. 448, above.

[57] Inevitably so, since s.323 bans the transactions instead of merely requiring. as s.324 does, that they be disclosed. But the spouse or children have a defence if they can prove that they

section 328 does so by requiring the director himself to notify and imposes no liability on the spouse or children. The broad effect of section 328 is that sections 324 and 325 are to be construed as if any reference in them to a director's interest included any interest of his spouse or infant children. It matters not that the director himself has no personal interest or whether or not he has tipped them off; his only protection is that, if they have acted without telling him, he will not have to notify the company until he finds out.[58]

By section 329 a further obligation is imposed on listed companies. If a notification relates to shares or debentures listed on the Stock Exchange,[59] the company must, before the end of the next working day,[60] notify the Exchange of that matter and the Exchange may publish it in any way it thinks fit. This not only helps the Exchange to detect breaches of its Model Code[61] but helps also in relation to its role as detector of possible offences under the insider dealing legislation. Finally, Schedule 7 to the Act requires that information about directors' interests be included in the directors' report or the annual accounts.[62]

So comprehensive is the disclosure obligation described above that it generates a large number of disclosure obligations, both by directors to their companies and by companies to the Exchange, often in relation to insignificant interests. In consequence, the DTI has recently proposed that directors of companies whose shares are publicly traded (where the main problem lies) should be free to aggregate minor transactions and disclose them only when a certain threshold is reached or at the end of the financial year (whichever was the sooner).[63] It is hoped thereby to focus attention on those transactions which are of real significance to the market. This proposal could perhaps be seen as a slight shift away from the deterrence of insider trading as the rationale for the disclosure obligation and towards that of "market transparency" (discussed in the following Chapter). Only relatively large changes of interest are of importance when what is at issue is the level of economic incentive the directors have to promote the price of the company's securities or their ability to influence the company's actions.

---

had no reason to believe that the other spouse or their father or mother was a director of the company: s.327(1).

[58] See nn. 38 and 39, above.

[59] Or any other recognised investment exchange other than an overseas exchange within the meaning of the Financial Services Act, *e.g.* A.I.M.

[60] This is not quickly enough for the Stock Exchange which requires notification "without delay": *Listing Rules*, para. 16.4.

[61] See p. 453, below.

[62] paras 2, 2A and 2B, but see n. 53, above.

[63] DTI, *Disclosure of Directors' Shareholdings: A Consultative Document*, August 1996. The suggested threshold is £10,000 in value or 1 per cent of the company's share capital. Certain transactions would be added to the list of those exempt from disclosure.

DIRECT RESTRAINTS

We now turn to those provisions which aim at controlling directly the practice of insider trading. Pride of place in this section must be given to the provisions of Part V of the Criminal Justice Act 1993, which we shall have to analyse in some detail. Before that, however, we shall look briefly at the Stock Exchange's *Model Code for Securities Transactions by Directors* and, after considering the 1993 Act, we shall examine briefly the part played by regulations made under the Financial Services Act in controlling insider dealing.

(i) The Stock Exchange's model code

The Stock Exchange's *Model Code for Securities Transactions by Directors* is to be found in the Listing Rules.[64] This is not directly binding on directors but is a model which listed companies are required to adopt with such refinements as are thought necessary. In practice it is normally adopted virtually verbatim. The board of the listed company is required to adopt a code and to take "all proper and reasonable" steps to secure compliance with it, not only by directors of the company but also by directors of subsidiaries and by employees of the company or its subsidiaries who are likely by reason of their office or employment to be in possession of price-sensitive information in relation to the company. However, if there is a breach of the code adopted by any particular company, the duty which is breached is one owed by the director to the company, not to the Stock Exchange. The duty owed to the Stock Exchange is simply to adopt and enforce the code and that is a duty owed by the listed company. For this reason, in *Chase Manhattan Equities Ltd v. Goodman*[65] Knox J. refused to hold that the director who sold shares in breach of his company's code incurred for that reason any liability towards the market maker which purchased the shares.

The importance of the Code is that, in addition to emphasising that in no circumstance should directors deal when they are forbidden from doing so under the insider dealing legislation, it prescribes that they should not do so within a period of two months preceding the preliminary announcement of the company's annual results or of the announcement of the half-yearly results and should in relation to all dealings give notice beforehand to the board's chairman or a committee of directors appointed specifically for the purpose. Directors of

---

[64] Appended to Chap. 16 of the Stock Exchange's *Listing Rules*.

[65] [1991] BCLC 897. The force of the learned judge's argument seems not to be diminished by the fact that the obligation to comply with the Model Code is no longer required to be imposed on directors by board resolution, for it is still an obligation owed by the director to the company. See the *Listing Rules*, para. 16.18.

listed companies are wary of breaching these prescriptions for, if they are found out (which they will be unless they also breach the disclosure provisions of the Companies Act), they run the grave risk of finding themselves on the Exchange's blacklist of persons unacceptable as directors of listed companies.

(ii) The Criminal Justice Act 1993, Part V[66]

The original British legislation on insider dealing was contained in Part V of the Companies Act 1980 and was later consolidated in the Company Securities (Insider Dealing) Act 1985. However, as a result of the adoption by the European Community of Directive 89/592 co-ordinating regulations on insider dealing,[67] some amendment of the British law became necessary, and the Department of Trade and Industry also took the opportunity to simplify the 1985 Act in some respects. The result was Part V of the Criminal Justice Act 1993. The degree of amendment of the British law required by the Community Directive was in fact limited partly because the Directive in its Article 6 expressly states that it lays down only minimum standards, so that individual Member States are free to adopt more stringent measures,[68] and partly because the existing British legislation was one of the most advanced in the Community and, to some degree, provided a model for the Community legislation. Equally, the Department's goal of simplification was only partially achieved, though some useful steps were taken in this direction.[69] The truth is that simplification cannot be an overriding goal in this area: the social phenomena which could be regulated in the name of insider dealing come in many forms and the extent to which they should be regulated is a controversial matter among those likely to be affected by the legislation. Both features of the situation tend to be productive of complexity on the legislative front. During the course of the revision this was true, for example, of the debates over the criteria for determining when information has entered the public domain (and so is no longer subject to the prohibitions contained in the Act) and over the defences which should be made available to those who would otherwise be caught by the Act.[70]

---

[66] For an excellent general study of this Act and of the surrounding area of regulation see B. Hannigan, *Insider Dealing*, (2nd ed., London, 1994).

[67] [1989] O.J. L334/30 (November 18, 1989).

[68] Article 6 specifically mentions the possibility of extending the prohibition on insider dealing, beyond primary insiders, to "tippees", an extension which the British legislation has always made. See p. 466, below.

[69] In particular, the deletion of the association both of "inside information" with "confidential information" and of "insiders" (at least in some circumstances) with those likely to have access to confidential information are welcome steps. See pp. 629–631 of the fifth edition of this book and Davies, "The European Community's Directive on Insider Dealing" (1991) 11 O.J.L.S. 92.

[70] See pp. 459 and 471, below.

The upshot of the limited changes required by the Directive and of the limited possibilities for radical simplification was that Part V of the Criminal Justice Act 1993 is recognisably in the mould established by the 1980 Act, though it contains some interesting new features and has abandoned some old obfuscations.

(a) *Regulating markets*

Section 52(1) of the 1993 Act defines the central offence which it creates in the following terms: "An individual who has information as an insider is guilty of insider dealing if, in the circumstances mentioned in subsection (3), he deals in securities that are price-affected securities in relation to the information." This definition, however, conceals as much as it reveals, for it is much elaborated and qualified in the remaining sections of the Part. It is proposed in the following sections to try to elucidate the central elements of the offences created and of the defences available.

Pursuing the reference to section 52(3), contained in the above definition, reveals at once that the Act does not aim to control all dealings in shares where one of the parties has price-sensitive, non-public information in his or her possession. On the contrary, it is only when the dealing takes place "on a regulated market" and in certain analogous situations does the Act bite. If, say, the transaction occurs face-to-face between private persons, then the situation is outside the control of this particular legislation. The Act leaves regulated markets to be identified by statutory instrument and the Insider Dealing (Securities and Regulated Markets) Order 1994[71] stipulates that in the United Kingdom these are any markets established under the rules of the London Stock Exchange, the London International Financial and Futures Exchange, the London Securities and Derivatives Exchange and Tradepoint.

However, the legislation has always applied to certain "off-market" deals and these are now defined as those where the person dealing "relies on a professional intermediary or is himself acting as a professional intermediary".[72] Section 59 makes it clear that the profession in question must be that of acquiring or disposing of securities (for example, as a market maker[73]) or acting as an intermediary between persons who wish to deal (for example, as a stockbroker[74]), and that a person does not fall within the definition if the activities of this type

---

[71] S.I. 1994 No. 187, art. 10, as amended by S.I. 1996 No. 1561.

[72] s.52(3).

[73] A firm which has undertaken to make a continuous two-way market in certain securities, so that, in relation to those securities, it will always be possible to buy from or sell to the market maker, though, of course, at a price established by the market maker.

[74] Following the "Big Bang" on the Stock Exchange in 1986 it is no longer required that market makers and brokers be entirely distinct functions, though equally it is not required that brokers make a continuous two-way market in any particular securities. Some broking firms act as market makers as well; others do not.

are merely incidental to some other activity or are merely occasional. This approach to off-market dealing is rather broader (and simpler) than that adopted under the previous legislation, which confined liability to those situations where there was trading on an informal or inchoate market. Under the current legislation, reliance on a professional intermediary (as defined) or trading by a professional intermediary acting as such brings the trading within the Act, even though no element of an organised market can be shown to exist.

Despite this extension, which is in any event required by the Directive,[75] it seems that the main thrust of the legislation is the regulation of dealings on formalised markets, and that the extension was designed to prevent the evasion of such regulation, which might occur if trading were driven off formalised markets into less efficient, but, without the extension, unregulated forms. What does emerge clearly from this analysis is that the 1993 Act is at least as much a part of the law of securities regulation as it is of company law. As the preamble to the Directive put it, it is the public interest in securing the confidence of investors in the operation of the securities markets which provides the rationale for the legislation on insider dealing.[76] The new Act recognises[77] the logic of this view by extending its regulation to debt securities issued by public authorities[78] as well as to corporate securities.[79] This is a welcome extension, and, although required by the Directive, is one to which the Government in any event had committed itself in 1985.[80] The new Act also brings expressly within its scope futures contracts[81] and contracts for differences,[82] both of which may be the subject of trading which is distinct from the trading in the securities to which these contracts relate.[83]

---

[75] Art. 2(3).

[76] "Whereas the secondary market in transferable securities plays an important role in the financing of economic agents . . . whereas the smooth operation of that market depends to a large extent on the confidence it inspires in investors . . .''

[77] The securities to which the Act applies are those which are identified in its Sched. 2 and which satisfy the conditions set out in the 1994 Order. See s.54, and for the 1994 Order below, p. 457.

[78] Thus "gilts", *i.e.* debt instruments issued by the Government, and local authority bonds are included.

[79] Thus, the *name* of the 1985 Act—the Company Securities (Insider Dealing) Act—if nothing else, would have had to be changed.

[80] "Financial Services in the United Kingdom", Cmmd. 9472 (1985).

[81] A contract of the sale or purchase of securities at a future date.

[82] A contract not involving an agreement to transfer an interest in the underlying securities but simply to pay the difference between the price of the securities on a particular date and their price on a future date.

[83] Certain types of security are omitted, perhaps most obviously the purchase or sale of units in unit trusts, though shares in companies which operate investment trusts are within the scope of the Act. Presumably, the former were excluded on the pragmatic grounds that it was unlikely that a person would have inside information which would significantly affect the price of the units, which normally reflect widely diversified underlying investments, though query whether this is always the case with more focused unit trusts; whereas the latter were swept in under the general prohibition on insider dealing in shares. In any event, the Treasury has power to amend the list of securities contained in Sched. 2 (see s.54(2)).

The concentration of the prohibition on dealing on regulated markets also makes it much easier for the legislator to confine the sanction for breach to the criminal law, as both the current legislation and its predecessors do.[84] In addition to the other difficulties which surround the creation of a coherent civil remedy in this area, the fact that the trading has occurred on a public exchange means that the identity of the counterparty in the transaction with the insider is a matter of chance. In any liquid stock many thousands of persons may be trading in the market at the same time as the insider. To give a civil remedy to the person who happened to end up with the insider's shares and not to the others who dealt in the market at the same time in the security in question would be arbitrary, whilst to give a civil remedy to all relevant market participants might well be oppressive of the insider.[85] By confining the sanction to the criminal law, Parliament avoided the need to address these difficulties. Moreover, if the main argument against insider trading is that it undermines public confidence in the securities markets, the criminal law is capable of expressing the community's view of that public interest, provided it can be effectively enforced.[86]

Finally, in this section on the definition of markets a few words should be said about the international dimension of insider dealing. It is now extremely easy, technically, for a person in one country to deal in the shares of a company which are listed or otherwise open to trading in another country; or for a person to deal in shares of a company quoted on an exchange in his or her own country via instructions placed with a foreign intermediary. For the domestic legislator not to deal with this situation runs the risk that the domestic legislation will be circumvented wholesale. To apply the domestic sanctions irrespective of the foreign element, on the other hand, is to run the risk of creating criminal law with an unacceptable extra-territorial reach. The latter risk is enlarged by the Directive's requirement that the Member States must prohibit insider dealing in transferable securities "admitted to a market of a Member State"[87] and not just those admitted to its own markets. In line with this requirement, the 1994 Order extends the application of the Act to securities which are officially listed in or are admitted to dealing under the rules of any investment exchange established within any of the states of the European Economic Area.[88]

This clearly should not mean, however, that a French citizen dealing on the basis of inside information on the Paris *Bourse* or even on the Milan Exchange in the shares of a British company (or a company of any other nationality) is guilty of an offence under English law.

---

[84] See further below, p. 473.
[85] In some cases it might not even be possible to identify the counterparty.
[86] See further below, p. 473.
[87] Art. 5.
[88] Insider Dealing (Securities and Regulated Markets) Order 1994, arts. 4 and 9 and Schedule.

Consequently, section 62(1)[89] of the Act lays down the requirement of a territorial connection with the United Kingdom before a criminal offence can be said to have been committed in the United Kingdom. This requires the dealer or the professional intermediary to have been within the United Kingdom at the time any act was done which forms part of the offence or the dealing to have taken place on a market regulated in the United Kingdom.[90] Consequently, our French citizen will commit a criminal offence in the United Kingdom, only if the deal is transacted on a market regulated in the United Kingdom,[91] unless he or the professional intermediary through whom the deal is transacted is in the United Kingdom at the time of the dealing.[92] This approach does not eliminate all potential of the insider dealing legislation for extra-territorial effect, but it does limit it to situations where there is some substantial connection between the offence and the United Kingdom.

(b) *Regulating individuals*

A striking feature of the 1993 Act, like its predecessor, is that it regulates insider dealing on regulated markets or through professional intermediaries only by individuals. The Act does not use the more usual term "person" to express the scope of its prohibition, so that bodies corporate are not liable to prosecution under the Act. Corporate bodies were excluded, not because it was thought undesirable to make them criminally liable but because of the difficulties it was thought would be faced by merchant banks when one department of the bank had unpublished price-sensitive information about the securities of a client company and other departments had successfully been kept in ignorance of that information by a "Chinese Wall"[93] or otherwise. One of those other departments might deal in the shares, in which event the bank as a single corporate body would arguably have committed an offence had the Act applied to corporate bodies.

---

[89] Section 62(2) provides that in the case of the offences of encouraging dealing or disclosing inside information (see p. 469, below) either the encourager or discloser must be in the U.K. when he did the relevant act or the recipient of the encouragement or information must be.

[90] See above, p. 455.

[91] If French law adopts the same territorial rules as the U.K., the citizen would also commit a criminal offence under French law if he gave the instructions to deal from France. His liability in the U.K. would not depend, of course, upon the nationality of the company in whose shares on a U.K. regulated market the trading occurred.

[92] If the French citizen is in the U.K. at the relevant time, he will commit a criminal offence in the U.K. even if the trading occurs on a regulated market outside the U.K. but within the EEA. However, if the market is outside the EEA (say, New York or Tokyo) and involves no professional intermediary who is within the U.K. it would seem that the offence of dealing is not committed in the U.K., even if the instruction to deal is given by a person in the U.K. This is because the dealing will not have taken place on a regulated market within s.52(3) and the 1994 Order and will not have involved a professional intermediary who is within the scope of s.62. However, the offence of encouraging dealing may have been committed, the encourager being in the U.K. even if the person encouraged is not. See n. 89, above.

[93] An arrangement designed to prevent information in one part of a firm from being available to individuals working elsewhere in the firm.

However, it should be noted that these arguments were not regarded as decisive by those who drafted the regulatory regime for those authorised to carry on investment business under the Financial Services Act 1986. Their policy was to bring insider dealing, even by corporate bodies, within the scope of the regulatory prohibitions but then to deal expressly with the problem of attributed knowledge. Thus, Core Rule 28 of the Securities and Investment Board[94] provides that "a firm must not effect (either in the United Kingdom or elsewhere) an own account transaction when it knows of circumstances which mean that it, its associate, or an employee of either, is prohibited from effecting that transaction by the statutory restriction on insider dealing". Thus, by virtue of this Core Rule the statutory prohibition on insider dealing, which applies to the company's employees, is extended to the company itself. Breach of the rule opens up the company to the wide range of enforcement measures which are available to the SIB and the SFA under the Financial Services Act.[95] However, the point about knowledge is dealt with by Core Rule 36, which provides that "the firm is not . . . to be taken to act with knowledge if none of the relevant individuals involved on behalf of the firm acts with knowledge". Thus, the company will be liable only if those who deal on its behalf have the relevant knowledge and not if the knowledge is simply available in some other part of the firm but has not been communicated in fact to those who deal. Of course, many people are rightly sceptical about the efficiency of Chinese Walls, but that does not seem so much of a problem from the point of view of drafting liability rules in this context. If the Chinese Wall is in fact effective in preventing the flow of information to those who deal on the company's behalf, the company will escape liability under the FSA; if it is not, then the company is liable.

Finally, it should be noted that the Criminal Justice Act does not have the effect that no individual can be liable under it if the dealing in question is done by a company. Companies can act only through human agents, and, as we shall see below,[96] the Act's prohibition on dealing extends to procuring or encouraging dealing in securities. so if the individuals who move the company to deal do so on the basis of unpublished price-sensitive information, they may well have committed the criminal offence of procuring or encouraging the company to deal, even if the company itself commits no offence in dealing.

(c) Inside information

Issues surrounding the definition of inside information have always been controversial, and rightly so, for the essence of the offence is

---

[94] For a discussion of the role of the Core Rules see below, p. 478.
[95] See further below, p. 479.
[96] p. 469.

trading on the basis of information which is known to the trader but is not available to the market generally. The general principle is stated in the preamble to the E.C. Directive: investor confidence in security markets depends, it states, *inter alia* on "the assurance afforded to investors that they are placed on an equal footing and that they will be protected against the improper use of inside information". However, it is much easier to state this general principle than to cast it into precise legal restrictions. Placing investors "on an equal footing" cannot mean that all those who deal on a market should have the same information. Otherwise, there would be no incentive for investors and their advisers to spend time and resources investigating the prospects of particular companies or sectors of the economy, so as to make better informed investment decisions; and if this incentive were removed, investment decisions, and the market as a whole, would simply become less efficient. The aim of the legislation, therefore, should not be to eliminate all informational advantages, but to proscribe those advantages whose use would be improper, often because their acquisition was not the result of skill or effort but of the mere fact of holding a particular position. This general issue will be seen to recur in relation to all four of the limbs of the statutory definition of "inside information".

Section 56 defines inside information as information which:

(a) relates to particular securities or to a particular issuer of securities and not to securities generally or to issuers of securities generally,
(b) is specific or precise,
(c) has not been made public,
(d) if it were made public would be likely to have a significant effect on the price of any securities.

The first limb of the definition is the subject of a crucial clarification in section 60(4) that information shall be treated as relating to an issuer of securities "not only where it is about the company but also where it may affect the company's business prospects". This makes it clear that the definition of inside information includes information coming from outside the company, for example, that the government intends to liberalise the industry in which the company previously had a monopoly, as well as information coming from within the company, say, that the company is about to declare a substantially increased or decreased dividend or has won or lost a significant contract. This casts the net very widely, but it is difficult to see that any narrower formulation would have been effective. The first limb of the definition is, in effect, the threshold requirement for information to be treated as inside information. The fact that a piece of knowledge crosses this threshold does not mean it will be regarded as inside information, for it may be excluded by the other provisions of section 56 or by other sections of the Act. If, however, it does not fall within section 56(1)(a), as expanded by section 60(4), then it cannot be treated as inside information.

In fact, the first limitation on the scope of the definition of inside information is to be found in section 56(1)(a) itself. The information must relate to a particular securities or a particular issuer[97] or particular issuers of securities and not to securities or issuers generally. So information relating to a particular company or sector of the economy is covered, but not information which applies in an undifferentiated way to the economy in general. This is not an entirely easy distinction. It would seem to mean that knowledge that the government is, unexpectedly, to increase or decrease interest rates would fall within the definition because it has specific relevance to the price of gilts (government stocks) by indicating the rate at which the government is prepared to borrow money. On the other hand, possession of knowledge, good or bad, about the recent performance of the economy might not, even thought its release will cause the price of shares in general to rise or fall.

The second limb of the definition restricts the scope of inside information further. The information, in addition to what has been discussed in the previous paragraph, must be specific or precise.[98] The directive requires simply that the information be "precise",[99] but this was thought by Parliament to be possibly too restrictive, so the alternative of "specific" was added. The example was given of knowledge that a takeover bid was going to be made for a company, which would be specific information, but might not be regarded as precise if there was no knowledge of the price to be offered or the exact date on which the announcement of the bid would be made.[1]

However, the crucial effect of this restriction is that it should relieve directors and senior managers of the company and analysts who have made a special study of the company from falling foul of the legislation simply because they have generalised informational advantages over other investors, arising from their position in the one case and the effort they have exerted in the other. Having a better sense of how well or badly the company is likely to respond to a particular publicly known development does not amount to the possession of precise or specific information. But the subsection, rightly, is not intended to give companies a *carte blanche* to pass to analysts specific information about the company which has not been released to the market in

---

[97] The Act uses the term "issuer" rather than "company" because, as we have seen (above, p. 456), the Act applies not only to securities issued by companies but also to government securities or even, though this is unlikely, securities issued by an individual: s.60(2).

[98] s.56(1)(b).

[99] Art. 1.

[1] H.C. Debs., Session 1992–1993, Standing Committee B, col. 174, June 10, 1993. It seems that, on this argument, precise information will always be specific.

general. That this does happen was revealed by the Stock Exchange's censuring of a company in 1993 for revealing important information about a downgrading of profits to a group of analysts and institutional investors rather than to the market generally. The guidance subsequently produced by the Stock Exchange[2] stresses that non-public, price-sensitive information "must always be given to the market as a whole" (through the announcement mechanisms provided by the Exchange) and that such information must not be allowed "to seep into the public domain; companies sometimes attempt to justify this practice as a means of allowing a share price to adjust gradually to unexpected information. However, this is unfair to shareholders and potential investors and is unlikely to change the long-term impact of the information."[3]

The tension between the policy of encouraging communication between companies and the investment community and of stimulating analysts and other professionals to play an appropriate role in that process, on the one hand, and that of preventing selective disclosure of significant information to the detriment of shareholders who are not close to the market, on the other, is further revealed in section 58 of the Act, which deals with the problem of when information can be said to have been "made public". The Government initially proposed to leave the problem to be solved by the courts on a case-by-case basis, but came under pressure in Parliament to deal with the issue expressly. The pressure probably reflected the accurate perception that, with the broadening of the definition of "insider",[4] more weight would fall on the definition of "inside information" and especially this limb of the definition. Section 58 is not, however, a comprehensive attempt to deal with the issue. It stipulates four situations where the information shall be regarded as having been made public and five situations where the court may so regard it; otherwise, the court is free to arrive at its own judgment.[5]

The most helpful statement in section 58 from the point of view of analysts is that "information is public if . . . it is derived from information which has been made public".[6] It is clear that this provision was intended to protect analysts who derive insights into a company's prospects which are not shared by the market generally (so that the analyst is able to out-guess his or her competitors) where those insights are derived from the intensive and intelligent study of information which

---

[2] London Stock Exchange, *Guidance on the Dissemination of Price Sensitive Information*, February 1995.
[3] paras. 1 and 7.
[4] See p. 464, below.
[5] In the permissive cases the situation is, presumably, that the facts described in the subsections do not prevent the court from holding the information to have been made public, but whether the court in a particular prosecution will so hold will depend on the circumstances of the case as a whole.
[6] s.58(2)(d).

has been made public. An analyst in this position can deal on the basis of the insights so derived without first disclosing to the market the process of reasoning which has led to the conclusions, even where the disclosure of the reasoning would have a significant impact on the price of the securities dealt in. This seems to be the case even where the analyst intends to and does publish the recommendations after the dealing, *i.e.* there is what is called "front running" of the research.[7]

The utility of this subsection to the analyst and others is enhanced by the other provisions of section 58(2). Section 58(2)(c) comes close to providing an overarching test for whether information is "made public" by stating that this is so if the information "can readily be acquired" by those likely to deal in the relevant securities. In other words, the public here is not the public in general but the dealing public in relation to the securities concerned (which is obviously sensible) and, more controversially, the issue is not whether the information is known to that public but whether it is readily available to them. This is a more relaxed test than that applied under the previous legislation, which required knowledge.[8] The former test required those close to the market to wait before trading until the information had been assimilated by the investment community. Now it appears that trading is permitted as soon as the information can be readily acquired by investors, even though it has not in fact been acquired. In other words, a person who has advance knowledge of the information can react as soon as it can be "readily acquired" and reap a benefit in the period before the information is in fact fully absorbed by the market. This consequence of section 58(2)(c) is strengthened by the express provisions that publication in accordance with the rules of a regulated market or publication in records which by statute are available for public inspection mean that the information has been made public.[9]

However, the extent of the move away from knowledge in the current legislation should not be exaggerated. The test laid down in section 58(2)(c) is not that information is public if it is available to the relevant segment of investors but whether it "can readily be acquired" by them. That information could be acquired by investors, if they took certain steps, is surely not enough in every case to meet the test of

---

[7] However, such conduct is prohibited by Core Rule 25 of the SIB, subject to exceptions. Query also whether, even under the Criminal Justice Act, front-running a recommendation, not based upon any research but where its publication will have an impact on the price of the securities because of the reputation of the recommender, would be protected by s.58(2)(d). *cf. U.S. v. Carpenter* 791 F 2d 1024 (1986). The trader might have a defence under para. 2(1) of Sched. 1 to the Act, but that would depend upon his having acted "reasonably": see p. 472, below. Such conduct might in extreme cases even be a breach of section 47 of the FSA. See p. 433, above.

[8] Company Securities (Insider Dealing) Act 1985, s.10(b).

[9] s.58(2)(a) and (b) respectively. The former would cover publication on the Exchange's Regulatory News Service and latter documents filed at Companies House or the Patents Registry.

ready availability. One can foresee much dispute over what in addition
is required to make information readily available. Section 58(3) helps
with this issue to the extent of stating that certain features of the
information do not necessarily prevent it from being brought within
the category of information which "can be readily acquired". Thus,
information is not to be excluded solely because it is published outside
the United Kingdom, is communicated only on payment of a fee, can
be acquired only by observation or the exercise of diligence or expertise, or is communicated only to a section of the public. However, in
overall context of particular cases, information falling within these
categories may be excluded from the scope of "public information",
for instance because the information supplied for a fee is supplied to
a very restricted number of persons. To this extent, the legislation has
necessarily ended up adopting the Government's initial standpoint that
much would have to depend upon case-by-case evaluation by the
courts in the context of particular prosecutions.

The final limb of the definition of inside information is the requirement that it should be likely to have "a significant effect" on the price
of the securities, if it were made public.[10] The law has chosen not to
pursue those who will reap only trivial advantages from trading on
inside information. At first sight, the test would seem to present the
court (or jury) with an impossibly hypothetical test to apply. In fact,
in most cases, by the time any prosecution is brought, the information
in question will have become public,[11] and so the question will probably be answered by looking at what impact the information did in
fact have on the market when it was published. However, it would
seem permissible for an insider to argue in an appropriate case that
the likely effect of the information being made public at the time of
the trading was not significant, even if its actual disclosure had a
bigger effect, because the surrounding circumstances had changed in
the meantime.

(d) *Insiders*

We have already noted[12] the important restriction in the legislation
that insiders must be individuals. Beyond that, it might be thought that
nothing more needs to be said other than that an insider is a person in
possession of inside information. In other words, the definitional
burden in the legislation should fall on deciding what is inside
information and the definition of insider should follow as a secondary
consequence of this primary definition. The Government's consultative document on the proposed legislation[13] rejected this approach as

---

[10] s.56(1)(d).
[11] Insiders have little incentive to trade on the basis on inside information which will never
become public or will do so only far into the future.
[12] Above p. 458.
[13] DTI, *The Law on Insider Dealing*, 1989, para. 2.24.

likely to cause "damaging uncertainty in the markets, as individuals attempted to identify whether or not they were covered". This is not convincing. Either the definition of inside information is adequate or it ought to be reformed. If it is adequate, so that it can be applied effectively to those who are insiders under the Act, then it is not clear why it cannot be applied to all individuals, whether they meet the separate criteria for being insiders or not. If the definition of inside information is not adequate, it is not proper to apply it even to those who clearly are insiders under the legislation and it should be changed. In fact, the proposal that insiders should be defined as those in possession of inside information would to some extent reduce uncertainty, because the only question which would have to be asked is whether the individual was in possession of inside information and the additional question of whether the individual met the separate criteria for being classed as an insider would be irrelevant.

However, the Government stuck to its guns whilst simplifying the criteria which had been used in the earlier legislation and, following the Directive, expanding the category of insiders quite considerably.[14] By virtue of section 57(2)(a) two categories of insider are defined. The first are those who obtain inside information "through being" a director, employee or shareholder of an issuer of securities.[15] Although it is not entirely clear, it seems that the "through being" test is simply a "but for" test. If a junior employee happens to see inside information in the non-public part of the employer's premises, he or she would be within the category of insider, even if the duties of the employment do not involve acquisition of that information. On the other hand, coming across such information in a social context would not make the employee an insider, even though the information related to the worker's employer. In other words, there must be a causal link between the employment and the acquisition of the information, but not in the sense that the information must be acquired in the course of the employee's employment (though the latter remains a possible interpretation of the subsection). It may be thought that shareholders, who were excluded from the definition of insider in the previous legislation, are unlikely to obtain access to inside information "though being" shareholders, but this is in fact a likely situation in relation to large institutional shareholders, which may, either as a general practice or in specific circumstances, keep in close touch with at least the largest companies in their portfolios.

The second category of insider identified by section 57(2)(a) is the individual with inside information "through having access to the

---

[14] In particular, the requirement of "being connected with the company" has gone. See the Company Securities (Insider Dealing) Act, s.9.

[15] The relationship does not have to exist with the issuer of the securities which are dealt in. So a director of company A who is privy to his or her company's plans to launch a bid for company B is an insider in relation to the securities of company B (as well as those of A).

information by virtue of his employment, office or profession'',
whether or not the employment, etc., relationship is with an issuer.
Thus, an insider in this second category may be, or be employed by,
a professional adviser to the company[16]; an investment analyst, who
has no business link with an issuer; a civil servant or an employee of
one of the burgeoning regulatory bodies; or a journalist or other
employee of a newspaper or printing company.[17] Again, the question
arises about the exact meaning of the phrase ''by virtue of'': is it
again a simple ''but for'' test or does it mean ''in the course of''
(perhaps a slightly stronger suggestion in this second situation)? Even
if the latter interpretation is ultimately adopted, this second category
would be wide enough to embrace partners and employees of a merchant bank or solicitors' firm retained to advise an issuer on a particular matter, employees of regulatory bodies who are concerned with the
issuer's affairs, journalists researching an issuer for a story and even
employees of a printing firm involved in the production of documents
for a planned but unannounced takeover bid.[18] If the broader ''but
for'' test is adopted, then employees of these organisations, not
employed on the tasks mentioned, but who serendipitously come
across the information in the workplace, would be covered too.[19]

In practice, the need to define the exact scope of the second category
of insider is reduced by the third category, created in this country by
section 57(2)(b). In the United States persons in this third category are
distinguished from primary insiders by the use of the graphic expression ''tippee'',[20] but the British legislation lumps them in with primary
insiders. This third category consists of those who have inside
information ''the direct or indirect source of'' which is a person falling within either of the first two categories. Thus, subject to the point
about *mens rea* made in the next paragraph, the employee of a merchant bank who overhears a colleague talking about a takeover bid on
which the latter is engaged would be in all probability an insider in
the third category if he or she does not fall within the second

---

[16] Again one must remember that in the course of their professional duties such individuals may well obtain inside information in relation to a company other than the instructing company. Thus, employees of a merchant bank preparing a takeover bid would become insiders in relation to both the proposed bidder (*i.e.* the bank's client) and in relation to the target company.

[17] Of course, the journalist's employer may be a listed company, in which case he would seem to fall within the first category as well.

[18] *cf. U.S. v. Chiarella* 445 U.S. 222 (1980).

[19] An even more restrictive test would be in the course of an employment which is likely to provide access to inside information. Such a test would exclude the famous, if unlikely, example of the cleaner who finds inside information in a waste-paper basket. However, there seems to be no warrant in the Act or the Directive for such a restrictive test, which would come close to reinstating the clearly discarded test of s.9(b) of the 1985 Act.

[20] The guru of securities regulation, Professor Louis Loss of Harvard Law School, first used this expression and is rightly proud that the Oxford English Dictionary has credited him with this fact.

category.[21] This example also makes it clear that the more striking American terminology might be somewhat misleading. It does not matter whether the primary insider has consciously communicated the information to the secondary insider (*i.e.* "tipped the latter off"). Provided the latter has acquired the information from an inside source, even indirectly, he or she will fall within the scope of the Act; indeed, as in the example, the "tipper" may be entirely unaware that inside information has been communicated to anyone else.[22] Furthermore, a certain type of tipping will not in fact make the tippee liable for dealing. If the insider within the first two categories encourages another person to deal without communicating to that other person any inside information, the latter can deal without being exposed to liability under the Act.[23] In short, the focus of the legislation is on the holding of inside information which has come from an inside source; how that information came to be transmitted to the present holder did not concern the drafters of the Act but the fact of its transmission did.

Finally, the definition of having information "as an insider" in section 57 was used by the drafters of the legislation to achieve a second function, which is logically separate from the definition of an insider, but which is nevertheless crucial to the overall construction of the legislation. This was to impose a requirement of *mens rea* for liability under the Act, a not surprising pre-condition for criminal liability, but nevertheless one which has made enforcement of the legislation often difficult.[24] The requirement in this regard is a two-fold one: the accused must be proved to have known that the information in question was inside information (as discussed in the previous section) and that the information came from "an inside source", *i.e.* that he or she fell within one or other of the three categories discussed in this section. The latter requirement is likely to be difficult to meet in the case of persons falling within the third category,[25] especially if the argument is that the information came indirectly from the primary insider to the suspect via a chain of communications. Proving that a "sub-tippee" or even a "sub-sub-tippee" knew that the ultimate source of the information was a primary insider could be fraught with problems.

---

[21] The third category is also apt to cover shadow directors, who were not brought within the first category and might not fall within the second category either: an independent businessman or woman, who was a shadow director, might have neither employment, office nor profession.

[22] Moreover, since it is enough that the individual in the third category "has" the information from a source falling within the first or second categories, it does not matter either whether the "tippee" has solicited the information. Inadvertent acquisition of inside information is covered. This was a point of controversy under the previous legislation until cleared up by the House of Lords, in favour of liability. See *Attorney General's Reference (No. 1 of 1988)* [1989] A.C. 971.

[23] The tipper would be liable for encouraging the dealing. See below, p. 469.

[24] See p. 473, below.

[25] The fact that someone is a director will presumably raise a pretty strong prima facie case that he or she knew that fact, and so move the evidential burden to the director to disprove knowledge.

(e) *Prohibited acts*

What is an insider, with inside information and with the relevant *mens rea*, prohibited from doing? There are four prohibitions and, before describing them, it should be pointed out that they apply only where a person has information "as an insider", which requirement includes knowingly having the information as a result of falling within one or other of the three categories discussed under heading (d), above. However, it is not necessary that the accused should still fall within these categories at the time the prohibited act takes place. Once inside information has been acquired by an insider, the prohibitions apply even though the accused, say, resigns the directorship or employment through which he obtained the information.[26] On the other hand, if the information acquired ceases to be inside information, because it enters the public domain, the prohibitions of the Act will equally cease to apply. This demonstrates again that the focus of the Act is on the information inequality between the insider or former insider and the rest of the market.

First and most obviously, there must be no dealing in the relevant securities.[27] The relevant securities are those which are "price-affected", *i.e.* those upon the price of which the inside information would be likely to have a significant effect, if made public.[28] Dealing is defined as acquiring or disposing of securities.[29] Thus, a person who refrains from dealing on the basis of inside information is not covered by the legislation.[30] In principle, it is difficult to defend this exclusion since the loss of public confidence in the market will be as strong as in a case of dealing, if news of the non-dealing emerges. The exclusion was presumably a pragmatic decision based on the severe evidential problems which would face the prosecution in such a case. The dealing prohibition is broken quite simply by dealing; the Act does not require the prosecution to go further and prove that the dealing was motivated by the inside information, though the accused may be able to put forward the defence that he would have done what he did even if he had not had the information.[31] The Act covers dealing as an agent (not only as a principal) even if the profit from the dealing is thereby made by someone else, for one can never be sure that the profit made by the third party will not filter back to the trader in some form or other.

---

[26] This is the significance of prohibiting acts by a person who has information "as an insider", which s.57 makes clear refers to the situation at the time of the acquisition of the information, rather than the simpler formulation of prohibiting acts *by* an insider, which might well refer to the accused's status at the time of the prohibited acts.

[27] s.52(1).

[28] See s.56(2) and p. 464, above.

[29] s.55.

[30] So a person who acquires bad news about a company and so decides not to buy its shares or discovers good news and decides not to dispose of its shares is not caught.

[31] See below, p. 470.

And it covers agreeing to acquire or dispose of securities as well as their actual acquisition or disposal, and entering into or ending a contract which creates the security[32] as well as contracting to acquire or dispose of a pre-existing security.

Secondly, the insider is prohibited from procuring, directly or indirectly, the acquisition or disposal of securities by any other person. This is done by bringing this situation within the definition of dealing.[33] Procurement will have taken place if the acquisition is done by the insider's agent or nominee or a person acting at his or her direction, but this does not exhaust the range of situations in which procurement can be found.[34] Since the person procured to deal may well not be in possession of any inside information and the procurer has not in fact dealt, without this extension of the statutory meaning of "dealing" there would be a lacuna in the law.

Thirdly, there is a prohibition on the individual encouraging another person to deal in price-affected securities, knowing or having reasonable cause to believe that dealing would take place on a regulated market or through a professional intermediary.[35] Again, it does not matter for the purposes of the liability of the person who does the encouraging that the person encouraged commits no offence, because, say, no inside information is imparted by the accused. Indeed, it does not matter for these purposes that no dealing at all in the end takes place, though the accused must at least have reasonable cause to believe that it would. The existence of this offence is likely to discourage over-enthusiastic presentations by company representatives to meetings of large shareholders or analysts.

Finally, the individual must not disclose the information "otherwise than in the proper performance of the functions of his employment, office or profession to another person".[36] Unlike in the previous two cases, the communication of inside information is a necessary ingredient of this offence, but no response on the part of the person to whom the information is communicated need occur nor be expected by the accused. However, in effect, this element is built into the liability, for the accused has a defence that "he did not at the time expect any person, because of the disclosure, to deal in securities" on a regulated market or through a professional intermediary.[37] So, even if it occurs outside the proper performance of duties, disclosure which is not expected to lead to dealing will not result in liability, but the burden of proving the absence of the expectation falls on the accused.

[32] As is the case with derivatives.
[33] s.55(1)(b).
[34] s.55(4) and (5).
[35] s.52(2)(a).
[36] s.52(2)(b).
[37] s.53(3)(a).

(f) *Defences*[38]

The Act provides a wide range of defences, which fall within two broad categories. First, there are two general defences which carry on the task of defining the mischief at which the Act is aimed.[39] Secondly, there are the special defences, set out mainly but not entirely, in Schedule 1 to the Act, which frankly accept that in certain circumstances, usually involving financing techniques established in the City of London, the policy of prohibiting insider trading should be overborne by the values underlying the exempted practices. These special defences, which are foreshadowed in the preamble to the Directive, will be dealt with only briefly here.[40]

The more important of the general defences is that the accused "would have done what he did even if he had not had the information".[41] This defence replaces with a general formulation the specific defences which had existed in the former legislation in respect of liquidators, receivers, trustees, trustees in bankruptcy and personal representatives,[42] who, for example, may find themselves in the course of their offices advised to trade when in fact themselves in possession of inside information. Thus, a trustee, who is advised by an investment adviser to deal for the trust in a security in relation to which the trustee has inside information, will be able to do so, relying on this defence. But the defence applies more generally than that and would embrace, for example, an insider who dealt when he did in order to meet a pressing financial need or legal obligation. However, the accused will carry the burden of showing that his decision to deal at that particular time in that particular security was not influenced by the possibility of exploiting the inside information which was held.

The other general defence is that the accused did not expect the dealing to result in a profit attributable to the inside information.[43] This is considerably narrower than the defence in the 1985 Act which applied when the individual traded "otherwise than with a view to the making of a profit"[44] and many of the situations covered by this provision of the old law—for example, trading to meet a pressing financial need—will now fall under the first general defence discussed above.

---

[38] We have already dealt, in the previous paragraph, with one of the defences relevant to the disclosure offence.

[39] Though s.53 makes it clear that the burden of proof falls on the accused, thus obviating a possible ambiguity which was found by some in the previous legislation. See *R. v. Cross* [1991] BCLC 125.

[40] Sched. 1 may be amended by the Treasury by order (s.53(5)), presumably so that it may be kept current with developments in financing techniques.

[41] s.53(1)(c) and (2)(c). This defence does not apply to the disclosure offence, though it is an essential ingredient of that offence that the disclosure should not have occurred in the proper performance of the accused's functions.

[42] 1985 Act, ss.3(1)(b) and 7.

[43] s.53(1)(a). The same defence is provided, *mutatis mutandis*, in relation to the other offences by s.53(2)(a) and (3)(b). Making a profit is defined so as to include avoiding a loss: s.53(6).

[44] 1985 Act, s.3(1)(a).

Although the defence is general in the sense that it is not confined to particular business or financial transactions, the range of situations falling within it is probably quite narrow. The Government's attempts in the Parliamentary debates to produce examples of situations for which this defence was needed and which were at all realistic were not entirely convincing.[45]

The Act provides six special defences, two in the body of the Act and four in Schedule 1. One of those provided in the body of the Act appears to be a general defence and is to the effect that dealing is not unlawful if the individual "believed on reasonable grounds that the information had been disclosed widely enough to ensure that none of those taking part in the dealing would be prejudiced by not having the information".[46] In short, the defence is that, although the information had not been made public, it was widely enough disclosed to avoid harm to the others involved. In fact, however, this defence is aimed particularly at underwriting arrangements,[47] where those involved in the underwriting may trade amongst themselves on the basis of shared knowledge about the underwriting proposal but which information is not known to the market generally. The other defence provided in the body of the Act[48] concerns things done "on behalf of a public sector body in pursuit of monetary policies or policies with respect to exchange rates or the management of public debt or foreign exchange reserves". So reasons of state, relating to financial policy, trump market integrity.[49]

The four special defences provided in the Schedule do not extend to the disclosure of inside information. Where the defences apply, those concerned may trade or encourage others to do so but may not enlarge the pool of persons privy to the inside information. In all four cases, what are judged to be valuable market activities would be impossible without the relaxation of the insider dealing prohibitions. Thus, market makers[50] may often be in possession of inside information but would not be able to discharge their undertaking to maintain a continuous two-way market in particular securities if they were always subject to the Act. So paragraph 1 of Schedule 1 exempts acts done by a market maker in good faith in the course of the market-making business. More controversially, paragraph 5 does the same thing in relation to price stabilisation of new issues.[51] This is a more controver-

---

[45] H.C. Debs., Session 1992–1993, Standing Committee B, June 10, 1993. A suggestion was where the insider sold at a price which took into account the impact the (bad) information would have on the market when released.

[46] s.53(1)(b). s.53(2)(b) provides a similar defence in relation to the encouraging offence.

[47] On underwriting see above, p. 396.

[48] s.63, applying to all offences under the Act. Technically, s.63 does not provide a defence but rather describes a situation where the Act "does not apply".

[49] As Art. 2(4) of the Directive permits.

[50] See above, n. 73.

[51] On which see p. 435, above.

sial step because the activity of stabilising the price of new issues is itself a controversial matter. In order to qualify for this protection the stabilisation must be conducted in accordance with rules made under section 48 of the Financial Services Act 1986.[52]

The final two special defences relate to trading whilst in possession of "market information", which is, in essence, information about transactions in securities being contemplated or no longer contemplated or having or not having taken place. First, an individual may act in connection with the acquisition or disposal of securities and with a view to facilitating their acquisition or disposal where the information held is market information arising directly out of the individual's involvement in the acquisition or disposal.[53] An example is where the employees of a merchant bank advising a bidder on a proposed takeover procure the acquisition of the target's shares on behalf of the bidder but before the bid is publicly announced, in order to give the bidder a good platform from which to launch the bid. This defence would not permit the employees to purchase shares for their own account, because they would not then be acting to facilitate the proposed transaction out of which the inside information arose. Even so, permitting a bidder to act in this way is somewhat controversial for those who procure the purchase of the shares know that a bid at a price in excess of the current market price is about to be launched and those who sell out to the bidder just before the public announcement may feel that they have been badly treated.[54] Another situation covered by the provision is that of a fund manager who decides to take a large stake in a particular company. The manager can go into the market on behalf of the funds under management and acquire the stake at the best prices possible, without announcing in advance the intention to build up a large stake, which would immediately drive up the price of the chosen company's shares.

Under the second and more general "market information" defence the individual may act if "it was reasonable for an individual in his position to have acted as he did" despite having the market information.[55] This is so broadly phrased that it would seem wide enough to cover the situations discussed in the previous paragraph. The more

---

[52] As amended by the Financial Services Act 1986 (Stabilisation) Order 1988 (S.I. 1988 No.717), and see SIB Core Rule 29.

[53] para. 3.

[54] Nevertheless, the City Code on Takeovers and Mergers adopts the same approach as the Act. See Rule 4.1. However the potential bidder would have to comply with the statutory provisions on the disclosure of shareholdings. See pp. 484 *et seq.*, and Davies, "The Takeover Bidder Exemption and the Policy of Disclosure" in Hopt and Wymeersch (eds.), *European Insider Dealing* (London, 1991). Even so, the bid facilitation argument ought not to be employed to justify the purchase of derivatives where the aim of the purchase is simply to give the bidder as cash benefit rather than to take a step towards the acquisition of voting control: SIB, *Equity-related Derivatives*, Consultative Paper on Market Conduct, June 1996, pp. 6 and 12.

[55] para. 2(1). Some guidance on what is reasonable is given in para. 2(2).

specific provisions were included as well presumably in order to give comfort to those who would otherwise have had to rely on the general reasonableness provision and who might have wondered whether the courts would interpret it in their favour.

(iii) Enforcing the law

(a) *Criminal penalties and disqualification*

The Criminal Justice Act places exclusive reliance upon criminal sanctions for its enforcement. Section 63(2) states that no contract shall be "void or unenforceable" by reason only of an offence committed under the Act, a provision which was redrafted in 1993, it would seem, in order to close the loop-hole, as the Government saw it, identified in *Chase Manhattan Equities v. Goodman*.[56] Although the Act does not deal expressly with the question of whether a civil action for breach of statutory duty could be built on its provisions, it seems unlikely that the Act would be held to fall within either of the categories identified for this purpose in the case-law.[57]

The criminal sanctions imposed by the Act are, on summary conviction, a fine not exceeding the statutory maximum (currently £5,000) and/or a term of imprisonment not exceeding six months, and on conviction on indictment an unlimited fine and/or imprisonment for not more than seven years.[58] The power of the judge on conviction on indictment to impose an unlimited fine means that, in theory at least, the court could ensure that the insider made no profit out of the dealing.[59] Prosecutions in England and Wales may be brought only by or with the consent of the Secretary of State or the Director of Public Prosecutions. The Secretary of State occasionally consents to prosecutions being brought by the Stock Exchange, which maintains a computerised system for surveillance of dealings taking place on the Exchange.

It is difficult to make a wholly accurate assessment of the extent of the use of the criminal process in this area. Hannigan[60] suggests that from 1980 up to the end of the first quarter of 1994 there had been some 33 recorded[61] cases brought against some 51 individuals, of whom 14 pleaded guilty and only 9 of whom were convicted after pleading not guilty. The fines imposed by the courts were modest, as,

---

[56] [1991] BCLC 897, at 930–935, where the judge held that the previous legislative formulation did not prevent the court from holding a contract unenforceable when it had been concluded in breach of the 1985 Act's provisions.

[57] See especially *Lonrho Ltd v. Shell Petroleum Co. Ltd (No. 2)* [1982] A.C. 173, H.L.

[58] s.61.

[59] The Crown Court has power under the Criminal Justice Act 1988, as amended by the Proceeds of Crime Act 1995, to make an order confiscating the proceeds of crime, which could also be used to this end.

[60] *op.cit.* n.1, pp.118 *et seq.*

[61] That is, in the newspapers. It cannot be said how many cases the newspapers did not pick up.

however, were the profits reported to have been made by the insiders. Only one non-suspended custodial sentence was imposed. This suggests a rather modest rate of use of the criminal law to date.

In addition to the traditional criminal penalties which may be visited upon insiders, it seems that the disqualification sanction is available against some insiders in some cases, the effect of which is to disable the person disqualified from being involved in the running of companies in the future.[62] In *R. v. Goodman*[63] the Court of Appeal upheld the Crown Court's decision to disqualify, for a period of 10 years, a managing director convicted of insider dealing. The Crown Court had invoked section 2 of the Company Directors Disqualification Act 1986 which enables a court to disqualify a person who has been convicted of an indictable offence in connection with the management of a company. The Court of Appeal took a liberal view of what could be said to be "in connection with the management of the company", so as to bring within the phrase the managing director's disposal of his shares in the company in advance of publication of bad news about its prospects. It would seem, too, that a disqualification order could be made on grounds of unfitness under section 8 of the 1986 Act upon an application by the Secretary of State, following an investigation into insider dealing under section 177 of the Financial Services Act (see (b), below). In this case, conviction by a court of an indictable offence would not be a pre-condition to a disqualification order, but the court would have to be satisfied that the person's conduct in relation to the company made him unfit to be concerned in the management of a company and this section, unlike section 2, is capable of applying to insider dealing only by directors and shadow directors.

(b) *Investigation, national and international*

It was, or should have been, apparent to everyone that a regime of criminal sanctions for insider trading would operate effectively only if there was an efficient system of investigating cases of suspected insider dealing. In this context, it is odd that when the criminal law was first deployed against insider dealing in 1980, the well-established technique of appointing inspectors to investigate aspects of companies' affairs was not extended to this new area of regulation.[64] The defect was remedied only with the enactment of the Financial Services Act 1986, sections 177 and 178 of which provide for the appointment of inspectors by the Secretary of State where "there are circumstances suggesting" that an offence under the 1993 Act may have been committed. Of course, the existing inspection provisions covered some examples of insider trading, notably the powers to appoint inspectors

---

[62] See Chap. 24, below.
[63] [1993] 2 All E.R. 789, C.A.
[64] On company investigations in general, see Chap. 25, below.

to investigate share dealings by directors or their families[65] or to report on the membership of companies or the ownership of shares.[66] However, an inspection provision aimed directly at insider dealing was undoubtedly a useful addition to the enforcement armoury.

It is not usual for the Department to announce the appointment of inspectors under the FSA in particular cases and there is no provision for the publication of their reports, though the information contained in them may be communicated to the regulatory or criminal law authorities for the purposes of enforcement.[67] It may also be used directly by the Secretary of State to obtain a disqualification order.[68] The information to which the Department responds in setting up inspectors often comes in insider dealing cases from the Stock Exchange, which monitors price movements in listed securities in order to detect unusual shifts. At present, however, the Stock Exchange, like the Department, does not announce the initiation or conclusions of investigations it may undertake as a result of the unusual movements it detects. What is known, however, is that only a small proportion of the cases referred by the Exchange to the Department are then investigated further by the latter. In 1995–1996 28 cases were referred and inspectors were approved in 13 instances.[69]

The general considerations relating to the conduct of investigations are considered in Chapter 25 but what needs to be emphasised here are the wide inquisitorial powers which the inspectors have and the attempts which have been made to deal with the overwhelmingly likely fact that any sophisticated insider dealing activity will involve intermediaries established outside the United Kingdom, which may not be minded to co-operate with the inspectors appointed under the British legislation.

The inspectors may require any person who, they consider, is or may be able to give them relevant information to produce to them documents in his possession or control, to attend before them, possibly for examination on oath, and to give the inspectors all other reasonable assistance.[70] If the person called upon fails in any of these duties or fails to answer any question put by the inspectors, the latter cannot take punitive action themselves but may certify the fact to the court, which will inquire into the situation. If the court concludes that the

---

[65] Companies Act 1985, s.446, below, p. 696.

[66] ss.442 and 444. Today, appointments are sometimes made under both s.177 of the Financial Services Act and s.442 of the Companies Act, because of the powers in relation to the "freezing" of share which inspectors appointed under the latter section have in the case of non-co-operation. See p. 495, below.

[67] ss.179 and 180, especially s.180(1)(a) and (n). On the problematic nature of the relationship between the absence of a right to silence before the inspectors, confirmed in *Styr v. H.M. Advocate* 1994 S.L.T. 5, and the communication of the information obtained for the purposes of a prosecution, see pp. 699 *et seq.* below.

[68] s.180(1)(c).

[69] DTI, *Companies in 1995–96* (1996), Table 9.

[70] s.177(3) and (4), subject to the protection of legal professional privilege: s.177(7).

person had no reasonable excuse for the failure, the court may either punish him as if guilty of contempt of court or direct the Secretary of State to take steps to remove or restrict the person's present or future freedom to engage in investment business.[71] These are powerful sanctions: the non-co-operator may be subject to the substantial penalties for contempt of court[72] or may be deprived of his or her livelihood for failing to accede to the inspectors' requests. In *Re an Inquiry under the Insider Dealing Act*[73] a journalist refused to answer the inspectors' questions, in order to protect his sources, but was held not to have reasonable excuse for the failure because his answers were needed for the prevention of crime.[74] He was fined £20,000 (though presumably this was paid by his employers).

As far as investigations involving foreign intermediaries, especially foreign banks, are concerned, the Act contains a number of innovative provisions. First, the banker/client relationship is not by itself a good reason for not co-operating with the inspectors, if the Secretary of State has authorised the inspectors to impose the requirement to which the relationship of confidence between bank and client is put up as a defence. So, although the inspectors acting alone cannot override banking confidence, the Secretary of State can authorise them to do so.[75] Secondly, foreign bank secrecy laws do not constitute a reasonable excuse for non-co-operation with the inspectors where the foreign institution has been dealing on the instructions or on behalf of another person, unless the institution is in a position to reveal at least the identity of the person for whom it acted (though not any further details of the transactions). Moreover, the secrecy laws will not protect the foreign institution at all in relation to the British legislation if the institution might have obtained exemption from its law or the consent of the person for whom it acted for the disclosure of further information.[76] In other words, the foreign institution cannot simply rest on the foreign law without making good faith efforts to secure its release from the obligation of secrecy.

All this, however, would be of little avail if the British authorities were not in a position to apply effective sanctions against the foreign institutions. Here, the Secretary of State's powers are widely drawn. Where the Secretary of State uses the sanction of disqualifying the non-co-operator from becoming authorised to carry on investment business in the United Kingdom, he or she may also direct all authorised persons in the United Kingdom not to transact business

---

[71] s.178(1)–(3).

[72] Two years' imprisonment or an unlimited fine, as laid down in s.14 of the Contempt of Court Act 1981 and presumably applicable under the FSA.

[73] [1988] A.C. 660, H.L. See also *X Ltd v. Morgan-Grampion Ltd.* [1991] 1 A.C. 1, H.L.

[74] Applying by analogy s.10 of the Contempt of Court Act 1981.

[75] s.177(8). This provision applies equally to banks based in the U.K.

[76] s.178(6).

with or on behalf of the disqualified institution, *i.e.* to ''cold shoulder'' the non-co-operator.[77] Thus, provided the foreign institution does have an interest in maintaining its access to the financial markets in the United Kingdom, it is possible to apply effective sanctions against it.

However, it is clear that the British Government hopes to obtain information about the international aspects of insider dealing and of other financial market wrongs, not only by the imposition of sanctions under domestic legislation, but also through co-operation with the regulatory authorities of the countries involved. Article 10 of the E.C. Directive requires Member States to co-operate with one another and to exchange information in the carrying out of their obligations under the Directive, and Memoranda of Understanding to somewhat similar effect have been agreed between the United Kingdom, on the one hand, and the United States, Japan, Hong Kong, Switzerland and Australia, on the other, *i.e.* with many of the leading financial countries outside the European Union. Statutory powers enabling the United Kingdom to implement these European Community and international obligations, where the information requested is not readily to hand, are to be found in sections 82 to 91 of the Companies Act 1989.[78] These sections empower (now)[79] the Treasury and Secretary of State for Trade and Industry to act for the purpose of assisting an overseas regulatory authority[80] and confer powers very similar to those which inspectors have under the Financial Services Act provisions discussed above.[81] They thus include the power to require any person to attend before the government minister or (and presumably normally) any officer of the Department of Trade and Industry or any other competent person, to answer questions and to produce documents.[82] The origins of the legislation are indicated by the provision that, in deciding whether to exercise these powers, the Treasury has to take into account whether, should the case arise, the corresponding assistance would be given to the British authorities in the country of the requesting

---

[77] s.178(5).

[78] Corresponding provisions permitting cooperation with other regulatory authorities in respect of the Financial Services Act functions are to be found in ss.128A-C of that Act.

[79] See the Transfer of Functions (Financial Services) Order, S.I. 1992 No. 1315, art. 5, Sched. 3, para.3.

[80] This includes, but is not confined to, overseas authorities charged with the enforcement of rules against insider dealing: s.82(2). However, in deciding whether to respond positively to the request, the Treasury must take into account whether the inquiry relates to a breach of law or regulation which has ''no close parallel'' in the U.K. or involves the assertion of a jurisdiction not recognised in the U.K: s.82(4)(b). These issues are not likely to arise in relation to the enforcement by overseas regulators of rules deriving from E.C. Directives.

[81] At p. 475. Overseas regulatory authorities are also permitted recipients of information obtained by inspectors appointed under the FSA: Financial Services Act 1986, s.180(1)(qq).

[82] s.83 and 84. The Companies Act provides only criminal sanctions for non-compliance or for making deliberately false or misleading statements: s.85. However, under s.128C of the Financial Services Act the Secretary of State may exercise his powers of discipline and intervention for the purpose of assisting an overseas regulatory authority, under conditions similar to those governing the Companies Act powers.

authority.[83] In the most recent year for which information is available,[84] some 47 requests came from overseas regulatory authorities, mainly the Securities Exchange Commission in the United States, but 18 came under the provisions of the Insider Dealing Directive. In 3 of the 47 cases the powers under the 1989 Act had to be used to obtain the information requested, but none of the 3 was an insider dealing case.[85]

(iv) Liability under the Financial Services Act and civil sanctions

We have already noted[86] that the Criminal Justice Act 1993 does not seek to deploy civil sanctions in support of its prohibitions. We have also seen that the law relating to directors' fiduciary duties has little purchase on insider dealing, mainly because is directed more at the relationship of the insider with the source of the information than with the relationship between the insider and other market participants.[87] Yet there is an area of regulation of insider dealing which does carry with it the possibility of civil sanctions for breach of the rules. It is constituted by the Core Conduct of Business Rules laid down by the Securities and Investment Board for those authorised to engage in investment business, some of which are relevant to insider dealing.

The system of Core Rules was ushered in by amendments made to the Financial Services Act by the Companies Act 1989. The Rules apply to those, relatively few in number, who are authorised to engage in investment business directly by SIB itself. Under section 63A of the FSA, however, the Core Rules may be "designated", so that they apply directly also to those, the majority, who are authorised through their membership of one of the Self-Regulating Organisations (SROs). Breach of a designated rule is treated in the same way as a breach of a rule of an SRO. However, the SROs normally have power under section 63B to amplify, modify, adapt or even to waive the Core Rules. Consequently, the process of designation, which was carried out in 1991 and 1992, involved the Core Rules being reflected and expanded upon in the rulebooks of the SROs, especially for our purposes in the rulebook of the Securities and Futures Association (SFA). However, in one of those rapid changes of policy which has characterised regulation of financial services in the United Kingdom since the Big Bang,

---

[83] s.82(4)(a), and the requesting authority may have to contribute to the costs of the inquiry: s.82(6).

[84] DTI, *Companies in 1995–96*, p. 15.

[85] The Treasury made some 5 outgoing requests for information.

[86] Above, p. 473.

[87] Above, p. 445. The same point could be made about the developing law relating to breach of confidence, which could be relevant where confidential information is used for the purposes of insider dealing: the action lies in the hands of the confider.

in 1994 SIB announced that it intended to "de-designate" most of the Core Conduct of Business Rules, in order to give the SROs greater control over their rulebooks.[88] Thus, in the future the provisions in the rulebooks of the SROs may begin to diverge from those of the Core Rules. However, for ease of exposition we shall confine ourselves to the Core Rules of SIB and assume that the rules of the SROs, especially the SFA, follow a similar pattern.

We have already referred to Core Rule 28, which prohibits insider dealing by authorised firms,[89] and by Rule 28.2 firms must use their "best endeavours" to ensure that they do not effect transactions for clients who they know are prohibited from dealing by the Criminal Justice Act. We have also referred to Core Rule 25[90] which prohibits firms (subject to exceptions) from front-running research releases or recommendations to buy or sell securities. Core Rule 25 is supplemented by Core Rule 20, which requires firms to "deal with customer and with own account orders fairly and in due turn". This rule is aimed at a variety of dubious practices, but included among them is the practice of a firm dealing for its own account ahead of executing a customer order which it knows will have an impact on the price of a security. Finally, Core Rule 34 requires firms to take "reasonable steps" to ensure that its officers and employees act in accordance with the rules of the regulatory system and "the statutory restrictions on insider dealing".[91]

The whole range of FSA sanctions is available against those who break the Core Rules, included among which are two obviously civil sanctions. What light do they shed on the utility of civil sanctions in the area of insider dealing? The first civil sanction is the private right of action of a person who suffers loss as a result of the breach of a Core Rule to sue the person in breach for damages under section 62 of the Act.[92] Where the insider dealing takes place on a regulated market, the probably insuperable problem which will face any plaintiff

---

[88] This was done by SIB's Financial Services (Dedesignation) Rules and Regulations 1994. The power to designate remains in the Act. However, this may not be the end of the story. The most recent rumours involve yet another change of direction, *i.e.* integrating the SROs into SIB, thus reducing or even eliminating their independence: *Financial Times*, January 30, 1996, p. 1.

[89] Subject to a "Chinese Wall" defence in Core Rule 36. See p. 459, above.

[90] Above, n. 7.

[91] This Rule constitutes the regulatory basis for the internal compliance systems which investment firms have established, thus creating a new breed of compliance officers, employed by the firm but responsible for ensuring that it abides by the rules—a far from easy task for those without a split personality.

[92] In the case of most, and perhaps all, of the Core Rules mentioned above, the right of action would not be confined to private investors because the rule in question is "directed at ensuring" that trading on the basis of inside information does not take place: Financial Services Act 1986 (Restriction of Right of Action) Regulations 1991 (S.I. 1991 No. 489), para. 3(c). This is one of four categories where non-private investors can sue as well as private ones.

under section 62 is the need to show loss.[93] In the case of dealings on a liquid market, the trading by the insider will not have induced the potential plaintiff into the market; that is, the market in the shares existed independently of the insider's activities and whatever reasons the other person had for wishing to trade at that particular time, they too presumably were not influenced by the insider's activities, of which the potential plaintiff was no doubt unaware. So the plaintiff cannot argue that he or she would otherwise not have traded and so would not have incurred the loss in question.

Alternatively, the plaintiff may argue that, had the insider disclosed the information in question, the price of the securities bought or sold by the plaintiff would have been different, and so the plaintiff, although he would have traded, would have done so at a price which reflected the information which the insider possessed and in that way would have avoided a loss or made a profit.[94] The difficulty with this argument is that it mistakes the nature of the obligations imposed by the Core Rules cited above. They do not require disclosure of information; they prohibit trading whilst in possession of such information.[95] That is a prohibition which can be met as well by not trading as by disclosing the information. Indeed, in some cases it would be improper for the insider to disclose the information—for instance, where it is confidential. Had the insider simply stayed out of the market, the plaintiff would still have done what he did, and yet there would have been no breach of the Core Rules.[96] So there is a serious question about the causal relevance of the insider's activities to the plaintiff's loss. Nevertheless, despite these problems, section 62 may be of significance to dealings directly between market professionals which, as we have seen, are brought within the scope of the Criminal Justice Act[97] and thus of the Core Rules. In such a case it is not difficult to

---

[93] It would also be necessary, of course, to show that a Core Rule had been broken. Since the Rules quoted above impose obligations of firms, it does not follow that insider dealing by the employee of a firm is by itself a breach of a Rule, say, where the employee had dealt for his or her own account and the firm had taken reasonable steps to ensure compliance with the insider dealing provisions.

[94] It is unclear whether "loss" in s.62(1) includes failure to make a profit.

[95] Of course, there is a strong case for disclosure rules, both to reduce opportunities for insider dealing and more generally to promote the efficiency of stock markets. See in this regard Chapter 9, "Continuing Obligations" of the Stock Exchange's *Listing Rules*, which require, *inter alia*, the disclosure by a listed company to the Exchange of "major new developments in its sphere of activity which are not public knowledge which may . . . lead to a substantial movement in the price of its listed securities" (para. 9.1). The Traded Securities (Disclosure) Regulations 1994 (S.I. 1994 No. 188) make similar, but statutory, provisions in relation to securities, other than listed securities, which are traded on a regulated market in the U.K. for example, securities traded on the Alternative Investment Market. See pp. 498–500, below. But insider dealing prohibitions are not disclosure obligations.

[96] The insider's activities may have had a minor effect on the market price of the securities in which he dealt, but, in so far as this did happen, it presumably tended to move the shares towards their accurate value and so tended to reduce the plaintiff's loss.

[97] See p. 455, above.

imagine situations in which it could be said that, without the intervention of the insider, the plaintiff would not have dealt at that particular time and so at that particular price.[98]

The second civil sanction is provided by section 61 of the Act which enables the SIB, acting on behalf of investors as a class, to seek an order from the court that profits[99] made by an authorised person from a breach of the Core Rules be paid into court.[1] The focus here is on the disgorgement of the profits made in breach of the Rules, rather than on compensating other traders for losses suffered. However, the latter aspect emerges again once one moves to consider what is to be done with the money which has been paid into court. By virtue of section 61(6) it is to be paid out to or distributed among the "persons appearing to the court to have entered into the transaction" with the authorised person who made the profit, which in the case of insider dealing on a liquid market would be an entirely arbitrary fact. Who of all the traders in the security at the time the insider was active happened to deal with the insider is a pure matter of chance and it would seem odd that such chance should determine which of the many contemporaneous market participants should have the benefit of the insider's profits.[2]

Nevertheless, the idea of a general civil sanction, designed primarily to deprive the insider of the profits of the dealing rather than to compensate other traders, and not confined to those who are subject to the FSA, continues to command attention among those concerned with making the insider dealing laws more effective in practice. Such a sanction could be seen to have two advantages over the current criminal sanction. First, it would require a lower burden of proof, and, secondly, it could be made available to a much wider range of plaintiffs than the prosecuting authorities which have charge of the criminal sanction and the SIB under section 61 of the FSA. The idea proved

---

[98] In addition, in such a case the SIB would seem to have the power to seek an order from the court requiring the party in breach and any other party "knowingly concerned in the contravention" to take "such steps as the court may direct" to remedy the contravention: s.61(1). This is a restitutionary remedy, modelled on but not identical to the equitable remedy of rescission. See *S.I.B v. Pantell (No. 2)* [1993] Ch. 256, C.A., and p. 434, above. Of course, the other party might himself have access to the rescission remedy in equity, but only if the insider had made a misstatement, whereas the SIB's powers are based simply upon a breach of the Core Rules.

[99] Query whether avoiding a loss is included within the idea of making a profit.

[1] s.61(3)(a). Section 61(3)(b) extends this mechanism to sums representing losses or "other adverse effects" incurred by investors as a result of the breach, but this provision seems open to the objections discussed in relation to s.62.

[2] A possible way to finesse the problem would be to amend the law so as to provide for the distribution of the profit among all those dealing (in the opposite direction to the insider) in the relevant securities in the market at the time the insider dealt, a model adopted by the U.S. Insider Trading and Securities Fraud Enforcement Act 1988, (inserting a new s.20A into the Securities Exchange Act 1934). However, this runs the risk of dividing the profit among so many potential claimants that, at least in the absence of very effective class action procedures, no individual claimant has an incentive to commence an action.

attractive to the Trade and Industry Committee of the House of Commons,[3] but the Government rejected the idea of a "civil penalty" on the grounds that the criminal law constituted the "classical" way of expressing the public interest in penalising individuals who engaged in insider dealing.[4]

CONCLUSION

The Companies Act 1980 and, now, the Criminal Justice Act 1993 have firmly established in the United Kingdom the principle that trading on public markets whilst in the possession of price-sensitive, non-public information is unlawful. The latter Act, implementing the European Community Directive on insider trading, has clarified the rationale of such legislation as being the protection of public confidence in securities exchanges. However, the detection and prosecution of those engaged in insider dealing remains a problem with which it cannot yet confidently be asserted that the Stock Exchange and the Department of Trade and Industry have fully come to grips. So long as this continues to be the case, the search for an effective civil sanction to supplement the criminal penalty is unlikely to be abandoned, despite the formidable difficulties involved in fashioning such a remedy.

---

[3] Third Report, Session 1989–1990, *Company Investigations*, H.C. 36, paras. 158–159. And see B. Rider, "Policing Insider Dealing in Britain" in Hopt and Wymeersch (eds.), *op. cit.*, especially pp. 328–329.

[4] DTI, *Company Investigation: Government's Response to the Third Report of the Trade and Industry Committee*, Cm. 1149 (1991), p. 18.

CHAPTER 18

MARKET TRANSPARENCY

IN Chapter 16 we analysed the rules relating to the public offering of securities and saw that the main regulatory technique employed by the law was the requirement of complete and accurate disclosure of information relating to the securities on offer. But the investors' need for such information does not cease the moment the shares are in issue. Efficient secondary trading in the shares requires a continuing flow of information about the company and its securities. A substantial contribution to this need is made by the statutory requirement for annual reporting by the management to the shareholders about the progress of the company's business and the filing of those reports with the Registrar. These statutory provisions are analysed in Chapter 19, below, and are supplemented in the case of listed companies by a requirement to publish half-yearly reports.[1] However, relevant information cannot always await the occasion of the publication of annual or semi-annual reports, and in this Chapter we shall examine the legal rules relating to the publication of such information.

These rules are also relevant to the topic discussed in the previous Chapter, insider dealing. An indirect way of reducing the scale of insider dealing is to promote the rapid dissemination into the public arena of all relevant information relating to companies. The legal rules which we shall examine in this Chapter relate to two, rather different, matters. The first is disclosure of information about shareholdings in the company; the second is a more general obligation to disclose information of relevance to an assessment of the value of its securities.

DISCLOSURE OF SHAREHOLDINGS

In Part VI of the Companies Act there are two sets of provisions relating to the disclosure of interests in shares, one placing an automatic obligation to disclose on the shareholder and the other placing a power to trigger a disclosure obligation in the hands of the company. We shall consider the two sets of provisions separately. It is becoming clear that they are driven by somewhat different, if overlapping, rationales. Before doing that, however, it may be worthwhile indicating how the need for this legislation potentially arises, given that it is almost standard for British companies to issue registered rather than bearer

---

[1] *Listing Rules*, paras. 12.46–12.59.

shares, unlike in some other European countries.[2] However, the requirement that the shareholder's name be registered in the company's share register does not mean that the name of the beneficial owner needs to be registered. The use of nominee names has long been popular among big investors and now the dematerialisation of shares[3] may put some pressure upon even small investors to use nominees. But the problem is much more complex than just the separation of the legal and beneficial title to shares. Control over the rights attached to shares may be separated from both legal and beneficial ownership of them. Thus, to give but one example, a discretionary investment manager, by contract with its client, may have the power to exercise the rights attached to shares, for example the voting rights, or even the right to dispose of them, say, to a takeover bidder, whilst the legal title to the shares is vested in a nominee company appointed by the custodian of the securities and their beneficial ownership is that of a pension fund.

Automatic disclosure
The rationale

Persons with interests in the shares of a public company must disclose that fact once a starting threshold of (normally) 3 per cent is exceeded and must make further disclosure at each percentage point thereafter. Disclosure must be made within two working days. Unlike the provisions discussed in the previous chapter,[4] this obligation is placed upon all who hold the relevant interests and so is not confined to directors, but it is confined to interests in shares of public companies,[5] to shares and not debentures (and indeed to shares carrying voting rights)[6] and applies only once the 3 per cent threshold is reached.[7] These differences in the scope of the two sets of provision reflect a difference in underlying rationale and also the fact that the rationale for the provisions considered in this chapter is rather less focused.

In part, but only in small part, these provisions aim to deter insider dealing. Rather, the purpose of these provisions has traditionally been put as follows:

"A company, its members and the public at large should be entitled

---

[2] See p. 329, above.

[3] See above, p. 339.

[4] pp. 448–452, but a director may be caught by both sets of rules and so have to make two returns in relation to a single transaction.

[5] s.198(1).

[6] s.198(2).

[7] s.199(2)—or whatever other percentage the Secretary of State may substitute by regulation: s.210A. Neither set of provisions appears to catch "indirect" interests in shares arising from derivatives contracts, which give a person an economic exposure to movements in the price of shares, but no interest in the shares themselves. Where a person has an interest in shares, the existence of additional "indirect" interests may be relevant to the market. See SIB, *Equity-related Derivatives*, Consultation Paper on Market Conduct, June 1996, Chap. 3.

to be informed promptly of the acquisition of a significant holding in its voting shares ... in order that existing members and those dealing with the company may protect their interests and that the conduct of the affairs of the company is not prejudiced by uncertainty over those who may be in a position to influence or control the company."[8]

This statement explains the concentration in Part VI on voting shares, because it is disclosure of actual or potential control of the company which is aimed at, rather than dealing in its securities in general.

However, the statement might be thought to run together two rationales for the provisions. One is protection of the management of the company and, to some extent, its members, by making them aware of who is building up a stake in the company. The legislation here operates as an early-warning device about potential takeover bids in particular, a function to which the second set of provisions contained in Part VI (see below) is particularly directed. But the statement refers also to the protection of "the public", an aim which is furthered by the requirement that the company maintain a public register of the interests notified to it[9] and by the requirement of the *Listing Rules* that listed companies forward the details received from investors to the Exchange, which will then publish them to the market.[10] In this way the rules may be said to be promoting the conceptually separate goal of "market transparency".

The British rules requiring disclosure of shareholdings on the part of investors are of long standing. The principle of disclosure was introduced as a result of the recommendations of the Cohen Committee[11] in 1945 that the beneficial ownership of shares be publicly disclosed, and, over time, the starting threshold has been lowered, the speed of disclosure increased and the range of interests to be disclosed made more sophisticated. It might therefore be thought that the E.C. Directive[12] on the information to be published when a major shareholding in a listed company is acquired or disposed of would have little impact in the United Kingdom since it sets higher starting thresholds (10 per cent) and less speedy disclosure (seven calendar days) than the current British legislation, though it does contain a narrower set of exemptions

---

[8] Department of Trade, Disclosure of Interests in Shares, 1980, p. 2.

[9] ss.211 and 219.

[10] Via the Company Announcements Office: paras. 9.11 to 9.15. If by use of the s.212 procedure, discussed below, the company discovers a notifiable 3 per cent interest, that too must be disclosed to the Exchange. However, these provisions seem to be an inadequate transposition of the relevant E.C. Directive (see n. 12, below) which requires in Art. 4(1) that an obligation be placed upon the *investor* to notify the "competent authority", *i.e.* in the U.K. the Stock Exchange.

[11] Report of the Committee on Company Law Amendment, (1945) Cmd. 6659, pp. 39–45. It is to be noted that the domestic legislation has still not been lowered to the 1 per cent threshold recommended by that Committee.

[12] Directive 88/627, [1988] O.J. L348/62 (December 17, 1988).

from the duty to disclose than did the domestic legislation prior to the adoption of the Directive. Moreover, the obligations in the Directive are confined to listed companies, whereas the domestic legislation currently applies to all public companies, listed or not.

Although the domestic law has had to be amended in (rather complex) detail to bring it into at least partial compliance with the Directive,[13] the latter's more significant effect has been to spark off a fundamental review of the purposes of these disclosure rules. In particular, the emphasis in the Directive upon disclosure as an instrument to improve the functioning of the securities markets[14] has led the DTI to propose[15] that the "market transparency" rationale be given pre-eminence over the others. Crucially, this would mean that the automatic obligation of disclosure would in future be confined to listed companies and those whose shares are otherwise publicly traded (for example, on A.I.M.), so that the number of companies covered by the provisions would be reduced from some 12,000 public companies to some 2,500 listed and similar companies. The managements of the latter group of companies would thus still have the benefit of this form of early warning against takeover proposals but the managements of companies whose shares are not publicly traded would be to rely on taking the initiative under the second set of provisions contained in Part VI.

The details of the disclosure required

The basic principle is easy enough to state, though its detailed implementation had led to some horrendously complex rules. Once any person has acquired an interest in the prescribed proportion of the voting shares, he or she comes under an obligation to notify the company and thereafter to do so if there is any whole percentage point increase or decrease in that proportion.[16] The proportion is currently set at 3 per cent for most interests, but, for some interests previously exempt from the domestic disclosure regime but now brought within it by the E.C. Directive, the Directive's minimum level of 10 per cent has been chosen.[17] Despite the fact that the provisions relate only to shares carrying voting rights at any general meeting, the relevant percentage is not of the votes but of the nominal value of the shares carrying votes. When there is only one class of such shares, this would produce the same result, but it would not do so if, for example, there were two classes of different nominal values, but both carrying the same number of votes per share. Section 198(2)(a) is generally interpreted as going further than is needed to deal with that situation and

---

[13] The amendments to Part VI were made by S.I. 1993 No. 1819.
[14] See especially the preamble to the Directive.
[15] DTI, *Proposals for Reform of Part VI of the Companies Act 1985*, April 1995.
[16] ss.198–200.
[17] s.199(2) and (2A), notably investment fund managers and operators of unit trusts and other collective investment schemes.

to require notification if over 3 per cent of any class of voting shares is acquired, even if that is far less than 3 per cent of the total votes.

A shareholder may, however, have considerable difficulty in determining whether from time to time his shares do constitute 3 per cent or more of the issued voting share capital, particularly now that companies may purchase their own shares which thereupon cease to be issued share capital. Moreover, when directors have authority to issue more shares, the investor may not know how many have been issued. The problem has arisen in relation to the meaning of "issued" share capital. It now seems that shares are issued only when both they are allotted and the shareholder is registered as a member of the company,[18] but in large share issues it sometimes takes months before all the shares are finally registered. It makes a nonsense of the two-day disclosure time-limit if the obligation to disclose bites only upon registration, since the shareholder and the company will be bound to the share issue once the allotment becomes unconditional.

However, proposals to make the disclosure obligation bite at the earlier stage have run up against the objection that the shareholder may not know how many shares the company has allotted.[19] At present, the law provides a partial answer to these difficulties because it states that the obligation to disclose arises only when the shareholder knows or becomes aware that he has acquired an interest in shares or has ceased to be interested.[20] However, the Directive clearly imposes a disclosure obligation when the investor in the circumstances ought to have learnt of the relevant event, thought it limits the relevant events to the acquisition or disposal of shares.[21] This change may cause difficulties in knowing, for example, when within a group of companies the parent ought to disclose the group's aggregated holding in an outside company, if it has no system for holding that information centrally.

The rules relating to what has to be disclosed when the obligation arises and the compilation of a register of the information by the company[22] are broadly similar to the rules relating to disclosure by directors, and the observations made above[23] do not need to be

---

[18] *National Westminster Bank plc v. Inland Revenue Commissioners* [1995] 1 A.C. 119, H.L.

[19] See DTI, *Disclosure of Interests in Shares: The E.C. Major Shareholdings Directive*, February 1991, pp. 13–16; The Law Society, *Disclosure of Interests in Shares: The EC Major Shareholdings Directive*, Memorandum No. 252, April 1991, pp. 5–10; DTI, *op. cit.*, n. 15, pp. 20–21. The Department, correctly it is submitted, is still committed to finding a practical way to require disclosure at the earlier stage. A similar problem relates to interests which consist of the holding of warrants or convertibles, since such interests do not relate to issued share capital.

[20] s.198(1) (3).

[21] Art. 4(1). Thus, unlike the current domestic legislation, the Directive would not trigger a disclosure obligation if the company, say, repurchased its shares with the result that an investor, who did not participate in the repurchase programme, now held more than 3 per cent of the voting rights.

[22] ss.202, 211, 217 and 218.

[23] pp. 448–452.

repeated here. There is a similarly wide definition of an interest in shares,[24] similar provisions on notification of family and corporate interests,[25] and a list of interests to be designed disregarded.[26] However, the second important question for domestic law posed by the Directive is whether it should switch from the disclosure of interests generally in voting shares to the disclosure only of voting interests in such shares, which is all the Directive requires.[27] The DTI now proposes to make this shift on the grounds that it is voting control in which the company and the market is interested and that the change would permit some simplification of the law. Consequently, it is proposed to require disclosure of the "control, possession of and the right to acquire, voting rights, and the right to dispose of vote-carrying shares".[28] The last element of the proposal is an important one because it would catch the fund manager who has the right to dispose of vote-carrying shares, even where the manager does not have the right to vote them (though normally the manager does have this right by agreement with the client).

On the other hand, sections 204–206 have no counterpart in the provisions relating to directors' shareholdings. These sections are designed to prevent the evasion of the need to notify dealings by the use of what have come to be known as "concert parties". There is nothing illegal or improper in a number of persons acting in concert in attempting to acquire or to maintain control of a company. It becomes objectionable only if that fact is concealed and the holdings of each member of the concert party are not notified until they reach the 3 per cent threshold notwithstanding that in combination the holdings may have exceeded it long before. To prevent this evasion has been the aim of both the legislation and of the City Panel's *Code on Takeovers and Mergers*.

Unfortunately, it has not as yet proved possible to agree upon a definition of "concert party"[29] common to both the Act and the Code. As an introduction to the Act's provisions it is helpful to look first at the definition in the Code which is comparatively simple and more readily intelligible. It says[30]:

---

[24] s.208.
[25] s.203 and see pp. 448 and 451, above.
[26] s.209, a number of which now apply, thanks to the Directive, in relation to listed companies only if the interest does not involve the exercise or control of voting rights: s.209(3)(4).
[27] Art. 1(1).
[28] *op. cit.*, n. 15, p. 16.
[29] This is the convenient term used in the Code.
[30] *Code*, Section C.1. defining "acting in concert". Rule 5 of the Panel's *Rules Governing Substantial Acquisitions of Shares* (the SARs) is even simpler—"Where two or more persons act by agreement or understanding in the acquisition by one or more of them of shares carrying voting rights in a company, or rights over such shares, their holdings and acquisitions must be aggregated and treated as a holding or acquisition by one person for the purpose of the SARs. . . ." The Code and the SARs are not primarily concerned with notification (which is left to the Act) but with determining whether certain thresholds have been reached which require a standstill on further acquisitions or a mandatory general bid. See Chap. 29, below.

"Persons acting in concert comprise persons who, pursuant to an agreement or understanding (whether formal or informal) actively co-operate, through the acquisition by any of them of shares in a company, to obtain or consolidate control[31] . . . of that company", and it then goes on to provide that six categories of persons[32] are presumed to be acting in concert unless the contrary is proved. This has not been thought sufficiently precise or "judge-proof" for statutory provisions giving rise to criminal liability. Accordingly, the statutory definition is considerably more tortuous—and made the more so in that, unlike the Code, it does not set out to define "acting in concert" but rather to define an arrangement leading to acting in concert, the existence of which arrangement is required to be notified in addition to the dealings under it.

First, section 204(1) provides that in certain circumstances an obligation of disclosure may arise from an agreement, between two or more persons, which includes provision for the acquisition by any one or more of them of interests in voting shares of a particular public company. Two points arise from the wording of this subsection. First, the agreement must relate to the acquisition of shares. It does not apply to a voting or other agreement between existing shareholders unless that also requires them to acquire more shares.[33] This clearly does not satisfy Article 7, third indent, of the Directive, and the definition will have to be amended so as to embrace certain voting agreements not involving the acquisition of shares. Secondly, the subsection refers to the public company whose shares are to be acquired as "the target company". This is liable to mislead. On a takeover bid it is normal to describe the company whose shares are to be bid for as the target company. Hence the subsection at first glance appears to apply only if that is the company whose shares are to be acquired. That will usually be the case[34] but the subsection would bite also if, for example, public company A proposed to bid for the shares of public company B on a share-for-share basis and the members of the concert party agreed to support the market price of company A's shares by buying its shares and retaining them until the conclusion of the bid.[35]

---

[31] *i.e.* 30 per cent or more of the voting rights: *Code*, Section C.4.

[32] *i.e.* (i) a company and any others in the group, (ii) a company and any of its directors, (iii) a company and any of its pension funds, (iv) a fund manager and any of its discretionary managed clients, (v) a stockbroker or the financial adviser and persons under the same control, (vi) the directors of the target company.

[33] The interest must also be acquired in pursuance of the agreement: *Re Ricardo Group plc* [1989] BCLC 766.

[34] *e.g.* an agreement by the members of the concert party to support the offeror company by buying shares in the offeree company, and to accept the offer when made; or to support the offeree company by buying its shares and to retain them and not accept the offer (an example of the Code's "consolidation of control").

[35] But it would not cover an agreement to *sell* shares in company B in the hope of causing a fall in the market price of its shares, even if company A agreed to indemnify the members of the concert party from any loss they sustained.

However, subsequent subsections in some respects widen, and in others reduce, the ambit of subsection (1). Subsection (5) provides that "agreement" includes "any agreement or arrangement" and that "provisions of an agreement" include "undertakings, expectations or understandings" whether "express or implied and whether absolute or not".[36] Hence the "agreement" need not be an enforceable contract. But subsection (6) introduces a further refinement, somewhat similar to valuable consideration, by providing that section 204 does not apply to an agreement which is not legally binding "unless it involves mutuality in the undertakings, expectations or understandings of the parties to it".[37] This is somewhat mystifying since one would have supposed that if there was such "mutuality" there would be "valuable consideration" making the agreement "legally binding". The object, however, was apparently to make it clear that the mere fact that two or more persons have agreed that one or more of them shall buy and retain voting shares in a public company does not of itself constitute a concert party agreement.[38] Subsection (2)(a) says that the section applies only if the agreement "also includes provisions imposing obligations or restrictions on any one or more of the parties to it with respect to their use, retention or disposal of their interests in that company's shares acquired in pursuance of the agreement . . .".[39] And subsection (3) clarifies the meaning of "use" in subsection (2) by saying that it means "the exercise of any rights or of any control or influence arising from" the interests in shares acquired "including the right to enter into any agreement for the exercise or for the control of the exercise of any of those rights by another person". In other words, there must not only be an "agreement" to acquire but also agreement on the use that is to be made of the shares acquired.

No obligation of disclosure arises immediately an agreement has been entered into; it arises only on the first acquisition pursuant to the agreement by any of the parties to it.[40] Thereafter it continues, whether or not further acquisitions take place or the members of the concert party change or the agreement is varied, so long as the agreement continues to include provisions of any description mentioned in subsection (2)(a).

What the disclosure obligations are, is dealt with in sections 205 and 206. Under the former, each member of the concert party is taken

---

[36] *cf.* the Code's "agreement or understanding (whether formal or informal)".

[37] The subsection also excludes an underwriting or sub-underwriting agreement provided that that "is confined to that purpose and any matters incidental to it".

[38] *e.g.* Mr & Mrs A are advised by their stockbroker that shares are undervalued and it seems a likely target for a takeover bid. Mr & Mrs A buy such shares from the broker. This clearly ought not to be a "concert party agreement" between Mr & Mrs A and the broker. But if it is only subs. (6) that would exclude it (and not subs. (2) or (3)) it does not seem to do so because the agreement *was* "legally binding".

[39] It is this, surely, which would exclude the agreement in the previous note?

[40] s.204(2)(b).

for the purposes of disclosure under sections 198–203 to be interested not only in all shares acquired by any member of the concert party but also in any in which other members are interested apart from the concert party agreement.[41] Any notification which a party makes with respect to his interest must state that he is a party to a concert party agreement, must include the names and (so far as known to him) the addresses of the other parties and must state whether or not any of the shares to which the notification relates are shares in which he is interested by virtue of section 204 and, if so, how many of them.[42] And when he makes a notification that he has ceased to be interested in any such shares because he or another member of the concert party has ceased to be a member of the concert party, he must include a statement that he or that other person (identifying him) has ceased to be a member of the concert party.[43] Compliance with this obligation should enable the company and, as a result of its obligation to register notifications,[44] anyone inspecting the register, to ascertain that there is a concert party, who its members are and (though this may take some working out) how many shares the concert party has. But, because a shareholder is obliged to notify only if he knows of his interest,[45] that desired result will not be achieved unless each member of the concert party keeps the other members informed both of all his interests in voting shares of the company at the time of the entry into the concert party agreement and of all changes in his interests (other than those undertaken under the concert party agreement and therefore known to them). This, in effect, is what section 206 requires him to do in writing within two days[46] of his knowing.[47] Section 207 provides when, in such circumstances (or in others when he is deemed to be interested by having attributed to him the interests of another person[48]) he is to be treated as having knowledge.

To conclude this discussion of concert parties all that need be added is that, despite the differences in the Act's and the Code's definitions. in most cases what is a concert party for purposes of the one will be so for the purposes of the other. In both cases, the great difficulty for the regulatory authorities is to prove the existence of a concert party,

---

[41] s.205(1), (2) & (3). The effect appears to be that although, under s.204(2)(b), the arrangement becomes a concert party agreement once any interest in shares is acquired in pursuance of it, notification is not required unless and until the total holdings of the concert party members (whether acquired under the agreement or not) reach the 3 per cent threshold. The provisions would probably be more effective if they required any concert party agreement to be notified once it was entered into, all holdings and transactions of the parties thereafter to be notified.

[42] s.205(4).

[43] s.205(5).

[44] s.211.

[45] See p. 487, above.

[46] Reduced from the former five days by the 1989 Act.

[47] He is also required to notify them of any change of his address: s.206.

[48] *e.g.* his wife or infant children or a company which he controls.

particularly when the members of it operate outside the United Kingdom.

Before turning to the next set of statutory provisions, mention must
be made of two further sections. The first is section 210, subsection
(1) of which provides that, if a person authorises an agent to acquire
or dispose of voting shares of a public company, he must secure that
the agent will notify him immediately of all transactions which may
give rise to an obligation of disclosure under Part VI. Most private
investors are wholly unaware of this as, probably, are many of the
professional agents they employ. Stockbrokers executing their clients'
orders immediately notify the latter when they have done so—but an
investment manager may not do so until some time later. While a
private investor is unlikely, on his own, ever to reach the 3 per cent
threshold for disclosure, he might well join a concert party that did
so. It seems therefore that every transaction in voting shares of a public
company is one which "*may* give rise" to an obligation of disclosure
so that the agent ought always to notify the principal immediately—
and arguably commits an offence if he does not![49]

The other subsections of section 210 prescribe the penalties for contravention of the foregoing sections or for knowingly or recklessly
making false statements. One such penalty is that the Secretary of
State may direct that the shares in respect of which the offence
occurred shall be subject to restrictions under Part XV of the Act.[50]

Disclosure triggered by the company

If the provisions discussed in the previous section are complied
with, the management and others will know who are the beneficial
holders of stakes in the company above 3 per cent. However, it is a
big "if", especially if the nominee and beneficial holders are resident
outside the United Kingdom. They may be aware that shares are changing hands more rapidly because turnover in the shares on the Stock
Exchange has shot up or because the volume of transfers being registered in the company's share register has increased, but they may well
be unaware of precisely who or what is behind the higher level of
activity in the shares. Some public companies have resorted to self-
help by introducing into their articles provisions entitling them to
demand information on the beneficial ownership of shares and to
impose restrictions on shares in relation to which that information is
not forthcoming. Whether they have or not, all public companies are
now afforded statutory powers to this end by sections 212–216, which
are extensively used by managements of companies which regard

---

[49] See s.210(3)(d). But the court would probably think he had a "reasonable excuse" (*ibid.*)
unless the client had alerted him about what he was up to.
[50] See below, pp. 496–497.

themselves as potential bid targets. The DTI does not propose to limit these provisions to listed companies,[51] so these provisions could be said to promote not only market transparency but also the broader goal of enabling those involved with public companies, and crucially the incumbent management, to know who is in a position to influence their affairs.

Section 212 provides that a public company may serve notice on a person whom it knows to be, or has reasonable cause to believe to be, or to have been at any time during the three years immediately preceding the date of the notice, interested in voting shares of the company. The notice may require that person to confirm that fact and, if so, (a) to give particulars of his own past or present interest; (b) where the interest is a present interest and any other interest subsists or subsisted during the three year period at a time when his own interest did, to give particulars known to him of that other interest; or (c) where his interest is a past interest, to give particulars of the identity of the person to whom that interest was transferred.[52] In cases (a) and (b) the particulars to be given include the identity of persons interested and whether they were members of a concert party or there were any other arrangements regarding the exercise of any rights conferred by the shares.[53] The notice must conclude by requiring a response to be given in writing within such reasonable time as may be specified in the notice.[54] The initial notice will normally be sent to the person named on the membership register and, if he is the sole beneficial owner of the shares, he will normally say so (at any rate once the likely consequences of refusing to respond are explained to him). But in other cases the notice may merely be the beginning of a long and often abortive paper-chase. If he is a nominee he may well decline to say more than that, claiming that his duty of confidentiality forbids disclosure or, if the nominee is, say, a foreign bank, that the foreign law makes it unlawful to disclose. Ultimately, as a result of the possibility of the freezing and disenfranchisement of the shares,[55] the true ownership may be disclosed—but not always.[56] Such information regarding present interests in the shares as may be elicited as a result of the notice (or a succession of notices as the company follows the trail)

---

[51] *op. cit.*, n. 15, p. 27.

[52] s.212(1) and (2). "Interest" bears the same meaning as in ss.203–205 and 208 (but omitting any reference to the interests to be disregarded under s.209): s.212(5).

[53] s.212(3). In the light of the complications of the statutory provisions defining "interests" and "concert party agreements" a lengthy explanation accompanying the notice may be needed if the recipient (particularly if he is a foreigner) is to understand precisely what is being asked of him.

[54] If the time allowed is unreasonably short, the notice will be invalid: *Re Lonrho plc (No. 2)* [1989] BCLC 309 (which is *not* the same as the decision cited in nn. 82–83, below, also reported as *Re Lonrho plc (No. 2)* in [1990] Ch. 695.

[55] See s.216 and Part XV of the Act, below.

[56] In some cases the information sought has never been obtained and the shares have remained frozen.

must be entered on a separate part of the register maintained for the purposes of sections 198–202.[57]

The Act recognises that members of the company may have a legitimate interest in securing that the company exercises its powers under section 212 even if the board does not want it to (perhaps because the directors or some of them may fear that it may bring to light breaches by them of their obligations to notify their dealings under either or both of section 324 or sections 198–210). Hence, under section 214, members holding not less than one-tenth of the paid-up voting capital may serve a requisition stating that the requisitionists require the company to exercise its powers under section 212, specifying the manner in which those powers are to be exercised[58] and giving reasonable grounds for requiring the powers to be exercised in the manner specified.[59] It is then the company's duty to comply.[60] If it does not, the company and every officer of it who is in default is liable to a fine.[61]

On the conclusion of an investigation under section 214, the company, under section 215, has to prepare a report of the information received which has to be made available at the company's registered office within a reasonable time[62] after the conclusion of the investigation.[63] If it is not concluded within three months beginning on the day after the deposit of the requisition, an interim report on the information already obtained has to be prepared in respect of that and each succeeding three months.[64] Any report has to be made available for inspection at the registered office[65] and the requisitionists must be informed within three days of the report becoming available.[66]

In addition to the foregoing means of obtaining information about the true ownership of a company, the DTI may intervene in order to do so. In the first instance, if the Secretary of State is persuaded that there may be good reasons for intervening, he will probably institute preliminary investigations under the powers conferred on him by section 444. Under this he can require any person whom he has reasonable cause to believe to have, or to be able to obtain, information as to the present and past interests in a company's shares or debentures to give him the information.

---

[57] s.213; with the result that the register may contain entries in respect of holdings below the 3 per cent threshold. The entry is against the name of the registered holder and must state the fact that, and the date when, the requirement was imposed.

[58] In particular, of course, in respect of which shareholdings they require notices to be served.

[59] s.214(1) and (2).

[60] s.214(4). The duty arises "on the deposit of a requisition complying with this section" but presumably the company has a reasonable time within which to dispatch the notice or notices.

[61] s.214(5). Fining the officers in default makes sense; fining the company itself does not.

[62] Not exceeding 15 days: s.215(3).

[63] s.215(1). On the meaning of "concluded" see s.215(6).

[64] s.215(2)

[65] ss.214(7) and 219.

[66] s.215(5) and it must remain available for inspection at the registered office for at least six years: s.215(7).

If this fails to produce a satisfactory answer he may then appoint inspectors under section 442[67]. He may do so of his own volition[68] or, in the case of a company with a share capital, if application is made either by not less than 200 members or members holding not less than one-tenth of the issued shares, and, in the case of a company without share capital, if the application is by not less than one-fifth of the members.[69] A fully fledged investigation may afford the best chance of getting at the truth but it is expensive and time-consuming.[70] Hence, the amendments to the section made by the 1989 Act provide that the Secretary of State shall not appoint inspectors if he is satisfied that the members' application is vexatious and, if he does appoint, shall exclude any matter if satisfied that it is unreasonable for it to be investigated[71]; and he may require the applicants to give security to an amount not exceeding £5,000, or such other sum as he may specify,[72] for payment of the costs of the investigation.[73] Furthermore, if it appears to the Secretary of State that there are circumstances suggesting breaches of the sections relating to disclosure of dealings by directors or their families,[74] he may, under section 445,[75] appoint inspectors to investigate and report.

What makes the foregoing sections more effective than they would otherwise be, is that if a person is convicted of an offence under section 210[76] or there is difficulty in finding out the relevant facts on an investigation under section 442 or 444, he may by order direct that the securities concerned shall, until further notice, be subject to the restrictions of Part XV of the Act.[77] Similarly, if under section 212 a notice is served on a person who is or was interested in shares of the company and he fails to give any information required by the notice, the company may apply to the court for an order directing that the shares in question be subject to the restrictions of Part XV.[78] However, it should be noted that the information a company may require under section 212 is, perhaps not surprisingly, limited by what the person asked knows. If the company obtains no useful information, because

---

[67] As amended by the 1989 Act. This section is directed not merely to determining share and debenture ownership but "the true persons who are or have been primarily interested in the success or failure (real or apparent) of the company or able to control or materially to influence its policy": s.442(1).

[68] s.442(1).

[69] s.442(3) as inserted by the 1989 Act. He need not appoint if it appears to him that an investigation under s.444 would suffice: s.442(3C).

[70] See Chap. 25, below.

[71] s.442(3A).

[72] By statutory instrument subject to annulment by a resolution of either House of Parliament.

[73] s.442(3B). The costs will not necessarily have to be borne in full by the applicants; only "to such extent (if any) as the S. of S. may direct": s.439(5), as amended by the 1989 Act.

[74] See Chap. 17, pp. 448–452, above.

[75] As amended by the 1989 Act.

[76] See above, p. 492.

[77] See ss.210(5) and 445.

[78] s.216.

the person asked does not have it, there is no breach of section 212 and restrictions cannot be imposed on the shares. On the other hand, the Secretary of State may impose restrictions simply where he is having "difficulty in finding out the relevant facts" (section 445(1)). An order, whether by the Secretary of State or the court, can be made notwithstanding any power in the company's memorandum or articles enabling the company itself to impose similar restrictions.[79]

The restrictions of Part XV (sections 454–457) of the Act are that:

(a) any transfer of the shares, or, in the case of unissued shares, any transfer of the right to be issued with the shares and any issue of them, is void;
(b) no voting rights are exercisable in respect of them;
(c) no further shares may be issued in right of them or in pursuance of an offer made to their holder; and
(d) except in a liquidation, no payment by the company, whether as a return of capital or a dividend, may be made in respect of them.[80]

This is a draconian penalty,[81] which may be detrimental to wholly innocent parties, for example bona fide purchasers of, or lenders on the security of, the shares, and, as originally enacted, the provisions afforded them inadequate protection. Although the court or the Secretary of State has a discretion whether to make the order, since "the clear purpose [of Part VI of the Act] is to give public companies, and ultimately the public at large, a prima facie unqualified right to know who are the real owners of its voting shares", an order should normally be made if that knowledge has not been obtained.[82] If an order was made, it had to impose all four restrictions without any qualifications designed to protect innocent parties.[83] Moreover, although the court (or the Secretary of State if he has made the order) could, under section

---

[79] See ss.210(5), 216(2), 445(1). This seems to be a tacit recognition of the legality and effectiveness of such provisions which, as mentioned at p. 492, above, some companies have inserted in their articles. However, the *Listing Rules*, para. 13 (App. 1). 13 limit the restrictions the articles of a listed company may impose upon shareholders who do not comply with s.212.

[80] s.454(1). And see s.454(2) & (3).

[81] Made the more so since any attempt to evade the restrictions may lead to a heavy fine: s.455.

[82] See *Re Lloyd Holdings plc* [1985] BCLC 293; *Re Geers Gross plc* [1987] 1 W.L.R. 1649, C.A.; *Re Lonrho plc (No. 2)* [1990] Ch. 695. The words quoted are those of Nourse J. in *Re Lloyd Holdings* at 300, adopted by the C.A. in *Re Geers Gross* and by Peter Gibson J. in *Re Lonrho plc (No. 2)*.

[83] In *Re Lonrho plc (No. 2)* Peter Gibson J. expressed regret that the court had no power to make an order qualifying the restrictions, being "conscious of the severity of the order and the commercial inconvenience and hardship it may cause to innocent persons affected by the order": [1990] Ch. at 708. An advantage of providing powers in the articles is that they could be expressed more flexibly.

456, remove the restrictions,[84] this normally could be done only by removing all of them "if satisfied that the relevant facts about the shares have been disclosed to the company and no unfair advantage has accrued to any person as a result of the earlier failure to make that disclosure".[85] To this there were (and still are) two exceptions. If "the shares are to be transferred for valuable consideration[86] and the court (in any case) or the Secretary of State (if the order was made under section 210 or 445) approves the transfer", an order could be made that the shares should cease to be subject to the restrictions.[87] Further, the court, on application by the Secretary of State (unless the restrictions were imposed by the court under section 216) or by the company, might order the shares to be sold,[88] subject to the court's approval as to the terms of the sale,[89] and might then also direct that the shares should cease to be subject to the restrictions.[90]

Having regard to the observations of Peter Gibson J. in *Re Lonrho plc (No. 2)*[91] it was felt that something had to be done about the hardship to innocent third parties. The requisite amendments were made by The Companies (Dislosure of Interests in Shares) (Orders imposing restrictions on shares) Regulations 1991.[92] These enable the court or the Secretary of State, as the case may be, if satisfied that an order may otherwise unfairly affect the rights of third parties, to direct that specified acts by such persons or classes of persons shall not constitute a breach of the restrictions and such directions may be given on the making of the order or on a subsequent application to relax or remove the restrictions.[93] They also empower the court to make an interim order, unconditionally or on such terms as it thinks fit.[94]

---

[84] On the application of any person aggrieved by an order made by the Secretary of State or his refusal to make an order disapplying the restrictions, or by such a person or the company if the order was made by the court under s.216: s.456(1) and (2).

[85] s.456(3)(a).

[86] Originally this read "are to be sold". The C.A. in *Re Westminster Group plc* [1985] 1 W.L.R. 676 felt constrained to hold that this did not enable the court to permit a transfer of restricted shares to a takeover bidder since the offer was an "exchange" and not a "sale". Leave was given to appeal to the H.L., but was not pursued. However, the point was dealt with by an amendment in the 1989 Act.

[87] s.456(3)(b). But the court has a discretion whether to allow the transfer and whether or not also to remove the restrictions; in particular it may continue restrictions (c) and (d) either in whole or in part so far as they relate to rights acquired or offered prior to the transfer: see s.456(6).

[88] Here "sale" was not changed to "transferred for valuable consideration". The only transaction that can be *ordered* is a sale.

[89] s.456(4). The court may then make further orders relating to the conduct of the sale: s.456(5). The proceeds of sale have to be paid into court for the benefit of the persons who are beneficially interested in the shares who may apply for the payment out of their proportionate entitlement: s.457.

[90] But it does not have to remove them and may well continue restrictions (c) and (d) to the extent provided by s.456(6).

[91] See n. 83, above.

[92] S.I. 1991 No. 1646, made under powers conferred by the 1989 Act.

[93] See, in particular, the new ss.210(5A), 216(1B), 445(1A) and 456(1A).

[94] s.216(1A).

DISCLOSURE OF SIGNIFICANT EVENTS

Although the disclosure of beneficial interests in shares and of the *locus* of control of companies are matters of the greatest importance to those concerned with companies, there are many other matters about the company which may affect the market's assessment of the company. The rule with which this section is concerned is stated in the Admissions Directive[95] as follows: "The company must inform the public as soon as possible of any major new developments in its sphere of activity which are not public knowledge and which may, by virtue of their effect on its assets and liabilities or financial position or on the general course of its business, lead to substantial movements in the prices of its shares." Article 7 of the Insider Dealing Directive[96] extends the obligation to companies whose shares are traded on any public, regulated market.[97] One significant difference to be noted is, however, that the share disclosure provisions are concerned with the flow of information *to* the company (including its management) and the market, whereas the provisions dealt with in this section concern the flow of information *from* the company (and especially its management) and to the market.

As we have now learned to expect, effect is given to the Directives in the United Kingdom in relation to Listed Companies by appropriate provisions in the Stock Exchange's Listing Rules. This is done as part of the Continuing Obligations imposed upon listed companies, observance of which is stated to be necessary for "the maintenance of an orderly market in securities and to ensure that all users of the market have simultaneous access to the same information".[98] Failure to disclose as required may lead the Exchange to take one or more of the following steps: public or private censure of the issuer and its directors, publication itself of the necessary information and even suspension or cancellation of the issuer's listing.[99]

The Listing Rules require notification "without delay" to the Company Announcements Office of the information specified in the Admissions Directive, which information will normally be passed on by the Office to the market.[1] However, the Listing Rules extend the

---

[95] Council Directive 79/279; see above, p. 414. The principle is set out, somewhat obscurely, in Sched. C, para. 5(a) of the Directive.

[96] Council Directive 89/592. It should be noted that this article of the Directive is concerned not only with selective disclosure by the company, but also with non-disclosure.

[97] As defined in Art. 1(2) of the Directive.

[98] Chapter 9, "Scope". This statement thus acknowledges that timely disclosure serves both market transparency and anti-insider dealing goals.

[99] These are the general powers at the disposal of the Exchange, as set out in Chapter 1 of the *Listing Rules*.

[1] para. 9.1. The Stock Exchange has published *Guidance of the Dissemination of Price Sensitive Information*, February 1995, which puts some flesh on the bare bones of the obligations in the *Listing Rules*.

disclosure obligation to "changes in the company's financial condition or in the performance of its business or in the company's expectation of its performance" where the changes are known to the issuer's directors and are likely to lead to a substantial movement in the price of the listed securities.[2] This would include disclosure of the fact that, say, Christmas trading was below expected levels and that this will have a major impact upon profits, something which might not qualify as a "major new development" under the first rule.

In the design of any rules relating to the disclosure of events, there are two problems which have to be faced. One is to define the point at which the event has crystallised and so triggers the disclosure obligation. If impending developments or matters under negotiation are disclosed too soon, their completion may be jeopardised and the market possibly given information whose value is difficult to assess because it relates to inchoate matters. The Listing Rules both relieve the issuer of the obligation to disclose in such circumstances and permit the issuer to make selective disclosure in confidence to those involved in the impending development or negotiation, including representatives of the employees and trade unions, unless the information ceases to be confidential, in which case a public announcement must be made.[3]

The second problem is that public disclosure of adverse developments may make it more difficult for the issuer to handle them. The Listing Rules permit the Exchange to give a dispensation from the publication to the market of information which has been given to it by an issuer if publication "might prejudice the company's legitimate interests".[4] It is right that the issuer should not be the judge of when this is the case, but the Exchange will no doubt have some difficult issues to deal with. Should it require publication of the company's discovery that an employee has been committing the issuer to unauthorised futures contracts if the company has a reasonable chance of unwinding the positions without great loss if the employee's activity is kept secret, but a much worse chance of so doing if there is immediate publication of the facts?

In the case of securities which are not listed but are nevertheless traded on a recognised investment exchange, such as A.I.M., the situation is governed by the Traded Securities (Disclosure) Regulations 1994.[5] These impose the first, but not the second, of the disclosure obligations mentioned above in relation to listed issuers on those

---

[2] para. 9.2. In addition to these general disclosure obligations, there are a number of specific events of which disclosure to the market is required by the Listing Rule, for example, the existence of major holdings in shares discussed above.

[3] paras. 9.4 and 9.5.

[4] para. 9.8. This exception is derived from para. 5(b) of Schedule C to the Admissions Directive.

[5] S.I. 1994 No. 188. Reg. 2 defines the securities to which it applies in such a way as to exclude listed securities.

issuers and securities governed by the Regulations, subject to the "legitimate interests" exception. The Regulations do not deal expressly with the problem of impending developments.

Conclusion

Disclosure obligations perform a number of different functions. Disclosure of information to the company may forewarn incumbent management against takeovers or help shareholders and others to know where they stand. Disclosure by the company may be an effective way of reducing the opportunities for insider dealing by speeding the transmission of information into the public domain. In this case, it may be easier to identify investors who have suffered loss as a result of tardy disclosure than it is with insider dealing on securities markets, where, as we saw in Chapter 17, failure to disclose is not the essence of the wrongdoing. However, the civil aspects of non-disclosure obligations, except in relation to the freezing of shares, have remained as undeveloped as they have in the insider dealing area. Finally, and most generally, the rapid and continuous supply of information to the market is an essential pre-requisite for the efficient operation of securities markets, as the Admissions Directive recognises.

Part Six

SHAREHOLDER AND CREDITOR PROTECTION

INTRODUCTION

This Part contains what is at the heart of many company law courses in universities. The general issue is how far the law makes the controllers of companies accountable to those who have invested in them,[1] whether as shareholders or as creditors. In this part three main legal techniques to promote such accountability are discussed. The first, more fully considered in Chapters 19 and 20, is the provision to the public of full, accurate and verified information about the company. The aim is to put those who are about to invest in the company in a position to assess the company's business before they commit themselves and to enable those who have invested to keep track of the performance of the company.

Secondly, the controllers of companies may be required to report to those who have invested in the company, to submit themselves to periodic re-election and to seek shareholder approval for certain types of corporate decision. The obligatory structures of company law have the shareholders mainly in mind when this technique is used (see Chapter 21) but it is possible, at least to some degree, to replicate these provisions by contract for the benefit of creditors, by appropriate covenants in the loan instrument.

Thirdly, and most famously, the law may seek to secure the accountability of controllers to the shareholders, creditors and perhaps others, by imposing legal duties on the directors, notably fiduciary duties to promote the interests of the company and, less strongly, at least in the past, to conduct the company's affairs competently. The imposition of duties is one thing; their enforcement another. Despite a battery of enforcement mechanisms, including traditional civil litigation, administrative measures, and new statutory powers for the courts to remedy "unfair prejudice" or to disqualify "unfit" directors, few people are content with the resulting situation. This area has been the subject of a recent and comprehensive Law Commission survey which has put forward various suggestions for reform.[2]

The conflict in the above situations is between company controllers and investors in the company who do not share in the control position. Often that is synonymous with a conflict between directors, on the one

---

[1] The employees, who have invested "human capital" in the enterprise, may gain some tangential benefit from the provisions discussed in this Part, but it cannot be said that the law was designed with their interests centrally in mind.

[2] Law Commission, *Shareholder Remedies*, Consultation Paper No. 142, 1996, which was published too late for detailed consideration in this edition.

hand, and shareholders (or creditors), on the other. But the controllers may owe their position of power not only to their directorships but also to their ownership of shares in the company. In such cases there may be a conflict between one group of shareholders and another. In some such cases the shareholders may have anticipated the possibility of conflict among themselves and have provided mechanisms in the company's constitution to deal with it when it arises. In other cases it may be left to general company law to deal with the issue. Company law has always found it more difficult to identify the principles upon which the actions of controlling shareholders, the "owners" of the company, should be regulated than those which should regulate the actions of controlling directors, who are regarded as mere "agents" of the company.

CHAPTER 19

PUBLICITY AND ACCOUNTS

On the basis that "forewarned is forearmed" the fundamental principle underlying the Companies Acts has been that of disclosure. If the public and the members were enabled to find out all relevant information about the company, this, thought the founding fathers of our company law, would be a sure shield. The shield may not have proved quite so strong as they had expected, and in more recent times it has been supported by offensive weapons, such as inspections or investigations instigated by the Department of Trade and Industry.[1] But, basically, disclosure still remains the principal safeguard on which the Companies Acts pin their faith, and every succeeding Act since 1862 has added to the extent of the publicity required, although, not unreasonably, it varies according to the type of company concerned.

This publicity is mainly secured in four ways:

(a) by official notification in the *Gazette*;
(b) by provisions for registration at Companies House;
(c) by compulsory maintenance of various registers and the like by the company; and
(d) by compulsory disclosure of the financial position in the company's published accounts and by attempting to ensure their accuracy through a professional audit.

In these ways, and in certain others of less importance which will be referred to briefly, members and the public (which, for practical purposes, means creditors and others who may subsequently have dealings with the company and become its members or creditors) are supposed to be able to obtain the information which they need to make an intelligent appraisal of their risks, and to decide when and how to exercise the rights and remedies which the law affords them.

OFFICIAL NOTIFICATION

This is a concept relatively new to English company law having been introduced by section 9 of the European Communities Act 1972 to comply with the First Company Law Directive. As a result of that and later Directives there are now many cases in which the Registrar must

[1] See Chap. 25, below.

cause to be published in the *Gazette*[2] notice that he has received for registration various types of documents.[3] The notice merely records the name and registered number of the company, the nature of the document and the date of its receipt. To see the document itself it will be necessary to resort to Companies House or the company in question. Nor is it an effective method of notifying the members, creditors or the general public, few of whom read the *Gazette*.[4] When it is thought vital that members or creditors should receive notice, the Act requires them to be given notice by the company; in relation to the general public the best that can be done is to require publication in newspapers.

REGISTRATION AT COMPANIES HOUSE

The most common method of obtaining information about a company is by searching its file at Companies House in Cardiff or London (or Edinburgh if the company is registered in Scotland). Most of the information (and more besides) could be obtained from the company itself but generally the first step will be to apply to Companies House. At one location it is possible to inspect not only the file of the company known to the searcher but also those of any related companies that this inspection reveals. And, especially perhaps, it enables searches to be undertaken without any of the companies knowing about it.

It is unnecessary, and would make tedious reading, to list all the sections of the Act which require a company to deliver documents for registration. Many such sections have been mentioned already. Here it suffices to say that the aim is to ensure that a company is required to do so when it is thought that the matter is one that the public needs to know. Hence, a search of its file should enable reasonably up-to-date information to be obtained on such matters as: its constitution (the memorandum and articles, as amended); its officers; the address of its registered office[5], its issued share capital[6]; charges on its property[7]; and, in most cases, its latest annual accounts.[8]

Subject to the payment of a fee prescribed from time to time by

---

[2] The London or the Edinburgh *Gazette* according to the place of registration of the company: s.744.

[3] s.711 (which lists the documents in question).

[4] It is not read by the populace but is scanned by credit agencies and the like.

[5] This is important since it is there that process can be served upon it.

[6] The returns of allotments (see Chap. 11 at p. 238, above) will show to whom the shares were originally allotted but not in whose names they are now registered as a result of transfers; for that, inspection of the membership register is needed unless the latest annual return (see below) is sufficiently recent for the searcher's purpose.

[7] This may give a more reliable indication of creditworthiness, or the lack of it, than the filed accounts which are unlikely to be as up-to-date.

[8] See below at pp. 511 *et seq.*

statutory instrument,[9] any person is entitled to inspect and to obtain copies of "any records kept by the registrar for the purposes of the Companies Acts"[10]; no distinction is drawn between the rights of members and inspection by other persons.[11] And a copy of any registered document, duly certified by the Registrar "is in all legal proceedings admissible in evidence as of equal validity with the original document and as evidence of any fact stated therein of which oral evidence would be admissible".[12]

ANNUAL RETURNS

In addition to the documents which have to be delivered to the Registrar shortly after[13] the occurrence of the events which they record, every company is required to make an Annual Return. As well as a means of publicising information this is a document of some importance administratively, since without it the register would be cluttered, to a greater extent than it is, with files of moribund companies[14] abandoned by their members. Failure to file the annual return alerts the Registrar and enables him to take appropriate steps leading to the companies' removal from the register.[15]

As a source of information, the return collates much that should have been delivered for registration when the relevant transactions occurred, so that a searcher may find it unnecessary to search back beyond the latest annual return on the file. It also enables some additional or more recent[16] information to be obtained. The 1989 Act substituted a new and somewhat simplified Chapter III (Annual Return) for that in the original Part XI of the 1985 Act. Briefly summarised the effect of the new Chapter is as follows:

Every company, whether or not it is required to file annual accounts, must deliver to the Registrar successive returns in the prescribed form made up to its "return date", *i.e.* the anniversary of its incorporation

---

[9] s.708.

[10] s.709 (inserted by the 1989 Act) subs.(1).

[11] Nor could there be, since the Registry's official are not in a position to check the credentials of searchers or of those on whose behalf they are acting (more often than not searches will be undertaken by solicitors, articled clerks or by professional agencies).

[12] s.709(3).

[13] A helpful reform would be to standardise so far as possible the periods within which the various documents are supposed to be delivered; at present they vary greatly, and often for no obvious reason, between 7, 14, 21 and 28 days and "one month".

[14] Such companies should not be confused with "dormant companies" (see below, pp. 532–533) which may have legitimate reasons for remaining registered.

[15] Also the fee for registering the return may help to finance Companies House. But the present fee can barely cover the cost of registering and hardly seems large enough to discourage people from allowing their moribund companies to cumber to register.

[16] *e.g.* the annual return should be delivered within 28 days after the "return date" to which it is made up whereas the annual accounts, even if filed timeously, are likely to be made up to a date some seven months before (and more in the case of private companies).

or, if its last return was made up to a different date, the anniversary
of that date. This must be signed by a director or the secretary of the
company and must be delivered within 28 days after the return date.[17]
If a proper return is not so delivered the company is guilty of an
offence and liable to a fine and a daily default fine so long as the
contravention continues.[18] And any director or the secretary of the
company is similarly liable unless he shows that he took all reasonable
steps to avoid the commission or continuance of the offence.[19]

Section 364 specifies the "general" information which the return
must state. This includes the address of the company's registered
office[20] and particulars of the directors[21] and secretary.[22] It also, and
this is new, includes "the type of company and its principal business
activities",[23] the type to be "given by reference to the classification
prescribed for the purposes of this section",[24] while the principal business activities "may be given by reference to categories of any prescribed system of classifying business activities".[25] Also new is the
requirement that a private company which has elected under the substituted section 252 to dispense with the laying of accounts before a
general meeting or, under section 366A, to dispense with the holding
of annual general meetings, must so state in the return.[26]

If the company has a share capital, in addition to the general
information the return must give the "particulars of share capital and
shareholders" specified in section 364A. This enables much the same
information to be obtained as that obtainable from the company's
membership register[27] but only as at the return date. If up-to-date particulars are needed, the searcher will have to inspect, or obtain a copy

---

[17] s.363(1) and (2).
[18] s.363(3). The contravention continues until there is delivered a return which complies both in
form and content: s.363(2) and (5)(a).
[19] s.363(4). This however is but one of the many sanctions that can be invoked: see n. 30, below.
And note that under the Company Directors Disqualification Act, Sched. I, para. 4(*f*), failure
to make annual returns is one of the matters relevant to determination of unfitness of directors,
whilst s.3 of that Act makes "persistent" default in complying with the returns requirement
in itself a ground for disqualification. See below, pp. 682 and 689.
[20] s.364(1) and (a).
[21] And (optimistically—see Chap. 7, pp. 182–183) includes a shadow director although he is
not an authorised signatory of the return: s.365(3).
[22] s.364(1)(c)–(f). The DTI has proposed (Disclosure of Directors' and Company Secretaries'
Particulars, February 1997) a reduction in the particulars to be provided in these cases. In
particular, the home addresses would no longer have to appear in the public register, though
a service address would and the Registrar would still have to be given the home address.
[23] s.364(1)(b).
[24] s.364(2). See The Companies (Forms Amendment No. 2 and Companies Type and Principal
Business Activities) Regs. (1990 S.I. No. 1766) made on the authority of no less than eight
sections of the Act.
[25] s.364(3). See The Companies (Forms Amendment No.2 and Companies Type and Principal
Business Activities) Regs.
[26] s.364(1)(i). See below, pp. 521 and 567.
[27] s.364A(3)–(6). Subs. (6) relieves companies of the need to include a full replica of the membership register more often than once every three years so long as all changes have been
stated in each of the two preceding returns.

of, the company's membership register. But, to enable the searcher to know where the register is kept, if that is not at the registered office, the general part of the return has to state where that is.[28] In the case of a company without share capital the return will give no particulars of the members; to ascertain that, resort must be to the company.

However, section 365(1) empowers the Secretary of State by regulations[29] to "make further provision as to the information to be given in a company's annual return, which may amend or repeal the provisions of sections 364 and 364A". So further changes seem likely.

The principal weakness of these provisions is that companies (especially, but not exclusively, private ones) are deplorably dilatory in delivering returns to the Registrar so that at any one time a majority of companies are in arrear to a greater or lesser extent. However, a few years ago a blitz on such companies was mounted[30] with the result that there has been some improvement. Nevertheless, if a creditor, with grounds for suspecting that a company is in financial difficulties, makes a search he is all too likely to find that no recent annual returns or accounts have been filed.

COMPANIES' REGISTERS AND RECORDS

Most of the information obtainable from Companies House can instead be obtained from the company and so can further information especially if the searcher is a member of the company. Nevertheless, a member, even of a private company, unless he is also a director, is not entitled, as he would be if he were a member of a partnership, to inspect the books and records of the company except to the extent that the Act specifically provides.[31] But there are an increasing number of documents and registers which he, and, indeed, other persons, are entitled to inspect (in the case of a member generally without payment) and to obtain copies on payment. These include, for example,

---

[28] s.364(1)(g) and likewise as to any register of debenture-holders: *ibid.*, (h).

[29] To be made by statutory instrument subject to annulment by a resolution of either House of Parliament: s.365(2).

[30] In England and Wales in 1990–1991 there were 3,050 prosecutions and 1,581 convictions for failure to forward annual returns (and 5,680 prosecutions and 3,030 convictions for failure to deliver accounts), 3,356 directors of 2,208 companies were involved in proceedings relating to annual returns and accounts and 1,864 directors of 1,284 companies were convicted. However, by 1995–1996 the number of prosecution for failing to file annual returns had dropped to 884 and for failure to deliver accounts to 2,297: *Companies in 1995–96*, Table D3. If companies are as dilatory in replying to correspondence as they are in filing returns they may find that the Registrar has struck them off the register under s.652 as "defunct," with serious and expensive consequence even if they succeed in getting restored to the register under s.653. See pp. 846–851, below. A further weapon in the authorities' armoury is s.713 which can lead to defaulting companies and directors finding themselves in contempt of court.

[31] Hence in *Butt v. Kelson* [1952] Ch. 197, C.A. it was held that the beneficial owners of shares of a company could not compel the trustee, who was a director of the company, to produce the company's books for their inspection.

directors' contracts of service,[32] and the registers of:—the directors and secretary,[33] directors' holdings of, and dealings in, the company's securities,[34] and (in the case of a public company) the register of 3 per cent shareholders.[35] The last two registers afford important information, not obtainable from Companies House, in relation to beneficial ownership and not just registered ownership, and are particularly valuable to a searcher who suspects that some major transaction (*e.g.* a takeover bid) is in the offing. Furthermore, the register of charges which the company is required to maintain may be more illuminating than that at Companies House since the company must also keep copies of any instrument creating a charge requiring registration with the Registrar.[36] Both the register and the copies are open to inspection by any creditor[37] or member without payment and by any other person on payment, copies being obtainable on payment.[38]

The maximum fees that companies can charge for inspection or copies are now prescribed by regulations (the former practice of stating them in the primary legislation did not work well in an inflationary climate) and these regulations[39] clarify the obligations of companies regarding inspection and copies.

OTHER METHODS

Before turning to the all-important accounts, mention must be made of other methods whereby information about a company is required to be disseminated. One which the Act employs in relation to information which can be briefly conveyed, is to require it to appear on all business communications of the company. Thus its name, number, the fact that its liability is limited (if such be the case) and the address of its registered office must be stated on all business letters or order forms. Again, if the company is listed, it will be subject to additional duties to keep its security holders and, indeed

---

[32] s.318. These can be inspected by any member without payment, but not by any other person. see below, p. 630.

[33] s.288–290 These can be inspected by any person without payment and copy may be obtained, in the case of a member, without payment.

[34] s.325 and Sched. 13, Part IV, paras. 25 and 26. The position is the same as in n. 33. See above, pp. 450–451.

[35] See above, p. 485. Here again the position is the same regarding inspection and copies (see s.219) save for the limited exception in s.211(9).

[36] ss.406–407.

[37] This equating of creditors with members is unusual but makes sense here. Note, however, that neither "creditor" nor "member" includes a person who is contemplating becoming a creditor or member: if he searches, as he should before he has committed himself, he will have to pay if the company insists.

[38] s.408.

[39] The Companies (Inspection and Copying of Registers, Indices and Documents) Regs. 1991 (1991 S.I. No. 1998) made under s.723A: see p. 334, above.

the public, informed of all major developments and if it does not the Exchange may publish the information.[40]

Apart from legally required publicity there is media publicity which may occur whether the company wants it to or not.[41] All the national newspapers and many of the provincial ones now devote an increasing number of columns to "City" or "Business" matters. The columnists have keen noses for scandals and once their interest is aroused they follow the scent with sleuth-like pertinacity and commendable disregard of the risks of suits for defamation.[42] The result may be that, what a company had hoped to treat as a minor domestic matter which could be brushed under the carpet, is exposed to the harsh light of day. This may not always be in the best interests of the company but as, on the whole, the Press acts in this area[43] with reasonable restraint, it generally is in the best interests of investors and the public.

Finally, it should be pointed out that one of the grounds on which under section 432[44] the Secretary of State may appoint inspectors to investigate and report on the affairs of a company is that "the company's members have not been given all the information with respect to its affairs which they might reasonably expect"[45]—whether or not that information is such that they have an express statutory right to be told it. A failure to give such information might also be relevant on a petition to wind up the company on the "just and equitable" ground[46] or to grant relief on the ground that the affairs of the company are being conducted in a manner unfairly prejudicial to members.[47]

ACCOUNTS

A staggering transformation has occurred in the course of the twentieth century in the ambit of statutory provisions regarding company accounts, as will be apparent to anyone who compares the exiguous

---

[40] See Chap. 18, above, and the *Listing Rules*, para. 9.1. And note s.329 of the Act which imposes an obligation on listed companies to notify the Stock Exchange of any reported transaction in its listed shares which a director is required to report to the company under s.324 or 328 (for entry on the register maintained under s.325: see n. 34, above) and expressly empowers the Exchange to publish it.

[41] It will welcome publicity only if the news is good but in that event it will probably have to pay for its inclusion as an advertisement.

[42] This attitude may not always be shared by their editors or the papers' proprietors. The only special protection that newspapers have is that fair and accurate reports of general meetings of public companies and quotations from most documents circulated to its members are not actionable in the absence of malice so long as any reasonable explanation or correction is published: Defamation Act 1996, s.15 and Sched. 1. This adds little to the general defences of justification, fair comment and qualified privilege. However, even if the paper decides not to publish, the journalist may alert the regulatory authorities.

[43] In contrast with exposure of sexual peccadilloes, when there tends to be an assumption that it must be in the public interest to publish whatever appeals to the prurient interests of the public.

[44] See Chap. 25 at p. 696.

[45] s.432(2)(d).

[46] Insolvency Act, s.122(1)(g). See Chap. 27, below, at pp. 749–751.

[47] Companies Act, s.459. See Chap. 27, below, at pp. 742–746.

provisions in the 1908 Act with the profusion of sections and Schedules in the Companies Act 1985 as amended, supplemented and rearranged by the 1989 Act. This has resulted from the recognition:

(a) that the price of limited liability ought to be the maximum possible disclosure of information regarding the company's financial position,
(b) that within the European Community that information ought to be presented in a standardised fashion so that like can be compared with like irrespective of the Member State in which the company was incorporated, but
(c) that some concessions regarding (a) should be afforded to small companies so as to relieve them of burdens and expense that they might find intolerable.[48]

All this Chapter attempts is to offer guidance on how to find the way through the statutory provisions[49] which, understandably, tend to be expressed in accountants' language rather than that of lawyers.

The United Kingdom chose dutifully to implement the Fourth Directive on Company Accounts without waiting, as some other Member States did, for the adoption of the Seventh Directive on Group Accounts. Hence, when the latter was implemented by the 1989 Act, Part VII of the Act and the related Schedules needed copious revision and the opportunity was seized to undertake a major rearrangement of the Schedules.[50] Despite taking two bites, the implementation of the Directives was achieved with less trauma than in some other Member States whose existing requirements were less advanced than those of the United Kingdom. Particularly was this so because the British accountancy profession played a more constructive role in the preparatory stages of the two Directives than our professional bodies had hitherto taken in relation to E.C. proposals. We even succeeded in securing the adoption of our basic principle that accounts must present

---

[48] The extent of proposition (c) is controversial since the failure-rate of small companies is greater.

[49] Reference has already been made to some of the relevant provisions particularly in Chap. 8 in relation to group accounts, in Chaps. 11 and 12 in relation to raising and maintaining capital and to dividends, and in Chap. 16 in relation to public issues. This Chapter concentrates on accounts as a means of publicising information and on those statutory provisions on the construction of which lawyers are likely to be asked to advise.

[50] After further amendment by S.I. 1997 No. 220, these Schedules now are Sched. 4 (form and content of company accounts); Sched. 4A (form and content of group accounts); Sched. 5 (disclosure of information: related undertakings); Sched. 6 (disclosure of information: emoluments and benefits of directors and others); Sched. 7 (matters to be dealt with in directors' reports); Sched. 8 (form and content of accounts prepared by small companies); Sched. 8A (form and content of abbreviated accounts of small companies delivered to the Registrar); Scheds. 9 and 9A (special provisions for banking and insurance companies and groups), and Sched. 10A (supplementary provisions on parent and subsidiary undertakings).

a "true and fair view"—notwithstanding that we were unable to explain precisely what that expression meant.

Accounting records

This Chapter concentrates primarily on accounts as a means of publicising information and hence on the annual accounts through which that publicity is achieved. But Part VII of the Act starts with a prescription of a company's obligation to maintain current accounting records; and logically enough, because, although these are not open to inspection by members or the public,[51] unless they are kept it will be impossible for the company to produce verifiable annual accounts. Hence, section 221 provides that every company shall keep records sufficient to show and explain the company's transactions, to disclose, with reasonable accuracy at any time, its financial position and to enable its directors to ensure that any balance sheet and profit and loss account will comply with the provisions of Part VII.[52]

The records must contain day-to-day entries of all money received or expended and of the matters to which that related and a record of the company's assets and liabilities.[53] If the company's business involves dealing in goods, the records must also contain a statement of stock held at the end of the financial year and statements of stocktakings from which that was prepared, and, except in the case of goods sold in the ordinary course of retail trade, statements of all goods sold or purchased, in sufficient detail to enable the other party to be identified.[54]

A company which has a subsidiary undertaking to which these requirements do not apply[55] must take all reasonable steps to secure that the subsidiary keeps such records as will enable the directors of the parent company to ensure that any balance sheet and profit and loss account prepared under Part VII complies with the Act's requirements.[56]

Failure to comply with the section renders every officer of the company[57] who is in default guilty of an offence[58] unless he shows that he acted honestly and that, in the circumstances in which the company's business was carried on, the default was excusable.[59]

Section 222 provides that accounting records are at all times to be

---

[51] See p. 509, above.
[52] s.221(1).
[53] s.221(2).
[54] s.221(3).
[55] *e.g.* because it is a foreign subsidiary or a partnership.
[56] s.221(4).
[57] But not the company itself.
[58] Punishable by fine or imprisonment or both: s.221(6).
[59] s.221(5).

open for inspection by officers of the company.[60] If any such records are kept outside Great Britain,[61] there must be sent to Great Britain (and be available for inspection there by the officers) records which will disclose with reasonable accuracy the position of the business in question at intervals of not more than six months and will enable the directors to ensure that the company's balance sheet and profit and loss account comply with the Act.[62] All required records must be preserved for three years if it is a private company or for six years if it is a public one.[63]

Annual accounts

Part VII then turns to matters concerning annual accounts. Sections 222–225 prescribe how a company's "financial year" is to be determined. Despite its name it is not a calendar year or, necessarily, a period of 12 months. What period it is depends on its "accounting reference period" as determined in accordance with section 223, which in turn depends on its "accounting reference date" (ARD), which is the date in each calendar year on which the company's accounting reference period (ARP) ends. Unless the company chooses otherwise, the company's ARD will now be the anniversary of the last day of the month in which the company was incorporated.[64] However, the company may choose a new ARD for the current and future ARPs and even for its immediately preceding one.[65] This it may well want to do for a variety of reasons; for instance, if the company has been taken over and wishes to bring its ARD into line with that of its new parent.[66] The new ARD may operate either to shorten or to lengthen the ARP within which the change is made,[67] but in the latter case the company may not normally extend the ARP to more than 18

---

[60] 222(1). For this reason, accountants may not exercise a lien for unpaid fees over such documents: *DTC(CNC) Ltd v. Gary Sargeant & Co.* [1996] 1 BCLC 529. And note the even wider rights of the auditors (s.389A(1)) and of the DTI or inspectors under Part XIV of the Act on which see below Chap. 25, below.

[61] *e.g.* because the company has a branch outside Great Britain.

[62] s.222(2) and (3). The penalty for non-compliance is the same as that in s.221: s.222(4).

[63] s.222(5). An officer of the company is liable to imprisonment or a fine or both if he fails to take all reasonable steps to secure compliance or intentionally causes any default. If there has been villainy, destroying all records of it is all too likely.

[64] s.224(3A), inserted by the Companies Act (Miscellaneous Accounting Amendments) Regulations 1996 (S.I. 1996 No. 189) for companies incorporated after April 1, 1996.

[65] s.225. This section applies no matter when the company was incorporated.

[66] Indeed, in this particular situation, in order to promote the production of group accounts, the directors of the parent company are under a presumptive duty to ensure that the financial years of subsidiaries coincide with that of the parent: s.223(5).

[67] s.225(3).

months[68] and may not normally engage in the process of extending the ARP more than once every five years.[69] These are necessary safeguards against obvious abuses. The company's financial year then corresponds to its ARP, as fixed according to the above rules, except that the directors have a discretion to make the financial year end at any point up to seven days before or seven days after the end of the ARP.[70]

Form and content of annual accounts

Section 226 imposes on the directors of every company the duty to prepare for each financial year of the company a balance sheet and a profit and loss account (its "individual accounts"[71]) and section 227 imposes a like duty on directors of a company which is a parent company additionally to prepare a consolidated balance sheet and profit and loss account ("group accounts"[72]) The basic and overriding principle is that the balance sheets must give a true and fair view, in the case of individual accounts "of the state of affairs of the company at the end of the financial year"[73] and in the case of group accounts "of the state of affairs as at the end of the financial year of the undertakings included in the consolidation as a whole, so far as it concerns the members of the company".[74] Similarly, the profit and loss accounts must give a like view of the profit or loss of the company or of the undertakings included in the consolidation for the financial year again "so far as it concerns the members". These latter words may be thought puzzling; accounts are intended to protect creditors as well as members. But so long as English law refuses to recognise that parent companies are under a legal as well as a moral obligation to meet the debts of their subsidiaries the group accounts are largely irrelevant so far as creditors are concerned since they normally have resort only against the individual company with which they have dealt.

Subject to the foregoing, the form and content of the balance sheets and profit and loss accounts and additional information provided by

---

[68] s.225(6), unless an administration order is in force in relation to the company, presumably because the administrator, who is responsible to the court, can be trusted in a way the directors cannot.

[69] s.225(4), unless an administration order is in force (see previous note) or the step is taken to make parent and subsidiary companies' ARPs coincide, or the Secretary of State permits it.

[70] s.223(2) and (3).

[71] s.226(1).

[72] s.227(1) & (2).

[73] s.226(2).

[74] s.227(3).

way of notes[75] must comply with Schedule 4[76] in relation to individual accounts and with Schedule 4A[77] in relation to group accounts.[78] Pursuant to the Directives' aim to promote comparability of the accounts of companies of the various Member States, companies are required to adopt one of two prescribed formats for the balance sheet and one of four for the profit and loss account but in doing so they may use either the prescribed "historical cost accounting rules"[79] or the "alternative accounting rules" which pay greater recognition to the impact of inflation by a type of current cost accounting.

Such is the importance attached to the true-and-fair principle that, when compliance with the relevant Schedule and other provisions of the Act would not be sufficient to give a true and fair view, the necessary additional information must be given in the accounts or notes to them.[80] And if, in special circumstances, compliance with a provision of the Schedules would be inconsistent with the requirement to give a true and fair view, the directors must depart from that provision to the extent necessary, giving, in a note to the accounts, particulars of the departure and the reasons for, and effect of, it.[81]

Although normally every parent company must prepare consolidated group accounts which must include all its subsidiary undertakings, there are narrowly defined exceptions. Under section 228 when a parent company is itself a subsidiary and its immediate parent is established under the law of a Member State, it may, if certain conditions are fulfilled, be exempt from the requirement to prepare group accounts. But these conditions are strict. The exemption applies only (a) if the company is a wholly owned subsidiary or (b) if the parent holds more than 50 per cent of its shares and the other shareholders[82] have not served notice requesting the preparation of group accounts[83] and the company's securities are not listed on a stock exchange in any Member State.[84] Moreover, strict conditions are laid down[85] to ensure that the company is included in consolidated accounts drawn up and

---

[75] Scheds. 4 and 4A and later sections of the Act provide for what information must or may be in notes instead of in the accounts themselves and Scheds. 5 and 6 make additional provisions for notes, the proliferation of which has been a feature of the last 50 years.

[76] Which was amended but not wholly replaced by the 1989 Act.

[77] Newly inserted by the 1989 Act. Essentially, Sched. 4 applies with adaptations, Sched. 4A, para. 1(1) providing that: "Group accounts shall comply so far as practicable with the provisions of Sched. 4 as if the undertakings included in the consolidation ('the group') were a single company" and para. 6 providing for the elimination of inter-group transactions.

[78] ss.226(3) and 227(4).

[79] Which most English companies choose.

[80] ss.226(4) & 227(5).

[81] ss.226(5) & 227(6).

[82] Holding more than half of the remaining shares or 5 per cent of the total shares: s.228(1)(b).

[83] s.228(1).

[84] s.228(3).

[85] ss.228(2).

audited in accordance with the Seventh Directive and made available to the British public.

Similarly, in certain circumstances a subsidiary may, under section 229, be omitted from the consolidation. This is so, for example, if its inclusion is not material for the purposes of giving a true and fair view[86] or if, in effect, the parent is not able to exercise dominance over the subsidiary[87] or holds its interest in the subsidiary exclusively with a view to resale,[88] or the information necessary for group accounts cannot be obtained without disproportionate delay or expense.[89] And a subsidiary must be excluded from the consolidation if its activities are so different from those of the rest of the group that its inclusion would be incompatible with the obligation to give a true and fair view.[90]

Under section 230, certain derogations from the provisions of Schedule 4 apply to the individual accounts of a parent which is required to prepare consolidated accounts (and has done so) thereby rendering those provisions otiose.

Section 231 requires information specified in Schedule 5 to be given in notes to the accounts regarding what are referred to in the headings to the section and the Schedule as "related undertakings"—an expression which the Act does not define but which includes parent and subsidiary undertakings,[91] associated undertakings,[92] joint ventures, and undertakings in which the company has a substantial holding.[93] Similarly, section 232 requires the information specified in Schedule 6, regarding the emoluments and other benefits of directors and their associates, to be given in notes to the accounts.[94]

The annual accounts must be approved by the directors and signed on behalf of the board by a director.[95] If the approved accounts do not comply with the Act, every director who was a party to their approval and who knows that they do not comply or is reckless as to whether or not they comply is guilty of an offence and every director at the time the accounts were approved is taken to be a party to their

---

[86] s.229(2). But two or more undertakings may be excluded on this ground only if taken together they are immaterial: *ibid.*

[87] s.229(3)(a).

[88] s.229(3)(c).

[89] s.229(3)(b).

[90] s.229(4).

[91] Defined in s.258 and Sched. 10A. See Chap. 8 at pp. 160–161, above.

[92] Defined in Sched. 4A para. 20 and dependent on the holding of a "participating interest" as defined in s.260: see Chap. 8 at p. 160, above.

[93] See Chap. 8, *ibid.*

[94] Thereby supplementary Part X of the Act (enforcement of fair dealing by directors). See below, p. 630.

[95] s.233(1). The signature must be on the balance sheet (s.233(2)) and every published copy of it must state the name of the signatory (s.233(3)). The copy delivered to the Registrar must also be signed on behalf of the board by a director (though not necessarily the same one): s.233(4).

approval unless he shows that he took all reasonable steps to prevent their approval.[96] Furthermore, if there is a breach of the requirements as to signature of the balance sheet, the company and every officer in default is guilty of an offence.[97]

The directors' report

Under section 234 the directors must, in addition, prepare a report for each financial year. This must contain a fair review of the development of the business of the company and its subsidiaries during the financial year and the position at the end of it, must state what amount (if any) they recommend should be paid as dividend, and what amount (if any) they propose to carry to reserves.[98] In addition it must give the names of all persons who at any time during the financial year were directors of the company and describe the principal activities of the company and its subsidiaries and any changes therein during the course of the year.[99] Furthermore, it must give additional information on the matters mentioned in Schedule 7 to the Act.[1]

Schedule 7[2] is divided into a number of parts, some of which require information which goes far beyond the purely financial. Thus Part III requires information to be given about the employment, training and promotion of disabled persons, and Part V about "employee involvement", *i.e.* the extent to which employees are systematically given information, consulted, and encouraged to join employee share schemes. None of these is relevant to an appraisal of the company's financial position. Nor, indeed is the requirement in Part I for separate disclosure of the amounts of charitable or political donations; in view of the minimal amounts needed to trigger this requirement and the modest amounts normally donated, they would very rarely be material to a true and fair view of its financial affairs.[3] In fact, Schedule 7 is increasingly resorted to by

---

[96] s.233(5). A director whose primary defence is that he did not know and was not reckless would be ill-advised to attempt to show alternatively that he took all reasonable steps to prevent approval since unless he knew or suspected that the accounts did not comply he would have no reason for trying to prevent their approval.

[97] s.233(6).

[98] s.234(1).

[99] s.234(2).

[1] s.234(3) & (4).

[2] As amended by the 1989 Act, generally in minor respects only but note paras. 2, 2A, 2B and 5A.

[3] Nor does disclosure of political contributions do much to assuage the resentment of the trade unions that they can contribute (generally to the Labour Party) only out of a separate political fund, which must be periodically approved in a secret ballot of the membership as a whole and from contributions to which individual members may contract out, even if the membership as a whole has approved the establishment of the fund, whereas companies can contribute (generally to the Conservative Party directly or indirectly) with no more than subsequent disclosure.

governments, not for the purpose of financial disclosure, but in order to expose to public gaze matters which government is unwilling to regulate prescriptively but which it hopes, perhaps optimistically, will be either promoted or contained (as the case may be) through the pressures of public opinion. A recent example of this is the addition to Schedule 7 that the company, if public, must disclose its policy on the payment of creditors.[4]

The auditors' report

The final document that has to accompany the annual accounts is the auditors' report thereon. This has to be addressed to the company's members[5] and to state whether in the auditors' opinion the annual accounts have been properly prepared in accordance with the Act and, in particular, whether they give a true and fair view.[6] The report must also state whether the auditors consider that the information given in the director's report is consistent with that in the annual accounts and, if they are not satisfied, they must say so in the report.[7] In preparing this report they must carry out such investigations as will enable them to form an opinion on (a) whether proper accounting records have been kept by the company[8] and whether proper returns adequate for their audit have been received from branches which they have not visited[9] and (b) whether the company's individual accounts are in agreement with the accounting records and returns.[10] If they are not of those opinions they must say so.[11] If they have failed to obtain all the information and explanations which, to the best of their knowledge and belief, are necessary for the purpose of their audit, their report must so state. Moreover, if the requirements of Schedule 6 (disclosure of emoluments and benefits of directors) are not complied with in the accounts, "the auditors shall include in their report, so far as they are

---

[4] Added by the Companies Act 1985 (Miscellaneous Accounting Amendments) Regulations 1996 (SI. 1996 No. 189), reg. 14. See further, DTI, *Tackling Late Payment: Stating Payment Practice in the Directors' Report*, June 1996, proposing a further extension to embrace practice as well as policy.

[5] s.235(1).

[6] s.235(2).

[7] s.235(3).

[8] See s.221, above.

[9] This would include records required from branches outside Great Britain under s.222 above, but is not restricted to them. A company with retail outlets throughout Britain may need initially to keep some records at each branch and although these may be collated at the head office the auditors will need to satisfy themselves that the accounts at head office are based on adequate and accurate returns from the branches.

[10] The group accounts will be based in those of the individual undertakings in the group and not all of them will necessarily be audited by the same firm.

[11] s.237(1) and (2).

reasonably able to do so, a statement giving the required particulars".[12]

The auditors' report must state the names of the auditors and be signed by them[13] and their names must be stated on all issued copies of the report.[14] The copy delivered to the Registrar must also be signed by the auditors.[15] And, now that the Act expressly recognises that a firm, as such, may be appointed[16] and that, increasingly, accountancy firms are incorporated, it is expressly stated that what is then required is a signature in the name of the firm by a person authorised to sign on its behalf.[17]

Publicity of accounts and reports

The next group of sections deals with the various types of publicity that have to be given to the annual accounts and reports. It starts with section 238 but it may be more illuminating to start here with section 240 which draws a distinction between the publication of "statutory accounts" (*i.e.* the annual accounts and reports considered above, copies of which have to be delivered to the Registrar under section 242) and "non-statutory accounts" (*i.e.* any other purported balance sheet or profit and loss account dealing with a financial year[18] of the company or group).[19] Section 240 seeks to ensure that recipients of the latter will not confuse them with statutory accounts. If a company publishes[20] any of its statutory accounts they must be accompanied by the auditors' report[21] and if it is required to prepare statutory group accounts it may not publish its (statutory) individual accounts unless they are accompanied by its statutory group accounts.[22] In contrast,

---

[12] s.237(4). This is an extension of the normal role of auditors. It is the directors' responsibility to prepare full and accurate accounts—not the auditors'. But this subs. requires the auditors in effect to correct the accounts.

[13] s.236(1).

[14] s.236(2).

[15] s.236(3).

[16] See Chap. 20, below. It had long been the general practice to appoint in the firm name but only as a result of the 1989 Act is it fully recognised that the firm may be "a person corporate or unincorporate".

[17] s.236(5). If there is a contravention of subs. (1) (2) or (3) the company and any officer of it who is in default is guilty of an offence and liable to a fine.

[18] Half-yearly financial statements, which are required by the Exchange's *Listing Rules* in the case of listed companies, are not "statutory" nor are they "non-statutory accounts" since they do not relate to a financial year.

[19] s.240(5).

[20] For the purposes of the section, "a company shall be regarded as publishing a document if it publishes, issues or circulates it, or otherwise makes it available for public inspection in a manner calculated to invite members of the public generally, or any class of members of the public, to read it": s.240(4). This clearly covers the methods of publication dealt with below— and others besides (*e.g.* a radio or TV advertisement announcing the publication of annual accounts and where they can be inspected).

[21] s.240(1). Or the report required by ss.249A(2) and 249C. See below, pp. 530 *et seq.*

[22] s.240(2).

any publication of non-statutory accounts must be accompanied by a statement indicating: (a) that they are not statutory accounts, (b) whether statutory accounts have been delivered to the Registrar, (c) whether the auditors have reported on those statutory accounts, and (d) whether any such report was qualified or contained a statement under section 272 or 273.[23] An auditors' report under section 235 must not be published with any non-statutory accounts.[24] The sections to which we next turn are concerned with publication of the "statutory" accounts only.

First, section 238(1) provides that any member, holder of the company's debentures[25] and any person who is entitled to receive notice of general meetings shall, not less than 21 days before the accounts are to be laid before the general meeting under section 241, be sent copies of them. This is subject to the minor exceptions in subsections (2) and (3), and to adaptations when a private company has validly elected under section 252 to dispense with laying of accounts before general meetings or when shareholders of listed companies have elected under section 251[26] to receive summary financial statements instead. If copies are sent less than 21 days before, they may be deemed to have been duly sent if so agreed by all the members entitled to attend and vote.[27]

Secondly, section 239 entitles any member or debenture-holder to be furnished, on demand and without charge, with a copy of the last accounts in addition to that to which he is entitled under section 238.[28]

Thirdly, under section 241 the statutory accounts must be laid before the company in general meeting (unless the company is a private one which has elected to dispense with this requirement under section 252). Section 244 provides that this normally has to be done within 10 months after the end of the accounting reference period to which the accounts relate (if it is a private company) or within seven months (if it is a public one).[29] But there are variations in respect of the first accounting reference period if that is longer than twelve months,[30] or on a change of the accounting reference date if the effect is to shorten the ARP,[31] or in the case of a company carrying on business or having interests outside the British

---

[23] s.240(3). The same rules apply to an accountant's report under s.249A(2).

[24] s.240(3). The same applies to a s.249A(2) report.

[25] In this and the later sections "debenture" is clearly used in its popular sense of a series of debentures or debenture stock and would not include a mortgage or one of the company's properties: see Chap. 13 at pp. 322–324, above.

[26] See below, at pp. 524–526.

[27] s.238(4).

[28] If he wants any more copies he can, of course, get them (on payment) from Companies House.

[29] s.244(1).

[30] s.244(2).

[31] s.244(4).

Isles.[32] Moreover, the Secretary of State may allow an extension in special circumstances.[33]

Fourthly, copies of the annual accounts and reports have to be delivered to the Registrar under section 242. This has to be done before the end of the time allowed for laying them before the general meeting[34] and if any of the documents is not in the English language a certified translation must be annexed.[35]

Compliance with section 242 is the most important of the four since it is the one which makes the statutory accounts available to the general public. While all four have provisions for penalties for non-compliance, those in section 242, as supplemented by section 242A, are the most stringent. If the requirements of section 242 are not complied with on time, any person who was a director immediately before the end of the time allowed is liable to a fine and, for continued contravention, to a daily default fine.[36] Furthermore, under subsection (3) if the directors fail to make good the default within 14 days after the service of a notice requiring compliance,[37] the court, on the application of the Registrar or any member or creditor of the company, may make an order directing the directors or any of them to make good the default within such time as may be specified[38] and may order them to pay the costs of and incidental to the application. Any person charged with an offence under the section has a defence if he can prove that he took all reasonable steps for securing that the accounts were delivered in time.[39] But, to spike the guns of barrack-room lawyers, it is expressly stated that it is not a defence to prove that the documents prepared were not in fact prepared in accordance with the Act.[40]

To these criminal sanctions against directors, section 242A adds civil penalties against the company. The amount of the penalty, recoverable by the Registrar, varies according to whether the company is private or public and to the length of time that the default

---

[32] s.244(3).

[33] s.244(5).

[34] s.242(1) and (2). In the case of a private company which has dispensed with laying they must be delivered to him before they are sent to the members and others under s.238 above: s.252(3).

[35] s.242(1). Except that in the case of a company whose memorandum states that it is to be registered in Wales, other than a listed company, it is the Registrar rather than the directors who has to obtain the translation: the Companies (Welsh Language Forms and Documents) Regulations 1994 (S.I. 1994 No. 117). Note also s.243 under which in some circumstances the accounts of a foreign or unincorporated subsidiary undertaking that have been excluded from consolidation under s.229(4) may have to be delivered as well.

[36] s.242(2).

[37] The subsection does not say who may serve such a notice so presumably anyone can: but in practice it is likely to be the Registrar who does so—though the subs. makes it pretty clear that a member or creditor certainly could.

[38] If they fail to do so they will be in contempt of court and liable to imprisonment.

[39] s.242(4).

[40] s.242(5). A similar express provision appears in s.241 (above) and in s.242A (below).

continues; the minimum being £100 for a private company and £500 for a public company when the default is for not more than three months and the maximum £1000 for a private and £5,000 for a public company when the default exceeds 12 months.[41] There are obvious attractions in affording the Registrar an additional weapon in the form of a penalty recoverable by civil suit to which there is no defence once it is shown that accounts have not been delivered on time.[42] But in principle it seems inexcusable to penalise the company for breach of a duty not owed by it but by its directors and intended to protect, among others, the company and its members.[43]

Revision of defective accounts

Another innovation by the 1989 Act was the introduction of statutory provisions regarding the correction of defective accounts. It has never been doubted that if directors discover that the accounts that they have presented are defective they can, and should, correct them. But there had been no statutory provisions regarding it. Now we have such provisions concerning both voluntary revisions (section 245) and revisions under compulsion (sections 245A–245C).

Section 245 provides that if it appears to the directors that any annual accounts of the company or any directors' report[44] did not comply with the provisions of the Act, they may prepare revised accounts or a revised report.[45] If copies of the previous accounts or report have been laid or delivered the revisions must be confined to the correction of those respects in which they did not comply with the Act and the making of any consequential alterations.[46] The section provides that the Secretary of State may make provisions by regulations in relation to revised accounts and reports[47] which, in particular, may:—make different provisions according to whether the previous documents are replaced or merely supplemented by a statement of corrections; deal with the functions of the auditors or reporting accountants; require the directors to take specified steps in relation to circulation to members and others entitled under section 238; laying

---

[41] s.242A(2).

[42] The civil penalties under s.242A apply only to late filing of the annual accounts, but the DTI has proposed an extension of the principle to late filing of the annual return: DTI, *The Functions of the Registrar of Companies*, August 1996, para. 4.23.

[43] The company could, presumably, sue the directors to recover its loss resulting from their default. But unless the company goes into liquidation, administration or receivership this will not happen.

[44] Obviously they cannot revise the *auditors'* report.

[45] s.245(1).

[46] s.245(2).

[47] s.245(3).

before a general meeting and delivery to the Registrar; and the application of provisions of the Act (including penalties).[48]

Under section 245A, where copies of the annual accounts have been sent out, laid, or delivered to the Registrar and it appears to the Secretary of State that there is or may be a question whether they comply with the Act, he may give notice to the directors indicating the respects in which it appears to him that the question may arise[49] and specifying a period of not less than one month for the directors to give him explanations or prepare revised accounts.[50] If at the end of the specified period, or such longer period as he may allow, they have not satisfied him in one way or the other, the voluntary process ends and he may apply to the court.[51]

Section 245B provides that, as an alternative to an application to the court by the Secretary of State, such an application may be made "by any person authorised by him for the purposes of this section".[52] In either case, the court may declare that the accounts do not comply and may order the directors to prepare revised accounts. The order may give directions on: auditing, the revision of the directors' report or any summary financial statement,[53] steps to be taken to bring the order to the notice of persons likely to rely on the original accounts, and on such other matters as the court thinks fit.[54]

Finally, section 245C deals with the authorisation of "any other person" for the purposes of section 245B. The Secretary of State may authorise any person appearing to him:—(a) to be "fit and proper", and (b) to have an interest in, and satisfactory procedures directed to, securing compliance by companies with the accounting provisions and for receiving and investigation complaints.[55] Authorisation may be general or in respect of particular classes of case.[56] Such authorisation has been conferred on the Financial Reporting Review Panel,[57] a subsidiary of the Financial Reporting Council.[58]

---

[48] s.245(4). See the Companies (Revision of Defective Accounts and Reports) Regs. 1990 (S.I. 1990 No. 2570).

[49] s.245A(1).

[50] s.245A(2).

[51] s.245A(3). The section can be invoked in relation to revised accounts as well as to the original versions: s.245A(4).

[52] s.245B(1). Notice of the application must be given to the Registrar by the applicant: s.245B(2).

[53] See s.251, below.

[54] s.245B(3). And the court may order that all or part of the costs and expenses shall be borne by such of the directors as were party to the approval of the defective accounts (which every director at the time when they were approved is deemed to be unless he shows that he took all reasonable steps to prevent their being approved): s.245B(4). But the court should have regard to whether a director knew or ought to have known that the accounts did not comply and may exclude one or more of the directors from the order or require payment of different amounts by different directors: s.245B(5).

[55] s.245C(1).

[56] s.245C(2).

[57] S.I. 1991 No. 13.

[58] The body, supported by public funds, is independent of the professional accountancy bodies, and has the wider remit of promoting best practice in financial reporting.

Exemptions, exceptions and special provisions

The 1989 Act substituted a new Chapter II, headed as above, in Part VII of the Act. It is mainly concerned with concessions to smaller companies and with the special treatment (not dealt with here) of banking and insurance companies and groups. But it also includes an interesting innovation in relation to companies listed on the Stock Exchange and to this we turn first.

Summary financial statements

Under the new section 251, a company, any of whose shares are officially listed, need not, in such circumstances as are specified by regulations[59] and subject to complying with conditions so specified, send copies of the accounts and reports to members, debenture-holders or those entitled to receive notice of general meetings[60] but may instead send them a summary financial statement,[61] derived from the company's annual accounts and directors' report, in such form and containing such information as may be specified in the regulations.[62] In fact, various conditions are laid down in the section itself; in particular that the nature of the document must be made clear, and that it must contain a statement by the company's auditors of their opinion on whether the statement is consistent with the accounts and reports and complies with the section and the regulations. It must also state whether the auditors' report was qualified or unqualified and, if it was qualified, must set out the report in full with any further material needed to understand the qualification.[63] Use of the section is purely optional and even if the company adopts it, each entitled person must be sent copies of the full accounts and reports if he wants to receive them.[64]

The importance that the Government place on this section is shown by the fact that it was among the first provisions of the 1989 Act to be brought into operation and the initial regulations made under it were among the first to be published. The commendable objectives were (a) to present private investors[65] with a document which they

---

[59] The Companies (Summary Financial Statements) Regs. (S.I. 1992 No. 3075).

[60] s.251 was extended to all those entitled under s.238 to receive copies of accounts and reports by the Companies Act 1985 (Amendment of Sections 250 and 251) Regs. (S.I. 1992 No. 3003).

[61] s.251(1).

[62] s.251(3). s.240 (above) does not apply: s.251(7). See the Companies (Summary Financial Statement) Regs. 1995 (S.I. 1995 No. 2092).

[63] If it contained a statement unders s.237(2) or (3) that too must be set out: s.251(4).

[64] s.251(2). And the regulations may make provisions as to the manner in which it is to be ascertained whether a member wishes to receive them: *ibid.*: see reg. 6.

[65] Institutional and professional investors will obviously wish to continue to receive the full accounts.

might find more helpful to them than the full statutory accounts, (b) reduce an appalling waste of paper, since undoubtedly a great many such investors consign the glossy brochures containing the accounts to their waste-paper baskets after only the most cursory of glances (if any) and, perhaps, (c) to reduce the company's postage—though it is unlikely that any saving on that could be commensurate with the cost of preparing an additional document and, in effect, having it audited.

It will be interesting to see whether these objectives are attained. As regards the first, it seems unlikely. A perusal of the Schedules to the Regulations suggests that the summary will be a pretty lengthy one and expressed in equally impenetrable accountants' and lawyers' jargon. What most private investors need is not a summary (which is generally less intelligible than the document it summarises) but an explanation; and this they will not get. This is openly admitted by the Regulations which require that the summary must include a statement in a prominent position to the effect that the summary financial statement does not contain sufficient information to allow as full an understanding of the results and state of affairs of the company as would be provided by the full annual accounts and reports.[66] And the statement encourages those who have received it to ask in addition for the free copy of the latest statutory accounts by requiring that it must contain a conspicuous statement of their rights under section 239.[67]

As for the conservation aim, there will initially be a greater, not a lesser, consumption of paper. If persons entitled under section 238 to the full documents are to be persuaded to be content with the summary, it will be necessary to obtain his or consent, either in a circulation undertaken expressly for the purpose or as part of the circulation of the annual accounts.[68] In either case a postage-paid card on which the member can respond must be included. If there is no response, the member will be deemed to have opted for the summary statement.[69] Hence there is likely there after to be some saving of paper in future years[70] so long as most people do not also demand copies of the full accounts under section 239. But one cannot help thinking that a far greater contribution to the preservation of the world's rain forests would be made if companies could be persuaded to make their annual brochures less glossy and to print them on recycled paper.

The other points to note on the Regulations is that advantage cannot

---

[66] Reg. 7(3).

[67] *ibid.*

[68] Regs. 5 and 6. One listed insurance company was reported to have used this as a reason to remove from shareholders the right to vote on the annual accounts, but later changed its mind after criticism from institutional investors. See p. 563, below, and *The Financial Times*, April 3, 1997, p. 24 and April 4, p. 1.

[69] Regs. 5(1)(a) and 6(1)(a).

[70] Mainly, one suspects, because a great many will fail to return the card. But each subsequent summary statement must be accompanied by a pre-paid card entitling them to obtain full accounts: reg. 5(h).

be taken of the section if a provision, "however expressed," of the company's memorandum or articles or debenture instrument requires copies of the full accounts to be sent or which prohibits the sending of summary financial statements.[71] The summary must also state who signed it on behalf of the board.[72]

Small and medium-sized companies or groups

The first sections of Chapter II of Part VII replace, with amendments, the concessions to smaller companies originally afforded by the 1981 Act in respect of the content of their accounts, as permitted by the Fourth Company Law Directive. The scope of these sections was extended by regulation in 1992 and further exemptions, removing the need for an audit, were added by regulation in 1994. We shall look first at the sections dealing with content (as amended). To qualify as "small" or "medium-sized" in any financial year a company must meet the qualifying conditions in that year and its previous financial year (if there was one).[73] These conditions in the case of individual company accounts are that the company must satisfy at least two of three requirements relating to the maximum size of: (i) its turnover, (ii) its "balance sheet total"[74] and (iii) the average number of its employees during the year.[75]

Even if it meets these conditions, it will not be entitled to the concessions unless, at no time during the year, has it, or any member of the group of which it is a member, been a public company, a banking or insurance company or an authorised person under the Financial Services Act[76] and, if it is a parent company, unless the group qualifies as a small or medium-sized group.[77] The conditions for qualification as a small or medium-sized group are broadly similar except that the maximum size of each of the three criteria is greater.[78]

If, in accordance with the foregoing, a company is eligible as a small or medium-sized company, the concessions to which it is entitled are:

(a) exemption from the requirements of paragraph 36A of Schedule 4;

---

[71] Reg. 3(1).

[72] Reg. 7(2).

[73] s.247(1) and (2).

[74] In effect, the value of its gross assets as shown in the balance sheet.

[75] s.247. The maxima permitted are greater for qualification as "medium-sized" than for "small" but the extent of the concessions much less: see below. A "small" company is currently one with a turnover of not more than £2.8m, a balance sheet total not exceeding £1.4m and having no more than 50 employees. For a "medium-sized" company the figures are £11.2m, £5.6m and 250: s.247(3).

[76] s.247A(1) and (2).

[77] s.247A(3).

[78] ss.248 and 249.

(b) exemptions to the extent provided by sections 246 and 246A and
     Schedule 8A[79] with respect to the delivery of individual accounts
     to the Registrar under section 242;
(c) exemption from the requirement to prepare group accounts in
     respect of a year in which the group headed by the company is a
     small or medium-sized group; and
(d) in the case of small companies only, exemption from the require-
     ment to produce full accounts to the extent provided by section
     246 and Schedule 8.

Only (a) (b) and (d) require a brief explanation. As regards (a), the
new paragraph 36A of Schedule 4 provides:
   "It shall be stated whether the accounts have been prepared in
   accordance with applicable accounting standards and particulars of
   any material departure from those standards and the reason for it
   shall be given."
For many years the Accounting Standards Committee (the ASC) of
the accountancy bodies had been producing valuable Statements of
Standard Accounting Practice (SSAPs) and had done its best to ensure
that they were observed—not always successfully since the Statements
had no statutory recognition.[80] Now they have. A later section (section
256) defines them as "statements of standard accounting practice
issued by such body or bodies as may be prescribed by regulations"
and goes still further by empowering the Secretary of State to make
grants,[81] "to or for the purposes of bodies concerned with (a) issuing
accounting standards, (b) overseeing and directing the issuing of such
standards or (c) investigating departures from such standards or from
the accounting requirements of this Act and taking steps to secure
compliance with them".[82] As a result, the former ASC has been converted into another recognised body, the Accounting Standards Board,
as another subsidiary company of the Financial Reporting Council.[83]
The case for exempting small and medium-sized companies from the
obligation to comply with the Standards does not appear to be particularly strong; but exempted they are.[84]

---

[79] As substituted by the Companies Act 1985 (Accounts of Small and Medium-sized Companies
    and Minor Accounting Amendments) Regulations 1997 (S.I. 1997 No. 220).
[80] Except to the extent that they embodied "generally recognised accounting principles" which
    Sched. 4 sometimes requires to be observed but which are rather different from "Standards".
[81] This represents a considerable U-turn by the Government which had insisted that the regu-
    latory bodies set up under the Financial Services Act should be financed from fees payable
    by those regulated. There, the only support from public funds is in relation to the Tribunal
    plus a pump-priming loan by the Bank of England to SIB, now being repaid out of SIB's
    fee-generated income.
[82] s.256(3).
[83] See n. 58, p. 524, above.
[84] This is done expressly in the case of medium-sized companies by s.246A(2) and in the case
    of small companies by making their accounts subject to their own Sched. 8 rather than the
    general Sched. 4. This does not necessarily mean that they will ignore the standards; if the

As regards (b), it should be noted that all it does is to permit small and medium-sized companies to prune the accounts to be delivered to the Registrar and thus made public. Far from relieving the companies from burdens and expense, it adds to them; for those companies that take advantage of it will have to prepare two distinct sets of accounts and reports, the full version to circulate to their members and the expurgated version to be made available to the general public.[85] In 1993/4 only half of the small companies on the register took advantage of the opportunity to file abbreviated accounts, apparently because it costs some £100 to £250 to convert the full accounts to abbreviated form.[86] What it does, in effect, is to enable such companies to conceal from outsiders detailed information regarding profitability and turnover, something of which they have a (much exaggerated) fear that it will be used by their competitors to the company's disadvantage. It represents, however, a retreat from the basic principle that the price of limited liability should be full financial disclosure—a principle which after a long struggle, was adopted in the 1967 Act. This retreat goes far in relation to small companies because, under section 246(5), they are wholly exempt from delivering copies of the profit and loss account[87] and the directors' report[88] while the balance sheet and the information that has to be given in notes to the accounts can be substantially abbreviated.[89] In contrast, under section 246A, medium-sized companies have to deliver a copy of the full balance sheet, and a profit and loss account which, however, can combine various items prescribed by Schedule 4 under a single item (gross profits)[90] and can omit particulars of turnover.[91]

It is only when one turns to (d) that one finds the legislation addressing what many proponents of small businesses ultimately seek, namely, a reduction in the amount of information which has to be incorporated into any version of the company's accounts, thus reducing the level of disclosure even to shareholders. It is argued that the format required by the Act for a company's accounts was set with

---

accounts are professionally prepared and audited it is likely that the standards will be observed by those companies which want small to be beautiful.

[85] Moreover, under s.246(8) a company wishing to take advantage of the exemptions will have to add to the balance sheet which it delivers a statement that advantage is being taken of the exemptions and under s.247B the auditors are required to make a special report to the Registrar stating that in their opinion the company is so entitled and that the accounts are properly prepared in accordance with the relevant Schedule. That special report must reproduce the full text of the auditors' report if it was qualified and must contain any further matter necessary to understand the qualification. These requirements are now less onerous than they were before they were reduced by S.I. 1997 No. 220.

[86] DTI, *Accounting Simplifications: A Consultative Document*, 1995, para. 4.14.

[87] s.246(5)(a).

[88] s.246(5)(b).

[89] Sched. 8A.

[90] s.246A(3)(a).

[91] s.246A(3)(b).

large companies in mind and that it is over-elaborate for the needs of shareholders of small companies. Although a number of the disclosure requirements, applying on the face of it to all companies, do in fact exempt small companies because there is a threshold built into the requirement itself,[92] it was argued that a more thorough-going look at the problem was required. In 1992 the Government accepted this argument to some extent by introducing what is now section 216 and Schedule 8,[93] which modify the requirements for other companies relating to full accounts, set out in Schedule 4, and the directors' report, set out in Schedule 7. These provisions permit small companies to combine various headings in the full accounts (for example, to make no distinction between freehold, long leasehold and short leasehold property), to omit certain information (for example, deferred taxation), and to shorten the directors' report by not commenting on, for example, the dividend recommended or the amount to be carried to reserves or measures taken to promote the participation of employees. If a company takes advantage of the provisions, its balance sheet must contain a statement to the effect that the accounts or the report have been compiled in accordance with the special provisions applying to small companies.[94]

Micro companies

One should not allow oneself to be misled about the numerical significance of the statutory definition of the "small" company. The DTI has estimated that some 870,000 of the total of 957,000 companies on the register in 1995 fell within the statutory definition of "small".[95] There is therefore scope for argument that there should be further relaxation of the accounting requirements for very small or "micro"[96] companies, where there is no divorce between ownership and control. This issue arose in the perhaps surprising context, not of a further relaxation of the disclosure requirements as such, but of the proposed removal of the requirement to have the statutory accounts audited. In the middle of the 1980s the Government had come out in favour of the retention of the statutory audit for all companies and had therefore opposed, along with other Member States, proposals at Community level to make the exemption of small companies from this

---

[92] For example, the requirement in para. 9 of Sched. 7 to disclose in the directors' report the company's policy with regard to disabled persons applies only to companies employing more than 250 employees.

[93] This was achieved in the Companies Act 1985 (Accounts of Small and Medium-sized Enterprised and Publication of Accounts in ECUs) Regulations 1992 (S.I. 1992 No. 2452), implementing Council Directive 90/604.

[94] s.246(8).

[95] DTI, *Accounting Simplification: A Consultative Document*, 1995, para. 3.6.

[96] See the influential article by J. Freedman and M. Godwin, "The Statutory Audit and the Micro Company—An Empirical Investigation" [1993] J.B.L. 105.

requirement mandatory.[97] What caused a revival of the issue were the additional costs generated by the implementation in the Companies Act 1989 of Council Directive 84/253 on auditors' qualifications,[98] which was alleged to have a disproportionate impact on the audit costs of very small firms. Despite the opposition from some users of accounts, notably the Inland Revenue and some banks, on this occasion the deregulatory pressure was successful and new sections 249A to E were introduced into Part VII.[99]

In fact, the new sections introduced two forms of exemption from the audit requirement. A company which qualifies as a small company, as defined above,[1] and which in addition has a balance sheet total of not more than £1.4 million and an annual turnover or not more than £90,000 is totally exempt from the audit requirement.[2] This is so unless members holding at least 10 per cent of any class of shares by notice in writing delivered to the company within the appropriate time limits require the company to obtain an audit of the accounts for the relevant year.[3] Where the exemption applies and is used, the directors must confirm in a statement attached to the balance sheet that the company was entitled to the exemption, that no effective notice has been delivered requiring an audit and that the directors acknowledge their responsibilities for ensuring that the company keeps accounting records[4] and for preparing accounts which give a true and fair view of the state of the company's affairs.[5]

The total exemption has been made available on a rather more generous scale than was originally envisaged.[6] In particular, the turnover level for qualification has been set at £90,000 rather than at the level of £37,600, as originally envisaged. Moreover, the Act now goes further by providing a qualified exemption for small companies whose turnover does not exceed £350,000 in the relevant year.[7] The overall

---

[97] DTI, *Accounting and Audit Requirements for Small Firms: A Consultative Document*, 1985 and *Consultative Document on Amending the Fourth Company Law Directive on Annual Accounts*, 1989. The Fourth Directive, however, permits Member States to exempt small companies from the audit.

[98] See below, p. 539.

[99] By the Companies Act 1985 (Audit Exemption) Regulations 1994 (S.I. 1994 No. 1935).

[1] See above, p. 527. This means that public companies, authorised persons under the FSA, etc., are excluded from the exemption, a restriction made explicit by s.249B(1).

[2] s.249A(3). It may seem unnecessary to repeat in this section the requirement as to balance sheet total since the same figure is contained in s.247(3) as part of the definition of a small company. However, its significance is that the criteria for qualifying as a small company could be relaxed, say for publication purposes, without altering the criteria for total exemption from the audit. It might not be thought appropriate to relieve from the audit a company which had substantial assets even if little in the way of income.

[3] s.249B(2). 10 per cent of the members is the relevant proportion in the case of a company without share capital.

[4] See above, p. 513.

[5] s.249B(4).

[6] DTI, *Audit and Accounting Requirements for Very Small Companies*, 1993, para. 6.3.

[7] s.249A(2) and (4). This figure was chosen apparently because it is the figure was chosen apparently because it is the figure below which cash accounting is permitted for VAT. In the

result is to exempt some 500,000 companies, wholly or by means of the qualified exemption, from the need for a statutory audit.[8] This exemption is a qualified one because for the obligation to have the accounts audited is substituted an obligation to have the accounts reported on by an accountant.[9] The reporting accountant, who must be professionally qualified, must state whether the accounts are in accordance with the company's accounting records and whether, having regard to those records, the accounts have been drawn up in accordance with the Act's requirements for companies of that size.[10] In essence, the distinction between the accountant's report and the full audit is that in the former case the company's accounting records are taken on trust and are not independently verified. However, it must be doubted whether such a restriction of the accountant's functions will save more than half the cost of an audit, and some estimates put the cost saving even lower.

It seems unlikely that even the above reforms constitute the end of the road for deregulation in this area. In 1995 the DTI consulted over a further range of accounting simplifications.[11] Of course, this is not a subject over which the Member States of the Community have an entirely free hand. As we have seen, the basic rules in this area are set by the Fourth and Seventh Company Law Directives. For example, the requirement that all companies produce accounts is laid down in the Fourth Directive. However, the Fourth Directive, as amended, permits for small companies greater modification of the full obligations applying to the accounts prepared for shareholders than the United Kingdom has yet made use of, and the United Kingdom clearly retains control over matters not regulated by Community law. Moreover, Community law itself is not static and in recent years the policy of promoting small and medium-sized companies, usually for their job-creation potential, has had its impact upon the Fourth and Seventh Directives. Thus, the modifications introduced in 1992 in relation to shareholders' accounts were made possible by the adoption at Community level of Directive 90/604,[12] and Council Directive 94/8[13] has

---

case of charities the gross income figure is chosen, rather than turnover, and is set at £250,000: s.249A(5).

[8] DTI, *op cit.*, n. 95, para. 4.1.

[9] The rule enabling 10 per cent of the members to demand a full audit applies in this case also: s.249B(2). The DTI has consulted recently over a proposal to raise the total audit exemption limit to £350,000 and to abolish the reporting accountant's report: DTI, *Small Companies Audit Exemption: Consultation on Proposed Amendments*, January 1997.

[10] s.249C(2). The reporting accountant must also state that in his opinion the company is entitled to the qualified exemption from the statutory audit: s.249C(3).

[11] See the document cited in n. 95, above. It contains some 50 proposals for accounting simplification, a few of which have already been implemented in the Companies Act (Miscellaneous Accounting Amendments) Regulations 1996 (S.I. 1996 No. 189). See also n. 9, above.

[12] O.J. L317/57, the preamble stating that "the administrative procedures imposed on small and medium-sized undertakings should be simplified".

[13] O.J. L82/33.

raised of the financial ceilings for small and medium-sized enterprises, though advantage has not yet been taken of this in the United Kingdom.

Dormant companies

A further, and less controversial, type of company which can totally dispense with the provisions of the Act relating to auditing of the accounts is a so-called "dormant company". Under section 250 it is treated as dormant "during a period in which . . . there is no transaction which is required by section 221[14] to be entered in the company's accounting records; and a company ceases to be dormant on the occurrence of such a transaction".[15] The most obvious and common example of such a company is a "shelf company" [16] while it remains on the shelf. But there may be legitimate reasons for incorporating a company which is intended to remain dormant indefinitely or for retaining on the register a company which for the time being has ceased to carry on business but which the members may wish to use at some time in the future for the same or some different business.

Unlike "micro" companies, a dormant company does not obtain the exemption merely by being dormant. In addition it must have passed a special resolution making itself "exempt"[17] and that resolution may not be passed if it is a banking or insurance company or an authorised person under the Financial Services Act.[18] However, not only is the dormant company then entitled to the exemption from auditing but, if it would have been entitled to the exemptions of a small company under section 246 but for the fact that it is a member of an ineligible group, it will also be entitled to those exemptions[19] until it ceases to be dormant or no longer qualifies to make itself exempt under section 250.[20]

It hardly needs saying that, if there is no audit, there will not be any auditors' report to be sent to members, laid before a general meeting, or delivered to the Registrar. This is recognised in the section[21] which, however, requires the copy of the balance sheet delivered to

---

[14] See above, p. 513.

[15] s.250(3). "For this purpose there shall be disregarded any transaction arising form the taking of shares by a subscriber to the memorandum in pursuance of an undertaking of his in the memorandum": *ibid.*

[16] See Chap. 6 at p. 110, above.

[17] s.250(1).

[18] s.250(2). Every authorised person under the FSA is required to keep audited accounts whether he is an individual, a partnership or a company.

[19] s.250(4)(d).

[20] s.250(5).

[21] s.250(4)(a) (b) & (c). s.249E makes similar provision in the case of exempted companies.

the Registrar to state immediately above the signature that the company was dormant throughout the year.[22]

Private companies: dispensing with laying accounts

The elective regime for private companies introduced by the 1989 Act[23] enables a private company to elect to dispense with the laying of accounts and reports before a general meeting in accordance with section 241.[24] So long as the documents have been sent to all those entitled to attend a general meeting in accordance with section 238,[25] it is a pointless farce to require a formal general meeting to be held in order that they may be "laid" unless a member wants to raise questions about them at a meeting,[26] or the auditors want to have an opportunity of talking to the members about them. Hence section 252 provides that a private company (whether or not small or medium-sized) may elect (by elective resolution in accordance with section 379A)[27] to dispense with the laying of accounts,[28] and this dispensation applies in respect of the financial year in which the election is made and to subsequent financial years so long as it remains in force.[29] References in other provisions of the Act to laying of accounts are then to be read as references to the sending of copies under section 238.[30]

However, the rights of any member or of the auditors to insist on a general meeting are entrenched by section 253. This requires that the accounts sent to members under section 238 shall be sent not less than 28 days before the end of the period allowed for laying and delivery of them[31] and shall be accompanied by notice of their right to require them to be laid before a general meeting.[32] Before the end of the 28 days any member or auditor may serve notice on the company requiring a meeting to be held for that purpose.[33] If the directors do not, within a further 21 days, proceed duly to convene the meeting,[34] the

---

[22] s.250(4)(c). The Registrar should also have received a copy of the special resolution under s.380(4).

[23] See Chap. 5 at p. 94, above.

[24] See p. 521, above.

[25] *ibid.*

[26] In the case of smaller private companies he can usually do so without the need for a formal meeting.

[27] On which see Chap. 5 at p. 91, above.

[28] s.252(1).

[29] s.252(2). When it ceases to have effect, s.241 applies to the financial year in which that occurs and subsequent financial years: s.252(4).

[30] s.252(3).

[31] Under ss.238 and 242, above. Under those sections the period allowed is not less than 21 days before.

[32] s.253(1). Formal notice to the auditors is not needed: they will have copies of the accounts and will know of the elective resolution and what their rights are.

[33] s.253(2).

[34] Which they shall be deemed not to have done if they give notice convening a meeting but for a date more than 28 days from the notice: s.253(6).

person who gave notice may himself do so.[35] The meeting must be convened in the same way, as nearly as possible, as that in which meetings are to be convened by the directors and must be held not later than three months from the date of service of the notice.[36] Any reasonable expenses incurred by the person who gave notice have to be made good by the company and recouped by the company out of any fees or other emoluments of the directors in default.[37]

Unlimited companies

In general, the accounting provisions of Part VII of the Act apply to every company, limited or unlimited. But in the case of the latter, it has been recognised that as regards the obligation, now in section 242, to deliver accounts and reports to the Registrar (thus making them available to the public), they (like partnerships) are entitled to exemption. However, inroads into that exemption, have been made when they are part of a group. Section 254(1) provides that the directors of an unlimited company are not required to deliver accounts and reports to the Registrar if certain conditions are met.[38] These conditions are that at no time during the relevant accounting reference period:

(a) has the company been, to its knowledge, a subsidiary undertaking of an undertaking which was then limited, nor
(b) have there been, to its knowledge, rights exercisable by or on behalf of two or more limited undertakings which if exercisable by one of them would have made the company a subsidiary of it, nor
(c) has the company been a parent company of an undertaking which was then limited.[39]

The reason for the inclusion of ''to its knowledge'' in (a) and (b) and its exclusion from (c) is that a subsidiary could well be ignorant, through no fault of its own, that it is a subsidiary, whereas a parent company ought to know what subsidiaries it has. The object of (b) is to require delivery of the accounts of an unlimited company if two or more limited companies would, if they had been a single entity, have been the parent of the unlimited company under the criteria in section 258,[40] although technically the unlimited company is not a subsidiary of any of them.

---

[35] s.253(3).
[36] s.253(4).
[37] s.253(5).
[38] s.254(1).
[39] s.254(2).
[40] On which see Chap. 8 at pp. 160–161.

The only other exclusion from the exemption is that it does not apply if at any time during the relevant accounting period the unlimited company carried on business as the promoter of a trading stamp scheme within the meaning of the Trading Stamps Act 1964.[41] To single out such companies seems curious; one would have thought that there is a stronger case for excluding unlimited companies which are authorised persons under the Financial Services Act.[42]

Banking and insurance companies

The remaining sections[43] of Chapter II of Part VII deal with the special provisions applying to banking and insurance companies. These may prepare their accounts in accordance with Schedules 9 and 9A (as amended) instead of Schedule 4.

Supplementary provisions

The 1989 Act added a new Chapter III, under the above heading, to Part VII. This contains section 256 (accounting standards) already referred to in this Chapter.[44] It also contains sections 258 and 259 which, in conjunction with Schedule 10A, define "parent and subsidiary undertakings" and section 260, defining "participating interest". These have been dealt with in Chapter 8, above.[45] Attention should, however, be drawn to sections 257 and 261. The former affords the Secretary of State the widest powers to modify, by Regulations, any of the provisions of Part VII.[46] If they are made more onerous an affirmative resolution of each House of Parliament is needed[47]: if not, they are effective unless annulled by a resolution of either House.[48] Section 261 clarifies the position of notes to the accounts: references in the Act to the accounts include any notes to the accounts containing information which the Act requires to be given and which it requires or allows to be given in a note to the accounts.[49] Such notes may be included in the accounts or in separate documents annexed thereto.[50]

---

[41] s.254(3).
[42] As in ss.246(3), 248(2), 250(2). The other exclusions in those sections are unlikely to be relevant in relation to s.254 (an unlimited company cannot be a public company) but an unlimited company (or a partnership) could be an authorised person and might well be a subsidiary undertaking in a group. If so, the public should surely be entitled to access to its accounts?
[43] ss.255–255D.
[44] See p. 528, above.
[45] At p. 160, above.
[46] s.257(1) and (4).
[47] s.257(2).
[48] s.257(3).
[49] s.261(2).
[50] s.261(3).

Conclusion

There is no doubt that members and creditors (actual or potential) of companies are afforded ample opportunities to obtain a great deal of financial and other information about the companies concerned. What is questionable is whether they make the best use of this information, particularly of that which, if they were competent to extract it, could be deduced from the companies' published accounts. This may not matter too much if they have professional advisers on whom they could rely. These advisers are more likely to be accountants, rather than lawyers whose principal role in this respect is likely to be in advising on the interpretation of the statutory provisions rather than on the financial state of the companies which the information reveals. But any worthwhile advice on the latter is dependent on the accuracy of the information disclosed. Hence the importance of audits by competent and independent auditors—to which we turn in the next Chapter.

CHAPTER 20

AUTORS

MANY references to the role of auditors have been made in earlier Chapters[1] and it has been stressed that their role is a vital one. If reliance is to be placed on accounts, it is essential that they should be true and fair and that is more likely to be the case if someone independent of the company has vetted them and certified that they are. If, however, that certification is to be relied on, the scrutineer must be competent as well as independent. Hence the Companies Acts have attempted to ensure that company auditors are both.

In the original version of the Companies Act 1985, provisions relating to audits and auditors were to be found in Part VII, and in Part XI, Chapter V. They still are. But, in addition, in implementation of the Eighth Company Law Directive on the qualifications of company auditors, the 1989 Act not only amended Part VII and Part XI, Chapter V, but also contained in its Part II some 30 sections dealing with eligibility to be appointed as a company auditor. In contrast with most of the provisions of the 1989 Act, its Part II did not make textual amendments to, or insertions in, the Companies Act 1985; these sections are self-standing substantive provisions. What will happen to them when and if there is a new official consolidation of the Companies Act is unclear. But it will not be a happy solution if there is, say, a consolidated Companies Act which excludes, but leaves on the statute-book, an emasculated Companies Act 1989 consisting of 30 sections numbered 24 to 54.[2]

The main purposes of these sections[3] "are to secure that only persons who are properly supervised and appropriately qualified are appointed company auditors, and that audits by persons so appointed are carried out properly and with integrity and with a proper degree of independence".[4] Subsequent sections then deal successively with eligibility, recognition of supervisory bodies and of professional qualifications, duties of recognised bodies, offences, and "supplementary provisions". The general effect is to subject auditors to a somewhat similar regime to that applying to authorised persons under the Financial Services Act (or to insolvency practitioners under the Insolvency

---

[1] Especially in Chaps. 11, 12 and 19. Note, however, that "micro" companies are now exempted from the statutory audit. See above, pp. 530–532.

[2] At any rate unless that residue of the Act is renamed the Companies (Eligibility of Auditors) Act (cf. the Company Securities (Insider Dealing) Act) or the Company Auditors Qualification Act (cf. the Company Directors Disqualification Act).

[3] Which follow immediately ss.1–23 substituting new sections of Part VII of the 1985 Act.

[4] 1989 Act, s.24(1).

Act). All that can be attempted in this Chapter is a description of the salient points. It should, however, be pointed out by way of introduction that in fact it does not resemble the financial services regime as closely as was originally envisaged. The sections follow the precedent of the Financial Services Act by conferring functions on the Secretary of State and then, by section 46, empowering him to delegate nearly all of them to a body corporate established for the purpose. On delegation to it, this would have resulted in there being a body corresponding to SIB under the Financial Services Act, which would perform the role of recognition and surveillance of the lower-tier bodies corresponding to the SROs and RPBs under that Act. In the light of the extent to which the accountancy bodies[5] already collaborated in matters of mutual concern it was thought that they would welcome this solution. But in fact they did not.

Hence, for the foreseeable future there will be no general delegation of the Secretary of State's functions under these sections and section 46 can be ignored. Instead, the new regulatory bodies,[6] are recognised by, and are answerable to, the Secretary of State.

ELEGIBILITY OF AUDITORS

A person is eligible for appointment as auditor of a company only if he is a member of a recognised supervisory body and is eligible for the appointment under the rules of that body.[7] A register must be kept and be open to public inspection of those eligible for appointment as auditors.[8]

As already mentioned,[9] an individual or a firm[10] may now be appointed as auditor.[11] Section 26 of the 1989 Act deals with the effect of an appointment of a partnership, which under English law (but not Scottish) is not a legal person. Despite that, an appointment of a firm is, unless the contrary appears, an appointment of the partnership as

---

[5] *i.e.* the Institute of Chartered Accountants in England and Wales, the Institute of Chartered Accountants of Scotland, the Chartered Association of Certified Accountants, the Chartered Institute of Management Accountants and the Institute of Chartered Accountants in Ireland (which covers both the Republic and N. Ireland) which collaborate through the Consultative Committee of Accountancy Bodies (the C.C.A.B.).

[6] Including the new Financial Reporting Review Panel and the Financial Reporting Council mentioned in Chap. 19 at p. 524, above.

[7] 1989 Act. s.25(1). The four bodies mentioned in n. 5, above, plus the Association of Authorised Public Accountants are recognised as supervisory bodies.

[8] Companies Act 1989 (Register of Auditors and Information about Audit Firms) Regulations 1991 (S.I. 1991 No. 1566). These require one of the recognised bodies to keep an overall register and each recognised body to make publicly available information about each firms eligible for appointment under its rules.

[9] See Chap. 19 at p. 519, above.

[10] 1989 Act s.25(2).

[11] In that Act (and in this Chapter) "he" and "him" are used whether the person is an individual or a firm.

such and not of the individual partners[12] and, when the composition of the partnership changes, the appointment extends to the successor partnership so long as its composition is substantially the same and it succeeds to substantially the same practice.[13] The same applies if the partnership ceases and a former partner, who is eligible, succeeds to the practice.[14] Where no one succeeds under the foregoing provisions, the appointment may, with the consent of the company, be extended to a partnership or other person eligible for the appointment which succeeds to the business of the former partnership (or to such part of the business as is agreed by the company to include the appointment).[15]

A person is ineligible for appointment on the ground of lack of independence if he is an officer or employee[16] of the company or a partner or employee of such an officer or employee or, in the case of the appointment of a partnership, if any member of the partnership is ineligible on these grounds. And he is also ineligible if any of these grounds apply in relation to any associated undertaking[17] of the company.[18]

Clearly an employer–employee relationship is far from being the only type of relationship which might impair the independence of the auditors, *e.g.* a debtor–creditor relationship or a substantial shareholding in the company[19] might do so. Hence section 27(2) empowers the Secretary of State to specify by regulations such connections "between him and any associate[20] of his and the company or any associated undertaking of it" which will also render him ineligible.

No person may act as a company auditor if he is ineligible for appointment,[21] and if he becomes ineligible he must vacate office and

---

[12] 1989 Act, s.26(2).

[13] *ibid.*, s.26(3)(a) and (4).

[14] *ibid.*, s.26(3)(b) and (4).

[15] *ibid.*, s.26(5). In the text, the paraphrase of s.26 has distinguished between changes of composition and cessations, since this seems helpful to an understanding of a somewhat complicated section. The section does not do so since, technically, any change in composition causes a cessation of the former partnership. The whole section would be unnecessary (with the possible exception of subs.(5)—and the Scots presumably manage happily without that) if English law had had the sense to follow the Scots by recognising the legal personality of a partnership.

[16] s.27(1) expressly states that, for this purpose, an auditor is not to be regarded as an "officer or employee". This hardly needs saying, for it was he was he would become ineligible once appointed. The definition of "officer" in the Companies Acts ("officer—includes a director, manager or secretary": 1985 Act, s.744) might seem to exclude auditors. Nevertheless, they have been held to be "officers" in a number of corporate contexts; *Mutual Reinsurance Co. Ltd v. Peat Marwick Mitchell & Co.* [1997] 1 BCLC 1, C.A.; *Re London & General Bank (No. 1)* [1895] 2 Ch. 166, C.A.; *Re Kingston Cotton Mills (No. 1)* [1896] 1 Ch. 6, C.A.

[17] *i.e.* a parent or subsidiary undertaking of the company or a subsidiary undertaking of any parent undertaking of the company: 1989 Act s.27(3).

[18] *ibid.*, s.27(1).

[19] Though the shareholding might make the auditor a more diligent watchdog over the members' interests—but members are not the only people whose interests he should protect.

[20] As defined in *ibid.*, s.52.

[21] 1989 Act, s.28(1).

forthwith give notice in writing to the company that he has vacated office by reason of ineligibility.[22] Contravention is an offence punishable by a fine[23] which may increase daily if he continues to act though ineligible.[24]

If an auditor proves to have been ineligible during any part of his audit, the Secretary of State may direct the company to appoint another (eligible) auditor in his place, either to carry out a second audit or to review the first and to report (giving reasons) whether a second audit is needed.[25] If a second audit is recommended, the company must comply.[26] The Registrar has to be sent a copy of the direction and of any report and the provisions of the 1985 Act applying to the first audit apply to the second "so far as is practicable".[27] If the original auditor knew that he was ineligible the company is entitled to recover from him any costs incurred in complying with the direction or recommendation.[28] But if the company has failed to comply with the direction or recommendation it is liable to a fine on a basis similar to that applying to the ineligible auditor.[29]

EDUCATIONAL QUALIFICATIONS

There is a marked difference between the regulation of the financial services industry (except in respect of those firms that are authorised by virtue of membership of recognised professional bodies) and that of the accountancy profession when acting as company auditors. In the case of the former it is, unfortunately, not yet possible to prescribe educational training and qualifying examinations as an essential precondition in all cases of "fitness and properness" for authorisation. But section 30–34 and Schedules 11 and 12 to the 1989 Act do this in respect of company auditors.[30]

---

[22] *ibid.*, s.28(2).

[23] *ibid.*, s.28(3). It is a defence for him to show that he did not know and had no reason to believe that he was ineligible: *ibid.*, s.28(5). This might well be shown when the ineligibility flowed from action by the company or by one of its associated undertakings or by one of his partners or associates.

[24] *ibid.*, s.28(4).

[25] *ibid.*, s.29(1).

[26] *ibid.*, s.29(2).

[27] *ibid.*, s.29(3) and (4). The extent of the practicability will depend on whether the ineligibility is discovered before the accounts and reports have been sent out, laid and delivered to the Registrar. If it is, the statutory provisions can be fully complied with by substituting the second auditor's report for the first's. Even if it is too late for that, the report of the second auditor has to be delivered to the Registrar (see s.29(3)) and presumably copies should be sent to the members—at any rate if it differs from the first auditors' report.

[28] *ibid.*, s.29(7).

[29] *ibid.*, s.29(5).

[30] It is also possible to do so relation to the authorisation of insolvency practitioners under Part XIII of the Insolvency Act 1986 and this is done to the extent that the recognised professional body that authorises them must, as a condition of recognition, have adequate rules ensuring that applicants for authorisation "meet acceptable requirements as to education and practical training and experience": Insolvency Act, ss.391(2)(b) and 393(2)(b). There is, however,

In addition to being a member[31] of a supervisory body which has been recognised in accordance with section 30, as supplemented by sections 35–53 and Schedule 11,[32] a person is not eligible for appointment as a company auditor unless he holds "an appropriate qualification". For this purpose sections 31–34, as supplemented by sections 35–53 and Schedule 12, deal with recognised qualifying bodies and recognised professional qualifications.

The role of the *qualifying* bodies is to provide courses and examinations in accountancy leading to an approved qualification. A body may apply to the Secretary of State for an order declaring a qualification offered by it to be a recognised professional qualification. But an order will not be made unless the Secretary of State is satisfied that the requirements of Schedule 12 regarding entry, theoretical instruction, professional experience, examinations[33] and rules regarding monitoring are met.[34] There is no reason why a recognised supervisory body should not also be a recognised qualifying body.

However, a recognised professional qualification is not the only available "appropriate qualification". A "grandfather" provision was needed to prevent all those formerly qualified from having to qualify anew. Hence, section 31 of the 1989 Act provides that a person qualified under the former section 389(1) before 1990 by virtue of membership of one of the four, then-recognised, accountancy bodies remains qualified[35] and that a person so qualified under that section, otherwise than by virtue of such membership, shall be treated as holding an approved qualification for 12 months from the date when section 25 came into force (1 October 1991) and shall continue thereafter to be so treated if, within that time, he notified the Secretary of State that he wished to retain the benefit of his qualification.[36]

---

nothing comparable to the detailed statutory prescription in ss.30–34 and Scheds. 11 and 12 of the 1989 Act.

[31] "Membership" includes "persons who, whether or not members of the body, are subject to its rules in seeking appointment or acting as company auditors": 1989 Act, s.30(2).

[32] Supervisory bodies will not be recognised unless they have rules and resources for effective monitoring and enforcement and for investigation of complaints: Sched. 11, Part II.

[33] The subjects on which theoretical knowledge must be tested by examinations, part at least of which must be written, may be prescribed by regulations made by the Secretary of State under Sched. 12, para. 7: see The Company Auditors (Examinations) Regs: S.I. 1990 No. 1146. These seem innocuous but the extent of the control which could be exercised by the Secretary of State for *Trade and Industry* over courses and examinations "requiring a standard of attainment at least equivalent to that required to obtain a degree from a university or similar establishment in the U.K." (Sched. 12, para. 7(1)) may cause shivers to run down academic spines. But note that exemption from subjects in the examination may be granted to someone who "has passed a university or other examination of equivalent standard in that subject or holds a university or equivalent qualification in it": Sched. 12, para. 7(2).

[34] *ibid.*, para. 9.

[35] 1989 Act, s.31(1)(a).

[36] *ibid.*, s.31(2). But note that a person previously qualified only under the "grandfather" provision in the 1967 Act remains qualified only for the audit of unquoted companies: *ibid.*, s.34(1) and (2). And other enactments (*e.g.* the FSA) referring to eligibility for appointment as a company auditor do not include such a person: s.34(4).

In addition, section 33 provides a further type of recognised qualification of which section 31[37] has to take account. Under section 33
the Secretary of State may declare that a person qualified to audit
accounts under the law of a specified country outside the United Kingdom, or one who holds a specified professional qualification recognised under the law of such a country, shall be regarded as holding
"an approved overseas qualification".[38] Such approval is dependent
on satisfying the Secretary of State that the overseas qualification
affords an assurance of professional competence equivalent to that
afforded by a recognised professional qualification[39] and the declaration may be made subject to his holding additional qualifications
ensuring that he has an adequate knowledge of United Kingdom law
and practice relevant to the audit of account.[40]

Attention must be drawn to certain provisions in Schedule 11 which
provide the answer to a question which may have puzzled readers.
When, as will normally be the case, a firm, corporate or unincorporated, is appointed as auditors, how does one ensure that the firm is
qualified not only by membership of a recognised supervisory body
(which presents no difficulty) but also by compliance with the educational and training requirements of a recognised qualifying body? One
cannot educate or train a firm; but only individual members of it. This
is not, as one would have expected, dealt with in a section of the 1989
Act itself but by paragraphs 4 and 5 of Schedule 11. These provide
that the supervisory body as a condition for its recognition must have
rules which ensure that a person is not eligible for appointment unless,
in the case of an individual, he holds an appropriate qualification and
that, in the case of a firm: (i) the individuals responsible for company
audit work on behalf of the firm hold appropriate qualifications[41], and
(ii) the firm is controlled by qualified persons.[42] A firm which has
ceased to comply may, however, be permitted to remain eligible for
not more than three months.[43] "Controlled by qualified persons"
means that a majority of the members hold appropriate qualifications
and, when the firm is managed by a management body, that a majority
of that body is qualified also.[44]

The foregoing covers only a part of the provisions of Part II of the

---

[37] *ibid.*, s.31(1)(c).
[38] *ibid.*, s.33(1).
[39] *ibid.*, s.33(2).
[40] *ibid.*, s.33(4).
[41] The register referred to in n. 8, above, must list, in the case of firms, the individuals who hold
appropriate qualifications and who are responsible for company audit work on behalf of the
firms.
[42] *ibid.*, Sched. 11 para. 4(1). This does not prevent the supervisory body from imposing more
stringent requirements: para. 4(2).
[43] para. 4(3). Thus giving it the opportunity, on a change in its membership, to make arrangements whereby it will comply.
[44] para. 5, of which the text is a brief summary omitting various qualifications.

1989 Act[45] but is sufficient, perhaps, to convey an impression of this new system for ensuring that auditors are properly qualified and which has now replaced section 389 of the Companies Act 1985.[46]

APPOINTMENT OF AUDITORS

We now turn to the new and amended sections 384–394A which sections 118–123 of the 1989 Act insert as Chapter V of Part XI (Auditors) of the 1985 Act.[47]

The first set of sections deals with appointment of auditors. Every company, other than a dormant or "micro" one, must appoint an auditor or auditors.[48] Except in the case of a private company which has elected to dispense with the laying of accounts[49] or with annual appointments,[50] this must be done at each general meeting at which the accounts and reports are to be laid and the appointment must be from the conclusion of that meeting until the conclusion of the next such meeting.[51] This is designed not merely to emphasise that it is to the members that auditors are to report and to ensure that the company has auditors at all times, but also to enhance the auditors' independence from the directors. However, the first auditors of the company must be appointed before the first general meeting at which accounts are to be laid and accordingly the first auditors may be, and, in practice invariably are, appointed by the directors[52] to hold office until that general meeting when the directors will recommend reappointment and the meeting, almost invariably, will agree. Normally, those auditors will continue to be reappointed until they wish to retire or the directors want to get rid of them.

In the case of a private company which has elected to dispense with laying of accounts, the foregoing provisions are adapted by requiring appointment within 28 days after the day on which copies of the accounts are to be sent to members under section 238.[53]

A private company may elect (by an elective resolution under sec-

---

[45] They confer powers on the S. of S. to ensure compliance by the recognised bodies (ss.37–41), and include matters such as offences (ss.41–44), fees (s.45), and prevention of restrictive practices (s.47 and Sched. 14, which provides a regime analogous to that applying to recognised SROs under the FSA).

[46] See The Companies Act 1989 (Eligibility for Appointment as Company Auditor) (Consequential Amendments) Regs. S.I. 1991 No. 1997.

[47] Hereafter references to sections are to those of the 1985 Act, as so amended, unless the contrary is stated.

[48] s.384. See pp. 530–533, above. s.388A applies to prescribe how auditors are to be appointed if a company ceases to be exempt from the requirement to appoint auditors.

[49] Under s.252, above, Chap. 19, p. 521.

[50] Under s.386, below.

[51] s.385(1) and (2).

[52] s.385(3). If they fail to do so, a general meeting may: s.385(4).

[53] s.385A. But see subs. (2) and (3) if notice is given under s.253(2) requiring the accounts for a particular year to be laid.

tion 379A) to dispense with the obligation to appoint auditors annually.[54] If such an election is in force, the auditors, once appointed, are deemed to be reappointed for each succeeding financial year unless a resolution has been passed under section 293[55] ending their appointment.[56] If, an election ceases to be in force, the auditors then holding office continue to do so until others are appointed under section 385 or 385A.[57] If, then or thereafter, they cease to hold office, no account can be taken of any loss of the opportunity of further deemed reappointment in assessing the amount of any compensation or damages payable for loss of office.[58]

In default of any appointment of auditors when they are required, the Secretary of State may appoint to fill the vacancy and the company must give notice to him, within one week of the end of the time for appointing auditors, that his power to do so has become exercisable.[59] In addition, the directors or the company in general meeting may fill a casual vacancy[60] and until it is filled the surviving or continuing auditor or auditors may continue to act.[61] If a casual vacancy is to be filled by a resolution of the general meeting or by a resolution to reappoint a person who was appointed by the directors, "special notice"[62] has to be given to the company and it must give notice of it to the person proposed to be appointed and, if the casual vacancy was caused by the resignation of an auditor, to him also.[63]

Subsection (1) of section 388A states the obvious—that a dormant or "micro" company which is exempt from the provisions of Part VII of the Act relating to audit of accounts is also exempt from the obligation to appoint auditors. The subsequent subsections deal with the less obvious question of precisely what occurs if the exemption ceases. In the normal situation, where accounts have to be laid,[64] the directors may appoint auditors at any time before the next general meeting at which accounts are to be laid and the auditors so appointed hold office until the conclusion of that meeting.[65] If, however, the company is a

---

[54] s.386(1).
[55] See below. Or unless a resolution has been passed under s.250 dispensing with audits as a "dormant company": see Chap. 19 at p. 533, above.
[56] s.386(2).
[57] s.386(3).
[58] s.386(4). If account were taken of it, the auditors would be paid more just because the company had elected to dispense with annual reappointment.
[59] s.387.
[60] s.388(1). In practice the directors will do so.
[61] s.388(2). If a firm has been appointed in accordance with the provisions of s.25 of the 1989 Act, the effect of its s.26 (see above, p. 539) will normally be to minimise the risk of there being a casual vacancy.
[62] *i.e.* 28 days' notice to the company of the intention to move it: s.379, on which see Chap. 21 at p. 575, below, and *cf.* Chap. 9 at p. 189.
[63] s.388(3) and (4).
[64] *i.e.* when s.385, above, applies.
[65] s.388A(2) and (3).

private company which has elected to dispense with laying,[66] the directors may appoint at any time before the expiration of the period provided by section 385A[67] and the auditors hold office until the end of that period.[68] If the directors fail to appoint, the company in general meeting may do so.[69]

RIGHTS OF AUDITORS

Section 237 in Part VII of the Act[70] having imposed statutory duties on the auditors in relation to the preparation of their reports, sections 389A and 390, as inserted in Chapter V of Part XI,[71] confer on them statutory rights which they need in order to perform these duties. Under section 389A they have a right of access at all times to the company's books, accounts and vouchers and are entitled to require from the company's officers such explanations as they think necessary for the performance of their duties as auditors[72] and an officer (but not any other person) commits an offence if he knowingly or recklessly makes to the auditors a statement which conveys or purports to convey any information or explanation which is misleading, false or deceptive in any material particular.[73] Similarly, a subsidiary undertaking incorporated in Great Britain and the auditors of that body are under a duty to give to the auditors of any parent company such information and explanations as they require for the purposes of their duties as auditors of that parent company.[74] Moreover, a parent company having a subsidiary undertaking not incorporated in Great Britain must, if required by its auditors to do so, take such steps as are reasonably open to it to obtain such information and explanations from the subsidiary.[75]

Under section 390, auditors are entitled to receive all notices and other communications relating to general meetings, to attend any general meeting and to be heard on any part of the business which concerns them as auditors.[76] In view of the fact that most private companies are likely to use written resolutions in accordance with section 381A rather than those passed at a meeting and that many of them

---

[66] *i.e.* when s.385A, above, applies.
[67] Or the beginning of the general meeting if one has been demanded; s.388A(2) and (4).
[68] Or the end of the meeting: s.388A(4).
[69] s.388A(5).
[70] See Chap. 19, p. 520, above.
[71] On a new consolidation an effort really ought to be made to bring the sections relating to duties and rights together in one Chapter of the Act.
[72] s.389A(1).
[73] s.389A(2).
[74] s.389A(3). The subsidiary, its officers in default and its auditors may commit an offence if they do not comply. If the offence is by an unincorporated body (*e.g.* an auditing partnership) s.734 applies (*i.e.* it is treated as if it was incorporated): s.389A(5).
[75] s.389A(4). The parent and its officers in default commit an offence if they fail to comply.
[76] s.390(1).

will elect to dispense with laying accounts before general meetings, this would be ineffective as a means of strengthening the role of the auditors as watchdogs of the members' interests unless the auditors could insist upon a meeting being held. Hence, in relation to laying accounts, section 253(2), as we have seen,[77] entitles an auditor to insist on a meeting being held. However, as far as written resolutions are concerned, the Act no longer gives the auditors the right to insist that a meeting be held on matters which concern them as auditors. The new section 381B[78] merely requires, on pain of criminal sanctions, that the auditors be notified of a proposed written resolution, but the validity of the resolution is not affected if notice is not given. Some of the risk associated with this change is removed by the prohibition on the use of the written resolution machinery for the removal of auditors,[79] though the prohibition does not extend to resolutions appointing other auditors at the expiry of the existing appointees' term of office. Here, the existing auditors have to make do with notice of what is proposed, but they may find it difficult to secure the circulation to the members of any statement they may wish to make under section 394[80] before the written resolution not reappointing them is adopted, especially as the members may now unanimously dispense with the 21 days' notice of written resolutions.[81]

As regards public companies, the value of the auditors' right to attend meetings is diminished by the fact that, as we shall see later,[82] the result of the meeting will, in practice, generally be determined by proxy votes lodged before the meeting is held. Hence the right is virtually worthless unless the auditors are able to get their views across to the members before proxies are lodged. This, as we shall see,[83] they may be able to do if they are prepared to resign or if it is proposed to remove them.

REMUNERATION OF AUDITORS

Section 390A provides that when auditors are appointed by a general meeting[84] (which, under sections 384–388[85] sooner or later they will generally have to be) their remuneration shall be fixed by the company in general meeting or in such manner as the general meeting shall

---

[77] Chap. 19 at p. 534, above.
[78] Inserted by the Deregulation (Resolutions of Private Companies) Order 1996 (S.I. 1996 No. 1471).
[79] Sched. 15A, para. 1(b).
[80] See below, p. 530.
[81] s.379A (2A).
[82] Chap. 21, below.
[83] Below, pp. 549–552.
[84] The effect of s.381A(4) is presumably that this includes a case when a private company has appointed by a written resolution under that section.
[85] Above pp. 544–546.

determine.[86] This, too, is intended to emphasise that the auditors are the members' watchdogs rather than the directors' lapdogs. But in practice it serves little purpose since the members normally adopt a resolution proposed by the directors to the effect that the remuneration shall be agreed by the directors. And when the auditors are appointed by the directors or the Secretary of State, the remuneration is to be fixed by them or him.[87] A more effective protection, perhaps, is that the amount of the remuneration, which includes expenses and benefits in kind (the monetary value of which has to be estimated) has to be shown in a note to the annual accounts,[88] thus enabling the members to criticise the directors if the amount seems to be out of line.[89]

The new section 390B recognises that very frequently the directors will arrange for the firm of auditors to undertake advisory or similar functions in addition to that of auditing, that for this they will be separately and additionally remunerated, and that section 390A does not require disclosure of the amount of that remuneration. Hence, section 390B empowers the Secretary of State to make regulations[90] requiring the disclosure of remuneration of auditors or their associates "in respect of services other than those of auditors in their capacity as such". Unfortunately this section does not tackle the root of the problem[91] which is that undertaking such services may be incompatible with their independence as auditors and that, even if it is not, it will increase the value to the firm of the auditorship and thus make the firm the more reluctant to do anything which will render it likely that the board of directors will seek to get rid of them as auditors. This problem is one that the supervisory bodies, and the Secretary of State, should tackle and it is to be hoped that they will. Unless it is tackled, the supervisory bodies will not have "adequate rules and practices" designed to ensure that persons are not appointed company auditors in circumstances in which they have any interest likely to conflict with the proper conduct of their audit—a condition for recognition as a supervisory body.[92]

---

[86] s.390A(1).

[87] s.390A(2).

[88] s.390A(3), (4) and (5).

[89] Generally, they criticise only if the amount seems abnormally high; they should perhaps be more alarmed if it is abnormally low.

[90] See the Regs. made by S.I. 1991 No. 2128 which, however, do not apply to small and medium-sized companies. See above, p. 526.

[91] An increasingly worrying problem as the major firms of accountants, themselves or through associated companies, offer a full range of financial and even some legal services to their corporate clients, the profits from which may be greater than that earned from audit work.

[92] 1989 Act, Sched. 11, para. 7(1). Another vexed question is in what circumstances the auditors, notwithstanding their duty of confidentiality, should immediately inform the regulatory authorities of misbehaviour that they have detected. If directors are party to a fraud, informing the board will merely alert the culprits. s.109 of the FSA and S.I. 1994 No. 526 require auditors to report to regulators under that Act matters relevant to the fitness of authorised persons or to the protection of investors by the regulator.

REMOVAL AND RESIGNATION OF AUDITORS

As in the case of directors,[93] "a company may be ordinary resolution at any time remove an auditor from office notwithstanding anything in any agreement between it and him".[94] But in relation to the removal of an auditor, special safeguards are needed not only to protect him, but to protect the company from being deprived of an auditor whose fault in the eyes of the directors may be that he has rightly not proved subservient to their wishes. Hence, not only has special notice[95] to be given to the company of a resolution to remove an auditor or not to reappoint him,[96] but notice of the proposed resolution has to be given to the auditor and to the person who is to be appointed in his place.[97] The auditor is entitled to make written representations which, if received in time, have to be sent to the members with the notice of the meeting,[98] and which, if not received in time, have to be read out at the meeting.[99] If the resolution is passed, he still retains his rights under section 390, above, in respect of the general meeting at which his term of office would otherwise have expired or at which it is proposed to fill the vacancy caused by his removal.[1] Nor does his removal deprive him of any right to compensation or damages to which he may be entitled under the contract between him and the company in respect of the termination of his appointment as auditor or any appointment terminating with that as auditor.[2]

In other words, a company cannot remove an auditor against his will without facing a serious risk of a row at the general meeting (and, in the case of a listed company, adverse press publicity) and, probably, payment of compensation.

It has been argued that this indefinite entrenchment of the existing auditors is not desirable, since it is liable to lead to an excessively cosy relationship between the company's management and the auditors, and that accordingly there should be a prescribed maximum period for which the same firm can hold office. But, so far, that argument has not prevailed.

However, no auditor will want to retain office if relations between

---

[93] s.303. See Chap. 9 at pp. 188–192, above.
[94] s.391(1). If such a resolution is passed, the company must within 14 days give notice of it to the Registrar: s.391(2).
[95] In accordance with s.379.
[96] s.391A(1).
[97] s.391A(2).
[98] The auditor should ensure that it is received in time since otherwise members may return proxy forms before they see his representations.
[99] s.391A(3) (4) and (5). But see subs.(6) regarding restraint by the court if the section is being abused "to secure needless publicity for defamatory matter". This is less likely than under the corresponding s.304(4) when a director is removed under s.303.
[1] s.391(4).
[2] s.391(3).

him and the management of the company have become seriously strained. It is therefore essential that he should not resign his office without ensuring that any matters which have caused him concern will not be brushed under the carpet. Hence section 392 provides that, although an auditor may resign by depositing a notice in writing to that effect at the company's registered office, the notice is not effective unless it is accompanied by the statement required by section 394.[3] The latter section provides that where an auditor ceases to hold office for any reason,[4] he shall deposit at the company's registered office a statement of any circumstances connected with his ceasing to hold office which he considers should be brought to the attention of members or creditors, or, if he considers that there are no such circumstances, a statement to that effect.[5] If the statement is of circumstances which the auditor considers should be brought to the attention of members or creditors, the company must, within 14 days of its deposit, either send copies of it to any person who, under section 238,[6] is entitled to be sent copies of the accounts,[7] or apply to the court[8] and notify the auditor that it has done so.[9] Unless the auditor receives such a notification within 21 days, he must, within a period of a further seven days, send a copy of the statement to the Registrar[10] thus making it available to creditors and the public generally. If the company applies to the court which is satisfied that the auditor is using the statement to secure needless publicity for defamatory matter, it must direct that the statement need not be sent out and may order the company's costs to be paid, in whole or in part, by the auditors.[11] The company must then send to members or debenture-holders a statement setting out the effect of the order.[12] If the court is not so satisfied, the company must within 14 days of the decision send copies of the auditor's statement to members, debenture-holders and any of the persons

[3] s.392(1). A copy of the notice must be sent to the Registrar within 14 days of its deposit: s.392(3). An effective notice ends the auditor's term of office on the date of its deposit or such later date as may be specified in it: s.392(2).
[4] Except, presumably, if he is an individual and he dies. It may have been thought that this can be ignored now that auditors are likely to be a firm which has two or more partners or is a body corporate. It is also unlikely that the circumstances of his death will be such as should be brought to the attention of members or creditors—unless, say, a fraudulent employee of the company whom he was about to expose had laced his mid-morning coffee with a lethal dose of poison.
[5] s.394(1). In cases of failure to seek reappointment the statement has to be deposited not less than 14 days before the time allowed for next appointing auditors and in other cases (except that of resignation) within 14 days after he ceases to hold office: s.394(2).
[6] See Chap. 19 at p. 520, above.
[7] This includes members and debenture-holders but not other creditors.
[8] s.394(3).
[9] s.394(4).
[10] s.394(5).
[11] s.394(6).
[12] *ibid.*

entitled to receive notice of general meetings,[13] and notify the auditor who must thereupon send the Registrar a copy of his statement.[14] Failure of the auditor or the company to comply is an offence.[15]

Furthermore, where an auditor's notice of resignation is accompanied by a statement of circumstances which he considers should be brought to the attention of members or creditors, he may under section 392A deposit with the notice a signed requisition calling upon the directors forthwith to convene an extraordinary general meeting for the purpose of receiving and considering such explanation of the circumstances of his resignation as he may wish to place before the meeting.[16] He may also require the company to place before that meeting (or one at which his term of office would have expired but for his resignation) his statement of the circumstances.[17] The directors must convene the meeting promptly, and, in the notice of it, state the fact that the statement has been made and send a copy of it to every member if it is received in time.[18] Hence, persuading auditors to retire or not to stand for reappointment cannot be effectively used as a means of muzzling the auditors.

Finally, section 393 empowers any member of a private company which has elected to dispense with the annual reappointments to deposit at the registered office of the company not more than one notice in each financial year proposing that the appointment of the auditors be brought to an end.[19] The directors must thereupon convene a meeting for a date not later than 28 days after the deposit of the notice to consider a resolution enabling the meeting to decide whether the auditors' appointment should be ended.[20] If the decision is that it should, the auditors are deemed not to be reappointed on the next occasion when otherwise they would be so deemed under section 386.[21] Indeed, if the member's notice was deposited within 14 days after the accounts and reports were sent to members under section 238, any deemed reappointment for the year following that to which those accounts related ceases to have effect.[22] This section prevails

---

[13] This would include the new auditor (if he had been appointed) and any continuing joint auditor.

[14] s.394(7).

[15] See s.394A for details.

[16] s.392A(1) and (2).

[17] s.392A(3).

[18] s.392A(4) and (5). If this statement was received too late for the company to comply, the auditor can require it to be read at the meeting and this is without prejudice to his right to be heard orally, in accordance with s.390, as if he was still the auditor: s.392A(6) and (8). There is the customary power of the court to ban defamatory matter: s.392(7).

[19] s.393(1).

[20] s.393(2). If the directors fail to do so, the member may, as under s.253 (Chap. 19 at p. 534), himself convene the meeting and recover from the company his reasonable expenses: s.393(4) (5) and (6).

[21] s.393(3).

[22] *ibid.*

notwithstanding any agreement to the contrary between the company
and its auditors and, as under section 386(4),[23] no compensation or
damages are payable to the auditors by reason of the appointment
being terminated under it.[24]

AUDITORS' NEGLIGENCE

Having reviewed, in this and the previous Chapter, the statutory provisions relating to company accounts and their audit, something needs
to be said about the auditors' potential civil liability if they are negligent in the performance of their duties. Although it is the directors
who are responsible for the published accounts, the auditors are more
likely to be worth powder-and-shot[25] if they can be shown to have
been negligent in certifying the accuracy of those accounts. Moreover,
in contrast with directors, they are required to display the care and
skill of professionals.

Hence at any one time in recent years, actions against auditors
attempting to recover billions of pounds or dollars have been proceeding not only in England but in countries from Hong Kong in the East
to the Pacific Coast of North America in the West. The reported
decisions in common law jurisdictions were reviewed by the House
of Lords in *Caparo Industries plc v. Dickman*[26] and, as a result of its
unanimous decision, the ambit of the duty of care owed by auditors
has been somewhat clarified so far as English law is concerned—and
in a way which will give greater comfort to auditors[27] than to investors.

The House of Lords' examination of the statutory framework for
company accounts and audits led them to the following conclusions.
The statutory provisions establish a relationship between those
responsible for the accounts (the directors) or for the report (the
auditors) and some other class or classes of persons and this relationship imposes a duty of care owed to those persons. Among these "persons" is the company itself, to which, apart altogether from the statutory provisions, the directors are in a fiduciary relationship and the
auditors in a contractual relationship by virtue of their employment by
the company as its auditors.

However, the statutory provisions do not establish such a relationship with everybody who has a right to be furnished with copies of

---

[23] See p. 545, above.

[24] s.393(7).

[25] Especially because they will be covered by professional indemnity insurance though it is
becoming more difficult and expensive to obtain full cover.

[26] [1990] 2 A.C. 605, H.L. The preliminary issue on which *Caparo* reached the H.L. was
whether, on the facts pleaded, a claim against the auditors could succeed. Two directors were
also being sued for alleged fraud.

[27] Less so, perhaps, to the big international firms which also operate in countries that take a
wider view of the scope of the duty of care (*e.g.* N. Zealand and some states of the USA).

the accounts or report or, *a fortiori*, with everybody who has a right to inspect, or obtain, copies of them. If a relationship other than with the company[28] is to be established under the statutory provisions, it can be only with members (and perhaps debenture-holders) and, even in their case, the scope of the resulting duty of care extends only to the protection of what, for the moment, may be described as those persons' corporate powers to safeguard their interests in the company. That does not include their powers to buy further shares in the company even if it is a perusal of the annual accounts and reports that led them to do so.[29]

In so far as a duty of care is owed to members as a result of the statutory provisions it is owed to them collectively, not individually, and in practice will normally be enforced by an action by the company which, if successful, will restore it, and hence its members collectively, to the position that they would have been in had the breach of duty not occurred.

To establish a duty of care to members which is greater in scope than this, or to establish any duty of care to other persons there must be an additional "special" relationship with the person who suffered loss as a result of relying on the accounts or report. To succeed in establishing that, the plaintiff (who in this case will be the person or class of persons who have so relied—and not the company itself) must show that the defendant knew that the accounts and report:

"would be communicated to the plaintiff either as an individual or as a member of an identifiable class, specifically in connection with a particular transaction or transactions of a particular kind (*e.g.* in a prospectus inviting investment[30]) and that the plaintiff would be very likely to rely on it for the purpose of deciding whether or not to enter upon that transaction or upon a transaction of that kind".[31]

---

[28] Even *vis-à-vis* the company, the issue of a "special relationship" may arise if the auditors are not its auditors but those of another company in the group. But the duty should be easily established where the auditor's report was made for the purpose of producing group accounts: *Barings plc v. Coopers & Lybrand, The Times*, December 6, 1996, C.A., but *cf. BCCI (Overseas) Ltd v. Price Waterhouse, ibid.*, February 10, 1997.

[29] This was the specific point that had to be determined in *Caparo*. The C.A. had held unanimously that auditors owed no duty of care to members of the public who, in reliance on the accounts and reports, bought shares (in the absence of a special relationship—see below) but, by a majority, that they did owe such a duty to existing shareholders who, in such reliance, bought more shares. The H.L. held unanimously that, in the absence of a "special relationship", a duty of care did not extend to either.

[30] As pointed out in Chap. 16, above at pp. 429–430 the statute law on prospectus liability has gone beyond the common law which will normally be irrelevant. But it remains highly relevant where the statute does not apply. See *Al-Nakib Investments Ltd v. Longcroft* [1990] 1 W.L.R. 1390. and the comment thereon at pp. 438–439, above.

[31] *Per* Lord Bridge at 621E–F. This was clearly the unanimous view, adopting the dissenting judgment of Denning L.J. in *Candler v. Crane Christmas & Co.* [1951] 2 K.B. 164, C.A. (which already had been adopted unanimously by the H.L. in *Hedley Byrne & Co. v. Heller* [1964] A.C. 465) and affirming the decision of Millett J. in *Al Saudi Banque v. Clark Pixley* [1990] Ch. 313, but rejecting the wider views expressed in *JEB Fasteners Ltd v. Marks Bloom & Co.* [1981] 3 All E.R. 289 and in *Twomax Ltd v. Dickson, McFarlane & Robinson,*

Caparo thus represented a firm rejection by the House of Lords of the proposition that negligent auditors were liable to those who it was reasonable to foresee would rely on the audited accounts and who suffered loss as a result of such reliance.[32] Instead, the House confined the common law duty of care within the statutory framework set by the Companies Act for company accounts and their audit, which by itself is a policy which has much to commend it.[33] What was surprising to a company lawyer about *Caparo* was the narrow view taken by the court of the purposes Parliament had in mind when steadily expanding over the century the disclosure provisions of the Act and especially when requiring ever greater levels of public disclosure of financial reports rather than just their circulation to members and other current investors in the company.

No doubt, a full explanation of the decision would require it to be set in an analysis of broader trends in the law of tort concerning compensation for negligently caused economic loss.[34] What follows is simply some comments upon the criteria for the establishment of a "special relationship" which will, exceptionally, take the case outside the narrowly conceived statutory boundaries of the purposes of the audit and give rise to a duty of care towards those who have suffered loss as investors in the company, whether as shareholders or creditors. Not surprisingly, the litigation subsequent to *Caparo* has been concerned with defining the limits of this proposition, with establishing, as it were, what, in addition to simply conducting a negligent audit, a defendant has to know or to do if his or her firm is to be civilly liable to investors who have suffered loss as a result of reliance on the misleading accounts. In the words of Lord Bridge in *Caparo*[35] the "salient feature" of the cases where such liability should be imposed was that

"the defendant giving the advice or information was fully aware of the nature of the transaction which the plaintiff had in contemplation, knew that the advice or information would be communicated to him directly or indirectly and knew that it was very likely that

---

1982 S.C. 113, and by the majority of the N.Z.C.A. in *Scott Group Ltd v. McFarlane* [1978] N.Z.L.R. 553. *cf. Smith v. Eric S. Bush* [1990] 1 A.C. 831, H.L. where, applying a similar test of proximity and foresight, it was held that a surveyor employed by a building society or local authority owed a duty of care to the purchaser/mortgagor of a house as well as to the mortgagee for whom the survey was undertaken.

[32] Contrast the decision of the New Zealand Court of Appeal in *Scott Group Ltd v. McFarlane* [1978] NZLR 553.

[33] For a similar refusal to use the common law to supplement the statutory framework but within an analysis of the statutory purposes which seems more faithful to the legislative intent (in this case the New Zealand Securities Act 1978) see *Deloitte Haskins & Sells v. National Mutual Life Nominees* [1993] A.C. 774, P.C.

[34] See, for example, Stapleton, "Duty of Care and Economic Loss: A Wider Agenda" (1991) 107 L.Q.R. 249.

[35] At 620–621.

the plaintiff would rely on that advice or information in deciding whether or not to engage in the transaction in contemplation''.

Somewhat as in *Caparo* itself, subsequent courts have often had to commit themselves to a view of the ''purpose'' of a document in which the auditors knew their statement about the accounts would be included. The courts have held that the purpose of a prospectus issued in connection with a rights issue is to induce subscriptions of shares but not purchases of shares in the market.[36] This limited view of the purpose of a prospectus has been criticised above,[37] though it has to be said that it has the support of high, if old, authority.[38] On the other hand, in *Morgan Crucible Co. plc v. Hill Samuel Bank*[39] the Court of Appeal thought it arguable that the purpose of defence documents issued in connection with a takeover bid, which contained references to the earlier audited accounts, was not simply to encourage the shareholders of the target to resist the bid but might also include that of persuading the bidder to increase its bid. Although this would be a matter for evidence at the trial, at least the Court of Appeal was prepared to contemplate that the regulatory scheme established in the City Code on Takeovers and Mergers could embrace this wider purpose. It was accepted, however, that the mere publication of the audited accounts in the normal way before the bidder emerged could not found a claim. The distinction between this case and *Caparo* thus seems to be that

''mere foreseeability that a potential bidder may rely on the audited accounts does not impose on the auditor a duty of care to the bidder, but if the auditor is expressly made aware that a particular identified bidder will rely on the audited accounts or other statements approved by the auditor, and intends that the bidder should so rely, the auditor will be under a duty of care to the bidder for the breach of which he may be liable.''[40]

Following this line of reasoning, the Court of Appeal in a later case[41]

---

[36] *Al-Nakib Investments (Jersey) Ltd v. Longcroft* [1990] 1 W.L.R. 1390, not in fact a case involving the auditors of the company but rather its directors, but the principles seem equally applicable.

[37] Above, pp. 438–439.

[38] In the shape of *Peek v. Gurney* (1873) L.R. 6 H.L. 377.

[39] [1991] Ch. 295, C.A., noted by Percival (1991) 54 M.L.R. 739. See below, p. 799. Would this reasoning be applicable not only to the bidder but also a potential ''white knight''? Note that in any event the Court seemed to regard the directors' and auditors' duty to the shareholders of the target company as unproblematic, since the defence document was clearly intended to influence their investment decisions.

[40] *Galoo Ltd v. Bright Grahame Murray* [1994] 1 W.L.R. 1360 at 1382, C.A. See also *Anthony v. Wright* [1995] 1 BCLC 236.

[41] See previous note. If the claim were made out at the trial, the measure of the plaintiffs' loss would be presumably the difference between the amount paid for the shares and their value at the time of acquisition, but no more, the auditors thus not being liable for any fall in the value of the shares subsequent to the purchase, even if it could be shown that, had the accounts been accurate, the plaintiffs would not have bought the shares at all: *South Australia Asset Management Corporation v. York Montague Ltd* [1996] 3 W.L.R. 87, H.L.

also refused to strike out a claim by a successful bidder against the auditors of the target company when the bidder's agreement with the target's shareholders expressly envisaged, as was allegedly known to and intended by the auditors, that the price to be paid to the shareholders for a 51 per cent holding in the company would be calculated on the basis of the audited accounts which the target was in the process of producing. On the other hand, a claim for compensation in relation to the later purchase of, in effect, the balance of the shares was struck out because it was not pleaded that the auditors knew that the bidder would rely on the accounts for this purpose or that the auditors intended it to do so.

The post-*Caparo* cases thus suggest that auditors are by no means completely in the clear in terms of their civil liability to investors in and lenders to the company, but that what needs to be established as a basis for such liability is the auditors' knowledge and acceptance of the purpose for which the plaintiff is to rely on the company's accounts. This approach gives bidders and lenders,[42] who might otherwise be unable to establish the beginnings of a claim, an incentive to bring themselves into a closer relationship with the auditors and, in particular, to ask them to repeat their support for the company's accounts in the specific context of the share purchase or loan which is in contemplation. Although a somewhat feeble attempt to deploy this strategy was held to be unsuccessful in *James McNaughton Paper Group v. Hicks Anderson & Co.*,[43] it was found to be effective in *ADT Ltd v. BDO Binder Hamlyn*[44] and liability was put on the basis of an assumption of responsibility on the part of the auditors towards the prospective bidder. This decision led to the largest ever damages award by a British court against auditors, the sum being over £100 million when costs were included.

Many of the post-*Caparo* decisions arose out of applications to strike out plaintiffs' claims. Consequently, they proceeded on the assumption that the allegations made in the pleadings were true and the question for the court was whether, on that basis, they disclosed a cause of action in law. The cases, therefore, did not approach the issues which arise once a duty of care has been found, such as the appropriate standard of care to be required of auditors, whether the accounts were in fact relied upon by the plaintiff[45] and whether the

---

[42] For examples of lenders whose claims have foundered in the light of the Caparo principle see *Al Saudi Banque v. Clark Pixley* [1990] 1 Ch.313 and *Berg Sons & Co. Ltd v. Mervyn Hampton Adams* [1993] BCLC 1045.

[43] [1991] 2 Q.B. 113, C.A.

[44] [1996] BCC 808. An appeal was subsequently compromised for a payment of £53m—within the firm's insurance cover: *The Financial Times*, February 22, 1997, p. 4. See also *Peach Publishing Ltd v. Slater & Co.* [1996] BCLC 751.

[45] See the analysis of the company's claim in *Berg Sons & Co. Ltd v. Mervyn Hampton Adams*, cited in n. 42.

auditors' negligence caused loss to the plaintiff and, if so, to what extent that loss should be recompensed.

As far as the standard of care is concerned, it is clear in law, though often not accepted in the commercial world, that the auditor is not a guarantor of the accuracy of the directors' accounts. Indeed, in an old case the auditor was given a broad discretion to rely on information provided by management, so long as no suspicious circumstances arose which should put the auditor on inquiry.[46] However, the force of this proposition depends in considerable part on how willing the courts are to find that no circumstances had arisen which were suspicious, and there is some evidence that modern courts take a more demanding line than their predecessors.[47] Moreover, some dicta suggest that, even in the absence of suspicious circumstances, modern auditing standards might require auditors to do more of their own motion. As Lord Denning once put it, the auditor, in order to perform his task properly, "must come to it with an inquiring mind—not suspicious of dishonesty, I agree—but suspecting that someone may have made a mistake somewhere and that a check must be made to ensure that there has been none".[48] Given the extensive development by the Accounting Standards Board[49] in recent years of Statements of Standard Accounting Practice and Financial Reporting Standards and by the Auditing Practices Board of Auditing Standards, it would be surprising if the courts were not guided to a very large degree by those standards in determining the standard of care at common law for auditors.[50] Thus, there is available to auditors much greater certainty about what the duty of care requires of them than is the case for some professionals.

Finally, a comment on the questions of causation and measure of damages.[50a] These questions did not arise directly in *Caparo* and little was said about them in the speeches. But they raise intractable problems in the present context. The fact that the published accounts do not show a true and fair view, despite the auditors' report, does not cause either the company or the shareholders collectively any immediate pecuniary loss. All it does is to deprive them of knowledge which might have afforded them an opportunity to take remedial action to

---

[46] *Re Kingston Cotton Mill (No. 2)* [1896] 2 Ch. 279, C.A., where the auditors relied on certificates as to levels of stock which were provided by the managing director which for years had grossly overstated the true position.

[47] See *Re Thomas Gerrard & Son Ltd* [1967] 2 All E.R. 525, where the discovery of altered invoices, it was held, should have caused the auditors to carry out their own check on the stock.

[48] *Formento (Sterling Area) Ltd v. Selsdon Fountain Pen Co. Ltd* [1958] 1 W.L.R. 45, H.L. and see also the remarks of Pennycuick J. in *Re Thomas Gerrard* (cited in previous note).

[49] See above, p. 528.

[50] As Woolf J. was in *Lloyd Cheyham & Co. Ltd v. Littlejohn & Co.* [1987] BCLC 303.

[50a] In addition to the problems discussed in the text see on the causation and measurement problems which arise on a negligently advised share-exchange acquisition: F. Oditah (1996) 112 L.Q.R. 424.

recover losses already incurred by the company, and, more importantly in practice, to prevent a continuance of mismanagement or fraud. The pecuniary value to be placed on that lost opportunity depends upon the degree of likelihood that action would have been taken and that it would have led to recovery of damages or cessation of the malpractice. Often that likelihood will be minimal, especially when those at fault included the directors. Then, it would seem, to establish any loss the plaintiff would have to show on the balance of probabilities that, had, say, the auditors' report been properly qualified, action would have been taken which would have led to the removal of the directors. And to recover any substantial damages, the plaintif would further have to establish a probability that the ill-consequences of the former directors' negligent or fraudulent reign would have been effectively remedied. The difficulties of establishing all this are obvious.

The difficulties may be less when individuals in a special relationship have rights of action. But they may arise there too. Thus in *JEB Fasteners Ltd v. Marks Bloom & Co.*,[51] Woolf J. held that, although all the conditions necessary for success other than causation had been established, the plaintiff failed on that since he would have entered into the transaction (a takeover) even if the accounts on which he had relied had presented a wholly true and fair view of the company's financial position, his main object having been to secure the managerial skills of two executive directors.[52] And in *Caparo*, Lord Bridge suggested that if a shareholder in a listed company suffered a loss as a result of selling his shares at an undervalue attributable to an undervalue of the company's assets in the audited accounts, the loss would be caused not by reliance on the auditors' report but by the "depreciatory effect of the report on the market value of the shares before ever the decision of the shareholder to sell was taken."[53] Similarly, but with greater plausibility, the Court of Appeal held in *Galoo Ltd v. Bright Grahame Murray*[54] that no loss was caused to the company itself, whether in contract or in tort, when it continued to trade on the basis of negligently optimistic audit reports rather than going into receivership, because the continued trading provided the opportunity for the incurring of the additional losses, but did not "cause" them as a matter of legal causation.

Despite, and indeed in part because of, the case-law developments

---

[51] [1981] 3 All E.R. 289; *affd.* on other grounds [1983] 1 All E.R. 583, C.A.

[52] Who, in fact, resigned!

[53] [1990] 2 A.C. at 627A. The result seems to be that (a) if the shareholder is able to have his "sell" order executed before the market has reacted to the accounts, he will have suffered no loss by relying on the account, while (b) if it is not executed until after the market has reacted, that reaction has broken the chain of causation between his reliance and his loss. This amounts to saying that reliance on the accounts by one type of recipient of them (the market-makers) destroys the causal connection between reliance and loss in relation to others (the members). Can that really be right?

[54] See n. 40, above.

noted above, the law relating to the liability of auditors is likely to continue to evolve. In the late 1980s, when concerns about the potential liability of auditors and the cost and availability to them of professional indemnity insurance were at their height, the Government appointed a study team which made various suggestions for reform.[55] Although some of the concerns about liability to shareholders and third parties have been dealt with in the *Caparo* decision, the above cases show that there is still the temptation and the possibility for plaintiffs, especially successful but then disappointed takeover bidders, to seek damages against the auditors on the basis that the acquired company turned out to be less valuable than the accounts had suggested. The potential exposure of the accounting firm in such cases is then many times greater than the audit fee and there is, moreover, a considerable incentive for plaintiffs to concentrate their fire on the insured accountants rather than the usually uninsured previous directors of the company who may not be worth powder-and-shot but who may have been responsible for the negligence or even fraud which the auditors failed to uncover.

Some of the suggestions put forward in the Likierman report have been implemented by the legislature or the courts, though not the most radical ones. Section 310 was amended by the Companies Act 1989 so as expressly to permit the purchase by companies of indemnity insurance for their directors and officers (and, indeed, auditors).[56] The theory here was that the availability of other insured defendants would take some of the burden off the shoulders of the auditors, though the change would seem to do nothing to reduce the likelihood of litigation (perhaps the opposite) and would not reduce the overall level of risk which the insurance market had to absorb. Moreover, the British law still stops short of following the New Zealand example of making directors' and officers' insurance compulsory,[57] so that the availability of alternative or additional insured defendants will be a function of the willingness of companies to buy such insurance for their directors.

A further proposed reform of section 310, permitting auditors to contract to limit or even exclude their liability to the company, has not been implemented, though, as we have seen, the company can now purchase insurance to indemnify the auditor in respect of his liability to the company.[58] Since section 310 was introduced in order to combat abuses arising out of such exclusions when corporate practice in this

---

[55] DTI, *Professional Liability: Report of the Study Teams*, 1989 (the Likierman Report). This dealt with the liability of surveyors and professionals engaged in the construction industry as well as with auditors.

[56] s.310 is discussed more fully below at pp. 623–626. The section, even as amended, does not permit indemnification in cases of fraud, of course, nor would such insurance be available.

[57] Companies Act 1955 (NZ), s.204, which also permits the company to contract to exclude the liability of directors and officers.

[58] This reform would might also require reform or, at least, elaboration of the "reasonableness" test of the Unfair Contract Terms Act 1977 in such cases.

area was unregulated, it is clear that any amendment to section 310 would have to be accompanied by safeguards for the shareholders. Moreover, such clauses would not do much to protect auditors against third-party claims arising in the bid situations discussed above and in analogous situations.

Perhaps the most radical of the Likierman ideas was the reform in general of the law relating to joint and several liability. This issue was referred to the Law Commission which in a consultative document came out against the substitution of proportionate liability for joint and several liability.[59] Although it is undoubtedly true that auditors have a deep-seated emotional objection to joint and several liability on the grounds that they are often, in practice, made liable for the whole of the plaintiff's loss, even though they were only partly to blame for it, the Commission did not think it justifiable to shift the risk of the co-tortfeasors' insolvency onto the plaintiff, either in general or where, as in the case of auditors, the auditor's liability often stems from the failure to detect the torts of the other joint tortfeasors, usually the directors.[60] For somewhat similar reasons, the Law Commission was not in favour of a statutory cap on the liability of auditors which, unlike a contractual limit negotiated under a reformed section 310, would apply to all plaintiffs and not just the company.[61]

In relation to auditing firms, however, the issue of joint and several liability arises in another context, that is, not only among those who

---

[59] DIT, *Feasibility Investigation of Joint and Several Liability by the Common Law Team of the Law Commission*, 1996. The proposal was considered only in the area of non-personal injury. Joint and several liability means that all the defendants are individually liable for the whole of the plaintiff's loss and the principle is applied in English law even to tortfeasors who have acted independently, provided they have caused the same indivisible damage to the same plaintiff. Proportionate liability would mean that independent tortfeasors would be liable only for their share of the plaintiff's loss, as is already the case in English law where tortfeasors acting independently cause *different* damage to the plaintiff. A tortfeasor who is made liable for the whole of the plaintiff's loss as a result of being jointly and severally liable can recover contributions from the other tortfeasors, if they have the resources: Civil Liability (Contribution) Act 1978.

[60] *ibid.*, Chap. 3 and pp. 30–33 but *cf.* Stapleton, "Duty of Care: Peripheral Parties and Alternative Opportunities for Deterrence" (1995) 111 L.Q.R. 301, 310–314. A minor clarification which the courts have effected is that the Law Reform (Contributory Negligence) Act 1945 applies where the defendant is in breach of a contractual duty of care, so that it does not matter in such cases whether the client company sues the auditor in tort or in contract. In either case, if the company through its directors has been negligent, its recovery will be reduced proportionately. See *Forsikringsaktieselskapet Vesta v. Butcher* [1989] A.C. 852. However, for a strong argument that, following *Caparo*, the auditors' duties are owed to the shareholders and they ought not to be able to reduce the company's recovery on behalf of the shareholders by praying in aid the negligence of the directors, see Stapledon, "The AWA case and the availability to auditors of the 'defence' of contributory negligence" (1995) 13 C. & S.L.J. 513.

[61] Feasibility Investigation (n. 59, above), pp. 46–49: "We can find no principled arguments for a capping scheme—it simply benefits defendants at the expense of plaintiffs." Nor had the Likierman report been in favour of this solution: *op. cit.*, p. 40 though such a scheme, based on a multiple of the fee charged, has been introduced in New South Wales: New South Wales Professional Standards Act 1994.

have caused the plaintiffs' loss but also among the partners of the firm of which the negligent audit partner is a member. The principle that all partners are jointly and severally liable to outsiders for the civil wrongs of any other partner committed in the ordinary course of business is a basic principle of English partnership law. The 1989 Act altered the law by permitting auditors to be incorporated bodies.[62] Although incorporation would preserve the individual wealth of the non-negligent partners, it would not prevent a large claim from having a catastrophic effect on the accountancy business itself. In any event, incorporation proved unattractive, apparently for tax reasons, though the large accountancy firms have show interest in a form of limited partnership which, unlike the current British Limited Partnership Act 1907, does not restrict the active participation in the firm of those partners whose liability is limited.[63]

CONCLUSION

The final part of this Chapter can be summed up in one sentence: Anyone involved, either as plaintiff or defendant, in a suit based upon alleged negligence in the preparation or auditing of the annual accounts has stepped into a minefield which, despite *Caparo*, has still not been comprehensively mapped.

However, the earlier part of the Chapter has shown that the status of company auditors has, in the course of this century, been transformed from that of somewhat toothless strays given temporary houseroom once a year, to that of trained rottweilers, entitled to sniff around at any time and, if need be, to bite the hands that feed them. As a result, the quality of most company audits has improved, even if the likelihood of recovery, in cases where audits are defective, has not.

---

[62] s.53(1): "'firm' means a body corporate or a partnership".
[63] "A limited partner shall not take part in the management of the partnership business and shall not have power to bind the firm": s.6(1). Moreover, the partnership may not consist entirely of limited partners: s.4(2). See above, pp. 82 and 97. However, in the face of a modern limited partnership law being introduced in Jersey and the threat of the big accounting firms moving off-shore, the DTI launched similar proposals for professional partnerships: DTI, *Limited Liability Partnership*, February 1997.

CHAPTER 21

GENERAL MEETINGS

INTRODUCTION

"The formal relationship between the shareholders and the board of directors is that the shareholders elect the directors, the directors report on their stewardship to the shareholders and the shareholders appoint the auditors to provide the external check on the directors' financial statements. Thus the shareholders as owners of the company elect the directors to run the business on their behalf and hold them accountable for its progress" (Report of the Committee on the Financial Aspects of Corporate Governance, 1992, para. 6.1).

IN this way the Cadbury Committee Report began its analysis of the accountability of boards to shareholders. It is an analysis in which the role of the general meeting of the shareholders might be expected to figure largely. Indeed, the Committee recommended that "both shareholders and boards of directors should consider how the effectiveness of general meetings could be increased and as a result the accountability of boards to all their shareholders strengthened" (para. 6.8). There are, however, two main reasons which might be put forward for thinking that the Committee's description of the current relationship between directors and shareholders and (implicitly) of the role played by the general meeting in this relationship is somewhat idealised, as perhaps the Committee's recommendations for the strengthening of the effectiveness of general meetings recognise. We shall look briefly at these two reasons in turn.

(a) *Regulation by the articles*

First, although the picture painted by the Committee may represent reality in some companies, it is by no means a requirement of company law that this be the case. The shareholders in public companies may indeed elect the directors, but the Companies Act does not require directors to be appointed in this way. In fact, the Act says nothing about how directors are to be selected. Article 73 of the current version of Table A, which is in any event only a model and may be excluded in any particular case, envisages the periodic retirement and re-election of members of the board, by requiring at every general meeting after the first that "one-third of the directors who are subject to retirement by rotation . . . shall retire from office". This makes it clear that there may be directors, and no limit is placed on their number, who are not subject to retirement by rotation and to whom the requirement of periodic re-election does not apply. There are in fact good commercial reasons for not requiring all directors to be elected by the shareholders or to be subject to periodic re-election by them. For example, a major lender to the company may insist on board representation as a method of protecting its investment.[1] However, this should not disguise the fact that the way in which this need is currently accommodated in company law is by giving companies a very broad discretion to avoid shareholder election of directors.

More generally, despite the growing number of transactions for which shareholder consent is required by either the Companies Act or the Listing Rules of the Stock Exchange,[2] which consent can often conveniently be obtained at the annual general meeting, the Act still does not state what business is required to be transacted at the annual general meetings (AGMs) of the company, though it does require such a meeting to be held. Even such central matters as the directors' report, the annual accounts and the auditors' report thereon do not have to be considered by the AGM but this is perhaps a quibble since they do have to be put before the company, normally, on an annual basis.

More to the point is that section 241 requires only that these documents be laid before the company on an annual basis and not, as many shareholders undoubtedly think and as the articles or practice of many companies require, that the shareholders be asked to resolve whether they approve of the accounts or not. Again, the general opportunity for shareholders to ask questions about all aspects of the company's business, which many companies allow under the agenda item adopting the report and accounts, is one which is there because companies choose to make it available and not because the Companies Act requires it. In practice, annual general meetings of the company will consider resolutions to declare dividends, to approve the accounts and the directors' and auditors' reports, make appointments to the board in the place of those retiring, and appoint and fix the remuneration of the auditors.

Nor should it be supposed that all shareholders, not even all ordinary shareholders, necessarily have the right to attend and vote at general meetings of the company or, even if they do, that they have voting rights as extensive as those attached to other shares which apparently carry the same level of risk. As we have seen, the rights to be attached to classes of shares, including the right to attend general meetings and the number of votes to be attached to the shares, are matters for the company to determine in its articles of association or in the terms of issue of the shares. The exclusion of preference shareholders from voting rights, except in limited circumstances, is common and the issuance of non-voting equity shares is not unknown, though it is fiercely opposed by institutional shareholders.[3] Thus, "shareholder

---

[1] On the position of such "nominee" directors, see below, p. 609.
[2] Especially in the case of major or "related-party" transactions. See pp. 635–640, below.
[3] See pp. 314–315, above.

democracy'', which is in any event a democracy of shares rather than of shareholders, is, or may be, an imperfect one. Company law does not require equal voting rights for shares carrying the same risk nor equivalent rights for shares of different classes of risk. All that, once again, is a matter for the company to determine.[4]

In short, the effectiveness of the general meeting is to a large degree in the hands of the company itself, and, indeed, in the hands of the management of the company, in the sense that central elements of what the meeting does and how it does them are controlled by the articles of association of the company in question. Although the amendment of those articles is itself a matter for the shareholders in general meeting, the influence of the management of the company in promoting proposals for change should not be underestimated. This situation gives rise to two questions of general principle. First, should the legislature continue to leave so much of the task of regulating meetings in the hands of the companies themselves or should it lay down a stronger framework of statutory rules, which would be either mandatory or alterable only to a limited degree? Secondly, how should companies themselves exercise the powers which the legislature has left with them?

As far as the first question is concerned, there has been a slight tendency since the Report of the Cohen Committee in 1945 for the legislature to reduce the discretion of companies themselves, especially, as we shall see,[5] in relation to shareholders' rights to propose resolutions for consideration at general meetings or to vote by proxy. Nevertheless, a very wide power to regulate the business and conduct of meetings remains with companies themselves. As to the second question, the thrust of the Cadbury Report would seem to be that companies should use the powers at their disposal to strengthen the role of the shareholders. Certainly, very few companies confine the rights of the shareholders assembled in general meeting as tightly as the Act would apparently permit them to do. Nevertheless, in recent years the realisation by single-issue protest groups of the publicity value to be obtained from vigorous use of shareholder rights at general meetings, not stopping short in a minority of cases of disruption of those meetings, has caused some companies which have been the target of such activities to propose the restriction of the rights that shareholders have traditionally enjoyed under the articles of associ-

---

[4] In *Re Savoy Hotel Ltd* [1981] Ch. 351 the company had created A and B shares, ranking *pari passu* except in relation to voting rights, with the effect that the holders of the B shares, who owned 2.3 per cent of the equity, could exercise 48.55 per cent of the votes. The additional voting rights may be confined to certain types of resolution, for example, the "golden share" held by the Government after some recent privatisations may operate so as to allow the Government to out-vote *all* other shareholders on certain specified resolutions: see Graham (1988) 9 Co. Law. 24.

[5] Below, pp. 575–581, below.

ation. Proposals have ranged from restricting attendance rights to shareholders who have held the shares for at least 12 months or who hold shares with a certain minimum value to ending voting on a show of hands at company meetings, so that all votes would be cast in advance of the meeting itself, or not putting forward a resolution to approve the company's accounts.

These developments have called into question the legitimacy of the traditional policy of leaving so much of the regulation relating to meetings to the company itself. It is sometimes difficult to determine whether the managements of companies making proposals to restrict shareholder participation at general meetings are more concerned to protect themselves from legitimate adverse criticism (for example, about the levels of executive remuneration) than to ensure the orderly conduct of business. For this reason, some companies would prefer any change in the status quo to be achieved by legislation rather than by amendments to the articles, even though the latter method would be legally effective, because such change would have greater legitimacy if embodied in legislation.

(b) *The willingness of shareholders to participate*

Ever since Berle and Means wrote their classic study of patterns of share ownership in large American corporations in the 1930s,[6] it has been common to think that shareholders are not in general interested in using the rights which the law or the company's articles confer upon them to hold the management of their company to account. The authors' thesis was that in large companies shareholdings had become so widely dispersed that it was not worth the while of most shareholders to devote time, effort and resources to seeking to change the policies of the managements which they thought were ineffective. The return on their relatively small investment, which success might bring, would be outweighed by the certain costs of seeking to achieve such change in a large company where co-ordination of shareholder action would be intensely difficult. Since large companies were likely to be listed on a stock exchange, the alternative and cheaper responses of accepting a takeover offer or simply selling in the market the shares in the company with whose management one had become disenchanted were likely to prove more attractive. Shareholders in large companies were thus "rationally apathetic" towards their general meeting rights.

Whether this was ever an entirely correct picture is controversial, but in any event it has been altered by the concentration over recent decades of shares in public companies in the hands of institutional

---

[6] A.A. Berle and G.C. Means, *The Modern Coporation and Private Property* (revised ed., New York, 1968).

investors, especially pension funds and insurance companies.[7] Institutional shareholders now hold about 60 per cent of the equity shares of companies listed on the London Stock Exchange, and this implies a considerable re-concentration of shareholdings. Although it is unusual for an institution to hold more than 5 per cent of the equities of the largest quoted companies, nevertheless the situation is one in which a small group of institutional shareholders can often bring decisive influence to bear on the management of ailing companies. Of course, they may not always wish to do so. Even institutional shareholders will not exercise their general meeting rights simply for the sake of it. If a takeover offer provides a cheaper remedy for the problem, they may be inclined to accept that, rather than take on the incumbent management of the under-performing company themselves. Nevertheless, "shareholder activism" on the part of the institutions is now a bigger part of the corporate scene than it was, say, 20 years ago, and it is an activity which is crucially underpinned by the rights of shareholders at general meetings. Although most intervention by institutional shareholders takes place in private and will move into the public arena of the general meeting only if private pressure is unsuccessful, the pressure which the institutions can bring to bear privately depends in large part upon the prospect of their being able to get their way in the public meeting if the private pressures are unsuccessful. No doubt, the crucial factors, if it comes to a public fight between the incumbent management and the institutional shareholders, are the ability of an ordinary majority of the shareholders at any time to remove the directors under the provisions of section 303,[8] coupled with the institutions' long-held opposition to non-voting equity shares. Nevertheless, the detailed legal rules governing the holding and conduct of meetings of shareholders can also be significant if it comes to a public fight. When all is going well, the institutional shareholders tend not to attend and to leave the AGM to the pressure groups and querulous individual shareholders, so that many managing directors regard the AGM "as presently constituted as an expensive waste of time and money".[9] But that is to underestimate its value, at least in the background, when things are not going well.

It should be made clear that all that has been said above assumes a separation between ownership and control, *i.e.* that, as is typical in a big company, the shareholders are a large group of people who have

---

[7] See P.L. Davies, "Institutional Investors in the United Kingdom" in T. Baums *et al* (eds.), *Institutional Investors and Corporate Governance* (1994); E. Boros, *Minority Shareholder Remedies* (Oxford, 1995), Chap. 3; and G.P. Stapledon, *Institutional Shareholders and Corporate Governance* (Oxford, 1996), Chap. 2.

[8] Above, pp. 188–192.

[9] City/Industry Working Group, *Developing a Winning Partnership* (the Myners Report), 1995, p. 14. Some reformers have proposed that institutional investors be obliged to vote at, though presumably not to attend, shareholder meetings.

delegated the conduct of the company's affairs to a smaller group of managers. If, as in a small company, the directors and the shareholders are the same people, it is rather nonsensical to insist on the role of the general meeting as against the directors and managers of the company. This is now recognised by section 366A which permits a private company to elect to dispense with the holding of annual general meetings by a unanimous resolution of all those entitled to attend the shareholders meeting at which the elective resolution is passed.[10] However, any member may, by notice to the company, require that a meeting be held, even after the election has been made, so that the resolution shifts the burden of taking the initiative to summon the meeting rather than dispensing entirely with the need to hold one. Moreover, the requirement of unanimity of all those entitled to attend, not just of those attending, ensures in practice that only in companies where shareholders and directors are virtually identical groups will such elections be made. We now turn to examine the rules governing meetings of the company.

The annual general meeting

The Act provides that a company shall in each year (*i.e.* each calendar year, not every 12 months[11]), hold an annual general meeting specified as such in the notices convening it,[12] and not more than 15 months must elapse between one annual general meeting and the next.[13] But it suffices if the first annual meeting is held within 18 months of formation even though this is not in the first or second year of incorporation.[14] If, when an AGM should be held, there is default in doing so[15] not only are the company and any officers in default liable to fines, but the Secretary of State on the application of any member may call or direct the calling of a meeting[16] which, normally, will be deemed to be an AGM.[17]

The AGM is the one occasion when members usually have an opportunity of meeting the directors and of questioning them on the accounts, on their report, and on the company's financial position and prospects. It is at this meeting that, normally, a proportion of the directors will retire and come up for re-election, and at which the

---

[10] s.379A. The company may also elect to dispense with laying accounts and reports before a general meeting (s.252) and with the annual election of auditors (s.386). See above, pp. 93–95.

[11] *Gibson v. Barton* (1875) L.R. 10 Q.B. 329.

[12] s.366(1).

[13] s.366(3).

[14] s.366(2).

[15] If an AGM is held after the prescribed time, voting rights are determined as at the actual date of the meeting; not as they would have been if the meeting had been held at the proper time: *Musselwhite v. Musselwhite & Sons Ltd* [1962] Ch. 964.

[16] s.367. It may give directions about the conduct of the meeting: subss.(1) & (2).

[17] s.367(4) & (5).

members may be able to try to exercise their only real power over the board—that of dismissal. Moreover, it may afford members an opportunity of moving resolutions on their own account. Most of these things could, of course, be done at other general meetings, but the members who want to raise these matters may not be able to insist upon the convening of other meetings. The AGM is valuable to them because the directors can be made to hold it whether they want to or not.

It must be emphasised that the business of an annual general meeting need not be restricted to the ordinary matters specified above. The AGM is a general meeting, and anything that can be done at a general meeting can be undertaken at the AGM. There is, for example, no reason why a special resolution or an extraordinary resolution should not be considered.[18]

Extraordinary general meeting

A company's regulations commonly provide that any meeting other than the AGM shall be called an extraordinary general meeting, and that it may be convened by the directors whenever they think fit. In the absence of any further statutory requirement the regulations would probably stop there, for the management would like nothing better than to be able to call meetings when it suited them, but to be under no obligation to do so when it did not. But the Act provides[19] that the directors must convene a meeting on the requisition of holders of not less than one-tenth of the paid-up capital carrying voting rights.[20] If they fail to do so within 21 days of the deposit of the requisition, the requisitionists, or any of them representing more than half of the total voting rights of all of them, may themselves convene the meeting,[21] and their reasonable expenses must be paid by the company and recovered from fees payable to the defaulting directors.[22] A former weakness of this provision was that, although the directors would be in default unless they took prompt steps to convene a meeting, there was nothing to stop them from convening it for a date in the distant future. This abuse, however, was at long last put right by the 1989 Act which inserted a new subsection providing that the directors shall be deemed

---

[18] This point is emphasised for there seems to be a widespread belief that the AGM should be restricted to ordinary business and that if, *i.e.* a special or extraordinary resolution is to be considered, an extraordinary general meeting should be convened even if this is to be held at the same time and place.

[19] s.368(1): "Notwithstanding anything in its articles."

[20] Or, if the company has no share capital, members representing not less than one-tenth of the voting rights s.368(2). Note that in the case of a company with a share capital in which some shares have more than one vote no regard is paid to this so far as concerns powers to requisition a meeting.

[21] s.368(4).

[22] s.368(6).

not to have duly convened a meeting if they convene it for a date more than 28 days after the date of the notice.[23] Moreover, under section 370(1) and (3) if the company's articles make no provision for calling general meetings by members, two or more members holding not less than one-tenth of the issued share capital (whether or not they have voting rights) or, if the company does not have a share capital, not less than 5 per cent of the members may call a meeting without having to requisition one.

These provisions work reasonably well in the case of small private companies, but in a public company with a large and dispersed membership it may be a matter of considerable difficulty and expense for one member to enlist the support of sufficient of his fellow-members to be able to make a valid requisition. The requisition must state the objects of the meeting[24] and, unless the articles otherwise provide, it will be impossible to insist on anything else being included in the notice of the meeting.[25]

As we have seen, the Secretary of State may cause an AGM to be held if the directors fail to convene it. A wider power, exercisable in respect of either type of general meeting, is conferred on the court "if for any reason it is impracticable to call a meeting . . . in any manner in which meetings of that company may be called or to conduct the meeting in manner prescribed by the articles or this Act". This power may be exercised by the court "of its own motion or on the application—(a) of any director of the company or (b) of any member who would be entitled to vote at the meeting" and the meeting can be "called, held and conducted in any manner the court thinks fit". The "court may give such ancillary or consequential directions as it thinks and these may include a direction that one member of the company present in person or by proxy be deemed to constitute a meeting".[26] However, the court will not use its powers under section 371 to override a quorum provision which is part of a shareholders' agreement designed to protect a minority shareholder and which has the effect of giving him a class right to be present at any valid shareholders' meeting.[27] On the other hand, where the court takes the view that the provisions of the articles are being cynically exploited by a group of shareholders in a way which was not intended by those who drafted them, it may exercise its section 371 powers in the broadest way. Thus, in

---

[23] s.368(8). Thus, 28 years (and six Companies Acts) later, implementing a recommendation of the Jenkins Committee (Cmnd. 1749, para. 458). The Scottish courts had reached this result by use of s.459: *McGuinness v. Bremner* 1988 S.L.T. 891. See p. 745, below.

[24] s.368(3).

[25] *Ball v. Metal Industries Ltd,* 1957 S.C. 315. Section 376, below, does not help because it applies only to resolutions to be moved at AGMs.

[26] s.371(1) & (3). *cf.* s.367. above, which confers similar powers on the S. of S. in respect of AGMs only.

[27] *Harman v. BML Group Ltd* [1994] 1 W.L.R. 893, C.A., and see further below, pp. 727–732.

Re British Union for the Abolition of Vivisection[28] a company whose articles required personal attendance in order to vote had had a general meeting badly disrupted by a minority of members, and the committee feared that other members would in future be deterred from attending. On an application by a majority of the committee the court ordered that a meeting be held to consider a resolution for the abolition of the personal attendance rule, at which meeting the personal attendance rule itself would not apply and personal attendance would be permitted only to the members of the company's committee.

These provisions go some way towards solving the problems which can arise when the members of a small private company have been reduced to one or none.[29] But what seems to be needed is to widen the class of those who may apply to the court, which (unless the company is involved in litigation before it) will not act "on its own motion" because it will know nothing about the matter. As a minimum, it ought, surely, to be expressly provided that "member" includes the personal representative of a deceased member. The provisions can also be used if it is clear that, were a meeting to be held on the requisition of a member, the other members would render it abortive by ensuring that there was no quorum.[30]

As pointed out in relation to directors' meetings,[31] thanks to modern technology it is no longer necessary that a meeting should require all those attending to be in the same room. If more turn up than had been foreseen, a valid meeting can still take place if proper arrangements have been made to direct the overflow to other rooms with adequate audio-visual links enabling everyone to participate in the discussion to the same extent as if all had been in the same room.[32] But this, it seems, does not go quite so far as it may in relation to meetings of directors who are allowed to regulate their proceedings with greater freedom and less formality. In their case there seems no difficulty in regarding them as having resolved on something if they do so as a result of a discussion between them conducted on audio-visual links

---

[28] [1995] 2 BCLC 1.

[29] Normally, "meeting" pre-supposes at least two persons getting together: *Sharp v. Dawes* (1876) 2 Q.B.D. 26., C.A. (where the only member present solemnly proposed a vote of thanks to himself as chairman!); *Re London Flats Ltd* [1969] 1 W.L.R. 711 and *Re Shanley Contracting Ltd* (1980) 124 Sol. J. 239 (notwithstanding that the one member held proxies from others). But *cf. East v. Bennett Bros* [1911] 1 Ch. 163 (where one member held all the shares of a class) and *Neil M'Leod & Sons Ltd*, 1967 S.C. 16 (which Oliver J. in *Re Shanley Contracting Ltd* declined to follow).

[30] *Re El Sombrero Ltd* [1958] Ch. 900 where the applicant shareholder held 900 of the company's 1,000 shares, the remaining 100 being held by the two directors whom the applicant wished to remove in exercise of his statutory powers under what is now s.303. The court directed that one member present in person or by proxy should constitute a quorate meeting. But *cf.* n. 27, above.

[31] Chap. 9 at p. 195, n. 22 above.

[32] *Byng v. London Life Association Ltd* [1990] Ch. 170, C.A. See below pp. 591–594.

however physically far apart they may have been. It is more difficult to regard a decision of the members arrived by a like method as having been taken at *a* general meeting. However, in the case of a private company, much the same result could be achieved through the use of written resolutions and fax machines so long as all the members agreed to the resolutions.[33]

Notice of meetings

Prior to the 1948 Act, the length of notice of meetings, and how and to whom notice should be given, depended primarily on the company's regulations. The only statutory regulation which could not be varied was that 21 days' notice was required for a meeting at which a special resolution was to be proposed. In other cases the Act of 1929 provided that, unless the articles otherwise directed (which they rarely did) only seven days' notice was needed. This left far too short a time for opposition to be organised.[34] Hence, it is now provided by section 369 of the 1985 Act that any provision of a company's articles shall be void in so far as it provides for the calling of a meeting by a shorter notice than 21 days' notice in writing in the case of an annual general meeting or a meeting for the passing of a special resolution, or 14 days' notice in writing in other cases.[35] The company's articles may provide for longer notice but they cannot validly provide for shorter.[36] However, if a meeting is called on shorter notice than the Act or the articles prescribe, it is deemed to be duly called if so agreed, in the case of an AGM, by all the members entitled to attend and vote and, in the case of an extraordinary meeting by "a requisite majority",[37] *i.e.* "a majority holding not less than 95 per cent of the shares giving a right to attend and vote at the meeting; or, in the case of a company not having a share capital, 95 per cent of the total votes of all the members.[38] This applies even if a special resolution is to be passed[39] so long as the members appreciate that they are being asked to consent to short notice of that resolution.[40] Moreover, as a result of amendments made by the 1989 Act, a private company may, by an elective

---

[33] s.381A.
[34] Particularly as the period might be reduced still further by provisions requiring proxy forms to be lodged in advance of the meeting.
[35] Seven days in the case of unlimited companies: s.369(1).
[36] s.369(2). There has been disagreement between the English and the Scottish courts on whether "days" means "clear days" (*i.e.* excluding the day of giving the notice and the day on which the meeting is to be held). The English courts hold that it does: *Re Hector Whaling* [1936] Ch. 208.
[37] s.369(3).
[38] s.369(4).
[39] s.369(2) makes this clear and it is repeated in s.378(3)
[40] *Re Pearce Buffalo Ltd* [1960] 1 W.L.R. 1014.

resolution,[41] reduce the prescribed 95 per cent to not less than 90 per cent.[42]

Apart from prescribing the minimum periods of notice and that it must be in writing, the Act leaves it to the company's articles to provide how it shall be given. What it does, however, is to say that in so far as the articles of the company do not make other provision in that behalf "notice shall be served on every member of it in the manner in which notices are required to be served by Table A (as for the time being in force)".[43] Hence, except to the extent that companies make "other provision in that behalf" they will, as regards giving of notice, be required to comply with Table A 1985 or, as that is amended or replaced, with the then current version, while remaining in respect of other matters subject to the Table A at the date of incorporation (to the extent that they have adopted it or, in the case of companies limited by shares, not excluded it).[44] The reason, presumably, for adopting this half measure rather than making statutory provisions is that, had the latter been done, the provisions would have had to deal with exceptional cases (such as that where holders of share-warrants to bearer are entitled to attend and vote).[45] Table A can and does ignore such cases and assumes that the company's register of members will give the names and addresses of all members. It deals comprehensively with that[46] but with that only; if companies behave exceptionally it is left to them to make appropriate provisions in their articles.

The salient points to note in the present Table A provisions are:

(i) Notice may be given to a member personally[47] or by sending it by post addressed to him at his registered address or by leaving it at that address. Notices to joint shareholders are to be given to the one first named in the register and this is sufficient notice to all joint holders. A member whose registered address is outside the United Kingdom is entitled to receive notice only if he gives the company an address within the United Kingdom at which notices may be given to him.[48]

(ii) If a member attends the meeting, in person or by proxy, he is deemed to have received notice;[49] and if, before a transferee of shares

---

[41] Under s.379(A).

[42] ss.369(4) and 378(3). It will be appreciated that in the case of a typical small private company there would often not be a 95 per cent majority if one member did not consent. And that will be so even with the reduction to 90 per cent.

[43] s.370(4) and (2).

[44] Which is liable to be overlooked by companies with Table A arts, earlier than the current one.

[45] The usual practice is to give notice by a newspaper advertisement. On listed companies see the *Listing Rules*, paras. 13(App 1).18 and 19.

[46] Arts. ss.111–125.

[47] *i.e.* by handing it to him (not telling him orally for the Act requires notice in writing).

[48] Art. 112.

[49] Art. 113.

is entered on the register, notice has been given to someone through whom the transferee derives title, that is effective notice to the transferee.[50]

(iii) Proof that an envelope containing a notice was properly addressed, prepaid and posted is conclusive that that notice was given; and the notice shall be deemed to be given[51] at the expiration of 48 hours[52] after the envelope containing it was posted.[53]

These regulations may be thought to give greater weight to the administrative convenience of the company than to the protection of members (but that is what articles of association often do) and especially is this so in the light of article 39[54] of Table A which provides that the accidental omission to give notice of a meeting to, or the non-receipt of a notice by, any person entitled to receive notice shall not invalidate the proceedings at that meeting."[55]

Contents of notices

The notice will obviously have to say where the meeting is to be held and on what day and time. If, having dispatched the notices, the company finds it necessary to alter the arrangements it will have to notify members of the change before the expiration of the minimum period of notice prescribed by the Act or the articles of the company. The members are entitled to that length of notice in order to make arrangements to attend if they want to and it does not follow that a member who, say, has arranged to attend a meeting at the Barbican at 12 noon will be able instead to attend it at the Cafe Royal at 2.30 p.m.[56]

The notice, equally obviously, will have to indicate the object of the meeting; unless a member knows that, he cannot be expected to decide whether or not to attend. But how specific must the notice be? If the meeting is an AGM at which all that is to be undertaken is what former Tables A described as "ordinary business",[57] all that is necessary is to list those matters. If, however, resolutions on other matters are to be proposed it is customary to set out the resolutions

---

[50] Art. 114.
[51] Under the original version this was followed by "unless the contrary is proved" but these words were deleted by S.I. 1985 No. 1052.
[52] This is optimistic even for 1st Class post (but it was "24 hours" under Table A 1948).
[53] Art. 115.
[54] There is a similar provision in earlier Tables.
[55] This, of course, would not cover the deliberate omission to give notice to a troublesome member, nor does it cover a deliberate omission based on a mistaken belief that a member is not entitled to attend the meeting: *Musselwhite v. Musselwhite & Son Ltd* [1962] Ch. 964. But, if the omission is "accidental", it applies even if the meeting is called to pass a special resolution: *Re West Canadian Collieries Ltd* [1962] Ch. 370.
[56] See *Byng v. London Life Association Ltd.* [1990] Ch. 170, C. A., below, pp. 591–594.
[57] The distinction between "ordinary" and "special" business of an AGM has disappeared from Table A 1985.

verbatim and to indicate that they are to be proposed as special, extraordinary, elective, or ordinary resolutions as the case may be. In the
case of special and extraordinary resolutions it has been held that the
effect of section 378, defining such resolutions, is that the notice must
specify "either the text or the entire substance of the resolution".[58] In
relation to other matters all that seems to be necessary is a fair statement of "the general nature of the business to be transacted"[59] in
sufficient detail to enable the members to decide whether or not to
attend and vote.[60] But the directors should ensure that, if the effect of
the proposed business will be to confer a personal benefit on the directors, that should be made clear either in the notice or in a circular[61]
sent with it.[62]

Notice of members' resolutions

In times past, the requirement of notice rendered largely illusory
the power of individual shareholders to move their own resolutions at
AGMs, for there was no way in which they could compel the board
to include notice of them in the notice of the meeting. Hence they
might have themselves to undertake the task of giving notice—a
laborious and expensive operation in relation to a widely held public
company. Only if they were able to requisition a meeting could they
be sure that the notice given by the board would include their resolutions.[63]

Their position is now strengthened by section 376.[64] Under that
section members representing not less than one-twentieth of the total
voting rights or 100 members holding shares on which there has been
paid up an average sum per member of not less than £100[65] may
require the company to give notice of their resolutions which can then
be considered at the next AGM.[66] The section ensures that notice of
the resolution will be given to members[67] and that the directors cannot
argue that the nature of the resolution is not one that could properly

---

[58] *Re Moorgate Mercantile Holdings Ltd* [1980] 1 W.L.R. 227 at 242F. This related to a special
  resolution but the wording of the section is identical in all material respects as regards extraordinary resolutions and, seemingly, elective resolutions under s.379A(2)(a).

[59] Table A 1985, art. 38.

[60] Contrast *Choppington Collieries Ltd v. Johnson* [1944] 1 All E.R. 762, C.A. with *Batchellor &
  Sons v. Batchellor* [1945] Ch. 169.

[61] On circulars. See below, p. 576.

[62] *Kaye v. Croydon Tramways Co.*. [1989] 1 Ch. 358, C.A.; *Tiessen v. Henderson* [1899] 1 Ch.
  861; *Baillie v. Oriental Telephone Co.* [1915] 1 Ch. 503; *Prudential Assurance v. Newman
  Industries Ltd (No. 2)* [1981] Ch. 257, [1982] Ch. 204, C.A.

[63] And then only if their resolutions were set out in their requisition: see p. 568, above.

[64] Re-enacting s. 140 of the 1948 Act.

[65] *i.e.* normally half the number required to requisition a meeting under s.368, above, but here
  regard is had to multiple voting rights: *cf.* p. 568, n. 20, above.

[66] s.376(1)(a) and (2).

[67] s.376(3), (4) and (5). But less detail is required in relation to members not entitled to notice
  of the meeting: s.376(5).

be dealt with at an AGM.[68] However, the company is not bound to give notice unless the conditions stated in section 377 are met. These conditions are that the requisition, duly signed, must be deposited at the registered office of the company at least six weeks before the AGM[69] and a sum tendered which is reasonably sufficient to meet the company's expenses in giving effect to it.[70]. The requirement that the requisitionists pay the costs of the circulation of the resolution and any accompanying statement was though by the House of Commons Select Committee on Employment[71] to be a significant barrier to shareholders' use of their section 376 powers. Although the additional costs to the company (and therefore to the requisitionists) would be slight if the company included the resolution with its ordinary AGM mailing, to ensure this course of action was adopted would require the requisitionists to find out about and then fit in with the company's timetable, about which the company is not obliged to inform them. If the matter which caused the requisitionists to wish to propose a resolution was something in the AGM mailing itself, then the costs of circulation might be very high and, indeed, they might not even be able to meet the requirement of six weeks' notice. Certainly, section 376 is rarely invoked to circulate resolutions and the Committee thought that its use would be promoted if the company were required to pay the expenses of circulation.[72]

Special notice

As we have seen, in certain circumstances a type of notice, unimaginatively and unhelpfully designated "special notice", has to be given, the principal example[73] being when it is proposed to remove a director or to remove or not to reappoint the auditors. In the light of the discussion of these examples in Chapters 9[74] and 20[75] respectively, little more needs to be said here except to emphasise that special notice

---

[68] s.376(6). In the USA where, under the Federal Securities Legislation, stockholders may have still wider powers to bring their resolutions before general meetings, companies frequently attempt to frustrate efforts of "consumer", "equal opportunity" or "environmental" activists to move resolutions on the company's practices by arguing that they are not matters which can be discussed at general meetings. s. 376 (6) would appear to render this unarguable here and pressure groups have raised such issues at AGMs—though less frequently than in the USA.

[69] But the board cannot frustrate the requisitionists by convening a meeting for less than six weeks after the deposit of the requisition: s.377(2).

[70] s.377(1).

[71] First Special Report on the Remuneration of Directors and Chief Executives of the Privatised Utilities, Session 1994–1995, H.C. 159.

[72] As the company may choose, but is not obliged, to do: s.376(1). At the time of writing the DTI is consulting over the Committee's proposal: *Shareholder Communications at the Annual General Meeting*, April 1996.

[73] For another, see s.293(5) relating to the appointment or reappointment of a director aged over 70.

[74] At pp. 188–192.

[75] At pp. 549–552.

is a type of notice very different from that discussed hitherto in this chapter. It is not notice of a meeting given *by* the company but notice given *to* the company of the intention to move a resolution at the meeting. Under section 379, where any provision of the Act requires special notice of a resolution, the resolution is ineffective unless notice of the intention to move it has been given to the company at least 28 days before the meeting.[76] The company must then give notice (in the normal sense) of the resolution, with the notice of the meeting or, if that is not practicable,[77] either by newspaper advertisement or by any other method allowed by the articles, at least 21 days before the meeting.[78] All this achieves in itself is to ensure that the company and its members have plenty of time to consider the resolution but, as we have seen, in the two principal cases where special notice is required[79] supplementary provisions enable protective steps to be taken by the directors or auditors concerned. Under this heading it is also to be noted that the company's articles may require notice of certain types of resolution to be given to the company in advance of the meeting, and this requirement may limit shareholders' freedom of action at the meeting itself. For example, article 76 of Table A provides that no person shall be appointed as a director at a meeting of the company unless he or she is a director retiring by rotation, a person recommended by the board or a person of whose proposed appointment the company has been given at least 14 days' (and not more than 35 days') notice, together with the proposed appointee's consent. At the general meeting of such a company it is thus not open to dissenting shareholders to put forward an alternative candidate for director on the spur of the moment, though it appears that the board could do so.

Circulars

In practice, the notice of a meeting will be of a formal nature but, if anything other than ordinary business is to be transacted, it will be accompanied by a circular explaining the reasons for the proposals and giving the opinion of the board thereon. Normally, therefore, the circular will be a reasoned case by the directors in favour of their own proposals or in opposition to proposals put forward by others. In deciding whether the nature of the business has been adequately

---

[76] s.379(1). This applies whether the resolution is proposed by the board or by a member. But the notice is effective if the meeting is called for a date 28 days or less after special notice has been given, s.379(3).

[77] *e.g.* if notices of the meeting have already been despatched.

[78] s.379(2). But it seems that this notice has to be given only if the resolution is to be put on the agenda and that the mover cannot compel the company to do this unless he can and does invoke s.376, above: *Pedley v. Inland Waterways Ltd* [1971] 1 All E.R. 209, *sed quaere.*

[79] See nn. 74 and 75, above.

described, the notice and circular can be read together.[80] But the circular must not misrepresent the facts; there have been many cases in which resolutions have been set aside on the ground that they were passed as a result of a "tricky" circular.[81]

If there is opposition to the board's proposals, the opposers will doubtless wish to state their case and a battle of circulars will result. It is here, however, that the superiority of the board's position becomes manifest. Even if the directors do not directly control many votes, they are for the moment in control of the company and they can get their say in first and use all the facilities and funds of the company in putting their views across. They will have had all the time in the world in which to prepare a polished and closely reasoned circular and with it they will have been able to dispatch stamped and addressed proxy forms in their own favour. And all this, of course, at the company's expense.[82]

Until the 1948 Act members opposing the board's resolution or proposing their resolutions had none of these advantages and, even now, only timid steps have been taken towards counteracting the immense advantage enjoyed by those in possession of the company's machinery. Such steps as have been taken are included in sections 376 and 377. As we have already seen, section 376 entitles members holding one-twentieth of the votes or 100 members holding shares on which there has been paid up an average of £100 each, to use the company's machinery for circulating resolutions to be moved at AGMs. It further entitles them to require the company to circulate statements not exceeding 1,000 words in length[83] with respect to any business to be dealt with at *any* meeting.[84] Members can therefore now use the company's machinery for the dispatch of circulars whether in support of their own resolutions or in opposition to any proposals of the board. In the case of circulars it suffices if the requisition is deposited with the company not less than a week before the meeting.[85]

In practice, however, this provision is of limited value. The expense

---

[80] *Tiessen v. Henderson* [1899] 1 Ch. 861 at 867; *Re Moorgate Mercantile Holdings Ltd* [1980] 1 W.L.R. 227 at 242F.

[81] *Kaye v. Croydon Tramways Co.* [1898] 1 Ch. 358, C.A.; *Tiessen v. Henderson* [1899] 1 Ch. 861; *Baillie v. Oriental Telephone Co.* [1915] 1 Ch. 503, C.A.; and see *Prudential Assurance v. Newman Industries Ltd (No. 2)* [1981] Ch. 257; [1982] Ch. 204, C.A. In the case of listed shares there is a further safeguard in the requirement that copies (and sometimes drafts) of circulars shall be sent to the Stock Exchange: see *Listing Rules*, paras. 14.2–14.4.

[82] *Peel v. L.N.W. Ry* [1907] 1 Ch. 5, C.A. For an excellent description of the relative weakness of the opposition, see *per* Maugham J. in *Re Dorman Long & Co.* [1934] 1 Ch. 635 at 657–658.

[83] Contrast the vaguer formula in the provisions relating to removal of auditors or directors where representations are to be "not exceeding a reasonable length".

[84] s.376(1)(b). As under the provisions relating to auditors and directors the court can excuse the company from circulating matter designed to "secure needless publicity for defamatory matter": s.377(3).

[85] s.377(1)(a)(ii).

still has to be borne by the members[86]—unless the company otherwise resolves[87]—and no substantial saving will result from the use of the company's facilities except in the case of a circular which can go out at the same time as the notices. In other cases (for example, when the circulars are designed to oppose proposals already forwarded by the board), little extra cost will be incurred by acting independently of the company and this will have a number of advantages. It will avoid any difficulty in obtaining sufficient requisitionists and will prevent delay, which may be fatal if notices of the meeting have already been dispatched. It will also obviate the need to cut the circular to 1,000 words and will enable the opposition to accompany it with proxies in their own favour.[88] Moreover, and from a tactical point of view this is vital, the board will not obtain advance information about the opposition's case, nor be able to send out at the same time a circular of its own in reply.

Hence members determined to do battle with the board may be better advised to disregard section 376 in relation to circulars. But, whether they do so or not, they start with severe handicaps, the least of which is that they will have to draw on their own funds, not on those of the company. Victory normally goes to those who first state their case and first solicit proxies. Unless the board is so foolish as to part with the initiative by failing to comply with a valid requisition for a meeting, it is almost invariably the board that will strike the first blow. In a public company with a large and dispersed membership this is normally sufficient to ensure victory.[89]

Proxies

It will have been apparent from the foregoing that proxies play a vital part in modern company meetings. At common law attending and

---

[86] s.376(1). The House of Commons Select Committee on Employment (above, p. 575) did not make any recommendation about the costs of shareholder circulars where no resolution was put forward by them.

[87] *ibid.* The company is likely so to resolve if the members' resolution is passed (which is unlikely) and may conceivably do so even if it is lost. In cases where it has not so resolved there have sometimes been disputes on precisely what are properly to be regarded as "the company's expenses in giving effect" to the requisition. *e.g.* does it include the costs of a circular opposing the members' resolution? It ought not to.

[88] There is clearly no reason why the members' circular should not invite recipients to cancel any proxies previously given to the board but it seems that the company could refuse to despatch the members' proxy forms unless, perhaps, the words in them were counted against the 1,000 words allowed.

[89] The only effective opposition is likely to come from institutional investors who probably hold large blocks and whom the board will endeavour to woo. Where those institutions are hostile small shareholders may obtain protection under their umbrella. But *cf. Re Old Silkstone Collieries Ltd* [1954] Ch. 169, C.A. (at 191–192), for a case where their approbation was likely to lull the other shareholders into unwarranted apathy. In the U.K., attempts to form investor protection associations to protect the interests of private investors have not proved successful.

voting had to be in person,[90] but it early became the normal practice to allow these duties to be undertaken by an agent or "proxy".[91] Until the 1948 Act, however, the right to vote by proxy at a meeting of a company was dependent upon express authorisation in the articles. In practice this was almost invariably given; but not infrequently it was limited in some way, generally by providing that the proxy must himself be a member. Where there was such a limitation the scales were further tilted in favour of the board, for a member wishing to appoint a proxy to oppose the board's proposals might find difficulty in locating a fellow member prepared to attend and vote on his behalf. It has also been customary to provide that proxy forms must be lodged in advance of the meeting. While this is a reasonable provision, in as much as it is necessary to check their validity before they are used at the meeting,[92] it too could be used to favour the board if the period allowed for lodging was unreasonably short. Moreover, as already pointed out, it had become the practice for the board to send out proxy forms in their own favour with the notice of the meeting and for these to be stamped and addressed at the company's expense.

For all these reasons, although proxy voting gave an appearance of stockholder democracy, this appearance was deceptive and in reality the practice helped to enhance the dictatorship of the board. In recognition of this the Stock Exchange requires that listed companies shall send out "two-way" proxies, *i.e.* forms which enable members to direct the proxy whether to vote for or against any resolution.[93]

The statutory provisions relating to proxies are now to be found in section 372 of the Act. Any member entitled to attend and vote at a meeting is entitled to appoint another person (whether a member of the company or not) as his proxy to attend and vote instead of himself and, in the case of a private company, to speak at the meeting.[94] But, unless the articles otherwise provide: (a) this does not apply to a com-

---

[90] *Harben v. Philips* (1883) 23 Ch.D 14, C.A., and see *Woodford v. Smith* [1970] 1 W.L.R. 806, *per* Megarry J. at 810.

[91] The word "proxy" is used indiscriminately to describe both the agent and the instrument appointing him.

[92] In the USA, where there is no such practice, the meeting may be deliberately prolonged for days in order to enable more proxy votes to be obtained by high-pressure solicitation.

[93] *Listing Rules*, paras, 9.26, 13.28 and 13.29. Notwithstanding recommendations that this should be a statutory requirement in all cases (*e.g.* by the Jenkins Committee, Cmnd. 1749, para. 464) it still is not. But Table A 1985 includes two forms of proxy, one of which gives the proxy complete discretion (art. 60) and the other, a two-way proxy which can be used "where it is desired to afford members an opportunity of instructing the proxy how he shall act" (art. 61).

[94] s.372(1). The Jenkins Committee recommended that this should apply also to a public company: Cmnd. 1749, para. 463. But this recommendation has not been implemented, apparently because it is feared that meetings would be unduly prolonged if professional advocates could be briefed to represent the various factions at a meeting of a public company. This seems rubbish for, so long as action is taken in time to ensure that the advocate will be entered on the register before the meeting, all each faction needs to do is to transfer one share to its advocate.

pany not having a share capital,[95] (b) a member of a private company is not entitled to appoint more than one proxy to attend on the same occasion[96] and (c) a proxy is not entitled to vote except on a poll.[97]

The shareholders must be informed of their rights to attend and vote by proxy in the notice convening the meeting.[98] Moreover, if proxies are solicited at the company's expense the invitation must be sent to all members entitled to attend and vote[99]; the board cannot invite only those from whom it expects a favourable response. Finally, it is no longer permissible to provide that proxy forms must be lodged more than 48 hours before a meeting or adjourned meeting.[1]

It cannot be said, however, that these provisions have done much to curtail the tactical advantages possessed by the directors. They still strike the first blow and their solicitation of proxy votes is likely to meet with a substantial response before the opposition is able to get under way. Even if their proxies are in the "two-way" form, many members will complete and lodge them[2] after hearing but one side of the case, and only the most intelligent or obstinate are likely to withstand the impact of the, as yet, uncontradicted assertions of the directors. It is, of course, true that once opposition is aroused members may be persuaded to cancel their proxies, for these are merely appointments of agents and the agents' authority can be withdrawn[3] either expressly or by personal attendance and voting.[4] But in practice this rarely happens.

Articles commonly provide that a vote given by a proxy shall be effective notwithstanding the revocation, by death or otherwise, of the authority, provided that the company has not received notice of the revocation,[5] and they sometimes specify that such notice must be received not later than so many hours before the meeting. Such provisions are clearly effective as between the company and the member, and it has even been held that the company must disregard notice of

---

[95] If the articles of a guarantee company follow Table C 1985 they will "otherwise provide": see arts. 1 and 8.

[96] Table A 1985 otherwise provides: art. 59.

[97] s.372(2). He can, however, demand a poll: see below.

[98] s.372(3).

[99] s.372(6). Overruling as regards registered companies *Wilson v. L.M.S. Ry* [1940] Ch. 393, C.A.

[1] s.372(5). Hence proxies may now validly be lodged between the original date of the meeting and any adjournment for more than 48 hours.

[2] Encouraged by the fact that postage is prepaid. Most two-way proxies provide that if neither "for" nor "against" is deleted the proxy will be used as the proxy thinks fit (*i.e.* as the board wish): Table A 1985, art. 61. The Stock Exchange requires this to be expressly stated: *Listing Rules*, para. 13.28(d).

[3] Unless it is an "authority coupled with an interest" (*e.g.* when given to a transferee prior to registration of his transfer) or is an irrevocable power of attorney under the Power of Attorney Act 1971, s.4.

[4] *Cousins v. International Brick Co.* [1931] 2 Ch. 90, C.A.

[5] Table A 1985, art. 63.

revocation received out of time.[6] On the other hand, it does not prevent the member from attending and voting in person and the company must then accept his vote instead of the proxy's.[7] And, on ordinary agency principles, it is clear that as between the member and his proxy a revocation is always effective if notified to the proxy before he has voted.[8]

The final question of interest relating to proxies is whether they are compelled to exercise the authority conferred upon them. Unless there is a binding contract or some equitable obligation compelling them to do so, the answer appears to be in the negative. Normally there is only a gratuitous authorisation imposing no positive obligation on the agent, but merely a negative obligation not to vote contrary to the instructions of his principal if he votes at all.[9] But there may be a binding contract, if, for example, the proxy is to be remunerated. Or there may be a fiduciary duty, if, for example, the proxy is the member's professional adviser. Although the directors are not normally in a fiduciary relationship to individual members, it seems that if they are appointed proxies and instructed how to vote they must obey their instructions.[10] If it were otherwise the two-way proxy would be valueless, for the board would only use the favourable proxies and ignore the others. Similarly, anyone who solicits proxies stating that he will use them in a certain way or as instructed, will, it is thought, be under a legal obligation to do as he has stated. But failing any such statement or definite instructions from his principal he will have a discretion and if he exercises it in good faith he will not be liable, whichever way he votes or if he refrains from voting.

Corporations' representatives

Since a company or other corporation is an artificial person which must act through agents or servants, it might be supposed that, when a member is another company, it could attend and vote at meetings only by proxy. This, however, is not so. Section 375 provides that a body corporate may, by a resolution of its directors or other governing body,[11] authorise such person as it thinks fit to act as its representative

---

[6] *Spiller v. Mayo (Rhodesia) Development Co. Ltd* [1926] W.N. 78.

[7] *Cousins v. International Brick Co.*, above.

[8] Unless the agency is irrevocable, see n. 3, above.

[9] This was discussed, but not decided, in *Oliver v. Dalgleish* [1963] 1 W.L.R. 1274, which also left open the question of how far the company is concerned to see whether the proxy is obeying his instructions.

[10] *Per* Uthwatt J. in *Second Consolidated Trust v. Ceylon Amalgamated Estates* [1943] 2 All E.R. 567 at 570. So held in the case of proxies solicited under an order of the court in connection with a scheme of arrangement in *Re Dorman Long & Co.* [1934] Ch. 635 (this case contains an admirable discussion of the general problems of proxy voting). But in both the cases the proxy holders were present at the meeting; *quaere* whether they can be compelled to attend: see [1934] Ch. 664–665.

[11] *e.g.* its liquidator: *Hillman v. Crystal Bowl Amusements Ltd* [1973] 1 W.L.R. 162.

at meetings of companies of which it is a member (or creditor) and that the representative may exercise the same powers as could the body corporate if it were an individual.[12] It is therefore preferable for a company to attend and vote by representative rather than by proxy, for the representative is in a stronger position since he may speak even at meetings of public companies, and vote on a show of hands as well as on a poll. However, the company may appoint only a single person as its representative, and this may be inconvenient in the case of a nominee company, holding shares on behalf of beneficial owners with a variety of views on the matters at issue. Alternatively, the company may appoint multiple proxies, at least for meetings of public companies, but proxies have no right to speak or vote on a show of hands.

Conduct of meetings

The discussion under this heading is focused primarily on meetings of public companies. Small private companies in most cases are likely to take advantages of the concessions in the 1989 Act and to pass any needed resolutions by written resolutions and to dispense even with AGMs. But, even so, they may not always be able to avoid holding meetings. Written resolutions are effective only if signed by, or on behalf of, all the members who would be entitled to attend and vote if a meeting was held,[13] and cannot be used in relation to a resolution under section 303 removing a director or under section 391 removing an auditor.[14-15] An elective resolution also has to be agreed to by all the members entitled to attend and vote and, even if it is, it will not necessarily prevent a member from insisting on an AGM.[16] Hence dispensing with meetings presupposes continued harmony between the members. All too often this breaks down at some stage in the lives of private companies, and the meetings, which will then have to be held to attempt to resolve the disagreements, are likely to be particularly bitter. The observance of the rules will then be just as important as in relation to public companies.

In relation to public companies, although the result of any disputed resolution is in reality generally determined in advance through the system of proxy votes, the meeting still has to be held. At the meeting the board and the opposition will have an opportunity of repeating the arguments already expressed in their circulars, often succeeding in generating a surprising amount of heat considering that both sides know that it is little more than shadow-boxing; little, but nevertheless more, for a mistake at the meeting may still dash the cup of victory

---

[12] This is really a statutory example of an officer acting as an organ of the company rather than as a mere agent.

[13] s.381A.

[14-15] s.381A(7) and Sched. 15A, Part I.

[16] s.366A(3).

from the lips of the triumphant party since a breach of the regulations governing the conduct of the meeting may cause any resolutions passed to be invalid.[17]

Nor are meetings merely a means of passing resolutions, they also give the members an opportunity of asking questions either out of a genuine desire for information for its own sake, or as a tactical move in the next stage of the battle. However, the shareholder's legal entitlements to ask questions are very limited, even if most companies do in fact permit a general "question and answer" session, usually on the resolution to adopt the directors' report and accounts, and even if institutional shareholders are doubtless able to get their questions answered privately without the need for a general meeting. At common law, questions must be kept within the scope of the business on the agenda. There is no statutory right to ask general questions at the AGM nor even a right for shareholders to table a question to be asked at the AGM after seeing the annual report and accounts, even though those documents might be thought likely to generate questions. The current statutory law, as we have seen, operates largely in terms of shareholder resolutions or the distribution of circulars in response to the board's resolutions and ignores the potential value of a statutory right to ask questions, despite the Parliamentary pedigree which this method of democracy enjoys.

Of course, meetings may be, and most often are, held when there is no battle at all, and here they afford an opportunity for the management to report to the members and for the latter to congratulate or commiserate with the former on the results of their labours. Unhappily, meetings are rarely attended by more than a handful of members unless there is some dispute, and then the only real excitement arises from the attempts by the party that has lost the battle of circulars to trap the other into some formal irregularity or into revealing information which may enable the validity of the notices to be attacked as misleading or incomplete.

It is therefore necessary in relation to all types of company to ensure that the rules for the conduct of meetings are scrupulously observed. What these rules are will depend on the regulations of the company construed in the light of the common law as to the conduct of meetings generally. Here attention can be drawn only to the most important matters which will require attention.

Quorums

The first essential is to ensure that a quorum is present, for without a quorum no resolutions can be passed. The Act provides that two members personally present constitute a quorum, but permit the art-

---

[17] For a recent example, see *Byng v. London Life Association Ltd*, below, pp. 591–594.

icles to lay down a different requirements, except that, in the case of a private company having only one member, that one member constitutes the quorum, no matter what the articles say.[18] It is not clear whether, if the articles are silent on the question, a quorum must remain present throughout or whether it suffices if it is present at the beginning of the meeting. Under the wording of earlier Tables A,[19] the English courts held that it sufficed that a quorum was present at the time when the meeting began,[20] even though some members left before all the business had been conducted (provided that at least two remained so that it could still be regarded as a meeting).[21] But under the wording of Table A 1985[22] it is clear that a quorum must be present throughout. As, however, it is the English practice to prescribe very small quorums,[23] except in relation to class meetings,[24] this is of not great importance in the case of general meetings of public companies though it can be in relation to those of private ones. Table A 1985 also provides that if a quorum is not present within half an hour of the time appointed, or if the meeting becomes inquorate, the meeting shall stand adjourned to the same day in the next week at the same time, and place, or to such time and place as the directors shall determine.[25]

Chairman

The next step is to provide a chairman to preside over the meeting. Who he or she shall be depends on the company's articles and if those are silent the members present may elect a chairman.[26] Table A 1985 sensibly takes the view that the chairman ought to be a member of the board and accordingly provides that the chairman of the board, or, in his absence some other director nominated by the directors, shall pres-

---

[18] ss.370 and 370A.

[19] "No business shall be transacted at any general meeting unless a quorum is present *at the time when the meeting proceeds to business*" (italics supplied): Table A 1948, art. 53.

[20] *Re Hartley Baird Ltd* [1955] Ch. 143, not following *Henderson v. James Outtit & Co. Ltd* (1894) 21 R (Ct. of Sess.) 674. Sc.

[21] *Re London Flats Ltd* [1969] 1 W.L.R. 711.

[22] Art. 40 (which omits the words italicised in the former article quoted at n. 19.) and art. 41 which says that the meeting shall be adjourned if during the meeting a quorum ceases to be present.

[23] Under Table A 1985, "two persons entitled to vote upon the business to be transacted each being a member or a proxy for a member or a duly authorised representative of a corporation": art. 40. If the articles make no provision, two members personally present are a quorum: s. 370(4). *cf* the USA where large quorums are commonly required and it is not unknown for a disgruntled minority, whose presence is needed for a quorum, if it expects to be outvoted to stay away or to walk out before the vote—which has been known to lead to fisticuffs.

[24] See below, p. 594.

[25] Art. 41. Table A 1948, art. 54, distinguishes between meetings requisitioned by members (which are dissolved if a quorum is not present within half an hour) and others (which stand adjourned as in the text above) and which adds that the members present at the adjourned meeting shall constitute a quorum (but presumably only if there are at least two).

[26] s.370(5).

ide but if neither is present (and willing to act) within 15 minutes after the time appointed, the directors present shall elect one of their number, and, if only one is present, he shall be chairman if willing.[27] Only if all this fails to produce a willing member of the board[28] will the members present have any say in the matter.

The position of chairman is an important and onerous one, for he will be in charge of the meeting and will be responsible for ensuring that its business is properly conducted. As chairman, he owes a duty to the meeting, not to the board of directors, even if he is a director. He should see that the business of the meeting is efficiently conducted and that all shades of opinion are given a fair hearing. This may entail taking snap decisions on points of order, motions, amendments and questions, often deliberately designed to harass him, and upon the correctness of his ruling the validity of any resolution may depend.[29] He will probably require the company's legal adviser to be at his elbow, and this is one of the occasions when even the most cautious lawyer will have to give advice without an opportunity of referring to the authorities.[30]

Resolutions

A reader who has got this far will appreciate that a meeting may have to deal with any one or more of four types of resolution—ordinary, extraordinary, special and, in the case of a private company, elective. But it may be helpful to remind him or her of the differences between them.

An ordinary resolution is one passed by a simple majority of those voting, and is used for all matters not requiring another type of resolution under the Act or the articles. An extraordinary resolution is one passed by a three-fourths majority but no special period of notice is needed.[31] Under the Act an extraordinary resolution is required only for certain matters connected with winding up,[32] or when class meetings are asked to agree to a modification of class rights.[33] A special resolution is also one passed by a three-fourths majority, but 21 days'

---

[27] Table A 1985, art. 42. Table A 1948 is substantially to the same effect.

[28] Which is unlikely unless all the directors have travelled together to the meeting and met with a serious accident or delay on the way.

[29] For the sort of situation with which the chairman may have to cope if the members of a public company turn up in far larger numbers than the board has foreseen, see the recent case of *Byng v. London Life Association Ltd* [1990] Ch. 170, C.A. (below, pp. 591–594) where his well-meaning efforts were in vain and the company had to convene a new meeting.

[30] He should appear to be sure of his ground even if he is not and pray that the rule in *Foss v. Harbottle* (below, Chap. 23, pp. 660 *et seq.*) will make it difficult for any of his rulings to be effectively attacked.

[31] s.378(1).

[32] See especially Insolvency Act. s.84(1)(c).

[33] s.125(2)(b).

notice must be given of the meeting at which it is to be proposed.[34] A special resolution is required before any important constitutional changes can be undertaken; and as a result of the legislation in the 1980s the number of such cases has greatly increased. In the case of both extraordinary and special resolutions the notice of the meeting must specify the intention to propose the resolution as an extraordinary or a special resolution, as the case may be.[35]

In all these three cases the requisite majority is of the members entitled to vote and actually voting either in person or by proxy where proxy voting is allowed. This may and, in the case of a public company normally will, be much less than a majority of the total membership, and may even be less than a majority of the members present at the meeting, for those who refrain from voting are ignored.[36] To take an extreme case: A meeting of a company with 500,000 preference shares without voting rights, and 500,000 ordinary shares each with one vote, is attended only by five ordinary shareholders, four with one share each and one with a hundred shares. If on a poll a resolution is voted for by three of the holders of one share and against by the fourth shareholder with one share, the holder of the hundred shares abstaining, the resolution will have been duly carried even if it is an extraordinary or special resolution, notwithstanding that only three out of a total of one million shares, three out of 500,000 total votes and three out of 104 votes exercisable at the meeting, have actually been polled in its favour. As we shall see later,[37] the procedure of voting on a show of hands, unless a poll is effectively demanded, may produce even greater anomalies.[38]

In relation to the new type of "elective resolution" (relevant only to private companies[39]) the position is very different. Such a resolution is ineffective unless the resolution is agreed to at the meeting, in person or by proxy, by all the members entitled to attend and vote at the meeting.[40] In other words, there must be unanimous agreement of

---

[34] s.378(2). But shorter notice can be agreed to by a majority of 95 per cent in nominal value of holders of shares giving a right to attend and vote or, in the case of a company not having a share capital, a majority of not less than 95 per cent of the total voting rights at the meeting of all members: s.378(3). A private company may elect, by an elective resolution, that not less than 90 per cent will suffice: *ibid.*

[35] s.378(1) and (2).

[36] s.378(5) states this expressly as regards extraordinary and special resolutions and the same applied to the simple majority needed for ordinary resolutions.

[37] Below, p. 589.

[38] So may multiple votes attached to the shares of a particular holder: *Bushell v. Faith* [1970] A.C. 1099, H.L.

[39] And, under s.379A(1), enabling them to elect to relax the requirements on the duration of the directors' authority to allot shares (s.80A); to dispense with the laying of accounts (s.252); to dispense with holding AGMs (s.366A); to reduce the majority required to agree to short notice of meetings (ss.369(4) and 378(3)); to dispense with annual appointment of auditors (s.386); or to dispense with such other requirement as may be specified by regulations made under the 1989 Act s.117.

[40] s.379(2). It may be revoked by an ordinary resolution: s.379A(3).

all members entitled to vote whether or not they are present or represented at the meeting.

Amendments to proposed resolutions

Problems on amending a resolution notified in the notice of the meeting may arise in two circumstances. The first is where the proposer of the resolution wants to amend it prior to the meeting. This will be possible only if it is practicable to give valid notice of the amended resolution. That is most unlikely if the proposer is a member rather than the board and unlikely even if the proposer is the board unless the company has a small membership willing to consent to short notice under section 369(3) and (4) or section 373(3). Normally, there is nothing that can be done except either to withdraw the resolution (and start all over again) or to seek to amend the resolution at the meeting. Obviously the latter alternative would be preferred, if practicable.

The second circumstance is where a member wishes to move at the meeting an amendment to a resolution proposed by the board, by another member or by himself. This, one might have supposed, would be entirely legitimate so long as the amendment was not such as to take the resolution beyond the scope of the business notified to the members in the notice of the meeting. However, as a result of the decision of Slade J. in *Re Moorgate Mercantile Holdings Ltd,*[41] it seems that, in relation to special, extraordinary and elective resolutions, no amendment can be made if it in any way alters the substance of the resolution as set out in the notice. Grammatical and clerical errors may be corrected, or words translated into more formal language, and, if the precise text of the resolution was not included in the notice,[42] it may be converted into a formal resolution, provided always that there is no departure whatever from the substance as stated in the notice.[43]

The learned judge thought that his decision was desirable on policy

---

[41] [1980] 1. W.L.R. 227. The case concerned the confirmation of a special resolution reducing the company's share premium account which had been "lost". The notice of the meeting proposed that the whole of it (£1,356,900.48) "be cancelled". Before the meeting was held it was realised that £327.17 resulting from a recent share issue could not be said yet to have been "lost". Accordingly, at the meeting the resolution was amended and it was resolved that the share premium a/c be reduced to £327.17. Confirmation was refused on the ground that the resolution had not been validly passed. But in a later case (unreported, but see (1991) 12 Co. Law at 64, 65), where the facts were virtually identical, a reduction was confirmed because the "substance" (*i.e.* the amount of the reduction) remained unchanged.

[42] Rather surprisingly, Slade J. thought that the language of what is now s.378(2) did not require this be done (at 240–241A). But that of s.379A(2), which requires notice of a meeting to pass an elective resolution to state "the terms of the resolution," (see above, p. 586) seems to demand that the actual resolution be stated. In all three cases it is good (and almost universal) practice to do so.

[43] At 242C.

grounds,[44] as well as being demanded by the terms of the Act, and that it would prevent the substantial embarrassment to the chairman of the meeting and to any persons holding "two-way" proxies on behalf of absent members,[45] that any less strict rule would cause. This, however, ignores the greater embarrassment which the company may face if the legal position is not understood at the time and put right by starting again. The company will then act upon the resolution until, sometime in the future, a disgruntled member seeks to take advantage of its invalidity. The company will then have to fall back on the uncertain defences of laches, acquiescence or waiver.[46] As a result of the companies' legislation of the 1980s there are now many more than the "about ten circumstances"[47] where special resolutions are needed and it is not unlikely that some, which companies believe to have been passed, are technically invalid. At present thousands of private companies are passing elective resolutions. If the notice is of a single such resolution dispensing with all five requirements[48] which can be dispensed with under section 379A but at the meeting this is amended by, say, deleting the election in respect of section 80A, the resolution will, it seems, be invalid.[49]

Slade J. emphasised that his decision had no relevance to ordinary resolutions and that in relation to them the criteria for permissible amendments might well be wider.[50] This is clearly so if the precise terms of the resolution are not set out in the notice but come within a statement of "the general nature of the business to be transacted at the meeting".[51] But even if the terms of an ordinary resolution are set out in the notice it seems that some amendments may be made at the meeting, and that if the chairman refuses to allow a permissible amendment to be moved the resolution will be invalid.[52] It is submitted that an amendment is permissible if, but only if, the amended resolution is such that no member who had made up his mind whether or not to attend and vote and, if he had decided to do so, how he should vote, could reasonably adopt a different attitude to the amended version.[53] The criticisms of that test by Slade J.[54] apply equally to an ordinary resolution but it is difficult to find any other test short of

---

[44] At 242A–243.

[45] At 243F.

[46] For these deep waters, see Chap. 8 at pp. 176–177, above.

[47] [1980] 1 W.L.R. at 242H.

[48] See n. 39, above.

[49] If the company realises this it can easily put matters right by, for example, getting all the members to sign a written resolution under s.381A—but it is unlikely that it will realise that it needs to do so.

[50] At 242H, citing *Betts & Co. Ltd v. Macnaghten* [1910] 1 Ch. 430.

[51] Table A 1985, art. 38.

[52] *Henderson v. Bank of Australasia* (1980) 45 Ch.D. 330, C.A.

[53] This was the advice given to the chairman in the *Moorgate* case; see [1980] 1 W.L.R. at 230A.

[54] *ibid.*, at 243D–G.

applying to ordinary resolutions that applied to special and extraordinary resolutions, *i.e.* that no amendment of substance, however trivial, may be made. And does the suggested test really face the chairman and two-way proxy-holders with the substantial embarrassments that Slade J. foresees?[55]

There may, nevertheless, be one type of ordinary resolution to which the stricter rule applies. This is when special notice of the resolution is required. The wording of section 379 bears a close resemblance to that of sections 378 and 379A and makes it arguable that no amendment of substance, however trivial, can be made to the resolution stated in the special notice. Hence, if, say, special notice has been given of a single resolution to remove all the directors[56] (under section 303) or both of two joint auditors (under section 391A), an amendment seeking to exclude from the resolution some or one of them may be impermissible. If so, this seems a regrettable emasculation of such powers as members have (and which the relevant sections were intended to enhance) and also seems unfair to the directors or auditors whom the members may wish to retain.[57] Even where an amendment to an ordinary resolution may be proposed on the above principles, the company's articles may aim to restrict the shareholders' freedom, say by providing that, where the text is fully set out in the notice of the meeting, the Chairman has a discretion not to consider amendments of which at least 48 hours' notice in writing has not been given to the company.

Voting

Unless the company's regulations otherwise provide, voting is in the first instance on a show of hands, *i.e.* those present indicate their views by raising their hands. Recognising the limitations of human anatomy, regulations generally provide for one vote only per person on a show of hands, irrespective of the number of shares held. Moreover, there is no statutory obligation to allow proxy votes on a show of hands and it is not usual to do so.[58] For both these reasons the result on a show of hands may give a very imperfect picture of the true

---

[55] If the articles say (as does Table A, art. 82) that directors' fees shall be such as "the company may by ordinary resolution determine" and the directors give notice of an ordinary resolution to increase the fees by £10,000 p.a., surely a member should be entitled to move an amendment to reduce the increase (though the directors clearly should not be permitted to move an amendment to increase it further)?

[56] This seems to be permissible—the singular "director" includes the plural—and s.292 relates only to voting on *appointments*, not to *removals*.

[57] Nor should proxy holders have any doubts on how they should vote. If instructed to vote for the resolution they would vote against the amendment but, if that was passed, for the amended resolution. If instructed to vote against, they would vote for the amendment but against the resolution as amended. If given a discretion they would exercise it.

[58] Unless the proxy holders are physically segregated from the members personally present it may, in a well-attended meeting, be difficult to enforce this in practice.

opinion of the meeting. If the resolution is uncontroversial a vote by show of hands will probably suffice and will save time and trouble, and on such matters the chairman's statement that the resolution is carried will normally be undisputed.[59] But on any disputed question a poll will almost certainly be demanded[60] by a member, or by the chairman if a resolution proposed by the board has been defeated on a show of hands (as may well be the case since it is probably only the opposition which will have attended in person in any strength). It is therefore of considerable importance to decide whether such a demand is effective.

The regulations of companies invariably direct that a demand by the chairman shall be effective.[61] This again strengthens the position of the directors, for they run no risk of not being able to use their full voting power. Further, the Act[62] provides that the articles must not exclude the right to demand a poll on any question, other than the election of a chairman or the adjournment of the meeting; nor must they make ineffective a demand by not less than five members having a right to vote, or by members representing not less than one-tenth of the total voting rights or holding shares having a right to vote on which a sum has been paid up equal to not less than one-tenth of the total sum paid up on all the shares conferring that right. Further, a proxy may demand or join in demanding a poll. This makes it impossible for the articles to hamstring a sizeable opposition by depriving them of their opportunity to exercise their full voting strength. Nevertheless, it may still mean that the members who on a poll can outvote all the others will (if fewer than five) never have an opportunity of doing so because they cannot effectively demand a poll. If, in the example given at page 586, above, the four holders with one share each had voted in favour and the holder of 100 shares had voted against, the special resolution would have been validly passed on a show of hands and the unfortunate dissentient would have had no right (unless the articles were more liberal than the Act) to demand a poll so as to reverse this decision. If a member wants to be absolutely safe, he should split his holdings among five nominees.[63] It is, however, the

---

[59] s.378(4) provides, in the case of special and extraordinary resolutions, that the chairman's declaration shall be conclusive. Table A 1985, art. 47, provides generally that the chairman's decision when recorded in the minutes shall be conclusive.

[60] It is a question of construction of the relevant article whether a poll can be demanded before there has been a vote on a show of hands: *Carruth v. I.C.I.* [1937] A.C. 707, H.L. at 754–755; *Holmes v. Keyes* [1959] Ch. 199, C.A.

[61] Table A 1985, art. 46.

[62] s.373. In the absence of anything in the regulations any member may demand a poll (*R. v. Wimbledon Local Board* (1882) 8 Q.B.D. 459, C.A.), and, of course, the articles may be more generous than s.373: see Table A 1985, art. 46 which entitles two members, rather than the statutory five, to demand a poll.

[63] It will be no use appointing five different proxies, for these will all represent one member and only be counted as one for the purpose of demanding a poll. Indeed, in the particular example quoted, the only result would be that the member would have disfranchised himself completely since his vote would not be counted at all on the show of hands!

duty of the chairman to exercise his right to demand a poll so that effect is given to the real sense of the meeting, and, if he realised what the position was, it seems that he would be legally bound to direct a poll to be taken.[64]

If a poll is demanded the company's articles may provide how it shall be taken; if they do not the chairman will have to decide. Usually the members and proxies present will sign lists or slips indicating whether they vote for or against and the number of votes that they are polling.[65] In the case of a small private company this should present no problem; the poll can be taken, the result declared and the meeting then proceed to the next item on the agenda. But in the case of a large public company this will probably not be practical. Hence the detailed regulations of this matter in Table A.[66]

It will be noted (a) that the need to check proxy forms and votes cast makes it impossible to have a secret ballot[67] and (b) that, unless the articles specifically provide for it,[68] voting by postal ballot is not permissible.[69] The latter may be thought strange since clearly such a referendum would be a better way of obtaining the views of the members. But the fiction is preserved that the result is determined after oral discussion at a meeting, although everybody knows that in the case of public companies the result is normally determined by proxies lodged before the meeting, is held.[70]

Adjournments

One situation in which it may be necessary to adjourn is when the meeting is inquorate; this has been dealt with above[71] and presents few problems. What may present many is the converse case where those attending the meeting are too many rather then too few, and the meeting becomes chaotic. It is this situation that has given rise to litigation in recent years. Before dealing with the reported cases, of

---

[64] *Second Consolidated Trust v. Ceylon Amalgamated Estates* [1943] 2 All E.R. 567. In this case the chairman held proxies (without which there would have been no quorum) which if voted would have defeated the resolutions passed on a show of hands.

[65] They are not bound to exercise all their votes nor need they vote them all in the same way: s.374. This is designed to enable trustees or nominees to give effect to the directions of the beneficial owners.

[66] See Table A 1985, arts. 48–53. Future references to Table A are to that of 1985 unless otherwise stated.

[67] But the identity of the voters will not be known by the directors if independent scrutineers are appointed.

[68] Which is unusual except in the case of clubs or other associations formed as companies limited by guarantee.

[69] *McMillan v. Le Roi Mining Co.* [1906] 1 Ch. 338.

[70] As was well said in an American case (*Berendt v. Bethlehem Steel Corp.* (1931) 154 A. 321 at 322), statements made to a meeting of proxy holders fall "upon ears not allowed to hear and minds not permitted to judge: upon automatons whose principals are uninformed of their own injury".

[71] At p. 583.

which the latest is *Byng v. London Life Association Ltd*[72] (where the earlier decisions were reviewed by the Court of Appeal), it should be emphasised that an adjournment of a meeting is to be distinguished from an abandonment of it.[73] In the latter case the meeting ends. If a new meeting is convened, new business, as well as any unfinished at the abandoned meeting, may be undertaken so long as proper notice is given of both. In contrast, if a meeting is adjourned, the adjourned meeting can undertake only the business of the original meeting[74] or such of it not been completed at that meeting. Indeed, it was thought necessary specifically to provide by what is now section 381 of the Act that where a resolution is passed at an adjourned meeting it shall "for all purposes be treated as having been passed on the date on which it was in fact passed and is not to be deemed to be passed on any earlier date".[75]

On the means whereby a meeting may be adjourned, article 45 of Table A 1985, provides that:

"The chairman may, with the consent of a meeting at which a quorum is present[76] (and shall if so directed by the meeting) adjourn the meeting from time to time and from place to place, but no business shall be transacted at an adjourned meeting other than business which might properly have be transacted at the meeting. When a meeting is adjourned for 14 days or more, at least seven clear days notice shall be given specifying the time and place of the adjourned meeting and the general nature of the business to be transacted. Otherwise it shall not be necessary to give any such notice."

As there was a similar article in Tables A 1929 and 1948 it can safely be assumed that it, or something to the same effect, is likely to be found in the articles of nearly all existing companies. The effect of the first part of the article is that normally it rests with the members present in person or by proxy at the meeting to decide whether the meeting shall be adjourned. The chairman can suggest that the meeting shall be adjourned and, if the members consent (by a show of hands or on a poll if validly demanded), the meeting will then stand adjourned. Alternatively the members can resolve on a adjournment on the motion of a member and, if this is passed, again the meeting will stand

---

[72] [1990] Ch. 170, C.A.

[73] One of the criticisms of the chairman in *Byng's* case was that he had not given sufficient consideration to the possibility of abandoning rather than adjourning.

[74] See Table A, art. 45, below. But a meeting can be adjourned despite the fact that it was not a meeting at which any substantive resolution could be passed: see *Byng's* case, above. This must be right for otherwise an inquorate meeting could not be adjourned, as all Tables A have provided that they can.

[75] Were it otherwise, the company might unavoidably contravene the obligation to deliver to the Register a copy of the resolution within 15 days of its passage, as required, in the case of a considerable number of resolutions, under s.380.

[76] On the position where a quorum is not present, see p. 583, above.

adjourned, since the meeting will then have "directed" the chairman to adjourn it. Basically this gives effect to the common law rule under which the chairman has no general right to adjourn a meeting if there are no circumstances preventing its effective continuance.[77] However, the primary duty of the chairman is to ensure, so far as possible, that the meeting conducts its business in an orderly manner and if, say, tempers have become heated and the proceedings are in danger of becoming unruly, the chairman has a common law power and duty to adjourn the meeting to allow tempers to cool. But the power and duty must be exercised bona fide for the purpose of facilitating the meeting and not as a ploy to prevent or delay the taking of a decision to which the chairman objects.[78]

Is, then, the effect of an article corresponding to Table A 1985, article 45, to exclude this common law power to adjourn, on the basis that *inclusio unius, exclusio alterius*? In *Byng*'s case, the Court of Appeal held that it is not. But, reversing the decision at first instance, the court held, nevertheless, that the chairman's adjournment was an invalid exercise of the chairman's common law powers. There, the meeting had been convened for the morning in one part of London, but, the booked premises proving totally inadequate for the number of members wishing to attend, it was adjourned by the chairman for a larger venue in another part of London in the afternoon. Although the chairman's decision was taken in good faith, it was not a reasonable one because he had not taken into account the fact that the main business of the meeting—to approve or not approve a proposed merger— could be taken at any time within the following five months, and so it would have been possible to have adjourned for a longer period or even to have abandoned the meeting and started again, which would probably have enabled those many members who had attended the morning meeting but could not attend the afternoon meeting to be present when the substantive business was finally discussed. In response to this decision some companies have amended their articles so as to give the chairman a wider express power of adjournment without the consent of the meeting than the common law envisages.

It will be noted that, under the final part of Table A article 45, no notice has to be given if a meeting is adjourned for less than 14 days. Clearly if the adjournment is a temporary one and the meeting is resumed at the same place on the same day, this is fair enough; but otherwise it seems unfair to members who may, perhaps through no fault of their own, have found themselves unable to attend the meeting as they had intended. As a result they may not know that it has been

---

[77] *National Dwellings Society v. Sykes* [1897] 3 Ch. 159; *John v. Rees* [1970] Ch. 345 (which concerned, not a company meeting, but one of a Divisional Labour Party); *Byng v. London Life Assoc. Ltd*, above. n. 72.

[78] If the chairman purports to adjourn for such a reason, the meeting may elect another chairman and continue: *ibid*.

adjourned and may be prevented from exercising their rights to attend the adjourned meeting. If the meeting has attracted the interest of the media they may find out in time. But not necessarily; for example, if in *Byng*'s case, a member, delayed in transit to the meeting, had not reached the Barbican until after 1 p.m. and had found the cinema deserted (the officers of the company then being on their way to the Café Royal), he would have assumed that the meeting had been concluded.

Class meetings

In addition to general meetings it may be necessary to convene separate meetings of classes of members or debenture-holders (for example, to consider variation of rights) or of creditors (for example, in connection with a reconstruction or in a winding up). Here again, the rules to be observed will depend on the company's articles construed in the light of the general law relating to meetings. Statute law is generally silent, but sections 372 (proxies), 374 (voting on a poll), 375 (representation of corporations) and 381 (resolutions passed at an adjourned meeting) are expressed to cover also meetings of any class of members (but not debenture-holders) and section 125, on variation of class rights of shareholders,[79] contains specific provisions regarding class meetings for that purpose. The main point to note is that whereas the prescribed quorums for general meetings are minimal, those for class meetings are usually substantial in respect of the proportion of capital which has to be represented.[80] In practice, very similar arrangements are incorporated in debenture trust deeds to regulate the conduct of meetings of debenture-holders.

At class meetings all members other than those of the class ought to be excluded, but if for convenience a joint meeting is held of the company and all separate classes, followed by separate polls, the court will not interfere if no objection has been taken by anyone present.[81]

Minutes of meetings

Section 382 requires every company to cause minutes of all proceedings of general meetings[82] to be entered in books kept for that purpose.[83] Such minutes, if purporting to be signed by the chairman

---

[79] Dealt with in Chapter 26.
[80] Under s.125, two persons holding or representing by proxy at least one-third in nominal value of the issued shares of the class: s.125(6)(a). But at an adjourned meeting one person holding shares of the class or his proxy suffices: *ibid*. This makes sense only if the adjournment is because there was no quorum at the original meeting.
[81] *Carruth v. I.C.I* [1937] A.C. 707, H.L.
[82] And of directors' meetings.
[83] s.382(1).

of the meeting or of the next succeeding meeting, are evidence of the proceedings[84] and, until the contrary is proved, the meeting is deemed to be duly convened and held.[85] Section 382A now further provides that when a written resolution is agreed to in accordance with section 381A, a record of it shall be entered in the minute book in the same way as minutes of proceedings of a general meeting[86] and that any such record, if purporting to be signed by a director or the secretary of the company, shall be evidence of the proceedings in agreeing to the resolution which, until the contrary is proved, shall be deemed to have complied with the requirements of the Act.[87]

The minute-books of meetings must be kept at the company's registered office and be open to inspection there by any member without charge. A member is also entitled to obtain a copy of such minutes on payment of a prescribed charge.[88] However, the minute-books are not open to the public; they form part of the company's internal administration. Nevertheless, it is to be noted that although minute-books are not open to the public, an ever-increasing number of resolutions, whether or not recorded in the minute-books, become available to the public because, under section 380, copies of them have to be sent to the Registrar within 15 days. This applies not only to resolutions passed at general meetings but to agreements of all the members which would otherwise have to be passed by a special, extraordinary or elective resolution[89] and not only to those resolutions but also to some ordinary resolutions and directors' resolutions.[90] Moreover (and this tends to get overlooked), a copy of any such resolution or agreement for the time being in force must be embodied in or annexed to every copy of the articles issued thereafter.[91]

Nominee shareholders

At various points in this Chapter we have referred to difficulties which may face a shareholder which is a nominee (usually a nominee company) in making use of the shareholders' rights in respect of

---

[84] s.382(2). But not conclusive, as they are when the chairman has declared that a special or extraordinary resolution has been passed or defeated on a show of hands: s.378(4) above, p. 590, n. 59. Table A, art. 47 extends that to such a declaration on any type of resolution so long as it is minuted. In *Kerr v. Mottram Ltd* [1940] Ch. 657, Simonds J. held that an article purporting to extend conclusiveness to signed minutes of any matter was effective in the absence of fraud. But his reasoning (that because the forerunner of s.374(4) had that effect so must an article which went considerably further) is unconvincing.
[85] s.382(4).
[86] s.382A(1)
[87] s.382A(2)
[88] s.383 as amended.
[89] s.380(4) (bb), (c), (d).
[90] s.380(4)(e)–(k).
[91] s.380(2).

meetings. The fundamental problem is, of course, that the statute and the articles confer rights upon the registered shareholder (*i.e.* the nominee) and not upon the person who has the beneficial interest in the shares.[92] However, in the case of a bare nominee, it would seem that the corporate governance rights of the shareholder should be exercised as the beneficial owner, not as the nominee, thinks best, and yet the statute does nothing to bring this about. This may be thought not to matter. In the case of institutional investors this result is achieved in practice. Although the right to vote is usually delegated by the institution to the fund manager and the shares are registered in a nominee company of the fund manager, the relationship between the institution and the manager is such that the nominee's rights can readily be exercised in accordance with the beneficial owner's wishes, if the latter so desires. On the other hand, private investors in the past have generally not used nominees.

However, pressures are now building upon private investors to hold their shares through nominees, partly because of the introduction of CREST.[93] By taking this step, however, the investor loses the right automatically to receive the company's annual report and accounts (though a set can always be obtained from the Registrar or, more likely, the company) and the right to attend, speak and vote at meetings of the company. In one situation, that relating to shares (as opposed to units in a unit trust) held under a Personal Equity Plan, where the plan manager or its nominee must be the registered holder of the shares, the manager is obliged, for a fee, to make available to investors who wish it copies of the annual report and accounts and to arrange for them to attend and vote at shareholders' meetings (albeit as a proxy rather than as a member in his or her own right).[94] The Government is currently consulting on the feasibility of extending this right generally to private investors whose shares are held by custodians in nominee accounts, by placing such an obligation either on the company or on the custodian.[95]

CONCLUSION

General meetings are intended to be the means whereby the members exercise control over the management. In the case of small private companies, where there is generally no separation of "ownership" and "control", formal general meetings rarely perform a useful purpose and the reforms instituted by the 1989 Act, enabling such com-

[92] *cf.* s.360, discussed at p. 333, above.
[93] See pp. 339–340, above.
[94] Personal Equity Plan Regulations 1989 (S.I. 1989 No. 469), reg. 4.
[95] DTI and H.M. Treasury, *Private Shareholders: Corporate Governance Rights*, November 1996.

panies, if all the members agree, to pass any needed resolution by agreeing to them in writing and to dispense even with AGMs, are eminently sensible. But, if and when there ceases to be identity between membership and directorship, their general meetings are more likely than in the case of large public companies to prove an effective way of enabling the majority of the members to exercise control over the directors and, in the last resort, to remove and replace them. Only if the directors hold a majority of the votes in general meeting will they be able to ignore the wishes of the members.

In contrast, in relation to public listed companies, general meetings have proved a singularly ineffective way of making directors answerable to the general body of members who have no wish to play any role in the administration of the company and who, in most cases, will not attend general meetings unless their investment has proved so disappointing that they relish the opportunity of attending a meeting to tell the company's management what they think of it. Even then, most of them will decide instead to cut their losses by selling their shares if that is still possible. It is only institutional shareholders that the directors have to fear; if they get together the board can probably be ousted. Subject to that and to the risk of an unwelcome takeover bid, the boards of widely held public companies are self-perpetuating oligarchies which control the general meeting rather than it controlling them.

This, however, does not mean that the need to hold general meetings fulfils no useful purpose. Directors of public companies do not relish the prospect of facing embarrassing questions[96] from shareholders at the AGM (however ill-attended it may be) and that may operate as a mild deterrent against directorial excesses. But as a means of making the board answerable to an informed membership or of ensuring that members have an effective veto on major corporate action it is wholly ineffective—though the legislature seems to assume the contrary by adding ever more circumstances where the consent of a general meeting is required.

---

[96] *e.g.* "if as the accounts show, the company's profits have halved why have the directors' emoluments been increased far beyond the rate of inflation?"

CHAPTER 22

DIRECTORS' DUTIES

THE preceding Chapter has dealt with the means whereby investors can exercise such control as they have over the company by attending and voting at meetings. But, as we saw in an earlier Chapter,[1] the general meeting is merely one of the company's two primary organs and most of the company's powers are not vested in it but in the board of directors. And, as we also saw, the directors exercise these powers either directly or through managers appointed by them. It is therefore of vital importance to see what duties are owed by directors and managers in the exercise of their powers. It is to this that we now turn.

It is often stated that directors are trustees and that the nature of their duties can be explained on this basis. It is easy to see how this idea arose. Prior to 1844 most joint stock companies were unincorporated and depended for their validity on a deed of settlement vesting the property of the company in trustees.[2] Often the directors were themselves the trustees and even when a distinction was drawn between the passive trustees and the managing board of directors, the latter would quite clearly be regarded as trustees in the eyes of a court of equity in so far as they dealt with the trust property.

With directors of incorporated companies the description "trustees" was less apposite but it was not unnatural that the courts should extend it to them by analogy. For one thing, the duties of the directors should obviously be the same whether the company was incorporated or not; for another, courts of equity tend to apply the label "trustee" to anyone in a fiduciary position. Nevertheless, to describe directors as trustees seems today to be neither strictly correct nor invariably helpful.[3] In truth, directors are agents of the company rather than trustees of it or its property. But as agents they stand in a fiduciary relationship to their principal, the company. The duties of good faith which this fiduciary relationship imposes are virtually identical with those imposed on trustees, and to this extent the description "trustee" still has validity. It is when we turn to the duties of care and skill that the trustee analogy breaks down. The duty of the trustees of a will or settlement is to be cautious and to avoid risks to the trust fund. The managers of a business concern must, perforce, take risks in an attempt to earn profits for the company and its members. Hence the duties of directors can conveniently be discussed under two heads: (1) fiduciary

---

[1] Chap. 9.
[2] Chaps. 2 and 3.
[3] *Re City Equitable Fire Insurance Co.* [1925] Ch. 407, *per* Romer J. at 426.

duties of loyalty and good faith (analogous to the duties of trustees *stricto sensu*), and (2) duties of care and skill (differing fundamentally from the duties of normal trustees).

FIDUCIARY DUTIES

General equitable principle

The basic principle is the same as that applying to any other fiduciary and discussed in works on Trusts and Agency. Such duties have, indeed, already been dealt with briefly in connection with another type of fiduciary peculiar to company law, the promoter.[4] But the relevant rules have received particular elaboration in relation to directors and the practical importance of the subject makes it desirable to discuss it here in greater detail.[5]

In the first place it should be noted that whereas the authority of the directors to bind the company as its agents normally depends on their acting collectively as a board,[6] their duties of good faith are owed by each director individually. One of several directors will not as such be an agent of the company with power to saddle it with responsibility for his acts, but he will be a fiduciary of it. To this extent, directors again resemble trustees who must normally act jointly but each of whom severally owes duties of good faith towards the beneficiaries.

Secondly, the fiduciary duties are owed to the company and to the company alone. The difficulties which may be caused by treating a metaphysical entity as the beneficiary, in whose interests the directors must act, are referred to later.[7] Here it suffices to emphasise that, in general, the directors owe no duties to the individual members as such, or, *a fortiori*, to a person who has not yet become a member—such as a potential purchaser of shares in it. This principle is regarded as firmly established by the much-criticised decision in *Percival v. Wright*,[8] where directors purchased shares from their members without revealing that negotiations were in progress for a sale of the undertaking at a favourable price.[9] This, however, does not mean that directors can never stand in a fiduciary relationship to the members; they well

---

[4] Chap. 7, above.

[5] An attempt in the 1978 Companies Bill to codify directors' duties proved abortive, to the regret of those who believe that a comprehensive statutory restatement of those duties would make it more likely that they are observed; a belief strengthened by the fact that the main reason for giving up the attempt was the impossibility of obtaining agreement of the legal profession on precisely what the duties are.

[6] Chaps. 9 & 10, above.

[7] Below, pp. 602–605.

[8] [1902] 2 Ch. 421. This applies even if all the shares are owned by a holding company with which the directors have service contracts: *Bell v. Lever Bros.* [1932] A.C. 161, H.L.

[9] The actual decision may be defensible because the shareholders had approached the directors and asked them to buy their shares.

may if they are authorised by the latter to negotiate on their behalf with, for example, a potential takeover bidder.[10] And something far less than the establishment of an agency relationship may suffice, particularly, as an important New Zealand decision illustrates,[11] in the case of a family company, "depending upon all the surrounding circumstances and the nature of the responsibility which in a real and practical sense the director has assumed towards the shareholder".[12] The courts are most likely to recognise a fiduciary duty owed by directors to individual shareholders in the context of advice given by the directors to the members as to whether they should sell their shares to a bidder, though such fiduciary duties are likely to be narrower than those owed to the company.[13]

The *Percival v. Wright* rule was severely criticised by the Cohen Committee,[14] and forthrightly rejected by the Jenkins Committee in one of its bolder moods.[15] After much vacillation, the 1980 Act[16] provided criminal sanctions against directors (and other "insiders") who make use of price-sensitive information in dealings in their companies' securities but this in no way modified the general principle that it is to the company, and not to its members individually,[17] or to anyone else, that the directors stand in a fiduciary relationship. It seems that directors of a holding company do not even owe duties to its subsidiary, at any rate when that has an independent board of directors.[18]

Thirdly, these duties, except in so far as they depend on statutory provisions expressly limited to directors, are not so restricted but apply equally to any officers of the company who are authorised to act on its behalf[19] and in particular to those acting in a manager-

---

[10] *Briess v. Woolley* [1954] A.C. 333, H.L. See also *Allen v. Hyatt* (1914) 30 T.L.R. 444, P.C.

[11] *Coleman v. Myers* [1977] 2 N.Z.L.R. 225, N.Z.C.A. In the Supreme Court (*ibid.*) Mahon J. had held that *Percival v. Wright* was wrongly decided but the C.A. distinguished it.

[12] *Per* Woodhouse J. at 324. And see his elaboration at 324–325 and *per* Cooke J. at 330. Their views were adopted by Browne-Wilkinson V.-C. in *Re Chez Nico (Restaurants) Ltd* [1991] BCC 736 at 750.

[13] *Re A Company* [1986] BCLC 382: if directors chose to give advice, they must ensure it was "given with a view to enabling the shareholders . . . to sell, if they so wish, at the best price" (*per* Hoffmann J.).

[14] Cmd. 6659, paras. 86 and 87.

[15] Cmnd. 1749, paras. 89 and 99(b)

[16] See now the Criminal Justice Act 1993, above, Chap. 17.

[17] Even to a member who is the controlling shareholder such as the holding company: *Pergamon Press Ltd v. Maxwell* [1970] 1 W.L.R. 1167. And if the subsidiary's directors merely act in the interests of the holding company ignoring those of the minority shareholders, those shareholders may have a remedy under s.459 (see Chap. 27): *Scottish Co-operative Wholesale Society v. Meyer* [1959] A.C. 324, H.L.

[18] *Lindgren v. L. & P. Estates Ltd* [1968] Ch. 572, C.A. But *cf.* the dicta of Lords Simonds and Keith in *Scottish Co-operative Wholesale Society v. Meyer*, at 343 and 362.

[19] *i.e.* to those who are the company's agents, and who therefore stand in fiduciary capacity towards it, as opposed to those who are merely its employees, who do work for it but do not act on its behalf. That the latter's duties of good faith are somewhat less extensive seems clearly established: *Bell v. Lever Bros.* [1932] A.C. 161, H.L. But employees, too, owe duties of fidelity which in most respects amount to much the same: *cf. Reading v. Att.-Gen.* [1951] A.C. 507, H.L; *Sybron Corporation v. Rochem Ltd* [1984] Ch. 112, C.A. These, however,

ial capacity.[20] Fourthly, the duties attach from the date when the director's appointment takes effect[21] but do not necessarily cease when his appointment ends; for example, he may be restrained from using to the prejudice of the company confidential information acquired when he was a director.[22]

In applying the general equitable principle to company directors four separate rules have emerged. These are: (1) that directors must act in good faith in what they believe to be the best interests of the company; (2) that they must not exercise the powers conferred upon them for purposes different from those for which they were conferred; (3) that they must not fetter their discretion as to how they shall act; and (4) that, without the informed consent of the company, they must not place themselves in a position in which their personal interests or duties to other persons are liable to conflict with their duties to the company.

1. *Acting in good faith*

In most cases compliance with the rule that directors must act honestly and in good faith is tested on common-sense principles, the court asking itself whether it is proved that the directors have not done what they honestly believed to be right, and normally accepting that they have unless satisfied that they have not behaved as honest men of business might be expected to act. Directors are required to act "bona fide in what they consider—not what a court may consider—is in the interests of the company . . .".[23] On the face of it, this duty is simply to display subjective good faith. But, notwithstanding that it is for the directors and not the court to consider what is in the interests of the company, they may breach that duty, notwithstanding that they have not acted with conscious dishonesty where they have failed to direct their minds to the question whether a transaction was in fact in the interests of the company. A good illustration of this is afforded by *Re W. & M. Roith Ltd.*[24] There the controlling shareholder and director

---

depend upon the normal law of the contract of employment and present no peculiarities in the company law field.

[20] This sentence, in an earlier edition, was approved by the Canadian Supreme Court in *Canadian Aero Service v. O'Malley* (1973) 40 D.L.R. (3d) 371 at 381.

[21] In *Lindgren v. L. & P. Estates Ltd*, above n. 18, the C.A. rejected an argument that a "director-elect" is in a fiduciary relationship to the company.

[22] See *Industrial Development Consultants Ltd v. Cooley* [1972] 1 W.L.R. 443; *Canadian Aero Services Ltd v. O'Malley*, above n. 20; *Island Export Finance Ltd v. Umunna* [1986] BCLC 460 (where it was pointed out that otherwise "a director, provided he does nothing contrary to his employers' interests while employed, may with impunity conceive the idea of resigning so that he may exploit some opportunity of the employers and, having resigned, proceed to exploit it for himself ").

[23] *Per* Lord Greene M.R. in *Re Smith & Fawcett Ltd* [1942] Ch. 304 C.A., at 306.

[24] [1967] 1 W.L.R. 432. But *cf. Charterbridge Corp. v. Lloyds Bank* [1970] Ch. 62, where the directors of a company forming part of a group had considered the benefit of the group as a whole without giving separate consideration to that of the company alone. It was held that "the proper test . . . in the absence of actual separate consideration must be whether an intelli-

wished to make provision for his widow. On advice he entered into a service agreement with the company whereby on his death she was to be entitled to a pension for life. On being satisfied that no thought had been given to the question whether the arrangement was for the benefit of the company and that, indeed, the sole object was to make provision for the widow, the court held that the transaction was not binding on the company.[25]

But what exactly is meant by saying that they must act in the interests of the company? Despite the separate personality of the company it is clear that directors are not expected to act on the basis of what is for the economic advantage of the corporate entity, disregarding the interests of the members.[26] They are, for example, clearly entitled to recommend the payment of dividends to the members and are not expected to deny them a return on their money by ploughing back all the profits so as to increase the size and wealth of the company. If, as will normally be the case, the directors themselves are shareholders, they are entitled to have some regard to their own interests as shareholders and not to think only of the others. As it was happily put in an Australian case, they are "not required by the law to live in an unreal region of detached altruism and to act in a vague mood of ideal abstraction from obvious facts which must be present to the mind of any honest and intelligent man when he exercises his powers as a director".[27]

Until the 1980 Act it seemed that the only interests to which the directors were entitled to have regard were the interests of the members. As it had become a cliché, repeated in the chairman's speech at almost every AGM of a public company, that "this company recognises that it has duties to its members, employees, consumers of its products and to the nation", this was somewhat anachronistic and was modified, but only in relation to employees, under what are now sections 309 and 719 of the Act and section 187 of the Insolvency Act 1986. The two latter sections have been dealt with sufficiently in Chapter 10.[28] What is relevant in the present context is section 309.

---

gent and honest man in the position of a director of the company concerned could ... have reasonably believed that the transactions were for the benefit of the company": at 74.

[25] Following *Re Lee, Behrens & Co. Ltd* [1932] 2 Ch. 46. See also *Alexander v. Automatic Telephone Co.* [1900] 2 Ch. 56, C.A.; but cf. *Lindgren v. L. & P. Estates Ltd* [1968] Ch. 572, C.A., where it was held that there had been no failure to consider the commercial merits.

[26] In connection with members voting in general meetings, Evershed M.R. in *Greenhalgh v. Arderne Cinemas* [1951] Ch. 286, C.A., said, at 291, "the phrase ιthe company as a whole' does not (at any rate in such a case as the present) mean the company as a commercial entity as distinct from the corporators". This seems equally true in the present context.

[27] *Mills v. Mills* (1938) 60 C.L.R. 150, Aust. H.C., *per* Latham C.J. at 164; cf. Dixon J. at 185–186.

[28] At pp. 219–220, above. They empower a company to make gratuitous provision for employees on the cessation of a company's business even though that "is not in the best interests of the company."

Under that, the matters to which directors[29] are to have regard in the performance of their functions "include the interests of the company's employees in general, as well as the interests of its members".[30] However, subsection (2) provides that: "Accordingly the duty imposed by this section on the directors is owed by them to the company (and the company alone) and is enforceable in the same way as any other fiduciary duty owed to a company by its directors" which means that the employees as such have no means of enforcing it. Indeed, it may be that one effect of section 309 is to dilute directors' accountability to shareholders rather than to strengthen their accountability to employees.[31]

This grudging recognition that the interests of the company include those of its workforce has been supplemented by both judicial dicta and legislative provision which accept that, when the company is insolvent or is nearing insolvency, the interests of the shareholders should be supplemented, even replaced, by those of the creditors. The clearest recognition of this argument in the English courts is to be found in *West Mercia Safetywear Ltd v. Dodd*,[32] where the rationale offered for this development was that in insolvency the creditors "become prospectively entitled, through the mechanism of liquidation, to displace the power of the directors and the shareholders to deal with the company's assets".[33] This suggests that the directors' duties should be seen as being owed to those who have the ultimate financial interest in the company: the shareholders when the company is a going concern and the creditors once the company's capital has been lost. Two points should be noted about this development. First, the rationale offered gives no warrant for regarding the directors as owing duties to the creditors individually. The duty is owed to the creditors as a group through the mechanism of their interests being identified as constituting the company's interests as insolvency approaches.[34] Secondly, the significance of the doctrine is that it opens up the possibility of challenges at common law to dispositions by management when insolvency is in prospect (even when the dispositions have been ratified by the shareholders) which reduce the pool of assets available to satisfy the creditors. However, there are a number of statutory provi-

---

[29] Including shadow directors: s.309(3).

[30] s.309(1).

[31] *cf. Re Saul D. Harrison & Sons plc* [1995] 1 BCLC 14, C.A, where s.309 was prayed in aid to undermine the shareholder petitioning under s.459 (at 25).

[32] [1988] BCLC 250, C.A. *cf. Re Welfab Engineers Ltd* [1990] BCLC 833: when insolvency threatens, the directors may not take a course of action which will clearly leave the creditors in a worse position, but they are not bound to give creditors' interests absolute priority.

[33] This is the rationale contained in the dictum of Street C.J. in *Kinsela v. Russell Kinsela Pty Ltd (in liq.)* (1986) 4 NSWLR 222, which was quoted with approval in the English case.

[34] In this respect the dictum of Lord Templeman in *Winkworth v. Edward Baron Development Co. Ltd* [1986] 1 W.L.R. 1512 at 1517 goes too far and seems not to have been followed by subsequent courts.

sions which also enable such a challenge to be mounted,[35] to which have recently been added the provisions on wrongful trading by directors,[36] whose central purpose is to protect creditors from managerial self-interest or worse in situations of incipient insolvency. Perhaps because of the existence of these statutory provisions, the common law developments have not proceeded very rapidly.

However, when considering the question of whose interests it is legitimate for the directors of a company to pursue, it is also crucial to distinguish between ends and means. Even if, in a going concern, the company's interests are those of the shareholders (with some regard having to be paid to the employees), it will do the shareholders no good if the company has dissatisfied customers, faces an antagonistic central or local government and has angry pressure groups disrupting its annual general meetings. In other words, much action which on the face of it promotes the interests of non-shareholder groups can easily be justified by management as necessary for the furthering of the interests of the shareholders. The point was made a long time ago, albeit in the context of *ultra vires*, by Bowen L.J., who said: "The law does not say that there are to be no cakes and ale, but there are to be no cakes and ale except such as are required for the benefit of the company."[37] This point is perhaps at the basis of the remarks made by company chairmen, mentioned above.

Furthermore, it seems that the directors are not bound to any particular time-frame within which to promote the shareholders' interests; on the contrary, they must take into account both the long- and the short-term interests of the shareholders and strike a balance between them.[38] And, as we have noted, the duty on the directors is a subjective one. In short, it is up to the directors, not the court, to identify the interests of the shareholders; it is up to the directors, not the court, to identify the period over which the goal of promoting the shareholders' interests can most appropriately be achieved; and it is up to the directors to decide how far the promotion of the shareholders' interests

---

[35] For example, the rules relating to preferences or transactions at an undervalue (I.A. 1986, ss. 238–241). For these reasons Sealy (Note, [1988] C.L.J. 175) has doubted the need for the common law development, but *cf.* Grantham "The Judicial Extension of Directors' Duties to Creditors" [1991] J.B.L. 1.

[36] Discussed above at pp. 153–155 and below at pp. 642–643. Also of great practical significance are the revised provisions on disqualification of directors on grounds of unfitness: below, Chap. 24.

[37] *Hutton v. West Cork Ry.* (1883) 23 Ch.D. at 673. For this reason directors can normally justify modest, business-related political or charitable donations on the part of their companies, though the broader public policy issues arising out of such donations are recognised in the requirement of Schedule 7 that such donations be disclosed in the directors' report: see above, p. 518.

[38] See Counsel's Opinion quoted in the Report by Mr Milner Holland of an investigation under s.165(b) of the Companies Act 1948 into the affairs of the Savoy Hotel Ltd and the Berkeley Hotel Company Ltd, Board of Trade, 1954. This somewhat obscure source has long been regarded as the *locus classicus* on this point.

requires corporate largess to be expended upon others (including, of course, themselves).[39] In these circumstances, it is hardly surprising that it is in fact very difficult to show that the directors have broken their duty of good faith, except in egregious cases or cases where the directors, obligingly, have left a clear record of the thought processes leading up to the challenged decision.[40]

2. *Proper purpose*

The weakness of the "good faith" test places greater weight on the remaining limbs of directors' fiduciary duties, which have an objective basis. In terms of directors' powers, usually conferred upon them by the articles of association, one can distinguish between the directors' failure to follow the express terms of the articles and their exercising a power, which has been conferred by the articles, for an improper purpose. The former duty, which may not be properly categorised a breach of fiduciary duty,[41] is of long standing and is now recognised by sections 35(3) and 35A(5) in relation respectively to the memorandum and articles of association.[42]

The greater controversy has surrounded the notion of directors exercising powers for an improper purpose. Often the improper purpose

---

[39] The "no conflict of duty and interest" rule, discussed below, does something, though it is debatable how much, to control the expenditure of corporate resources on the directors themselves.

[40] That the directors now have to take into account the interests of the employees only makes proof of breach of duty even more difficult. See n. 31, above. The classic case where the directors did all too clearly reveal their reasoning is *Dodge v. Ford Motor Co.* 170 N.W. 668 (1919). Henry Ford openly took the view that the shareholders had been more than amply rewarded on their investment in the company and so proposed to declare no further special dividends but only the regular dividends (of some 60 per cent per annum!) in order to reduce the price of the cars, to expand production and "to employ still more men, to spread the benefits of this industrial system to the greatest possible number, to help them build up their lives and their homes" (at 683). This was held to be "an arbitrary refusal to distribute funds that ought to have been distributed to the stockholders as dividends" (at 685). Would s.309 mean a different decision would be reached in the U.K.?

[41] Note, however, that in *Bishopsgate Investment Management Ltd (in liq.) v. Maxwell (No. 2)* [1993] BCLC 814 at 831–833 Chadwick J. regarded the director's failure to ensure that stock transfers were carried out in accordance with the procedures set out in the company's articles as a breach of the director's fiduciary duties and held him liable to indemnify the company in respect of the losses caused to it by the unauthorised transfers, though it is not entirely clear whether the simple failure to follow the procedures set out in the articles constituted the breach or whether it was the director's failure to consider whether the transfers were in the best interests of the company. In the latter case, the decision becomes one on good faith. In the C.A. ([1994] 1 All E.R. 261) the breach seems to have been regarded as acting for improper purpose in the second sense identified in the text!

[42] s.35(3): "It remains the duty of the directors to observe any limitation on their powers flowing from the company's memorandum." s.35A(5): "Nor does [s.35A(1)] affect any liability incurred by the directors . . . by reason of the directors exceeding their powers." In *Hogg v. Cramphorn* [1967] Ch. 254 the directors purported to issue shares with ten votes attached per share, in a situation where the articles did not give the directors power to attach more than one vote per share. The court held that the attempt to attach more votes was simply ineffective, a decision which did not necessarily require a finding of breach of duty on the part of the directors.

will be to feather the directors' own nests or to preserve their own control, in which event it will be a breach of the duty, already considered, to act honestly for the benefit of the company as a whole. But it is clear that, notwithstanding that directors have acted honestly for what they believe to be the benefit of the company, they may nevertheless be liable if they have exercised their powers for a purpose different from that for which the powers were conferred upon them.[43]

The legal position was reviewed by the Privy Council in *Howard Smith Ltd v. Ampol Ltd*,[44] which considered the decisions on this subject of courts throughout the Commonwealth. It concerned, as have most of the cases, the power of directors to issue new shares.[45] It was argued that the only proper purpose for which such a power could be exercised was to raise new capital when the company needed it.[46] This was rejected as too narrow.[47] It might be a proper use of the power to issue shares to do so to a larger company in order to secure the financial stability of the company[48] or as part of an agreement relating to the exploitation of mineral rights owned by the company.[49] If so, the mere fact that the incidental (and desired) result was to deprive a shareholder of his voting majority or to defeat a takeover bid would not be sufficient to make the purpose improper.[50] But if, as in the instant case, the purpose was found to be simply and solely to dilute the majority voting power so as to enable an offer to proceed which the existing majority was in a position to block,[51] the exercise of the power would be improper despite the fact that the directors were not motivated by a desire to obtain some personal advantage. Moreover, when:

---

[43] See *Howard Smith Ltd v. Ampol Ltd* [1974] A.C. 821, P.C. at 834, citing *Fraser v. Whalley* (1864) 2 H.C.M. & M. 10; *Punt v. Symons & Co. Ltd* [1903] 2 Ch. 506; *Piercy v. S. Mills & Co. Ltd* [1920] 1 Ch. 77; *Ngurli v. McCann* (1954) 90 C.L.R. 425, Aust. H.C.; *Hogg v. Cramphorn Ltd* [1967] Ch. 254 at 267. The "improper purpose" test, as a requirement distinct from subjective good faith, has been rejected, however, in British Columbia: *Teck Corporation Ltd v. Millar* (1973) 33 D.L.R. (3d) 288.

[44] Above, n. 43. The judgment was delivered by Lord Wilberforce.

[45] This particular example should have become less common in the light of ss.80, 89–96 restricting the authority of directors to issue shares: see Chap. 13 at pp. 304–313, above. But the principle applies generally. For examples in relation to other powers, see, *Stanhope's Case* (1866) L.R. 1 Ch.App. 161, and *Manisty's Case* (1873) 17 S.J. 745 (forfeiture of shares); *Galloway v. Halle Concerts Society* [1915] 2 Ch. 233 (calls); *Bennett's Case* (1854) 5 De G.M. & G. 284 and *Australian Metropolitan Life Asscn. Co. Ltd v. Ure* (1923) 33 C.L.R. 199, Aust. H.C. (registration of transfers); *Hogg v. Cramphorn Ltd*, above (loans). See also *Lee Panavision Ltd v. Lee Lighting Ltd* [1992] BCLC 22, C.A.

[46] This has often been assumed and the directors had apparently been so advised and sought, unsuccessfully, to show that this was their purpose.

[47] At 835–836.

[48] *Harlowe's Nominees Pty Ltd v. Woodside Oil Co.* (1968) 121 C.L.R. 483, Aust. H.C.

[49] *Teck Corp. Ltd v. Miller* (1972) 33 D.L.R. (3d) 288, B.C. Sup.Ct.

[50] The test is what the substantial or primary purpose was: *Hirsche v. Sims* [1894] A.C. 654, P.C.; *Hindle v. John Cotton Ltd*, 1919 56 S.L.T. 625; *Mills v. Mills* (1938) 60 C.L.R. 150, Aust. H.C.

[51] Or, conversely, to block a bid: *Winthrop Investments Ltd v. Winns Ltd* [1975] 2 N.S.W.L.R. 666, N.S.W., C.A.

"a dispute arises whether directors . . . made a particular decision for one purpose or for another, or whether, there being more than one purpose, one or another purpose was the substantial or primary purpose, the court . . . is entitled to look at the situation objectively. . . . If it finds that a particular requirement, though real, was not urgent or critical at the relevant time, it may have reason to doubt, or discount, the assertions of individuals that they acted solely to deal with it, particularly when the action they took was unusual or even extreme."[52]

Perhaps the greatest puzzle in this area is to know by what criteria the courts judge whether a particular purpose is proper. This is generally stated to be a matter of construction of the articles of association.[53] Hence, the test is an objective one, even if it is applied to the directors' subjective motivations. In *Smith v. Ampol*, however, the clause giving the directors power to issue shares was drawn in the widest terms. The "purposes" limitation which the Privy Council read into the directors' powers derived not from a narrow analysis of that clause, but from placing the share issue power within the company's constitutional arrangements as a whole, as demonstrated by the terms of its memorandum and articles of association.[54] It follows that in a different type of company with a different constitution, in which, say, ownership and control were not separated, a broader view might be taken of the directors' powers under the articles. This seems to be the explanation of the decisions in *Re Smith and Fawcett Ltd*,[55] where the clause in question was widely construed so as to produce the effect equivalent to the partnership rule of strict control over the admission of new members. Similarly, in a company limited by guarantee and formed for the pur-

---

[52] At 832.

[53] *Re Smith and Fawcett Ltd* [1942] Ch. 304 at 306.

[54] "The constitution of a limited company normally provides for directors, with powers of management, and shareholders, with defined voting powers having to appoint the directors, and to take, in general meeting, by majority vote, decisions on matters not reserved for management. Just as it is established that directors, within their management powers, may take decisions against the wishes of majority shareholders, and indeed that the majority of shareholders cannot control them in the exercise of these powers while they remain in office . . . so it must be unconstitutional for directors to use their fiduciary powers over the shares in the company purely for the purpose of destroying an existing majority, or creating a new majority which did not previously exist. To do so is to interfere with that element in the company's constitution which is separate from and set against their powers" ([1974] A.C. 821, P.C. at 837). This principle was applied by the Court of Appeal in *Lee Panavision Ltd v. Lee Lighting Ltd* [1992] BCLC 22 where the incumbent directors entered into a long-term management agreement with a third party knowing that the shareholders were proposing to exercise their rights to appoint new directors.

[55] [1942] Ch. 304, C.A., where in a quasi-partnership company it was held that the directors, in exercising a power to refuse to register a transfer of shares, could "take account of any matter which they conceive to be in the interests of the company . . . such matters, for instance, as whether by their passing a particular transfer the transferee would obtain too great a weight in the councils of the company or might even perhaps obtain control". (at 308) In modern law the position would now have to be considered in the light of any "legitimate expectations" enforceable under s.459. See below, pp. 742–745.

pose of campaigning for the adoption of a particular policy in a certain area of social life, it was held that the directors' powers to expel members with contrary views should not be cut down on the grounds that the directors were seeking to control the composition of the general meeting.[56]

3. *Unfettered discretion*

We now turn to certain further objective standards which must be complied with notwithstanding the presence of good faith and proper motive. Before dealing, under the next head, with the more important of these, there is one which is often ignored but which appears to exist and to need mention. Since the directors' powers are held by them as fiduciaries of the company they cannot, without the consent of the company, fetter their future discretion. Thus, it seems clear as a general principle, despite the paucity of reported cases on the point,[57] that directors cannot validly contract (either with one another or with third parties) as to how they shall vote at future board meetings or otherwise conduct themselves in the future.[58] This is so even though there is no improper motive or purpose (thus infringing the previous rules) and no personal advantage reaped by the directors under the agreement (thus infringing the succeeding rule).

This, however, does not mean that if, in the bona fide exercise of their discretion, the directors have entered into a contract on behalf of the company, they cannot in that contract validly agree to take such further action at board meetings or otherwise as are necessary to carry out that contract. As was said in a judgment of the Australian High Court[59]:

> "There are many kinds of transaction in which the proper time for the exercise of the directors' discretion is the time of the negotiation of a contract and not the time at which the contract is to be performed. . . . If at the former time they are bona fide of opinion that it is in the best interests of the company that the transaction should be entered into and carried into effect, I can see no reason in law why they should not bind themselves to do whatever under the transaction is to be done by the board."[60]

Indeed, it may be that if there is a voting agreement between all the members and directors which provides that they shall vote together at

---

[56] *Gaiman v. National Association of Mental Health* [1971] Ch. 317.

[57] But see *Clark v. Workman* [1920] 1 Ir.R. 107 and an unreported decision of Morton J. in the *Arderne Cinema* litigation, below, Chap. 26, at pp. 712–714 and the Scottish decision in *Dawson International plc v. Coats Paton plc*, 1989 S.L.T. 655 (1st Div.) where it was accepted that an agreement by the directors would be subject to an implied term that it did not derogate from their duty to give advice to the shareholders which reflected the situation at the time the advice was given.

[58] Contrast the position of shareholders who may freely enter into such voting agreements: below, pp. 729–732.

[59] *Thorby v. Goldberg* (1964) 112 C.L.R. 597, Aus.H.C.

[60] *ibid., per* Kitto J. at 605–606.

all meetings, whether general meetings or directors' meetings, the parties to it will be bound *inter se*,[61] and only if there are other members or directors will they be able to complain.[62] The principle in *Thorby v. Goldberg* was recently applied by the Court of Appeal in *Cabra Estates plc v. Fulham Football Club*,[63] so as to uphold an elaborate contract which the directors had entered into on behalf of the company for the redevelopment of the football ground and under which, *inter alia*, the club was entitled to some £11 million and the directors had agreed to support any planning application the developers might make during the coming seven years. This is surely correct: if individuals may contract as to their future behaviour in these matters, it is desirable that companies should be able to do so too. The application of the "no fettering" rule would make companies unreliable contracting parties and perhaps deprive them of the opportunity to enter into long-term contracts which would be to their commercial benefit.

It may be wondered what is left of the "no fettering" rule after this decision and whether the decided cases cannot be rationalised as applications of the bona fides principle. However, the principle may still have a role to play where the directors purport to contract as to the advice they will give to the shareholders in the future on a matter which lies within the shareholders' power of decision[64] (in contrast to the situation where the conclusion of the substantive contract lies within the power of the directors). This qualification might be justified on the basis that shareholders are peculiarly dependent upon the advice of their directors and that they might find themselves in a poor position to take the decision which had been put in their hands, if they were given directors' advice which did not reflect the situation as the directors saw it at the time it fell to the shareholders to take their decision.

A somewhat similar problem could arise in relation to "nominee" directors, *i.e.* directors not elected by the shareholders generally but appointed by a particular class of security holder or creditor to protect their interests. English law solves such problems by requiring nominee directors to ignore the interests of the nominator,[65] though it may be

---

[61] *cf.* Menzies J., *ibid.* 616.

[62] This was discussed, but not clearly settled, by the Canadian Supreme Court in *Ringuet v. Bergeron* [1960] S.C.R. 672, where the majority held the voting agreement valid because, in their view, it related only to voting at general meetings. The minority held that it extended also to directors' meetings and was void, but they conceded that the position might have been different had all the members originally been parties to the agreement: see at 677.

[63] [1994] 1 BCLC 363, C.A., noted by Griffiths in [1993] J.B.L. 576.

[64] *John Crowther Group plc v. Carpets International* [1990] BCLC 460; *Rackham v. Peek Foods Ltd* [1990] BCLC 895 and the *Dawson* case cited above, n. 57. Even here it must be accepted that the shareholders may in consequence lose a commercial opportunity which would otherwise be open to them. See the discussion below at pp. 786–788.

[65] *Boulting v. ACTT* [1963] 2 Q.B. 606 at 626, *per* Lord Denning M.R.; *Kuwait Asia Bank EC v. National Mutual Life Nominees Ltd* [1991] 1 A.C. 187, P.C. The latter case shows that this principle has the advantage of not making the nominator liable for any breaches of duty to the company by the nominee director.

doubted how far this injunction is obeyed in practice. The Ghana Companies Code 1973 adopts what might be regarded as the more realistic line by permitting nominee directors to "give special, but not exclusive, consideration to the interests" of the nominator, but even this formulation would not permit the "mandating" of directors and thus the creation of a fettering problem.

On much the same principle, the board must not, in the absence of express authority, delegate their discretions to others.[66] But in practice wide authority to delegate is invariably conferred by the articles.[67]

4. *Conflict of duty and interest*

As fiduciaries, directors must not place themselves in a position in which there is a conflict between their duties to the company and their personal interests or duties to others. Good faith must not only be done but must manifestly be seen to be done, and the law will not allow a fiduciary to place himself in a position in which his judgment is likely to be biased and then to escape liability by denying that in fact it was biased. It will be convenient to consider its application in three connections. And first, in relation to transactions with the company, where it has received its most detailed working out.

(a) **Transactions with the company.** By the middle of the nineteenth century it had been clearly established that the trustee-like position of directors was liable to vitiate any contract which the board entered into on behalf of the company with one of their number. This principle receives its clearest expression in *Aberdeen Ry v. Blaikie*[68] in which a contract between the company and a partnership of which one of the directors was a partner was avoided at the instance of the company, notwithstanding that its terms were perfectly fair. Lord Cranworth L.C. said on that occasion[69]:

"A corporate body can only act by agents, and it is, of course, the duty of those agents so to act as best to promote the interests of the corporation whose affairs they are conducting. Such agents have duties to discharge of a fiduciary nature towards their principal. And it is a rule of universal application that no one, having such duties to discharge, shall be allowed to enter into engagements in which he has, or can have, a personal interest conflicting, or which possibly may conflict, with the interests of those whom he is bound to protect. . . . So strictly is this principle adhered to that no question is allowed to be raised as to the fairness or unfairness of a contract so entered into. . . ."

---

[66] *Cartmells' Case* (1874) L.R. 9 Ch.App. 691.
[67] See Chap. 9 above, at p. 197.
[68] (1854) 1 Macq.H.L. 461, H.L. Sc.
[69] At 471–472.

Later cases have added little to the general principle thus enunciated.[70]
It applies not only to transactions directly with the directors but also
to those in which they are in any way interested, whether because they
benefit personally, however indirectly, or because they are subject to
a conflicting duty.[71] The principle is the same as that applying to promoters and already discussed,[72] but the burden of it falls more heavily
upon directors. Promoters can enter into transactions with the company
if they make full disclosure of all material facts either to an independent board or to the members of the company. Any transaction which
the company then enters into with the promoter will be valid and
enforceable. The same applies to a transaction with any agent of the
company other than a director.[73] But the directors themselves cannot
escape so easily. Disclosure to themselves is ineffective even if the
interested directors refrain from attending and voting, leaving an independent quorum to decide, for the company has a right to the unbiased
voice and advice of every director.[73a] Hence, in the absence of express
provision in the company's articles, the only effective step is to make
full disclosure to the members of the company and to have the contract
entered into or ratified by the company in general meeting.

This need for approval in general meeting was expressly recognised
by section 29 of the first Joint Stock Companies Act of 1844. However, this section disappeared from the Act of 1856, to be replaced
only by an article in the optional Table[74] to the effect that any director,
directly or indirectly interested in any contract with the company
(except an interest merely as shareholder of another company) should
be disqualified and vacate office—a provision borrowed from the provisions in the Companies Clauses Consolidation Act of 1845.[75] Similar
provisions for disqualification have caused difficulty in the case of
public authorities; they seem even less appropriate in the case of
purely commercial ventures. Yet they remained in all Tables A until
the 1948 Act.

It is not surprising that these strict rules were not acceptable to the

---

[70] Except to recognise that, as we shall see below, the duty may, within limits, be waived or
modified by provisions in the company's articles.
[71] *Transvaal Lands Co. v. New Belgium (Transvaal) Land and Development Co.* [1914] 2 Ch.
488, C.A.; *Boulting v. ACTAT* [1963] 2 Q.B. 606, C.A., *per* Upjohn L.J. at 635–638. The rule
is for the protection of the company and cannot be used by the director as a shield to protect
himself against a third party: *Boulting v. ACTAT.*
[72] Above, Chap. 7, pp. 133–136.
[73] *e.g.* the company's solicitor: see *Regal (Hastings) Ltd v. Gulliver* [1942] 1 All E.R. 378;
[1967] 2 A.C. 134n., H.L., below, p. 615.
[73a] See *Benson v. Heathorn* (1842) 1 Y. & C.C.C. 326, *per* Knight-Bruce V.-C. at 341–342, and
Imperial Mercantile Credit Asscn. v. Coleman (1871) L.R. 6 Ch.App. 558, C.A., *per* Hather-
ley L.C. at 567–568.
[74] Then Table B (art. 47) which later became Table A.
[75] ss.85–87. These provisions were borrowed from the Municipal Corporations Act 1835, s.28;
it was not unnatural to apply to statutory companies running public utilities the same rules as
those for local authorities.

business community. Hence, it soon became the practice to attempt to modify them by provisions in the articles. So far as the disqualifying rules were concerned this was easy; they had no common law or equitable basis and all that was necessary was to exclude or modify Table A. And in the case of registered companies formed under the 1948 and subsequent Acts not even that is needed, for the post-1948 Tables omit the former disqualifying clause.

The basic equitable principle was, and is, the more serious snag. Contracts with directors, such as service agreements, became increasingly common, and contracts in which the directors were interested, for example as directors of another company, more common still. And the directors were unwilling to suffer the delay, embarrassment and possible frustration entailed by having to submit all such contracts to the company in general meeting. But just as the normal restraints on trustees can be modified by express provisions in the will or deed under which they were appointed,[76] so (within limits) can the normal fiduciary duties of directors be modified by express provision in the company's constitution. Such provisions have become common-form in the articles of registered companies.

Alarmed by the increasing ambit of these clauses, the legislature intervened.

(i) Statutory duty to declare interests. Section 149 of the 1929 Act placed directors under a duty to declare their interests in a contract or proposed contract with the company at a meeting of the directors. This section became section 199 of the 1948 Act and an amended version, which extends its ambit from "contracts" to "contracts, transactions or arrangements" and applies to shadow directors, is now section 317 of the 1985 Act. Discussion of its precise terms is left until later in this Chapter,[77] when the various statutory extensions of the general equitable principle are dealt with. Here it is only necessary to note that the only express sanction securing its observance is that the errant director is liable to a fine[78] but that nothing in the section "prejudices the operation of any rule of law restricting directors from having an interest" in transactions with the company.[79]

The inter-relation between this section and the general equitable principle was considered by an unusually strong Court of Appeal[80] in *Hely-Hutchinson v. Brayhead Ltd*[81] and by the House of Lords in

---

[76] The most common example is a "charging clause" enabling professional trustees and their firms to charge fees for acting as trustees or executors.

[77] See pp. 627–630, below.

[78] s.317(7).

[79] s.317(9).

[80] Lord Denning M.R. and Lords Wilberforce and Pearson.

[81] [1968] 1 Q.B. 549, C.A.

Guinness v. Saunders.[82] In both, the articles of association provided (as do Tables A 1948[83] and 1985[84]) that a director might be interested in, and should not be liable to account to the company for benefits resulting from, transactions with the company provided that he disclosed his interest in accordance with the section. In both cases he had entered into such a transaction without declaring his interest. Both decisions accept that if a director fails to declare his interest the transaction is voidable at the instance of the company and any benefits received by the director are recoverable by the company if it acts while it is still possible to restore both parties to their former positions.[85] It is also implicit in the judgments that if he has duly declared his interest[86] the transaction will not be voidable, despite the fact that the company has not specifically consented to his placing himself in a position where his interest conflicts with his duty to the company.

What these cases do not make wholly clear, however, is what the position is if the director has not declared his interest and the enabling article makes no reference to his duty to do so. Earlier editions of this book[87] took the view that in those circumstances the contract would be voidable under the equitable principle since, although articles could contract out of the need for the ad hoc consent by the company, they could not contract out of the statutory duty. That seems to be the view of most of the judges in the two cases.[88] But Lord Goff in *Guinness*

---

[82] [1990] 2 A.C. 663. H.L. This was one of the many cases—civil and criminal—arising from the hotly contested takeover battle for Distillers which Guinness won. Mr Ward, an American lawyer and a Guinness director, had played a valuable role as a member of the ad hoc committee of the board set up to plan Guinness's strategy and tactics. After the victory he submitted an invoice for special remuneration of £5.2m, based on an agreement by the committee that, if the Guinness bid was successful, he should be remunerated at the rate of 0.2 per cent of the value of the bid. The £5.2m was paid to him but when the full board learnt of it they caused Guinness to sue Mr Ward for its recovery and, at first instance and in the C.A., obtained summary judgment on the ground that he had not disclosed his interest in accordance with s.317: [1988] 1 W.L.R. 863, C.A. In the H.L. it was held that Guinness could not succeed on this ground because, as in the *Hely-Hutchinson* case, *restitutio in integrum* was no longer possible. However, the appeal was dismissed on a new ground; namely that, under Guinness's articles, remuneration of directors could be determined only by the board and could not be delegated to a committee. Hence there was no contract with Mr Ward, the £5.2m belonged in equity to Guinness and had to be restored. Nor had he any legal entitlement to a *quantum meruit* or to an "equitable allowance" under *Boardman v. Phipps*; below, p. 651.

[83] Art. 84.

[84] Art. 85. This does not specifically mention s.317 but says: "Subject to the provisions of the Act and provided that he has disclosed to the directors the nature and extent of any interest of his, a director may . . ."

[85] Which in both cases it was not.

[86] And complied with any other conditions in the articles; *e.g.* that he should not vote (or be counted in the quorum) on any matter in which he is interested: see Table A 1985, arts. 94, 95. As regards listed companies, see *Listing Rules*, para. 13 (App 1). 20.

[87] 4th ed., p. 586. This issue arises only where the enabling article excludes the normal equitable rule. Otherwise, the director would be caught by that: s.317(9). But the exclusion of the equitable duty is precisely the purpose of enabling articles, and most companies' articles contain them, at least as regards directors' contracts with the company.

[88] In *Hely-Hutchinson v. Brayhead, per* Lord Denning [1968] 1 Q.B. at 585; and *per* Lord Wilberforce, *ibid.* at 589, but perhaps not of Lord Pearson. In *Guinness v. Saunders, per* Fox

v. Saunders and, perhaps, Lord Pearson in *Hely-Hutchinson v. Brayhead* took a rather different view which, although it led to the same result in the cases before them, would lead to a different one in the circumstances presently under consideration. Lord Pearson said[89]:

"It is not contended that section 199[90] in itself affects the contract. The section merely creates a statutory duty of disclosure and imposes a fine for non-compliance. But it has to be read in conjuction with [the article]. If a director makes or is interested in a contract but fails to disclose his interest, what happens to the contract? Is it void or is it voidable at the option of the company, or is it still binding on both parties, or what? I think the answer must be supplied by the general law, and the answer is that the contract is voidable at the option of the company."

In *Guinness v. Saunders*, Lord Goff, having quoted that dictum, said[91]

"On this basis I cannot see that a breach of section 317 ... had itself any effect upon the contract[92] between Mr Ward and Guinness. As a matter of general law to the extent that there was a failure by Mr Ward to comply with his duty of disclosure *under the relevant articles*[93] of Guinness ... the contract was no doubt voidable under the general law to which Lord Pearson refers."

It would seem to follow that if the article did not make it a condition that the interest should have been declared,[94] Lord Goff would hold that the contract would be unimpeachable, even though the interest was not declared. That seems to be a regrettable conclusion and one which the legislature surely could not have intended. It would mean that a director could profit at the expense of the company notwithstanding that he had breached his statutory duty as a director.[95] It may be, however, that too much is being read into the different formulations. In both of the cases the articles required compliance with the section and the judges did not have to consider what the position

---

L.J. (with whose judgment Glidewell L.J. and Sir Frederick Lawton concurred) at [1988] 1 W.L.R. 868, 869 (see especially "It seems to me that section 317(1) must be regarded as imposing a duty which has consequences in the civil law in addition to the penalty of a fine:" at 869G); *per* Lord Templeman (with whose speech Lords Keith and Brandon concurred) at [1990] 2 A.C. 694D. It is impossible to tell whose side Lord Griffith is on as he expressed agreement with the speeches of both Lords Templeman and Goff.

[89] [1968] 1 Q.B. at 594.
[90] Of the 1948 Act which was then the relevant one.
[91] [1990] 2 A.C. at 697.
[92] This was said at the stage of his speech where he was dealing with the effect of the breach of s.317 and before he concluded that there was no contract with Mr Ward.
[93] Italics supplied.
[94] As article 85 of Table A 1985 does. But there is nothing to stop companies from adopting articles which do not, though the decision in *Cowan de Groot Properties Ltd v. Eagle Trust plc* [1992] 4 All E.R. at 762–764 suggests the courts will require explicit wording if the articles are to be construed in this way.
[95] The possibility of having to pay a fine is an inadequate preventative particularly as it is unlikely that he will be prosecuted.

would otherwise have been and may well not have directed their minds to it.[96]

(ii) Disclosure of misconduct. This seems a convenient place to mention another curious feature of the fiduciary duties of directors. One might have supposed that these duties required disclosure by the directors of their own misconduct at any rate where that was relevant to any proposed transaction between the company and the directors. Yet the leading case of *Bell v. Lever Bros. Ltd*[97] is taken to have determined that they are under no such duty. What makes this the more anomalous is that executive directors may be under a duty to disclose the misconduct of other employees, even though in so doing they may inevitably have to disclose their own.[98]

(b) Use of corporate property, opportunity or information. Another, and most important, consequence of the principle, that directors must not place themselves in a position where their fiduciary duties conflict with their personal interests, is that they must not, without the informed consent of the company, use for their own profit the company's assets, opportunities or information. And this prohibition is one that it has not proved so easy to avoid by provisions in the company's articles.[99]

Misuse of corporate assets generally presents no particular problem[1]; even the most unsophisticated director should realise that he must not use the company's property as if it was his own (although even this is frequently overlooked or ignored in a "one-man" company). It is misuse of corporate information or a corporate opportunity—in practice the two are likely to overlap—which gives rise to difficulties. A decision which illustrates both the questions which may arise and the extreme severity of the law is that of the House of Lords

---

[96] It is clear from a subsequent case that the apparent divergence of views is causing difficulties. In *Lee Panavision Ltd v. Lee Lighting Ltd* [1991] B.C.C. 620, (Harman J. and C.A.) Harman J. discussed it (at 626F–627H) but the C.A. declined an invitation to do so (at 637E, G).

[97] [1932] A.C. 161, H.L. The company which, in ignorance that the directors had misbehaved so seriously that the company would have been entitled to dismiss them summarily (and would have done so), was held to be not entitled to recover the substantial sums paid to them on their retirement. See also *Horcal v. Gatland* [1984] I.R.L.R. 288, C.A.

[98] *Sybron Corpn. v. Rochem Ltd* [1984] Ch. 112, C.A. following *Swain v. West (Butchers) Ltd* [1936] 3 All E.R. 261, C.A.

[99] An article such as art. 85 of the 1985 Act might be effective in some situations, but not in all, and only if the director "has disclosed to the directors the nature and content of any material interest of his" which, as the cases discussed below illustrate, it is not very likely that he will be able and willing to do.

[1] Except the problem of knowing when "corporate assets" end and "corporate information" or "corporate opportunity" begin. The present law does not clearly draw a distinction between them and the decisions frequently treat the latter as "belonging" to the company, *i.e.* as being its "property" or "asset". As we shall see, the distinction may be important in relation to authorisation or ratification by the company.

in *Regal (Hastings) Ltd v. Gulliver*.[2] The facts, briefly, were as follows: Company A owned a cinema and the directors decided to acquire
two others with a view to selling the whole undertaking as a going
concern. For this purpose they formed company B to take a lease of
the other two cinemas. But the lessor insisted on a personal guarantee
from the directors unless the paid-up capital of company B was at
least £5,000 (which in those days was a large sum). The company was
unable to subscribe more than £2,000 and the directors were not willing to give personal guarantees. Accordingly the original plan was
changed; instead of company A subscribing for all the shares in company B, company A took up 2,000 and the remaining 3,000 were
taken by the directors and their friends. Later, instead of selling the
undertaking, all the shares in both companies were sold, a profit of £2
16s. 1d. being made on each of the shares in company B. The new
controllers then caused company A to bring an action against the
former directors to recover the profit they had made.

It will be observed that this claim was wholly unmeritorious. Recovery by the company would benefit only the purchasers, who, if the
action was successful, would recover an undeserved windfall resulting
in a reduction in the price which they had freely agreed to pay.[3] It
also appears that the directors had held a majority of the shares in
company A so that there would have been no difficulty in obtaining
ratification of their action by the company in general meeting[4]; but
acting, as it was conceded they had, in perfect good faith and in full
belief in the legality and propriety of their actions it had not occurred
to them to go through this formality. It was also clear that the directors
had not deprived the company of any of its property[5] (unless information can be regarded as property[6]), or, seemingly, robbed it of an
opportunity which it might have exercised for its own advantage; the
3,000 shares in company B had never been the company's property
and, on the facts as found, the company could not have availed itself
of the opportunity to acquire them. Because of this, the court of first
instance and a unanimous Court of Appeal had dismissed the action.
But a unanimous House of Lords reversed this decision. Following
the well-known cases on trustees[7] it was held that the directors were
liable to account once it was established "(i) that what the directors

---

[2] [1942] 1 All E.R. 378: [1967] 2 A.C. 134n. A case which, because it was decided during the
War and then reported only in the All E.R., was frequently overlooked until it was included
in the L.R. 25 years later.
[3] Only one of their Lordships seemed to be disturbed by this—Lord Porter at [1967] 2 A.C.
157.
[4] See the cogent editorial note in [1942] 1 All E.R. at 379. It was conceded that had this been
done, there could have been no recovery: see further on this question, pp. 644–648, below.
[5] Thus bringing the case within the "corporate asset" basis of liability.
[6] On this vexed question, see the differing views of the Law Lords in *Boardman v. Phipps*
[1967] 2 A.C. 46, H.L.: below, p. 619.
[7] Notably the leading case of *Keech v. Sandford* (1726) Sel. Cas. Ch 61.

did was so related to the affairs of the company that it can properly be said to have been done in the course of their management and in utilisation of their opportunities and special knowledge as directors; and (ii) that what they did resulted in a profit to themselves.''[8]

This may well be thought to be carrying equitable principles to an inequitable conclusion. Nor does this account exhaust the anomalies inherent in the decision. The chairman (and, apparently, the dominant member) of the board, instead of agreeing himself to subscribe for shares in company B, had merely agreed to find subscribers for £500. Shares to that value had, accordingly, been taken up by two private companies of which he was a member and director, and by a personal friend of his. It was accepted that the companies and friend had subscribed beneficially and not as his nominees and, accordingly, he was held not to be under any liability to account for the profit which they had made.[9] The company's solicitor also escaped; though he had subscribed for shares and profited personally he could retain his profit because he had acted with the knowledge and consent of the company exercised through the board of directors. The directors themselves could avoid liability only if a general meeting had ratified, but the solicitor, not being a director, could rely on the consent of the board. And this despite the fact that the board had acted throughout on his advice. Hence the two men most responsible for what had been done escaped liability, while those who had followed their lead had to pay up.

What seems wrong with the application of the basic principle in this case is that recovery was not from all the right people and, more especially, was in favour of quite the wrong people.[10] Had it not been for the change of ownership it might well have been equitable to order restoration to the company, thus, in effect, causing the directors' profits to be shared among all the members. Certainly it is generally salutary to insist that directors shall not derive secret benefits from their trust. And it is probably well that this should apply whether or not any actual loss is suffered by the company, and whether or not it is deprived of an opportunity of benefiting itself. To allow directors to decide that the company shall not accept the opportunity and then to accept the opportunity themselves might impose too great a strain on their impartiality.

Of the many subsequent decisions that have followed or commented on the *Regal* case, three are of particular interest: *Industrial Develop-*

---

[8] *Per* Lord MacMilan at [1967] A.C. 153.
[9] The companies and friend had not been sued. Could recovery have been obtained from them had they been joined as parties?
[10] Some American jurisdictions, in like circumstances, allow what is there known as ''pro rata recovery'' by those shareholders who have not profited. We, unfortunately, lack any such procedure.

ment Consultants v. Cooley,[11] *Canadian Aero Service v. O'Malley*[12] (a decision of the Canadian Supreme Court in which the judgment was delivered by Laskin J.—later the C.J.) and *Boardman v. Phipps.*[13] The facts in the first two cases were very similar. In both the companies concerned had been eager to obtain, and in negotiation for, highly remunerative work in connection with impending projects. In both it was unlikely that the companies would have obtained the work, but in each there was a director whose expertise the undertaker of the project was anxious to obtain. Accordingly, each of the directors concerned resigned his office and later joined the undertaker of the project, in *Cooley* directly, in *Canadian Aero Service* indirectly through a company formed for the purpose which entered into a consortium with the undertaker. In both they were held liable to account for the profits which they made.[14]

In *Cooley* liability was based on misuse of information,[15] the defendant having, while managing director, obtained information and knowledge that the project was to be revived and deliberately concealed this from the company and taken steps to turn the information to his personal advantage. It was irrelevant that the approach had been made to him and that his services were being sought as an individual consultant and would be undertaken free from any association with the company.[16] "Information which came to him while he was managing director and which was of concern to the plaintiffs and relevant for the plaintiffs to know, was information which it was his duty to pass on to the plaintiffs."[17] It might be remarkable that the plaintiffs should receive a benefit which "it is unlikely that they would have got for themselves had the defendant complied with his duty to them" but "if the defendant is not required to account he will have made a large profit as a result of having deliberately put himself into a position in which his duty to the plaintiffs who were employing him and his personal interests conflicted."[18]

---

[11] [1972] 1 W.L.R. 443 (Roskill J.)

[12] [1973] 40 D.L.R. (3d) 371 (Can. S.C.).

[13] [1967] 2 A.C. 46, H.L.

[14] In *Canadian Aero Service* the award of $125,000 was described as "damages" but was upheld on the basis that it should be "viewed as an accounting for profits or, what amounts to the same thing, as based on unjust enrichment": (1973) 40 D.L.R. (3d) at 392.

[15] Roskill J. presumably chose this rather than the more obvious loss of opportunity because the chance that the company could have secured the opportunity was minimal: Roskill J. assessed it at not not more than 10 per cent: [1972] 1 W.L.R. at 454.

[16] So that, "in one sense, the benefit . . . did not arise because of the defendant's directorship: indeed, the defendant would not have got this work had he remained a director": [1972] 1 W.L.R. at 451.

[17] *ibid.* Would it follow that, even if the defendant had not used the information himself, he would have been liable in damages for breach of duty if the company could have proved that it suffered loss as a result of the failure to disclose? Suppose he had been a director of two companies to each of which the information was relevant: would he have been liable to both if he did not disclose to either and liable to one if he disclosed to the other?

[18] At 453.

In *Canadian Aero Service*, the decision was based firmly on misuse of a corporate opportunity. On this Laskin J. said[19]:

"An examination of the case-law … shows the pervasiveness of a strict ethic in this area of the law. In my opinion this ethic disqualifies a director or senior officer from usurping for himself or diverting to another person or company with whom or with which he is associated a maturing business opportunity which his company is actively pursuing[20]; he is also precluded from so acting even after his resignation where the resignation may fairly be said to be prompted or influenced by a wish to acquire for himself the opportunity sought by the company, or where it was his position with the company rather than a fresh initiative which led him to the opportunity which he later acquired."

It seems, however, that he would have favoured a flexibility, greater than English case law allows, when testing the conduct of directors against "the general standards of loyalty, good faith and the avoidance of a conflict of duty and self-interest".[21]

In the third case, *Boardman v. Phipps*,[22] the two defendants were not company directors but a trustee and the solicitor to the trust who had acted as agents of the trustees in relation to a company in which the trust had a substantial but minority shareholding that was not proving a satisfactory investment. They eventually decided that the best course would be to try to obtain control of the company by making a takeover bid for the other shares and, if that was successful, then to make a capital distribution. As there were obvious difficulties in the trustees using the trust fund in bidding, they obtained, as they thought, the informal consent of all the trustees and beneficiaries to bid on their own behalf and at their own expense. Unfortunately they did not, as the court held, adequately explain their proposed course of action to the plaintiff, one of the beneficiaries. After long and skilful negotiations with the other shareholders they succeeded in acquiring their shares at prices between £3 and £4 10s. per share (mainly the latter). Thereafter the company made distributions totalling £5 17s. 6d. per share which still left each share worth, on asset value, more than £3 per share. Hence the trust, with 8,000 shares, did well; but the defendants, with some 22,000 shares, did even better—making a profit of over £75,000. It was held, following *Regal*, that they had to account

---

[19] (1973) 40 D.L.R. (3d) at 382.

[20] But *quaere* whether the company need be "actively pursuing" it. See below, p. 621.

[21] At 391, where he enumerated some of the many factors which in his view were relevant. *cf.* Gareth Jones in (1968) 84 L.Q.R. 472 who argues persuasively that fiduciaries should not be liable to account unless they have not acted honestly or they have been unjustly enriched. Contrast Beck in Ziegel (ed.), *Studies in Canadian Company Law*, Vol. II (Toronto, 1973), Chap. 5.

[22] n. 13, above.

to the plaintiff for a proportion of that profit corresponding to his fraction of the beneficial interest (8/15s.) in the trust fund.

One question which these decisions do not answer but which was posed in *Regal*, is: Does the equitable principle involve "the proposition that, if the directors bona fide decide not to invest their company's funds in some proposed investment, a director who thereafter embarks his own money therein is accountable for any profits he may derive therefrom?"[23] The one circumstance in which it is clear that there is no such liability is where the company has duly authorised the act of the director; *i.e.* has not merely decided that the company shall not avail itself of the information or opportunity but also decided that the director may. However, although that authority could be conferred by the board on an officer of the company who is not a director,[24] the board cannot confer it on the directors themselves; only the general meeting, or the agreement of all the members entitled to vote, can do so. But suppose it is not all the directors who want to take advantage of the opportunity but only one (or some) of them. Can the board effectively authorise him to do so? There is powerful support from the Privy Council decision in *Queensland Mines Ltd v. Hudson*,[25] for the view that it can. There, "the board of the company knew the facts, decided to renounce the company's interest . . . in the venture and assented to Mr Hudson [the managing director] doing what he could with [it] at his own risk and for his own benefit".[26] It was held that, although the venture ultimately proved profitable, the managing director was not liable to account. This has been criticised on the ground that the decision should have been taken either by a completely independent board with Hudson playing no part or by the general meeting.[27] Normally, no doubt, that is correct but on the facts it seems an over-technical objection since the only members of the company were two companies, each represented on the board and fully aware of the company's "early interest in the venture and of the manner and circumstances of the company's escape".[28]

It is therefore submitted that if the board has taken a bona fide decision that the company should reject the opportunity on its merits,

---

[23] *Per* Lord Russell (quoting Greene M.R.) at [1967] A.C. 152.
[24] *New Zealand Netherlands Society v. Kuys* [1973] 1 W.L.R. 1127, P.C. where an opportunity to publish a newspaper had come to the secretary of an incorporated society as a result of his position. With full knowledge of the facts the society, which initially provided some financial support, had agreed that it should be published by him beneficially and at his own risk.
[25] [1978] 52 A.L.J.R. 379, P.C. In this case, unlike *Regal, Cooly, Canadian Aero* and *Boardman*, there had been a bona fida decision that the company should renounce the opportunity on its merits. In the other cases the opportunity was not taken up on the alleged, but dubious, ground that it was impossible for the company to do so.
[26] Lord Scarman at 403.
[27] (1979) 42 M.L.R. 711.
[28] Lord Scarman at 404.

it may then permit one (or more) of its members to take it up.[29] If, however, that director has any intention to ask for permission he should declare his interest at the meeting and absent himself from the discussion of the matter. Failing that, the board's decision to consent should be submitted for ratification, after full disclosure of material facts, by a general meeting or by all the members entitled to attend and vote.

Suppose, however, that at the time of the directors' meeting the director had no intention of taking up the opportunity, but subsequently decided that he would like to do so. It is submitted that he cannot without full disclosure of all material facts (which may well be different from those at the time of the company's decision to renounce) and that, if still a member of the board, he should play no part in its deliberations on the matter.

A final set of issues English courts may ultimately have to consider concerns the criteria for identifying the opportunities for the personal exploitation of which the director must seek the company's permission. In *Cooley* and *O'Malley*, as we have noted, this was not a live issue because in both cases the company was actively pursuing the opportunities in question. However, it would seem unduly limited to confine the law's conception of "corporate opportunities" to such cases, with the consequent exclusion of opportunities which fall within the company's existing or prospective business activities, even though the company has not identified the particular opportunity in question as one it wished to take up.[30] This test would not bring all business opportunities which came to the notice of a director within the scope of the duty, no matter how tangentially they were related to the company's current business operations or plans, but it would recognise that the director's fiduciary duty was co-extensive with his or her function of promoting the business interests of the company, as conceived by its senior management at the time. In the case of directors holding multiple directorships, this development could give rise to some tricky problems of how the director is to deal equitably with all the companies of which he or she is a director. A starting point might be to require the director to obtain the approval of all the companies within whose "line of business" the opportunity in question fell, though it would be for consideration whether it would be open to the director to give priority, in the case of a person holding executive and non-executive directorships, to the interests of the company where the director was an executive. The director might be permitted to seek the approval of this company first, thus giving it, if it decided to seek the

---

[29] But, in such circumstances, a court is likely to take a deal of persuading that the board's decision to reject the opportunity was taken bona fide in the interests of the company rather than in that of their fellow director—especially if he has a powerful personality.

[30] Courts in the United States have gone this far, under what is generally referred to as the "line of business" test. See Note (1960–1961) 74 Harv. L.R. 765.

opportunity itself, a lead over the other companies with which the director was connected. Whilst acknowledging the difficult issues which arise here, which are analogous to those discussed in the next section, it is submitted that the English courts should not restrict the scope of directors' duties in respect of corporate opportunities to those particular ones already identified by the company as opportunities it wishes to acquire.

(c) Competing with the company. One of the most obvious examples of a situation which might be expected to give rise to a conflict between a director's interests and his duties is where he carries on or is associated with a business competing with that of the company. Certainly a fiduciary without the consent of his beneficiaries is normally strictly precluded from competing with them and this is specifically stated in the analogous field of partnership law.[31] Yet, strangely, it is by no means clear on the existing case law that a similar rule applies to directors of a company.[32] Indeed, it is generally stated that it does not, and there appears to be a definite, if inadequately reported, decision that a director cannot be restrained from acting as a director of a rival company.[33] And it has been said that "What he could do for a rival company he could, of course, do for himself."[34] This view is becoming increasingly difficult to support. It has been held that the duty of fidelity flowing from the relationship of master and servant may preclude the servant from engaging, even in his spare time, in work for a competitor,[35] notwithstanding that the servant's duty of fidelity imposes lesser obligations than the full duty of good faith owed by a director or other fiduciary agent. How, then, can it be that a director can compete whereas a subordinate employee cannot? Moreover it has been recognised that one who is a director of two rival concerns is walking a tight-rope and at risk if he fails to deal fairly with both.[36]

In arguing that a director who carries on a business which competes with that of his company inevitably places himself in a position where his personal interest will conflict with his duty to the company, it is not being contended that he will necessarily have breached his fiduciary duty; he will not if the company has consented so long as he

---

[31] Partnership Act 1890, s.30.

[32] It clearly does not apply to members, even in a private company, for members, as such, are not fiduciaries, though such conduct might give rise to a remedy under s.429. See Chap. 27, below.

[33] *London & Mashonaland Exploration Co. v. New Mashonaland Exploration Co.* [1891] W.N. 165, approved by Lord Blanesburgh in *Bell v. Lever Bros.* [1932] A.C. 161 at 195, H.L.

[34] *Per* Lord Blanesburgh, *ibid.*

[35] *Hivac Ltd v. Park Royal Scientific Instruments Ltd* [1946] Ch. 169, C.A. If correct it must apply to an executive director: see *Scottish Co-op Wholesale Society Ltd v. Meyer* [1959] A.C. 324, H.L., *per* Lord Denning at 367.

[36] See *per* Lord Denning in *Scottish Co-op Wholesale Society v. Meyer*, above, at 366–368. This concerned an application under what is now s.459 (on which see Chap. 27, below) but Lord Denning obviously had doubts whether the *Mashonaland* case was still good law.

observes his subjective duty to the company by subordinating his interests to those of the company. Nor is it being suggested that there is anything objectionable in his holding other directorships so long as all the companies have consented if their businesses compete. But in both cases consent is unlikely if he is a full-time executive director or if the extent of the competition is substantial. And even if the consent is given the director is likely to be faced with constant difficulties in avoiding breaches of his subjective duty of good faith to the company or companies concerned. He may be able to subordinate his personal interests to those of a single company but it is less easy to reconcile conflicting duties to more than one company. Nor would a reformed rule be inconsistent with the modern emphasis on a more important role for non-executive directors, who are often executive directors of other companies. Even if executive directors are regarded as a good source of non-executive talent for other companies (which some would question), a reformed rule would simply require executive directors not to become non-executives of *competing* companies, which they are, in fact, rarely asked to become.

STATUTORY INTERVENTIONS

Although the equitable principle has not been codified, there has been considerable statutory intervention regarding particular applications of it, notably in what are now sections 310 to 347 of the Act.

Section 310

Section 310[37] is the successor to section 205 of the 1948 Act. Prior thereto it had been generally accepted that provisions in articles might effectively exempt officers of the company from liability to it provided, at any rate, that the officers were not guilty of fraud or wilful default.[38] Now this section provides that "any provision, whether contained in a company's articles or in any contract with the company or otherwise",[39] which purport to exempt any officer or auditor of a company from, or to indemnifying him against, "any liability which by virtue of any rule of law would otherwise attach to him in respect of any negligence, default, breach of duty or breach of trust of which he may be guilty in relation to the company" shall, except as provided in subsection (3)[40] be void.[41] On the face of it, this seems clearly to ban

---

[37] Implementing a recommendation of the Greene Committee: (1926) Cmd. 2657, paras. 46 & 47.
[38] See *Re City Equitable Fire Insurance Co.* [1925] Ch. 407.
[39] It is not clear whether "or otherwise" relates to "with the company" or to "any provision". If to the latter it would seem to ban such provisions in members' or directors' resolutions.
[40] See below, pp. 625–626.
[41] s.310(1) and (2).

provisions in articles such as those which, as we have seen, purport to exempt directors from the most likely applications of the duty not to place themselves in a position in which their personal interests or duties to others may conflict with their duties to the company. But these provisions have continued to appear in Tables A 1948 and 1985 and, as such, must presumably be taken to be valid and effective—as, indeed, highly authoritative decisions have assumed.[42] How a provision, such as Table A 1985, article 85, can be reconciled with section 310 has led to a considerable volume of literature[43] but not to any explanation by the English courts until Vinelott J. wrestled with it in the case of *Movitex Ltd v. Bulfield*.[44]

His explanation draws a distinction between (1) "the overriding principle of equity" that "if a director places himself in a position in which his duty to the company conflicts with his personal interest or duty to another, the court will set aside the transaction without enquiring whether there was any breach of duty to the company" and (2) the director's "duty to promote the interests of [the company] and when the interests of [the company] conflicted with his own to prefer the interests of [the company]". While any proposed modification of (2) would infringe section 310, the shareholders of the company in formulating the articles can exclude or modify the application of (1) "the overriding principle of equity". In doing so they do not exempt the director from, or from the consequences of, a breach of duty owed to the company.[45]

Earlier editions of this book[46] accepted that there was a distinction between (a) the overriding principle that a director must not place himself in a conflicting position and (b) the director's subjective duty to act bona fide in the interests of the company. They also accepted that, seemingly, the former (but not the latter) could be excluded or modified by the articles. To that extent the views expressed were in accord with those of Vinelott J. (though, in contrast with his, they failed to offer any rational explanation of how that could be reconciled with section 310). But his conclusions go much further. If it be a fact that a director is under no *duty* not, without the company's consent, to place himself in a position where his interests conflict with his duty, then it presumably follows that, even if there is no contracting-out in the articles, the director's only duty is to declare his interest (with liability to a fine if he does not) under section 317 when it applies.[47]

[42] See, *e.g. Hely-Hutchinson v. Brayhead* and *Guinness v. Saunders*, above, pp. 612–615.
[43] See, in addition to the company law textbooks, Baker [1975] J.B.L. 181; Birds (1976) 39 M.L.R. 394; Parkinson [1981] J.B.L. 335; and Gregory (1982) 98 L.Q.R. 413.
[44] [1988] BCLC 104.
[45] *ibid.*, 120–121d.
[46] 4th ed., p. 601.
[47] See above. It does not apply unless the conflict arises from a director's interest in "an actual or proposed contract, transaction or arrangement with the company": see below, p. 627.

Hence, it would seem that if the director has placed himself in a position where a serious conflict is inevitable, the company will not be able immediately to dismiss him without liability to pay damages for breach of his service agreement if he has one. To avoid that liability it will have to wait until it can prove that the director has actually breached his duty to prefer the company's interests to those of himself or of others to whom he owes duties. This seems an undesirable conclusion on policy grounds.[48]

The fact is that at present it seems impossible to reconcile section 310 with exclusions of the "overriding equitable principle" by articles such as articles 85 and 86 of Table A 1985 without doing violence to the section and producing undesirable results. A possible solution might be to translate those articles (appropriately amended) into sections of the Act itself and to amend section 310 so as to exclude from its ambit any transactions permitted under those sections. If section 317 was also amended to meet the criticisms made below[49] this would produce a result defensible on policy grounds.[50]

A further query that has arisen in relation to section 310 is whether subsections (1) and (2) apply only to exemptions and indemnifications from liability to the company or also to indemnifications by the company of liabilities incurred to third parties by an officer or auditor acting in relation to the company. The better view is that, reading the section as a whole,[51] they apply to the latter also; but some take the opposite view and it would be well to remove any doubt.

As a result of the 1989 Act, subsection (3) now provides, first, that the section does not prevent a company from purchasing and maintaining for an officer or auditor insurance against any liability under subsections (1) and (2). This was inserted as a result of representations that public companies were finding it difficult to persuade people to accept directorships in the light of increased risks of liability (for example, for "wrongful trading" under subsection 214 of the Insolvency Act 1986) unless the companies could offer (and pay for) insurance against such risks.[52] If a company does take out such insurance that must be disclosed in the directors' annual report.[53]

---

[48] But it is perhaps reconciliable with the dictum of Cranworth L.C. in *Aberdeen Ry. v. Blaikie* (see above) and would seem to be the position if there is a contracting-out in the articles wide enough to cover the type of conflict (but then at least there is a semblance of "consent" by the company).

[49] See below at pp. 627–630.

[50] And the result for which Birds contends (*loc. cit.*, n. 43, above) but which cannot, surely be achieved without statutory intervention.

[51] Particularly having regard to the new subs.(3) inserted by the 1989 Act: see below.

[52] This is, to come extent, beneficial to the companies since without insurance the errant directors are less likely to be worth powder-and-shot. The case for allowing companies to insure their auditors is less obvious, for auditors will be covered by their own professional indemnity insurance, the cost of which will be indirectly borne by their clients out of the fees charged. If two rival insurance companies cover the risk it may make life more difficult for auditors. On the general impact of s.310 on auditors see above, p. 559.

[53] Sched. 7, para. 5A, inserted by s.137(2) of the 1989 Act.

Secondly, subsection (3) provides that the section does not prevent a company from indemnifying an officer or auditor against any liability incurred by him in defending any proceedings (civil or criminal) in which judgment is given in his favour or he is acquitted, or if the court grants him relief under section 144(3) or (4)[54] or under section 727.[55]

Enforcement of fair dealing

Part X of the Act contains sections, most of which are derived from those in the 1980 Act, designed to render more effective the "enforcement of fair dealing by directors",[56] This it does in three ways. First, an increased number of transactions with directors are prohibited outright; secondly, certain transactions with directors require the prior approval of the general meeting; and thirdly, increased disclosure is required of transactions undertaken with or by the directors. In general, the sections apply only to directors (not to other officers) but, as so often, "directors" includes "shadow directors", except that, for the purposes of most of the sections[57] in Part X, "a body corporate is not to be treated as a shadow director of any of its subsidiary companies *by reason only*[58] that the directors of the subsidiary are accustomed to act in accordance with its directions or instructions."[59]

(a) **Tax-free emoluments.** Section 311 makes it unlawful for a company to pay remuneration to a director (whether as a director or otherwise) free of income tax or varying according to his income tax or his tax rate. Apart from the difficulty of calculating precisely what the company would be liable to pay[60] a provision for such payments is objectionable since what appeared to be a modest remuneration could prove to be exorbitant. Hence, any provision for such a payment takes effect as if the net sum for which it purports to provide was a gross sum subject to income tax.[61]

Sections 312–316 relate to payments to directors, ostensibly as com-

---

[54] See Chap. 11 at p. 250, n. 11, above.
[55] The court's general power to grant relief to officers or auditors who have acted honestly and reasonably and ought fairly to be excused. See p. 652, below.
[56] The words of the heading of Part X.
[57] *i.e.* ss.319, 320–322 and 330–346.
[58] Italics supplied. This wording implies that the parent company could be a shadow director of the subsidiary if there were other reasons. But it is difficult to see how, since "shadow director" is defined as a person in accordance with whose directions or instructions the directors of the company are accustomed to act" (s.741(2)). Hence, unless directors are so accustomed a person cannot be a shadow director.
[59] s.741(3).
[60] It would depend on the precise terms of the provision, his other income and his family situation and in calculating his taxable income the net sum would have to be grossed-up since the benefit he received by having it paid net of tax would be a taxable benefit.
[61] Which means that his remuneration would probably be less than it would have been had he not tried it on.

pensation for loss of office, on the occasion of a transfer of undertakings or a takeover. They are dealt with in Chapter 29.[62]

(b) Declarations of interest. Section 317, relating to declarations of interests, has already been referred to more than once in this Chapter,[63] but it needs to be looked at in greater detail, if only to indicate its inadequacies.

Section 317(1) provides that it is the duty of a director, who is in any way, whether directly or indirectly, interested in a contract or proposed contract with the company, to declare the nature of his interest at a meeting of the directors of the company. This subsection refers only to "contracts" and, moreover, to contracts "with the company", Hence, on its own, it covers only one of the many situations in which a director may have an interest conflicting with that of the company. However, as a result originally of the 1980 Act, it has been widened considerably by what are now subsections (5) and (6). The former provides that a reference in the section to a "contract" includes "any transaction or arrangement (whether or not a contract) made or entered into on or after 22nd December 1980". The latter adds that for the purposes of the section a transaction described in section 330[64] made by a company for a director or a "connected person"[65] of that director shall be treated (whether or not it is prohibited by section 330) as a transaction or arrangement in which the director is interested.[66] Accordingly a declaration of interest is now required more often. But the section still does not apply to all conflict situations. It applies only to interests in transactions or proposed transactions *with* the company and to transactions described in section 330 that are *by* the company. It would not apply, for example, to the use of a corporate opportunity or of corporate information which is not, or has not reached the stage of becoming, a transaction or proposed transaction with the company.

All that subsection (1) requires is a declaration at a meeting of directors of "the nature of" the director's interest (not of all material facts or even of the extent of his interest). On the other hand, it appears to require a declaration even if the extent of the interest is so minimal as to be immaterial. However, if the company has an article corresponding to article 85 of Table A 1985 a director will be permitted to have personal interests in company transactions but only "subject to the provisions of the Act and provided that he has disclosed to the

---

[62] At pp. 812–815, below.

[63] Particularly in connection with its inter-relationship with provisions in the articles enabling directors to be interested in transactions notwithstanding the equitable principle: see pp. 612–615, above.

[64] The effect of that section is dealt with below at pp. 637–640.

[65] As defined in s.346.

[66] Accordingly in this book when citing or summarising the provisions of s.317, "transactions" has been substituted for "contracts".

directors the nature and extent of any material interest of his'', The
result appears to be that he will then have to comply with section 317
and also to disclose to the board the extent of his interest if material.

Section 317(2) provides that in the case of a proposed transaction
the declaration shall be made at the meeting of the directors at which
the question of entering into the transaction is first taken into consideration or, if the director was not at that meeting, at the next meeting
held after he became so interested. It has often been assumed[67] that
the effect of this is that a declaration of interest is required only if the
transaction is one that is "taken into consideration by the directors"—
which, of course, is unlikely except in the case of major transactions.
But that view is thought to be mistaken. The duty imposed by subsection (1) is not so qualified. And subsection (2) goes on to say that, in
a case where the director becomes interested in a transaction after it
is made, the declaration shall be made at the first meeting of the directors after he becomes interested—again without any reference to
whether the transaction has been, or is to be, "taken into consideration
by the directors", Hence it is thought that a declaration is required in
the case of all relevant transactions whether or not they would otherwise come before the board.

However, subsection (3) provides an avenue which directors can
take to protect themselves from breaching the statutory duty. It provides that a general notice given to the directors of the company by a
director to the effect: (a) that he is a member of a specified company
or firm and is to be regarded as interested in any transaction after the
date of the notice with that company or firm, or; (b) that he is to be
regarded as interested in any transaction after the date of the notice
with a specified person who is "connected" with him within the
meaning of section 346,[68] is deemed to be a sufficient declaration of
interest.

Under subsection (4) that is so only if notice is given at a meeting
of the directors or the director takes reasonable steps to ensure that it
is brought up and read at the next directors' meeting. Even so there is
an undoubted weakness.[69] If all that the director needs to do is to
declare that he is a member of another company and that suffices in
respect of all subsequent transactions, he will not have to add, if that

---

[67] *e.g.* in earlier editions of this book and in the Report of the Jenkins Committee which made
recommendations accordingly, Cmnd 1949, paras. 95 and 99(c). The view now stated in the
text received the support of Lightman J. in *Neptune (Vehicle Washing Equipment) Ltd v.
Fitzgerald* [1996] Ch. 274.

[68] In effect, members of his immediate family and companies which he or they control.

[69] A weakness not to be found in art. 86(a) of Table A 1985. And art. 86(b) sensibly provides,
as s.317 does not, that an interest of which a director has no knowledge and of which it is
unreasonable to expect him to have knowledge, shall not be as an interest of his. At present
we have a defective s.317 improved by an optional Table A if companies choose to adopt it;
not a satisfactory solution.

be the case, then or subsequently, that, say, he is also a director whose remuneration varies with the company's annual profits. Nor, it seems, if at the time of the notice he held only 100 shares and mentioned that in the notice, would he have to give notice if he increased his holdings even if that gave him a controlling interest.

In addition to the doubts one may have about the efficacy of the general notice in producing full disclosure of the nature of the director's interest, it is possible to be sceptical about the protective value for shareholders of disclosure, even full disclosure, to fellow directors, who may be inclined to take a more lenient view of conflicts of interest than would the shareholders. This is especially likely where the other directors entertain hopes of similarly lenient treatment should they themselves have to disclose a conflict in the future.[70] The apotheosis of meaningless disclosure was reached in *Neptune (Vehicle Washing Equipment) Ltd v. Fitzgerald*,[71] where it was held that the section was capable of applying to a sole director (*i.e.* that a single director could constitute a meeting for the purpose of section 317), who should therefore make a declaration to himself, which, indeed, supposing the company secretary were not present, he could even do silently! The alternative argued for by the plaintiffs in that case, that the disclosure in such a situation should be to the shareholders because the decision on the contract should revert to them,[72] has a lot to commend it.

The question of the value of disclosure to the board has also troubled the courts in recent years, but in the sense of making them reluctant to hold that a transaction was not binding[73] on the company where the failure to disclose was "purely technical", *i.e.* full disclosure would clearly not have altered the decision which was in fact taken. In *Runciman v. Walter Runciman plc*,[74] where the interest which had not been declared at a meeting of the board was in fact known to all the other members of the board and where, rather as in *Regal Hastings*,[75] a successful takeover bidder for the company was seeking to take advantage of the earlier non-disclosure to dismiss the managing director cheaply, the judge held that he had a discretion not to set aside the managing director's service contract, despite the non-compliance with the disclosure requirements. This novel doctrine, which, however, has been referred to favourably by the Court of

---

[70] For example, where the matter is something which routinely affects all or many directors over time. This is one reason why the disclosure provisions have been made more rigorous in relation to directors' remuneration. See below, pp. 630–635.

[71] [1996] Ch. 274.

[72] On the grounds that a pre-condition for effective board action, *i.e.* compliance with s.317, could not be met. See above, pp. 187–188.

[73] These were cases where the enabling article (see above, p. 612) required compliance with the statutory disclosure requirements.

[74] [1992] BCLC 1084.

[75] Above, p. 615.

Appeal,[76] may avoid the imposition of sanctions for the omission of a "mere incantation", but does nothing to put in place effective disclosure provisions.

Of the remaining subsections it is only necessary to mention that subsection (8) applies the section to shadow directors with appropriate adjustments to the method of making the declaration of interest, and that subsection (9) states that the section does not derogate from any rule of law restricting directors from having an interest in transactions with the company.

(c) Restraints on directors' remuneration. Sections 318 and 319 deal with the obvious openings for abuse flowing from the fact that, whereas the members of the company have some control over directors' fees, they had, until recently, none over the total emoluments paid to a director in the form of salaries, bonuses, contributions to pension schemes and compensation for loss of office.[77] Members could, of course, glean some information from the annual accounts[78] but there was precious little they could do about it beyond complaining at the AGM that it was grossly excessive in total and that the emoluments of the chairman and chief executive were positively obscene. In effect, the directors could vote themselves long-term service agreements in the case of executive directors, and generous contracts for consulting and similar services in the case of non-executives. Now some restraints are imposed by these two sections on the liberality with which directors assess the value of each other's services.

Section 318 requires every company to keep a copy of the service agreement (but not of an agreement for services) of each director[79] of the company or its subsidiary or a memorandum of its terms if the agreement is not in writing.[80] The copy or memorandum must be kept either at the registered office, or at the place where its register of members is kept, or at its principal place of business if that is situated in that part of Great Britain in which the company is registered.[81] All such copies and memoranda must be kept at the same place[82] and the company must notify the Registrar of the place where they are kept.[83] The copies and memoranda must be open to inspection by any member

---

[76] *Lee Panavision Ltd v. Lee Lighting Ltd* [1992] BCLC 22. C.A., at 33. In the *Neptune* case, which was a decision on an application for summary judgment, this issue was left to the trial judge. See also *Re Dominion International Group (No. 2)* [1996] 1 BCLC 572 at 598–600.

[77] Except when ss.312–315 apply, on which see Chap. 29 at pp. 812–815.

[78] s.232 and Sched.6: see Chap. 19, above at p. 517.

[79] Including a shadow director.

[80] s.318(1). This does not apply if the contract requires the director to work wholly or mainly outside the U.K. but the company must then keep instead a memorandum giving the director's name and the provisions of the contract relating to its duration: s.318(5). There is also an exception for contracts having less than 12 months to run: s.318(11).

[81] s.318(3).

[82] s.318(2).

[83] s.318(4).

of the company without charge.[84] If inspection is refused the court may order an immediate inspection.[85] In practice not much use is made of the rights of inspection conferred by this section even in the case of public companies.[86] More use would no doubt be made of it if the right to inspect were extended from members to employees, to whose interests the directors are required to have regard in the exercise of their duties to the company[87]; but any such proposal would undoubtedly cause howls of protest as a gross breach of confidentiality.

More effective, however, is section 319. This prohibits any term whereby any director is to be employed, whether under a contract of service *or for services*,[88] which may last for more than 5 years without being terminable[89] by the company or terminable only in specified circumstances,[90] unless the term is first approved by a resolution of the company in general meeting.[91] If approval is sought, a written memorandum of the proposed agreement has to be made available for inspection without charge by members at the company's registered office during a period of not less than 15 days before the meeting and at the meeting itself.[92] If a term, prohibited in the absence of approval in general meeting, is included in the agreement in contravention of the section, the term is void to the extent that it contravenes the section and the agreement is terminable at any time by reasonable notice by the company.[93]

Since directors of public companies have a rooted antipathy to exposing their service agreement to debate and possible rejection by a general meeting of the members, this has largely eradicated long-term service agreements not determinable by the company until the directors reach retirement age or later. Legal ingenuity has, however, devised agreements, popularly known as the "five year roller", which are not caught by the section but which ensure that, when and if they are terminated by the company, the agreement will always have about five years to run.

---

[84] s.318(7).

[85] s.318(9). And the company and every officer in default are liable to fines for any contravention of the section: s.318(8).

[86] In the case of small private companies there will probably not be any prior agreements regarding emoluments: the member-directors will just decide from time to time how much to pay themselves.

[87] s.309, above, p. 602.

[88] s.319(7)(a): italics supplied.

[89] *i.e.* terminable without that being a breach of contract: see Chap. 9 at pp. 190–192, above.

[90] s.319(1) and (2). In the case of a director of a holding company it applies to any employment within the group (as defined in s.319(7)(b)) and "director" includes a shadow director (s.319(7)) other than the holding company: s.741(3).

[91] s.319(3). But note the restriction in s.319(4) on the types of "company" to which it applies and that it does not apply to a wholly owned subsidiary—when it would be farcial.

[92] s.319(5). Although only members are entitled to inspect it (and are not entitled to take copies) it may be difficult to prevent its salient points being leaked to and published by the Press.

[93] s.319(6).

In addition to the two sections discussed immediately above, other provisions of the Act require *post hoc* disclosure to shareholders and, directly or indirectly, to the public at large of the remuneration and other benefits conferred upon directors, notably Schedule 6 requiring some information on these matters to be included in the directors' report.[94] However, the inadequacy of the overall statutory controls was demonstrated by the public outcry at the end of 1994 about the levels of directors' remuneration, especially, but not exclusively, in the recently privatised utility companies. There the directors seemed to have awarded themselves generous salaries and stock option packages, even though the successful running of those monopolies (as they still largely were) required no great entrepreneurial flair, but only the rigorous institution of cost-cutting measures, notably the dismissal of significant numbers of employees. Like the problem, the solution, too, was largely privatised. The Government being unwilling to pick up this hot potato, it was left to the Confederation of British Industry, with tacit Government support, to set up a "study group" under Sir Richard Greenbury, whose report[95] has been implemented largely by amendments to the Stock Exchange's continuing obligations for listed companies,[96] though some amendments to Schedule 6 have been made.[97]

The terms of reference of the Greenbury Committee required it to produce a Code of Practice on directors' remuneration, which now appears as an annex to the Stock Exchange's Listing Rules and which is intended to replace the guidance in this area previously issued by the Cadbury Committee[98] and by various groupings of institutional investors. The Listing Rules put listed companies under varying degrees of pressure to comply with the different sections of the Code. For our purposes four aspects of the Code deserve mention. First, Section A of the Code attempts to solve, or at any rate reduce, the acute conflicts of interest in the area of directors' remuneration by requiring[99] companies to establish "remuneration committees", con-

---

[94] On the directors' report see above, pp. 517–518. s.325(3) also requires the register of directors' interests (see above, p. 450) to contain information about share options granted to directors.

[95] Directors' Remuneration: Report of a Study Group chaired by Sir Richard Greenbury, 1995.

[96] On the continuing obligations see above, p. 416.

[97] The Company Accounts (Disclosure of Directors' Emoluments) Regs. 1997 (S.I. 1997 No. 570), enhancing disclosure of gains made on the exercise of share options or under long-term incentive schemes and of pension contributions on the director's behalf. The statutory changes are clearly thought subordinate to the changes to the *Listing Rules*, though they will have especial importance for unlisted companies.

[98] Report of the Committee on the Financial Aspects of Corporate Governance, 1992. See above, p. 191.

[99] para. 12.43(w) of the *Listing Rules* requires a listed company incorporated in the U.K. to state in the annual report whether it has complied with Section A and to "explain and justify" any areas of non-compliance. So a company could refrain from setting up an appropriate remuneration committee, if it were prepared to accept the resulting public opprobrium. All the provisions of the *Listing Rules* which implement the Greenbury Committee's recommendations apply, not surprisingly, only to listed companies incorporated in the U.K. Listed compan-

sisting entirely of non-executive directors, to determine both the company's general remuneration policy and the remuneration packages of individual executive directors. The remuneration committee is to report directly to the general meeting, rather than to the board as a whole. So those directors personally interested in the remuneration decisions are wholly removed from decision-making on these matters.[1] Secondly, Part B of the Code requires[2] full disclosure to the general meeting of all elements of each individual director's remuneration package, including details of incentive schemes and of pension entitlements earned during the year. The Act already requires disclosure of much of this information, though the Code adds to the Act's requirements, notably in the areas of pensions (where establishing the appropriate basis of disclosure has proved very controversial) and of any performance criteria upon which incentive schemes are conditioned. Probably more important in Section B is the requirement of *ex ante* disclosure of the remuneration policy which the remuneration committee has adopted and which will guide its decisions in the future on remuneration matters. It is to be noted, however, that companies do not have to seek the approval by the shareholders of the remuneration policy by putting forward a resolution for its adoption.

However, thirdly, shareholder approval is required for "new long-term incentive schemes (including share option schemes)".[3] Share option schemes, which are now rather out of favour, involve the granting to executives of (usually) rights to subscribe in the future for shares in the company at a price fixed at the time the option is granted, so that if the company's shares appreciate in value, the executives will be a position to exercise the options and make a profit. Although the Act does not apply its pre-emption provisions to employee share schemes (which include executive share schemes),[4] the Listing Rules have long required shareholder approval for employees' share schemes which may involve the issue of new shares. And rightly so, for the essence of such schemes is that shares are issued at less than

---

ies incorporated outside the U.K. have these matters regulated by the law of the place of incorporation. This shows how in this instance securities market law is being used to fill a deficiency in company law.

[1] Under art. 94 of Table A, directors may be present at decisions on their remuneration, though they may not vote on the decision or be counted in the quorum. Since the new requirement amounts to compulsory delegation of an area of decision-making from the board to a committee of the board, some companies may have to amend their articles of association so as to permit it. For companies with 1985 Table A articles a simple decision by the board to delegate is all that is required: art. 72.

[2] para. 2.43 (x) (ii) of the *Listing Rules* requires companies to give "full consideration" to the provisions of Section B, but para. 12.43 (x) also requires of its own motion (and not just by reference to the Code) disclosure of the precise details of individual remuneration packages.

[3] Code, para. B12, implemented in the *Listing Rules*, paras. 13.13–13.17.

[4] s.89(5). If it did, the shareholders would in effect have a vote on the share option scheme by way of a vote on a resolution to disapply the pre-emption provisions. See above, pp. 305–313.

the prevailing market price at the time the options are exercised and so such schemes are inherently dilutive of the interests of the existing shareholders.[5] This requirement has now been extended to all long-term incentive schemes, whether taking the particular form of a share option scheme or not, since all long-term incentive schemes involve either a future commitment of corporate resources or dilution of the shareholders' equity or both.

Fourthly, and finally, the Code recommends certain substantive restrictions on some forms of directors' remuneration, though this is done in sections C and D of the Code, which are not usually made binding on listed companies by the Listing Rules. In particular, grants under long-term incentive schemes should "be subject to challenging performance criteria",[6] the frequent absence of which had brought share option schemes into disrepute. An increase in the price of the shares might reflect simply a rise in the stock market as a whole, rather than an especially good performance by the company in question, whose relative position in the market might even have declined. Where stock options are issued, they should not be exercisable in less than three years, should not be exercisable in a block and the exercise price should not be less than the market price at the date of grant of the option.[7] Fixed-term contracts or notice periods should not normally exceed one year[8] (in contrast to the five years required for shareholder approval under section 319) which is a crucial matter when it comes to calculating the compensation of directors forced to depart. However, this provision of the Code is enforced by the Listing Rules only to the extent of requiring disclosure of situations where the recommendation has not been complied with.[9]

Four comments may be made on the Greenbury Committee and its aftermath. First, it adds less to the previous Stock Exchange requirements than might appear at first sight, since the Exchange was already committed to a high degree of disclosure and a significant role for shareholders. Secondly, the Report demonstrates a distaste for statutory regulation on the part of both industrial and financial interests and the Government. The Committee states that "statutory controls . . .

---

[5] Shareholder approval is not required for share option schemes or other long-term incentive schemes which are open to all or substantially all the issuer's employees (provided that the employees are not coterminous with the directors), presumably on the grounds that the wide scope of the scheme is protection against directorial self-interest: para. 13.13A. Nor is shareholder approval required for schemes confined to an individual director and designed "in unusual circumstances" to facilitate the retention or recruitment of that individual.

[6] Code, para. C8.

[7] Code, paras. C6, C9 and C10. The last provision is in fact enforced by the *Listing Rules*, by way of a requirement for shareholder approval in such cases: paras. 13.30–13.32.

[8] Code, para. D2.

[9] para. 12.43 (x) (vii). However, the Cadbury Code requires that directors' service contracts "should not exceed three years without shareholders' approval" and para. 12.43(j) of the *Listing Rules* requires companies to report annually on the extent of their compliance with that Code also. On the Cadbury Code see above, p. 191.

would be at best unnecessary and at worst harmful'' but do not seek to demonstrate why the same degree of regulation as is now embodied in the Listing Rules would become unnecessary or harmful if embodied in statute and thus applied, say, to all public companies.

Thirdly, the role of non-executive directors is further enhanced, the Greenbury Committee taking forward a trend begun by the Cadbury Committee. Both Committees emphasise the supervisory role of the non-executive directors, the Greenbury Committee in the particular area of directors' remuneration, the Cadbury Committee more generally. One begins to wonder whether the traditional British objections to the two-tier board (separate supervisory and management boards) are sustainable, given the growing division of functions within the single board. The debate is becoming less one about the appropriateness of the division of function and more one about whether the supervisory function is better discharged within a single-tier or a two-tier arrangement.[10]

Finally, although the tone of the Greenbury Report is suggestive of restraint in the setting of executive pay, it remains to be seen whether the new arrangements will make much difference. Early indications are that non-executive directors, who are often executives of other companies, are not noticeably more tough on levels of directors' remuneration or stricter on the formulation of performance criteria than boards as a whole, and that mobilising shareholder action over such matters still faces all the difficulties associated with collective action.

(d) Substantial property transactions. Sections 320–322 require substantial property transactions with directors to be approved in advance by the company in general meetings. Under section 320(1), except as provided in section 321, a company is prohibited from entering into any arrangement whereby a director[11] of the company or its holding company, or a person connected with[12] such a director, is to acquire[13] from the company or the company is to acquire from any such person, one or more non-cash assets[14] ''of the requisite value'', unless the arrangement is first approved by a resolution of the company in general meeting and, if the director or connected person is a director of the holding company, by a resolution in general meeting of that company. Under subsection (2) the present ''requisite value'', is anything exceeding £100,000 or 10 per cent of the company's net assets if more

---

[10] For a strong argument that this function is better discharged within a reformed unitary board see G. Owen, *The Future of Britain's Boards of Directors: Two Tiers or One*, Board for Chartered Accountants in Business, 1995.

[11] Again including a shadow director.

[12] Defined in s.346.

[13] Defined in s.739(2) as including the creation or extinction of an estate or interest in, or right over, any property and the discharge of any person's liability other than for a liquidated sum.

[14] Defined in s.739(1) as meaning ''any property or interest in property other than cash''.

than £2,000.[15] It has been said of section 320: "The thinking behind that section is that if directors enter into a substantial commercial transaction with one of their number, there is a danger that their judgment may be distorted by conflicts of interest and loyalties, even in cases of no actual dishonesty . . . It enables members to provide a check . . . it does make it likely the matter will be more widely ventilated, and a more objective decision reached."[16]

To the need for approval in general meetings there are exceptions in section 321. The only ones needing mention[17] are: (a) inter-group transfers when the property is to be acquired by a holding company from one of its wholly owned subsidiaries, or vice versa, or by one wholly owned subsidiary from another wholly owned subsidiary of that holding company,[18] and (b) arrangements entered into by a company which is being wound up otherwise than by a members' voluntary winding-up.[19]

Section 322 in effect provides that an arrangement which contravenes section 320, or any transaction entered into in pursuance of it, is to be treated much as it would be under the general equitable principle when there has been no modification of that principle by provisions in the company's articles; *i.e.* it is voidable at the instance of the company unless it is too late to avoid it[20] or the arrangement has been affirmed within a reasonable time by a general meeting.[21] Indeed, much of the statutory material in Part X only makes sense against a background in which the articles of companies routinely disapply the basic equitable principle in many areas of conflict of interest.[22]

Under subsection (3) the other party and any director of the company who authorised the arrangement, or any transaction in pursuance of it, is liable to account to the company for any gain which he has made, and (jointly and severally with any others liable under the section) is also liable to indemnify the company from any loss resulting from the arrangement or transaction. Subsection (3) is without prejudice to any liability imposed otherwise than under it and the

[15] The original figures were doubled by S.I. 1990 No. 1393 made under s.345. The value of the net assets is to be determined by the latest accounts or, if none have been laid, by reference to its called-up share capital: s.320(2).
[16] *British Racing Driver's Club Ltd v. Hextall Erskine & Co. (a firm)* [1996] 3 All E.R. 667 at 681–682. The case is a good illustration of the operation of both the dangers and their remedy.
[17] s.321(1) corresponds to s.319(4) mentioned in n. 91, above.
[18] s.321(2)(a).
[19] s.321(2)(g). *i.e.* in a winding-up in which the liquidator will not have been appointed by the members on the nomination of the directors.
[20] s.322(1) and (2)(a) and (b).
[21] s.322(2)(c). When the director is concerned as director of the holding company affirmation is required of both a general meeting of the company party to the transaction and a general meeting of its holding company.
[22] For example, art. 85 of Table A: "Subject to the provisions of the Act, and provided he has disclosed to the directors the nature and extent of any material interest of his, a director . . . may be a party to, or otherwise interested in, any transaction or arrangement with the company or in which the company is interested . . ."

liability arises whether or not the arrangement or transaction has been avoided in pursuance of subsection (1).[23] However, under subsection (2), if the company has been indemnified, pursuant to subsection (3), for the loss or damage suffered by it, it cannot subsequently avoid the contract even though *restitutio in integrum* is still possible.[24]

It will be noted that the section does not preclude the director from voting as a member at a general meeting to approve or affirm. But, in the case of a listed company, the Stock Exchange may require him not to.[25]

Section 322A was inserted by the 1989 Act as a result of its reforms of the law relating to *ultra vires*. As such it has already been dealt with in Chapter 10.[26] Here all that is necessary is a reminder that it relates to transactions (cash or non-cash) in which the parties include the company and a director of the company or its holding company or a person connected with such a director or a company with which the director is associated.[27] If the transaction exceeds the powers conferred on the board by the company's constitution, the transaction is voidable at the instance of the company and the director[28] must account for his gains—essentially as under section 322.

Sections 323–329 are dealt with in the Chapter on insider dealing.[29] However, it should here be pointed out that they play a wider role in that, by requiring disclosure of the holdings of, and dealings in, the securities of the company by its directors or their families, they may afford valuable information in judging the extent to which the directors are fulfilling their duty to subordinate their personal interests to that of the company.

(e) Loans, quasi-loans and credit transactions. Restraints on making loans to directors date back to the 1948 Act, but sections 330–344 extend them, especially in relation to public companies.

Subject to the exceptions in sections 332–338,[30] section 330(2) and (3) prohibit a company from making a loan to a director of it or of its holding company or from entering into any guarantee[31] or providing any security in connection with a loan made by any person to such a

---

[23] s.322(4).
[24] And if an arrangement contravening s.320 has been entered into with a person connected with a director, the director is not liable under subs. (3) if he shows that he took all reasonable steps to secure the company's compliance with the section: s.322(5). Nor is the connected person, or another director who authorised the arrangement or transaction, if he shows that, at the time the arrangement was made, he did not know the relevant circumstance constituting the contravention: s.322(6).
[25] *Listing Rules*, para. 11.5(a).
[26] At pp. 217–218.
[27] "Connected" and "associated" are defined in s.346.
[28] Or connected or associated person.
[29] At pp. 448–452.
[30] s.330(1).
[31] Which includes an indemnity: s.331(2).

director.[32] Further, a "relevant company" (*i.e.* any company which is part of a group which contains a public company[33]) is prohibited from:

(a) making what the Act calls a "quasi-loan",[34] to a director of the company or of its holding company;
(b) making a loan or quasi-loan to a person connected with such a director; or
(c) entering into any guarantee or providing any security in connection with a loan or quasi-loan made by any other person to such a director or connected person.[35]

The object of extending the prohibition, so far as relevant companies are concerned, is to catch transactions resulting in debts to the company which are not technically "loans". Essentially, quasi-loans are transactions, to which the company is a party, resulting in a director or his connected person obtaining some financial benefit for which he is liable to make reimbursement to the company. If, for example, a public company agrees that its managing director may at all times retain £50,000 of the company's money to provide a "float" out of which to meet expenses of worldwide trips on the company's business (instead of his having to reclaim expenses from the company) that will be an unlawful quasi-loan.[36]

Section 330(4) similarly prohibits a company from entering into a "credit transaction" with such director or his connected person or from guaranteeing or providing security in connection with a credit transaction with him by any other person. A credit transaction is one under which the director or his connected person is supplied with goods or sold land under a hire-purchase agreement or conditional sale agreement; or in which land or goods are let or hired out to him in return for periodical payments, or land, goods or services are supplied to him on the understanding that full payment is to be deferred.[37]

Section 330(6) prohibits the company from arranging the assignment to it, or the assumption by it, of any rights, obligations or liabilities of a transaction which, if entered into by the company, would have contravened subsection (2), (3) or (4). Nor, under section 330(7), may a company take part in any arrangement whereby another person

---

[32] s.330(2).

[33] s.331(6) which defines "relevant company" rather more elaborately than in the text.

[34] Defined, in a complicated fashion, in s.331(3) which describes the company as "the creditor" and the director or his connected person as "the borrower". The text attempts to describe the effect of the statutory definitions in terms more immediately intelligible. This, it is hoped, redners it unnecessary, in relation to either quasi-loans or credit transactions, to go into the intricacies of s.331(9).

[35] s.330(3).

[36] But it would not have been unlawful if the float had been more modest and s.337 (below) had been complied with.

[37] s.331(7).

enters into a transaction which, if it had been entered into by the company, would have contravened section 330(2), (3), (4) or (6), and the other person pursuant to the arrangement obtains any benefit from the company or group.

Finally, section 330(5) provides that for the purpose of sections 330–346 "director" includes a shadow director.[38]

To each of these prohibitions, sections 332–338 provide certain exceptions. In a book of this sort it is not necessary to go into detail. It suffices to say that their general effect is to exclude certain transactions which are small,[39] short-term,[40] intra-group,[41] or in the ordinary course of the company's business and on its normal terms,[42] but provided, in most cases, that the aggregate amount or value of that transaction and of that outstanding on earlier such transactions (the "relevant amounts") does not exceed a prescribed figure.[43] Section 339 prescribes how the "relevant amounts" are to be ascertained and section 340 how the "value" of transactions is to be determined.

Specific mention should, however, be made of section 337. This says that a company is not prohibited by section 330 "from doing anything to provide a director with funds to meet expenditure incurred or to be incurred by him for the purposes of the company or for the purpose of enabling him properly to perform his duties as an officer of the company."[44] But it then severely limits that concession by requiring either that prior approval of the general meeting is obtained after disclosure of the matters stated in subsection (3)[45]; or, if such approval is not given at or before the next AGM, that the funds will be repaid within six months after the AGM. Moreover, a relevant company must not enter into any such transactions if the aggregate of the relevant amounts exceeds £20,000.[46] Hence, there is now a curb on the abuses, disclosed in several Inspectors' reports, whereby directors draw freely on the company's funds, making it difficult to determine at any time precisely what is the extent of their indebtedness to the company.

---

[38] But, as in the following sections, excluding a holding company: s.741(3).

[39] See s.334 as regards small loans.

[40] See s.332 as regards short-term quasi-loans.

[41] See s.333 as regards intra-group loans and s.336 as regards transactions for the benefit of the holding company.

[42] See s.335 and, as regards money-lending companies, s.338.

[43] The figures in the original version of the Act have been at least doubled (to account for inflation) either by the 1989 Act or by 1990 S.I. No. 1393 and are at the time of writing: in ss.332(1) and 334(1), £5,000; in s.335(1), £10,000; in s.337(3), £20,000; and in s.340(7), £100,000.

[44] s.337(1). Nor does it "prohibit a company from doing anything to enable a director to avoid incurring such expenditure": s.337(2). But most such "things" (*e.g.* supplying him with a company car) would not normally be transactions caught by s.330.

[45] *i.e.* the purpose of the expenditure, the amount provided by the company and the extent of the company's liability under any connected transaction: s.337(4).

[46] s.337(3).

Under section 341, breaches of section 330 give rise to civil remedies[47] similar to those under section 322 (for breaches of section 320) and under section 322A. There are also criminal penalties under section 342.

Generally, the types of transaction mentioned in section 330 which are lawfully undertaken under the exceptions will require to be disclosed in the annual accounts.[48]

COMMON LAW DUTIES OF CARE AND SKILL[48a]

This is an area of the law relating to directors' duties which is, at last, beginning to undergo a profound change. Traditionally, the law has demonstrated a striking contrast between the directors' heavy duties of loyalty and good faith and their light obligations of skill and diligence. Recent decisions in England, and even more so in Australia,[49] suggest that laxness of the law in relation to skill and diligence is a thing of the past. The courts have been influenced by the development of more demanding statutory standards for directors whose companies are facing insolvency[50] and have developed the general common law requirements by analogy to those specific statutory provisions. The courts may also have been influenced by the increasing emphasis upon the importance of the role of the non-executive director in governmental and semi-official reports, such as the Cadbury and Greenbury Reports.[51] These reports suggest that even non-executive directors should not be seen and should not see themselves as mere figureheads.

The traditional view is to be found in a stream of largely nineteenth-century cases which culminated in the decision in 1925 in *Re City Equitable Fire Insurance Co.*[52] Those cases seem to have framed the

---

[47] The company is entitled to avoid the transaction, to indemnity against loss, and to recovery of profits made by the director or his connected person.

[48] Under Sched. 6 of the Act. Special provisions apply in relation to disclosure by banking companies: ss.343–344.

[48a] Both common law and equity developed duties of care, which historically were based upon different standards of care and were in other respects different. Today the tendency is to amalgamate the rules arising from these two sources, in favour of the common law rules. More important is the recognition that a person who is a fiduciary and who acts negligently does not, without more, commit a breach of fiduciary duty. A negligent act does not necessarily involve a breach of the duties of loyalty and good faith, and, where it does not, the plaintiff's remedy will sound normally in damages and he or she will not have access to the remedies made available for breaches of fiduciary duty. See *Bristol and West Building Society v. Mothew* [1996] 4 All E.R. 698, C.A. and below, pp. 649–652.

[49] See the fully argued reasoning of the majority of the Court of Appeal of New South Wales in *Daniels v. Anderson* (1995) 16 ACSR 607, on the decision in which at first instance see the illuminating analysis by Stapledon, "The AWA Case: Non-Executive Directors, Auditors and Corporate Governance Issues in Court" in Prentice and Holland (eds.), *Contemporary Issues in Corporate Governance* (Oxford, 1993).

[50] Principally the wrongful trading provisions to be found in s.214 of the Insolvency Act 1986.

[51] See above, pp. 193 and 632.

[52] [1925] Ch. 407, a decision of the C.A. but always quoted for the judgment of Romer J. at first instance, because the appeal concerned only the liability of the auditors.

directors' duties of skill and care with non-executive rather than executive directors in mind and, moreover, on the basis of a view that the non-executive director had no serious role to play within the company but was simply a piece of window-dressing aimed at promoting the company's image.[53] The result was a conceptualisation of the duty in highly subjective terms. The proposition was famously formulated by Romer J. in the *City Equitable* case that "a director need not exhibit in the performance of his duties a greater degree of skill than may reasonably be expected from a person of *his* knowledge and experience."[54] The courts were also influenced by a model of corporate decision-making which gave the shareholders effective control over the choice of directors. If the shareholders chose incompetent directors, that was their fault and the remedy lay in their hands. As we have seen,[55] that is no longer an accurate picture of the degree of control exercised by shareholders over boards of directors in most public companies.

The proposition formulated by Romer J. is highly inappropriate for executive directors, appointed to their positions and paid large, sometimes very large, sums of money for the expertise which they assert they can bring to the business. Of course, it may well be possible to hold such directors to an objective standard of skill and care via the express and implied terms in the service contract under which they took up their executive position. In relation to employees, even though they are lower down in the hierarchy than directors, the common law has long recognised that, if an employee holds him- or herself out as having a particular skill, the employee will be held to an objective standard of reasonableness in its exercise.[56] However, this method of approach does nothing to improve the standards of skill and care required of non-executive directors, for whom the only relevant rules are those relating to directors.

The beginnings of the modern approach can be found in *Dorchester Finance Co. v. Stebbing*,[57] where Foster J. held that the proposition of Romer J., quoted above, applied only to the exercise by a director of his skill. This duty was to be distinguished from his duty of diligence, where what was required was "such care as an ordinary man might

---

[53] The most famous example of this is perhaps *Re Cardiff Savings Bank* [1892] 2 Ch. 100, where the Marquis of Bute, whose family, despite its Scottish antecedents, owned, indeed had largely rebuilt, Cardiff Castle, was appointed president of the Bank at the age of six months and attended only one meeting of the board in his whole life. He was held not liable.

[54] At 427 (emphasis added). This test contains *an* objective element because the director could be held liable for failing on a particular occasion to live up to the standard of which he or she is in fact capable of reaching, but the stronger element in the proposition is the subjective one, meaning that the director can never be required to achieve a standard higher than that which he or she is personally capable of reaching. See further, below.

[55] Above, Chap. 21.

[56] *Lister v. Romford Ice and Cold Storage Co. Ltd* [1957] A.C. 555, H.L.

[57] Decided in 1977 but fully reported only in 1989: [1989] BCLC 498.

be expected to take on his own behalf''. This is an objective test and one pitched at a reasonably high level, since presumably an ordinary man will be diligent in the promotion of his own affairs. Although *Dorchester Finance* was an easy case—without inquiring to what purpose the money was to be paid, the negligent non-executive directors were in the habit of signing blank cheques to be filled in later by the executive director—the principle underlying it suggests that the old cases on non-attendance at board meetings may not be a good guide to the current law.[58]

However, the line between an (objective) duty of diligence and a (subjective) duty to exercise skill is not always easy to draw, nor in principle should such a line be drawn. Consequently, it is highly significant that in two recent cases[59] Hoffmann J. has expressed the view that both elements of the duty of care are to be assessed objectively. He explicitly adopted as an accurate expression of the common law the test contained in section 214(4) of the Insolvency Act in relation to wrongful trading.[60] This is that an assessment of what the director should have done or known is to be based on what a ''a reasonably diligent person having both (a) the general knowledge, skill and experience that may reasonably be expected of a person carrying out the same functions as are carried out by that director in relation to the company and (b) the general knowledge, skill and experience that that director has''.

The crucial difference between the statutory formulation and that of Romer J. is that in the latter the director's subjective level of skill sets the standard required of the director,[61] whereas under the former the director's subjective level does so only if it improves upon the objective standard of the reasonable director. Limb (a) of the statutory formula sets a standard which all directors must meet and it is not one dependent on the particular director's capabilities; limb (b) adds a subjective standard which, however, can operate only to increase the level of care required of the director.[62]

What does this all mean or not mean for directors? First, although

---

[58] See *Re Cardiff Savings Bank*, above, n. 53, where Stirling J. said that ''neglect or omission to attend meetings is not, in my opinion, the same thing as neglect or omission of a duty which ought to be performed at those meetings'' (at 109). This seems a pernicious doctrine since it exposes to a greater risk of liability the director who turns up and participates in the decision as against the one who absents himself entirely.

[59] *Norman v. Theodore Goddard* [1991] BCLC 1027 (where the judge was ''willing to assume'' that s.214 of the Insolvency Act represented the common law) and *Re D'Jan of London Ltd* [1994] 1 BCLC 561 where the director was found negligent on the basis of an objective test, though it has to be said that the director could probably have been found liable on the facts on a subjective test of diligence (he signed an insurance proposal form without reading it).

[60] See above, p. 153.

[61] See n. 54, above.

[62] The section attributes to the director the knowledge, skill and experience of *both* the reasonable man and the particular director in question, so the latter is important only when it *adds* to the attributes of the reasonable person.

directors, executive and non-executive, may be on the way to becoming subject to a uniform and objective duty of care, what the discharge of that duty requires in particular cases will not be uniform. As the statutory formulation itself recognises, what is required of the director will depend on the functions which have been assigned[63] to him or her, so that there will be variations, not only between executive and non-executive directors[64] but also between different types of executive director (and equally of non-executives) and between different types and sizes of company.

Secondly, the imposition of an objective duty of care does not necessarily require a directorship to be regarded as a profession. The vexed issue of what constitutes a profession does not have to be addressed; all that is required is an assessment of what is reasonably required of a person having, as the statute puts it, the knowledge, skill and experience which a person in the position of the particular director ought to have. Given the enormous range of types and sizes of companies, it would be odd if all directors were to be regarded as professional. On the other hand, as was pointed out by the Court of Appeal of New South Wales, an objective approach does require even non-executive directors, as a minimum, to "take reasonable steps to place themselves in a position to guide and monitor the management of the company".[65] The days of the wholly inactive or passive director would thus seem to be numbered—or, at least, a director who is so runs a high risk of being held negligent.

Thirdly, much of what was said by Romer J. in 1925 remains good law. In particular his proposition—that "in respect of all duties that, having regard to the exigencies of business, and the articles of association, may properly be left to some other official, a director is, in the absence of grounds for suspicion, justified in trusting to that official to perform such duties honestly"[66]—is an inevitable reflection of the fact that companies are organisations, sometimes very big organisations, the running of which may require a large staff. In the recent cases of *Daniels v. Anderson* and *Norman v. Theodore Goddard*,[67] where objective tests were applied, at least some of the directors

---

[63] See in this respect s.214(5) which refers to functions entrusted to the director as well as those actually carried out.

[64] Note how in *Daniels v. Anderson*, above, n. 49, the non-executive directors were held not liable for the failure to discover the foreign exchange frauds being committed by an employee, but the chief executive officer was so held.

[65] *Daniels v. Anderson*, above, n. 49, at 664. The language of monitoring fits in well with the views of the Cadbury and Greenbury Committees on the proper role for the board of directors, but it suggests that thought ought to be given to the wording of art. 70 of Table A, which states that it is the business of the board to manage the company, which in the case of large companies it clearly is not.

[66] Above, n. 52 at 429. See also *Dovey v. Cory* [1901] A.C. 477, H.L. But the matter must not be delegated to an obviously inappropriate employee or official, as was the case in *Re City Equitable* itself.

[67] Above, n. 59.

escaped liability as a result of the application of this proposition. By
defining the extent to which delegation is permitted, the courts will be
demarcating the point at which guidance and monitoring cease and
operational activity begins.

Fourthly, it follows from the inevitable acceptance of extensive delegation, at least in large companies, that directors cannot be guarantors
that everything is going well within the company. Subordinate
employees may be fraudulent or negligent and the directors may not
discover this in time, but this does not necessarily mean that they have
been negligent. That conclusion will depend on the facts of the situation. Further, although nearly all decided English cases have arisen
out of alleged failures by directors to act or to act effectively, negligence suits could arise where the directors have clearly acted, but with
disastrous consequences for their company. Here too, however, since
companies are in business to take risks, the fact that a business venture
does not pay off and even leads the company into financial trouble
does not necessarily indicate negligence, though it may encourage the
shareholders to replace the directors. In the United States, where an
objective standard for directors' competence is well established, the
"business judgment" rule generally operates to relieve the directors
of liability in such cases.[68] In other words, the acceptance by the courts
that the standard of care is objective still leaves open the question of
the level at which that standard should be pitched. In particular, one
may expect the courts to be alive to the probability that they are better
at dealing with conflicts of interest than with the assessment of business risks and to the desirability of avoiding the luxury of substituting
the courts' hindsight for the directors' foresight.

Finally, as with auditors,[69] showing breach of a duty of care is one
thing; showing that the loss suffered by the company was a consequence of the breach of duty may be quite another. Thus, the true
explanation of the finding of no liability in *Re Denham & Co.*[70] is
only in part that the director was entitled to rely on others. Equally
important was the judge's view that, even if the director had made the
inquiries he should have made, he would probably not have discovered
the fraud.

RATIFICATION OF BREACHES OF DUTY

It is a normal principle of the law relating to fiduciaries that those to
whom the duties are owed may release those who owe the duties
from their legal obligations and may do so either prospectively or

---

[68] Despite the unusual decision in *Smith v. Van Gorkom* 488 A.2d 858 (1985) imposing liability
where the directors decided to merge their company with another. See generally, R.C. Clark,
Corporate Law, (Boston, 1986), pp. 123–129.

[69] See above, p. 557.

[70] (1883) 25 Ch.D. 752, on which see Stapledon, *op. cit.* n. 49, at p. 206. The classic statement
of the problem is that by Learned Hand J. in *Barnes v. Andrews* 298 F. 614, 616–617 (1924).

retrospectively, provided that full disclosure of the relevant facts is made to them in advance of the decision. Consequently, it has long been recognised that an ordinary majority of the shareholders in general meeting may release the directors from many of their fiduciary duties, provided at least that the company is a going concern.[71] Indeed, as we have seen above,[72] the courts have tentatively accepted that in some limited cases even the board of directors may grant a release from an individual director's duties, though those circumstances should remain limited in view of the potential for "mutual back-scratching" among directors.

Ratification[73] does not involve the shareholders taking the decision in question but rather their deciding whether to adopt a decision taken, albeit in breach of duty, by the directors. Consequently, ratification by the shareholders is not inconsistent with articles of association which deprive the shareholders' meeting of most managerial powers and confer them instead on the board.[74] Ratification has a twin effect: it operates so as to make binding on the company a transaction which might otherwise be impeachable as having been entered into in breach of fiduciary duty and so as to release the directors from liability to the company for breach of duty. In the case of *ultra vires* transactions the statute now distinguishes between these two effects of the ratification process and requires separate resolutions for each,[75] but at common law a simple resolution to "ratify" a transaction seems to have both effects.[76]

However, the courts have stopped short of accepting the proposition that all breaches of directors' duties may be ratified by an ordinary majority of the shareholders in general meeting.[77] The main reason for

---

[71] The significance of the tentative recognition by the courts that the company's interests are the interests of the creditors when insolvency threatens is precisely that it throws doubt upon the power of the shareholders to continue to ratify breaches of the directors' duties. It seems to be assumed that the statutory recognition of the interests of the employees has not affected the power of the shareholders to ratify breaches of duty, though it is not clear why this should be in a case where the breach consists of a failure to consider the interests of the employees. See further above, pp. 603–604.

[72] p. 620.

[73] The term refers technically to post-breach approval by the shareholders, but will be used in this section, unless the context otherwise requires, to refer to approval in advance by the shareholders of the directors' proposed course of action.

[74] *Bamford v. Bamford* [1970] Ch. 212, C.A. On the division of powers between shareholders and the board, see p. 183, above.

[75] s.35(3), though the third party will be protected, whether there is ratification or not, if the company has entered into a legal obligation to do the "*ultra vires*" act: s.35(1) and (2). Note also that s.35 requires a special resolution to relieve the directors from liability for embarking upon an *ultra vires* transaction. See pp. 212–213, above.

[76] There is a lot to be said for the statutory approach, since the considerations which are relevant to the two decisions are not identical. See Yeung, "Disentagling the Tangled Skein: the Ratification of Directors' Actions" (1992) 66 A.J.L.R. 343. But presumably at common law the resolution could be expressly framed so as to achieve the first but not the second result.

[77] In this Chapter we are not concerned with the impact of the classification of the breach as between these two categories upon the right of the individual shareholder to sue to enforce the company's rights. For a discussion of this thorny issue see below, pp. 670–676.

this reluctance seems to be the fact that the shareholders are not subject to fiduciary duties (even of a less extensive kind than those applying to directors) when voting on resolutions to ratify the directors'
actions[78] and, furthermore, that it is open to the directors who are in
breach of duty to cast their votes as shareholders in favour of the
forgiveness of the breaches of duty committed by them as directors.
On the contrary, it has been repeatedly laid down that votes are proprietary rights, to the same extent as any other incidents of the shares,
which the holder may exercise in his own selfish interests even if these
are opposed to those of the company.[79] He may even bind himself by
contract to vote or not to vote in a particular way and the contract will
be enforced by injunction.[80]

It is perhaps not surprising that the courts have been reluctant to
accept that directors, who have *de jure* or, more likely, *de facto* control
over the general meeting, can disregard their fiduciary duties provided
only that they have the front to disclose their wrongdoing to the shareholders and to force through an approving resolution. However, identifying the limits which the courts have placed on the power of the
shareholders to ratify breaches of fiduciary duty is not an easy task.
The most commonly formulated proposition is that a majority of the
shareholders may not by resolution expropriate to themselves company property, because the property of the company is something in
which all the shareholders of the company have a (pro rata) interest.
Consequently, a resolution to ratify directors' breaches of duty which
would offend against this principle is ineffective (unless, presumably,
all the shareholders of the company agreed to the resolution and any
relevant capital maintenance rules were complied with).[81] But it is a
principle easier to formulate than apply, because of the ambiguities
surrounding the meaning of ''property''.

The principle was applied in *Cook v. Deeks*,[82] in which the directors
had diverted to themselves contracts which they should have taken up
on behalf of the company. By virtue of their controlling interests they
secured the passing of a resolution in general meeting ratifying and
approving what they had done. It was held that they must be regarded

---

[78] This proposition needs to be qualified where the shareholders are voting, not on a ratification
resolution, but to amend the articles of the company or to alter class rights. See Chap. 26,
below.

[79] *North-West Transportation v. Beatty* (1887) 12 App.Cas. 589, P.C.; *Burland v. Earle* [1902]
A.C. 83, P.C.; *Goodfellow v. Nelson Line* [1912] 2 Ch. 324; *Northern Counties Securities Ltd
v. Jackson & Steeple Ltd* [1974] 1 W.L.R. 1133. The contrary views of Vinelott J. in *Prudential Assurance Co. Ltd v. Newman Industries Ltd (No. 2)* [1981] Ch. 257, to the effect that
interested shareholders may not vote on ratification resolutions must be regarded as heretical.
See Wedderburn (1981) 44 M.L.R. 202.

[80] See below, p. 731.

[81] See *Re Halt Garage (1964) Ltd* [1982] 3 All E.R.1016; *Aveling Barford Ltd v. Perion Ltd*
[1989] BCLC 626; *Rolled Steel Products (Holdings) Ltd v. British Steel Corporation* [1986]
Ch. 246 at 296.

[82] [1916] 1 A.C. 554, P.C.

as holding the benefits of the contracts on trust for the company, for "directors holding a majority of votes would not be permitted to make a present to themselves".[83] The same may apply when the present is not to themselves but to someone else.

Where, then, is the line to be drawn between those cases where shareholder action is improper, and those in which shareholder action has been upheld? How, in particular, can one reconcile *Cook v. Deeks* with the many cases in which the liability of directors has been held to disappear as a result of ratification in general meeting, notwithstanding the use of their own votes?[84] Why, in *Regal (Hastings) Ltd v. Gulliver*,[85] did the House of Lords say that the directors would not have been liable to account for their profits had the transaction been ratified, while, in *Cook v. Deeks*, the Privy Council made them account notwithstanding such ratification? A satisfactory answer, consistent with common sense and with the decided cases, is difficult (and perhaps impossible) to provide.[86]

The solution may be that a distinction is to be drawn between (i) misappropriating the company's property and (ii) merely making an incidental profit for which the directors are liable to account to the company. *Cook v. Deeks* came within (i) for it was the duty of the directors to acquire the contracts on behalf of the company and accordingly when they themselves acquired them they did so as constructive trustees of the company. On the other hand, in *Regal (Hastings) Ltd v. Gulliver* the directors did not misappropriate any property of the company; they had instead profited from information acquired as directors of the company and made use of an opportunity of which the company might have availed itself.

Beyond the proposition that ratification is not effective where it would amount to misappropriation of corporate property, it is difficult to formulate any further limitations which command general consent. It is sometimes said that breach of the directors' duties to act bona fide in the interests of the company cannot be ratified by ordinary resolution of the shareholders. Certainly, this would be odd where the breach consists of failure to take account of the interests of the employees (as is required by section 309) or of the creditors, since that would mean release of the duty by the persons other than those to whom it is owed.[87] However, it is not obvious that release should

---

[83] At 564.

[84] *e.g. N.W. Transportation Co. v. Beatty* (1887) 12 App.Cas. 589. P.C.; *Burland v. Earle* [1902] A.C. 83, P.C.; *A. Harris v. Harris Ltd*, 1936 S.C. 183 (Sc.); *Baird v. Baird & Co.*, 1949 S.L.T. 368 (Sc.).

[85] [1942] 1 All E.R. 378; [1967] 2 A.C. 134n., H.L., above, pp. 615 *et seq.*

[86] It has troubled a number of other writers: see, in particular, Wedderburn [1957] Cam.L.J. 194; [1958] *ibid.* 93; Afterman, *Company Directors and Controllers* (Sydney, 1970), pp. 149 *et seq.*; Beck, in Ziegel (ed.), *Studies in Canadian Company Law*, Vol. II (Toronto, 1973). pp. 232–238, and Sealy [1967] C.L.J. 83, pp. 102 *et seq.*

[87] s.309(2) says that the duty "is enforceable in the same way as any other fiduciary duty owed to a company by its directors", but that proposition does not address the issue of ratifiability.

never be permitted where it is the interests of the shareholders which have been ignored by the directors, and the Court of Appeal in *Bamford v. Bamford*[88] proceeded on the assumption that such ratification was possible. For example, if the directors have simply failed to consider whether a particular transaction was in the interests of the shareholders,[89] there would seem to be no reason why it should not be open to the shareholders in general meeting to conclude that, on consideration, it was and so ratify it.[90]

In some Australian cases it has been suggested that the improper purposes doctrine applies to shareholder decisions, including ratification decisions.[91] Even if this is in principle possible, the shareholders should not be subject to the same duty in this regard as directors. As we have seen,[92] as against directors that doctrine aims to prevent them taking out of the hands of the shareholders decisions which rightly belong with the latter, notably decisions on the success or failure of takeover bids. It is entirely consonant with this approach that the shareholders by a majority should be free to decide on the bidder's fate.[93] The development of a notion of improper purposes *vis-à-vis* decision-making by the shareholders relates in fact to a difficult but rather different question of how one identifies the personal rights of individual shareholders which are not subject to the control of the majority. That is a matter to which we shall return in the next Chapter.

In short, in English law, at least, it would seem that a wide range of breaches of duty by directors may be ratified, whether arising out of lack of bona fides, improper purposes, conflict of interest or negligence,[94] provided that no dishonesty or expropriation of corporate property is involved in the transactions which are approved.

---

[88] [1972] Ch. 212. Both judgments delivered in the Court of Appeal referred to the case as one of lack of bona fides, though in fact Plowman J. at first instance characterised it more accurately as an "improper purposes" case.

[89] See above, p. 601.

[90] It would be different if actual dishonesty were involved: *Atwood v. Merryweather* (1867) L.R. 5 Eq. 464n.

[91] *Ngurli Ltd v. McCann* (1953) 90 C.L.R. 425; *Residues Treatment and Trading Co. Ltd v. Southern Resources Ltd (No. 4)* (1988) 51 SASR 196; *Colarc Pty Ltd v. Donarc Pty Ltd* (1991) 4 ACSR 155, discussed by Boros, *Minority Shareholder Remedies* (Oxford, 1995), pp. 200–203.

[92] Above, pp. 605 *et seq.*

[93] See below, p. 782. If the shareholders purport to interfere with powers which are within the exclusive jurisdiction of the directors, the law long ago developed principles to deal with this which do not depend on the idea of improper purposes. See above, pp. 183 *et seq.*

[94] The view implicit in *Daniels v. Daniels* [1978] Ch. 406 that the directors' negligence was not ratifiable, in contrast to the view taken in *Pavlides v. Jensen* [1956] Ch. 565, seems to be the consequence of the fact that in the former, unlike the latter, case, there was misappropriation of corporate property.

REMEDIES FOR BREACH OF DUTY

The remedies for breaches of the fiduciary duties discussed above, including situations where the directors, individually or collectively, have acted beyond the authority conferred upon them by the company's constitution, may be listed as follows:

(a) injunction or declaration;
(b) damages or compensation;
(c) restoration of the company's property;
(d) rescission of the contract;
(e) account of profits;
(f) summary dismissal.

(a) Injunction or declaration. These are primarily employed where the breach is threatened but has not yet occurred. If action can be taken in time, this is obviously the most satisfactory course. However, as we have seen above in relation to *ultra vires* situations,[95] if the remedy is to be used effectively by an individual shareholder, he or she will need to be well informed about the proposals of the board, which in all but the smallest companies will often not be the case. An injunction may also be appropriate where the breach has already occurred but is likely to continue or if some of its consequences can thereby be avoided.[96]

(b) Damages or compensation. Damages are the appropriate remedy for breach of a common law duty of care; compensation is the equivalent equitable remedy granted against a trustee or other fiduciary to compel restitution for the loss suffered by his breach of fiduciary duty. In practice, the distinction between the two has become blurred, and probably no useful purpose is served by seeking to keep them distinct. We have touched above[97] on the potentially difficult issues of remoteness of damage which can occur with this liability. All that needs to be added is that all the directors who participate in the breach[98] are jointly and severally liable with the usual rights of contribution *inter se*.[99]

---

[95] s.35(2), above, pp. 211–212.
[96] For example, to enjoin the delivery up of confidential documents improperly taken away by a former director: *Measures Bros. v. Measures* [1910] 2 Ch. 248, C.A.; *Cranleigh Precision Engineering Ltd v. Bryant* [1965] 1 W.L.R. 1293.
[97] p. 644.
[98] Either actively or by subsequent acquiescence in it: *Re Lands Allotment Co.* [1894] 1 Ch. 616, C.A. Merely protesting will not necessarily disprove acquiescence: *Joint Stock Discount Co. v. Brown* (1869) L.R. 8 Eq. 381.
[99] Civil Liability (Contribution) Act 1978. The application of the principle of joint and several liability is discussed more fully above at pp. 560 *et seq.* in relation to auditors.

(c) Restoration of property. Since directors are regarded as trustees of such of the company's property as has or should have come under their control,[1] it may be recovered *in rem* from them in so far as it is traceable, either in law or in equity. This includes not only property reduced into the company's possession but also property which it was the directors' duty to acquire for the company or perhaps give the company the opportunity of acquiring. But apparently it does not include all profits made by a director or other agent for which the company has a right to call upon him to account. These profits and the investments made with them will not be regarded as belonging in equity to the company unless they flowed from a use of the company's property. As we noted above,[2] the line between these two categories is not easy to draw, nor in particular is the question of when information is property one to which the courts have given consistent answers.[3]

(d) Rescission of contracts. An agreement with the company that breaks the rules relating to contracts in which directors are interested[4] may be avoided, provided that the company has done nothing to indicate an intention to ratify the agreement after finding out about the breach of duty,[5] that *restitutio in integrum* is possible and that the rights of bona fide third parties have not supervened.[6] Indeed, it may be doubted how strong a bar *restitutio in integrum* really is, given the wide powers the court has to order financial adjustments when directing rescission.[7]

(e) Accounting for profits. This liability may arise either out of a contract made between a director and the company[8] or as a result of some contract or arrangement between the director and a third person.[9] In the former case, accounting is a remedy additional to avoidance of the contract and is normally available whether or not there is rescission. However, if a director has sold his own property to the company, the

---

[1] *Re Forest of Dean Coal Co.* (1879) 10 Ch.D. 450.

[2] pp. 646–648, and see generally Oakley, "Proprietary Claims and their Priority in Insolvency" [1995] C.L.J. 377.

[3] See the contrasting views on this matter expressed by the judges in *Phipps v. Boardman* [1967] 2 A.C. 46, H.L.

[4] Above, pp. 610 *et seq.*

[5] *Lagunas Nitrate Co. v. Lagunas Syndicate* [1899] 2 Ch. 392, C.A., a case concerning promoters' liability, but the operative principles are the same.

[6] *Transvaal Lands Co. v. New Belgium (Transvaal) Land & Development Co.* [1914] 2 Ch. 488, C.A.

[7] This is certainly the case when fraud is involved and perhaps even when it is not: *Erlanger v. New Sombrero Phosphate Co.* (1873) 3 App. Cas. 1218, H.L.; *Spence v. Crawford* [1939] 3 All E.R. 271, H.L.; *Armstrong v. Jackson* [1917] 2 K.B. 822; *O'Sullivan v. Management Agency and Music Ltd* [1985] Q.B. 428, C.A.

[8] *Imperial Mercantile Credit Association v. Coleman* (1873) L.R. 6 H.L. 189.

[9] For example, in relation to the use of corporate information or opportunity discussed above, pp. 615–622.

right to an account of profits will be lost if the company elects not to rescind or is too late to do so.[10] When the profit arises out of a contract between the director and a third party there will be no question of rescinding that contract at the instance of the company, since the company is not a party to it. Here an account of profit will be the sole remedy.

As we have seen, in neither case does recovery of the profit depend on proof of any loss suffered by the company; it is recoverable not as damages or compensation but because the company is entitled to call upon the director to account to it. However, in the case of trustees, where the profit arises out of transactions with a third party, it has been usual to make an allowance in the account to provide a reasonable remuneration (including a profit element) for the work carried out by the trustee in effecting the transaction.[11] However, in *Guinness v. Saunders*[12] the House of Lords were minded to apply a stricter rule to directors, partly because it was always open to the company to make an award of remuneration to the errant director, if it so wished, and partly because the payment of remuneration would encourage directors to put themselves in a position of conflict, knowing that, even if they were brought to account, they would be handsomely rewarded for their efforts.[13]

(f) Summary dismissal. The right which an employer has at common law to dismiss an employee who has been guilty of serious misconduct has no application to the director as such.[14] However, it could be an effective sanction against executive directors and other officers of the company, since it may involve loss of livelihood rather than simply of position and directors' fees, and has been so used in some cases of insider dealing.[15]

---

[10] *Re Ambrose Lake Tin Co.* (1880) 11 Ch.D. 390, C.A.; *Re Cape Breton Co.* (1885) 29 Ch.D. 795, C.A. (affd. *sub nom. Cavendish Bentinck v. Fenn* (1887) 12 App. Cas.652, H.L.); *Ladywell Mining Co. v. Brookes* (1887) 35 Ch.D. 400, C.A.; *Gluckstein v. Barnes* [1900] A.C. 240, H.L.; *Re Lady Forrest (Murchison) Gold Mine* [1901] 1 Ch. 582; *Burland v. Earle* [1902] A.C. 83, P.C.; *Jacobus Marler v. Marler* (1913) 85 L.J.P.C. 167n; *Hely-Hutchinson v. Brayhead Ltd* [1968] 1 Q.B. 549, C.A.

[11] *Phipps v. Boardman* [1967] 2 A.C. 46, H.L.; *O'Sullivan v. Management Agency and Music Ltd* [1985] Q.B. 428, C.A.

[12] [1990] 2 A.C. 663.

[13] The first argument seems a little disingenuous, whilst the second, as Lord Goff recognised (at 701) is applicable to all fiduciaries and leads to the conclusion that the decision in *Phipps v. Boardman* (see n. 11, above) should be regarded as confined to "the unusual circumstances of that case". See the criticisms of Beatson and Prentice in (1990) 106 L.Q.R. 365.

[14] The right which the shareholders have under s.303 to remove a director at any time by ordinary resolution (see above, pp. 188–191) could be prayed in aid, and the articles sometimes provide that a director must resign if called upon by a majority of the board to do so.

[15] See above, Chap. 17. The statutory law of unfair dismissal will afford the executive director some procedural protection, but is likely to take the same view as the common law on the substantive merits of the dismissal for serious breach of fiduciary duty.

Like the trustee,[16] the director and any officer of the company (including the auditor) has the possibility of appealing to the court to prevent the full application to him or her of the remedies outlined above. Under section 727 the court has a discretion to relieve against liability for negligence, default, breach of duty or breach of trust, provided that it appears to the court that the director has acted honestly and reasonably and that, having regard to all the circumstances, he ought to be excused. However, the section is not available in respect of third-party (as opposed to corporate) claims against the director,[17] and, more important for present purposes, will not be applied even to corporate claims where that would be inconsistent with the purposes underlying the rule imposing the liability against which relief is sought.[18] Finally, we have noted above[19] that since 1989 it has been lawful for the company to purchase insurance for its directors and officers in respect of the same liabilities as are listed in section 727, but in this case presumably without the limitations which the courts have built into the latter section.[20]

Liability of third parties

Despite the wide range of civil remedies which exist to support the substantive law of directors' duties, it is to be doubted whether in many cases the directors are in fact worth suing, at least if they are uninsured. They may once have had property belonging to the company but, by the time the company finds this out, may have it no longer. They may have made large profits which they should account to the company, but may well have spent them by the time the writ arrives. Companies are therefore likely to want to identify some more stable third party, often a bank, which is worth powder-and-shot, either instead of or in addition to the directors.[21]

But under what conditions may the company hold a third party liable in connection with a breach of duty by the directors? This has in fact become a highly complex and confused area of law, and only the briefest sketch of the relevant principles can be attempted here. Some light has been shed by a recent decision of the Privy Council. It has long been recognised that there are two bases of third-party liability, one resting on receipt by the third party of company property and the other resting on complicity by the third party in the director's

---

[16] Trustee Act 1925, s.61.
[17] *Customs and Excise Commissioners v. Hedon Alpha Ltd* [1981] Q.B. 818, C.A.
[18] *Re Produce Marketing Consortium Ltd* [1989] 1 W.L.R. 745 (excluding in this case liability for wrongful trading—above, p. 153—from the ambit of s.727).
[19] pp. 625–626.
[20] There seems no reason why the company should not purchase insurance, if it wishes, against third party claims or in respect of wrongful trading by its directors, though in the latter case it may well be that such insurance is not in fact freely available.
[21] See, for example, *Selangor United Rubber Estates v. Cradock (No. 3)* [1968] 1 W.L.R. 1555.

breach of duty. The main conceptual contribution of the Privy Council in *Royal Brunei Airlines Sdn. Bhd. v. Tan*[22] was to make it clear that the principles supporting the imposition of liability in these two situations are different from one another.

In the case of complicity in the breach, which the court helpfully termed "accessory" liability, the liability is a reflection of a general principle of the law of obligations. This imposes liability upon third parties who assist or procure the breach of a duty or obligation owed by another, the liability of the third party being enforceable by the person who is the beneficiary of the duty whose performance has been interfered with.[23] Since the liability is imposed on the third party to protect the beneficiary (in our case, the company), the liability of the third party should not depend, as had previously been thought, upon the director having acted dishonestly. Provided there has been a breach of duty by the director, whether committed knowingly or not, the third party will be liable to the company if it has acted dishonestly. The focus is on the fault of the third party, not on the fault of the director. The effect of the decision is to expand the boundaries of the liability of third parties as accessories, though some doubt still remains over the precise tests for assessing the dishonesty of the third party.[24]

In the case of solvent and respectable third parties, however, accessory liability is less likely[25] to be available on the facts than an argument based upon "knowing receipt" of the company's property, at least if the term "knowing" is given a wide enough connotation. The essence of this claim is restitutionary. Company property has been transferred to the third party in breach of the directors' fiduciary duties and the company seeks the imposition of a constructive trust upon the third party to secure the return of the value of that property to the company, even if the third party no longer has the property or its identifiable proceeds in its hands.[26] A common situation found in the

---

[22] [1995] 2 A.C. 378, P.C., noted by Birks [1996] LMCLQ 1 and Harpum (1995) 111 L.Q.R. 545. The facts of the case did not raise an issue of directors' duties. In fact, the fiduciary duty in question was owed by the company and the principle of accessory liability was used to make the director liable to the plaintiff for the *company's* breach of duty. But the principle of the case is clearly of general application.

[23] See at 387. The principle is most familiar in the guise of the tort of inducing breach of contract, though this is not to say that "assistance" and "procurement" are identical concepts. Although the courts often refer to third parties who are liable as accessories in relation to breaches of directors' duties as "constructive trustees", it would seem that their liability is personal, not proprietary, and that the language of constructive trusts could be abandoned here. See Birks, "The Recovery of Misapplied Assets" in McKendrick (ed.), *Commercial Aspects of Trusts and Fiduciary Obligations* (Oxford, 1992) at pp. 153–154.

[24] Even here it should be noted that the Privy Council was innovative: dishonesty was an objective, not a subjective, matter and consisted in "not acting as an honest person would in the circumstances" (at 389).

[25] Which is not to say that the first basis of liability is never available: see *Canada Safeway Ltd v. Thompson* [1951] 3 D.L.R. 295.

[26] If the third party does still have the property or its identifiable proceeds to hand, then a proprietary constructive trust or tracing claim may be possible. Otherwise, the liability

cases is one where the directors have used the company's assets in
breach of the statutory prohibition on the provision of financial assistance towards the purchase of its shares, and the assets in question
have passed through the hands of a third party.[27]

The scope of this liability depends heavily upon the degree of
knowledge on the part of the third party which is requisite to
trigger it, an issue which has been much discussed in the courts in
recent years, usually be reference to the five-point scale of knowledge established by Peter Gibson J.[28] Although the issue is far
from settled, the tendency of the recent decisions has been not to
impose liability on the basis of constructive knowledge in ordinary
commercial transactions, on the grounds that the doctrine of constructive knowledge presupposes an underlying system of careful
and comprehensive investigation of the surrounding legal context,
which is typical of property transactions but atypical of commercial
transactions (including the non-property aspects of commercial property transfers).[29] If this line of authority eventually wins out, as it
is submitted it should and as would be consistent with the declining
importance of constructive knowledge in company law,[30] then third
party liability will depend upon showing actual knowledge of the
directors' breach of duty or wilful shutting one's eyes to the obvious
or wilful and reckless failure to make such inquiries as an honest
and reasonable person would make, *i.e.* inferred but not constructive
knowledge.[31] Thus, in *Eagle Trust plc v. SBC Securities Ltd (No.
2)*[32] the managing director had wrongfully used the company's
assets to discharge obligations incurred by him under a sub-
underwriting agreement entered into in connection with a rights
issue by the company. The underwriters, into whose hands the
company's monies eventually came, were held not liable on the
knowing receipt basis, because they did not know or suspect that
the money paid over by the managing directors was the company's
money.

---

imposed under the constructive trust seems to be personal, and again it is doubtful whether
the language of "constructive trust" is really needed. See Birks, *op. cit.*, pp. 154–156.

[27] See above, pp. 263–279, and *Belmont Finance Corporation v. Williams Furniture Ltd (No.
2)* [1980] 1 All E.R. 393, C.A.

[28] In *Baden v. Société Générale pour Favoriser le Développment du Commerce et de l'Industrie
en France S.A.* [1993] 1 W.L.R. 509n.

[29] See *Eagle Trust plc v. SBC Securities Ltd* [1993] 1 W.L.R. 484; *Cowan de Groot Properties
Ltd v. Eagle Trust plc* [1992] 4 All E.R. 700; *Eagle Trust plc v. SBC Securities Ltd (No. 2)*
[1996] 1 BCLC 121.

[30] See above, Chap. 10.

[31] These are the first three categories of the *Baden* case. The disfavoured other two categories
are knowledge of circumstances which would indicate the facts to an honest and reasonable
man and knowledge of circumstances which would put an honest and reasonable person on
inquiry. The second category must certainly be excluded if constructive knowledge is not to
be a basis for liability. The line between the first category and wilful and reckless failure to
make inquiries may not be so easy to draw.

[32] Above, n. 29.

Illustration in relation to bribes

The possible interrelation of the various orders described above is usefully illustrated in relation to the rather special case of bribes. The courts have always taken a strict line here, even though the definition of a "bribe" for these purposes does not connote a corrupt motive, on the part of either giver or receiver. It is enough that there has been the payment of money or the conferment of another benefit upon an agent whom the payer knows is acting as an agent for a principal in circumstances where the payment has not been disclosed to the principal.[33] The rules about bribes are prophylactic, designed to combat the tendency of such payments to corrupt the devotion of the agent to the promotion of the interests of the principal, and so do not require proof that the principal's interests were in fact harmed. In this respect, these rules achieve the same objective as those discussed above[34] relating to conflicts of duty and interest or secret profits.

Where a bribe has been paid to a director or other agent of the company, the company may rescind the contract between it and the third party, whether the briber is the third party or the third party's agent (*e.g.* where the third party is another company).[35] In addition, or instead, both the briber and the director or other agent are jointly and severally liable in damages in fraud to the company, the amount of the recovery depending upon proof of actual loss.[36] Alternatively, the company may hold both the director and the briber jointly and severally liable to pay the amount of the bribe to the company as money had and received to its use, this liability being naturally not dependent upon proof of loss. Against the director, such a personal liability to account is straightforward: the bribe is akin to a secret profit made out the director's position. Against the briber it is a rather peculiar remedy, though one which seems to be established.[37] However, the company must choose between the remedies of damages and account, the choice no doubt depending on the amount of the provable loss which the company suffered as a result of the bribe, though it need not do so until judgment.[38]

---

[33] *Industries and General Mortgage Co. Ltd v. Lewis* [1949] 2 All E.R. 573. In particular, though the payer must know that he is dealing with an agent, he need not know or intend that the payment not be disclosed to the principal. It is enough if it is in fact not disclosed: *Taylor v. Walker* [1958] 1 Lloyd's Rep. 490; *Logicrose Ltd v. Southend United F.C. Ltd* [1988] 1 W.L.R. 1257.

[34] pp. 610–623.

[35] *Taylor v. Walker*, above, n. 33; *Shipway v. Broadwood* [1899] 1 Q.B. 369, C.A. There is not space here to explore the complications which may arise when the briber is also the director of a company and makes unauthorised use of that company's assets to effect the bribe.

[36] *Mahesan v. Malaysia Government Officers' Co-operative Housing Society Ltd* [1979] A.C. 374 at 381, P.C. The cause of action appears to lie in fraud even in the absence of a corrupt motive on the part of the briber.

[37] *ibid.*, at 383.

[38] *ibid.*, and *United Australia Ltd v. Barclays Bank Ltd* [1941] A.C. 1, H.L. Where the briber is or acts on behalf of a supplier, the damages are unlikely to be less than the amount of the

In *Attorney-General for Hong Kong v. Reid*[39] the Privy Council
took the further step of recognising a proprietary remedy by way of a
constructive trust in favour of the company (or other principal) against
the director or other agent in respect of the bribe. The significance of
the provision of this remedy in addition to the personal remedy to
account for money had and received is that the company may claim
any profit made by the director through the use of the bribe (whilst
falling back on the personal claim if the investment has been
unprofitable) and that the company's claim will prevail over those of
the unsecured creditors in the event of the director's insolvency. The
recognition of a proprietary claim in respect of assets which are neither
company assets nor assets which the director was under a duty to
obtain for the company could have far-reaching consequences.[40]

CONCLUSION

The law relating to directors' duties appears at first sight to consist of
strong rules about honesty and the absence of conflicts of interest, but
weak rules about competence—the legal expression, if you like, of a
view of the director as a gentlemanly amateur. However, on closer
examination, the picture is more complicated. On the one hand, the
courts have sought to initiate a move away from the low standards of
skill and diligence required of directors by the nineteenth-century
judges. On the other, the fiduciary duties turn out to be to a significant
extent avoidable by the directors. Perhaps the real difficulty revealed
by this chapter, as so often in company law, is the fact that the shareholders' meeting cannot be guaranteed to act as an independent check
on management. In theory, strict fiduciary duties which are capable of
being relaxed generally by provisions in the articles or ad hoc by
resolutions of the general meeting ought to provide an attractive balance of shareholder protection and commercial flexibility. However,
directors who have *de jure* or *de facto* control over the shareholders'
meeting may be able to exercise those powers not so much to that

---

bribe, since presumably the supplier would have been prepared to reduce its price to the
company by the amount paid to the director. However, the damages could be more, as where
the briber has passed on only part of its inflated profit to the person bribed.

[39] [1994] 1 A.C. 324, P.C., declining to follow *Metropolitan Bank v. Heiron* (1880) 5 Ex.D.
319, C.A. and *Lister & Co. v. Stubbs* (1890) 45 Ch.D. 1, C.A.

[40] Academic comment has been generally unfavourable. See Gardner [1995] C.L.J. 60; Cowan,
Edmunds and Lowry [1996] J.B.L. 22; Pearce [1994] LMCLQ 189; Rotherham [1977] CFILR
43; but *cf.* Oakley [1995] C.L.J. 377 and Nolan (1994) Co.Law. 3. The last named suggests
that *Reid* stands for the principle that a proprietary remedy should be available in all cases of
profits made by fiduciaries through the abuse of confidential information or of their fiduciary
position, a principle that would have great import for the problems of corporate information
and corporate opportunity, discussed above at pp. 615–622. There is some support for this
view in dicta of the Vice-Chancellor in *Attorney General v. Blake* [1996] 3 All E.R. 903,
though the judge would have regarded himself as bound by *Lister v. Stubbs*, a decision of the
Court of Appeal, as against the decision of the Privy Council.

end as simply to relieve themselves of what they see as inconvenient constraints. Neither the interventions by the legislature to restore the equitable principles of disclosure and shareholder approval nor the common law's own restrictions on the scope of ratification have reached to the heart of this problem. As we shall see in the next Chapter, it is an issue which besets the enforcement of directors' duties even more than it affects their substantive formulation and application.

CHAPTER 23

THE ENFORCEMENT OF DIRECTORS' DUTIES AND THE PRINCIPLE OF MAJORITY RULE

WE have seen in the previous Chapter that the fiduciary duties of directors are owed to the company, and only exceptionally to shareholders individually. Although there is debate as to whether the shareholders' collective interests should always be seen as lying behind "the company", especially when insolvency threatens,[1] the proposition set out in the previous sentence does lead naturally to the further proposition that decisions whether to enforce the company's rights[2] should also be taken by the appropriate organ of the company, rather than by an individual shareholder. Under the management article[3] of most companies, that organ would appear to be at first sight the board of directors, but where the directors, or even only some of them, are the alleged wrongdoers, that solution is hardly appropriate.[4] So, despite what the articles may say about the directors having general powers of management, the decision whether to sue must be one for the general meeting,[5] unless there is another management organ, independent of the directors, to which decision may safely be entrusted. This is likely to be the case if the company is insolvent and a liquidator has been appointed.[6] Indeed, in such a case it would seem positively inept to leave the decision in the hands of the general meeting, since

---

[1] See above, p. 602.

[2] It is a mistake, of course, to suppose that it is always in the interests of the person to whom legal duties are owed to enforce those rights.

[3] See, for example, art. 70 of Table A, 1985.

[4] Where the directors are *not* the alleged wrongdoers, however, the problem discussed in this Chapter simply does not arise: *Watts v. Midland Bank plc* [1986] BCLC 15 (alleged wrongdoer was a receiver appointed by a debenture-holder).

[5] See *Alexander Ward & Co. Ltd v. Samyang Navigation Co. Ltd* [1975] 1 W.L.R. 673 at 679, *per* Lord Hailsham L.C., quoting with approval a passage from the third edition of this book at pp. 136–137.

[6] *Ferguson v. Wallbridge* [1935] 3 D.L.R. 66, P.C.; *Fargro Ltd v. Godfroy* [1986] 1 W.L.R. 1134. In *Barrett v. Duckett* [1995] 1 BCLC 243, C.A. the principle was even extended to deny the possibility of bringing a derivative action to a shareholder who turned down the opportunity to put the company into liquidation: "As the company does have some money which might be used in litigating the claims, it is in my opinion manifest that it is better that the decision whether or not to use the money should be taken by an independent liquidator rather than by [the shareholder]" (at 255 *per* Peter Gibson L.J.). Although these cases concerned the availability of the derivative action, it is submitted that the principle behind them is that it is appropriate for the liquidator to take the decision rather than the shareholders, whether individually or collectively.

in insolvent liquidation it is the creditors' interests which should predominate.[7]

However, the law cannot concern itself simply with identifying the situations where the shareholders collectively, rather than the directors, should be entrusted with the decision on litigation to enforce the company's rights. As we saw at the end of the previous Chapter, when discussing the issue of ratification, the wrongdoing directors may have *de jure* or *de facto* control over the general meeting, in which case for the law to entrust the decision on litigation to the general meeting may not be very different from leaving it with the directors at board level, and the result would seem equally inappropriate. So it might be thought that the rule should be that, if the directors have control, *de facto* or *de jure*, over the general meeting, some third person or body of persons should be empowered to enforce the company's rights. Within the traditional *dramatis personae* of company law, the only available candidates for this privilege would seem to be the independent[8] shareholders (either individually or collectively). However, English law has not adopted this simple rule. Driven by fears that such a rule would generate a multiplicity of suits against companies and encourage wasted litigation, it has a developed a much more elaborate and restrictive set of criteria for determining when an individual[9] shareholder may sue to enforce the company's rights against the wrongdoing directors. Those criteria are referred to compendiously as the "rule in *Foss v. Harbottle*",[10] after the case in which the principle was first clearly articulated that the decision on suit ought normally be taken by the majority of the shareholders in general meeting.

The rule in *Foss v. Harbottle* has been vigorously criticised by commentators over the years, and the question of its reform has recently been referred to the Law Commission.[11] It has been said to restrict too narrowly the individual shareholder's power to enforce the company's rights; to have resulted in an overly complex body of rules; to pursue

[7] However, in the case of the employees' interests s.309(2) positively embraces a similar ineptness by providing that the duty under the section "is owed to the company ... and is enforceable in the same way as any other fiduciary duty owed to a company by its directors". In short, the employees, or their representatives, have no role as such in decisions about enforcement, even though the substantive duty is owed, apparently, to them.

[8] That is, those against whom no wrongdoing is alleged, though it may well be difficult to identify which shares are controlled by the wrongdoers. This is a strong argument in favour of vesting the right to sue in such cases on behalf of the company in any individual shareholder. See Wedderburn (1981) 44 M.L.R. 202.

[9] For the moment we shall assume that the question is whether the role of third party enforcer of the company's rights should be given to the individual shareholder, for that is the question traditionally discussed, though we shall see below (p. 674) that recently the courts have been concerned with the role of the independent shareholders as a whole.

[10] (1843) 2 Hare 461. The classic analysis of the rule is by Wedderburn in [1957] C.L.J. 194 and [1958] C.L.J. 93.

[11] For a brief discussion of its proposals, see the end of this Chapter.

inconsistent policies; and to have been extended beyond its proper scope. There is force, even much force, in these criticisms.[12] It is certainly true that it is impossible to present a coherent account of the law in this area which is consistent with all the decided cases—and it should be admitted at once that the views presented in this chapter do not achieve that impossible feat. Yet it is a body of law to which the courts are attached, not simply because it is well established, but because it is seen by them as performing a valuable function.[13]

That function can perhaps best be expressed as the preservation of the corporate and collective nature of the company. A decision to litigate the company's rights is a decision to commit the company's resources to a particular end, in competition with, presumably, other claims on those resources.[14] It is a protection for both shareholders and creditors that such decisions should only exceptionally lie in the hands of individual shareholders, whose views on the merits and desirability of the litigation may not be shared by the members as a whole. So the law must balance the need to take decisions on corporate matters collectively and the equally important desideratum of not permitting errant directors to stifle suits arising out of their own wrongdoing. It can hardly be denied that the rule at present gives undue weight to the former objective and that reform in necessary, but it would be equally wrong not to recognise that the rule addresses a real problem in company law and "is fundamental to any rational system of jurisprudence".[15]

Personal Rights and Corporate Rights

The above description of the problem underlying the rule in *Foss v. Harbottle* has been couched in terms of the enforcement by individual shareholders of duties owed by directors to their company. Where the duty is owed to the shareholder personally, whether by the directors or by the company, the above analysis ought to be irrelevant. If the shareholder is also the right-holder, it would seem in principle to be

---

[12] For a vigorous but by no means unrepresentative exposition of these criticisms, see Sealy, "Problems of Standing, Pleading and Proof in Corporate Litigation" in Pettet (ed.), *Company Law in Change* (London, 1987).

[13] For recent examples of judicial attachment to the rule see *Prudential Assurance Co. Ltd v. Newman Industries (No. 2)* [1982] Ch. 204, C.A.; *Smith v. Croft (No. 2)* [1988] Ch. 114; and *Barrett v. Duckett* [1995] 1 BCLC 243, C.A.

[14] This is so even when the individual shareholder commences the action. See *Wallersteiner v. Moir (No. 2)* [1975] Q.B. 373, C.A. and below, pp. 666 *et seq.* The fact that the litigation is expected to pay off handsomely does not alter the fact that, in the absence of a contingent fee system, which has supported so much corporate litigation in the United States, a decision to litigate is a decision to use corporate resources to run a risk, which may be high or low, against an expected return, which may be great or small. s.58 of the Courts and Legal Services Act 1990 introduced a limited form of the contingent fee into this country, but no order has yet been made applying the mechanism to derivative actions.

[15] As it was rather grandiloquently put in the *Prudential* case, above n. 13 at 210.

entirely a matter for his or her discretion whether the right is enforced. So much is indeed recognised in the cases,[16] but it is also true to say that the rule in *Foss v. Harbottle* was extended at an early stage to embrace the principle that "an individual shareholder cannot bring an action in the courts to complain of an irregularity (as distinct from an illegality) in the conduct of the company's internal affairs if the irregularity is one which can be cured by a vote of the company in general meeting".[17]

This is at first sight a surprising extension, for in such cases what is being complained of is not necessarily a wrong done to the company. However, the basis of the extension is that an irregularity is, by definition, something which can be "cured" by a vote of the ordinary shareholders in general meeting. As we shall see below, the parallel idea that many breaches of directors' duties are ratifiable[18] has provided a rationale for the courts' holding that such breaches cannot be complained of by an individual shareholder on behalf of the company. Thus, as Wedderburn put it, there may be two parts to the rule in *Foss*, one applying to wrongs to the company and the other to internal irregularities, but "the limits of that Rule run along the boundaries of majority rule".[19]

However, this leaves the student of this branch of the law in the position of having to distinguish infringements of the shareholder's personal rights, where the shareholder can sue free of *Foss v. Harbottle* considerations, from mere internal irregularities, where the constraints of the rule operate to the full. This is an area where it is strongly arguable that the rule has been over-extended, especially in the crucial case of breaches of the company's constitution. We have seen in an earlier Chapter[20] that section 14 constitutes the memorandum and articles of association a contract between the company and each shareholder. Consequently, where the memorandum or articles confer rights upon the shareholder, they should be enforceable by the shareholder without regard to the rule. Indeed, where the shareholder

---

[16] "The gist of the case is that the personal and individual rights of membership of each of them have been invaded by a purported, but invalid, alteration of the tables of contributions. In those circumstances, it seems to me the rule in *Foss v. Harbottle* has no application at all, for the individual members who are suing sue, not in the right of the union, but in their own right to protect from invasion their own individual rights as members": *Edwards v. Halliwell* [1950] 2 All E.R. 1064 at 1067, C.A., a trade union case but the *Foss* rule is applicable, not only to companies, but also to "any legal entity which is capable of suing in its own name and which is composed of individuals bound together by rules which give the majority of them the power to bind the minority" (*per* Romer J. in *Cotter v. National Union of Seamen* [1929] Ch. 58). See also *Heron International Ltd v. Lord Grade* [1983] BCLC 244 at 261–263, C.A.

[17] *Prudential*, above n. 13 at 210. The extension took place as early as the decision in *Mozley v. Alston* (1847) 1 Ph. 790.

[18] See above, pp. 644–648.

[19] [1957] C.L.J. at 198.

[20] Above, pp. 115–122.

invokes section 14, the situation would appear to be one where the member, far from seeking to enforce the company's rights against a third party, is in fact seeking to uphold his or her own rights against the company. Further, if one accepts the argument, adumbrated in the earlier Chapter,[21] that the shareholder has a general right to have the affairs of the company conducted in accordance with the articles of association, then any breach by the company of the articles would be a breach of the shareholder's personal rights.

However, the courts have not taken this simple, if bold, line, but rather have confusingly applied the category of internal irregularities to some (but by no means all) breaches of articles conferring rights upon the shareholder. The importance, if not the nature, of the distinction is shown by two ultimately irreconcilable cases from the 1870s, *MacDougall v. Gardiner*[22] and *Pender v. Lushington*,[23] in the former of which the decision of the chairman of the shareholders' meeting wrongfully (*i.e.* in breach of the articles) to refuse a request for a poll was held to be an internal irregularity, whilst in the latter the refusal of a chairman to recognise the votes attached to shares held by nominee shareholders was held to infringe their personal rights. Each decision has spawned a line of equally irreconcilable authorities. In truth, there is a conflict here between proper recognition of the contractual nature of the company's constitution[24] and the traditional policy of non-interference by the courts in the internal affairs of companies. As Smith has suggested,[25] ultimately the only satisfactory solution is to choose which policy is to have priority; moreover, it is surely clear today that it ought to be the former. It can hardly be argued in modern law that it is an example of excessive interference by the courts to hold a company (or any other association) to the procedures which it itself has adopted in its constitution for its internal decision-making (until such time as it decides to change those internal rules according to the procedures set down for that to occur).[26] Indeed, it might even be suggested that effective protection of this procedural entitlement of members is basic to any satisfactory system of company law.[27]

---

[21] Above, p. 120. For judicial acceptance of this argument, see *Wise v. USDAW* [1996] IRLR 609.

[22] (1875) 1 Ch.D. 13.

[23] (1877) 6 Ch.D. 70.

[24] Or the union's rule-book.

[25] R.J. Smith, "Minority Shareholders and Corporate Irregularities" (1978) M.L.R. 147.

[26] This argument would lack force only if, as is *not* usually the case for companies or, indeed, most associations, the procedure for amending the rules on how decisions are to be taken was the same as the one for taking substantive decisions. *cf.* the discussion of the "special majority exception" below, p. 672.

[27] Such a statement would surely be regarded as uncontroversial if made in relation to trade union law. *cf. Kahn-Freund's Labour and the Law*, (3rd ed., London, 1983), pp. 286 *et seq.* The courts do not lack techniques for dealing with members whose complaints are purely "technical", *i.e.* where it is clear that the same result would have been arrived at even if the proper procedure had been followed: *Harben v. Phillips* [1974] 1 W.L.R. 638.

Part of the confusion may have arisen because of a failure to appreciate that the same situation may give rise to wrongs both by and against the company, and the individual shareholder's position will vary according to which wrong he seeks to redress. A parallel can be drawn between breaches of the articles and *ultra vires* acts, where this distinction has been recognised in the decisions and, now, in the statute. If the directors embark upon an *ultra vires* transaction, they will be in breach of their duty to the company, but so will the company be in breach of its section 14 contract with the shareholder. So the company appears as both wrongdoer and victim, as section 35 recognises.[28] However, if the shareholder sues to enforce his or her own rights, he or she must ensure that the relief sought is consonant with the right asserted,[29] and that corporate relief is not sought unless the conditions of the rule in *Foss v. Harbottle* are satisfied.[30] Thus, in *Taylor v. NUM (Derbyshire Area)*[31] the plaintiff successfully sued his trade union[32] in a personal capacity to obtain an injunction restraining the officials of the union from continuing an *ultra vires* strike, but failed in his claim for an order requiring the same officials to restore to the union the funds already expended on the strike, because he did not meet the requirements of the rule in *Foss v. Harbottle*. The same analysis may often be applicable to breaches of the articles.[33] In other words, the company may be regarded as breaching its contract with the member if it seeks to act upon a resolution improperly passed and should be restrainable by the member, but for the loss (say the wasted costs of organising the meeting) caused to the company by the chair of the meeting in not conducting it in accordance with the company's regulations, the company is the proper plaintiff.[34]

However, personal rights may be found elsewhere than in the articles and so the scope of the argument that *Foss v. Harbottle* has no application to personal rights has a rather broader ambit. Although the company's constitution is the main source of rights for the shareholder against the company, it is not the exclusive source of such rights, especially if the shareholder is prepared to cast his or her net wider

---

[28] Contrast s.35(2) and (3), above, pp. 212–213.

[29] That will normally be injunctive relief to restrain future breaches of the constitution.

[30] Where corporate relief is sought, the company will need to be joined to the action against the directors. For further discussion of the problem of bringing both personal and derivative actions see below, p. 667.

[31] [1985] BCLC 237. For the application of the distinction between personal and derivative actions to companies in an *ultra vires* context, see *Moseley v. Koffyfontein Mines* [1911] 1 Ch. 73, C.A.

[32] See n. 16, above.

[33] But note *Devlin v. Slough Estates Ltd* [1983] BCLC 497, refusing to recognise that the particular article in question, relating to the preparation of the company's accounts, conferred a right upon individual shareholders (as contrasted with "the company").

[34] There is some suggestion in the language used in *MacDougall v. Gardiner* and *Pender v. Lushington* (see above, nn. 22 and 23), respectively, that the decisions are to be explained on the basis that the two courts simply fastened on two different legal aspects of a single situation.

and sue the directors as well as, or instead of,[35] the company. The shareholder may have rights derived from the general law, as was the case in *Prudential* itself, where the shareholder asserted the directors were liable in the tort of conspiracy as against the members of the company as well as the company itself. There seems to be no principled reason against the enforcement of such actions, though the remedies may have to be carefully tailored so as to avoid double recovery.[36] Exceptionally,[37] the shareholder may be owed a fiduciary duty directly by the directors, in which case the *Foss* rule would seem irrelevant since the shareholder is suing to enforce his own, not the company's, fiduciary rights. Indeed, the rule would be substantially undermined if the courts were to expand the range of duties owed by directors to shareholders directly. However, so long as the courts remain attached to the policies underlying the rule, it is unlikely that this will happen, and so directors' advice to shareholders on the exercise of the rights attached to their shares will probably remain the prime area for the recognition of direct fiduciary duties.[38]

If an extension of the direct duties is to be made, the most likely candidate is the duty upon directors not to act for an improper purpose, the legitimate purposes being defined by reference to the articles.[39] Although it is usual to see breach of this duty not as a breach of the articles but as an abuse of power conferred by them, nevertheless Hoffmann J. took the view in *Re A Company*[40] that where shares were issued for an improper purpose, "the true basis of the action is an alleged infringement of the petitioner's individual rights as a shareholder."[41] This view was echoed and elaborated by the Full Court of the Supreme Court of South Australia, where the right of the shareholder was said to be the right to have the voting power of the shares undiminished by improper actions on the part of the directors.[42] Such a development would loosen the standing requirements upon individual shareholders seeking to enforce this duty, at least where the impropriety related to the issue of shares, whilst possibly casting upon them the full cost of so doing.[43] However, it is still not clear whether the

---

[35] In this case it would seem to be unnecessary for the company to be a party to the litigation.

[36] See below, p. 667.

[37] See above, pp. 599–600.

[38] See above, p. 600.

[39] See above, pp. 605–608.

[40] [1986] BCLC 82.

[41] At 84, the effect of which in this case was to deprive the petitioner of any claim to financial assistance from the company for the bringing of the claim. Even if the right is analysed as a personal one, so that the company is a true defendant, it may be too harsh a consequence to conclude that the company has no interest in, and so should never pay for, litigation designed to rectify procedural defects arising during its internal decision-making processes. Such litigation could be a valuable check upon abuse of authority be directors: see n. 27, above.

[42] *Residues Treatment and Trading Co. Ltd v. Southern Resources Ltd (No. 4)* (1988) 14 A.C.L.R. 569.

[43] See n. 41, above.

plaintiff's ultimate success in improper purposes actions is dependent on the views of the majority.[44] If it is, then the recognition of a personal right in this area remains a partial one.

In general, it is submitted that the rule in *Foss* ought to have no application to the enforcement of rights conferred upon the shareholder or member personally. The difficult issue is not so much that proposition as the question of when, outside the articles, company law ought to recognise that shareholders have such rights as against the company or its directors.

PERSONAL, REPRESENTATIVE, DERIVATIVE AND CORPORATE ACTIONS

It will have become clear by now that the rule in *Foss v. Harbottle* is part of our law of civil procedure. The main question which it seeks to address is one of *locus standi*: in what circumstances may an individual shareholder seek to enforce a right which is vested, not in him- or herself, but in the company? Before proceeding to address that issue directly, some brief elaboration of the types of action to be found in this area of law is necessary.

We have argued above that, if the right in question is vested in the shareholder personally, the rule should have no application. Equally, the form of the action in such cases needs little further comment. The shareholder is the plaintiff and the person owing the duty to the shareholder, perhaps the company, is the defendant. However, it may be—indeed, it is likely to be so—that the defendant's action, of which complaint is made, infringed the rights of a number of shareholders and not just the plaintiff's rights. In such a case the plaintiff may (but is not obliged to) sue in representative form on behalf of himself and all the other similarly situated members, as provided by Order 15, rule 12 of the Rules of the Supreme Court.[45] Indeed, it is desirable that this be done, since the judgment will be binding on all those represented and the threat of a multiplicity of actions will be reduced.

This is all fairly straightforward. The confusion in this area begins to emerge when one considers the form in which an action by an individual shareholder to enforce the company's rights is required to

---

[44] In *Hogg v. Cramphorn* [1967] Ch. 254. the individual shareholder was allowed to sue but judgement in his favour was suspended whilst a general meeting of the shareholders was called to consider approving the directors' actions, which they in fact did, so that the litigation was ultimately fruitless. And in *Bamford v. Bamford* [1970] Ch. 212, C.A., it was held that the improper issue of shares was ratifiable.

[45] Rule 12 provides: "(1) Where numerous persons have the same interest in any proceedings ... the proceedings may be begun ... and continued by ... any one or more of them as representing all or as representing all except one or more of them ... (3) A judgment or order given in proceedings under this rule shall be binding on all the persons as representing whom the plaintiffs sue ..."

be cast. It has two misleading aspects. The first is that it is required to be brought in representative form,[46] even though it is the company, rather than the other shareholders, whom the plaintiff represents. The utility of the requirement is, of course, that all the other shareholders are bound by the result of the action. Secondly, although the action is brought on behalf of the company, the company appears as a defendant, so that the action takes the form of a representative action by the plaintiff shareholder on behalf of himself and all the other shareholders, other than the alleged wrongdoers, against the alleged wrongdoers and the company. Although it is easy to appreciate that the company is joined as a defendant in order that it may be bound by and benefit from the judgment and that it cannot be made a plaintiff if neither the board nor the general meeting have consented to this,[47] nevertheless it is highly misleading to find that an action to enforce the company's rights takes the form, apparently, of an action against the company! It also follows from the above analysis that nothing can be deduced from the representative form of the action about the rights which are being enforced. It may be a "true" representative action to enforce personal rights held by a group of shareholders or it may be an action to enforce the company's rights—and equally the company may be a real or a nominal defendant.

The confusion likely to arise from the above was not helped by the terminology previously employed to describe the action on behalf of the company. The phrase "minority shareholder's action" obscured rather than revealed the nature of the rights being enforced, and it was therefore a step forward when the Court of Appeal in *Wallersteiner v. Moir (No. 2)* in 1975 introduced from United States law the alternative phrase, "derivative action".[48] Although the new description did not alter the procedural requirements described above, it did articulate much more clearly the essence of what is happening in these cases: the individual shareholder is enforcing a right which is not his or hers but rather is "derived from" the company. The new description has taken root and is even reflected in the Supreme Court Rules, where a derivative action is defined as one "begun by writ by one or more shareholders of a company where the cause of action is vested in the company and relief is accordingly sought on its behalf".[49]

The significance of *Wallersteiner v. Moir*, however, goes beyond the adoption of a more accurate terminology. By acknowledging the

---

[46] Unless the defendants do not object to the lack of representative form: *Wallersteiner v. Moir (No. 2)* [1975] Q.B. 373, C.A.

[47] *Spokes v. Grosvenor Hotel* [1897] 2 Q.B. 124, C.A. and *Beattie v. Beattie Ltd* [1938] Ch. 708 at 718, *per* Lord Greene M.R. If the company has ceased to exist and cannot be resuscitated (see p. 848, below), no action can be brought on its behalf: *Clarkson v. Davies* [1923] A.C. 100, P.C.; *Ferguson v. Wallbridge* [1935] 3 D.L.R. 66, P.C.

[48] Above, n. 46.

[49] Ord. 15, r.12A(1).

true nature of the right being asserted, the court was led to remove, or at least reduce, one of the major impediments to actions by individual shareholders to enforce corporate rights. This was that the cost of the action was carried by the plaintiff shareholder, whilst recovery would be ordered in favour of the company.[50] This injustice was partially remedied in *Wallersteiner* where the Court of Appeal recognised that in appropriate cases the shareholder should be indemnified by the company against the costs of bringing the action on the company's behalf. The revised procedure has been formalised to some extent in a new Supreme Court Rule, which, while expressly authorising the court to give the plaintiff an indemnity against costs out of the assets of the company on such terms as it thinks appropriate,[51] also expressly requires the court's approval for the continuance of a derivative action where the defendant has indicated an intention to resist the claim.[52] So the price of the possibility of the company's financial support for the claim is a greater degree of supervision by the court over its conduct by the individual shareholder. However, the court's approval is required for all derivative actions, not just those where an indemnity order is made. The need to obtain the approval is thus added to the standing requirements of *Foss v. Harbottle*.[53] A further, and important, example of court control is that the order for an indemnity will often require the plaintiff to refer back to the court for approval any offer of settlement of the suit, thus reducing the possibilities for "gold-digging" claims against the company, which are settled on terms advantageous to the plaintiff shareholder but which do not reflect the value of the company's rights.[54]

Thus, we can see that the "ownership" of the rights being protected in, respectively, personal and derivative actions lies in very different hands, despite the confusing similarity of the procedural forms in which those rights may be asserted. On the other hand, we have also seen that the same set of facts may give rise to infringements of both

---

[50] Given the way costs are taxed, this meant that the plaintiff would be out of pocket, even if he won, unless the company chose to make up the difference, whilst the costs risk facing the plaintiff at the outset of the litigation was enormous, so that only the most promising of cases were likely to be litigated under the old rules about costs.

[51] It is still unclear whether the courts regard the indemnity as a form of legal aid and thus as subject to a means test (see *Smith v. Croft* [1986] 2 All E.R. 551 at 565) or, and it is submitted correctly, as a reflection of the rights being protected in the action: *Jaybird Group Ltd v. Greenwood* [1986] BCLC 319 at 328.

[52] Ord. 15, r.12A(2) and (13).

[53] And, conversely, the reform proposals of the Law Commission (below, pp. 676–678) can be seen as involving the substitution of judicial discretion for the standing rules. For an example of the present procedure, see *Cooke v. Cooke* [1997] BCC 17, where in a joint writ action and s.459 petition the judge stayed the derivative action on the grounds that all the issues between the parties could be more conveniently handled under the petition.

[54] See *The Supreme Court Practice 1995*, Vol. 1, p. 233. Any indemnity granted is likely to have to be renewed and reviewed as the litigation proceeds. In appropriate cases the shareholder, as the company's agent, should hold payments received for dropping an action on trust for the company.

the shareholders' and the company's rights. The question is thus bound to arise as to whether personal and corporate rights may be asserted in the same action. It used to be thought that this was not possible, but in *Prudential Assurance Co. Ltd v. Newman Industries Ltd (No. 2)*[55] Vinelott J. permitted it a first instance. The Court of Appeal did not dissent from this view but did hold that the personal claim was misconceived on the facts, because the only relevant loss suffered consisted in a diminution in the value of the plaintiff's shares, which was simply a reflection of the loss allegedly inflicted on the company by the defendants. To allow the plaintiff to recover personally in that situation might impose double recovery on the defendants; moreover, the nature of the corporate enterprise indicated that the company should be the sole holder of the cause of action in such a case.[56] It would thus seem that personal and derivative actions may be joined, if they arise out of the same events, but that the plaintiff may seek a remedy in the personal action only in respect of the harm inflicted directly upon him.[57]

There are other minor differences between the personal and the derivative action, arising out of the differences in the rights protected. A derivative action, since it enforces the company's rights, may be initiated by a shareholder even though it relates to matters which occurred before he or she became a member,[58] whereas in relation to an action to enforce the member's personal rights it is difficult to envisage circumstances where this could arise, since the rights in question presumably were acquired only upon admission as a member of the company. Further, since the derivative action is an invention of equity to allow enforcement of the company's rights, it is available only as a matter of the court's discretion. The plaintiff will be disqualified from bringing a claim if he or she does not come to court with

---

[55] [1981] Ch. 257 at 303–304.

[56] [1982] Ch. 204 at 222–224. With respect, this seems correct. The company should recover in respect of the loss inflicted on it and, if there is to be a distribution to the shareholders, that should be the result of a corporate decision, not of a decision to litigate taken by an individual shareholder. *cf. George Fischer (Great Britain) Ltd v. Multi Construction Ltd* [1995] 1 BCLC 260, C.A., where the court held that the *Prudential* principle did not apply when assessing the remoteness of damage (in contrast to the determination of whether the plaintiff had a cause of action). To have applied the principle in this case would have meant that neither company nor shareholder recovered for the loss inflicted. See also *R.P. Howard Ltd & Richard Alan Witchell v. Woodman Matthews and Co.* [1983] BCLC 117. Both cases perhaps also demonstrate the fact that there is little point in insisting on the argument made in the text where the plaintiffs hold all the shares in the company.

[57] The point was neatly illustrated by *Heron International Ltd v. Lord Grade* [1983] BCLC at 261–263, where the Court of Appeal distinguished between the harm inflicted on the company's assets by the assumed recklessness of the directors (recoverable only in a derivative action) and the harm suffered directly by the shareholders individually though their resulting inability to accept a higher takeover offer for their shares (assertable in a personal action with which "*Foss v. Harbottle* has nothing whatever to do").

[58] *Seaton v. Grant* (1867) L.R. 2 Ch.App. 459; *Bloxham v. Metropolitan Ry* (1868) L.R. 3 Ch.App. 337. But the plaintiff must be a shareholder when the action is brought: *Birch v. Sullivan* [1957] 1 W.L.R. 1247.

"clean hands", for example, if the plaintiff has participated in the wrong of which complaint is made.[59] The claim may also not be allowed to proceed if the court forms the view that it is being pursued for an ulterior purpose and not bona fide for the benefit of the company.[60]

In the *Prudential* litigation the Court of Appeal[61] introduced a further procedural limitation on the derivative action. Since the rule is, as we have seen, essentially one of *locus standi*, the Court thought that the standing of the plaintiff to bring the derivative action should be decided as a preliminary matter before the trial of the action. Although an apparently plausible view, taken in order to save costs, it is in fact a precept which is very difficult to implement. As we shall see below, the availability of the derivative action depends substantially on the nature of the wrongs alleged to have been committed by the defendants against the company. If the preliminary investigation is to proceed on the assumption that the plaintiff's pleadings are factually correct (as in a striking-out action), it will be relatively easy for the plaintiff to meet the standing conditions and the requirement of a preliminary investigation of this point will lose much of its point. If, on the other hand, this assumption is not to be made, then the difficulty will arise which afflicts many interlocutory proceedings, namely, that of determining how extensive the investigation of the plaintiff's allegations should be. If it is too extensive, the alleged advantages of the preliminary investigation will be lost.[62]

We have not yet dealt with corporate actions. Since the whole purpose of this chapter is to identify situations in which corporate rights may be asserted by individual shareholders, rather than the company, it may be thought unnecessary to describe the form in which actions by the company are brought. However, two comments should be made. First, an individual shareholder might seek to sue in the name of the company rather than derivatively on its behalf. If this course of action is taken, the defendants will apply to strike out the claim on the grounds that the plaintiff does not have the authority to use the company's name in litigation, and the court will normally suspend proceedings whilst a meeting of the shareholders is convened to decide whether the litigation shall continue in the company's name.[63] Although this procedure is of no use to the individual shareholder when it is clear that the wrongdoers have control of the general meet-

---

[59] *Whitwam v. Watkin* (1898) 78 L.T. 188; *Towers v. African Tug Co.* [1904] 1 Ch. 558, C.A.; cf. *Moseley v. Koffyfontein Mines Ltd* [1911] 1 Ch. 73, C.A.

[60] *Nurcombe v. Nurcombe* [1985] 1 W.L.R. 370; *Barrett v. Duckett* [1995] 1 BCLC 243, C.A.

[61] Above, n. 56.

[62] cf. *American Cyanamid v. Ethicon* [1975] A.C. 396, H.L., which demonstrates that the simple formula that the court should investigate so far as is necessary to establish whether the plaintiff has made out a *prima facie* case disguises, rather than solves, the problem set out in the text.

[63] *Danish Mercantile Co. Ltd v. Beaumont* [1951] Ch. 680, C.A.; *Airways Ltd v. Bowen* [1985] BCLC 355.

ing, it is a mechanism which can be used if the shareholder wishes to put the matter before the general meeting and cannot meet the statutory criteria for requisitioning a meeting.[64] However, it is a high risk strategy: if the meeting does not support the litigation, the plaintiff and, unusually, the solicitors to the plaintiff will be liable to the defendants for the costs of the litigation.[65]

Secondly, if, as all too often happens, the directors' breaches of duty lead to the winding-up of the company, the controlling directors will be replaced by a liquidator who may not exhibit the same inhibitions about suing the directors in respect of their breaches, if it is thought that there is a good chance of recovery. Indeed, in this situation, section 212 of the Insolvency Act 1986 provides a summary procedure under which the liquidator may apply to the court for an order that those previously involved in the management of the company restore assets to the company or contribute to its assets by way of compensation. This is the so-called "misfeasance" procedure, but it can now be invoked in any case of "breach of any fiduciary or other duty in relation to the company", including, therefore, negligence, and not just where the managers have misapplied the company's assets. In practice, it is a significant method of enforcing the duties of directors.

CONDITIONS FOR ACCESS TO THE DERIVATIVE ACTION

We are now at last in a position to address the central issue of this Chapter: in what circumstances may an individual shareholder seek to enforce the company's rights on its behalf through a derivative action? Bearing in mind our previous warning that it is impossible to reconcile all the decided cases with any simple set of propositions, it is nevertheless submitted that the cases best support the following statements. They are that, first, the individual shareholder may not sue to enforce the company's rights if the wrong in question is one which is ratifiable by the company in general meeting by ordinary resolution. Secondly, even if the wrong is not ratifiable as being a "fraud on the minority", the derivative action may not be brought unless the wrongdoers are in control of the company and (possibly) may not be brought in the case of any non-ratifiable wrong unless the majority of the independent shareholders support the bringing of the action.[66]

Before turning to the cases it is as well to make some remarks on the policies which might be though to underlie these propositions. The first proposition tends to support the principle of majority rule, for it

---

[64] See above, p. 568.

[65] *Newbiggin Gas Co. v. Armstrong* (1880) 13 Ch.D. 310, C.A.; *La Compagnie de Mayville v. Whitley* [1896] 1 Ch. 788, C.A.

[66] In essence this is the view put forward by Wedderburn in his seminal articles in the 1950s, elaborated in the light of *Smith v. Croft (No. 2)* [1988] Ch. 114: see above, n. 10.

requires the dissatisfied shareholder to go to the general meeting and to try to persuade it to commence the litigation, and deprives the individual of standing to commence the action him- or herself. On the other hand, this is a very partial or negative support for majority rule, for it prevents the individual from suing but does nothing to guarantee that the matter will in fact be put before the general meeting. The rule is that the individual cannot sue if the wrong is ratifiable, *not* that he cannot do so if it has been ratified.[67]

It is suggested that a substantial element in the courts' acceptance of the first proposition set out above rests not on support for majority rule but on the desire to avoid wasted litigation. Where the wrong is ratifiable, there is a risk that the litigation will prove fruitless in the sense that some time after its commencement, and perhaps not until judgment, the shareholders will ratify the wrong and thus deprive the litigation of its basis. That will involve wasted costs, both for the parties involved in the litigation[68] and for the taxpayer, in the sense of the non-recoverable costs of running the court system. As was said in the early "internal irregularities" cases, if the matter is one which is under the control of the majority, "there can be no use in having a litigation about it, the ultimate end of which is only that a meeting has to be called, and then ultimately the majority gets its wishes".[69]

When the wrong is not ratifiable, the argument as to wasted litigation falls away, and the matter becomes more straightforwardly one of identifying the appropriate body or person to initiate the litigation. What the second proposition above reflects is the desire, even with non-ratifiable wrongs, to have decisions on litigation taken collectively where an appropriate collective body is available to take them. If the wrongdoers are not in control of the general meeting, it is said, that body may safely be left to decide whether to litigate or not over "fraud" (though once again the rule does nothing to ensure that the shareholders collectively actually give their mind to the matter). Recently, a decision at first instance by a respected judge has taken this principle to the extent of giving a role in the litigation decision to the "majority of the independent minority", even when the wrong-

---

[67] Vinelott J. at first instance in the *Prudential* case was in favour of ratification as the test, but neither the authorities nor the Court of Appeal in that case (see above, n. 56) support him. In *Hogg v. Cramphorn Ltd* [1967] Ch. 254 the plaintiff shareholder was allowed to sue, even though the wrong was ratifiable. However, this seems to have been a personal action, not that that by itself renders the result any more explicable. See above, p. 664.

[68] Including possibly the company itself after the decision in *Wallersteiner v. Moir (No. 2)*. See n. 46, above.

[69] *MacDougall v. Gardiner* [1875] 1 Ch.D. 13 at 25, C.A. This argument, of course, ignores the point made in the previous paragraph, namely that the "use" might be that a different rule would place pressure on the wrongdoers to put the matter before the general meeting, rather than just sheltering behind *Foss*. This would be the case, for example, if the individual could sue unless the wrong had been ratified.

doers are in control of the general meeting and so that body cannot, as such, be left with the decision on litigation.[70]

(a) Ratifiable wrongs

The first proposition was formulated by Jenkins L.J. in *Edwards v. Halliwell*,[71] in a dictum which was recognised in the *Prudential* litigation[72] as the best modern formulation of the rule in *Foss v. Harbottle*. He said that "where the alleged wrong [done to the company] is a transaction which might be made binding on the company or association of persons and all its members by a simple majority of the members, no individual member of the company is allowed to maintain an action in respect of that matter . . .". Once the notion of ratifiability as a bar to the derivative action has been articulated, much of the rest of the learning surrounding the Rule falls into place. In particular, some, if not all, of the so-called "exceptions" to the Rule appear as situations in which the wrong is not ratifiable by a simple majority of the members. Let us look at the three situations which were identified in the dictum of Jenkins L.J. in *Edwards v. Halliwell* as ones where the individual could sue derivatively. These were the *ultra vires*, special majorities and "fraud on the minority" cases.[73]

Ultra vires cases are ones where it is clear that the wrong to the company cannot be ratified by ordinary resolution. Before the reforms of 1989 *ultra vires* acts could not be ratified at all and now they need a special resolution.[74] As we have noted above,[75] since the *ultra vires* act will involve a breach of the section 14 contract *by* the company, as well as a wrong done to it by the directors, this is a situation in which personal and derivative actions, each with its appropriate remedy, may lie, though our concern here is with the derivative action. The special majority category, which now embraces acts outside the company's objects clause, has been justified on the grounds that otherwise "the effect would be to allow a company acting in breach of its

---

[70] *Smith v. Croft (No. 2)* [1988] Ch. 114, discussed further below at p. 673.

[71] Above n. 16, at 1066. It is clear that the judge was talking about wrongs to the company, for he added: "In my judgment, it is implicit in the rule that the matter relied on as constituting the cause of action should be a cause of action properly belonging to the general body of corporators . . . as opposed to a cause of action which some individual member can assert in his own right."

[72] Above, nn. 55 and 56.

[73] It may be wrong to think that the categories of non-ratifiable wrongs is closed. In *Hodgson v. NALGO* [1972] 1 W.L.R. 130 it was held that the individual member could sue in respect of a matter within the control of the majority, if in practical terms it was impossible for the majority to express their view before the matter became moot.

[74] s.35(3); see above, p. 212. It is probably right to include within the *ultra vires* class those cases where the statute imposes restrictions upon the company's powers, for example, in relation to a return of capital (see Chap. 11, above). In such cases, the rule that ratification is not permitted at all often still obtains.

[75] p. 663. See also *Smith v. Croft (No. 2)* [1988] Ch. 114 at 169–170.

articles to do *de facto* by ordinary resolution that which according to its own regulations could only be done by special resolution".[76] It is clearly consistent with the first proposition articulated above.

Finally, there are the controversial and mis-named instances of "fraud on the minority". Although there may be some cases[77] which are inconsistent with this view, it does seem to be correct to state that a fraud[78] is not a wrong done to the shareholders but is a wrong done to the company and that what distinguishes a fraud from other non-fraudulent wrongs is whether the breach of duty can be ratified by the shareholders by ordinary resolution.[79] Certainly, it is true to say that only if a wrong can be identified in relation to which the individual may sue derivatively, even though the wrong is ratifiable, will a "true" exception to the rule in *Foss v. Harbottle* have been identified. For the moment, the matter must remain uncertain, though Megarry V.-C. in *Estmanco v. G.L.C.*[80] was prepared to say that the "it may be" that the guiding principle underlying the rule "may come to be whether an ordinary resolution of the shareholders could validly carry out or ratify the act in question".

(b) Non-ratifiable wrongs

It was suggested in the second proposition formulated above that, even where the wrong is not ratifiable, the courts have not accepted that the individual shareholder should be free to initiate litigation on the company's behalf, for there may still be an appropriate collective body which can be entrusted with this decision. The force of this argument has always been accepted in the case of "fraud on the minority" by the addition of the rider that the individual can sue only if the wrongdoers are not in control of the general meeting, for in that case the decision, it is said, can be left to the general meeting.[81] However, more recently, in the important case of *Smith v. Croft (No. 2)*[82] Knox J. extended the principle, albeit not strictly as a matter of *locus standi*, and applied it beyond the situation of "frauds". Let us look first, however, at the traditional rule.

In recent years there has been some relaxation of the courts' understanding of what constitutes control and thus some loosening of the

---

[76] *Edwards v. Halliwell*, above, n. 16 at 1067; *Cotter v. National Union of Seamen* [1929] 2 Ch. 58.

[77] Notably *Alexander v. Automatic Telephone Co.* [1900] 2 Ch. 56, though query whether the case did not involve the expropriation of corporate property.

[78] It is clear that the word "fraud" is here being used in its equitable rather than its common law sense, connoting dishonesty.

[79] Wedderburn [1958] C.L.J. at 96–106. The rules relating to ratification of directors' breaches of duty are discussed above at pp. 644–648.

[80] [1982] 1 W.L.R. 2 at 11.

[81] *Edwards v. Halliwell*, above, n. 16 at 1067.

[82] [1988] Ch. 114.

locus standi requirements for the derivative suit. English law has never insisted that a general meeting be called upon, and be shown to have refused, to institute proceedings, provided wrongdoer control could be demonstrated in other ways.[83] However, in *Pavlides v. Jensen*[84] the judge seemed to think of control in terms of *de jure* control, *i.e.* control of at least a majority of the votes capable of being cast at a general meeting. Yet in the *Prudential* case, the Court of Appeal[85] referred to control in much more wide-ranging and realistic terms, as embracing "a wide spectrum extending from an overall absolute majority of votes at one end to a majority of votes at the other end made up of those likely to be cast by the delinquent himself plus those voting with him as a result of influence or apathy". The reference to apathy in particular would seem to bring in situations of control exercised by directors over the general meeting through the advantages afforded to them by the proxy voting system.[86]

At the same time, however, as the courts were relaxing the requirements of wrongdoer control, Knox J. in *Smith v. Croft (No. 2)*[87] set about giving greater prominence to the principle that majority decisions on litigation were preferable to putting the matter wholly into the hands of an individual shareholder, whose views on this matter might not be representative of the other shareholders. Even where the individual shareholder met the standing requirements of *Foss v. Harbottle*, it was now suggested, he or she did not have the right to initiate litigation if the majority of the independent minority of shareholders were against the litigation.[88] This development of the principle of majority rule was effected by drawing a distinction between the standing rules of *Foss* and the freedom of the company through an appropriate mechanism to compromise litigation or to decide not to initiate it. If the company validly decided not to sue, the individual shareholder would not be able to initiate litigation, even if he met the standing requirements of *Foss*, because he or she could not be a better position to sue that the company itself. In determining whether the "company" did wish to initiate litigation, the court should have regard to the views of the majority of the independent minority shareholders.

If the decision in *Smith v. Croft (No. 2)* is followed, it will have a destructive impact upon the derivative action. It is clear that Knox J. saw his reasoning as being applicable equally to frauds and to corpor-

---

[83] *Atwool v. Merryweather* (1867) L.R. 5 Eq. 464n; *Mason v. Harris* (1879) 11 Ch.D. 97 at 108; *Alexander v. Automatic Telephone Co.*, above, n. 77 at 69.

[84] [1956] Ch. 565.

[85] Above, n. 56 at 219.

[86] See above, pp. 578–581.

[87] [1988] Ch. 114, noted by Prentice (1988) 104 L.Q.R. 341; the distinction on which the case is based seems to have been first articulated in *Taylor v. NUM*, above, n. 31, noted by Davies [1985] J.B.L. 318.

[88] It is unclear whether plaintiff or defendant carries the burden of proof on this issue.

ate actions arising out of *ultra vires* cases. In these cases no derivative action will lie if the majority of the minority oppose the action (or even, perhaps, if it cannot be shown that the majority of the minority support the action). This novel restriction represents a considerable tightening of the conditions which must be met by an individual share-holder who wishes to enforce the company's rights; indeed, it could be said to constitute the most significant development of the rule since it was first fully formulated in the second half of the nineteenth century.

The conceptual legal basis of the decision is the distinction drawn between ratifying a breach of duty (so that it ceases to be a wrongful act) and deciding not to sue in respect of the wrong. Whereas under the old law identification of a non-ratifiable act allowed in the derivative action (subject to proof of wrongdoer control, at least in fraud cases),[89] we now learn that the possibility (or is it the fact?) of an appropriate, if minority, group of shareholders[90] deciding not to enforce the company's rights will prevent action by the individual, even if the wrong is not ratifiable. The fundamental flaw, it is suggested, lies in the drawing of precisely this distinction between decisions to ratify and not to sue. The old law implicitly accepted that deciding not to sue was the functional equivalent, at least for these purposes, of ratification, so that the same rules should determine in both cases whether action by the individual was permitted or collective decision-making was required. There may be a case for seeking to identify an appropriate independent organ which can decide whether to enforce the company's rights against wrongdoing controllers, but that objective should not be achieved on the basis of yet further conceptual refinements. More to the point, perhaps, any such innovations should not operate simply by making the bringing of litigation more difficult. If an independent body is to have the decision over suit, should there not be some guarantee that it will meet and decide whether to sue and should it not have power to sue not only in relation to non-ratifiable but also ratifiable wrongs?

The truth of the matter, it is suggested, is that the courts' views about the utility of the derivative action have undergone a fundamental shift.[91] In the *Prudential* litigation[92] the Court of Appeal brutally

---

[89] It has always been rather unclear why the test of wrongdoer control did not have to be met for derivative actions in *ultra vires* cases, since there too the general meeting could have been left to decide whether to initiate litigation. Perhaps this was another instance of confusion between individual and corporate rights. However, the application of the "majority of the independent minority" test to *ultra vires* actions will overtake this previous liberality in no uncertain way.

[90] Although the facts of the case presented the minority shareholders as the appropriate independent element, it is clear that Knox J. did not exclude an independent board from that function.

[91] Sealy, *op. cit.*, p. 2 refers to "a marked judicial antipathy, even hostility, towards the minority shareholder who comes before the court as a litigant".

[92] Above, nn. 55 and 56.

rejected the attempts of Vinelott J. at first instance to liberalise the standing rules, mainly, it would seem, because the case appeared to them as one where the shareholder had embroiled the company in litigation to enforce its rights which was a misconceived use of resources and left the company worse off, even though its rights were vindicated. Similar echoes can be found in the comments of Knox J. on counsel's proposition, which would have been uncontroversial under the old law, that "once control by the defendants is established the views of the rest of the minority as to the advisability of the prosecution of the suit are necessarily irrelevant". This the judge found "hard to square with the concept of a form of pleading originally introduced on the ground of necessity alone in order to prevent a wrong going without redress".[93] So the derivative action is not to be regarded as a normal part of the enforcement apparatus of the law, but as a weapon of last resort.

It is also consistent with these developments that courts in recent years have rejected the flexibility that was offered to them in the shape of a further (and genuine) exception to the rule in *Foss v. Harbottle*, namely one that operates when the "justice" so requires.[94] Dicta supporting such an exception can be found in the old cases, though it has to be said that they had not hardened into a generally accepted exception and such a provision gives, by its nature, only uncertain guidance to litigants.

In short, influenced by a small number of cases where the corporate benefit of the litigation attempted to be pursued derivatively was far from clear, the courts have not only rejected attempts to loosen the standing rules but have thrown that process into reverse by placing new and significant barriers in the way of the shareholder acting without majority support. It was suggested above that the rule in *Foss v. Harbottle* has to maintain a balance between ensuring the enforcement of directors' duties and preserving the collective nature of corporate decision-making. It is strongly arguable that the balance of advantage has now swung too much in favour of the latter objective, and that reform is now required to rebalance the rule.

CONCLUSION

In fact, the flag of reform has been run up the mast by the Law Commission[95] whose recent report has proposed for legislation an even bolder version of the "simple rule" mentioned at the beginning of

---

[93] Above, n. 87 at 185.
[94] See *Prudential*, above, n. 56, at 327 and *Estmanco*, above, n. 80, at 10–11 but *cf. Ruralcorp Consulting Pty Ltd v. Pynery Pty Ltd* (1996) 21 ACSR 161, Sup. Ct. Vic., and the Law Commission's proposals, below.
[95] Law Commission, *Shareholders' Remedies*, Consultation Paper No. 142, 1996.

this Chapter as having been rejected by the current case law. Their suggested principle is that a member should "be able to bring and subsequently maintain a derivative action to enforce any cause of action vested in the company against any person arising out of any breach or threatened breach of duty by any director".[96] Ratifiability would no longer be a bar to a derivative action (so that the range of breaches of which a member could complain derivatively would be expanded to include, in particular, simple negligence) and even in relation to non-ratifiable breaches the position of the minority would be improved because wrongdoer control would not have to be demonstrated and the adverse views of any independent minority would no longer prevent the bringing of such an action. In fact, without more, the stated principle would simply add the individual shareholder to the list of those capable of enforcing the company's rights in relation to breaches of directors' duties.

On the other hand, the Commission professes itself committed to the principles that "a member should be able to maintain proceedings about wrongs done to the company only in exceptional circumstances" and that "shareholders should not be able to involve the company in litigation without good cause . . . Otherwise the company may be 'killed by kindness', or waste money and management time in dealing with unwarranted proceedings."[97] In other words, the competing considerations for and against derivative actions are still thought to be the same, but the Commission proposes to strike a different balance among them and to use a different mechanisms to strike that balance. Instead of the rules of standing (albeit often unclear rules) of *Foss v. Harbottle* the Commission proposes judicial discretion to determine whether any particular piece of derivative litigation should proceed. Building on precedents from other common law jurisdictions which have reformed their standing rules and on the embryonic supervisory role of the courts under Rules of the Supreme Court,[98] the Commission proposes that the leave of the court be required to continue a derivative action commenced under its new principle, the court's decision being based on its view of all the relevant circumstances.[99] Although the court would have to look at the strength of the case, the applicant's good faith, the interests of the company, whether the wrong was ratifiable or had been ratified, the views of any independent organ of the company and the availability of alternative remedies, these would be no more than factors and would be defined in such a way as to maximise the court's discretion.[1]

---

[96] *ibid.*, para. 16.1.
[97] *ibid.*, para. 14.1.
[98] See p. 667, above.
[99] Chap. 15 of Law Commission, *Shareholders' Remedies*, above, n. 95.
[1] Presumably, effective ratification of a ratifiable wrong would mean the action would not be allowed to proceed, as would also be the case if the court formed the view that the action had no realistic prospect of success.

The question, therefore, is how the judges would exercise their new-found discretion. On the one hand, the modern Chancery judges have a good record of developing the discretion conferred upon them by the statutory unfair prejudice remedy,[2] albeit only after the legislature had reiterated its invitation to the courts to intervene by reformulating the original statutory provisions of 1947 in 1980. On the other hand, recent decisions by the courts[3] suggest that the courts see much merit in the arguments against enforcement by individual shareholders of the company's rights. Much is likely to depend, therefore, on how enthusiastic the judges perceive Parliament to have been about any reform which emerges from the Law Commission's consultative document.

[2] See Chap. 27, below.
[3] See n. 13, above.

CHAPTER 24

DISQUALIFICATION OF DIRECTORS

IN the previous Chapter we considered the difficulties which lie in the path of those wishing to enforce the company's rights *vis-à-vis* wrongdoing directors by way of traditional litigation in the civil courts. In this Chapter we examine another type of litigation, which aims to protect the public in the future by placing a prohibition on a wrongdoing director being involved for a period of time in the management of companies, rather than aiming at recovery of assets or compensation for the company. Although in some cases it is open to any member or creditor of the company to apply to the court for the imposition of a disqualification order upon a director and in other cases a disqualification order may be imposed by the court as an ancillary measure in litigation, the leading role in initiating applications for orders is in fact played by the Department of Trade and Industry and its agencies, especially the Insolvency Agency. In other words, in this area of law the public interest in the enforcement of appropriate standards of conduct upon directors and others involved in the management of companies is recognised in the very design of the legislation.

The situations in which a court may or must impose a disqualification order are now collected together in the Company Directors Disqualification Act 1986. However, that Act does not give the courts a general power to disqualify errant directors. Rather, the law on this topic had expanded in a rather haphazard way since the Second World War so as to generate a range of specific instances where disqualification may or must be imposed by the courts. The specific instances can best be analysed as falling within the following categories:

(a) commission of a serious offence, usually involving dishonesty, in connection with the management of a company;
(b) being found liable to make a contribution to the assets of the company on grounds of fraudulent or wrongful trading;
(c) failure to comply with the provisions of the companies' or insolvency legislation relating to the filing of documents with the Registrar;
(d) being found to be unfit to be concerned in the management of a company either on the basis of one's conduct as a director of a company which has become insolvent or on the basis of material discovered in an official investigation of a company.

Of the above, the last category is perhaps the most pertinent in relation to the enforcement of directors' duties. Thus, the 1986 Act[1] requires a court considering the issue of unfitness to take into account "any misfeasance or breach of any fiduciary or other duty by the director in relation to the company"[2] and "any misapplication or retention by the director of, or any conduct by the director giving rise to an obligation to account for, any money or other property of the company". The last category is also the one which has given rise to the greatest quantity of litigation, and we shall examine it first, after having briefly described the analogous but separate provisions relating to bankrupts acting as directors.

Bankrupts

The prohibition on undischarged bankrupts acting as directors or being involved in the management of companies can be traced back to the Companies Act 1928. Although bankruptcy does not necessarily connote any wrongdoing, the policy against permitting those who have been so spectacularly unsuccessful in the management of their own finances taking charge of other people's money is so self-evident that it has not proved controversial. The prohibition is contained in section 11 of the 1986 Act, and the main point of interest about it for present purposes is that it is an automatic disqualification, not dependent upon the making of a disqualification order by the court. However, the disqualification is not absolute, because the bankrupt may apply to the court for leave to act even though bankrupt.[3]

In other words, the statute really reverses the burden of action, by placing it upon the bankrupt to show that he or she may be safely involved in the management of companies rather than upon some state official to demonstrate to a court that the bankrupt ought not to be allowed to act. However, opposition to the use of this technique, when the government proposed in the Insolvency Bill 1985 to use it in the case of the directors of insolvent companies,[4] proved so strong that all other cases of disqualification contained in the 1986 Act require an order of the court.[5] This method of proceeding at least makes it easier

---

[1] paras. 1 and 2 of Schedule 1. A number of other matters are mentioned as relevant in the Schedule, especially when the company is insolvent, and in any event the Schedule does not aim to set out an exhaustive list of relevant matters.

[2] See, for example, *Re Looe Fish Ltd* [1993] BCLC 1160, (director issued shares to keep himself and his faction in control of the company); *Re Godwin Warren Control Systems plc* [1993] BCLC 80 (failure of director to disclose his interest in a transaction between his company and a third party); *Re Dominion International Group plc (No. 2)* [1996] 1 BCLC 572 (failure to act bona fide in the interests of the company); *Re Continental Assurance Co. of London plc* [1977] 1 BCLC 48 (negligence).

[3] s.11(1).

[4] See Hick, "Disqualification of Directors—Forty Years On" [1988] J.B.L. 27 at 35 and 38–40.

[5] Even under s.12, relating to county court administration orders, an order of the court, if not a disqualification order, is required.

to create and maintain a register of those against whom disqualification orders have been made.[6]

Disqualification orders

So the central instrument in the courts' hands under the 1986 Act is the disqualification order. It would obviously be too limited for such an order to prohibit a person from acting as director of a company, since there are many ways of controlling a company's management without being a director of the company. So the prohibition extends to the positions of liquidator, administrator and receiver as well and, generally, to "in any way, directly or indirectly, be[ing] concerned or tak[ing] part in the promotion, formation or management of a company".[7] The courts have taken a broad approach to what being concerned or taking part in the management of a company may embrace.[8]

Adherence to a disqualification order, once made, is secured by criminal penalties[9] and, probably much more important, by personal liability for the debts and other liabilities of the company incurred during the time the disqualified person was involved in its management in breach of the order. This demonstrates that it is misuse of the facility of limited liability which lies at the basis of disqualification orders. Personal liability is also extended to any other person involved in the management of the company who knowingly acts on the instructions of a disqualified person.[10] Conversely, entrusting the management of a company to someone known to be bankrupt or disqualified might well be a basis for disqualifying the entrusting director on grounds of unfitness.[11]

The rigour of the prohibition imposed by the Act is mitigated by two factors. First, as we shall see below, the disqualification is for a limited period of time, and the maximum period of time (15 years)

---

[6] See p. 690, below.

[7] s.1(1). If a court makes a disqualification order, it must cover all the activities set out in s.1(1), but the court could give the disqualified director limited leave to act despite the order. See *Re Gower Enterprises (No. 2)* [1995] 2 BCLC 201 and *Re Seagull Manufacturing Co. Ltd* [1996] 1 BCLC 51 and below, p. 682.

[8] Management of a company is thought to require involvement in the general management and policy of the company and not just the holding of any post labelled managerial, though in small companies it may not be possible to distinguish between policy-setting and day-to-day management: *R. v. Campbell* (1983) 78 Cr.App.R 95, C.A. (acting as a management consultant); *Drew v. Lord Advocate* 1996 S.L.T. 1062.

[9] ss.13 and 14. The equivalent offence in relation to acting when bankrupt has been held to be one of strict liability (*R v. Brockley* (1993) 92 Cr.App.R. 385, C.A.) and the arguments used to support that conclusion would seem equally applicable to the offence of acting when disqualified.

[10] s.15. This section applies also to breaches of the prohibition on undischarged bankrupts, imposed by s.11. The various people made personally liable by s.15 are jointly and severally liable with each other and with the company and any others who are for any reason personally liable: s.15(2).

[11] See *Re Moorgate Metals Ltd* [1995] 1 BCLC 503 and below, p. 682.

will be imposed only in the most serious cases. Secondly, as with bankrupts, the prohibition may be relaxed by the court. In the case of disqualification on grounds of unfitness under section 6, it is the practice to consider such applications at the same time as the disqualification order is made.[12] The leave granted, which obviously must not be so wide as to undermine the purposes of the Act, often relates to other companies of which the applicant is already a director, which are trading successfully and whose future success is thought to be dependent on the continued involvement of the applicant. Often the leave is made conditional upon other steps being taken to protect the public, such as the appointment of an independent director to the board.[13]

Disqualification on grounds of unfitness

There are two provisions of the 1986 Act relating to disqualification on this ground, the initiative in both cases lying with the Secretary of State. Under section 6 the Secretary of State (or the Official Receiver in the case of a company being wound up by the court) may apply to the court to have a director[14] or shadow director[15] of an insolvent[16] company disqualified; and under section 8 the Secretary of State may do so, whether the company is insolvent or not, if he decides it is in the public interest to apply after consideration of the results of an official investigation of the company.[17] The former section, which will be considered in this Chapter, has the unique feature that, if unfitness is established to the satisfaction of the court, disqualification is mandatory (for a period of two years, though the court may impose a longer period).[18] Thus, although City opposition fought off the idea of automatic disqualification in the case of directors of insolvent

---

[12] *Secretary of State for Trade and Industry v. Worth* [1994] 2 BCLC 113, C.A., which indeed puts the applicant under some costs pressure to apply then, if his application is based on circumstances existing at the time of the order.

[13] *Re Cargo Agency Ltd* [1992] BCLC 686; *Re Chartmore Ltd* [1990] BCLC 673. The practice has been followed in Scotland despite doubts whether the power to give leave confers upon the courts the power to specify conditions: *Secretary of State for Trade and Industry v. Palfreman* [1995] 2 BCLC 301. If the conditions attached by the court are not strictly complied with, the director is in breach of the disqualification order and so exposed to personal liability: *Re Brian Sheridan Cars Ltd* [1996] 1 BCLC 327.

[14] Including a *de facto* director, *i.e.* a person who acts as a director even though he has not been validly appointed as a director or even though there has been no attempt at all to appoint him as director: *Re Lo-Line Electric Motors Ltd* [1988] Ch. 477; *Re Richborough Furniture Ltd* [1996] 1 BCLC 507. Of course, in this last situation it may be difficult to establish on the facts whether the respondent has been acting as a director.

[15] s.22(4) and (5).

[16] A company is insolvent if it goes into liquidation with insufficient assets to meet its liabilities, if an administration order has been made in relation to the company or if an administrative receiver is appointed: s.6(2).

[17] See the following Chapter, especially at pp. 702–703. s.8 will not be considered further here.

[18] s.6(1) and (4)—the maximum period is 15 years.

companies, the Government managed to avoid leaving the issue entirely to the discretion of the courts.[19]

Moreover, it should be noted that section 6 does not permit the court to disqualify *any* person whose conduct seems to the court to make him or her unfit to be a director. Only directors (including *de facto* and shadow directors) may be disqualified. The legislation may thus be said to embody the idea that everyone is entitled to one bite at the cherry in terms of becoming a director. The law's control operates only after, and not in advance of, the respondent's taking up the position of director.

Before embarking upon an analysis of section 6 and the case law it has generated, it is necessary to address an underlying question about the purpose of the section. That it is there to protect the public against being involved, whether as shareholders or, more likely, as creditors, with companies run by people who have shown themselves to be unfit to be directors is clear.[20] What is less clear is how that protection is to be effected. The issue has arisen recently in relation to the calculation of the period of disqualification. Should that be assessed on a forward- or a backward-looking basis? In other words, is the question which the court has to answer, for what period in the future will the director be a danger to the public? Or is the question, how far below the conduct expected of a director did the respondent fall in the activities which have been examined by the court? After some lack of clarity in the cases[21] the Court of Appeal seems now to have opted for the latter approach. In other words, the public is to be protected by the imposition of sanctions on directors for falling below the standard required by section 6, the sanction being gradated according to the seriousness of the director's lapse.[22] As we have noted, the minimum and maximum periods of disqualification under section 6 are set at two and 15 years respectively. In *Re Sevenoaks Stationers (Retail) Ltd*[23] the Court of Appeal divided that period into three brackets, though it cannot be said that it drew the dividing line between them very clearly.[24]

---

[19] The scope of s.6 was much influenced by chapter 45 of the Report of the Review Committee on Insolvency Law and Practice, Chairman Sir Kenneth Cork, Cmnd. 8558 (1982). The predecessor of s.6 (s.9 of the Insolvency Act 1976) had required involvement in two companies which had gone insolvent within five years of one another before disqualification on grounds of unfitness could be imposed.

[20] *Re Sevenoaks Stationers (Retail) Ltd* [1991] Ch. 164 at 176, C.A.

[21] The earlier cases are examined by Finch in (1993) 22 I.L.J. 35.

[22] *Re Grayan Building Services Ltd* [1995] Ch. 241, C.A. In this case the Court of Appeal held that the respondent could not reduce the period of disqualification by showing that, despite past shortcomings, he was unlikely to offend again. Such evidence, however, could be taken into account on an application for leave.

[23] Above, n. 20.

[24] The court distinguished between a top bracket of over ten years for "particularly serious" cases; a middle bracket of six to ten years for serious cases "which do not merit the top bracket"; and a minimum bracket "not very serious" cases.

The role of the Insolvency Service

When recommending what is now section 6, the Cork Committee[25] said that its aim was to "replace by a far more rigorous system the present ineffective provisions ...". The effectiveness in practice of section 6 can be said to depend upon two matters. The first is the assiduity of the Insolvency Service, an executive agency of the DTI, in bringing applications for disqualification orders before the court; and the second is the courts' approach to section 6, especially their interpretation of the central concept of unfitness.

In order to maximise the chances of applications being made, the Cork Committee[26] recommended that applications by liquidators or, with leave, other creditors should be permitted, and so confining applications to the Secretary of State and the Official Receiver was regarded at the time of the passage of the Insolvency Act 1985 as a retrograde step. There are two reasons why the Insolvency Service might not prove effective. The first is lack of information about directors' conduct, especially when the company is being wound up voluntarily, so that the Official Receiver is not involved.[27] This is addressed by the imposition of a requirement on liquidators, administrators and receivers to report to the Secretary of State on the conduct of directors and shadow directors of companies for whose affairs they are responsible, if they think such conduct falls within section 6,[28] though the quality of the information provided is not always high.[29]

Secondly, there was doubt about the quantity and quality of the resources the DTI would devote to the enforcement of the legislation. Although the early efforts of the Insolvency Service were criticised,[30] by the middle of the 1990s it was securing the disqualification of some 400 directors a year, about 40 per cent on reports from Official Receivers, the remainder on reports from insolvency practitioners.[31] Nevertheless, it is clear that the Service still experiences difficulties in commencing insolvency applications within the two year period

---

[25] Above, n. 19 at para. 1809.

[26] *ibid.*, para. 1818.

[27] In Scotland, where there are no Official Receivers, even compulsory liquidations are handled by insolvency practitioners and the potential scope of the problem is accordingly greater.

[28] s.7(3) and the Insolvent Companies (Reports on Conduct of Directors) Rules 1996 (S.I. 1996 No. 1909) and the Insolvent Companies (Reports on Conduct of Directors)(Scotland) Rules 1996 (S.I. 1996 No. 1910). The Secretary of State may also take the initiative to ask for information, including the production of documents (s.7(4)), something most often done, presumably, when the report under s.7(3) suggests unfitness but does not contain enough detail to form the basis of an application.

[29] See Wheeler, "Directors' Disqualification: Insolvency Practitioners and the Decision-making Process" (1995) 15 L.S. 283.

[30] National Audit Office, *The Insolvency Service Executive Agency: Company Director Disqualification*, H.C. 907, 1993

[31] Insolvency Service, *Annual Report 1994–95*, p. 11. 67 per cent of disqualification orders were in the lowest bracket; 30 per cent in the middle bracket; and 3 per cent in the highest bracket. See n. 24, above. In 1996 946 directors were disqualified as unfit.

permitted by the statute[32] and in prosecuting them with sufficient vigour to avoid striking out on grounds of delay.[33]

Breach of commercial morality

As far as the role of the courts is concerned, it seems possible to divide the cases in which the courts have found unfitness into two rough categories.[34] However, it must be remembered that the concept of unfitness is open-ended, so that it cannot be claimed that all potential, or even actual, disqualification applications can be forced into one or other of these categories. Further, in the nature of things, many disqualification cases display aspects from both categories. Nevertheless, it is thought that identifying the two categories is a useful starting point, if nothing more.

The first category, breach of commercial morality, has at its centre the idea of conducting a business at the expense of its creditors. A leading example, though only an example, of such conduct was described by the Cork Committee in terms of a person who sets up an undercapitalised company, allows it to become insolvent, forms a new company (often with assets purchased at a discount from the liquidator of the old company), carries on trading much as before, and repeats the process perhaps several times, leaving behind him each time a trail of unpaid creditors.[35]

More generally, the courts have been alert to find unfairness where the directors have apparently attempted to trade on the backs of their creditors.[36] Part II of Schedule I indeed requires the court, when assessing unfitness, to have regard to the extend of the directors' responsibility for the company becoming insolvent, for the failure of the company to provide goods or services which have already been paid for or for giving a preference to one group of creditors over another or entering into a transaction at an undervalue.[37] It was thought at one time that particular obloquy attached to directors who attempted to trade out their difficulties by using as capital in the business monies

---

[32] s.7(2). The court may give leave to commence the application out of time, though the Secretary of State must show a good reason for any extension: *Re Copecrest Ltd* [1994] 2 BCLC 284, C.A.

[33] *Re Manlon Trading Ltd* [1996] Ch. 136, C.A. The National Audit Office, above, n. 30, p. 18, found that the Insolvency Service in most cases took nearly the full two-year period permitted to bring an application and that up to a further four years might elapse before a disqualification order was made, during which period the director was free to carry on business with limited liability.

[34] "Those who trade under the regime of limited liability and who avail themselves of the privileges of that regime must accept the standards of probity and competence to which the law requires company directors to conform" (*per* Neill L.J. in *Re Grayan Building Services Ltd*, above, n. 22).

[35] Cork Committee, para. 1813. This is the so-called "Phoenix" syndrome. For examples in the subsequent case law see *Re Travel Mondial (UK) Ltd* [1991] BCLC 120; *Re Linvale Ltd* [1993] BCLC 654; *Re Swift 736 Ltd* [1993] BCLC 1.

[36] *Re Keypak Homecare Ltd* [1990] BCLC 440.

[37] paras. 6–8.

owed to the Crown by way of income tax, national insurance contributions or VAT, on the grounds that the Crown was an involuntary creditor. Although that view has been rejected by the Court of Appeal, the same court has affirmed that, in relation to any creditor, paying only those creditors who pressed for payment and taking advantage of those creditors who did not in order to provide the working capital which the company needed, was a clear example of unfitness.[38] If the directors of the financially troubled company were at the same time paying themselves salaries which were out of proportion to the company's trading success (or lack of it), the likelihood of a disqualification order being made is only increased.[39]

Recklessness and incompetence

In the previous section the cases on unfitness highlighted the improper treatment by directors of the creditors of the company. The cases considered in this section focus on the recklessness or incompetence of the directors' conduct of the business. It may often be that the creditors are the ones who suffer from the maladministration, but here it is the competence of the directors which is at issue, rather than the fact that they have improperly used monies owed to creditors to finance the business, or otherwise acted improperly in relation to the creditors. In many cases, of course, both aspects of unfitness can be found.

The early cases put liability on the basis of recklessness,[40] but more recently it has been said that "incompetence or negligence to a very marked degree"[41] would be enough. The danger which the courts have to avoid in this area is that of treating any business venture which collapses as evidence of negligence. To do so would be to discourage the taking of commercial risks, which must be the life-blood of corporate activity. As we have seen above in relation to the common law duty of care,[42] however, creating a space for proper risk-taking is no longer thought to require relieving directors of all objective standards of conduct. Thus, in *Re Richborough Furniture Ltd*[43] a director was disqualified for three years, on the basis of "lack of experience, knowledge and understanding ... She did not have enough experience or knowledge to know what she should do in the face of the problems of pressing creditors, escalating Crown debts and lack of capital. It seems that she was not sufficiently skilful as regards the accounts functions

---

[38] *Re Sevenoaks Stationers (Retail) Ltd* [1991] Ch. 164, C.A.; *Secretary of State for Trade and Industry v. McTighe (No. 2)* [1996] 2 BCLC 477, C.A.
[39] *Re Synthetic Technology Ltd* [1993] BCC 549; *Secretary of State v. Van Hengel* [1995] 1 BCLC 545.
[40] *Re Stanford Services Ltd* [1987] BCLC 607.
[41] *Re Sevenoaks Stationers (Retail) Ltd*, above, at 184.
[42] pp. 640–644, above.
[43] [1996] 1 BCLC 507.

to see that the records were inadequate." It seems likely that disqualification of incompetent directors is a more effective remedy than actions for breach of the director's ratifiable common law duty of care.[44]

In this area, particular importance is attached by the courts to failure by directors to file annual returns, produce audited accounts and to keep proper accounting records.[45] These are the practical expressions of a more general view that all directors must keep themselves *au fait* with the financial position of their company and make sure that it complies with the reporting requirements of the Companies legislation, for otherwise they cannot know what corrective action, if any, needs to be taken.[46] Although this duty may fall with particular emphasis on those responsible for the financial side of the company, all directors must keep themselves informed about the company's basic financial position.[47]

On the other hand, seeking and acting on competent outside advice when financial difficulties arise will be an indication of competence, even if the plan recommended does not pay off and the company eventually collapses.[48] It should also be remembered that the courts have required a "marked degree" of negligence before declaring a director unfit. There is a contrast here with wrongful trading[49] where a director can be held liable, once insolvency threatens, unless he can show that he "took *every* step with a view to minimising the potential loss to the company's creditors as . . . he ought to have taken".[50] It is suggested that this contrast is explained by the fact that a disqualification order can often have the effect of depriving the director of his livelihood and that, once unfitness is found, a two-year disqualification is mandatory. Under the Insolvency Act, on the other hand, no order as to contribution need be made, even if the director was guilty of

---

[44] Above, pp. 644–648.

[45] These may be ingredients in a finding of unfitness, even though, as we see below, p. 689, non-compliance with the reporting requirements of the legislation is a separate ground of disqualification, albeit only for up to five years.

[46] *Re Firedart Ltd* [1994] 2 BCLC 340; *Re New Generation Engineers Ltd* [1993] BCLC 435.

[47] *Re City Investment Centres Ltd* [1992] BCLC 956; *Secretary of State v. Van Hengel* [1995] 1 BCLC 545; *Re Majestic Recording Studios Ltd* [1989] BCLC 1; *Re Continental Assurance Co. of London plc* [1977] 1 BCLC 48.

[48] *Re Douglas Construction Services Ltd* [1988] BCLC 397. Conversely, ignoring a plan produced by outside accountants is likely to be characterised as "obstinately and unjustifiably backing [the director's] own assessment of the company's business": *Re GSAR Realisations Ltd* [1993] BCLC 409.

[49] Above pp. 153–155.

[50] s.214(3). Of course, keeping an insolvent company going can be grounds for disqualification for being unfit but only in strong cases. See, for example, *Re Living Images Ltd* [1996] 1 BCLC 348, where the directors were aware of the company's parlous condition and keeping it going was described as "a gamble at long odds" and "the taking of unwarranted risks with creditors' money", so that there was a lack of probity involved and not just negligence. *cf.* the refusal to make a disqualification order in *Re Dawson Print Group Ltd* [1987] BCLC 601; *Re Bath Glass Ltd* [1988] BCLC 329; *Re CU Fittings Ltd* [1989] BCLC 556; and *Secretary of State v. Gash* [1997] 1 BCLC 341.

wrongful trading, and if an order is made, it can be carefully matched to the director's fault.[51]

Moreover, although section 6 is triggered by the insolvency of the company, the inquisition into the director's conduct can go back into any part of his activities as director, whether before or after the threat of insolvency arose, and indeed may embrace his conduct as director of any other company, whether or not that other company has become insolvent.[52] Under the Insolvency Act, by contrast, the duty in question only attaches once the director ought to have realised there was no reasonable prospect of the company avoiding insolvent liquidation and it relates only to his conduct after that point.

Serious offences

The remaining provisions of the 1986 Act permit, but do not require, the court to disqualify a director, on various grounds. These will be dealt with briefly, partly because they have not generated as much controversy as the unfitness ground, and partly because the disqualification provisions are being used in these cases in support of aspects of the corporate framework other than directors' duties as considered in the immediately preceding chapters.

In relation to serious offences, there are two routes to a disqualification order, depending upon whether the person concerned has actually been convicted of an offence. If there has been a conviction, a disqualification order may be made against a person, whether a director or not, who has committed an indictable offence in connection with the promotion, formation, management, liquidation or striking off of a company or in connection with the receivership or management of its property.[53] Usually, the disqualification will be ordered by the court by which the person is convicted and at the time of his or her conviction. Thus, in 1994–1995 courts made 44 disqualification orders following convictions in prosecutions initiated by the Insolvency Service. However, if the convicting court does not act, the Secretary of State or the liquidator or any past or present creditor or member of the company in relation to which the offence was committed, may apply to any court having jurisdiction to wind up the company to impose the disqualification.[54] Here, too, the courts have taken a wide view of what "in connection with the management of the company" means in this context.[55]

Where there has not been a conviction, but the company is being

---

[51] s.214(1): the court "may declare that [the director] is to be liable to make such contribution (if any) to the company's assets as the court thinks proper".

[52] s.6(1).

[53] s.2.

[54] s.16(2).

[55] *R. v. Goodman* [1994] 1 BCLC 349, C.A. (insider dealing by a director in the shares of his company—see above, p. 474); *R.v. Georgiou* (1988) 4 BCC 625; *R. v. Ward, The Times*, April 10, 1997 (conspiracy to defraud by creating a false market in shares during a takeover bid—see above, p. 435 and below, p. 775).

wound up, then if it appears that a person has been guilty of the offence[56] of fraudulent trading or has been guilty as an officer[57] of the company of any fraud in relation to it or any breach of duty as an officer, then the court having jurisdiction to wind up the company may impose a disqualification order.[58]

Disqualification in connection with civil liability for fraudulent or wrongful trading

In addition to the array of orders which the court may make under sections 213 and 214 of the Insolvency Act 1986 in cases of fraudulent or wrongful trading,[59] section 10 of the Disqualification Act adds the power to make a disqualification order. The court may act here on its own motion, that is, whether or not an application is made to it by anyone for an order to be made.

Failure to comply with reporting requirements

Again, there are separate provisions according to whether the person to be disqualified has been convicted or not. If he or she has been convicted of a summary offence in connection with a failure to file a document with or give notice of a fact to the Registrar, then the convicting court may disqualify that person if in the previous five years he has had at least three convictions (including the current one) or default orders against him for non-compliance with the reporting requirements of the Companies and Insolvency Acts.[60] If the current conviction were on indictment, then the provisions of section 2 (above) would apply, though naturally, where the current conviction is summary, the fact that the earlier convictions were on indictment does not prevent the convicting summary court from disqualifying.[61]

Where there has been no conviction, the Secretary of State and the others mentioned in section 16(2)[62] may apply to the court having jurisdiction to wind up the companies in question for disqualification orders to be made on the grounds that the respondent has been "persistently in default" in complying with the reporting requirements of the Companies and Insolvency Acts.[63] The "three convictions or defaults in five years" rule applies here too, but without prejudice to proof of persistent default in any other manner.[64] Since the offences

---

[56] Under s.458 of the Companies Act.

[57] Also included are the usual cast of liquidators, receivers and managers: s.4(1)(b).

[58] s.4, upon application by those listed in s.16(2). It is unclear whether the breach of duty referred to must involve the commission of a criminal offence.

[59] See above, pp. 151–155, but the court is not obliged to disqualify; *cf.* n. 50, above.

[60] s.5. Those listed in s.16(2) may apply for a disqualification order to be made.

[61] Contrast the wording of subsections (1) and (2) of s.5.

[62] Above, text attached to n. 54.

[63] s.3.

[64] s.3(2).

involved in these sections may be only summary ones, the maximum period of disqualification is limited to five, instead of the usual 15, years. Nevertheless, the fact that these provisions are in the Act at all is a testimony to the importance attached recently to timely filing of accounts and other documents. However, the improvement recorded in this area may be due more to the introduction of late filing penalties than the disqualification orders, of which only seven were made by magistrates in 1994–1995 in relation to failures to deliver.[65]

Register of disqualification orders

Crucial to the effective operation of the disqualification machinery is that publicity should be given to the names of those who have been disqualified. Thus, the Act requires the Secretary of State to create such a register on the basis of information supplied by court officials, which register is open to public inspection.[66] In 1995–1996 903 disqualification orders were notified to the Secretary of State, of which 718 related to unfitness, one to wrongful trading, three to investigations and 181 to the remaining provisions of the Disqualification Act lumped together.[67]

Conclusion

For many years the disqualification provisions of the successive Companies Acts seemed to make little impact. Important in principle as a technique for dealing with corporate wrongdoing of one sort or another, especially on the part of directors, the practical consequences of the provisions were limited. The combination of the substantive reforms recommended by the Cork Committee and of acceptance by Government that the promotion of small, and not-so-small, businesses needed to be accompanied by action to raise the standards of directors' behaviour and to protect the public from the scheming and the incompetent, has at last brought the disqualification provisions to the fore. Although the workings of the Insolvency Agency are still not beyond improvement, its activities probably do far more to protect the interests of shareholders and creditors than the recent developments in the common law of directors' duties, whether by recognition of the interests of the creditors or by way of the development of an objective standard of care.[68]

---

[65] *Companies in 1994–95*, pp. 18–19.
[66] s.18 and the Companies (Disqualification Orders) Regulations 1986 (S.I. 1986 No. 2067).
[67] *Companies in 1995–96*, Table D1.
[68] See pp. 603 and 640, above.

CHAPTER 25

BREACH OF CORPORATE DUTIES: ADMINISTRATIVE REMEDIES

MANY other countries have recognised that the abuse of corporate power cannot be adequately constrained by leaving it to the company's members to ensure that the controllers behave and to take action in the courts if they do not. They have accordingly set up governmental agencies to exercise a supervisory role, sometimes conferring legislative and judicial, as well as administrative, functions on those agencies. But few of them (not even the United States, which has in the SEC the most powerful of such agencies) have gone so far as we have in empowering them to launch inquisitorial raids on corporate (and even unincorporated) bodies. The fact that we have gone further is not necessarily grounds for pride; it is partly due to the still primitive state of our version of derivative actions and to the appalling cost of litigation in England (not effectively mitigated by Legal Aid and aggravated by our rule that the losing party pays both his and the winner's costs and by our refusal hitherto to countenance contingent fees). Be that as it may, the fact is that Draconian powers have increasingly been vested in the Secretary of State and the Department of Trade and Industry now has a sizeable Investigations and Enforcement Directorate which frequently conducts the initial inquisition though it may be hived-off later to outside inspectors, normally a Q.C. and a chartered accountant. Those subject to these powers, having largely failed to obtain any amelioration of them in the domestic courts, have mounted challenges under the European Convention on Human Rights, as we shall see below.

Originally, appointment of outside inspectors was the only power that the Secretary of State had. But an announced appointment of inspectors is likely in itself to cause damage to the company. Hence the Department was reluctant to appoint unless a strong case for doing so could be made out and it normally made inquiries of the board of directors before doing so. Though such inquiries might cause the board to take remedial action, they might equally well provide an opportunity for evidence to be destroyed or fabricated. Hence, on the recommendation of the Jenkins Committee,[1] power to require the production of books and papers was added by the 1967 Act, a power which can be exercised with less publicity[2] and which may suffice in itself or

---

[1] Cmnd. 1749, paras. 213–219.

[2] The Department does not normally announce that it has mounted such an investigation and all information about it is regarded as confidential. This has its disadvantages. If a team of officials is going through the company's books and papers this cannot be concealed from its

lead to a formal appointment of inspectors if the facts elicited show that that is needed. This power, now conferred by section 447 of the Act[3] is by far the one most commonly exercised.[4] It and the provisions regarding appointment of inspectors under the Companies Act are now to be found in its Part XIV (sections 431–453).

1. Investigations of companies' documents

Under section 447 (2)–(3) the Secretary of State may, at any time if he thinks there is good reason to do so, give directions to any company requiring it, at such time and place as are specified in the direction, to produce such documents[5] as may be specified[6] or authorise an officer of his, on producing, if required, evidence of his authority, to produce to that officer any documents which the officer may specify.[7] In practice the latter course is adopted since it avoids the risk of the documents being destroyed or doctored; the officer will arrive without warning[8] at the company's registered office (or wherever else the documents are believed to be held).[9] When it appears to the Secretary of State or to the officer authorised by him that the documents concerned are in the possession of some person other than the company, he has the like power to require that person to produce them.[10] About three-quarters of these investigations are prompted by allegations of fraudulent trading, theft or acting as a director whilst disqualified or a bankrupt.[11]

The requirement to produce documents includes power, if they are produced, to take copies of them or extracts from them and to require any person who produces them, or any other person who is, or was in the past, an officer or employee of the company to provide an explana-

---

employees and will soon become known to the Press, thus putting the company under a cloud which may never be dispersed because the ending of the inquiries will not normally be announced or their results ever be published, notwithstanding that the conclusion may be that all is well with the company.

[3] As amended by the 1989 Act, s.63(1)–(7).

[4] In 1995/1996 389 investigations were commenced under s.447, but only one under the other investigatory sections of the 1985 Act: *Companies in 1995–96*, Table 2. For investigations into insider dealing under the FSA, see above, pp. 474–476.

[5] The 1989 Act substituted "documents" for "books or papers" and defined "documents" in a new subs.(9) as including "information recorded in any form and, in relation to information recorded otherwise than in legible form, the power to require its production includes power to require the production of a copy in legible form" (*e.g.* a computer print-out).

[6] s.447(2).

[7] s.447(3).

[8] The investigation is an administrative act to which the full rules of natural justice do not apply: *Norwest Holst Ltd v. Secretary of State* [1978] Ch. 201, C.A., at 224. But "fairness" must be observed and directions to produce should be clear and not excessive: *R. v. Trade Secretary, ex p. Perestrello* [1981] 1 Q.B. 19 (a case which illustrates the problems that may be met if the documents are not held in the U.K.).

[9] The officer may be accompanied by a policeman with a search warrant: see s.448, below.

[10] s.447(4). But this is without prejudice to any lien that the possessor may have.

[11] *Companies in 1995–96*, Table 7.

tion of them and, if they are not produced by the person asked, to state to the best of his knowledge where they are.[12]

Failure to comply with any requirement is an offence punishable by a fine[13] but it is a defence to a charge of failure to produce documents, to prove that they were not in the accused's possession or control and that it was not reasonably practicable for him to comply with the requirement.[14] Criminal sanctions are imposed by sections 450 and 451 on any officer of the company who is privy to the falsification or destruction of a document relating to the company's affairs or who furnishes false information.

Section 448,[15] was replaced and strengthened by the 1989 Act.[16–17] Formerly it applied only to investigations under what is now section 447. But now it applies also to any investigations under Part XIV of the Act, *i.e.* to those by outside inspectors as well. It nevertheless seems better to deal with it before turning to inspectors because the full implications of section 447 cannot otherwise be appreciated.

Under subsection (1) of section 448, a Justice of the Peace, if satisfied on information given on oath by the Secretary of State, or by a person appointed or authorised to exercise powers under Part XIV, that there are on any premises documents, production of which has been required under that Part and which have not been produced, may issue a search warrant.

Under that subsection a search warrant cannot be issued unless there has first been a requirement to produce the documents sought. The company thus forewarned, could destroy the documents before the search took place. Hence, the 1989 Act added a new subsection (2) under which a warrant may be issued if the J.P. is satisfied: (a) that there are reasonable grounds for believing that an indictable offence has been committed and that there are on the premises documents relating to whether the offence has been committed, (b) that the applicant has power under Part XIV to require the production of the

---

[12] s.447(5). Any statements he makes may be used in evidence against him: s.447(8).

[13] s.447(6). The offence is subject to: s.732 (restricting prosecution to the S. of S. or the DPP or with their consent), s.733 (making officers of bodies corporate liable if they connived at, or caused by their neglect, an offence by the body corporate) and s.734 (enabling prosecutions to be brought against unincorporated bodies in the name of the body).

[14] s.447(7). s.449 contains detailed provisions regarding the security and confidentiality of documents and information produced under s.447 and the uses to which they can be put.

[15] Note also that there is a power under s.721 whereby (on application of the DPP, the S. of S. or the police) a High Court judge, if satisfied that there is reasonable cause to believe that any person, while an officer of a company, has committed an offence in its management and that evidence of the commission is to be found in any books or papers of, or under the control of, the company, may make an order authorising any named person to inspect the books and papers or require an officer of the company to produce them: see *Re A Company* [1980] Ch. 138, C.A. (reversed by H.L. *sub nom. Re Racal Communications Ltd* [1981] A.C. 374, because, under the express provisions of subs.(4), there can be no appeal from the judge and it was held that this included cases where he had erred on a point of law—and, having discovered that other judges had taken a different view, had volunteered leave to appeal!)

[16–17] 1989 Act, s.64.

documents, and (c) that there are reasonable grounds for believing that if production was required it would not be forthcoming but the documents would be removed, hidden, tampered with or destroyed. Though narrowly circumscribed by the need to satisfy the J.P. of conditions (a)–(c), this enables the search for the documents to be undertaken by the police rather than by the (possibly self-interested) officers of the company.

Part XIV contains further provisions common to both Departmental investigations and to inspections but these are left until after a description of the latter. What should be emphasised, however, is that an investigation by the Department's officials under section 447 is very far from being merely a preliminary step towards the appointment of inspectors if the documentary evidence thus discovered justifies that. On the contrary, in most cases it will be the only investigation undertaken and will lead either to a decision that no further action is needed or that some follow-up action should be taken in accordance with (4), below. The time taken to decide may vary from a few days to several months and while it continues the officials will probe deeply and in a way which from the viewpoint of the company is just as traumatic as a formal inspection.

2. Investigations by inspectors
When inspectors can be appointed

In a wide range of circumstances the Secretary of State is empowered to appoint "one or more competent inspectors[18] to investigate the affairs[19] of a company and to report on them in such manner as he directs." He has a discretion whether or not to do so, except that he must appoint if the court by order declares that the affairs of the company ought to be so investigated.[20]

Under section 431 he may appoint on the application of: (a) in the case of a company with a share capital, not less than 200 members or of members holding not less than one-tenth of the issued shares; (b) in the case of a company not having a share capital, not less than one-fifth of the persons on the company's register of members; or (c)

---

[18] As already mentioned, the usual appointees are a Q.C. and a chartered accountant but less expensive mortals may be appointed in the rarer case when the DTI appoints in relation to a private company.

[19] *i.e.* its business, including its control over its subsidiaries, whether that is being managed by the board of directors or an administrator, administrative receiver or a liquidator in a voluntary liquidation: *R. v. Board of Trade, ex p. St Martins Preserving Co.* [1965] 1 Q.B. 603.

[20] s.432(1). This seems to make the S. of S.'s refusal to appoint reviewable by the court if an application is made to it by anyone with *locus standi* and to enable a court, in proceedings before it (*e.g.* on a petition under s.459), to make an order declaring that the company's affairs ought to be investigated by Inspectors. There was formerly another situation in which the S. of S. had to appoint, *i.e.* if the company passed a special resolution declaring that its affairs ought to be so investigated, but this was removed by the 1981 Act.

in any case, the company itself.[21] However, appointments under this
section hardly ever occur.[22] This is due not only to the fact that before
appointing under the section the Secretary of State may require applicants to give security to an amount not exceeding £5,000 for payment
of the costs of the investigation[23] but also because the application has
to be supported by evidence that the applicants have good reason for
the application.[24] If they have, the Secretary of State will normally
have power to appoint of his own motion under section 432(2), below,
and it is far better for those who have good reasons to draw them to
the attention of the Department, requesting that there should be an
appointment under that section. Proceeding thus avoids the danger,
inherent in section 431, that the malefactors in the company will
tamper with the evidence once they learn of possible action under that
section and thus frustrate effective intervention by the Department
under either sections 447–448 or section 432(2).

Section 432(2) empowers the Secretary of State to appoint
inspectors[25] if it appears to him that there are circumstances suggesting
one (or more) of four grounds, the first two of which are:

"(a) that the company's affairs are being conducted or have been
conducted with intent to defraud creditors or the creditors of
any other person or otherwise for a fraudulent or unlawful
purpose or in a manner which is unfairly prejudicial to some
part of its members[26]; or

(b) that any actual or proposed act or omission of the company
(including an act or omission on its behalf) is or would be so
prejudicial, or that the company was formed for any fraudulent or unlawful purpose."

These, it will be observed, adopt the wording of sections 459 and
460 except that, presumably by an oversight, the 1989 Act omitted
here to change "some part of the members" (at the end of (a)) to
"members generally or some part of the members",[27] but in addition

---

[21] s.431(2)(c). This was added on the deletion by the 1981 Act of the former provision, compelling the S. of S. to appoint if the company resolved by special resolution (see n. 20, above)
and enables an application to be instigated by a resolution of the board or, if it refuses to do
so, by an ordinary resolution of the company in general meeting.

[22] There were no appointments under it in the years 1991–1996. *Companies in 1995–96*, Table 2.

[23] s.431(4). The £5,000 can be altered by statutory instrument. In the 1948 Act it was only £100
which, even then, would not have kept a competent Q.C. and chartered accountant happy for
the time that most inspections take.

[24] s.431(3).

[25] Even if the company is in the course of being voluntarily wound up: s.432(3).

[26] "Member" includes a person to whom shares have been transmitted by operation of law:
s.432(4).

[27] Arguably, with the absurd result that, strictly speaking, the S. of S. should not appoint
inspectors if he thinks that *all* the members are unfairly prejudiced and therefore cannot,
despite the alteration made to ss.459 and 460 (see Chap. 27 at p. 737, below) act under (a)
unless he has also acted under s.447 or 448! Since, however, the precise grounds on which
he has acted do not have to be stated (see *Norwest Holst v. Trade Secretary* [1978] Ch. 201,
C.A.) the omission is probably of no practical importance.

it enables him to appoint where the company has been operated with intent to defraud creditors or was formed or conducted for a fraudulent or unlawful purpose.

In addition an appointment may be made on the ground:

"(c) that persons concerned with the company's formation or the management of its affairs have in connection therewith been guilty of fraud, misfeasance or other misconduct towards it or towards its member; or

(d) that the company's members have not been given all the information with respect to its affairs which they might reasonably expect."[28]

Under a new subsection (2A), inserted by the 1989 Act, inspectors may be appointed on terms that any report they make is not for publication, in which case section 437, below, does not apply. Since, under that section, a report does not have to be published unless the Secretary of State thinks fit, it might be thought that subsection (2A) was unnecessary. But it has two advantages: it protects the Secretary of State from pressure to publish even though he is advised that that might prejudice possible criminal prosecutions, and it makes it clear to the proposed appointees that they will not be able to bask in publicity resulting from their efforts.[29]

In recent years, appointments under section 432(2) have become less common than they were before the introduction of the powers dealt with under (1) above,[30] which, except in major cases, normally suffice and produce results more rapidly and at less expense.

In addition to the powers of investigation dealt with above, Part XIV of the Act includes provisions regarding investigations of company ownership (sections 442–444) and of dealings in the company's securities (section 446). These, together with the power in section 177 of the Financial Services Act, to investigate insider dealing are considered elsewhere.[31]

Conduct of inspections

The Act itself contains a number of sections on the conduct of inspections. Under section 433, if inspectors, appointed to investigate the affairs of a company, think it necessary for the purposes of their

---

[28] The wording of this implies that members may "reasonably expect" more information than that to which the Act entitles them. But it seems that s.432(2) does not entitle the Secretary of State to appoint merely because the directors or officers of the company appear to have breached their duties of care, skill or diligence: see *SBA Properties Ltd v. Cradock* [1967] 1 W.L.R. 716 (which, however, was concerned with an action by the S. of S. under what is now s.438, below).

[29] It may also tend to make the officers of the company more co-operative.

[30] 8 such investigations were commenced in the years 1991–1992 to 1995–1996: *Companies in 1995–96*, Table 2.

[31] pp. 474 *et seq.* and 494 *et seq.*, where the important new powers of investigation on behalf of overseas regulators are discussed.

investigation to investigate also the affairs of another body corporate in the same group they may do so and report the results of that so far as it is relevant to the affairs of the company.[32] Under section 434[33] inspectors have powers, similar to those of officers of the Department under section 447 (above), to require the production of documents.[34] They may also require any past or present officer or agent of the company to attend before them and otherwise to give all assistance that he is reasonably able to give.[35] In addition, they may examine any person on oath[36] and any answer may be used in evidence against him.[37] If any person fails to comply with their requirements or refuses to answer any question put to him by the inspectors for the purposes of the investigation, the inspectors may certify that fact in writing to the court[38] which will thereupon inquire into the case and may punish the offender in like manner as if he had been guilty of contempt of court.[39]

The inspectors may, and, if so directed by the Secretary of State, shall, make interim reports and, on the conclusion of the investigation, must make a final report.[40] If so directed by the Secretary of State, they must also inform him of any matters coming to their knowledge during their investigation.[41] When criminal matters have come to light and been referred to the appropriate prosecuting authorities, the inspectors can be directed to discontinue or curtail the scope of their investigation and, in that event, a final report will be made only if the inspectors were appointed under section 432(1) in pursuance of an order of the court[42] or if the Secretary of State so directs.[43]

The Secretary of State may, if he thinks fit, forward a copy of any report to the company's registered office and, on request and payment of a prescribed fee, to any member of the company or other body corporate which is the subject of the report, to any person whose

---

[32] Most major corporate scandals involve the use of a network of holding and subsidiary companies, the extent of which may only become apparent during the course of the investigation: s.433 avoids the need for a formal extension of the inspectors' appointment each time they unearth another member of the group.

[33] As amended by the 1989 Act, s.56.

[34] s.434(1), (2) and (6).

[35] s.434(1) and (2).

[36] s.434(3).

[37] s.434(5). Whether or not he was on oath: *London Securities Ltd v. Nicholson* [1980] 1 W.L.R. 948 (not following *Karak Rubber Co. v. Burden* [1971] 1 W.L.R. 1748). See also *R. v. Seelig, R. v. Spens* (at p. 699, below). The evidence is equally admissible in civil proceedings: see *London Securities v. Nicholson* [1980] 1 W.L.R. 948 where evidence given by the company's auditors to Inspectors was held admissible against the auditors in subsequent proceedings against them by the company for their alleged negligence.

[38] s.436(1) (as substituted by the 1989 Act, s.56).

[39] s.436(2). See on this the discussion of the comparable provision on an investigation of insider dealing under the FSA, ss.177 and 178: above Chap. 17 at pp. 475–476.

[40] s.437(1).

[41] s.437(1A) inserted by the FSA.

[42] In which event a copy of the report will be sent to the court: s.437(2).

[43] s.437(1B) and (1C) inserted by the 1989 Act, s.57.

conduct is referred to in the report, to the auditors, to the applicants for the investigation[44] and to any other person whose financial interests appear to be affected by matters dealt with in the report.[45] And he may (and generally will, though not until after any criminal proceedings have been concluded[46]) cause the report to be printed and published.[47]

In addition to the foregoing statutory provisions, a number of other matters have been established by practice and case law. Although the inspectors may be expected to be somewhat more independent and impartial than the Secretary of State or his minions exercising powers under section 447 in the belief that there is good reason for doing so, they too are not regarded as exercising a judicial role but an administrative one. Nevertheless, though the full rules of "natural justice" do not apply, they must act fairly. This involves letting witnesses know of criticisms made against them (assuming that the inspectors envisage relying on, or referring to, those criticisms in their report) and giving them adequate opportunity of answering. But the inspectors are not bound to show them a draft of the parts of their report referring to them, so long as they have had a fair opportunity of answering any criticisms of their conduct. Inspectors are free to draw conclusions from the evidence about the conduct of individuals, but should do so only with restraint.[48-49]

Inspectors sit in private but allow witnesses to be accompanied by their lawyers—although the latter's role is limited since the questioning is undertaken by the inspectors and neither the witness nor his lawyers can cross-examine other witnesses. Although the range of persons whom the inspectors may question is very wide,[50] the Act provides that such persons cannot be compelled to disclose or produce any information or document which they would be entitled to refuse on grounds of legal professional privilege except that lawyers must disclose the names and addresses of their clients.[51] A banker's duty of confidentiality is protected more narrowly. Under section 452(1A) and (1B),[52] nothing in sections 434, 443, or 446 requires any person to

---

[44] This is not relevant to inspections under s.432(2) when the S. of S. appoints of his own motion.

[45] s.437(3).

[46] For an unsuccessful attempt to force the S. of S. to publish while criminal proceedings were still being considered: see *R. v. Secretary of State, ex p. Lonrho* [1989] 1 W.L.R. 525, H.L.

[47] s.437(3)(c). Thus making the reports available for purchase from H.M.S.O. by any member of the public so long as the reports remain in print. They often make fascinating reading for anyone interested in "the unacceptable face of capitalism".

[48-49] *Re Pergamon Press Ltd* [1971] Ch. 388, C.A.; *Maxwell v. DTI* [1974] Q.B. 523, C.A. See generally, DTI, *Investigation Handbook*.

[50] Especially in investigations under s.442 (see s.443(2)), s.444 and under s.177 of the FSA.

[51] s.452. This applies to DTI investigations as well as to inspections and there are comparable provisions in the FSA and other legislation providing for investigations or inspections.

[52] Inserted by the 1989 Act. Under s.69 under the widened exceptions the bank may find itself compelled to disclose information relating to the accounts of customers who are not themselves under investigation. Again there are comparable provisions in the other legislation.

disclose anything in respect of which he owes an obligation of confidence by virtue of carrying on the business of banking, unless (a) the person to whom the duty is owed consents, or (b) the duty is owed to the company or other body under investigation, or (c) the making of the requirement is authorised by the Secretary of State, or (d) it is the bank itself that is under investigation.

The main criticisms levelled against the conduct of investigations concern the inquisitorial nature of the process and, in particular, the relationship between the proceedings before the inspectors and possible subsequent criminal proceedings against those subject to interrogation under the Companies Act. Although the criminal law has now moved away from the observance of a general right to silence in criminal trials, in the sense that a suspect or accused who remains silent may have adverse inferences drawn from his silence,[53] in relation to company investigations the law goes, and always has gone, very much further in putting pressure on those summoned before the inspectors to give evidence which may incriminate them. Attempts by those affected by these rules to persuade the domestic courts to ameliorate the statutory provisions have largely failed, and the focus of litigation has moved to the European Court of Human Rights.

As a result of the domestic litigation,[54] the position appears to be as follows. A person interrogated by the inspectors must answer their questions, on pain of being held in contempt of court, even if the effect of those answers is to incriminate him or her; in carrying out an investigation an inspector is not an investigating officer and so is not bound by the codes made under the Police and Criminal Evidence Act 1984, for example, as to the administration of cautions[55]; the answers given to the inspectors may be given in evidence in subsequent criminal proceedings against those interrogated, subject to the discretion of the judge at the criminal trial to exclude such evidence on grounds of unfairness under section 78 of the 1984 Act; and, finally, that the criminal trial judge should not use his discretion under section 78 so as to restore a right to silence which Parliament intended to remove, so that exclusion of the answers will happen only occasionally.[56]

The most critical proposition is the third one stated above, namely the use of the compelled answers as evidence in subsequent criminal proceedings. Even if this were not permitted, however, there would

---

[53] Criminal Justice and Public Order Act 1994.

[54] *Re London United Investment plc* [1992] Ch. 576, C.A.; *R. v. Seelig* [1992] 1 W.L.R. 148, C.A.; *R. v. Saunders* [1996] 1 Cr.App.R. 463, C.A., interpreting ss.434 and 436.

[55] The conclusion might be different if the inspectors were appointed under s.177 of the Financial Services Act to carry out investigations as to whether breaches of the insider dealing laws had occurred. See pp. 474 *et seq.*, above.

[56] In the *Guinness* trial, for example, the judge excluded only the transcripts of the interviews which took place after the accused were charged with the offences for which they were later tried.

still be an issue of principle to be considered, because the compelled answers might lead the prosecuting authorities, via the inspectors, to other, already existing, evidence which they may wish to use in the criminal proceedings. The issue of principle would be whether the law should prohibit "derivative" as well as direct use of evidence emerging from the compelled testimony before the inspectors. On the approach taken by the domestic courts, of course, the secondary issue of principle did not arise because the courts were prepared to permit even direct use of the compelled evidence at the criminal trial.

The pattern of rules established in relation to company investigations can be said to reflect the legal rules to be found more generally in the area of financial and corporate fraud.[57] Thus, under section 236 of the Insolvency Act 1986 those being judicially examined in relation to the affairs of an insolvent company must answer even incriminatory questions put to them and those answers are admissible in subsequent criminal proceedings.[58] A rather different pattern is found in relation to the Director of the Serious Fraud Office, perhaps because the investigations here are necessarily with a view to prosecution. Here the Director's questions must be answered, but the answers may not be given in evidence in subsequent criminal proceedings.[59] Thus, only derivative use may be made of answers given to the Director.[60]

However, whether one is considering the full or the qualified freedom of the prosecution to make use of compelled testimony, the question arises why it is necessary in these cases to depart from the normal rules applicable in criminal trials. The answer cannot be put on the basis that the crimes arising in these contexts are necessarily more serious than those, such as rape and murder, arising outside them. The argument must be one based on the difficulties of obtaining evidence about the commission of financial wrongdoing, especially where the wrongdoing has an international element. However, in an application concerning the rulings of the judge in the *Guinness* case,[61] the European Commission on Human Rights refused to accept that "varying degrees of fairness apply

---

[57] See generally Smith, "The Right to Silence in Cases of Serious Fraud" in Birks (ed.), *Pressing Problems in the Law*, Vol. I (Oxford, 1995), p. 75.

[58] *Bishopsgate Investment Management v. Maxwell* [1993] Ch. 1, C.A.; *Re Arrows (No. 4)* [1995] 2 A.C. 75 at 92–93, though these rules may not apply to the informal procedure under s.235 where time is of the essence and those investigated must therefore be given an incentive to co-operate with the liquidator, receiver or administrator (*ibid.*, pp. 101–102). But the full rules apply elsewhere in the financial field by virtue of the FSA 1986, ss.94 (unit trusts) and 105 (persons carrying on investment business); ss.41–44 of the Banking Act 1987—see *Riley v. Bank of England* [1992] Ch. 475, C.A.; and s.44 of the Insurance Companies Act 1982.

[59] Criminal Justice Act 1987, s.2(2) and (8) and *R. v. Director of the Serious Fraud Office ex parte Smith* [1993] A.C. 1, H.L.

[60] It is anomalous that the restriction on direct use does not apply to documents supplied compulsorily to the Director, even if the document consists of a record of answers given compulsorily to questions from another official (*e.g.* a liquidator) which questions, if asked by the Director himself, could not be the subject of direct use: *Re Arrows (No. 4)* [1995] 2 A.C. 75, H.L.; *cf. Soden v. Burns* [1996] 2 BCLC 636.

[61] See n. 56, above.

to different categories of accused in criminal trials".[62] Since the Commission thought that the privilege against self-incrimination was an essential element in the guarantee of a fair trial under article 6 of the Convention, it found the United Kingdom to be in violation. The European Court of Human Rights took the same view.

The issue has also been fully considered by the Constitutional Court of South Africa in the context of South African provisions analogous to the British ones relating to examinations in insolvency.[63] The decision is interesting for the views expressed on the use of derived evidence, an issue not considered by the European Court. Whilst holding that the constitutional guarantee of freedom and security of the person required a prohibition on the direct use of compelled testimony, the Court thought that the correct balance between the public interest in the investigation of the affairs of insolvent companies and protection of the constitutional right could be achieved by giving the trial judge a discretion to exclude existing evidence to which the prosecution was led by the compelled testimony. Even so, evidence which could not have been obtained or the significance of which would not have been appreciated without the compelled testimony should normally be excluded.[64]

Inspections have been criticised also for taking too long. Attempts have been made to meet this criticism, for example by requiring inspectors to report within 12 months which, however, they are unlikely to succeed in doing if one of them is a busy o.c. who is not prepared to devote himself full-time to the task.[65] A major improvement here has been the increased use of investigations by the Department's officials (rather than full-fledged inspections) but even these may sometimes take many months.

Despite the foregoing, and other legitimate criticisms of investigations and inspectors, they seem to be the most effective method yet devised to detect corporate misconduct and to bring to book the perpetrators of it.[66]

---

[62] *Ernest Saunders v. United Kingdom* (1994) 18 E.H.R.R. CD 23. The Commission's adjudication was upheld by the European Court of Human Rights, so changes to the British law or practice will now be necessary. See *Saunders v. United Kingdom, The Times Human Rights Law Report*, December 18, 1996. The impact of the judgment is likely to be felt particularly in relation to prosecutions for insider trading on the basis of inspectors' reports: see pp. 474–477, above.

[63] *Ferreira v. Levin* 1996 (1) SA 984.

[64] At 1065–1072, following the Supreme Court of Canada in *Thomson Newspapers Ltd v. Director of Investigation and Research* (1990) 67 D.L.R. (4th) 161 and *RJS v. The Queen* (1995) 121 D.L.R. (4th) 589. Thus, the prosecution may use independent evidence to which the compelled testimony leads them, provided that the compelled testimony was not the only way of discovering it or appreciating its significance.

[65] Greater use of solicitors, who can more easily delegate other tasks to their partners and staff, might help.

[66] For a recent review of them, see the Third Report of the House of Commons' Trade and Industry Committee, *Company Investigations*, session 1989–90, H.C. 36, to which the government replied in DTI, *Company Investigations* Cm. 1149 (1990).

3. Liability for costs of investigations

Under section 439, the expenses of any investigation under Part XIV of the Act[67] are to be defrayed in the first instance by the DTI,[68] but may be recoverable from persons specified in that section, there being treated as expenses such reasonable sums as the Secretary of State may determine in respect of general staff costs and overheads.[69] The persons from whom costs are recoverable include: anyone successfully prosecuted as a result of the investigation[70]; any body corporate in whose name proceedings are brought under section 438[71] to the extent of the amount or value recovered[72]; any body corporate dealt with in an inspectors' report when the inspectors were not appointed on the Secretary of State's own motion[73] unless the body corporate was the applicant or except so far as the Secretary of State otherwise directs.[74] Where inspectors were appointed under section 431 or 442(3) the applicants are liable to the extent, if any, that the Secretary of State directs.[75]

4. Follow-up to investigations

Following an investigation, the Secretary of State has a number of powers. Apart from the obvious one of causing prosecutions to be mounted against those whose crimes have come to light, which prosecutions may be mounted by the Investigation and Enforcement Directorate itself or by others, such as the Serious Fraud Office, the Secretary of State may petition under section 8 of the Disqualification Act for the disqualification of a director or shadow director on grounds of unfitness.[76] He may also petition under section 460 for an order under section 461 if unfair prejudice to all or some of the company's members has been revealed.[77] Alternatively or in addition, he may petition

---

[67] Which is the case of inspections are likely to be heavy; the Atlantic computers investigation cost £6.5m. and the consolidated goldfields one nearly £4m.: *Companies in 1994–95*, Table 8, and the total costs to the companies and their officers were probably as great or greater.

[68] This is subject to the power to require security for costs on an appointment of inspectors under the rarely used s.431 above.

[69] s.439(1) as substituted by s.59 of the 1989 Act.

[70] s.439(2).

[71] On which see (4) below.

[72] s.439(3).And a person ordered to pay costs in a civil action brought under s.438 may also be ordered to pay or contribute to the payment of the costs of the investigation which led to the action: s.439(2).

[73] But under s.431 (above) or s.442(3) (see p. 494, above).

[74] s.439(4).

[75] s.439(5) as substituted by s.59 of the 1989 Act. Inspectors appointed otherwise than on the S. of S.'s own motion may, and shall if so directed, include in their report a recommendation about costs: s.439(6). Note also the provisions regarding rights to indemnity or contribution (s.439(8) and (9)) and that the costs may include costs in respect of proceedings under s.438.

[76] See above, p. 682.

[77] See Chap. 27 at p. 736, below.

for the winding-up of the company under what is now section 124A[78] of the Insolvency Act 1986. Under that section if it appears to him as a result of any report or information obtained under Part XIV of the Companies Act[79] that it is expedient in the public interest that a company should be wound up, he may present a petition for it to be wound up if the court thinks it just and equitable. Some 13 companies were wound up on the Secretary of State's petition in 1995–1996.[80]

Furthermore, if, from any report made or information obtained under Part XIV, it appears to the Secretary of State that any civil proceedings ought, in the public interest, to be brought by any body corporate, he may, under section 438, himself bring such proceedings in the name and on behalf of the body corporate,[81] indemnifying it against any costs or expenses incurred by it in connection with the proceedings.

As a result of these follow-up powers, the company, its members and its creditors may find that their causes of complaint are ended, or rectified so far as possible, without any further action on their part. But, if not, they should obtain, from the inspectors' report, information of assistance to them should they choose to launch proceedings. Under section 441[82] a copy of any report of inspectors appointed under Part XIV, certified by the Secretary of State to be a true copy, is admissible in any legal proceedings "as evidence of the opinion of the inspectors in relation to any matter contained in the report and, in proceedings on an application under section 8 of the Company Directors Disqualification Act 1986,[83] as evidence of any fact stated therein".[84] The importance of this, however, seems slight; the real value of an inspectors' report to a potential litigant is that it will enable him to identify the sources of the evidence on which the inspectors reached their conclusions, which may enable him to obtain from those sources the evidence he needs.

---

[78] Inserted by the 1989 Act, s.60(3).

[79] Or under s.94, 105, or 177 of the FSA (or after fraud investigations under s.2 of the Criminal Justice Act 1987 or the Criminal Justice (Scotland) Act 1987 or as a result of information gleaned under s.83 of the 1989 Act in assisting an overseas regulatory agency).

[80] *Companies in 1995–96*, p. 14.

[81] This he can do without first having to petition under s.460, above, and obtaining a court order under s.461(2)(c).

[82] As amended by the Insolvency Acts 1985 and 1986 and the 1989 Act.

[83] See Chap. 24 at p. 682.

[84] Ascertaining the precise meaning of earlier versiosn of this section caused the courts some difficulty:see *Re Travel and Holiday Clubs Ltd* [1967] 1 W.L.R. 711; *Re SBA Properties Ltd* [1967] 1 W.L.R. 789; *Re St Piran Ltd* [1981] 1 W.L.R. 1300; and *Savings & Investment Bank v. Gasco* [1984] 1 W.L.R. 271 Nor is the present version much clearer except that it appears to rule out any reliance on the report as evidence of facts except in relation to s.8 of the Company Directors Disqualification Act. The same status has now been extended to information provided to inspectors appointed under s.447 to examine the company's documents, where the Secretary of State subsequently applies for a disqualification order: *Re Rex Williams Leisure plc* [1994] Ch. 350, C.A. Such information is normally confidential but can be disclosed for the purposes set out in s.449.

CONCLUSIONS

The conclusions to be drawn from this Chapter and Chapter 23 are, it is thought:

(1) If a member has a clear case for saying that a company has breached a duty owed to him personally, so that he has a personal right of action falling completely outside the rule in *Foss v. Harbottle*, it may be sensible for him to sue the company in a personal action. Otherwise he should not resort to the courts until he has drawn the matter to the attention of the DTI with a request that the Secretary of State exercise his investigatory powers;

(2) If that request does not elicit a favourable response[85] he should in no circumstances bring a *derivative* action.[86] If he brings any action it should be by way of a petition under section 459 coupled, if that is a remedy acceptable to him, with a petition for winding-up on the just and equitable ground. See Chapter 27, below. A threat to petition may often lead to remedial action being voluntarily taken by the company or to a settlement out of court;

(3) If the company is listed, a member will be well advised to cut his losses by selling his shares—assuming that he can do so without committing the offence of insider dealing—rather than to litigate. But, if the company is a private one, a sale may not be a practical alternative.

---

[85] As it may not; more applications are refused than are granted and there will be reluctance to intervene if the company concerned is a small private company of little public interest.

[86] The alleged advantage of being able to obtain a *Wallersteiner v. Moir* costs order (which has diminished in the light of *Smith v. Croft (Nos. (1) and (2)*, see Chap. 23, above) does not outweigh its disadvantages.

CHAPTER 26

CONTROLLING MEMBERS' VOTING

INTRODUCTION

ALTHOUGH it is now formally possible to create "one-person" companies,[1] it is a characteristic of most companies that they act as vehicles for bringing together and putting to use the capital contributions of a number, sometimes an enormous number, of individuals and institutions, who become the shareholders of the company. As we have seen,[2] it is common in all but the smallest companies to confer a wide power of management of the company upon the board of directors, but the company law does not permit the complete delegation to the board of all decisions affecting the company, and drafters of articles of association may choose in any event not to make full use of the possibilities of delegation which the law permits.

It follows, therefore, that some important decisions affecting the company will have to be taken by the shareholders meeting together, and the question naturally arises as to the principle upon which decisions of the shareholders shall be binding. As we have seen in an earlier Chapter,[3] the principle adopted in British company law, as in the company laws of most countries, is the principle of majority rule: sometimes rule by a simple majority; in the case of important decisions more often rule by a majority of three-quarters of the shareholders present and voting. To require as the general rule that there be unanimity among the shareholders would make decision-making impossibly difficult in large companies, though it may be feasible in the case of small companies or joint ventures, as we shall see in our discussion of self-help later in this Chapter.

Although some degree, perhaps a large degree, of protection is conferred upon dissentients by the requirement of a "super-majority" for certain types of decision, there will always be the potential for a minority to be outvoted if anything less than unanimity in decision-making is permitted. The question to be explored in this Chapter and the next, accordingly, is what legal steps a minority can take to protect itself from majority decisions of which it disapproves. The primary emphasis is on *ex post* protection in the shape of a legal challenge to

---

[1] See above, pp. 149–150. Of course, it has long been possible to do so through the use of nominee shareholders.
[2] Above, pp. 183–187.
[3] Chap. 21, above, pp. 585–587.

the decision on the part of a minority which has actually been out-voted. As important in practice, however, are *ex ante* protections, for example, requirements for a separate meeting of, and assent by, the group of shareholders whose rights or interests are particularly at stake in the decision or for a particular decision to be taken on the basis of unanimity or only with the assent of a particular shareholder. As we shall see, some such *ex ante* devices are to be found in the Companies Act and others the shareholders themselves may try to create by way of self-help.

In practice, the factual situations to be discussed in this Chapter may well overlap with those discussed in the immediately preceding Chapters. The majority of the shareholders may dominate the board and seek to ignore the minority's interests not only as shareholders but also as directors. However, as we shall see, at common law signi-ficantly different legal principles apply to decisions taken by directors and those taken by shareholders, and so it seems sensible to begin by dealing with the two aspects of the situation separately. Moreover, in some cases, as in many large public companies, the directors have no significant shareholdings,[4] so that their domination of the company depends entirely on their position as directors. In that situation, the rules relating to directors, as discussed in the immediately preceding Chapters, would appear to be the only relevant ones. However, as we shall see when in the next Chapter we examine the scope of the statut-ory remedy against unfairly prejudicial conduct on the part of the controllers of companies, this remedy deals with all aspects of control-lers' conduct, whether as shareholders or as directors. In the next Chapter, therefore, the concerns of both the preceding Chapters (on directors' duties) and of this Chapter (on controls on shareholder decision-making) will come together.

Underlying the detailed rules discussed below is the question of the nature of the shareholder's interest in the company, a matter upon which we have touched earlier in the book.[5] Some courts have viewed that relationship as proprietary, others as contractual. Even when there is agreement as to the nature of that interest, there may disagreement about the consequences of the characterisation. For example, as we shall see, from the characterisation of the interest as proprietary some courts draw the conclusion that the majority should be free to exercise their voting rights as they wish; others that there are limits on the extent to which the minority's rights may be altered. Even if the char-acterisation chosen is the contractual one, implying a lower degree of legal protection, there may be disagreement about the nature of the

---

[4] Significant, that is, in terms of control of the general meeting, rather than significant in terms of their own remuneration.
[5] Above, pp. 299–302.

contractual right. As we have seen,[6] the contract created by the articles under section 14 is in many ways an unusual one, being in principle capable of alteration by majority vote of the shareholders. Is there a core of the shareholders' contractual rights which is not open to alteration or are all aspects of the contract defeasible by vote of the majority? Can the shareholders contract out of their right to alter the articles?

THE STARTING POINT

Scattered throughout the reports are statements that members must exercise their votes "bona fide for the benefit of the company as a whole",[7] a statement which suggests that they are subject to precisely the same basic principle as directors. But, it seems, this is highly misleading, and the decisions do not support any such rule as a universal principle. On the contrary, it has been repeatedly laid down that votes are proprietary rights, to the same extent as any other incidents of the shares, which the holder may exercise in his own selfish interests even if these are opposed to those of the company.[8] He or she may even bind him- or herself by contract to vote or not to vote in a particular way and his contract may be enforced by injunction.[9]

In all these respects the position of the shareholder is in striking contrast with that of the director. If it were the case that the general meeting could only operate in a few residual matters reserved to it by the company's constitution[10] this would not be unduly serious. But, as we have seen,[11] the general meeting is regarded as having power to act in place of the board if for any reason the board cannot function. If, therefore, a proper quorum cannot be obtained at a directors' meeting or there is a deadlock on the board, the general meeting may act instead.[12] Furthermore, what would otherwise be a breach of the directors' duties may, as we have seen,[13] in some circumstances be authorised or ratified by the company in general meeting. This may be so although the transaction relates to the ordinary management of the company and is therefore primarily a matter for the board of dir-

---

[6] Above, pp. 116–122.

[7] The original source of this oft-repeated but misleading expression seems to be Lindley M.R. in *Allen v. Gold Reefs of W. Africa* [1900] 1 Ch. at 671.

[8] *North-West Transportation Co. v. Beatty* (1887) 12 App.Cas. 589, P.C.; *Burland v. Earle* [1902] A.C. 83, P.C.; *Goodfellow v. Nelson Line* [1912] 2 Ch. 324.

[9] *Greenwell v. Porter* [1902] 1 Ch. 530; *Puddephatt v. Leith* [1916] 1 Ch. 200—in which a mandatory injunction was granted.

[10] See Chap. 9, above.

[11] *ibid.*

[12] *Barron v. Potter* [1914] 1 Ch. 895; *Foster v. Foster* [1916] 1 Ch. 532; *Alexander Ward & Co. Ltd v. Samyang Navigation Co. Ltd* [1975] 1 W.L.R. 673, H.L. But see *Breckland Holdings Ltd v. London & Suffolk Properties Ltd* [1989] BCLC 100.

[13] See above, Chap. 22.

ectors.[14] As a result, the activities of general meetings may indirectly extend over the whole sphere of the company's operations, and ultimate control revert to shareholders who are free from duties of good faith to which the directors are subject.

What is more startling still is that the directors themselves, even though personally interested, can vote in their capacity of shareholders at that general meeting.[15] And this is so even as regards the transactions which, under Part X of the Act,[16] require the prior approval of the company in general meeting.[17] As a consequence, when the directors have *de facto* control they can, subject to what follows, disregard their fiduciary duties at their pleasure, provided that they are prepared openly to disclose what they propose to do, and force through a confirming resolution by the exercise of their own votes supplemented, if need be, by their control of the proxy voting machinery. It is true that if the transaction to be ratified is one which has increased their voting power the court may order that the increased votes shall not be exercised but it will not, apparently, prevent them from exercising their original votes.[18]

Clearly, therefore, some restraint must be put on the power of those able to command a majority vote. And in fact it is clear that, in some circumstances, the courts will intervene to annul[19] the resulting resolution.

RATIFICATION OF BREACHES OF DUTY

We have considered this issue in an earlier Chapter[20] and do not need to repeat that analysis here. Suffice it to say that the conclusions there arrived at were that breaches of duty by directors were in principle ratifiable by an ordinary majority of the shareholders, but that ratification was not possible if the breach of duty involved the expropriation

---

[14] *Irvine v. Union Bank of Australia* (1877) 2 App.Cas. 366, P.C.; *Grant v. UK Switchback Ry.* (1888) 40 Ch.D. 135, C.A.; *Hogg v. Cramphorn Ltd* [1967] Ch. 254; *Bamford v. Bamford* [1970] Ch. 212, C.A.

[15] *N.W. Transportation Co. v. Beatty* above; *Burland v. Earle* [1902] A.C. 83 at 93, P.C.; *Harris v. A. Harris Ltd*, 1936 S.C. 183 (Sc.); *Baird v. Baird & Co.*, 1949 S.L.T. 368 (Sc.). And see the remarkable case of *Northern Counties Securities Ltd v. Jackson & Steeple Ltd* [1974] 1 W.L.R. 1133 where it was held that although, to comply with an undertaking given by the company to the court, the directors were bound to recommend the shareholders to vote for a resolution they, as shareholders, could vote against it, if so minded.

[16] See Chap. 22 at pp. 623–640, above.

[17] For the rare statutory exceptions, see ss.164(5) and 174(2) under which a shareholder whose shares are to be purchased by the company must refrain from voting on the resolutions approving such a purchase: Chap. 11 at pp. 255 and 260, above.

[18] *Hogg v. Cramphorn Ltd*, above; *Bamford v. Bamford*, above. See also Beck (1975) 53 Can. Bar Rev. 771 at 785–787.

[19] It seems clear that a resolution only impeachable as a fraud on the minority is merely voidable and will be valid until successfully attacked: *cf. Borland's Trustee v. Steel Bros.* [1901] 1 Ch. 279 and the observations thereon in *Brown v. British Abrasive Wheel Co.* [1919] 1 Ch. 290.

[20] Above, pp. 644–648.

of corporate property or acting by the directors with actual dishonesty. Ratification in such a case would amount to a fraud on the minority. In these cases, the interests of the minority are protected by depriving the majority of the power to take the decision.[21]

ALTERATION OF THE ARTICLES

This has been an important area of conflict between the interests of the majority and of the minority. Section 9 of the Companies Act 1985 declares that, subject to certain conditions, the articles of a company are alterable by special resolution.[22] The section itself thus contains a procedural protection for the minority in the shape of a "super-majority" requirement for the passage of a resolution for the alteration of the articles. Further, a substantive limit is placed on the powers of the majority by section 16, which provides that a member is not bound by an alteration (whether of the memorandum or articles) after the date upon which he or she became a member if its effect is to require the member to take more shares in the company than the number held on the date of the alteration or in any other way increases the member's liability to contribute to the company's share capital or otherwise pay money to the company. However, since the substantive limitation addresses only a narrow category of alterations and the procedural hurdle may be overcome by a majority holding three-quarters of the shares present and voting at the meeting, it is perhaps not surprising that proposed alterations to the articles have been a steady source of litigation over the years, especially, but not exclusively, where the majority propose to expropriate the shares held by the minority.

In contrast to the law on the ratification of directors' duties, where minority protection has taken the form of removing the decision from the hands of the majority, in this area the question is how far the majority, in taking the decision, are subject to some version of the duty to act bona fide for the benefit of the company as a whole.[23] In other words, even when what is at issue is expropriation, this form of control does not absolutely prohibit alteration of the articles, but subjects the majority's reasons to judicial review. We shall examine, first, the expropriation cases and, secondly, other examples of alterations adverse to the interests of the minority.

Resolutions to expropriate members' shares

It is in fact unclear how far the majority must here consider the interests of the company. The relevant authorities start with *Brown v.*

---

[21] It is a little unclear whether in these cases the shareholders cannot act at all or whether, as is submitted ought to be the case, unanimity is required.

[22] Above, pp. 116–117.

[23] See n. 7, above.

British Abrasive Wheel Co.,[24] a decision at first instance in which a public company was in urgent need of future capital which shareholders, holding 98 per cent of the shares, were willing to put up but only if they could buy out the 2 per cent minority. Having failed to persuade the minority to sell, they proposed a special resolution adding to the articles a provision to the effect that any shareholder was bound to transfer his shares upon a request in writing of the holders of 90 per cent of the shares. Although such a provision could have been validly inserted in the original articles,[25] and although the good faith of the majority was not challenged, it was held that the addition of such a provision in order to enable the majority to expropriate the minority could not be for the benefit of the company as a whole but was solely for the benefit of the majority. Hence an injunction was granted restraining the company from passing the resolution.

This decision, however, was almost immediately "distinguished" by the Court of Appeal in *Sidebottom v. Kershaw, Leese & Co. Ltd.*[26] There, a director-controlled private company had a minority shareholder who had an interest in a competing business. Objecting to this, the company passed a special resolution adding to the articles a provision empowering the directors to require any shareholder who competed with the company to sell his shares at a fair value to nominees of the directors. This was upheld on the basis that it was obviously beneficial to the company. In contrast, shortly thereafter in *Dafen Tinplate Co. v. Llanelly Steel Co.*,[27] it was held at first instance that a resolution inserting a new article empowering the majority to buy out any shareholder as they thought proper, was invalid as being self-evidently wider than could be necessary in the interests of the company.

So far, all the decisions had implied that a resolution adding to the articles a provision enabling the shares of a member to be expropriated would be upheld only if it was passed bona fide in the interests of the company and that this was to be judged not just by the members but also by the court. However, in *Shuttleworth v. Cox Bros. Ltd*,[28] a case concerning not expropriation of shares but the removal of an unpopular life director, the Court of Appeal, in upholding the validity of a resolution inserting in the articles a provision that any director should vacate office if called upon to do so by the board, held that it was for the members, and not the court, to determine whether the resolution is for the benefit of the company and that the court will intervene only

---

[24] [1919] 1 Ch. 290.
[25] *Phillips v. Manufacturers Securities Ltd* (1917) 116 L.T. 209; in *Borland's Trustees v. Steel Bros.* [1901] 1 Ch. 279 an even wider article was inserted with the agreement of all the members.
[26] [1920] 1 Ch. 154, C.A.
[27] [1920] 2 Ch. 124.
[28] [1927] 2 K.B. 9, C.A.

if satisfied that the members have acted in bad faith.[29] If the same applies to expropriation of shares, it is difficult to understand why what is now section 429 of the Act[30] was needed. That section[31] enables a takeover bidder who has acquired 90 per cent or more of the target company's shares to acquire compulsorily the remainder. There would have been no need for that section if a bidder, having acquired a controlling interest, could then cause the target company to insert in its articles a similar power. But, as we shall see[32] "the beliefs or assumptions of those who frame Acts of Parliament" are an unsafe guide to what the law actually is. More significant, perhaps, are the decision and observations of the Court of Appeal in *Re Bugle Press*.[33] There the holders of 90 per cent of the shares, who wished to buy out the remaining 10 per cent but who must have been advised not to attempt to proceed by the simple expedient of inserting an enabling power in the articles, formed another company and then made a bid for the shares of the company. This offer was accepted, not surprisingly, by the majority and, when the minority rejected it, the bidder purported to exercise the power under section 209 of the 1948 Act (corresponding to section 429 of the present Act).[34] The court refused to countenance this, declaring that to allow existing shareholders to use the section as a device to get rid of a minority whom they did not happen to like would be contrary to "fundamental principles of company law".[35]

The issue was recently reviewed by the High Court of Australia in *Gambotto v. WCP Ltd*,[36] where it was proposed to alter the articles to allow a 90 per cent shareholder to acquire the shares of minority shareholders at a certain price. Following its famous inter-war decision, *Peter's American Delicacy Co. Ltd v. Heath*,[37] the Court refused, rightly it is submitted, to regard the "bona fide in the interests of the company" test as a useful one in the context of a conflict between two groups of shareholders as to how their respective rights and liabilities should be adjusted. However, the Court was equally unwilling to leave the issue to (super-) majority rule, coupled with a

---

[29] The court conceded that if the resolution was such that no reasonable man could consider it for the benefit of the company as a whole that might be a ground for finding bad faith. *ibid.* at pp. 18, 19, 23, 26 & 27. Another, it is submitted, would be if the majority was trying to acquire the shares of the minority at an obvious undervalue.

[30] Formerly s.209 of the 1948 Act.

[31] Dealt with in Chap. 29 at pp. 807–809, below.

[32] In relation to the discussion of *Cumbrian Newspapers Group v. Cumberland and Westmorland Herald* [1987] Ch 1; see below, pp. 718–720.

[33] [1961] Ch. 270, C.A.

[34] On s.429, see p. 807, below.

[35] *ibid.*, *per* Evershed M.R. at 287 and Harman L.J. at 287, 288. But it is not easy to detect any such "fundamental principle" in Evershed's judgment in *Greenhalgh v. Arderne Cinemas* [1951] Ch. 286; see below.

[36] (1995) 127 A.L.R. 417.

[37] (1939) 61 C.L.R. 457.

requirement of good faith on the part of the majority. There was still an objective test which had to be applied, even if the price was fair, which the majority found in the notion of proper purposes.[38] This meant that expropriation of shares could be used to save the company from "significant detriment or harm" (as in *Sidebottom v. Kershaw, Leese and Co. Ltd*) but not to "advance the interest of the company as a legal and commercial entity or those of the majority, albeit the great majority, of the incorporators" (as in this case where acquisition of the minority shares would have conferred very considerable tax advantages on the majority shareholder). "English authority", presumably *Shuttleworth v. Cox Bros. Ltd*, was disapproved on the grounds that "it does not attach sufficient weight to the proprietary nature of a share".[39] An alternative view of the share as an investment in the shape of a series of financial entitlements, notably to future dividends, would be more favourable to the notion of compulsory acquisition at a fair price by a good faith majority. This approach is perhaps reflected in the view of the minority judge who was unimpressed by the distinction between harm and benefit, drawn by the majority, but agreed in the result, on the basis that the proponents of the change had not demonstrated the price to be a fair one.

Other resolutions

Although it is difficult to draw a hard and fast line between resolutions to expropriate shares and resolutions which alter the shareholders' rights adversely, the courts have from time to time suggested that the controls on shareholder voting in the latter case are less strict. To what extend do the decisions suggest that there is a general obligation upon shareholders when voting on resolutions to alter the articles (or, indeed, upon other classes of resolution) to vote bona fide in the interests of the company?

An attempt to answer these questions was made by the Court of Appeal in *Greenhalgh v. Arderne Cinemas Ltd*.[40] This case marked the conclusion of a 10-year battle between the plaintiff, Greenhalgh, and one Mallard and his associates who had enlisted the aid of Greenhalgh when the company needed financial support. As a result Greenhalgh then became the controlling shareholder and a director. However, after a few years, thanks to an adroit series of manoeuvres orchestrated by Mallard (which had already led to no less than six

---

[38] See also above, p. 664, for another example of the attachment of the Australian courts to the idea of proper purposes in the context of shareholder action.

[39] At 425–426.

[40] [1951] Ch. 286, C.A. and [1950] 2 All E.R. 1120 where the judgment of Evershed M.R. is reported more fully.

actions, three of which had been taken to the Court of Appeal)[41] Greenhalgh had been ousted from his control and his seat on the board. But he was still a shareholder and, as such, had pre-emptive rights under the articles if any other shareholder wanted to sell to a non-member. This the Mallard faction now wished to do because Mallard had negotiated a deal with another entrepreneur to take over the company. To enable the deal to go through, they had to circumvent Greenhalgh's pre-emptive rights and this they sought to do by amending the articles by a special resolution which provided that, despite the pre-emptive rights, "any member may, with the sanction of an ordinary resolution . . . transfer his shares . . . to any person named in such resolution as the proposed transferee and the directors shall be bound to register any transfer which has been so sanctioned". Having secured the passage of this special resolution, they then passed an ordinary resolution sanctioning transfers to the purchaser. Thereupon Greenhalgh instituted this, his seventh, action, claiming a declaration that the resolutions were invalid as a fraud on the majority and had not been passed bona fide in the interests of the company as a whole. This, too, went to the Court of Appeal.

In his judgment,[42] Evershed M.R., though critical of the conduct of Mallard, held first that the resolutions were not a fraud on the minority. He then went on to consider whether the resolutions were nevertheless invalid as not having been passed bona fide in the interests of the company, clearly assuming that, if not, they would be invalid on that ground. This, if correct, seems to put paid to the belief that bona fides has to be shown only if the transaction would otherwise have been a fraud on the minority. In a dictum which has been widely cited in judgments throughout the Commonwealth, he said[43]:

"In the first place, I think it is now plain that 'bona fide for the benefit of the company as a whole' means not two things, but one thing.[44] It means that the shareholder must proceed on what, in his honest opinion, is for the benefit of the company as a whole. The second thing is that the phrase, 'the company as a whole' does not (at any rate in such a case as the present) mean the company as a commercial entity, distinct from the corporators; it means the corporators as a general body. That is to say, the case may be taken of an individual hypothetical member and it may be asked whether

---

[41] The three are: *Greenhalgh v. Mallard* [1943] 2 All E.R. 234, C.A.; *Greenhalgh v. Arderne Cinemas Ltd* [1946] 1 All E.R. 512, C.A.; and *Greenhalgh v. Mallard* [1947] 2 All E.R. 255, C.A. A fuller account of the whole saga was recounted in earlier editions (4th edn at pp. 624–627) but is omitted here as largely of historical interest only; it is thought that today anyone treated as Greenhalgh was would be able to nip it in the bud by invoking s.459: see Chap. 27, below.

[42] With which Asquith and Jenkins L.JJ. concurred.

[43] [1951] Ch. at 291.

[44] *i.e* not "(i) bona fide" and (ii) "for the benefit of the company as a whole" but a single "bona fide for the company as a whole".

what is proposed is, in the honest opinion of those who voted in its favour, for that person's benefit.''

This formula seems to be the same as that applying to directors[45] except that the "hypothetical member" is a novel refinement. On the face of it, what this is saying is that, whenever members vote on a resolution, they must ask themselves whether the proposal is beneficial not only to themselves but to a hypothetical member who, presumably, has no personal interest apart from that of being a member and (if such be the case) a shareholder.[46] If their honest answer is that it would not be in the hypothetical member's interest they should vote against (if they vote at all) and, presumably, if their answer is that it would be for the hypothetical member's interest they should vote for it (if they vote at all), even though convinced that it would be against their own interests. If that is correct, the only safe course seems to be for every member to refrain from voting unless he is satisfied that he is the paradigm hypothetical member—for no one has yet suggested that a member is bound to exercise his votes.[47]

One can see that such a conclusion might conceivably be reasonable (a) in relation to a small family concern which was, in reality, an incorporated partnership and (b) in relation to directors voting as members at general meetings. But in other situations it seems utterly unrealistic. Even if the onus of proof that members had not asked themselves the suggested question was placed on those attacking the validity of the resolution, there would be little difficulty in the case of a resolution voted on at a meeting of a large public company in finding numerous Sids and Aunt Agathas honest enough to confess that it had never occurred to them to ask themselves anything of the sort. The impracticability of the formula suggested by Evershed M.R. seems to have worried him; for he went on to say:

"I think that the matter can, in practice, be more accurately and precisely stated by looking at the converse and by saying that a special resolution of this kind would be liable to be impeached if the effect of it were to discriminate between the majority shareholders and the minority shareholders, so as to give the former an advantage of which the latter were deprived.''

That, however, seems to go to the other extreme; for all it appears to do is to reiterate that members of the same class must generally be treated alike. That principle[48] seems to have no connection with the

---

[45] See Chap. 22, above.

[46] This interpretation was expressly adopted by McLelland J. in *Australian Fixed Trusts Pty Ltd v. Clyde Industries Ltd* [1959] S.R. (N.S.W.) 33 at 56.

[47] In this respect there would seem to be a difference between the position of a member and that of a director at a directors' meeting; the latter, if present at the meeting, could not, by abstaining, evade his duty to act in the interests of the company.

[48] But which Goulding J., in *Mutual Life v. Rank Organisation* [1985] BCLC 11, held did not mean that there could be no discrimination so long as directors acted fairly as between different shareholders.

concept of "bona fide in the interests of the company" unless what Evershed M.R. meant was that resolutions could be impeached if they were intended to enable the majority to deprive the minority (but not the majority) of an advantage. But clearly he did not mean that. In all the expropriation cases that is precisely what the majority had done. In some, it was held that the resolution could not be impeached since it was in the interests of the company as a whole, while in others the resolution was impeached because it was not in the company's interests. In none was there any overt distinction, in the resolution itself, discriminating against the minority.

In the instant case the court held that, whichever of the Evershed tests was applied, the resolutions were unimpeachable. Faced with that and the earlier decision of the Court of Appeal in *Shuttleworth v. Cox*, one might have supposed that the last nail had been driven into the coffin of bona fides in relation to members' resolutions. Not so. *Re Holders Investment Trust*[49] concerned a capital reduction scheme requiring the confirmation of the court. Confirmation was refused because the resolution of a class meeting of the preference shareholders had been passed as a result of votes of trustees who held a large block of the preference shares but a still larger block of ordinary shares. Had the refusal been on the ground that the court was not satisfied that the scheme was fair to both classes there would have been nothing remarkable about the decision; as we shall see later[50] the courts, which normally regard a majority vote of members as cogent evidence that the scheme is fair, are rightly hesitant to do so where the majority vote of one class has resulted from the votes of members who also belong to another class. But Megarry J. approached the matter on the basis that he first had to be satisfied that the resolution of the preference shareholders had been validly passed bona fide in the interest of that class. He held that it had not, because the trustees had taken advice as to how, as trustees, they should vote and had been advised that in the interest of their beneficiaries they should vote for the resolution. This they did, admittedly without any consideration of what was in the best interest of the preference shareholders as a whole.[51] This case is also interesting in that it confirms the view taken in an earlier case[52] that, in relation to class meetings, it is the interest

---

[49] [1971] 1 W.L.R. 583.

[50] Chap. 28.

[51] Contrast *Rights & Issues Investments Trust v. Stylo Shoes Ltd* [1965] Ch. 250 where there was an unsuccessful attack on the validity of a resolution which, on the issue of further shares to one class, increased the votes of another class to preserve the existing balance of control. That other class had refrained from voting and the court, adopting the terminology both of the then version of the present s.459 and of Evershed's alternative formula, held that there had been no "oppression" of, or "discrimination" against, some part of the members. Both classes had decided that it was for the benefit of the company to preserve the existing balance.

[52] *British American Nickel Corp. v. O'Brien* [1927] A.C. 369, P.C. which seems to suggest that the obligation of a class member to consider the interest of the class as a whole is greater than that of a member voting at a general meeting to consider the interest of the company as

of the class rather than that of "the company as a whole" that has to be considered. In that respect, therefore, there is another difference between members and directors since the latter have to exercise their powers in the interest of the company as a whole even if they are appointed by the members of a particular class.

More remarkable, perhaps, is the later and much criticised decision of Foster J. in *Clemens v. Clemens Bros. Ltd.*[53] That case concerned a private company in which the plaintiff held 45 per cent of the shares and her aunt, who, unlike the plaintiff, was one of the five directors (and the dominant one) held 55 per cent. Resolutions were passed at a general meeting, by the aunt's votes, to issue further shares to the other directors and to trustees of an employees' share-ownership scheme. The result was to reduce the plaintiff's holding to under 25 per cent, thereby depriving her of her negative control through her power to block a special or extraordinary resolution and reducing the value of her pre-emptive rights under the articles if another shareholder wished to sell. Foster J. set the resolutions aside saying[54]:

"They are specifically and carefully designed to ensure not only that the plaintiff can never get control of the company but to deprive her of what has been called her negative control. Whether I say that these proposals are oppressive to the plaintiff, or that no one could reasonably believe that they are for her benefit, matters not."

Here, in effect, the judge substituted for Evershed's hypothetical member an actual minority member and held that the majority had to consider whether the resolutions were for her benefit. In reaching this rather startling conclusion the judge was obviously influenced by section 210 of the 1948 Act (the predecessor of the present section 459) as his reference to "oppression" shows. But the plaintiff was not proceeding under section 210 and at that time would probably not have succeeded had she done so. But now she could succeed under section 459 if the court was satisfied, as Foster J. obviously was, that the resolutions were "unfairly prejudicial" to her.

What conclusions (if any) can be drawn from the foregoing discussion of the case law? Only, it is submitted, that the twin concepts of "fraud on the minority" and "bona fide in the interests of the company" are obsolete and meaningless in relation to activities by members. They were invented by the judges to curb the worst excesses of majority rule and at the time of their invention they were needed in the light of the then statute law. Now, however, because of recent

---

a whole. There seems to be no reason why that should be so and there is nothing in the judgment of Megarry J. to suggest that there is any such difference.

[53] [1976] 2 All E.R. 268. See the note in (1977) 40 M.L.R. 71 where his decision is described as "heart-warming" (at 71) but as subverting "the present basis of the law by displacing the principles of majority rule" (at 73).

[54] At 282.

statutory reforms[55] they are needed no longer. In most cases anything that they achieve can be achieved better by a petition under section 459. The only advantage of applying directly for an injunction or declaration rather than by petition under section 459 is that, when suing in a derivative action on behalf of the company,[56] the plaintiff may be able to obtain immediate security for his costs, whereas under section 459 he apparently cannot do so unless and until the court authorises him (as it can[57]) to bring civil proceedings in the name and on behalf of the company. That disadvantage could be removed by a simple amendment to section 459 or to the rules of court. Unless and until that is done, there is no great harm in allowing proceedings for an injunction or declaration to continue, so long as the courts cease to base their decisions on the vague concept of fraud on the minority and the wholly unrealistic pretence that it is meaningful to require members (except perhaps of a quasi-partnership private company) to ask themselves when they vote whether they are doing so for the benefit of the company as a whole.

In all the cases reviewed above, if the courts, instead of having to ask themselves whether there was a fraud on the minority or whether the resolution had been passed "bona fide in the interests of the company", had simply had to consider whether the members or some of them were being unfairly prejudiced, it can scarcely be doubted that they would have found that an easier question to answer. Indeed, in the more recent of the cases reviewed above they have come very close to asking themselves just that.

ALTERATION OF CLASS RIGHTS

The power of the majority under section 9 to alter the articles is expressly subject to "the provisions of this Act". Among those provisions are sections 125 to 127 which afford protection to minorities in relation to their "class rights". The protective technique deployed in these sections consists of requiring the separate consent of the class, usually by way of a 75 per cent majority, to any proposal to alter the articles in such a way as would vary their class rights. Although, as we have just seen,[58] this provision itself creates the potential for minority oppression within the class, nevertheless it is a very important protective technique. Without it, the protected class might be swamped by

---

[55] These include not only s.459 but also provisions protecting shareholders, *e.g.* on issues of new equity shares: see Chap. 13 at pp. 305–313, above—though pre-emptive rights are inadequately protected in the case of private companies as they can too easily be excluded.

[56] See Chap. 23 at pp. 666–667, above.

[57] See s.461(2)(c).

[58] Above, p. 715.

the votes of other classes of shareholders.[59] Indeed, they might not otherwise have any say in the matter at all, if, for example, they were preference shareholders without voting rights. The alteration of their right would otherwise be a matter entirely for the ordinary shareholders.

Sections 125 to 127 were introduced in 1980 and were intended to clear up a problem which existed before that date about the correct procedure for the variation of class rights contained in the articles. It was clear before 1980 that if the articles contained a procedure for the variation of class rights, that procedure had to be followed if a variation was to be validly effected. Moreover, Table A (for example, article 4 of the 1948 version) contained a variation of class rights procedure which, no doubt, was incorporated into the articles of many companies formed under that Act. That article required "the consent in writing of the holders of three-fourths of the issued shares of that class or . . . the sanction of an extraordinary resolution passed at a separate general meeting of the holders of the shares of that class". Where, however, article 4 was excluded, it was unclear whether class rights were not variable at all without the consent of each individual shareholder affected or whether they could be varied simply by using the normal variation procedure set out in section 9, which would give the minority members of the class very little protection.[60] Although the legislation now addresses the issue directly, section 125 applies only to companies "whose share capital is divided into shares of different classes". Accordingly, and oddly, the old uncertainty continues in relation to the variation of class rights in companies without a share capital.[61]

Section 125 begins by explaining that: "This section is concerned with the variation of rights attaching to any class in a company whose share capital is divided into shares of different classes."[62] This clearly covers the normal situation in which a company's share capital is expressly divided into separate classes. But does it also cover cases where nominally the shares are of the same class but special rights are conferred on one or more members without attaching those rights to any particular shares held by that member or members? This was the question facing Scott J. in the *Cumbria Newspapers* case.[63] Two com-

---

[59] For judicial deployment of the same protective technique within the statutory provisions for schemes of arrangement, see *Re Hellenic and General Trust Ltd* [1976] 1 W.L.R. 123 (below, p. 765).

[60] For example, under the articles of association of the particular company, the class affected by the proposal might have no right to attend and vote at a general meeting of the company. Nevertheless, in *Cumbria Newspapers Group Ltd v. Cumberland & Westmorland Herald Ltd* [1987] Ch. 1, Scott J. took the view that this was the position, but by then the legislation had been altered.

[61] But see the previous note and below, pp. 726–727.

[62] s.125(1).

[63] Above, n. 60.

panies, publishing rival provincial weekly newspapers in an area where it had become apparent that only one was viable, entered into an arrangement designed to ensure that one of the companies (company A) would publish that one newspaper but that it would issue 10 per cent of its ordinary share capital[64] to the other company (company B). Company B was anxious to ensure that the paper should remain locally owned and controlled and to this end the articles of company A were amended in such a way as to confer on company B pre-emptive rights in the event of any new issue of shares by company A or on a disposal by other shareholders of their shares in company A. These rights were not attached to any particular shares but on company B by name. Further, another new article provided that: "If and so long as [company B] shall be the holder of not less than one-tenth in nominal value of the issued ordinary share capital of" company A, company B "shall be entitled from time to time to nominate one person to be a director of" company A. Company A's articles had adopted article 4 of Table A 1948.[65] 18 years later, company A's directors proposed to convene a general meeting to pass a special resolution deleting the relevant articles. Company B thereupon applied to the court for a declaration that company B's rights were class rights that could not be abrogated without its consent and for an injunction restraining company A from convening or holding the meeting to pass the special resolution.

Scott J. pointed out that special rights contained in articles could be divided into three categories.[66] First, there are rights annexed to particular shares. The classic example of this is where particular shares carry particular rights not enjoyed by others, *e.g.* in relation to "dividends and rights to participate in surplus assets on a winding up".[67] These clearly were "rights attached to [a] class of shares" within the meaning of section 125(1) and article 4 of Table A 1948. He also held that this category would include cases where rights were attached to particular shares issued to a named individual but expressed to determine upon transfer by that individual of his shares.

The second category was where the articles purported to confer rights on individuals not in their capacity as members or shareholders.[68] Rights of this sort would not be class rights for they would not be attached to any class of shares.[69] But company B's rights did not fall within this class; the articles in question were "inextricably

---

[64] It also had preference shares but nothing turned on that. Clearly an attempt to vary their rights would have been subject to the equivalent of s.125 from 1981 onwards.

[65] Quoted on p. 718, above.

[66] [1987] 1 Ch. at 15A–18A.

[67] At 15.

[68] He instanced *Eley v. Positive Life Assurance Co.* (1875) 1 Ex.D. 20, on which see Chap. 6 at p. 118, above. It seems clear that in such a case the individual will have no enforceable rights in the absence of an express contract with the company additional to the articles.

[69] At 16A–E.

connected with the issue to the plaintiff[70] and the acceptance by the plaintiff of the ordinary shares in the defendant".[71]

This left the third category: "rights that, although not attached to any particular shares were nonetheless conferred upon the beneficiary in the capacity of member or shareholder of the company".[72] In his view, rights conferred on company B fell into this category.[73] But did they come within the words in section 125(1) "rights attaching to any class of shares"? After an analysis of the various legislative provisions and of the anomalies which would result if they did not,[74] he concluded that the legislative intent must have been to deal comprehensively with the variation or abrogation of shareholders' class rights and that he should therefore construe section 125 as applying to categories one and three.[75] He accordingly granted the declaration sought.[76]

This decision is greatly to be welcomed since it makes admirable sense. The pity of it is that there is no way in which sections 125 and 127 can be construed as applying to class rights in companies without a share capital.

The effect of sections 125–127

Section 125(2) deals with the most common situation, *i.e.* that in which the rights are attached to a class of shares otherwise than by the memorandum. If the articles do not contain provisions with respect to the variation[77] the rights may nevertheless be varied[78] but only if (a) the holders of three-quarters in nominal value of the issued shares of that class consent in writing or (b) an extraordinary resolution passed at a separate general meeting of the holders of shares of that class sanctions the variation and (c) in either case, any additional requirements, however imposed,[79] are complied with. In other words,

---

[70] *i.e.* company B.

[71] At 16G.

[72] At 16A–17A.

[73] At 17. He instanced as other examples, *Bushell v. Faith* [1970] A.C. 1099 (above, p. 189) and *Rayfield v. Hands* [1960] Ch. 1. (above, p. 118).

[74] At 18A–22B.

[75] At 22F, G.

[76] But he refrained from granting an injunction on the ground that this would "prevent the company from discharging its statutory duties in respect of the convening of meetings" (instancing s.368—though there had not in fact been any requisition by its members under this section). The result was therefore that company A could hold the meeting if it wished but, if the resolution was passed, it would nevertheless be ineffective in the light of the declaration unless company B consented.

[77] Since there is no variation of rights clause in Table A 1985, this is likely to become increasingly common.

[78] In this section and in any variation of rights clause in the company's memo. or arts. "variation" includes "abrogation" except when the context otherwise requires: s.125(8).

[79] *i.e.* whether in the memo., or arts. (which would be unlikely since it is difficult to envisage how there could be any such requirement without that being "a provision with respect to the variation") or in the terms of issue, a resolution or an agreement.

what was formerly the optional article 4 of Table A 1948 is now a statutory provision applying in this situation in the absence of an express variation of rights clause. Moreover, under subsection (3), in two circumstances the provisions of subsection (2) have to be complied with even if there is provision in the memorandum or articles for the variation. This is so if the variation of the rights is connected with either the giving, variation, revocation or renewal of an authority to the directors to allot shares under section 80,[80] or with a special resolution for a formal reduction of capital under section 135.[81] In either of these cases the company cannot take advantage of a more lax variation of rights clause in its memorandum or articles (or insert such a clause)[82] in order to remove or reduce the rights of a class in relation to the authority or reduction.

Subsection (4) starts with the situation: (a) where rights are attached by the memorandum and the articles contain a variation of rights clause which had been included in the articles at the time of the company's incorporation, or (b) with that in which the rights are attached, *otherwise than in the memorandum*, and the articles contain a variation of rights clause *whenever first so included*. In either case, so long as the variation is not connected with either of the two transactions referred to in subsection (3)(c), the rights can be altered in accordance with the provision in the articles.

If, however, the rights are attached by the memorandum and neither it nor the articles contain provision with respect to their variation, then, under subsection (5), they can be varied only if all the members[83] of the company agree to the variation. In other words, class rights may be entrenched in the memorandum without declaring them to be unalterable,[84] but simply by failing to provide a mechanism for their variation. This, it will be noted, requires not merely the consent of the class of shareholders whose rights are to be varied but of all members of the company. And that is a valuable protection because one of the weaknesses of that afforded by class meetings is that if one class (say, the ordinary shareholders) would benefit by the variation of the rights of another (the preference shareholders) those who hold both classes may, at the meeting of the preference shareholders, out-vote those who do not.[85]

---

[80] See Chap. 13, p. 304, above.
[81] See Chap. 11, pp. 247–251, above and Chap. 28 at pp. 757–762, below.
[82] See s.125(7), below.
[83] The use here of "members" rather than "shareholders" is presumably to take account of the few remaining companies limited by guarantee and having a share capital (where some members may not be shareholders) and to exclude the need for consent of holders of share-warrants to bearer unless the articles treat them as members.
[84] See p. 728, below.
[85] In which event, however, if the variation is connected with a transaction requiring the court's consent it may be refused: see, *e.g. Re Holders Investment Trust* [1971] 1 W.L.R. 583, above, p. 715.

Moreover, by subsection (7), any alteration of a variation of rights clause in a company's articles or the insertion into the articles of any such clause is to be treated as a variation of class rights. This, of course, does not preclude the alteration or insertion of such a provision by special resolution at a time when there is only one class of shares. But, once there is another class, class consents in accordance with the foregoing will be needed.

Finally, as an additional precaution it is expressly provided by subsection (6) that the provisions of section 369 (length of notice of meetings), section 370 (meetings and votes), sections 376 and 377 (circulation of members' resolutions) and the provisions of the articles as to general meetings[86] shall, so far as applicable and with such modifications as are necessary, apply to any meetings required by the section, or otherwise, in relation to variation of rights. This is subject to the exception that the quorum, other than at an adjourned meeting, shall be two persons holding or representing by proxy one-third in nominal value of the issued shares of the class or at an adjourned meeting[87] one person holding shares of the class or his proxy and that any holder or his proxy may demand a poll.

Section 126 merely states the obvious, that nothing in section 125(2)–(5) derogates from the powers of the court under sections 4–6,[88] 54,[89] 425,[90] 427,[91] or 459–461.[92]

Section 127, however, is of greater interest. It affords a dissenting minority of not less than 15 per cent of the issued shares of a class[93] whose rights have been varied in manner permitted by section 125, a right to apply to the court to have the variation cancelled.[94] Application must be made within 21 days after the consent was given or the resolution passed but can be made by such one or more of their number as they appoint in writing.[95] Once such an application is made the variation has no effect unless and until it is confirmed by the court.[96] If, after hearing the applicant "and any other persons who apply to be heard and appear to the court to be interested",[97] the court is satisfied

---

[86] On all of which see Chap. 21, above.

[87] As suggested above (Chap. 21, p. 594, n. 80) this ought to be amended to make it clear that it applies only if the adjournment was because of the absence of a quorum.

[88] Chap. 10 at pp. 210–211, above.

[89] Chap. 6 at pp. 124–125, above.

[90] Chap. 28 at pp. 762–767, below.

[91] *ibid.*

[92] Chap. 27, below.

[93] Provided that they have not consented to or voted in favour of the resolution—an unfortunately worded restriction which effectively rules out nominees who have not exercised all their votes in one way.

[94] s.127(1) and (2).

[95] s.127(3).

[96] *ibid.*

[97] This clearly includes representatives of other classes affected and of the company.

that the variation would unfairly prejudice[98] the shareholders of the class represented by the applicant, it may disallow the variation but otherwise must confirm it.[99] It is expressly provided that "the decision of the court is final",[1] which presumably means that it cannot be taken to appeal.[2]

The dearth of reported cases on section 127, and earlier versions of it, suggests that applications under it are used rarely if at all. Nevertheless, it probably serves a useful purpose in specifically drawing the attention of boards of directors to the need to ensure that variations of class rights treat classes fairly. But should they ignore that warning they are more likely to face an application under sections 459–461 rather than under section 127.

What constitutes a "variation"

What the various sections do not make clear is precisely what constitutes a variation of class rights. Indeed they obfuscate that by referring in one section[3] to a variation of "the special rights of any class" but elsewhere to a variation of "the rights attached to a class of shares".[4] The use of the former expression in section 17 seems on the face of it to imply that class rights attached by the memorandum are protected only to the extent that they are rights unique to that class (unless they are protected by an express provision prohibiting their alteration). In the light of section 125, however, that seems not to be the case. That section, however, has not removed all anomalies and uncertainties. Prior to the enactment of the section it seems to have been widely assumed that variation of class rights in accordance with an article equivalent to Table A 1948, article 4, required class consent only of the class whose rights were being altered in a manner adverse to that class. Thus, if there were two classes of ordinary shares, one of which had restricted voting rights or none at all, the separate consent of that class was not necessary if what was proposed was the

---

[98] This is the same expression as that used on ss.459–461 (see Chap. 27, below) which would seem to provide a better alternative remedy not demanding 15 per cent support and strict time limits and with a wider range of orders that the court can make.

[99] s.127(4). The company must within 15 days after the making of an order forward a copy to the Registrar: s.127(5).

[1] s.127(4).

[2] This was certainly the intention of the Greene Committee on whose recommendation the section was based: Cmd. 2657, para. 23. But the need for speedy finality seems no greater than on an application under ss.459–461 in which there is no such provision and cases can be taken to the H.L. But if the application is struck out on the ground that subs. (3) is not complied with, that can be taken to appeal and was in *Re Suburban Stores Ltd* [1943] Ch. 156, C.A. See also *Re Sound City (Films) Ltd* [1947] Ch. 169 which seems to be the only officially reported case on s.127 and its predecessors. Cases in which it might have been invoked (*e.g. Rights & Issues Investment Trust v. Stylo Shoes Ltd* [1965] Ch. 250) have been taken instead under ss.459–461 or earlier versions of those sections.

[3] s.17(2)(b).

[4] ss.125 and 127. See also Table A 1948, art. 4.

enfranchisement of their shares without any reduction of their other rights in order to compensate the other class for the reduction in their proportion of voting power.[5] But it is very difficult to believe that "variation" (even if coupled with the statement that it includes "abrogation") can reasonably be construed as "*adverse variation*" and it is submitted that, to avoid any subsequent attack on the validity of the resolution, the formal consent of the benefited class should be obtained.

What, however, was more serious, was the extraordinarily narrow construction placed by the courts on what constituted a variation of rights. The House of Lords in *Adelaide Electric Co. v. Prudential Assurance*[6] held that the alteration in the place of payment of a preferential dividend from England to Australia did not vary the rights of the preference shareholders notwithstanding that the Australian pound was worth less than the English. A subdivision[7] or increase[8] of one class of shares was held not to vary the rights of the other notwithstanding that the result was to alter the voting equilibrium of the classes. When preference shares were non-participating as regards dividend but participating as regards capital on a winding up or reduction of capital, a capitalisation of undistributed profits in the form of a bonus issue to the ordinary shareholders was not a variation of the preference shareholders' rights notwithstanding that the effect was to deny them their future participation in those profits on winding up or reduction.[9] A reduction of capital by repayment of irredeemable preference shares in accordance with their rights on a winding up was not regarded as a variation or abrogation of their rights[10]; nor was an issue of further shares ranking *pari passu* with the existing shares of

---

[5] Nor, it seems, would the separate consent of a class with one vote per share be needed if another with one vote per hundred shares was to be given one vote per share. On the construction placed by the courts on the meaning of "variation" (see the cases cited in nn. 7–8, below), their rights to one vote per share would not be "varied".

[6] [1934] A.C. 122, H.L.

[7] *Greenhalgh v. Arderne Cinemas* [1946] 1 All E.R. 512, C.A., where the result of the subdivision was to deprive the holder of one class of his power to block a special resolution.

[8] *White v. Bristol Aeroplane Co.* [1953] Ch. 65, C.A.; *Re John Smith's Tadcaster Brewery Co.* [1953] Ch. 308, C.A.

[9] *Dimbula Valley (Ceylon) Tea Co. v. Laurie* [1961] Ch. 353. And see the startling decision in *Re Mackenzie & Co. Ltd* [1916] 2 Ch. 450 which implies that a rateable reduction of the nominal preference and ordinary capital (which participated *pari passu* on a winding up) did not modify the rights of the preference shareholders notwithstanding that the effect was to reduce the amount payable to them by way of preference dividend while making no difference at all to the ordinary.

[10] *Scottish Insurance Corp. v. Wilson & Clyde Coal Co.* [1949] A.C. 462, H.L.; *Prudential Assurance Co. v. Chatterly Whitfield Collieries* [1949] A.C. 512, H.L., and this is so even if they are participating as regards dividends: *Re Saltdean Estate Co. Ltd* [1968] 1 W.L.R. 1844; *House of Fraser v. AGCE Investments Ltd* [1987] A.C. 387, H.L.Sc. (this, of course, does not apply if they are expressly given special rights on a reduction of capital). But contrast *Re Old Silkstone Collieries Ltd* [1954] Ch. 169, C.A. where confirmation of the repayment was refused because it would have deprived the preference shareholders of a contingent right to apply for an adjustment of capital under the coal nationalisation legislation.

a class.[11] And, where there were preference and ordinary shares, an issue of preferred ordinary shares ranking ahead of the ordinary but behind the preference was not a variation of the rights of either existing class.[12]

Presumably the courts will continue to follow this restrictive interpretation of variation of rights clauses in memoranda and articles and will apply it in relation to section 125, for there is nothing in the wording of that section which constrains them to do otherwise. It is true that the decisions suggest that the terms of variation of rights clauses could be expressed so as to afford protection against action additional to a variation or abrogation as construed by the courts. Thus, in the wake of the decisions on reduction of capital referred to in the previous paragraph, it has become common to introduce special provisions into a company's articles to protect preference shareholders. In *Re Northern Engineering Industries plc*[13] a clause in the articles deeming a reduction of capital to be a variation of rights was upheld and enforced when the company proposed to cancel its preference shares. But very clear wording will have to be used if such a provision is to be construed as affording any greater safeguards. In *White v. Bristol Aeroplane Co.*[14] and *Re John Smith's Tadcaster Brewery Co.*,[15] the relevant clauses referred to class rights being "affected, modified, dealt with or abrogated". At first instance Danckwerts J.[15a] held that bonus issue to the ordinary shareholders could not be made without the consent of the preference shareholders because, although their rights would not be abrogated or varied, they would be "affected" since their votes would be worth less in view of the increased voting power of the ordinary shareholders. But the Court of Appeal reversed his decisions. They said that the rights of the preference shareholders would not be affected; the rights themselves—to one vote per share in certain circumstances—remained precisely as before. All that would occur was that their holders' enjoyment of those rights would be affected. If that eventuality was to be guarded against, more explicit wording would have to be used.

It seems, therefore, that if section 125 is effectively to prevent class rights from being "affected as a matter of business"[15b]—which one

---

[11] This is expressly provided in Table A 1948, art. 5 (but not in Table A 1985). But the position seems to be the same in the absence of express provision: see the cases cited above, but contrast *Re Schweppes Ltd* [1914] 1 Ch. 322, C.A., which, however, concerned s.45 of the 1908 Act, which forbade "interference" with the "preference or special priviledge" of a class.

[12] *Hodge v. James Howell & Co.* [1958] C.L.Y. 446, C.A., *The Times*, December 13, 1958.

[13] [1994] 2 BCLC 704, C.A.

[14] [1953] Ch. 65, C.A.

[15] [1953] Ch. 308, C.A.

[15a] Only his judgement in the latter case is fully reported: see [1952] 2 All E.R. 751.

[15b] The words are those of Greene M.R. in *Greenhalgh v. Arderne Cinemas* [1946] 1 All E.R. at 518.

would have supposed is what businessmen would want—it is necessary to find a formula for a variation of rights clause which will
expressly operate in any event which affects any class of shareholders
(as opposed to the rights attached to their shares) or the enjoyment of
their rights (as opposed to the rights themselves). In the absence of
such a clause in Table A, adoption of such clauses is unlikely. This
seems less than satisfactory. In every case where the voting equilibrium is upset it is clear that class rights are "affected as a matter of
business", and it is strange to protect a class from having its votes
halved while refusing to protect it when the votes of the other class
are doubled; the practical effect is the same in both cases.

Class rights of members not shareholders

As we have seen,[16] the Act does nothing to clarify the position
regarding the variation of class rights of members who are not shareholders. As a result the present position in their case seems to be as
follows:
(1) The only relevant statutory provision remains section 17(2) under
    which "special rights", if attached to a class of members by the
    memorandum, cannot be varied or abrogated under section 17.
    Unless "special rights" is to be interpreted as meaning rights
    unique to the class (which, in the light of section 125 it clearly
    does not mean if the rights are attached to shares and which, it is
    submitted, it cannot mean here either[17]) the result is that members'
    class rights, if attached by the memorandum, can be altered only
    to the extent permitted under the case law prior to the 1948 Act.
    That established that such alterations of class rights were permiss-
    ible only in accordance with a variation of rights clause in the
    memorandum or, perhaps, in the original articles registered with
    the memorandum.[18] Hence, it seems that that remains the position.
    If the class rights in the memorandum are varied under such a
    variation of rights clause, dissenting members will have a right to
    apply for its cancellation under section 127 but not under section
    17(1) and (3) since that applies only to "alterations made under

---

[16] p. 718, above.
[17] If it did, it would presumably mean that those unique rights could not be varied under s.17
    but that other class rights could unless that was prohibited by the memorandum.
[18] *Re Welsbach Gas Light Co.* [1904] 1 Ch. 87, C.A. where the memo expressly referred to
    variation in accordance with a provision in the articles. Two Scottish cases went further,
    holding that it sufficed if the clause was in the original articles: *Oban Distilleries Ltd* (1903)
    5 F. 1140; *Marshall Fleming & Co. Ltd,* 1938 S.C. 873. Since the Scottish view has been
    adopted by the legislature in s.125(4)(a), the English courts can be expected to follow suit.
    Whether they would feel able also to adopt by analogy s.125(5), validating a variation agreed
    to by all the members, is less clear but unanimous agreement plus the abolition of *ultra vires*
    has presumably produced the same result.

this section''[19] and the alteration would not have been so made. This, however, is of little moment since a member, if unfairly prejudiced, will have a better remedy under sections 459–461.

(2) If, however, class rights are not attached by the memorandum but by the articles (the more usual situation) or otherwise[20] then, assuming that the courts follow the dicta of Scott J., in the *Cumbrian Newspapers* case[21] on the position prior to the enactment of section 125, the company will be able to vary the rights by a special resolution[22] and without the need for class consents. If however, the articles contain a variation of rights clause, even if it is expressed as enabling (rather than as restricting) as in former Tables A, then "it may fairly be said to be implicit . . . that rights cannot be varied . . . otherwise than by the procedure thus laid down".[23] That, at least, gives the members of the class some protection. And, in any event, they have the protection of sections 459–461 if they are able to establish that a variation is unfairly prejudicial to them.

The contrasts between variation of class rights of shareholders and of members who are not shareholders are highly anomalous. Particularly is this so when, as is usual, the rights are set out in the articles and the articles do not contain a variation of rights clause (as will become increasingly common since neither Table A nor Table C contains such a clause). Whereas in the *Cumbrian* case class consents were required and, under section 125, would have been required even if there had been no express variation of rights clause, had the company been one without a share capital, class consents would not have been needed. Yet the protection which the class rights were designed to protect were essentially of voting rights and board representation, both of which are equally important whether or not the company has a share capital.[24]

SELF HELP

A potential minority shareholder, reading the previous pages, would be justified in feeling somewhat gloomy about the extent to which his or her interests are truly protected by the rules there analysed. Where class rights are not involved, the scope of the objective controls upon the voting decisions of the majority is still very unclear. Where class

---

[19] This seems to be the effect of the application of s.5(1) by s.17(3).

[20] *e.g.* under the terms of issue.

[21] [1987] Ch. 1: see above.

[22] On which the class affected may not be entitled to vote.

[23] [1987] Ch. at 19D.

[24] And there is no reason why a newspaper should not be published by a company without share capital—many companies limited by guarantee are in fact publishers of journals.

rights are involved, the situation is rather better, especially in the light of the new statutory provisions and the decision of Scott J. in the *Cumbria Newspapers* case, but the class rights procedure still has its weaknesses, notably the limited view taken by the courts of what constitutes the variation of a class right, and, even when it works properly, the procedure still leaves a minority within a class exposed to adverse decisions. Therefore, there is a considerable incentive to shareholders themselves to provide, in advance of a dispute arising, for a substantive or procedural rule which will govern the case.

The Act itself suggests one way forward, by offering the possibility that a provision may be entrenched by including it in the memorandum of association, rather than in the articles. Section 2(7) provides that a company may not alter the conditions contained in its memorandum except to the extent and in the ways expressly provided in the Act. In fact, the Act does expressly provide for the alteration of most provisions of the memorandum. Relevant to the current discussion is section 17 which allows for the alteration by special resolution[25] of any provision of the memorandum which could have been included in the articles. That provision is subject, however, to the proviso that it does not operate where the memorandum itself prohibits alteration of the provision or provides a more demanding procedure for alteration than that laid down in section 17 itself.[26]

So the possibility arises of entrenching a provision by including it in the memorandum and declaring it to be unalterable or, say, alterable only with the assent of X. However, the drawback of this way of proceeding is its inflexibility. At the same time as this procedure takes the provision out of the hands of the majority, it also renders it unalterable even if the proponents of its entrenchment subsequently desire a change. A provision declared to be unalterable cannot be changed except by way of a scheme of arrangement under section 425,[27] which will hardly be practicable in many cases.[28] Consequently, it may be preferable to proceed by means of an agreement existing outside the articles, the parties to which may be the members *inter se* or the interested members and the company or both. That contract will then be freely alterable if all the parties to it agree. The legal problem here is rather how to be sure that the initial agreement is legally binding. Where the contract is with the company, one is faced with two appar-

---

[25] And possible appeal to the court to have the alteration cancelled, as in the case of an alteration of the objects clause: see above, p. 210.

[26] s.17(2)(b). Nor may section 17 be used if it would involve a variation or abrogation of class rights, even if alteration is not expressly forbidden in the memorandum. See above, p. 721.

[27] See below, pp. 762 *et seq.*

[28] In the case of an alteration being permissible only with the consent of X, X will have a class right, so that s.17 will not be available to deprive X of his veto, even if alteration is not expressly forbidden. See n. 26, above. Here, in addition to a scheme of arrangement, it is possible to alter the class right through the unanimous consent of all the members of the company (s.125(5)), though that will often not be a practical procedure either.

ently conflicting principles: first, that a company, like any other person, cannot with impunity break its contracts and, secondly, that a company cannot contract out of its statutory power under section 9 to alter its articles by special resolution.

The second proposition was recently considered by the House of Lords in *Russell v. Northern Bank Development Corporation Ltd.*[29] It was clear to their lordships that "a provision in a company's articles which restricts its statutory power to alter those articles is invalid"[30] and they applied that principle to the agreement before them, existing outside the articles among the shareholders and to which the company purported to be a party. That agreement provided that no further share capital should be created or issued in the company without the written consent of all the parties to the agreement. Consequently, it would seem that the company cannot validly contract independently of the articles not to alter those articles—or, indeed, not to alter the provisions of its memorandum.[31] However, that proposition is heavily qualified by two further propositions which may render the initial proposition ineffective in practice, at least for those who are well advised.

The first qualification is that the principle of invalidity, laid down in *Russell*, does not apply where the company has entered into a previous contract on such terms that for the company to act upon its altered article would involve it in a breach of the prior contract. In this situation the term of the earlier contract, which would be breached if the company acted upon the altered article, is not invalid. The *Russell* principle is not relevant here because the term in the earlier contract is not broken when the company alters its articles, but only when it acts upon the altered article. Thus, in *Southern Foundries (1926) Ltd v. Shirlaw*[32] the company altered its articles so as to introduce a new method of removing directors from office and then used the new method to dismiss the managing director in breach of his 10-year service contract. The managing director successfully obtained damages for wrongful dismissal. The provision as to the term of the service agreement was thus clearly held by the House of Lords to be valid. Lord Porter said: "A company cannot be precluded from altering its articles thereby giving itself power to act upon the provisions of the altered articles—but so to act may nevertheless be a breach of contract if it is contrary to a stipulation in a contract validly made before the alteration."[33]

---

[29] [1992] 1 W.L.R. 588, H.L. See Sealy [1992] C.L.J. 437; Davenport (1993) 109 L.Q.R. 553; Riley (1993) 44 N.I.L.Q. 34; Ferran [1994] C.L.J. 343.

[30] At 593.

[31] In this case what was proposed was an increase in the company's authorised capital laid down in the memorandum. Whether the quoted principle applies to all powers conferred on the company by the statute is unclear.

[32] [1940] A.C. 701, H.L.

[33] At 740–741.

The unresolved issue in relation to this first qualification is whether a plaintiff seeking to enforce his or her contractual rights against the company's acting on the alteration is confined to the remedy of damages or whether and, if so, how far injunctive relief is available to enforce the earlier contract. In *Baily v. British Equitable Insurance Co.*[34] the Court of Appeal granted a declaration that to act on the altered article would be a breach of the plaintiff's contractual rights. More surprisingly, in *British Murac Syndicate Ltd v. Alperton Rubber Co Ltd*[35] Sargant J. went so far as to grant an injunction to restrain an alteration of the articles which would have contravened the plaintiff's contractual rights. Although Sargant J.'s decision is generally regarded as based upon a misunderstanding of the previous authorities, some sympathy with this approach was expressed by Scott J. in the *Cumbria Newspapers* case,[36] where he said that he could "see no reason why [the company] should not, in a suitable case, be injuncted from initiating the calling of a general meeting with a view to the alteration of the articles." To the extent that injunctive relief is made available in this way not simply to restrain acting upon the altered article but to restrain the operation of the machinery for effecting the alteration itself, the notion that the company cannot validly make a direct contract not to alter its articles becomes hollow. Such an extension of injunctive relief would also contradict the dictum of Lord Porter in *Shirlaw*[37]: "Nor can an injunction be granted to prevent the adoption of the new articles." However, injunctive relief merely to prevent an acting upon the new articles would not fall foul of this principle.

The second qualification is that an agreement among the shareholders as to how they will exercise the voting rights attached to their shares is not caught by the principle that a company cannot contract out of its statutory powers to alter its articles or memorandum. This rule was applied to save the agreement in *Russell*, the House of Lords benignly severing the company from the agreement in question. Lord Jauncy said that "shareholders may lawfully agree *inter se* to exercise their voting rights in a manner which, if it were dictated by the articles, and were thereby binding on the company, would be unlawful".[38] The plaintiff was granted a declaration as to the validity of the agreement, and it seems that their lordships would have been happy to grant an injunction had the plaintiff objected substantively to the course of action proposed by the company, as against wishing to establish the

---

[34] [1904] 1 Ch. 373, C.A.
[35] [1915] 2 Ch. 186. The case concerned the right of the plaintiff, under both the articles and a separate contract, to appoint two directors to the board so long as he held 5,000 shares in the company. Today, after the *Cumbria Newspaper* decision (see p. 718, above) the plaintiff would be protected as the holder of a class right.
[36] Above, n. 60, at 24.
[37] Above, n. 32.
[38] [1992] 1 W.L.R. at 593.

principle that his consent to the change was required.[39] This conclusion flows from the more general proposition that the vote attached to a share is a property right which the shareholder is prima facie entitled to exercise and deal with as he or she thinks fit.[40]

Of course, a members' agreement is less effective than one which binds the company as well. Its initial conclusion is feasible only if there is a relatively small number of shareholders whose consent is necessary to the effective operation of the agreement, and on a subsequent transfer of a shareholding covered by the agreement the new shareholder will not be bound without his or her express adherence to the agreement among the other shareholders.[41] Nevertheless, the shareholders' agreement does play an important role in entrenching unanimous shareholder agreement for important changes to the company's financial or constitutional arrangements in situations such as management buy-outs, venture capital investments and joint ventures.[42] Not only can the shareholders'agreement be used to avoid the rule that the company cannot contract out of its power to alter its constitution, but also the enforcement of shareholder agreements outside the articles does not fall foul of the restrictions on the enforcement of the articles of association as a contract or the rule in *Foss v. Harbottle*.[43]

At the end of this analysis it may be thought that there is little practical impact left of the principle that a company may not contract out of its power to alter its articles or memorandum, at least for those who are aware of the problem when they draft the agreements designed to secure the consent of all or some of the shareholders to such changes. In this situation it may be thought desirable to introduce a greater degree of simplicity by abandoning the underlying rule which has been so heavily qualified. However, the present situation does have some merit in conducing to genuine shareholder consent to departures from majority rule. If restrictions on constitutional changes contained in the articles were freely allowed, then consent on the part

[39] *ibid.*, at 595.
[40] On the enforcement of shareholder agreements see *Greenwell v. Porter* [1902] 1 Ch. 530 and *Puddephatt v. Leith* [1916] 1 Ch. 200, where a mandatory injunction was granted to compel a shareholder to vote in accordance with his agreement. Some shareholder agreements may make their adherents "concert parties" within the meaning of Part VI of the Act (see pp. 488 *et seq*; above) and so require registration of their holdings and dealings.
[41] *cf. Greenhalgh v. Mallard* [1943] 2 All E.R. 234, C.A. Of course, the selling shareholder may be contractually bound to secure the adherence of the acquiring shareholder, but even so it is difficult to make the arrangement completely water-tight by purely contractual means, especially at the remedial level.
[42] G. Stedman and J. Jones, *Shareholders' Agreements* (2nd ed., London, 1990). If the power which it is sought to control is one which is exercisable by the board of directors, it may in addition be necessary to alter the articles so as to shift the power in question to the general meeting or to provide for its exercise by the board only with the consent of the general meeting.
[43] On the former, see p. 118, above, and on the latter p. 660, above.

of shareholders to such restrictions would often be entirely formal, arising simply out of the shareholder's becoming a member on the terms of the articles.[44] Assuming that the courts are correct in their view that alteration of the articles and memorandum by majority decision is the appropriate principle for most companies, the current rules which permit that situation to be negated where, but only where, some or all of the shareholders consciously agree that an alternative principle (say, unanimous shareholder agreement) suits them better, has a lot to commend it.[45]

Finally, it should be noted that protection of minority shareholders may be provided by self-help techniques other than the shareholders' voting agreement. Closely associated with, but more sophisticated than, the voting agreement is the voting trust, not uncommon in the United States but less common in the United Kingdom. Under this, in effect, voting rights are separated from the financial interest in the shares, the former being held and exercisable by trustees while the latter remains with the shareholders. Other techniques are available which may involve alterations to the articles rather than agreements outside the articles. Examples are the introduction of weighted voting rights for the shareholder(s) to be protected (after the decision in *Bushell v. Faith*[46]) or of a quorum requirement that the shareholder(s) to be protected be present, so that they can in effect veto the proposal by absenting themselves.[47]

DEBENTURE-HOLDERS' RIGHTS

The protection of the rights of the other type of investor—the debenture-holder—is obviously much greater than that of a member's rights under the articles since a debenture confers contractual rights independent of the company's articles. It is, nonetheless, possible that those contractual rights might be affected as a result of the exercise by the company or the general meeting of its statutory powers. If, for example, the debenture provided that the holder should be entitled to appoint a director of the company and if a provision to that effect was inserted in the company's articles, a question similar to that discussed in relation to shareholders might arise on whether an attempt to delete

---

[44] "Not one percent of intending shareholders read the articles before applying for or accepting a transfer of shares, and a shareholder does not expect to find that he has entered into a special contract waiving his statutory rights" *per* Byrne J. in *Re Peveril Gold Mines Ltd* [1898] 1 Ch. 122 at 126.

[45] Of course, shareholders not party to the agreement may feel aggrieved about its operation in practice, but they will have their remedy under s.459: see below, Chap. 27.

[46] [1970] A.C. 1099, H.L., see p. 189, above.

[47] *Harman v. BML Group Ltd* [1994] 1 W.L.R. 893, C.A., where the quorum requirement was upheld against an application under s.371, even though it was contained in a shareholders' agreement rather than the articles. See above, p. 569.

that provision could be restrained by injunction.[48] But this would rarely be a live question for the breach would normally entitle the debenture-holder to require his debt security to be repaid and, if it was secured by a charge on the company's property, to enforce his security. This he would do rather than sue for damages for the breach. While the value of his rights may depend on the continued prosperity of the company, particularly if the debenture is unsecured loan stock, he is normally not subject, as is a shareholder, to any serious possibility that his rights will be varied by the company by corporate action without his consent.

To this, however, there are two exceptions. The first is that, if the debenture is one of a series or is debenture stock, its terms may provide for the variation of the holders' rights with the consent of a prescribed majority of the holders or an extraordinary resolution of the holders. In such a case, while he will not be vulnerable to action by the company or its members as such, he will be vulnerable to that of the requisite majority of his fellow debenture-holders who may have interests conflicting with his because they are also shareholders or directors. In such circumstances he will not have the protection of sections 459–461 which apply only to "members".[49] However, as we have seen,[50] where there is a series of debentures or debenture stock there will almost invariably be independent trustees who should ensure that any proposed variations are fair and are fully and fairly explained in the circulars seeking the needed consents.

The second exception is that the powers of a debenture-holder to enforce his security may be seriously curtailed if the court makes an administration order under Part II of the Insolvency Act 1986.[51] Such an order will not be made if a debenture-holder has already appointed an administrative receiver unless the court is satisfied that the debenture-holder has consented to the order being made or is not satisfied that the security under which the administrative receiver was appointed could not be challenged under certain provisions[52] of that Act.[53] If, however, an order is made, any administrative receiver must vacate office as must a receiver of any part of the company's property if the administrator requires him to do so.[54] Thereafter, so long as the administration order remains in force there is a complete moratorium

---

[48] Even if it could, it seems clear that an injunction could not be granted to restrain the general meeting from removing his nominated director under s.303.

[49] Nor, of course, will ss.125–127 afford protection (they apply only to shareholders).

[50] Above, Chap. 13 at pp. 325–326.

[51] See Chap. 30 at pp. 821–825.

[52] *i.e.* Insolvency Act ss.238–240 (transactions at an undervalue or preferences); s.242 (gratuitous alienations); s.243 (unfair preferences); or s.245 (avoidance of floating charges): see *ibid.*, and Chap. 15, above.

[53] *ibid.*, s.9(3).

[54] *ibid.*, s.11(1)(b) and (2).

on any type of enforcement against the company without the consent of the administrator or the leave of the court.[55]

While an administration order does not destroy or vary the debenture-holder's rights, it does mean that his powers to enforce those rights are suspended and that any realisation of the property on which he has a charge will not rest with him or with an insolvency practitioner chosen by him (and whose primary aim will be to realise it at a price sufficient to discharge the debenture) but with one appointed by the court, whose primary aim will normally be to achieve "the survival of the company, and the whole or any part of its undertaking, as a going concern"[56] and so that if any parts of the undertaking have to be disposed of, it will be on the best terms obtainable in the interests of creditors and members as a whole.

VARIATIONS UNDER RECONSTRUCTIONS

This Chapter has concentrated on variation of investors' rights under what may be termed internal corporate action. As we shall see in a later Chapter,[57] variations may also occur under formal reductions of capital or schemes of arrangement involving, normally, court confirmation. All that needs mention at this stage is that there too emphasis is placed on protection of class rights and that "classes" in that context may have a wider connotation than it has in relation to classes of members in the context of this Chapter.

[55] *ibid.*, s.11(3).
[56] *ibid.*, s.8(3)(a).
[57] Chap. 28, below.

CHAPTER 27

UNFAIR PREJUDICE

INTRODUCTION

SECTION 459, the first of only three sections which constitute Part XVII of the Act, provides that any member may petition[1] the court for relief on the grounds that

"the company's affairs are being or have been conducted in a manner which is unfairly prejudicial to the interest of its members generally or some part of the members (including at least himself) or that any actual or proposed act or omission of the company (including any act or omission on its behalf) is or would be so prejudicial."

It is clear that the section is wide enough to catch the activities of controllers of companies, whether they conduct the business of the company through the exercise of their powers as directors or as shareholders or both. The section may even apply to the conduct of corporate groups. Although the conduct of a shareholder, even a majority shareholder, of its own affairs is excluded from the section, nevertheless where a parent company has assumed detailed control over the affairs of its subsidiary and treats the financial affairs of the two companies as those of a single enterprise, actions taken by the parent in its own interest may be regarded as acts done in the conduct of the affairs of the subsidiary.[2] The "outside" shareholders in the subsidiary may thus use the section to protect themselves against exploitation by the majority-shareholding parent company.

Thus, this statutory remedy is capable of ranging very widely over the conduct of corporate affairs. It embraces control of both shareholders' voting powers, examined in the immediately preceding Chapter, and directors' powers, examined in the four Chapters before that. The section posed, moreover, when introduced in its modern form in 1980, a very considerable challenge to the traditionally non-interventionist attitudes of the judges in relation to the internal affairs

---

[1] The procedure for petitions is governed mainly by the Companies (Unfair Prejudice Applications) Proceedings Rules 1986 (S.I. 1986 No. 2000), but also by the Rules of the Supreme Court, the County Court Rules and the practice of the High Court, where not inconsistent with the 1986 Rules. For earlier helpful analysis of this Part, see Prentice (1988) 8 O.J.L.S. 55 and Riley (1992) 55 M.L.R. 782.

[2] *Nicholas v. Soundcraft Electronics Ltd* [1993] BCLC 360, C.A., expanding upon the approach taken in *Scottish Co-operative Wholesale Society Ltd v. Meyer* [1959] A.C. 324, H.L. by not confining the principle to companies engaged in the same type of business. See also *Re Dominion International Group (No. 2)* [1996] 1 BCLC 634.

of companies.[3] The extent to which the modern judges have thrown off that traditional attitude is one of the main underlying themes of this Chapter. It will be suggested that what we have witnessed is a partial revolution in judicial attitudes.

When an administration order is in force,[4] section 459 is supplemented by section 27 of the Insolvency Act 1986, permitting any creditor or member to petition the court[5] on the grounds that the administrator's management of the company's "affairs, business and property" has been unfairly prejudicial to the company's members or creditors as a whole or some class of them. Finally, section 460 permits the Secretary of State to petition if, as a result of an investigation carried out into a company,[6] he concludes that the affairs of the company have been carried on in a way that is unfairly prejudicial to the members (or some part of them).

It is clear that the sections were drafted in deliberately wide terms. They have therefore presented to the courts an initial problem of defining their scope. It is suggested that three main questions have arisen. First, should the sections be seen as simply aimed at providing a more effective way of remedying harms which, independently of the sections, are in any case unlawful? This may be termed the "independent illegality" issue. The competing view, which, as we shall see, has been adopted by the courts and which constitutes one of their most important contributions to the development of the provisions, is that the sections are not concerned simply with better remedies but, in addition, are designed to render unlawful some types of conduct which, apart from the sections, are not in any way unlawful. This approach launches the courts upon a voyage of discovery. Deprived of the familiar landmarks of established illegalities, what criteria should the courts deploy in determining whether conduct is unfairly prejudicial, *i.e.* unlawful? This is the second main issue which has faced the courts and it is the one which has absorbed the greatest amount of judicial thought and effort. It is upon the courts' handling of this issue that the suggestion that there has been a partial revolution in judicial attitudes largely depends.

However, whether or not the courts extend the range of unfairly

---

[3] See the lament of the Lord President (Cooper) in *Scottish Insurance Corporation v. Wilsons & Clyde Coal Company*, 1948 S.C. 376, quoted below at p. 759, n. 18.

[4] For administration orders, see below, pp. 817–833. An unfair prejudice challenge may also be made to proposals adopted by way of a company voluntary arrangement (see s.6 of the Insolvency Act 1986 and below, pp. 768–770) but the court's powers are here confined to setting aside the proposals adopted at the creditors' meeting and ordering meetings to consider revised proposals.

[5] The Bank of England or the Deposit Protection Board may also petition.

[6] See Chap. 25, above. A petition under s.460 may be instead of or in addition to a petition by the Secretary of State to have the company wound up under s.124A of the Insolvency Act (see pp. 702–703, above) but it is notable that the Company Act power does not require the Secretary of State to be of the opinion that the public interest would be furthered by the bringing of an unfair prejudice petition.

prejudicial conduct beyond conduct which is independently unlawful, there remains an important issue of the relationship between the unfair prejudice remedy and the derivative action. When a wrong has been committed against the company, may a shareholder leap over the restrictions of the rule in *Foss v. Harbottle*[7] by presenting a petition founded upon unfair prejudice? Or are the unfair prejudice petition and the derivative action aimed at redressing different wrongs and, if so, how does one distinguish between them? It is this issue with which we shall begin.[8]

UNFAIR PREJUDICE AND THE DERIVATIVE ACTION

It may seem odd at first sight that a right of petition vested in the individual member or creditor may be used to secure the redress of wrongs done to the company, especially those committed by its directors. The problem does not arise if the conduct of which the petitioner complains consists of a breach of the articles, for section 14 constitutes the articles a contract between the member and the company.[9] But the directors' duties are owed, normally, to the company, not individual shareholders. However, the sections are drafted so as to protect the *interests* of the members and not just their rights,[10] and it cannot be denied that a wrong done to the company may affect the interests of its members. Before the introduction by the 1989 Act of the words "of its members generally" into section 459, there was an argument that a wrong done to the company, which affected all the members equally, fell outside the section,[11] but that argument is no longer available.

The Jenkins Committee, whose report recommended the introduction of the unfair prejudice remedy, envisaged that it would have a role in relation to wrongs to the company. "In addition to these direct wrongs[12] to the minority, there is the type of case in which a wrong is done to the company itself and the control vested in the majority is wrongfully used to prevent action being taken against the wrongdoer. In such a case the minority is indirectly wronged."[13] There are a number of reported cases under the current legislation in which petitions have been entertained by the courts where the wrongdoers' con-

---

[7] Analysed in Chap. 23, above.

[8] For a penetrating analysis of the problem in a Canadian context, see MacIntosh, "The Oppression Remedy: Personal or Derivative?" (1991) 70 Can. Bar Rev. 29.

[9] To allow a petition in these circumstances may further undermine the "internal irregularities" limb of *Foss v. Harbottle*, but it has been argued above (pp. 660–665) that that limb ought to have no application to breaches of the articles.

[10] A point to which the courts have attached some importance. See below, p. 740.

[11] The argument was accepted by Vinelott J. in *Re Carrington Viyella plc* (1983) 1 BCC 98, 951, though the exact scope of the point was never finally settled.

[12] "Direct wrongs" are considered below at p. 741.

[13] Report of the Company Law Committee, Cmnd. 1749 (1962), para. 206.

duct consisted wholly or partly of wrongs done to the company.[14] The courts have even gone so far as to refuse to accept that the actual availability of a derivative action constitutes a bar to an unfair prejudice petition.[15] As Hoffmann L.J. (as he then was) has said: "Enabling the court in an appropriate case to outflank the rule in *Foss v. Harbottle* was one of the purposes of the section."[16]

What, however, is an "appropriate case"? There is something of a mystery here. In our discussion of the rule in *Foss v. Harbottle* we noted that there were recent decisions by the courts which seemed to display approval of the restrictive standing requirements for shareholders to bring derivative actions and which had insisted upon, even reinforced, those requirements.[17] It is impossible to believe that all the policies underlying restrictions on the derivative action fall away when the action is commenced by petition rather than by writ. An attempt to address this difficult problem was made by Millett J. in *Re Charnley Davies Ltd (No. 2)*,[18] which involved a petition under section 27 of the Insolvency Act claiming that the administrator had broken his duty of care to the company by selling its business at an undervalue and ought to pay compensation to the company. Whilst holding that on the facts there had been no breach of duty, he nevertheless went on to consider in dicta the relationship between a petition based on unfair prejudice and the derivative action.

The learned judge thought that, just as an allegation of independent illegality was not necessary to found a successful petition,[19] so also an allegation that the controllers had broken their duties to the company was not sufficient to found one. Just as in an *ultra vires* case there may be more than one legal dimension of the same set of facts,[20] so also in a case of breach of duty more generally the same facts may give rise to a complaint both of breach of duty owed to the company, which is prosecuted by the company (or by a shareholder suing derivatively, where that is allowed), and of unfair prejudice, which is prosecuted by a petitioning shareholder. If the shareholder wishes to com-

---

[14] *Re Stewarts (Brixton) Ltd* [1985] BCLC 4; *Re London School of Electronics* [1986] Ch. 211; *Re Cumana Ltd* [1986] BCLC 430 (all involving various forms of diversion of the company's business to rival companies in which the majority were interested, *i.e.* situation of the type found in *Cook v. Deeks* [1916] 1 A.C. 553, P.C., above, p. 646); *Re A Company, ex p. Glossop* [1988] 1 W.L.R. 1068 (exercise of directors' powers for an improper purpose); *Re Saul D. Harrison & Sons plc* [1995] 1 BCLC 14 (failure of directors to act bona fide in the interests of the company). In not all these cases was the allegation in question made out on the facts.

[15] *Re A Company (No. 5287 of 1985)* [1986] 1 W.L.R. 281; *Re Stewarts (Brixton) Ltd*, above, n. 14; *Lowe v. Fahey* [1996] 1 BCLC 262.

[16] *Re Saul D Harrison & Sons plc*, above n. 14 at 18.

[17] Notably *Prudential Insurance v. Newman Industries (No. 2)* [1982] Ch. 204, C.A. ' above, p. 669) and *Smith v. Croft (No. 2)* [1988] Ch. 114 (above, p. 674).

[18] [1990] BCLC 760.

[19] See below, p. 740.

[20] So that both a personal and a derivative action may lie, but each subject to its appropriate conditions. See above, p. 663.

plain simply of the breach of duty by the directors, this cannot be done by petition. The shareholder must sue instead on behalf of the company and subject to the standing restrictions of *Foss v. Harbottle*. In the petition the gist of the action is not the wrong done to the company but the disregard by the controllers of the interests of the minority.

As in the *ultra vires* cases, however, the difficult questions of which complaint the petitioner is seeking to make and of whether the petition is the appropriate vehicle seem to turn very largely on the nature of the remedy sought. In *Re Charnley Davies* the petition sought compensation for the company, for which, it was said, an unfair prejudice petition was inappropriate, whereas a claim that the controllers purchase the petitioners' shares at an appropriate price would have indicated that the gist of the complaint was unfair prejudice to the minority.[21] In short, the suggestion is that, whilst an unfair prejudice petition may be founded, wholly or partly, on breaches of duty owed by directors to the company, the relief that may be claimed in a petition is confined personal remedies and may not include corporate relief.[22]

On the one hand, this approach might be thought to fit in well with the view of the Jenkins Committee that the harm to the shareholders in such cases is "indirect" and that the wrong to them consists, not in the wrong done to the company, but in the controllers' use of their position to prevent action being taken to redress the wrong done to the company. On the other hand, it sits rather oddly with the fact that one of the remedies which the statute expressly empowers the court to grant to a successful petitioner is to "authorise civil proceedings to be brought in the name and on behalf of the company by such person or persons and on such terms as the court may direct".[23] This provision suggests that recovery *for the company* is in principle a proper outcome of a petition based on unfair prejudice. If so, then should not corporate relief be granted by the court without the need for a separate action on behalf of the company where, as a result of the petition, it is clear to the court against which person[24] the remedy ought to be ordered, *i.e.* precisely the claim which was made in *Re Charnley Davies*? And, if this is accepted, is it not also the case that an unfair prejudice petition may indeed act so as to "outflank" the rule in *Foss*

---

[21] This is, of course, a remedy very commonly sought by s.459 petitioners (see below, p. 747). On this basis the judge thought that the refusal to strike out the petition in *Re A Company (No. 5287 of 1985)*, above, n. 15, was correct. It is not clear what its equivalent should be in a petition against an administrator.

[22] *cf.* the somewhat similar approach taken to the personal action in the *Prudential* case, above, p. 667.

[23] s.461(2)(c).

[24] It is clear that the court may make orders against persons who are no longer members of the company or who have never been members if, nevertheless, they have been knowingly involved in or have benefited from the conduct of which complaint is made: *Re A Company (No. 5287 of 1985)*, above, n. 15; *Re Little Olympian Each-Ways Ltd (No. 3)* [1995] 1 BCLC 636; *Lowe v. Fahey* [1996] 1 BCLC 262.

v. Harbottle, the discretion of the court at the remedial level[25] being substituted for the *locus standi* provisions of that rule?[26]

INDEPENDENT ILLEGALITY

We now turn to the question of whether it is a necessary ingredient of a successful petition on the basis of unfair prejudice that the petitioner should allege that the controllers' acts were independently unlawful. We will examine that issue together with another limiting factor, the "qua member" requirement, which was inherited from earlier legislation. Section 459 is not the first attempt by Parliament to provide a statutory remedy for the protection of minorities. Section 210 of the 1948 Act was aimed at the same objective, but achieved very limited success because of both limitations in its drafting and narrow interpretation by the courts. Many of those restrictions were removed when the remedy was cast into its modern form in 1980. Most notably, the test for intervention ceased to be "oppression" of the minority by the controllers and became instead that of "unfair prejudice", a clear indication that Parliament intended the courts to take a more active role.

However, the legislature did not deal expressly with two limitations which the courts had built into the oppression remedy by way of interpretation. The first was that section 210 was interpreted as applying only to oppression of the petitioner qua member and not in any other capacity. In an early decision under section 459 it seemed that this restriction was going to be transposed with full effect,[27] but it is clear now that the courts take a more flexible view of the requirement. The point is an important one, for under section 210 a very common form of minority oppression, namely expulsion of the minority from a position on the board, could not give rise to a remedy, for that was oppression *qua* director, not *qua* member.[28] It is now clear that, although the qua member restriction remains as part of section 459, it is much more flexibly interpreted, so that its practical significance is very much reduced. It is now accepted that the interests of a member, at least in a small company, may be affected by his or her expulsion from the board, whether because it was expected that the return on investment

---

[25] Under s.461. See below, p. 747.

[26] Stapledon (in (1993) 67 A.L.J. 575) argues that the court ought to authorise proceedings in the name of the company once the petitioner has shown that the company has an arguable case, unless the respondents can show it is not in the interests of the company that the litigation be brought (and he proposes an equivalent test where the petition seeks substantive corporate relief directly). This would turn s.459 into something like the Canadian statutory derivative action, where the court's discretion is the determining factor. See also p. 676, above, for the Law Commission's proposals to like effect.

[27] *Re A Company* [1983] Ch. 178.

[28] *Re Lundie Bros.* [1965] 1 W.L.R. 1051; *Re Westbourne Galleries* [1970] 3 All E.R. 374.

would take the form of directors' fees or because a board position, even in a non-executive role, may be necessary to monitor and protect the member's investment.[29]

The second restriction suggested by judicial interpretation of section 210, although perhaps less well established than the "qua member" requirement, was encapsulated by the definition of "oppression" by the House of Lords as conduct which was "burdensome, harsh *and wrongful*" (emphasis added).[30] This was the point which gave rise to the notion that the oppression section was aimed only at providing better remedies for existing wrongs, and it offered another reason for not regarding the expulsion of the minority from the board as oppress-ive: in most cases the removal was an exercise of the majority's statut-ory powers under section 303.[31] The Jenkins Committee recommended that the restriction, if it existed, should be removed,[32] and the courts, from an early stage, have interpreted the substitution of the words "unfairly prejudicial" as intended to achieve that result. "The concept of unfairness which was chosen by Parliament as the basis of the jurisdiction under section 459 in my judgment cuts across the distinc-tion between acts which do or do not infringe the rights attached to the shares by the constitution of the company."[33]

So by the middle of the 1980s the two judicial interpretations which had hobbled section 210 had been rejected by the courts in their application of section 459. These were crucial steps, without which the new section might well have been consigned to the limited place which its predecessor had occupied. They put the courts in a position to tackle the second of the tasks envisaged for the new remedy by the Jenkins Committee, that of dealing with reprehensible acts done "directly" to the minority by those in control.[34] However, they were only ground-clearing steps; they gave no clear indication of the nature of the judicial construction which was to be built in the space so cleared.

In modern law, giving courts the power by statute to control the exercise of discretion by persons or institutions on grounds of "unfairness" is hardly novel.[35] Yet such open-ended legislation,

---

[29] *Re A Company* [1986] BCLC 376; *Re Haden Bill Electrical Ltd* [1995] 2 BCLC 280.

[30] *Scottish Co-operative Wholesale Society Ltd v. Meyer* [1959] A.C. 324.

[31] Above, p. 188.

[32] *op. cit.*, para. 203.

[33] *Per* Hoffmann J. in *Re A Company (No. 8699 of 1985)* [1986] BCLC 382 at 387. This was the position at which the courts had arrived some years previously in the case of petitions to wind up the company. See *Ebrahimi v. Westbourne Galleries Ltd* [1973] A.C. 360, H.L., below, p. 749.

[34] *op. cit.*, paras. 203–206. In this respect it is important to note that petitions may be brought by those to whom shares have been transferred or transmitted by operation of law, for example, personal representatives, the weakness of whose position apart from the section was noted by the Jenkins Committee and has been referred to above, pp. 353–354.

[35] See, for example, the law relating to unfair dismissal of employees by employers, introduced in 1971 and now contained in the Employment Rights Act 1996.

which in effect involves a sharing of the legislative function between Parliament and the courts, always presents the courts with the challenge of how to develop on a case-by-case basis the criteria by which the imprecise concept of "fairness" can be given operational content. As we remarked above, the challenge was particularly acute for the courts in relation to the unfair prejudice remedy, for the tradition of the courts was not to interfere in the internal affairs of companies. It is to the issue of how that challenge has been met by the courts that we now turn.

LEGITIMATE EXPECTATIONS

The important step taken by the courts, as described in the previous section, can be characterised by saying that they recognised that section 459 protects expectations and not just rights. Borrowing from public law, it is sometimes said that the section protects the "legitimate expectations" of the petitioner.[36] Whatever the language used, the difficult issue is to distinguish those expectations of the petitioner which are to be classified as "legitimate" and so as deserving of legal recognition and protection, from those expectations which the petitioner may harbour as a matter of fact but which the courts will not protect. It is suggested that the decisions of the courts to date have succeeded in identifying one clear class of legitimate expectation and have hinted at a range of other situations where section 459 may be prayed in aid but without developing any of them in a comprehensive way. We shall begin with the clearly established category of legitimate expectation.

Informal arrangements among the members

This category of legitimate expectation has been described as follows: it "arises out of a fundamental understanding between the shareholders which formed the basis of their association but was not put into contractual form".[37] What this principle recognises is that the totality of the agreement or arrangement among the members of the company may not be captured in the articles of association. This may be so for a number of reasons, but predominantly, it is suggested, because of a desire to avoid transaction costs when establishing a company or when admitting a new person to membership of the company. It will be cheaper to adopt some standard, or only slightly modified, form of articles rather than to bargain out in detail and then incorporate into the articles a customised set of rules dealing with

---

[36] *Re Saul D. Harrison & Sons plc* [1995] 1 BCLC 14 at 19, *per* Hoffmann L.J.
[37] *ibid.*, at 19.

every aspect of the company's present and likely future method of operation, the future being in any case inherently unpredictable. This is especially likely to be the case for small "quasi-partnership" companies where the incorporators[38] know each other well and may have worked out a successful method of operation when trading in unincorporated form and whose translation into a formal document they would see as a needless expense.[39] When things eventually go wrong—and small companies emulate marriages in the frequency and bitterness of their breakdown—the articles may seem almost irrelevant to the petitioner's sense of grievance.

The range of expectations which may be protected in this way is open-ended, though the one most commonly protected is undoubtedly the petitioner's expectation that he or she would be involved in the management of the company through having a seat on the board.[40] It is important to grasp, however, that this category of legitimate expectation does depend on the factual demonstration that an informal agreement or arrangement did exist outside the articles and supplementing them with the expectation relied upon. The "starting point"[41] of the court's analysis will be the articles of association and "something more" will be required to move the court from the view that "it can safely be said that the basis of association is adequately and exhaustively laid down in the articles".[42] If that factual demonstration cannot be made, the petitioner's case will fail.[43] It follows from this that this category of protected expectations is almost wholly confined to small, even very small, companies. Beyond "quasi-partnership" companies it becomes increasingly difficult to demonstrate that all the members of the company were parties to the informal arrangement, and, if they were not, the court is unlikely to enforce it, on the grounds

---

[38] Though the legitimate expectation normally arises when the company is formed, it may arise at a later date, for example, when the petitioner becomes a member: *Tay Bok Choon v. Tahanson Sdn Bhd* [1987] 1 W.L.R. 413, P.C. Equally, a legitimate expectation based on informal agreement among all the members is most often recognised in a quasi-partnership company, but may arise in any small company, whether the company is to be operated as an incorporated partnership or not: *Re Elgindata Ltd* [1991] BCLC 959.

[39] The matter will be different in the case of a joint venture between two large companies. The joint venture may be small in terms of the number of its members but if its capital is large the legal costs of hammering out a comprehensive agreement may be only a very small fraction of that capital.

[40] So that s.459 may qualify, not only the formal articles, but also the statutory powers of the majority under s.303. In this respect the s.459 decisions reinforce the decision of the House of Lords in *Bushell v. Faith*, above, p. 189.

[41] *Re Saul D. Harrison*, above, n. 36 at 18.

[42] *Ebrahimi v. Westbourne Galleries Ltd*, above, n. 33, at 379.

[43] See *Re Saul D. Harrison*, above, n. 36, itself but also *Re Posgate and Denby (Agencies) Ltd* [1987] BCLC 8; *Re A Company* [1987] BCLC 562; *Re A Company* (1988) 4 BCC 80; *Re Ringtower Holdings plc* (1989) 5 BCC 82; *Currie v. Cowdenbeath Football Club Ltd* [1992] BCLC 1029; *Re J.E. Cade & Sons Ltd* [1992] BCLC 213; *Murray's Judicial Factor v. Thomas Murray & Sons (Ice Merchants) Ltd* [1993] BCLC 1437 at 1455.

that the non-involved members are entitled to rely on the registered constitution of the company.[44]

So the strict legal rights of the majority, deriving from the articles of association or the Companies Act, may be subject to "equitable considerations"[45] which channel and restrict the discretion which the majority would otherwise have, where it can be shown that the members came together on the basis that those legal rights should not be entirely freely exercisable. It is suggested that putting the proposition in this way enables us to explain both the vigour with which the courts have developed this aspect of unfair prejudice and the limited conceptual nature of the development. As we have already said, the difficulty for the courts, when they abandon illegality as the touchstone of unfairness, is that the choice of criteria for judging whether section 459 has been broken seems to be at large. The "informal arrangement" category of unfair prejudice provides a partial answer to this problem. The courts can claim to be, and indeed are, using as the criteria for judging unfairness the standards laid down, albeit informally, by the members themselves, and the judges can thus avoid the more challenging task of developing their own criteria. These considerations explain, it is suggested, the emphasis in the *Ebrahimi* case[46] that the equitable considerations do not flow simply from the nature of the company as a quasi-partnership but require "something more" in the shape of proof of the existence of an informal agreement concerning, say, the participation by the minority in the management of the company. As we have seen, this requirement has been fully absorbed into the case law under section 459. The company's formal constitution is the "starting point" for judicial analysis because "keeping promises and honouring agreements is probably the most important element of commercial fairness".[47] Informal qualifications and supplements to the written constitution must be proved to have been agreed. And even when they are proved, the "extended" agreement sets the boundaries of the courts' intervention. Thus, in *Re J.E. Cade and Son Ltd*[48] Warner J. denied the proposition that "where such equitable considerations arise from agreements or understandings between the shareholders dehors the constitution of the company, the court is free to superimpose on the rights, expectations and obligations springing from those agreements or understandings further rights and

---

[44] *Re Blue Arrow plc* [1987] BCLC 585; *Re Tottenham Hotspur plc* [1994] 1 BCLC 655. See also above, p. 117, for the operation of the same considerations in relation to the courts' interpretation of the articles of association.

[45] *Ebrahim's* case, above, n. 33.

[46] [1973] A.C. at 379. This was a winding-up case, but, as we shall see below at p. 749, similar considerations apply there too and the winding-up case law has strongly influenced the development of this category of unfair prejudice.

[47] *Re Saul D. Harrison*, above, n. 36, at 18.

[48] Above, n. 43.

obligations arising from its own concept of fairness. There can in my judgment be no such third tier of rights and obligations.''

In short, in this category of unfair prejudice petitions the court is still dealing with and enforcing the parties' agreements, formal and informal. The charge of unwarranted intervention by the courts in the internal affairs of companies can be easily rebutted, because it is the members' own standards which the courts are purporting to enforce.[49] On the other hand, because, at least in small companies, the articles systematically fail to capture the full agreement between the members, the development of this case law has brought company law into much greater touch with corporate reality and, as the amount of litigation shows, has addressed a previously unmet legal need.

Other categories of unfair prejudice

Although the case law is dominated by the informal arrangement category of unfair prejudice, the wording of the section in no way permits the courts to confine its scope to such cases. However, beyond informal arrangements or allegations that the controllers have committed breaches of their fiduciary duties, the issue of how to set the bounds of the courts' intervention arises in an acute way. Probably for this reason alone, no further, clearly defined categories of unfair prejudice can be found in the case law, though one can find a number of cases where allegations of unfair prejudice have been accepted outside the two categories mentioned above. An examination of these categories is of particular importance in assessing the significance of section 459 outside the small company field.

A feature of some of them is reasoning by analogy from established standards, that is, using the unfair prejudice provisions to extend established rules into adjacent areas where the provisions do not formally apply. Thus, in *Re A Company*[50] the judge used the provisions of the City Code on Takeovers and Mergers as guide to what section 459 required the directors of a target company should do by way of communication with their shareholders, even though the target was a private company and so outside the formal scope of the Code.[51] In *McGuinness v. Bremner plc*[52] the judge found a useful analogy in article 37 of the current version of Table A, even though the company in question had not adopted that version, when deciding whether delay on

---

[49] This is not to deny that the degree of proof which the court requires of the informal arrangement may vary according to whether the alleged arrangement is usual or unusual in the type of company in question.

[50] [1986] BCLC 382. See also *Re St Piran Ltd* [1981] 1 W.L.R. 1300.

[51] See below, p. 782. The Code was used only as a guide. In particular, the judge borrowed from the Code the proposition that any advice given by the directors should be given in the interests of the shareholders, but he did not borrow the further proposition that the directors were obliged to give the shareholders their view on the bid.

[52] [1988] BCLC 673.

the part of the directors in convening a meeting requisitioned by the petitioners was unfairly prejudicial. Again, such reasoning by analogy plays a useful role in defending the courts against the charge of unwarranted or inexpert interference.

However, an appropriate analogy will not be available in all cases. Then the court may have to face the task of developing its own criteria of fairness. For example, the company may have adopted a policy of paying only low dividends, although financially able to do better and even though the controllers have been able to obtain an income from the company by way of directors' fees. Is that unfairly prejudicial to the interests of the non-director shareholders, even in the absence of any informal understanding as to the level of dividend pay-outs? The courts have shown themselves willing to entertain such claims under section 459, but have not yet had to adjudicate on their merits.[53] The issue could be approached on the basis that the court undertakes the task of working out the appropriate distribution policy for the company (or for companies of a that type), which seems unlikely, or by asking the question whether the policy in question unfairly discriminated between the insiders with their directorships and the outsiders who were only shareholders.

Somewhat similar issues arise in relation to allegations of incompetence by directors falling short of breach of duty. Here, however, the courts have shied away from setting standards, except in obvious cases of serious mismanagement,[54] but if the arguments made in an earlier Chapter[55] about the changing standards of skill and care required of directors are correct, this approach may need reconsideration, if only because one would then be in the world of a wrong done to the company.

Prejudice and unfairness

In a number of cases the courts have stressed that the section requires prejudice to the minority which is unfair and not just prejudice *per se*. In some cases this is simply another way of putting the point that only legitimate expectations are protected by the section, not every factual expectation which the petitioner may entertain. Thus, a shareholder who needs the money may be prejudiced by the failure of the company to adopt a scheme for the return of capital to its shareholders, but it does not follow that there was anything unfair in

---

[53] *Re Sam Weller Ltd* [1990] Ch. 682, where the judge refused to strike out the claim. The case was largely concerned with the now irrelevant issue of whether the dividend policy affected all the shareholders equally: *cf. Re A Company, ex p. Glossop* [1988] 1 W.L.R. 1068.

[54] *Re Elgindata Ltd* [1991] BCLC 959, criticised by Stapledon in (1993) 14 Co. Law. 94; *Re Macro (Ipswich) Ltd* [1994] 2 BCLC 354; *Re Saul D. Harrison & Sons plc* [1995] 1 BCLC 14 at 31.

[55] Above, pp. 640–644.

the company's decision to retain the capital in the business, in the absence of a formal or informal understanding that the company's capital would be returned at a certain point in its life.[56]

In other and more interesting cases the petitioner appears to have a prima facie case for the protection of section 459, but his conduct means that he or she is not granted relief. There is no requirement that the petitioner come to the court with clean hands, but the petitioner's conduct might mean that the harm inflicted upon him was not unfair or that the relief granted should be restricted.[57] Again, the petitioners may have consented to, and even benefited from, the company being run in a way which would normally be regarded as unfairly prejudicial to their interests[58]; or they might have shown no interest in pursuing their legitimate interest in being involved in the company.[59]

The test of whether the prejudice was unfair is an objective one, but this means no more than that unfair prejudice may be established even if the controllers did not intend to harm the petitioners.[60] The question is whether the harm which the petitioner has suffered is something he or she is entitled to be protected from. It has been suggested that a fall in the value of the petitioners' shares is a touchstone of unfairness, but this seems to be incorrect. The exclusion of the petitioners' from the management of the company in breach of his legitimate expectation of involvement would not necessarily have any impact upon the value of the company's shares, whilst, on the other hand, those shares might fall in value as a result of a managerial misjudgement which was in no way unfair to the petitioner.[61]

REMEDIES

Section 461 gives the court a wide remedial discretion to "make such order as it thinks fit for giving relief in respect of the matters complained of".[62] In addition to this general grant, four specific powers are given to the court by section 461(2), of which undoubtedly the most commonly used is an order that the petitioners' shares be pur-

---

[56] *Re A Company* [1983] Ch. 178, as explained in *Re A Company* [1986] BCLC 382 at 387.

[57] *Re London School of Electronics* [1986] Ch. 211.

[58] *Jesner v. Jarrad Properties Ltd* [1993] BCLC 1032 (Inner House).

[59] *Re R.A. Noble & Sons (Clothing) Ltd* [1983] BCLC 273.

[60] *Re Bovey Hotel Ventures Ltd*, unreported, but this view is set out and approved at [1983] BCLC 290; *Re Saul D. Harrison & Sons plc*, above, n. 36 at 17.

[61] *Rutherford, Petitioner* [1994] BCC 876 at 879 and above.

[62] Equivalent provisions are to be found in s.27 of the Insolvency Act 1986, but that section includes an express power to make interim orders which in principle the court cannot do under s.461 (*Re A Company* [1987] BCLC 574; *cf. Ferguson v. MacLennan Salmon Co. Ltd* 1990 S.L.T. 658). On the other hand, there are certain restrictions on the courts' powers under s.27 which are designed to protect the operation of the Insolvency Act's mechanisms for rescuing the company: s.27(3). See pp. 830–832, below.

chased by the controllers or the company.[63] The reason for the popularity of this remedy, with both petitioners and the courts, is linked to the fact that, as we have seen, the notion of unfair prejudice is most firmly established in relation to quasi-partnership companies. Where business and, often, personal relations between quasi-partners have broken down, they are, as in a marriage, incapable of reconstitution by a court, for which the only issue upon which it can effectively operate is the terms of the separation. A share purchase order gives the petitioner an opportunity to exit from the company with the fair value of his or her investment, something which, in the absence of a court order, is often not available to the shareholder in a small company, because no potential purchasers of the shares are available or, even if they were, because of pre-emption rights[64] in the articles in favour of the other shareholders, *i.e.* the controllers.

The crucial question in this buy-out process is how is the court to assess the fairness of the price to be paid for the shares. Two important issues have emerged in the valuation process. The first is whether the petitioner's shareholding should be valued *pro rata* to the total value of the company or whether its value should be discounted on the basis that it is *ex hypothesi* a minority holding and so does not carry with it control of the company. In *Re Bird Precision Bellows Ltd*[65] it was established the principle was *pro rata* valuation because the buy-out had been forced upon the minority by the unlawful acts of the controllers. However, the court accepted that, if the petitioner's conduct had not been blameless,[66] the value of the shareholding might be discounted for its minority status. Further, if the petitioner had bought the shareholding at a price which reflected its minority status[67] or it had devolved upon him or her by operation of law, the full *pro rata* value might not be appropriate.

The court's powers of valuation will normally override any provisions of the company's articles on this matter, at least where they are less favourable to the minority. At one time it was thought that the minority could, in effect, be forced to use the share-purchase and associated valuation provisions in the articles, where they existed, on the grounds that an offer by the controllers to purchase on the basis set

---

[63] s.461(2)(d). In the latter case the company's share capital must be reduced. The statutory power is widely enough drawn to include an order that the minority purchase the majority's shares, which has occasionally been ordered: *Re Brenfield Squash Racquets Club Ltd* [1996] 2 BCLC 184. The other specific powers are the authorisation of proceedings to be brought in the company's name (s.461(2)(c) and above, p. 739); requiring the company to do or refrain from doing an act (s.461(2)(b)); and regulating the conduct of the company's affairs in the future (s.461(2)(a)). Whatever remedy is contemplated, the court must choose what is appropriate at the time it is granted: *Re A Company* [1992] BCC 542.

[64] Above, p. 305.

[65] [1984] Ch. 419 (Nourse J.), approved on appeal: [1986] Ch. 658.

[66] See *Re D.R. Chemicals* (1989) 5 BCC 37 and above, p. 747.

[67] *Re Elgindata Ltd* [1991] BCLC 959 at 1007.

out in the articles deprived their previous conduct of its quality of unfair prejudice.[68] Although motivated by a laudable desire to encourage the parties to settle their differences without coming to court, the approach suffered from the fact that the articles often did not guarantee the minority *pro rata* valuation. It now seems to have been abandoned although an open offer on a *pro rata* basis, which would give the petitioner all he could reasonably expect if the petition were successful, will make it an abuse of process for the petitioner to continue.[69]

The second issue concerns timing. The value put on shares, whether on a *pro rata* or on a discounted basis, will often crucially depend on when the value of the company is assessed. The courts have given themselves the widest discretion to choose the most appropriate date, which may be the date of the presentation of the petition but equally may be an earlier or later date. The court's choice will be influenced strongly be a desire to avoid the valuation reflecting the harm done to the company by the conduct of which the petitioner rightly complains.[70]

WINDING-UP ON THE JUST AND EQUITABLE GROUND

A company may be wound up compulsorily by the court on a petition presented to it by a contributory[71] if the court is of the opinion that it is just and equitable to do so. This provision, now contained in section 122(1)(g) of the Insolvency Act 1986, has a long pedigree in the law relating to companies, and the power can be traced back to the Joint Stock Companies Winding-up Act 1848. The provision was influenced by the (then uncodified) partnership law and was originally used

---

[68] *Re A Company, ex p. Kremer* [1989] BCLC 365.

[69] *Virdi v. Abbey Leisure Ltd* [1990] BCLC 342; *Re A Company, ex p. Holden* [1991] BCLC 597; *Re A Company* [1996] 2 BCLC 192.

[70] *Re O.C. (Transport) Services Ltd* [1984] BCLC 251; *Re London School of Electronics* [1986] Ch. 211; *Re Macro (Ipswich) Ltd* [1994] 2 BCLC 354 at 409–410. This can be achieved either by taking a valuation date before the conduct complained of had its effect on the company or by taking a more recent figure and trying to estimate what the value of the company would have been, had the unfair prejudice not occurred.

[71] s.124(1). Petitions may also be brought by creditors, directors or the company itself, though such applications are rare. The Secretary of State may petition under s.124A on the basis of information received as a result of an investigation into the company's affairs. See above, p. 703. The term "contributory" includes even a fully paid-up shareholder provided he or she has a tangible interest in the winding up, which is usually demonstrated by showing that the company has a surplus of assets over liabilities, though that will not be required if the petitioner's complaint is that the controllers failed to provide the financial information from which that assessment could be made: see *Re Rica Gold Washing Co.* (1879) 11 Ch.D. 36; *Re Bellador Silk Ltd* [1965] 1 All E.R. 667; *Re Othery Construction Ltd* [1966] 1 W.L.R. 69; *Re Expanded Plugs Ltd* [1966] 1 W.L.R. 514; *Re Chesterfield Catering Ltd* [1977] Ch. 373 at 380; *Re Land and Property Trust Co. plc* [1991] BCC 446 at 448; *Re Newman & Howard Ltd* [1962] Ch. 257; *Re Wessex Computer Stationers Ltd* [1992] BCLC 366; *Re A Company* [1995] BCC 705. The Jenkins Committee recommended (para. 503(h)) that any member should be entitled to petition, presumably on the grounds that this remedy was aimed primarily at protecting minorities rather than at winding up companies.

mainly in cases where the company was deadlocked. In the course of this century it has been moulded by the courts into a means of subjecting small private companies to equitable principles derived from partnership law when they were in reality incorporated partnerships. As we have seen, the apotheosis of this use of the section, the decision of the House of Lords in *Ebrahimi v. Westbourne Galleries Ltd*,[72] was highly influential in the courts' development of their powers under section 459. Despite its remarkable substantive development, the provision always suffered from a weakness at the remedial level: if the company was prospering, presenting a "just and equitable" petition was tantamount to killing the goose that might lay the golden egg. So long as the alternative remedy was hobbled by the restrictive wording and interpretation of section 210 of the Companies Act 1948, the winding-up petition was better than nothing. But, with the introduction of the unfair prejudice remedy, one may wonder what its appropriate role in the scheme of things now is.

Part of the answer to this question lies in purely tactical considerations on the part of the petitioner. A winding-up petition triggers section 127 of the Insolvency Act 1986, which requires the court's consent for any disposition of the company's property after the petition is presented. This ability to paralyse, or at least disrupt, the normal running of the company's business adds to the negotiating strength of the petitioner but is hardly legitimate if a section 459 petition could give him or her all that is required. Consequently, a Practice Direction[73] seeks to discourage the routine joining of winding-up petitions to unfair prejudice claims, unless a winding-up remedy is what is genuinely sought. The force behind the Practice Direction is provided by section 125(2) of the Insolvency Act 1986, to the effect that the court need not grant a winding-up order if it is of the opinion that some alternative remedy is available to the petitioners and that they have acted unreasonably in not pursuing it.[74] It would not seem an unreasonable use of this power for the courts to insist that, where a more flexible section 459 remedy is available, the petitioner should be confined to it. That would be a natural consequence of the fact that the statutory alternative to a winding-up order has finally come of age.

However, another part of the answer lies in the fact that the grounds for winding up seem to be wider than the grounds for an unfair prejudice petition, even after the importation into the latter of the reasoning

---

[72] Above, n. 33.
[73] Chancery 1/90, [1990] 1 W.L.R. 490. See *Re A Company* (No. 004415 of 1996), unreported, January 22, 1997, where the judge struck out the alternative petition for winding up on the just and equitable ground on the basis that there was no reasonable prospect that the trial judge would order a winding up as against a share purchase under s.461.
[74] The alternative remedy need not be a legal one. For example, it may be an offer to purchase the petitioner's shares on the same basis as the court would order on an unfair prejudice petition: *Virdi v. Abbey Leisure Ltd* [1990] BCLC 342.

in *Ebrahimi*. There are reported cases in which the court has denied a petition based on unfair prejudice, because of the conduct of the petitioner, but has granted a winding-up order on the grounds that mutual confidence among the quasi-partners had broken down.[75] In other words, the mere fact of breakdown is sufficient to ground a winding-up order,[76] whereas an unfair prejudice petition is seen as requiring some assessment of the comparative blameworthiness of petitioners and controllers. It is a somewhat odd result that, if a remedy is thought to be needed in this situation, the court is once again confined to the strait-jacket of winding-up.

CONCLUSION

The burden of the argument in the previous part of this Chapter has been to the effect that the statutory unfair prejudice remedy has achieved a substantial improvement in the position of minority shareholders, at least within small companies. The Law Commission's review,[77] whilst largely agreeing with that conclusion at the level of the substantive law, thought that the provisions could be criticised as having led to "costly, cumbersome litigation",[78] where the disputes were not settled out of court. This was because allegations of unfairness opened up a potentially wide-ranging historical investigation into the affairs of the company, during which many allegations and counter-allegations were canvassed, a process which was necessarily costly in terms of days in court.

The Law Commission therefore suggested three cumulative ways of attacking this defect. The first, about which it would be inappropriate to expand upon in this book, was more effective management by the court of the conduct of unfair prejudice petitions.[79] The second was the development for smaller companies of an additional unfair prejudice remedy which would cover only some of the ground of section 459 but would raise fewer issues of fact and so be cheaper to try.[80] The model put forward by the Law Commission for consultation

---

[75] *Re R.A. Noble (Clothing) Ltd*, above, n. 59, and *Jesner v. Jarrad Properties Ltd*, above, n. 58. See also *Re Full Cup International Trading Ltd* [1995] BCC 682, where the judge found himself in the presumably unusual position of being unable to fashion an appropriate remedy under s.461 but of being prepared to wind up the company.

[76] Though it should be noted that it is a requirement of a petitioner for a "just and equitable" winding-up order that he or she comes to the court with clean hands (*cf.* the position in relation to unfair prejudice petitions, above, p. 747), so that if the breakdown is wholly the result of the petitioner's conduct, relief will be denied: *Ebrahimi v. Westbourne Galleries Ltd* [1973] A.C. 360 at 387 *per* Lord Cross.

[77] Law Commission, *Shareholder Remedies*, Consultation Paper No. 142, 1996.

[78] para. 14.5.

[79] Chap. 17, here drawing heavily on the approach suggested in *Access to Justice, Final Report to the Lord Chancellor on the Civil Justice System in England and Wales*, 1996 ("the Woolf Report").

[80] Chap. 18.

would give the petitioner a right to be bought out on a non-discounted basis (but no other remedy) where the unfair act complained of was exclusion from management and there was an informal arrangement or agreement that the excluded person should participate (but no other unfairness could be remedied under the new procedure) and where the company was a private company with no more than five members and had been formed on the basis of personal relationship involving mutual confidence (*i.e.* where the company was a quasi-partnership). Although the new procedure would supplement, not replace, section 459, it would embrace the vast majority of cases where petitioners are successful under the present provisions. It must be wondered whether the effect of its introduction would be to entrench the view that the radicalism of the unfair prejudice remedy should be confined to small companies and that its operation outside this sphere should be exceptional.

Thirdly, and building on the attempts under the existing legislation to encourage disputing shareholders to use self-help provisions contained in the articles,[81] the Commission suggests the incorporation of additional regulations in Table A which would provide a "no-fault" exit route for dissatisfied shareholders or for the use of arbitration rather than the courts to resolve disputes or to provide an agreed basis for the valuation of shares.[82] Although this approach would work most effectively where a company adopted all three model articles, there is no proposal to give the new model regulations any different status from the rest of Table A,[83] so that no one company would be obliged to adopt any or all of them. Indeed, the first model article,[84] which would give to the shareholders to whom it applied a right to be bought out, possibly at any time, on the basis of an agreed valuation process, could have considerable financial implications for the company or the other members. Consequently, it is proposed that, even if the company's articles contained the exit right machinery, the right would not become effective unless it were attached by resolution to particular shares. In this case, therefore, a positive decision by the company would be needed to make the mechanism active; mere failure to exclude this regulation from the company's articles would not be sufficient to give any shareholder the right to be bought out. The likely level of take-up of this proposal is difficult to gauge.

---

[81] See p. 748, above.
[82] Chap. 19.
[83] On which see above, p. 107.
[84] Applying to private companies with fewer than 10 members.

Part Seven

COMPANIES IN TRAUMA

INTRODUCTION

THIS final Part is concerned with certain major operations which a company may wish, or be forced, to undergo but which the law regards as so fundamental as to require special procedures and a measure of independent supervision. The less traumatic of these operations, dealt with in Chapters 28 and 29, do not necessarily imply that the company is terminally ill; it, or at any rate its business, may well survive—though often under different control. In contrast, those operations referred to in Chapter 30 (administrations and liquidations) are undertaken, in the case of administrations, when major surgery is needed if the company is to have any hope of survival, or, in the case of liquidations, when there are good reasons for voluntary or involuntary euthanasia.

The discussion here of these matters is in outline only (each is a vast subject, demanding a volume to itself). Especially is this so in the case of Chapter 30 which deals with matters now recognised as insolvency law rather than company law and with the relevant statutory provisions in the Insolvency Act 1986 and not in the Companies Act 1985. They have, nevertheless, implications for company law, especially in relation to shareholder and creditor protection dealt with in Part Six—but, in contrast with that Part, with particular (but not exclusive) emphasis on creditor, rather than shareholder, protection.

CHAPTER 28

RECONSTRUCTIONS

ONE difficulty in dealing with the major operations with which this Chapter is concerned is the looseness of English legal terminology in this area. The operations are variously described as reductions, reconstructions, reorganisations, schemes of arrangement, amalgamations, mergers, de-mergers, buy-outs, etc. etc. But none of those expressions is a term of art with a clearly defined meaning distinguishing one such transaction from another. In general the expression "reconstruction", "reorganisation", or "scheme of arrangement" is employed when only one company is involved, the last of these terms being more commonly used when the rights of creditors are varied as well as those of the shareholders. Under an "amalgamation" or "merger" two or more companies are merged either by the acquisition of their undertakings and assets by one of them or by a newly incorporated company or, more commonly, by one such company acquiring a controlling shareholding in the others.[1] In English practice most mergers are achieved through takeovers, dealt with in Chapter 30. The Act contains various sections under which the above transactions may be carried out subject to prescribed safeguards which in the case of listed companies may be supplemented by Rules of the Stock Exchange.

1. REDUCTIONS OF CAPITAL

As we saw from Chapter 11, the Act imposes restraints on the extent to which a limited company with a share capital can reduce that capital. As a general principle it can do so only by a formal reduction of capital confirmed by the court in accordance with sections 135–141.[2] But today a private company will rarely need to resort to that procedure. The main situation in which such a company might wish to reduce capital is when it needs to buy out a retiring member of the company or to return to the personal representatives of a deceased member his share of the capital, but has insufficient profits available for dividend to enable it to do so except out of capital. As pointed out in Chapter 11,[3] when companies were empowered to purchase their own shares

---

[1] In contrast with the practice in the civil law countries of the E.C., mergers by transfers of undertakings and assets are unusual: here the normal *modus operandi* is by acquisitions of share capital and most commonly by an agreed or hostile takeover bid (hostile bids are at present virtually impracticable in most other E.C. countries).

[2] Part V, Chap. IV of the Act.

[3] At pp. 247–251, above.

special concessions were made to private companies to enable them to do so out of capital and without the need for a formal reduction.[4] However, in the case of public companies formal reductions may well be necessary or desirable especially in the light of the stricter rules regarding payment of dividends.[5]

Formal reductions are undertaken under Chapter IV of Part V of the Act. The company must be authorised by the articles to reduce capital. This presents no problems; in the unlikely event that the company is not so authorised, it merely has to alter its articles by a special resolution conferring that authority. It must then pass a special resolution to reduce its share capital and this it may resolve to do "in any way".[6] But the Act envisages that it will normally be either (a) by reducing or extinguishing the amount of any uncalled liability on its shares,[7] or (b) by cancelling any paid up share capital "which is lost or unrepresented by available assets",[8] or (c) by paying off any paid-up share capital which is in excess of the company's wants. So far as is necessary, it will alter its memorandum by reducing the amount of its share capital and of its shares accordingly.[9]

The company must then apply to the court for an order confirming the resolution.[10] The procedure varies according to whether existing creditors of the company will be affected. This they will be in cases (a) and (c). Then, and in any other case which involves a diminution of liability in respect of unpaid share capital or the payment to any shareholder of any paid up capital and in which the court, having regard to the special circumstances, so directs,[11] a somewhat complicated and expensive procedure, outlined in section 136(3)–(5),[12] may have to be followed to ensure that all creditors have been notified and given an opportunity to object. The difficulty of identifying every one of a fluctuating body of trade creditors is, however, generally avoided by satisfying the court that a sufficient sum has been deposited, or

---

[4] ss.171–177.
[5] See Chap. 12, above.
[6] s.135(1).
[7] In the unlikely event (see pp. 237–238, above) of its having uncalled capital.
[8] Technically share capital (a notional liability) cannot be "lost" (see Chap. 11, above) but may well be "unrepresented by available assets". However, this does not seem to have bothered the courts which have interpreted "lost" to mean that the value of the company's net assets has fallen below the amount of its capital (*i.e.* its issued share capital, and, if any, its share premium a/c and capital redemption reserve) and that this "loss" is likely to be permanent. If it is likely to be temporary only the court may nevertheless confirm the reduction but may require to company to set up an equivalent non-distributable reserve: see *Re Jupiter House Investments Ltd* [1985] 1 W.L.R. 975 (where that was required) and *Re Grosvenor Press plc* [1985] 1 W.L.R. 980 (where, as is more usual, it was not).
[9] s.135(2). No alteration of the memo will be needed if share premium a/c or capital redemption reserve only are being reduced because neither will be stated in the memo.
[10] s.136(1).
[11] s.136(2) and (6).
[12] And amplified by R.S.C., Ord. 102.

been guaranteed by a bank or insurance company, to meet the claims of all creditors.

The court, if satisfied that every existing creditor has consented or that his debt or claim has been discharged or secured, may then make an order confirming the reduction on such terms and conditions as it sees fit.[13] But if any creditor has been overlooked and was ignorant of the reduction proceedings and, after the reduction, was not paid and the company goes into insolvent liquidation, the court on the application of that creditor may order members, whose uncalled liability has been reduced, to contribute, as if it had not been, to the extent necessary to pay the creditor.[14] Section 138 contains provisions ensuring that the confirming order is duly registered at Companies House (it does not take effect until it is) and advertised. And section 139 provides that if the effect of the reduction is that the nominal amount of the allotted share capital of a public company is below the "authorised minimum",[15] the order shall not be registered unless the court otherwise directs or the company is first re-registered as a private company (the court may authorise it to be so re-registered without the need for a further special resolution). As a result of the foregoing provisions, existing creditors should be fully protected and future creditors not put at serious risk.[16]

The principal purposes of requiring confirmation by the court are (a) to ensure that the prescribed formalities have been strictly observed and (b) that the reduction treats the company's shareholders fairly. The courts have little difficulty with their role in relation to (a) and perform it with what may seem to be excessive strictness.[17] But in relation to (b), although they constantly affirm that their discretion to confirm will not be exercised unless the reduction is fair and equitable,[18] in practice they normally confirm

---

[13] s.137(1). It may also direct that the company shall for a specified period add to its name after "Ltd", or "plc", the words "and reduced" (s.137(2)) but in practice this is never done at the present day.

[14] s.140. Note also that any officer of the company who wilfully conceals the name of a creditor, or misrepresents the nature or amount of his debt, or is a privy to either, is guilty of an offence: s.141.

[15] See p. 243, above.

[16] The latter can obtain knowledge of the company's new capital structure from its documents registered at Companies House, and are not regarded as entitled to any similar protection: *Re Grosvenor Press plc*, n. 8, above.

[17] See, *e.g. Re Moorgate Mercantile Holdings* [1980] 1 W.L.R. 227 (Chap. 21 at pp. 587–589, above) and *Re Barry Artist Ltd* [1985] 1 W.L.R. 1305 (Chap. 8 at p. 176, above).

[18] As Lord President Cooper protested in the Court of Session in *Scottish Insurance Corp. v. Wilsons & Clyde Coal Company*, 1948 S.C. at 376: "Nothing could be clearer and more reassuring than those formulations of the duties of the court. Nothing could be more disappointing than the reported instances of their subsequent exercise. Examples abound of the refusal of the courts to entertain a plea that a scheme was not fair and equitable, but it is very hard to find in recent time any clear and instructive instance of the acceptance of such an objection."

provided that they are satisfied that the reduction treats the classes of shareholders in strict accordance with their rights, either as they formerly were or as varied in accordance with section 126(3) of the Act, which, as we have seen, demands stricter class consents for a variation if it is connected with a reduction of capital.[19] This, however, is not, as we have also seen,[20] an effective protection against what most people would regard as unfairness because of the narrow construction which the court have adopted in relation to what are class rights and their variation. Moreover, it seems to be clearly established that the courts still have a discretion to confirm a reduction which they regard as fair, even if it does not treat classes of shareholders in accordance with their rights, though in that event the onus of satisfying them that the reduction is fair will be on the applicant company.[21] Although it now seems unlikely that the courts would confirm a reduction so blatantly unfair as some of those in the past,[22] it is still difficult to find any English reported case in which confirmation has been refused on the sole ground that it was unfair.[23]

However, a reduction of capital is a very limited form of reconstruction and one which may, and often will, amount to no more than an adjustment of the amount of a company's capital to bring it into closer relationship with reality. While a reduction may have adverse consequences for shareholders, it cannot, on its own, do anything more fundamental. There are, however, other methods which can. One of them, which is not infrequently used in relation to private companies, is provided by what used to be section 287 of the Companies Act 1948 and is now sections 110 and 111 of the Insolvency Act 1986.

---

[19] Chap. 26 at pp. 717–727, above.

[20] Chap. 26 at pp. 723–726, above.

[21] *Carruth v. I.C.I. Ltd* [1937] A.C. 707, H.L.; *Re William Jones Ltd* [1969] 1 W.L.R. 146; *Re Holders Investment Trust* [1971] 1 W.L.R. 583.

[22] Such as that in *Re MacKenzie & Co.* [1916] 2 Ch. 450 where the effect of the special resolution, passed without the class consent of the preference shareholders, was to reduce the amount payable as their preferential dividend to the benefit of the ordinary shareholders!

[23] The nearest approaches are *Re Old Silkstone Collieries Ltd* [1954] Ch. 169 C.A., where confirmation was refused on the ground that the resolution did not treat the shareholders in accordance with their class rights but the C.A. went on to say that, even if it had, they would have regarded the reduction as unfair, and *Re Holders Investment Trust* (above, n. 21) where Megarry J. having held that the resolution of the class meeting was invalid as it had not been passed bona fide in the interests of the class (see Chap. 26 at pp. 715–716, above) accepted that he had a discretion, notwithstanding that, to confirm the reduction but refused to do so since he was satisfied that it was unfair. But the House of Lords still seems to cling to the belief that if shareholders are treated in accordance with their rights the reduction cannot be "unfair": *House of Fraser plc v. AGCE Investments Ltd* [1987] A.C. 387, H.L.Sc.

2. Reorganisation under Sections 110 and 111 of the Insolvency Act

Under this type of reorganisation the company concerned resolves first to go into voluntary liquidation[24] and secondly to authorise by a special resolution the liquidator to transfer the whole or any part of the company's business or property to another company[25] in consideration of shares or like interests in that company for distribution *in specie* among the members of the liquidating company. This procedure affords a relatively simple method of reconstructing a single company or of effecting a merger of its undertaking into that of another. In the former case, the other company will be incorporated with a capital structure different from that of the liquidating company and the liquidator will transfer its undertaking to the new company in consideration of an issue of its securities which will be distributed to the members of the liquidating company. A new company may also be formed when the procedure is adopted for the purposes of a merger of two or more existing companies. Alternatively, when the arrangement is essentially an agreed takeover by one existing company of another (or others) that existing company may buy the other's undertaking from its liquidator, paying for it by its securities which will be distributed *in specie* to the liquidating company's members.[26]

Use of this method has the advantage that confirmation by the court is not required.[27] But what it can achieve is somewhat limited. Creditors will be entitled to prove in the liquidation and the liquidator must ensure that their proved claims are met and cannot rely upon an indemnity given by the acquiring company.[28] And, although members' rights will be varied, since it is unlikely that rights under the securities of the other company will be identical with the members' former holdings, it is unsafe to make them seriously less attractive.[29] This is because section 111 provides that any member of the company who did not vote in favour of the special resolution may, within seven days

---

[24] Under the former s.287 it had to be a *members'* voluntary liquidation, *i.e.* one in which the directors have made a "declaration of solvency" declaring that all the company's debts will be paid in full within 12 months: see Chap. 30, below. It can now be employed also in a creditors' voluntary liquidation so long as it is sanctioned by the court or the liquidation committee (Insolvency Act, s.110(2)) but that sanction is unlikely to be given unless all creditors are paid in full.

[25] Whether or not the latter is a company within the meaning of the Companies Act: Insolvency Act, s.110(1).

[26] In practice, however, the existing company is much more likely to make a takeover bid to the shareholders of the other companies.

[27] Though the court's sanction may be needed if the company is to be woundup in a creditors' winding-up.

[28] *Pulsford v. Devenish* [1903] 2 Ch. 625. But the sale of the undertaking will be binding on the creditors who will not be able to follow the assets transferred to the transferee company: *Re City & County Investment Co.* (1879) 13 Ch.D. 475, C.A.

[29] *e.g* by replacing fully paid shares by those that are partly paid.

of its passing, serve a notice on the liquidator requiring him either to refrain from carrying the resolution into effect or to purchase his shares[30] at a price to be determined either by agreement or by arbitration.[31] It is normally essential if advantage is to be taken of stamp duty concessions that the membership of the old company and the new should be very largely the same. If a number of the members elect to be bought out[32] there is a grave risk that the reorganisation will have to be abandoned as prohibitively expensive.

3. SCHEMES OF ARRANGEMENT

More extreme types of reorganisation can be undertaken under sections 425–427A of the Companies Act 1985. Sections 425–427 replace the former sections 206–208 of the 1948 Act; section 427A (and Schedule 15B[33] which amplifies it) was inserted by the Companies (Mergers and Divisions) Regulations 1987[34] to implement the Third and Eighth Company Law Directives[35] on Mergers[36] and Scissions.[37] When it applies, considerably greater formalities and safeguards have to be observed than when sections 425–427 alone are relevant.

Section 425 describes the types of transactions to which it and the other sections apply as "compromises or arrangements between a company and its creditors or any class of them or its members or any class of them"[38] and "arrangement" is expressly stated to include a reorganisation of the company's share capital by the consolidation of shares of different classes or by the division of shares into shares of different classes or by both.[39] This, on the face of it, would suggest that it is wider in its scope than a reorganisation of type (2) only in

---

[30] This is an example, rare under U.K. law (but more widely used in some other common law jurisdictions) of protecting dissenting members by granting them "appraisal rights". The courts will not permit the company to deprive members of their appraisal rights under the section by purporting to act under powers in its memo. and arts. to sell its undertaking in consideration of securities of another company to be distributed *in specie*: *Bisgood v. Henderson's Transvaal Estates* [1908] 1 Ch. 743, C.A.

[31] If arbitration has to be resorted to, it has to be undertaken in accordance with the somewhat antiquated provisions of the Companies Clauses Consolidation Act 1845 (or, if the winding-up is in Scotland, under the corresponding Scottish Act of the same year). It is not a very satisfactory process because it involves determining what the member would have received on the hypothetical assumption that the liquidation had proceeded without any transfer of the undertaking.

[32] In the case of a widely held company there will, in addition, always be some shareholders who cannot be traced or who are too uninterested to do anything so that they too never become members of the new company.

[33] Originally numbered 15A but changed to 15B by the 1989 Act.

[34] S.I. 1987 No. 1991.

[35] See Chap. 4 at p. 55, above.

[36] Directive 78/885.

[37] Directive 82/89.

[38] s.425(1).

[39] s.425(6)(b).

that it can effect a compromise or arrangement with creditors and not merely with members. But that it is far wider is made clear by section 427 which deals specifically with compromises or arrangements under section 425 proposed for the purpose of or in connection with the reconstruction of any company or companies, or the amalgamation of two or more companies.[40] Indeed, the courts have construed "arrangement" as a word of very wide import[41] covering almost every type of legal transaction[42] so long as there is some element of give and take[43] and has the approval of the company (or companies) concerned, either through its board or through the members in general meeting.[44]

When the proposed scheme has been formulated, the first step is an application (normally *ex parte*) to the court by the company (or companies)[45] to which the compromise or arrangement relates for the court to order meetings, of the creditors or classes of creditors or members or classes of members, to be summoned.[46] This the court will generally do[47] and will give directions about the length of notice, the method of giving it and the forms of proxy. But it will not, at this stage, give directions or make any decisions on what is a class for this purpose. That is the responsibility of the applicants to determine—and it can be a difficult task, particularly so far as creditors are concerned. Apart from the obvious distinctions between secured debenture-holders, unsecured lenders and trade creditors, what precisely determines whether or not creditors are of the same "class"?[48] Nor is it necessarily simple even so far as members are concerned; for in this context "class" seems to mean something different from what it means elsewhere.[49] The consequences of failing to make a correct determination are serious; the court may refuse to sanction the scheme even though all the meetings have approved it by the requisite majority.

---

[40] s.427(2).

[41] *Re National Bank Ltd* [1966] 1 W.L.R. 819 at 829; *Re Calgary and Edmonton Land Co.* [1975] 1 W.L.R. 355 at 363; *Re Savoy Hotel Ltd* [1981] Ch. 351 at 359D–F.

[42] If it involves a reduction of capital, as if often will, this can be sanctioned without the need for separate proceedings under (1) above.

[43] *Re NFU Development Trust Ltd* [1972] 1 W.L.R. 1548 held that the court had no jurisdiction to sanction a scheme whereby all the members were required to relinquish their financial rights without any quid pro quo.

[44] *Re Savoy Hotel* above, n. 41, where in the course of the long-running battle to wrest control from the holders of a minority of the equity but a majority of the votes, a vain attempt was made to do so by seeking sanction for a scheme which neither the board nor a general meeting had approved.

[45] It can instead be made by any member or creditor (so long as the scheme has been approved by the company: see *Re Savoy Hotel* (above, nn. 41 and 44) but, if the company is in liquidation or an administrator has been appointed, it must be made by the liquidator or administrator.

[46] s.425(1).

[47] But, again, see *Re Savoy Hotel*, above, where the court refused to do so.

[48] The difficulty is particularly acute in the case of policyholders of an insurance company.

[49] *i.e.* in those discussed in Chap.13 and 26. Here, for example, if some shares of the same class are fully paid and others are not they will be separate "classes." And see *Re Hellenic Trust* [1976] 1 W.L.R. 132, below, n. 64.

Section 426[50] requires any notice sent out summoning the meetings to be accompanied by a statement explaining the effect of the compromise or arrangement and in particular stating any material interests of the directors (whether in their capacity of directors or otherwise) and the effect on those interests of the scheme in so far as that differs from the effect on the interests of others.[51] Where the scheme affects the rights of debenture-holders, the statement must give the like statement regarding the interests of any trustees for the debenture-holders.[52] If the notice is given by advertisement,[53] the advertisement must include the foregoing statements or a notification of where and how copies of the circular can be obtained[54] and on making application a member or creditor is entitled to be furnished with a copy free of charge.[55] If the scheme is approved at the meetings by a majority in number, representing three-fourths in value,[56] of its creditors and by members present and voting in person or by proxy, the scheme becomes binding on the company and all members and creditors (or all members of the class concerned) and, if the company is in liquidation, on the liquidator, so long as it is sanctioned by the court.[57] But its order sanctioning the scheme does not take effect until a copy is delivered to the Registrar and a copy of it has to be attached to every copy of the company's memorandum of association issued thereafter.[58]

The application for the court's approval is made by petition of the applicants and may be opposed by members and creditors who object to the scheme. In the oft-quoted words of Maugham J.,[59] the duties of the court are two-fold:

"The first is to see that the resolutions are passed by the statutory

[50] The corresponding earlier section (207) first appeared in the 1948 Act but long before that it was the invariable custom for the notices to be accompanied by a circular and the courts, before sanctioning, needed to be satisfied that it was full and fair and not in any way "tricky".

[51] s.426(1) & (2).

[52] s.426(4). If the interests of the directors or the trustees change before the meetings are held, the court will not sanction the scheme unless satisfied that no reasonable shareholder or debenture-holder would have altered his decision on how to vote if the changed position had been disclosed: *Re Jessel Trust Ltd* [1985] BCLC 119; *Re Minster Assets*, [1985] BCLC 200.

[53] Which will be the only way of notifying holders of share warrants to bearer or of bearer bonds. It may also be necessary to advertise for creditors.

[54] s.426(3).

[55] s.426(5). A default in complying with any requirement of the section renders the company and ever officer, liquidator, administrator, or trustee for debenture-holders liable to a fine unless he shows that the default was due to the refusal of another director or trustee for debenture-holders to supply the necessary particulars of his interest: s.426(6) & (7).

[56] In relation to creditors further difficulties may arise in valuing their claims and thus determining whether the majority does represent three-fourths in value. This is a problem met whenever this formula is employed in respect of creditors—as it is throughout the Insolvency Act.

[57] s.425(2). This will be so even if the scheme involves the commission of acts which would be unlawful on the company's part without the sanction of the court: *British and Commonwealth Holdings plc v. Barclays Bank plc* [1996] 1 W.L.R. 1, C.A.

[58] s.425(3). The latter requirement seems to be an unnecessarily cumbersome and unhelpful way of ensuring that subsequently issued copies of the memorandum reflect any changes of it made by the order.

[59] In *Re Dorman Long & Co.* [1934] Ch. 635.

majority in value and number ... at a meeting or meetings duly convened and held. The other duty is in the nature of a discretionary power[60] ... [W]hat I have to see is whether the proposal is such that an intelligent and honest man, a member of the class concerned and acting in respect of his interest, might reasonably approve."[61]

Its role, in other words, is very similar to that in the case of reductions of capital under (1) above. However, the courts tend to take their role more seriously and there is greater evidence of a reluctance to rely as heavily on the assumption that if creditors and members "are acting on sufficient information and with time to consider what they are about, and are acting honestly they are ... much better judges of what is to their commercial advantage than the court can be".[62] Nevertheless, when they are unhappy about a scheme there is the same tendency to try to find that there has been some flaw in the procedure rather than to exercise the discretionary power to refuse to sanction on the ground that the scheme is unfair. Although Lord Maugham (as Maugham J. had become) stressed in *Carruth v. I.C.I.*[63] that, in the exercise of the court's discretionary role, too much weight should not be placed on majority votes when it can be shown that "the majority of the class has voted, or may have voted, in the way it did because of its interests as shareholders of another class", the courts are likely to treat this as affecting the validity of the resulting resolutions[64] rather than to rely solely on their own independent judgment that the scheme is unfair.

An advantageous feature of a scheme of arrangement under section 425 is that when it involves the transfer of the whole or any part of the undertaking or property of one company (a "transferor company") to another (the "transferee company") the court may, by the order sanctioning the scheme or a subsequent order, make provision for the automatic transfer of the undertaking and of the property and liabilities[65] of any transferor company to the transferee company and for the

---

[60] *ibid.*, at 655.

[61] *ibid.*, at 657.

[62] *Per* Lindley L.J. in *Re English, Scottish & Australian Bank* [1893] 3 Ch. 385, C.A. at 409.

[63] [1937] A.C. 707, H.L. at 769.

[64] This they may do either by holding that the class had not voted bona fide in the interests of the class (as Megarry J. did in *Re Holders Investment Trust Ltd* [1976] 1 W.L.R. 583, on an unfair reduction of capital: see above) or, as Templeman J. did on a scheme of arrangement, by holding that proper meetings had not been convened and held because a wholly-owned subsidiary of the transferee company already holding 53 per cent of the shares to be acquired should not have been regarded as a member of the same class as the other shareholders and accordingly that the court had no jurisdiction to sanction: *Re Hellenic Trust Ltd* [1976] 1 W.L.R. 123. In both, the courts also declared that they would have declined to exercise a discretion to sanction; in the latter case on the interesting ground that although the scheme was eminently fair to shareholders generally it was not fair to compel those who did not want to, to sell their shares in circumstances where they could not have been compelled to do so under what is now section 429 (see Chap. 29 at pp. 807–809) had the transferee company made a takeover offer instead of proceeding by way of a scheme under s.425.

[65] As we have seen (Chap. 8 at p. 164, above), it was held in *Nokes v. Doncaster Amalgamated Collieries* [1940] A.C. 1014, H.L. that this did not permit the automatic transfer of contracts for personal services but this has, in effect, been reversed, at least in favour of employees, as

allotment or appropriation of the securities of the transferee company.[66] Furthermore, the order may provide for: the continuation of legal proceedings pending by or against any transferor company, the dissolution without winding-up of any transferor company, the provision to be made for any person who dissents from the scheme[67] and such other matters as are necessary to secure that the scheme is carried out.[68]

However, under the British practice, amalgamations and reconstructions are rarely carried out by means of transfers of undertakings even if section 425 is employed (rather than the more usual takeover bid) and, if the scheme can be carried out by means of transfer of shares rather than undertakings, that solution is likely to be adopted, especially if section 427A would otherwise apply. That section applies only if (a) the arrangement is proposed between a public company and its members or creditors, for the purposes of or in connection with a scheme for the reconstruction of any company or companies or their amalgamation; (b) the circumstances are as specified in one of three "Cases"; (c) the consideration envisaged for any transfers of undertakings is to be shares in the transferee company or companies receivable by the members of the transferor company or companies with or without a cash payment[69] and (d) the public company is not being wound up.[70] This provides considerable scope for framing the scheme in such a way that it will not have to comply with the considerably stricter requirements which are added to sections 425–427 when section 427A does apply.

The three "Cases" referred to in (b) are[71]:

Case 1. Where the undertaking, property and liabilities of the public company are to be transferred to another public company, other than one formed for the purpose of, or in connection with, the scheme.

Case 2. Where the undertakings, property and liabilities of each of two or more public companies, including the one in respect of which the arrangement is proposed, are to be transferred to a company (whether or not a public company) formed for the purpose of, or in connection with, the scheme.

Case 3. Where, under the scheme, the undertaking, property and liabilities of the public company are to be divided among, or trans-

---

a result of the Transfer of Undertakings (Protection of Employment) Regs. 1981 (S.I. 1981 No. 1794), as subsequently amended.

[66] s.427(1)–(3)(b). Thus obviating the need to incur the burden and expense of fomal transfers and conveyances.

[67] Thus enabling the court, if it sees fit, to protect the appraisal rights that the dissentients would have had if the scheme had been carried out under s.110, above. But not much use seems to have been made of this.

[68] s.427(3)(c)–(f).

[69] s.427A(1).

[70] s.427A(4).

[71] s.427A(2).

ferred to, two or more companies each of which is either a public company or a company formed for the purposes of, or in connection with, the scheme.[72]

If the scheme is one to which section 427A applies, sections 425–427 have effect subject to the provisions of section 427A and of the lengthy and detailed Schedule 15B.[73] Here it suffices to say that the major additional requirements[74] are:

1. Normally, a draft scheme has to be drawn up by the boards of all the companies concerned, a copy delivered to the Registrar and the latter has to publish a notice of its receipt in the *Gazette*. All this must be done at least one month before the meetings are held.[75]

2. What has to be stated in the board's circulars required by section 426 is considerably amplified.[76]

3. In addition, there generally have to be separate written reports on the scheme to the members of each company by an independent expert appointed by that company or, if the court approves, a single joint report to all companies by an independent expert appointed by all of them.[77] This requirement of an independent report is perhaps the most valuable of the additional requirements. It should help both the members and creditors and the courts in the exercise of their discretionary power to refuse their sanction.[78]

Finally, it should be noted that, when a scheme of arrangement is designed to effect a merger, the Panel and the Code on Takeovers and Mergers, described in the next Chapter, may have a role to play. The Panel's role, however, will then be ancillary to that of the court and will mainly be concerned to ensure that the documentation (as opposed to the timetable) complies with the Code's Rules and that the parties lodge their circulars with it. In such cases the court, as it were, performs the role of referee and the Panel that of linesman.

---

[72] *i.e.* that type of de-merger known on the continent as a "scission" and referred to in the Act as a "division".

[73] As renumbered, and amended in minor respects, by the 1989 Act.

[74] The details differ somewhat according to the "Case" within which the scheme falls, the main differences being between those within Case 1 or 2 (mergers) and Case 3 (divisions).

[75] Sched. 15B, para. 2.

[76] *ibid.*, para. 4.

[77] *ibid.*, para. 5. The matters to be dealt with in the report are specified in some detail. In some respects it resembles the report required (also as a result of E.C. Directives) when a public company makes an issue of shares paid-up otherwise than in cash: see Chap. 11 at pp. 240–241, above.

[78] As the Scottish courts would, it is believed, confirm from their experience of employing such aid. The English courts are likely to have the auditors' reports and, sometimes, an independent valuation of property but, in circumstances where s.427A does not apply, they are unlikely to have the help of anything comparable to the reports required by Sched. 15B.

4. VOLUNTARY ARRANGEMENTS UNDER PART I OF THE INSOLVENCY ACT

Schemes of arrangement under (3) are available to companies which are insolvent or teetering on the brink of it. But the Cork Committee[79] felt that something simpler and quicker was needed to enable such companies to avoid or escape from insolvent liquidation by making a composition with their creditors. They expressed the view that an arrangement on the lines that they proposed was "only likely to be used, first, where for some reason it is not appropriate to appoint an administrator and secondly where the scheme is a simple one involving a composition or moratorium or both for the general body of creditors which can be formulated and presented speedily." They were "convinced that the facility to promote such arrangements without the obligation to go to the court will prove of value to small companies ...".[80] Accordingly, Part I of the Insolvency Act 1986 provides such a facility, termed the Company Voluntary Arrangement (CVA).

In contrast with the other types of arrangements discussed in this Chapter, this type is primarily designed simply to enable a company to make an arrangement with its creditors. Essentially it relates to insolvency law and the statutory provisions are appropriately included in the Insolvency Act rather than the Companies Act.[81] Hence no attempt is made here to describe the procedure in detail. Only a few comments only need be made.

The first is that although the new type of voluntary arrangement is undoubtedly somewhat simpler than a scheme under section 425, it is not all that simple. The deceptively brief seven sections of Part I cannot be fully understood without reference to the detailed and lengthy Part 1 of the Insolvency Rules 1986.[82] If employed in an attempt to stave off liquidation or the appointment of an administrator, it will be successful only if the creditors by a similar majority to that under section 425 resolve to accept the proposed arrangement and, even if they do, it is all too likely to leave the company without adequate working capital (unless the members are prepared to put up more). If the creditors do not approve, it will merely have added a further step prior to liquidation or administration, and quite an expensive one since a qualified insolvency practitioner has

---

[79] 1982 Cmnd. 8558, paras. 400–430.

[80] Cmnd. 8558, para. 430. Their recommendations were an adaptation of those relating to individuals implemented in Part VIII of the I.A. 1986.

[81] The same seems less appropriate in relation to arrangements under s.110 of the Insolvency Act: see (2), above. There, as we have seen, the primary aim is to enable a solvent company to reorganise or to amalgamate with another and the fact that a voluntary liquidation is involved is purely incidental.

[82] 1986 S.I. No. 1925 (as amended).

to be engaged as the "nominee" who undertakes the tasks of reporting to the court on the board's proposals, of summoning the meetings, under the court's directions, and of implementing the arrangement if approved. Instead of often being a means of avoiding liquidation or administration, as the Cork Committee envisaged,[83] it seems likely to prove more valuable as an additional option available to a liquidator or administrator who may use it to effect an early settlement with the creditors,[84] leading possibly to the salvage of the company's business.

Although the Cork Committee described their recommended voluntary arrangement as one that could be achieved "without the obligation to go to the court", as enacted this is true only in the sense that, in contrast with section 425, the court does not have to confirm the voluntary arrangement; there is, however, always some court involvement and plenty of opportunities for others.[85] Unless the company is already in liquidation or under administration, a serious weakness is that, until approval of the arrangement, there is no moratorium on the rights of creditors to enforce their claims. After the board decides to seek a voluntary arrangement it will take weeks before the meetings are held to consider the proposals and during that time the company will be at risk of action by creditors that may scupper the proposals. Nor, even if the proposals are approved, will the voluntary arrangement deprive a secured creditor of his right to enforce his security or a preferred creditor of his right to be paid in priority to non-preferred creditors and to be treated as favourably as other preferred creditors unless, in either case, the creditor agrees.[86]

In response to criticisms of this sort, the Government proposed,[87] in 1995 to introduce (when legislative time could be made available) an additional form of voluntary arrangement which would be available only to small companies[88] which were not in administration or liquidation. The crucial and novel feature of this additional form of

---

[83] See above.
[84] In that case the liquidator or administrator himself will formulate the proposed arrangement and may act as the "nominee". He may then summon the meetings without reference to the court and undertake the implementation of the arrangement if the meetings approve it. But the Act and the Rules enable the court or the liquidator or administrator to appoint other qualify insolvency practitioners for the whole or part of the nominee's role.
[85] See Insolvency Act, ss.2, 3, 4(6), 5(3) & (4), 6, 7(3) & (5). In particular, even if the arrangement is approved by the requisite majority of members and creditors, it may be challenged in court on the ground that there has been some material inregularity in connection with the meetings or that it unfairly prejudices the interests of any creditor or member thus, in effect, extending s.459 in this case from members to creditors: *ibid.*, s.6.
[86] *ibid.*, s.4(3) and (4).
[87] See the Insolvency Service, *Revised Proposals for a New Company Voluntary Arrangement Procedure*, April 1995 and DTI, *Company Voluntary Arrangements*, Press Notice P/95/839, November 1995, putting forward a more limited set of proposals for legislation than that envisaged by the Insolvency Service.
[88] As defined in s.247.

voluntary arrangement is that it would involve a moratorium on the enforcement of debts which would be binding on all creditors, including secured creditors, thus, it is hoped, removing the prospect of inter-creditor competition to recover their debts whilst the company established whether a rescue package, entered into by the creditors as a whole, was feasible. Although the machinery for establishing this new CVA would be set in motion by the company's directors, who would remain in charge during the rescue attempt, the interests of the creditors during the process would be protected by a number of mechanisms. For example, only if a nominee certified to the court that there was a reasonable prospect of the CVA being successful would the court grant the application for a moratorium; the nominee would supervise the conduct of the directors during the moratorium; and if the nominee at any time became of the opinion that there was no longer a reasonable prospect of the CVA working out, he should withdraw his consent to act and thus bring it to an end. During the moratorium, creditors, including secured creditors, would not be able to enforce their security, but assets subject to fixed or crystallised floating charges would not be able to be disposed of without the consent of the charge-holder or of the court. Any rescue package adopted by the creditors, which would require a 75 per cent majority, could not affect the right of a secured creditor to enforce the security once the CVA came to an end, unless the creditor consented to the change. Even so, these proposals do not deal with all the criticisms made above. In particular, the process of obtaining a court order to establish the CVA would be sufficiently lengthy and public that the holder of a floating charge would probably learn what was afoot and might prevent the establishment of a CVA by appointing an administrative receiver.[89] At the time of writing it is unclear whether the Government intends to deal with this problem by also introducing a requirement that a floating charge-holder give the company five working days' notice of intention to appoint an administrative receiver, during which period a CVA could be set up instead. In general, it may be queried whether the proposals are sufficiently radical in swinging the balance of advantage away from protection of the existing rights of creditors and towards the continuation of companies as going concerns to make the CVA of substantially greater importance among the procedures for dealing with insolvent companies.[90]

---

[89] See p. 769, above.

[90] Contrast the rather more extensive powers of the administrator, which are dealt with in Chap. 30, pp. 817–833, below, though that procedure, too, is at risk of being stymied by the appointment of an administrative receiver.

OTHER METHODS

Finally, a further method of achieving a merger or a change of control[91] is by means of a takeover bid and this is, in fact, the most common method and the one of greatest interest. As such it deserves treatment in a Chapter to itself. But, before affording it one, it should, perhaps, be pointed out that occasionally a scheme of arrangement (method (3) above) may be invoked after a takeover bid has succeeded but not the extent that had been hoped: *e.g.* although control in the sense of 50 per cent plus of the voting rights has been secured, it has not resulted in the target company becoming a wholly owned subsidiary of the offeror company. In those circumstances the new controllers may seek to achieve that through a later scheme of arrangement.

[91] The latter can, of course, sometimes be achieved by an existing minority shareholder or a consortium of shareholders persuading a general meeting to exercise its power under s.303 of the Act to remove the present directors and to appoint nominees of the shareholder or consortium in their place. Also, the company's bankers in their capacity of secured creditors may enforce their security by appointing an administrative receiver (see Chap. 15, above) and thus obtain control, but that is not designed to reconstruct the company but to ensure that the bank has priority over other creditors in the company's expected insolvent liquidation.

CHAPTER 29

TAKEOVERS

As we saw in the previous Chapter, mergers or changes of control may be achieved by method (2)[1] or (3)[2] outlined in that Chapter but that by far the most common method is by a takeover bid. The growth of that phenomenon is one of the most conspicuous and controversial developments of the post-war years both in the United Kingdom and other common law countries and one in which the United Kingdom was a pioneer.[3]

The *modus operandi* differs fundamentally from those employed for mergers under methods described in Chapter 28 in that those require corporate action of the companies concerned usually by resolutions in general meetings of all of them. A takeover bid need not. Assuming that there are no restrictions in a company's constitution on the rights of its shareholders to sell their shares,[4] if an offer is made to any shareholder he is able to accept it if he thinks fit. If, as a result, a majority of the voting shares are acquired by the offeror, there will be a change of control of the company[5] and, if the offeror is another company[6] it will become the parent and holding company of the group consisting of the two companies—which we will here describe as the "offeror company" and the "target company".[7] Furthermore, if the price offered is to be satisfied, wholly or partly, in securities of the offeror company, there will be a merger of the offeror and target companies similar in effect to one undertaken under method (2) or (3) described in Chapter 28.

The fact that a takeover may need no corporate action by the target company[8] has made it difficult for takeovers to be adequately

---

[1] *i.e.* under s. 110 of the Insolvency Act: see pp. 761–763, above.

[2] *i.e.* under ss.425–427A of the Companies Act: see pp. 763–767, above.

[3] In the USA in the 1950s, takeovers, already common in the U.K., were rarely used to obtain control of another company, the popular method being a "proxy fight" with the incumbent board in an attempt to oust it. Now takeovers there are as common as they are in the U.K.— though still, probably, not regulated as effectively and, certainly, very differently.

[4] As there almost certainly will be in the case of private companies.

[5] The succesful offeror will be able to remove the former board (s.303) and install his own nominees.

[6] As it generally will be and as the following account assumes it is.

[7] The legislation and the Code on Takeovers and Mergers prefers "offeror" and "offeree" (a recipe for typing errors). If the offer is unwelcome, the target's board will describe the offeror as a "predator".

[8] It will, of course, require such action by the offeror company but so long as (a) that company does not have to increase its share capital, (b) that general authority to issue it has been conferred on the board, and (c) that the "Super Class I" requirements of the Stock Exchange's *Listing Rules* do not require approval by a general meeting, only the board of directors need

controlled by provisions in the Companies Act; and, indeed, provisions in that Act specifically directed to takeovers[9] are still sparse, consisting of sections 314–316 and sections 428–430F.[10] In fact, it could be said (with some exaggeration) that the Act deals with the "before" and the "after" but not with the bid itself. Thus, as we have seen above in Chapter 18,[11] the Act contains a mechanism whereby the management of a potential bid target may seek to ascertain who is building up a stake in the company, perhaps in order to launch an offer to the target's shareholders. And we shall see later on in this Chapter that, once the bid is over, the Act enables the new controller in some circumstances to mop up the shares of the minority who have unsuccessfully resisted the offer and, equally, enables the minority to insist on being bought out. The Act also regulates, though not very effectively, compensation payments to the departing management of the target, but otherwise the conduct of bids is at first sight remarkably free of regulation, and in the 1950s and 1960s bidders took full advantage of their freedom.[12] Alarmed by what was happening,[13] a City working party published in 1959 a modest set of "Queensberry Rules" entitled *Notes on Amalgamation of British Businesses*, which was followed in 1968 by a more elaborate *City Code on Takeovers and Mergers* and the establishment of a Panel[14] to administer and enforce it. It is this Code which has since constituted the main body of "legislation"[15] relating to takeovers, with the Companies Act[16] and the Financial Services Act,[17] and rules and regulations made thereunder, performing an accessory role.

The Code has now grown to a formidable size and to do justice to it demands a large volume.[18] Here all that can be attempted is a brief description of the Panel and the Code, and an indication of the application of the Code's Principles and Rules to each stage of a takeover.

---

be involved—and on a contested bid the directors may throw the company's money around without consulting their own shareholders.

[9] But it does contain provisions which are highly relevant, particularly those on disclosure of shareholdings and dealings (on which see Chap. 18, above) and those on financial assistance (on which see Chap. 11 at pp. 263, *et seq.*, above). The insider dealing provisions are also highly relevant (see Chap. 17).

[10] On them see pp. 805, *et seq.*, below.

[11] pp. 492, *et seq.*

[12] A. Johnston, *The City Take-over Code* (Oxford, 1980), Chapters 1–4.

[13] Which, in some cases, was horrendous, with rival bidders badgering each of the target's shareholders by night and day telephone calls offering him a special price because, so it was falsely alleged, only his holding was needed to bring that bidder's acceptances to over 50 per cent. In one case the result was that the bidder who eventually succeeded paid prices ranging from £2 to £15 per share.

[14] During the brief life of the "umbrella" Council for the Securities Industry (the CSI) the Panel became "an arm" of the CSI.

[15] Albeit neither primary nor secondary *statutory* legislation: see below.

[16] See above.

[17] See in particular its ss.47, 47A, 56, & 57.

[18] The "bible" is *Weinberg & Blank—Takeovers and Mergers* (5th ed., London, 1989).

The Panel

The membership of the Panel consists of a chairman, two deputy chairmen and three "non-representative" members (two of whom are industrialists), each nominated by the Governor of the Bank of England, and of representatives of the relevant professional or commercial associations and the Self-regulating Organisations (SROs) recognised under the Financial Services Act, and of the Stock Exchange. The day-to-day work is undertaken by an Executive, headed by a Director-General and three Deputy Directors-General. Most of its members[19] are recruited on secondment for two or three years from City institutions but the Deputy Directors-General have served for many years (and will be sorely missed when they decide to retire). The Panel itself normally meets only when there is an appeal to it by an involved party from a ruling given by the Executive on the application of the Code to a current bid (or where the Executive itself has referred a difficult point to the Panel) or where the Executive has instituted disciplinary proceedings for an alleged breach of the code, such proceedings being heard by the Panel rather than the Executive. In addition there is an Appeal Committee (headed by a Chairman who has held high judicial office) to which there can be resort by those disciplined for a breach of the Code (or in certain other specified circumstances) or if the Panel grants leave.

The Panel's role is that of a self-regulating body performing legislative, executive and judicial functions. Its status differs from that of the recognised SROs established under the Financial Services Act (or under the Companies Act in relation to auditors or the Insolvency Act in relation to insolvency practitioners) since it is wholly free from any outside surveillance by the DTI or Securities and Investment Board (SIB)[20] and is the only remaining relic of pure and unsupervised City self-regulation. As such it is something of an anomaly in the post "Big Bang" era and, despite the fact that it has performed its roles with conspicuous success (and to general, if not unanimous, approval), it is questionable whether it will be able for long to retain its present status. Indeed, it may well have to change as a result of the proposed E.C. Directive on Takeovers. The European Court of Justice insists upon Directives being implemented by Member States in such a way that their provisions are "legally enforceable"; rules which do not have the force of law may not be regarded as meeting that criterion. The Panel fears that any change in its status would destroy what it regards as its great merits—its ability to act speedily, informally, and flexibly and to waive or adjust its Rules to meet the needs of peculiar

---

[19] Including the Director-General.
[20] More or even than the Stock Exchange which, in its role of "competent authority", is subject to DTI surveillance and, in its role of a recognised investment exchange, to that of SIB also.

circumstances. These fears seem exaggerated; there is no reason why a statutory body should not act likewise so long as the statute is worded so as to permit it to do so.

A more real fear on the part of the Panel is that the requirements of European Community law will make it easier for those dissatisfied with its rulings to challenge them in the courts, and to do so in the course of the bid itself. The Panel has always set great store by its ability to give binding rulings on the meaning of the Code during the currency of even the most bitterly contested bids and thus to avoid the U.S. pattern of regular resort to the courts: the arbiters of the success or otherwise of the bid should be the shareholders of the target company and not the judges. Although the latest version of the proposed Thirteenth Company Law Directive attempts to take account of the United Kingdom's position by specifically permitting the supervisory authority for takeover bids, which each Member State must establish, to delegate its powers to other authorities, including "private bodies",[21] it is not clear that this is enough to solve all the problems of recourse to the courts during bids. The exact scope in this context of the principle of Community law, that rights intended to be created for individuals (including companies) by directives must be capable of effective enforcement in the national courts, remains uncertain.[22]

However, even without the advent of principles of Community law, the status of the Panel as a body wholly outside the purview of the courts has changed significantly in recent years—though in a manner which it has found wholly acceptable. It has been held[23] that the Panel is subject to judicial review but that the courts should be reluctant to nullify its decisions and should normally content themselves with a retrospective review in order to give guidance on how the Panel should proceed in future cases (*i.e.* the court should not normally intervene in the course of the bid), or to remedy any unfairness done in the exercise of the Panel's disciplinary functions.[24] Furthermore, the Panel

---

[21] Com. (95) 655 final, Art. 4(1).

[22] The competing arguments are displayed in the evidence to and the report of the House of Lords Select Committee on the European Communities, Session 1995–1996, 13th Report, *Takeover Bids*, H.L.100, July 1996.

[23] See *R. v. Takeover Panel, ex p. Datafin plc* [1987] Q.B. 815, C.A.; *R. v. Takeover Panel, ex p. Guinness plc* [1990] 1 Q.B. 146, C.A. See Cane, "Self Regulation and Judicial Review" [1987] C.J.Q. 324. The latter arose out of the battle between Guinness and the Argyll Group to take over Distillers to which reference has been made already: see in particular Chap. 22 at pp. 612–615, above. The C.A.'s judgments in both cases repay reading as admirable discussions of the nature of the Panel and its roles. See also in like vein *R. v. Takeover Panel, ex p. Fayed* [1992] BCC 524, C.A.

[24] In the *Guinness* case the Panel, while the takeover battle was being waged, had dismissed for lack of evidence Argyll's allegation that a concert party of Guinness and some of its supporters had brought Distillers' shares at a higher price than the bid resulting in a breach of Rule 11 of the Code. A year later the Panel reopened the matter as a result of evidence obtained by inspectors appointed by the DTI. Guinness sought judicial review, alleging unfair procedure by the Executive in connection with the renewed hearings. The court dismissed the complaint (as it had in *Datafin*) though it felt that the Executive had displayed some lack of sensitivity

is now designated as an authority with whom regulatory authorities under the Financial Services Act may exchange information and to which documents or information obtained under section 447 or 448 of the Companies Act[25] may be passed.[26] In the light of these developments[27] the Panel is now clearly recognised by the courts, the legislature and the Government as a public body performing public functions on behalf of the State.[28]

Linked to the Panel's status as a self-regulatory body is the question of what sanctions are available to enforce its decisions. Ever since the Panel was established, it has been debated how it could be given effective and appropriate sanctions which were under its own control.[29] The Panel itself may administer only private reprimand or public censure, which are not likely to be effective against those who do not share the Panel's view of what is proper conduct in this field. For more pressing measures it is dependent on the action of other regulatory authorities, such as the Department of Trade and Industry or the Stock Exchange. However, these bodies, even if willing to act, may not have appropriate sanctions at their disposal. Thus, the refusal, discontinuance or suspension of listing of a company by the Stock Exchange is certainly a powerful sanction, but it might be more painful to the innocent shareholders than to the guilty controllers of the company who have caused the company to break the Code. In one notorious case such action by the Exchange proved singularly ineffective, despite belated undertakings by the guilty party to behave in future.[30]

Recently, however, the Panel has been given clearer access to the sanctions available under the Financial Services Act in respect of those people who need the authorisation of the regulatory authorities to engage in investment business. It is likely that these sanctions can be deployed so as to put pressure not only on those, such as merchant banks, who advise the companies engaged in takeover battles, but also

---

and wisdom. The ultimate result of the renewed hearings by the Panel was that Guinness was ordered to pay Distillers' former shareholders additional sums to make up the price to what it would have been had the Rules been complied with.

[25] See Chap. 25 at p. 692, above.

[26] Financial Services (Disclosure of Information) (Designated Authorities No. 2) Order 1987 (S.I. 1987 No. 859).

[27] See also *R. v. Spens* [1991] 1 W.L.R. 624, C.A. where it was held that although the construction of documents is normally a question of fact for the jury, the Code "sufficiently resembles legislation as to be likewise regarded as demanding construction of its provisions by a judge": at 632 F.

[28] With the result, presumably, that individuals may be able to invoke the proposed Directive on Takeovers in suits against the Panel even if it is not fully implemented by U.K. legislation by the prescribed date. See Chap. 4 at pp. 54–55, above.

[29] Johnson, *The City Take-over Code*, pp. 53–54.

[30] Concerning St Piran Ltd see the Annual Reports of the Panel for 1981 and 1984. See also *Re St Piran Ltd* [1981] 1 W.L.R. 1300, C.A., where intervention by the Secretary of State was saved from futility only because a shareholder in the company was prepared to bring a petition for the winding-up of the company on the just and equitable ground. On suspension and discontinuance of listing, see pp. 414–416, above.

on the companies themselves and their directors to comply with the provisions of the Code. The scheme which has been put in place, however, takes considerable pains to give the Panel a veto over the use of these sanctions and to reduce the risk of legal challenges involving the Code arising in the courts. The scheme makes use of the amendment introduced in 1989 whereby the SIB may issue statements of principle with respect to the conduct of those engaged in investment business, which conduct may include compliance with "a code . . . issued by another person, as for the time being in force".[31] On January 19, 1995 the SIB endorsed the Takeover Code for the purposes of its Principle 3, relating to market conduct.

Although failure to comply with a SIB Principle (and any endorsed Code) does not give rise to actions for damages or render any transaction invalid,[32] such failure does open the way to two very significant types of action being taken by the regulatory authorities. First, disciplinary action may be taken against regulated persons, normally by the relevant SRO, which action includes a temporary or permanent ban on a person's working in investment business, whether as a principal or as an employee.[33] Secondly, and in practice likely to be more important, the SIB may exercise the powers of "intervention" set out in Chapter VI of Part I of the Act. In the expressive colloquialism of the industry the SIB may order authorised persons to "cold shoulder" (*i.e.* not to deal with) those who have broken the Code, even though those to whom the order is addressed are not themselves in breach.[34] In this way the reach of the sanctions under the FSA is considerably extended. However, to protect the primacy of the Panel in this field, disciplinary or intervention action may be taken by the SIB or a SRO only at the request of the Panel.[35] Finally, the role of the courts is maintained at a low level, not only by the exclusion of the damages remedy in all cases involving SIB Principles, but also by the express deletion of the power to apply to the court for an injunction from the list of possible disciplinary actions in the case of a breach of the takeover code.[36]

The Code

The Code, the current edition of which was published in December 1996, is now a substantial looseleaf volume of some 180 pages. In the same binders are the *Rules Governing Substantial Acquisitions of*

---

[31] Financial Services Act 1986, s.47A(1) and (2) and SIB, Financial Services (Statement of Principle) (Endorsement of Codes and Standards) Instrument 1995.
[32] s.47A(3).
[33] s.47A(4).
[34] s.64(1) (a).
[35] s.47A(5) (b) and SIB, n. 31, above, para. 5.
[36] *ibid.*, para. 6, disapplying what would otherwise be the power under section 61(1) of the FSA.

Shares (SARs) for which the Panel is also now responsible and which is closely related to the Code.

The Code consists of an informative Introduction, ten General Principles, definitions of shorthand expressions used in the Rules, the Rules and four Appendices. There are 38 Rules, most of which are divided into several sub-rules. Moreover, in most cases each Definition, Rule or sub-rule has Notes appended, many of which are prescriptive and not just explanatory. The same is true of the four Appendices.

The distinction between the General Principles and the Rules is explained in the Introduction. The Principles are essentially a codification of good standards of commercial behaviour applying in relation to all takeovers. Some of the Rules are examples of the application of those Principles; others are rules of procedure designed to govern specific types of takeover. Both the Principles and the Rules are to be interpreted so as to achieve their underlying purpose, observing their spirit as well as their letter, which the Panel may modify or relax if it considers that in particular circumstances it would operate unduly harshly or inappropriately.[37] When in doubt whether a proposed course of conduct is in accordance with the Code, parties and their advisers are encouraged to consult the Panel's Executive in advance.[38]

The scope of the Code is wide. It covers all types of mergers (including those effected by a scheme of arrangement and offers by a parent companies for shares in subsidiaries[39]) in which control[40] of a target company is to be obtained or consolidated,[41] and the target company is a public company (whether listed or unlisted) considered by the Panel to be resident in the United Kingdom, the Channel Islands or the Isle of Man.[42] It also applies when the target company is a private company, but only if, within the past 10 years:

(a) its equity capital has been listed on the Stock Exchange;

(b) dealings in its equity capital have been advertised on a regular basis for at least six months;

(c) its equity capital has been afforded facilities for dealings on the A.I.M. or other investment exchange; or

(d) it has filed a prospectus for the issue of its equity shares.[43]

---

[37] Introduction, para. 3(a).

[38] *ibid.*, para. 3(b).

[39] Though the Panel and the Code will then be constrained by the role played by the court and by ss.425–427A: see Chap. 28 at pp. 762–767, above.

[40] Which is defined as a holding shares carrying 30 per cent or more of the voting rights (*i.e.* voting rights attributable to the share capital which are currently exercisable at a general meeting: Definitions at p. C6) irrespective of whether that gives *de facto* control: *ibid.*, at p. C4. It normally does not apply to bids for non-voting, non-equity shares.

[41] Introduction, para. 4(*b*).

[42] *ibid.*, para. 4(*a*). However, it does not apply to Open-ended Investment Companies, which can now be created under the Open-ended Investment Companies (Investment Companies with Variable Capital) Regulations 1996 (S.I. 1996 No. 2827). Residence is normally tested by where the company was incorporated and has its head office and central administration.

[43] *ibid.*

Other private companies are left to the relevant provisions of the Financial Services Act and the rules and regulations made thereunder.

The basic objectives of the Code are to ensure that the shareholders of the target company are treated fairly and equally[44] and that the decision on the acceptability of the offer is made by the shareholders of the target company (and not, say, by its management). In this connection the shareholders must be given all the information they need in order to decide whether or not to accept the bid. But neither the Panel nor the Code is concerned with the merits of the bid, either in the sense of whether it is one that the shareholders should accept or of whether it is in the public interest that the merger should take place. The former is a question to be answered by the shareholders themselves and the latter by the Office of Fair Trading, the Monopolies and Mergers Commission and the DTI or the European Commission in relation to major "cross-border" mergers.[45]

The SARs

The first step taken by anyone minded to make a takeover bid for a company is likely to be to ensure that he has a sufficiently substantial shareholding in it to act as a launching pad. It is here that the *Rules Governing Substantial Acquisitions* (the SARs), rather than the Code, may be relevant.

The SARs were promulgated as a result of a "dawn raid" in 1980 in which brokers acting for two mining companies succeeded in obtaining in a few minutes a further 11 per cent of the shares of another such company (in which the two companies already held over 13 per cent) by announcing on the floor of the Exchange that they were buyers at a price which was 18 per cent above the current market price. This was regarded as unfair to shareholders since only the institutional ones were, in practice, able to take advantage of the offer.[46] Hence, an effort was made by the CSI (which published the SARs) and by the Stock Exchange (through instructions to its members), to ensure that nothing comparable occurred again. The result of the SARs (and of the statutory provisions now requiring disclosure of 3 per cent shareholdings[47]) is to reduce the possibility of surreptitious acquisitions and to ensure that any substantial acquisition of voting capital, except from a single shareholder, must be made either by a takeover

---

[44] And not, *e.g.*, as they were treated in the pre-Code cases mentioned in n. 13 at p. 773, above.

[45] Under Rule 12 it must be a condition of the offer that it lapses if it is referred to the national or European competition authorities and, except in relation to mandatory bids (below, p. 789), there is no obligation to revive the bid even if it is given clearance on competition grounds. The possibility of referral may depress the target company's share below the offer price and thus allow the offeror to acquire them cheaply.

[46] It also breached the spirit of the Code if it was intended as the first step in a takeover of control.

[47] See Chap. 18 at pp. 483 *et seq.*, above.

bid in accordance with the Code or by a tender offer under Rule 4 of the SARs.[48]

The SARs ensure that the tender offer is made in a way which will give all the shareholders time to take advice and to accept the offer if they want to, and to afford the company's board a breathing space to take stock of the position. The SARs do not apply if the offeror has announced a firm intention to make a bid for control; if it has, the Code applies. In practice a tender offer is unlikely to be made if it is intended soon to follow it by a full bid, for the effect of the advertised tender offer which, if it is to succeed, will need to be at a price above the current market one, will cause the latter to rise, at least for so long as the market thinks that a full bid may be in the offing.[49]

The SARs are appended to the Code and, since the demise of the CSI, the Panel is responsible for them.

The Code's Rules

In discussing the Code's Rules we start with the period prior to the actual making of the offer and deal with it rather more fully than with what occurs thereafter. This is because the former period is likely to face the directors with particularly intractable problems which raise interesting questions on the relationship between the self-regulating Code and general common law and equitable principles. The Code Rules which apply only to this period are those in its Section D (Rules 1–3) but there are Rules in other Sections that are relevant also.

Preparing to bid

Under Rule 1, the first approach to the target company must be to its board or its advisers. In practice, apart altogether from this Rule, the offeror would normally wish to make such an approach, principally in the hope that discussions will lead to the takeover proceeding as an agreed takeover which will be less expensive and more likely to succeed than a hostile one. The offeror may also hope thereby to obtain further financial information about the target.[50] On such an approach

---

[48] The type of tender offer required by the SARs resembles that described in Chap. 16 at p. 398, above, except that the offeror invites the shareholders to sell instead of to buy. It may be at a fixed price or subject to a maximum price. In the latter case, if the offer is over-subscribed, a "striking price" will be determined as described in Chap. 16: see SARs, Rule 4.

[49] This may suit an offeror buying as an investor or speculator but not one who is contemplating a full bid since it may mean that if that bid is to have any chance of success the price will have to be in excess of that paid on the tender offer.

[50] Although General Principle 2 and Rule 20 forbid the furnishing of information to some shareholders which is not available to all shareholders, both permit the furnishing of information in confidence by the target company to the offeror or vice versa. Under Rule 20.2 any information given to one offeror or potential offeror must on request be given to another even if the latter is less welcome. But some discrimination against the less-welcomed is permitted because it will have to specify precisely what information it wants and is not entitled, by asking in general terms, to receive all the information given to a favoured competitor: Rule

the identity of the ultimate offeror must be disclosed and the board is entitled to be satisfied that it will be in a position to implement an offer in full.

Rule 2.1 emphasises the need for absolute secrecy before any public announcement is made[51] and Rule 2.2 requires such an announcement to be made:

(a) when there is a firm intention to make an offer (that intention[52] not being subject to any pre-condition);
(b) immediately upon any acquisition being made by the offeror or those acting in concert with the offeror which triggers an obligation to make an offer under Rule 9,[53]
(c) when, after an approach to the target, it becomes the subject of rumour and speculation or there is an untoward movement in its share price[54];
(d) when the like occurs prior to the approach and there are reasonable grounds for concluding that it was due to the offeror's actions, whether through inadequate security, purchase of shares, or otherwise;
(e) when discussions are about to be extended beyond a very restricted number of people; or
(f) when, instead of the normal situation in which the initiative has been taken by a potential offeror, a shareholder (or shareholders) or the board of the target company is seeking a purchaser of its shares carrying 30 per cent or more of the voting rights and the company is the subject of rumour and speculation or an untoward movement has occurred in its share price or the range of potential purchasers is about to be increased beyond a very restricted number.[55]

Once an announcement is made[56] "the offer period" will begin[57] and with it the stricter rules regarding dealings in the shares of the parties.[58]

20.2, n. 1. See, however, Rules 20.2, n. 2 and 20.3, designed to counteract the head-start that those mounting a management buy-out will inevitably have over any other competing offeror. Such buy-outs give rise to particular difficulties throughout in view of the inevitable conflicts of interest.

[51] If it is not, insider dealing is almost inevitable. It frequently occurs.

[52] The offer itself will almost certainly be "conditional", *i.e.* on its acceptance by a stated proportion of the target's shareholders (normally 90 per cent or such lesser proportion exceeding 50 per cent as the offeror may elect to accept).

[53] See below, p. 789.

[54] A movement upward of 10 per cent or more is regarded as "untoward": Rule 2.2, Note.

[55] Of these, (f) did not appear in editions prior to that of 1990.

[56] The responsibility for an announcement will be that of the offeror prior to an approach to the target's board but thereafter the primary responsibility will normally be that of the target's board and the offeror must not attempt to prevent it from making an announcement or requesting the the Stock Exchange temporarily to suspend listing: Rule 2.3.

[57] See Definitions at C. 6.

[58] See Section E of the Code: below, pp. 788–789.

The board of the offeror will hope that there will be no need to make an announcement until it is possible to make a fuller and firmer announcement[59] under Rule 2.5. This must not be made unless the offeror has every reason to believe that it can and will be able to implement that offer.[60] The reason why the offeror will seek to avoid any earlier announcement is that once any announcement is made the target company will be "in play", as a result of which another bidder may emerge leading to a hotly contested and extremely expensive battle.[61] Hence the offeror will try to negotiate with the target's board so that the first announcement can be that under Rule 2.5 as an agreed takeover with, ideally, a "lock-out" agreement whereby the directors undertake to accept the offer in respect of their own holdings and not to encourage, or collaborate with, any other potential offeror. This, however, the target's directors are unlikely to agree to unless they are satisfied that a takeover by someone is unavoidable and that they have negotiated the best price that is reasonably obtainable. If not, they will seek a "white knight" that will offer better terms and will not agree to recommend the bid unless and until they have failed.

The duties of the target's board

In relation to the duties of the target's board at this stage the Code contains a number of relevant provisions. Under Rule 3.1 the board is required to obtain competent independent advice[62] on any offer and the substance of that advice must be made known to the shareholders.[63] Independent advice is regarded as of particular importance on a management buyout or an offer by controlling shareholders.[64] The directors should not recommend the acceptance of any offer unless the advice is that the offer is a fair one—and not necessarily even then. Nor need all the directors take the same view: if the board of the target "is split in its views of an offer, the directors who are in a minority should also publish their views" and "the Panel will normally require that

---

[59] This announcement (in contrast with that under Rule 2.2, (which may amount to no more than that talks are taking place which may lead to a bid: (see Rule 2.4)) bears much the same relationship to the full offer documents (which, if all goes well, will be posted shortly after) as does a mini-prospectus to a full prospectus on an issue of shares: see Chap. 16 at p. 414, above.

[60] The financial advisers to the offeror also bear responsibilities in this connection: Rule 2.5. In the report of inspectors appointed to investigate the Al Fayeds' takeover of House of Fraser (the owner of Harrods) the advisers were criticised for not having investigated the offeror's financial resources sufficiently thoroughly.

[61] The target's shareholders are likely to obtain the best price for their shares if there is a battle between rival bidders in which each, in the excitement of the fray, increases its offer with reckless abandon (and scant regard to the interests of *its* shareholders).

[62] Normally from a merchant bank not disqualified under Rule 3.3.

[63] A similar obligation applies to the board of the offeror when the offer is made in a "reverse takeover" (*i.e.* one in which the offeror may need to increase its issued voting equity share capital by more than 100 per cent: see n. 2 to Rule 3.2) or when the directors are faced with a conflict of interests: Rule 3.2.

[64] Rule 3.1, n. 1.

they be circulated by the [target] company".[65] If there are any lock-out arrangements such as those mentioned above, these will be referred to in the announcement under Rule 2.5, the notes to which caution that the word "agreement" should be used with the greatest care and not give the impression that persons have committed themselves (for example, to accept in respect of their own shares) when in fact they have not, and that references to commitments to accept must specify in what circumstances (if any) they will cease to be binding.[66]

In addition, General Principles 7 and 9 are relevant. The former says that after a bona fide offer has been communicated to the board of the target or the board has reason to believe that it is imminent, no action may be taken by the board without the approval of the company in general meeting which could result in the offer being frustrated or to shareholders being denied an opportunity to decide on its merits.[67] This makes it difficult for the existing controllers to erect any of the defences[68] against being ousted from control by an unwelcome takeover unless they have succeeded in doing so, well in advance of a threatened takeover.[69] General Principle 7 thus lays down a particularly strict rule. Unlike the common law relating to improper purposes,[70] the Principle requires shareholder approval for any action proposed by the directors of the target company which could have the result of preventing the shareholders of the target company from deciding on the merits of the bid. Whether the directors of the target had this purpose in mind or whether it was their predominant purpose in proposing the action in question is beside the point under the Principle. The Principle looks to consequences, not to purposes.

Rules 21 and 37.3 spell out some common situations where the approval of the shareholders will be required, for example, in relation to share issues; acquisition or, more likely, disposals of target com-

---

[65] Note 2 to Rule 25.1.

[66] Notes 1 and 3 to Rule 2.5.

[67] This, however, seems to be restricted to internal corporate action of the sort specified in Rule 21 and it is not regarded as breached by lobbying the OFT, the Monopolies and Mergers Commission, the European Commission or the DTI seeking to persuade them to take action which will lead to the offer lapsing as a result of Rule 12 below.

[68] Those most commonly employed in the U.K. are through non-voting or weighted voting equity share capital and service agreements which will entitle directors to "golden parachutes" if they are removed. In the USA a wider and ever-increasing number of defences (with picturesque names—"poison pills", "crown jewels", "PacMan", "shark repellent", etc., etc.,) are to be found. Attempts to employ them have given rise to much litigation.

[69] Note also Principle 8 which warns that "Rights of control must be exercised in good faith and the oppression of a minority [the Code has not caught up with the legislation's preference for 'unfairly prejudicial' as a substitute for 'oppression'] is wholly unacceptable": hence approval of the shareholders in general meeting (even if one can be convened in time) will not necessarily be effective. See also Code, Appendix 3 (Directors' Responsibilities and Conflicts of Interest).

[70] See pp. 605–608, above.

pany assets of a "material amount"[71]; entering into contracts other than in the ordinary course of business (which may include the declaration and payment of interim dividends); and the redemption or purchase of shares.[72] But Principle 7 covers any frustrating action, whether specifically mentioned in the Rules or not, and it has been held by the Panel to cover even the initiation of litigation on behalf of the target once an offer is imminent.[73] The overall effect of the Principle is to reduce the defensive tactics available to the management of the target company to three main categories: attempting to convince the shareholders that their future is better assured with the incumbent management than with the bidder, to persuade the competition authorities, at national or Community level,[74] that the bid ought to be referred on public interest grounds, and to encourage another bidder to come forward as a "white knight" and make an alternative offer to the shareholders. In all three situations the directors of the target are thrown back on their powers of persuasion; in all three cases the final decision on the success of these defensive moves rests with others. The inability of the management of the target company to block unwelcome takeover offers and, conversely, the wide freedom of offerors to make an offer over the heads of the incumbent management and against its wishes to the shareholders of the target (the so-called "hostile bid") is a distinctive and controversial feature of takeover regulation in the United Kingdom, which is not shared by the legal systems of other Member States of the European Community or even, to the same extent, of the United States.[75]

Principle 9 is also of particular importance. It declares that the directors of both the offeror and target companies:

"must always, in advising their shareholders act only in their capacity as directors and not have regard to their personal or family shareholdings or to their personal relationships with the company. It is the shareholders' interests taken as a whole, together with those of employees and creditors which should be considered . . . Directors of the [target] company should give careful consideration before they enter into any commitment . . . which would restrict their freedom to advise their shareholders in the future. Such com-

---

[71] On which see note 2 to Rule 21.

[72] Of course, the management of the target company may, and often do, promise as part of their defence to the bid to carry out one or more of these actions after their shareholders have rejected the offer.

[73] See Panel Statement 1989/7, *Consolidated Gold Fields* and Panel Statement 1989/20, *BAT Industries*, which explore the complications which arise when the litigation is initiated in a foreign jurisdiction by a partially owned subsidiary or when the "litigation" takes the form of enthusiastic participation in regulatory hearings.

[74] See n. 67, above.

[75] See n. 68, above and Davies, "Defensive Measures: The Anglo-American Approach" (now somewhat dated on the U.S. side) and Schaafsma, "Defensive Measures: The Continental Approach" both in Hopt and Wymeersch (eds.), *European Takeovers: Law and Practice* (London, 1992).

mitments may give rise to conflicts of interest or result in a breach of the directors' fiduciary duties.''

The overall result seems to be that although the Panel obviously dislikes lock-outs it does not actually ban them[76] but leaves their legality to be determined by the courts on the basis of general legal and equitable principles.[77] But what is the effect of those principles?

The common feature of the cases discussed below is that there were, actually or potentially, two competing bidders for the shares of the target company. The general body of the shareholders, if they were minded to accept any bid at all, may be assumed to wish to accept the higher offer. What are the duties of the directors in such a situation? Two somewhat different propositions have been discussed in the recent cases. The first, and bolder, is the proposition that directors of the target company are under a duty, at least in certain circumstances, to take positive steps, including steps in relation to their own shares, to ensure that their shareholders are able to accept the higher of two competing offers. In *Heron International Ltd v. Lord Grade*[78] there were two competing bids for a company whose directors held over 50 per cent of the shares and where, unusually for a public company, the consent of the directors was required for the transfer of shares. The directors had given irrevocable undertakings to accept what turned out to be the lower bid and stood by those undertakings, so that the higher bidder was defeated.

In the resulting litigation the Court of Appeal declared that:

"Where directors have decided that it is in the best interests of a company that the company should be taken over and there are two or more bidders the only duty of the directors, who have powers such as those in Article 29, is to obtain the best price. The directors should not commit themselves to transfer their own voting shares to a bidder unless they are satisfied that he is offering the best price reasonably available."[79]

This dictum clearly suggests that the directors' freedom to assent their own shares to the bidder favoured by them is restricted by their duty as directors to the other shareholders. In *Re A Company*,[80] where a similar issue arose in the context of a section 459 petition but involving this time a small private company, Hoffmann J., however, refused to accept "the proposition that the board must inevitably be under a positive duty to recommend and take all steps within their power to

---

[76] Indeed, it expressly recognises that: "Shareholders in companies which are effectively controlled by the directors must accept that in respect of any offer the attitude of their board will be decisive": Note 1 to Rule 25.1. And see Note 5 to Rule 4 which permits directors and financial advisers to deal in such securites contrary to the advice they have given to shareholders so long as they give public notice of their intentions and an explanation.

[77] Admirably summarised in General Principle 9, above.

[78] [1983] BCLC 244, C.A.

[79] At 265.

[80] [1986] BCLC 382.

facilitate whichever is the highest offer'', especially where that alleged duty restricted the directors' freedom of action in relation to their own shares. Their duty went no further than requiring them not to exercise their powers under the articles so as to prevent those other share-holders, who wished to do so, from accepting the higher offer, and requiring them, if they gave advice to the shareholders, to do so in the interests of those shareholders and not in order to further the bid pre-ferred by the directors. The view of Hoffmann J. seems more in accord with generally accepted principles and with the Code which, as we have seen, draws a distinction between advice to the shareholders, which is subject to fiduciary duties, and what the controllers decide to do with their own shareholdings.

In the above cases, the directors were faced with the question of what to do in the face of a competing bidder which had actually emerged. However, even where there is only one bid on the table or in prospect, the possibility of a competing bid may well be in the mind of the first bidder. The initial bidder may wish to secure from the directors of the target company a legally binding undertaking to recommend the bid to the shareholders of the target and not to encour-age or co-operate with any ''white knight'' which may emerge as a rival. Indeed, the initial bidder may not be willing to make a bid for the target unless such assurances are forthcoming. This situation has given rise to discussion of the second proposition, namely that dir-ectors may not effectively limit their discretion to act in whatever way seems to them at any given time to be in the best interests of the company, and so cannot give legally binding undertakings of the type sought by the initial bidder. If a subsequent bid emerges, it is said, the directors of the target must be free to co-operate with the second bidder and recommend its bid to the shareholders if that subsequently seems to them to be in the best interests of their shareholders.

It is true that the courts exhibit some reluctance to regard undertak-ings of this sort, given by the incumbent management, as intended by the parties to have contractual force. In *Dawson International plc v. Coats Paton plc*[81] Lord Prosser in the Outer House of the Court of Session held that the actions of the parties could be fully explained by their desire to act in accordance with the Code and that it was not necessary to attribute contractual effect to their undertakings and promises in order to give them binding force.[82] Consequently, an action by the initial bidder for damages for wasted expenditure, based on breach of contract, against the target company when the latter's directors did co-operate with and recommend a subsequent and higher

---

[81] [1991] BCC 278.
[82] ''Each party having these obligations under the code, it appears to me less necessary to search for a contract, as a basis and explanation for either the one party feeling obliged to do particu-lar things, or for the other party relying upon them being done.''

bid, failed. Although a remarkable example of deference by the courts to the regulatory primacy of the Code and the Panel in this area, the decision is based on no stronger a doctrinal foundation than the lack of intention of the parties to create contractual relations. As such, it would seem open to circumvention through the use of sufficiently explicit language on the part of the bidder and the directors of the target, making clear their determination indeed to establish contractual relations between themselves.

A more challenging attack on lock-out agreements can be based on the duty of directors not to fetter their discretion.[83] In *John Crowther Group Ltd v. Carpets International plc*[84] an offer for the shares of a wholly owned subsidiary of the defendant company[85] was conditional, under the Stock Exchange's rules, on the approval of the shareholders of the parent company, whose directors undertook "to use all reasonable endeavours" to secure the necessary consents. When a subsequent and higher bid emerged, the directors recommended that bid and, as in the *Coats Paton* case, were sued for breach of contract by the initial bidder. Vinelott J. held that "it must have been understood by all that if the undertaking was to use reasonable endeavours to procure the passing of the resolution it was necessarily subject to anything which the directors had to do in pursuance of their fiduciary duty", in particular the duty "to make full and honest disclosure to shareholders before they vote" on a resolution. Thus, the directors had not in fact broken the contract with the initial bidder.

It is rather unclear from the judgment of Vinelot J. whether he regarded the term allowing the directors to advise against the initial bid as one implied in fact, arising out of the factual matrix within which the parties contracted (in which case it would be open to the parties in a future case to exclude the implication by express words), or whether it was a necessary implication to save the contract from unenforceability. Without such an implied term, it might be said, such agreements would be unenforceable as having been concluded, to the knowledge of both sides, in breach of the directors' duty not to fetter their discretion.[86] However, as was pointed out above,[87] it is not always easy to distinguish an agreement in which the directors fetter their

---

[83] See pp. 608–610, above.

[84] [1990] BCLC 460, an interlocutory decision of Vinelott J. in which he followed the earlier decided but later reported decision of Templeman J. in *Rackham v. Peek Foods Ltd* [1990] BCLC 895.

[85] The offer was thus outside the terms of the City Code.

[86] cf. *Wilton Group plc v. Abrams* [1991] BCLC 315 and see the concession by counsel in interlocutory proceedings in the *Coats Paton* case: [1990] BCLC 560 at 563–564 (Inner House). Of course, not all elements of a typical lock-out agreement are in breach of the directors' duty not to fetter their discretion. For example, an agreement on the part of the target company not to seek a "white knight" might be unobjectionable, even if the directors could not refuse to co-operate with one which in fact emerged.

[87] At p. 609, above.

discretion from one in which they exercise it. Suppose the directors undertook in absolute terms to recommend a bid to their shareholders in an agreement with a company which was not otherwise willing to bid for the target, where the target was in desperate need of a merger and where the directors genuinely thought that there was no prospect of another bidder emerging.[88] In *Fulham Football Club v. Cabra Estates*[89] the Court of Appeal, responding to these sorts of arguments, took the view that, although the *Crowther* case might be right on its facts, it should not be regarded "as laying down a general proposition that directors can never bind themselves as to the future exercise of their fiduciary powers".

The upshot of the cases is to leave the law in a considerable state of confusion, especially as to how far the outcomes were contingent on the facts of the particular disputes or how far controlled by the operation of rules of law out of which the parties are not free to contract. Clarity could come either from a review of the whole area by the House of Lords or from the Panel making the Code more specific on the acceptability of lock-out agreements (or, of course, from both sources). In the meantime the only safe form of lock-out agreement seems to be one concluded with substantial shareholders who are not directors of the company.[90]

Dealings in shares

Section E of the Code imposes certain prohibitions on dealings in the securities of the companies concerned. Prior to the "offer period"[91] the main prohibition is that flowing from the insider dealing legislation[92] as a result of which anyone with knowledge of the possible takeover will be in possession of price-sensitive unpublished information. This, as we have seen, will not prevent the offeror from continuing to purchase shares of the target but will prevent the target company or any officers of either company from doing so on their own account.[93] However, the Code places restrictions, supplementing those of the SARs, on the extent to which the potential offeror, even before the offer period, may continue to increase its holdings of voting shares in the target. Under Rule 5.1, except as permitted by Rule 5.2,

[88] Apart from the form of the undertaking this hypothetical is not so far from the actual facts of the *Coats Paton* case.

[89] [1994] 1 BCLC 363, C.A. The case concerned an agreement made for a substantial consideration by the football company with a property developer whereby the former undertook to maintain a particular attitude towards planning proposals in relation to land owned by the development company but leased to the football company, from which agreement the football company subsequently wished to resile.

[90] *cf. Hasbro UK Ltd v. Harris* [1994] BCC 839.

[91] Which, as we have seen, starts when an announcement is made of a proposed or possible offer.

[92] See Chap. 17 at p. 472, above. Rule 4.1 of the Code reflects this.

[93] This puts the target company's directors at a temporary disadvantage in defending themselves against an unwelcome bid.

a person who, with others acting in concert with it,[94] holds shares which confer less than 30 per cent of the voting rights of a company may not acquire further voting shares if that would result in the holding of shares conferring 30 per cent or more of the votes.[95] Similarly, if between 30 per cent and 50 per cent is already held, no more than an additional 1 per cent of the voting rights may be acquired in any period of 12 months.[96] This, however, is subject to the exceptions in Rule 5.2 of which the most important are (i) an acquisition from a single shareholder if it is the only acquisition within any period of seven days,[97] and (ii) when the acquisitions are an agreed prelude to an agreed takeover offer.[98]

Once the "offer period"[99] starts and has not ended, the offeror and persons acting in concert with it must not sell any securities in the target company.[1] Moreover, during that period disclosure of dealings, additional to and stricter than that required by the Act, comes into operation.[2]

Mandatory bids

Hitherto we have assumed that the bid is a voluntary one, made by the offeror because it wants to. But it will sometimes have to make a general offer whether it wants to or not—and perhaps at a price higher than it would have contemplated offering. General Principle 10 provides that when control of a company is acquired by a person, or persons acting in concert, a general offer to all other shareholders is normally required and that a similar obligation may arise if existing control is further consolidated.[3] This Principle is spelt out in Rule 9,

---

[94] On concert parties see Chap. 18 at pp. 488–489, above.

[95] This bans acquisition of control unless Rule 5.2 applies.

[96] This restricts consolidation of control, again unless Rule 5.2 applies.

[97] Rule 5.2(a). But generally no further acquisitions may then be made (Rule 5.3) and the acquisition must be immediately notified to the Stock Exchange and the Panel (Rule 5.4).

[98] Rule 5.2(b), (c) and (d). As Note 2 to Rule 5.2 points out, an acquisition permitted by Rule 5.2 may result in an obligation to make an offer under Rule 9: see "mandatory offers", below. And presumably so might acquisitions covered by Rule 5.1 even if not permitted by Rule 5.2 unless the Panel chose instead to order the acquirer to dispose of the shares concerned.

[99] See Definitions, p. C.6.

[1] Doing so might well be a criminal offence under s.47(2) of the FSA, if the object was to rig the market by causing a fall in the quoted price of the target's shares, thus making the offer more attractive; or under the insider dealing legislation if information available to the offeror suggested that its offer would not succeed and it wanted to "make a profit or avoid a loss" by selling before the quoted market price fell back when the offer lapsed.

[2] In particular 1 per cent shareholdings (instead of 3 per cent) must be disclosed (Rule 8.3) and all dealings by the parties or their "associates" (as defined in Definitions at p. C.3) must be disclosed to the Panel and, generally, to the Stock Exchange (and, sometimes, to the Press) no later than noon on the business day following the transaction. Dealings in derivatives must also be disclosed: Note 2 to Rule 8.

[3] It adds that if an acquisition is contemplated as a result of which a person may incur such an obligation, he must, before making such an acquisition, ensure that he can and will be able to continue to implement such an offer.

which also ensures that General Principle 1 (that all shareholders of the same class of a target company must be treated similarly by an offeror) is observed in relation to the general offer.

Under Rule 9.1 when:

(a) any person acquires shares which (with any shares held or acquired by any persons acting in concert with him) carry 30 per cent or more of the voting rights of a company; or

(b) any person who, with persons acting in concert with him, already holds not less than 30 per cent but not more than 50 per cent of the voting rights and who, alone or with persons acting in concert with him, acquires in any period of 12 months additional shares carrying more than 1 per cent of the voting rights,[4] then,

unless the Panel otherwise consents, such person must extend offers on the basis set out in Rules 9.3–9.5 to the holders of any class of equity share capital *whether voting or non-voting* and also to the holders of any class of *voting non-equity in which any member of the concert party holds shares*. Offers for the different classes of equity share capital must be comparable[5] and the Panel should be consulted in advance.

The effect of this is that, once acquisitions have secured "control" (circumstance (a)) or substantial acquisitions have been made to consolidate control (circumstance (b)) a general offer must be made, thus giving shareholders an opportunity of quitting the company and sharing in the price paid for the control or its consolidation. Generally the terms of the offer will have to be the same as those which the offeror would have to include if it made a voluntary bid. But in some respects the requirements are stricter. A mandatory bid must not contain any conditions other than that it is dependent on acceptance being such as to result in the bidder holding 50 per cent of the voting rights[6]; on a

---

[4] The wording of (a) and (b) is very similar to that of Rule 5.1, above, restricting acquisitions. The differences are (i) that Rule 5.1 applies to acquisitions of shares or rights to shares, whereas, in general, Rule 9.1 applies only to acquisitions of shares (but see Note 13 to Rule 9.1) and (ii) that Rule 5.1 is subject to specified exceptions in Rule 5.2 whereas Rule 9.1 is subject only to a blanket "except with the consent of the Panel". A Note on such "dispensations" is appended at the end of Rule 9.

[5] For the meaning of "comparable" see Note 1 to Rule 14.1 applicable to all offers, whether voluntary or mandatory. In relation to non-voting equity (in which a bidder may not be interested unless it wants to ensure that the target company will become its wholly owned subsidiary) the ratio between the offer values of voting and non-voting must normally be based on the average of the respective mid-market prices over the course of the six months preceding the offer period. This should prevent the non-voting being unduly penalised by the widening of the difference between the market prices for the two classes once there are rumours of a takeover.

[6] Rule 9.3. But, when the offer comes within the provisions for a possible reference to the Monopolies and Mergers Commission or the European Commission, it must be a condition of the offer that it will lapse if that occurs. But, in contrast with voluntary offers (Rule 12),

voluntary offer, there may well be further conditions.[7] Furthermore, a mandatory offer must be a cash offer, or with a cash alternative, in respect of each class of shares and at the highest price paid by the offeror or a member of his concert party within the past 12 months[8]; on a voluntary offer this is so only if shares were purchased for cash and carried 10 per cent or more of the voting rights of that class, or if the Panel considers that it is necessary in order to give effect to General Principle 1.[9]

Where directors of the target company (or their close relatives and family trusts) sell shares to a purchaser as a result of which the purchaser is required by Rule 9 to make a mandatory offer, the directors must ensure that, as a condition of the sale, the purchaser undertakes to fulfil its obligations under Rule 9 and, except with the consent of the Panel, the directors must not resign from the board until the closing date of the offer or the date when it becomes wholly unconditional, whichever is the later.[10] Nor, except with the consent of the Panel, may a nominee of the offeror be appointed to the board of the target company or exercise the votes attached to any shares it holds in the target company until the formal offer document has been posted.[11]

Section P of the Code (Rule 37) is also relevant. It will be appreciated that, if the target company redeems or purchases its own voting shares, the effect will be to increase the percentage of voting rights carried by the shareholdings of the directors and persons acting in concert with them if their shares are not among those redeemed or purchased. Under Rule 37.1 this will be treated as an acquisition by them and, if their holdings are substantial, may give rise to an obligation to make a mandatory bid. The Panel will normally waive that obligation, but only if there is a vote of the independent shareholders and the procedure set out in the Code's Appendix 1 (the "whitewash" guidance note) is followed.[12] If, however, the board of the target company has reason to believe that an offer may be imminent, from then on and during the course of a takeover, no redemption or purchase of

---

it *must* be revived if the merger is allowed and, if it is prohibited, the Panel may require the offeror to reduce its holdings to below 30 per cent: Rule 9.4, Note 1.

[7] *e.g.* on a share for share offer that it is conditional on the passing of a resolution by members of the offeror to increase its issued capital.

[8] Rule 9.5. Unless the Panel agrees to an adjusted price in a particular case: see Rule 9.5, Note 3.

[9] Rule 11.1. Then, too, the Panel has a discretion to agree an adjusted price: Rule 11.2.

[10] Rule 9.6. On "closing dates" see Rule 31, below at pp. 800–802.

[11] Rule 9.7. It may seem surprising that this is permissible earlier than under Rule 9.6 but it must be remembered that the obligation to make a mandatory offer cannot arise unless the offeror already holds at least 15 per cent of the votes and it might be unfair to disenfranchise the offeror once it has complied with its obligations to make a general offer.

[12] For the procedure, which is detailed and stringent, see the Appendix. It also applies if the Panel is to be asked to waive an obligation to make a mandatory offer resulting from an issue of new securities as consideration for an acquisition or a cash injection, or in fulfilment of an obligation to underwrite the issue of new securities.

its own shares[13] may take place without the approval of the members in general meeting.[14]

The mandatory bid rule is a very strong expression of the Code's principle that all shareholders in the target company must be treated equally upon a change of control. Underlying the principle is the view that the prospects of minority shareholders in a company depend crucially upon how the controllers of the company exercise their powers and that the provisions of company law proper, even after the enactment of the new "unfair prejudice" provisions of the Companies Act,[15] are not capable of protecting minority shareholders against unfair treatment, at least not in all cases. Consequently, when there is a change of control of a company, all the shareholders should be given an opportunity to leave the company and to do so on the same terms as have been obtained by those who have sold the shares which constitute the new controlling block. The availability of this opportunity should not be dependent on the new controller wishing to make a general offer for the shares of the target, but is to made available by the Code on a compulsory basis in all cases of change of control by acquisition of shares.[16]

It should be noted that there are two aspects of the Rule under discussion. The first is the opportunity for all shareholders to exit the company upon a change of control by selling their shares to the new controller, and the second is the opportunity to do so on the same terms as have obtained by those who sold to the holder of the 30 per cent block. Of these two aspects it is the second which is the more controversial. In particular, the latter aspect of the Rule makes it impossible for the holder of an existing controlling block of shares to obtain any premium for control upon the sale of the shares. Since the purchaser of the block will know that the Code requires it to offer the same price to all shareholders, the purchaser is forced to divide the consideration for the company's securities rateably among all the shareholders.[17] In the United Kingdom, where shareholdings in listed companies are widely dispersed, this is probably not an important issue, but in countries where family shareholdings in even listed companies are of significant size, the Rule might operate as a disincentive

---

[13] An obvious defence ploy in the case of a hostile bid. See p. 784, above.

[14] Rule 37.3.

[15] Above, Chap. 27.

[16] Of course, 30 per cent is only a rough approximation of the point at which a change of *de facto* control of a company occurs. In the early versions of the Code the figure was set at 40 per cent, but it was reduced to 30 per cent in 1974. However, a precise percentage makes the Rule easier to operate than would a case-by-case examination of whether a particular shareholder had acquired sufficient shares in a particular company to enable it to control that company.

[17] Rule 16 (see p. 794, below) prevents the offeror from circumventing this rule by attaching non-pecuniary advantages to the offer made to some shareholders which are not available to all shareholders.

to transfers of control out of the family. Unable to obtain a premium for control, the existing controllers may simply prefer not to sell.[18]

Terms of offers

Section G of the Code contains four Rules (10–13), relating to voluntary offers, on matters which, in relation to mandatory offers, are dealt with in Rule 9. Rule 10 prescribes that it must be a condition of any offer for voting equity share capital which, if accepted in full, would result in the offeror holding over 50 per cent of the voting rights of the target company, that it will not be declared unconditional as to acceptances unless the offeror has acquired or agreed to acquire (either pursuant to the offer or otherwise) 50 per cent of the voting rights attributable to (a) the equity share capital alone and (b) the equity share capital and the non-equity share capital combined.[19] It does not specifically state that this may be waived by the Panel but Note 1 makes it clear that, in exceptional circumstances, the Panel may be prepared to do so.

Rule 11, dealing with when a cash offer is required, has already been summarised when dealing with mandatory bids.[20] Rule 12 provides that where an offer (a) comes within the statutory provisions for possible reference to the Monopolies and Mergers Commission or (b) would give rise to a concentration with a Community dimension within the scope of the E.C. Regulation[21] it must be a term of the offer that it will lapse if there is a reference under (a) or proceedings by the European Commission under (b) before the first closing date of the offer or before it is declared unconditional whichever is the later. As we have seen, by virtue of Rule 9.4, this applies equally to mandatory offers. Rule 12(c) also provides that, except in the case of mandatory offers, the offeror may make the offer conditional upon a decision that there shall be no such references or proceedings or upon that decision being on terms satisfactory to the offeror. When the offer lapses as a result of (a) or (b) the Panel will normally consent to a new offer being made once the merger has been allowed to go forward, without having to wait the normal period of 12 months.[22]

---

[18] In this context it is interesting that the most recent version of the proposed E.C. Directive on takeover bids (see p. 775, n. 21, above), whilst requiring a bid where a person acquires one-third of the voting rights, does not specify the level at which the mandatory bid must be made. The freedom to offer a lower price than that obtained by the holder of the controlling block does much to remove the sting of the mandatory bid rule, whilst also, of course, considerably qualifying the principle of equal treatment of shareholders.

[19] *cf.* Rule 9.3.

[20] See p. 791, above.

[21] 4064/89: and see p. 779, n. 45, above. Rule 12 does not cause offers to lapse if they have to be conditional on approval of the takeover by foreign regulatory agencies (*e.g.* Federal or State agencies in the USA). These agencies may take a considerable time to reach a decision, thus playing havoc with the time-limits prescribed by the Code and forcing the Panel to grant extensions.

[22] See Rule 35.1 (below) and Note (a)(iii) thereto.

Rule 13 provides that an offer must not be subject to conditions which depend solely on subjective judgments by the directors of the offeror or the fulfilment of which is in their hands.[23]

Section H of the Code (Rules 14–18) relates to terms of offers whether voluntary or mandatory. Under Rule 14, when an offer is made for more than one class of shares, separate offers must be made for each class,[24] and when the target company has more than one class of equity share capital a "comparable" offer[25] must be made for each, whether it carries voting rights or not. The offer for non-voting equity should not be made conditional upon any particular level of acceptance unless the offer for the voting equity shares is conditional upon acceptance of the offer for the non-voting equity.[26] Classes of non-equity need not be the subject of an offer except on a mandatory bid under Rule 9 or when Rule 15 applies.[27] The latter Rule requires that on an offer for equity share capital an appropriate offer or proposal must be made to holders of securities convertible into equity shares.[28]

Except with the consent of the Panel, the offeror may not make any special arrangements, either during an offer or when one is reasonably in contemplation, whereby favourable conditions are offered to some shareholders which are not extended to all of them.[29]

Partial offers

Under the Code's Section O (Rule 36) the Panel's consent is needed for partial offers.[30] Consent will normally be given if the offer could not result in the offeror holding 30 per cent or more of the voting rights of the target company.[31] If it could result in the offeror holding more than 30 per cent but less than 100 per cent, consent will not normally be granted if the offeror or its concert party has acquired, selectively or in significant numbers, shares in the target company during the previous 12 months or if any shares were acquired after the

---

[23] Note 1 to the Rule concedes that an element of subjectivity may be unavoidable but Note 2 says that an offeror should not invoke any condition so as to cause the offer to lapse unless the circumstances are of material significance to the offeror in the context of the offer (thus precluding the offeror from taking advantage of an immaterial non-fulfilment to extricate itself from the takeover).

[24] Rule 14.2. Thus ensuring that a holder of two classes can accept one and reject the other.

[25] See Rule 14.1, Note 1: see p. 790, n. 5, above.

[26] If it is, notwithstanding n. 24, above, a holder of both should act similarly in respect of both.

[27] Rule 14.1

[28] It should not normally be made conditional on any particular level of acceptances. It may however be put to the security holders by way of a scheme to be considered at a stockholders' meeting: Rule 15(d).

[29] Rule 16, Note 1 makes it clear that this bans the not-unknown practice of buying a holding with an undertaking to make good to the seller any difference between the sale price and the higher price of any successful subsequent bid. It also covers cases where a shareholder of the target company is to be remunerated for the part he has played in promoting the offer ("a finder's fee").

[30] *i.e.* those in which the offeror bids for a proportion only of the shares or a class of shares.

[31] Rule 36.1.

partial offer was reasonably in contemplation.[32] Nor, without consent, may any member of the concert party purchase any further shares within 12 months after a successful partial bid.[33] If the offer is one which could result in the offeror holding not less than 30 per cent and not more than 50 per cent of the voting rights, the offer must state the precise number of shares bid for and the offer must not be declared unconditional unless acceptances are received for not less than that number.[34] And, most importantly, any offer, which could result in the offeror holding more than 30 per cent, must not merely be conditional on the specified number of acceptances but also on approval of the offer by shareholders holding over 50 per cent of the voting rights not held by the offeror and persons acting in concert with it.[35] This consent need not be given at a meeting[36] and is normally secured, as permitted by the Rule, by means of a separate box on the form of acceptance.

Furthermore an offer which could result in the offeror holding shares carrying over 49 per cent of the votes must contain a prominent warning that, if the offer succeeds, the offeror will be free, subject to Rule 36.3, to acquire further shares without incurring an obligation to make a mandatory offer.[37] Each shareholder must be able to accept in full for the relevant proportion of his holding and if shares are tendered in excess of this proportion they must be scaled down rateably.[38] When an offer is made for a company with more than one class of equity capital which could result in the offeror acquiring 30 per cent or more of the votes, a "comparable" offer must be made for each class.[39]

These rules of the Code display an obvious antipathy to partial offers, even though equality of treatment is apparently maintained by the Rule that all shareholders who accept the offer must have the same proportion of their holdings acquired by the bidder. In consequence, partial bids are infrequent, though not unknown. There seem to be two reasons for the Panel's dislike of partial bids. First, if they could be made without restriction, they would constitute an obvious way around the mandatory bid requirement. Or, to put it another way, the mandatory bid requirement operates so as to convert partial bids into full bids in all cases where a successful partial bid results in the bidder holding

---

[32] Rule 36.2.

[33] Rule 36.3.

[34] Rule 36.4.

[35] Rule 36.5. This may occasionally be waived if 5 per cent of the rights are held by a single shareholder: *ibid.*

[36] It might be difficult to achieve the 50 per cent plus at a meeting, even though proxy voting is permitted. Nor will it always be easy to obtain by the "box" method because those who are not going to accept will probably not return the acceptance forms and the majority needed is a majority of the whole and not, as in the case of most resolutions, of those voting.

[37] Rule 36.6.

[38] Rule 36.7.

[39] Rule 36.8.

more than 30 per cent of the target's voting shares.[40] In giving consent to a partial bid the Panel is in fact waiving the mandatory bid requirement.

Secondly, the partial bid, when allowed, is thought to put undue pressure on shareholders to accept the offer. There will be a change of control if the bid is successful, but the existing shareholders will remain members of the target company, at least as to part of their shareholdings. They may well regard this as unsatisfactory: hence the requirement that shareholders should have the double opportunity to vote outlined above. Shareholders may vote to accept the offer in relation to the relevant proportion of their shares, thus preserving their position as far as possible if the bid does go through, whilst voting against the bid as a matter of principle. The partial bid will be successful only if the bidder obtains at least 50 per cent approval in relation to each question.[41]

At a more general level, the Rules on partial bids do something to counteract the ease with which hostile bids may be mounted in the United Kingdom.[42] Although the Code makes it difficult for the management of the target to block a bid addressed to their shareholders, the disfavouring of partial bids means that normally the bidder must offer to acquire the whole of the equity share capital of a company if it wishes to obtain control through a takeover.[43] The Code frowns upon the acquisition of control "on the cheap" through an offer to purchase only a part of the target's equity capital.

The offer period

Having attempted to describe and explain the major matters relevant to the preparation of the offer we now turn to a briefer description of what then happens and of which Rules then have to be complied with.[44]

The offer document

Rule 30 provides that the offer document should normally be posted within 28 days of the announcement of a firm intention to make the

---

[40] Conversely, as Rule 36.1 suggests, where the partial bid would result in the offeror holding less than 30 per cent of the target's shares, this objection to the partial bid falls away.

[41] See Rule 36.5, discussed above. For discussion of how this issue in handled in relation to general bids, see Rule 31.4 and pp. 801 and 810, below.

[42] See p. 772, above.

[43] The fact that all classes of equity capital must be bid for, whether or not the shares carry voting rights (see Rule 14.1), again suggests that the Code is solicitous of the interests of shareholders whose prospects may be adversely affected by a change of control.

[44] In doing so we shall diverge from the order in which the Rules appear in the Code to an even greater extent than hitherto. The Panel, like all legislative draftsmen, is inhibited from altering the order, and thereby the numbering, since practitioners will have become accustomed to it and will not be pleased if it is changed. The writer of an explanatory textbook is not so inhibited.

bid. If it is not, the Panel must be consulted.[45] The board of the target company should advise its shareholders of its views on the offer as soon as practicable thereafter and normally within 14 days.[46]

The offer will, of course, be a longer and more detailed document than any announcement that may have been made under Rules 2.2 or 2.5.[47] Especially is this so if the offeror or target company is listed, for it will then have to comply with the *Listing Rules*[48] as well as with the Code. Moreover, unless the offer is a pure cash offer—and most are share-for-share offers[49] although generally with a cash alternative—the offer document will, in effect, be an offer to buy the shares of the target company, demanding full details about that offer, and an offer to pay the purchase price by shares in the offeror company, demanding[50] listing particulars[51] giving details about that company and those shares. On a pure cash offer the detailed information about the offeror's shares will not be needed, but information about the offeror will. In many cases a cash alternative will be provided not by the offeror itself but by the offeror's merchant bank that is underwriting the issue. In that event, this "cash underwritten alternative" will be referred to in the offeror's offer document but probably in such a way as to emphasise that it is a "separate offer".[52]

After a general statement in Rule 23 that shareholders must be given sufficient information and advice to enable them to reach a properly informed decision as to the merits or demerits of an offer and early enough to decide in good time,[53] Rule 24 (divided into 13 sub-Rules) states what financial and other information the offer document must be contain and Rule 25 (divided into five sub-Rules) what information must be contained in circulars giving advice by the target company's board. The information required is very much what one would expect in the light of the nature of the documents.

In the case of an agreed recommended takeover with no rival bidders, no more may need stating than the Code requires. But, in the case of a hostile bid or where there are two or more rival bids, each

---

[45] Rule 30.1.
[46] Rule 30.2.
[47] See pp. 780–782, above.
[48] See its Chapter 10.
[49] Which the Code describes as "securities exchange offers": Definitions at p. C.7 There are many reasons why the bidder would generally prefer a pure share-for-share offer if it could get away with it; not the least being that, unless the offeror is cash-rich, it will be easier and cheaper to issue paper than to raise the cash.
[50] Which the Code frequently insists upon (see above) and which institutional shareholders will expect.
[51] See Stock Exchange, *Listing Rules*, Chap. 10.46–10.50 and Chap. 5. If the shares are not listed (nor to be listed) then no prospectus is required: the Public Offers of Securities Regulations 1995 (S.I. 1995 No. 1537), reg. 7(2)(k).
[52] See pp. 801 and 805, below.
[53] This does not mean that if advised to accept they should promptly do so; on the contrary, they should leave it to the last possible date since, until it is declared unconditional as to acceptances, it is always possible that a rival higher bid will be made.

of the companies involved will probably want to make optimistic profit forecasts about itself[54] and to rubbish those of the others. All profit forecasts are unreliable and those made in a takeover battle more unreliable than usual. Hence Rule 28 (with nine sub-Rules) lays down stringent conditions about them. In particular, the forecast "must be compiled with scrupulous care and objectivity by the directors whose sole responsibility it is" but "the financial advisers must satisfy themselves" that it has been so compiled.[55] The assumptions on which the forecast is based must be stated both in the document and in any press release.[56] Except on a pure cash offer, the forecast must be reported on by the auditors or consultant accountants (and sometimes by an independent valuer[57]) and sent to the shareholders[58] and, if any subsequent document is sent out, the continued accuracy of the forecast must be confirmed.[59] All this is wholly admirable but the evidence does not suggest that it has made such forecasts significantly more reliable. Somewhat similar requirements apply when a valuation of assets is given in connection with an offer.[60] These valuations tend to vary according to whether it is in the interests of the company which engages the "independent" valuer that the value should be high or low; but at least the valuer of real property is likely to have more objective evidence to guide him in the form of prices recently paid for comparable properties.

Although there has not been space here to discuss the details, it is clear that the Code attaches the highest importance to the provision to shareholders of complete and accurate information about the bid and any defence to it. This is emphasised in General Principle 5 which states that any information document addressed to shareholders "must, as is the case with a prospectus, be prepared with the highest standards of care and accuracy". Without such guarantees, the Code's purpose of placing the decision on the commercial acceptability of the offer in the hands of the shareholders of the target company might seem unrealistic, as might the Panel's own refusal to make any assessment of the commercial merits of the bid.[61]

Naturally, the sanctions normally available to the Panel may be deployed where there has been a breach of the Code's provisions relating to the disclosure of information. However, this is an area in which the Code intersects with the general law, in the sense that there may well be

---

[54] The offeror will not need to do so on a pure cash offer for all the shares; but the target will.
[55] Rule 28.1. Statements about the expected financial benefits of a takeover may fall short of constituting profit forecasts, but they are now regulated in a similar manner under new Note 8 to Rule 19.1 (see Panel Statement 1997/5).
[56] Rule 28.2 (and see the Notes thereto).
[57] Rule 28.3.
[58] Rule 28.4.
[59] Rule 28.5.
[60] Rule 29.
[61] See p. 779, above.

legal remedies available to shareholders who have suffered loss as a result of inaccurate or incomplete information provided in the course of a takeover bid.[62] We have already noted that in some situations the bidder may have to issue listing particulars, as specified by the Stock Exchange. Inaccurate or incomplete statements in the listing particulars may trigger the liability of those responsible for the particulars, as laid down in sections 150 *et seq.* of the Financial Services Act 1986, to pay compensation to those who suffer loss thereby, unless the absence of negligence can be proved by the defendant in question.[63]

This liability under the Financial Services Act can attach only to documents issued by the bidder which fall within the category of listing particulars. Applying generally, that is, to both bidder and target documentation, is the common law liability for negligent misstatement, which, even after the decision of the House of Lords in *Caparo Industries plc v. Dickman*,[64] would seem to impose liability upon the issuers of documentation in the course of takeover bids towards the shareholders of the target company, to whom it is clearly addressed, where such shareholders act in reliance upon the information to either reject or accept the offer made.[65] Indeed, in the post-*Caparo* case of *Morgan Crucible & Co. v. Hill Samuel & Co.*[66] the Court of Appeal refused to strike out a claim by the bidding company that inaccurate statements made by the target company in the course of a bid had been intended to cause the bidder to raise its bid, which it had done to its detriment. There may also be a general criminal liability arising under section 47 of the Financial Services Act, which prohibits in section 47(1) the intentional or reckless making of a false "statement, promise or forecast", *inter alia*, for the purpose of inducing shareholders of the target company to sell or not to sell[67] their shares. In subsection (2) it goes further and applies criminal liability for the negligent creation of a false or misleading impression as to the price or value of shares if this is done for the purpose of inducing a person to, *inter alia*, dispose or not to dispose of securities.[68]

---

[62] A further safeguard of compliance with the Code is that many documents issued in the course of takeover bids, though not pure defence documents, constitute "investment advertisements" within the scope of section 57 of the Financial Services Act 1986 and so must be issued or approved by a person authorised under the Act to carry on investment business, normally a merchant bank.

[63] See pp. 428 *et seq.*, above. The bidder might also be liable in damages under s.2(1) of the Misrepresentation Act 1976 (unless it could disprove negligence) or to have its contract with the accepting shareholders rescinded in equity, though in both cases this could apply only between the bidder and the target company shareholders and where the shareholders had accepted the bidder's offer.

[64] [1990] 2 A.C. 605. See pp. 552 *et seq.*, above.

[65] Proving that the negligent misstatement caused the plaintiff the loss in question may be, of course, a very difficult matter. See *JEB Fasteners Ltd v. Marks Bloom & Co.* [1981] 3 All E.R. 289 (above, p. 558).

[66] [1991] Ch. 295, C.A. See p. 555, above.

[67] So the subsection applies to defence documents as well.

[68] See pp. 433 *et seq.*, above.

Acceptances

An offer must initially be open for acceptance for at least 21 days.[69] If this is later extended, a new date must be specified unless the offer has already become unconditional as to acceptance, in which case it may be left open until further notice which must be not less than 14 days' notice to shareholders who have not accepted.[70] There is no obligation to extend an offer the conditions of which have not been met by the closing date,[71] but once it has been declared unconditional as to acceptances it must remain open for acceptance for not less than 14 days after the date on which it would otherwise have expired.[72] Apart from that, however, if it is stated that the offer will not be further extended, only in exceptional cases will the Panel allow it to be extended.[73] And, except with the consent of the Panel, an offer may not be declared unconditional as to acceptances after 60 days from its initial posting.[74]

In some cases the offer may be revised, sometimes more than once. This is particularly likely to occur if there is a contested takeover between two or more bidders. In such circumstances each rival bidder, having already incurred considerable expense, is likely to go on raising its bid and trying to get its new one recommended by the board of the target. Even if it loses the battle, it will at least be able to recover part of the expenses out of the profit it will make by accepting the winner's bid in respect of its own holdings. Moreover, even if there is no contest, an offeror may be forced to increase its bid if it or its associates or members of its concert party have acquired shares at above the price of its offer.[75]

If an offer is revised, it must be kept open for at least 14 days after the revised offer document is posted.[76] All shareholders who have

---

[69] Rule 31.1. The date so stated is the "first closing date" which has importance in connection with a number of Code Rules.

[70] Rule 31.2.

[71] Rule 31.3.

[72] Rule 31.4. Once non-acceptors know that the takeover is going to be consummated, whether they like it or not, they may well change their minds and this Rule gives them that opportunity. In other words, this Rule enables a shareholder, who dislike the bid, to maintain his opposition up until the point when it becomes clear that the majority of the shareholders do not take the same view, without fear of being locked into a minority position when the bid succeeds. This beneficial effect is rather diluted by the Code's failure to insist on the principle in relation to alternatives offers (see p. 801). For the statutory provisions, see p. 810. If, unusually, the offer was unconditional as to acceptances from the outset the extension is not necessary so long as the position is made clear: Rule 31.4.

[73] Rule 31.5. This is not merely because the offeror should not break its promises but to prevent shareholders being pressurised into accepting before the current closing date by false statements that they will lose all chance of availing themselves of the offer unless they accept before that date.

[74] Rule 31.6. But see ss.430A and B in Part XIIIA of the Companies Act (below, pp. 807, *et seq.*) the effect of which may be that non-acceptors get a further chance.

[75] See Rules 6, 9 and 11, above.

[76] Rule 32.1.

accepted the original offer are entitled to the revised consideration[77] and new conditions must not be introduced except to the extent necessary to implement an increased or improved offer and with the prior consent of the Panel.[78]

In general, the foregoing Rules[79] apply equally to alternative offers in which the target's shareholders are given the option of accepting various types of consideration (*e.g.* shares, convertible debentures, non-convertible debentures, cash or combinations or different proportions of these).[80] In other words, the shareholders retain their options so long as the offer remains open. But where the value of a cash alternative provided by third parties (*i.e.* a "cash underwritten alternative" mentioned above[81]) is more than half the maximum value of the primary share option, the offeror is not obliged to keep that offer open, or to extend it, if not less than 14 days' written notice to shareholders[82] is given reserving the right to close it on a stated date.[83] The reason for this is that the underwriters will be reluctant to agree to remain at risk for an indeterminate period.[84] A disadvantage to an offeror in a contested bid of extending its offer is that under Rule 34 an acceptor must be entitled to withdraw his acceptance after 21 days from the first closing date of the initial offer, unless by that time the offer has become unconditional as to acceptances. If, therefore, an offeror extends its offer beyond that date it runs the risk that some of those who have accepted its offer will withdraw and switch to the competitor.

Under Rule 17.1, by 8.30 a.m. on the business day following that on which an offer is due to expire or on which it has become unconditional as to acceptances or is revised or extended, an offeror must make an announcement (and, except when the target company is not listed, must inform the Stock Exchange) stating the total number of shares or rights over shares: (a) for which acceptances of the offer have been received, (b) which were held before the offer period and (c) which have been acquired or agreed to be acquired during the offer period. The announcement must specify the percentages of the relevant classes of share capital represented by the figures. Moreover, if any general statements are made by the offeror or its advisers about acceptances, Note 2 to the Rule requires that such an announcement is to be made immediately. Hence, if only to be able to comply, the offeror

---

[77] Rule 32.3.
[78] Rule 32.4.
[79] *i.e.* those in Rules 31 and 32.
[80] Rule 33.1
[81] See p. 797, above.
[82] This does not apply to a cash alternative provided to satisfy Rule 9: Rule 33.2, Note 2.
[83] Rule 33.2. But such a notice must not be given if a competing offer has been announced until the competitive situation ends. And the procedure must have been clearly stated in the offer documents and acceptance forms: Rule 24.13.
[84] For the position under Part XIIIA of the Act see pp. 809, *et seq.*

needs to be in a position at all times to state what the precise position is regarding acceptances and other acquisitions. This is not as easy as it may sound[85] and cases have occurred in which an offer has been declared unconditional as to acceptances when, because of double counting, it should not have been. Notes to Rules 9 and 10 and the *Receiving Agents' Code of Practice*[86] in Appendix 4 to the Code are designed to reduce the risk of such disasters.

Solicitation during the offer period

The advent of the Code and the Panel has in itself done much to reduce the risk of misconduct in the course of takeovers. But recent developments have added a new dimension to the opportunities for high-pressure salesmanship, resort to which is an almost irresistible temptation in the case of a hostile or, especially, a contested take-over. Whereas formerly the only means of communication with the target's shareholders were via written circulars, newspaper advertisements, and meetings with, and calls upon them by visits or telephone, we now have in addition audio and television broadcasting and (as the United States has long had) firms specialising in the art of persuading reluctant shareholders. It is increasingly common for the services of such firms to be recruited by the parties or their financial advisers. Rule 19 of the Code is designed to curb the excesses which may result (and sometimes have done).

The sub-Rules of particular interest include Rule 19.4 which prohibits the publication of an advertisement connected with an offer unless it falls within one of nine categories, and, with two exceptions,[87] it is cleared with the Panel in advance. The Panel does not attempt to verify the accuracy of statements,[88] but if it subsequently appears that any statement was inaccurate the Panel may, at least,[89] require an immediate correction.[90] This pre-vetting, however superficial, is a powerful disincentive to window-dressing and to "argument or invective".[91] The Rule applies not only to press advertisements (which must

---

[85] It demands the collaboration of the target company (which will not be given with enthusiasm to an unwelcome or unfavoured offeror) and, usually, of the Stock Exchange, plus efficient organisation, supported by modern technology and professional skills on the part of the offeror.

[86] Drawn up by the Panel in consultation with the CBI, the banks, and the Institute of Chartered Secretaries and Administrators.

[87] A product advertisement, not bearing on the offer (which is not really an exception), and advertisements in relation to schemes of arrangement (when the relevant regulator is the court): see Chap. 28 at p. 763, above.

[88] Time constraints do not permit this to be done; the Panel requires only 24 hours to consider the proof of the advertisement which must have been approved by the company's financial adviser: Rule 9.4, Note 1.

[89] It may also impose a disciplinary penalty.

[90] Rule 19.4, Note 2.

[91] Specifically excluded from exceptions (iii) and (iv) to Rule 19.4.

not include acceptance or other forms[92]) but also to television, radio, video, audio-tapes and posters[93] and in each case the advertisement must "clearly and prominently" identify the party on whose behalf it is being published.[94]

The Rule, however, covers only advertising material of which there will be a record. The greater danger arises from unrecorded oral communications, which cannot be vetted in advance or scrutinised afterwards. However, an attempt is made to control these. Rule 19.5 provides that, without the consent of the Panel, campaigns in which shareholders are contacted by telephone may be conducted only by "staff of the financial advisers who are fully conversant with the requirements of, and their responsibilities under, the Code", and it adds that only previously published information which remains accurate and not misleading may be used, and that "shareholders must not be put under pressure and must be encouraged to consult their financial advisers". However, in recognition, no doubt, that the parties will have selected their financial advisers on the basis of their financial expertise and reputation rather than their ability to woo, the Panel may consent to the use of other people, subject to the Panel's approval of an appropriate script which must not be departed from, even if those rung up ask questions which cannot be answered without doing so, and to the operation being supervised by the financial adviser.[95]

Telephone campaigns of the kind envisaged in Rule 19.5 are examples of the practice known as "cold-calling". If the calls are intended to induce those called upon to accept the offer they are clearly banned by section 56 of the Financial Services Act (though probably not if the aim is to persuade them to reject it[96]) except to the extent permitted by regulations made by SIB. However, it has been agreed that it would be preferable to leave the regulation in the context of takeovers to the Panel. Accordingly, SIB's Common Unsolicited Calls Regulations, which came into force on September 1, 1991, provide by Regulation 6 that the statutory restrictions "are lifted to the extent that the call . . . is made by or under the supervision of an authorised person and in connection with or for the purposes of a takeover or substantial acquisition which is subject to the Takeover Code or to requirements in another member State which afford equivalent protection to investors in the United Kingdom".

---

[92] Rule 19.4, Note 5.

[93] Rule 19.4, Note 4.

[94] Rule 19.4, Note 3.

[95] Rule 19.5, Note 1. It is difficult to see how the financial adviser can supervise effectively unless it insists upon all calls made being recorded on tape; but the Rules and Notes do not require or suggest that.

[96] The curious wording of s.56 means that calls are banned only if they result in an "investment agreement" or are made to procure the entry into such an agreement. An agreement to accept a takeover offer is clearly an "investment agreement" as defined in s.44(9); but an agreement to reject it seemingly is not.

With effect from the same date the Panel amended the Code. A new Rule 4.3 provides that any person proposing to contact a private individual or small corporate shareholder with a view to seeking an irrevocable commitment to accept *or refrain from accepting* an offer or contemplated offer must consult the Panel in advance. A Note to Rule 4.3 states that the Panel will need to be satisfied that the proposed arrangements will provide adequate information as to the nature of the commitment sought and a realistic opportunity to consider whether or not it should be given and with time to take independent advice. It adds that the financial adviser will be responsible "for ensuring compliance with all relevant legislation and other regulatory requirements".[97] Furthermore, Note 3 to Rule 19.5 has been amended so that it now reads: "In accordance with Rule 4.3, the Panel must be consulted before a telephone campaign is conducted with a view to gathering irrevocable commitments in connection with an offer. Rule 19.5 applies to such campaigns although, in appropriate circumstances, the Panel may permit those called to be informed of details of a proposed offer which has not been publicly announced. Attention is, however, drawn to General Principles 2 and 4." Short of a total ban on cold-calling this seems to regulate it in this context as satisfactorily as is reasonably possible—assuming that financial advisers can be relied on to observe the Rules.

Rule 19.6 says that parties, if interviewed on radio or television, should seek to ensure that the interview, when broadcast, is not interspersed with comments or observations made by others in the course of a different interview. It also provides that joint interviews or public confrontations between representatives of the contesting parties should be avoided.

The more serious problem, arising from meetings with shareholders or those who are likely to advise them, is dealt with in Rule 20.1 which provides that "information about companies involved in an offer must be made equally available to all shareholders as nearly as possible at the same time and in the same manner".[98] Despite this, meetings with institutional shareholders, individually or through their professional bodies, are likely to be held, as, often, are meetings with financial journalists and investment analysts and advisers. Note 3 to the Rule permits this, "provided that no material new information is forthcoming and no significant new opinions are expressed". If that really is strictly observed, one wonders why anybody bothers to attend such meetings.[99] But many do, and when a representative of the financial

---

[97] This warning ought to frighten the financial adviser!

[98] This does not preclude the issue of circulars to their own investment clients by brokers or advisers provided that the circulars are approved by the Panel.

[99] The risk of new information being given out on a partial basis in such cases materialised in the Kvaerner bid for AMEC, where a financial public relations company employed by the target made statements in closed meetings about the targets future profits which had not been

adviser or corporate broker of the party convening the meeting is present (as he must be unless the Panel otherwise consents), he generally seems able to confirm in writing to the Panel (as the Note requires) that this Rule was observed. If such confirmation is not given, a circular to shareholders (and, in the later stages, a newspaper advertisement also) must be published giving the new information or opinions supported by a directors' responsibility statement.

The post-offer period

Except with the consent of the Panel, when an offer[1] has been withdrawn or has lapsed, neither the offeror nor any person who has acted or now is acting in concert with it, may, within the next 12 months: (a) make another offer for the target company, (b) acquire any shares of the target company which would require an offer to be made under Rule 9, or (c) acquire any shares in the target company if the result would be a holding of over 49 per cent but less than 50 per cent of the voting rights of the target.[2] Similar restrictions apply following a partial offer which could result in a holding of not less than 30 per cent and not more than 50 per cent of the target's voting rights and whether or not the offer has been declared unconditional.[3] Furthermore, if a person or concert party following a takeover offer holds 50 per cent or more of the voting rights it must not, within six months of the closure of the offer, make a second offer, or acquire any shares from the shareholders on better terms than those under the previous offer.[4] These provisions prevent the offeror from continuously harassing the target and, while the maximum waiting period is only 12 months, it may enable the target's board to strengthen its defences against further hostile bids by the offeror.

Companies Act provisions

Although in general the Companies Act itself does not regulate the conduct of takeover bids it does nevertheless contain two sets of provisions[5] primarily directed to takeovers. Indeed, one such set[6] relates exclusively to them and, as a result of the Financial Services Act,[7] which substituted a revised version of the sections concerned, now appears in a new Part XIIIA of the Companies Act under the heading

---

contained in the defence document: Panel statement 1995/9. The P.R. company was censured by the Panel and dismissed by the target.
[1] Or even if no offer has been made but an announcement has been made implying that one is contemplated: Rule 35.1(b).
[2] Rule 35.1(a).
[3] Rule 35.2.
[4] Rule 35.3.
[5] *i.e.* ss.312–316 and 428–430F.
[6] ss.428–430F.
[7] FSA, s.172.

"Takeover offers". This new Part contains the provisions which have germinated from section 155 of the 1929 Act, enacted when takeovers were in their early infancy and when the Panel and the Code were undreamt of. In Part XIIIA that short and simple section has become no less than nine distinctly complicated ones.

The basic objectives are simple enough. When, as a result of a takeover offer, an offeror has acquired nine-tenths of the share capital of the target company, or nine-tenths of any class of it, then:

(i) the offeror is enabled to acquire the remaining one-tenth on the same terms,[8]
(ii) any shareholder who has not accepted the offeror's offer is enabled to require the transferor to acquire his shares on the same terms.[9]

However, it could be misleading to leave it at that and attention must be drawn to various refinements and qualifications.

Scope of Part XIIIA

In contrast with the Code, Part XIIIA applies to takeovers of any type of company within the meaning of the Act whether it is public or private. As in the case of the Code, the offeror need not be a company though in practice it will usually be a body corporate[10] (or in some cases two or more[11]). The definition of "takeover offer" is somewhat different from that of the Code. It means, for the purposes of Part XIIIA, "an offer to acquire all the shares, or all the shares of any class or classes,[12] in a company (other than shares which at the date of the offer are already held by the offeror[13]) being an offer on terms which are the same in relation to all the shares to which the offer relates, or, where those shares include shares of different classes, in relation to all the shares of each class."[14]

In *Re Chez Nico (Restaurants) Ltd,*[15] Browne-Wilkinson V.-C. held that this definition had to be construed strictly, since Part XIIIA enabled a bidder who had acquired 90 per cent of the shares to expropriate the remaining shares, and that accordingly the Part

---

[8] ss.429, 430.
[9] ss.430A, 430B.
[10] But it could be an unincorporated body, *e.g.* the trustees of a pension fund.
[11] See s.430D on joint offers.
[12] Hence it does not apply to "partial offers": but, where the Code applies, the Panel would not be likely to allow a partial offer which might lead to the acquisition of 90 per cent.
[13] This includes shares which the offeror has contracted to acquire, but not contracts to accept the offer when made unless the holder has received a payment: s.428(5). Note s.430E regarding shares held by "associates" of the offeror.
[14] s.428(1); "shares" here means shares allotted at the date of the offer but the offer may include shares to be allotted before a specified date: s.428(2).
[15] [1992] BCLC 192.

operated only if the bidder had made an "offer" in the contractual sense of the word. In the instant case two directors of the company who were its major shareholders had circulated the other shareholders inviting them to offer to sell their shares to them and indicating the price that those directors would be prepared to pay if they accepted the offers. As a result, the directors succeeded in acquiring over 90 per cent and then sought to acquire the remainder. On an application by one of the remaining shareholders under section 430C (below) the court declared that the directors were not entitled to do so, since they had not made any "offer" but instead had invited the shareholders to do so.

While this produced the right result in this instant case,[16] the importation into company law of the subtle distinctions drawn by the law of contract seems regrettable; in company law many transactions are described as "offers" or "offerings" when strictly they are invitations to make offers.[17] Moreover, the decision has adverse consequences for a minority shareholder who, instead of wanting to remain a shareholder in the taken-over company, wishes to exercise his rights under section 430A to be bought out; the effect of the decision is that he will not be entitled to do so if the bidder has proceeded as the directors did in this case.[18]

Attention must also be drawn to another curious effect of this definition of "takeover offer". There is everything to be said for a statutory requirement that a bidder should offer "terms which are the same in relation to all the shares . . . to which the offer relates",[19] thus adopting the Code's General Principle 1. But putting this requirement in the definition of "takeover offer" again has the effect of depriving the non-accepting minority of their right to be bought out under section 430A if the bidder has failed to observe it.

Buy-out right of offeror

This is dealt with in sections 429 and 430. Subsection (1) of section 429 relates to cases where the takeover has been for shares of one

---

[16] See pp. 811–812, below.

[17] Browne-Wilkinson V.-C. emphasised that his decision was only on the meaning of "takeover offer" for the purposes of Part XIIIA and that he had no doubt that what had occurred would be a takeover offer for the purposes of many statutory or non-statutory provisions. This is certainly true of the non-statutory Code. Indeed, the Panel had treated the *Chez Nico* takeover as subject to the Code (the company had been a plc at the time of the circularisation and remained subject to the Code after its conversion to a private company since, while a public company, it had made a public (BES) offering) but the only penalty that the Panel had imposed was to criticise the two directors for their ignorance of, and failure to observe, the Code: see at p. 200. The decision, however, seems to cast some doubt on whether section 314, below, would have applied—as clearly it ought to.

[18] But if he could not apply to the court under s.430C, below, he could petition under s.459 as a member "unfairly prejudiced".

[19] An exception to this requirement is permitted if the law of a foreign country precludes an offer there of consideration in the form specified or precludes it except on compliance with unduly onerous conditions, but only if the foreign shareholders are enabled to receive other

class and subsection (2) to those in which it has been for two or more classes. If the offeror has acquired or contracted to acquire by virtue of acceptances of the offer not less than nine-tenths in nominal value[20] of the shares or class, it may give notice[21] to holders of the shares to which the offer relates but which have not been acquired or contracted to be acquired, stating that the offeror desires to acquire them. In calculating whether the requisite 90 per cent has been obtained, shares held by the offeror prior to the offer period are ignored; these were not "acquired by virtue of acceptance of the offer". But purchases which he makes during the offer period will be treated as having been so acquired if the price paid does not at that time exceed the value of the consideration specified in the offer or the offer is subsequently revised so that it no longer does so.[22]

The effect of the notice is, under section 430, that the offeror becomes bound to acquire the shares on the final terms of the offer. If the offer gave shareholders alternative choices of consideration (*e.g.* shares or a cash alternative), the notice must offer a similar choice and state that the shareholder may, within six weeks from the date of the notice, indicate his choice by a written communication to the offeror and must also state which consideration will apply in default of his indicating a choice.[23] This applies whether or not any time limit or other conditions relating to choice in the offer can still be complied with and even if (a) the offer chosen is not cash and the offeror is no longer able to provide it or (b) it was to have been provided by a third party[24] who is no longer bound or able to provide it.[25] The remainder of section 430[26] prescribes in detail the procedures that has to be adopted to ensure that the shares which the offeror is bound to acquire

consideration of substantially equivalent value: s.428(3) and (4). Hence the offeror has to find a way of treating them fairly.

[20] In contrast with the Code, it is the proportion of the share capital (not that of the voting rights) which counts. The main aim of s.429 is to enable and encourage a 100 per cent takeover resulting in the target becoming the offeror's wholly owned subsidiary instead of one in which there is a small minority to the embarrassment of the parent and the attendant risks to the minority.

[21] A notice may not be given unless, within four months from the initial date of the takeover offer, the requisite proportion has been obtained and cannot be given later than two months after that proportion was obtained: s.429(3). An additional ground for the decision in *Chez Nico* was that the two directors had not observed this timetable. The notice must be given in the prescribed manner (Form No. 429(4)) and when the offeror gives the first notice he must send a copy of it to the target company with a statutory declaration in the prescribed form (Form No. 429 dec.) stating that the conditions have been satisfied: s.429(4).

[22] s.429(8). In other words, the offeror cannot count towards the 90 per cent shares which he acquires by offering more than the final offer price but can count those which he was able to buy at less than that price.

[23] s.430(3).

[24] *i.e.* on a "cash underwritten alternative": see above, pp. 791 and 793.

[25] s.430(4). This adopts and codifies the effect of the decision of Brightman J. in *Re Carlton Holdings Ltd* [1971] 1 W.L.R. 918, interpreting the corresponding, but less explicit, provisions of s.209(1) of the 1948 Act. But arguments still rage: see below

[26] subss. (5)–(15).

are transferred to it and that the consideration that it is bound to pay reaches the shareholders concerned.[27]

Sell-out rights of shareholders

These are dealt with in sections 430A and 430B which are broadly similar to sections 429 and 430 except that it is the non-acceptors of the takeover offer who can require the offeror to buy them out. There are, however, significant differences of wording. The rights of the offeror under section 429 arise only if as a result of acceptances (or deemed acceptances[28]) nine-tenths of the relevant share capital[29] has been acquired. But the rights of non-acceptors to require the offeror to buy them out arise whenever "at any time before the end of the period within which the offer can be accepted . . . (a) the offeror has by virtue of acceptances of the offer acquired or contracted to acquire some (but not all) of the shares to which the offer relates, and (b) those shares, with or without any other shares in the [target] company which he has acquired or contracted to acquire, amount to not less than nine-tenths in value of" the relevant share capital.[30] Hence, the rights arise if at the closure of the offer the holdings of the offeror total 90 per cent or more; and rightly so, for what concerns the shareholder is whether he wants to remain a minority shareholder in a company of which the offeror holds 90 per cent, however that may have been acquired.

Within one month of the closure of the offer, the offeror must give notice, in the prescribed manner,[31] to each shareholder who has not accepted the offer, of the rights exercisable by him under the section and if the notice is given before the closing date of the offer it must state that the offer is still open for acceptance.[32] The notice may specify a period, not being less than three months from the closing date of the offer, within which the rights must be exercised.

Section 430B, on the effect of the shareholder's requirement that his shares be acquired, is, *mutatis mutandis*, identical with subsections (1)–(4) of section 430.[33] In particular, the same provisions relating to alternative offers apply.[34] It is in this case, rather than in relation to

---

[27] The main problem that has had to be solved is that many of the non-acceptors of the offer will probably be untraceable. The solution adopted causes the offeror little trouble: see subss. (5)–(8), but the target company may have to maintain trust accounts for 12 years or earlier winding up and then pay into court: subss. (9)–(15).

[28] See s.429(8) above.

[29] s.429(1) and (2). But see s.430C(5), below.

[30] s.430A(1) and (2). There is no equivalent of s.429(8).

[31] On Form 430A.

[32] s.430A(3). This does not apply if the offeror has already given the shareholder a notice under s.429: s.430A(5).

[33] Provisions corresponding to s.430(5)–(13) are not needed since the shareholder has identified himself and is a willing seller.

[34] A point specifically left open by Brightman J. in *Re Carlton Holdings Ltd*, above, p. 808, n. 25.

section 429,[35] that the need to provide a choice of all the original
alternatives (including a cash underwritten alternative) is so unpopular
with offerors and their advisers. And it is, perhaps, rather remarkable
and not altogether easy to reconcile with the provisions of the Code.
As we have seen, under the Code an offer has to remain open for at
least 14 days after it becomes unconditional as to acceptances.[36] However, an offeror is not obliged to keep most types of cash underwritten
alternatives open if it has given notice to shareholders that it reserves
the right to close them on a stated date being not less than 14 days
after the date on which the written notice is given.[37] The effect of
section 430B(3) and (4) is virtually to keep all the offer open for
considerably longer than is required under the Code in all cases where
the offer has been 90 per cent successful. And clearly the parties
cannot contract out of the statutory provisions. Nor can the Panel or
the Code waive them.

However, it is sometimes argued that sections 430B(3) and (4) do
not apply if the cash alternative is described in the offeror's offer
document as a separate offer by the underwriting merchant bank. In
the light of the section that argument seems unsustainable. The fact is
that, as the section and the Code clearly recognise, the offeror's
"offer" may and probably will contain a number of separate offers
and that some of those offers may be made by third parties. The only
way, it is submitted, in which offerors and their merchant banks might
be able to achieve their aim is by making no mention at all of a cash
underwritten alternative hoping that an independent merchant bank,
not acting on behalf of, or paid for its services by, the offeror will
come forward and make an offer on its own account to the target's
shareholders to buy the shares of the offeror received on the takeover.
That is a somewhat unlikely scenario.

Applications to the court

In relation to both buy-outs and sell-outs there is a right to apply to
the court under section 430C. Its subsection (1) provides that where
the offeror has given a notice to a shareholder under section 429, the
shareholder may within six weeks from the date of the notice apply to
the court which (a) may order that the offeror shall not be entitled or
bound to acquire the shares or (b) specify terms of acquisition different
from those of the offer.[38] Under subsection (3), when a shareholder
exercises his rights under section 430A an application may be made
either by the shareholder or the offeror and the court may order that

---

[35] Where the offeror does not have to exercise his rights unless it wants to.
[36] Rule 31.4. See pp. 800–801, above.
[37] Rule 33.2.
[38] When an application is pending the procedure for completing the acquisition is suspended:
s.430C(2).

the terms on which the offeror shall acquire the shares shall be such as the court thinks fit.

At one time, there were a considerable number of such applications, mainly under subsection (1), but with rare exceptions all unsuccessful.[39] It is therefore not surprising that in recent years there seem to have been fewer. Indeed, it may be questioned whether there is any need for section 430C in view of sections 459–461. However, section 430C does something to encourage its use by providing specifically that "no order for costs or expenses shall be made against a shareholder[40] unless the court considers that the application was unnecessary, improper or vexatious" or that there has been unreasonable delay in making the application or unreasonable conduct in the shareholder's conduct of the proceedings.[41] This may be regarded as an advantage over proceeding by way of section 459.

Subsection (5) provides that, when an offer has been accepted to the extent necessary for entitling the offeror to give notice under section 429, the court may, on the application of the offeror, permit it to give notice under section 430C notwithstanding that it has been unable after reasonable inquiry to trace one or more of the non-accepting shareholders but the shares that the offeror has acquired or contracted to acquire by virtue of acceptances and those already held by the offeror amount to not less than 90 per cent. But the court must be satisfied that the consideration is fair and reasonable, and that it is just and equitable to do so having regard to the number of shareholders who have been traced but who have not accepted the offer. If such an order is made, the effect is to enable the offeror to invoke section 429 when its total holdings are such as would entitle the shareholders to invoke their rights under section 430A.

On the wording of section 430C it is clear that the court has a discretion whether or not to make an order. In *Re Chez Nico (Restaurants) Ltd*[42] Browne-Wilkinson V.-C. made some interesting and helpful observations on how he would have exercised his discretion in that case had it been necessary for him to do so. He indicated that he would unhesitatingly have refused to make an order in favour of the two directors having regard to their failure to observe the rules

---

[39] The usual fate of applications attacking transactions approved by a substantial majority. The courts on applications under the forerunner of the present Part XIIIA seemed to regard it as scarcely believable that there could be anything wrong with a bid accepted by 90 per cent. For a rare exception see *Re Bugle Press Ltd* [1961] Ch. 434, C.A. where what is now s.429 was being abused rather than used: see p. 711, above. More recently, the courts have seemed willing to investigate the basis upon which the majority came to their conclusion: *Re Lifecare International plc* [1990] BCLC 222.

[40] In fact it had not been the practice of the courts to order shareholders to pay costs. As in the case of appearing in opposition to a scheme of arrangement, it was generally felt that their appearance was helpful to the court which would otherwise hear only one side of the argument.

[41] s.430C(4).

[42] [1992] BCLC 192; see p. 806, above.

of the Code to which the transaction was subject. On the general duties of disclosure by directors in a takeover situation he expressed his agreement with the views of the New Zealand Court of Appeal in *Coleman v. Myers*[43] on *Percival v. Wright*[44] but said that it was unnecessary to decide whether, under the general law, the directors were, in the circumstances, under a duty to make full disclosure to the shareholders; the takeover was subject to the Code's rules and the directors had failed to disclose in accordance with its rules. While the Code "does not have the force of law, in considering for the purpose of section 430C whether the court should exercise its discretion, the Code is a factor of great importance".[45] This is a welcome supplement to the views expressed by Lord Prosser in *Dawson International v. Coats Patons*[46] on the inter-relation of the general law and the Code.

The remaining sections of Part XIIIA deal with certain specific points which, in the past, have caused difficulty. It had been held by the Privy Council on an appeal from Australia that a section similar to the former section 209 of the 1948 Act did not apply when the offer was made by a consortium of offerors.[47] This loophole has now been closed[48] by section 430D which provides that Part XIIIA shall apply with the needed modifications specified in that section.[49] Section 430E deals with the position when shares are held or acquired not by the offeror but by its "associates" as widely defined in its subsections (4)–(8).[50] And, finally, section 430F provides that "shares" shall include securities convertible[51] into, or entitling the holder to subscribe for, shares and that "shareholder" includes the holders of such securities.[52]

Sections 314–316

These sections are in Part X of the Act (Enforcement of Fair Dealing by Directors). They are preceded by sections 312 and 313, the first of which makes it unlawful for a company to give a director of the company any payment by way of compensation for loss of office or as consideration for or in connection with his retirement from office, without particulars of the proposed payment (including its amount) being disclosed to members of the company and the proposal

---

[43] See Chap. 22 at p. 600, above.
[44] *ibid.*
[45] [1992] BCLC 192 at 209. See also *Re St Piran Ltd* [1981] 1 W.L.R. 1300, 1307.
[46] See pp. 786–787, above.
[47] *Blue Metal Industries Ltd v. Dilley* [1970] A.C. 827, P.C.
[48] As it was more promptly in Australia.
[49] For the Code's treatment of joint offers, see Rule 4, Note 2.
[50] *cf.* the Code's definition: Definitions p. C.2 and 3.
[51] For the Code's treatment of convertibles, see Rule 5.1, Note 4, Rule 6, Note 6, Rule 9.1, Note 10, and Rule 15.
[52] But they do not have to be treated as shares of the same class as that into which they are convertible; nor do different types of securities have to be treated as shares of the same class merely because they are convertible into the same class of share.

being approved by the company. Section 313 similarly declares it to be unlawful, without such disclosure being made and such approval given, if in connection with the transfer of the whole or any part of the undertaking or property of the company any payment (*by whomsoever made*) is to be made to a director by way of compensation for loss of office or in connection with his retirement. However, neither of these sections is specifically directed to takeovers and neither is likely to be relevant to takeovers of the type dealt with in this chapter.[53]

However, section 314 is specifically directed to takeovers as its side-note indicates—although the word "takeover" is not used in the section itself. It applies when there has been a transfer of shares of a company resulting from:

"(a) an offer made to the general body of shareholders; or
(b) an offer made by or on behalf of some other body corporate with a view to the company becoming its subsidiary or a subsidiary of its holding company; or
(c) an offer made by an individual with a view to his obtaining the right to exercise or control the exercise of not less than one third of the voting power at any general meeting; or
(d) any other offer which is conditional on acceptance to a given extent"[54]

and a payment is to be made (whether by the company or the offeror or by anyone else) to a director of the company "by way of compensation for loss of office or as consideration for or in connection with his retirement from office".[55]

When that is so, it is the director's duty to take all reasonable steps to secure that particulars of the proposed payment are disclosed in or with the offer document sent to the shareholders.[56] If he fails to do so, he is liable to a fine (as is any person who has been properly required to include those particulars and has failed to do so).[57] The real deterrent, however, is not the risk of a fine but the consequences flowing from section 315. This provides that if (a) the director's duty is not complied with, or[58] (b) the payment is not, before the transfer of shares, approved by a meeting of the holders of shares to which the offer

---

[53] s.312 is irrelevant because the wider s.314 will apply and s.313 because it will not apply since the takeover will normally be by transfer of shares, not of the company's undertaking or property. But both may be relevant to arrangements undertaken by method (2) or (3) dealt with in Chap. 28.

[54] s.314(1). Though (a), (b) or (c) would almost certainly be a "takeover offer" for the purposes of the Code or Part XIIIA of the Act, this would not necessarily be so in the case of (d).

[55] *ibid.* For the extended meaning of these quoted words see s.316, below.

[56] s.314(2).

[57] s.314(3).

[58] The, grammatically correct, disjunctive "or" in s.315(1) has led some readers to suppose that, if the director has performed his duty under (a), approval under (b) is not required. This, of course, is not so: both must be complied with.

related,[59] any sum received by the director is held by him in trust for those who have sold their shares as a result of the offer.[60] Here, therefore, the legislation has avoided the absurdity illustrated in *Regal (Hastings) Ltd v. Gulliver*,[61] by providing restitution to those truly damnified, rather than to the company when, in effect, it would result in an undeserved reduction of the price that the successful offeror has paid. Instead, under section 314, the director becomes a trustee for the former shareholders who have sold.

Although sections 312–315 are all expressed to relate only to payments made "for loss of office" or "in connection with retirement from office", the meaning of these expressions is widened in some respects and narrowed in others by section 316. Under its subsection (1) if a payment is made to a director who has lost, or retired from, office in pursuance of any arrangement made either as part of the agreement for the transfer or within one year before or two years after it, and the offeror or target company was privy to the arrangement, the payment is deemed, unless the contrary is shown, to be one to which the sections apply. Furthermore, under subsection (2), if the price to be paid to any such director for his shares is in excess of the price obtainable by other shareholders or if any other valuable consideration is given to the director, the excess price or the value of the consideration is deemed to be a payment caught by the sections.[62]

However, these extensions are counterbalanced by subsection (3) which provides that sections 312 to 315 do not include any bona fide payment by way of damages for breach of contract or by way of pension[63] in respect of past services. Hence, so long as the directors have rolling five-year service agreements it is normally possible to pay them adequate "golden parachutes" without having to get prior approval from the shareholders. Especially is this so because it has been held, by the Privy Council on an appeal concerning the equivalent to what is now section 312 of the British Act, that that section does not apply to payments due under a contract with the company, but only to uncovenanted benefits,[64] nor to payments, whether contrac-

---

[59] And of "other members of the same class". When the target company has only one class of shares the meeting will be a general meeting of the company. In other cases subs. (2) makes appropriate provisions for class meetings.

[60] s.315(1). The expenses of distributing the sum among those former shareholders must be borne by the director.

[61] See Chap. 22 at pp. 615–617, above.

[62] This means of evasion by paying more for the shares of a retiring director is unlikely to be tried if the Code applies since it would normally lead to the offer price having to be raised. And for the same reason, if the offeror wants to retain certain directors of the target they will not be paid more for their shares to persuade them *not* to resign, though that would not be caught by the sections.

[63] Widely defined: see s.316(3). It appears that the pension payment does not have to be a contractual entitlement.

[64] *Taupo Totara Timber Co. v. Rowe* [1978] A.C. 537, P.C. In the instant case the director's service contract provided that, if the company were taken over, he could within twelve months resign from the company and become entitled to a lump-sum payment of five times his annual

tual or not, made in connection with the loss of an office held in conjunction with the directorship, for example a managing directorship. If this reasoning applies to section 314, it is highly undesirable. The second part of the above proposition would render the section inapplicable to compensation paid to executive directors qua executives, where it is most needed. Indeed, this dictum[65] seems to render almost superfluous the saving in section 316(3) for any "bona fide payment by way of damages for breach of contract", since the most obvious source of such damages is the executive's service contract. Even the force of the first part of the proposition, excluding contractual payments, may need to be reconsidered in its application to section 314, in the light of 316(2)[66] which deems valuable consideration given to a director in connection with a takeover to have been a payment made to him by way of compensation for loss of office or as consideration for or in connection with his retirement from office.

Section 316(4) specifically states that nothing in sections 313 to 315 "prejudices the operation of any rule of law requiring *disclosure*[67] to be made . . . of payments made or to be made to a company director". It does not, however, say anything about its not prejudicing any rule of law requiring prior agreement of the members in general meetings to such payments but, in the absence of bad faith on the part of the board, there does not seem to be any such requirement apart from sections 313 to 315.[68]

The loopholes with which the sections are riddled enable their obvious purpose to be easily defeated and they are in need of urgent review.

CONCLUSION

This Chapter has not attempted to answer the hotly disputed question of whether, on balance, takeovers are a "good thing" or a "bad thing". However, it is clear that the form of regulation of takeovers adopted in the United Kingdom does facilitate shifts in control achieved in this way. Especially important in this regard are the restrictions imposed by the Code on the defensive steps which are open to the management of the target company and its insistence that

---

salary! Such provisions should not be regarded as a New Zealand peculiarity, however. *The Financial Times* (July 23, 1996, p. 19) reported that the chief executive of a listed U.K. company would be entitled to three years' salary and fringe benefits (some £12 million) if he left the company within a year of a change of control.

[65] In the *Rowe* case itself, since the payment was due contractually, the court did not have to address itself to what the legal position would have been, had this not been so, but the payment had been made in relation to the loss of executive position rather than directorial office.

[66] See p. 814, above. Section 316(2) does not apply to s.312.

[67] Italics supplied.

[68] See Chap. 22, above.

the shareholders of the target should not be denied the opportunity to decide on the merits of the bid.[69] In other countries it is easier for the incumbent management to take steps to defend itself against unwelcome bids, though not necessarily to the point of preventing them entirely.[70] The argument in favour of the regime adopted by the Code is that it provides a cheap and effective method of keeping management on their toes and protects shareholders from management slackness or self-dealing—or, in any event, provides a method for the shareholders to exit the company on acceptable terms if such managerial misbehaviour produces a takeover bid. Moreover, the Code seems to reflect in this respect the dominance of the institutional shareholders in the United Kingdom, which, even in pre-bid situations, where the Code does not apply, have set their faces against the adoption of defensive devices by the management of potential takeover targets.[71] However, it is perhaps easy to overestimate the beneficial effect upon management performance of the threat of the takeover bid,[72] which is not to say that the takeover bid has no role to play in the British system of corporate governance. Moreover, it might be very unwise to put the decision on the fate of the takeover bid entirely in the hands of the management of the target company when it is their discharge of their managerial functions which may be the main issue of contention in the bid. Going beyond these considerations of shareholder and management relations, however, is the broader question of the impact of takeovers on the public interest and on the interests of those other than the current shareholders whom company law now recognises as having an interest in the company, notably the employees.[73] This leads into the much wider subject of whether the current pattern of regulation of takeovers is part of a broader institutional structure which encourages "short-termism" on the part of the management of British companies, to the detriment of all those with a stake in the efficient running of the British economy. That, however, is a debate which cannot be embarked upon here.

[69] See Paul, "Corporate Governance in the Context of Takeovers of U.K. Public Companies" in Prentice and Holland (eds.), *Contemporary Issues in Corporate Governance* (Oxford, 1993), especially at pp. 139–143.

[70] See Davies, "Defensive Measures: The Anglo-American Approach" (now somewhat dated on the U.S. side) and Schaafsma, "Defensive Measures: The Continental Approach" in Hopt and Wymeersch (eds.), *European Takeovers: Law and Practice* (London, 1992).

[71] See Davies, "Institutional Investors in the United Kingdom" in Prentice and Holland (eds.), *op. cit.*, especially at pp. 85–87.

[72] See Coffee, "Regulating the Market for Corporate Control" (1984) 84 *Columbia Law Review* 1145.

[73] See p. 602, above.

CHAPTER 30

ADMINISTRATIONS, WINDINGS-UP AND DISSOLUTIONS

ALTHOUGH as pointed out in Chapter 5,[1] one of the advantages of a body corporate is that it can live forever, most companies do not. Indeed in times of economic rescession they are put to death with alarming frequency because they are unable to pay their debts. If that is their only offence death may seem an unnecessarily extreme penalty (we don't hang individuals who have gone bankrupt). But until the Insolvency Act 1986[2] we had no formal system, such as the South African "judicial management", the Australian "official management", or the American Chapter 11 of the Bankruptcy Act, whereby an attempt can be made to nurse back to health a company presently unable to pay its debts owing to cash flow or similar difficulties. Now we have something similar and the first part of this Chapter deals with that, leaving the funeral rites of liquidation to be described, in brief outline only, in the second and third parts.

1. ADMINSTRATION ORDERS

Background

This new alternative to liquidation or winding up (the two expressions are used indiscriminately) implements recommendations of the Cork Committee,[3] which were based on its belief in the beneficial results flowing from the appointment, by the holder of a floating charge, of a receiver and manager (now called an "administrative receiver") which has been dealt with in Chapter 15.[4] In most cases an ailing company will have granted its bankers a floating charge over all its undertaking and assets and if it becomes unable to meet its

---

[1] At pp. 85–87, above.
[2] In this Chapter (except in relation to the last Part on Dissolution) it is the Insolvency Act (not the Companies Act) which is referred to as "the Act" and references to sections are to those of that Act unless the context otherwise requires.
[3] *The Report of the Review Committee on Insolvency Law and Practice*, (1982) Cmnd. 8558.
[4] At pp. 382, *et seq.* It is still possible to appoint a receiver and manager who will not be an administrative receiver within the meaning of the Act because the floating charge and the appointment do not cover "the whole or substantially the whole of the company's property or such of it as would have been substantially the whole of that property but for the fact that some other person has been appointed as receiver", *e.g.* by the holder of a fixed charge on some part of it: s.29(2).

obligations the first step will normally be for the bank[5] to appoint an administrative receiver.[6] Since the latter's "primary duty is to realise the assets in the interests of the debenture-holder and his powers of management are really ancillary to that duty",[7] the administrative receiver will, quite properly, tend to concentrate on realising sufficient of the assets to enable the preferred creditors[8] to be paid and the indebtedness to the debenture-holder and the costs of the receivership to be discharged. This, in most cases, will leave little (if anything) to be handed over to a liquidator. Admittedly in a few cases the receiver may have managed so skilfully that the company is restored to solvency and he can then be discharged and the company not put into liquidation—but that is very unusual.

However, the Cork Committee regarded the power to appoint administrative receivers as having been "of outstanding benefit to the general public and to society as a whole" since "in some cases they have been able to restore an ailing enterprise to profitability and return it to its former owners", and "in others, to dispose of the whole or part of the business as a going concern"[9] so that, in either case, "the preservation of the profitable parts of the enterprise has been of advantage to the employees, the commercial community, and the general public".[10] The Committee was "satisfied that in a significant number of cases, companies have been forced into liquidation and potentially viable businesses capable of being rescued have been closed down for want of a floating charge under which a receiver and manager could have been appointed".[11] Accordingly, its recommended solution was that the court should be empowered to appoint an administrator, whether or not there was a holder of a floating charge entitled to appoint an administrative receiver, but that the rights of such a holder to appoint an administrative receiver should be preserved so long as the holder elected to do so before an administration order was made.

As a result of the implementation of these recommendations we have a solution which more closely resembles the South African

---

[5] In recent years the banks have been criticised for allegedly acting precipitately, thereby causing companies to be put into receivership followed by liquidation when they might have survived if the banks had not stepped in prematurely.

[6] Alternatively, in the case of a company with debenture stock, the trustees for the debenture stockholders may appoint.

[7] *Per* Hoffmann J. in *Gomba Holdings v. Homan* [1986] 1 W.L.R. 1301 at 1305C.

[8] They have to be paid by the receiver in priority to the holder of the floating charge: see Chap. 15 at pp. 382 *et seq.*, above.

[9] This, however, can be done in a liquidation since the liquidator is empowered to carry on the business of the company so far as may be necessary for its beneficial winding up, but the sanction of the court is needed in the case of compulsory liquidations: ss.165, 167 and Sched. 4, para. 5.

[10] Cmnd 8558, para. 495.

[11] *ibid.*, para. 496.

"judicial" or Australian "official" management (neither of which seems to have been particularly successful as a rescue operation) rather than the American Chapter 11, which has proved more successful and which affords the ailing company a complete and often lengthy moratorium in respect of its debts. However, the new administration procedure is being used to a greater extent than was expected.[12]

Although the objective of administration is to provide generally something similar to administrative receiverships, there are important differences between the two. Administrators can be appointed only by the court and they are officers of the court who, under the supervision of the court, act in the interests of the company as a whole and in the public interest in its survival if possible. An administrative receiver, in contrast, is normally appointed out of court by the holder of a floating charge and then he is not an officer of the court. And even if he is appointed by the court, his primary duty remains that of realising the company's assets in the interests of the holder of the floating charge.[13]

The statutory provisions relating to administrations are in Part II (sections 8–27) of the Insolvency Act, which, as in relation to receiverships and liquidations, is supplemented by the detailed Insolvency Rules.[14]

When administration can be ordered

The appointment of an administrator requires an order of the court and is necessarily a somewhat more formal and expensive procedure than the appointment by a floating charge holder of an administrative receiver.[15] Section 8(1) provides that the court may make such an order if it is satisfied that the company is unable to pay its debts[16] (or is likely to become so, so that there is no need to wait until the company is *in extremis*) and that the appointment of an administrator would be likely to achieve one or more of the purposes stipulated in the statute as proper purposes for an administration.[17] These are, as

---

[12] Because it was thought that, if the company's bankers had a floating charge, they would normally prefer to appoint their own administrative receiver. The fact that now they sometimes seem to be willing to refrain from doing so if administration is proposed may be partly due to sensitivity to the criticisms referred to in n. 5, above. They also now have the assurance that whoever is appointed will be a qualified and licensed insolvency practitioner and not just someone friendly towards the company's management.

[13] But the Act has done something to ensure that the general body of creditors are kept informed about what the administrative receiver is doing: see ss.47–49. The position of the administrator and of the administrative receiver are compared and contrasted by Anderson, (1996) 12 *Insolvency Law and Practice* No. 7 at p. 9 and No. 2 at p. 54.

[14] S.I. 1986 No. 1925, as amended. The rules relating to administration specifically are in Part II.

[15] See above, p. 382.

[16] As defined in s.123.

[17] The court's order must specify the purpose(s) for which the administration order is made.

provided in section 8(3), the survival of the company and[18] the whole
or any part of its undertaking as a going concern; the achievement of
a voluntary arrangement under Part I of the Act[19]; the sanctioning by
the court of a scheme of arrangement[20]; or the more advantageous
realisation of the company's assets than could be effected by a winding
up. In practice, most applications are made on the first and fourth
grounds.

After some initial hesitation the courts seem to have rejected the
view that the court has to be satisfied on the balance of probabilities
that the suggested purpose will be achieved in favour of the less
demanding test that there must be a "real prospect" that the purpose
or purposes will be achieved.[21] The point is an important one, for the
higher hurdle materially increases the costs (as well as decreasing the
chances) of securing an administration order, especially by encouraging applicants to commission an extensive report by an independent
person in support of the application.[22]

There are, however, further restrictions on the jurisdiction to grant
an order.[23] Winding up and administration are mutually exclusive procedures for dealing with insolvent companies. Accordingly, an administration order cannot be made if the company has gone into liquidation,[24] though equally there can be no winding up during the currency
of an administration order.[25] In principle, the same situation prevails
in respect of an administrative receiver. If the holder of the floating
charge has actually appointed an administrative receiver, the court may
not appoint an administrator as well, unless the holder consents or the
court is satisfied that the security under which the administrative
receiver was appointed is impeachable; on the other hand, once an
administrator has been appointed by the court, the charge-holder may
not appoint an administrative receiver.[26]

However, since the appointment by a charge-holder of an administrative receiver is a simple and speedy private act, involving the exer-

---

[18] It is thought that this is in fact a statement of two separate purposes: the survival of the
company as a going concern or the survival of the whole or part of its undertaking as a going
concern (in the other hands); otherwise this is a very stiff hurdle.

[19] See pp. 768–770, above.

[20] See pp. 762–767, above.

[21] *Re Harris Simmons Ltd* [1989] 1 W.L.R. 368; *Re Primlaks (UK) Ltd* [1989] BCLC 734; *cf.*
Re Consumer & Industrial Press Ltd [1988] BCLC 177.

[22] Provision is made for such reports by Rule 2.2 but they are not mandatory and the Chancery
Division judges have sought to encourage concise reports not based on protracted and expensive investigation: *Practice Note* [1994] 1 W.L.R. 160.

[23] In addition to the matters dealt with in the text insurance companies are excluded from the
administration procedure: s.8(4)(a).

[24] s.8(4).

[25] s.11(1)(a).

[26] ss.9(3) and 11(3)(b). If the court exceptionally appoints an administrator even though an
administrative receiver is in place, then the latter will vacate office on the former's appointment: s.11(1)(b).

cise of powers set out in the instrument creating the security,[27] and since five days' notice[28] of the petition for the appointment of a administrator has to be given to various parties, including the person who is or may be entitled to appoint an administrative receiver,[29] the effect of the provisions is to give the holder of a floating charge (normally a bank) a veto over the appointment of an administrator. On receipt of the notice the holder of the floating charge, who has not yet exercised its right of appointment, can normally do so, if it so wishes, before the petition for an administrator is heard. Although the courts have regarded themselves as having the power to abridge the five-day period in cases of urgency[30] or even to make an appointment in relation to an intended petition,[31] the courts have not sought to exercise these powers so as to deprive the charge-holder of the opportunity to pre-empt the administration petition by appointing an administrative receiver.[32]

Petitions for the appointment of an administrator may be presented by the company, acting pursuant to a resolution passed in general meeting, its directors[33] or a creditor or creditors (including contingent and prospective creditors)[34] or all or any of them, together or separately.

Effect of the application

During the period beginning with the presentation of the petition and ending with the making of an order or the dismissal of the petition there is a limited moratorium. Under section 10 no resolution may be passed for voluntary winding up or order made for compulsory winding up by the court.[35] Nor may any steps be taken to enforce any security[36] over the company's property or to repossess goods in its possession under a hire purchase agreement[37] or to take any legal

---

[27] See p. 382, above.

[28] Rule 2.7.

[29] Rule 2.6.

[30] *Re A Company (No. 00175 of 1987)* [1987] BCLC 467.

[31] *Re Gallidoro Trawlers Ltd* [1991] BCLC 411.

[32] This point was made explicitly in the *Re A Company* case; in *Re Gallidoro Trawlers* the issue did not arise since it was the bank which was seeking the appointment of an administrator.

[33] Acting by resolution of the board or unanimously without a resolution: *Re Equiticorp International plc* [1989] 1 W.L.R. 1010.

[34] Or indeed the clerk of a magistrates' court to enforce fines imposed on the company: s.9(1) as amended by Criminal Justice Act 1988.

[35] s.10(1)(a). This, however, does not preclude the presentation of a petition for winding up (see s.10(2)(a)) and in a number of cases the court has been faced at the hearing with petitions for both winding up and administration and has had to decide which (if either) it should order. But no further steps can be taken on the winding up petition until that for the administration order has been heard: *Re A Company (No. 001992 of 1988)* [1988] BCLC 9.

[36] Widely defined in s.248. The definition has even been held to include a landlord's right of re-entry; *Exchange Travel v. Triton* [1991] BCLC 396.

[37] Which, for the purposes of both ss.10 and 11, include conditional sale agreements, chattel leasing agreements and retention of title agreements: s.10 (4).

process against the company or its property except with the leave of the court.[38] But this, as we have seen, does not prevent the appointment of an administrative receiver or the carrying out by him of his functions until his appointor consents to the making of the administrative order.[39]

Effect of the order

On the making of an administration order a more extensive moratorium then comes into effect. Under section 11(3) during the period that the administration order remains in force: (a) no resolution may be passed or order made for the winding-up of the company; (b) no administrative receiver of the company may be appointed; (c) no other steps may be taken to enforce any security on the company's property or to repossess goods in the possession of the company under a hire-purchase agreement; and (d) no other proceedings and no execution or other legal process may be taken or continued and no distress may be levied against the company or its property; unless, in case (c) or (d), the administrator consents or the court grants leave on such terms as the court may impose.

It is section 11(3)(c) and (d) that has caused administrators and their advisers particular difficulty. Fortunately they now have some guidance from the two leading cases on administrations, namely the Court of Appeal judgments in *Bristol Airport plc v. Powdrill*[40] and, especially, *Re Atlantic Computer Systems (No. 1).*[41] These cases are also of importance in relation to administrations generally for they stress the need for a purposive construction of Part II of the Insolvency Act paying regard to the mischiefs identified by the Cork Committee and which that Part was intended to cure. That is admirable. But unfortunately it does not provide a ready answer to all the problems arising from situations dealt with by section 11(3)(c) and (d) in which there is a potential conflict between the purposes of the legislation, *i.e.* (i) that creditors, secured or unsecured, shall not exercise their rights in a way which might frustrate the purpose of the administration and (ii) that, nevertheless, such creditors must be treated fairly and, if secured, should not find their status reduced to that of unsecured creditors.

In *Atlantic Computer Systems* the Court of Appeal was disturbed by the increasing number of applications to the courts for leave. It considered that it was the intention of the legislation that, in the first, and ideally the final, instance, such matters should be dealt with by

[38] s.10(1)(b) and (c).
[39] s.10(2)(b) and (c) and s.10(3).
[40] [1990] Ch. 744, C.A. A case not devoid of humorous facts in which an airport attempted to exercise its statutory right to retain the aircraft of an airline under administration until it had been paid all airport dues payable in respect of the period before its going into administration.
[41] [1992] Ch. 505, C.A.

the administrator on applications to him for consent. But this, it recognised, was unlikely to occur unless administrators and their legal
advisers had clearer guidance on what is the approach of the courts
when application for leave is made so that administrators could adopt
the same approach in dealing with applications for consent. Accordingly, with some reluctance, the Court proceeded to give such guidance in what it described as 12 "general observations", hoping
thereby that applications to the court would become the exception
rather than the rule.[42] The following two paragraphs attempt to
summarise the effect of those observations.[43]

Since the prohibitions in section 11 are intended to assist the administrator to achieve the purpose of the administration, it is for the person
who seeks leave (or consent) to make out a case for being granted it.
If leave is unlikely to impede the achievement of that purpose, leave
should normally be given. In other cases it is necessary to carry out a
balancing exercise, weighing the legitimate interests of the applicant
and those of the other creditors of the company.[44] In carrying out that
exercise the underlying principle is that an administration should not
be conducted at the expense of those who have proprietary rights
which they are seeking to exercise, except to the extent that this may
be inevitable if the purpose of the administration is to succeed and
even then only to a limited extent. Thus, it will normally be a sufficient
ground for granting leave if significant loss would otherwise be suffered by the applicant, unless the loss to others would be significantly
greater. In assessing the respective losses all the circumstances relating
to the administration should be taken into account[45] and regard paid
to how probable they are likely to be. The conduct of the respective
parties may sometimes also be relevant.[46]

Similar considerations apply to decisions regarding imposing terms.
Powers to do so are expressly conferred when the court grants leave
and, although section 11 makes no express provision when leave is
refused, the court has power to do so, directly by giving directions to
the administrator under section 17, or in response to an application by
the administrator under section 14, or in exercise of its control over
officers of the court. Alternatively, the court may do so indirectly by
ordering that the applicant shall have leave unless the administrator is
prepared to take steps in the administration specified by the court.
Cases where leave is refused on undertakings being given by the

[42] [1991] BCLC at 632a–e.
[43] *ibid.* at 632–634.
[44] Citing *Royal Trust Bank v. Buchler* [1989] BCLC 130 at 135. See also *Re David Meek Plant Ltd* [1994] 1 BCLC 680 (where, in addition, the court gave a broad meaning to "goods in the company's possession under any hire purchase agreement")
[45] See observation (6) at 663(e)(f) of which the text, above, is a somewhat inadequate summary.
[46] Citing, at 663, *Bristol Airport v. Powdrill*, where leave was refused because the applicant airport had benefited from the administration and delayed in seeking to enforce its right of retention.

administrator are likely to be frequent. The court's observations on terms and its expressed belief that observance by administrators of the guidance will make applications to the courts exceptional necessarily imply that an administrator when granting consent is empowered to impose terms on the applicant and when refusing consent is empowered to give undertakings. This is indeed an admirable example of the use of a purposive construction, for neither is expressly provided in section 11,[47] which confers such powers only on the court when granting leave. So long as administrators follow the guidelines, applications to the court should be greatly reduced and needed only when mutually acceptable terms cannot be agreed by applicants and administrators. In cases where the applicant is the holder of a fully secured fixed or floating charge there should normally be no difficulty in obtaining agreement that the applicant will delay enforcing his security for a reasonable time to enable the administrator to plan his strategy.[48]

However, not every form of litigation or action by creditors falls within the scope of the moratorium created by section 11(3). In *Air Ecosse Ltd v. Civil Aviation Authority*[49] proceedings by non-creditors were held to lie outside the scope of the moratorium even though the action in question (administrative proceedings by a regulatory body to review the company's fitness to hold an operating licence) could have a devastating effect upon the company's ability to carry on its business. Even in relation to creditors, certain self-help remedies, not amounting to the enforcement of security, seem to fall outside the moratorium, the most important example being the right of set-off.[50] Nor, of course, does an unpaid creditor of a company in administration have an obligation to continue with supplies or to make further advances unless contractually or statutorily[51] required to do so.[52] Thus, the moratorium may protect the company in administration from pressure from its existing creditors, but it falls far short of guaranteeing that the administrator will be able to carry on the business effectively during the administration. That is likely to require fresh funding and

---

[47] Contrast s.15, below.
[48] See [1991] BCLC at 634d, C.A.
[49] 1987 S.L.T. 751.
[50] *Electro Magnetic (S) Ltd v. Development Bank of Singapore* [1994] 1 S.L.R. 734. See also *Re Olympia & York Canary Wharf Ltd* [1993] BCLC 453 (service of notice on company in administration making time the essence of a contract and, later, accepting the company's repudiatory breach did not amount to the commencement of proceedings or other legal process), explaining *Exchange Travel Agency Ltd v. Triton Property Trust plc* [1991] BCLC 396 (peaceable re-entry by landlord for non-payment of rent by company in administration was not commencement of legal process but did amount to enforcement of a security).
[51] *cf.* s.233, relating to supplies of gas, water and electricity.
[52] *Leyland DAF Ltd v. Automotive Products plc* [1994] 1 BCLC 245, C.A., where the supplier refused further supplies unless paid for those already delivered.

the availability (or not) of such funding is one of the matters the court needs to consider when deciding whether to appoint an administrator.[53]

Powers of administrators

The administrator (a) may do all such things as may be necessary for the management of the affairs, business and property of the company and (b) without prejudice to the generality of (a) he has all the powers specified in Schedule 1 to the Act.[54] That Schedule confers 22 specific powers on administrators[55] and a "catch-all" power "to do all other things incidental to the exercise of the foregoing powers". In effect, therefore, the administrator[56] has all the powers normally vested in the board of directors. The directors do not necessarily vacate office, but the administrator has power to remove any director of the company, to appoint any person to be a director of it and to call any meeting of the members or creditors of the company.[57] Hence, the administrator can retain directors, executive or non-executive, if he thinks they might be useful, and indeed should ensure that there is the minimum number of directors to fulfil their obligations under the Companies Act regarding calling of AGMs and the like to the extent that these duties are not performed by him. But "any power conferred on the company or its officers whether by this Act or the Companies Act or by the memorandum or articles of association, which could be exercised in such a way as to interfere with the exercise by the administrator of his powers, is not exercisable except with the consent of the administrator . . .".[58]

In exercising his powers the administrator is deemed to act as the company's agent,[59] and, in contrast with an administrative receiver,[60] he is not personally liable on contracts which he enters into on the company's behalf. However, the Act contains an alternative mechanism for ensuring that the administrator secures the discharge of the obligations he causes the company to incur. When the administrator

---

[53] Practice Note, above, n. 22.

[54] s.14(1).

[55] These are the same powers as s.42 confers on administrative receivers except, in their case, to the extent that the powers are inconsistent with the debenture under which they were appointed: see Chap. 15 at p. 385, above.

[56] Who may apply to the court for directions in relation to any particular matter arising in connection with the carrying out of his functions: s.14(3).

[57] s.14(2). The power to remove directors may have a chilling effect upon directors' willingness to apply for the appointment of an administrator.

[58] s.14(4).

[59] s.14(5). This gives him or her the protection of s.727 of the Companies Act 1985 (see p. 652, above and *Re Home Treat Ltd* [1991] BCLC 705). But his relationship with the company is not that of its agent or servant: he is an officer of the court, not of the company.

[60] Who, despite the fact that he too acts as agent, is personally liable on contracts he enters into unless they provide to the contrary: s.44(1); see Chap. 15 at p. 387, above.

relinquishes office, undischarged liabilities are charged on the company's assets and rank ahead of any floating charge or the administrator's own remuneration.[61] A person dealing with an administrator in good faith and for value is not concerned with whether the administrator is acting within his powers.[62] This would seem to afford third parties much the same protection as they would have obtained, prior to the administration, under the new sections 35–35B of the Companies Act but only so long as in addition to acting in good faith they have given value.[63] In order that persons dealing with the company realise that it is under administration, section 12 requires that every invoice, order for goods or business letter on which the name of the company appears shall also contain a statement that the affairs, business and property of the company are being managed by an administrator.

Finally, section 15[64] significantly adds to the importance of the moratorium under section 11(3)[65] by enabling the administrator to sell company property free of third party interests in the shape of the floating charge and, even more important, subject to court approval, to dispose of a third party's property in the company's possession, that is, where the company has granted a fixed charge or holds property under a hire purchase agreement, etc. Thus, third parties may find not only that they cannot repossess their property but that the administrator has disposed of it. The first power arises where any part of the company's property is subject to a charge which, when created, was a floating charge.[66] In such a case the administrator is, under subsections (1), (3) and (4), empowered to dispose of the property as if it was not subject to the charge but the holder of the charge has the same priority in respect of any property of the company representing, directly or indirectly, the property disposed of. In effect the charge is treated as if it is still an uncrystallised floating charge so that the administrator can sell the property free from the charge which then attaches to the proceeds of sale.

When, however, the property is subject to any other type of "security" or is held by the company under a "hire-purchase agreement",[67] the more complicated provisions of subsections (2) and (5)–(8) apply.

---

[61] s.19(5). For the application of this rule in relation to adopted employment contracts see, *Powdrill v. Watson* [1995] 2 A.C 394, H.L., partially reversed by the Insolvency Act 1994, and Pollard (1995) 24 I.L.J. 141.

[62] s.14(6).

[63] Which is not a condition of ss.35–35B of the Companies Act: see Chap. 10, above. Presumably it was thought that as the company is insolvent this additional condition was needed to protect creditors.

[64] Adapted to Scotland by s.16.

[65] See pp. 822–824, above.

[66] *i.e.* it applies notwithstanding that the charge may have crystallised as a result of the administration order or the appointment of an administrative receiver or a receiver and manager, prior to the administration order.

[67] Once again defined, in subs. (9), as including "conditional sale agreements, chattel leasing agreements and retention of title agreements". See generally Oditah and Zacaroli [1977] CFILR 29.

Under subsection (2), where, on application by the administrator, the court is satisfied that the disposal (with or without other assets) of the property would be likely to promote the purpose or one of the purposes specified in the administration order, the court may by order authorise the administrator to dispose of the property as if it were not subject to the security or to the rights of the owner under the hire-purchase agreement. The court has a discretion whether or not to make such an order and it has been held that in deciding whether or not to do so it should undertake a balancing exercise similar to that on applications under section 11, to decide whether the hardship to the security-holder or owner of the goods of making an order would outweigh the detrimental effect on the achievement of the purposes of the administration.[68] Even if the security is a fixed charge the hardship to the holder should be slight. It must be a condition of an order that the net proceeds of the disposal (and, if they prove to be less than the court determined would be realised on a sale in the open market by a willing vendor, such sums as are required to make up the deficiency) have to be applied towards discharging the sums secured.[69] In effect, therefore, the security is retained and the only detriment to the security-holder is that he cannot control the timing of the realisation of his security which will be undertaken by the administrator, probably as part of a larger disposal, instead of by the security holder as a single transaction.

Duties of the administrators

In contrast with the detailed provisions regarding the administrator's powers, all the Act says about his general duties is in one short section 17. However, the general principle underlying this Part of the Act is that administration is a procedure for the benefit of the general body of creditors and is controlled by them. So the main obligation laid upon the administrator is to produce proposals for consideration by the creditors and to implement them, if approved. Section 17 provides that the administrator shall on his appointment take into his custody or control all the property to which the company is, or appears to be, entitled[70]; shall manage its affairs, business and property in accordance with any directions of the court prior to the approval of proposals in accordance with section 24, below; and thereafter in accordance with those proposals[71]; and shall summon a meeting of creditors if requested by one-tenth in value of the creditors or if directed by the court.[72] In addition, specific duties are imposed on him as regards:

[68] *Re ARV Aviation Ltd* [1989] BCLC 664.
[69] See subsection (6) for the position when two or more securities are involved.
[70] s.17(1).
[71] s.17(2).
[72] s.17(3).

giving information about his appointment to the company's creditors and the Registrar[73]; obtaining a statement of affairs from officers and employees of the company[74]; and, within three months (or such longer period as the court may allow), sending to the Registrar, the company's members and creditors a statement of his proposals for achieving the purpose or purposes specified in the order and to lay this before a meeting of creditors.[75] If the meeting approves his proposals (with any modifications that he accepts) he must report the result to the court and give notice to the Registrar and to other persons prescribed by the Rules.[76] Thereafter, if the administrator proposes to make any revisions which appear to him to be substantial, he must convene another meeting of creditors and obtain their approval.[77] At a meeting summoned under section 23 which approves the proposals, the meeting may, if it thinks fit, establish a creditors' committee which may require the administrator to attend before it at any reasonable time and to furnish it with such information relating to the carrying out of his functions as it may reasonably require.[78]

If, however, the administrator's proposals are not approved at the meeting summoned under section 23, this must similarly be reported and the court may "discharge the administration order and make such consequential provision as it thinks fit, or adjourn the hearing conditionally or unconditionally, or make an interim order or any other order that it thinks fit".[79] Normally it will obviously be necessary that the company is put into insolvent liquidation—and as soon as possible. Indeed, except when the efforts of the administrator have enabled the company itself to survive as a solvent going concern, the administration will have to be succeeded by a liquidation if only because (except when the administrator has achieved a successful voluntary arrangement[80]) an administrator has no power to make distributions of dividends to creditors. This is commonly regarded as a great weakness of Part II. And, unfortunately, the wording of the Act and the Rules implies that the winding-up will be a compulsory liquidation by the court—the most expensive method.

However, ways have been found for reducing the expense. Almost

---

[73] s.21.
[74] s.22.
[75] s.23.
[76] s.24(1)–(4).
[77] s.25.
[78] s.26. This is a somewhat emasculated version of what the Cork Committee recommended; *i.e.* that the creditors "should be required to nominate a Committee which will take office if the court confirms the Order appointing an Administrator or directs that the company should be placed in some form of insolvency proceedings": Cmnd. 8558, para. 513.
[79] s.24(5). If the administration order is discharged, the administrator must send to the Registrar a copy of the order discharging it: s.24(6).
[80] Under Part I of the Act: see Chap. 28 at pp. 768–770, above.

invariably the liquidator appointed will be the former administrator[81] and the courts have proved willing in an increasing number of cases to countenance a voluntary winding-up notwithstanding the wording of the Act—again adopting a "purposive" approach, this time to reduce the very real danger that the additional expense of preceding a liquidation by an administration will frustrate the legislative aim by discouraging the use of administrations.

Discharge or variation of administration orders

Section 18 provides that the administrator may at any time apply to the court for the administration order to be discharged or to be varied so as to specify an additional purpose.[82] And he must make an application if "(a) it appears to him that the purpose or each of the purposes specified in the order either has been achieved or is incapable of achievement[83]; or (b) he is required to do so by a meeting of the company's creditors summoned for the purpose".[84] If the order is discharged or varied the administrator must within 14 days send an office copy to the Registrar of Companies and is liable to a fine if he fails to do so without a reasonable excuse.[85]

Vacation of office

The administrator may at any time be removed from office by the court and may, in prescribed circumstances,[86] resign by giving notice to the court.[87] He must also vacate office if he ceases to be qualified to act as an insolvency practitioner in relation to the company or if the administration order is discharged.[88] And, since administrators must be

---

[81] s.140 expressly empowers the court to do so where a winding-up order is made immediately upon the discharge of the administrator.

[82] s.18(1).

[83] The wording of this suggests that he is not bound to apply if two or more purposes were specified unless and until it appears to him that both or all purposes have been achieved or are incapable of achievement (if he had to apply when any one of them was achieved or was incapable of achievement "any" would surely have been used instead of "each").

[84] s.18(2). On an application under s.18 the court's powers are the same as those under s.24(5) when a report to it is made under that section (see above).

[85] s.18(4) and (5).

[86] The Rules (r.2.53) prescribe ill-health, intention to cease practice as an insolvency practitioner, conflict of interest or a change of personal circumstances which make it impractical to continue to act; but the court may grant leave on other grounds.

[87] s.19(1).

[88] s.19(2). s.19(4) and (5) contain provisions (similar to those applying to receivers) for protecting his rights in respect of remuneration due and indemnity out of the assets of the company in respect of liability on contracts. The latter is less important than in the case of receivers because he will be personally liable only if he has expressly agreed (see p. 825, above) as he may have had to.

appointed as individuals, his death will also cause a vacation of his office.[89]

When the office is vacated the administrator is released "from all liability both in respect of acts or omissions of his in the administration and otherwise in relation to his conduct as administrator",[90] with effect from, in the case of death, the date when notice is given to the court in accordance with the Rules[91] and in any other case such time as the court may determine.[92] The reason why the date of his release may be later than the date of vacation of office is to ensure that, if liquidation is to follow, the administrator is not released *qua* administrator until he or someone else is appointed as liquidator.

Unfair prejudice by administrator

Given the administrator's substantial powers to interfere with what would otherwise be the rights of creditors, it is perhaps not surprising that Parliament provided an express statutory mechanism for judicial review of the fairness of the administrator's conduct. This is done in the final section 27 of Part II of the Act which affords a remedy similar to sections 459–461 of the Companies Act.[93] It provides that:

"*At any time when an administration order is in force a creditor* or member[94] may apply to the court by petition for an order under this section on the ground:

(a) that the company's affairs, *business and property* are being *managed*, or have *been managed, by the administrator* in a manner which is unfairly prejudicial to the interests of its *creditors* or members generally or of some part of its creditors or members (including at least himself) or

(b) that any actual or proposed act or omission of *the administrator* is or would be so prejudicial.*"*[95]

This, in substance, is identical with section 459(1) except as regards the words italicised which differ from those in section 459(1) in order

---

[89] This is another reason why firms of practitioners favour joint appointments of two or more of their members: if only one is appointed the firm risks losing the remunerative work on his death.

[90] s.20(2). But it does not relieve him from potential liability to the summary remedy, against delinquent directors, administrators *et al.*, under s.212: s.20(3).

[91] Under r.2.54 notice may be given by the deceased's personal representatives, a partner in the deceased's firm who is a qualified insolvency practitioner or by "any person producing to the court the relevant death certificate or a copy of it."

[92] s.20(1).

[93] See Chap. 27, above. Apart from s.27 the court will expect the administration to adhere to certain standards of conduct by virtue of his status as an officer of the court. *Re Atlantic Computer Systems (No. 1)* [1992] Ch. 505.

[94] Which, as in s.459, includes a person to whom shares have been transmitted by operation of law: see s.250; a general provision (which the Companies Act lacks) applying for the purposes of Parts I–VII of the Act.

[95] s.27(1). Italics supplied.

to adapt it appropriately to the period when the business and property of the company are being managed by an administrator. The important change is that, in contrast with section 459, it provides a remedy which is available to creditors as well as members. It should be noted, however, that, in order to use it, the creditors or members must petition while the administration order is in force. Once the order is discharged it will be too late. But, while it is in force, section 27 supersedes section 459 of the Companies Act, even so far as members are concerned, unless the administrator consents or the court grants leave for a petition under the latter section to be commenced or continued.[96]

Section 27 also provides that an order under it shall not prejudice or prevent the implementation of a voluntary arrangement under Part I of the Act or any scheme of arrangement sanctioned under section 425 of the Companies Act Act[97]; or the implementation of any proposals approved under section 24 or 25[98] if the application is made more than 28 days after the approval.[99] On the other hand, it is expressly provided that "nothing in section 15[1] is to be taken as prejudicing applications under" section 27.[2] The effect of this seems to be that, notwithstanding that the court has made an order under section 15(2) authorising the administrator to dispose of property free from a charge thereon or from the rights of the owner under a hire-purchase agreement, the chargee or owner may petition under section 27 on the ground that the disposition was unfairly prejudicial to him. This is despite the protection afforded him by section 15(4) or (5) and despite the fact that the court authorised the disposition after deciding that achievement of the purposes of the administration outweighed any detriment to him. This at first glance seems strange but is designed to enable the applicant to complain that the transaction was carried out in a manner unfairly prejudicial, if he does so in time.

The orders that the court can make on an application under section 27 are broadly similar to those that can be made under section 461 of the Companies Act on an application under its section 459. They start similarly with a general power to "make such order as it thinks fit for giving relief in respect of the matters complained of"[3] and then four particular examples are given.[4] The four are: (a) regulating the future management by the administrator; (b) requiring the administrator to refrain from doing or continuing to do, or from omitting to do, an act

---

[96] No power is conferred on an administrator himself to invoke s.459 (it is not "legal proceedings in the name and on behalf of the company" within the meaning of the Act, Sched. I. para. 5).

[97] On which see Chap. 28, above.

[98] Above, p. 827.

[99] s.27(3).

[1] See pp. 826–827, above. The same applies in respect of s.16, the Scottish equivalent of s.15.

[2] s.27(5).

[3] s.27(2).

[4] s.27(4).

in respect of which the petitioner has complained[5]; (c) requiring the summoning of a meeting of creditors or members to consider such matters as the court directs; and (d) discharging the administration order and making consequential provisions.[6] There is nothing similar to the Companies Act, section 461(2)(c) authorising civil proceedings to be taken on behalf of the company (which may seem surprising since the act complained of might be a refusal by the administrator to sue on behalf of the company but the omission is presumably because the court could order him to sue under section 27(2) or by exercising its inherent jurisdiction over officers of the court). Nor is there anything similar to section 461(2)(d) providing for a purchase of the petitioner's shares (which is presumably not regarded as appropriate in the circumstances of an administration of an insolvent company).

Conclusion

Although the administration procedure had its origins in the proposal of the Cork Committee to extend what it saw as the benefits of the administrative receivership to all insolvent companies,[7] the legislation enacting the idea in fact puts the administrator in some respects in a stronger position that the administrative receiver. The most striking features of the administration procedure turn out to be the moratorium, without court consent, on the enforcement of rights by creditors (which does not obtain in the case of an administrative receivership but rather is drawn from analogy with the powers of the liquidator)[8] and the ability of the administrator to sell company property free of third-party rights and, with court sanction, to dispose of third-party property (where the administrative receiver's powers[9] are more limited). Nevertheless, appointments of receivers, although not negligible in number, are much fewer than appointments of administrative receivers: in 1995 168 of the former as against 1,845 of the latter.[10] Obviously, in large part this is the result of the reluctance of banks to allow an administrator, with responsibilities to the creditors as a whole, to be appointed in place of an administrative receiver, who is much more the creature of the appointing charge-holder. However, when reviewing the operation of the current procedures in 1993, the Insolvency Service stopped short of recommending that the current

---

[5] (a) and (b) correspond with Companies Act, s.461(2)(a) and (b).
[6] (c) and (d) have no counterparts in s.461.
[7] Above, p. 817.
[8] See below, pp. 833 *et seq.* Moreover, in *Re Atlantic Computer Systems plc (No. 1)* [1992] Ch. 505 at 527–528 the Court of Appeal was disposed to think that the courts should be less protective of third-party interests when exercising their discretion in administrations than in liquidations, on the ground that the former was an interim and temporary regime.
[9] s.43. See p. 386, above.
[10] (1996) 12 *Insolvency Law and Practice* No. 4 at 139.

right of veto be removed or circumscribed, whether in relation to the present procedure or the additional administration procedure which it proposed.[11] The second main drawback of the present procedure is perceived to be its expense, especially at the stage of application to the court for the appointment of an administrator.[12] The Insolvency Service Consultative Document proposed the introduction of an additional administration procedure which would be available upon a simple filing with the court for an administrator to be appointed and without any court scrutiny of the grounds for the appointment. The new procedure would be limited, however, to 28 days (extendible to a maximum of three months with the consent of three-quarters in value of the creditors) and its main purpose would be for the administrator to establish whether a survival plan for the company was feasible rather than, as at present, for the plan to be formulated before an application is made.[13] However, no legislative steps have been taken to implement these proposals.[14]

2. WINDING-UP

Despite the fact that administrations relate more to insolvency law than to company law, they have been dealt with relatively fully in the first part of this Chapter because of their novelty and interest and the fact that if they succeed in their primary aim they may enable the company to survive as a solvent concern. This second part of the Chapter is concerned with the winding-up process that normally has to be undertaken before a company is dissolved. The provisions relating to this are now to be found almost exclusively[15] in the Insolvency Act and Part IV of the Insolvency Rules,[16] and not in the Companies Act; and rightly so where the company is insolvent. But, although insolvency is the most common reason for winding up, it is far from being the only one and, when the company is fully solvent, it seems, on the face of it, somewhat illogical to treat the process as part of insolvency law rather than company law. The reason why the legisla-

---

[11] Insolvency Service, *Company Voluntary Arrangements and Administration Orders: Consultative Document*, October 1993, paras. 5.7 and 6.6.
[12] See p. 820, above.
[13] *ibid.*
[14] For the Chancery Court's response, see n. 22, above.
[15] But see Companies Act, ss.651–658, below at pp. 846 *et seq.*
[16] Both eschew the use of the word "members" and substitute "contributories", thus giving the misleading impression that it means only members who are called upon to contribute because their shares are partly paid (or in the case of guarantee companies because of the minimal amounts that they have agreed to contribute on a winding-up). To avoid this impression, here "members" has been substituted; but readers should be warned that that too is not wholly accurate for "contributories" also includes past members unless they ceased to be members more than 12 months before the commencement of the winding-up: see ss.74 and 76 and *Re Anglesea Collieries* (1866) L.R. 1 Ch. 555, C.A. and *Re Consolidated Goldfields of New Zealand* [1953] Ch. 689.

tion relating to liquidation of solvent companies is in the Insolvency Act is probably to avoid duplicating those many provisions that apply whether or not the company is insolvent—to repeat them in the Companies Act would have added substantially to the length of the combined legislation.[17] But it can also be justified as realistic. Once a company goes into liquidation, the distinction between shareholders and creditors becomes more than usually difficult to draw; the members' interests will, in effect, have become purely financial interests deferred to those of the creditors.

Types of winding-up

The basic distinction is between voluntary winding-up and compulsory winding-up by the court.[18] But voluntary windings-up and subdivided into two types—members' voluntary winding-up and creditors' voluntary winding-up. In relation to companies registered under the Companies Acts which are dealt with in Part IV of the Insolvency Act,[19] Chapters I and VII–X of that Part relate to all three types, except where it is otherwise stated, Chapters II and V relate to both types of voluntary winding-up, Chapter III relates only to members' voluntary winding-up, Chapter IV only to creditors' voluntary winding-up and Chapter VI only to winding-up by the court. This arrangement of the sections is not exactly "user friendly" for it means that, to grasp which sections apply to the type of winding-up with which one is concerned, it is necessary to refer to various Chapters of Part IV. Nor is life made easier because other Parts of the Act may also be relevant: for example Part VI on "miscellaneous provisions" and Part VII on "interpretation for first group of Parts".

As their names imply, an essential difference between compulsory winding-up by the court and voluntary winding-up is that the former does not necessarily involve action taken by any organ of the company itself, whereas voluntary winding-up does. The essential difference between members' and creditors' winding-up is that the former is possible only if the company is solvent, in which event the company's members appoint the liquidators, whereas, if it is not, its creditors have the whip hand in deciding who the liquidator shall be. In all three

---

[17] Duplication has not been avoided without some infelicities, not made any happier by the insertion by the Insolvency Act of a new s.735A in the Companies Act under which references in the latter to "this Act" are deemed to include references to a substantial number of sections of the Insolvency Act (and, in some cases, to the whole of the Company Directors' Disqualification Act).

[18] There used to be a further (hybrid) type of voluntary winding-up subject to the supervision of the court, but this had ceased to be used and was abolished by the reforms of 1985/1986.

[19] In relation to the winding-up of "unregistered companies" (on which see Chap. 6 at pp. 127–130, above) winding-up by the court is the only method allowed: see Part V of the Act. A company incorporated outside Great Britain which has been carrying on business in Britain may be wound up as an unregistered company notwithstanding that it has ceased to exist under the law of the country of incorporation: s.225.

cases, the winding-up process is not exclusively directed towards realising the assets and distributing the net proceeds to the creditors and, if anything is left, to the members, according to their respective priorities; it also enables an examination of the conduct of the company's management to be undertaken. And this may result in civil and criminal proceedings being taken against those who have engaged in any malpractices thus revealed[20] and in the adjustment or avoidance of various transactions.[21]

Winding-up by the court

Under section 122 of the Act a company may be wound up by the court[22] on one or more of seven specified grounds. Of these grounds, by far the most important is ground (f), that the company is unable to pay its debts, and the next most important ground (g), that the court is of the opinion that it is just and equitable that the company should be wound up. The latter has been dealt with in Chapter 27 (where we saw that it may be used as a remedy in cases where members are being unfairly prejudiced or there is a deadlocked management) and in Chapter 25 (where we saw that it may be invoked by the Secretary of State following the exercise by him of his investigatory powers). The presence of a minority protection remedy in the Insolvency Act is, in fact, something of an anomaly. It should be noted that the company itself can opt for winding-up by the court, since ground (a) is that the company has by special resolution resolved that the company be so wound up. But normally that is the last thing that those controlling the company will want; it is the most expensive type of winding-up and the one in which their conduct is likely to be investigated most thoroughly.[23]

Section 123 affords creditors owed more than £750 a simple means of establishing ground (f), that the company is unable to pay its debts.[24] As in the case of administration orders, creditors are among those who may petition[25] and this they are likely to do once it becomes widely known that the company is in financial difficulties[26]; like a petition for the bankruptcy of an individual, a petition for winding-up is the creditors' ultimate remedy. The company itself or its directors[27]

---

[20] See Part IV, Chap. X of the Act.

[21] See Part VI, ss.238–246.

[22] Normally the High Court, but the county court of the district in which the company has its registered office has concurrent jurisdiction if the company's paid-up capital is small and if that county court has jurisdiction in relation to bankruptcy of individuals: s.117.

[23] But it might be used if the court is already involved because the liquidation of the company is part of a scheme requiring its sanction in accordance with Chap. 28, above.

[24] By serving a "statutory notice" in accordance with s.123(1)(a).

[25] s.124. As may the clerk of a magistrates' Court: *cf.* n. 34, p. 821, above.

[26] Until then each may try to obtain judgment and levy execution thus getting ahead of the pack.

[27] Prior to the 1985/1986 statutory reforms, it was held, somewhat surprisingly, that directors could not apply: *Re Emmerdart Ltd* [1979] Ch. 540. Now they can. For the interpretation of "the directors" see *Re Equiticorp International plc* [1989] 1 W.L.R. 1010.

or members[28] may petition but the court will be reluctant to grant it on ground (f) if it is opposed by a majority of the creditors.

If a winding-up order is made, the first step needing to be taken will be to appoint a liquidator to whom, as in all types of winding-up, the administration of the company's affairs and property will pass. In contrast with an individual's trustee in bankruptcy its property does not vest in him[29]; but the control and management of it and of the company's affairs do and the board of directors, in effect, becomes *functus officio*. A liquidator may, indeed, be appointed before a final order is made, for at any time after the presentation of a winding-up petition the court may appoint a provisional liquidator, normally the official receiver attached to the court.[30]

The important role played by official receivers in compulsory liquidations in England and Wales[31] is perhaps the major difference between compulsory and voluntary liquidations.[32] Official receivers are officers of the Insolvency Service, an Executive Agency of the DTI, attached to courts having bankruptcy jurisdiction.[33] Not only will an official receiver normally be the provisional liquidator (if one is appointed) but he will generally be the initial liquidator and often will remain the liquidator throughout. On the making of a winding-up order[34] he automatically becomes liquidator by virtue of his office and will remain so unless and until another liquidator is appointed.[35] He may succeed in ridding himself of the office by summoning separate meetings of the creditors and of the members for the purpose of

---

[28] But unless the membership has been reduced below two, a member cannot apply unless his shares were originally allotted to him or have been held and registered in his name for at least six months during 18 months prior to the commencement of the winding up (on which see below) or have devolved on him through the death of a former holder: s.124(2). This is designed to prevent a disgruntled person (*e.g.* an ex-employee) from buying a share and then bringing a winding-up petition (or threatening to do so).

[29] Unless the court so orders, as it may: s.145(1).

[30] s.135.

[31] Scotland manages without them but when the Government, in a desire to reduce civil service manpower and public expenditure, proposed to remove their role in individual bankruptcy there was bitter opposition (not least from the Cork Committee: see Cmnd. 8558, Chap. 14) and the proposal was dropped.

[32] In the latter, their role is principally in relation to disqualification of directors under the Directors Disqualification Act (on which see Chap. 24 at p. 684, above). They also play a major role in relation to individual bankruptcies which always require a court order, there being nothing comparable to voluntary liquidation except that the individual concerned may, and often will, file his own petition.

[33] Official receivers have the unique distinction of being entitled to act as liquidators notwithstanding that they are not licensed insolvency practitioners under Part XIII of the Act: ss.388(5) and 389(2).

[34] Except when it is made immediately upon the discharge of an administration order or when there is a supervisor of a voluntary arrangement under Part I of the Act (on which see Chap. 26, above at pp. 768–770) when the former administrator or the supervisor of the arrangement may be appointed by the court as liquidator: s.140.

[35] s.136(1) and (2).

appointing another liquidator.[36] And if that does not succeed[37] he may decide to refer the need to appoint another liquidator to the Secretary of State who may appoint.[38] But, whenever any vacancy occurs, he again becomes the liquidator until another is appointed.[39]

Whether or not the official receiver becomes the liquidator he has important investigatory powers and duties. When the court has made a winding-up order he may require officers, employees and those who have taken part in the formation of the company to submit to him a statement as to the affairs of the company verified by affidavit.[40] It is his duty to investigate the causes of the failure, and to make such report, if any, to the court as he thinks fit.[41] He may apply to the court for the public examination of anyone who is or has been an officer, liquidator, administrator, receiver or manager of the company or anyone else who has taken part in its promotion, formation or management and must do so, unless the court otherwise orders, if requested by one-half in value of the creditors or three-quarters in value of the members.[42] And if he is not the liquidator, the person who is must give him all the information and assistance that he reasonably requires for the exercise of his functions.[43]

On the making of a winding-up order the winding-up is deemed to have commenced as from the date of the presentation of the petition (or, indeed, if the order is made in respect of a company already in voluntary winding-up, as from the date of the resolution to wind up voluntarily[44]). This dating back is important since it can have the effect of invalidating property dispositions[45] and executions of judgments[46] lawfully undertaken during the period between the presentation of the petition and the order,[47] and of affecting the duration of the periods prior to "the onset of insolvency" in which, if certain transactions are undertaken, they are liable to adjustment or avoidance in the event of winding-up or administration.[48]

Once a liquidator is appointed, the process of the winding-up

---

[36] See s.136(4) and (5). The nominee of the creditors prevails unless, on application to the court, it otherwise orders (s.139) which it is unlikely to do if the company is insolvent.

[37] Which it may not since both creditors and members may be happy to leave the liquidation to the official receiver since that may prove less expensive.

[38] s.137.

[39] s.136(3).

[40] s.131. See also ss.235 and 236.

[41] s.132.

[42] ss.133 and 134. It is this public examination that is the most dreaded ordeal, particularly if the company is sufficiently well known to attract the attention of the general public and the Press. But there is a similar provision in relation to individual bankruptcy (s.290) and there is no reason why those who have chosen to incorporate their businesses should escape it.

[43] s.143.

[44] s.129.

[45] s.127.

[46] s.128.

[47] Which may be considerable if hearings are adjourned, as is not infrequent.

[48] See ss.238–245.

proceeds very much as it would in the case of a voluntary liquidation since the objective is identical and his functions are the same as those in voluntary windings up, namely[49] "to secure that the assets of the company are got in, realised, and distributed to the company's creditors[50] and, if there is a surplus, to the persons entitled to it".[51] The main difference is that, in a winding-up by the court, the liquidator in the exercise of his powers under Schedule 4 to the Act will more often require to obtain sanction of the court before entering into transactions and that throughout he will be subject to the surveillance of the official receiver acting, in effect, as an officer of the court.

Voluntary windings-up

In contrast with winding up by the court, voluntary winding up always starts with a resolution of the company. In the unlikely event of the articles fixing a period for the duration of the company[52] or specifying an event on the occurrence of which it is to be dissolved,[53] all that is required is an ordinary resolution in general meeting.[54] Otherwise, what is required is a special resolution that the company be wound up voluntarily,[55] or an extraordinary resolution "to the effect that it cannot, by reason of its liabilities, continue its business, and that it is advisable to wind up".[56] The reason for the resort to an extraordinary resolution is that although it, like a special resolution, requires to be passed by a three-fourths majority of those voting, the meeting can be convened on 14 days' notice rather than 21 and speed may be of the essence when the company is insolvent.[57] Each of these resolutions is subject to section 380 of the Companies Act (*i.e.* a copy of it has to be sent to the Registrar within 15 days[58]) and the company must give notice of the resolution by advertisement in the *Gazette* within 14 days of its passing.[59] A voluntary winding-up is deemed to commence on the passing of the resolution[60]; there is no "relating

---

[49] s.143(1).

[50] Giving priority, of course, to preferred creditors as set out in Sched. 6 to the Act.

[51] Normally the members (except in the case of non-profit-making or charitable companies) in accordance with their class rights on a winding-up.

[52] This is rare but Charters of incorporation of limited duration are not uncommon.

[53] It is possible to conceive of circumstances in which this might be done: *e.g.* when a partnership converts to an incorporated company because its solicitors and accountants advise that this would be advantageous tax-wise, the partners might wish to ensure that it could be dissolved by a simple majority if they were later advised that it would be better to revert to a partnership.

[54] s.84(1)(a).

[55] s.84(1)(b).

[56] s.84(1)(c).

[57] In relation to companies with a very small number of like-minded members this is of theoretical importance only for they will agree on short notice under s.369(3) of the Companies Act and, if a private company, act by a written resolution under its section 381A.

[58] s.84(3).

[59] s.85(1). In Chap. 19 at p. 507, n. 13, above, mention was made of the apparently irrational differences between times allowed for notifications; here we have an example.

[60] s.86.

back'' as there is in the case of winding-up by the court. As from the commencement of the winding-up, the company must cease to carry on its business, except so far as may be required for its beneficial winding-up,[61] and any transfer of shares, unless made with the sanction of the liquidator, is void, as is any alteration in the status of the members.[62]

Members' winding-up

The most important question which the directors of the company will have had to consider prior to the passing of the resolution is whether they can, in good conscience and without dire consequences to themselves, allow the voluntary winding-up to proceed as a members', as opposed to a creditors', winding-up. In order for that to occur they, or if there are more than two of them, the majority of them, must, in accordance with section 89, make at a directors' meeting[63] a statutory declaration (the "declaration of solvency") to the effect that they have made a full inquiry into the company's affairs and that, having done so, they have formed the opinion that the company will be able to pay its debts in full, together with interest at the "official rate",[64] within such period, not exceeding 12 months from the commencement of the winding-up, as may be specified in the declaration.[65]

The declaration is ineffective unless:

(a) it is made within five weeks preceding the date of the passing of the resolution, and
(b) it embodies a statement of the company's assets and liabilities as at the latest practicable date before the making of the declaration.[66]

If a director makes the declaration without having reasonable grounds for believing that the company will be able to pay its debts with interest within the period specified in the declaration he is liable to fines and imprisonment,[67] and if the debts are not so paid it is presumed, unless the contrary is shown, that he did not have reasonable grounds for his opinion.[68] It therefore behoves the directors to take the utmost

---

[61] s.87(1).
[62] s.88. Contrast the wording of the comparable s.127, above, in relation to winding-up by the court; that avoids also any disposition of the company's property (unless the court otherwise orders) which s.88 does not.
[63] This, on the face of it rather curious, use of a board meeting as a venue for the making of statutory declarations ensures that all the directors know what is going on.
[64] *i.e.* whichever is the greater of the interest payable on judgment debts or that applicable to the particular debt apart from the winding-up: ss.189(4) and 251.
[65] s.89(1). In practice the declaration will play safe and not specify a shorter period than 12 months even if the directors expect that it will be shorter.
[66] s.89(2). The declaration must be delivered to the Registrar within 15 days immediately following the passing of the resolution: s.89(3) and (4).
[67] s.89(4).
[68] s.89(5).

care and to seek professional advice before they make the declaration. Especially is this so because, even if the winding-up is a members' one, a licensed insolvency practitioner will have to be appointed as liquidator and he is likely to detect whether the declaration was over-optimistic long before the expiration of the 12 months. Formerly, small private companies could, and often did, appoint as liquidator one of the directors and, in effect, continued to proceed much as they would have when a partnership was being dissolved. This is no longer possible[69]; despite the efforts begun by the 1989 Act to reduce the burdens on private companies, the Insolvency Act has increased their burdens as regards winding-up even if they are quasi-partnerships.

If the professional liquidator becomes of the opinion that the company will not be able to pay its debts within the stated period, he must summon a meeting of the creditors and supply them with full information in accordance with section 95 and, as from the date when the meeting is held, the winding-up is converted under section 96 from a members' to a (insolvent) creditors' voluntary winding-up.[70] So long, however, as the liquidator shares the view of the directors (and if they are wise they will have consulted him, as their proposed nominee, before they made the declaration) all should proceed smoothly as a members' winding-up. The company in general meeting will appoint one or more liquidators for the purpose of winding up the company's affairs and distributing its assets[71] whereupon "all the powers of the directors cease except so far as a general meeting or the liquidator sanctions their continuance".[72] If a vacancy in the office of liquidator "occurs by death, resignation or otherwise" the company in general meeting may, subject to any arrangement with the creditors,[73] fill the vacancy.[74] If the winding-up continues for more than a year,[75] the liquidator must summon a general meeting at the end of the first and any subsequent year or at the first convenient date within three months from the end of the year or such longer period as the Secretary of State may allow.[76] The liquidator must lay before the meeting an account of

---

[69] But see below at pp. 846–848 for the possible resort to s.652 of the Companies Act.

[70] Indeed, it may become a winding-up by the court, for a winding-up order may be made notwithstanding that the company is already in voluntary winding-up and an official receiver, as well as the other persons entitled under s.124, may present a petition: s.124(5). But unless the court, on proof of fraud or mistake, directs otherwise, all proceedings already taken in the voluntary winding-up are deemed to have been validly taken: s.129(1).

[71] s.91(1).

[72] s.91(2). As they probably will.

[73] This reference to "creditors" is presumably to cover the case where the members' voluntary winding-up forms part of a reorganisation of one of the types dealt with in Chap. 28 above, in which creditors are involved.

[74] s.92(1). The meeting to do so may be convened by any continuing liquidators if there was more than one or by a member: s.92(2).

[75] Which it may, because although the creditors should be paid within 12 months the subsequent distribution of the remaining assets or their proceeds does not have to be completed within any prescribed time.

[76] s.93(1).

his acts and dealings, and of the conduct of the winding-up during the year.[77]

When the company's affairs are fully wound up the liquidator must "make up"[78] an account of the winding-up, showing how it has been conducted and the company's property disposed of, and must call a final meeting of the company for the purpose of laying before it the account and giving an explanation of it.[79] The fact that this meeting is being called is something which is of wider interest than to members alone for, as we shall see,[80] it will lead to the final dissolution of the company. The Act provides that it shall be called by advertisement in the *Gazette*, specifying its time, place and object and published at least one month before the meeting.[81] Within one week after the meeting he must also send the Registrar a copy of the account and make a return to him of the holding of the meeting.[82]

Creditors' winding-up

Here, in contrast with members' winding-up, the company is assumed to be insolvent and it is the creditors in whose interests the winding-up is undertaken and they who have the whip hand. If no declaration of solvency has been made, the company must cause a meeting of its creditors to be summoned for a day not later than the fourteenth day after the resolution for voluntary winding-up is to be proposed and cause notices to be sent by post to the creditors not less than seven days before the date of the meeting and must advertise it once in the *Gazette* and once at least in two newspapers circulating in the locality in which the company's principal place of business in Great Britain was situated during the previous six months.[83] This must state either (a) the name of a qualified insolvency practitioner[84] who, before the meeting, will furnish creditors with such information as they may reasonably require or (b) a place where, on the two business days before the meeting, a list of the company's creditors will be available for inspection free of charge.[85] Further, the directors must prepare a statement of the company's affairs verified by affidavit and cause it to be laid before the creditors' meeting. The directors must

---

[77] s.93(2).

[78] These are the words used in the section but they are not intended to countenance fictitious accounts as they might suggest.

[79] s.94(1).

[80] See pp. 844–846, below.

[81] What is surprising is that neither the Act nor the Rules seem to require the liquidator to give written notice to the members. If he does not, it is not surprising that the final meeting is frequently inquorate.

[82] s.94(3) and (4). If a quorum is not present the liquidator must send instead a return that the meeting was duly summoned and that no quorum was present.

[83] s.98(1).

[84] In practice he will probably be the person that the directors intend to propose to the company meeting for appointment as liquidator.

[85] s.98(2).

also nominate one of their number to preside at the creditors' meeting—an unenviable task which it is the nominee's duty to perform.[86]

At the respective meetings the creditors and the company may nominate a liquidator and if the creditors do so he becomes the liquidator, unless, on application to the court by a director, creditor or member, it directs that the nominee of the company shall be liquidator instead of, or jointly with, the creditors' nominee, or it appoints some other person instead of the creditors' nominee.[87] Provisions, similar in effect, apply when a members' winding-up is converted to a creditors' winding-up because the liquidator concludes that the company's debts will not be paid in full within the 12 months, except that the obligations of the directors have to be undertaken by the incumbent liquidator.[88]

In a creditors' voluntary winding-up,[89] or in a winding-up by the court,[90] the creditors may decide at their initial or a subsequent meeting to establish what used to be called a ''committee of inspection'' but which the Act now calls a ''liquidation committee'', and, in the case of a creditors' winding-up, may appoint not more than five members of it.[91] If they do so, the company in general meeting may also appoint members not exceeding five in number.[92] However, if the creditors resolve that all or any of those appointed by the general meeting ought not to be members of the committee, the persons concerned will not be qualified to act unless the court otherwise directs.[93]

The functions of a liquidation committee are to be found in the Rules rather than the Act and for present purposes can be summarised by saying that they give the liquidator the opportunity of consulting the creditors and the members without having to convene formal creditors' and company meetings and also provide additional means whereby the creditors and members can keep an eye on the liquidator. In the latter respect, liquidation committees are, perhaps, likely to be more valuable in creditors' voluntary windings-up (rather than in windings-up by the court) owing to the lesser role played by official receivers.

It may be thought somewhat anomalous that, when the company is insolvent, the members should have equal (or any) representation on the liquidation committee. But the Cork Committee rejected the argu-

---

[86] s.99.

[87] s.100.

[88] ss.95 and 96.

[89] s.101, and, when a members' is converted to a creditors' winding-up, s.102.

[90] s.141.

[91] s.101(1). In the case of windings-up by the court the position under s.141 and Chapter 12 of Part 4 of the Rules is somewhat different and is designed to ensure that, when the official receiver is the liquidator, the committee's functions are performed instead by the DTI's Insolvency Service and that, if the liquidator is some other person, it is left to him to decide whether to convene a meeting of creditors to establish a liquidation committee (unless one-tenth in value of the creditors require him to do so).

[92] s.101(2).

[93] s.101(3).

ment that they should not, because "it is rarely possible to assess the interest of shareholders at the outset of proceedings".[94] This is certainly true. What at the commencement of the winding-up would seem to be a clear case of the company's liabilities greatly exceeding its assets (so that the shareholders have no prospective stake in the outcome of the winding up) may turn out otherwise if the winding-up is prolonged.[95]

In other respects a creditors' winding-up proceeds up to and including the final meetings in much the same way as in a members' winding-up.

Conclusion

No attempt has been made here to deal with the many important matters which may arise in the course of winding-up, whether by the court or voluntarily; for example how creditors "prove" their debts (dealt with in detail by the Rules rather than by the Act). However, a word ought to be said about the position of secured creditors in order to draw attention to the difference between their position on a winding up compared with that during an administration. As we saw, in the latter, unless they have taken steps to enforce their security prior to the administration, they may be in difficulties in doing so while it lasts.[96] In contrast, on a winding-up, a secured creditor is in the enviable position of having the choice of realising his security and, if this does not raise sufficient to pay him in full, to prove for the balance, or to surrender his security for the benefit of the general body of creditors and prove for the whole debt.[97] Normally, of course, he will adopt the former option.[98]

However, as emphasised in Chapter 15,[99] when his security is a floating charge he may be adversely affected by a winding-up (or administration) both because of the inherent nature of such a charge and of the statutory provisions relating to its subordination to the claims of preferred creditors and those relating to adjustment of prior transactions and in particular, avoidance under section 245 of the Act. And it is not only holders of *floating* charges who may find themselves adversely affected. Although section 245 applies only to floating

[94] Cmnd. 8558, para. 939.
[95] But, unless it is, the reverse is at present likely to be the case, resulting in members' windings-up having to be converted into creditors' (or to winding-up by the court).
[96] See pp. 822–824, above.
[97] Rule 4.88. If the winding up follows an administration in which the administrator has exercised his powers under s.15 (above, pp. 826–827) it would seem that the effect of s.15(4) and (5) will be to preserve the security-holder's rights by treating the sums mentioned in those subsections as the security in the winding-up.
[98] Unless he is an unusually altruistic creditor or he wants to maximise his votes at a creditors' meeting.
[99] At pp. 382 *et seq.*, above.

charges, any persons who have obtained benefits from the company prior to the winding-up (or administration) may find themselves deprived of them under section 238 as "transactions at an under-value"[1]; or, under section 239, as "preferences"[2]; or, under section 244, as "extortionate credit transactions".

3. DISSOLUTION

After winding-up

In contrast with the formalities attendant on the birth of a company,[3] its death takes place with a singular absence of ceremony. In the case of voluntary liquidations, once the liquidator has sent to the Registrar his final account and return,[4] on the expiration of three months from their registration the company is deemed to be dissolved,[5] unless the court, on the application of the liquidator or any other person who appears to the court to be interested, makes an order deferring the date of dissolution.[6]

Normally the position is much the same where the winding-up is by the court. The liquidator, once it appears to him that the winding-up is for all practical purposes complete, must summon a final meeting of creditors[7] which receives the liquidator's report on the winding-up and determines whether he shall be released.[8] The liquidator then gives notice to the court and to the Registrar that the meeting has been held and of the decisions (if any) of the meeting. When the Registrar receives the notice he registers it and, unless the Secretary of State, on the application of the official receiver or anyone else who appears to be interested, directs a deferment,[9] the company is dissolved at the end of three months from that registration.[10]

If the official receiver is the liquidator the procedure is the same except that registration is of a notice from the official receiver that

---

[1] Or in Scotland as "gratuitous alienations": see s.242.

[2] In Scotland "unfair preferences": see s.243.

[3] See Chap. 6, above.

[4] In accordance with s.94 (members' voluntary) or s.106 (creditors' voluntary).

[5] s.201(1) and (2).

[6] s.201(3). It is then the duty of the applicant to deliver an office copy of the order to the Registrar for registration: s.201(4).

[7] The relevant statutory provisions appear to apply to windings up by the court on any ground and whether or not the company is insolvent and not to require any final meeting of the company (as in a voluntary liquidation). If this is correct, it is very curious. In a winding-up on the petition of a member on the ground that it is just and equitable, if the company's creditors have been fully paid it is only the members who will have any interest in the result of the winding-up.

[8] ss.146 and 172(8).

[9] s.205(3). An appeal to the court lies from any such decision of the Secretary of State: s.205(4).

[10] s.205(1) and (2).

the winding-up is complete.[11] However, there is a sensible procedure whereby he may bring about an early dissolution if it appears to him that the realisable assets are insufficient to cover the costs of the winding-up[12] and that the affairs of the company do not require any further investigation.[13] He must, before doing so, give at least 28 days' notice of his intention to the company's creditors and members and to an administrative receiver if there is one,[14] and, with the giving of that notice, he ceases to be required to undertake any of his duties other than to apply to the Registrar for the early dissolution of the company.[15] On the registration of that application the company becomes dissolved at the end of three months[16] unless the Secretary of State, on the application of the official receiver or any creditor, member or administrative receiver,[17] gives directions to the contrary before the end of that period.

The grounds upon which the application to the Secretary of State may be made are (a) that the realisable assets are in fact sufficient to cover the expenses of the winding-up or (b) that the affairs of the company do require further investigation,[18] or (c) that for any other reason the early dissolution of the company is inappropriate.[19] And the directions that may be given may make provision for enabling the winding-up to proceed as if the official receiver had not invoked the procedure or may include a deferment of the date of dissolution.[20]

There are no similar provisions for early dissolution on a voluntary winding-up; once the company has resolved on voluntary winding-up it is expected to go through with it. But if there is a vacancy in the liquidatorship and no one can be found who is willing to accept the office because there is clearly not enough left to pay the expenses of continuing it (no insolvency practitioner will accept office in such circumstances unless someone is prepared to pay him), it is difficult to see how the Registrar could do other than to strike the company off the register as a defunct company, under section 652 of the Companies Act—as, indeed, that section specifically recognises. To that section

---

[11] s.205(1)(b).

[12] In Scotland (lacking official receivers) there is a procedure for early dissolution on this ground alone but it involves an application to the court: s.204.

[13] s.202(1) and (2).

[14] s.202(3).

[15] s.202(4).

[16] s.202(5).

[17] There is an apparent inconsistency between s.202(5) which says that the application can be made by the official receiver "or any other person who appears to the Secretary of State to be interested" and s.203(1) which says that it must be by one of the persons mentioned in the text above. Presumably the Secretary of State will not regard any other person as "interested".

[18] Neither of which is likely to be accepted by the Secretary of State if the official receiver has concluded the contrary.

[19] s.203(2).

[20] s.203(3). There can be an appeal to the court against the S. of S.'s decision: s.203(4).

we now turn because it affords a method whereby a small company can, in practice, often be inexpensively dissolved without any formal winding-up. Although it appears in a chapter of the Companies Act headed "matters arising subsequent to winding up" (which therefore has been left in that Act and not transferred to the Insolvency Act) section 652 is in fact something that is extensively used when there has been no winding-up.

Defunct companies

Under section 652, if the Registrar has reasonable cause to believe that a company is not carrying on business or in operation, he may send to the company a letter inquiring whether that is so.[21] If within a month of sending the letter he does not receive a reply he shall, within 14 days thereafter, send a registered letter referring to the first letter and stating that no answer to it has been received and that, if an answer to the second letter is not received within one month from its date, a notice will be published in the *Gazette* with a view to striking the company's name off the register.[22] If the Registrar receives a reply to the effect that the company is not carrying on business or is not in operation, or if he does not, within one month of sending the second letter, receive any reply, he may publish in the *Gazette* and send to the company by post a notice that at the expiration of three months from the date of the notice the name of the company will, unless cause to the contrary is shown, be struck off the register and the company will be dissolved.[23] At the expiration of the time mentioned in the notice, the Registrar may, unless cause to the contrary is shown, strike the company off the register and publish notice of this in the *Gazette*, whereupon the company is dissolved.[24]

As mentioned in Chapter 19,[25] this section is most commonly used when what has afforded the Registrar reasonable cause to believe that the company is not carrying on business or in operation is the fact that it is in arrear with the lodging of its annual returns and accounts. When so used by the Registrar, it is both a method of inducing those companies that are operating in breach of their filing obligations to mend their ways as well as a method of clearing the register of companies which are indeed defunct. It can, however, specifically be used to deal with the situation referred to above when winding-up proceedings have been started but insufficient resources are available to com-

---

[21] Companies Act, s.652(1). For meticulous details about how letters and notices are to be addressed, see s.652(7).
[22] *ibid.*, s.652(2). From hereon references to "the Act" are to the Companies Act 1985 unless the context otherwise requires.
[23] s.652(3).
[24] s.652(5).
[25] At p. 509 at n. 30, above.

plete them. Section 652(4) says that where the Registrar has reasonable cause to believe either that no liquidator is acting or that the affairs of the company are fully wound up and that the returns required to be made by the liquidator have not been made for a period of six consecutive months, the Registrar shall publish in the *Gazette* and send to the company or the liquidator (if any) a like notice which causes the company to be dissolved.

Moreover, section 652 used to provide companies with a method of dissolving without the expense of a formal winding-up and especially without the appointment of an insolvency practitioner to oversee the process: the directors of a company which had ceased trading would simply write to the Registrar inviting him to exercise his powers under the section to it strike off. Under the Deregulation and Contracting Out Act 1994,[26] perhaps somewhat ironically, this practice has been formalised in new sections 652A–F and it is understood that the Registrar has discontinued the old practice and will in future entertain only formal applications for striking-off under the new procedure. The new sections in large part replicate the old practice, so the change has helped to make this course of action more transparent. However, the new procedure is confined to private companies in a way that the old practice was not.[27]

The procedure enables a company, which has not traded[28] during the previous three months, to apply by its directors (or a majority of them)[29] to the Registrar for the company to be struck off. The directors must ensure that notice of the application is given to a list of persons laid down in section 652B(6), who include, notably, its creditors (contingent and prospective creditors being embraced within the term),[30] its employees, the managers and trustees of any pension fund and its members. On receipt of the application the Registrar publishes a notice in the *Gazette* stating that he may strike the company off and inviting any person to show cause why he should not. Not less than three months later the Registrar may strike the company off and, on publication of a notice to this effect in the *Gazette*, the company is dissolved.[31] The purpose of requiring notice to be given by the directors is obviously to see if the people most likely to object to the striking-off in fact oppose this course of action, but the legislation lays down no particular procedure which the Registrar must follow in dealing with objections. The fact that the company has creditors clearly does not debar it from using this procedure (otherwise the Act

---

[26] s.13 and Sched.5, which came into force on July 1, 1995.
[27] A public company wishing to avail itself of the new procedure would need to reincorporate as a private company.
[28] What this involves (or rather does not involve) is set out in some detail in s.652B.
[29] s.652A(2).
[30] s.652D(8).
[31] s.652A(3)–(5).

would not require notice to be given to creditors) but it is not intended to be used in place of liquidation where the company has substantial assets or liabilities outstanding at the time of application.[32]

The range of matters which the Registrar must keep in mind upon an application under section 652A is much reduced by the provision that dissolution under the procedure does not inhibit the enforcement of any liability of the erstwhile company's directors, managing officers or members, so that these people cannot escape their common law or statutory duties by causing their company to be dissolved. Moreover, a company dissolved under the new procedure, like companies dissolved in other ways, may be restored to the register in certain circumstances,[33] a topic to which we now turn.

Resurrection of dissolved companies

A contrast between the death of an individual and that of a company is that, without divine intervention but merely by an order of the court, a dissolved company can be resurrected. The courts have found some difficulty in making sense of the statutory provisions empowering them to perform this miracle, particularly because the legislature has, for some reason, chosen to provide two distinct means: one under what is now section 651 of the Companies Act and the other under what is now its section 653. Most people reading the two sections would unhesitatingly conclude that section 651 applies when the company has been dissolved following a formal winding-up[34] and section 653 when it has been dissolved under section 652A.[35] This was certainly the view of Lord Blanesburgh, in *Morris v. Harris*,[36] who said of the predecessor of section 651 that it was "clearly confined to cases where the dissolution succeeds the complete winding up of the company's affairs and cannot take effect at all except at the instance, or with the knowledge, of the liquidator, the company's only executive officer". However, in *Re Belmont & Co. Ltd*,[37] in which this dictum seems not to have been cited, Wynn Parry J. decided that so long as the applicant could bring himself within the list of those entitled to apply to the court under both sections, he could choose either. In the subsequent case of *Re Test Holdings (Clifton) Ltd*[38] Megarry J. was persuaded by counsel for the Registrar to follow that decision, which

---

[32] If the company has assets and the application is successful, these will become *bona vacantia* upon the dissolution of the company: s.654.

[33] s.653 was amended by the addition of new ss.(2A) to (2D) so as specifically to cater for companies dissolved under the new procedure.

[34] See s.651(1) which refers to application by "the liquidator".

[35] See s.653(2) and (2A) which specifically refer to striking-off under s.652 and s.652A respectively.

[36] [1927] A.C. 252, H.L. at 269.

[37] [1950] Ch. 10.

[38] [1970] Ch. 285.

had been relied on in many later cases. He did, however, express doubts on whether the sections reflected a coherent policy and suggested that when the Companies Act was next revised, consideration might with advantage be given to that point. Notwithstanding the many subsequent revisions, that suggestion has been taken up only to the extent that the changes made by the Companies Act 1989 to section 651 (but not also to section 653) make sense only on the assumption that the legislature accepts that an applicant does have a choice of either section.

The absence of a "coherent policy" in sections 651 and 653 is vividly illustrated in *Re Wood & Martin Ltd*[39] and *Re Thompson & Riches Ltd.*[40] In both of these cases the companies concerned had been dissolved as a result of action by the Registrar under what is now section 652. In the first, the company, in blissful ignorance of this (notwithstanding the communications sent to it by the Registrar) purported to pass a resolution for a voluntary winding-up, appointing a "liquidator" who had proceeded to realise the assets. When he discovered the flaw in his appointment he applied, under what is now section 651, as "the liquidator of the company or any other person appearing to the court to be interested", for the dissolution to be declared void. Megarry J. held that, although it was necessary to make sense of the section to construe "liquidator" as including a former liquidator, it was impossible to construe it as including someone who, in law, had never been the liquidator. However, it did appear that he was an "other person interested" and he accordingly made the order applied for.

In *Re Thompson & Riches Ltd* the applicant for an order was a member of the company who, in ignorance (shared, apparently, by all concerned, including the court) of the fact that the company had been struck off, had obtained an order for the winding-up of the company by the court and the appointment of the official receiver as provisional liquidator. Presumably it was the official receiver who discovered that the company had long since been struck off. The fact that the winding-up was compulsory (rather than voluntary, as in *Re Wood & Martin*) added a complication, since section 652(6)(b) says that nothing in its subsection (5) "affects the power of the court to wind up a company the name of which has been struck off the register", Technically, therefore, the winding-up order was not void. Slade J. held that what the applicant should have done was to "follow the common practice adopted in the light of the decision in *Re Cambridge Coffee Room Association Ltd*[41] by asking for: (1) rescission of the existing winding-up order; (2) liberty to amend his petition so as to include an

[39] [1971] 1 W.L.R. 293.
[40] [1981] 1 W.L.R. 682.
[41] [1952] 1 All E.R. 112, where a similar situation had arisen (it is all too common).

application for restoration of the name of the company to the register; (3) an order for such restoration; and (4) a new winding-up order",[42] Instead of adopting this course, the applicant had applied[43] under the predecessor of section 651. Slade J., though he thought it would have been preferable to apply under section 653,[44] accepted that in the light of the earlier cases the applicant was entitled to apply under section 651 and he made an order declaring the dissolution void.

In most cases, therefore, applicants will have the choice of applying under either section 651 or 653. The differences between their wording (though less so between their substance) are great. Section 651 provides first that where a company has been dissolved the court may, on the application of the liquidator[45] or any other person appearing to the court to be interested, make an order in such terms as it thinks fit declaring the dissolution to be void. If an order is made "such proceedings may be taken as might have been taken if the company had not been dissolved". The use of the word "proceedings" suggests that all the draftsman was contemplating were legal proceedings by or against the company. But the effect is certainly wider than that since it causes any property of the company which may have vested in the Crown as *bona vacantia* on the company's dissolution to revest in the company.[46] On the other hand, the House of Lords[47] has held that it does not, as does an order under section 653,[48] have the effect of validating transactions by or with the company during the period between its dissolution and its restoration. If an order is made, it is the duty of the applicant to deliver an office copy to the Registrar for registration[49] and the applicant will be liable to fines if he fails to do so.[50]

However, a major contrast between the two sections relates to the limitation periods applied to each. Under section 651, applications must be brought within two years, except in certain cases relating to

---

[42] [1981] 1 W.L.R. at 687A.

[43] Presumably as a "person interested".

[44] Which he could have done as an "aggrieved member": see s.653(1) and (2) below.

[45] s.651(1). As Megarry J. had pointed out in *Re Wood & Martin*, above, once the company is dissolved it cannot have a "liquidator" which therefore must be construed as "former liquidator".

[46] s.655. Indeed, it has been said that a common purpose of a s.651 order is to permit distribution of an asset which was overlooked in the liquidation (*Re Servers of the Blind League* [1960] 1 W.L.R. 564) but the procedure is equally available to enable a creditor to make a claim not previously made: *Stanhope Pension Trust Ltd v. Registrar of Companies* [1994] 1 BCLC 628, C.A; *Re Oakleague Ltd* [1995] 2 BCLC 624.

[47] *Morris v. Harris* [1927] A.C. 252.

[48] See s.653(3) which provides that on the delivery to the Registrar of an office copy of the order made under that section "the company is deemed to have continued in existence as if its name had not been struck off".

[49] As the Registrar should be joined as a respondent unless the company is in liquidation (*Re Test Holdings Ltd*, above, n. 38, *Re Wood & Martin*, above, n. 39, and *Re Thompson & Riches Ltd*, above, n. 40) this hardly seems necessary except where the company is in liquidation.

[50] s.651(3).

personal injuries,[51] whereas applications under section 653 can be made up to 20 years after the dissolution.

Turning, then, to section 653. The wording of this is very different and superficially much simpler—though the effect seems to be much the same. It does not say that the court may declare the dissolution to be void but instead provides that if a company or any member or creditor of it feels aggrieved by the company having been struck off, he may apply before the expiration of 20 years from the publication in the *Gazette* of the notice under section 652, and the court may, if satisfied that the company was at the time of the striking-off carrying on business or in operation, or otherwise that it is just that the company be restored to the register, order the company's name to be restored.[52] This differs from section 651 (where the application must be made by the liquidator "or any other person appearing to the court to be interested") and is somewhat strange since, although one can reasonably construe "member or creditor" as meaning a "former member or creditor", it is more difficult to see how a non-existent company can "feel aggrieved" or how it can "apply".[53] In practice, however, so long as "creditor" includes a contingent or prospective creditor,[54] those who can apply as aggrieved members or creditors are likely to be the same as "any other person appearing to the court to be interested" who may apply under section 651. And the "otherwise that it is just that the company be restored to the register" seems to afford the court the same wide discretion as under section 651.

Finally, section 653(3) provides that "on an office copy of the order being delivered to the Registrar for registration the company is deemed to have continued in existence as if its name had not been struck off and the court may by the order give such directions and make such provisions as seem just for placing the company and all other persons in the same position (as nearly as may be) as if the company's name had not been struck off."

---

[51] See s.141 of the Companies Act 1989, overruling the effect of *Bradley v. Eagle Star Insurance Co. Ltd* [1989] A.C. 957, H.L., and *Re Mixhurst Ltd* [1994] 2 BCLC 19, where the judge held that the new s.651(6) gave him no power to declare that the period between dissolution and the order declaring the dissolution void should not count for the purposes of limitation periods other than those relating to personal injury and falling within s.651(5).

[52] s.653(1) and (2). See *Re Priceland* [1997] BCC 207. The typical "just cause" is to enable the applicant to bring a claim against the company or a third party which can be enforced only if the company is restored. If the striking off was effected under s.652A the application must be made by the Secretary of State in the public interest or by a person entitled to receive notification of the company's original application to be struck off (see above, p. 847), and the grounds for restoration, in addition to justice, are that the company was not entitled to make the application or that the applicant was not given the notice to which he or she was entitled: s.653(2B)–(2D).

[53] Presumably it is envisaged that the former directors or members could cause the presently non-existent company to apply as if it had not been dissolved.

[54] As Megarry J., in *Re Harvest Lane Motor Bodies Ltd* [1969] 1 Ch. 457, held that it did. But apparently it does not include a transferee or assignee subsequent to the dissolution: *Re Timbique Gold Mines Ltd* [1961] Ch. 319. But he could, perhaps, apply under s.651 as a "person appearing to the court to be interested".

INDEX